Lecture Notes in Computer Science 12436

More information about this series at http://www.springer.com/series/7412

Mingxia Liu · Pingkun Yan ·
Chunfeng Lian · Xiaohuan Cao (Eds.)

Machine Learning in Medical Imaging

11th International Workshop, MLMI 2020
Held in Conjunction with MICCAI 2020
Lima, Peru, October 4, 2020
Proceedings

Springer

Editors
Mingxia Liu
University of North Carolina at Chapel Hill
Chapel Hill, NC, USA

Pingkun Yan
Rensselaer Polytechnic Institute
Troy, NY, USA

Chunfeng Lian
University of North Carolina at Chapel Hill
Chapel Hill, NC, USA

Xiaohuan Cao
United Imaging Intelligence
Shanghai, China

ISSN 0302-9743 ISSN 1611-3349 (electronic)
Lecture Notes in Computer Science
ISBN 978-3-030-59860-0 ISBN 978-3-030-59861-7 (eBook)
https://doi.org/10.1007/978-3-030-59861-7

LNCS Sublibrary: SL6 – Image Processing, Computer Vision, Pattern Recognition, and Graphics

This Springer imprint is published by the registered company Springer Nature Switzerland AG
The registered company address is: Gewerbestrasse 11, 6330 Cham, Switzerland

Preface

The 11th International Workshop on Machine Learning in Medical Imaging (MLMI 2020) was held in Lima, Peru, on October 4, 2020, in conjunction with the 23rd International Conference on Medical Image Computing and Computer-Assisted Intervention (MICCAI 2020).

In the face of artificial intelligence making significant changes in both academia and industry, machine learning has always played a crucial role in the medical imaging field, including, but not limited to, computer-aided detection and diagnosis, image segmentation, image registration, image fusion, image-guided intervention, image annotation, image retrieval, image reconstruction, etc. The main scope of this workshop was to help advance the scientific researches within the broad field of machine learning in medical imaging. This workshop focused on major trends and challenges in this area and presented original works aiming to identify new cutting-edge techniques and their uses in medical imaging. The workshop facilitated translating medical imaging research, boosted by machine learning, from bench to bedside. Topics of interests included deep learning, generative adversarial learning, ensemble learning, sparse learning, multi-task learning, multi-view learning, manifold learning, and reinforcement learning, with their applications to medical image analysis, computer-aided detection and diagnosis, multi-modality fusion, image reconstruction, image retrieval, cellular image analysis, molecular imaging, digital pathology, etc.

Along with the great advances in machine learning, MLMI 2020 received an unprecedentedly large number of papers (101 in total). All the submissions underwent a rigorous double-blinded peer-review process, with each paper being reviewed by at least two members of the Program Committee, composed of 60 experts in the field. Based on the reviewing scores and critiques, the 68 best papers (67.3%) were accepted for presentation at the workshop and chosen to be included in this Springer LNCS volume. It was a tough decision and many high-quality papers had to be rejected due to the page limit of this volume.

We are grateful to all Program Committee members for reviewing the submissions and giving constructive comments. We also thank all the authors for making the workshop very fruitful and successful.

September 2020

Mingxia Liu
Pingkun Yan
Chunfeng Lian
Xiaohuan Cao

Organization

Workshop Organizers

Mingxia Liu   University of North Carolina at Chapel Hill, USA
Pingkun Yan   Rensselaer Polytechnic Institute, USA
Chunfeng Lian   University of North Carolina at Chapel Hill, USA
Xiaohuan Cao   United Imaging Intelligence, China

Steering Committee

Dinggang Shen   University of North Carolina at Chapel Hill, USA
Kenji Suzuki   University of Chicago, USA
Fei Wang   Huami Inc., USA

Program Committee

Ehsan Adeli   Stanford University, USA
Sahar Ahmad   University of North Carolina at Chapel Hill, USA
Ulas Bagci   University of Central Florida, USA
Xiaohuan Cao   United Imaging Intelligence, China
Heang-Ping Chan   University of Michigan Medical Center, USA
Liangjun Chen   University of North Carolina at Chapel Hill, USA
Liyun Chen   Shanghai Jiaotong University, China
Yuanyuan Gao   Rensselaer Polytechnic Institute, USA
Dongdong Gu   United Imaging Intelligence, Hunan University, China
Hao Guan   University of North Carolina at Chapel Hill, USA
Yu Guo   Tianjin University, China
Kelei He   Nanjing University, China
Yasushi Hirano   Yamaguchi University, Japan
Jiashuang Huang   Nanjing University of Aeronautics and Astronautics, China
Yuankai Huo   Vanderbilt University, USA
Khoi Huynh   University of North Carolina at Chapel Hill, USA
Won-Ki Jeong   Ulsan National Institute of Science and Technology, South Korea
Xi Jiang   University of Electronic Science and Technology of China, China
Zhicheng Jiao   University of Pennsylvania, USA
Biao Jie   University of North Carolina at Chapel Hill, USA
Ze Jin   Tokyo Institute of Technology, Japan
Gang Li   University of North Carolina at Chapel Hill, USA
Chunfeng Lian   University of North Carolina at Chapel Hill, USA

Mingxia Liu	University of North Carolina at Chapel Hill, USA
Yunbi Liu	University of North Carolina at Chapel Hill, USA
Janne Nappi	Massachusetts General Hospital, USA
Masahiro Oda	Nagoya University, Japan
Yongsheng Pan	Northwestern Polytechnical University, China
Sanghyun Park	Daegu Gyeongbuk Institute of Science and Technology, South Korea
Kilian Pohl	SRI International, USA
Liangqiong Qu	Stanford University, USA
Gerard Sanroma-Guell	Bayer, Germany
Hongming Shan	Rensselaer Polytechnic Institute, USA
Heung-Il Suk	Korea University, South Korea
Jian Sun	Xi'an Jiaotong University, China
Satish Viswanath	Case Western Reserve University, USA
Lei Wang	University of Wollongong, Australia
Li Wang	University of North Carolina at Chapel Hill, USA
Linwei Wang	Rochester Institute of Technology, USA
Mingliang Wang	Nanjing University of Aeronautics and Astronautics, China
Sheng Wang	Shanghai Jiao Tong University, China
Shuai Wang	University of North Carolina at Chapel Hill, USA
Dongming Wei	Shanghai Jiao Tong University, China
Jie Wei	Northwestern Polytechnical University, China
Zhengwang Wu	University of North Carolina at Chapel Hill, USA
Xuanang Xu	University of North Carolina at Chapel Hill, USA
Pingkun Yan	Rensselaer Polytechnic Institute, USA
Erkun Yang	University of North Carolina at Chapel Hill, USA
Fan Yang	Inception Institute of Artificial Intelligence, UAE
Wanqi Yang	Nanjing Normal University, China
Dongren Yao	Institute of Automation Chinese Academy of Sciences, China
Qian Yu	Nanjing University, China
Jun Zhang	Tencent, China
Li Zhang	Nanjing Forestry University, China
Lichi Zhang	Shanghai Jiao Tong University, China
Yi Zhang	Sichuan University, China
Fengjun Zhao	Northwest University, China
Sihang Zhou	National University of Defense Technology, China
Tao Zhou	Inception Institute of Artificial Intelligence, UAE
Qikui Zhu	Wuhan University, China

Contents

Temporal-Adaptive Graph Convolutional Network for Automated Identification of Major Depressive Disorder Using Resting-State fMRI

Dongren Yao[1,2,3], Jing Sui[1,2]([envelope]), Erkun Yang[3], Pew-Thian Yap[3],
Dinggang Shen[3]([envelope]), and Mingxia Liu[3]([envelope])

[1] Brainentome Center and National Laboratory of Pattern Recognition,
Institute of Automation, Chinese Academy of Sciences, Beijing 100190, China
jing.sui@nlpr.ia.ac.cn
[2] University of Chinese Academy of Sciences, Beijing 100049, China
[3] Department of Radiology and BRIC, University of North Carolina at Chapel Hill,
Chapel Hill, NC 27599, USA
Dinggang.Shen@gmail.com, mxliu@med.unc.edu

Abstract. Extensive studies focus on analyzing human brain functional connectivity from a network perspective, in which each network contains complex graph structures. Based on resting-state functional MRI (rs-fMRI) data, graph convolutional networks (GCNs) enable comprehensive mapping of brain functional connectivity (FC) patterns to depict brain activities. However, existing studies usually characterize static properties of the FC patterns, ignoring the time-varying dynamic information. In addition, previous GCN methods generally use fixed group-level (e.g., patients or controls) representation of FC networks, and thus, cannot capture subject-level FC specificity. To this end, we propose a Temporal-Adaptive GCN (TAGCN) framework that can not only take advantage of both spatial and temporal information using resting-state FC patterns and time-series but also explicitly characterize subject-level specificity of FC patterns. Specifically, we first segment each ROI-based time-series into multiple overlapping windows, then employ an adaptive GCN to mine topological information. We further model the temporal patterns for each ROI along time to learn the periodic brain status changes. Experimental results on 533 major depressive disorder (MDD) and health control (HC) subjects demonstrate that the proposed TAGCN outperforms several state-of-the-art methods in MDD vs. HC classification, and also can be used to capture dynamic FC alterations and learn valid graph representations.

1 Introduction

Major depression disorder (MDD), one of the largest mental diseases, affects as many as 300 million people annually. Patients suffer this debilitating illness from

© Springer Nature Switzerland AG 2020
M. Liu et al. (Eds.): MLMI 2020, LNCS 12436, pp. 1–10, 2020.
https://doi.org/10.1007/978-3-030-59861-7_1

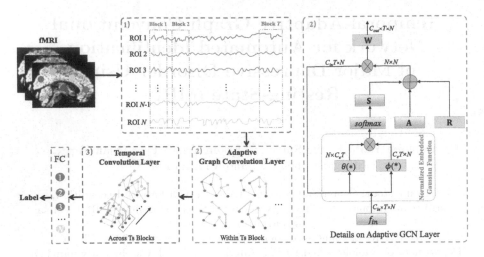

Fig. 1. Illustration of the proposed Temporal-Adaptive Graph Convolutional Network (TAGCN) and details on adaptive GCN layer. The whole framework contains 3 parts: 1) Using step-wise slice windows to generate several time series blocks. 2) Applying an adaptive GCN layer to construct flexible brain functional connectivity topology structure within each block. 3) Employing a temporal convolutional layer to extract dynamic information between blocks on one ROI. With the output of temporal convolutional layer, a fully-connected layer is employed to predict MDD classification (with N-dimensional input and the class label as output). As shown in the right panel, three types of matrix (i.e., **A**, **R**, and **S**), Normalized Embedded Gaussian function (i.e., θ, and ϕ) and several simple operations constitute the whole adaptive GCN layer. $\oplus$ and $\otimes$ denote the element-wise summation and matrix multiplication operations. Pink boxes present those parameters are learnable while blue boxes denote fixed parts.

depressed mood, diminished interests, and impaired cognitive function [1,2]. Despite many efforts have been made from different areas such as basic science, clinical neuroscience, and psychiatric research, the pathophysiology of MDD is still unclear. In addition, conventional diagnosis of MDD often depends on a subjective clinical impression from Diagnostic and Statistical Manual of Mental Disorders (DSM) criterion and treatment responses. Recently, many researchers have developed various computer-aided diagnostic tools based on noninvasive neuroimaging techniques to better understand the neurobiological mechanisms underpinning this mental disorder [3–5].

Among various neuroimaging techniques, resting-state functional magnetic resonance imaging (rs-fMRI) can depict large scale abnormality or dysfunction on brain connectivity networks by measuring the blood-oxygen level in the brain [6,7]. This technology has been widely used to identify MDD from healthy controls (HCs) [4,8]. Most of the existing rs-fMRI based studies hold an implicit but strong assumption that the brain functional connectivity network is *temporal stationary* through the whole scanning period, by relying on static functional connectivity (FC) networks. Therefore, these methods ignore the temporal dynamic information of brain FC networks, which can not well monitor the changes of macroscopic neural activities underlying critical aspects of cognitive/behavioral disorders [9,10]. Spectral graph convolutional neural networks (GCNs) have been used to explicitly capture topological information for learning useful representations of brain FC networks [11,12]. However, conventional GCNs generally use fixed *group-level* rather than *subject-level* adjacent matrix to model the relationships among different brain regions, failing to capture the time-varying information in fMRI data. Intuitively, it is interesting to capture subject-level specificity of functional connectivities to boost the performance of automated MDD identification.

In this paper, we propose a Temporal-Adaptive Graph Convolutional Network (TAGCN) to extract both static and dynamic information of brain FC patterns for MDD identification, as shown in Fig. 1. Specifically, we first extract rs-fMRI time-series signals from each specific region-of-interest (ROI), and employ fixed-size sliding windows to divide time-series data into multiple overlapped blocks. For each block, an adaptive graph convolutional layer is subsequently used to generate a flexible connectivity matrix, which can help model multilevel semantic information within the whole time series. After that, convolution operations on each ROI along different blocks are used to capture temporal dynamics of the complete time series. Finally, a fully connected layer followed by a softmax function is used for MDD classification. Experimental results on 533 subjects from an open-source MDD dataset demonstrate the effectiveness of our TAGCN in capturing dynamic FC alteration and learning valid graph representations. Also, our TAGCN achieves better performance than several state-of-the-art methods in the task of MDD vs. HC classification. To the best of our knowledge, this is among the first attempt to use an end-to-end GCN model to capture adaptive FC topology for automated MDD diagnosis.

2   Method

2.1   Data and fMRI Pre-processing

A total of 533 subjects from an open-source MDD dataset [13] with rs-fMRI data are used in this work, including 282 MDD subjects and 251 healthy controls (HCs) recruited from the Southwest University. For each scan, the TR (repetition time) is $2,000\,ms$, TE (echo time) is $30\,ms$, slice thickness is $3.0\,mm$, and time points are $242\,s$. The demographic information of the studied subjects is provided in Table 1.

Each rs-fMRI scan was pre-processed using the Data Processing Assistant for Resting-State fMRI (DPARSF) [14]. Specifically, we first discard the first ten time points, followed by slice timing correction, head motion correction, regression of nuisance covariates of head motion parameters, white matter, and cerebrospinal fluid (CSF). Then, fMRI data are normalized with an EPI template in the MNI space, and resampled to the resolution of $3 \times 3 \times 3\,mm^3$, followed by spatial smoothing using a $6\,mm$ full width half maximum Gaussian kernel. Finally, the Harvard-Oxford atlas, with 112 pre-defined regions-of-interest

4 D. Yao et al.

Table 1. Demographic information of studied subjects in the MDD dataset. M: Male; F: Female; Y: Yes; N: No; D: Lack of record; Mean ± Standard deviation.

Category	Sex	Age	Education	First Period	On Medication	Duration of Illness
MDD	99M 183F	38.7 ± 13.6	10.8 ± 3.6	209(Y)/49(N) 24(D)	124(Y)/125(N) 33(D)	50.0 ± 65.9 35(D)
HC	87M 164F	39.6 ± 15.8	13.0 ± 3.9	-	-	-

(ROIs) including cortical and subcortical areas, are nonlinearly aligned onto each scan to extract the mean time series for each ROI.

2.2 Proposed Temporal-Adaptive Graph Convolutional Network

As shown in Fig. 1, our model aims to capture temporal and graph topology information to identify MDD subjects from HCs based on rs-fMRI time series. Denote a subject as $\mathbf{X} = (\mathbf{x}_1, \mathbf{x}_2, \cdots, \mathbf{x}_N)^T \in \mathbb{R}^{N \times M}$, where $\mathbf{x}_n \in \mathbb{R}^M$ ($n = 1, \cdots, N$) contains all time-series information at the n-th ROI. Here, $N = 112$ and $M = 232$ denote the number of ROIs and the time-points, respectively. The slicing window size L is set to 25 TR (i.e., 50 s) and the stride of slide window is set to 10 TR (i.e., 20 s). To reduce the overlap of the last two blocks, we discard the first TR and generate $T = 10$ blocks for each subject.

Spectral Graph Convolutional Network. Spectral Graph Convolutional Network (GCN) has recently shown its superiority in learning high-level graph features from brain fMRI data [11,12,15]. Denote f_{in} and f_{out} as the input and output of a GCN, respectively. The simplest spectral GCN layer [16] can be formulated as:

$$f_{out} = \mathbf{W} f_{in}(\hat{\mathbf{D}}^{-0.5} \hat{\mathbf{A}} \hat{\mathbf{D}}^{-0.5}), \tag{1}$$

where $\hat{\mathbf{D}}$ denotes the $N \times N$ degree matrix (with N representing the number of ROIs), and $\mathbf{W}$ denotes the learnable weighted matrix for those connected vertices. Here, $\hat{\mathbf{A}} = \mathbf{A} + \mathbf{I}$, where $\mathbf{A}$ and $\mathbf{I}$ denote the adjacent matrix and an identity matrix, respectively. However, in the definition of spectral graph convolution, the localized first-order approximation makes the nodes i and j share the same parameter if the node j is directly connected to i. To enable specifying different weights to different nodes in a neighborhood, a Graph Attention (GAT) [17] layer is further proposed, with its definition shown in the following:

$$f_{out} = \mathbf{W} f_{in}(\bar{\mathbf{D}}^{-\frac{1}{2}} \hat{\mathbf{A}} \bar{\mathbf{D}}^{-\frac{1}{2}}) \odot \mathbf{M}, \tag{2}$$

where $\bar{\mathbf{D}}$ is a $N \times N$ degree matrix that only adds constant small numbers to avoid empty rows. $\odot$ denotes the dot product and $\mathbf{M}$ is an attention map which presents the importance of each node/vertex/ROI. However, both the conventional spectral GCN layer and GAT layer still highly depend on the construction of brain functional connectivity topology, while each fMRI scan is usually treated as a complete/fully-connected graph.

Adaptive Graph Convolutional Layer. To solve the problem caused by the fixed topology of brain functional connectivity, we employ a new adjacent matrix $\mathbf{A} + \mathbf{R} + \mathbf{S}$ to generate an end-to-end learning module. The definition of the adaptive graph convolutional layer is shown as follows:

$$f_{out} = \mathbf{W} f_{in} (\mathbf{A} + \mathbf{R} + \mathbf{S}). \tag{3}$$

where the definitions of $\mathbf{A}$, $\mathbf{R}$ and $\mathbf{S}$ are shown below.

The matrix $\mathbf{A}$ is an $N \times N$ adjacency matrix, which determines whether a connection exists between two ROIs (i.e., vertices). Specifically, we first calculate the mean FC matrix of all training subjects within the same time-series block and then construct a k-Nearest Neighbour (KNN) graph by connecting each vertex with its top k nearest neighbors (with the Pearson's correlation coefficient as the similarity metric).

The matrix $\mathbf{R}$ is an $N \times N$ adjacency matrix, which is parameterized and optimized in the training process with other tunable parameters. It is a data-driven matrix without any constraint, through which one can learn graphs more individualized for different topology information between different time-series blocks. Although the attention matrix $\mathbf{M}$ in Eq. (2) can model the existence and strength of connections between two ROIs, the dot operation $\odot$ leads to that those zero elements in the adjacent matrix $\mathbf{A}$ always be 0 (i.e., not affected by $\mathbf{M}$). Different from the attention matrix $\mathbf{M}$, $\mathbf{R}$ is learned in a data-driven manner, and thus, is more flexible.

The matrix $\mathbf{S}$ is used to learn the topology information of brain functional connectivity in each time-series block. We employ a normalized embedding Gaussian function [18] to calculate the similarity of two ROIs in $\mathbf{S}$. Specifically, this function determines whether two ROIs (e.g., r_i and r_j) should be connected and also the connection strength if the connection exists, defined as follows:

$$r_{i,j} = f(r_i, r_j) = \frac{e^{\theta(r_i)^T \phi(r_j)}}{\sum_{n=1}^{N} e^{\theta(r_i)^T \phi(r_n)}}, \tag{4}$$

where $r_{i,j}$ is the element of $\mathbf{S}$ and $\theta(*)$ and $\phi(*)$ are two embedding functions. These two embedding functions map the input feature map ($C_{in} \times T \times N$) into the size of ($C_e \times T \times N$), where C_{in}, C_e and T denote the numbers of channels, embedding size and temporal blocks, respectively. We use the 1×1 convolutional layer as the embedding function. After rearranging the new feature maps into the shape of $N \times C_e T$ and $C_e T \times N$, a $N \times N$ matrix $\mathbf{S}$ is generated by multiplying them. The element r_{ij} in the matrix $\mathbf{S}$ denotes the similarity of two ROIs (i.e., r_i and r_j) that is normalized to $[0, 1]$. Details on adaptive graph convolutional layer are shown in the right panel of Fig. 1.

Temporal Convolutional Layer. For the temporal dimension, since the number of blocks is fixed as $T = 10$ (as mentioned in Sect. 2.2), we perform the graph convolution similar to the traditional convolution operation. Specifically, a $K_t \times 1$

convolution operation is employed to work on the output feature maps calculated from adaptive graph convolutional layer, where K_t is the kernel size of the temporal dimension. The kernel size is set as $K_t = 3$ empirically.

Implementation. We optimize the proposed TAGCN model via the Adam algorithm, with the learning rate of 0.001, the number of epochs of 200, and the mini-batch size of 5. For a new test subject, our TAGCN costumes about 8.6 seconds to predict its class label (i.e., MDD or HC) using a single GPU (NVIDIA GTX TITAN 12 GB).

3   Experiment

Experimental Setup. We evaluate the proposed TAGCN on the MDD dataset based on a 5-fold cross-validation strategy. The performance of MDD identification from age-matched HCs is measured by four metrics, i.e., accuracy (ACC), sensitivity (SEN), specificity (SPE), and area under the ROC curve (AUC).

Competing Method. We first compare the proposed TAGCN method with two baseline methods based on static FC matrices, i.e., (1) support vector machine (**SVM**) with Radial Basis Function kernel, and (2) Clustering Coefficients (CC) with SVM (**CC+SVM**). CC not only measures the clustering degree of each node in a graph but also can be treated as a feature selection algorithm. Hence, we employ SVM with and without CC to discriminate MDD from HCs based on their static FC matrices. Specifically, each static FC matrix (corresponding to a specific subject) is constructed based on the Pearson's correlation between the whole time series of each pair of pre-defined ROIs. The SVM method direct perform classification based on the static FC matrix. The CC+SVM method is associated with the degree of network sparsity, where the sparsity parameter is chosen from $\{0.10, 0.15, \cdots, 0.40\}$ according to cross-validation performance. The parameter C in SVM with RBF kernel is chosen from $\{0.80, 0.85, \cdots, 3.00\}$ via cross validation, and we use default values for the other parameters.

We also compare our TAGCN with two state-of-the-art GCN methods, including (1) **sGCN** [16] shown in Eq. 1, and (2) **GAT** [17] shown in Eq. 2. Both networks are tested on static FC matrices generated from rs-fMRI. Li et al. [19] found that spectral GCN models can be explained as a special form of Laplacian smoothing which employs features of each vertex as well as its neighbors. In order to use brain functional network more effectively, we construct a KNN graph, instead of fully-connected graphs which cannot capture the *node-centralized local topology* via spectral GCNs, by connecting each vertex with its k-nearest neighbors to model the node-centralized local topology. It should be noted that the graph topology (reflected by vertices and their connectivity) of such a group-level (rather than subject-level) KNN graph is shared by all subjects. The parameter k for constructing KNN graphs is chosen from

Method	Accuracy (Std)	Sensitivity(Std)	Specificity(Std)
SVM	0.628±0.023	0.636±0.026	0.618±0.070
CC+SVM	0.636±0.030	0.683±0.073	0.625±0.069
sGCN	0.682±0.017	0.714±0.016	0.662±0.043
GAT	0.701±0.022	0.722±0.034	0.690±0.029
TAGCN	**0.738±0.048**	**0.762±0.024**	**0.705±0.031**

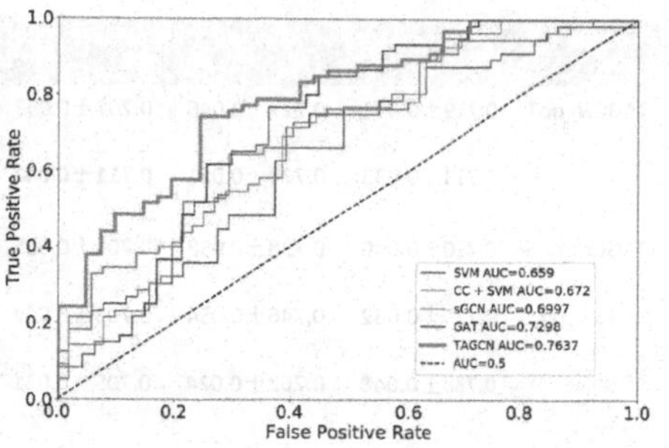

Fig. 2. Three indexes (i.e., accuracy, sensitivity, and specificity), ROC curves and related AUC values of five different methods in the task of MDD vs. HC classification.

$\{1, 2, \cdots, 30\}$. These networks contain 3 graph convolutional layers and one fully-connected layer. Besides, these 3 graph convolutional layers share the same size of inputs to make sure that features can be well explained. The number of heads on GAT is chosen from $\{2, 3, \cdots, 6\}$ via cross validation. The parameter of attention dropout is 0.6 and the negative slope of leaky ReLU is 0.2.

Result. In the left panel of Fig. 2, we report the disease classification results achieved by 2 traditional machine learning methods (*i.e.*, SVM and CC+SVM), 2 GCN methods (*i.e.*, sGCN and GAT) and our TAGCN. We further show the ROC curves and AUC values of these methods in the right panel of Fig. 2. From Fig. 2, one can have the following interesting observations. *First*, GCN-based models are superior to traditional methods (including SVM and CC+SVM) significantly. For instance, these traditional methods (without considering graph topology information) achieve at least 5% lower performance than other GCN-based models. This demonstrates the necessity and effectiveness of exploiting graph topology on FC. *Second*, GAT (with different weights to different nodes/ROIs in a neighborhood) outperforms sGCN, which means GAT might conquer the negative influence of using group-level adjacent matrix. *Besides*, our proposed adaptive learning strategies with flexible brain connectivity topology structure achieve better performance than GAT and sGCN. It implies that modeling subject-level functional connectivity topology structure helps capture discriminative features than group-level topology structure.

Ablation Study. To evaluate the contributions of our proposed three matrices and temporal learning strategy, we further compare TAGCN with its four types of variants, including (1) **TAGCN_noT** based on static FC matrix, i.e., ignoring temporal dynamic information, (2) TAGCN without the KNN adjacency matrix **A** in Eq. 3, denoted as **TAGCN_noA**, (3) TGCN without the randomly initial adjacency matrix **R** (**TAGCN_noR**), and (4) TGCN without the similarity matrix **S** (**TAGCN_noS**). For the fair comparison, all GCN-related layers in

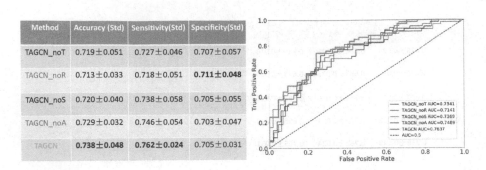

Method	Accuracy (Std)	Sensitivity(Std)	Specificity(Std)
TAGCN_noT	0.719±0.051	0.727±0.046	0.707±0.057
TAGCN_noR	0.713±0.033	0.718±0.051	**0.711±0.048**
TAGCN_noS	0.720±0.040	0.738±0.058	0.705±0.055
TAGCN_noA	0.729±0.032	0.746±0.054	0.703±0.047
TAGCN	**0.738±0.048**	**0.762±0.024**	0.705±0.031

Fig. 3. Three indexes (i.e., accuracy, sensitivity, and specificity), ROC curves and related AUC values of our TAGCN and its four variants in the task of MDD vs. HC classification.

six GCN methods(without GAT) are followed by a batch Normalization (BN) layer and a ReLU layer. The experimental results are shown in Fig. 3.

Figure 3 suggests that TAGCN with temporal information promotes the classification results, compared with TAGCN_noT using the static FC matrix. This confirms that dynamic fluctuation in FCs also contributes to discriminating MDD from HCs. *In addition*, TAGCN_noR achieves the highest specificity without random **Matrix R**, indicating that topological information based on KNN may pay more attention on abnormal FC. *Also*, three variants of TAGCN (i.e., TAGCN_noR, TAGCN_noS, and TAGCN_noA) yield comparable results with TAGCN, suggesting that three matrices (i.e., **R**, **S**, and **A**) in Eq. (3) provide complementary useful information for MDD identification.

As shown in the right of Figs. 2 and 3, our proposed TAGCN achieves good ROC performance and the best AUC value when compared to the competing methods. These results further suggest the efficiency of TAGCN in MDD vs. HC diagnosis.

4   Conclusion

In this paper, we propose a temporal-adaptive graph convolution network (TAGCN) to mine spatial and temporal information using rs-fMRI time series. Specifically, the time-series data are first segmented with fixed sliding windows. Then, an adaptive GCN module is employed to generate unfixed topological information, by mainly focusing on each specific sliding window. We further model the temporal patterns of each ROI within the whole time series to learn periodic changes of the brain. The proposed TAGCN can *not only* learn completed data-driven based graph topology information *but also* effectively capture dynamic variations of brain fMRI data. Instead of sharing one group-level adjacent matrix, TAGCN with an adaptive GCN layer takes subject-level topological information (i.e, self adjacent matrix) into consideration. Experimental results on the MDD dataset demonstrate that our method yields state-of-the-art performance in identifying MDD patients from healthy controls.

In the current work, we only focus on using rs-fMRI data to capture subject-level connectivity topology. Actually, other modalities (e.g., structure MRI and diffusion tensor imaging) can also help uncover the neurobiological mechanisms of MDD by providing more direct structural connectivity topology. In future, we will extend TAGCN to multi-modal brain imaging data. Moreover, it is interesting to design other strategies to generate and segment fMRI time-series to take advantage of temporal dynamics.

Acknowledgements. This work was partly supported by NIH grant (No. MH108560).

References

1. Organization, W.H., et al.: Depression and Other Common Mental Disorders: Global Health Estimates. World Health Organization, Technical report (2017)
2. Otte, C., et al.: Major depressive disorder. Nat. Rev. Dis. Primers **2**(1), 1–20 (2016)
3. Gray, J.P., Müller, V.I., Eickhoff, S.B., Fox, P.T.: Multimodal abnormalities of brain structure and function in major depressive disorder: a meta-analysis of neuroimaging studies. Am. J. Psychiatry. **177**(5), 422–434 (2020)
4. Gao, S., Calhoun, V.D., Sui, J.: Machine learning in major depression: from classification to treatment outcome prediction. CNS Neurosci. Ther. **24**(11), 1037–1052 (2018)
5. Sui, J., et al.: Multimodal neuromarkers in schizophrenia via cognition-guided MRI fusion. Nat. Commun. **9**(1), 1–14 (2018)
6. Jie, B., Liu, M., Shen, D.: Integration of temporal and spatial properties of dynamic connectivity networks for automatic diagnosis of brain disease. Med. Image Anal. **47**, 81–94 (2018)
7. Zhang, D., Huang, J., Jie, B., Du, J., Tu, L., Liu, M.: Ordinal pattern: a new descriptor for brain connectivity networks. IEEE Trans. Med. Imaging **37**(7), 1711–1722 (2018)
8. Li, G., et al.: Identification of abnormal circuit dynamics in major depressive disorder via multiscale neural modeling of resting-state fMRI. In: Shen, D., et al. (eds.) MICCAI 2019. LNCS, vol. 11766, pp. 682–690. Springer, Cham (2019). https://doi.org/10.1007/978-3-030-32248-9_76
9. Wang, M., Lian, C., Yao, D., Zhang, D., Liu, M., Shen, D.: Spatial-temporal dependency modeling and network hub detection for functional MRI analysis via convolutional-recurrent network. IEEE Transactions on Biomedical Engineering. IEEE (2019)
10. Jiao, Z., et al.: Dynamic routing capsule networks for mild cognitive impairment diagnosis. In: Shen, D., et al. (eds.) MICCAI 2019. LNCS, vol. 11767, pp. 620–628. Springer, Cham (2019). https://doi.org/10.1007/978-3-030-32251-9_68
11. Yao, D., et al.: Triplet graph convolutional network for multi-scale analysis of functional connectivity using functional MRI. In: Zhang, D., Zhou, L., Jie, B., Liu, M. (eds.) GLMI 2019. LNCS, vol. 11849, pp. 70–78. Springer, Cham (2019). https://doi.org/10.1007/978-3-030-35817-4_9
12. Ktena, S.I., et al.: Metric learning with spectral graph convolutions on brain connectivity networks. NeuroImage **169**, 431–442 (2018)

13. Yan, C.G., et al.: Reduced default mode network functional connectivity in patients with recurrent major depressive disorder. Proc. Nat. Acad. Sci. **116**(18), 9078–9083 (2019)
14. Yan, C.G., Wang, X.D., Zuo, X.N., Zang, Y.F.: DPABI: data processing & analysis for (resting-state) brain imaging. Neuroinform. **14**(3), 339–351 (2016)
15. Parisot, S., Ktena, S.I., Ferrante, E., Lee, M., Guerrero, R., Glocker, B., Rueckert, D.: Disease prediction using graph convolutional networks: application to autism spectrum disorder and Alzheimer's disease. Med. Image Anal. **48**, 117–130 (2018)
16. Kipf, T.N., Welling, M.: Semi-supervised classification with graph convolutional networks. arXiv preprint arXiv:1609.02907 (2016)
17. Velivcković, P., Cucurull, G., Casanova, A., Romero, A., Lio, P., Bengio, Y.: Graph attention networks. arXiv preprint arXiv:1710.10903 (2017)
18. Shi, L., Zhang, Y., Cheng, J., Lu, H.: Two-stream adaptive graph convolutional networks for skeleton-based action recognition. In: Proceedings of the IEEE Conference on Computer Vision and Pattern Recognition, pp. 12026–12035. IEEE (2019)
19. Li, Q., Han, Z., Wu, X.M.: Deeper insights into graph convolutional networks for semi-supervised learning. In: Thirty-Second AAAI Conference on Artificial Intelligence. (2018)

Error Attention Interactive Segmentation of Medical Image Through Matting and Fusion

Weifeng Hu[1], Xiaofen Yao[2], Zhou Zheng[1], Xiaoyun Zhang[1(✉)],
Yumin Zhong[2(✉)], Xiaoxia Wang[2], Ya Zhang[1], and Yanfeng Wang[1]

[1] Cooperative Medianet Innovation Center, Shanghai Jiao Tong University,
Shanghai, China
xiaoyun.zhang@sjtu.edu.cn
[2] Shanghai Children's Medical Center, Shanghai, China
zhongyumin@scmc.com.cn

Abstract. Deep learning-based interactive segmentation has attracted research interest recently since it can smartly utilize user interactions to refine a coarse automatic segmentation to get higher accuracy for clinical use. Current methods usually transform user clicks to geodesic distance hint maps as guidance, then concatenate them with the raw image and coarse segmentation, and feed them into a refinement network. Such methods are insufficient in refining error region, which is a key capability required for interactive segmentation. In this paper, we propose Error Attention Interactive network with Matting and Fusion to auto-extract guide information of mis-segmentation region from two branches and transfer it into main segmentor. We first design Region Matting to obtain foreground and background mattings from coarse segmentation. And then we adopt the features extracted by two branches trained on above mattings as guidance. Attention-Fusion is further proposed to transfer the guidance to main segmentor effectively based on attention mechanism and feature concatenation. Experimental results on BraTS 2015 and our Neuroblastoma datasets have shown that our method significantly outperforms state-of-the-art methods, with the advantage of fewer interactions.

Keywords: Interactive medical image segmentation · Error attention · Attention fusion · Region matting

1 Introduction

Image segmentation is an essential building block in computer aided diagnosis and surgical planning, etc. Manual segmentation by experts can ensure annotation quality but is tedious and time consuming. Automatic segmentation such as recent U-net [1] has achieved significant progress, but the accuracy and performance robustness are still not good enough for clinical application. Interactive

© Springer Nature Switzerland AG 2020
M. Liu et al. (Eds.): MLMI 2020, LNCS 12436, pp. 11–20, 2020.
https://doi.org/10.1007/978-3-030-59861-7_2

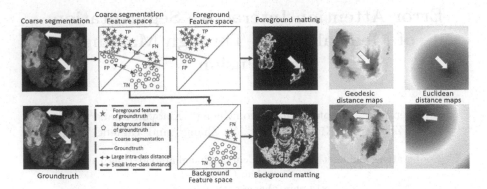

Fig. 1. The large intra-class distance and small inter-class distance cause mis-segmentation. Region matting makes network see only foreground/background of image according to coarse segmentation, which ignores large intra-class distance. Meanwhile, histogram equalization is applied to mattings in order to expand small inter-class distance. Compared with region mattings and Geodesic, Euclidean distance maps, region mattings can easily distinguish error areas that arrow points. While Geodesic, Euclidean distance maps hardly find mis-segmentation regions in large red area. (Color figure online)

segmentation takes advantage of users' knowledge in an interactive way to overcome the challenges faced by manual and automatic methods, and offers a good trade-off between required human effort and segmentation robustness [5]. However, existing interactive segmentation methods still need much interaction to acquire improvement for clinical application.

Early interactive segmentation methods such as Graph Cuts [8], GeoS [10], and Random Walks [11], mainly consider hand-crafted low-level features, and require a relatively large amount of user interactions because of medical image's low-contrast intensity and ambiguous boundaries. Recently, using deep CNNs to improve interactive segmentation has also attracted increasing interests. With the input of an initial segmentation and interactive information, such as clicks [6], contour [7], bounding box [9] from doctors, an interactive segmentation network can automatically refine the initial segmentation to a better one, and this process is repeated until we get a satisfactory result. Thus, there are two key issues in learning based interactive segmentation: (1) How to obtain and express the interactive hints information effectively from doctor's interactions, which is generally referred to as "hint map generation" ; (2) How to design an appropriate network to effectively utilize these interactive hint maps to improve coarse segmentation while with fewer interactions and faster response.

Currently, learning based interactive segmentation such as [2,3] usually transform doctor's positive and negative clicks into two distance maps. As shown in Fig. 1, the Euclidean distance map [2] treats each direction equally and does not take the image context into account. In contrast, the geodesic distance map in DeepIGeoS [3] helps to better differentiate neighboring pixels with different appearances. However, as is pointed out in recent works [14] that without edge information, using geodesic distance alone may fail in areas where the grayscale difference between foreground and background is not significant. In other words, geodesic distance map is suitable for whole segmentation but weak in distinguish mis-segmentation areas. In [3,4], the generated hint maps are directly concatenated with raw image and coarse segmentation as the input of segmentation network for refinement. This scheme is simple and can not make full use of certainty information indicated by clicks.

To address above issues, we propose Error Attention interactive network with Matting and Fusion. It contains a main segment or to predict complete segmentation and two branches to extract error region guided information which help main segmentor to pay more attention on mis-segmentation. Firstly, to rectify the mis-segmentation more easily, we propose region matting that obtains foreground and background mattings from coarse segmentation as input of two branches to better extract guidance compared to using only geodesic distance map. Through separating feature space into foreground/background feature space, region matting can ignore large intra-class distance which causes incorrect segmentation, to distinguish mis-segmentation more easily. After that, histogram equalization is applied to mattings to expand small inter-class distance. As shown in Fig. 1, the contrast of grayscale between error and correct region is more obvious in mattings than whole image. Moreover, we design Attention-Fusion module which fuses the guided feature and main segmentor's feature to refine mis-segmentation. Attention-Fusion adopts a learned fusion strategy, where the feature of main segmentor will be complemented by the guided information in error area. And the guide information will be maintained to keep more detail in incorrect segmentation for improvement by being concatenated to main segmentor.

The contributions of our interactive segmentation are summarized as:

- We propose an Error Attention interactive network with Matting and Fusion(EAMF) to extract error region guided information in two branches which guides main segmentor to refine mis-segmentation.
- Through Region Matting(RM), we obtain a better representation of guidance by training two branches to effectively express the interaction. In order to effectively utilize the guided information, Attention-Fusion(AF) module is proposed to complement feature in main segmentor with guided feature from two branches by attention-based mechanism.
- Experimental results on the public BraTS 2015 and our Neuroblastoma datasets validate that our method has advantages of better segmentation refinement performance, and has fewer interactive iterations.

2   Methodology

The overall workflow of our proposed interactive segmentation is similar to DeepIGeoS [3], where a coarse segmentation (obtained by a segmentation network such as U-net [1]) will be refined with the provided interactions until we get a satisfactory segmentation. The proposed Error Attention Interactive Network with Matting and Fusion is depicted in Fig. 2. We adopt U-net(64channel)

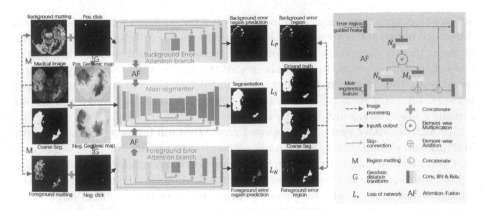

Fig. 2. The proposed EAMF network structure. Region mattings are used as input of branches to help to extract guided features in error areas easily. Main segmentor receives error region attention features to obtain an improved refined segmentation. AF is used in each layer of encoders.

as our main segmentor. We denote I as medical image, P as coarse prediction. C_f and C_b represent the set of pixels belonging to foreground and background interaction(clicks), respectively. First of all, foreground matting map M_f and background matting map M_b are computed according to coarse segmentation, concatenated with clicks as input of error attention branches to extract guided feature which concentrates more on mis-segmentation. Then the guided feature is fused to main segmentor to guide it by supplementing details about incorrect area. To keep a whole view of segmentation in main segmentor, following the generated method of [3], foreground/background geodesic distance map G_f/G_b is computed. We concatenate coarse segmentation, whole image, geodesic distance maps as input of main segmentor for whole object prediction. Afterwards the guided feature guides the main segmentor to better refined in incorrect segmentation by paying attention to error region, fusing whole view information and mis-segmentation detailed information(Attention-Fusion).

Region Matting. Feature distance between intra-class is greater than inter-class, which leads to mis-segmentation. If we take the whole image into account, the large intra-class distance will still affect refinement. To address this problem, we propose region matting to get foreground matting map M_f and background matting map M_b to ignore large intra-class distance. Through histogram equalization, the mattings' grayscale contrast is enhanced to expand small inter-class distance. The formulation can be described as: $M_f = h(P \cdot I), M_g = h((1 - P) \cdot I)$, where $h(\Delta)$ means histogram equalization of images. Moreover, region matting can guarantee that foreground/background clicks guide the refinement only in background/foreground region to avoid mixing of guidance.

Attention-Fusion. In previous work, [15] uses emendation network to predict mis-segmentation region. And error region prediction is used to emendate the coarse segmentation for an improved segmentation performance. However, the inaccurate error prediction needs further improvement. Therefore, we consider to extract feature from error region attention segmentor's encoder as guided feature instead of using error region prediction directly. Feature attention and concatenation are efficient ways to transmit low level detail information of network. Thus, we fuse guidance $f_g \in R^{H \times W \times C}$ with main segmentor features $f_s \in R^{H \times W \times C}$ in each layer of encoder. It first extracts the common parts between f_g and f_s by element-wise multiplication and then combines them with original f_s by element-wise addition. To maintain detail of mis-segmentation, f_g is further concatenated with f_s. As shown in Fig. 2, the whole process can be formulated as follows:

$$f_s = concat(f_s + M_s(N_s(f_s) * N_g(f_g)), f_g) \tag{1}$$

where each of $M_s(\Delta), N_s(\Delta), N_g(\Delta)$ is the combination of convolution, batchnorm and relu. Attention-Fusion is used in each layer of encoder to guide the refinement. We also analyse the feature before output of main segmentor by using t-SNE [16] in mis-segmentation region for demonstrating the effectiveness of our proposed network in experiment.

Loss function. As shown in Fig. 2, our network is supervised like DeepIGeoS [3]. Differently, the false positive region Y_{fp} and false negative region Y_{fn} are calculated from groundtruth $Y \in \{0,1\}$ and coarse prediction $P \in \{0,1\}$: $Y_{fn} = Q(Y - P)$, $Y_{fp} = Q(P - Y)$, where $Y - P \in \{0, 1, -1\}$ and $Q(\Delta)$ means that pixel values greater than 0.5 are set to 1, and others are set to 0. Suppose the output of background branch is $\tilde{Y}_{fn}$, output of foreground branch is $\tilde{Y}_{fp}$. The output of main segmentor is $\tilde{Y}$. We calculate loss as follows:

$$L_P = -\sum_i \left[(Y_{fn})_i \left(\log \tilde{Y}_{fn} \right)_i + (1 - (Y_{fn})_i) \log \left(1 - \left(\tilde{Y}_{fn} \right)_i \right) \right] \tag{2}$$

$$L_N = -\sum_i \left[(Y_{fp})_i \left(\log \tilde{Y}_{fp} \right)_i + (1 - (Y_{fp})_i) \log \left(1 - \left(\tilde{Y}_{fp} \right)_i \right) \right] \tag{3}$$

$$L_S = -\sum_i \left[Y_i \log \tilde{Y}_i + (1 - Y_i) \log \left(1 - \tilde{Y}_i \right) \right] \tag{4}$$

$$L_{Total} = L_S + w \cdot (L_P + L_N) \tag{5}$$

Where L_S means the loss of main segmentor, L_P / L_N means the loss of background/foreground error attention branch. ω is the weight for balance branches' loss and main segmentor's loss, we set $\omega = 0.1$ in our experiments.

3   Experiments

Datasets. BraTS15: Brain Tumor Segmentation Challenge 2015 (BraTS)[12] provides a dataset for brain tumor segmentation in magnetic resonance images. We use 157 cases Fluid-attenuated Inversion Recovery (FLAIR) images to train and test. We use 58 cases to train coarse segmentation, and 59 cases to train interactive segmentation, and use 40 cases to test.

NB Dataset: A neuroblastoma segmentation dataset which consists of 430 cases CT scans of children is established by expert doctors from Shanghai Children's Medical Center with a manually-annotated label. The intra-slices resolution is 512x512, and the number of slices varies from 67 to 395 and the voxel size is 0.49x0.49x1.24 mm^3 in average. We only use 110 cases to train and test. We use 20 cases to train coarse segmentation, and 60 cases to train interactive segmentation, and use 30 cases to test.

Implementation Details and Evaluation Metrics. The caorse segmentation is obtained by training a U-net [1] under supervision. In order to prove the robustness of our method, we set a good coarse segmentation and a bad coarse segmentation in different datasets (83.31 DSC in BraTS15 and 54.80 DSC in NB dataset). We automatically simulate user interactions to train EAMF network. Coarse segmentation is compared with the ground truth to find mis-segmentation regions. Then the user interactions on mis-segmented regions are simulated by randomly sampling one pixel location in mis-segmented region, and at most 3 positive and negative clicks are provided at each step for an image. Specifically, the clicks are randomly selected in the largest 3 mis-segmentation regions which is similar to the behavior of user interaction. Our network is trained in an end to end manner, the main segmentor and two branches are trained simultaneously. Dice Similarity Coefficient (DSC), Hausdorff Distance(HD)(mm) and Average Surface Distance (ASD)(mm) are used as the evaluation metrics. As for interactive segmentation task, click number and the response time for network are also important indicators which we also evaluated.

Comparative Experiment. As shown in Table 1, our proposed EAMF is compared with DeepiIGeoS [3] (R-net + CRF + Geodesic), U-net [1](64channel) with different hint maps (Euclidean, Geodesic), U-net with large channel (128channel) has the same parameter size as EAMF. EAMF sets U-net(64) as main segmentor(backbone). And two branches are U-net(32). Compared to Emendation, Emendation-net, among different ways of using guide information(result/feature), EAMF, which extracts error guided feature in separate error attention branches and then fuses it, shows superiority. Region matting shows a better refined segmentation by using matting as input compared to using whole image.

Figure 3 presents the segmentation results of different interactive methods. With the provided positive (yellow) or negative(red) clicks, our method can refine the coarse segmentation to obtain a satisfactory result which is close to the ground truth. After coarse segmentation, we can see that mis-segmentation regions show significant difference in grayscale to correct area, which called large intra-class. If the refined network takes the whole image as input, it will yield the similar result to coarse segmentation because the large intra-class distance. For example, it is shown in top and middle rows that under-segmentation area shows darker grayscale compared with correct-segmentation. By region matting,

Table 1. Comparison with different methods in one step with three clicks. Eu/Geo means using Euclidean/Geodesic distance map as input. 64/128 means the numbers of channel of U-net. W/M means using the whole image/matting as input to predict mis-segmentation. In Emendation, we train only error attention branches independently, using error region prediction to correct coarse segmentation directly. Emendation-net sets coarse segmentation, whole image, geodesic distance maps and mis-segmentation prediction as input of U-net for refinement.

| Datasets | Brats15 | | | NB | | | Time(s) |
Methods	DSC	HD	ASD	DSC	HD	ASD	
Coarse Seg	83.31	10.37	1.634	54.80	15.78	2.714	-
DeepIGeoS [3]	89.44	5.57	0.389	82.54	6.65	0.393	0.51
U-net(Eu-64)	85.55	9.48	0.752	74.29	14.91	1.211	0.15
U-net(Geo-64)	89.01	5.87	0.426	81.73	6.92	0.387	**0.07**
U-net(Geo-128)	89.58	5.51	0.384	83.03	6.64	0.517	0.10
Emendation(W)	87.64	6.01	0.375	81.23	6.88	0.474	0.08
Emendation(M)	89.84	5.62	0.305	82.98	6.57	0.406	0.08
Emendation-net(W)	88.82	5.83	0.410	81.84	6.73	0.404	0.09
Emendation-net(M)	90.38	5.53	0.279	83.99	6.22	0.384	0.09
EAMF(W)	90.45	5.41	0.256	85.37	6.26	0.325	0.12
EAMF(M)	**91.89**	**4.77**	**0.248**	**87.24**	**5.29**	**0.316**	0.12

EAMF refines under-segmentation area and don't take correct-segmentation into account. Therefore, EAMF can refine under-segmentation area better. In bottom rows, the red clicks indicate over-segmentation area. After refinement, another over-segmentation appeared around the tumor that is in bottom right corner of image in U-net, DeeoIGeoS and Emendation-net. Through matting foreground area, the red click will not cause over-segmentation in background area. With region matting to ignore large intra-class distance and histogram equalization to expand inter-class distance, EAMF can distinguish mis-segmentation better.

t-SNE Analysis. As shown in Fig. 4, we apply t-SNE to features before output of U-net(64). For each patient, we randomly select a slice and randomly sample pixels which are around and in error region, in those slices. For each image, we have features $f \in R^{H \times W \times C}$, And each pixel $i \in H \times W$ has C dim feature and label $\in \{0, 1\}$. Suppose mis-segmentation $E = Y_{fp} + Y_{fn}$. In order to have positive and negative samples in each error area, 5×5 dilated kernel is used in region E to obtain pixel around and in error region. It can be shown that in and around error region, our method shows more features aggregation, and splits foreground and background more effectively.

Numbers of Iteration and Ablation Study. In Fig. 5, for the first interaction step, our EAMF network shows the biggest improvement. With more interaction iterations, our method achieves higher accuracy and shows more improvement.

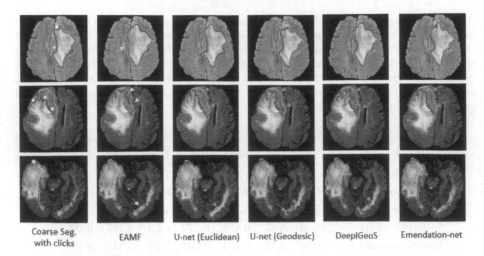

Coarse Seg.   EAMF   U-net (Euclidean)   U-net (Geodesic)   DeepIGeoS   Emendation-net
with clicks

Fig. 3. Visualization of different methods. Green curve is the predicted segmentation, yellow curve is groundtruth. Cyan arrow shows EAMF better refined area and orange arrow shows mis-refined area of other methods. (Color figure online)

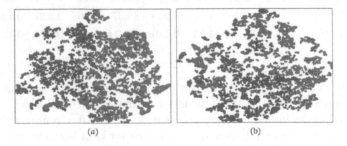

Fig. 4. The t-SNE visualization of mis-segmentation features in BraTS15 dataset. (a)/(b) is result of our method/U-net(64).

The ablation experiment results shown in Table 2 shows improvement of each module in our network. BEB, FEB means background error attention branch, foreground error attention branch, respectively. Atten means that only Auto-Attention is used to fuse features without concatenation. Concat means that the guide information are transferred only by concatenation.

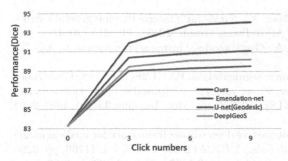

Fig. 5. Performance improvement in continuous interaction.

Table 2. Ablation Experiments.

Module				Brats15	NB
BEB	FEB	Atten	Concat	DSC	DSC
Backbone-Unet(64)				89.01	83.03
✓			✓	90.90	84.21
✓	✓		✓	89.87	84.63
✓	✓		✓	91.25	86.43
✓	✓	✓		91.38	86.21
✓	✓	✓	✓	91.89	87.24

4 Conclusion

In this work, we propose a novel Error Attention interactive network with Matting and Fusion. Our method transfers error region guide information into main segmentor to achieve better refined segmentation. Region Matting and Fusion are proposed to extract and fuse guide information. The experimental results show that our proposed method performs better than the state-of-the-art methods.

References

1. Ronneberger, O., Fischer, P., Brox, T.: U-Net: convolutional networks for biomedical image segmentation. In: Navab, N., Hornegger, J., Wells, W.M., Frangi, A.F. (eds.) MICCAI 2015. LNCS, vol. 9351, pp. 234–241. Springer, Cham (2015). https://doi.org/10.1007/978-3-319-24574-4_28
2. Xu, N., Price, B., Cohen, S., Yang, J., Huang, T.S.: Deep interactive object selection. In: The IEEE Conference on Computer Vision and Pattern Recognition (CVPR), pp. 373–381. IEEE (2016)
3. Wang, G., Zuluaga, M.A., Li, W., et al.: DeepIGeoS: a deep interactive geodesic framework for medical image segmentation. IEEE Trans. Pattern Anal. Mach. Intell. 41(7), 1559–1572 (2018)
4. Lei, W., Wang, H., Gu, R., Zhang, S., Zhang, S., Wang, G.: DeepIGeoS-V2: deep interactive segmentation of multiple organs from head and neck images with lightweight CNNs. In: Zhou, L., et al. (eds.) LABELS/HAL-MICCAI/CuRIOUS -2019. LNCS, vol. 11851, pp. 61–69. Springer, Cham (2019). https://doi.org/10.1007/978-3-030-33642-4_7
5. Zhao, F., Xie, X.: An overview of interactive medical image segmentation. In: Annals of the BMVA, pp: 1–22 (2013)
6. Haider, S. A., et al.: Single-click, semi-automatic lung nodule contouring using hierarchical conditional random fields. In: ISBI, (2015)
7. Xu, C., Prince, J.L.: Snakes, shapes, and gradient vector flow. TIP 7(3), 359–369 (1998)
8. Boykov, Y., Jolly, M.P.: Interactive graph cuts for optimal boundary region segmentation of objects in N-D images. In: ICCV, pp: 105–112 (2001)

9. Rother, C., Kolmogorov, V., Blake, A.: "GrabCut": interactive foreground extraction using iterated graph cuts. ACM Trans. Graph. **23**(3), 309–314 (2004)
10. Criminisi, A., Sharp, T., Blake, A.: GeoS: geodesic image segmentation. In: ECCV, pp: 99–112 (2008)
11. Grady, L.: Random walks for image segmentation. PAMI **28**(11), 1768–1783 (2006)
12. Menze, B.H., Jakab, A., Bauer, S., et al.: The multimodal brain tumor image segmentation benchmark (BRATS). IEEE Trans. Med. Imaging **34**(10), 1993–2024 (2014)
13. Zhou, B., Chen, L., Wang, Z.: Interactive deep editing framework for medical image segmentation. In: Shen, D., et al. (eds.) MICCAI 2019. LNCS, vol. 11766, pp. 329–337. Springer, Cham (2019). https://doi.org/10.1007/978-3-030-32248-9_37
14. Price, B.L., Morse, B., Cohen, S.: Geodesic graph cut for interactive image segmentation. In: 2010 IEEE Computer Society Conference on Computer Vision and Pattern Recognition, San Francisco, CA, pp. 3161–3168. IEEE (2010)
15. Xie, Y., Lu, H., Zhang, J., Shen, C., Xia, Y.: Deep segmentation-emendation model for gland instance segmentation. In: Shen, D., et al. (eds.) MICCAI 2019. LNCS, vol. 11764, pp. 469–477. Springer, Cham (2019). https://doi.org/10.1007/978-3-030-32239-7_52
16. Maaten, L.V.D., Hinton, G.: Visualizing data using t-SNE. J. Mach. Learn. Res. **9**(Nov), pp. 2579–2605 (2008)

A Novel fMRI Representation Learning Framework with GAN

Qinglin Dong[1], Ning Qiang[2], Jinglei Lv[3], Xiang Li[1,6], Liang Dong[5], Tianming Liu[4], and Quanzheng Li[1,6(✉)]

[1] Center for Advanced Medical Computing and Analysis, Department of Radiology, Massachusetts General Hospital and Harvard Medical School, Boston, MA, USA
li.quanzheng@mgh.harvard.edu
[2] School of Physics and Information Technology, Shaanxi Normal University, Xi'an, China
[3] School of Biomedical Engineering & Sydney Imaging, Brain and Mind Centre, The University of Sydney, Camperdown, Australia
[4] Cortical Architecture Imaging and Discovery Lab, Department of Computer Science and Bioimaging Research Center, The University of Georgia, Athens, GA, USA
[5] Google, Menlo Park, United States
[6] MGH & BWH Center for Clinical Data Science, Boston, MA, USA

Abstract. Modeling the mapping between mind and brain is the key towards understanding how brain works. More specifically, the question can be formatted as modeling the posterior distribution of the latent psychological state given the observed brain, and the likelihood of brain observation given the latent psychological state. Generative adversarial network (GAN) is known for learning implicitly distributions over data which are hard to model with an explicit likelihood. To utilize GAN for the brain mapping modeling, we propose a novel representation learning framework to explore brain representations of different functions. With a linear regression, the learned representations are interpreted as functional brain networks (FBNs), which characterize the mapping between mind and brain. The proposed framework is evaluated on Human Connectome Project (HCP) task functional MRI (tfMRI) data. This novel framework proves that GAN can learn meaningful representations of tfMRI and promises better understanding of the brain function.

Keywords: GAN · fMRI · Functional brain networks

1 Introduction

Among the many available imaging techniques, non-invasive brain imaging techniques are showing great promises to reveal the intrinsic functional architecture of the brain. Functional magnetic resonance imaging (fMRI) records spontaneous fluctuations in the brain, yielding blood oxygenation level dependent (BOLD) based data [1–9]. By revealing the synchronization of distant neural systems via correlations in neurophysiological

---

Q. Dong and N. Qiang – Equally contribution to this work.

© Springer Nature Switzerland AG 2020
M. Liu et al. (Eds.): MLMI 2020, LNCS 12436, pp. 21–29, 2020.
https://doi.org/10.1007/978-3-030-59861-7_3

measures of brain activity, functional brain networks (FBNs) have emerged as fundamental, organizational elements of human brain architecture [6–9]. Reconstruction and interpretation of FBNs from fMRI data, either resting state fMRI or task-based fMRI, has been under extensive active research in the past decade. In the neuroimaging and brain mapping communities, researchers have proposed a variety of computational methods and tools for brain network mapping. Among the data-driven methods, machine learning methodologies have played a central role in advancing both brain network reconstruction methods and their neuroscientific interpretations. These methods include general linear model (GLM) [4, 10], independent component analysis (ICA) [11–14] and sparse dictionary learning (SDL) [15–20].

Recently, deep learning has attracted much attention in the fields of machine learning and data mining and there have been growing bodies of literature that adopted deep learning models into fMRI data modeling and associated applications. However, two challenges emerged while the deep learning being applied to neuroimaging data. The first challenge is overfitting caused by data paucity. Considering the tremendous dimension of fMRI volumes, which can be more than 200K voxel per frame (MNI152 template) [21] and much more than a typical neuroimage dataset size, the overfitting can be serious. The second challenge is the lack of high-quality label. The fMRI data is unsupervised in nature since the psychological label is coarse-grained and no accurate frame-wise label is given, plus the complex co-activities of multiple intrinsic FBNs. Compared to discriminate models like convolutional neural networks (CNN) [22–24] and recurrent neural networks (RNN) [25, 26], generative models outperforms on smaller dataset and are promising to address the mentioned problems at the same time [27]. Deep generative models like variational autoencoder (VAE) and GAN have already been proposed to be applied to biomedical images [28–34] to solve the challenge of insufficient neuroimaging data, however, their powerful ability of representation learning is highly overlooked [30, 32, 34–36]. In the context of fMRI, an approximate posterior over the latent brain signal source is a physiological representation of fMRI data, more specifically, an FBN. In this paper, aiming to model the representations from fMRI data, a framework based on GAN is designed and the representation learned with the deep generative models is fully investigated.

2   Methods

The proposed computational framework is shown in Fig. 1. In Sect. 2.1, tfMRI data of all subjects are registered to a standard space and concatenated after preprocessing. In Sect. 2.2, a GAN model consists of a generator and a discriminator and is trained in an adversarial way. In Sect. 2.3, the GAN is trained layer-wisely on a large-scale task tfMRI dataset. The trained discriminator encodes representation of the real fMRI data and can be further interpreted as human brain function networks.

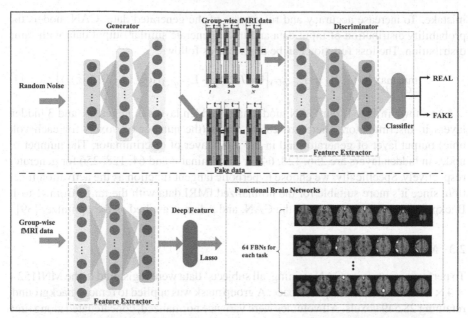

Fig. 1. Illustration of representing learning of tfMRI data by GAN. (a) Preprocessed fMRI volumes are temporally concatenated as input. (b) A GAN with 6 layers is trained with fMRI volumes, generating 64 features. (c) The feature extracted by the discriminator are visualized in the standard brain space.

2.1 Dataset and Preprocessing

The HCP task fMRI dataset is a systematic and comprehensive brain mapping collection of connectome-scale over a large population [37]. In the HCP Q3 public release, 900 subjects' tfMRI datasets are available. Among these 900 subjects, 35 are excluded from our experiment due to incomplete data of all tasks for consistency. In this paper, our experiments are based on the emotion task fMRI data of the HCP Q3's 865 subjects.

The acquisition parameters of emotion tfMRI data are as follows: 90×104 matrix, 220 mm FOV, 72 slices, TR = 0.72 s, TE = 33.1 ms, flip angle = 52°, BW = 2290 Hz/Px, in-plane FOV = 208×180 mm, 2.0 mm isotropic voxels. For tfMRI images, the preprocessing pipelines included skull removal, motion correction, slice time correction, spatial smoothing, global drift removal (high-pass filtering). These steps are implemented by FSL FEAT [38].

2.2 Generative Adversarial Networks (GAN)

In this paper, we take advantage of the advances in generative model and propose a novel framework based on GAN. GAN is a generative model trained with an adversarial process, in which we simultaneously train two models: a generative model G and a discriminative model D. The adversarial process corresponds to a minimax two-player game and the generator G is to maximize the probability of discriminator D making a mistake. To increase accuracy and robustness of the generated data, GAN models the probability distribution of input data and try to generate similar output data with same distribution. The loss function can be described as follows:

$$\min_{G} \max_{D} V(G, D) = E_{x \sim p(x)}\big[\log D(x)\big] + E_{z \sim q(z)}\big[\log(1 - D(G(z)))\big] \qquad (1)$$

As shown in Fig. 1, our GAN model has 3 hidden layers in generator and 3 hidden layers in discriminator. There are 28546 nodes (the number of voxels for each volume) output layer of generator and in the input layer of discriminator. The number of nodes in hidden layers are 256, 128, 64 for discriminator and 64, 128, 256 for generator respectively. Specifically, we choose hyperbolic tangent function as the activation function, since it's more suitable for the normalized fMRI data with the range from -1 to 1. Backpropagation is used to train the GAN, and Adam is applied as the optimizer [39].

2.3 Model Training

To perform group-wise GAN training, all subjects' data were registered to the MNI152 4 $\times$ 4 $\times$ 4 mm^3 standard template space. A group mask was applied to remove background, retaining 28,549 voxels. All volumes were variance normalized, concatenated along time dimension and shuffled. Each run of emotion processing consists of 176 frames, thus with 865 subjects it yields 152,250 volumes in total.

All hyperparameters of the three layers are set as the same. To start with training, the weights and biases are initialized from a Gaussian with zero-mean and a standard deviation of 0.01. To reduce overfitting and improve generalization, L1 regularization is applied to weight. In each iteration, the weight regularization is calculated, and its gradient is applied to update weights with a 0.1 weight decay rate. In the context of fMRI, L1 regularization also smooths the feature and improves interpretability.

To improve the gradient flow, the batch normalization technique is applied to each hidden layer, which explicitly forces the activations to be unit gaussian distributed. The volumes are divided into mini batches with a size of 5. Mini batches take the advantage of GPU boards better and accelerate training with a proper size. However, if the batch size is too large, it may end up with less efficiency or even not converging, unless learning rate is decreased even larger. With a learning rate of 0.001, full cohort of data is trained with 200 epochs for full convergence on one NVIDIA Quadro M4000 GPU.

2.4 GAN Derived FBNs

In this paper, the emotion task is investigated in which setting the participants are presented with blocks of trials that ask them to decide either which of two faces presented on the bottom of the screen match the face at the top of the screen, or which of two shapes presented at the bottom of the screen match the shape at the top of the screen. The faces have either angry or fearful expressions.

To explore the representation on the emotion task fMRI data, we apply Lasso regression to estimate sparse coefficient matrix which is used to build spatial maps. As shown in Fig. 1, the group-wise fMRI data X is fed into the trained encoder, yielding the latent variables Z is from the output of encoder. Next, the FBNs W are derived from latent variables and group-wise input via Lasso regression as follow:

$$W = min\|Z - XW\|_2^2 + \lambda\|W\|_1 \tag{2}$$

After Lasso regression, W is regularized and transposed to a coefficient matrix, then each row of coefficient matrix is mapped back to the original 3D brain image space, which is the inverse operation of masking in data preprocessing. Thus, 32 functional networks are generated and interpreted in a neuroanatomically meaningful context. All the functional networks are thresholded at $Z > 2.3$ after transformation into "Z-scores" across spatial volumes.

3 Results

3.1 Functional Brain Network Interpretation

By visual inspection, these networks can be well interpreted, and they agree with domain knowledge of functional network atlases in the literature, especially emotion network. To quantitatively evaluate the performance of GAN in modeling tfMRI data, a comparison study between GAN and GLM methods is provided in this section. The GLM-based activation detection result is performed individually using FSL FEAT and group-wise averaged. Task designs are convoluted with the double gamma hemodynamic response function and set as the repressors of GLM. The contrast-based statistical parametric mapping was carried out with T-test and $p < 0.05$ (with cluster correction) is used to reject false positives. All the functional networks are thresholded at $Z > 2.3$ after transformation into "Z-scores" across spatial volumes.

To compare the functional networks derived by these two methods, the spatial overlap rate is defined to measure the similarity of two spatial maps. The spatial similarity is defined by the overlap rate (OR) between two functional networks $N^{(1)}$ and $N^{(2)}$ as follows, where n is the volume size:

$$OR(N^{(1)}, N^{(2)}) = \frac{\sum_{i=1}^{n}|N_i^{(1)} \cap N_i^{(2)}|}{\sum_{i=1}^{n}|N_i^{(1)} \cup N_i^{(2)}|} \tag{3}$$

With the similarity measure defined above, the similarities $OR(N_{GAN}, N_{GLM})$ between the GAN derived functional networks N_{GAN} and the GLM derived functional networks N_{GLM} are quantitatively measured. Comparisons of pairs by these two methods are shown in Fig. 4 and Fig. 5, and the quantitative overlap rate numbers are shown in the O/R columns. This result demonstrated that GAN could identify GLM-derived networks very well, suggesting the effectiveness and meaningfulness of our GAN model (Fig. 2).

Emotion Task-Fear Activation

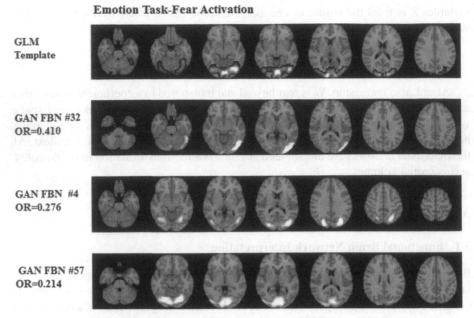

Fig. 2. Illustration of task related networks out of the 64 GAN-derived networks. The overlap rate (OR) shows the similarities between the GAN derived networks and the GLM derived network template (benchmark).

3.2 Intrinsic FBNs from GAN

In our experiment results, it is also observed that the intrinsic FBNs is continuously dynamically active even when subjects are doing task, which provides evidence supporting the conclusion in [3]. With the similarity measure defined above, the similarities $OR(N_{GAN}, N_{RSN})$ between the GAN derived functional networks N_{GAN} and functional template networks N_{RSN} from [3] are quantitatively measured. Comparisons of pairs of N_{GAN} and N_{RSN} are shown in Fig. 3, and the quantitative overlap rate numbers are shown on the sides. The first network includes supplementary motor area, sensorimotor cortex, and secondary somatosensory cortex, which suggests that inspired by the emotion, the subjects may have given rise to potential motor imagination. The second network includes several medial–frontal areas, including anterior cingulate and para cingulate, suggesting that inhibition, emotion or perception may be invoked. The third network includes the superior temporal gyrus, Heschl's gyrus, and posterior insular, which suggests that the auditory function is activated during the task. The fourth network includes medial, occipital pole, and lateral visual areas, which corresponds to the visual processing activity in the experiment.

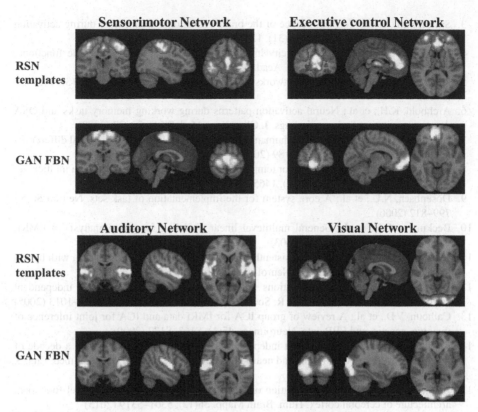

Fig. 3. Some illustrative pairs of networks showing he similarities between the GAN derived functional networks and the resting state network (RSN) template measured with overlap rate.

4   Discussions

This paper is among the earliest studies that explore modeling fMRI with adversarial network, to our best knowledge. With a group-wise experiment on massive fMRI data, the proposed model shows its capability to learn functional network. A comparison study of GAN with GLM and RSN template showed that the networks learned by GAN are meaningful and can be well interpreted. One limitation of our current approach is that vanilla GAN is also known for hard to train and the Wasserstein GAN (WGAN) [40] can help relieve the problem. One promising future study is to apply the encoder representation and corresponding functional connectivity as biomarkers to brain disorder identification such as Alzheimer's disease, ADHD, Autism, etc.

References

1. Huettel, S.A., et al.: Functional Magnetic Resonance Imaging, vol. 1. Sinauer Associates Sunderland, MA (2004)
2. Shimony, J.S., et al.: Resting-state spontaneous fluctuations in brain activity: a new paradigm for presurgical planning using fMRI. Acad. Radiol. **16**(5), 578–583 (2009)

3. Smith, S.M., et al.: Correspondence of the brain's functional architecture during activation and rest. Proc. Nat. Acad. Sci. **106**(31), 13040–13045 (2009)
4. Kanwisher, N.: Functional specificity in the human brain: a window into the functional architecture of the mind. Proc. Nat. Acad. Sci. **107**(25), 11163–11170 (2010)
5. Pessoa, L.: Understanding brain networks and brain organization. Phys. Rev. **11**(3), 400–435 (2014)
6. Archbold, K.H., et al.: Neural activation patterns during working memory tasks and OSA disease severity: preliminary findings. J. Clin. Sleep Med. **5**(01), 21–27 (2009)
7. Barch, D.M., et al.: Function in the human connectome: task-fMRI and individual differences in behavior. Neuroimage **80**, 169–189 (2013)
8. Binder, J.R., et al.: Mapping anterior temporal lobe language areas with fMRI: a multicenter normative study. Neuroimage **54**(2), 1465–1475 (2011)
9. Dosenbach, N.U., et al.: A core system for the implementation of task sets. Neuron **50**(5), 799–812 (2006)
10. Beckmann, C.F., et al.: General multilevel linear modeling for group analysis in FMRI. Neuroimage **20**(2), 1052–1063 (2003)
11. McKeown, M.J.: Detection of consistently task-related activations in fMRI data with hybrid independent component analysis. NeuroImage **11**(1), 24–35 (2000)
12. Beckmann, C.F., et al.: Investigations into resting-state connectivity using independent component analysis. Philos. Trans. R. Soc. Lond. B Biol. Sci. **360**(1457), 1001–1013 (2005)
13. Calhoun, V.D., et al.: A review of group ICA for fMRI data and ICA for joint inference of imaging, genetic, and ERP data. Neuroimage **45**(1), S163–S172 (2009)
14. Calhoun, V.D., et al.: Multisubject independent component analysis of fMRI: a decade of intrinsic networks, default mode, and neurodiagnostic discovery. IEEE Rev. Biomed. Eng. **5**, 60–73 (2012)
15. Jiang, X., et al.: Sparse representation of HCP grayordinate data reveals novel functional architecture of cerebral cortex. Hum. Brain Mapp. **36**(12), 5301–5319 (2015)
16. Lv, J., et al.: Holistic atlases of functional networks and interactions reveal reciprocal organizational architecture of cortical function. IEEE Trans. Biomed. Eng. **62**(4), 1120–1131 (2015)
17. Li, X., et al.: Multple-demand system identification and characterization via sparse representations of fMRI data. In: Biomedical Imaging (ISBI), 2016 IEEE 13th International Symposium on. IEEE (2016)
18. Ge, F., et al.: Exploring intrinsic networks and their interactions using group wise temporal sparse coding. In: Biomedical Imaging (ISBI 2018), 2018 IEEE 15th International Symposium on. IEEE (2018)
19. Ge, F., et al.: Deriving ADHD biomarkers with sparse coding based network analysis. In: 2015 IEEE 12th International Symposium on Biomedical Imaging (ISBI). IEEE (2015)
20. Zhao, Y., et al.: Connectome-scale group-wise consistent resting-state network analysis in autism spectrum disorder. NeuroImage Clin. **12**, 23–33 (2016)
21. Grabner, G., Janke, A.L., Budge, M.M., Smith, D., Pruessner, J., Collins, D.L.: Symmetric atlasing and model based segmentation: an application to the hippocampus in older adults. In: Larsen, R., Nielsen, M., Sporring, J. (eds.) MICCAI 2006. LNCS, vol. 4191, pp. 58–66. Springer, Heidelberg (2006). https://doi.org/10.1007/11866763_8
22. Huang, H., et al.: Modeling task fMRI data via mixture of deep expert networks. In: Biomedical Imaging (ISBI 2018), 2018 IEEE 15th International Symposium on. IEEE (2018)
23. Huang, H., et al.: Modeling task fMRI data via deep convolutional autoencoder. IEEE Trans. Med. Imaging **37**(7), 1551–1561 (2018)
24. Zhao, Y., et al.: 4D modeling of fMRI data via spatio-temporal convolutional neural networks (ST-CNN). In: IEEE Transactions on Cognitive and Developmental Systems. IEEE (2019)

25. Li, Q., et al.: Simultaneous spatial-temporal decomposition of connectome-scale brain networks by deep sparse recurrent auto-encoders. In: Chung, A.C.S., Gee, J.C., Yushkevich, P.A., Bao, S. (eds.) IPMI 2019. LNCS, vol. 11492, pp. 579–591. Springer, Cham (2019). https://doi.org/10.1007/978-3-030-20351-1_45
26. Wang, H., et al.: Recognizing brain states using deep sparse recurrent neural network. In: IEEE transactions on medical imaging. IEEE (2018)
27. Ng, A.Y., et al.: On discriminative vs. generative classifiers: a comparison of logistic regression and naive bayes. In: Advances in neural information processing systems, (2002)
28. Calimeri, F., Marzullo, A., Stamile, C., Terracina, G.: Biomedical data augmentation using generative adversarial neural networks. In: Lintas, A., Rovetta, S., Verschure, P.F.M.J., Villa, A.E.P. (eds.) ICANN 2017. LNCS, vol. 10614, pp. 626–634. Springer, Cham (2017). https://doi.org/10.1007/978-3-319-68612-7_71
29. Nie, Dong., et al.: Medical image synthesis with context-aware generative adversarial networks. In: Descoteaux, M., Maier-Hein, L., Franz, A., Jannin, P., Collins, D.L., Duchesne, S. (eds.) MICCAI 2017. LNCS, vol. 10435, pp. 417–425. Springer, Cham (2017). https://doi.org/10.1007/978-3-319-66179-7_48
30. Chen, X., et al.: Infogan: interpretable representation learning by information maximizing generative adversarial nets. In: Advances in neural information processing systems, (2016)
31. Costa, P., et al.: Towards adversarial retinal image synthesis. arXiv preprint, (2017) arXiv:1701.08974
32. Dimsdale-Zucker, H.R., et al.: Representational similarity analyses: a practical guide for functional MRI applications. In: Handbook of Behavioral Neuroscience, Elsevier. pp. 509–525 (2019)
33. Guibas, J.T., et al.: Synthetic medical images from dual generative adversarial networks. arXiv preprint, (2017) arXiv:1709.01872
34. Radford, A., et al.: Unsupervised representation learning with deep convolutional generative adversarial networks. (2015)
35. Bengio, Y., et al.: Representation learning: a review and new perspectives. **35**(8), 1798–1828 (2013)
36. Bengio, Y., et al.: Representation learning: a review and new perspectives. IEEE Trans. Pattern Anal. Mach. Intell. **35**(8), 1798–1828 (2013)
37. Barch, D.M., et al.: Function in the human connectome: task-fMRI and individual differences in behavior. Neuroimage **80**, 169–189 (2013)
38. Jenkinson, M., et al.: Fsl. Neuroimage **62**(2), 782–790 (2012)
39. Kingma, D.P., et al.: Adam: a method for stochastic optimization. arXiv preprint, (2014) arXiv:1412.6980
40. Arjovsky, M., et al.: Wasserstein gan, (2017)

Semi-supervised Segmentation with Self-training Based on Quality Estimation and Refinement

Zhou Zheng[1], Xiaoxia Wang[2], Xiaoyun Zhang[1(✉)], Yumin Zhong[2(✉)], Xiaofen Yao[2], Ya Zhang[1], and Yanfeng Wang[1]

[1] Cooperative Medianet Innovation Center, Shanghai Jiao Yong University, Shanghai, China
xiaoyun.zhang@sjtu.edu.cn
[2] Shanghai Children's Medical Center, Shanghai, China
zhongyumin@scmc.com.cn

Abstract. Building a large dataset with high-quality annotations for medical image segmentation is time-consuming and highly depends on expert knowledge. Therefore semi-supervised segmentation has been investigated by utilizing a small set of labeled data and a large set of unlabeled data with generated pseudo labels, but the quality of pseudo labels is crucial since bad labels may lead to even worse segmentation. In this paper, we propose a novel semi-supervised segmentation framework which can automatically estimate and refine the quality of pseudo labels, and select only those good samples to expand the training set for self-training. Specifically the quality is automatically estimated in the view of shape and semantic confidence using variational auto-encoder (VAE) and CNN based network. And, the selected labels are refined in an adversarial way by distinguishing whether a label is the ground truth mask or not at pixel level. Our method is evaluated on the established neuroblastoma(NB) and BraTS18 dataset and outperforms other state-of-the-art semi-supervised medical image segmentation methods. We can achieve a fully supervised performance while requiring ∼4x less annotation effort.

Keywords: Medical image segmentation · Semi-supervised learning · Quality estimation and refinement

1 Introduction

Recently, deep Fully Convolutional Neural networks (FCN) [1] have gained much popularity in the medical image segmentation because of its ability to learn the most discriminative pixel-wise features. Based on the encoder-decoder structure of FCN, U-Net [2] proposes a skip connection between the encoder and decoder layers which can utilize the low level features to improve the segmentation. However, supervised learning requires laborious pixel-level annotation which is very

© Springer Nature Switzerland AG 2020
M. Liu et al. (Eds.): MLMI 2020, LNCS 12436, pp. 30–39, 2020.
https://doi.org/10.1007/978-3-030-59861-7_4

time-consuming and needs expert knowledge. In practice, usually only a small set of data with pixel-level annotations are affordable while most of the data left unlabeled. Semi-supervised learning(SSL) aims to solve this challenge by exploring the potential of unlabeled data to improve the performance of a segmentation model.

Because of the characteristics of fuzzy texture structure, low-contrast intensity and limited amount of data, medical image segmentation is extremely challenging in learning based semi-supervised setting, and some methods have been proposed to address the problem. The work in [3,4] have explored the consistency of transformation between labeled and unlabeled data, where a consistency loss is incorporated into the loss function and provides regularization for training the network. Another direction in semi-supervised segmentation is co-training [5–7], which tries to improve segmentation with the assistance of other auxiliary tasks. Also, transfer learning is adopted in semi-supervised segmentation such as [8,9] by employing external labeled data sets via domain adaption.

One practical direction for semi-supervised learning is self-training [10] which is the earliest SSL approach and became popular in deep learning schemes [15, 16]. In this setting, after finishing the supervised training stage of a segmentation model, it is possible to continue the learning process on new unlabeled data by creating pseudo labels for the unlabeled data. However, the quality of the generated pseudo labels is not guaranteed for retraining the segmentation model, which limits their potential for improvements from the data with pseudo label and sometimes even makes the updated model worse. The work in [11] just selects the confident region in the segmentation map to train the network which focuses more on the background area and ignores the tumor region. Such method can limit the negative impact of bad pseudo labels but it can not make full use of the unlabeled data.

In this paper, we propose a novel self-training method which can automatically estimate and refine the quality of pseudo labels, and select only those good samples to expand the data set for retraining the segmentation network. The quality of the pseudo label is estimated from the view of shape confidence and semantic confidence. The former estimates the shape matching between the prediction map and the label mask, while the latter evaluates the semantic matching between the prediction map and the raw image. By ranking the quality of the predicted segmentation, we choose the top K samples as the pseudo labels. In considering that the selected pseudo labels may still have some obvious mis-segmentation for possible improvement, we further refine the label in an adversarial way by distinguishing whether it is the ground truth mask or not at pixel level. After quality estimation and refinement, the samples with good quality pseudo labels are added to expand the training set, which is then utilized to retrain and update the segmentation network. This process can be iterated until to a satisfied result. In addition, the refinement network can also be employed during inference to obtain a refined and better segmentation.

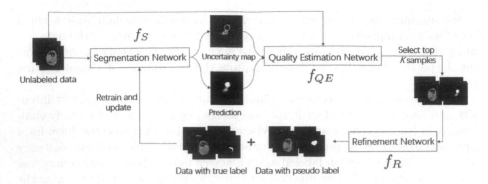

Fig. 1. Overview of the architecture of our proposed semi-supervised approach.

In this work, our contributions can be summarized as follows:

- We propose a novel semi-supervised segmentation method which can automatically estimate the quality of a segmentation and refine it in an adversarial way. Then a segmentation model can be retrained by the expanded dataset with the selected good pseudo labels in a self-training way.
- We design a robust quality estimation network by estimating the shape confidence and the semantic confidence with Variational Auto-encoder(VAE) and VGG [12] based network. Also, a refinement network is proposed to refine the generated pseudo label for higher quality expanded dataset.
- We establish a neuroblastoma segmentation dataset which contains 430 cases of young children's CT with manually-annotated label by doctors. Experiments on NB and BraTS18 dataset demonstrate the robustness and effectiveness of our method compared to other semi-supervised methods.

2 Method

2.1 Overview

The overview structure of our proposed framework is shown in Fig. 1 which consists of three modules: segmentation f_S, quality estimation f_{QE} and refinement f_R.

Given a set of labeled data $X_L = \{x_L^1, x_L^2, ..., x_L^m\}$ with corresponding label $Y_L = \{y_1, y_2, ..., y_m\}$ and a large set of unlabeled data $X_U = \{x_U^1, x_U^2, ..., x_U^n\}$, we can generate pseudo label Y_U' and uncertainty map U for X_U with f_S. However, the quality of generated pseudo label Y_U' is not guaranteed for retraining the segmentation model. The addition of good quality training data can improve the performance of the segmentation model greatly so we need to filter the pseudo label Y_U' to ensure that the model can obtain a high-quality subset Y_{sub}' and X_{sub}' to expand the training data. To this end, we design a quality estimation module f_{QE} which can provide a reliable estimation about the quality of the pseudo label Y'_U. In considering that the selected pseudo labels may still have some obvious mis-segmentation for possible improvement, we introduce a refinement module f_R to refine the pseudo labels Y'_{sub} in an adversarial way. Our goal is to retrain the segmentation model f_S from training data $X_T = X_L \cup X'_{sub}$, training label $Y_T = Y_L \cup Y'_{sub}$ in a self-training way. We repeat the above steps till to obtain a final model f_S with expected results.

2.2   Network Architecture and Loss Functions

Quality Estimation Module: A segmentation network is very vulnerable to the quality and quantity of annotations as it implements segmentation at pixel level. This quality estimation module can provide a reliable estimation about the quality of the predicted segmentation or the pseudo label Y'_U so we can use it to select a subset Y'_{sub} of Y'_U to expand the training dataset.

We consider the quality of the pseudo label from the view of shape confidence and semantic confidence. As shown in Fig. 2(a), we utilize a VAE for shape representation learning where the encoder learns a low dimensional space for the underlying distribution of the shape prior such as the continuity and boundary smoothness etc. We utilize the latent vector z to distinguish whether it is the real mask or the prediction map in order to provide a shape confidence of the prediction map.

We also introduce the semantic confidence network which looks into the relationship between the prediction map and its surrounding tissue to evaluate the semantic matching between the prediction map and the input image. Besides the original image and the segmentation map, we also feed the semantic confidence network with the uncertainty map U produced by the segmentation network to provide it with information about the uncertainty region in the segmentation map. VGG16 [12] is the backbone architecture of the semantic confidence network.

We then fuse the shape and semantic confidence to form the final quality by several FC layers. We adopt mean absolute error loss L_q, binary cross entropy loss L_d and mean square error loss L_{vae} to train the semantic and fusion branch, discriminator and VAE respectively.

$$L_q = |q - y| \tag{1}$$

$$L_d = -(y_z \log(D(z)) + (1 - y_z) \log(1 - D(z))) \tag{2}$$

$$L_{vae} = \sum |x'_i - x_i| + KL(p(z|x)\|q(z)) \tag{3}$$

Where q is the quality output, y is the true DSC, z is the latent vector of the VAE and y_z is $\{0,1\}$ where 0 for prediction and 1 for label, x_i and x'_i is the input and reconstruction data, $q(z) \sim N(0, I)$.

Refinement Module: The selected pseudo labels may still have some obvious mis-segmentation, so we design a refinement module to refine the pseudo labels in

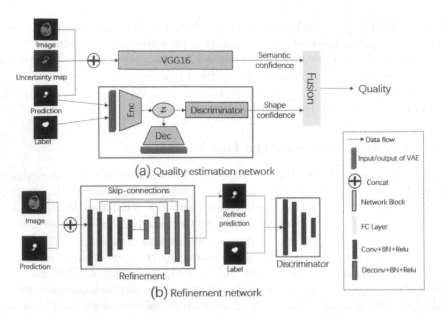

(a) Quality estimation network

(b) Refinement network

Fig. 2. (a) Quality estimation network consists of two branches. One is to estimate the shape matching by distinguish the latent vector z of prediction and label while reconstructing them, the other is to estimate the semantic matching between the prediction and the image from VGG16. Two confidences are fused by FC layers to form the estimated quality. (b) Refinement network is to improve the prediction by adversarial learning.

an adversarial way as shown in Fig. 2(b). Our generator utilizes the U-Net [2] as the backbone and takes the original image and the corresponding segmentation map as input and outputs a refined map. Different from the typical discriminator which discriminates the map at the image level, we propose a fully convolutional discriminator like [13] that learns to differentiate the predicted probability maps from the ground truth segmentation distribution at pixel level.

We train the refinement network f_R by minimizing a weighted joint of binary cross entropy and adversarial loss L_r:

$$L_r = -((y_i \log(f_R(x_i)) + (1 - y_i) \log(1 - f_R(x_i))) + \lambda L_{adv}) \tag{4}$$

$$L_{adv} = \mathbb{E}_{y_i \sim Y}[\log(D(y_i))] + \mathbb{E}_{y_i' \sim Y'}[\log(1 - D(y_i'))] \tag{5}$$

where L_{adv} is the adversarial loss, λ is the weighted coefficient.

Segmentation Module: The architecture of the segmentation module is same to U-Net [2] which has skip-connections, allowing the transfer of low-level features from the encoder to the decoder. It accepts the image and produces a segmentation probability map with an uncertainty map which is sent to the quality estimation network f_{QE}. The objective function L_s of this module is a sum of binary cross entropy L_{bce} and the Kullback–Leibler divergence loss L_{kl} which can provide a distribution constraint between mask Y and prediction P.

$$L_{bce} = -(y_i \log(f_S(x_i)) + (1 - y_i) \log(1 - (f_S(x_i)))) \quad (6)$$

$$L_{kl} = y_i * (log(y_i/p_i)) \quad (7)$$

$$L_s = L_{bce} + L_{kl} \quad (8)$$

The output uncertainty map $U = \{u_i\}$ is obtained from the prediction map P by calculating the margin between the positive and negative probability $u_i = 1 - |p_i - (1 - p_i)|$, where p_i is the predicted probability for pixel x_i.

2.3 Training Strategy

Our entire algorithm is summarized in Algorithm 1. To improve the performance of our core quality estimation module f_{QE}, we can pre-train it on any public datasets and tranfer it to our target dataset. The training of f_{QE} follows that the VAE and discriminator are firstly trained with L_{vae} and L_d respectively, and then train the CNN network and fusion layers with L_q by fixing the VAE and discriminator.

Algorithm 1. Training process of our method.

Step 1: Pre-train f_{QE} with any public datasets.

Step 2: Train f_S, f_R and fine-tune f_{QE} with labeled data X_L, Y_L by Eq.1 – Eq.8.

Step 3: Generate pseudo label Y'_U for X_U with f_S. Select a subset Y'_{sub} and refine it by f_{QE} and f_R respectively.

Step 4: Expand train dataset $X_T = X_L + X'_{sub}$, $Y_T = Y_L + Y'_{sub}$. Retrain and update f_S with X_T, Y_T.

Step 5: Repeat step 3 and step 4 for several iterations.

---

3 Experiment Results

3.1 Dataset and Implementation Details

NB Dataset: We establish a neuroblastoma segmentation dataset which consists of 430 CT scans of children, with a manually-annotated label by expert doctors from **Shanghai Children's Medical Center**. The dataset is divided into two parts: training set (344 cases) and testing set (86 cases). The intra-slices resolution is 512×512, and the number of slices varies from 67 to 395 and the voxel size is $0.49 \times 0.49 \times 1.24mm^3$ in average.

BraTS18 Dataset [17]: 210(train:160, test:50) MRI scans from patients with high grade glioma and 75(train:60, test:15) MRI scans from patients with low grade glioma are split into training set and testing set. To simplify comparison between different segmentation methods, we perform binary classification and segment only the whole tumor with the FLAIR sequence.

Table 1. Experiment results on NB dataset by different methods.

Labeled (unlabeled)	33(311)			106(238)			169(175)			344(0)		
Methods	DSC	HD	ASD	DSC	HD	ASD	DSC	HD	ASD	DSC	HD	ASD
U-Net	54.76	24.49	3.54	68.21	17.69	0.82	71.85	16.65	0.88	77.91	14.09	0.80
MASSL [5]	63.94	18.53	1.67	72.72	17.41	1.07	74.92	14.88	0.84	-	-	-
ASDNet [11]	65.39	21.01	1.43	72.93	17.47	1.41	75.88	14.45	0.66	-	-	-
TCSM [4]	68.15	17.55	1.12	73.09	17.31	1.08	76.70	13.98	0.81	-	-	-
Ours	**71.79**	**17.46**	**1.09**	**77.64**	**15.13**	**0.78**	**80.01**	**13.44**	**0.61**	-	-	-

Implementation Details: The proposed method is implemented on a NVIDIA GeForce GTX1080Ti GPU in Keras [14]. The adaptive moment estimation optimizer(ADAM) and weight decay are used. The initial learning rate is set to be 0.001, 0.0001 and 0.001 for segmentation module and quality estimation module and refinement module respectively. The coefficient λ is set to be 1 and the number of iterations is 3 in our experiment as the results remain stable when the number of iteration is greater than 3 so we just set it to be 3 for simplicity. In our experiment, K has an important impact on the results. If K is too small, the selected data with pseudo label won't be enough. If K is too large, it will lead to an increase of low-quality data with pseudo labels, so we set K to be 50% for balance. When segmenting NB(BraTS18) dataset, we pre-train f_{QE} on BraTS18(NB) dataset.

3.2   Quantitative and Qualitative Analysis

Metrics: Dice Similarity Coefficient (DSC), Hausdorff Distance(HD) and Average Surface Distance (ASD) are used as the evaluation metrics. For fair comparison, 5-fold cross validation is employed.

We compare with the backbone U-Net [2] and other state-of-the-art semi-supervised segmentation methods TCSM [4], MASSL [5], ASDNet [11]. Some methods are not originally used for binary segmentation and we re-implement all above methods and apply them to our experiment dataset. In Table 1, our methods can outperform other methods at least 3.64%, 4.55% and 3.31% in DSC with 10%, 30%, 50% of labeled data. Besides using quality estimation to guarantee the quality of the pseudo label, the refinement module is reused in the inference to get a better result and Kullback–Leibler divergence is adopted in the loss function which is proved effective in segmentation, so we can achieve a competing performance with only 106 labelled data to a fully supervised model with 344 labelled data.

We further investigate the robustness of our proposed semi-supervised segmentation algorithm on BraTS18 dataset. In Table 2, we achieve a DSC of 78.03%, 80.31% and 80.61% with 20, 50 and 110 labeled data, with obvious margin compared with other methods. Futhermore, we can reach a fully supervised performance with only 50 labeled data.

Table 2. Experiment results on BraTS18 dataset by different methods.

Labeled (unlabeled)	20(200)			50(170)			110(110)			220(0)		
Methods	DSC	HD	ASD	DSC	HD	ASD	DSC	HD	ASD	DSC	HD	ASD
U-Net	70.17	17.99	2.46	72.82	17.77	2.39	74.42	17.59	2.17	80.28	15.38	1.97
MASSL [5]	76.35	19.97	2.82	77.34	17.36	2.44	78.26	16.32	1.88	-	-	-
ASDNet [11]	75.47	17.59	2.75	77.18	18.20	2.32	78.59	15.10	2.21	-	-	-
TCSM [4]	74.25	17.58	**2.01**	78.24	15.34	1.88	79.41	15.86	**1.38**	-	-	-
Ours	**78.03**	**15.47**	2.24	**80.31**	**14.74**	**1.75**	**80.61**	**14.68**	1.59	-	-	-

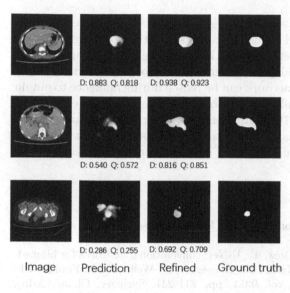

D: 0.883 Q: 0.818   D: 0.938 Q: 0.923

D: 0.540 Q: 0.572   D: 0.816 Q: 0.851

D: 0.286 Q: 0.255   D: 0.692 Q: 0.709

Image   Prediction   Refined   Ground truth

Fig. 3. Visual results of quality estimation and refinement on NB dataset(D: DSC Q: Estimated Quality).

Table 3. Ablation study of our method on NB and BraTS18 dataset with 169 and 110 labeled data. We evaluate the efficiency of each component in our method (Selecting strategy, shape confidence branch, semantic confidence branch and refinement module).

Data	NB	BraTS18
Methods	DSC	DSC
U-Net	71.85	74.42
U-Net+All unlabeled without selection	69.87	72.93
U-Net+random 50% selection	70.56	73.75
U-Net+Shape	75.94	77.69
U-Net+Shape+ Semantic	78.13	79.05
U-Net+Shape+ Semantic+Refinement	**80.01**	**80.61**

Visual results on NB dataset are also presented in Fig. 3, which illustrates the effectiveness of the quality estimation and refinement modules. The second and third column indicate that the refinement module can produce a better prediction with higher DSC and more accurate segmentation. The DSC and Quality under the prediction and refined prediction show the quality estimation module can provide a reliable quality with less than 10% estimation error.

Ablation Study: We analyze the efficiency of each component in our proposed method by performing five ablation studies on NB and BraTS18 dataset as Table 3 shows. First, we examine the effect of using all unlabeled data and randomly selecting 50% of unlabeled data with pseudo labels to expand the training set. From the fourth and fifth row of the table, the DSC even decreases to 69.87%, 70.56% from 71.85% in NB and 72.93%, 73.75% from 74.42% in BraTS18 for many low-quality pseudo labels have been added to the train set. Then we analyse the performance of the shape confidence branch, semantic confidence branch and refinement module. We can see the DSC increases to 75.94%, 78.13%, 80.01% in NB and 77.69%, 79.05%, 80.61% in BraTS18 respectively. The results show that the quality estimation module has the greatest improvement on the proposed framework.

4   Conclusion

In this paper, we propose a novel semi-supervised segmentation with self-training based on quality estimation and refinement. We select the good segmentation samples to expand the training set by estimating their quality and refine them in an adversarial way by distinguishing the generated pseudo label with the ground truth. Moreover, the refinement network can be reused during inference to obtain more accurate segmentation result. Our method is evaluated on the established neuroblastoma(NB) and BraTS18 dataset and outperforms other state-of-the-art semi-supervised medical image segmentation methods. We can achieve a fully supervised performance while requiring ∼4x less annotation effort.

References

1. Long, J., et al.: Fully convolutional networks for semantic segmentation. In: CVPR, pp. 3431–3440 (2015)
2. Ronneberger, O., Fischer, P., Brox, T.: U-Net: convolutional networks for biomedical image segmentation. In: Navab, N., Hornegger, J., Wells, W.M., Frangi, A.F. (eds.) MICCAI 2015. LNCS, vol. 9351, pp. 234–241. Springer, Cham (2015). https://doi.org/10.1007/978-3-319-24574-4_28
3. Baur, C., Albarqouni, S., Navab, N.: Semi-supervised deep learning for fully convolutional networks. In: Descoteaux, M., Maier-Hein, L., Franz, A., Jannin, P., Collins, D.L., Duchesne, S. (eds.) MICCAI 2017. LNCS, vol. 10435, pp. 311–319. Springer, Cham (2017). https://doi.org/10.1007/978-3-319-66179-7_36
4. Li, X., et al.: Transformation consistent self-ensembling model for semi-supervised medical image segmentation. arXiv preprint (2019). arXiv:1903.00348
5. Chen, S., Bortsova, G., García-Uceda Juárez, A., van Tulder, G., de Bruijne, M.: Multi-task attention-based semi-supervised learning for medical image segmentation. In: Shen, D., et al. (eds.) MICCAI 2019. LNCS, vol. 11766, pp. 457–465. Springer, Cham (2019). https://doi.org/10.1007/978-3-030-32248-9_51
6. Peng, J., et al.: Deep co-training for semi-supervised image segmentation. arXiv preprint (2019). arXiv:1903.11233
7. Zhou, Y., Wang, Y., et al.: Semi-supervised multi-organ segmentation via multi-planar co-training. arXiv preprint (2018). arXiv:1804.02586
8. Fu, Y., et al.: More unlabelled data or label more data? a study on semi-supervised laparoscopic image segmentation. In: Wang, Q., et al. (eds.) DART/MIL3ID -2019. LNCS, vol. 11795, pp. 173–180. Springer, Cham (2019). https://doi.org/10.1007/978-3-030-33391-1_20

9. Cui, W., et al.: Semi-supervised brain lesion segmentation with an adapted mean teacher model. In: Chung, A.C.S., Gee, J.C., Yushkevich, P.A., Bao, S. (eds.) IPMI 2019. LNCS, vol. 11492, pp. 554–565. Springer, Cham (2019). https://doi.org/10. 1007/978-3-030-20351-1_43
10. You, X., Peng, Q., Yuan, Y., Cheung, Y.M., Lei, J.: Segmentation of retinal blood vessels using the radial projection and semi-supervised approach. Pattern Recognit. **44**(10–11), 2314–2324 (2011)
11. Nie, D., Gao, Y., Wang, L., Shen, D.: ASDNet: attention based semi-supervised deep networks for medical image segmentation. In: Frangi, A.F., Schnabel, J.A., Davatzikos, C., Alberola-López, C., Fichtinger, G. (eds.) MICCAI 2018. LNCS, vol. 11073, pp. 370–378. Springer, Cham (2018). https://doi.org/10.1007/978-3-030-00937-3_43
12. Simonyan, K., Zisserman, A.: Very deep convolutional networks for large-scale image recognition. arXiv preprint (2014). arXiv:1409.1556
13. Hung, W.-C., et al.: Adversarial learning for semi-supervised semantic segmentation. arXiv preprint (2018). arXiv:1802.07934
14. Keras: Deep learning library for theano and tensorflow (2015). http://keras.io
15. Zhang, Y., Yang, L., Chen, J., Fredericksen, M., Hughes, D.P., Chen, D.Z.: Deep adversarial networks for biomedical image segmentation utilizing unannotated images. In: Descoteaux, M., Maier-Hein, L., Franz, A., Jannin, P., Collins, D.L., Duchesne, S. (eds.) MICCAI 2017. LNCS, vol. 10435, pp. 408–416. Springer, Cham (2017). https://doi.org/10.1007/978-3-319-66179-7_47
16. Radosavovic, I., Dollár, P., Girshick, R., Gkioxari, G., He, K.: Data distillation: towards omni-supervised learning. In: CVPR, pp. 4119–4128 (2018)
17. Menze, B.H., et al.: The multimodal brain tumor image segmentation benchmark (BRATS). IEEE TMI **34**(10), 1993–2024 (2015)

3D Segmentation Networks for Excessive Numbers of Classes: Distinct Bone Segmentation in Upper Bodies

Eva Schnider[1]([⊠]), Antal Horváth[1], Georg Rauter[1], Azhar Zam[1], Magdalena Müller-Gerbl[2], and Philippe C. Cattin[1]

[1] Department of Biomedical Engineering, University of Basel, Allschwil, Switzerland
{eva.schnider,antal.horvath,georg.rauter,azhar.zam,m.mueller-gerbl,
philippe.cattin}@unibas.ch
[2] Department of Biomedicine, Musculoskeletal Research, University of Basel, Basel, Switzerland

Abstract. Segmentation of distinct bones plays a crucial role in diagnosis, planning, navigation, and the assessment of bone metastasis. It supplies semantic knowledge to visualisation tools for the planning of surgical interventions and the education of health professionals. Fully supervised segmentation of 3D data using Deep Learning methods has been extensively studied for many tasks but is usually restricted to distinguishing only a handful of classes. With 125 distinct bones, our case includes many more labels than typical 3D segmentation tasks. For this reason, the direct adaptation of most established methods is not possible. This paper discusses the intricacies of training a 3D segmentation network in a many-label setting and shows necessary modifications in network architecture, loss function, and data augmentation. As a result, we demonstrate the robustness of our method by automatically segmenting over one hundred distinct bones simultaneously in an end-to-end learnt fashion from a CT-scan.

Keywords: 3D segmentation · Deep learning · Many label segmentation

1 Introduction

The segmentation of distinct bones from CT images is often performed as an intermediate or preprocessing task for planning and navigation purposes to provide semantic feedback to those systems. It is also crucial for the evaluation of the progress of bone diseases [7], or for the quantification of skeletal metastases [17]. In Virtual Reality (VR) tools [5,14], the distinct segmentation of bones permits more fine-grained control over rendered body parts and can serve an educational purpose by teaching skeletal anatomy. Due to its distinctive high Hounsfield unit (HU) values in CT images, cortical bone tissue can be segmented approximately using thresholding. However, random intensity variations and the relatively low HU value of squamous bones hinder accurate results [18].

© Springer Nature Switzerland AG 2020
M. Liu et al. (Eds.): MLMI 2020, LNCS 12436, pp. 40–49, 2020.
https://doi.org/10.1007/978-3-030-59861-7_5

For a precise segmentation, or the separation of individual bones, more elaborate methods are needed. For the analysis and segmentation of single bones, statistical shape or appearance models are applied [19,21,22]. For whole skeletons, atlas segmentations using articulated joints have been used in mice [1], and for human upper bodies [7]. A combination of shape models and convolutional neural networks (CNN) have been employed in [17] to segment almost fifty distinct bones. Their multi-step approach consists of an initial shape model corrected landmark detection, followed by a subsequent voxel-wise segmentation. Solely CNN based methods have been used for full-body bone tissue segmentation, without labelling of individual bones [13], and for segmentation of bones of groups, such as vertebrae [23]. To our knowledge, no simultaneous segmentation of all distinct bones of a human upper body by the use of CNNs has been published so far.

Fully automated methods driven by CNNs have shown great results for various tasks in medical image analysis. They excel at pathology detection [2,10,11] as well as at segmenting anatomical structures [9,16,20] for a wide array of body regions and in both 2D and 3D. In conjunction with data augmentation, good results have been reported even when training networks on as little as 1–3 fully annotated scans [3,4]. However, in typical 3D medical image segmentation tasks, distinctions are made for a handful or up to a dozen classes. Many established methods developed for a few classes fail when dealing with the over hundred classes for our particular case, or are not practical anymore due to restrictions in computational time and memory.

In this work, we present, which kinds of preprocessing, network choice, loss function and data augmentation schemes are suitable for 3D medical image segmentation with many labels at once, using the example of distinct bone segmentation in upper bodies. Our contributions are: 1) We discuss essential adaptions concerning network choice and data augmentation when performing 3D segmentation in a many-label setting. 2) We examine different sampling strategies and loss functions to mitigate the class imbalance. 3) We present results on a 3D segmentation task with over 100 classes, as depicted in Fig. 1.

2   Methods

Segmenting many classes simultaneously in 3D comes at a cost in computational space and time. In the following, we discuss how this affects and limits not only

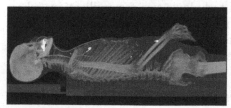

Fig. 1. Left: maximum intensity projection of one of our upper body CT-scans. Right: the manual target segmentation depicting 125 different bones with individual colours. (Color figure online)

the possibilities in network design but also renders certain loss functions and data augmentation schemes impractical. We present the methods that worked under the constraints imposed by the many-class task and rendered distinct bone segmentation from upper body CT scans possible.

2.1 Limitations Imposed by Many-Label 3D Segmentation Tasks

Limitations in computational resources, particularly in GPU RAM size, ask for a careful design of 3D segmentation networks. There are many existing architectures optimised for typical GPU memory sizes. They generally support input patches in the range of 64^3 px to 128^3 px and feature only few network layers at the costly full resolution – mainly input and classification layers. The full resolution classification layer becomes much bigger in the presence of a high number of classes N_c, since its size is given by $H \times W \times D \times N_c$, where H, W, and D represent the output patches' spatial dimensions.

One possibility to counter the computational challenges would be splitting of the task into different groups of bones and learning one network per group. Such an ensemble approach has its own downsides, however. There is much overhead needed to train not one, but many networks for the tasks. Apart from training, the added complexity also increases resources and time needed during inference [15]. Even if resorting to such an approach, both hands alone would sum up to 54 bones (sesamoid bones not included), and therefore considerations about simultaneous segmentation of many bones remain an issue.

2.2 Network Design

For the segmentation task, we use No-New-Net [10]. This modification of the standard 3D U-Net [4] achieves similar performance with less trainable parameters, thus increasing the possible size of input patches and allowing us to capture more global context for our task. We were able to use input and output patches of spatial size 96^3 px on a 8 GB, 128^3 px on a 12 GB, and of size 160^3 px on a 24 GB GPU. Even the latter is nowhere near the original size of our CT-scans, the extent of which is 512 px for the smallest dimension. The disparity between scan and patch size means that we can use only a minuscule part of the volume at once and consequently loose information on the global context and surrounding of the subvolume. However, using patches is akin to random cropping of the input and an established technique even for applications where the cropping is not necessary for GPU memory reasons. All in all, we have to balance the increasing information loss of extracting smaller volumes with the enhanced data augmentation effect of more aggressive cropping.

2.3 Fast Balancing Many-Class Segmentation Loss

As a consequence of the unusually large classification layer, any byte additionally spent for representing a single voxel label in the final prediction is amplified millionfold. Using a dense representation of the prediction instead of a sparse one will tip the balance easily towards an out-of-memory error. We thus use sparse representations of the class-wise predictions and ground truths for computation of the loss. To counter the high imbalance in the number of voxels per class, we use the multi-class cross-entropy loss in conjunction with a Dice similarity coefficient (DSC) loss over all classes $c \in C$: We chose to use an unweighted linear combination of the two, following the implementation given in [10]:

$$\mathcal{L}_{\text{X-Ent + DSC}} := \mathcal{L}_{\text{X-Ent}} + \sum_{c \in C} \mathcal{L}_{\text{DSC}}^c. \tag{1}$$

2.4 Resourceful Data Augmentation

We utilise various data augmentation techniques to increase the variety of data the network encounters during training. We use random sampling of the input patch locations in two flavours: Uniform random sampling returns every possible patch with the same probability. With balanced sampling, every class has the same probability of being present in the chosen subvolume. Balanced sampling results in high variability in the field of views of the (input) patches while asserting to repeatedly present all bones, even small ones, to the network.

Much like random cropping, many of the other prevalent techniques in 3D segmentation such as affine transformations, elastic deformations, and changes in brightness and contrast can be employed unhindered in the many-label setting. Contrarily, some augmentation schemes – notably MixUp [24] and its variants – work with dense labels and losses, thus causing tremendous inflation of the classification layer size and loss calculation time. We, therefore, omit the latter kind of data augmentation and concentrate on the first kind.

2.5 Implementation Details

Our experiments are built on top of the NiftyNet [8] implementation of the No-New-Net [10]. We modified the network architecture only in the number of channels of the classification layer, to account for the different amount of classes. We used the Leaky ReLU activation function with a leak factor of 0.02, and instance normalisation. In contrast to the No-New-Net publication [10], we were only able to fit a batch size of 1 due to the high memory demands of our many-class case. We optimised our networks using Adam [12] with a learning rate of 0.001 and ran 20 000 iterations of training.

3   Experiments

For lack of publicly available data sets with many-label distinct bone segmentation, our experiments are conducted on an in-house data set, consisting of five CT scans and their voxel-wise segmentation into 126 classes. To counter the low number of labelled images, we use 5-fold cross-validation throughout.

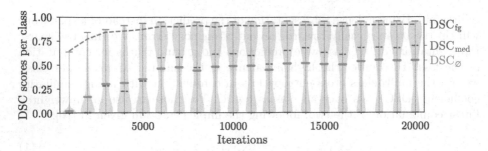

Fig. 2. Development of DSC scores (see subsect. 3.2) over the course of training. The distribution of per-class DSC scores is indicated by the violins (grey area). Additionally, the mean, median, and foreground DSC scores (3), are provided.

3.1 Data Set and Preprocessing

The five CT scans were taken and annotated by our university's anatomical department. The resulting voxel-wise segmentation consists of 126 classes – one for each kind of bone in the scans, plus background. The scans were taken from individual subjects aged 44–60, three of whom were female, two male. The field of view starts at the top of the skull and includes the area below until approximately mid-femur. All subjects lie on their backs, arms either resting on the lap or crossed over the stomach, a posture variation that makes the segmentation task harder. The size of each scan was $512 \times 512 \times H$, where the value of H ranges from 656 to 1001. In-plane resolutions vary from $0.83\,\text{mm} \times 0.83\,\text{mm}$ to $0.97\,\text{mm} \times 0.97\,\text{mm}$ while inter-plane spacing ranges from 1.0 mm to 1.5 mm.

To be able to capture more body context within an input patch, we resampled our data to 2 mm per dimension – approximately half the original resolution – resulting in volumes of $214 - 252 \times 215 - 252 \times 477 - 514$. We used bilinear interpolation for the scans and nearest neighbour interpolation for the label volume.

3.2 Evaluation

To evaluate the network's ability to correctly label and delineate each bone, we use the DSC of individual classes c in all our experiments: $\text{DSC}_c = \frac{2|P_c \odot G_c|}{|P_c| + |G_c|}$, where P_c and G_c represent the pixel-wise binary form of the prediction of class c and the corresponding ground truth. To obtain a combined score for a whole group of bones over all cross-validation sets, we provide the median DSC. We furthermore provide the distance from the median to the upper and lower uncertainty bound, which correspond to the 16 and 84 percentile. If certain bones are not detected at all, i.e. their DSC equals 0, they are excluded to not distort the distribution. Instead, we provide the detection ratio

$$\text{dr} := \frac{\#\text{ bones with DSC} > 0}{\#\text{ all bones}}. \tag{2}$$

Table 1. Comparison of segmentation performance per model. We provide the median DSC, the uncertainty boundaries, along with the detection ratio dr (2) for each group of bones, and the median foreground DSC (3) for all bones combined. Time per training iteration normalised by batch size.

Method	Segmentation performance for groups of bones											Time
	Spine		Ribs		Hands		Large bones		All			
	DSC	dr	DSC	dr	DSC	dr	DSC	dr	DSC	dr	fg	s
96_{bal}	$0.79^{+0.11}_{-0.26}$	1	$0.52^{+0.31}_{-0.26}$	1	$0.48^{+0.31}_{-0.38}$	0.54	$0.83^{+0.07}_{-0.19}$	1	$0.68^{+0.19}_{-0.43}$	0.79	0.84	2.1
$96_{bal,xent}$	$0.81^{+0.09}_{-0.39}$	1	$0.53^{+0.21}_{-0.27}$	1	$0.42^{+0.37}_{-0.35}$	0.57	$0.87^{+0.05}_{-0.09}$	1	$0.66^{+0.21}_{-0.40}$	0.80	0.90	1.1
$128_{unif,d}$	$0.80^{+0.09}_{-0.20}$	1	$0.62^{+0.20}_{-0.32}$	1	$0.52^{+0.21}_{-0.42}$	0.41	$0.90^{+0.04}_{-0.04}$	1	$0.73^{+0.16}_{-0.38}$	0.73	0.89	5.2
$128_{bal,d}$	$0.80^{+0.11}_{-0.28}$	1	$0.54^{+0.23}_{-0.35}$	1	$0.58^{+0.27}_{-0.46}$	0.51	$0.84^{+0.07}_{-0.17}$	1	$0.71^{+0.18}_{-0.48}$	0.77	0.85	5.3
$160_{bal,d}$	$0.82^{+0.09}_{-0.17}$	1	$0.58^{+0.21}_{-0.27}$	1	$0.67^{+0.18}_{-0.39}$	0.58	$0.88^{+0.04}_{-0.11}$	1	$0.75^{+0.14}_{-0.38}$	0.80	0.88	8.8
$160_{bal,xent,d}$	$0.83^{+0.09}_{-0.25}$	1	$0.58^{+0.23}_{-0.29}$	1	$0.55^{+0.28}_{-0.41}$	0.59	$0.90^{+0.04}_{-0.08}$	1	$0.75^{+0.15}_{-0.43}$	0.81	0.89	3.7
2D U-Net$_{2c}$	–	–	–	–	–	–	–	–	–	–	0.91	0.4
2D U-Net$_{126c}$	$0.45^{+0.24}_{-0.30}$	0.87	$0.34^{+0.26}_{-0.27}$	0.94	$0.36^{+0.33}_{-0.26}$	0.23	$0.82^{+0.08}_{-0.19}$	1	$0.49^{+0.29}_{-0.37}$	0.61	0.86	0.4

Additionally, we provide the foreground (fg) DSC of all bone tissue combined. In this case no distinctions between bones are made. We define the DSC_{fg} using foreground ground truth and prediction $G_{fg} := \bigvee_{\substack{c \in C \\ c \neq bg}} G_c$ and $P_{fg} := \bigvee_{\substack{c \in C \\ c \neq bg}} P_c$. Assuming mutually exclusive class segmentations we can compute

$$DSC_{fg} := \frac{2|P_{fg} \odot G_{fg}|}{|P_{fg}| + |G_{fg}|} = \frac{2|\overline{P_{bg}} \odot \overline{G_{bg}}|}{|\overline{P_{bg}}| + |\overline{G_{bg}}|}, \tag{3}$$

using only the background segmentation. In this equation, $\overline{P_{bg}}$ denotes the logic complement of the binary predication for the background class bg, and $\overline{G_{bg}}$ denotes the respective ground truth.

We employ cross-validation using five different data folds, each comprising of three scans for training, one for validation and one for testing. The validation set is used for adjusting the hyperparameters and monitoring convergence. Within every cross-evaluation fold, we use a different scan for the final testing.

4   Results and Discussion

To evaluate the contributions of different patch sizes, sampling strategies, data augmentation schemes and loss functions, we present quantitative results in Table 1. We investigate input patch sizes of 96, 128, and 160 px per dimension, chosen through balanced sampling **bal** or uniform sampling **unif**. The subscript **xent** stands for the use of the cross-entropy loss function alone instead of the full loss (1). With **d** we denote data augmentation with elastic deformations.

Not least because of the small data set available, there is considerable variance within the DSC scores of a given model and bone group, which impedes direct comparison of different models. No single model outperforms all others, although bigger patch sizes correspond to higher total scores. As for class imbalances, we note that the two models trained with a uniform sampler have the

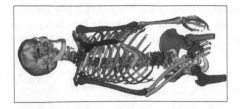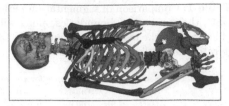

Fig. 3. Qualitative segmentation results created using $160_{bal,d}$ and two exemplary CT scans for which no manual labels exist. The 3D views were created with 3D Slicer [6] and show an interpolated version of the data.

lowest detection ratio for bones in the hands. The balanced sampler thus seems to benefit the detection and segmentation of tiny bones. We indicate the time needed for one iteration of training. To ensure a fair comparison, we averaged 100 iterations trained on the same machine under stable conditions. Patch sizes profoundly influence the time needed per iteration. The resulting times range from close to 1 second for a patch of size 96^3 up to almost 9 seconds for patches sized 160^3. The loss function also influences the training time considerably, with pure cross-entropy taking only half as long as the combined loss function.

Because many of our limitations in computational resources stem from the combination of a 3D network with a large number of classes, we additionally provide the results obtained using a 2D U-Net. We trained this network as specified in [13] who used it successfully for non-distinct bone segmentation of whole-body CT images. This network leads to good results for the 2-class case (2D U-Net$_{2c}$), but it does not scale well to bone distinction, as our results of a 2D U-Net$_{126c}$ – trained on the primary task – suggest.

A comparison with existing methods is made in Table 2. Since code and data sets are not publicly available, we compare the published results for different bones with our own. While the atlas method presented in [7] exhibits the best segmentation performance, their inference takes 20 min. They also require manual intervention if used on CT images that show only parts of an upper body. The two-step neural network presented in [17] was trained on 100 data sets and evaluated on 5. For the sacrum and L3, both our work and [17] show similar results. For bones that have a high chance of being confused with the ones below and above, their use of a shape model for landmark labelling and post-processing helps to keep scores for ribs and vertebrae high. It is, however, not clear how easily their approach could be adapted to accommodate for the segmentation of further bones, e.g. hands.

Qualitative results using two scans of unlabelled data are depicted in Fig. 3.

Table 2. Comparison of segmentation results for an end-to-end trained neural network approach (this work, model 160_{bal}), a hybrid approach using neural networks and shape models for landmark detection and a subsequent neural network for segmentation [17], and a hierarchical atlas segmentation [7].

DSC	This work		Lindgren et al. [17]		Fu et al. [7]	
	Median	Range	Median	Range	$\varnothing_c$	Std
Th7	0.64	0.22-0.94	0.86	0.42-0.89	0.85	0.02
L3	0.89	0.72-0.94	0.85	0.72-0.90	0.91	0.01
Sacrum	0.86	0.80-0.92	0.88	0.76-0.89	–	–
Rib	0.38	0.19-0.58	0.84	0.76-0.86	–	–
Sternum	0.74	0.59-0.87	0.83	0.80-0.87	0.89	0.02
Inference time for 1 scan (min)	∼ 1		–		∼ 20	
Distinct bones (#)	125		49		62	
In-plane resolution (mm)	2		3.27		0.97	
Slice thickness (mm)	2		3.75		1.5-2.5	

5   Summary and Conclusion

We tackled the task of segmenting 125 distinct bones at once in an upper-body CT scan, using an end-to-end trained neural network and only three fully labelled scans for training. We provide network architectures, loss functions and data augmentation schemes which make this computationally singular task feasible. While not all problems are solved, we showed how balanced sampling and a suitable choice of the loss function help to deal with the class imbalance inherent to our task. Despite a lack of training data, we obtained median DSC scores of up to 0.9 on large bones, 0.8 on vertebrae, which compares well with other works that segment various bones of the upper body simultaneously. More problematic are ribs, which tend to be confused with one another, an issue where shape models certainly could help. As for the hands, many of the tiny bones are not detected at all, which suggests the need for more fine-grained methods for this particular set of bones. In terms of inference time, the complete labelling of a scan takes roughly one minute, which would be fast enough to be used to create initial guesses of a more accurate atlas method. More manually labelled scans would certainly improve the generalisation capacity of our networks and the statistical significance of our comparisons. Using our results on momentarily unlabelled data as priors, we expect a drastic decrease in the time needed for further manual annotations.

Acknowledgements. This work was financially supported by the Werner Siemens Foundation through the MIRACLE project. We thank Mireille Toranelli for acquiring the scans and providing the ground truth labelling.

References

1. Baiker, M., et al.: Fully automated whole-body registration in mice using an articulated skeleton atlas. In: 2007 4th IEEE International Symposium on Biomedical Imaging: From Nano to Macro, pp. 728–731. IEEE (2007)
2. Bilic, P., et al.: The liver tumor segmentation benchmark (lits). arXiv preprint (2019). arXiv:1901.04056
3. Chaitanya, K., Karani, N., Baumgartner, C.F., Becker, A., Donati, O., Konukoglu, E.: Semi-supervised and task-driven data augmentation. In: Chung, A.C.S., Gee, J.C., Yushkevich, P.A., Bao, S. (eds.) IPMI 2019. LNCS, vol. 11492, pp. 29–41. Springer, Cham (2019). https://doi.org/10.1007/978-3-030-20351-1_3
4. Çiçek, Ö., Abdulkadir, A., Lienkamp, S.S., Brox, T., Ronneberger, O.: 3D u-net: learning dense volumetric segmentation from sparse annotation. In: Ourselin, S., Joskowicz, L., Sabuncu, M.R., Unal, G., Wells, W. (eds.) MICCAI 2016. LNCS, vol. 9901, pp. 424–432. Springer, Cham (2016). https://doi.org/10.1007/978-3-319-46723-8_49
5. Faludi, B., Zoller, E.I., Gerig, N., Zam, A., Rauter, G., Cattin, P.C.: Direct visual and haptic volume rendering of medical data sets for an immersive exploration in virtual reality. In: Shen, D., et al. (eds.) MICCAI 2019. LNCS, vol. 11768, pp. 29–37. Springer, Cham (2019). https://doi.org/10.1007/978-3-030-32254-0_4
6. Fedorov, A., et al.: 3D slicer as an image computing platform for the quantitative imaging network. Magn. Reson. Imaging 30(9), 1323–1341 (2012)
7. Fu, Y., Liu, S., Li, H.H., Yang, D.: Automatic and hierarchical segmentation of the human skeleton in CT images. Phys. Med. Biol. 62(7), 2812–2833 (2017)
8. Gibson, E., et al.: Niftynet: a deep-learning platform for medical imaging. Comput. Methods Programs Biomed. 158, 113–122 (2018)
9. Horváth, A., Tsagkas, C., Andermatt, S., Pezold, S., Parmar, K., Cattin, P.: Spinal cord gray matter-white matter segmentation on magnetic resonance AMIRA images with MD-GRU. In: Zheng, G., Belavy, D., Cai, Y., Li, S. (eds.) CSI 2018. LNCS, vol. 11397, pp. 3–14. Springer, Cham (2019). https://doi.org/10.1007/978-3-030-13736-6_1
10. Isensee, F., Kickingereder, P., Wick, W., Bendszus, M., Maier-Hein, K.H.: No newnet. In: Crimi, A., Bakas, S., Kuijf, H., Keyvan, F., Reyes, M., van Walsum, T. (eds.) Brainlesion: Glioma, Multiple Sclerosis, Stroke and Traumatic Brain Injuries, pp. 234–244. Springer International Publishing, Cham (2019)
11. Kamnitsas, K., et al.: Efficient multi-scale 3D CNN with fully connected CRF for accurate brain lesion segmentation. Med. Image Anal. 36, 61–78 (2017)
12. Kingma, D.P., Ba, J.: Adam: a method for stochastic optimization. arXiv preprint (2014). arXiv:1412.6980
13. Klein, A., Warszawski, J., Hillengaß, J., Maier-Hein, K.H.: Automatic bone segmentation in whole-body ct images. Int. J. Comput. Assist. Radiol. Surg. 14(1), 21–29 (2019)
14. Knodel, M.M., et al.: Virtual reality in advanced medical immersive imaging: a workflow for introducing virtual reality as a supporting tool in medical imaging. Comput. Vis. Sci. 18(6), 203–212 (2018). https://doi.org/10.1007/s00791-018-0292-3
15. Lee, S.W., Kim, J.H., Jun, J., Ha, J.W., Zhang, B.T.: Overcoming catastrophic forgetting by incremental moment matching. In: Advances in neural information processing systems, pp. 4652–4662 (2017)

16. Lessmann, N., van Ginneken, B., de Jong, P.A., Išgum, I.: Iterative fully convolutional neural networks for automatic vertebra segmentation and identification. Med. Image Anal. **53**, 142–155 (2019)
17. Lindgren Belal, S., et al.: Deep learning for segmentation of 49 selected bones in CT scans: first step in automated PET/CT-based 3D quantification of skeletal metastases. Eur. J. Radiol. **113**, 89–95 (2019)
18. Pérez-Carrasco, J.A., Acha, B., Suárez-Mejías, C., López-Guerra, J.L., Serrano, C.: Joint segmentation of bones and muscles using an intensity and histogram-based energy minimization approach. Comput. Methods Programs Biomed. **156**, 85–95 (2018)
19. Rahbani, D., Morel-Forster, A., Madsen, D., Lüthi, M., Vetter, T.: Robust registration of statistical shape models for unsupervised pathology annotation. In: Zhou, L., et al. (eds.) LABELS/HAL-MICCAI/CuRIOUS -2019. LNCS, vol. 11851, pp. 13–21. Springer, Cham (2019). https://doi.org/10.1007/978-3-030-33642-4_2
20. Ronneberger, O., Fischer, P., Brox, T.: U-net: convolutional networks for biomedical image segmentation. In: Navab, N., Hornegger, J., Wells, W.M., Frangi, A.F. (eds.) MICCAI 2015. LNCS, vol. 9351, pp. 234–241. Springer, Cham (2015). https://doi.org/10.1007/978-3-319-24574-4_28
21. Sarkalkan, N., Weinans, H., Zadpoor, A.A.: Statistical shape and appearance models of bones. Bone **60**, 129–140 (2014)
22. Seim, H., Kainmueller, D., Heller, M., Lamecker, H., Zachow, S., Hege, H.C.: Automatic segmentation of the pelvic bones from ct data based on a statistical shape model. VCBM **8**, 93–100 (2008)
23. Sekuboyina, A., et al.: Verse: a vertebrae labelling and segmentation benchmark. arXiv preprint (2020). arXiv:2001.09193
24. Zhang, H., Cisse, M., Dauphin, Y.N., Lopez-Paz, D.: mixup: beyond empirical risk minimization. arXiv preprint (2017). arXiv:1710.09412

Super Resolution of Arterial Spin Labeling MR Imaging Using Unsupervised Multi-scale Generative Adversarial Network

Jianan Cui[1,2], Kuang Gong[2,3], Paul Han[3], Huafeng Liu[1(✉)], and Quanzheng Li[2,3(✉)]

[1] State Key Laboratory of Modern Optical Instrumentation, College of Optical Science and Engineering, Zhejiang University, Hangzhou 310027, Zhejiang, China
`liuhf@zju.edu.cn`
[2] Center for Advanced Medical Computing and Analysis, Massachusetts General Hospital/Harvard Medical School, Boston, MA 02114, USA
`Li.Quanzheng@mgh.harvard.edu`
[3] Gordon Center for Medical Imaging, Massachusetts General Hospital/Harvard Medical School, Boston, MA 02114, USA

Abstract. Arterial spin labeling (ASL) magnetic resonance imaging (MRI) is a powerful imaging technology that can measure cerebral blood flow (CBF) quantitatively. However, since only a small portion of blood is labeled compared to the whole tissue volume, conventional ASL suffers from low signal-to-noise ratio (SNR), poor spatial resolution, and long acquisition time. In this paper, we proposed a super-resolution method based on a multi-scale generative adversarial network (GAN) through unsupervised training. The network only needs the low-resolution (LR) ASL image itself for training and the T1-weighted image as the anatomical prior. No training pairs or pre-training are needed. A low-pass filter guided item was added as an additional loss to suppress the noise interference from the LR ASL image. After the network was trained, the super-resolution (SR) image was generated by supplying the upsampled LR ASL image and corresponding T1-weighted image to the generator of the last layer. Performance of the proposed method was evaluated by comparing the peak signal-to-noise ratio (PSNR) and structural similarity index (SSIM) using normal-resolution (NR) ASL image (5.5 min acquisition) and high-resolution (HR) ASL image (44 min acquisition) as the ground truth. Compared to the nearest, linear, and spline interpolation methods, the proposed method recovers more detailed structure information, reduces the image noise visually, and achieves the highest PSNR and SSIM when using HR ASL image as the ground-truth.

Keywords: Arterial spin labeling MRI · Super resolution · Unsupervised deep learning · Multi-scale · Generative adversarial network

J. Cui and K. Gong—Contributed equally to this work.

© Springer Nature Switzerland AG 2020
M. Liu et al. (Eds.): MLMI 2020, LNCS 12436, pp. 50–59, 2020.
https://doi.org/10.1007/978-3-030-59861-7_6

1   Introduction

Arterial spin labeling (ASL) is a non-invasive magnetic resonance imaging (MRI) technique which uses water as a diffusible tracer to measure cerebral blood flow (CBF) [25]. Without a gadolinium-containing contrast agent, ASL is repeatable and can be applied to pediatric patients and patients with impaired renal function [2,19]. However, as the lifetime of the tracer is short—approximately the transport time from labeling position to the tissue—the data acquisition time is limited in a single-shot [1]. Thus, ASL images usually suffer from low signal-to-noise ratio (SNR) and limited spatial resolution.

Due to the great potential of ASL in clinical and research applications, developing advanced acquisition sequence and processing methods to achieve high-resolution, high-SNR ASL has been a very active research area. Regarding post-processing methods, non-local mean [7] and temporal filtering [21] has been developed to improve the SNR of ASL without additional training data. Partial volume correction methods [5,17,18] have also been proposed to improve the perfusion signal from ASL images with limited spatial resolutions. As for reconstruction approaches, parallel imaging [4], compressed sensing [12], spatial [20] or spatio-temporal constraints [8,23] have been proposed to recover high-SNR ASL images from noisy or sparsely sampled raw data.

Recently, deep learning has achieved great success in computer vision tasks when large number of training data exist. It has been applied to ASL image denoising and showed better results than state-of-the-arts methods [9,10,14,24, 26]. Specifically, Zheng et al proposed a two-stage multi-loss super resolution (SR) network that can both improve spatial resolution and SNR of the ASL images [16]. These prior arts mostly focused on supervised deep learning where a large number of high-quality ASL images are required. However, it is not easy to acquire such kind of training labels in clinical practice, especially for high-resolution ASL, due to the MR sequence limit and long acquisition time.

In this paper, we explored the possibility of using unsupervised Generative Adversarial Network (GAN) to perform ASL super-resolution. It does not require high-resolution ASL images as training labels and no extra training is needed. The main contributions of this work include:

(1) The low-resolution ASL image itself was used as the training label and only one single ASL volume was needed for GAN training. No training labels nor large number of datasets is needed. Registered T1-weighted image was fed to the network as a separate channel to provide anatomical prior information.
(2) Inspired by the pyramid structure of the sinGAN structure [22] which extracted features from multi-scales, our network consisted of multi-scale feature-extraction layers. After network training, generator of the last layer containing the finest scale information was used to generate the final super-resolution ASL image.
(3) Considering the noisy character of the ASL images, a super low-pass filter loss term was added as an additional loss item to reduce the image noise and stabilize the network training.

(4) The voxel size of the generated SR image can be adjusted at will as there
    is no requirement of zoom-in ratio and the proposed method is fully unsu-
    pervised.

2   Method

Diagram of the whole generative framework is shown in Fig. 1. It can be performed in two steps: multi-scale training and super-resolution generation.

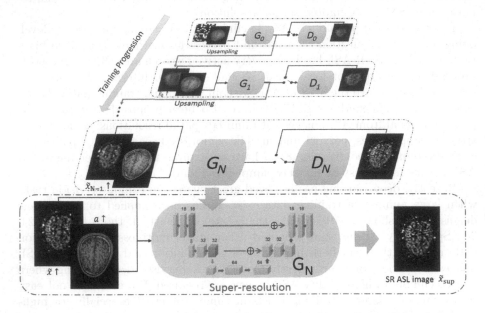

Fig. 1. Diagram of the proposed framework. The network contains multi-scale layers.
Each layer includes a generator and a discriminator.

2.1   Multi-scale Training Step

A pyramid of generators $\{G_0, ..., G_N\}$ was trained against an ASL image pyramid
of $x : \{x_0, ...x_N\}$ layer by layer progressively. Meanwhile, a T1-weighted image
pyramid of $a : \{a_0, ..., a_N\}$ was inserted to the generators in another channel
to provide anatomical information. The T1 image a was coregistered with the
low resolution (LR) ASL image x. x_n and a_n are downsampled from x and a
by a factor r^{N-n}. At the very beginning, spatial white Gaussian noise z_0 was
injected as the initial input of generator G_0. Then each generator accepted the
upsampled generative result $\widetilde{x}_{n-1}\uparrow$ from the upper layer as the input to generate
image $\widetilde{x}_n$ in a higher spatial resolution,

$$\widetilde{x}_n\uparrow = \begin{cases} G_0\left(z_0, a_0\right) & n = 0 \\ G_n\left(\widetilde{x}_{n-1}\uparrow, a_n\right) & 0 < n \leq N \end{cases}. \tag{1}$$

For each layer's training, the generator G_n intended to produce realistic image like the training label x_n to fool the associated discriminator D_n, while the discriminator was trained to distinguish the generated image $G_n(\tilde{x}_{n-1}\uparrow, a_n)$ from real x_n. All the generators and the discriminators share the same architectures which is a three-layer 3D Unet [6] and Markovian discriminator [13,15], respectively. Each generator used the upper-layer generator's parameters as the initial parameters. The network was trained by the Adam optimizer with a learning rate of 10^{-3}. 2000 epochs were run for each layer.

2.2 Super-Resolution Generation Step

The LR ASL image x was upsampled to $x\uparrow$ and concatenated with T1-weighted image of the same size: $a\uparrow$. Both $x\uparrow$ and $a\uparrow$ were supplied to the last generator G_N and the output of the generator G_N is the final SR ASL image. The multi-scale architecture has been verified by [22], which can recover structure features from the coarsest scale to the finest scale. After training, the generator G_N learned fine details and texture information from the last layer. Based on it, we can recover the missing structure details of the upsampled image $x\uparrow$.

$$\tilde{x}_{sup} = G_n(x\uparrow, a\uparrow). \tag{2}$$

2.3 Loss Function

Each GAN in the network was trained with the loss function which is combined by three part: adversarial loss, mean squared error (MSE) loss and low-pass filter loss,

$$\min_{G_n} \max_{D_n} L_{adv}(G_n, D_n) + \alpha L_{mse}(G_n) + \beta L_{lp}(G_n), \tag{3}$$

where α and β are the weighted parameters for MSE loss and Gaussian filter loss, respectively. The adversarial loss was WGAN-GP loss [11]. The MSE loss aims to improve Peak SNR (PSNR),

$$L_{rec} = \|G_n(\tilde{x}_{n-1}\uparrow, a_n) - x_n\|^2. \tag{4}$$

The low-pass filter loss term calculates the MSE between the generated image and the real image label after they pass a super low-pass filter F. This term can reduce the influence of noise and it is formulated as:

$$L_{lp} = \|F(G_n(\tilde{x}_{n-1}\uparrow, a_n)) - F(x_n)\|^2. \tag{5}$$

In this paper, we use Gaussian filter with a sigma of 5.

3 Experiment

3.1 Overall Design

Two experiments are designed to evaluate the performance of our proposed method. Firstly, we used low-resolution (LR) ASL image as the training label and generated normal-resolution (NR) ASL image. As the LR ASL image was down-sampled from NR ASL image, we can calculate peak SNR (PSNR) and structural similarity index (SSIM) for quantitative analysis. In the second experiment, we tried to generate SR image which has the same voxel size as the T1-weighted image by training NR ASL image. The second experiment can better show the practical usability of the proposed method.

3.2 Data Acquisition and Generation

The ASL MRI image was acquired from a healthy volunteer by a 3 T whole-body scanner (Magnetom Tim Trio, Siemens Healthcare, Erlangen, Germany) using pseudo-continuous ASL (pCASL) with bSSFP readout (total labeling duration: 1500 ms; post-labeling delay time: 1.2 s). The matrix size of the ASL MRI image is $128 \times 96 \times 48$ with a voxel size of $1.875 \times 1.875 \times 2.5 \, mm^3$ and TR/TE = $3.93/1.73 \, ms$. There are ASL images of two different spatial resolution consider-ing different acquisition time: 44 min for high-resolution ASL image and 5.5 min for normal-resolution ASL image. A three-plane localizer and a T1-weighted magnetization-prepared rapid gradient echo (MPRAGE) were performed after the ASL acquisition. The matrix size of the T1-weighted image is $224 \times 176 \times 256$ with a voxel size of $0.9766 \times 0.9766 \times 1mm^3$.

In order to verify the performance of the proposed method quantitatively, we generated the LR ASL image (matrix size: $64 \times 48 \times 48$; voxel size: $3.75 \times 3.75 \times 2.5 \, mm^3$) by downsampling the NR ASL image (5.5 min acquisition). As the T1-weighted image was paired with the upsampled ASL image during the train step and the super-resolution generation step, the T1 image was registered to different scales of the ASL image by Advanced Normalization Tools (ANTs) [3].

4   Results

In the first experiment, the network was trained using the LR ASL image (Fig. 2) as the training label. The super-resolution results were compared with the near-est interpolation, linear interpolation, and spline interpolation results, as shown in Fig. 2 (transaxial view) and Fig. 3 (coronal view). It can be seen that images of the proposed method have a good visual appearance with clear boundaries and low image noise. The quantitative results of PSNR and SSIM are shown in Table. 1. One interesting observation is that when using NR ASL image as the reference image, both linear and spline interpolation have better PSNR and SSIM than the proposed method. However, the proposed method achieves the highest PSNR and SSIM when using 44-min HR ASL image as the reference image. As the NR ASL image is still noisy and does not have as many details as the HR ASL image, this conflicting conclusion actually proves that the proposed method does utilize the structure information from T1-weighted image which can not be observed from the NR ASL image.

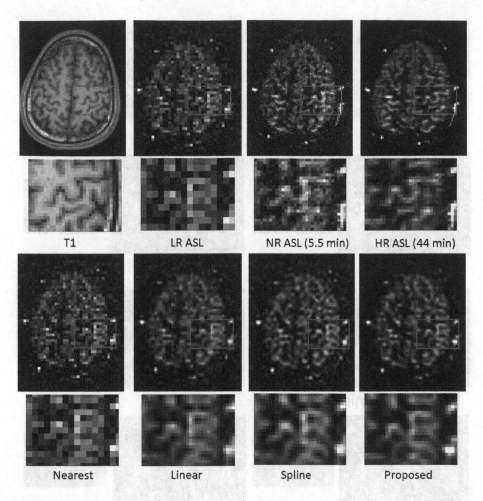

Fig. 2. Visual comparison (transaxial view) of different reference images and different super-resolution method results. The super-resolution was performed on LR ASL image in the first row.

For the second experiment, we trained the network by using the NR ASL image as the training label (Fig. 4), and then generated SR ASL image with the same voxel size ($0.9766 \times 0.9766 \times 1mm^3$) as the T1-weighted image. Successful super-resolution generation of this experiment can prove that this proposed framework can be applied to any existing ASL protocols by translating the voxel size and resolution to that of the T1-weighted image. There is no limit on the voxel-size ratio between the original ASL and the T1-weighted image, which is quite flexible. The results in transaxial view and sagital view shown in Fig. 4 demonstrates this point. The linear interpolation result was chosen for comparison as it has higher PSNR and SSIM than the nearest and spline interpolation in the quantification. The structure of the proposed result is sharp and clear while the linear interpolation result is a little bit blurred.

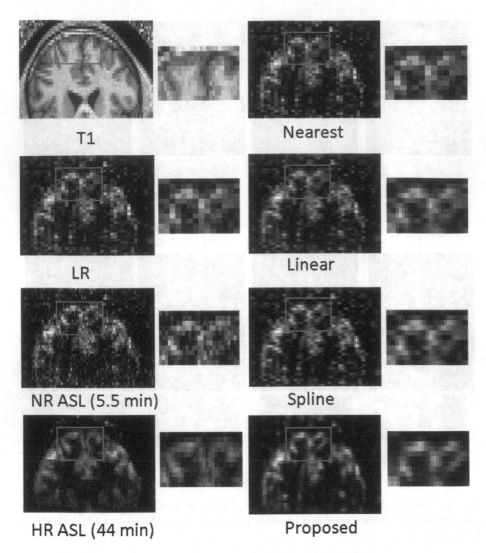

Fig. 3. Visual comparison (coronal view) of different reference images and different super-resolution method results. The super-resolution was performed on LR ASL image in the first row.

Table 1. Quantitative results using NR ASL and HR ASL as reference

Groundtruth	NR ASL		HR ASL	
	PSNR	SSIM	PSNR	SSIM
Nearest	31.5249	0.7507	30.9289	0.5320
Linear	**33.6745**	**0.8158**	32.9041	0.5851
Spline	32.8720	0.7816	32.1518	0.5536
Proposed	32.5795	0.7795	**33.3723**	**0.6488**

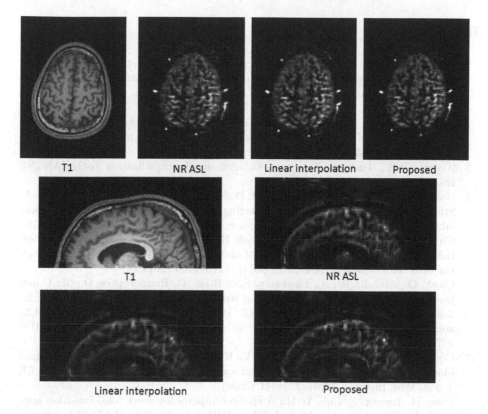

Fig. 4. Visual comparison of different reference images and different super-resolution method results. The super-resolution was performed on NR ASL image in the first row.

5   Conclusion

In this paper, we proposed an unsupervised multi-scale GAN framework for ASL image super-resolution. Corresponding T1-weighted image inserted into the network works as an anatomical prior to guide the ASL super-resolution generation process. After being trained layer by layer progressively, the last-layer generator can capture the finest feature to produce realistic super-resolution images. In-vivo results show that the proposed framework can simultaneously improve spatial resolution while also reducing the image noise with the help of low-pass-filter loss term. Our future work will focus on more quantitative analysis of the generated CBF map as well as more data evaluations.

Acknowledgement. This work is supported in part by the National Key Technology Research and Development Program of China (No: 2017YFE0104000, 2016YFC1300302), and by the National Natural Science Foundation of China (No: U1809204, 61525106, 81873908, 61701436).

References

1. Alsop, D.C., et al.: Recommended implementation of arterial spin-labeled perfusion MRI for clinical applications: a consensus of the ISMRM perfusion study group and the European consortium for ASL in dementia. Magn. Reson. Med. **73**(1), 102–116 (2015)
2. Amukotuwa, S.A., Yu, C., Zaharchuk, G.: 3D pseudocontinuous arterial spin labeling in routine clinical practice: a review of clinically significant artifacts. J. Magn. Reson. Imaging **43**(1), 11–27 (2016)
3. Avants, B.B., Tustison, N., Song, G.: Advanced normalization tools (ANTS). Insight j **2**(365), 1–35 (2009)
4. Boland, M., Stirnberg, R., Pracht, E.D., Kramme, J., Viviani, R., Stingl, J., Stöcker, T.: Accelerated 3D-grase imaging improves quantitative multiple post labeling delay arterial spin labeling. Magn. Reson. Med. **80**(6), 2475–2484 (2018)
5. Chappell, M.A., Groves, A.R., MacIntosh, B.J., Donahue, M.J., Jezzard, P., Woolrich, M.W.: Partial volume correction of multiple inversion time arterial spin labeling MRI data. Magn. Reson. Med. **65**(4), 1173–1183 (2011)
6. Çiçek, Ö., Abdulkadir, A., Lienkamp, S.S., Brox, T., Ronneberger, O.: 3D U-net: learning dense volumetric segmentation from sparse annotation. In: Ourselin, S., Joskowicz, L., Sabuncu, M.R., Unal, G., Wells, W. (eds.) MICCAI 2016. LNCS, vol. 9901, pp. 424–432. Springer, Cham (2016). https://doi.org/10.1007/978-3-319-46723-8_49
7. Coupé, P., Yger, P., Prima, S., Hellier, P., Kervrann, C., Barillot, C.: An optimized blockwise nonlocal means denoising filter for 3-D magnetic resonance images. IEEE Trans. Med. Imaging **27**(4), 425–441 (2008)
8. Fang, R., Huang, J., Luh, W.M.: A spatio-temporal low-rank total variation approach for denoising arterial spin labeling MRI data. In: 2015 IEEE 12th International Symposium on Biomedical Imaging (ISBI), pp. 498–502. IEEE (2015)
9. Gong, E., Pauly, J., Zaharchuk, G.: Boosting SNR and/or resolution of arterial spin label (ASL) imaging using multi-contrast approaches with multi-lateral guided filter and deep networks. In: Proceedings of the Annual Meeting of the International Society for Magnetic Resonance in Medicine, Honolulu, Hawaii (2017)
10. Gong, K., Han, P., El Fakhri, G., Ma, C., Li, Q.: Arterial spin labeling MR image denoising and reconstruction using unsupervised deep learning. NMR Biomed. e4224 (2019)
11. Gulrajani, I., Ahmed, F., Arjovsky, M., Dumoulin, V., Courville, A.C.: Improved training of wasserstein gans. In: Advances in neural information processing systems, pp. 5767–5777 (2017)

12. Han, P.K., Ye, J.C., Kim, E.Y., Choi, S.H., Park, S.H.: Whole-brain perfusion imaging with balanced steady-state free precession arterial spin labeling. NMR Biomed. **29**(3), 264–274 (2016)
13. Isola, P., Zhu, J.Y., Zhou, T., Efros, A.A.: Image-to-image translation with conditional adversarial networks. In: Proceedings of the IEEE conference on computer vision and pattern recognition, pp. 1125–1134 (2017)
14. Kim, K.H., Choi, S.H., Park, S.H.: Improving arterial spin labeling by using deep learning. Radiology **287**(2), 658–666 (2018)
15. Li, C., Wand, M.: Precomputed real-time texture synthesis with markovian generative adversarial networks. In: Leibe, B., Matas, J., Sebe, N., Welling, M. (eds.) ECCV 2016. LNCS, vol. 9907, pp. 702–716. Springer, Cham (2016). https://doi.org/10.1007/978-3-319-46487-9_43
16. Li, Z., et al.: A two-stage multi-loss super-resolution network for arterial spin labeling magnetic resonance imaging. In: Shen, D., et al. (eds.) MICCAI 2019. LNCS, vol. 11766, pp. 12–20. Springer, Cham (2019). https://doi.org/10.1007/978-3-030-32248-9_2
17. Liang, X., Connelly, A., Calamante, F.: Improved partial volume correction for single inversion time arterial spin labeling data. Magn. Reson. Med. **69**(2), 531–537 (2013)
18. Meurée, C., Maurel, P., Ferré, J.C., Barillot, C.: Patch-based super-resolution of arterial spin labeling magnetic resonance images. Neuroimage **189**, 85–94 (2019)
19. Pedrosa, I., et al.: Arterial spin labeling MR imaging for characterisation of renal masses in patients with impaired renal function: initial experience. Eur. Radiol. **22**(2), 484–492 (2012)
20. Petr, J., Ferré, J.C., Gauvrit, J.Y., Barillot, C.: Denoising arterial spin labeling MRI using tissue partial volume. In: Medical Imaging 2010: Image Processing, vol. 7623, p. 76230L. International Society for Optics and Photonics (2010)
21. Petr, J., Ferré, J.C., Gauvrit, J.Y., Barillot, C.: Improving arterial spin labeling data by temporal filtering. In: Medical Imaging 2010: Image Processing, vol. 7623, p. 76233B. International Society for Optics and Photonics (2010)
22. Shaham, T.R., Dekel, T., Michaeli, T.: Singan: learning a generative model from a single natural image. In: Proceedings of the IEEE International Conference on Computer Vision, pp. 4570–4580 (2019)
23. Spann, S.M., Kazimierski, K.S., Aigner, C.S., Kraiger, M., Bredies, K., Stollberger, R.: Spatio-temporal TGV denoising for asl perfusion imaging. Neuroimage **157**, 81–96 (2017)
24. Ulas, C., Tetteh, G., Kaczmarz, S., Preibisch, C., Menze, B.H.: DeepASL: kinetic model incorporated loss for denoising arterial spin labeled MRI via deep residual learning. In: Frangi, A.F., Schnabel, J.A., Davatzikos, C., Alberola-López, C., Fichtinger, G. (eds.) MICCAI 2018. LNCS, vol. 11070, pp. 30–38. Springer, Cham (2018). https://doi.org/10.1007/978-3-030-00928-1_4
25. Williams, D.S., Detre, J.A., Leigh, J.S., Koretsky, A.P.: Magnetic resonance imaging of perfusion using spin inversion of arterial water. Proc. Nat. Acad. Sci. **89**(1), 212–216 (1992)
26. Xie, D., et al.: Denoising arterial spin labeling perfusion MRI with deep machine learning. Magn. Reson. Imaging **68**, 95–105 (2020)

Self-recursive Contextual Network for Unsupervised 3D Medical Image Registration

Bo Hu, Shenglong Zhou, Zhiwei Xiong[✉], and Feng Wu

University of Science and Technology of China, Hefei, China
zwxiong@ustc.edu.cn

Abstract. In this paper, we propose a self-recursive contextual network for unsupervised 3D medical image registration. Current learning-based registration methods refine an initial deformation field either through cascaded stages or in a coarse-to-fine manner, which improve results at the cost of a rapidly increased number of parameters. Aiming to achieve both elevation of performance and reduction of parameters, we design a novel pyramid structure with a self-recursive scheme and contextual components. Specifically, we adopt a weight-sharing generator to refine the deformation fields recursively across different levels of the pyramid. Meanwhile, we introduce a spatial pyramid pooling module in the feature extractor to capture richer contextual information, as well as a dilated receptive module for the post-processing of the deformation field. Evaluated on two benchmark datasets for 3D medical image registration, our method outperforms the state-of-the-art pyramid network with 39% less parameters, and competes to multi-stage cascaded registration networks with significantly less parameters and faster running speed.

Keywords: Medical image registration · Self-recursive · Contextual

1 Introduction

Deformable registration targets at estimating the anatomical non-linear correspondence between a pair of 3D images, which plays an important role in medical image analysis such as multi-modality image fusion [9] and brain atlas creation [7]. When analyzing 3D image pairs from diverse viewpoints captured at different times, one image (termed moving image) needs to be transformed to another image (termed fixed image), according to the correspondence (termed deformation field) generated by a registration model. Such transformation is useful for comparison of structures and understanding of variability.

B. Hu and S. Zhou—Contributed equally.

Electronic supplementary material The online version of this chapter (https://doi.org/10.1007/978-3-030-59861-7_7) contains supplementary material, which is available to authorized users.

M. Liu et al. (Eds.): MLMI 2020, LNCS 12436, pp. 60–69, 2020.
https://doi.org/10.1007/978-3-030-59861-7_7

Traditional methods [2,3,12] consider the registration procedure as an optimization problem for each image pair. After generating the deformation field through an established model, parameters are updated iteratively based on a designed similarity measure function. Nevertheless, optimization for every image pair is extremely time-consuming and computationally expensive. Recently, learning-based methods [14,17,19,25] leveraging convolutional neural networks (CNNs) are developed to overcome the above drawback while advancing the performance. Under the framework of deep learning, registration can be defined as a global parametric function that is optimized given a set of image pairs, which is at a speed orders of magnitude faster than before.

Due to the expensive cost of manual annotation such as anatomical landmarks, however, the application of supervised learning-based approaches encounters inevitable limitations. On the other hand, relying on the constraint of image similarity coordinated with spatial smoothness of deformation fields, unsupervised registration methods have attracted extensive research attention. Balakrishnan et al. [5] proposed VoxelMorph consisting of an encoder-decoder CNN to generate deformation fields. While speeding up the registration procedure significantly, it just achieves similar performance compared with traditional methods. Hu et al. [15] introduced a pyramid network with a dual-stream feature extractor and a series of deformation field generators. This pyramid structure takes advantage of the coarse-to-fine recursive refinement across multi-scale features, and gives higher accuracy than VoxelMorph. Still, it only adopts individual deformation generators in different levels and neglects the contextual information. Zhao et al. [24] cascaded the registration subnetworks named as VTN with an additional invertibility loss, then extended the cascaded structure to 10-stage [23] by constraining the similarity loss between the last warped moving image and the fixed image. Through refining the deformation fields by repeating subnetworks recursively, this cascaded method further improves the performance compared with one single subnetwork. Yet the downside of it is also obvious, the linear growth of trainable parameters consume tremendous resources, which restricts its application scenarios. Meanwhile, the increase of registration time poses a trade-off between accuracy and efficiency. Therefore, it is highly expected to simultaneously elevate the registration performance and reduce the burden of parameters.

In this paper, we propose a novel feature pyramid structure called Self-Recursive Contextual Network, which boosts the registration performance of 3D medical images with much less parameters. Our key observation is that, instead of using individual deformation field generators across different feature levels in the pyramid, deploying one weight-sharing generator can obtain promising accuracy while requiring much less parameters, where the deformation fields are recursively produced in a coarse-to-fine manner. To further explore the potential of this feature-based structure, we introduce abundant contextual information in 3D image registration, which is more contextually complicated than 2D image registration. A Spatial Pyramid Pooling (SPP) module is first used in the dual-stream feature extractor, which supplements more representative features for the following operation. Besides, a receptive module consisting of dilated convolutions is deployed for the post-processing of the deformation field, also in a self-recursive manner. Evaluated on two benchmark datasets for 3D medical image registration, brain MRI (LPBA) and liver CT (SLIVER), our method outperforms the state-of-the-art pyramid network with 39% less parameters, and competes to multi-stage cascaded registration networks with significantly less parameters and faster running speed.

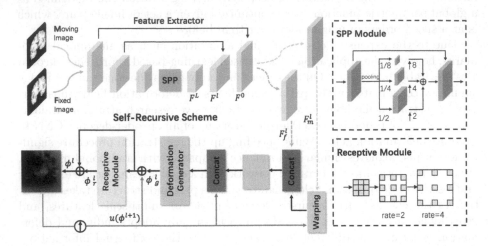

Fig. 1. Workflow of our method. We feed moving and fixed images respectively to the feature extractor with the Spatial Pyramid Pooling (SPP) module to obtain feature representations. Deformation fields are recursively produced by one deformation generator and one receptive module, where black and red lines indicate forward and recursive directions. Dashed boxes are detailed designs of two contextual components.

2   Method

3D medical image registration aims to determine a deformation field ϕ that warps a moving image $I_m \in \mathbb{R}^3$ to a fixed image $I_f \in \mathbb{R}^3$, so that the warped image $I_m \circ \phi$ can be similar to I_f ($\circ$ denotes the warping operation). The deformation field ϕ is typically determined by minimizing an energy function as

$$\phi = \arg\min_{\phi} \mathcal{L}_{sim}(I_f, I_m \circ \phi) + \mathcal{L}_{smooth}(\phi), \tag{1}$$

where $\mathcal{L}_{sim}$ quantifies the similarity between the fixed image and the warped image, and $\mathcal{L}_{smooth}$ is a regularization term to enforce spatial smoothness.

Figure 1 presents a complete workflow of our proposed network and its main components. Firstly, we feed I_m and I_f into a **feature extractor E** with the SPP module separately, and obtain L-level pyramids of feature representations $F_f = \{F_f^0, ..., F_f^L\}$ and $F_m = \{F_m^0, ..., F_m^L\}$, where the 0-th level means the full resolution and the L-th level is the coarsest one. After that, we generate deformation fields $\Phi = \{\phi^0, ..., \phi^L\}$ in a coarse-to-fine manner, by reusing a weight-sharing **generator** G and a weight-sharing **receptive module** R. At last, we can get the final deformation ϕ^0 for registering the moving image.

2.1   Self-recursive Scheme

A regular pyramid network recursively generates deformation fields with different generators at different levels. In order to realize the self-recursive scheme, our main manipulation is to set the deformation generator G and the receptive module R to share weights respectively across different pyramid levels, and refine the deformation fields using a residual aggregation. Obtained a pair of F_f^l and F_m^l from weight sharing feature extractor E separately at the l-th level, we use trilinear interpolation to upsample the deformation ϕ^{l+1} by a factor of 2 from a coarser level as $u(\phi^{l+1})$, and utilize it to get the warped moving feature $F_m^l \circ u(\phi^{l+1})$ by the spatial transform layer [16].

Then, we feed the concatenation of $\{F_f^l, F_m^l \circ u(\phi^{l+1}), u(\phi^{l+1})\}$ to the generator G, which merges information from both feature and deformation domains. Specifically, we employ a $1 \times 1 \times 1$ convolution layer after the concatenation of $\{F_f^l, F_m^l \circ u(\phi^{l+1})\}$, making the output features of the concatenation have the equal number of channels across different levels. Then we concatenate the output features and $u(\phi^{l+1})$ as the input for G. At the coarsest level of the pyramid, there is no deformation yet so we just concatenate the fixed and moving features. The $1 \times 1 \times 1$ convolution used here guarantees the channel dimensions of input features to G across different pyramid levels are consistent. G contains four 3D convolutions followed by leaky ReLU activations with the same kernel size of $3 \times 3 \times 3$, which generates a deformation field ϕ_g as

$$\phi_g^l = G(F_f^l, F_m^l \circ u(\phi^{l+1}), u(\phi^{l+1})). \tag{2}$$

Adopting the residual aggregation, ϕ_g^l and $u(\phi^{l+1})$ are summed up for the receptive module R to generate a deformation field ϕ_r, which is detailed in Sect. 2.2. Finally, the deformation field ϕ^l at this level is obtained as

$$\phi^l = \phi_g^l + \phi_r^l + u(\phi^{l+1}). \tag{3}$$

Through the residual aggregation, the network can learn the deformation easier.

The above procedure is repeated across different levels of the pyramid while the deformation is refined from coarse to fine. If we take Eq. (2) into Eq. (3), and regard the joint operation of G and R as GR while omitting the upsampling as it is an constant operation, the whole process of our network can be depicted as

$$\begin{aligned} \phi^0 &= \boldsymbol{GR}(F_f^0, F_m^0, \phi^1) \\ &= \boldsymbol{GR}(F_f^0, F_m^0, \boldsymbol{GR}(F_f^1, F_m^1, \phi^2)) = \cdots \cdots \\ &= \boldsymbol{GR}(F_f^0, F_m^0, \boldsymbol{GR}(F_f^1, F_m^1, \cdots, \boldsymbol{GR}(F_f^L, F_m^L))). \end{aligned} \tag{4}$$

As an end-to-end network, the weight-sharing generator G and receptive module R are jointly trained at multiple levels, fusing information at each level and leading to better generalization. This compact network using the self-recursive scheme reduces parameters while maintaining promising performance.

2.2 Contextual Components

For better capturing contextual information in the self-recursive network, we design two contextual components in the feature extraction stage and the deformation post-processing stage respectively.

Feature Extractor with SPP. A regular pyramid network extracts features from input images using a series of strided 3D convolutions [19] or a 3D U-net structure [15], and here we choose a light U-net as the base extractor E. We equip the 3D U-net with L downsampled and upsampled convolutions with kernel size of $3 \times 3 \times 3$ and $4 \times 4 \times 4$ respectively, while the stride of them is 2 and L is set to 4. We then introduce a 3-level spatial pyramid pooling [22] (SPP) module in the extractor E to capture richer contextual features, which locates at the end of the encoder in U-net. As shown in Fig. 1, the SPP module employs average poolings with kernel size 2, 4, 8 separately. It then convolves and upsamples the pooling features to the original scale. After that, we average these features as the input of the decoder in U-net to generate feature representations.

Receptive Module. Instead of directly treating ϕ_g from generator G as the final output at each level, we present a novel receptive module R to post-process the deformation. The input for R is ϕ_g and the second last feature F_g of G, and the output deformation can be depicted as $\phi_r = R(F_g, \phi_g)$. ϕ_r is then used for the residual aggregation described in Sect. 2.1. Specifically, we construct R with four $3 \times 3 \times 3$ dilated convolutions [11] followed by leaky ReLU, and the spatial kernel of each convolution is $3 \times 3 \times 3$. As shown in Fig. 1, we set different dilation rates as 1, 2, 4 in order. Dilated convolutions enlarge the receptive field without introducing any more parameters which recovers more details for the post-processing of deformation field.

2.3 Training Strategies

Loss Function. Our total loss consists of two parts, the affine loss and the deformable loss. Our proposed network focuses on the deformable part. Before an image pair is sent to it, an affine registration subnetwork identical to [23] is used to predict linearly affine transformation parameters. This subnet is essential in preventing the gradients from exploding and ensuring training stability with its affine loss including negative local cross correlation (NLCC) loss, total variation loss, orthogonality loss and determinant loss as in [23]. Deformable loss obeys the formulation in equation (1), where L_{sim} is in the form of the NLCC loss and L_{smooth} is the total variation loss.

Training Parameters. We employ the Adam optimizer with the first momentum of 0.9, the second momentum of 0.999. The training stage runs for 10^5 iterations. The initial learning rate is 10^{-4}, which is halved after 6×10^4 steps and again after 8×10^4 steps. Our model is implemented in TensorFlow and we set the batch size as 4 on 4 GPUs of NVIDIA TITAN XP.

3 Experiments and Results

Datasets. We train and test our model on public benchmark datasets with two types of 3D scans: brain MRI and liver CT. For brain MRI, we use ADNI [20], ABIDE [8], and ADHD [6] which contain 2302 samples in total for training, and use LPBA [21] for testing. LPBA consists of 40 scans and corresponding segmentation ground truth with 56 manually labeled anatomical structures. For liver CT, we train our network on MSD [1] and BFH [24], and test on SLIVER [13]. We select the most relevant 933 scans of liver in MSD and the whole BFH for our experiments. SLIVER contains 20 scans which are annotated with segmentation ground truth for key position areas.

Data Preprocessing. Both brain MRI and liver CT scans are resampled into $128 \times 128 \times 128$ voxels after cropping. Brain MRI scans are processed by removing the skulls with FreeSurfer [10] and liver CT scans are cropped into bounding boxes by a threshold-based algorithm following [23].

Evaluation Metrics. We choose the atlas-based registration strategy for brain scans, where the first image of LPBA is fixed as an atlas with all other images aligning to it. Liver scans are evaluated for subject-to-subject registration, where 20×19 image pairs are generated from SLIVER. These settings are inherited from [23] for a fair comparison. During test, we evaluate different models by the Dice Similarity Coefficient (DSC) which is a common metric for registration methods [5]. We compute the average DSC of all anatomical structures. Besides, we utilize the average landmark distance (abbreviated as Dist) as an auxiliary metric in SLIVER.

Evaluation on Brain MRI. To verify the effectiveness of our method, we first investigate the performance on 3D brain MRI images. We regard the affine result in [23] as the lower-bound of deformable registration, and compare our method with traditional methods such as ANTs SyN [3,4] and Elastic B-spline [18]. Representative one-stage encoder-decoder registration methods, VoxelMorph [5] and VTN [23], are also included for comparison. Besides, we reimplement a state-of-the-art one-stage pyramid registration method according to [15] (abbreviated as Pyramid). Moreover, we compare our with multi-stage cascaded methods reported in [23], such as 10-stage VTN and 5-stage VoxelMorph.

Table 1 provides DSC results for all methods. As can be seen, our method improves the performance at a much faster running speed compared with ANTs

Table 1. Quantitative results on the brain dataset LPBA.

Methods	DSC(%)	Params(M)	Time(s)
Affine only	62.8 ± 1.7	-	-
ANTs SyN	70.8 ± 3.9	-	748 (CPU)
Elastic B-spline	67.5 ± 1.3	-	115 (CPU)
VoxelMorph	68.8 ± 1.5	1.2	0.25 (GPU)
VTN	68.6 ± 1.4	107.8	0.24 (GPU)
Pyramid	71.1 ± 1.3	5.4	0.61 (GPU)
5-VoxelMorph	70.8 ± 1.5	5.7	1.27 (GPU)
6-VTN	71.2 ± 1.4	646.6	1.43 (GPU)
10-VTN	**71.6** ± 1.3	1077.7	2.39 (GPU)
Ours	**71.6** ± 1.3	3.3	0.70 (GPU)

SyN and Elastic B-spline. Meanwhile, our method outperforms Voxel-Morph and VTN by a large margin, and also improves the performance over the state-of-the-art Pyramid with 39% less parameters (Note that, for a similar DSC improvement, 10-VTN uses 66.7% more parameters over 6-VTN). For cascaded networks, our method performs better than 5-VoxelMorph with 57% of its parameters. It is even competitive to 10-VTN with only 0.3% of its parameters. Besides, we also evaluate the diffeomorphism property in terms of the percentage of non-positive pixels in the Jacobian determinant. As a representative, Pyramid is 0.6% while ours is 0.19% (the lower, the better). Figure 2 visualizes those methods for an example in the dataset, where our method performs the best (on par with 10-VTN) in terms of the overlap of segmentation results.

Evaluation on Liver CT. We further conduct experiments on another 3D image type of liver CT. The comparison methods are the same as those in MRI experiments. Compared with traditional methods, our method achieves 4.8% DSC improvement over ANTS SyN and 3.3% over Elastic. Figure 3 plots the performance of different learning-based methods. As one-stage methods, VoxelMorph (with 1.1M parameters) achieves 91.3% DSC and 13.1 Dist and VTN (107.8M) achieves 91.4% DSC and 13.0 Dist. Our method (3.3M) reaches the highest DSC 94.3% and the lowest Dist 11.1 among one-stage methods while using a small number of parameters. Especially, compared with the state-of-the-art Pyramid (5.4M), our method notably improves DSC and reduces Dist with 39% less parameters. For cascaded methods, our method competes to 3-VTN (323.3M) and 4-VoxelMorph (4.6M) in DSC, while outperforming 5-VoxelMorph (5.7M) and competes to 8-VTN (862.2M) in Dist.

Ablation. We provide an ablation study on the brain dataset LPBA to confirm the effectiveness of three key components in our method: SPP in feature extractor, self-recursive scheme (termed SR) and receptive module (termed RM).

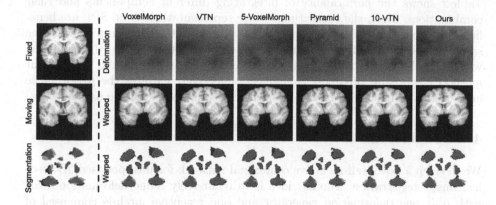

Fig. 2. Visualization of an example in the brain dataset LPBA. Left: fixed image, moving image and 9 selected anatomical structures with overlaps of them. Right: The first row shows the generated deformation fields of different methods, the second row shows the corresponding warped moving images, and the third row shows the overlaps (red) of fixed image segments (green) and warped moving image segments (blue). (Color figure online)

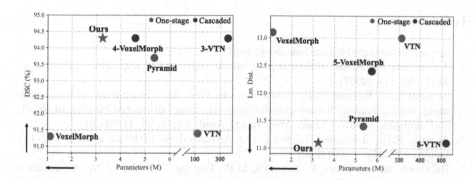

Fig. 3. Performance on the liver dataset SLIVER. Horizontal axis: number of parameters. Vertical axis: left is DSC and right is the landmark distance. Arrow direction: better tendency of each metric.

Table 2. Ablation study on the brain dataset LPBA.

LPBA	Pyramid	+SPP	+SR	+SR+RM	+SR+RM+SPP
DSC (%)	71.1	71.4	70.9	71.3	71.6
Params (%)	0	+0.9	−42.3	−39.9	−39.0

Table 2 shows the performance of integrating different components and their combinations. First, the contextual feature representations from SPP are beneficial for the pyramid registration. Second, compared to slight drop in DSC, the significant reduction of parameters from SR is more attractive. Further equipped with RM, the performance already exceeds the original Pyramid. Finally, our method comprising three key components effectively elevates the performance and greatly reduce the number of parameters compared with the baseline.

4 Conclusion

We develop a novel self-recursive contextual network for unsupervised 3D medical image registration. The key idea is to recursively refine deformation fields with only one deformation generator and one receptive module composed of dilated convolutions. We also introduce the SPP module into the feature extractor for capturing richer contextual information. Experimental results on MRI and CT benchmark datasets demonstrate that our registration network offers an elegant solution jointly considering performance and model size.

Acknowledgement. This work was supported in part by Key Area R&D Program of Guangdong Province with grant No. 2018B030338001 and the Fundamental Research Funds for the Central Universities under Grant WK2380000002.

References

1. https://decathlon-10.grand-challenge.org/
2. Ashburner, J.: A fast diffeomorphic image registration algorithm. Neuroimage **38**(1), 95–113 (2007)
3. Avants, B.B., Epstein, C.L., Grossman, M., Gee, J.C.: Symmetric diffeomorphic image registration with cross-correlation: evaluating automated labeling of elderly and neurodegenerative brain. Med. Image Anal. **12**(1), 26–41 (2008)
4. Avants, B.B., Tustison, N., Song, G.: Advanced normalization tools (ANTs). Insight j **2**(365), 1–35 (2009)
5. Balakrishnan, G., Zhao, A., Sabuncu, M.R., Guttag, J., Dalca, A.V.: An unsupervised learning model for deformable medical image registration. In: Proceedings of the IEEE Conference on Computer Vision and Pattern Recognition, pp. 9252–9260 (2018)
6. Bellec, P., Chu, C., Chouinard-Decorte, F., Benhajali, Y., Margulies, D.S., Craddock, R.C.: The neuro bureau ADHD-200 preprocessed repository. Neuroimage **144**, 275–286 (2017)
7. Chakravarty, M.M., Bertrand, G., Hodge, C.P., Sadikot, A.F., Collins, D.L.: The creation of a brain atlas for image guided neurosurgery using serial histological data. Neuroimage **30**(2), 359–376 (2006)
8. Di Martino, A., et al.: The autism brain imaging data exchange: towards a large-scale evaluation of the intrinsic brain architecture in autism. Mol. Psychiatry **19**(6), 659–667 (2014)
9. Du, J., Li, W., Lu, K., Xiao, B.: An overview of multi-modal medical image fusion. Neurocomputing **215**, 3–20 (2016)

10. Fischl, B.: Freesurfer. Neuroimage **62**(2), 774–781 (2012)
11. Fisher Yu, V.K.: Multi-scale context aggregation by dilated convolutions. In: International Conference on Learning Representations (2016)
12. Glocker, B., Komodakis, N., Tziritas, G., Navab, N., Paragios, N.: Dense image registration through MRFs and efficient linear programming. Med. Image Anal. **12**(6), 731–741 (2008)
13. Heimann, T., et al.: Comparison and evaluation of methods for liver segmentation from CT datasets. IEEE Trans. Med. Imaging **28**(8), 1251–1265 (2009)
14. Heinrich, M.P.: Closing the gap between deep and conventional image registration using probabilistic dense displacement networks. In: Shen, D., et al. (eds.) MICCAI 2019. LNCS, vol. 11769, pp. 50–58. Springer, Cham (2019). https://doi.org/10.1007/978-3-030-32226-7_6
15. Hu, X., Kang, M., Huang, W., Scott, M.R., Wiest, R., Reyes, M.: Dual-stream pyramid registration network. In: Shen, D., et al. (eds.) MICCAI 2019. LNCS, vol. 11765, pp. 382–390. Springer, Cham (2019). https://doi.org/10.1007/978-3-030-32245-8_43
16. Jaderberg, M., Simonyan, K., Zisserman, A., et al.: Spatial transformer networks. In: Advances in Neural Information Processing Systems, pp. 2017–2025 (2015)
17. Kim, B., Kim, J., Lee, J.-G., Kim, D.H., Park, S.H., Ye, J.C.: Unsupervised deformable image registration using cycle-consistent CNN. In: Shen, D., et al. (eds.) MICCAI 2019. LNCS, vol. 11769, pp. 166–174. Springer, Cham (2019). https://doi.org/10.1007/978-3-030-32226-7_19
18. Klein, S., Staring, M., Murphy, K., Viergever, M.A., Pluim, J.P.: Elastix: a toolbox for intensity-based medical image registration. IEEE Trans. Med. Imaging **29**(1), 196–205 (2009)
19. Liu, L., Hu, X., Zhu, L., Heng, P.A.: Probabilistic multilayer regularization network for unsupervised 3D brain image registration. In: Shen, D., et al. (eds.) International Conference on Medical Image Computing and Computer-Assisted Intervention, pp. 346–354. Springer, Heidelberg (2019). https://doi.org/10.1007/978-3-030-32245-8_39
20. Mueller, S.G., et al.: Ways toward an early diagnosis in alzheimer's disease: the Alzheimer's disease neuroimaging initiative (ADNI). Alzheimer's Dementia **1**(1), 55–66 (2005)
21. Shattuck, D.W., et al.: Construction of a 3D probabilistic atlas of human cortical structures. Neuroimage **39**(3), 1064–1080 (2008)
22. Zhao, H., Shi, J., Qi, X., Wang, X., Jia, J.: Pyramid scene parsing network. In: Proceedings of the IEEE Conference on Computer Vision and Pattern Recognition, pp. 2881–2890 (2017)
23. Zhao, S., Dong, Y., Chang, E.I., Xu, Y., et al.: Recursive cascaded networks for unsupervised medical image registration. In: Proceedings of the IEEE International Conference on Computer Vision, pp. 10600–10610 (2019)
24. Zhao, S., Lau, T., Luo, J., Eric, I., Chang, C., Xu, Y.: Unsupervised 3D end-to-end medical image registration with volume tweening network. IEEE J. Biomed. Health Inform. (2019)
25. Zhou, S., et al.: Fast and accurate electron microscopy image registration with 3D convolution. In: Shen, D., et al. (eds.) MICCAI 2019. LNCS, vol. 11764, pp. 478–486. Springer, Cham (2019). https://doi.org/10.1007/978-3-030-32239-7_53

Automated Tumor Proportion Scoring for Assessment of PD-L1 Expression Based on Multi-Stage Ensemble Strategy

Yuxin Kang[1], Hansheng Li[1], Xin Han[1], Boju Pan[2], Yuan Li[3], Yan Jin[3], Qirong Bu[1], Lei Cui[1(✉)], Jun Feng[1(✉)], and Lin Yang[1(✉)]

[1] School of Information Science and Technology, Northwest University, Xi'an 710127, Shaanxi, China
{leicui,fengjun,linyang}@nwu.edu.cn
[2] Peking Union Medical College Hospital, Beijing, China
[3] Fudan University Shanghai Cancer Center, Shanghai, China

Abstract. Tumor Programmed Death-Ligand 1 (PD-L1) expression is a crucial biomarker to identify tumor patients who may have an enhanced response to anti-Programmed Death-1 (PD-1)/PD-L1 treatment. Tumor proportion score (TPS) is an indicator to describe the frequency of PD-L1 expression and is essential for selecting from different tumor therapies. In this paper, we propose a novel deep learning-based framework for automated tumor proportion scoring. Specifically, we introduce the clinical diagnosis process to our framework. The framework consists of a cellular localization network (C-Net) and a regional segmentation network (R-Net). The C-Net is dedicated to classifying cells and generating TPS, and R-Net learns to distinguish tumor regions from their normal counterparts. The predictions made by R-Net can, in turn, be used to refine the TPS. We have consolidated the visual TPS from multiple pathologists for clinical verification. Concordance measures computed on a set of WSI provide evidence that our method matches visual scoring from multiple pathologists (**MAE = 7.405, RMSE = 11.25, PCCs = 0.9305, SRCC = 0.967**).

1 Introduction

Tumors can evade the immune system via the exploitation of inhibitory checkpoint pathways that suppress antitumor T-cell responses [1]. In the Programmed Death-1 (PD-1) and Programmed Death-Ligand 1 (PD-L1) pathway, the PD-L1 expressed by tumor cells (TC) binds to PD-1, inhibiting T-cell receptor signaling and blocking antitumor immune response [1,2]. Antibodies targeting PD-1 or PD-L1 can block this interaction, thus resuming antitumor response [1]. Meanwhile, tumor PD-L1 expression is a key biomarker to identify tumor patients who may respond to treatment using PD-1 or PD-L1 inhibitors [1,3,12]. Tumor

---

Y. Kang and H. Li—Equally-contributed.

© Springer Nature Switzerland AG 2020
M. Liu et al. (Eds.): MLMI 2020, LNCS 12436, pp. 70–79, 2020.
https://doi.org/10.1007/978-3-030-59861-7_8

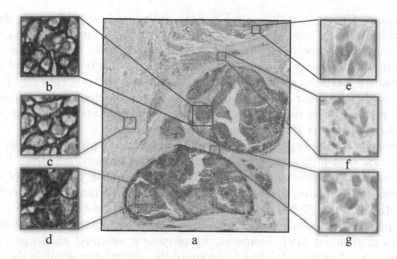

Fig. 1. The different types of regions on a low magnification scale and various types of cells on a high magnification scale. (a) the PD-L1 WSI on a low magnification scale. (b) TC(+). (c) histocytes. (d) necrotic cells. (e) negative tumor cells (TC(−)). (f) stromal cells. (g) lymphocytes.

proportion score (TPS) is the ratio of the number between the count of positive tumor cells (TC(+)) and the count of TC on PD-L1 whole slide image (WSI) [2]. TPS is also an indicator to describe the tumor PD-L1 expression and essential for selecting tumor therapy options [2,3]. However, manually calculate TPS is a time-consuming process and also prone to error due to the number of cell nuclei ranges from several thousands to even millions in the whole slide image (WSI) [6]. Hence, it is desirable to design an automated tumor proportion scoring method for the scarce pathologists.

Recently, many researchers have proven that deep learning-based methods show the ability to estimate TPS automatically [1,2,6], and these methods can be divided into two main categories: regional area-ratio based and cellular count-ratio based. **Regional area-ratio based** methods often employ region segmentation to distinguish the TC region from other regions based on regional information [1,2] and estimate TPS by calculating the ratio between region area of TC(+) and TC. However, the method is not precise enough because clinical guidelines require that TPS should be calculated based on tumor cellular count [4,5]. **Cellular count-ratio based** methods refer to those directly extract cellular information on a high magnification scale to localize and count the cells [6]. Further efforts for more accurate cell classification is still expecting.

In clinical diagnosis, as shown in Fig. 1 (b–g), PD-L1 expression is not only restricted to the membrane of TC but also existed in histocytes and necrotic cells [4]. This may lead to potential mistakes even for those experienced pathologists if they just distinguish on high magnification. And we will not rule out that this may be the reason why cellular-ratio based methods are not in an excellent performance. Uniquely, as shown in Fig. 1 (a), pathologists approximately distinguish the TC region from other regions firstly with the distinguishable regional information on the lower magnification scale and then zoom in the higher magnification for accurate cell counting. Such a process works best to prevent both false positive and false negative (e.g., histocytes and necrotic cells) by fusing the regional-and-cellular information. However, an automated tumor proportion scoring method based on both regional and cellular information has not been proposed yet as far as we know.

Motivated by the experience of the clinical diagnosis process, our primary contribution is to propose a novel automated tumor proportion scoring framework based on a multi-stage ensemble strategy. We utilize the merits of both categories stating above, to design our framework, which composed of a cellular localization network (C-Net) and a regional segmentation network (R-Net). The C-Net predicts the cellular count-ratio based TPS by locating and classifying the cells of an input WSI. Moreover, we propose a weighted pixel-wise cross-entropy as loss function of C-Net to promote the algorithm trained in the right direction. The R-Net learns a probability map that distinguishes tumor regions from their normal counterparts. The predicted map is used to emendate the predicted cellular mask for an improved scoring performance. Extensive experimental cellular results show significant improvement by using our C-Net. We further consolidate the visual TPS from multiple pathologists' research to make sure of clinical verification. Concordance measures computed on a set of WSIs provide evidence that regional information is indispensable, and our solution matches visual scoring per multiple pathologists' perspective.

2   Methodology

The proposed framework consists of two main parts: (1) cellular localization and elementary TPS calculation using fully convolutional networks, in which a weighted pixel-wise cross-entropy is proposed (Sect. 2.1); (2) a synchronized regional segmentation branch to refine the TPS (Sect. 2.2);

2.1   Cellular Localization

Cellular Localization aims to utilize fully convolutional networks (e.g. FCN [13] and U-Net [7]) predict the positions of key points defined on the nucleus. The networks consist of an encoder and decoder that are symmetrically connected through skip connections. However, the excessive decoding processes significantly increase algorithm parameters, and the global loss can't guide each convolution kernels to extract more useful cellular information. This will result in difficulty for the network to be trained on the right direction.

Different from FCN and U-Net, S^3Net [12] has shown high performance, which is redesigned with a high-efficiency decoder that restores the resolution of the encoded features. S^3Net utilizes the deep supervision method and transition block to let the shallower convolution kernels extract more semantic features,

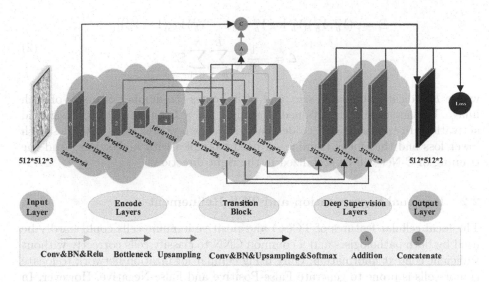

512*512*3

256*256*64

128*128*256

64*64*512

32*32*1024

16*16*1024

128*128*256

128*128*256

128*128*256

512*512*2

512*512*2

512*512*2

512*512*2

| Input Layer | Encode Layers | Transition Block | Deep Supervision Layers | Output Layer |

Conv&BN&Relu   Bottleneck   Upsampling   Conv&BN&Upsampling&Softmax   Addition   Concatenate

Fig. 2. The architecture of C-Net.

which are critical for prediction. Hence, we use S^3Net as the basic model for C-Net. The architecture of our proposed C-Net is shown in Fig. 2. C-Net predicts one identical-sized heat map $\hat{y}$, from where larger values mean these pixels are more close to cell centers. To mitigate the effects of image noise, we suppress the pixels with values less than $\eta \cdot max(\hat{y})$, where $\eta \in [0,1]$ by assigning them zeros. Then we locate cell centers by seeking local maxima on the suppressed prediction map.

Weighted Pixel-Wise Cross-Entropy Loss: Tumor cells are close and/or adhesive, which is easy to cause the network to recognize multiple cells as one cell. Meanwhile, the cross-entropy is ineffective since the point-level annotation can't represents cells with rupturing membranes or missing nucleus. To better identify the tumor cells individually and inspired by the weight matrix in the focal loss [9], we construct a weight matrix φ which effectively increases the loss of those difficult cells during training. It can also be understood as a kind of difficult sample mining. The weight φ is defined as

$$\varphi(Y_b^i, \hat{Y}_b^i) = \lambda||Y_b^i - \hat{Y}_b^i||^\gamma. \tag{1}$$

where $\hat{Y}_b^i$ denotes the ground truth of the pixel i in flattened b^{th} image and Y_b^i is the predicted probability. Lin, Tsung-Yi et al. [9] utilized tunable focusing parameters to balance the importance of positive/negative examples in focal loss [9]. Hence, we also utilize two tunable focusing parameter λ and γ to weight the importance of matrix φ for the weighted pixel-wise cross-entropy loss $\mathcal{L}$, respectively. In our experiments we set $\lambda = 3$ and $\gamma = 3$. Specifically, φ will make the false prediction pixels with a higher loss. Accordingly, the $\mathcal{L}$, can be formulated as

$$\mathbb{E} = \varphi(Y_b^i, \hat{Y}_b^i)[Y_b^i \log \hat{Y}_b^i + (1 - Y_b^i) \log(1 - \hat{Y}_b^i)],$$

$$\mathcal{L} = -\frac{1}{B}\frac{1}{N}\sum_{b=1}^{B}\sum_{i=1}^{N}\mathbb{E}. \tag{2}$$

where B indicates the batch size, and N indicates the number of pixels of each image. Further, each Y_b^i is obtained by using $1 \times 1 \times 1$ convolutions with sigmoid activation. In this sense, we guide the C-Net down-weight easy examples with lower loss and thus focus training on hard examples with higher loss. And the training of C-Net will be stabilized in the right direction.

2.2   Regional Segmentation and TPS Refinement

The local cellular features of TC(+) and positive immune cells could hardly be used by both pathologists and a common CNN to classify cells correctly without sufficient context information. Only using cellular localization network to locate tumor cells is prone to generate False-Positive and False-Negative. However, In PD-L1 images, the knowledge of clinical diagnosis is tumor cells usually cluster into obvious regions on a low magnification scale. Hence, we propose to use R-Net to improve C-Net to avoid problems in localization task due to lack of context information for local features. As mentioned above, we first use the R-Net to generate a tumor region probability map on a low magnification scale. Specifically, we employ the DeeplabV3+ [10] pre-trained on ImageNet as the basic model for R-Net and use Cross-entropy loss to monitor the performance of R-Net. The larger values in the map indicate a high probability of the region being a tumor. Then we use the map to weight the feature map in the C-Net during testing. To adapt the input size and high magnification scale of the localization algorithm, we further extract patches of the tumor region probability map with a stride of 512 pixels and utilize global average pooling to combine the

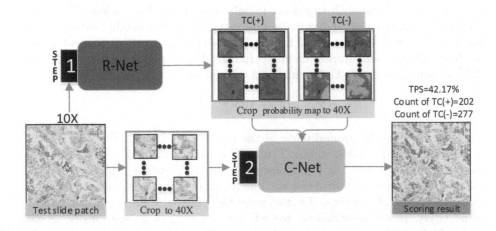

Fig. 3. The technical pipeline of our proposed framework.

neighborhood spatial features. Finally, we introduce the concurrent operation to embed regional information into cellular information and yield the feature map $\mathcal{C}$. The process of obtaining $\mathcal{C}$ can be expressed as follow:

$$\mathcal{C} = T \oplus (T \otimes P). \tag{3}$$

Where T is the decoded cellular-level semantic features from the transition block of C-Net and P is the tumor region probability map, $\oplus$ and $\otimes$ mean adding and multiplying in element-wise, respectively. By this, the non-tumor cell features will be suppressed, and the non-tumor cell will get a minimal probability value after the activation layer. The technical pipeline of our proposed framework as shown in Fig. 3.

3   Experiments and Results

3.1   Datasets and Experimental Design

The dataset contains 100 PD-L1 WSIs which is provided from 3 pathology departments. We utilized 30 WSIs to sample patch for annotating. The other 70 WSIs to evaluate the clinical effectiveness. The dataset contains three scale level tags, namely: Cell, Region, and Clinical. Cell tags are labeled on 300 patches of size 512×512 from 30 WSIs, which indicates the type of TC in the 40x magnification scale and consists of 17660 TC(+) and 15643 TC(−). Region tags are labeled on 160 patches of size 512×512 from 30 WSIs, which indicates the type of tumor region in the 10x magnification scale and consists of 272 TC(+) regions and 584 TC(−) regions. Meanwhile, the patches of cell tags and the region tags are extracted non-repetitively. Clinical tags are labeled on the other 70 WSIs, which indicates the TPS of each WSI and is utilized to evaluate the clinical effectiveness against pathologists.

To alleviate the overfit of deep neural networks, we employed the online data augmentation techniques, including random rotation, shear, shift, zoom of width and height, whitening and horizontal and vertical flips to enlarge the training set. We optimized both C-Net and R-Net used the momentum optimizer with a batch size of 4, an initial learning rate of 0.001, the maximum epoch of 200. We set 20% of both Cell tags and Region tags aside to monitor the performance of both networks and 20% for testing.

3.2   Evaluation Metrics

We evaluated the results of localization algorithm using four metrics provided by [11], including (1) the accuracy of the detection of tumor cells (Object F1 Score); (2) the mean absolute error of the count of tumor cells (MAE); (3) the root mean squared error of the count of tumor cells (RMSE); (4) the mean absolute percent error of the count of tumor cells (MAPE). Meanwhile, we evaluated the clinical effectiveness using five metrics, which are MAE, RMSE, MAPE, the Pearson product-moment correlation coefficient (PCCs), and Spearman's rank correlation coefficient (SRCC).

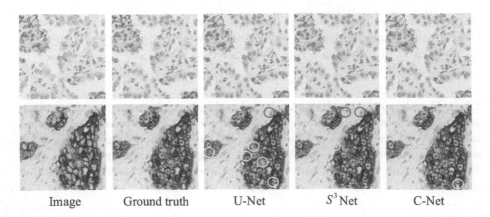

| Image | Ground truth | U-Net | S^3Net | C-Net |

Fig. 4. Visualization of tumor cells localization results of two cases selected from the Cell datasets. TC(+) and TC(−) are highlighted by different colors (e.g., red and green). The yellow circle and blue circle are representing the false negative, and false positive. (Color figure online)

3.3   Results

Results of Quantitative Verification: Mi et al. [6] which reported the best performance so far for automated tumor proportion scoring. Comparing the proposed C-Net against Mi et al. [6], U-Net and S^3Net, and verified the effectiveness of weighted pixel-wise cross-entropy loss on the Cell tags, we listed the obtained average performance of these models in Table 1. In dealing with close tumor cells, based on the construction of the proposed weighted pixel-wise cross-entropy loss, the C-Net is able to identify different tumor cells individually which helps achieve the best performance in the Object F1 Score, MAE, RMSE and MAPE on the validation data of Cell datasets. Meanwhile, due to the norm in the proposed loss strengthens to supervise the close tumor cells, the performance of the C-Net in terms of the object-level recall would be improveed significantly. We visualized two patch images and the corresponding localization results obtained by different deep models, together with the ground truth, in Fig. 4.

Results of Consistency Verification: We also evaluated the importance of regional information for our automated tumor proportion scoring and the clinical effectiveness of framework against two experienced pathologists' research on the Clinical dataset. The obtained average performance in Table 2 reveals that our method consistently surpasses the other three methods by large margins overall metrics and are more close to the scores of two pathologists. Specifically, the local cellular features of TC(+) and positive immune cells could hardly be used by a common CNN to classify cells correctly. Benefits from the R-Net, which provide contextual information while classifying similar cells. The results show that R-Net can significantly improve the performance of each localization network. Meanwhile, we visualized 6 PD-L1 WSIs and the TPS calculation results obtained by both C-Net and R-Net in Fig. 5.

Table 1. Comparison our C-Net with U-Net and S^3Net on the cell dataset.

Method	F1 score			MAE			RMSE			MAPE		
	TC(+)	TC(−)	Avg	TC(+)	TC(−)	Avg	TC(+)	TC(−)	Avg	TC(+)	TC(−)	Avg
Mi [6]	0.56	0.57	0.565	40.27	24.34	32.31	52.76	28.99	40.86	44.61	53.17	45.61
U-Net	0.58	0.64	0.61	39.71	20.01	29.86	48.93	26.01	37.37	43.82	42.85	43.34
S^3Net	0.68	0.71	0.695	30.07	17.52	23.795	42.68	23.53	33.105	33.82	38.16	35.99
C-Net	**0.75**	**0.78**	**0.765**	**19.01**	**10.41**	**14.71**	**27.21**	**17.21**	**22.21**	**24.19**	**23.34**	**23.765**

Table 2. Comparison with three methods and two trained pathologists on the clinical dataset.

Method		Pathologist1				Pathologist2			
	R-Net	MAE	RMSE	PCCs	SRCC	MAE	RMSE	PCCs	SRCC
Pathologist1	-	0	0	1	1	**4.43**	**8.51**	**0.970**	**0.977**
Pathologist2	-	**4.43**	**8.51**	**0.970**	**0.977**	0	0	1	1
Mi [6]	-	12.34	17.82	0.834	0.921	13.62	18.43	0.825	0.917
Mi [6]	✓	9.64	15.71	0.882	0.927	11.22	17.35	0.902	0.925
U-Net	-	10.22	15.45	0.865	0.936	9.82	13.72	0.874	0.945
U-Net	✓	8.83	14.48	0.904	0.937	10.05	15.30	0.898	0.934
S^3Net	-	8.18	13.46	0.905	0.945	8.77	13.28	0.902	0.946
S^3Net	✓	7.65	12.73	0.928	0.956	7.88	12.35	0.927	0.959
C-Net	-	8.00	12.19	0.906	0.951	8.69	13.29	0.904	0.947
C-Net	✓	**7.55**	**11.82**	**0.933**	**0.965**	**7.26**	**10.68**	**0.928**	**0.969**

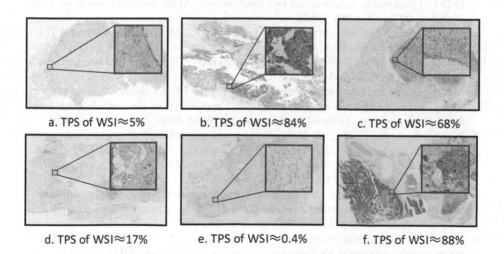

a. TPS of WSI≈5%   b. TPS of WSI≈84%   c. TPS of WSI≈68%

d. TPS of WSI≈17%   e. TPS of WSI≈0.4%   f. TPS of WSI≈88%

Fig. 5. Visualization of TPS calculation results of our method. TC(+) and TC(−) are highlighted by different colors (e.g., red and green). (Color figure online)

4   Conclusion

A PD-L1 computer-aided automatic scoring tool has been urgently needed in the current clinical diagnosis. In this work, we propose a novel TPS scoring framework that combines the pathologist's diagnosis processing knowledge in the first time. The framework consists of two networks: C-Net for TPS calculation and R-Net for TPS refinement. Moreover, we enlighten the weighted pixel-wise cross-entropy to promote C-Net in the right direction. Concordance measurements provide evidence that regional information is indispensable, and our method matches visual scoring from multiple pathologists' research.

Ackowlegement. Hereby the authors would like to thank appreciate the support from the Medical Diagnosis team at AstraZeneca for their scientific comments on this study. This work is financially supported by National Natural Science Foundation of China (No. 61701404) and partially supported by Major Program of National Natural Science Foundation of China (No. 81727802), Natural Science Foundation of Shaanxi Province of China (No. 2020JM-438).

References

1. Widmaier, M., et al.: Comparison of continuous measures across diagnostic PD-L1 assays in non-small cell lung cancer using automated image analysis. Mod. Pathol. 1–11 (2019)
2. Kapil, A., et al.: Deep semi supervised generative learning for automated tumor proportion scoring on NSCLC tissue needle biopsies. Sci. Rep. **8**(1), 1–10 (2018)
3. Taylor, C.R., et al.: A multi-institutional study to evaluate automated whole slide scoring of immunohistochemistry for assessment of programmed death-ligand 1 (PD-L1) expression in non-small cell lung cancer. Appl. Immunohistochem. Mol. Morphol. **27**(4), 263–269 (2019)
4. McLaughlin, J., et al.: Quantitative assessment of the heterogeneity of PD-L1 expression in non-small-cell lung cancer. JAMA Oncol. **2**(1), 46–54 (2016)
5. Ettinger, D.S., et al.: Non-small cell lung cancer. NCCN clinical practice guidelines in oncology (NCCN Guidelines) (2019)
6. Mi, H., et al.: A quantitative analysis platform for PD-L1 immunohistochemistry based on point-level supervision model. In: Proceedings of the 28th International Joint Conference on Artificial Intelligence, pp. 6554–6556. AAAI Press (2019)
7. Ronneberger, O., Fischer, P., Brox, T.: U-net: convolutional networks for biomedical image segmentation. In: Navab, N., Hornegger, J., Wells, W.M., Frangi, A.F. (eds.) MICCAI 2015. LNCS, vol. 9351, pp. 234–241. Springer, Cham (2015). https://doi.org/10.1007/978-3-319-24574-4_28
8. Abraham, N., Khan, N.M.: A novel focal tversky loss function with improved attention u-net for lesion segmentation. In: 2019 IEEE 16th International Symposium on Biomedical Imaging (ISBI 2019), pp. 683–687 (2019)
9. Lin, T.-Y., et al.: Focal loss for dense object detection. In: Proceedings of the IEEE international conference on computer vision, pp. 2980–2988 (2017)
10. Chen, L.-C., et al.: Encoder-decoder with atrous separable convolution for semantic image segmentation. In: Proceedings of the European conference on computer vision, pp. 801–818 (2018)

11. Ribera, J., Guera, D., Chen, Y., Delp, E.J.: Locating objects without bounding boxes. In: Proceedings of the IEEE Conference on Computer Vision and Pattern Recognition, pp. 6479–6489 (2019)
12. Yan, M., et al.: S^3 Net: trained on a small sample segmentation network for biomedical image analysis. In: 2019 IEEE International Conference on Bioinformatics and Biomedicine, pp. 1402–1408 (2019)
13. Long, J., Shelhamer, E., Darrell, T.: Fully convolutional networks for semantic segmentation. In: Proceedings of the IEEE conference on computer vision and pattern recognition, pp. 3431–3440 (2015)

Uncertainty Quantification in Medical Image Segmentation with Normalizing Flows

Raghavendra Selvan[1(✉)], Frederik Faye[2], Jon Middleton[2], and Akshay Pai[1,2]

[1] Department of Computer Science, University of Copenhagen, Copenhagen, Denmark
raghav@di.ku.dk
[2] Cerebriu A/S, Copenhagen, Denmark

Abstract. Medical image segmentation is inherently an ambiguous task due to factors such as partial volumes and variations in anatomical definitions. While in most cases the segmentation uncertainty is around the border of structures of interest, there can also be considerable inter-rater differences. The class of conditional variational autoencoders (cVAE) offers a principled approach to inferring distributions over plausible segmentations that are conditioned on input images. Segmentation uncertainty estimated from samples of such distributions can be more informative than using pixel level probability scores. In this work, we propose a novel conditional generative model that is based on conditional Normalizing Flow (cFlow). The basic idea is to increase the expressivity of the cVAE by introducing a cFlow transformation step after the encoder. This yields improved approximations of the latent posterior distribution, allowing the model to capture richer segmentation variations. With this we show that the quality and diversity of samples obtained from our conditional generative model is enhanced. Performance of our model, which we call *cFlow Net*, is evaluated on two medical imaging datasets demonstrating substantial improvements in both qualitative and quantitative measures when compared to a recent cVAE based model.

Keywords: Segmentation · Uncertainty · Normalizing flow · cVAE · chest CT · Vessels

1 Introduction

Medical image segmentation is inherently an ambiguous task and segmentation methods capable of quantifying uncertainty by inferring distributions over segmentations are therefore of substantial interest to the medical imaging community [7, 8, 25]. Estimating uncertainty from distributions over segmentations is closer to the clinical settings, than obtaining pixel-wise uncertainty estimates, where *whenever feasible* multiple expert opinions are used to ascertain downstream clinical decisions. Such consensus based decisions not only account

© Springer Nature Switzerland AG 2020
M. Liu et al. (Eds.): MLMI 2020, LNCS 12436, pp. 80–90, 2020.
https://doi.org/10.1007/978-3-030-59861-7_9

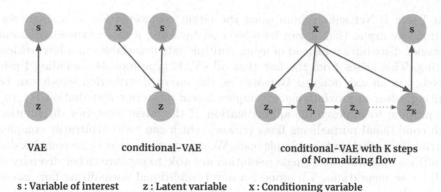

VAE   conditional-VAE   conditional-VAE with K steps
                                                          of Normalizing flow

s : Variable of interest   z : Latent variable   x : Conditioning variable

Fig. 1. Graphical model view of VAE and variations to it including the proposed cFlow Net (right)

for the aleatoric (inherent) and epistemic (modeling) uncertainties but also explain the inter-rater variability that is largely inevitable in medical image segmentation.

Remarkable strides in supervised medical image segmentation have been made with deep learning methods [4,20,26]. These methods, however, provide point estimates of segmentations – meaning a single segmentation mask per image – which limits our ability to quantify the uncertainty of said segmentations.

Bayesian deep learning methods offer a natural setting to infer distributions over segmentations. This has been explored to some extent for medical image segmentation in the spirit of Monte Carlo estimation where multiple hypotheses are explored by predicting segmentation masks with different dropout rates [5] or with an ensemble of models [21]. These methods can output a fixed number of samples with pixel level probability scores which can be a limitation.

Conditional variational autoencoders (cVAE) [23] belong to the class of conditional generative models. cVAEs can be used to obtain an unlimited number of predictions by sampling from a latent space conditioned on the input images. This model was adapted for medical image segmentation as the probabilistic U-Net (Prob. U-Net) [13] demonstrating the possibility of generating large number of plausible segmentations. The Prob. U-Net model fuses an additional channel obtained from the latent space to the final layer (at the highest resolution) of U-Net to obtain a variety of albeit less diverse and blurry segmentations when compared to the raters [3]. Quite recently, two models have sought to improve upon the Prob. U-Net [3,14]. Both these methods hypothesize that the blurriness and lack of diversity observed in samples obtained from Prob. U-Net is caused by the use of a single latent variable at the highest resolution. They propose using latent variables in a hierarchical fashion operating at different resolutions to make the model more expressive and demonstrate this to be helpful.

In this work, we focus on obtaining expressive latent representations that can yield diverse segmentations within the cVAE setting. While we agree with [3,14] that Prob. U-Net suffers from using the latent representation at a single resolution, we argue that it can be alleviated by using a more expressive latent posterior distribution instead of using multiple latent variables in a hierarchical setting. This arises from the fact that all cVAE type models, including Prob. U-Net, use an axis aligned Gaussian as the latent distribution which can be limiting when approximating a complex latent posterior distribution [11,19]. We propose to improve the approximation of the latent posterior distribution with conditional normalizing flows (cFlow) which can yield arbitrarily complex distributions starting from simple ones. We demonstrate that these complex distributions operating at a single resolution are able to capture richer diversity of realistic segmentations. We propose a novel conditional normalizing flow model – cFlow Net – and demonstrate the use of two types of normalizing flow transformations: Planar flows [19] and Generative Flows [10]. We evaluate the method on two medical imaging datasets: LIDC-IDRI [2] for detecting lesions in lungs from chest CT and for detecting retina blood vessels from on a new Retinal Vessel dataset created from three older datasets [6,16,24]. We compare the performance of our model with deterministic U-Net [20] and Prob. U-Net demonstrating significant improvements on both quantitative (generalized energy distance and dice) and qualitative measures.

2   Background and Problem Formulation

Image segmentation tasks can be formulated in a conditional generative model setting with the objective of estimating the conditional distribution $p(\mathbf{s}|\mathbf{x})$, where $\mathbf{x} \in \mathbb{R}^{H \times W \times C}$ and $\mathbf{s} \in \{0,1\}^{H \times W}$ are the input images and corresponding binary segmentations, respectively, of dimensions H, W with C channels. This has been approached using the conditional VAE formulation where the conditional distribution $p(\mathbf{s}|\mathbf{x})$ is approximated by introducing dependency on a d-dimensional latent variable $\mathbf{z} \in \mathbb{R}^d$ [13,23], as shown in Fig. 1 (center).

The cVAE objective minimizes the KL divergence between the true latent posterior distribution $p(\mathbf{z}|\mathbf{s}, \mathbf{x})$ and its variational approximation $q(\mathbf{z}|\mathbf{s}, \mathbf{x})$ resulting in an objective of the form [23]:

$$\mathcal{L}_{\text{cVAE}} = -\mathbb{E}_{q_\phi(\mathbf{z}|\mathbf{s},\mathbf{x})}\left[\log p_\theta(\mathbf{s}|\mathbf{z}, \mathbf{x})\right] + \text{KL}\left[q_\phi(\mathbf{z}|\mathbf{s}, \mathbf{x})||p_\psi(\mathbf{z}|\mathbf{x})\right] \tag{1}$$

The first term is the expected conditional log-likelihood (CLL) under the variational distribution $q_\phi(\mathbf{z}|\mathbf{s}, \mathbf{x})$ and the second term can be seen as the regularization forcing the posterior distribution to match the conditional prior distribution $p_\psi(\mathbf{z}|\mathbf{x})$. In cVAE, the posterior density is modeled as a diagonal Gaussian density for tractability reasons: $q_\phi(\mathbf{z}|\mathbf{s}, \mathbf{x}) = N(\mathbf{z}; \boldsymbol{\mu}_\phi, \boldsymbol{\sigma}_\phi^2)$. The mean $\boldsymbol{\mu}_\phi$ and variance $\boldsymbol{\sigma}_\phi^2$ are predicted using an encoder network parameterized by ϕ. The decoder and prior networks are parameterized by θ and ψ, respectively.

Normalizing flows can be used to transform simple base distributions into complex ones using a sequence of bijective transformations (the flow chain) with easy to compute Jacobians [17,19]. They basically extend the change of variable rule to transform a base distribution into a target distribution in K successive steps. Normalizing flows can transform a simple base distribution $p(\mathbf{z}_0)$ into an arbitrarily complex target distribution, $p(\mathbf{z}_K)$, by composing complex flow transformations with simpler flow steps [17].

Consider one such bijective transformation T composed of K steps:

$$T = T_K \circ T_{K-1} \circ \cdots T_1. \tag{2}$$

Forward evaluation of this flow chain, transforming $\mathbf{z}_0 \to \mathbf{z}_K$, can be written as:

$$\mathbf{z}_k = T_k(\mathbf{z}_{k-1}) \quad \text{for } k = 1 \ldots K \tag{3}$$

where $\mathbf{z}_0$ is distributed according to the base distribution $p(\mathbf{z}_0)$.

Reverse evaluation of the flow chain, transforming $\mathbf{z}_K \to \mathbf{z}_0$, can be written as:

$$\mathbf{z}_{k-1} = T_k^{-1}(\mathbf{z}_k) \quad \text{for } k = K \ldots 1. \tag{4}$$

The transformed distribution, $p(\mathbf{z}_K)$, is obtained from the base distribution, $p(\mathbf{z}_0)$, adjusted by the inverse absolute Jacobian determinant of the flow transformation. For a single flow step k:

$$p(\mathbf{z}_k) = p(\mathbf{z}_{k-1}) \left| \frac{\partial T_k(\mathbf{z}_{k-1})}{\partial \mathbf{z}_{k-1}} \right|^{-1} = p(\mathbf{z}_{k-1}) \left| J_{T_k}(\mathbf{z}_{k-1}) \right|^{-1} \tag{5}$$

where $J_{T_k}(\mathbf{z}_{k-1})$ denotes the Jacobian determinant. The complete transformation using the full flow chain in log domain is given by

$$\log p(\mathbf{z}_K) = \log p(\mathbf{z}_0) + \log \left| \prod_{k=1}^{K} J_{T_k}^{-1}(\mathbf{z}_{k-1}) \right| = \log p(\mathbf{z}_0) - \sum_{k=1}^{K} \log \left| J_{T_k}(\mathbf{z}_{k-1}) \right|, \tag{6}$$

where the last equality follows from $\log \left| J_{T_k}^{-1} \right| = \log \left| J_{T_k} \right|^{-1} = -\log \left| J_{T_k} \right|$.

3 Methods

When using cVAE-like models for medical image segmentation tasks, it is assumed that the diversity of segmentations is captured with the latent posterior distribution. However, using a simple distribution such as an axis-aligned Gaussian to approximate the latent posterior distribution can be too restrictive and might not be sufficiently expressive to capture richer variations. This is noticeable in the Prob. U-Net model [13] where the segmentations are blurry and lack diversity [3,14]. It is in this context that normalizing flows can be used to improve the flexibility of the approximate posterior density to capture a richer diversity of high quality segmentations.

If we denote the approximate posterior density output by the encoder network as the base distribution, $q(\mathbf{z}_0|\mathbf{s}, \mathbf{x})$, using the latent variable $\mathbf{z}_0$, then using the idea of normalizing flows in Sect. 2 can yield more expressive posterior densities. If the base distribution is transformed using a flow chain of K steps according

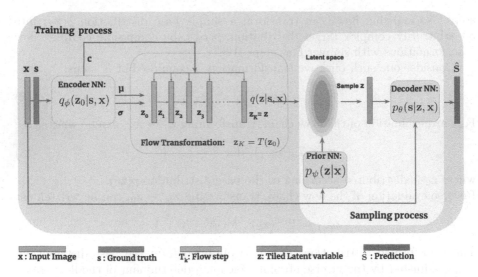

Fig. 2. Proposed cFlow Net model. (Training) The training process takes the reference segmentations **s** and the image data **x** as input to the encoder, which predicts the mean μ and standard deviation σ of the base distribution along with the context vector **c** for the flow transformation. The flow transformation block transforms the base distribution, $q_\phi(\mathbf{z}_0|\mathbf{s},\mathbf{x})$ to an approximation of the target posterior distribution $q(\mathbf{z}|\mathbf{s},\mathbf{x})$ in K steps. The latent space is jointly learned by minimizing the KL divergence between the transformed posterior distribution $q(\mathbf{z}|\mathbf{s},\mathbf{x})$ and the conditional prior $p_\psi(\mathbf{z}|\mathbf{x})$. (Sampling) The sampling process involves obtaining samples from the conditional prior which is used with the input image together to be decoded in the decoder $p_\theta(\mathbf{s}|\mathbf{z},\mathbf{x})$ to obtain the segmentation $\hat{\mathbf{s}}$. After training the model, only the sampling part of the network is used for inference.

to Eq. (2), then the transformed distribution after K steps with $\mathbf{z} = \mathbf{z}_K$ can be written using Eq. (6) as:

$$\log q(\mathbf{z}|\mathbf{s},\mathbf{x}) = \log q(\mathbf{z}_K|\mathbf{s},\mathbf{x}) = \log q(\mathbf{z}_0|\mathbf{s},\mathbf{x}) - \sum_{k=1}^{K} \log \left| J_{T_k}(\mathbf{z}_{k-1}|\mathbf{x}) \right|. \quad (7)$$

It can be shown that the modified objective for the conditional flow-based model becomes (see Sect. 6.1 in the online supplementary material [22]):

$$\mathcal{L}_{\text{cFlow}} = -\mathbb{E}_{q_\phi(\mathbf{z}_0|\mathbf{s},\mathbf{x})} \left[\log p_\theta(\mathbf{s}|\mathbf{z}_K,\mathbf{x}) \right]$$
$$+ \text{KL}\left[q_\phi(\mathbf{z}_0|\mathbf{s},\mathbf{x}) || p_\psi(\mathbf{z}_K|\mathbf{x}) \right] - \mathbb{E}_{q_\phi(\mathbf{z}_0|\mathbf{s},\mathbf{x})} \left[\sum_{k=1}^{K} \log \left| J_{T_k}(\mathbf{z}_{k-1}|\mathbf{x}) \right| \right]. \quad (8)$$

Note that the expectation is with respect to the *base* distribution of the normalizing flow $q_\phi(\mathbf{z}_0|\mathbf{s},\mathbf{x})$. The KL divergence is similar to the term for cVAE in Eq. 1 except for an additional term due to the log determinant of the Jacobian terms in Eq. (7).

Planar Flows: In this work we use planar flows introduced in [19] modified to be conditioned on the input image $\mathbf{x}$ with each step of the flow:

$$\mathbf{u}_k, \mathbf{w}_k, b_k = f_k(\mathbf{x}) \tag{9}$$

$$T(\mathbf{z}_k|\mathbf{x}) = \mathbf{z}_{k-1} + \mathbf{u}_k h(\mathbf{w}_k^T \mathbf{z}_{k-1} + b_k) \tag{10}$$

where $\{\mathbf{u}_k, \mathbf{w}_k \in \mathbb{R}^L, b_k \in \mathbb{R}\}$ are learnable parameters predicted by a conditioning neural network $f_k(\cdot)$ similar to the conditioning network used in [15], L is the dimensionality of the latent space and $h(\cdot)$ is an element-wise non-linearity such as *tanh* with derivative $h'(\cdot)$. The Jacobian determinant for the planar flow step T_k is given by

$$\left| J_{T_k}(\mathbf{z}_{k-1}|\mathbf{x}) \right| = \left| 1 + \mathbf{u}_k^T \psi_k(\mathbf{z}_{k-1}) \right| \quad \text{where } \psi_k(\mathbf{z}_{k-1}) = h'(\mathbf{w}_k^T \mathbf{z}_{k-1} + b_k)\mathbf{w}_k. \tag{11}$$

The conditioning on the flow chain is introduced through the context vector $\mathbf{c}$ which is dependent on $\mathbf{x}$. The context vector $\mathbf{c} \in \mathbb{R}^H$ of dimension H is also predicted by the encoder network. The proposed cFlow Net model is visualized in Fig. 2.

Note that at inference, to sample multiple segmentations only the *Sampling Process* part of the model is used. Given an image $\mathbf{x}$, the prior network can be used to obtain multiple latent variable samples $\mathbf{z}$ which are then decoded by the decoder network to output multiple segmentations for the input image.

4   Experiments and Results

4.1   Data

All experiments are performed on two publicly available datasets. Both datasets comprise labels from at least two raters used to quantify the performance of all models. We use a training-validation-test split of 60:20:20 for both datasets.

LIDC-IDRI Dataset: The LIDC-IDRI dataset consists of 1018 thoracic CT scans with four raters annotating the lesions in them [2]. We use patches of size 128×128 centered on lesions similar to the procedures followed in [3,13] to obtain $15,096$ patches in total. The preprocessed data is obtained from [12].

Retinal Vessel Dataset: As a secondary dataset we create a new dataset derived from three older retinal vessel segmentation datasets: DRIVE [24], STARE [6] and CHASE [16]. Each of these datasets has a subset of images with labels from two raters. We collected images with two raters from these three datasets, extracted retinal masks when there were none and resized them such that all images are of height 512 px. This yields 68 images of which 20 are of size 620×512 px and the remaining 48 are 512×512 px. All images have vessel annotations from two raters. (Figure 4 in online supplementary material [22]).

Table 1. Performance comparison of all models. Higher is better for Dice and lower is better for -CLL and d^2_{GED}. Significant differences are shown in bold.

Models	LIDC dataset					Retina dataset				
	All raters		Single rater			All raters		Single rater		
	-CLL	d^2_{GED}	-CLL	d^2_{GED}	Dice	-CLL ($\times 10^3$)	d^2_{GED}	-CLL ($\times 10^3$)	d^2_{GED}	Dice
Det.U-Net [20]	–	–	–	–	**0.727**	–	–	–	–	0.624
Prob.U-Net [13]	52.1	0.279	238.9	0.579	0.698	4.738	0.905	4.495	0.946	0.616
cFlow Net (Planar)	**47.3**	**0.204**	89.0	0.288	0.713	**4.436**	**0.884**	4.482	0.877	0.632
cFlow Net (Glow)	49.2	0.302	217.0	0.547	0.704	4.482	0.901	4.488	0.878	0.620

4.2   Experiments and Results

The proposed cFlow Net model is compared with the probabilistic U-Net [13], and additionally with the deterministic U-Net [20] for the single rater setting. Other than the cFlow Net model described in Sect. 3 with planar flows [19], we additionally report the cFlow model with conditional generative flow model which uses the Glow transformation steps [10,15] (Sect. 6.2 in the online supplementary material [22]).

Performance of the models in the multiple annotator setting is evaluated based on the generalized energy distance (d^2_{GED}) which captures the diversity of samples obtained from the generative models when compared to the annotators. It is given by

$$d^2_{GED}(P_R, P_M) = 2\mathbb{E}\Big[d(\mathbf{s}, \hat{\mathbf{s}})\Big] - \mathbb{E}\Big[d(\mathbf{s}, \mathbf{s}')\Big] - \mathbb{E}\Big[d(\hat{\mathbf{s}}, \hat{\mathbf{s}}')\Big], \tag{12}$$

where $\mathbf{s}, \mathbf{s}'$ are samples from the ground truth distribution, P_R, comprising different raters, $\hat{\mathbf{s}}, \hat{\mathbf{s}}'$ are samples from the generative distribution, P_M, learned by the model and $d(\cdot)$ is 1-IoU (intersection-over-union) measure. Additionally, we report the negative conditional log likelihood (-CLL $= -\log p(\mathbf{s}|\mathbf{x})$) approximated with 128 samples (Sect. 6.3 in the online supplementary material [22]) and the dice accuracy for the single rater settings.

Both variants of the cFlow Net models use $K = 4$ flow steps. The *decoder* network in the cFlow Net and Prob. U-Net was a deterministic U-Net with 4 resolutions identical to the ones used in [13]. Architectures of both *encoder* and *prior* networks were similar to the encoding path of the decoder network. In addition to predicting the mean μ and variance σ^2, the encoder network in the cFlow Net model outputs a context vector $\mathbf{c}$ of dimension $H = 128$ which is input to the *flow transformation* block as illustrated in Fig. 2. The conditioning network $f_k(\cdot)$ is a three layered multi-layer perceptron (MLP) with 8 hidden units. Latent space dimension of $L = 6$ was used for the Prob. U-Net and the cFlow Net models. All the models were trained using a batch size of 96 and a learning rate of 10^{-4} with the Adam optimizer [9]. The models were trained for a maximum of 300 epochs and training convergence was assumed when there was no improvement in validation loss for 20 epochs. Models with the best validation

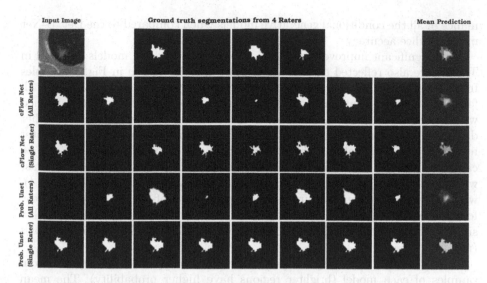

Fig. 3. Qualitative results showing the segmentation diversity of the cFlow Net model and Prob. U-Net for one scan from LIDC-IDRI test set. First row shows the input image, segmentation masks from the four raters; Rows 2 and 3 are samples from cFlow Net model when trained with all and a single (first) rater; Rows 4 and 5 show samples from the Prob. U-Net model for all and single rater setting. Mean prediction over all samples are shown in the last column (brigher regions correspond to higher probability).

loss was used to evaluate the performance on test set reported in Table 1. The experiments were run using PyTorch [18] on a single Tesla K80 GPU with 12GB memory. The computation time for both variants of the cFlow Net models on LIDC dataset was 250s, and about 30s on the Retinal Vessel dataset per training epoch. The average CO_2 footprint of developing and training the baseline and proposed models is estimated to be 22.3 kg or equivalently about 180 km traveled by a car, measured using Carbontracker [1].

4.3   Results and Discussion

Performance of all the models on test set of both the datasets are reported in Table 1. Within each dataset we report the performance when compared to *All Raters* and a *Single Rater*. Statistically significant improvement in performance (based on paired sample t-tests with $p < 0.05$) when compared to other models are highlighted in bold.

The proposed cFlow Net (Planar) model is consistently better than the baseline Prob. U-Net model on the LIDC dataset in d^2_{GED} and -CLL measures. The performance of the cFlow Net (Planar) model in the *Single Rater* setting shows a large improvement when compared to Prob. U-Net model. This is also demonstrated in Fig. 3 seen as more realistic and diverse samples generated only by training only on a single (the first) rater. There is a small reduction in performance of all the conditional generative models when compared to the Det. U-Net model in dice accuracy.

The significant improvements in d^2_{GED} for the cFlow Net models reported in Table 1 are also reflected qualitatively in the samples shown in Fig. 3. Samples from cFlow Net (row 2) are not only able to capture the variations amongst all four raters (row 1) but the remainder samples appear plausible. When trained with a single rater (row 3), the cFlow Net model is still able to capture a richer diversity of segmentations. As annotations are available from only a single rater in majority of applications, this behaviour of the cFlow Net of being able to capture diverse segmentations from single rater is desirable. This is in contrast with the samples from Prob. U-Net even when trained with all raters (row 4), where the samples appear blurry and are unable to reflect the diversity of the four raters. This lack of diversity becomes more pronounced when trained with a single rater, as the Prob. U-Net model outputs almost identical looking samples (row 5).

In the last column of Fig. 3 we also show the mean prediction obtained from samples of each model (brighter regions have higher probability). The mean predictions from the cFlow Net model trained on a single rater could be more informative than the mean prediction from Prob. U-Net trained on a single rater. This further strengthens our argument that improving the approximation to the latent posterior distribution with conditional normalizing flows helps capture meaningful uncertainty with the possibility of sampling unlimited number of diverse segmentations.

A similar trend is also observed with the Retinal Vessel dataset. This is a far more challenging dataset as the images are acquired differently and the quality of annotations vary between the six annotators. This is captured as higher d^2_{GED} and -CLL across all models. Even within this setting, the cFlow Net models fare better than the Prob. U-Net model in both the single and multiple rater experiments. There was no significant difference in dice accuracy between any of the methods indicating the stochastic generative components of the proposed models do not affect segmentation accuracy.

5   Conclusion

We proposed a novel conditional generative model based on conditional normalizing flows to quantify uncertainty in segmentations. The use of cFlow steps improved the approximation of the latent posterior distribution, captured in the smaller negative conditional log likelihood values and also manifested in the diversity of samples. The primary contribution in this work is the incorporation of conditional normalizing flows for handling high dimensional data such as medical images. The *flow transformation* block is modular and can be easily replaced with any suitable normalizing flow providing access to a rich class of improved conditional generative models [17]. We demonstrated this feature of cFlow Net with two types of normalizing flow transformations: Planar [19] and Glow [10] with promising performance.

Acknowledgements. We thank Oswin Krause and the Medical Image Analysis group at DIKU for fruitful discussions and valuable feedback.

References

1. Anthony, L.F.W., Kanding, B., Selvan, R.: Carbontracker: tracking and predicting the carbon footprint of training deep learning models. In: ICML Workshop on Challenges in Deploying and monitoring Machine Learning Systems (2020). https://arxiv.org/abs/2007.03051
2. Armato III, S.G., et al.: Lung image database consortium: developing a resource for the medical imaging research community. Radiology **232**(3), 739–748 (2004)
3. Baumgartner, C.F., et al.: PHiSeg: capturing uncertainty in medical image segmentation. In: Shen, D., et al. (eds.) MICCAI 2019. LNCS, vol. 11765, pp. 119–127. Springer, Cham (2019). https://doi.org/10.1007/978-3-030-32245-8_14
4. Çiçek, Ö., Abdulkadir, A., Lienkamp, S.S., Brox, T., Ronneberger, O.: 3D U-Net: learning dense volumetric segmentation from sparse annotation. In: Ourselin, S., Joskowicz, L., Sabuncu, M.R., Unal, G., Wells, W. (eds.) MICCAI 2016. LNCS, vol. 9901, pp. 424–432. Springer, Cham (2016). https://doi.org/10.1007/978-3-319-46723-8_49
5. Gal, Y., Ghahramani, Z.: Dropout as a Bayesian approximation: representing model uncertainty in deep learning. In: International Conference on Machine Learning, pp. 1050–1059 (2016)
6. Hoover, A., Kouznetsova, V., Goldbaum, M.: Locating blood vessels in retinal images by piecewise threshold probing of a matched filter response. IEEE Trans. Med. imaging **19**(3), 203–210 (2000)
7. Jensen, M.H., Jørgensen, D.R., Jalaboi, R., Hansen, M.E., Olsen, M.A.: Improving uncertainty estimation in convolutional neural networks using inter-rater agreement. In: Shen, D., et al. (eds.) MICCAI 2019. LNCS, vol. 11767, pp. 540–548. Springer, Cham (2019). https://doi.org/10.1007/978-3-030-32251-9_59
8. Kendall, A., Gal, Y.: What uncertainties do we need in Bayesian deep learning for computer vision? In: Advances in Neural Information Processing Systems, pp. 5574–5584 (2017)
9. Kingma, D.P., Ba, J.: Adam: A method for stochastic optimization. arXiv preprint arXiv:1412.6980 (2014)
10. Kingma, D.P., Dhariwal, P.: Glow: generative flow with invertible 1x1 convolutions. In: Advances in Neural Information Processing Systems, pp. 10215–10224 (2018)
11. Kingma, D.P., Salimans, T., Jozefowicz, R., Chen, X., Sutskever, I., Welling, M.: Improved variational inference with inverse autoregressive flow. In: Advances in Neural Information Processing Systems, pp. 4743–4751 (2016)
12. Knegt, S.: A Probabilistic U-Net for segmentation of ambiguous images implemented in PyTorch (2018). https://github.com/stefanknegt/Probabilistic-Unet-Pytorch
13. Kohl, S., et al.: A probabilistic u-net for segmentation of ambiguous images. In: Advances in Neural Information Processing Systems, pp. 6965–6975 (2018)
14. Kohl, S.A., et al.: A hierarchical probabilistic u-net for modeling multi-scale ambiguities. In: Workshop on Medical Imaging Meets NeurIPS (2019)
15. Lu, Y., Huang, B.: Structured output learning with conditional generative flows. In: ICML Workshop on Invertible Neural Networks, Normalizing Flows, and Explicit Likelihood Models (2019)

16. Owen, C.G., et al.: Retinal arteriolar tortuosity and cardiovascular risk factors in a multi-ethnic population study of 10-year-old children; the child heart and health study in england (chase). Arteriosclerosis Thrombosis Vasc. Biol. **31**(8), 1933–1938 (2011)
17. Papamakarios, G., Nalisnick, E., Rezende, D.J., Mohamed, S., Lakshminarayanan, B.: Normalizing flows for probabilistic modeling and inference. arXiv preprint arXiv:1912.02762 (2019)
18. Paszke, A., et al.: Pytorch: an imperative style, high-performance deep learning library. In: Advances in Neural Information Processing Systems, pp. 8024–8035 (2019)
19. Rezende, D.J., Mohamed, S.: Variational inference with normalizing flows. arXiv preprint arXiv:1505.05770 (2015)
20. Ronneberger, O., Fischer, P., Brox, T.: U-net: convolutional networks for biomedical image segmentation. In: Navab, N., Hornegger, J., Wells, W.M., Frangi, A.F. (eds.) MICCAI 2015. LNCS, vol. 9351, pp. 234–241. Springer, Cham (2015). https://doi.org/10.1007/978-3-319-24574-4_28
21. Rupprecht, C., et al.: Learning in an uncertain world: representing ambiguity through multiple hypotheses. In: Proceedings of the IEEE International Conference on Computer Vision, pp. 3591–3600 (2017)
22. Selvan, R., Faye, F., Middleton, J., Pai, A.: Uncertainty quantification in medical image segmentation with Normalizing Flows (Supplementary material). arXiv preprint arXiv:2006.02683 (2020)
23. Sohn, K., Lee, H., Yan, X.: Learning structured output representation using deep conditional generative models. In: Advances in Neural Information Processing Systems, pp. 3483–3491 (2015)
24. Staal, J., Abràmoff, M.D., Niemeijer, M., Viergever, M.A., Van Ginneken, B.: Ridge-based vessel segmentation in color images of the retina. IEEE Trans. Med. Imaging **23**(4), 501–509 (2004)
25. Wilson, R., Spann, M.: Image Segmentation and Uncertainty. Wiley, Hoboken (1988)
26. Zhou, T., Ruan, S., Canu, S.: A review: deep learning for medical image segmentation using multi-modality fusion. Array 100004 (2019)

Out-of-Distribution Detection for Skin Lesion Images with Deep Isolation Forest

Xuan Li[1(✉)], Yuchen Lu[2], Christian Desrosiers[3], and Xue Liu[1]

[1] McGill University, Montreal, Canada
{xuan.li2,xue.liu}@mcgill.ca
[2] Universite de Montreal, Montreal, Canada
yuchen.lu@umontreal.ca
[3] ETS Montreal, Montreal, Canada
christian.desrosiers@etsmtl.ca

Abstract. In this paper, we study the problem of out-of-distribution (OOD) detection in skin lesion images. Publicly available medical datasets have a limited number of lesion classes compared to the number of possible diseases in real-life clinical applications. It is thus essential to develop methods that leverage available disease classes in existing datasets to detect previously-unseen types in an unsupervised manner. Toward this goal, we propose an unsupervised and non-parametric OOD detection approach, called DeepIF, which learns the normal distribution of features in a pre-trained CNN using Isolation Forests. We conduct comprehensive experiments on two different datasets and compare our DeepIF against four baseline models. Results demonstrate state-of-the-art performance of our proposed approach on the task of detecting unseen skin lesions.

1 Introduction

Deep convolution neural networks (CNNs) have shown outstanding potential in dermatology for skin cancer detection and classification [4,5,24]. While such models have achieved high classification accuracy on various benchmark datasets, their use for automatic differential diagnosis is hindered by the diversity of skin diseases in real-life clinical applications. For instance, the well-known HAM10000 dataset [22] contains eight different skin lesion classes in its training set, whereas the actual number of known skin lesion types and subtypes can be in the thousands [4]. It is therefore essential to develop methods that can leverage the limited types of disease in existing datasets to detect previously-unseen diseases in an unsupervised manner, a problem known as out-of-distribution (OOD) detection. A simple yet powerful strategy for OOD image detection is to model the distribution of features from a pre-trained CNN with a parametric model like a Gaussian [11], and then use this model to estimate the normality score of new examples. While this strategy achieves good performance for detecting OOD images in standard datasets like CIFAR10 and SVHN, it is poorly suited for the

© Springer Nature Switzerland AG 2020
M. Liu et al. (Eds.): MLMI 2020, LNCS 12436, pp. 91–100, 2020.
https://doi.org/10.1007/978-3-030-59861-7_10

problem of skin lesion detection, where inter-class variability is low yet intra-class differences can be significant.

To address this limitation, we propose a novel OOD detection framework based on Isolation Forest (IF) [13]. This anomaly detection method, building on the well-known idea of decision tree ensembling, is based on the intuition that abnormal samples are scarce and are different from normal samples, thus they can be classified in leaf nodes of a decision tree with fewer splits. Compared to most unsupervised anomaly detection approaches, IF has the advantage of being non-parametric, and requires no assumption about the distribution or family of normal samples. Moreover, it has a low computational complexity and can be used in scenarios where training samples are few and have high dimensionality.

We introduce a non-parametric and scalable OOD detection method called *DeepIF*, which estimates the normality score of skin lesion images by training IFs on the features of a pre-trained deep CNN. Our contributions are as follows:

- To our knowledge, this is the first application of Isolation Forest for OOD image detection on features from a pre-trained deep CNN. Unlike the majority of existing OOD techniques, it is non-parametric and can be added to any classification model without having to re-train this model. Our method also differs from other OOD approaches by using intermediate features instead of the network output. This enables it to learn more meaningful differences between normal samples and outliers.
- We present a comprehensive evaluation of DeepIF on two large and very different skin lesion datasets, i.e. HAM10000 [22] and DermNet [17], and show that our method outperforms four recently-proposed OOD detection approaches.

2   Related Works

In recent years, a broad range of approaches have been proposed for OOD detection. The work in [7] introduces a simple heuristic applying a threshold on the softmax probability of a deep network for the predicted class. The ODIN approach, proposed by Liang et al. [12], uses softmax temperature scaling and adversarial input perturbation to make softmax scores of in-distribution and out-of-distribution examples better separated. As described in [16], softmax-based methods suffer from the problem that OOD images are forced to be divided over known classes. Based on the assumption that features computed by a pre-trained network follow a class-conditional Gaussian distribution, Lee et al. [11] obtain improved performance for OOD and adversarial sample detection by measuring the Mahalanobis distance in the predicted class distribution. Our method can be seen as a non-parametric extension of this last approach, which is more suitable to the high complexity and variability of skin lesion images. In [21], a one-class kernel Support Vector Machine (SVM) is trained on features from a deep neural net to perform anomaly detection. In this paper, we show that our DeepIF method outperforms these existing approaches on tasks where unseen labels are present.

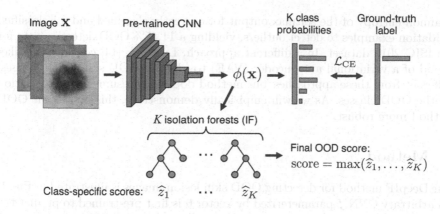

Fig. 1. Proposed DeepIF method for detecting OOD skin lesion images.

In [3], Devries et al. use an auxiliary loss function to generate a confidence score in another branch of the network. This loss function encourages the network to identify examples for which its prediction is unsure. The main challenge, however, is setting the task versus confidence loss hyper-parameter, which can have a large impact on results and whose optimal value greatly varies from one dataset to another. Vyas et al. [23] train an ensemble of classifiers in a self-supervised manner, considering a random subset of training examples as OOD data and the rest as in-distribution data. A margin-based loss is proposed to impose a given margin between the mean entropy of OOD and in-distribution samples. A drawback of this approach is the need to train multiple deep networks, which significantly increases computational times and memory requirements. In [16], Masana et al. use metric learning to derive an embedding space where samples from the same in–distribution class form clusters that are separated from other in–distribution classes and OOD samples. An important limitation of this approach is that it requires to have a large set of OOD samples during training. The method in [18] uses transfer learning as a general abnormality detection for medical images. Likewise, Hentrycks et al. [8] use an auxiliary dataset to model OOD samples and minimize the objective during training along with the original in-distribution objective. In a follow-up work [9], they show that adding self-supervised training loss to the original supervised loss can increase the robustness of OOD detection. Finally, [20] uses the likelihood ratio between the output probability of two deep networks, the first one modeling in-distribution data and the second capturing background statistics, as measure of normality. While these approaches require modifying the original training algorithm, our method is more flexible as it only needs a pre-trained network and can use a black-box algorithm for training.

Most of the above studies have focused on natural images. As shown in our experiments, methods designed for such images perform poorly on skin lesion images which have less inter-class variability. So far, only a few works have investigated OOD detection for images of skin lesions. Pacheco et al. [19] use the mean

Shannon entropy of the softmax output for correctly classified and misclassified validation examples to detect outliers, yielding a 11.45% OOD detection rate for the ISIC 2019 dataset. In a different approach, Lu et al. [14] consider the likelihood of a variational autoencoder (VAE) to identify OOD skin lesion images. Different from these approaches, our method does not presume any distribution for the OOD classes. As we will empirically demonstrate, this makes our OOD method more robust.

3   Method

Our DeepIF method for detecting OOD skin lesion images is illustrated in Fig. 1. An arbitrary CNN f parameterized by vector θ is first pre-trained to predict the K normal classes in the training data. Given an image $\mathbf{x}$, the CNN outputs a vector $f(\mathbf{x}; \theta) \in [0, 1]^K$ of class probabilities. To explain our method, we suppose the CNN computes a representation $\phi(\mathbf{x})$ comprised of convolutional features, which is then converted to the output vector with a linear transformation producing a vector of logits, followed by a softmax:

$$f(\mathbf{x}; \theta) = \text{softmax}(\mathbf{W} \cdot \phi(\mathbf{x})). \tag{1}$$

Although any suitable loss function can be considered, we suppose that cross-entropy is used to train the network. Let $\mathcal{D}_{\text{train}} = \{(\mathbf{x}_i, y)\}_{i=1}^N$ be the set of training images $\mathbf{x}_i$ and their corresponding normal class label $y \in \{1, \ldots, K\}$, the loss function is defined as

$$\mathcal{L}_{\text{CE}}(\theta; \mathcal{D}_{\text{train}}) = -\frac{1}{N} \sum_{i=1}^N \sum_{k=1}^K \mathbb{1}[y_i = k] \log f_k(\mathbf{x}_i; \theta) \tag{2}$$

Given a pre-trained network, our method uses the network's latent representation $\phi(\mathbf{x})$ to detect OOD samples. Toward this goal, we use a two-step approach similar to the one proposed in [11]. In the first step, the representation vectors of training examples are used to learn a model of in-distribution classes. Then, the learned model is used on the representation vectors of test examples to compute their normality scores. OOD examples are found by applying a threshold on the scores or via a ranking strategy.

The approach in [11] uses a Gaussian to model the distribution of each normal class. For OOD detection, they calculate the Mahalanobis distance between the representation vector of a test example and the mean vector of each class, and use the smallest distance among all classes as the normality score. As shown in our results, a simple uni-modal Gaussian distribution is not expressive enough to capture the complex distribution of representations from skin lesion images. To overcome this problem, our method instead leverages the non-parametric Isolation Forest (IF) algorithm, which builds on the idea of decision tree ensembling. In IF, a set of decision trees is constructed by splitting the data points in the training set. To build a tree, at each node, a random feature from a subset of features, the size of which is controlled by hyper-parameter N_f, is selected.

Then, a random value between the minimum and maximum values of that feature is chosen to split data points. A node is considered to be a leaf node when it reaches a specified maximum depth or the number of data points at that node is less or equal to a specified number. We construct a total of N_e decision trees to form our IF.

The application of IF for OOD detection is based on the idea that OOD data points are few and different, thus should be separable from in-distribution data on some features with fewer splits. Hence, by averaging the splits in the IF, OOD data points should have a smaller number of splits compared to the in-distribution data points. In the proposed method, we build K different IF models, one for each of the normal classes in the training data. Once these IF models are constructed, we calculate the normality score of a test example $\mathbf{x} \in \mathcal{D}_{\text{test}}$ with respect to class k as

$$z_k = -2^{-\mathbb{E}[P_k^e(\phi(\mathbf{x}))]/P_k^{\text{avg}}} + 0.5. \tag{3}$$

Here, $P_k^e(\phi(\mathbf{x}))$ is the number of tree nodes (i.e., path length) traversed by $\phi(\mathbf{x})$ from the root node to the terminal leaf node of the e-th decision tree in the IF of class k. Moreover, $\mathbb{E}[P_k^e(\phi(\mathbf{x}))]$ is the average of path lengths across all trees in the IF of class k, and P_k^{avg} is the average path length for training representation in the same IF. The intuition is that anomaly data points have extreme values on certain features, so they can be easily isolated within shorter paths. Thus, $\mathbb{E}[P_k^e(\phi(\mathbf{x}))]$ would be small for abnormal data points, resulting in small z_k close to -0.5, whereas in-distribution data points would have large $\mathbb{E}[P_k^e(\phi(\mathbf{x}))]$ close to P_k^{avg}, resulting in a z_k close to 0.5.

The representation $\phi(\mathbf{x})$ of test examples $\mathbf{x}$ is fed to the IF model of each class to obtain normality scores $\{z_1, \ldots, z_K\}$. To compare examples on the same scale, we then normalize these score as follows:

$$\widehat{z}_k = \frac{z_k - \text{mean}(z_1, \ldots, z_K)}{\text{std}(z_1, \ldots, z_K)}. \tag{4}$$

Last, the final normality score is computed as the maximum value of class-specific scores, i.e.

$$\text{score}(\mathbf{x}) = \max(\widehat{z}_1, \ldots, \widehat{z}_K). \tag{5}$$

Since the class with highest normality score is the one to which $\mathbf{x}$ most likely belongs, a low maximum score indicates that $\mathbf{x}$ can be still easily separated from its most similar samples.

4 Experiments

Datas and Setup. Our OOD detection method is evaluated on two different datasets: HAM10000 [22] and DermNet [17]. The HAM10000 dataset contains skin lesion images taken from dermoscopes. The training set contains 25,331 images from 8 lesion classes: Melanoma (MEL), Melanocytic nevus (NV), Basal cell carcinoma (BCC), Actinic keratosis (AK), Benign keratosis (BKL), Dermatofibroma (DF), Vascular lesion (VASC), Squamous cell carcinoma (SCC). For each experiment, we hold out 1 class as the Anomaly Class, which we refer to as an *OOD set*. We pre-train the network with the remaining 7 classes as in a regular classification task. For each of the 7 classes, a 90% − 10% split is made for the training and validation sets. We treat the validation set as in-distribution set.

The DermNet dataset comprises skin lesion images taken from standard cameras and thus has a distribution completely different from HAM10000. The training set contains 22,494 images from 23 lesion classes. We treat 4 classes having less than 500 images each (Cellulitis-Impetigo, Hair-Diseases, Contact-Dermatitis, and Urticaria-Hives) as a single OOD set, and pre-train the network on the other 19 classes. The same 90% − 10% split is made on each of the 19 classes for the training and validation sets. Once more, the validation set is used as in-distribution set.

Evaluation Metrics. We adopt the same metrics as in other studies on OOD detection [3,11,12]: area under the ROC curve (AUROC); area under the precision recall curve where in-distribution is specified as the positive (AUPR in); area under the precision recall curve where OOD is specified as the positive (AUPR out); true negative rate (TNR) when the true positive rate is as high as 95% (TNR95TPR). In the latter, the TNR is computed as TN/(TN+FP), where TN is the number of true negative and FP the number of false positives. We also show the classification accuracy on the validation dataset.

Implementation Details. We pre-train the skin lesion classification network with a standard approach: an image resized to 224×224 is fed into a ResNet152 [6] to get the predictions for each class. Cross-entropy loss is calculated and back-propagated to the network. SGD is adopted to optimize the network with a learning rate of 1e-4. We train the network 200 epochs with a batch size of 32. In the training stage, the OOD set is held out, and treated as an anomaly class. Once the training procedure finishes, the parameters of the network are fixed throughout the rest of the procedures. For constructing the IF models, we empirically set N_e to be 200, and N_f to be 1.0. Final scores for in-distribution and OOD sets are stored separately for evaluation.

Baselines. As our goal is having a detection algorithm that is agnostic to the specific training algorithm, we compare directly with baselines that can be conveniently added to existing models without the need to re-train. We thus compare our method against three baselines supporting this setup: the Mahalanobis distance approach using the implementation from [10], the One-class SVM from [21], and the VAE approach in [14] which measures the normality score based on reconstruction error. We also compare to a strong baseline Confidence learning [3], which learns to predict the confidence score in joint training with the regular classification task. We use the implementation from [2] but keep the same pre-trained network as our DeepIF.

Table 1. Results on the HAM10000 dataset. We report the mean performance across 8 experiments, each one using a different class as hold-out OOD set. Except for accuracy on the validation set (Val. Acc), all metrics are measure on the OOD test set.

Method	AUROC	AUPR in	AUPR out	TNR at 95% TPR	Val. Acc %
DeepIF (ours)	**0.7560**	**0.7527**	**0.7255**	**0.2091**	**90.3**
Mahalanobis [10]	0.5771	0.5728	0.5516	0.0672	
OCSVM [21]	0.6073	0.7224	0.6110	0.0548	
VAE [14]	0.5315	0.5418	0.5054	0.0357	
Confidence [3]	0.6783	0.7137	0.6315	0.1238	86.1

Table 2. Result on the DermNet dataset. We treat 4 diseases (having less than 500 images each) as a single OOD dataset. Except for accuracy on the validation set (Val. Acc), all metrics are measure on the OOD test set.

Method	AUROC	AUPR in	AUPR out	TNR at 95%TPR	Val. Acc %
DeepIF (ours)	**0.6908**	**0.6933**	**0.6498**	**0.1125**	**71.44**
Mahalanobis [10]	0.5761	0.5882	0.5472	0.0637	
OCSVM [21]	0.5065	0.4816	0.3144	0.0148	
VAE [14]	0.6002	0.6067	0.5666	0.0622	
Confidence [3]	0.6208	0.6492	0.5820	0.0855	60.11

5   Results

5.1   Comparison to Baselines

Results for the HAM10000 and DermNet datasets are shown in Table 1 and Table 2, respectively. Our DeepIF method outperforms all tested baselines on all metrics for both datasets. Specifically, we obtain large AUROC improvements of 0.1789 for HAM10000 and 0.1147 for DermNet, compared to the Mahalonbi distance baseline. This confirms our hypothesis that parametric OOD detection approaches are less suitable when there is huge intra-class diversity and low inter-class variability. Our method also yields a significantly better performance than VAE and OCSVM.

Although the Confidence learning approach is a strong baseline, as it is jointly trained with the regular classification task, our DeepIF method still achieves better results on all metrics and datasets. Additionally, we find that using this baseline decreases the classification performance on validation data, with a 4.2% drop in mean accuracy for HAM10000 and a 11.3% drop for DermNet. We believe that learning to predict confidence adds an extra requirement to the training process which can hurt performance for the main task. An OOD framework like ours, that is independent from the training procedure, has the advantage of

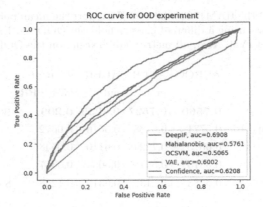

Fig. 2. ROC curves for OOD experiments on DermNet. DeepIF (blue curve) achieves the highest ROC performance compared with other baselines. (Color figure online)

Table 3. Result of DeepIF on HAM10000 using features from different layers of the pre-trained network. $L_{logit-j}$ refers to the j-th layer before the logits.

Layer	AUROC	AUPR in	AUPR out	TNR at 95% TPR
$L_{logit-1}$	**0.7560**	**0.7527**	**0.7255**	**0.2091**
$L_{logit-2}$	0.5763	0.6076	0.5502	0.0673
$L_{logit-3}$	0.5520	0.5508	0.5352	0.0607
$L_{logit-4}$	0.5293	0.5243	0.5296	0.0770

preserving the model performance. The ROC curves for 5 approaches in Fig. 2 also validate that DeepIF has the best performance differentiating in-distribution and OOD data.

5.2 Analysis of Hidden Representations

Our proposed DeepIF uses hidden representations from the last convolutional layer, as it should contain the richest information. In this experiment, we analyze the effect of using representations from different layers $L_{logit-j}$, where $j = \{1, 2, 3, 4\}$ is the distance to the layer of logits. The results shown in Table 3 on HAM10000, confirm that employing the last convolutional layer provides the best performance, and that this performance drops as we use features in shallower layers. However, performance metrics similar to those of baselines can also be obtained from these shallower layers, demonstrating the power and flexibility of our proposed method.

6 Discussion and Conclusion

In this paper, we studied the problem of OOD detection on medical image datasets where intra-class difference is large and inter-class variability is low. We proposed a non-parameteric framework based on Isolation Forests which learns the normal distribution of features from a pre-trained CNN and then predicts the normality of test examples based on the path length from root to leaf nodes in decision trees. Our framework is agnostic to the pre-training tasks, and thus can be easily applied to any existing classification model to perform OOD detection. We evaluated our approach on two large skin lesion datasets of very different distributions: HAM10000 [22] which containts dermoscopic images, and DermNet [17] comprised of camera images. Experiments show our approach to achieve state-of-the-art performance for differentiating in-distribution and OOD data.

To further validate our method, we aim to cover a broader range of medical image datasets where there exists huge intra-class diversity, for instance, Diabetic Retinopathy, CT, and MRI datasets. Moreover, while our DeepIF focuses on image data, our method can be easily transferred to other non-image data, such as electric medical records data, or time sequence data including electroencephalogram (EEG) and electrocardiogram (ECG). In future work, we would also like to compare our DeepIF with more non-parametric algorithms such as Dirichlet Process Mixture Model (DPMM) [1] or a self-organizing network [15].

References

1. Blei, D.M., Jordan, M.I., et al.: Variational inference for dirichlet process mixtures. Bayesian Anal. **1**(1), 121–143 (2006)
2. DeVries, T.: Learning confidence for out-of-distribution detection in neural networks (2018). https://github.com/uoguelph-mlrg/confidence_estimation
3. DeVries, T., Taylor, G.W.: Learning confidence for out-of-distribution detection in neural networks. arXiv preprint (2018). arXiv:1802.04865
4. Esteva, A., et al.: Dermatologist-level classification of skin cancer with deep neural networks. Nature **542**(7639), 115–118 (2017)
5. Han, S.S., et al.: Deep neural networks show an equivalent and often superior performance to dermatologists in onychomycosis diagnosis: automatic construction of onychomycosis datasets by region-based convolutional deep neural network. PloS one **13**(1), e0191493 (2018)
6. He, K., Zhang, X., Ren, S., Sun, J.: Deep residual learning for image recognition. In: Proceedings of the IEEE conference on computer vision and pattern recognition, pp. 770–778 (2016)
7. Hendrycks, D., Gimpel, K.: A baseline for detecting misclassified and out-of-distribution examples in neural networks. arXiv preprint (2016). arXiv:1610.02136
8. Hendrycks, D., Mazeika, M., Dietterich, T.: Deep anomaly detection with outlier exposure. arXiv preprint (2018). arXiv:1812.04606
9. Hendrycks, D., Mazeika, M., Kadavath, S., Song, D.: Using self-supervised learning can improve model robustness and uncertainty. In: Advances in Neural Information Processing Systems, pp. 15637–15648 (2019)

10. Lee, K.: A simple unified framework for detecting out-of-distribution samples and adversarial attacks (2019). https://github.com/pokaxpoka/deep_Mahalanobis_detector
11. Lee, K., Lee, K., Lee, H., Shin, J.: A simple unified framework for detecting out-of-distribution samples and adversarial attacks. In: Advances in Neural Information Processing Systems, pp. 7167–7177 (2018)
12. Liang, S., Li, Y., Srikant, R.: Enhancing the reliability of out-of-distribution image detection in neural networks. In: 6th International Conference on Learning Representations, ICLR 2018 (2018)
13. Liu, F.T., Ting, K.M., Zhou, Z.H.: Isolation forest. In: 2008 Eighth IEEE International Conference on Data Mining, pp. 413–422. IEEE (2008)
14. Lu, Y., Xu, P.: Anomaly detection for skin disease images using variational autoencoder. arXiv preprint (2018). arXiv:1807.01349
15. Marsland, S., Shapiro, J., Nehmzow, U.: A self-organising network that grows when required. Neural Netw. 15(8–9), 1041–1058 (2002)
16. Masana, M., Ruiz, I., Serrat, J., van de Weijer, J., Lopez, A.M.: Metric learning for novelty and anomaly detection. arXiv preprint (2018). arXiv:1808.05492
17. Oakley, A.: Dermnet new zealand (2016)
18. Ouardini, K., et al.: Towards practical unsupervised anomaly detection on retinal images. In: Wang, Q., et al. (eds.) DART/MIL3ID -2019. LNCS, vol. 11795, pp. 225–234. Springer, Cham (2019). https://doi.org/10.1007/978-3-030-33391-1_26
19. Pacheco, A.G., Ali, A.R., Trappenberg, T.: Skin cancer detection based on deep learning and entropy to detect outlier samples. arXiv preprint (2019). arXiv:1909.04525
20. Ren, J., et al.: Likelihood ratios for out-of-distribution detection. In: Advances in Neural Information Processing Systems, pp. 14680–14691 (2019)
21. Ruff, L., et al.: Deep one-class classification. In: International conference on machine learning, pp. 4393–4402 (2018)
22. Tschandl, P., Rosendahl, C., Kittler, H.: The ham10000 dataset, a large collection of multi-source dermatoscopic images of common pigmented skin lesions. Sci. Data 5, 180161 (2018)
23. Vyas, A., Jammalamadaka, N., Zhu, X., Das, D., Kaul, B., Willke, T.L.: Out-of-distribution detection using an ensemble of self supervised leave-out classifiers. In: Proceedings of the European Conference on Computer Vision (ECCV), pp. 550–564 (2018)
24. Zhang, X., Wang, S., Liu, J., Tao, C.: Towards improving diagnosis of skin diseases by combining deep neural network and human knowledge. BMC Med. Inform. Decis. Making 18(2), 59 (2018)

A 3D+2D CNN Approach Incorporating Boundary Loss for Stroke Lesion Segmentation

Yue Zhang[1,2], Jiong Wu[1], Yilong Liu[2], Yifan Chen[3], Ed X. Wu[2], and Xiaoying Tang[1(✉)]

[1] Department of Electrical and Electronic Engineering,
Southern University of Science and Technology, Shenzhen, China
tangxy@sustech.edu.cn
[2] Department of Electrical and Electronic Engineering,
The University of Hong Kong, Hong Kong, China
[3] School of Life Science and Technology, University of Electronic Science
and Technology, Chengdu, China

Abstract. Dice loss is the most widely used loss function in deep learning methods for unbalanced medical image segmentation. The main limitation of Dice loss is that it weighs different parts of the to-be-segmented region of interest (ROI) equally, which is inappropriate given that the fuzzy boundary is typically more challenging to segment than central parts. A recently-proposed boundary loss weighs different parts of an ROI according to their distances to the ROI's boundary, thus providing complementary information to Dice loss. However, boundary loss can not be directly applied to patch-based 3D convolutional neural networks (CNNs), significantly limiting its utility. In this paper, we proposed and validated a two-stage 3D+2D framework making use of 3D CNN for spatial information extraction and also boundary loss to complement the typically-used generalized Dice loss, for segmenting stroke lesions from magnetic resonance (MR) images. A 3D patch-based fully convolutional network was firstly used to learn local spatial features. And then the to-be-segmented MR image and the probability map predicted from the trained 3D model were sliced and fed into a 2D network with a joint loss combining boundary loss and generalized Dice loss. We evaluated the proposed method on a publicly-available dataset consisting of 229 T1-weighted MR images. The proposed approach yielded an average Dice score of 56.25% and an average Hausdorff distance of 27.14 mm, performing much better than existing state-of-the-art stroke lesion segmentation methods.

Keywords: Stroke lesion segmentation · Convolutional neural network · Boundary loss · 3D+2D

© Springer Nature Switzerland AG 2020
M. Liu et al. (Eds.): MLMI 2020, LNCS 12436, pp. 101–110, 2020.
https://doi.org/10.1007/978-3-030-59861-7_11

1   Introduction

Stroke is a serious manifestation of various cerebrovascular diseases and is one of the main causes of death and disability [1]. Accurate stroke lesion segmentation from magnetic resonance (MR) images is important for computer-aided diagnoses of stroke and also stroke rehabilitation [2,3]. For example, quantifying the overlap between stroke lesions and brain functional regions is helpful for evaluating a patient's condition [4–6]. Manual labeling by radiologists requires professional knowledge and is time-consuming, subjective, and prone to inconsistency among different raters. Over the past few years, many fully-automatic and semi-automatic stroke lesion segmentation methods have been proposed. These methods can be broadly divided into two categories: traditional methods [7–11] (such as fuzzy clustering [8] and random forest classification [9]) and methods based on convolutional neural networks (CNNs) [12–15]. Traditional methods typically make use of hand-crafted features, and thus have limited segmentation performance. Recently, CNN-based methods has become one of the mainstreams [16–20].

Stroke lesion segmentation is an unbalanced medical image segmentation task, wherein Dice loss [21], namely negative Dice score, is the most widely used loss function in CNN-based stroke lesion segmentation methods. However, a lower Dice loss does not always guarantee a better segmentation. For example, Fig. 1(b) is intuitively more accurate than both Fig. 1(c) and Fig. 1(d). However, Dice scores of Fig. 1(c) and Fig. 1(d) are both higher than that of Fig. 1(b). This may be due to the fact that Dice weighs different parts of a to-be-segmented region of interest (ROI) equally, which is inappropriate given that the fuzzy boundary is typically more challenging to segment than central parts. More specifically, human annotations at the boundary are highly subjective and thus the loss function should have lower weights on the boundary and higher weights on the central regions. Recently, Hoel et al. proposed a boundary loss making use of a distance metric on the contour space [22]. The boundary loss of Fig. 1(b) is lower than that of Fig. 1(c) and Fig. 1(d), indicating that a neural network with boundary loss will have penalty on cases like Fig. 1(c) and Fig. 1(d). The main limitation of boundary loss is that it cannot be applied to patch-based methods because of the distance-based definition. 3D CNNs are mostly inputted by patches rather than whole volumes [23–25], as limited by 3D data sample size and GPU memory, and thus boundary loss generally cannot be applied to 3D CNNs which have a strong spatial information extraction ability. In such context, it is of great importance to design a pipeline taking the advantage of boundary loss and meanwhile capturing spatial information via 3D CNN.

In this paper, we propose a two-stage 3D+2D CNN framework that makes use of 3D CNN for spatial information extraction and also boundary loss to complement the typically-used Dice loss. A two-input U-shape structure incorporating attention block is designed to fuse multi-level features. We conduct both quantitative and qualitative evaluations of the proposed pipeline on a publicly-available dataset for stroke lesion segmentation [26].

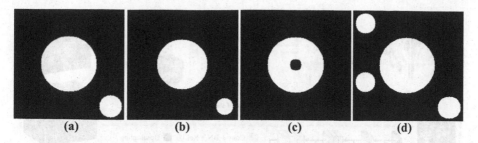

Fig. 1. An example used to demonstrate the superiority of boundary loss over Dice loss. (a) ground truth (b)–(d) different segmentation results.

2   Method

As shown in Fig. 2, the training procedure of the proposed pipeline consists of two stages. At the first stage, a 3D U-shape fully convolutional network (3D U-Net) is trained using 3D patches which are randomly selected from 3D volumes via the dense sampling strategy [24], i.e., the centers of half patches are located within stroke lesions and those of the other half are located within the background. At the second stage, the training images go through the trained 3D U-Net via sliding-window sampling. Afterwards, the predicted probability map and the to-be-segmented MR image are sliced and fed into a 2D neural network, which is built based on U-Net [16,27]. The additional probability input is encoded by separate convolution and max pooling to generate multi-level feature maps, which are then fused and inputted to the U-Net backbone through attention blocks [28,29].

Attention Block. As shown in Fig. 2, the attention block is fed by two feature maps: assistant input $F_{l-1}^{(1)}$ encoded from probability map and master input $F_{l-1}^{(2)}$ encoded from MR image. We firstly apply convolution operation $\mathcal{C}$ with a 1×1 filter to $F_{l-1}^{(1)}$ and $F_{l-1}^{(2)}$, yielding $F_l^{(1)}$ and $F_l^{(2)}$. After that, we apply subtraction and addition to $F_l^{(1)}$ and $F_l^{(2)}$ and then convolution operation $\mathcal{C}$ and element-wise ReLU $\mathcal{R}$ to $F_l^{(1)} + F_l^{(2)}$ and $F_l^{(1)} - F_l^{(2)}$. The processed feature maps are added and then activated by a sigmoid operation σ to obtain weight ω. In summary, ω is produced from two feature maps via

$$\omega = \sigma(\mathcal{R}(\mathcal{C}(\mathcal{C}(F_{l-1}^{(1)}) - \mathcal{C}(F_{l-1}^{(2)}))) + \mathcal{R}(\mathcal{C}(\mathcal{C}(F_{l-1}^{(1)}) + \mathcal{C}(F_{l-1}^{(2)})))). \tag{1}$$

Finally, the output of the attention block is obtained by an element-wise multiplication $\omega \cdot F_{l-1}^{(2)}$.

Loss Function. We train our 2D network using a loss combining generalized Dice loss and boundary loss

$$\mathcal{L}_{total} = \alpha \mathcal{L}_D + (1 - \alpha)\mathcal{L}_B. \tag{2}$$

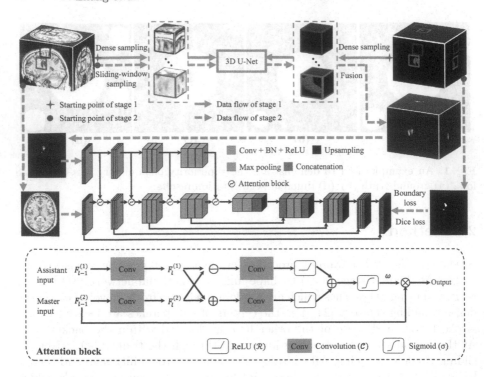

Fig. 2. Illustration of the two-stage strategy and architecture of the two-input 2D CNN with attention blocks.

Let N denote the total number of pixels, the generalized Dice loss function is defined as

$$\mathcal{L}_D = -2\frac{\sum_{l=1}^{2} \omega_l \sum_{n=1}^{N} s_\theta(l,n) \cdot g(l,n)}{\sum_{l=1}^{2} \omega_l \sum_{n=1}^{N} s_\theta(l,n) + g(l,n)}, \tag{3}$$

where $s_\theta(l,n) \in [0,1]$ is the softmax probability value of the nth pixel, θ denotes parameters of the neural netork, $g(l,n) \in \{0,1\}$ is the binary ground truth value of the nth pixel, $\omega_l = 1/(\sum_{n=1}^{N} g(l,n))^2$. We use G to represent a ground truth binary mask defined in a 2D space Ω and ∂G to denote its boundary. Let q_n denote the location of the nth pixel in space Ω, the level-set representation $\phi_G : \Omega \to \mathbb{R}$ can be obtained by

$$\phi_G(q_n) = \begin{cases} -D_G(q_n), & \text{if } q_n \in G \\ D_G(q_n), & \text{otherwise,} \end{cases} \tag{4}$$

where $D_G : \Omega \to \mathbb{R}^+$ evaluates the Euclidean distance between q_n and the nearest point $z_{\partial G}$ on the contour ∂G by $D_G(q_n) = ||q_n - z_{\partial G}||_{L^2}$. The boundary loss is computed as

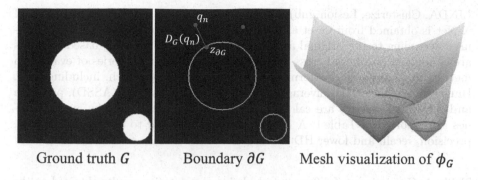

Ground truth G Boundary ∂G Mesh visualization of ϕ_G

Fig. 3. An example to demonstrate the definition of boundary loss.

$$\mathcal{L}_B = \frac{1}{N} \sum_{n=1}^{N} s_\theta(n) \phi_G(q_n). \tag{5}$$

The boundary loss can be considered as a weighted average of ϕ_G. Given the ground truth example in Fig. 1(a), Fig. 3 shows its boundary ∂G and mesh visualization of its level-set reprentation ϕ_G. The boundary loss of Fig. 1(b) is lower that of Fig. 1(c) and Fig. 1(d) because the missing central part in Fig. 1(c) and the extra parts in Fig. 1(d) are penalized with more weights than the missing edge in Fig. 1(b).

Implementation Details. The input window size is set as $49 \times 49 \times 49$ for 3D experiments and 224×192 for 2D experiments. The stride size used at both the second training stage and the testing stage is $15 \times 15 \times 15$. At the second training stage, only slices containing stroke lesions in the ground truth (training) or the 3D U-Net segmentation (testing) are used. During training, the value of α in Eq. (2) is initially set to be 1, and is decreased by 0.01 after each epoch until reaching a value of 0.01 [22].

3 Experimental Results

3.1 Dataset

The proposed method is evaluated on the Anatomical Tracing of Lesions After Stroke (ATLAS) dataset [26]. All images have been rigidly aligned to a same template by registration and have been normalized to be of the same image size ($233 \times 197 \times 189$) and voxel size ($1\,\text{mm}^3$). To accommodate the input size of the 2D model, we centrally crop all axial image slices from 233×197 to 224×192.

3.2 Comparisons with State-of-the-art Methods

We compare the proposed method with existing methods evaluated on the same ATLAS dataset in Table 1. The results of the four classical methods (ALI,

LINDA, Clusterize, Lesion_gnb) are obtained from Ito et al. [7] and the result of
X-Net is obtained from Qi et al. [12]. The 2D U-Net and 3D U-Net are configured according to the original articles [16,17]. All deep learning-based methods
are conducted in a 5-fold cross-validation fashion. We use a series of evaluation
metrics to quantify the performance of the proposed approach, including Dice,
Hausdorff distance (HD), average symmetric surface distance (ASSD), precision
and recall. All metrics are calculated for each 3D image and the average values are reported in Table 1. A better model is supposed to obtain higher Dice,
precision, recall, and lower HD and ASSD.

Table 1. Comparisons of different stroke lesion segmentation results obtained on the
ATLAS dataset. ↓ indicates that the smaller the better.

Method	Dice [%]	HD↓[mm]	ASSD↓[mm]	Precision [%]	Recall [%]
ALI [8]	36	61.55	14.38	31	55
LINDA [9]	45	42.07	12.68	50	52
Clusterize [10]	23	75.00	13.59	16	**79**
lesion_gnb [11]	39	58.00	10.49	30	69
X-Net [12]	48.67	–	–	60.00	47.52
2D U-Net [16]	45.54	65.30	20.63	50.65	51.31
3D U-Net [17]	52.96	38.80	10.33	60.90	54.97
Ours ($\mathcal{L}_D$)	54.53	28.76	7.88	64.87	55.22
Ours ($\mathcal{L}_B$)	52.14	31.74	10.34	**66.21**	50.14
Ours ($\mathcal{L}_D+\mathcal{L}_B$)	**56.25**	**27.14**	**5.90**	62.89	59.35

We also evaluate different loss function settings, i.e., generalized Dice loss
alone, boundary loss alone and the joint loss in Eq. (2). Compared with the
results from generalized Dice loss alone, the results from boundary loss alone
are worse. This is because the gradient descent process may be trapped on a
saddle point if using boundary loss alone [22]. The proposed method performs
the best if we use the joint loss function combining boundary loss and generalized
Dice loss.

With respect to Dice, the proposed method has the highest mean score of
56.25%, which is 3.29% higher than the second-highest result (3D U-Net). Meanwhile, compared to 3D U-Net, the HD/ASSD of the proposed method is largely
reduced from 42.75 mm/12.54 mm to 27.14 mm/5.90 mm, all differences of which
are statistically significant (p < 0.05 from paired Student's t-tests). It can be
observed that deep learning-based methods have relatively lower recall but higher
precision and Dice compared with traditional methods. For example, the Clusterize method is the best in terms of recall, but its Dice and precision are the lowest,
indicating that Clusterize misclassifies a lot of non-lesion areas to be lesions. In
summary, the proposed method yields the highest recall in deep learning-based

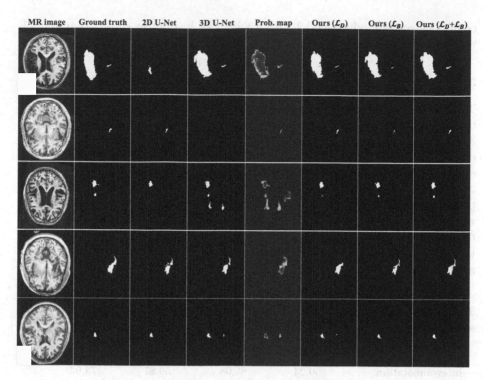

Fig. 4. Representative examples of segmentation results on the ATLAS dataset.

methods and ranks the best in Dice, HD, ASSD among all methods. The average inter-rater Dice/HD scores for ATLAS dataset are 73%/25.29 mm [26]. The proposed method achieves comparable HD score with inter-rater.

3.3 Qualitative Comparisons

The prediction results of different methods are illustrated in Fig. 4, As shown in the first row of Fig. 4.

2D U-Net fails to segment large stroke lesions but 3D U-Net can successfully segment them. The proposed method (last three columns) largely benefits from the probability map output of 3D U-Net. The binary segmentation results of 3D U-Net are obtained using 0.5 as the threshold. As shown in the second row of Fig. 4, although the segmentation from 3D U-Net is empty, the probability map is not empty and there are probability values (less than 0.5) in the lesion area. This false negative can not be removed by simply decreasing the threshold, as there are also false positive from 3D U-Net such as the example in the third row of Fig. 4. The proposed method can correct the aforementioned errors by using the probability map from 3D U-Net to generate assistant features. As shown in the fourth row of Fig. 4, the proposed method with boundary loss alone can successfully preserve the general skeleton of a lesion but lose some pixels at the edge. The corresponding model with a joint loss has better results than models with only a single loss.

3.4 Further Analysis

To simulate the subjectivity of human annotations, we employ erosion/dilation to the ground truth slice-by-slice using square kernels with sizes of 2×2 and 3×3. We first compute Dice between the original ground truth and that after erosion/dilation (see the second row of Table 2). It can be observed that even small changes at the boundary can significantly impact the segmentation accuracy, which may be the main reason for low inter-rater Dice. To evaluate the performance of different methods with human annotations of different biases, we then measure Dice between segmentation results and the processed ground truth (see the third to seventh rows of Table 2). The proposed method performs the best under different level of biases, indicating its robustness to errors in ground truth annotations.

Table 2. The Dice scores for results obtained from different methods using human annotations with different level biases.

	Original	Erode(2×2)	Dilate(2×2)	Erode(3×3)	Dilate(3×3)
Inter-annotation	-	80.24	85.08	59.87	73.94
2D U-Net	45.54	42.39	43.33	37.57	40.76
3D U-Net	52.96	49.18	49.74	43.83	46.65
Ours ($\mathcal{L}_D$)	54.53	51.46	51.41	45.58	47.85
Ours ($\mathcal{L}_B$)	52.14	51.07	48.25	**47.06**	44.45
Ours ($\mathcal{L}_D+\mathcal{L}_B$)	**56.25**	**51.78**	**53.59**	46.31	**50.54**

4 Conclusion

To simultaneously make use of spatial and positional information in 3D MR images, we proposed and validated a novel and fully-automatic stroke lesion segmentation method by integrating 3D patch-based and 2D slice-based neural networks. The novel pipeline effectively combines boundary loss and generalized Dice loss, and is robust to human annotation errors. We demonstrated that our proposed method had better segmentation performance than existing methods evaluated on the ATLAS dataset.

Acknowledgement. This study was supported by the Shenzhen Basic Research Program (JCYJ20190809120205578), the National Key R&D Program of China (2017YFC0112404) and the National Natural Science Foundation of China (81501546).

References

1. Johnson, W., Onuma, O., Owolabi, M., et al.: Stroke: a global response is needed. Bull. World Health Organ. **94**(9), 634 (2016)
2. Pinto, A., Mckinley, R., Alves, V., et al.: Stroke lesion outcome prediction based on MRI imaging combined with clinical information. Front. Neurol. **9**, 1060 (2018)
3. Cramer, S.C., Wolf, S.L., Adams Jr., H.P., et al.: Stroke recovery and rehabilitation research: issues, opportunities, and the National Institutes of Health StrokeNet. Stroke **48**(3), 813–819 (2017)
4. Burke Quinlan, E., Dodakian, L., See, J., et al.: Neural function, injury, and stroke subtype predict treatment gains after stroke. Ann. Neuro. **77**(1), 132–145 (2015)
5. Crinion, J., Holland, A.L., Copland, D.A., Thompson, C.K., Hillis, A.E.: Neuroimaging in aphasia treatment research: quantifying brain lesions after stroke. Neuroimage **73**, 208–214 (2013)
6. Tipirneni, S.A., Christensen, S., Straka, M., et al.: Prediction of final infarct volume on subacute MRI by quantifying cerebral edema in ischemic stroke. J. Cereb. Blood Flow Metab. **37**(8), 3077–3084 (2017)
7. Ito, K.L., Kim, H., Liew, S.L.: A comparison of automated lesion segmentation approaches for chronic stroke T1-weighted MRI data. Hum. Brain Mapp. **40**(16), 4669–4685 (2019)
8. Seghier, M.L., Ramlackhansingh, A., Crinion, J., Leff, A.P., Price, C.J.: Lesion identification using unified segmentation-normalisation models and fuzzy clustering. NeuroImage **41**(4), 1253–1266 (2008)
9. Pustina, D., Coslett, H.B., Turkeltaub, P.E., Tustison, N., Schwartz, M.F., Avants, B.: Automated segmentation of chronic stroke lesions using LINDA: lesion identification with neighborhood data analysis. Hum. Brain Mapp. **37**(4), 1405–1421 (2016)
10. De Haan, B., Clas, P., Juenger, H., Wilke, M., Karnath, H.O.: Fast semi-automated lesion demarcation in stroke. NeuroImage Clin. **9**, 69–74 (2015)
11. Griffis, J.C., Allendorfer, J.B., Szaflarski, J.P.: Voxel-based Gaussian naïve Bayes classification of ischemic stroke lesions in individual T1-weighted MRI scans. J. Neurosci. Methods **257**, 97–108 (2016)
12. Qi, K., et al.: X-Net: brain stroke lesion segmentation based on depthwise separable convolution and long-range dependencies. In: Shen, D., et al. (eds.) MICCAI 2019. LNCS, vol. 11766, pp. 247–255. Springer, Cham (2019). https://doi.org/10.1007/978-3-030-32248-9_28
13. Zhou, Y., Huang, W., Dong, P., et al.: D-UNet: a dimension-fusion U shape network for chronic stroke lesion segmentation. IEEE/ACM Trans. Comput. Biol. Bioinform (2019)
14. Xue, Y., Farhat, F.G., Boukrina, O., et al.: A multi-path 2.5 dimensional convolutional neural network system for segmenting stroke lesions in brain MRI images. NeuroImage Clin. **25**, 102118 (2020)
15. Yang, H., et al.: CLCI-Net: cross-level fusion and context inference networks for lesion segmentation of chronic stroke. In: Shen, D., et al. (eds.) MICCAI 2019. LNCS, vol. 11766, pp. 266–274. Springer, Cham (2019). https://doi.org/10.1007/978-3-030-32248-9_30
16. Ronneberger, O., Fischer, P., Brox, T.: U-Net: convolutional networks for biomedical image segmentation. In: Navab, N., Hornegger, J., Wells, W.M., Frangi, A.F. (eds.) MICCAI 2015. LNCS, vol. 9351, pp. 234–241. Springer, Cham (2015). https://doi.org/10.1007/978-3-319-24574-4_28

17. Wu, J., Zhang, Y., Tang, X.: A multi-atlas guided 3D fully convolutional network for MRI-based subcortical segmentation. In: ISBI, pp. 705–708. IEEE (2019)
18. Maier, O., Menze, B.H., von der Gablentz, J., Häni, L., et al.: ISLES 2015-A public evaluation benchmark for ischemic stroke lesion segmentation from multispectral MRI. Med. Image Anal. **35**, 250–269 (2017)
19. Chen, H., Dou, Q., Yu, L., Qin, J., Heng, P.A.: VoxResNet: deep voxelwise residual networks for brain segmentation from 3D MR images. NeuroImage **170**, 446–455 (2018)
20. Zhang, Y., Wu, J., Liu, Y., Chen, Y., Wu, X., Tang, X.: MI-UNet: multi-inputs UNet incorporating brain parcellation for stroke lesion segmentation from T1-weighted magnetic resonance images. IEEE J. Biomed. Health Inform. (2020)
21. Milletari, F., Navab, N., Ahmadi, S.A.: V-net: fully convolutional neural networks for volumetric medical image segmentation. In: 3DV, pp. 565–571. IEEE (2016)
22. Kervadec, H., Bouchtiba, J., Desrosiers, C., et al.: Boundary loss for highly unbalanced segmentation. In: MIDL, pp. 285–296 (2019)
23. Kamnitsas, K., Ledig, C., Newcombe, V.F., et al.: Efficient multi-scale 3D CNN with fully connected CRF for accurate brain lesion segmentation. Med. Image Anal. **36**, 61–78 (2017)
24. Dolz, J., Desrosiers, C., Ayed, I.B.: 3D fully convolutional networks for subcortical segmentation in MRI: a large-scale study. NeuroImage **170**, 456–470 (2018)
25. Lian, C., Zhang, J., Liu, M., et al.: Multi-channel multi-scale fully convolutional network for 3D perivascular spaces segmentation in 7T MR images. Med. Image Anal. **46**, 106–117 (2018)
26. Liew, S.L., Anglin, J.M., Banks, N.W., et al.: A large, open-source dataset of stroke anatomical brain images and manual lesion segmentations. Sci. Data **5**, 180011 (2018)
27. Li, C., Sun, H., Liu, Z., Wang, M., Zheng, H., Wang, S.: Learning cross-modal deep representations for multi-modal MR image segmentation. In: Shen, D., et al. (eds.) MICCAI 2019. LNCS, vol. 11765, pp. 57–65. Springer, Cham (2019). https://doi.org/10.1007/978-3-030-32245-8_7
28. Vaswani, A., Shazeer, N., Parmar, N., et al.: Attention is all you need. In: NIPS, pp. 5998–6008 (2017)
29. Wu, J., Zhang, Y., Tang, X.: A joint 3D+2D fully convolutional framework for subcortical segmentation. In: Shen, D., et al. (eds.) MICCAI 2019. LNCS, vol. 11766, pp. 301–309. Springer, Cham (2019). https://doi.org/10.1007/978-3-030-32248-9_34

Linking Adolescent Brain MRI to Obesity via Deep Multi-cue Regression Network

Hao Guan, Erkun Yang, Li Wang, Pew-Thian Yap, Mingxia Liu[✉],
and Dinggang Shen[✉]

Department of Radiology and BRIC, University of North Carolina at Chapel Hill,
Chapel Hill, NC 27599, USA
mxliu@med.unc.edu, Dinggang.Shen@gmail.com

Abstract. Adolescent obesity has become a significant public health problem for the potential risk of various diseases in later life. Recent biomedical studies have revealed that obesity is associated with structural changes in the brain. Thus the computer-aided analysis of adolescent obesity based on brain MRI is of great clinical value. While previous methods typically rely on hand-crafted MRI features for obesity prediction, we propose to link adolescent obesity and brain MRI through a deep learning framework. The newly released brain MRI data from the large-scale Adolescent Brain Cognitive Development (ABCD) study has paved the way for such an exploration. In this paper, we propose a deep multi-cue regression network (DMRN) for MRI-based analysis of adolescent obesity. Specially, in DMRN, we first design a feature encoding network to automatically extract high-dimensional features from brain MR images, followed by a regression network to predict Body Mass Index (BMI) scores for obesity analysis. To take advantage of other prior knowledge of studied subjects, our DMRN framework further explicitly incorporates the demographic information (e.g., waist circumference) of subjects into the learning process. Experiments have been conducted on 3,779 subjects with T1-weighted MRIs from the ABCD dataset. The results have provided some useful findings: (1) we consolidate the relationship between adolescent obesity and brain MRI as well as demographic information through a deep learning model; (2) we use visualization method to explain the prediction results by highlighting potential biomarkers in the brain MR images that are associated with adolescent obesity.

1 Introduction

Adolescent obesity has become a significant public health problem, which is estimated to affect millions of young people worldwide [1,2]. Adolescents who are obese have a potential risk of poor diseases in later life, such as heart diseases, diabetes and various cancers [3,4]. While obesity is primarily characterized by weight gain, a recent study suggests that it is related to structural changes of the brain which may trigger impairments in the nerve system [5]. However, a

© Springer Nature Switzerland AG 2020
M. Liu et al. (Eds.): MLMI 2020, LNCS 12436, pp. 111–119, 2020.
https://doi.org/10.1007/978-3-030-59861-7_12

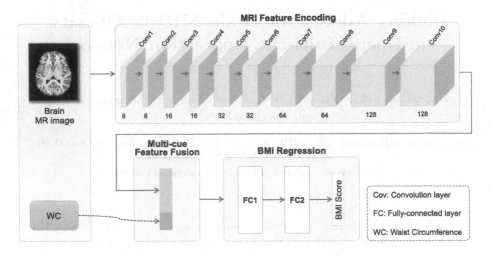

Fig. 1. Overview of the proposed deep multi-cue regression network (DMRN) for adolescent obesity prediction based on structural MR images, including (1) MRI feature encoding, (2) multi-cue feature fusion, and (3) BMI regression. The input data include the brain MR image and the demographic information (i.e., waist circumference, WC) of each subject, while the output is the BMI score.

clear association between adolescent brain structure and obesity still remains an open problem currently. Therefore, it is of great clinical value to conduct more in-depth research on such correlation to bridge the gap.

Structural magnetic resonance imaging (MRI) has been widely used in brain morphology analysis due to its sensitivity and high spatial resolution [6–10]. In this work, we investigate the association between brain structural changes and adolescent obesity, based on a recently released large-scale MRI dataset, i.e., the NIH Adolescent Brain and Cognitive Development (ABCD) [11]. The ABCD dataset is currently the largest longitudinal study of over 11,000 young people aged 9–10 from 21 research sites across the United States. As the newly released and largest dataset of adolescent brain MRIs, the ABCD dataset has paved the way for further pushing forward the research on exploring the relationship between adolescent obesity and the corresponding brain structural changes. Among the various indicators of obesity, the Body Mass Index (BMI) is the most widely-used measurement which has been used by the World Health Organization (WHO) for clinical diagnosis of obesity [12]. Since BMI is easily calculated and reliable for indicating obesity, BMI is used as the clinical indicator of obesity in our analysis.

In the literature, several machine learning methods have been proposed to analyze obesity [13,14]. However, these methods only used facial or body images to train the model, which could not essentially reflect the relationship between obesity and its biological causes (e.g., structural changes of the brain). In addition, existing studies generally rely on small-scale datasets, which greatly limits the scope and depth of the analysis. Based on the large-scale ABCD dataset, some research has been conducted to study the relationship between adolescent obesity and brain structure [15]. However, they merely rely on demographic information of subjects, and do not investigate the association between obesity with brain MR images.

In this paper, we intend to link brain structural MRI to adolescent obesity through a deep learning framework. To this end, we propose a deep multi-clue regression network (DMRN) to predict BMI scores of subjects, as illustrated in Fig. 1. As can be seen from this figure, the proposed DMRN consists of three key components: (1) a *MRI feature encoding* module that extracts feature representations of the input MR images, (2) a *multi-cue feature fusion* module that fuses MRI features and demographic information, and (3) a *BMI regression* module that predicts BMI scores for measuring obesity. Different from previous studies, our DMRN can automatically extract informative MRI features which are associated with obesity, without requiring any hand-crafted representations or expert knowledge. Especially, DMRN is able to explicitly incorporate the demographic information (e.g., waist circumference) of subjects into the learning process, which is expected to further improve the prediction performance by introducing more prior knowledge of studied subjects.

The major contributions of this work is two-fold. *First*, we introduce a simple but effective deep model to a novel application, i.e., studying structural changes in adolescent brains that are linked to obesity. To the best of our knowledge, this is among the first attempt to link adolescent obesity to brain MRI on such a large-scale (i.e., 3,779 subjects) adolescent brain MRI dataset. *Besides*, we employ a visualization method to analyze the network outputs by highlighting potential obesity-related biomarkers in MRIs. The results can offer valuable information for related research and encourage the development of AI models for adolescent obesity analysis.

2   Method

2.1   Materials and Image-Processing

A total of 3,779 T1-weighted brain MR images of adolescents aged 9–10 and their corresponding raw adolescent anthropometrics scores (i.e., weight, height, waist circumference, and age) from the ABCD dataset were downloaded and included in our study. As the obesity indicator, BMI is calculated based on the ratio of weight and height (all the original weight and height scores are measured and offered by the ABCD study) as follows:

$$BMI = 703 \times \frac{weight}{height^2} \qquad (1)$$

where weight and height are measured by pound (*lb*) and inch (*in*), respectively.

All T1-weighted MR images were pre-processed through a standard pipeline, including (1) anterior commissure-posterior commissure alignment, (2) skull stripping, (3) intensity correction, (4) linear alignment with the Colin27 template, (5) image normalization and background removal, and (6) intensity inhomogeneity correction using N3 algorithm. Finally, all the pre-processed MR images had the same size of $181 \times 217 \times 181\,\mathrm{mm}^3$ with the spatial resolution of $1 \times 1 \times 1\,\mathrm{mm}^3$.

2.2 Proposed Method

As shown in Fig. 1, the proposed deep multi-cue regression network (DMRN) consists of three modules: (1) MRI feature encoding, (2) multi-cue feature fusion, and (3) BMI regression. In the following, we first present the detail of each module, and then introduce the visualization method and implementation of DMRN.

MR Feature Encoding. As illustrated in the top panel of Fig. 1, we exploit a 3D convolutional neural network as the backbone to extract feature representations of each input MRI (with the whole image as the input). Specifically, the MRI feature encoding backbone contains ten convolutional (Conv) layers (size: $3 \times 3 \times 3$) to extract local-to-global representations of brain MRIs. The filter numbers of these sequential Conv layers are 8, 8, 16, 16, 32, 32, 64, 64, 128, and 128, respectively. The stride for each Conv layer is set to 1, and each Conv layer is followed by batch normalization and rectified linear unit (ReLU). To reduce over-fitting and increase receptive field, down-sampling operations (with the stride of $2 \times 2 \times 2$) are plugged into four Conv layers (i.e., Conv2, Conv4, Conv6, Conv8 and Conv10), respectively. As a plug-in module, the MRI feature encoding backbone can be replaced with any other network architectures, e.g., residual blocks.

Multi-cue Feature Fusion. To take advantage of other prior knowledge (e.g., demographic information) of studied subjects, we incorporate the demographic factor, i.e., waist circumference (WC), into the learning process. As shown in the bottom left panel of Fig. 1, we concatenate the waist circumference with the learned MR feature vector of the convolution layers. Here, the WC value is encoded as a vector (ranging from 0 to 1). Then, the concatenated feature vector is further fed into a regression module for BMI prediction.

Regression Module for BMI Prediction. With the multi-cue representations (i.e., concatenation of MRI features and WC) as input, two successive fully-connected layers are employed for BMI score estimation. Let $\mathcal{X} = \{X_i\}_{i=1}^{N}$ and $\mathbf{y} = \{y_i\}_{i=1}^{N}$ represent the feature representations and ground-truth BMI scores of N training subjects, respectively. For the i-th subject X_i ($i = 1, \cdots, N$), we denote its BMI score as y_i. The proposed model aims to link the input and the obesity measurement scores via a non-linear mapping $\phi \colon \mathcal{X} \to \mathbf{y}$, with the objective function defined as follows:

$$\min_{\mathbf{W}} \frac{1}{N} \sum_{X_i \in \mathcal{X}} (y_i - \phi(X_i, \mathbf{W}))^2 \qquad (2)$$

where $\mathbf{W}$ denotes the parameters of the DMRN model.

Visualization of Discriminative Regions. We use a visualization method [16] to show potential biomarkers in brain MR images that are associated with obesity. The results can be used as a useful complement to MRI analysis by experts and help to interpret the prediction results of DMRN. To this end, we calculate the gradient of the output feature maps of DMRN (w.r.t. each input brain MR image). The gradient can describe how the output varies when a specific voxel value changes, thus indicating the contributions of different brain regions for predicting BMI scores. In the training process, the gradient can be easily calculated by the back-propagation algorithm.

Implementation. The proposed DMRN model was implemented using Python based on PyTorch. The input of the network was linearly-aligned brain MR image (size: $181 \times 217 \times 181$) and a demographic factor (i.e., waist circumference), while the output was the estimated BMI score. At the training phase, the Adam optimizer was adopted with a mini-batch size of 2 and a learning rate of 1×10^{-3}. A dropout rate of 0.5 was used to prevent over-fitting. The network was trained in an end-to-end manner for 30 epochs.

3 Experiment and Discussion

Experimental Setup. A total of 3, 779 subjects with T1-weighted MRIs from ABCD are included in the experiments. All these subjects are partitioned into three subsets, including a training set (60%), a validation set (20%), and a test set (20%), and such data partition is fixed[1]. Based on the training set, we construct a specific model and save the trained model that achieves the smallest validation loss on the validation set. The model is then applied to the independent test set. To evaluate the performance of BMI prediction, two metrics are used in the experiments, including (1) mean square error (MSE), and (2) mean absolute error (MAE). For these two metrics, lower values indicate better performance.

The proposed DMRN is first compared with two conventional machine learning method using different hand-crafted features, including (1) support vector regressor (SVR) using ROI features (gray matter volume in 90 ROIs defined in AAL template) [17], and (2) SVR using WC as features. We further compare DMRN with two deep learning models, including (1) AlexNet [18] and (2) Vox-CNN [19]. Specifically, the AlexNet consists of five $3 \times 3 \times 3$ Conv layers (with the channel numbers of 64, 64, 128, 128, and 256, respectively), followed by three fully-connected layers for regression. The VoxCNN contains ten $3 \times 3 \times 3$ Conv

---

[1] https://sibis.sri.com/abcd-np-challenge/.

Table 1. Results of BMI prediction achieved by the proposed method and several other methods on the ABCD dataset.

Method	Validation Result		Testing Result	
	MSE	MAE	MSE	MAE
ROI+SVR	19.26	5.05	19.50	5.12
WC+SVR	22.57	6.01	22.32	5.95
AlexNet	18.61	4.95	18.05	4.88
VoxCNN	17.33	4.25	16.98	4.01
DMRN-MRI	15.16	3.06	15.06	3.09
DMRN (Ours)	**14.80**	**3.01**	**14.01**	**2.87**

layers (with the channel numbers of 8, 8, 16, 16, 32, 32, 32, 64, 64, and 64, respectively), followed by two fully-connected layers for regression. We also compare our DMRN with its variant (called DMRN-MRI) that uses only MRIs as input. For the fair comparison, all deep learning methods share the same input MR images and ground-truth BMI scores, while our DMRN also uses a demographic factor (i.e., WC) as input.

Results of BMI Prediction. The experimental results achieved by six different methods on the ABCD dataset for BMI prediction are listed in Table 1. From Table 1, one can observe that the proposed DMRN achieves relatively higher precision, with consistently better performance than the other methods.

Based on the results, we can draw the following conclusions. *First*, a deep learning model (e.g., our DMRN) for BMI prediction could be trained from brain MR images, by automatically learning MRI features. This also implies that the adolescent obesity and brain structure have some correlation. Without hand-crafted analysis with prior expert knowledge, deep learning for MRI-based BMI prediction has offered a new perspective to mine the relationship between obesity and brain structure. *Second*, these results indicate that our deep network is relatively suitable for the task of BMI prediction compared to the other two CNN models. This implies that the task-oriented feature encoding and multi-cue feature fusion strategy are helpful to learn informative feature representations to boost the prediction performance of BMI.

Obesity-Related Brain Regions in MRI. Previous studies have revealed that obesity is associated with certain regions of the brain. Note that our method is totally based on automated learning from brain MR images (without any neuroscience knowledge). To understanding the output of the proposed deep network, we aggregate saliency maps learned by our method on the whole cohort (grouped by high BMI > 40 and low BMI < 10 [12]) to visualize obesity-related patterns in MRIs. The result is shown in Fig. 2.

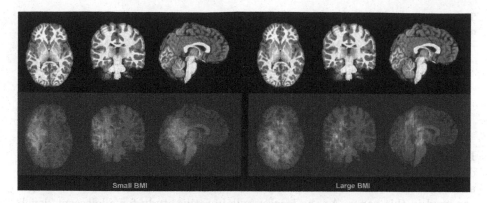

Fig. 2. Relevance heatmaps generated by our deep multi-cue regression network (DMRN) for BMI score prediction. The highlighted parts (in yellow color) indicate the ares that are more closely related to obesity. (Color figure online)

From Fig. 2, it can be observed that different brain regions have different contributions to obesity in terms of BMI prediction. In addition, Fig. 2 shows that brain regions that are closely associated with obesity may have some differences between the cohorts with different BMI scores.

Ablation Study. To investigate the impact of demographic information and the role of our multi-cue fusion strategy for BMI prediction, we conduct several ablation experiments based on two variants of DMRN. Note that height and weight information are highly correlated with ground-truth BMI (see Eq. 1), and BMI is the output, thus they are not used in the ablation study.

First, we analyze the impact of multi-cue fusion strategy, by removing waist circumference (WC) from DMRN. That is, we train the network solely based on MR images and denote this variant as "DMRN-MRI", with results shown in Table 1. From Table 1, we can see that DMRN with WC information performs better than DMRN-MRI that uses only MR images. This implies that the proposed multi-cue fusion strategy (for fusing MRI and WC) helps to improve the performance of BMI prediction, and WC is positively correlated with obesity. This is consistent with the findings of some related research studies [20].

We further investigate whether the age information is helpful in BMI prediction. Specifically, we replace the WC value with age (in months) as demographic information in DMRN, and denote this variant with "DMRN-Age". We encode the age (normalized into the range of $[0,1]$) with MR features in the multi-cue fusion module, with experimental results reported in Table 2. Table 2 shows that the age information does not impact the prediction significantly, suggesting that there is no obvious correlation between obesity and age. This is different from the cases in some other type of diseases caused by brain impairment, such as Alzheimer's disease and autism spectrum disorder.

Table 2. Results of BMI prediction achieved by two variants of the proposed DMRN on the ABCD dataset.

Method	Validation Result		Testing Result	
	MSE	MAE	MSE	MAE
DMRN-MRI	15.16	3.06	15.06	3.09
DMRN-Age	**15.13**	**3.05**	**15.03**	**3.02**

Limitations and Future Work. Even though our DMRN is effective in predicting adolescent obesity, there are still several limitations that need to be addressed in the future. *First*, only T1-weighted structural brain MR images are used in this paper. As the largest collaborative study for adolescent development, the ABCD dataset consists of multi-modal neuroimaging data, such as T2-weighted structural MRI, Diffusion tensor imaging (DTI), and functional MRI (fMRI). It is interesting to extend our DMRN to a multi-modal version to take advantage of those multi-modal neuroimages, which will be our future work. *Second*, we equally treat subjects from 21 research centers in the ABCD database, ignoring the differences in data distribution among multiple imaging centers. Considering that such data heterogeneity may have a negative impact on the robustness of the learned model, we plan to develop advanced data adaptation techniques [21,22] to handle this challenging problem. *Third*, to improve the prediction precision, more complex CNN architectures (e.g., residual or dense networks) could be used as backbones to more efficiently encode MR images, which will also be studied in future.

4 Conclusion

In this paper, we developed a deep multi-cue regression network (DMRN) for MRI-based analysis of adolescent obesity in terms of BMI. The proposed DMRN consists of a MRI feature encoding module, a multi-cue feature fusion module, and a BMI regression module. Besides the input MRI, DMRN can also explicitly incorporate two demographic factors (i.e., waist circumference and age) into the learning process. Experiments were performed on the newly released ABCD dataset which offers a relatively large number of adolescent brain MRIs. Experimental result suggest that the BMI can be reliably predicted based on brain MR images via DMRN, thus demonstrating the association between adolescent obesity and brain structure. Besides, we also visualize the learned heatmaps in the brain MR images to indicate important imaging biomarker that may be associated with obesity.

References

1. Abarca-Gómez, L., et al.: Worldwide trends in body-mass index, underweight, overweight, and obesity from 1975 to 2016: a pooled analysis of 2416 population-based measurement studies in 128.9 million children, adolescents, and adults. Lancet **390**(10113), 2627–2642 (2017)

2. Ogden, C.L., Carroll, M.D., Kit, B.K., Flegal, K.M.: Prevalence of childhood and adult obesity in the United States, 2011–2012. Jama **311**(8), 806–814 (2014)
3. Biro, F.M., Wien, M.: Childhood obesity and adult morbidities. Am. J. Clin. Nutr. **91**(5), 1499–1505 (2010)
4. Arnold, M., et al.: Obesity and cancer: an update of the global impact. Cancer Epidemiol. **41**, 8–15 (2016)
5. Li, N., Yolton, K., Lanphear, B.P., Chen, A., et al.: Impact of early-life weight status on cognitive abilities in children. Obesity **26**(6), 1088–1095 (2018)
6. Giedd, J.N., et al.: Brain development during childhood and adolescence: a longitudinal MRI study. Nat. Neurosci. **2**(10), 861–863 (1999)
7. Liu, M., Zhang, D., Shen, D.: Relationship induced multi-template learning for diagnosis of Alzheimer's disease and mild cognitive impairment. IEEE Trans. Med. Imaging **35**(6), 1463–1474 (2016)
8. Liu, M., Zhang, J., Adeli, E., Shen, D.: Landmark-based deep multi-instance learning for brain disease diagnosis. Med. Image Anal. **43**, 157–168 (2018)
9. Pan, Y., Liu, M., Wang, L., Xia, Y., Shen, D.: Discriminative-region-aware residual network for adolescent brain structure and cognitive development analysis. In: Zhang, D., Zhou, L., Jie, B., Liu, Mingxia (eds.) GLMI 2019. LNCS, vol. 11849, pp. 138–146. Springer, Cham (2019). https://doi.org/10.1007/978-3-030-35817-4_17
10. Liu, M., Zhang, J., Lian, C., Shen, D.: Weakly supervised deep learning for brain disease prognosis using MRI and incomplete clinical scores. IEEE Trans. Cybern. **50**(7), 3381–3392 (2019)
11. Volkow, N.D., et al.: The conception of the abcd study: from substance use to a broad NIH collaboration. Dev. Cogn. Neurosci. **32**, 4–7 (2018)
12. Garvey, W.T.: The diagnosis and evaluation of patients with obesity. Curr. Opin. Endocr. Metab. Res. **4**, 50–57 (2019)
13. Jiang, M., Shang, Y., Guo, G.: On visual BMI analysis from facial images. Image Vis. Comput. **89**, 183–196 (2019)
14. Dantcheva, A., Bremond, F., Bilinski, P.: Show me your face and i will tell you your height, weight and body mass index. In: ICPR, pp. 3555–3560 (2018)
15. Ronan, L., Alexander-Bloch, A., Fletcher, P.C.: Childhood obesity, cortical structure, and executive function in healthy children. Cereb. Cortex **30**(4), 2519–2528 (2019)
16. Simonyan, K., Vedaldi, A., Zisserman, A.: Deep inside convolutional networks: visualising image classification models and saliency maps. In: ICLR (2014)
17. Drucker, H., et al.: Support vector regression machines. In: NIPS, pp. 155–161 (1997)
18. Krizhevsky, A., Sutskever, I., Hinton, G.E.: Imagenet classification with deep convolutional neural networks. In: NIPS, pp. 1097–1105 (2012)
19. Korolev, S., Safiullin, A., Belyaev, M., Dodonova, Y.: Residual and plain convolutional neural networks for 3D brain MRI classification. In: ISBI (2017)
20. Walls, H.L., et al.: Comparing trends in BMI and waist circumference. Obesity **19**(1), 216–219 (2011)
21. Cheng, B., Liu, M., Shen, D., Li, Z., Zhang, D.: Multi-domain transfer learning for early diagnosis of Alzheimer's disease. Neuroinformatics **15**(2), 115–132 (2017)
22. Wang, M., Zhang, D., Huang, J., Yap, P.T., Shen, D., Liu, M.: Identifying autism spectrum disorder with multi-site fMRI via low-rank domain adaptation. IEEE Trans. Med. Imaging **39**(3), 644–655 (2019)

Robust Multiple Sclerosis Lesion Inpainting with Edge Prior

Huahong Zhang[1], Rohit Bakshi[2], Francesca Bagnato[3], and Ipek Oguz[1(✉)]

[1] Vanderbilt University, Nashville, TN 37235, USA
{huahong.zhang,ipek.oguz}@vanderbilt.edu
[2] Brigham and Women's Hospital, Boston, MA 02115, USA
[3] Vanderbilt University Medical Center and Nashville VA Medical Center,
Nashville, TN 37212, USA

Abstract. Inpainting lesions is an important preprocessing task for algorithms analyzing brain MRIs of multiple sclerosis (MS) patients, such as tissue segmentation and cortical surface reconstruction. We propose a new deep learning approach for this task. Unlike existing inpainting approaches which ignore the lesion areas of the input image, we leverage the edge information around the lesions as a prior to help the inpainting process. Thus, the input of this network includes the T1-w image, lesion mask and the edge map computed from the T1-w image, and the output is the lesion-free image. The introduction of the edge prior is based on our observation that the edge detection results of the MRI scans will usually contain the contour of white matter (WM) and grey matter (GM), even though some undesired edges appear near the lesions. Instead of losing all the information around the neighborhood of lesions, our approach preserves the local tissue shape (brain/WM/GM) with the guidance of the input edges. The qualitative results show that our pipeline inpaints the lesion areas in a realistic and shape-consistent way. Our quantitative evaluation shows that our approach outperforms the existing state-of-the-art inpainting methods in both image-based metrics and in FreeSurfer segmentation accuracy. Furthermore, our approach demonstrates robustness to inaccurate lesion mask inputs. This is important for practical usability, because it allows for a generous over-segmentation of lesions instead of requiring precise boundaries, while still yielding accurate results.

Keywords: Multiple sclerosis · Deep learning · Inpainting

1 Introduction

Multiple Sclerosis (MS) is a common autoimmune disease of the central nervous system characterized by focal demyelinating lesions visible on brain MRI. In the long term, the clinical progression of the disease is closely linked to brain atrophy, which makes the estimation of brain atrophy an important tool for longitudinal monitoring [11]. In order to measure the GM and WM atrophy, algorithms such

Electronic supplementary material The online version of this chapter (https://doi.org/10.1007/978-3-030-59861-7_13) contains supplementary material, which is available to authorized users.

© Springer Nature Switzerland AG 2020
M. Liu et al. (Eds.): MLMI 2020, LNCS 12436, pp. 120–129, 2020.
https://doi.org/10.1007/978-3-030-59861-7_13

as brain tissue classification and cortical surface reconstruction/thickness measurement are necessary. However, the presence of MS lesions is problematic for most automated algorithms and can lead to biased morphological measurements. To mitigate this problem, many lesion inpainting methods have been proposed [2–4,6,9,12–14,17,18]. These methods, whether conventional or deep-learning-based, consider the areas of lesions as "missing" during inpainting. Discarding the original lesion voxels is a common practice in MS lesion inpainting, and is consistent with the inpainting techniques in computer vision. Nevertheless, much structural information is lost when the lesion voxels are discarded. As a consequence, the algorithms are highly likely to produce inaccurate predictions if the lesion masks cross the tissue boundaries.

In this work, we re-consider the difference between the MS lesion inpainting and the general-purpose inpainting task in computer vision. We hypothesize that, specifically for MS lesion refilling (and potentially for other medical image inpainting tasks), the areas that require inpainting are not "missing" but rather contain information useful for inpainting and, thus, should not be discarded. Even though the lesions have different intensities than normal-appearing brain tissue, the structural information around lesions can and should be preserved. Therefore, we introduce the edge information from the input images as a prior.

Contributions. The main contributions of this paper are summarized below:

- Instead of considering the lesion areas as missing, we use the edge information extracted from the input image as a prior to guide the inpainting. This is more appropriate for MS inpainting as it preserves the shape and boundary of normal-appearing tissue around the lesions in the inpainted images. Different from [10] which infers the edges with an extra network, we believe the input image itself already contains the information for constraining the inpainting.
- Our method makes no assumptions about the characteristics of the lesions, which makes it suitable for both white matter lesions and gray matter lesions. This could also allow for the generalization to different modalities.
- We demonstrate that the proposed method can handle highly inaccurate lesion masks, which makes it robust to errors in lesion delineations. This reduces the dependence on highly accurate lesion segmentation, which is an elusive goal even for experts. Also, while incorrect lesion masks can cause artifacts for some methods such as FSL [2] and SLF [17], our method does not create such artifacts.
- The introduction of edge information as a prior to inpainting algorithms is architecture-agnostic. It can be readily used in conjunction with other deep learning algorithms, which may further improve performance.

2   Methods

2.1   Datasets and Pre-processing

We use an in-house dataset of 15 healthy controls and 40 patients with relapsing-remitting MS (RRMS) or secondary progressive MS (SPMS). At Brigham and

Women's Hospital, 3T T1-w MPRAGE and FLAIR images were acquired for each subject, at $1\,mm^3$ isotropic resolution. FLAIR images were co-registered to T1-w space [1]. All were skull-stripped with BET [15], followed by N4ITK [16].

In this paper, we refer to the healthy controls as original healthy control images (OHC) and the generated images as simulated lesion images (SL, see Sect. 3), in contrast to real lesion images (RL) from MS patients.

We use the original healthy control images (without any lesions, real or simulated) in the training phase. This forces the network to only learn the appearance of healthy tissue. In the test phase, we use the simulated lesion images (see Sect. 3) for both the qualitative and quantitative experiments; we also present qualitative results from the real lesion images.

2.2   Edge Detection

Due to the lack of ground truth pairs for training, a simple translation between the lesion and lesion-free images, e.g. using pix2pix [7], cannot be performed. Instead, the current inpainting methods consider the lesion areas as "missing" and train the network to infer the masked regions based on their surrounding areas. This idea is straightforward but causes the network to, by construction, ignore the lesion areas in the test phase, which means all the structure or shape information within the lesion masks is lost. Instead, our goal is to preserve such information in the test phase, while making no assumption on lesion appearance (e.g., a specific intensity profile relative to surrounding tissue) during training.

We use the classical Canny edge detector to extract the edge information from the lesion image. In Fig. 1, A-1 is a RL image, and A-2 is the corresponding edge map ($\sigma = 0.8$ for Gaussian filter, first step of edge detection). The boundaries between different brain tissues remain visible even when the lesions are present.

In the training phase, we use only OHC images. We provide random ROIs as the lesion mask, and the network has to learn to reconstruct the original T1w image. However, this means all the edges from the input will be preserved in the network output for the training set, whereas for the testing set, it is desirable that the edges from the lesion are ignored while the edges from tissue (e.g., WM/GM boundary) will be preserved. To alleviate this discrepancy, and to teach the model to ignore certain edges while preserving others, we use augmentations of the input edges during the training phase. This is illustrated in Fig. 1, where B-1 is a slice from OHC image, and B-2 is the corresponding edge map. By adding Gaussian noise to B-1 and detecting the edges from it, we get B-3, which contains some random edges compared to (B-2). We hypothesize that, with these augmentations, the network will learn to deal with the edges caused by the lesions.

2.3   Network Structure and Loss Functions

We adopted the network architecture described in [10] for MS inpainting. This network follows the encoder-decoder structure as shown in Fig. 2. Similar to the 2.5D methods in [19], the training input is the cropped 128×128 2D slices from

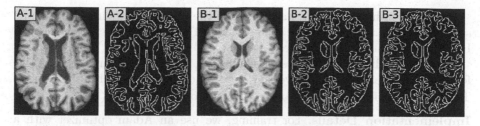

Fig. 1. Edge maps. (A-1) T1-w image with real lesions (RL) outlined in red; (A-2) Edges from A-1. (B-1) T1-w image of OHC; (B-2) Edges from B-1; (B-3) Edges after adding Gaussian noise to B-1. Orange pixels in (B-3) mark the newly generated edges. (Color figure online)

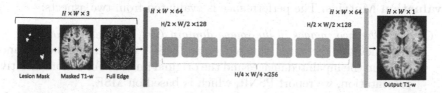

Fig. 2. Overview of the network architecture. The input is the concatenation of the binary lesion mask, the masked T1-w and edge detection of T1-w after adding random noise. The output is the inpainted T1-w image. Purple: 7×7 Convolution-SpectralNorm-InstanceNorm-ReLU; Green: 4×4 Convolution-SpectralNorm-InstanceNorm-ReLU layer, *stride* = 2 for down-sampling; Orange: residual blocks; Blue: similar to green, up-sampling; Gray: scaled *tanh*. (Color figure online)

all the 3 orientations and the test output is the consensus of the prediction from axial, coronal and sagittal views.

Our loss function is defined as $\mathcal{L}_{total} = \mathcal{L}_{rec} + 250\mathcal{L}_{style} + 0.1\mathcal{L}_{perceptual}$, where $\mathcal{L}_{rec}$ is the reconstruction loss, i.e., the pixel-wise L1 distance between the ground truth and the output image. $\mathcal{L}_{perceptual}$ and $\mathcal{L}_{style}$ are the perceptual loss and content loss introduced by [8], and they capture the difference of high-level features instead of raw images. We use perceptual loss and content loss to help the network generate realistic inpainting results with natural texture.

3   Experiments

Ground truth. Unlike lesion segmentation, which usually has gold standard lesion delineations, there is no gold standard for pairs of T1-w images with lesions and the corresponding lesion-free images. We thus use a lesion simulator on OHCs to evaluate in-painting methods: 1) the OHC image serves as 'ground truth' for what the corresponding inpainting result should look like, and 2) the tissue classification of the OHC image serves as 'ground truth' for the tissue classification of the corresponding inpainted images.

With our in-house dataset, we split 4/5 of the OHC subjects into the training set and 1/5 into the test set. We then obtained 11 SL-OHC pairs for the test set by simulating multiple SL images for each OHC image.

Using a publicly available lesion simulator[1], several lesion images with different lesion size, location and volume were generated for each healthy control. The lesion load followed a log-normal distribution $Log - N(log(15), \frac{log(3)}{3})$.

Implementation Details. For training, we use an Adam optimizer with a momentum of 0.5 and the initial learning rate (lr) of 0.0002. We use the initial learning rate for 100 epochs and let it decay to 0 within another 100 epochs. For validation, we choose the model with best F1 score (see below) for each fold. During training, we perform random lesion mask dilation for data augmentation.

Evaluation Metrics. The performance is evaluated from two aspects:

- *Compare the two images in the image domain (i.e., synthesis error).*
  - We calculate the mean squared error (MSE) to measure the distance between the inpainted images and the original images. For a more intuitive presentation, we report PSNR, which is based on MSE.
  - We compare the edge detection result between the output image and the ground truth images. To take both precision and recall into consideration, the F_1 score is calculated from the binary edge maps.
- *Compare the brain segmentation results (i.e., volume error and tissue overlap).* The brain segmentation results will be affected by MS lesions, however, the lesion filling methods are expected to reduce this effect. We use FreeSurfer [5] for segmentation.
  - Absolute volume difference (AVD) for WM and GM is computed as $AVD = \frac{|V_o - V_{gt}|}{V_{gt}} \times 100\%$ where V_o and V_{gt} are the volume of a given class in the segmentation of the inpainting output and the ground truth, respectively.
  - The F1 score and Jaccard similarity coefficient (IoU) over all classes are also reported to provide an overall evaluation of the segmentations.

With the exception of PSNR, all the metrics are reported on the lesion neighborhoods to focus on the changes caused by lesions, since there are practically no differences away from the lesion ROIs. The neighborhoods are defined by the dilation of lesion masks (3D dilation using octahedron kernel, $k = 5$).

Compared Methods. We compared our approach with three existing inpainting algorithms on T1-w images: the lesion filling tool included in FSL library [2], the SLF toolbox [17], and the recently proposed non-local partial convolutions (NLPC) inpainting method which is deep-learning-based [18]. Since NLPC is not publicly available, to make a fair comparison, we kept everything the same as our methods for training and evaluating NLPC except the network architecture.

---

[1] https://github.com/CSIM-Toolkits/LesionSimulatorExtension.

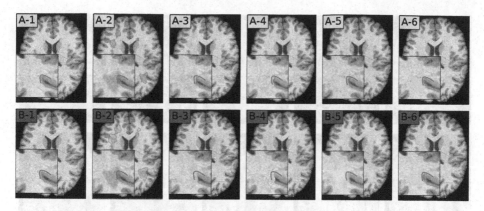

Fig. 3. Qualitative evaluation (simulated dataset). Group (A) uses "ground truth" lesion mask inputs. Group (B) uses dilated ($k = 3$) lesion mask inputs. (1) T1-w image of a healthy control; (2) T1-w image with lesions (lesion boundaries are marked in red); (3–6) Inpainted results using FSL, SLF, NLPC and our method, respectively. (Color figure online)

4 Results

Qualitative Analysis. The qualitative evaluation results are shown in Fig. 3.

In group (A), an OHC image (A1) and the corresponding lesion simulation results (A2) are shown. The inpainting results by FSL (A3), SLF (A4), NLPC (A5) and our proposed method (A6) are shown. Panel insets show a zoomed-in view near the lesion in temporal lobe. We note that SLF and FSL failed to preserve the brain structure of the sulcus by erroneously inpainting GM tissue. While for the deep-learning-based approaches, NLPC and the proposed method provide reasonable inpainting results. However, compared to NLPC, our method produced a more similar GM sulcus to the ground truth T1-w image.

Next, we explore the effect of inaccurate lesion delineations by dilating the input lesion masks. Group (B) contains the results filled with the dilated (k = 3) lesion masks. Similar results with dilation kernels k = 2 and k = 4 are presented in the appendix. In group (B), we can observe that SLF and FSL performance deteriorates because of the dilated masks. Additionally, because NLPC discards voxels within the lesion mask, it lacks adequate information and cannot preserve GM structure either. Our method, however, still presents results similar to ground truth and preserves the boundary between WM and GM.

In (A-5) and (A-6), we observe discontinuities between the inpainted regions and the surrounding tissue. This is due to the fusing of non-lesion regions of the input and the lesion regions of the output. Even though the lesion masks from the simulation are considered to be the 'ground truth', voxels outside the lesion mask can still contain abnormal intensities. This discontinuity disappears in group (B) since most abnormal voxels are included in the inpainted regions.

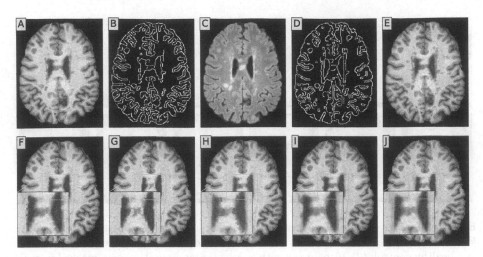

Fig. 4. Qualitative evaluation (real lesions). (A) T1-w image with real lesion; (B) Edge detection from A; (C) FLAIR image corresponding to (A); (D) Edge detection from C; (E) T1-w with segmented lesions (red pixels mark the boundary of lesions); (F–J) Inpainted results of FSL, SLF, NLPC, ours with T1-w edge and ours with FLAIR edge. (F–H) contain many small holes/artifacts, whereas our method avoids this problem. We note that the lesion between the lateral ventricles is missed by the lesion segmentation algorithm, and thus is not inpainted by any of the methods.

For some real lesion (RL) images, we observed that the lesions in the T1-w image can mislead the inpainting model by affecting the edges generated by the Canny edge detector. However, this can be solved by using the edge detection results from some other modalities (FLAIR, T2, etc) or their combinations. Qualitative results illustrating this extension are shown in Fig. 4. In this example, the lesion segmentation is obtained using [19]. This figure also contains examples of the artifacts generated by other inpainting methods. Our method provides the smoothest and most accurate boundaries after inpainting.

Quantitative Analysis. In Fig. 5, we show boxplots of the evaluation metrics described above. To demonstrate the effect of inaccurate lesion delineations, the x-axes are the dilation kernel sizes. We also report the same metrics for the simulated lesion images (without any inpainting) as a baseline.

In the image domain, our method has the best PSNR with all k values; its PSNR also decreases much slower than the other methods with increasing k-value. Even when k = 4, our method showed better PSNR than the simulated images. For the F1 score of the edge detection results, our method again decreases with the smallest slope among the methods. It falls under the lines of simulated images when k = 4, and we believe this is due to the variability of edge detection. The superior performance of our method on the other metrics supports this.

More importantly, for the metrics of segmentation results using FreeSurfer, our methods performed much better than the comparing methods. For the AVD

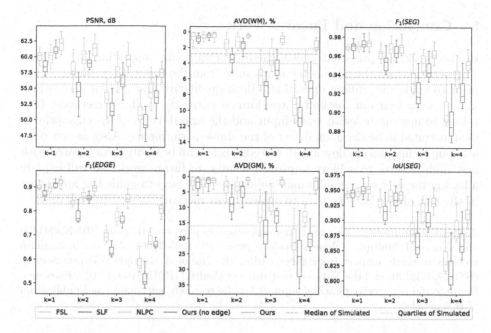

Fig. 5. Quantitative evaluation (simulated dataset). We report results for "ground truth" lesion mask input (no dilation, k = 1) and dilated lesion mask input (k = 2,3,4). The dotted lines are the medians and the quartiles of the simulated images.

of WM and GM, our method outperformed all other in-painting methods and the simulated images even when k = 4, which is not the case for any of the other methods. Interestingly, we noticed that the GM segmentation performance of our method when k = 2 is better than k = 1. We believe this is due to the discontinuity between the original lesion masks and the hypo/hyper-intense areas as discussed in the qualitative analysis. The F1 and Jaccard score over all the classes also prove the stable performance of our algorithm. Since our approach demonstrates stable performance, it allows the raters to segment in a more "aggressive" way, by deliberately oversegmenting instead of attempting to delineate precise boundaries, and our algorithm can ensure the performance of the inpainting. This can also be done by segmenting as usual and dilating the masks before inpainting.

As an ablation study, the results of our method without edge priors are also provided in Fig. 5. The no-edge experiments show similar performance to NLPC, and much lower than the with-edge results. This strongly supports our argument that the stability of our algorithm comes from the introduction of edge priors.

To provide another form of imperfect lesion mask, we used the state-of-the-art segmentation algorithm [19] to segment the lesions and inpainted using these imperfect masks. The results are in Appendix. Quantitative analysis for RLs is not possible since we don't have ground truth "lesion-free" images.

5 Conclusion and Future Work

In this work, we proposed a deep neural network for inpainting MS lesions. The network uses the edge detection results from the input T1-w image as the prior to guide the refilling operations. Both qualitative and quantitative experiments show that our method outperformed currently available methods. It is robust to inaccurate lesion mask input and the introduction of the edge prior is demonstrated to be the main driver of the stable performance. Also, as new deep learning techniques are developed, the edge prior can be easily incorporated with new architectures to achieve improved results. In future work, we will explore allowing the user to manually manipulate the edge map to guide the inpainting in the test phase. We also plan to evaluate our methods in longitudinal data.

Acknowledgements. This work was supported, in part, by NIH grant R01-NS094456 and National Multiple Sclerosis Society grant PP-1905-34001. Francesca Bagnato receives research support from Biogen Idec, the National Multiple Sclerosis Society (RG-1901-33190) and the National Institutes of Health (1R01NS109114-01). Francesca Bagnato did not receive financial support for the research, authorship and publication of this article.

References

1. Avants, B.B., Tustison, N.J., Song, G., Cook, P.A., Klein, A., Gee, J.C.: A reproducible evaluation of ANTs similarity metric performance in brain image registration. NeuroImage **54**(3), 2033–2044 (2011)
2. Battaglini, M., Jenkinson, M., De Stefano, N.: Evaluating and reducing the impact of white matter lesions on brain volume measurements. Hum. Brain Mapp. **33**(9), 2062–2071 (2012)
3. Ceccarelli, A., et al.: The impact of lesion in-painting and registration methods on voxel-based morphometry in detecting regional cerebral gray matter atrophy in multiple sclerosis. Am. J. Neuroradiol. **33**(8), 1579–1585 (2012)
4. Chard, D.T., Jackson, J.S., Miller, D.H., Wheeler-Kingshott, C.A.M.: Reducing the impact of white matter lesions on automated measures of brain gray and white matter volumes. J. Magn. Reson. Imaging **32**(1), 223–228 (2010)
5. Fischl, B.: FreeSurfer. NeuroImage **62**(2), 774–781 (2012)
6. Guizard, N., Nakamura, K., Coupé, P., Fonov, V.S., Arnold, D.L., Collins, D.L.: Non-local means inpainting of MS lesions in longitudinal image processing. Frontiers Neurosci. **9**, 456 (2015)
7. Isola, P., Zhu, J.Y., Zhou, T., Efros, A.A.: Image-to-image translation with conditional adversarial networks. (2016), arXiv: 1611.07004
8. Johnson, J., Alahi, A., Fei-Fei, L.: Perceptual losses for real-time style transfer and super-resolution. In: Leibe, B., Matas, J., Sebe, N., Welling, M. (eds.) ECCV 2016. LNCS, vol. 9906, pp. 694–711. Springer, Cham (2016). https://doi.org/10.1007/978-3-319-46475-6_43
9. Magon, S., et al.: White matter lesion filling improves the accuracy of cortical thickness measurements in multiple sclerosis patients: a longitudinal study. BMC Neurosci. **15**, 106 (2014). https://doi.org/10.1186/1471-2202-15-106

10. Nazeri, K., Ng, E., Joseph, T., Qureshi, F.Z., Ebrahimi, M.: Edgeconnect: Generative image inpainting with adversarial edge learning (2019)
11. Pellicano, C., et al.: Relationship of cortical atrophy to fatigue in patients with multiple sclerosis. Arch. Neurol. **67**(4), 447–453 (2010)
12. Prados, F., Cardoso, M.J., MacManus, D., Wheeler-Kingshott, C.A.M., Ourselin, S.: A modality-agnostic patch-based technique for lesion filling in multiple sclerosis. In: Golland, P., Hata, N., Barillot, C., Hornegger, J., Howe, R. (eds.) MICCAI 2014. LNCS, vol. 8674, pp. 781–788. Springer, Cham (2014). https://doi.org/10.1007/978-3-319-10470-6_97
13. Prados, F., et al.: A multi-time-point modality-agnostic patch-based method for lesion filling in multiple sclerosis. NeuroImage. **139**, 376–384 (2016)
14. Sdika, M., Pelletier, D.: Nonrigid registration of multiple sclerosis brain images using lesion inpainting for morphometry or lesion mapping. Human Brain Mapping **30**(4), 1060–1067 (2009)
15. Smith, S.M.: Fast robust automated brain extraction. Hum. Brain Mapp. **17**(3), 143–155 (2002)
16. Tustison, N.J., et al.: N4ITK: improved N3 bias correction. IEEE Trans. Med. Imaging **29**(6), 1310–1320 (2010)
17. Valverde, S., Oliver, A., Lladó, X.: A white matter lesion-filling approach to improve brain tissue volume measurements. NeuroImage Clin. **6**, 86–92 (2014)
18. Xiong, H., Tao, D.: Multiple Sclerosis Lesion Inpainting Using Non-Local Partial Convolutions.(2018), arXiv: 1901.00055
19. Zhang, H., et al.: Multiple sclerosis lesion segmentation with tiramisu and 2.5D stacked slices. In: Shen, D., et al. (eds.) MICCAI 2019. LNCS, vol. 11766, pp. 338–346. Springer, Cham (2019). https://doi.org/10.1007/978-3-030-32248-9_38

Segmentation to Label: Automatic Coronary Artery Labeling from Mask Parcellation

Zhuowei Li[1], Qing Xia[1(✉)], Wenji Wang[1], Zhennan Yan[2], Ruohan Yin[3], Changjie Pan[3], and Dimitris Metaxas[4]

[1] SenseTime Research, Beijing, China
xiaqing@sensetime.com
[2] SenseBrain Technology Limited LLC, San Jose, USA
[3] Changzhou No.2 People's Hospital, Changzhou, China
[4] Rutgers University, New Jersey, USA

Abstract. Automatic and accurate coronary artery labeling technique from CCTA can greatly reduce clinician's manual efforts and benefit large-scale data analysis. Current line of research falls into two general categories: knowledge-based methods and learning-based techniques. However, no matter in which fashion it is developed, the formation of problem finally attributes to tree-structured centerline classification and requires hand-crafted features. Here, instead we present a new concise, effective and flexible framework for automatic coronary artery labeling by modeling the task as coronary artery parsing task. An intact pipeline is proposed and two paralleled sub-modules are further designed to consume volumetric image and unordered point cloud correspondingly. Finally, a self-contained loss is proposed to supervise labeling process. At experiment section, we conduct comprehensive experiments on collected 526 CCTA scans and exhibit stable and promising results.

Keywords: Coronary artery labeling · Parsing · Point cloud · Deep learning.

1 Introduction

Cardiovascular disease has long been a leading death reason worldwide. Coronary computed tomography angiography (CCTA) as a non-invasive imaging technique for diagnosis of coronary artery diseases has been widely used by physicians and radiologists. In a standard workflow, one of the most crucial and fundamental step is to correctly label branches by their anatomical names. Automatic and accurate coronary artery labeling technique can greatly reduce clinician's manual efforts and benefit large-scale data analysis.

Electronic supplementary material The online version of this chapter (https://doi.org/10.1007/978-3-030-59861-7_14) contains supplementary material, which is available to authorized users.

© Springer Nature Switzerland AG 2020
M. Liu et al. (Eds.): MLMI 2020, LNCS 12436, pp. 130–138, 2020.
https://doi.org/10.1007/978-3-030-59861-7_14

Among multiple concerns in automatic coronary artery labeling, the main challenge related is large individual variances among subjects. Current line of research falls into two general categories: knowledge-based methods and learning-based techniques. However, no matter in which fashion it is developed, the formation of problem finally attribute to tree-structured centerline classification. Previous methods are either matching target centerlines with pre-defined reference model [1,3,4,15] or do segment-level classification using hand-crafted features [12,13]. Most recently, Dan wu et al. [13] employed bi-directional tree-lstm to fully exploit topological information contained within the tree-structure using some hand-crafted features. Now the question we proposed here is: Does tree-structured centerline contains all useful information? Especially when the input features are manually collected. Clinically, the anatomical naming of a coronary artery relies on it's functional effect that is for which cardiac field it supplies. Therefore, we conjecture that the scope of current methods may not contain all informative information and thus may be sub-optimal. Considering the fact that centerlines are commonly extracted using minimal-path or skeletonization algorithm from pre-segmentated masks or similar pixel-level representative space [5,6,8,12,16], so instead of dealing with centerlines, we here take a step back and reverse the order. We model the task as the coronary artery parsing problem and directly operate on coronary artery masks and then map back to centerlines for subsequent utilization. By doing so, we encode not only topological informations, but also morphological information and geometrical information as a whole. And the training ROIs are extensively enlarged comparing with pure centerline points. Moreover, the new pipeline can been implemented in an end-to-end deep-learning fashion without hand-crafted engineering.

In this paper, we demonstrate a new pipeline for automatic coronary artery labeling by constructing the task as parsing issue. Specifically, two sub-frameworks are proposed to consume volumetric images and point clouds correspondingly. A universal loss and voting strategy is designed for both sub-frameworks. Finally, we evaluate our proposed ideas and frameworks on collected CCTA scans and demonstrate promising results.

2 Methods

2.1 Mask Space and Input

Under mask space, all inputs have been readily divided and regrouped, thus the complexity of the learning process is largely downgraded. Since acquisition of coronary artery mask is also a prerequisite for extracting centerlines under common circumstances, it is an straightforward and labor-saving choice to build our framework on mask space instead of original space. In order to encode functional information of coronary artery, the mask of whole cardiac has also been extracted and merged with coronary artery mask. Then an isotropic patch with fixed size is center-cropped at mass center of coronary artery mask as the final input.

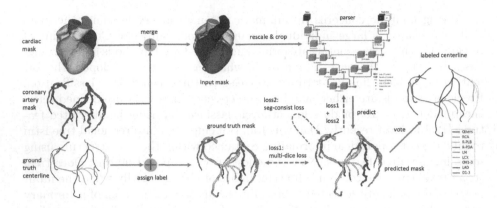

Fig. 1. General workflow for coronary artery parsing.

2.2 Volumetric Coronary Artery Parsing

Unlike objects in natural images, coronary artery branches in CTA image are revealed as tenuous and twisty tubular structure and they are all also tightly connected. This character makes anchor-based two-stage parsing techniques a failure in our case. Considering the fact that coronary arteries contain relative consistent components, here we model the task as multi-label segmentation task. In order to successfully extract structural information and stay robust against large individual variances, the most essential insight is to keep the view of the whole environment, that is the receptive field should contains whole input. So instead of cutting input volume into multiple cubes, here we down-sample the input to fit the memory. Due to the simplicity of mask space, large scale down-sampling operation is acceptable. Figure 1 elaborates the overall workflow of our proposed framework. As showed in Fig. 1, we employed a modified version of V-net [14] as our parser. Any other effective architecture can also substitute this backbone. During training, ground truth coronary artery mask is generated as follows: we first annotate tree-structured centerlines in segment-level, then each voxel in coronary artery mask is assigned with the same label as it's nearest centerline point. Since the problem formation has been set as multi-label segmentation (pixel-level classification), multi-categorical dice loss is deployed to supervise the learning process. Even though dice-loss provides a good supervision on categorical segmentation, it neglects geometrical and semantic informations. One of the most challenging issue under coronary artery mask parsing is the chaotic predictions within a branch. Especially at bifurcation area where multiple branches are bordered. In order to address this issue, a self-contained loss called seg-consist loss is proposed. The intuition behind the loss design is based on a prior cognition: *points' labels within the same coronary artery segment should be consist.* Formally, the loss is designed as:

$$Loss_{seg\_entropy} = \sum_{n=1}^{N} \lambda_n \left(\frac{\sum_{a \in A_n} -p(a|\mathbf{S_n}) \log_2 p(a|\mathbf{S_n})}{\log_2 |A_n|} \right) \qquad (1)$$

where A_n is the predicted label space for segment S_n and $p(a|S_n)$ is the probability of predicting label a within segment S_n. In general, normalized entropy of predicted labels within each segment is calculated, then entropies of all segments are weighted summed. We set $\lambda_n = \frac{1}{N}$ across our experiments to provide equal attentions for all segments regardless of their sizes. In general, our final loss function is defined as:

$$Loss = \alpha Loss_{multi\_dice} + (1 - \alpha)Loss_{seg\_entropy} \qquad (2)$$

α in Eq. (2) is experimentally set to 0.6.

2.3 Back to Centerline

Herein, a two-step voting strategy is developed naturally to map coronary artery masks back to centerlines. Specifically, the label for the target segment is defined as:

$$S_i = mode\{mode(D_{ij}), mode(D_{ij+1})...mode(D_{ij+n})\} \qquad (3)$$

Dij is the neighbor space of point j in segment i, In our framework, the neighborhood is set as a $3 \times 3 \times 3$ cube. To sum up, we perform a point-level voting following by a segment-level voting. By doing so, the final labeling result is impressively robust against noises and segmentation corruption. As long as the majority group remains correct, the final label will be sound. After assigning labels for all segments, segments with the same label will be extracted to compose final branches. In order to keep branch from breaking apart under exceptional situation, one step post-processing is performed to connect two separate segments if they have the same label and the segment between them is marked with different label.

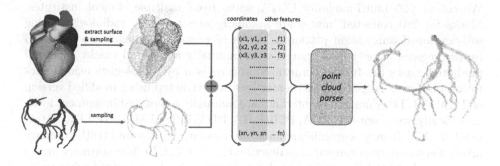

Fig. 2. Framework with point cloud input, voting step and loss calculation is omitted for the simplicity.

2.4 Point Cloud Extension

Despite the conciseness of proposed framework, it is in fact an computing and memory hungry implementation. Down-sampling and crop operations are needed to fit volumetric input into the GPU. The bottleneck causing this issue is the existence of vast less-informative background voxels. So here we also formulate parsing process from another perspective, instead of viewing input as volumetric image, we treat foreground masks as points cloud and get rid of backgrounds. Formally, we are aiming to assign k scores of k candidate categories for each point in a disordered $3D$ points set $\{P_i | i = 1, ..., n\}$. By doing so, down-sample and crop operations are no longer needed. Figure 2 displays point cloud version of our framework. Here we deploy PointNet/PointNet++ [9,10] as our point cloud parser. Since cardiac surface has already contains enough information, we keep only surface of the cardiac mask in order to save memories and speed up learning process. And above proposed seg-consist loss and two-step voting steps can be swiftly transferred to point cloud version without modification. Detailed comparisons between volumetric version and point cloud version are demonstrated in experiment section.

3 Experiments

This section will be organized in 3 subsections. We first introduce our dataset and metric used, then we present the configuration of our experiments and compare our results with other existing methods. Finally we substantiate our proposed ideas and heuristics by conducting ablation studies.

3.1 Dataset

We collect 526 multi-modality CCTA scans from multiple clinical institutes. Masks for 280 collected images are manually annotated by radiologists using self-developed annotation platform. Masks of remaining images are predicted by the segmentation model trained with manually annotated masks. Then all predicted masks are further scrutinized and revised by radiologists using annotation platform. Tree-structured centerlines are extracted using modified version of TEASAR [11]. Finally all centerlines are manually annotated in segment level. Specifically, we annotated RCA, PLB(R/L), PDA(R/L), LM, LAD, LCX, D1–2, OM1–2. All left-over segments are annotated as Others. Ground truth coronary artery masks are then generated as described in Sect. 2.2. Besides coronary artery masks, masks for whole cardiac are also collected, a model is trained using annotations from MM-WHS challenge [17]. Then masks of all 526 images are acquired increasingly using the similar strategy as mentioned above. The dataset is further split into 200 training set and 326 test set.

Our final results are evaluated in two ways, firstly a branch-level precision are judged manually by experts. Then a segment-level statistic result is evaluated using precision, recall and f1 score.

Table 1. Results of previous work comparing with ours, numbers here are the same as those collected by Wu et al [13]. P represents precision and R stands for recall. Our results reported here are in branch level, Ours-v is the volumetric version of our methods and Ours-pc is the point cloud version.

Study	Akinyemi et al. [1]	Yang et al. [15]	Gülsün et al. [4]	Cao et al. [2]	Wu et al. [13]	Ours-pc	Ours-v
Subject	52	58	37	83	44 (each fold)	326	326
Metric	R	P	P	P	P	P	P
LM	100.0	99.3	100.0	100.0	99.1	92.6	95.7
LAD(p/m/d)	97.4	93.4/86.8/93.4	99.2/97.1/100	93.6/85.8/95.4	96.9	99.7	99.1
LCX(p/m/d)	91.7	84.6/80.3	99.2/99.2/83.9	87.3/83.2	93.5	96.9	95.1
RCA(p/m/d)	98.9	97.8/94.1/92.7	100	85.1/82.3/92.5	96.0	96.9	97.6
D(1–2)	80.0	100/86.8	91.2/83.2	93.5/82.2	91.0	85.0	86.5
OM(1–2)	78.9	86.1/78.8	90.5/83.2	90.4/79.7	85.2	85.1	82.9
PLB(R/L)	86.5/ -	88.3/ -	91.2/89.7	89.8/85.7	82.7/65.9	94.0	95.5
R-PDA	65.0	94.1	94.8	96.6	79.8	87.5	89.6

3.2 Coronary Artery Mask Parsing

Volumetric input: As described in Sect. 2.1, we isotropically downsample masks to spacing 0.8 mm. Then a patch with size $144 \times 144 \times 144$ is cropped at ROI. Then extracted patches are feed into the parser. Seg-entropy loss and multi-dice loss co-supervise the training process. **Point cloud input:** Surfaces of cardiac masks are extracted using marching cubes [7]. Points in coronary artery mask are all saved. During training, 16384 points are sampled from each case, Among these points, half are randomly sampled from the coronary artery mask and others are sampled proportionally from the cardiac surfaces. All coordinates are transferred to relative coordinates according to coronary artery's mass center and input masks' labels are collected as extra features. Architectures for pointnet and pointnet++ remain the same as in original work except that seeds generated for pointnet++ are doubled due to the complexity of coronary artery mask. Then the point cloud parser is trained under joint supervision of NLL loss and seg-consist loss.

Table 1 shows results of our proposed framework comparing with other existing methods. Unlike other methods which are evaluated on relative small datasets or tested with many folds, we here train on 200 images and inference on 326 unseen data. A stable and promising result is exhibited.

3.3 Ablation Studies

At this section, we report segment-level result to eliminate compensatory effect of post-processing and potential manual deviation. Experiments are organized as follows: **(1) org-img:** We firstly parse coronary artery directly from raw image instead of mask space in order to demonstrate the complexity of the task in original space. **(2) cor:** Secondly, we input on coronary artery mask without cardiac masks to clarify the contribution of cardiac atlas information.**(3) cor+car:** Here merge two coronary artery mask and cardiac mask as final input.**(4)cc+loss:**

Table 2. Results of our ablation experiments. All metrics here are measured in segment level. P represents precision and R stands for recall.

	Metric	org-img	cor	cor+car	cc+loss	pc	pc+loss	pc!	pc!+loss
LM	P	76.4	89.8	89.9	92.8	83.1	87.9	88.4	89.6
	R	97.5	98.1	98.8	99.1	95.4	94.4	98.4	98.5
	F1	85.7	93.8	94.1	**95.8**	88.8	91.1	93.1	**93.8**
LAD	P	86.9	82.7	87.9	85.9	79.1	78.8	80.4	79.7
	R	95.3	97.5	96.8	97.1	91.6	91.2	94.8	94.2
	F1	90.9	89.5	**92.1**	91.2	84.9	84.6	**87.0**	86.3
LCX	P	86.3	83.9	84.8	89.6	88.6	87.3	90.7	91.8
	R	77.3	89.0	90.9	91.1	86.5	88.0	86.7	85.7
	F1	81.6	86.3	87.8	**90.3**	87.5	87.7	88.7	**88.7**
RCA	P	85.4	94.2	94.0	94.6	90.5	91.9	91.8	91.4
	R	94.1	95.5	95.9	95.5	89.0	92.5	92.5	92.6
	F1	89.5	94.8	95.0	**95.1**	89.8	92.2	**92.2**	92.0
D	P	88.3	84.1	88.1	87.1	81.9	88.3	88.7	87.3
	R	72.4	92.3	91.2	93.1	85.3	78.2	88.2	90.4
	F1	79.6	88.0	89.6	**90.0**	83.6	83.0	88.4	**88.8**
OM	P	78.2	82.9	84.7	87.2	88.2	86.8	84.7	85.5
	R	47.6	84.4	80.9	84.5	68.9	71.0	79.8	84.0
	F1	59.2	83.7	82.8	**85.8**	77.4	78.1	82.2	**84.7**
PLB	P	91.4	91.3	92.0	93.9	81.2	89.6	90.1	90.3
	R	90.5	93.8	92.9	92.7	92.6	88.4	88.7	91.1
	F1	91.0	92.5	92.4	**93.9**	86.5	89.0	89.4	**90.7**
PDA	P	85.3	82.9	82.2	84.4	81.2	72.8	76.9	79.9
	R	72.8	80.6	81.8	84.7	68.3	86.3	83.4	83.8
	F1	78.5	81.7	82.0	**84.7**	74.2	79.0	80.0	**81.8**
Avg.	P	84.8	86.5	88.0	89.4	84.2	85.4	86.5	86.9
	R	80.9	91.4	91.2	92.3	84.7	86.3	89.1	90.0
	F1	82.0	88.8	89.5	**90.8**	84.1	85.6	87.6	**88.4**

We finally add our proposed seg-consist loss to reach final proposed volumetric version of framework. As for point cloud extension, we transfer experiment set (3) to point cloud version using pointnet and pointnet++ noted as **(5) pc** and **(6) pc!** correspondingly. Then we integrate seg-consist to form **(5) pc+loss** and **(5) pc!+loss**.

As showed in Table 2, task is more challenging in original space than in mask space. Since gap between (2) and (3) is relative small. We conjecture that even though cardiac mask is informative, coronary artery mask itself has already contained most valuable information So even when the cardiac mask is

Table 3. Efficiency analysis between volumetric input and point cloud input. Train time calculates costs for training 1000 epochs on 200 training set

Object	GPU	Train Time (GPU hrs)	Infer Memory (MB)	Infer Time (s)
V-net	1060	197	3736	1.0 ± 0.1
PointNet	1060	8	938	0.03 ± 0.01
PointNet++	1060	42	3082	1.2 ± 0.1

not obtainable, our proposed framework will remain effective. Comparing with volumetric input, point cloud version achieves slightly inferior but compatible results. And no matter in which formation of parsing process, seg+consist loss is beneficial.

We further analyze efficiency in terms of both time and space for two formations. As listed in Table 3, point cloud version is much more space and time efficient. It serves as a good choice under limited memories or facing abundant training data.

4 Conclusion

In this paper, we present a new concise, effective and flexible framework for automatic coronary artery labeling by modeling the task as coronary artery parsing task. An intact pipeline is proposed and two paralleled sub-modules are further designed to consume volumetric image and unordered point cloud correspondingly. Finally, a self-contained loss is proposed to supervise labeling process. At experiment section, we conducted comprehensive experiments on collected 526 CCTA scans. Stable and promising results are exhibited.

References

1. Akinyemi, A., Murphy, S., Poole, I., Roberts, C.: Automatic labelling of coronary arteries. In: 2009 17th European Signal Processing Conference, pp. 1562–1566 (2009)
2. Cao, Q., et al.: Automatic identification of coronary tree anatomy in coronary computed tomography angiography. Int. J. Cardiovasc. Imaging **33**(11), 1809–1819 (2017). https://doi.org/10.1007/s10554-017-1169-0
3. Chalopin, C., Finet, G., Magnin, I.E.: Modeling the 3d coronary tree for labeling purposes. Med. Image Anal. **5**(4), 301–315 (2001). https://doi.org/10.1016/S1361-8415(01)00047-0
4. Gülsün, M.A., Funka-Lea, G., Zheng, Y., Eckert, M.: CTA coronary labeling through efficient geodesics between trees using anatomy priors. In: Golland, P., Hata, N., Barillot, C., Hornegger, J., Howe, R. (eds.) MICCAI 2014. LNCS, vol. 8674, pp. 521–528. Springer, Cham (2014). https://doi.org/10.1007/978-3-319-10470-6_65

5. Guo, Z., et al.: DeepCenterline: a multi-task fully convolutional network for centerline extraction. In: Chung, A.C.S., Gee, J.C., Yushkevich, P.A., Bao, S. (eds.) IPMI 2019. LNCS, vol. 11492, pp. 441–453. Springer, Cham (2019). https://doi.org/10.1007/978-3-030-20351-1_34
6. Jin, D., Iyer, K.S., Chen, C., Hoffman, E.A., Saha, P.K.: A robust and efficient curve skeletonization algorithm for tree-like objects using minimum cost paths. Pattern Recogn. Lett. **76**, 32–40 (2016)
7. Lorensen, W.E., Cline, H.E.: Marching cubes: a high resolution 3d surface construction algorithm. In: Proceedings of the 14th Annual Conference on Computer Graphics and Interactive Techniques. SIGGRAPH '87, Association for Computing Machinery, New York, NY, USA, pp. 163–169 (1987), https://doi.org/10.1145/37401.37422
8. Metz, C.T., Schaap, M., Weustink, A.C., Mollet, N.R., van Walsum, T., Niessen, W.J.: Coronary centerline extraction from ct coronary angiography images using a minimum cost path approach. Med. Phys. **36**(12), 5568–5579 (2009)
9. Qi, C.R., Su, H., Mo, K., Guibas, L.J.: Pointnet: deep learning on point sets for 3d classification and segmentation. In: Proceedings of the IEEE conference on computer vision and pattern recognition, pp. 652–660. IEEE (2017)
10. Qi, C.R., Yi, L., Su, H., Guibas, L.J.: Pointnet++: deep hierarchical feature learning on point sets in a metric space. arXiv preprint, (2017) arXiv:1706.02413
11. Sato, M., Bitter, I., Bender, M.A., Kaufman, A.E., Nakajima, M.: Teasar: tree-structure extraction algorithm for accurate and robust skeletons. In: Proceedings the Eighth Pacific Conference on Computer Graphics and Applications, pp. 281–449 (2000)
12. Wu, D., et al.: A learning based deformable template matching method for automatic rib centerline extraction and labeling in ct images. In 2012 IEEE Conference on Computer Vision and Pattern Recognition, pp. 980–987. IEEE (2012)
13. Wu, D., et al.: Automated anatomical labeling of coronary arteries via bidirectional tree LSTMs. Int. J. Comput. Assist. Radiol. Surg. **14**(2), 271–280 (2018). https://doi.org/10.1007/s11548-018-1884-6
14. Xia, Q., Yao, Y., Hu, Z., Hao, A.: Automatic 3D atrial segmentation from GE-MRIs using volumetric fully convolutional networks. In: Pop, M., et al. (eds.) STACOM 2018. LNCS, vol. 11395, pp. 211–220. Springer, Cham (2019). https://doi.org/10.1007/978-3-030-12029-0_23
15. Yang, G., et al.: Automatic coronary artery tree labeling in coronary computed tomographic angiography datasets. Computing in Cardiology, pp. 109–112. IEEE (2011)
16. Zheng, Y., Tek, H., Funka-Lea, G.: Robust and accurate coronary artery centerline extraction in CTA by combining model-driven and data-driven approaches. In: Mori, K., Sakuma, I., Sato, Y., Barillot, C., Navab, N. (eds.) MICCAI 2013. LNCS, vol. 8151, pp. 74–81. Springer, Heidelberg (2013). https://doi.org/10.1007/978-3-642-40760-4_10
17. Zhuang, X., Shen, J.: Multi-scale patch and multi-modality atlases for whole heart segmentation of MRI. Med. Image Anal. **31**, 77–87 (2016). https://doi.org/10.1016/j.media.2016.02.006. http://www.sciencedirect.com/science/article/pii/S1361841516000219

GSR-Net: Graph Super-Resolution Network for Predicting High-Resolution from Low-Resolution Functional Brain Connectomes

Megi Isallari and Islem Rekik[✉] (iD)

BASIRA Lab, Faculty of Computer and Informatics,
Istanbul Technical University, Istanbul, Turkey
irekik@itu.edu.tr
http://basira-lab.com

Abstract. Catchy but rigorous deep learning architectures were tailored for image super-resolution (SR), however, these fail to generalize to non-Euclidean data such as brain connectomes. Specifically, building generative models for *super-resolving a low-resolution brain connectome* at a higher resolution (i.e., adding new graph nodes/edges) remains unexplored —although this would circumvent the need for costly data collection and manual labelling of anatomical brain regions (i.e. parcellation). To fill this gap, we introduce GSR-Net (Graph Super-Resolution Network), the first super-resolution framework operating on graph-structured data that generates high-resolution brain graphs from low-resolution graphs. *First,* we adopt a U-Net like architecture based on graph convolution, pooling and unpooling operations specific to non-Euclidean data. However, unlike conventional U-Nets where graph nodes represent samples and node features are mapped to a low-dimensional space (encoding and decoding node attributes or sample features), our GSR-Net operates *directly* on a single connectome: a fully connected graph where conventionally, a node denotes a brain region, nodes have no features, and edge weights denote brain connectivity strength between two regions of interest (ROIs). In the absence of original node features, we initially assign identity feature vectors to each brain ROI (node) and then leverage the learned local receptive fields to learn node feature representations. Specifically, for each ROI, we learn a node feature embedding by locally averaging the features of its neighboring nodes based on their connectivity weights. *Second,* inspired by spectral theory, we break the symmetry of the U-Net architecture by topping it up with a graph super-resolution (GSR) layer and two graph convolutional network layers to predict a HR (high-resolution) graph while preserving the characteristics of the LR (low-resolution) input. Our proposed GSR-Net framework outperformed its variants for predicting high-resolution brain functional connectomes from low-resolution connectomes. Our Python GSR-Net code is available on BASIRA GitHub at https://github.com/basiralab/GSR-Net.

© Springer Nature Switzerland AG 2020
M. Liu et al. (Eds.): MLMI 2020, LNCS 12436, pp. 139–149, 2020.
https://doi.org/10.1007/978-3-030-59861-7_15

1   Introduction

Remarkable progress in diagnosing brain disorders and exploring brain anatomy has been made using neuroimaging modalities (such as MRI (magnetic resonance imaging) or DTI (diffusion tensor imaging)). Recent advances in ultra-high field (7 Tesla) MRI help show fine-grained variations in brain structure and function. However, MRI data at submillimeter resolutions is very scarce due to the limited number and high cost of the ultra-high field scanners. To circumvent this issue, several works explored the prospect of super-resolution to map a brain intensity image of low resolution to an image of higher resolution [1–3]. In recent years, advances in deep learning have inspired a multitude of works in image super-resolution ranging from the early approaches using Convolutional Neural Networks (CNN) (e.g. SRCNN [4]) to the state-of-the-art methods such as Generative Adversarial Nets (GAN) (e.g. SRGAN [5]). For instance, [6] used Convolutional Neural Networks to generate 7T-like MRI images from 3T MRI and more recently, [7] used ensemble learning to synergize high-resolution GANs of MRI differentially enlarged with complementary priors. While a significant number of image super-resolution methods have been proposed for MRI super-resolution, super-resolving brain connectomes (i.e., brain graphs) remains largely unexplored. Typically, a brain connectome is the product of a very complex neuroimage processing pipeline that integrates MRI images into pre-processing and analysis steps from skull stripping to cortical thickness, tissue segmentation and registration to a brain atlas [8]. To generate brain connectomes at different resolutions, one conventionally uses image brain atlas (template) to define the parcellation of the brain into N (depending on the resolution) anatomical regions of interest (ROIs). A typical brain connectome is comprised of N nodes where a node denotes a brain ROI and edge weights denote brain connectivity strength between two ROIs (e.g., correlation between neural activity or similarity in brain morphology) [9,10]. However, this process has two main drawbacks: (1) the computational time per subject is very high and (2) pre-processing steps such as registration and label propagation are highly prone to variability and bias [11,12].

Alternatively, given a low-resolution (LR) connectome, one can devise a systematic method to automatically generate a high-resolution (HR) connectome and thus circumvent the need for costly neuroimage processing pipelines. However, such a method would have to address two major challenges. *First*, standard downsampling/upsampling techniques are not easily generalizable to non-Euclidean data due to the complexity of network data. The high computational complexity, low parallelizability, and inapplicability of machine learning methods to geometric data render image super-resolution algorithms ineffective [13]. *Second*, upsampling (super-resolution) in particular is a notoriously ill-posed problem since the LR connectome can be mapped to a variety of possible solutions in HR space. Furthermore, while unpooling (deconvolution) is a recurring concept in graph embedding approaches, it typically focuses on graph embedding reconstruction rather than in the expansion of the topology of the graph [14]. Two recent pioneering works have tackled the problem of graph super-resolution

[15,16], however both share the dichotomized aspect of the engineered learning-based GSR framework, which is composed of independent blocks that cannot co-learn together to better solve the target super-resolution problem. Besides, both resort to first vectorizing LR brain graphs in the beginning of the learning process, thereby spoiling the rich topology of the brain as a connectome.

To address these limitations, we propose GSR-Net: the first geometric deep learning framework that attempts to solve the problem of predicting a high-resolution connectome from a low-resolution connectome. The key idea of GSR-Net can be summarized in three fundamental steps: (i) learning feature embeddings for each brain ROI (node) in the LR connectome, (ii) the design of a graph super-resolution operation that predicts an HR connectome from the LR connectivity matrix and feature embeddings of the LR connectome computed in (i), (iii) learning node feature embeddings for each node in the super-resolved (HR) graph obtained in (ii). First, we adopt a U-Net like architecture and introduce the Graph U-Autoencoder. Specifically, we leverage the Graph U-Net proposed in [14]: an encoder-decoder architecture based on graph convolution, pooling and unpooling operations that specifically work on non-Euclidean data. However, as most graph embedding methods, the Graph U-Net focuses on typical graph analytic tasks such as link prediction or node classification rather than super-resolution. Particularly, the conventional Graph U-Net is a *node-focused* architecture where a node n represents a sample and mapping the node n to an m-dimensional space (i.e., simpler representation) depends on the node and its attributes [17].

Our Graph U-Autoencoder on the other hand, is a *graph-focused* architecture where a sample is represented by a *connectome*: a fully connected graph where conventionally, nodes have no features and edge weights denote brain connectivity strength between two nodes. We unify both these concepts by learning a mapping of the node n to an m-dimensional space that translates the topological relationships between the nodes in the connectome as node features. Namely, we initially assign identity feature vectors to each brain ROI and we learn node feature embeddings by locally averaging the features of its neighboring nodes based on their connectivity weights. Second, we break the symmetry of the U-Net architecture by adding a GSR layer to generate an HR connectome from the node feature embeddings of the LR connectome learned in the Graph U-Autoencoder block. Specifically, in our GSR block, we propose a layer-wise propagation rule for super-resolving low-resolution brain graphs, rooted in spectral graph theory. Third, we stack two additional graph convolutional network layers to learn node feature embeddings for each brain ROI in the super-resolved graph.

2 Proposed GSR-Net for Brain Connectome Super-Resolution

Problem Definition. A connectome can be represented as $C = \{V, E, X\}$ where V is a set of nodes and E is a set of edges connecting pairs of nodes. The network nodes are defined as brain ROIs. The connectivity (adjacency)

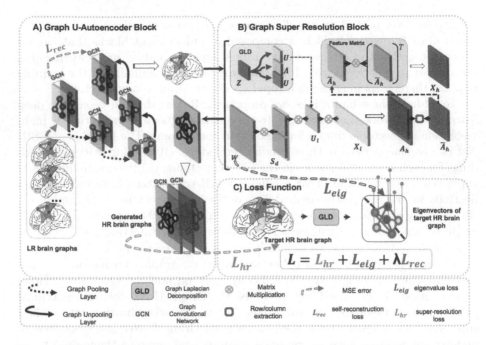

Fig. 1. *Proposed framework of Graph Super-Resolution Network (GSR-Net) for super-resolving low-resolution brain connectomes.* **(A) Graph U-Autoencoder Block.** Our Graph U-Autoencoder is built by stacking two encoding modules and two decoding modules. An encoding module contains a graph pooling layer and a graph convolutional network (GCN) and its inverse operation is a decoding module comprised of a graph unpooling layer and a GCN. Here, we integrate a *self-reconstruction loss* $\mathcal{L}_{rec}$ that guides the learning of node feature embeddings for each brain ROI in the LR connectome. **(B) Super Resolution Block.** The GSR Layer super-resolves both the topological structure of the LR connectome (connectivity matrix $\mathbf{A}_l$) and the feature matrix of the LR connectome ($\mathbf{X}_l$). To super-resolve $\mathbf{A}_l$, we propose the layer-wise propagation rule $\tilde{\mathbf{A}}_h = \mathbf{WS}_d\mathbf{U}_0^*\mathbf{Z}_l$, where $\mathbf{W}$ is a matrix of trainable filters that we enforce to match the eigenvector matrix of the HR graph via an *eigen-decomposition loss* $\mathcal{L}_{eig}$, $\mathbf{S}_d$ is the concatenation of two identity matrices, $\mathbf{U}_0$ is the eigenvector matrix of $\mathbf{A}_l$ and $\mathbf{Z}_l$ is the matrix of node feature embeddings of the LR brain graph generated in **(A)**. The propagation rule for the feature matrix super-resolution is: $\tilde{\mathbf{X}}_h = \tilde{\mathbf{A}}_h\tilde{\mathbf{A}}_h^T$. **(C) Loss function.** Our GSR-Net loss comprises a self-reconstruction loss $\mathcal{L}_{rec}$, super-resolution loss $\mathcal{L}_{hr}$ and eigen-decomposition loss $\mathcal{L}_{eig}$ to optimize learning the predicted HR connectome from a LR connectome.

matrix $\mathbf{A}$ is an $N \times N$ matrix (N is the number of nodes), where $\mathbf{A}_{ij}$ denotes the connectivity weight between two ROIs i and j using a specific metric (e.g., correlation between neural activity or similarity in brain morphology). Let $\mathbf{X} \in \mathbb{R}^{N \times F}$ denote the feature matrix where N is the number of nodes and F is the number of features (i.e., connectivity weights) per node. Each training subject s in our dataset is represented by two connectivity matrices in LR and HR domains denoted as $\mathbf{C}_l = \{\mathbf{V}_l, \mathbf{E}_l, \mathbf{X}_l\}$ and $\mathbf{C}_h = \{\mathbf{V}_h, \mathbf{E}_h, \mathbf{X}_h\}$, respectively. Given a brain graph C_l, our objective is to learn a mapping $f : (A_l, X_l) \mapsto (A_h, X_h)$, which maps C_l onto C_h.

Overall Framework. In **Fig** 1, we illustrate the proposed GSR-Net architecture including: **(i)** an asymmetric graph U-Autoencoder to learn the feature embeddings matrix Z_l for a LR brain graph by $f_l : (A_l, X_l) \mapsto Z_l$, **(ii)** a graph super-resolution (GSR) layer mapping LR graph embeddings Z_l and the LR connectivity matrix to a HR feature matrix and connectivity matrix by $f_h : (A_l, Z_l) \mapsto (\tilde{A}_h, \tilde{X}_h)$, **(iii)** learning the HR feature embeddings Z_h by stacking two graph convolutional layers as $f_z : (\tilde{A}_h, \tilde{X}_h) \mapsto Z_h$, and **(iv)** computing the loss function $\mathcal{L}$.

1. Graph U-Autoencoder. U-Net architectures have long achieved state-of-the-art performance in various tasks thanks to their encoding-decoding nature for high-level feature extraction and embedding. In the first step of our GSR-Net, we adopt the concept of Graph U-Nets [14] based on learning node representations from node attributes and we extend this idea to learning node representations from topological relationships between nodes. To learn node feature embeddings of a given LR connectome $C_l = \{V_l, E_l, X_l\}$, we propose a Graph U-Autoencoder comprising of a Graph U-Encoder and a Graph U-Decoder.

Graph U-Encoder. The Graph U-Encoder inputs the adjacency matrix $A_l \in \mathbb{R}^{N \times N}$ of $C_l = \{V_l, E_l, X_l\}$ (N is the number of nodes of C_l) as well as the feature matrix capturing the node content of the graph $X_l \in \mathbb{R}^{N \times F}$. In the absence of original node features, we assign an identity matrix $I_N \in \mathbb{R}^{N \times N}$ to the feature matrix X_l , where the encoder is only informed of the identity of each node. We build the Graph U-Encoder by stacking multiple encoding modules, each containing a graph pooling layer followed by a graph convolutional layer. Each encoding block is intuitively expected to encode high-level features by downsampling the connectome and aggregating content from each node's local topological neighborhood. However, as a *graph-focused* approach where the sample is represented by a connectome and the connectome's nodes are featureless, our Graph U-Encoder defines the notion of locality by edge weights rather than node features. Specifically, the pooling layer adaptively selects a few nodes to form a smaller brain graph in order to increase the local receptive field and for each node, the GCN layer aggregates (locally averages) the features of its neighboring nodes based on their connectivity weights.

Graph Pooling Layer. The layer's propagation rule can be defined as follows:

$$v = X_l^{(l)} u^{(l)} / \parallel u^{(l)} \parallel; indices = rank(v, k); \tilde{v} = sigmoid(v(indices));$$

$$\tilde{X}_l^{(l)} = X_l^{(l)}(indices, :); A_l^{(l+1)} = A_l^{(l)}(indices, indices); X_l^{(l+1)} = \tilde{X}_l^{(l)} \odot (\tilde{v}1_F^T)$$

The graph pooling layer adaptively selects a subset of nodes to form a new smaller graph based on their scalar projection values on a trainable projection vector u. First, we find the scalar projection of X_l on u which computes a one-dimensional v vector, where v_i is the scalar projection of each node on vector u. We find the k-largest values in v which are then saved as the indices of the nodes selected for the new downsampled graph. According to the indices found, we extract the feature matrix rows for each node selected $(\mathbf{X}_l^{(l)}(indices, :))$ as well as the respective adjacency matrix rows and columns to obtain the adjacency matrix of the downsampled graph: $\mathbf{A}_l^{(l+1)} = \mathbf{A}_l^{(l)}(indices, indices)$. Hence, this reduces the graph size from N to k : $\mathbf{A}_l^{(l+1)} \in \mathbb{R}^{k \times k}$. In the end, by applying a sigmoid mapping to the projection vector v, we obtain the gate vector $\tilde{v} \in \mathbb{R}^k$ which we multiply with $\mathbf{1}_F^T$ (one-dimensional vector with all F elements equal to 1). The product $\tilde{v}\mathbf{1}_F^T$ is then multiplied element-wise with $\tilde{\mathbf{X}}_l^{(l)}$ to control information of the selected nodes and obtain the new feature matrix of the downsampled graph $\mathbf{X}_l^{(l+1)} \in \mathbb{R}^{k \times F}$.

Graph U-Decoder. Similarly to Graph U-Encoder, Graph U-Decoder is built by stacking multiple decoding modules, each comprising a graph unpooling layer followed by a graph convolutional layer. Each decoding module acts as the inverse operation of its encoding counterpart by gradually upsampling and aggregating neighborhood information for each node.

Graph Unpooling Layer. The graph unpooling layer retracts the graph pooling operation by relocating the nodes in their original positions according to the saved indices of the selected nodes in the pooled graph. Formally, we write $\mathbf{X}^{(l+1)} = relocate(\mathbf{0}_{N \times F}, \mathbf{X}_l^{(l)}, indices)$, where $\mathbf{0}_{N \times F}$ is the reconstructed feature matrix of the new graph (initially the feature matrix is empty) . $\mathbf{X}_l^{(l)} \in \mathbb{R}^{k \times F}$ is the feature matrix of the current downsampled graph and the *relocate* operation assigns row vectors in $\mathbf{X}_l^{(l)}$ into $\mathbf{0}_{N \times F}$ feature matrix according to their corresponding indices stored in *indices*.

Graph U-Autoencoder for super-resolution. Next, we introduce our Graph U-Autoencoder which first includes a GCN to learn an initial node representation of the LR connectome. This first GCN layer takes as input $(\mathbf{A}_l, \mathbf{X}_l)$ and outputs $\mathbf{Z}_0 \in \mathbb{R}^{N \times NK}$: a node feature embedding matrix with NK number of features per node where K is the factor by which the resolution increases when we predict the HR graph from a LR graph (F is specifically chosen to be NK for reasons we explore in greater detail in the next section). The transformation can be defined as follows: $\mathbf{Z}_0 = \sigma(\hat{\mathbf{D}}^{-\frac{1}{2}}\hat{\mathbf{A}}\hat{\mathbf{D}}^{-\frac{1}{2}}\mathbf{X}_l\mathbf{W}_l)$, where $\hat{\mathbf{D}}$ is the diagonal node degree matrix, $\hat{\mathbf{A}} = \mathbf{A} + \mathbf{I}$ is the adjacency matrix with added self-loops and σ is the activation function. $\mathbf{W}_l$ is a matrix of trainable filter parameters to learn. Next, we apply two encoding blocks followed by two decoding blocks outputting $\mathbf{Z}_l \in \mathbb{R}^{N \times NK}$: $\mathbf{Z}_l = GraphUAutoencoder(\hat{\mathbf{A}}_l, \mathbf{Z}_0)$.

Optimization. To improve and regularize the training of our graph autoencoder model such that the LR connectome embeddings preserve the topological structure $\mathbf{A}_l$ and node content information $\mathbf{X}_l$ of the original LR connectome, we enforce the learned LR node feature embedding $\mathbf{Z}_l$ to match the initial node feature embedding of the LR connectome $\mathbf{Z}_0$. In our loss function we integrate a *self-reconstruction regularization term* which minimizes the mean squared error (MSE) between the node representation $\mathbf{Z}_0$ and the output of the Graph U-Autoencoder $\mathbf{Z}_l$: $\mathcal{L}_{rec} = \lambda\frac{1}{N}\sum_{i=1}^{N}||\mathbf{Z}_{0i} - \mathbf{Z}_{li}||_2^2$.

2. Proposed GSR layer. Super-resolution plays an important role in grid-like data but standard image operations are not directly applicable to graph data. In particular, there is no spatial locality information among nodes in graphs. In this section, we present a mathematical formalization of the GSR Layer, which is the key operation for predicting a high-resolution graph $\mathbf{C}_h$ from the low-resolution brain graph $\mathbf{C}_l$. Recently, [18] proposed a novel upsampling method rooted in graph Laplacian decomposition that aims to upsample a graph signal while retaining the frequency domain characteristics of the original signal defined in the time/spatial domain. To define our GSR layer, we leverage the spectral upsampling concept to expand the size of graph while perserving the local information of the node *and* the global structure of the graph using the spectrum of its graph Laplacian.

Suppose $\mathbf{L}_0 \in \mathbb{R}^{N \times N}$ and $\mathbf{L}_1 \in \mathbb{R}^{NK \times NK}$ are the graph Laplacians of the original low-resolution graph and high-resolution (upsampled) graph respectively (K is the factor by which the resolution of the graph increases). Given $\mathbf{L}_0$ and $\mathbf{L}_1$, their respective eigendecompositions are: $\mathbf{L}_0 = \mathbf{U}_0 \Lambda \mathbf{U}_0^*, \mathbf{L}_1 = \mathbf{U}_1 \Lambda \mathbf{U}_1^*$, where $\mathbf{U}_0 \in \mathbb{R}^{N \times N}$ and $\mathbf{U}_1 \in \mathbb{R}^{NK \times NK}$. In matrix form, our graph upsampling definition can be easily defined as: $x_u = \mathbf{U}_1 \mathbf{S}_d \mathbf{U}_0^* x$, where $\mathbf{S}_d = [\mathbf{I}_{N \times N} \mathbf{I}_{N \times N}]^T$, x is a signal on the input graph and x_u denotes the upsampled signal. We can generalize the matrix form to a signal $\mathbf{X}_l \in \mathbb{R}^{N \times F}$ with F input channels (i.e., a F-dimensional vector for every node) as follows: $\tilde{\mathbf{A}}_h = \mathbf{U}_1 \mathbf{S}_d \mathbf{U}_0^* \mathbf{X}_l$. To generate an $NK \times NK$ resolution graph, the number of input channels F of $\mathbf{X}_l$ should be set to NK. This is why the output of the Graph U-AutoEncoder $\mathbf{Z}_l$ (which is going to be the input $\mathbf{X}_l$ of the GSR Layer) is specified to be of the dimensions: $N \times NK$.

Super-Resolving the Graph Structure. To predict $\tilde{\mathbf{A}}_h$, we first predict the eigenvectors $\mathbf{U}_1$ of the ground truth high-dimensional $\mathbf{A}_h$. We formalize the learnable parameters in this GSR layer as a matrix $\mathbf{W} \in \mathbb{R}^{NK \times NK}$ to learn such that the distance error between the weights and the eigenvectors $\mathbf{U}_1$ of the ground truth high-resolution $\mathbf{A}_h$ is minimized. Hence, the propagation rule for our layer is: $\tilde{\mathbf{A}}_h = \mathbf{W} \mathbf{S}_d \mathbf{U}_0^* \mathbf{Z}_l$.

Super-Resolving the Graph node Features. To super-resolve the feature matrix or assign feature vectors to the new nodes (at this point, the new nodes do not have meaningful representations), we again leverage the concept of translating topological relationships between nodes to node features. By adding new nodes and edges while attempting to retain the characteristics of the original low-resolution brain graph, it is highly probable that some new nodes and edges will remain isolated, which might cause loss of information in the subsequent layers. To avoid this, we initialize the target feature matrix $\tilde{\mathbf{C}}_h$ as follows: $\tilde{\mathbf{X}}_h^{(l)} = \tilde{\mathbf{A}}_h^{(l)} (\tilde{\mathbf{A}}_h^{(l)})^T$. This operation links nodes at a maximum two-hop distance and increases connectivity between nodes [19]. Each node is then assigned a feature vector that satisfies this property. Notably, both the adjacency and feature matrix are converted to symmetric matrices mimicking realistic predictions: $\tilde{\mathbf{A}}_h = (\tilde{\mathbf{A}}_h + \tilde{\mathbf{A}}_h^T)/2$ and $\tilde{\mathbf{X}}_h = (\tilde{\mathbf{X}}_h + \tilde{\mathbf{X}}_h^T)/2$.

Optimization. To learn trainable filters which enforce the super-resolved connectome's eigen-decomposition to match that of the ground truth HR connectome (i.e., preserving both local and global topologies), we further add the *eigen-decomposition loss*: the MSE between the weights and the eigenvectors $\mathbf{U}_1$ of the ground truth high-resolution $\mathbf{A}_h$: $\mathcal{L}_{eig} = \frac{1}{N} \sum_{i=1}^{N} ||\mathbf{W}_i - \mathbf{U}_{1i}||_2^2$.

3. Additional graph embedding layers. Following the GSR layer, we learn more representative ROI-specific feature embeddings of the super-resolved graph by stacking two additional GCNs: $\mathbf{Z}_h^0 = GCN(\tilde{\mathbf{A}}_h, \tilde{\mathbf{X}}_h)$ and $\mathbf{Z}_h = GCN(\tilde{\mathbf{A}}_h, \tilde{\mathbf{Z}}_h^0)$. For each node, these embedding layers aggregate the feature vectors of its neighboring nodes, thus fully translating the connectivity weights to node features of the new super-resolved graph. The output of this third step constitutes the final prediction of the GSR-Net of the HR connectome from the input LR connectome. However, our predictions of the HR graph $\mathbf{Z}_h$ are of size $NK \times NK$ and our target HR graph size might not satisfy such multiplicity rule. In such case, we can add isotropic padding of HR adjacency matrix during the training stage and remove the extra-padding in the loss evaluation step and in the final prediction.

Optimization. Our training process is primarily guided by the *super-resolution loss* which minimizes the MSE between our super-resolved brain connectomes and the ground truth HR ones. The total GSR-Net loss function comprises the *self-reconstruction loss*, the *eigen-decomposition loss*, and the *super-resolution loss* and it is computed as follows:

$$\mathcal{L} = \mathcal{L}_{hr} + \mathcal{L}_{eig} + \lambda \mathcal{L}_{rec}$$
$$= \frac{1}{N} \sum_{i=1}^{N} ||\mathbf{Z}_{hi} - \mathbf{A}_{hi}||_2^2 + \frac{1}{N} \sum_{i=1}^{N} ||\mathbf{W}_i - \mathbf{U}_{1i}||_2^2 + \lambda \frac{1}{N} \sum_{i=1}^{N} ||\mathbf{Z}_{0i} - \mathbf{Z}_{li}||_2^2$$

3   Results and Discussion

Connectomic Dataset and Parameter Setting. We used 5-fold cross-validation to evaluate our framework on 277 subjects from the Southwest University Longitudinal Imaging Multimodal (SLIM) study [20]. For each subject, two separate functional brain networks with 160×160 (LR) and 268×268 (HR) resolutions were produced using two groupwise whole-brain parcellation approaches proposed in [21] and [22], respectively. Our GSR-Net uses Adam Optimizer with a learning rate of 0.0001 and the number of neurons in both Graph U-Autoencoder and GCN layers is set to NK. We empirically set the parameter λ of the self-reconstruction regularization loss to 16.

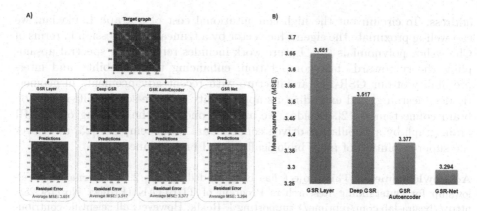

Fig. 2. *Comparison between the ground truth HR graph and the predicted HR graph of a representative subject.* We display in **(A)** the residual error matrix computed using mean squared error (MSE) between the ground truth and predicted super-resolved brain graph. We plot in **(B)** MSE results for each of the three baseline methods and our proposed GSR-Net.

Evaluation and Comparison Methods. We benchmark the performance of our GSR-Net against different baseline methods: **(1) GSR Layer:** a variant of GSR-Net where we remove both the graph Autoencoder (**Fig** 1–A) and the additional graph embedding layers. **(2) Deep GSR:** In this variant, first, the node feature embeddings matrix Z_l of the LR connectome is learned through two GCN layers. Second, this Z_l is inputted to the GSR Layer, and third we learn the node feature embeddings of the output of the GSR Layer (i.e., the super-resolved graph) leveraging two more GCN layers and a final inner product decoder layer. **(3) GSR-Autoencoder:** a variant of GSR-Net where we remove only the additional GCN layers. **Fig** 2–B displays the average MSE between the ground truth and predicted HR brain graphs by all methods. Our GSR-Net achieved the best super-resolution performance. For a representative subject, we also display the ground truth and predicted HR graphs by all methods along with their residual error. GSR-Net clearly achieves the lowest residual error. Building on this first work, we will further extend our GSR-Net architecture to predict brain connectomes at different resolutions from a low-resolution brain connectome, which can be leveraged in comparative connectomics [23] as well as charting the *multi-scale* landscape of brain dysconnectivity in a wide spectrum of disorders [10].

4 Conclusion

In this paper, we proposed GSR-Net, the first geometric deep learning framework for super-resolving low-resolution functional brain connectomes. Our method achieved the best graph super-resolution results in comparison with its ablated version and other variants. However, there are a few limitations we need to address. To circumvent the high computational cost of a graph Laplacian, we can well-approximate the eigenvalue vector by a truncated expression in terms of Chebyshev polynomials [24]. Future work includes refining our spectral upsampling theory towards fast computation, enhancing the scalability and interpretability of our GSR-Net architecture with recent advancements in geometric deep learning, and extending its applicability to large-scale multi-resolution brain connectomes [12]. Besides, we aim to condition the learning of the HR brain graph by a population-driven connectional brain template [25] to enforce the super-resolution of more biologically sound brain connectomes.

Acknowledgement. This project has been funded by the 2232 International Fellowship for Outstanding Researchers Program of TUBITAK (Project No:118C288, http://basira-lab.com/reprime/) supporting I. Rekik. However, all scientific contributions made in this project are owned and approved solely by the authors.

References

1. Bahrami, K., Shi, F., Rekik, I., Gao, Y., Shen, D.: 7T-guided super-resolution of 3T mri. Med. Phys. **44**, 1661–1677 (2017)
2. Chen, Y., Xie, Y., Zhou, Z., Shi, F., Christodoulou, A.G., Li, D.: Brain mri super resolution using 3d deep densely connected neural networks. In: 2018 IEEE 15th International Symposium on Biomedical Imaging (ISBI 2018), pp. 739–742. IEEE (2018)
3. Ebner, M., et al.: An automated framework for localization, segmentation and super-resolution reconstruction of fetal brain mri. NeuroImage **206**, 116324 (2020)
4. Dong, C., Loy, C.C., He, K., Tang, X.: Image super-resolution using deep convolutional networks (2014)
5. Ledig, C., et al.: Photo-realistic single image super-resolution using a generative adversarial network. In: Proceedings of the IEEE conference on computer vision and pattern recognition, pp. 4681–4690 (2016)
6. Bahrami, K., Shi, F., Rekik, I.: Convolutional neural network for reconstruction of 7T-like images from 3T MRI using appearance and anatomical features. In: International Conference on Medical Image Computing and Computer-Assisted Intervention, (2016)
7. Lyu, Q., Shan, H., Wang, G.: Mri super-resolution with ensemble learning and complementary priors. IEEE Trans. Comput. Imaging **6**, 615–624 (2020)
8. Bassett, D.S., Sporns, O.: Network neuroscience. Nat. Neurosci. **20**, 353 (2017)
9. Fornito, A., Zalesky, A., Breakspear, M.: The connectomics of brain disorders. Nat. Rev. Neurosci. **16**, 159–172 (2015)
10. Van den Heuvel, M.P., Sporns, O.: A cross-disorder connectome landscape of brain dysconnectivity. Nat. Rev. Neurosci. **20**, 435–446 (2019)
11. Qi, S., Meesters, S., Nicolay, K., ter Haar Romeny, B.M., Ossenblok, P.: The influence of construction methodology on structural brain network measures: a review. J. Neurosci. Methods **253**, 170–182 (2015)
12. Bressler, S.L., Menon, V.: Large-scale brain networks in cognition: emerging methods and principles. Trends Cognitive Sci. **14**, 277–290 (2010)
13. Cui, P., Wang, X., Pei, J., Zhu, W.: A survey on network embedding. IEEE Trans. Knowl. Data Eng. **31**(5), 833–852 (2017)

14. Gao, H., Ji, S.: Graph u-nets. In: Chaudhuri, K., Salakhutdinov, R., (eds.) Proceedings of the 36th International Conference on Machine Learning. Volume 97 of Proceedings of Machine Learning Research., Long Beach, CA, USA, PMLR, pp. 2083–2092 (2019)
15. Cengiz, K., Rekik, I.: Predicting high-resolution brain networks using hierarchically embedded and aligned multi-resolution neighborhoods. In: Rekik, I., Adeli, E., Park, S.H. (eds.) PRIME 2019. LNCS, vol. 11843, pp. 115–124. Springer, Cham (2019). https://doi.org/10.1007/978-3-030-32281-6_12
16. Mhiri, I., Khalifa, A.B., Mahjoub, M.A., Rekik, I.: Brain graph super-resolution for boosting neurological disorder diagnosis using unsupervised multi-topology connectional brain template learning. Med. Image Anal. **65**, 101768 (2020)
17. Scarselli, F., Gori, M., Tsoi, A.C., Hagenbuchner, M., Monfardini, G.: The graph neural network model. IEEE Trans. Neural Netw. **20**, 61–80 (2009)
18. Tanaka, Y.: Spectral domain sampling of graph signals. IEEE Trans. Signal Process. **66**, 3752–3767 (2018)
19. Chepuri, S.P., Leus, G.: Subsampling for graph power spectrum estimation. In: 2016 IEEE Sensor Array and Multichannel Signal Processing Workshop (SAM), pp. 1–5. IEEE (2016)
20. Liu, W., et al.: Longitudinal test-retest neuroimaging data from healthy young adults in southwest china. Scientific Data. **4**(1), 1–9 (2017)
21. Dosenbach, N.U., et al.: Prediction of individual brain maturity using fMRI. Sci. **329**, 1358–1361 (2010)
22. Shen, X., Tokoglu, F., Papademetris, X., Constable, R.: Groupwise whole-brain parcellation from resting-state fMRI data for network node identification. NeuroImage **82**, 403–415 (2013)
23. Van den Heuvel, M.P., Bullmore, E.T., Sporns, O.: Comparative connectomics. Trends Cognitive Sci. **20**, 345–361 (2016)
24. Hammond, D.K., Vandergheynst, P., Gribonval, R.: Wavelets on graphs via spectral graph theory. Appl. Comput. Harmonic Anal. **30**(2), 129–150 (2009)
25. Dhifallah, S., Rekik, I., Initiative, A.D.N., et al.: Estimation of connectional brain templates using selective multi-view network normalization. Med. Image Anal. **59**, 101567 (2020)

Anatomy-Aware Cardiac Motion Estimation

Pingjun Chen[1], Xiao Chen[2], Eric Z. Chen[2], Hanchao Yu[3],
Terrence Chen[2], and Shanhui Sun[2(✉)]

[1] University of Florida, Gainesville, FL 32611, USA
[2] United Imaging Intelligence, Cambridge, MA 02140, USA
shanhui.sun@united-imaging.com
[3] University of Illinois at Urbana-Champaign, Urbana, IL 61801, USA

Abstract. Cardiac motion estimation is critical to the assessment of
cardiac function. Myocardium feature tracking (FT) can directly estimate cardiac motion from cine MRI, which requires no special scanning procedure. However, current deep learning-based FT methods may
result in unrealistic myocardium shapes since the learning is solely guided
by image intensities without considering anatomy. On the other hand,
motion estimation through learning is challenging because ground-truth
motion fields are almost impossible to obtain. In this study, we propose a novel Anatomy-Aware Tracker (AATracker) for cardiac motion
estimation that preserves anatomy by weak supervision. A convolutional variational autoencoder (VAE) is trained to encapsulate realistic myocardium shapes. A baseline dense motion tracker is trained to
approximate the motion fields and then refined to estimate anatomy-
aware motion fields under the weak supervision from the VAE. We evaluate the proposed method on long-axis cardiac cine MRI, which has more
complex myocardium appearances and motions than short-axis. Compared with other methods, AATracker significantly improves the tracking
performance and provides visually more realistic tracking results, demonstrating the effectiveness of the proposed weakly-supervision scheme in
cardiac motion estimation.

Keywords: Anatomy aware · Motion estimation · Weak supervision.

1 Introduction

Accurate cardiac motion estimation plays a critical role in cardiac function
assessment, such as myocardium strain, torsion, and dyssynchrony, which have
been demonstrated as sensitive and early indicators of myocardial disorders [15].
Myocardial feature tracking (FT) can provide motion estimation from breath-
hold 2D cine MRI, which is recommended by the American Heart Association

P. Chen and H. Yu—This work was carried out during the internship of the author at
United Imaging Intelligence, Cambridge, MA 02140.

© Springer Nature Switzerland AG 2020
M. Liu et al. (Eds.): MLMI 2020, LNCS 12436, pp. 150–159, 2020.
https://doi.org/10.1007/978-3-030-59861-7_16

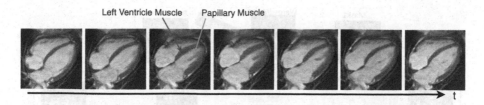

Fig. 1. Full cardiac cycle in Cine MRI. Example frames from a long-axis cine MRI show the heart motion starting from relaxation to contraction and then back to relaxation. The left ventricular (LV) muscle (V-shape dark region) undergoes large deformation during the cycle. Papillary muscle appears similar to the LV muscle.

(AHA) for clinical routine [13]. Cardiac MRI feature tracking (CMR-FT) [5,17] estimates time-varying cardiac motion from cine MRI that usually includes a complete cycle of cardiac contraction and relaxation, as shown in Fig. 1. Starting from an initial image frame (usually end-diastole ED) as a reference, the next frame in time as a source image is compared, and motion occurred in-between is estimated. Then the source image becomes a new reference frame, and the process is repeated for all the consecutive frames to obtain the motion for the full cardiac cycle.

CMR-FT is a challenging topic still under active investigation, as addressed e.g. in [11,17,18,20,22–24]. A conventional image registration based method was proposed in [17] to estimate left ventricle motion using 2D B-spline free form deformation (FFD). Vigneault *et al.* in [20] proposed to perform cardiac segmentation and then apply B-Spline registration on the boundary points to track myocardium. This approach requires additional segmentation work. Tracking only boundary points also limits the motion estimation accuracy since both image features inside and outside the myocardium are not considered. Recently, Krebs *et al.* in [11] presented a variational autoencoder based image registration algorithm for estimating motion field for two consecutive frames from cine CMR. The VAE encoder takes the two images and encode them into latent variables which generate cardiac deformations via decoder. Because myocardium has similar image appearances with neighboring tissues/organs such as the papillary muscle, mere image-based motion estimation will face severe ambiguity in these regions, which causes anatomically unrealistic tracked results. Qin *et al.* proposed to jointly learn motion estimation and segmentation using a supervised deep learning method [18]. Zheng *et al.* introduced a semi-supervised learning method for apparent flow estimation aiming for explainable cardiac pathology classification [24]. Both studies make use of raw MR images and cardiac segmentation together for accurate flow estimation.

In this study, we propose an end-to-end framework to estimate cardiac motion that is aware of the underlying anatomy through shape-constraints in a weakly supervision manner, coined as anatomy-aware tracker (AATracker). We first train an unsupervised CNN-based dense tracker as the baseline. We then train a convolutional VAE model that learns the latent space of realis-

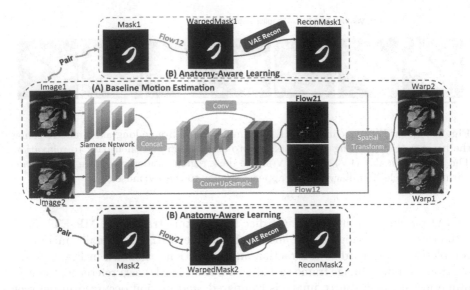

Fig. 2. The illustration of the baseline unsupervised motion estimation model and the weakly-supervised anatomy-aware model (AATracker). Module (A) presents the baseline, and Module (B) adds shape constraints to enhance the baseline motion estimation. Besides the image intensity loss and motion field regularization in the baseline model, loss between the warped mask with the VAE refined results (anatomy loss) and loss between the warped mask with its VAE reconstruction (reconstruction loss) are introduced in Module (B) to constrain the motion estimation for anatomy awareness.

tic myocardium shapes. We apply the trained VAE model to baseline-tracked myocardium and treat the anatomically reasonable myocardium masks from the VAE as self-learned shape constraints. The baseline model is further refined as AATracker using shape constraints for anatomy awareness. We evaluate the proposed method on the Kaggle Cardiovascular Disease dataset[1].

The main contributions of this work are as follows: (1) We present AATracker, an end-to-end anatomy-aware cardiac motion estimation model via weak supervision. (2) We employ VAE to constrain motion estimation for anatomy awareness. (3) AATracker significantly improves the performance of myocardium feature tracking compared to baseline and conventional methods.

2   Method

2.1   Unsupervised Motion Estimation

The network structure for baseline cardiac motion estimation is shown in the middle part of Fig. 2. Two images, source and target at different time points of cine MRI, are inputs to the network. Three main modules include a Siamese

---

[1] https://www.kaggle.com/c/second-annual-data-science-bowl/data.

network for mutual image feature extraction, a multi-scale decoder for flow field generation, and a spatial transform that warps the source image with the flow fields [3,9]. Unlike previous studies [2,12], the motion estimation framework here is symmetrical, inspired by traditional symmetric registration algorithms [1,21].

For an input image pair $(\mathcal{I}_1, \mathcal{I}_2)$, $\mathcal{F}_{12}$ is the flow field from $\mathcal{I}_1$ to $\mathcal{I}_2$, and $\mathcal{F}_{21}$ is the reverse. Using $\otimes$ as the warping operator, $\mathcal{I}_1' = \mathcal{F}_{12} \otimes \mathcal{I}_1$ and $\mathcal{I}_2' = \mathcal{F}_{21} \otimes \mathcal{I}_2$ are the warped results of $\mathcal{I}_1$ and $\mathcal{I}_2$ via the spatial transform, respectively. The loss function enforcing warping consistency is defined as $\mathcal{L}_{cons} = \|\mathcal{I}_1 - \mathcal{I}_2'\| + \|\mathcal{I}_2 - \mathcal{I}_1'\|$. We add Huber loss $\mathcal{L}_H = \mathcal{H}(\mathcal{F}_{12}) + \mathcal{H}(\mathcal{F}_{21})$ on the flow fields as the regularizer for motion smoothness [8]. The loss function for the baseline model is then formulated as:

$$\mathcal{L}_{base} = \mathcal{L}_{cons} + \lambda_H \mathcal{L}_H, \tag{1}$$

where λ_H is the Huber loss weight.

2.2 Myocardium Feature Tracking

We can now perform CMR-FT for cine MRI based on the motion estimation between consecutive frames, as shown in Fig. 3(A). We denote the flow field between the (n−1)-th and n-th frame as $\mathcal{F}_{(n-1)n}$. We compute the composite flow field $\hat{\mathcal{F}}_{1n}$ between the first and n-th frame using all intermediate motion fields:

$$\hat{\mathcal{F}}_{1n} = \begin{cases} \mathcal{F}_{12} & n = 2 \\ \hat{\mathcal{F}}_{1(n-1)} \oplus \mathcal{F}_{(n-1)n} & n > 2, \end{cases} \tag{2}$$

where $\oplus$ is a flow composite operator and $\mathcal{F}_{ik} = \mathcal{F}_{ij} \oplus \mathcal{F}_{jk} = \mathcal{F}_{ij} \otimes \mathcal{F}_{jk} + \mathcal{F}_{jk}$. Note that motion is estimated only between two neighboring frames to avert large feature changes due to image intensity drifting and severe deformation seen in cine MRI. Additionally, the calculation of composite flow always refers to the ED frame because myocardium semantic information (*i.e.*, segmentation mask) is usually given at the ED frame, either by cardiologists' annotation or computer-aided algorithms. Without the loss of generality, we assume the first frame is ED. The myocardium semantic information can thus be obtained by warping the first frame with the composite flow field $\hat{\mathcal{F}}_{1n}$.

We take a refinement step to compensate for potential accumulation error through tracking. Specifically, after the warping to the n-th frame $\mathcal{I}_n' = \hat{\mathcal{F}}_{1n} \otimes \mathcal{I}_1$, motion $\mathcal{F}_n^\delta$ is estimated between $\mathcal{I}_n'$ and $\mathcal{I}_n$. The final compensated motion between the first and the n-th frame is composed as $\hat{\mathcal{F}}_{1n}^* = \hat{\mathcal{F}}_{1n} \oplus \mathcal{F}_n^\delta$.

2.3 Anatomy-Aware Motion Estimation

Shape prior via VAE: The tracked myocardium using the above pipeline achieves fairly promising results. However, as the baseline model is mainly based on image intensity difference, the estimated motion can thus be severely affected by disturbances such as intensity-similar anatomies (*e.g.*, papillary muscle) and

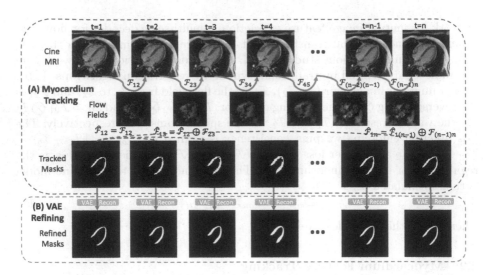

Fig. 3. Cine MRI myocardium tracking via motion estimation from consecutive frames and myocardium refining via VAE reconstruction. (A) describes the flow field composing procedure and the myocardium tracking based on the composite flow fields. (B) presents the refining of the tracked myocardium using VAE.

noises, which leads to tracked myocardium with unrealistic anatomy ("Tracked Masks" in Fig. 3(A)).

To solve this problem, we utilize convolutional VAE [6,7,16] to encode myocardium anatomy and enforce myocardium shape constraints (anatomy-awareness) in the motion estimation. Using available myocardium annotations, we train the VAE model to take the myocardium mask as input and reconstruct it. In addition to the reconstruction loss, the Kullback-Leibler Divergence (KLD) loss is used to enforce the latent space to conform to a standard normal distribution. Thus, the encoder's outputs are a mean vector and a standard deviation vector. During the training, we sample from this distribution based on the mean and the standard deviation and reconstruct myocardium shape from the sample via the decoder. We used the trained VAE model (both the encoder and the decoder) to correct unrealistic myocardium masks. Specifically, the mean latent variable representing expected myocardium manifold in the latent space given the input mask is used without sampling. The decoder can decode such a latent variable into a realistic shape. Figure 3(B) shows the reconstructed myocardium using the trained VAE model.

Weakly-Supervised Motion Estimation Using Shape Prior: For every cine MRI in the training dataset, we first use the baseline model to feature-track the myocardium to obtain coarse myocardium results for every image. The tracked myocardium through time, with possible unrealistic shapes, are then corrected by the VAE model, which are further used as anatomy constraints to improve the motion model. In this way, the motion estimation can mitigate the disturbances in images. Specifically, each input image pair $(\mathcal{I}_1, \mathcal{I}_2)$ now has its corresponding corrected myocardium $(\mathcal{M}_1, \mathcal{M}_2)$. We apply the flow fields $\mathcal{F}_{12}$ and $\mathcal{F}_{21}$ to their corresponding masks and obtain warped masks $\mathcal{M}_1' = \mathcal{F}_{12} \otimes \mathcal{M}_1$ and $\mathcal{M}_2' = \mathcal{F}_{21} \otimes \mathcal{M}_2$. We expect that a plausible flow field will preserve the anatomy after warping and therefore propose the anatomy loss function $\mathcal{L}_{anat}^M = |\mathcal{M}_1 - \mathcal{M}_2'| + |\mathcal{M}_2 - \mathcal{M}_1'|$.

Furthermore, we apply the VAE model to the warped masks $(\mathcal{M}_1', \mathcal{M}_2')$ and obtain their reconstructed masks $(\mathcal{M}_1^{recon}, \mathcal{M}_2^{recon})$. We enforce the warped masks to be close to their VAE reconstructions to constrain the motion estimation model further using the reconstruction loss $\mathcal{L}_{recon}^M = |\mathcal{M}_1' - \mathcal{M}_1^{recon}| + |\mathcal{M}_2' - \mathcal{M}_2^{recon}|$. We define the anatomy-aware motion estimation loss as:

$$\mathcal{L} = \mathcal{L}_{cons} + \lambda_H \mathcal{L}_H + \lambda_{anat} \mathcal{L}_{anat}^M + \lambda_{recon} \mathcal{L}_{recon}^M, \qquad (3)$$

where λ_H, λ_{anat}, and λ_{recon} are weights, and we denote this model as AATracker. Figure 2 presents examples for the aforementioned images, flow fields, and masks. After refining the baseline model, we then apply the AATracker to the pipeline in Fig. 3(A) to track myocardium. Since only the myocardium in the first frame needs annotation, and the rest are tracked and then corrected by VAE, the whole process is weakly-supervised. It is worth pointing out that ED frame annotation is available in clinical setup for CMR-FT application. Also note that the AATracker directly estimates cardiac motions that preserve the underlying anatomy. The anatomy-aware learning module (Fig. 2B) is only performed during the training stage to infuse the anatomical knowledge into the motion estimation network.

3   Experiments and Results

3.1   Implementation Details

We benchmark the proposed method on 1,137 2-chamber and 1,111 4-chamber cine MRI from Kaggle. Each cine is from one patient with 30 frames. Data is randomly split for training, testing and validation. The VAE model is trained on fully-annotated 100 cine (3000 frames). The motion estimation refinement is trained on another 300 cine with the first frame annotated, and is tested on another 45 fully-annotated cine (1,350 frames). The remaining data, without any annotation, are used for the unsupervised baseline model training, hyper parameters tuning and model selection. All images and annotated myocardium masks are rescaled to the same resolution and cropped into 192×192. The images are normalized into zero mean and unit standard deviation. Since no ground truth motion field is available, we evaluate the motion estimation based on the tracked myocardium with three commonly used metrics. The Dice similarity coefficient (DSC) measures the overlapping regions. The Hausdorff distance (HD) calculates the maximum distance between two boundaries, while the average symmetric surface distance (ASSD) calculates the average distance between two boundaries.

Table 1. Comparison of FFD, diffeomorphic demons, Baseline model, baseline with anatomy loss (Baseline+anat), baseline with reconstruction loss (Baseline+recon) and the AATracker. Dice Similarity Coefficient (DSC), Hausdorff Distance (HD), and Average Symmetric Surface Distance (ASSD) on 2- and 4-chamber cine MRI are shown in mean(std).

Long-Axis	Method	DSC	HD (mm)	ASSD (mm)
2-chamber	FFD	0.768 (0.054)	6.242 (1.556)	1.480 (0.310)
	Diffeomorphic Demons	0.791 (0.051)	6.265 (1.313)	1.370 (0.238)
	Baseline	0.834 (0.039)	6.389 (1.444)	1.203 (0.216)
	Baseline+anat	0.835 (0.048)	5.659 (1.285)	1.158 (0.209)
	Baseline+recon	0.835 (0.038)	6.163 (1.507)	1.190 (0.224)
	AATracker	**0.836** (0.048)	**5.604** (1.252)	**1.154** (0.206)
4-chamber	FFD	0.803 (0.039)	6.067 (1.339)	1.306 (0.238)
	Diffeomorphic Demons	0.813 (0.037)	6.936 (1.583)	1.274 (0.213)
	Baseline	0.861 (0.026)	6.228 (1.607)	1.062 (0.207)
	Baseline+anat	0.864 (0.026)	5.328 (1.185)	1.007 (0.163)
	Baseline+recon	**0.865** (0.025)	5.936 (1.615)	1.026 (0.197)
	AATracker	0.864 (0.028)	**5.303** (1.171)	**0.998** (0.160)

The implementation includes three aspects: baseline motion estimation, VAE, and AATracker. The baseline model is trained with λ_H as 0.02. We train the VAE model with extensive data augmentation, including vertical and horizontal flipping, and multi-angle rotation, and set the latent space as a 32-d representation. In the AATracker training, λ_H, λ_{anat}, and λ_{recon} are set as 0.04, 6.0, 1.2, respectively. We compare the AATracker with the baseline model and the two shape-constrained models employing either anatomy loss or reconstruction loss. We also compared to two conventional registration methods, multi-scale free form deformation (FFD) [10,14] and multi-scale diffeomorphic demons [19], that have been previously used for medical image motion estimation [4]. All models are trained and tested on a standard workstation equipped with Intel Xeon Bronze 3106 CPUs and a Nvidia Titan XP GPU.

3.2   Results and Discussions

Table 1 presents the quantitative results over compared methods. Both anatomy loss and reconstruction loss can boost the performance of the baseline, while the effect of anatomy loss is more noticeable. The anatomy-aware model AATracker with both losses attains the best performance. Compared with the baseline model, AATracker reduces HD by 12.3% and 14.9% on 2- and 4-chamber cine MRI, respectively. The accuracy improvements of utilizing deep-learning-based methods over conventional methods are consistent with existing studies [2,12]. Besides, the AATracker takes much less time (∼1.5 s) on average to estimate the

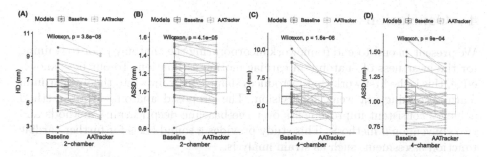

Fig. 4. Patient-wise comparison between the baseline model and AATracker on 2-chamber (A–B) and 4-chamber (C–D) cine MRI.

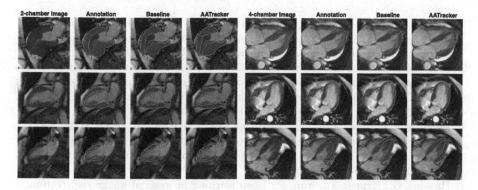

Fig. 5. Examples of myocardium annotation, baseline, and AATracker results.

motion than FFD (∼46.1 s) and diffeomorphic demons (∼25.2 s) for a cine MRI of typical size.

Figure 4 shows a patient-wise comparison between the baseline model and AATracker. On both 2- and 4-chamber evaluation, the p-values from the Wilcoxon signed-rank test are significant for the two boundary-based metrics HD and ASSD. This result demonstrates that AATracker consistently improves the myocardium tracking results. Figure 5 shows examples of tracked myocardium. The results of AATracker are visually more similar to the annotations. Most importantly, the anatomy-aware myocardium are more anatomically reasonable with smoother boundaries, demonstrating the effectiveness of the shape constraints.

Both Fig. 4 and Fig. 5 demonstrate the improved performance of the AATracker over baseline. These results indicate that AATracker preserves the anatomy structure during tracking. Arguably, DSC improvement is subtle after the motion estimation refinement. The main reason is that the myocardium boundary only accounts for a tiny part in the myocardium, and the refinement works mainly on the myocardium boundary without substantially affecting the overall myocardium shape. The reduction in ASSD is not as significant as HD, likely because ASSD is the average distance considering all boundary pixels while HD measures the worst error distance.

4   Conclusion

We present an end-to-end framework incorporating the anatomy prior to training for the awareness of anatomy in cardiac motion estimation. To our best knowledge, this is the first work that introduces shape constraints into the myocardium feature tracking via weak supervision. The proposed anatomy-aware method achieves consistent improvements over the baseline deep learning methods and two conventional methods. This study provides a sound basis for further cardiac function assessment, such as strain analysis.

References

1. Avants, B.B., Epstein, C.L., Grossman, M., Gee, J.C.: Symmetric diffeomorphic image registration with cross-correlation: evaluating automated labeling of elderly and neurodegenerative brain. Med. Image Anal. **12**(1), 26–41 (2008)
2. Balakrishnan, G., Zhao, A., Sabuncu, M.R., Guttag, J., Dalca, A.V.: An unsupervised learning model for deformable medical image registration. In: Proceedings of the IEEE conference on computer vision and pattern recognition, pp. 9252–9260. IEEE (2018)
3. Bertinetto, L., Valmadre, J., Henriques, J.F., Vedaldi, A., Torr, P.H.S.: Fully-convolutional siamese networks for object tracking. In: Hua, G., Jégou, H. (eds.) ECCV 2016. LNCS, vol. 9914, pp. 850–865. Springer, Cham (2016). https://doi.org/10.1007/978-3-319-48881-3_56
4. Haskins, G., Kruger, U., Yan, P.: Deep learning in medical image registration: a survey. Mach. Vision Appl. **31**(1), 8 (2020)
5. Heinke, R., et al.: Towards standardized postprocessing of global longitudinal strain by feature tracking-optistrain cmr-ft study. BMC Cardiovasc. Disord. **19**(1), 267 (2019)
6. Higgins, I., et al.: beta-vae: learning basic visual concepts with a constrained variational framework. Iclr **2**(5), 6 (2017)
7. Hou, X., Shen, L., Sun, K., Qiu, G.: Deep feature consistent variational autoencoder. In: 2017 IEEE Winter Conference on Applications of Computer Vision (WACV), pp. 1133–1141. IEEE (2017)
8. Huber P.J.: Robust Estimation of a Location Parameter. In: Kotz S., Johnson N.L. (eds) Breakthroughs in Statistics. Springer Series in Statistics (Perspectives in Statistics). Springer, New York, NY, (1992) https://doi.org/10.1007/978-1-4612-4380-9_35
9. Jaderberg, M., Simonyan, K., Zisserman, A., et al.: Spatial transformer networks. In: Advances in neural information processing systems, pp. 2017–2025 (2015)
10. Joshi, S., Pizer, S., Fletcher, P.T., Thall, A., Tracton, G.: Multi-scale 3-D deformable model segmentation based on medial description. In: Insana, M.F., Leahy, R.M. (eds.) IPMI 2001. LNCS, vol. 2082, pp. 64–77. Springer, Heidelberg (2001). https://doi.org/10.1007/3-540-45729-1_6
11. Krebs, J., Delingette, H., Mailhé, B., Ayache, N., Mansi, T.: Learning a probabilistic model for diffeomorphic registration. IEEE Trans. Med. Imaging **38**(9), 2165–2176 (2019)
12. Mansilla, L., Milone, D.H., Ferrante, E.: Learning deformable registration of medical images with anatomical constraints. Neural Netw., (2020)

13. WRITING   COMMITTEE   MEMBERS,   Hundley,   W.G.,   et   al.: Accf/acr/aha/nasci/scmr 2010 expert consensus document on cardiovascular magnetic resonance: a report of the american college of cardiology foundation task force on expert consensus documents. Circulation. **121**(22), pp. 2462–2508 (2010)

14. Modat, M., et al.: Fast free-form deformation using graphics processing units. Comput. Methods Programs Biomed. **98**(3), 278–284 (2010)

15. Muser, D., Castro, S.A., Santangeli, P., Nucifora, G.: Clinical applications of feature-tracking cardiac magnetic resonance imaging. World J. Cardiol. **10**(11), 210 (2018)

16. Pu, Y., et al.: Variational autoencoder for deep learning of images, labels and captions. In: Advances in neural information processing systems, pp. 2352–2360 (2016)

17. Puyol-Antón, E., et al.: Fully automated myocardial strain estimation from cine mri using convolutional neural networks. In: 2018 IEEE 15th International Symposium on Biomedical Imaging (ISBI 2018), pp. 1139–1143. IEEE (2018)

18. Qin, C., et al.: Joint learning of motion estimation and segmentation for cardiac mr image sequences. In: International Conference on Medical Image Computing and Computer-Assisted Intervention, Springer, pp. 472–480 (2018) https://doi.org/10.1007/978-3-030-00934-2_53

19. Vercauteren, T., Pennec, X., Perchant, A., Ayache, N.: Diffeomorphic demons: efficient non-parametric image registration. NeuroImage **45**(1), S61–S72 (2009)

20. Vigneault, D.M., Xie, W., Bluemke, D.A., Noble, J.A.: Feature tracking cardiac magnetic resonance via deep learning and spline optimization. In: International Conference on Functional Imaging and Modeling of the Heart, Springer, pp. 183–194 (2017) https://doi.org/10.1007/978-3-319-59448-4_18

21. Wu, G., Kim, M., Wang, Q., Shen, D.: S-hammer: hierarchical attribute-guided, symmetric diffeomorphic registration for mr brain images. Hum. Brain Mapp. **35**(3), 1044–1060 (2014)

22. Yu, H., Chen, X., Shi, H., Chen, T., Huang, T.S., Sun, S.: Motion pyramid networks for accurate and efficient cardiac motion estimation. arXiv preprint arXiv:2006.15710 (2020)

23. Yu, H., et al.: Foal: fast online adaptive learning for cardiac motion estimation. In: Proceedings of the IEEE/CVF Conference on Computer Vision and Pattern Recognition, pp. 4313–4323 (2020)

24. Zheng, Q., Delingette, H., Ayache, N.: Explainable cardiac pathology classification on cine mri with motion characterization by semi-supervised learning of apparent flow. Med. Image Anal. **56**, 80–95 (2019)

Division and Fusion: Rethink Convolutional Kernels for 3D Medical Image Segmentation

Xi Fang[1], Thomas Sanford[2], Baris Turkbey[3], Sheng Xu[4], Bradford J. Wood[4], and Pingkun Yan[1(✉)]

[1] Department of Biomedical Engineering and Center for Biotechnology and Interdisciplinary Studies, Rensselaer Polytechnic Institute, Troy, NY 12180, USA
yanp2@rpi.edu
[2] The State University of New York Upstate Medical University, Syracuse, USA
[3] Molecular Imaging Program, National Cancer Institute, National Institutes of Health, Bethesda, USA
[4] Center for Interventional Oncology, Radiology and Imaging Sciences, National Institutes of Health, Bethesda, USA

Abstract. There has been a debate of using 2D and 3D convolution on volumetric medical image segmentation. The problem is that 2D convolution loses 3D spatial relationship of image features, while 3D convolution layers are hard to train from scratch due to the limited size of medical image dataset. Employing more trainable parameters and complicated connections may improve the performance of 3D CNN, however, inducing extra computational burden at the same time. It is meaningful to improve performance of current 3D medical image processing without requiring extra inference computation and memory resources. In this paper, we propose a general solution, Division-Fusion (DF)-CNN for free performance improvement on any available 3D medical image segmentation approach. During the division phase, different view-based kernels are divided from a single 3D kernel to extract multi-view context information that strengthens the spatial information of feature maps. During the fusion phase, all kernels are fused into one 3D kernel to reduce the parameters of deployed model. We extensively evaluated our DF mechanism on prostate ultrasound volume segmentation. The results demonstrate a consistent improvement over different benchmark models with a clear margin.

Keywords: Division and fusion · Deep learning · Medical image segmentation

This work was partially supported by National Institute of Biomedical Imaging and Bioengineering (NIBIB) of the National Institutes of Health (NIH) under awards R21EB028001 and R01EB027898, and through an NIH Bench-to-Bedside award made possible by the National Cancer Institute.

M. Liu et al. (Eds.): MLMI 2020, LNCS 12436, pp. 160–169, 2020.
https://doi.org/10.1007/978-3-030-59861-7_17

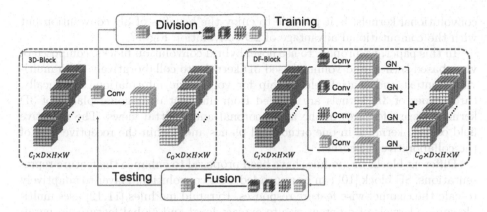

Fig. 1. Illustration of an Division-Fusion convolutional layer in training and valida-tion/testing. For efficient training, different kernels are divided from 3D kernels to extract both view-based context and volume-based image context. During testing, all kernels are fused into one single 3D kernel to reduce the inference time and alleviate the computational burden.

1 Introduction

Deep learning has been dominating the area of medical image computing. Specif-ically, deep convolutional neural network (CNN) based methods have been pro-posed and applied to a wide range of imaging modalities. Many medical imaging modalities like MRI (magnetic resonance imaging) and CT (computed tomog-raphy) produce images in 3D volumes, which contain 3D context information. 2D networks commonly used for analyzing natural images may not be suffi-cient. Prior studies dealing with volumetric data can be categorized into 2D and 3D-based approaches. Methods in the former group [1–3] are based on 2D con-volutions to extract 2D features from three orthogonal views. The features are then fused together to achieve segmentation. Although such 2D networks are computational efficient and easy to train, they may not take full advantage of 3D imaging for analysis. The second group of methods uses 3D convolutions and trains 3D CNNs directly over volumetric data [4–6]. However, the large search space of 3D kernel and the relatively small size of medical image dataset lead to insufficiently trained 3D CNNs when starting from scratch, as we know a key factor in training deep networks is to have plenty of training data [7,8].

To bridge the gap between 2D and 3D CNNs, hybrid approaches combining 2D and 3D features to extract context information have been proposed. For example, Some works [7,9] combine 2D and 3D features to improve learning efficiency. Xia et al. [8] use a 2D CNN to obtain a coarse segmentation and a 3D CNN to refine the result. Although empirically effective, the use of 2D CNN in those approaches comes with the intrinsic problem that 2D convolution loses 3D spatial relationship of image features. Given such challenges in medical image segmentation, we have to rethink a key component inside CNN – the convolutional kernels. Is it possible to enjoy the benefits of 3D convolution but with the computational advantage of 2D convolution Fig. 1?

In this paper, we propose to use novel hybrid convolution blocks, composed of view-based kernels and volume-based 3D kernels, to collaboratively learn multi-view context and spatial relationship for volumetric information. Specifically, three types of 3D kernels are divided from different orthogonal planes of 3D kernel to learn features in the axial, coronal and sagittal views. The receptive field of each kernel is in one orthogonal planes and within the receptive field of the collaborative 3D kernel.

Different blocks or modules have been proposed to enhance the feature representations. SE-block [10] can be appended after convolutional layer to adaptively rescale the channel-wise feature responses. Pyramid modules [11,12] uses multiple square kernels of different size to extract local and global features in parallel. However, compared to the baseline model, all these blocks bring additional parameters and computational cost. On the contrary, our method maintains the original network structure without inducing external parameter numbers when deploying the model. ACNet [13] introduces the additivity of convolutions and use asymmetric convolution to strengthen the skeleton of 2D convolution. In our work, we instead use different view-based kernels, which are commonly used in medical image computing to extract view-based features. All divided kernels in our proposed hybrid block can be fused into one 3D kernel. The hybrid kernel can produce the same outputs as the training time.

Since all kernels are "divided" from and "fused" into one 3D kernel, the method is coined as "Division-Fusion" (DF)-CNN. We test the proposed DF-CNN on an ultrasound volumetric image dataset for prostate segmentation. Prostate cancer is the leading cause of cancer related deaths in men [14]. Ultrasound, a versatile and real-time imaging modality, has been a routine imaging modalities for image-guided prostate cancer intervention. Automatic prostate segmentation of ultrasound image during intervention is crucial for the diagnosis and treatment [15]. Various methods have been proposed to improve the segmentation performance by employing more trainable parameters and complicated connections [16]. However, besides segmentation accuracy, the computational efficiency also plays a very important role in clinical applications [17]. Thus, in this paper, we demonstrate the performance of DF-CNN on this challenging problem of efficient prostate ultrasound volume segmentation. Our experimental results demonstrate that a significant improvement has been achieved over several benchmark models with the use of our DF mechanism for training. The major contributions of this work are summarized as follows.

1. We present a new hybrid convolution block to enhance volumetric feature space by combining both multi-view based features and 3D spatial features.
2. The proposed DF convolution can be easily plugged into different 3D network architectures to improve the performance.
3. Once trained, the filters are integrated for model deployment, which thus introduces neither extra parameters, nor computational burden, nor extra inference time compared to the original 3D CNN. Therefore, the testing phase gets free performance improvement over its 3D counterpart.

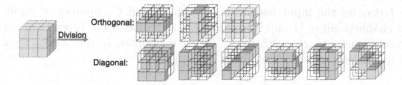

Fig. 2. Given a 3D kernel, different types of sparse 3D kernel can be divided from different orthogonal and diagonal planes. The 3D kernel (K-3D) directly learns 3D spatial information, and K-Axial, K-Sagittal, K-Coronal kernels extract planar information from axial, sagittal and coronal views respectively. 3D convolution of view-based kernel equals 2D convolution on corresponding plane and concatenating all 2D planar features.

2 Methods

In this section, we present the details of the proposed Division-Fusion (DF) mechanism for enhancing the feature representation of 3D convolution kernels. The proposed method consists of two phases, **Division** in the training phase and **Fusion** in the model deployment phase. During training, different view-based kernels and are **divided** from 3D kernels and efficiently trained by extracting features from different planes. When deploying the model, all kernels at a convolutional layer are **fused** into one 3D kernel for performance improvement without adding inference time.

2.1 Convolutional Kernels for Spatial and Multi-view Information

Convolutional kernel is the basic key component of CNN. 2D and 3D kernels are most common for 3D medical image processing. 2D kernels help extract slice-based features from either axial, or coronal, or sagittal view, while 3D kernels directly extract volumetric features.

Instead of using 2D kernel for view-based convolution, as shown in Fig. 2, nine types of sparse 3D kernel can be divided from orthogonal and diagonal planes of 3D kernel to extract view-based features on 3D feature maps. Division mechanism, takes any shape of kernel in 3D CNN to produce a collection of view-based kernels. Specifically, all these view-based convolution can be implemented by sparse 3D kernel. In this work, we use three view-based kernels divided from three orthogonal plane for axial, coronal and sagittal views. For three orthogonal view-based convolution and 3D convolution, they can be easily implemented with kernel size of $1 \times S_y \times S_z$, $S_x \times 1 \times S_z$, $S_x \times S_y \times 1$ and $S_x \times S_y \times S_z$.

2.2 Kernel Division for Efficient Training

For a convolutional layer with kernels $\{F^i | i = 1, \cdots, C_o\}$ in the size of $S_x \times S_y \times S_z$, the convolutional output of the i-th channel can be written as

$$O_i = \sum_{k=1}^{C_i} I_k * F_k^i, \tag{1}$$

where I denotes the input feature map with C_i and C_o number of input and output channels. Since Group Normalization (GN) has been shown to accelerate the training and reduce overfitting [18], it is adopted in our work. Then the convolutional output is updated from Eq. (1) to

$$O_i = \left(\sum_{k=1}^{C_i} I_k * F_k^i - \mu_i \right) \frac{\gamma_i}{\sigma_i} + \beta_i, \tag{2}$$

where σ_i, μ_i are the standard deviation and the mean values of the same group of channels, respectively. γ_i and β_i are trainable scale and shift to compensate the possible lost of representational ability.

In the Division stage, the input feature maps are operated in multiple branches. In each branch, features are extracted by one convolutional kernel with the same number of kernels. After normalization, the outputs of all the branches are summed up to get the output feature maps. So spatial context can be learned collaboratively via different kernels. Demonstrated in Sect. 2.1, three view-based kernels and one volume-based 3D kernel are used for parallel feature extraction.

$$O_i = O_i^A + O_i^S + O_i^C + O_i^{3D}, \tag{3}$$

where O_i^A, O_i^S, O_i^C, O_i^{3D} are the output feature map for i-th filter of axial, coronal, sagittal view-based and 3D kernels respectively.

The view-based convolutional kernels, which are computational efficient and extract useful local context information from multiple views. The summation operation enables aggregating multi-view context and spatial context to enhance the feature space of output feature maps.

2.3   Kernel Fusion

The receptive fields of the divided view-based kernels are completely within the receptive field of the original 3D kernel. Due to the additivity of convolutional kernel [13], all these four kernels can be fused into one single 3D kernel to reduce the number of model parameters by summing up all the aligned kernels to form a new 3D kernel. That is to say

$$I * F_A + I * F_S + I * F_C + I * F_{3D} = I * (F_A \oplus F_S \oplus F_C \oplus F_{3D}), \tag{4}$$

where F_A, F_S, F_C denotes kernels on axial, sagittal, coronal planes and F_{3D} denotes 3D volumetric kernel. $\oplus$ is the element-wise addition of weights onto the corresponding positions. During the Fusion phase, the parameters of group normalization are first fused into one convolution kernel in each branch.

$$O_i = \left(\sum_{k=1}^{C} I_k * \frac{\gamma}{\sigma} F_k^i \right) - \frac{\mu_i \gamma_i}{\sigma_i} + \beta_i \tag{5}$$

Then, all four kernels can be fused into one 3D kernel. According to Eq. 4, the weights in the i-th filter of fused 3D kernel can be computed by

$$F^i = \frac{\gamma_{A,i}}{\sigma_{A,i}} F_A^i \oplus \frac{\gamma_{S,i}}{\sigma_{S,i}} F_S^i \oplus \frac{\gamma_{C,i}}{\sigma_{C,i}} F_C^i \oplus \frac{\gamma_{3D,i}}{\sigma_{3D,i}} F_{3D}^i, \tag{6}$$

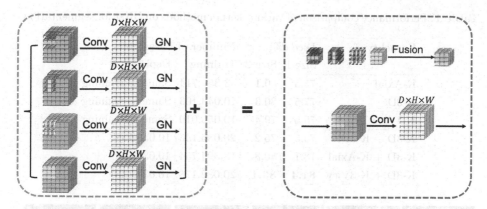

Fig. 3. For each kernel, the output feature maps of the i-th filter in size of are $D \times H \times W$. All outputs of these filters are summed up into the i-th channel outputs. By adding the weights of filters of each kernel onto the corresponding positions, the hybrid block can be fused into one 3D kernel.

$$b_i = -\frac{\mu_{A,i}\gamma_{A,i}}{\sigma_{A,i}} - \frac{\mu_{S,i}\gamma_{S,i}}{\sigma_{S,i}} - \frac{\mu_{C,i}\gamma_{C,i}}{\sigma_{C,i}} - \frac{\mu_{3D}^i\gamma_{3D}^i}{\sigma_{3D}^i} + \beta_{A,i} + \beta_{S,i} + \beta_{C,i} + \beta_{3D}^i, \quad (7)$$

In this way, for arbitrary i-th filter, weights from different convolution kernels and group normalization can be fused into one convolution kernel,

$$O_i^A + O_i^S + O_i^C + O_i^{3D} = \sum_{k=1}^{C} I_k * F_k^i + b_i, \quad (8)$$

The model using the newly fused 3D kernel produces the same outputs as doing the convolutions separately, as described by Eq. (3).

3   Experiments and Results

3.1   Materials and Implementation Details

In this paper, we focus on $3 \times 3 \times 3$ convolutional kernels. We extensively evaluated our method on prostate ultrasound volume dataset, which are composed of 41 ultrasound volumes that are labeled with prostate. 31 of them are used for training and 10 of them are used for validation. The resolution of these volumes varies from 0.47 mm to 0.71 mm. For preprocessing, we first resample all image volumes into a fixed resolution of 0.5 mm × 0.5 mm × 0.5 mm and then normalize all volumetric data into zero mean and unit variance. After preprocessing, voxel number along x-axis, y-axis, z-axis ranges are 186 to 264, 127 to 178, 116 to 284. During training, we randomly cropped sub-volumes from one volume. We choose two sub-volume size, $96 \times 96 \times 96$ and $112 \times 112 \times 112$ in our experiments. During inference, to segment one volume, we use overlapping windows to crop sub-volumes in the same size and stride is $32 \times 32 \times 32$ in voxel. The overlapping output probability maps are averaged to get the final segmentation result Fig. 3.

Table 1. Performance comparison of various kernel methods on UNet for segmentation.

Kernel type	Dice (%)		Number of Parameters	
	Size 1	Size 2	Training	Deployment
K-Axial	75.5	80.1	3,351,714	Same as training
K-3D	77.5	80.3	10,043,106	Same as training
K-3View	76.5	79.4	10,055,010	Same as training
K-3D + K-3D	75.5	75.2	20,086,146	10,039,138
K-3D + K-Axial	78.1	80.8	13,394,754	10,039,138
K-3D + K-3View	**81.4**	**83.1**	20,082,178	10,039,138

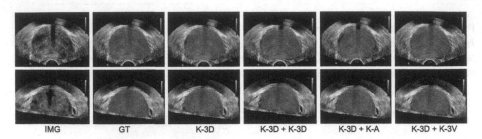

Fig. 4. From the left to right are image, ground truth, result of K-3D, K-3D + K-3D, K-3D + K-Axial, and K-3D + K-3View.

Our implementation is based on a open-sourced platform Pytorch [19]. All convolution operations are followed by the activation function ReLU [20]. Number of groups to seperate the channels is set to 32. For network training, we adopt Adam optimizer [21] with the initial learning rate of 0.0001, momentum of 0.9 and a mini-batch size of 1 on a NVIDIA V100 GPU maximum epoch number is 200. To compare the performance of segmentation model, dice coefficient, parameter numbers for training and deploying are used as evaluation criterion.

3.2   Results

To evaluate the performance of our proposed DF mechanism, we compare different combinations of kernels to demonstrate the effect of different kernels. We then conduct our method on different 3D network architectures. FCN [22], UNet [5] and ResUNet [23] are used in our experiments. All networks are 19-layer network. Max-pooling and Tri-linear upsampling operations are followed by every two convolutions in encoder part and decoder part respectively.

Effect of Convolutional Kernel. To demonstrate the effectiveness of our proposed DF mechanism, we use UNet as the network architecture and use different combinations of kernel for comparison. We use two sizes of sub-volume in the experiments (Size 1: $96 \times 96 \times 96$, Size 2: $112 \times 112 \times 112$). In Table 1, we

Table 2. Segmentation performance comparison of different methods.

Network	Dice (%)			Number of Parameters		
	3D	DF	↑	3D	Division	Fusion
FCN [22]	79.3	**80.0**	0.7	8,854,242	17,720,322	8,850,274
UNet [5]	80.3	**83.1**	2.8	10,043,106	20,098,050	10,039,138
ResUNet [23]	78.4	**82.0**	3.6	10,242,594	20,297,538	10,238,626

can see that K-3D + K-3D do not bring improvement for segmentation accuracy on single 3D kernel, the increased training parameters brings severe overfitting. On the contrary, K-Axial + K-3D outperforms single K-Axial and K-3D, which demonstrate the effectiveness of hybrid blocks. It is because view-based kernels are more computational efficient and provides useful view-based features. K-3View that extracts multi-view context information, obtained lower performance than K-3D. It is because of lack of spatial relationship. K-3View + K-3D that combine multi-view based features and 3D spatial features, outperforms all other combinations by clear margin Fig. 4.

Comparison with Benchmark Models. We further apply our method on 3D-FCN [22], 3D-UNet [5] and 3D-ResUNet [23] to show the robustness of our method. 3D UNet add skip connections to combine low and high level features. 3D ResUNet add shortcut connections across two continuous convolution layer to perform identity mapping [24]. In our network, it is fulfilled by a $1 \times 1 \times 1$ convolution. The size of the sub-volume is set to $112 \times 112 \times 112$. All these networks are trained from scratch in the same environment. The results show that our proposed mechanism can bring free improvement for all benchmark models with clear margin. With our DF mechanism, the dice of 3D FCN, 3D UNet and 3D ResUNet increase by 0.7%, 2.8% and 3.6%, respectively Table 2.

4 Conclusion

In this paper, we present a method called "Division-Fusion" to efficiently train 3D convolutions for volumetric medical image segmentation. During the Division, the network extracts both view-based and volume-based context in each layer. After training, all kernels can be fused into one 3D kernel. The proposed DF approach brings clear improvement over directly training 3D network. A possible explanation is that the parallel sparse kernels regularize the model training. The proposed DF method can be easily plugged into different networks and contribute performance improvement without inducing extra computational load when deployed. The benefit can be important for computational resource and time restricted applications, like image-guided intervention.

References

1. Mortazi, A., Burt, J., Bagci, U.: Multi-planar deep segmentation networks for cardiac substructures from MRI and CT. In: Pop, M., et al. (eds.) STACOM 2017. LNCS, vol. 10663, pp. 199–206. Springer, Cham (2018). https://doi.org/10.1007/978-3-319-75541-0_21
2. Moeskops, P., et al.: Deep learning for multi-task medical image segmentation in multiple modalities. In: Ourselin, S., Joskowicz, L., Sabuncu, M.R., Unal, G., Wells, W. (eds.) MICCAI 2016. LNCS, vol. 9901, pp. 478–486. Springer, Cham (2016). https://doi.org/10.1007/978-3-319-46723-8_55
3. Fang, X., Yan, P.: Multi-organ segmentation over partially labeled datasets with multi-scale feature abstraction. IEEE Trans. Med. Imaging, 1–1 (2020)
4. Milletari, F., Navab, N., Ahmadi, S.-A.: V-net: fully convolutional neural networks for volumetric medical image segmentation. In: 2016 Fourth International Conference on 3D Vision (3DV), pp. 565–571. IEEE (2016)
5. Ronneberger, O., Fischer, P., Brox, T.: U-Net: convolutional networks for biomedical image segmentation. In: Navab, N., Hornegger, J., Wells, W.M., Frangi, A.F. (eds.) MICCAI 2015. LNCS, vol. 9351, pp. 234–241. Springer, Cham (2015). https://doi.org/10.1007/978-3-319-24574-4_28
6. Zhu, Q., Du, B., Yan, P.: Boundary-weighted domain adaptive neural network for prostate MR image segmentation. IEEE Trans. Med. Imaging **39**(3), 753–763 (2019)
7. Li, X., Chen, H., Qi, X., Dou, Q., Fu, C.-W., Heng, P.-A.: H-DenseUNet: hybrid densely connected UNet for liver and tumor segmentation from CT volumes. IEEE Trans. Med. Imaging **37**(12), 2663–2674 (2018)
8. Xia, Y., Xie, L., Liu, F., Zhu, Z., Fishman, E.K., Yuille, A.L.: Bridging the gap between 2D and 3D organ segmentation with volumetric fusion net. In: Frangi, A.F., Schnabel, J.A., Davatzikos, C., Alberola-López, C., Fichtinger, Gabor (eds.) MICCAI 2018. LNCS, vol. 11073, pp. 445–453. Springer, Cham (2018). https://doi.org/10.1007/978-3-030-00937-3_51
9. Zheng, H., et al.: A new ensemble learning framework for 3D biomedical image segmentation. Proc. AAAI Conf. Artif. Intell. **33**, 5909–5916 (2019)
10. Hu, J., Shen, L., Sun, G.: Squeeze-and-excitation networks. In: Proceedings of the IEEE Conference on Computer Vision and Pattern Recognition, pp. 7132–7141 (2018)
11. He, K., Zhang, X., Ren, S., Sun, J.: Spatial pyramid pooling in deep convolutional networks for visual recognition. IEEE Trans. Pattern Anal. Mach. Intell. **37**(9), 1904–1916 (2015)
12. Chen, L.-C., Papandreou, G., Kokkinos, I., Murphy, K., Yuille, A.L.: Deeplab: semantic image segmentation with deep convolutional nets, atrous convolution, and fully connected CRFS. IEEE Trans. Pattern Anal. Mach. Intell. **40**(4), 834–848 (2017)
13. Ding, X., Guo, Y., Ding, G., Han, J.: Acnet: strengthening the kernel skeletons for powerful CNN via asymmetric convolution blocks. In: Proceedings of the IEEE International Conference on Computer Vision, pp. 1911–1920 (2019)
14. Siegel, R.L., Miller, K.D., Jemal, A.: Cancer statistics, 2019. CA Cancer J. Clin. **69**(1), 7–34 (2019)
15. Yan, P., Xu, S., Turkbey, B., Kruecker, J.: Discrete deformable model guided by partial active shape model for TRUS image segmentation. IEEE Trans. Biomed. Eng. **57**(5), 1158–1166 (2010)

16. Wang, Y., et al.: Deep attentive features for prostate segmentation in 3D transrectal ultrasound. IEEE Trans. Med. Imaging **38**(12), 2768–2778 (2019)
17. Yan, P., Xu, S., Turkbey, B., Kruecker, J.: Adaptively learning local shape statistics for prostate segmentation in ultrasound. IEEE Trans. Biomed. Eng. **58**(3), 633–641 (2010)
18. Wu, Y., He, K.: Group normalization. In: Proceedings of the European Conference on Computer Vision (ECCV), pp. 3–19 (2018)
19. Paszke, A., et al.: Automatic differentiation in PyTorch. In: NIPS 2017 Workshop Autodiff (2017)
20. Nair, V., Hinton, G.E.: Rectified linear units improve restricted boltzmann machines. In: Proceedings of the 27th International Conference on Machine Learning (ICML-10), pp. 807–814 (2010)
21. Kingma, D.P., Ba, J.: Adam: a method for stochastic optimization. arXiv preprint (2014). arXiv:1412.6980
22. Long, J., Shelhamer, E., Darrell, T.: Fully convolutional networks for semantic segmentation. In: Proceedings of the IEEE Conference on Computer vision and Pattern Recognition, pp. 3431–3440 (2015)
23. Yu, L., Yang, X., Chen, H., Qin, J., Heng, P.A.: Volumetric convnets with mixed residual connections for automated prostate segmentation from 3d MR images. In: Thirty-first AAAI Conference on Artificial Intelligence (2017)
24. He, K., Zhang, X., Ren, S., Sun, J.: Deep residual learning for image recognition. In: Proceedings of the IEEE Conference on Computer Vision and Pattern Recognition, pp. 770–778 (2016)

LDGAN: Longitudinal-Diagnostic Generative Adversarial Network for Disease Progression Prediction with Missing Structural MRI

Zhenyuan Ning[1,2], Yu Zhang[1(✉)], Yongsheng Pan[3], Tao Zhong[1,2], Mingxia Liu[2(✉)], and Dinggang Shen[2(✉)]

[1] School of Biomedical Engineering, Southern Medical University, Guangzhou 510515, China
yuzhang@smu.edu.cn
[2] Department of Radiology and BRIC, University of North Carolina at Chapel Hill, Chapel Hill, NC 27599, USA
mxliu@med.unc.edu, dinggang.Shen@gmail.com
[3] School of Computer Science and Engineering, Northwestern Polytechnical University, Xian 710072, China

Abstract. Predicting future progression of brain disorders is fundamental for effective intervention of pathological cognitive decline. Structural MRI provides a non-invasive solution to examine brain pathology and has been widely used for longitudinal analysis of brain disorders. Previous studies typically use only *complete baseline* MRI scans to predict future disease status due to the lack of MRI data at one or more future time points. Since temporal changes of each brain MRI are ignored, these methods would result in sub-optimal performance. To this end, we propose a longitudinal-diagnostic generative adversarial network (LDGAN) to predict multiple clinical scores at future time points using incomplete longitudinal MRI data. Specifically, LDGAN imputes MR images by learning a bi-directional mapping between MRIs of two adjacent time points and performing clinical score prediction jointly, thereby explicitly encouraging task-oriented image synthesis. The proposed LDGAN is further armed with a *temporal constraint* and an *output constraint* to model the temporal regularity of MRIs at adjacent time points and encourage the diagnostic consistency, respectively. We also design a weighted loss function to make use of those subjects without ground-truth scores at certain time points. The major advantage of the proposed LDGAN is that it can impute those missing scans in a task-oriented manner and can explicitly capture the temporal characteristics of brain changes for accurate prediction. Experimental results on both ADNI-1 and ADNI-2 datasets demonstrate that, compared with the state-of-the-art methods, LDGAN can generate more reasonable MRI scans and efficiently predict longitudinal clinical measures.

Electronic supplementary material The online version of this chapter (https://doi.org/10.1007/978-3-030-59861-7_18) contains supplementary material, which is available to authorized users.

1   Introduction

Structural magnetic resonance imaging (MRI) provides a feasible solution to potentially identify abnormal changes of the brain that could be used as biomarkers for automated diagnosis of brain diseases, such as Alzheimer's Disease (AD) and its prodromal stage (i.e., mild cognitive impairment, MCI) [1–5]. An interesting topic is to assess the stage of pathology and predict future progression of MCI by estimating longitudinal clinical scores of subjects based on MRI data [6,7]. However, missing data problem (e.g., incomplete MRI and ground-truth clinical scores) has been remaining a huge challenge for longitudinal diagnosis of brain diseases due to patient dropout and/or poor data quality.

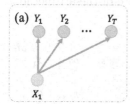 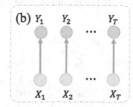 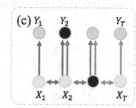

Fig. 1. Illustration of three learning strategies for MRI-based longitudinal diagnosis: (a) estimating baseline and T future clinical scores (i.e., $\{Y_1, Y_2, \cdots, Y_T\}$) using only baseline MRI (i.e., X_1); (b) estimating each score using its corresponding true MRI at the same time point; and (c) estimating scores at multiple time points using incomplete longitudinal MRI, where those missing MRIs (denoted as black circles) are imputed by a certain image synthesis method. Two-way arrows and one-way arrows represent image synthesis and diagnosis, respectively.

Existing learning-based methods often simply discard subjects without MRI or ground-truth scores at a certain time point, which results in limited training samples for learning reliable and robust models [8,9]. Recent effort has been devoted to taking advantage of all available subjects by using multi-view learning or data imputation techniques [2,7]. For example, a weakly-supervised densely connected neural network (WiseDNN) is proposed to perform longitudinal diagnosis for AD and MCI based on *complete baseline* MRI and incomplete clinical scores, as shown in Fig. 1 (a). However, these methods generally ignore temporal changes of brain MRIs and clinical scores, because only baseline MRIs are used to predict future clinical measures. It seems to be more reliable to predict clinical scores using MRIs at the same time point, as shown in Fig. 1 (b). On the other hand, even though several studies propose to directly impute missing data [2,10,11], they typically treat data imputation and disease diagnosis as two standalone tasks. Intuitively, integrating MRI synthesis and disease diagnosis into a unified framework is desirable, as illustrated in Fig. 1 (c).

In this work, we propose a longitudinal-diagnostic generative adversarial network (LDGAN) for joint longitudinal image synthesis and clinical score prediction based on incomplete MRIs and ground-truth clinical scores. As shown in

Fig. 2, the proposed LDGAN can jointly perform image synthesis and disease diagnosis at multiple (e.g., T) time points. Specifically, by using the current time-point MR images (e.g., X_t) as input, LDGAN is developed to synthesize MR images (e.g., $\tilde{X}_{t+1}$) at the next time point, through which imaging representations that reflect temporal changes of the brain over time can be simultaneously learned for diagnosis. Moreover, our LDGAN is armed with a temporal constraint (e.g., R_t^T) and an output constraint (e.g., R_t^C) to model the temporal regularity and encourage the diagnostic consistency, respectively. To make full use of all available subjects (even those without ground-true scores at a certain time point), a weighted loss function is further employed to train the network. Experimental results on ADNI-1 and ADNI-2 demonstrate that the proposed method can simultaneously generate reasonable MRI scans and efficiently predict longitudinal clinical scores, compared with several state-of-the-art methods.

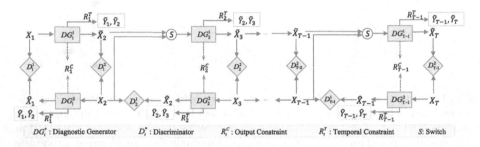

Fig. 2. Overview of the proposed LDGAN for joint image synthesis and clinical score prediction at multiple (i.e., T) time points based on incomplete MRI data, including 1) diagnostic generator (e.g., DG_1^1 and DG_1^2) for image synthesis, 2) discriminator (e.g., D_1^1 and D_1^2), and 3) temporal constraint (e.g., R_1^T) and output constraint (e.g., R_1^C). The switch (S) operation indicates that the input is a real image if it exists; otherwise, the input is a synthetic image.

2   Method

2.1   Problem Analysis

For the i-th subject, we denote $\{X_t^i, Y_t^i\}_{t=1}^T$ as its MRI scans and clinical scores at T time points. To avoid the time gap problem, we use MRI scans at the t-th time point to predict clinical scores at the t-th time point. Specifically, the longitudinal diagnostic model can be formulated as $\tilde{Y}_t^i = \Phi_t(X_t^i)$, where Φ_t and $\tilde{Y}_t^i$ are the regressor and the predicted score for i-th subject at the t-th time point, respectively. However, the predictor $\Phi_t(-)$ cannot be executed if X_t^i is missing. To address this issue, the straightforward way is to use the real MRI of i-th subject at another time point to generate a virtual X_t^i. Considering that AD/MCI are progressive neurodegenerative disorders, we assume that a missing

MRI scan at the next time point (e.g., X_{t+1}^i) can be synthesized by the real MRI scan at current time point (e.g., X_t^i), as shown in Fig. 1 (c).

Let G_t be the function to generate X_{t+1}^i from X_t^i, and D_t as the discriminator to distinguish whether the image is real or synthetic. Based on synthetic images, a diagnostic model at the t-th time point can be formulated as $\tilde{Y}_t^i \approx \Phi_t(G_t(X_t^i))$. Previous studies have shown that temporal changes of the brain are beneficial to longitudinal diagnosis [12–14]. Accordingly, we assume that MRI features that reflect the brain changes of can be jointly learned for diagnosis during the process of image generation, and denote such a joint image synthesis and diagnosis model as DG_t. With some constraint terms (denoted as $R(-)$), the longitudinal-diagnostic model with can be reformulated as

$$\tilde{Y}_t^i = \Phi_t(X_t^i) \approx DG_t(X_t^i), \quad s.t. \ R(DG_t, D_t). \tag{1}$$

To this end, we propose a longitudinal-diagnostic generative adversarial network (LDGAN) to jointly perform image synthesis and diagnosis at multiple time points, with the schematic illustration shown in Fig. 2. In the following, we first introduce LDGAN for joint image synthesis and diagnosis at two time points, and then extend it for the task with multiple time points.

2.2 LDGAN with Two Time Points

The architecture of LDGAN at two time points is illustrated in Fig. 3, which basically consists of diagnostic generator (e.g., DG_t), discriminator (e.g., D_t), and constraint operator (e.g., R_t^T and R_t^C), with the details given below.

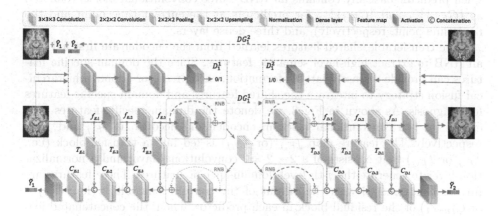

Fig. 3. Network architecture of LDGAN for two time-point image synthesis and clinical score prediction, including two longitudinal-diagnostic generators (e.g., DG_1^1 with X_1 as input and $\{\tilde{X}_2, \tilde{Y}_1, \tilde{Y}_2\}$ as output, and DG_1^2 with X_2 as input and $\{\hat{X}_1, \hat{Y}_1, \hat{Y}_2\}$ as output), and two discriminators (e.g., D_1^1 and D_1^2). RNB: residual network block.

Diagnostic Generator. The two time-point LDGAN has two diagnostic generators, i.e., $DG_1^1 : X_1^i \rightarrow \{\tilde{X}_2^i, \tilde{Y}_1^i, \tilde{Y}_2^i\}$ for the 1st time point and $DG_1^2 : X_2^i \rightarrow \{\hat{X}_1^i, \hat{Y}_1^i, \hat{Y}_2^i\}$ for the 2nd time point. Each diagnostic generator contains a shared encoder, a decoder, and two predictors, for joint image synthesis and prediction.

1) Shared Encoder. The shared encoder aims to extract source-domain-specific features and transferable features shared by source and target domains. Specifically, the shared encoder consists of a set of convolutional blocks and a residual network block (RNB). Three consecutive convolutional blocks are first used to extract MRI features, each of which containing a convolutional layer (with the kernel size of $3 \times 3 \times 3$) and a normalization layer. Between the first two blocks, a $2 \times 2 \times 2$ pooling layer is placed to perform feature reduction. The subsequent RNB consists of two convolutional blocks with the dropout rate of 0.8 and skip-connections. The RNB is used to generate shared feature maps for the source domain (e.g., $\mathcal{X}_1$) and the target domain (e.g., $\mathcal{X}_2$). And such feature maps are further used for image synthesis (via the decoder) and clinical score prediction (via two predictors).

2) Decoder. The decoder is constructed to learn target-domain-specific features and produce synthesized images based on feature maps produced by the encoder. The structure of the decoder is basically mirrored from the shared encoder, i.e., with an RNB followed by three convolutional blocks. In particular, the connective order of decoder is opposite to encoder and the pooling layer is replaced by an upsampling layer. A convolutional layer is further used to generate MRI scans in the target domain.

3) Predictor. Unlike previous predictors that are independent of image generation, the predictors in our LDGAN are embedded in the diagnostic generators. Each predictor basically contains an RNB, three convolutional blocks (denoted as $\{C_{E,j}\}_{j=1}^3$ and $\{C_{D,j}\}_{j=1}^3$ for predictors at the current time point and the next time point, respectively), and three dense layers.

The transferable/shared features learned from the encoder are first fed into an RNB to extract high-level semantic features. Since the domain-specific features can provide disease-related information, each predictor adopts a hierarchical fusion strategy to integrate the shared features and domain-specific features for diagnosis. As shown in Fig. 3, we denote the domain-specific features generated by j-th convolutional block in encoder and decoder as $f_{E,j}$ and $f_{D,j}$, respectively. The feature map $f_{E,j}$ (or $f_{D,j}$) is fed into a transfer block (i.e., $T_{E,j}$ or $T_{D,j}$) that consists of a $2 \times 2 \times 2$ convolutional layer and a normalization layer to generate the j-th level domain-specific features. These features are further concatenated with the output of the convolutional block (i.e., $C_{E,j+1}$ or $C_{D,j+1}$) or the residual block in each predictor. Then, the concatenated features are fed into the convolutional block (i.e., $C_{E,j}$ or $C_{D,j}$), whose output is concatenated with the $(j\text{-}1)$-level domain-specific features as the input of the next convolutional block (i.e., $C_{E,j-1}$ or $C_{D,j-1}$). Subsequently, a global pooling layer and three dense layers are used to predict the scores based on the features generated by the last convolutional block (i.e., $C_{E,1}$ or $C_{D,1}$). The loss function of the proposed diagnostic generator (with DG_1^1 for the current time point and DG_1^2 for the next time point) is defined as:

$$\mathcal{L}(DG_1^1, DG_1^2) = \mathcal{L}_{DG}(DG_1^1) + \mathcal{L}_{DG}(DG_1^2) + \lambda_c \mathcal{L}_C(DG_1^1, DG_1^2), \tag{2}$$

$$\mathcal{L}_{DG}(DG_1^1) = \mathbb{E}_{X_1^i \in \mathcal{X}_1} ||\log(D_1^2(G_1^1(X_1^i)))||_2 + \mathbb{E}_{X_1^i \in \mathcal{X}_1} ||P_1^{1,1}(X_1^i) - Y_1^i||_2$$
$$+ \mathbb{E}_{X_1^i \in \mathcal{X}_1} ||P_1^{1,2}(X_1^i) - Y_2^i||_2, \tag{3}$$

where G_1^1 is the generator, and $P_1^{1,1}$ and $P_1^{1,2}$ are the predictors for the 1st and 2nd time points in DG_1^1, respectively. Using Eq. (3), one can ensure that the synthetic images can be generated in a prediction-oriented manner by using both domain-specific features and shared features. Besides, the last term in Eq. (2) is defined as:

$$\mathcal{L}_C(DG_1^1, DG_1^2) = \mathbb{E}_{X_1^i \in \mathcal{X}_1} ||G_1^2(G_1^1(X_1^i)) - X_1^i||_2 + \mathbb{E}_{X_2^i \in \mathcal{X}_2} ||G_1^1(G_1^2(X_2^i)) - X_2^i||_2, \tag{4}$$

which is used to encourage each synthetic MR image to be consistent with its corresponding real MR image.

Discriminator. The proposed LDGAN contains two adversarial discriminators, i.e., D_1^1 and D_1^2, to distinguish whether the image is real or synthetic. Specifically, each discriminator contains three consecutive convolutional layers with LeakyReLU activation function and kernel size of $3 \times 3 \times 3$ to extract imaging features. By leveraging these features, three dense layers (with the neuron number of 16, 8, and 1, respectively) are used to perform identification. The loss function of the discriminator is defined as:

$$\mathcal{L}(D_1^1, D_1^2) = \mathbb{E}_{X_1^i \in \mathcal{X}_1} ||\log(D_1^1(X_1^i))||_2 + \mathbb{E}_{X_1^i \in \mathcal{X}_1} ||\log(1 - D_1^1(G_1^2(X_2^i)))||_2$$
$$+ \mathbb{E}_{X_2^i \in \mathcal{X}_2} ||\log(D_1^2(X_2^i))||_2 + \mathbb{E}_{X_2^i \in \mathcal{X}_2} ||\log(1 - D_1^2(G_1^1(X_1^i)))||_2. \tag{5}$$

Constraints. Our LDGAN includes a temporal constraint and an output constraint, both of which are used to constrain the output of two predictors. Specifically, the proposed temporal and output constraints are defined as:

$$R(DG_1^1, DG_1^2) = R^T(DG_1^1, DG_1^2) + \mu_c R^C(DG_1^1, DG_1^2), \tag{6}$$

where μ_c is the penalty coefficient, and the temporal constraint is defined as:

$$R^T(DG_1^1, DG_1^2) = \mathbb{E}_{X_1^i \in \mathcal{X}_1} \psi(\tilde{Y}_1^i, \tilde{Y}_2^i) + \mathbb{E}_{X_2^i \in \mathcal{X}_2} \psi(\hat{Y}_1^i, \hat{Y}_2^i), \tag{7}$$

where the term $\psi(A, B) = 0$ if A and B follows the time regularity of clinical scores (e.g., longitudinal increase in Clinical Dementia Rating and longitudinal decrease in Alzheimer's Disease Assessment Scale's Cognitive subscale); and $\psi(A, B) = ||A\text{-}B||_2$, otherwise. Equation 7 encourages the predicted scores to follow time regularity of clinical scores. The output constraint is defined as:

$$R^C(DG_1^1, DG_1^2) = \mathbb{E}_{X_1^i \in \mathcal{X}_1, X_2^i \in \mathcal{X}_2} ||\tilde{Y}_1^i - \hat{Y}_1^i||_2 + \mathbb{E}_{X_1^i \in \mathcal{X}_1, X_2^i \in \mathcal{X}_2} ||\tilde{Y}_2^i - \hat{Y}_2^i||_2, \tag{8}$$

which encourages the outputs of predictors for the same score at the same time point to be consistent.

2.3   LDGAN with Multiple Time Points

The LDGAN can be further extended to handle problems with multiple time points. As shown in Fig. 2, DG_1 is first developed to map X_1 to $\tilde{X}_2$, and predict the scores $\tilde{Y}_1$ and $\tilde{Y}_2$. Then, $\tilde{X}_2$ is used to complement X_2 as the input of DG_2 to synthesize $\tilde{X}_3$ and predict the scores $\tilde{Y}_2$ and $\tilde{Y}_3$. By that analogy, we can generate the missing images and its clinical scores. To make use of subjects without ground-truth clinical scores, a weighted loss function is designed in LDGAN to make use of all available subjects (even those with missing ground-true scores at a certain time point). Let $Y_t = [\mathbf{y}_{t,1}, \cdots, \mathbf{y}_{t,s}, \cdots, \mathbf{y}_{t,S}]$ denote S types of ground-truth clinical scores of all subjects at the t-th time point. The $\mathcal{L}_{DG}(DG_t^1)$ and $\mathcal{L}_{DG}(DG_t^2)$ in $\mathcal{L}(DG_t^1, DG_t^2)$ are written as:

$$
\begin{aligned}
\mathcal{L}_{DG}(DG_t^*) = &\mathbb{E}_{X_t^i \in \mathcal{X}_t} ||\log(1 - D_t^2(G_t^*(X_t^i)))||_2 + \mathbb{E}_{X_t^i \in \mathcal{X}_t} \mathbf{H}_t^i \times ||P_t^{*,1}(X_t^i) - Y_t^i||_2 \\
&+ \mathbb{E}_{X_t^i \in \mathcal{X}_t} \mathbf{H}_{t+1}^i \times ||P_t^{*,2}(X_t^i) - Y_{t+1}^i||_2,
\end{aligned} \tag{9}
$$

where $\mathbf{H}_t = [\gamma_{t,1}, \cdots, \gamma_{t,s}, \cdots, \gamma_{t,S}]$ is an indicator matrix that denotes whether X_t is labeled with clinical scores or not. To be specific, $\gamma_{t,s}^i = 1$ if the ground-true score $y_{t,s}^i$ is available for X_t^i; and $\gamma_{t,s}^i = 0$, otherwise. Finally, the adversarial loss of LDGAN with multiple time points is defined as:

$$
\mathcal{L} = \sum_{t=1}^{T} \mathcal{L}(DG_t^1, DG_t^2) + \mathcal{L}(D_t^1, D_t^2) + \eta_t R(DG_t^1, DG_t^2), \tag{10}
$$

where η_t is the penalty coefficient for the t-th time point. In the implementation, we first train D_t and DG_t with fixed predictors, iteratively. After that, we jointly train the generator and predictor in DG_t. The Adam solver is used as the optimizer, with a batch size of 2 and a learning rate of 0.001.

3   Experiment

Data and Experimental Setup. We evaluated LDGAN on subjects with longitudinal MRI from ADNI [15], including ADNI-1 and ADNI-2. Our goal is to predict three types of clinical scores at four time points, i.e., Baseline, the 6th month (M06), 12th month (M12), and 24th month (M24) after baseline. These clinical sores include: 1) clinical dementia rating sum of boxes (CDR-SB), 2) classic AD assessment scale cognitive subscale with 11 items (ADAS-Cog11), and 3) modified ADAS-Cog with 13 items (ADAS-Cog13). After removing subjects that exist in both ADNI-1 and ADNI-2 from ADNI-2, we obtain a total of 824 and 637 subjects from ADNI-1 and ADNI-2, respectively. All studied subjects have baseline MRI data, and only a part of them have M06/M12/M24 MRI data. The number of MRIs and clinical scores of studied subjects are summarized in the *Supplementary Materials*. For all MRI scans, we performed skull-stripping, intensity correction and spatial normalization. Hence, there is spatial correspondence between a set of MRIs at different time points for each subject. ADNI-1 and ADNI-2 are used as training and test sets, respectively.

Performance of MRI Generation. We first evaluate the quality of synthetic MR images generated by our LDGAN and two classical GAN models, i.e., 1) a conventional GAN [16], and 2) the cycle-consistent GAN (CGAN) [17]. It's worthy mentioning that the structures of GAN and CGAN are modified for 3D-input version based on [16] and [17]. Three metrics are used to measure the quality of generated images, including the mean absolute error (MAE), peak signal-to-noise ratio (PSNR), and structural similarity index measure (SSIM) [18]. All models are trained and tested based on the same datasets, namely, subjects in ADNI-1 for training, and subjects in ADNI-2 for testing. The quantitative results are listed in Table 1, from which one can observe that our LDGAN consistently outperforms the competing methods in terms of three metrics at all four time points. We further visually show real and synthetic MR images of a randomly-selected subject from ADNI-2 at four time points in Fig. 4. As can be seen from Fig. 4, our synthetic MR images look more similar to their corresponding real images when compared with other two models. These results demonstrate that our method can generate reasonable longitudinal MRI scans.

Table 1. Comparison of different methods in longitudinal MR image generation at four time points, in terms of MAE (%), SSIM (%), and PSNR.

Method	Baseline			M06			M12			M24		
	MAE	SSIM	PSNR	MAE	SSIM	PSNR	MAE	SSIM	PSNR	MAE	SSIM	PSNR
GAN	4.17	59.38	23.46	4.89	57.66	22.77	4.75	54.22	21.52	8.93	50.77	20.47
CGAN	3.78	62.43	25.83	4.33	58.75	25.62	4.59	54.72	25.04	8.24	51.49	21.42
LDGAN (Ours)	**2.45**	**66.65**	**28.82**	**3.14**	**60.81**	**27.19**	**3.53**	**56.91**	**26.42**	**6.39**	**54.04**	**21.60**

Table 2. Comparison of different methods in predicting three types of clinical scores at four time points using the same ADNI-1 and ADNI-2 datasets, in terms of RMSE.

Method	Baseline			M06		
	CDR-SB	ADAS-Cog11	ADAS-Cog13	CDR-SB	ADAS-Cog11	ADAS-Cog13
LMF [19]	1.922	5.835	8.286	2.394	7.640	10.060
WiseDNN [7]	1.619	5.662	**7.596**	2.016	6.238	8.649
LDGAN (Ours)	**1.572**	**4.980**	7.739	**1.986**	**6.008**	**8.380**
Method	M12			M24		
	CDR-SB	ADAS-Cog11	ADAS-Cog13	CDR-SB	ADAS-Cog11	ADAS-Cog13
LMF [19]	2.694	8.140	10.060	4.009	11.145	14.324
WiseDNN [7]	2.442	7.300	9.888	3.412	9.410	11.177
LDGAN (Ours)	**1.859**	**6.014**	**8.609**	**2.077**	**8.160**	**8.502**

Performance of Longitudinal Diagnosis. We further evaluate the performance of the proposed LDGAN in predicting three types of clinical scores (CDR-SB, ADAS-Cog11, and ADAS-Cog13) at four time points. We compare our model with two state-of-the-art methods, including 1) a model using landmark-based morphological features (LMF) [19], and 2) WiseDNN [7]. Note that LMF and WiseDNN use only baseline MRIs for longitudinal prediction, while our LDGAN

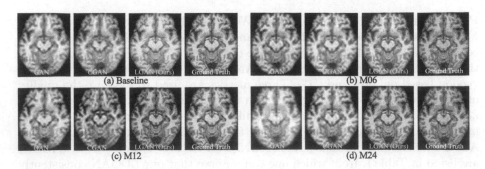

Fig. 4. Illustration of synthetic images generated by three methods and their corresponding ground-truth images at four time points for a subject from ADNI-2.

can use all available MRIs at multiple time points. For a fair comparison, these three methods are trained on ADNI-1 and tested on ADNI-2. The root mean square error (RMSE) is used to evaluate the effectiveness of all methods, with results reported in Table 2. From Table 2, we can observe that, in most cases, the proposed LDGAN obtains the best performance when compared with two competing methods, implying that generating prediction-oriented MRIs (as we do in LDGAN) helps promote the performance of longitudinal prediction.

4   Conclusion

In this work, we propose a longitudinal-diagnostic generative adversarial network (LDGAN) to predict multiple clinical scores at future time points using incomplete longitudinal MRI data. Specifically, LDGAN imputes MR images by jointly learning a bi-directional mapping between MRIs of two adjacent time points and performing clinical score prediction. In addition, the proposed LDGAN is armed with a temporal constraint and an output constraint to encourage the temporal consistency of MRIs at adjacent time points and the output consistency of predicted clinical scores, respectively. To make use of subjects without ground-truth clinical scores at a certain time point, we further design a weighted loss function to train LDGAN. Experimental results demonstrate that LDGAN can generate more reasonable MRI scans and efficiently predict longitudinal clinical scores.

References

1. Frisoni, G.B., Fox, N.C., Jack, C.R., Scheltens, P., Thompson, P.M.: The clinical use of structural MRI in Alzheimer disease. Nat. Rev. Neurol. **6**(2), 67–77 (2010)
2. Yuan, L., Wang, Y., Thompson, P.M., Narayan, V.A., Ye, J.: Multi-source feature learning for joint analysis of incomplete multiple heterogeneous neuroimaging data. NeuroImage **61**(3), 622–632 (2012)
3. Liu, M., Zhang, D., Shen, D.: Relationship induced multi-template learning for diagnosis of Alzheimer's disease and mild cognitive impairment. IEEE Trans. Med. Imaging **35**(6), 1463–1474 (2016)

4. Cheng, B., Liu, M., Shen, D., Li, Z., Zhang, D.: Multi-domain transfer learning for early diagnosis of Alzheimer's disease. Neuroinformatics 15(2), 115–132 (2017)
5. Liu, M., Zhang, J., Adeli, E., Shen, D.: Landmark-based deep multi-instance learning for brain disease diagnosis. Med. Image Anal. 43, 157–168 (2018)
6. Lei, B., Jiang, F., Chen, S., Ni, D., Wang, T.: Longitudinal analysis for disease progression via simultaneous multi-relational temporal-fused learning. Front. Aging Neurosci. 9(6), 1–6 (2017)
7. Liu, M., Zhang, J., Lian, C., Shen, D.: Weakly supervised deep learning for brain disease prognosis using MRI and incomplete clinical scores. IEEE Trans. Cybern. 50(7), 3381–3392 (2020)
8. Weiner, M.W., et al.: The Alzheimer's disease neuroimaging initiative: a review of papers published since its inception. Alzheimer's Dement. 9(5), e111–e194 (2013)
9. Jiang, P., Wang, X., Li, Q., Jin, L., Li, S.: Correlation-aware sparse and low-rank constrained multi-task learning for longitudinal analysis of Alzheimer's disease. IEEE J. Biomed. Health Inform. 23(4), 1450–1456 (2018)
10. Ritter, K., Schumacher, J., Weygandt, M., Buchert, R., Allefeld, C., Haynes, J.D.: Multimodal prediction of conversion to Alzheimer's disease based on incomplete biomarkers. Alzheimer's Dement.: Diagn. Assess. Dis. Monit. 1(2), 206–215 (2015)
11. Pan, Y., Liu, M., Lian, C., Zhou, T., Xia, Y., Shen, D.: Synthesizing missing PET from MRI with cycle-consistent generative adversarial networks for Alzheimer's disease diagnosis. In: Frangi, A.F., Schnabel, J.A., Davatzikos, C., Alberola-López, C., Fichtinger, G. (eds.) MICCAI 2018. LNCS, vol. 11072, pp. 455–463. Springer, Cham (2018). https://doi.org/10.1007/978-3-030-00931-1_52
12. Beason-Held, L.L., O Goh, J., An, Y., A Kraut, M., J O'Brien, R., Ferrucci, L.: A longitudinal study of brain anatomy changes preceding dementia in down syndromechanges in brain function occur years before the onset of cognitive impairment. J. Neurosci. 33(46), 18008–18014 (2013)
13. Jie, B., Liu, M., Liu, J., Zhang, D., Shen, D.: Temporally constrained group sparse learning for longitudinal data analysis in Alzheimer's disease. IEEE Trans. Biomed. Eng. 64(1), 238–249 (2016)
14. Pujol, J., et al.: A longitudinal study of brain anatomy changes preceding dementia in down syndrome. NeuroImage Clin. 18, 160–166 (2018)
15. Jack, C., Bernstein, M., Fox, N., et al.: The Alzheimer's disease neuroimaging initiative (ADNI): MRI methods. J. Magn. Reson. Imaging 27(4), 685–691 (2008)
16. Goodfellow, I., et al.: Generative adversarial nets. In: Advances in Neural Information Processing Systems, pp. 2672–2680 (2014)
17. Zhu, J.Y., Park, T., Isola, P., Efros, A.A.: Unpaired image-to-image translation using cycle-consistent adversarial networks. In: Proceedings of the IEEE International Conference on Computer Vision, pp. 2223–2232 (2017)
18. Hore, A., Ziou, D.: Image quality metrics: PSNR vs. SSIM. In: International Conference on Pattern Recognition, pp. 2366–2369. IEEE (2010)
19. Zhang, J., Liu, M., An, L., Gao, Y., Shen, D.: Alzheimer's disease diagnosis using landmark-based features from longitudinal structural MR images. IEEE J. Biomed. Health Inform. 21(6), 1607–1616 (2017)

Unsupervised MRI Homogenization: Application to Pediatric Anterior Visual Pathway Segmentation

Carlos Tor-Diez[1]([envelope]), Antonio Reyes Porras[1], Roger J. Packer[2,3], Robert A. Avery[4], and Marius George Linguraru[1,5]

[1] Sheikh Zayed Institute for Pediatric Surgical Innovation, Children's National Hospital, Washington, DC 20010, USA
ctordez@childrensnational.org
[2] Center for Neuroscience& Behavioral Health, Children's National Hospital, Washington, DC 20010, USA
[3] Gilbert Neurofibromatosis Institute, Children's National Hospital, Washington, DC 20010, USA
[4] Division of Pediatric Ophthalmology, Children's Hospital of Philadelphia, Philadelphia, PA 19104, USA
[5] School of Medicine and Health Sciences, George Washington University, Washington, DC 20037, USA

Abstract. Deep learning strategies have become ubiquitous optimization tools for medical image analysis. With the appropriate amount of data, these approaches outperform classic methodologies in a variety of image processing tasks. However, rare diseases and pediatric imaging often lack extensive data. Specially, MRI are uncommon because they require sedation in young children. Moreover, the lack of standardization in MRI protocols introduces a strong variability between different datasets. In this paper, we present a general deep learning architecture for MRI homogenization that also provides the segmentation map of an anatomical region of interest. Homogenization is achieved using an unsupervised architecture based on variational autoencoder with cycle generative adversarial networks, which learns a common space (i.e. a representation of the optimal imaging protocol) using an unpaired image-to-image translation network. The segmentation is simultaneously generated by a supervised learning strategy. We evaluated our method segmenting the challenging anterior visual pathway using three brain T1-weighted MRI datasets (variable protocols and vendors). Our method significantly outperformed a non-homogenized multi-protocol U-Net.

Keywords: MRI homogenization · Brain MRI segmentation · Deep learning

1 Introduction

Magnetic resonance imaging (MRI) provides anatomical information of soft tissues in a non-ionizing and non-invasive way. However, MRI intensities may lack interpretability

© Springer Nature Switzerland AG 2020
M. Liu et al. (Eds.): MLMI 2020, LNCS 12436, pp. 180–188, 2020.
https://doi.org/10.1007/978-3-030-59861-7_19

because they do not have a tissue specific unit. MRI units are dependent on the provider and protocol criteria, thus challenging the application of image segmentation and classification techniques. For example, the authors [1], obtained an error of 12,50% classifying MRI without homogenization. Therefore, normalizing MRI intensities is critical. As presented in [2], there are two types of intensity correction approaches: based on the properties of the MRI machine, and based on the imaged object. The first is focused on finding the static field inhomogeneity by testing different coils or calibrating with phantoms. The second consists of giving a standard unit to observed tissues. Despite its difficulty, the general preference in the literature is for the second approach, since it does not need additional acquisitions and steers to a more general solution.

Most MRI intensity normalization methods are based on histogram-matching techniques [3–5]. These methods usually use expensive preprocessing steps to make the histogram mapping structurally meaningful, such as non-rigid registration or patch-based approaches [6, 7]. Alternatively, Shinohara et al. [8] proposed a list of principles for defining biologically interpretable units and defined an efficient pipeline procedure with several simple steps. Deep learning has also been recently introduced to the MR homogenization. In [9], they applied several networks based on U-Net [10] to segment different structures. These networks were used to learn a subject-based histogram mapping, leading to a non-parametric normalization MRI method. In [11], authors replaced the popular MRI bias field correction, i.e., ITKN4 [12], by an artificial neural network. Finally, Jacobsen et al. [13] presented an evaluation of four intensity normalization methods based on their segmentation performance using a 3D fully convolutional neural network. These methods lack a general function that maps different input domains to a common space.

A few recent methods have presented neural networks to perform unsupervised image-to-image translation [14–16]. Liu et al. [14] introduced the concept of shared-latent space into the unpaired translation, which is a common space between datasets. In [15], they presented an efficient network called CycleGAN that avoids the common space by introducing cycle consistency. Using generative adversarial networks (GAN), this approach maps one image to another domain and re-maps this estimated image to the original space. In the UNIT architecture [16], the authors extended [14] by adding a variational autoencoder (VAE)— that helped learning the shared-latent space. In the medical image context, these techniques were used to synthesize images from one modality or sequence to another, such as synthesizing CT from and to MRI [17, 18] or T1- and T2-weighted MR images [19]. However, these works did not optimize the imaging protocol to a particular task.

Nevertheless, the amount of harmonization methods for diffusion-weighted MRI (dMRI) was recently rising [20–23]. The application of machine learning techniques improve the traditional methods and cope the re-projection of spherical harmonics basis, a common representation for dMRI. In [23], authors implemented a network based on residual network, obtaining harmonized images. Moyer et al. [22] presented a VAE in order to split the inter-scanner variability from the subject anatomy and be able to reconstruct it to any scanner protocol, similarly to the first part of UNIT [16]. In [21], they were focused on applying recent deep network blocks such as the multi-task learning to increase the algorithm effectiveness. Although all these methods present promising results, they lack for a specific application such as segmentation or registration. In addition, their application to conventional MRI scans, such as T1w or T2w, still have to be evaluated for future works. One example of this transition was presented in [29], reformulating the dMRI method [20] based on linear regression and empirical Bayes.

In this paper, we present an unsupervised network for general multi-protocol MRI homogenization to find the mapping of all images to a new and common protocol. We apply this novel concept to the challenging segmentation of the anterior visual pathway (AVP), which is thin (thickness around 2-3 mm), long and amorphous as it contains the chiasm, optic nerves and optic tracks. In addition, the AVP has variable shape between subjects and patients with disease, and shows poor contrast with respect to adjacent tissues. Without surprise, there are only a few methods designed to segment the AVP and they have struggled to be accurate [24–26], in part because they lack a robust multi-protocol strategy for segmentation. This is particularly challenging when datasets are small, which is the case of AVP images and pediatric applications in general.

We use our method to quantify the AVP, which is critical for the diagnosis, prediction and treatment of children with optic pathway glioma who are at risk for vision loss. Given the rare but serious nature of these gliomas, imaging data are very limited as patients are seen by different institutions using variable MRI protocols. Hence, we propose a novel approach to synthetize a common domain (intuitively representing an optimal MRI protocol) from limited and variable imaging data. The limitations of data availability is handled by orienting the brain MRI from different protocols that can be reliably read by the human observer to a common direction that can be accurately interpreted by a deep learning network. Thus, our main methodological contribution is the creation of an unpaired image-to-image network to synthesize a new common protocol that is concurrently optimized to perform an image analysis task, which in our example is the segmentation of the AVP. Based on UNIT [16], we generalize the number of input datasets, leading to increased combinations of intermediate results and therefore of the complexity of the cycle consistency. We handle this complexity with a new loss function that leverages the extra number of inputs to perform a more efficient training. In addition, the segmentation sub-network is directly connected to the common space provided by the VAE, thus training for one single domain while the network has multi-domain inputs. The general nature of our approach makes it applicable to other image analysis tasks that benefit from consistency in imaging protocols.

2   Method

2.1   Unsupervised Image-to-Image Translation (UNIT)

The UNIT deep-learning architecture [16] consists of two parts: one that creates a common space between image domains, and another that reconstructs each domain from the common space. The first part allows building a shared-latent space that finds the common features of the input datasets. The reconstruction part is made of different GANs for each input image domain that generate the reconstruction of each input dataset space from the shared-latent space.

UNIT was designed as a method to translate two datasets, or two protocols in our case. Let $\mathcal{X}_1$ and $\mathcal{X}_2$ be two MRI protocols. The goal of the unsupervised method is to find the joint distribution $P_{\mathcal{X}_1 \mathcal{X}_2}(x_1, x_2)$ with marginals $P_{\mathcal{X}_1}(x_1)$ and $P_{\mathcal{X}_2}(x_2)$. This step assumes that a variable z in a shared-latent space $\mathcal{Z}$ can represent both inputs with the same code and that both can be recovered separately. Let E_1 and E_2 be the encoders that map $\mathcal{X}_1$ and $\mathcal{X}_2$ to $\mathcal{Z}$. Then, we can reconstruct $\mathcal{X}_1$ and $\mathcal{X}_2$ from $\mathcal{Z}$ by a combination of a decoder and a generator. Given the G_1 and G_2 networks that generate $\mathcal{X}_1$ and $\mathcal{X}_2$ from $\mathcal{Z}$, the architecture uses adversarial discriminators, D_1 and D_2, to optimize the loss function $\mathcal{L}$ by a minimax game:

$$\arg \min_{E_1, E_2, G_1, G_2} \max_{D_1, D_2} L_{UNIT}(E_1, E_2, G_1, G_2, D_1, D_2) \tag{1}$$

At this stage, the architecture is equivalent to a classic autoencoder. Then, the architecture combines the sub-networks of different domains to create map functions that switch from one space to another. Let $F_{1\to 2}$ and $F_{2\to 1}$ be the mapping functions that map $\mathcal{X}_1$ to $\mathcal{X}_2$ and $\mathcal{X}_2$ to $\mathcal{X}_1$, respectively. These functions are defined by mixing the encoder and generator sub-networks of different domains, i.e. $F_{1\to 2} = G_2(E_1(.))$ and $F_{2\to 1} = G_1(E_2(.))$. By applying cycle consistency [15], the loss function terms $\mathcal{L}_{CC_1}$ and $\mathcal{L}_{CC_2}$ are computed such as $x_1 = F_{2\to 1}(F_{1\to 2}(x_2))$ and $x_2 = F_{1\to 2}(F_{2\to 1}(x_1))$, respectively.

Then, the loss function can be expressed as follows:

$$\begin{aligned}
\mathcal{L}_{UNIT} = &\mathcal{L}_{VAE_1}(E_1, G_1) + \mathcal{L}_{GAN_1}(E_1, G_1, D_1) + \mathcal{L}_{CC_1}(E_1, G_1, E_2, G_2) \\
&+ \mathcal{L}_{VAE_2}(E_2, G_2) + \mathcal{L}_{GAN_2}(E_2, G_2, D_2) + \mathcal{L}_{CC_2}(E_2, G_2, E_1, G_1).
\end{aligned} \tag{2}$$

2.2 Generalized UNIT (G-UNIT)

The UNIT architecture is limited to two image domains, and to translating these domains into each other. However, MRI data often originate from multiple protocols, which would involve retraining the shared-latent space $\mathcal{Z}$ for each new data domain. We propose a more efficient alternative to expand the network by including n datasets and allowing the simultaneous training of $\mathcal{Z}$ for all protocols. Thus, in G-UNIT, we generalize the loss function from Eq. (2) as follows:

$$\mathcal{L}_{G-UNIT} = \sum_{i=1}^{n} \mathcal{L}_{VAE_i}(E_i, G_i) + \mathcal{L}_{GAN_i}(E_i, G_i, D_i) + \mathcal{L}_{CC_i}(E_1, G_1, \ldots, E_n, G_n). \tag{3}$$

In addition, we introduce an initialization loss in the G-UNIT network. Since the image synthesis performance depend only on the loss cycle consistency term, the network does not optimize the latent space for the application as mentioned in [18]. If we consider that all our data are commonly oriented, the images from the same protocol should share the same contrast. To optimize the latent space for the application of the network, we add a term in the loss function that regularizes the image synthesis. Given an input image x_j acquired with the j-protocol, we implement the correlation coefficient loss function as follows:

$$\mathcal{L}_{init}(E_1, G_1, \ldots, E_n, G_n) = -\sum_{i=1}^{n} \sum_{j=1, j\neq i}^{n} \frac{(\hat{x}_{ij} - m_{x_{ij}})(x_j - m_{x_j})}{\sqrt{(\hat{x}_{ij} - m_{\hat{x}_{ij}})^2 (x_j - m_{x_j})^2}} \tag{4}$$

Where $\hat{x}_{ij}$ is the estimated j-protocol for image x_i, $\hat{x}_{ij} = G_j(E_i(x_i))$, and $m_{\hat{x}_{ij}}$ and m_{x_i} are the mean intensity of $\hat{x}_{ij}$ and x_j, respectively.

2.3 Generalized UNIT for Segmentation (G-UNIT-S)

To incorporate the segmentation into G-UNIT and use the homogenized and optimized MRI protocol, we apply the segmentation directly to the shared-latent space $\mathcal{Z}$. This allows our method to train only one sub-network for segmentation, making it robust against inter-protocol variations and allowing the use of the entire data pool for training. For this purpose, we propose a GAN to map the shared-latent space $\mathcal{Z}$ to the segmentation space $\mathcal{S}$ and we implement a segmentation cycle consistency term to train the shared-latent space toward the optimal protocol representation. Since $\mathcal{S}$ and $\mathcal{Z}$ are trained simultaneously, we assume that the creation of $\mathcal{Z}$ is optimized for the generation of $\mathcal{S}$, i.e. $\mathcal{Z}$ contains the representation of the optimal protocol for segmentation. Let G_S be the generator of segmentations that maps from the common space $\mathcal{Z}$ and D_S the discriminator. The loss function of the GAN is:

$$\mathcal{L}_S(G_S, D_S) = \mathcal{L}_{GAN_S}(G_S, D_S) + \mathcal{L}_{CC_S}(G_S, D_S) \tag{5}$$

Finally, the loss function of the G-UNIT-S method (Fig. 1) is:

$$\mathcal{L}_{G-UNIT\text{-}S}(E_1, G_1, \ldots, E_n, G_n, G_S, D_S) =$$
$$\mathcal{L}_{G-UNIT}(E_1, G_1, \ldots, E_n, G_n) + \lambda\mathcal{L}_{init}(E_1, G_1, \ldots, E_n, G_n) + \mathcal{L}_S(G_S, D_S) \tag{6}$$

where $\lambda = 1$ for the first epoch, and $\lambda = 0$ otherwise.

3   Experiments and Results

3.1   Data

Our approach is evaluated on multi-protocol brain MRI-data from three datasets. These datasets were acquired at three different centers: Children's National Hospital (CNH), Children's Hospital of Philadelphia (CHOP) and Children's Hospital of Colorado (CHC). Each center used a specific protocol and imaging device for all its acquisitions. More details about the imaging parameters are shown in Table 1.

3.2   Experiments and Results

As shown in Table 1, each dataset has a different acquisition plane and image resolution, which represents is an additional challenge to automate image analysis. We used rigid image registration to standardize the resolution between datasets, defining arbitrarily, the protocol with the highest resolution (CNH) as a reference. As a result, all images has a size of ($372 \times 324 \times 363$).

For training G-UNIT-S, datasets from each protocol have the same number of images, thus avoiding a skew in the generator bias. For our experiments, we used 18 3D T1-weighted MRIs, six from each clinical center, i.e., CNH, CHOP and CHC. The experiments are then performed by cross-validation using the leave-one-patient-out from each

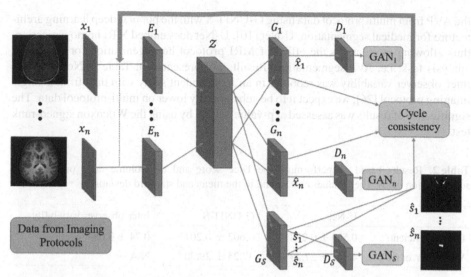

Fig. 1. Schematics of our proposed network G-UNIT-S. We consider n images $(x_1, \ldots, x_n)$ from protocols $\mathcal{X}_1, \ldots, \mathcal{X}_n$. $E_1, \ldots, E_n$ are the encoders that map to the shared-latent space $\mathcal{Z}$. The generators $G_1, \ldots, G_n$ reconstruct the image to the desired protocol. In addition, $G_{\mathcal{S}}$ generates the segmentation from $\mathcal{Z}$, i.e. for every protocol. With them, we can generate the reconstructions image $(\hat{x}_1, \ldots, \hat{x}_n)$, other protocols $(\hat{x}_{1j}, \ldots, \hat{x}_{nj})$ or segmentations $(\hat{s}_1, \ldots, \hat{s}_n)$. $D_1, \ldots, D_n$ and $D_{\mathcal{S}}$ are adversarial discriminators that regularize the results to be more realistic. All sub-networks are implemented as in [16].

Table 1. Properties of data used for our experiments grouped by acquisition center. TR- repetition time; TE- echo time.

Clinical Center	MRI Manufacturer	Acquisition Plane	TR/TE (ms)	Slice thickness (mm)	In-plane resolution (mm^2)
CNH	General Electric	Axial	600/10.5	0.60	0.41 × 0.41
CHOP	Siemens	Sagittal	1900/2.5	0.90	0.82 × 0.82
CHC	Philips	Coronal	8.3/3.8	1.00	0.94 × 0.94

protocol strategy. To train our network, we used 100 slices for each 3D image. Therefore, we used 1,500 inputs and 25 epochs per each training in the cross-validation.

We used the Wasserstein distance with the gradient penalty variant [23] to train our network, which ensures stability to the training process. Data were post processed to keep only the largest component of the segmentation and remove small areas of false positives. We evaluated the reconstructed (after using cycle consistency) and the ground-truth images using the mean absolute square difference, and we used the Dice coefficient and the volume error to evaluate the segmentations. We compared the segmentation of the AVP from multi-protocol data using G-UNIT-S with the popular deep learning architecture for medical segmentation, U-Net [10]. U-Net does embed MRI homogenization, thus allowing us to assess the effect of MRI protocol homogenization for the image analysis task, i.e. AVP segmentation. Results are presented in Table 2. Note that the inter-observer variability was reported in an independent study with data from a single imaging protocol [26]; we expect it to be substantially lower on multi-protocol data. The significance of results was assessed at p-value ≈ 0.05 by using the Wilcoxon signed-rank test.

Table 2. Results based on performing the Dice score and the volume error on estimated segmentation maps. These values correspond to the mean and standard deviation.

	U-Net	G-UNIT-S	Inter-observer variability
Dice coefficient	0.509 ± 0.223	0.602 ± 0.201	0.74 ± 0.08
Volume error (%)	$46.51 \pm 27.23\%$	$37.25 \pm 29.30\%$	N\A

G-UNIT-S significantly outperformed the U-Net network using images from small datasets of variable acquisition protocols. Moreover, since the AVP does not have a stable contrast in MRI and its structure is thin and small, this improvement is still far from the inter-observer variability. A shortcoming of our approach is the limited data used for training the network. However, this is not uncommon in rare diseases where clinical consortia are distributed over multiple clinical centers. In addition, the segmentation of AVP is challenging due to the shape and appearance of this anatomical structure. Our experiments indicate that multi-protocol image homogenization is essential for optimizing challenging image analysis tasks, and can significantly improve segmentation even for small datasets (Fig. 2).

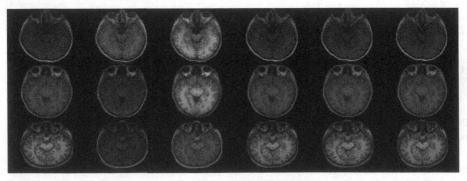

Fig. 2. Visual representation of results. From left to right: the original image, its transformation to other two protocols, the ground-truth segmentation and automated segmentations by U-Net and G-UNIT-S. From up to down: CNH, CHOP and CHC protocols.

4 Conclusion

We presented a general deep network architecture that homogenizes different imaging protocols, and optimizes their common representation for an image analysis task. We demonstrated its application with using brain MRI and anterior visual pathway segmentation. Our network, called G-UNIT-S, was designed to homogenize any number of datasets, which is critical for the analysis of small datasets that are acquired by multiple clinical centers using different imaging devices and protocols. G-UNIT-S also incorporates an extension to segment the AVP based on the representation of a new, optimized image protocol. This extension can be expanded to general image analysis applications. Our results demonstrated that G-UNIT-S significantly improves an image analysis task over the popular U-Net. In future work, we will incorporate different modalities of MRI such as the T2-weighted and FLAIR to provide complementary information about the AVP anatomy.

References

1. Collewet, G., Strzelecki, M., Mariette, F.: Influence of MRI acquisition protocols and image intensity normalization methods on texture classification. Magn. Reson. Imaging **22**, 81–91 (2004)
2. Vovk, U., Pernus, F., Likar, B.: A review of methods for correction of intensity inhomogeneity in MRI. IEEE Trans. Med. Imaging **26**, 405–421 (2007)
3. Nyul, L.G., Udupa, J.K., Zhang, X.: New variants of a method of MRI scale standardization. IEEE Trans. Med. Imaging **19**, 143–150 (2000)
4. Shah, M., et al.: Evaluating intensity normalization on MRIs of human brain with multiple sclerosis. Med. Image Anal. **15**, 267–282 (2011)
5. Sun, X., Shi, L., Luo, Y., Yang, W., Li, H., Liang, P., et al.: Histogram-based normalization technique on human brain magnetic resonance images from different acquisitions. BioMed. Eng. OnLine. **14**, 73 (2015)
6. Jager, F., Hornegger, J.: Nonrigid registration of joint histograms for intensity standardization in magnetic resonance imaging. IEEE Trans. Med. Imaging **28**, 137–150 (2009)
7. Roy, S., Carass, A., Prince, J.L.: Patch based intensity normalization of brain MR images. In: 2013 IEEE 10th International Symposium on Biomedical Imaging, pp. 342–345. IEEE (2013)
8. Shinohara, R.T., et al.: Statistical normalization techniques for magnetic resonance imaging. Neuroimage Clin. **6**, 9–19 (2014)
9. Zhang, J., Saha, A., Soher, B.J., Mazurowski, M.A.: Automatic deep learning-based normalization of breast dynamic contrast-enhanced magnetic resonance images. (2018), arXiv:1807.02152 [cs]
10. Ronneberger, O., Fischer, P., Brox, T.: U-Net: convolutional networks for biomedical image segmentation. In: Navab, N., Hornegger, J., Wells, W.M., Frangi, A.F. (eds.) MICCAI 2015. LNCS, vol. 9351, pp. 234–241. Springer, Cham (2015). https://doi.org/10.1007/978-3-319-24574-4_28
11. Simkó, A., Löfstedt, T., Garpebring, A., Nyholm, T., Jonsson, J.: A Generalized Network for MRI Intensity Normalization. (2019), arXiv:1909.05484 [eess]
12. Tustison, N.J., et al.: N4ITK: improved N3 bias correction. IEEE Trans. Med. Imaging **29**, 1310–1320 (2010)

13. Jacobsen, N., Deistung, A., Timmann, D., Goericke, S.L., Reichenbach, J.R., Güllmar, D.: Analysis of intensity normalization for optimal segmentation performance of a fully convolutional neural network. Z. Med. Phys. **29**, 128–138 (2019)
14. Liu, M.-Y., Tuzel, O.: Coupled generative adversarial networks. In: Advances in Neural Information Processing Systems, Curran Associates, Inc. **29**, pp. 469–477 (2016)
15. Zhu, J.-Y., Park, T., Isola, P., Efros, A.A.: Unpaired image-to-image translation using cycle-consistent adversarial networks. In: Presented at the Proceedings of the IEEE International Conference on Computer Vision, IEEE (2017)
16. Liu, M.-Y., Breuel, T., Kautz, J.: Unsupervised image-to-image translation networks. In: Advances in Neural Information Processing Systems, Curran Associates, Inc. **30**, pp. 700–708 (2017)
17. Wolterink, J.M., Dinkla, A.M., Savenije, M.H.F., Seevinck, P.R., van den Berg, C.A.T., Išgum, I.: Deep MR to CT synthesis using unpaired data. In: Tsaftaris, S.A., Gooya, A., Frangi, A.F., Prince, J.L. (eds.) SASHIMI 2017. LNCS, vol. 10557, pp. 14–23. Springer, Cham (2017). https://doi.org/10.1007/978-3-319-68127-6_2
18. Yang, H., et al.: Unpaired brain MR-to-CT synthesis using a structure-constrained cycleGAN. In: Stoyanov, D., et al. (eds.) DLMIA/ML-CDS -2018. LNCS, vol. 11045, pp. 174–182. Springer, Cham (2018). https://doi.org/10.1007/978-3-030-00889-5_20
19. Welander, P., Karlsson, S., Eklund, A.: Generative Adversarial Networks for Image-to-Image Translation on Multi-Contrast MR Images - A Comparison of CycleGAN and UNIT. (2018), arXiv:1806.07777 [cs]
20. Fortin, J.-P., et al.: Harmonization of multi-site diffusion tensor imaging data. NeuroImage. **161**, 149–170 (2017)
21. Blumberg, S.B., Palombo, M., Khoo, C.S., Tax, C.M.W., Tanno, R., Alexander, D.C.: Multi-stage prediction networks for data harmonization. In: Shen, D., et al. (eds.) MICCAI 2019. LNCS, vol. 11767, pp. 411–419. Springer, Cham (2019). https://doi.org/10.1007/978-3-030-32251-9_45
22. Moyer, D., Steeg, G.V., Tax, C.M.W., Thompson, P.M.: Scanner invariant representations for diffusion MRI harmonization. Magnetic Resonance in Medicine, (2020)
23. Koppers, S., Bloy, L., Berman, J.I., Tax, C.M.W., Edgar, J.C., Merhof, D.: Spherical harmonic residual network for diffusion signal harmonization. In: Bonet-Carne, E., Grussu, F., Ning, L., Sepehrband, F., Tax, C.M.W. (eds.) MICCAI 2019. MV, pp. 173–182. Springer, Cham (2019). https://doi.org/10.1007/978-3-030-05831-9_14
24. Noble, J.H., Dawant, B.M.: An atlas-navigated optimal medial axis and deformable model algorithm (NOMAD) for the segmentation of the optic nerves and chiasm in MR and CT images. Med. Image Anal. **15**, 877–884 (2011)
25. Yang, X., et al.: Weighted partitioned active shape model for optic pathway segmentation in MRI. In: Linguraru, M.G., et al. (eds.) CLIP 2014. LNCS, vol. 8680, pp. 109–117. Springer, Cham (2014). https://doi.org/10.1007/978-3-319-13909-8_14
26. Mansoor, A., et al.: Deep learning guided partitioned shape model for anterior visual pathway segmentation. IEEE Trans. Med. Imaging **35**, 1856–1865 (2016)
27. Gulrajani, I., Ahmed, F., Arjovsky, M., Dumoulin, V., Courville, A.C.: Improved training of wasserstein GANs. In: Advances in Neural Information Processing Systems, Curran Associates, Inc. **30**, pp. 5767–5777 (2017)
28. Fortin, J.-P., et al.: Harmonization of cortical thickness measurements across scanners and sites. NeuroImage. **167**, 104–120 (2018)

Boundary-Aware Network for Kidney Tumor Segmentation

Shishuai Hu[1,2], Jianpeng Zhang[2], and Yong Xia[1,2(✉)]

[1] Research & Development Institute of Northwestern Polytechnical University
in Shenzhen, Shenzhen 518057, China
yxia@nwpu.edu.cn
[2] National Engineering Laboratory for Integrated Aero-Space-Ground-Ocean Big
Data Application Technology, School of Computer Science and Engineering,
Northwestern Polytechnical University, Xi'an 710072, China

Abstract. Segmentation of the kidney and kidney tumors using computed tomography (CT) is a crucial step in related surgical procedures. Although many deep learning models have been constructed to solve this problem, most of them ignore the boundary information. In this paper, we propose a boundary-aware network (BA-Net) for kidney and kidney tumor segmentation. This model consists of a shared 3D encoder, a 3D boundary decoder, and a 3D segmentation decoder. In contrast to existing boundary-involved methods, we first introduce the skip connections from the boundary decoder to the segmentation decoder, incorporating the boundary prior as the attention that indicates the error-prone regions into the segmentation process, and then define the consistency loss to push both decoders towards producing the same result. Besides, we also use the strategies of multi-scale input and deep supervision to extract hierarchical structural information, which can alleviate the issues caused by variable tumor sizes. We evaluated the proposed BA-Net on the kidney tumor segmentation challenge (KiTS19) dataset. The results suggest that the boundary decoder and consistency loss used in our model are effective and the BA-Net is able to produce relatively accurate segmentation of the kidney and kidney tumors.

Keywords: Kidney and kidney tumor segmentation · Boundary detection · Deep learning · Computed tomography.

1 Introduction

Kidney tumor is one of the most deadly tumors in human urinary system [1]. Surgical removal of kidney tumors is regarded as curative, which generally relies on the accurate segmentation of kidneys and the tumors on contrast-enhanced abdominal CT images [2,5]. Since performing this segmentation task manually requires high concentration and expertise and is time-consuming and prone to operator-related bias, automated segmentation approaches are highly demanded to reduce the workloads and improve the efficiencies of medical professionals [7].

© Springer Nature Switzerland AG 2020
M. Liu et al. (Eds.): MLMI 2020, LNCS 12436, pp. 189–198, 2020.
https://doi.org/10.1007/978-3-030-59861-7_20

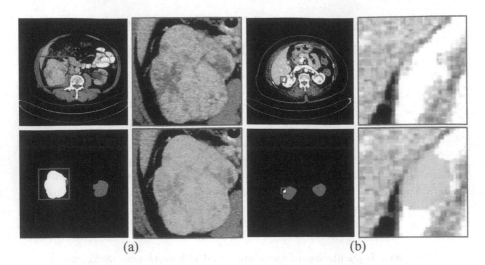

Fig. 1. (a) A large kidney tumor and (b) a small kidney tumor on CT slices. The top row shows the CT silces and enlarged tumor bounding boxes. The bottom row gives the ground truth of kidneys (gray) and kidney tumors (white) and shows the enlarged bounding boxes with tumors (green) overlaying on CT images. (Color figure online)

Although deep learning techniques have achieved remarkable success in medical image processing, automated segmentation of kidneys and the tumors on CT images, however, remains challenging for three major reasons. First, the sizes of kidney tumors vary significantly, resulting in either under-segmentation of large tumors or over-segmentation of small tumors. Second, the contrast between kidney tumors and their anatomical surroundings is extremely low (see Fig. 1), leading to error-prone tumor boundaries. Third, it is difficult to distinguish kidney tumors from kidney cysts due to their visual similarities.

Many research efforts have been devoted to address these issues. Hou et al. [9] proposed a triple-stage method to capture the global region features on low-resolution images and local region features on high-resolution images sequentially, and thus alleviated the difficulties caused by the diverse sizes of kidney tumors. Yu et al. [16] adopted crossbar patches to extract regional information of kidney tumors in vertical and horizontal directions simultaneously, and trained complemented horizontal sub-model and vertical sub-model to achieve the self-improvement of the model. Despite their improved performance, these methods focus merely on exploiting the abilities of deep convolutional neural networks (DCNNs) to extract continuity-based region information. It is commonly acknowledged that the discontinuity-based boundary information is also crucial for image segmentation [10,12,18], particularly the segmentation of kidney tumors, whose boundaries are hard to be detected due to the low-contrast between them and surrounding tissues and the visual similarity between them and kidney cysts. Therefore, several recent attempts have been made to complement the advantages of continuity-based segmentation and discontinuity-based boundary detection. Zhou et al. [18] introduced high-resolution skip connections and auxiliary contour regression to improve the performance on low-contrast image segmentation tasks. Jia et al. [10] incorporated a boundary decoder into the hybrid discriminative network (HD-Net), which accordingly has a shared encoder, a segmentation decoder, and a boundary decoder. Although achieving the top performance in prostate segmentation using magnetic resonance imaging, HD-Net not only prohibits the interaction between the segmentation and boundary decoders but also abandons the boundary decoder in the inference stage. To tackle this issue, Myronenko et al. [12] used a fusion layer to combine the boundary features with regional features before feeding them to the last layer for making the final segmentation. Despite the feature fusion, this model still ignores the interaction between segmentation and boundary detection, let alone the consistency between them. Since the boundary regions are the places where segmentation errors are prone to occur, we advocate the use of boundary information to facilitate the segmentation process and the adoption of the consistency between these two as extra supervision.

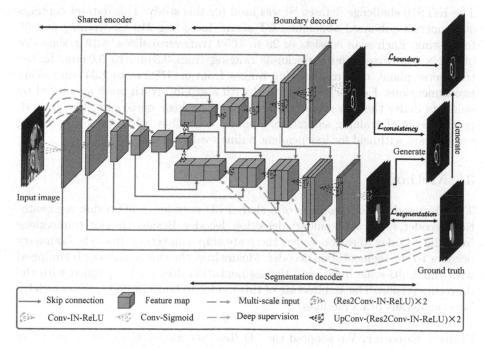

Fig. 2. Architecture of the proposed BA-Net

In this paper, we propose a boundary-aware network (BA-Net) for automated segmentation of kidneys and kidney tumors on contrast-enhanced CT scans. The BA-Net has a 3D encoder-decoder structure, consisting of a shared 3D encoder, a 3D region segmentation decoder, and a 3D boundary detection decoder. Besides the skip connections from the encoder to both decoders, we introduce extra skip connections from the boundary decoder to the segmentation decoder (see Fig. 2), which enables the use of boundary information that indicates the error-prone regions as a type of spatial attentions to assist the segmentation task. We also introduce a consistency loss to promote the output consistency between the segmentation and boundary decoders. Meanwhile, we employ the multi-scale input in the encoder and the deep supervision in the segmentation decoder.

The main contributions of this work include: (1) we combine the continuity-based region segmentation with discontinuity-based boundary detection and use the detected boundary information as that spatial attention to assist the segmentation decoder at multiple scales; (2) we introduce a consistency loss to ensure that the outputs of the segmentation and boundary decoders are consistent; and (3) we evaluate the proposed BA-Net on the KiTS19 [8] dataset and achieve one of the top performance as compared to those on the challenge leaderboard.

2   Datasets

The KiTS19 challenge dataset [8] was used for this study. This dataset contains 300 contrast-enhanced abdominal CT scans, including 210 for training and 90 for testing. Each scan consists of 29 to 1059 transverse slices, with a slice size of 512×512 voxels and a thickness ranging from 0.5 mm to 5.0 mm. In the transverse plane, the voxel spacing ranges from 0.4375 mm to 1.041 mm along two dimensions. Each scan is equipped with a ground-truth mask annotated by students under the supervision of experienced urologic oncologist. The ground-truth masks of training samples are public accessible, while those for testing samples are withheld for independent online evaluation.

3   Method

The proposed BA-Net consists of a shared 3D encoder, a 3D region segmentation decoder, and a 3D boundary detection decoder. Besides the skip connections from the encoder to each decoder, there are skip connections from the boundary decoder to the segmentation decoder. Meanwhile, the shared encoder is equipped with the multi-scale input, and the segmentation decoder is equipped with the deep supervision. The architecture of this model is shown in Fig. 2. We now delve into the details of its modules.

Shared Encoder. We adopted the 3D Res2Net model [6] as the backbone of our encoder, which is composed of five down-sample layers, each containing two Res2Net modules. To extract and use the context information at different scales, we incorporate the multi-scale input technique [4] to our encoder. Specifically, we use max-pooling followed by a convolutional block to generate muti-scale feature maps, and then add them to the feature maps of the encoder at each scale. In the meantime, to alleviate the potential of over fitting, we adopt instance normalization in all normalization layers of BA-Net.

Boundary Decoder. To improve the ability of BA-Net to boundary feature extraction, we add a 3D boundary decoder to explicitly extract the intra-slice information and predict the surface of the target, as shown in the top-right of Fig. 2. In contrast to the segmentation decoder, this decoder aims to extract the discontinuity-based inter-class discrimination of adjacent region and to provide the regularization to the predicted shape of the target. However, since the 3D surface only accounts for a tiny proportion of the input volume, predicting the surface is an extremely imbalanced problem. To address this issue, we make the surface of the target to at least a three-pixel thickness. Moreover, we add skip connections from boundary decoder to segmentation decoder so that the supervision signals from the region decoder can update the parameters of the boundary decoder (see Fig. 2).

Segmentation Decoder. Similar to 3D U-Net [3], the 3D segmentation decoder receives the high resolution features from the encoder. Nevertheless, these features, combined with up-sampled features, are not enough for accurate kidney tumor segmentation, especially around the vague boundaries with low inter-class discrimination features. Targeting at this problem, we use the features from boundary decoder introduced by skip connections to improve the feature representation ability of the segmentation decoder (see Fig. 2). Since the boundary regions are prone to segmentation error, the features from the boundary decoder provide the attention to the segmentation decoder, indicating where the model should allocate more computational resources. In addition, the kidney tumor segmentation also suffers from serious variation of tumor size. To address this issue, we adopt the deep supervision strategy. Specifically, we add an auxiliary output unit, which is composed of a $1 \times 1 \times 1$ convolution layer with the sigmoid activation, before the up-sample operation at each scale, and calculate loss between the auxiliary output and down-sampled ground truth.

Loss Functions. We jointly minimize weighted cross entropy loss and Dice loss [11] to optimize both decoders:

$$\mathcal{L} = \mathcal{L}_{dice} + \mathcal{L}_{ce}$$
$$= \frac{1}{C} \sum_{c=1}^{C} \omega_c (1 - \frac{2\sum_{i=1}^{V} p_i^c g_i^c}{\sum_{i=1}^{V}(p_i^c + g_i^c) + \varepsilon}) - \frac{1}{V} \sum_{i}^{V} \sum_{c}^{C} \omega_c g_i^c \log p_i^c \qquad (1)$$

where C and V represent the numbers of categories and voxels, respectively, p_i^c is the prediction score, g_i^c denotes the ground truth label, ε is a smooth factor, and ω_c is a balance factor.

We adopt $\omega_c = 1$ and $\omega_c = \log \frac{V}{V^c}$ for $\mathcal{L}_{segmentation}$ and $\mathcal{L}_{boundary}$, respectively, where V^c denotes the number of voxels which belong to class c.

To promote the consistency between the outputs of the segmentation decoder and boundary decoder, we design a consistency loss. We generate a boundary map from the output of the segmentation branch, and then calculate the weighted Dice loss and cross entropy loss between the output of the boundary branch and the generated boundary map. Thus, the consistency can be defined as follows

$$\mathcal{L}_{consistency} = \begin{cases} 0, & epoch < \frac{iter}{2}, \\ \mathcal{L}_{dice} + \mathcal{L}_{ce}, & epoch \geq \frac{iter}{2}. \end{cases} \qquad (2)$$

where $epoch$ denotes current training iteration number, $iter$ is the total training iterations. The balance factor we use in $\mathcal{L}_{consistency}$ is same as that in $\mathcal{L}_{boundary}$. Since the outputs of the two branches are unreliable in the early training stage, we only use the consistency loss in the late training stage.

Training and Inference. The boundary decoder and the segmentation decoder are trained at the same time in training stage via jointly minimizing $\mathcal{L}_{segmentation}$, $\mathcal{L}_{boundary}$, and $\mathcal{L}_{consistency}$. In the inference stage, we use a sliding window whose size is the same as that of the input. The stride of the sliding window is set to a quarter of the input size. Due to the ovrelap, each voxel may appear in multiple windows and its final class label is the average predictions made by the segmentation decoder.

Implementation Details. We clipped the Hounsfiled Unit (HU) values of the CT images to the range of $[-68, 286]$, and then linearly normalize HU values to $[0, 1]$. To alleviate the problem caused by the small proportion of the kidneys and kidney tumors in most of the CT images, we first utilized a 3D U-Net with large input image size (*i.e.*, $160 \times 160 \times 80$) to segment kidneys and kidney tumors at larger voxel size (*i.e.*, $1.5 \, \text{mm} \times 1.5 \, \text{mm} \times 3\text{mm}$) to generate the region of interest (ROI). The 3D U-Net we used consists of five down-sample layers and five up-sample layers, and was trained from scratch via jointly minimizing the cross entropy loss and Dice loss. We used the trained 3D U-Net to get the coarse segmentation mask, and then adopted connected component analysis based postprocessing to reduce false-positive area. The ROI was thereupon generated and re-sampled to a smaller voxel size of $1 \, \text{mm} \times 1\text{mm} \times 1\text{mm}$.

Subsequently, we applied data augmentation techniques, including random cropping, random rotation, random scaling, random flipping, random Gaussian noise addition, and elastic deformation to generate augmented input volumes with a size of $128 \times 128 \times 128$ voxels. Limited by the GPU memory, we set the batch size to 2. Using the trained BA-Net, we first generated the segmentation mask of the ROI, and then zero-padded the outside area of the ROI to get the final result. We utilized the PyTorch framework [13] to implement our mode on a desktop with a Nvidia Titan GPU (12G). We optimized the two networks using the Adam optimizer implemented in PyTorch with an initial learning rate of 0.0003, and adopted the default settings for other parameters. We trained BA-Net for at most 250 epochs with 250 batches per epoch.

Evaluation Metrics. Following the KiTS19 Challenge [8], we adopted the Dice score to measure the accuracy of kidney segmentation and tumor segmentation. The composite Dice is calculated according to the tumor Dice and kidney (including kidney tumor) Dice, shown as follows

$$S = \frac{1}{N} \sum_{i=0}^{N-1} \frac{1}{2}(Dice^i_{tumor} + Dice^i_{kidney}) \tag{3}$$

where N is the number of evaluated cases, and i represents ith case.

4   Results and Discussions

Table 1 gives the performance of our proposed BA-Net and ten top-ranking methods listed on the KiTS19 Challenge Leaderboard[1]. We highlighted the top-3 performance in red, green, and blue. It shows that the proposed BA-Net achieves the third highest kidney Dice, tumor Dice, and composite Dice on the testing dataset. Specifically, the kidney Dice achieved by our BA-Net is comparable to the highest one, while the tumor Dice we achieved is about 1.5% lower than the highest tumor Dice. The performance gap is largely due to the unsolved issues caused by the similar appearance between kidney tumors and kidney cysts.

Table 1. Comparison with ten methods on the KiTS19 Challenge dataset. Red, green, and blue fonts indicate the first-, second- and third-best results, respectively.

Method	Kidney Dice ↑	Tumor Dice ↑	Composite Dice ↑
Isensee et al	97.37%	85.09%	91.23%
Hou et al	96.74%	84.54%	90.64%
Mu et al	97.29%	83.21%	90.25%
Zhang et al	97.42%	83.06%	90.24%
Ma et al	97.34%	82.54%	89.94%
Liu et al	97.42%	82.31%	89.87%
Zhao et al	97.41%	81.81%	89.61%
Li et al	97.17%	81.61%	89.39%
Myronenko et al	97.42%	81.03%	89.23%
Chen et al	97.01%	81.03%	89.23%
Ours	97.39%	83.55%	90.47%

Ablation Study: The major uniqueness of the proposed BA-Net is two-fold: (1) using the boundary decoder for the discontinuity-based segmentation and providing the boundary prior to the segmentation decoder, and (2) using the consistency loss to force the outputs of both decoders converge to the same result. Besides them, the use of Res2Net modules and deep supervision also makes contributions to the performance of BA-Net. To verify this, we conducted

---

[1] http://results.kits-challenge.org/miccai2019/.

ablation studies on the training dataset using the five-fold cross validation, and displayed the results in Table 2. It shows that using Res2Net modules, deep supervision, boundary decoder and consistency loss improve the tumor Dice by 2.1%, 1.45%, 1.13%, and 2.19%, respectively, and improves the composite Dice by 1.15%, 0.83%, 0.79%, and 1.16%, respectively. The results proves the effectiveness of these techniques.

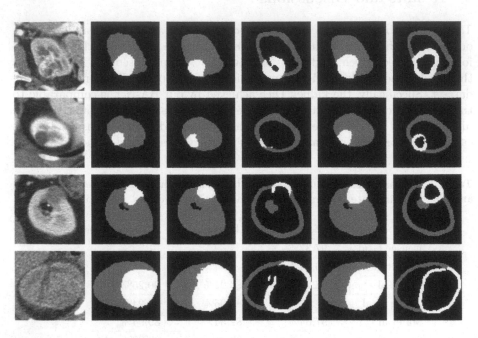

Fig. 3. Visualization of the results on four slices. From left to right: enlarged image, ground truth, and the output of segmentation decoder (w/o $\mathcal{L}_{consistency}$), boundary decoder (w/o $\mathcal{L}_{consistency}$), segmentation decoder, and boundary decoder. The Kidney and tumor are highlighted in gray and white, respectively.

Meanwhile, we visualize the segmentation results on four slices in Fig. 3. These results were obtained by the boundary decoder and segmentation decoder when using or without using the consistency loss. It reveals that the consistency loss can promote the output consistency between the segmentation and boundary decoders effectively.

Table 2. Results of ablation studies on the training dataset using the five-fold cross validation. R2M: Res2Net Modules, DS: Deep Supervision, BD: Boundary Decoder, and CLoss: Consistency Loss.

R2M	DS	BD	CLoss	Kidney Dice ↑	Tumor Dice ↑	Composite Dice ↑
×	×	×	×	96.10%	76.58%	86.34%
✓	×	×	×	96.30%	78.68%	87.49%
✓	✓	×	×	96.51%	80.13%	88.32%
✓	✓	✓	×	96.95%	81.26%	89.11%
✓	✓	✓	✓	**97.08%**	**83.45%**	**90.27%**

5   Conclusion

This paper proposes the BA-Net for kidney and kidney tumor segmentation on CT images, which extract the boundary information to facilitate the segmentation process and defines the consistency loss to push the boundary decoder and segmentation decoder towards generating the same result. This model was evaluated on the KiTS19 Challenge dataset and achieves promising performance. The results indicate that the boundary decoder and consistency loss used in BA-Net are effective. In our future work, we will improve the performance of this model via investigating more powerful backbone networks which have a better discriminatory ability to separate kidney tumors from kidney cysts.

Acknowledgment. This work was supported in part by the Science and Technology Innovation Committee of Shenzhen Municipality, China, under Grants JCYJ20180306171334997, in part by the National Natural Science Foundation of China under Grants 61771397, and in part by the Project for Graduate Innovation team of Northwestern Polytechnical University.

References

1. Bray, F., Ferlay, J., Soerjomataram, I., Siegel, R.L., Torre, L.A., Jemal, A.: Global cancer statistics 2018: GLOBOCAN estimates of incidence and mortality worldwide for 36 cancers in 185 countries. CA: Cancer J. Clin. **68**(6), 394–424 (2018)
2. Capitanio, U., Montorsi, F.: Renal cancer. Lancet **387**(10021), 894–906 (2016)
3. Çiçek, Ö., Abdulkadir, A., Lienkamp, S.S., Brox, T., Ronneberger, O.: 3D u-net: learning dense volumetric segmentation from sparse annotation. In: Proceedings of the International Conference on Medical Image Computing and Computer-Assisted Intervention (MICCAI), pp. 424–432 (2016)
4. Fang, X., Yan, P.: Multi-organ segmentation over partially labeled datasets with multi-scale feature abstraction. IEEE Transactions on Medical Imaging, pp. 1–1 (2020)
5. Ficarra, V., et al.: Preoperative aspects and dimensions used for an anatomical (padua) classification of renal tumours in patients who are candidates for nephron-sparing surgery. Eur. Urol. **56**(5), 786–793 (2009)

6. Gao, S., Cheng, M.M., Zhao, K., Zhang, X.Y., Yang, M.H., Torr, P.H.: Res2net: a new multi-scale backbone architecture. In: IEEE Transactions on Pattern Analysis and Machine Intelligence, (2019)
7. Heller, N., et al.: The state of the art in kidney and kidney tumor segmentation in contrast-enhanced CT imaging: results of the kits19 challenge. arXiv preprint, (2019) arXiv:1912.01054
8. Heller, N., et al.: The kits19 challenge data: 300 kidney tumor cases with clinical context, ct semantic segmentations, and surgical outcomes. arXiv preprint arXiv:1904.00445 (2019)
9. Hou, X., et al.: A triple-stage self-guided network for kidney tumor segmentation. In: Proceedings of the IEEE International Symposium on Biomedical Imaging (ISBI), pp. 341–344. IEEE (2020)
10. Jia, H., Song, Y., Huang, H., Cai, W., Xia, Y.: HD-Net: hybrid discriminative network for prostate segmentation in MR images. In: Shen, D., et al. (eds.) MICCAI 2019. LNCS, vol. 11765, pp. 110–118. Springer, Cham (2019). https://doi.org/10.1007/978-3-030-32245-8_13
11. Milletari, F., Navab, N., Ahmadi, S.A.: V-net: Fully convolutional neural networks for volumetric medical image segmentation. In: Proceedings of the International Conference on 3D Vision (3DV). pp. 565–571 (2016)
12. Myronenko, A., Hatamizadeh, A.: 3D kidneys and kidney tumor semantic segmentation using boundary-aware networks. arXiv preprint, (2019) arXiv:1909.06684
13. Paszke, A., et al.: Pytorch: An imperative style, high-performance deep learning library. In: Proceedings of the Advances in Neural Information Processing Systems, pp. 8024–8035 (2019)
14. Wu, Y., et al.: Vessel-Net: retinal vessel segmentation under multi-path supervision. In: Shen, D., et al. (eds.) MICCAI 2019. LNCS, vol. 11764, pp. 264–272. Springer, Cham (2019). https://doi.org/10.1007/978-3-030-32239-7_30
15. Xie, Y., Lu, H., Zhang, J., Shen, C., Xia, Y.: Deep segmentation-emendation model for gland instance segmentation. In: Proceedings of the International Conference on Medical Image Computing and Computer-Assisted Intervention (MICCAI), Springer. pp. 469–477 (2019) https://doi.org/10.1007/978-3-030-32239-7_52
16. Yu, Q., Shi, Y., Sun, J., Gao, Y., Zhu, J., Dai, Y.: Crossbar-net: a novel convolutional neural network for kidney tumor segmentation in CT images. IEEE Trans. Image Process. 28(8), 4060–4074 (2019)
17. Zhang, J., Xie, Y., Zhang, P., Chen, H., Xia, Y., Shen, C.: Light-weight hybrid convolutional network for liver tumor segmentation. In: Proceedings of the International Joint Conference on Artificial Intelligence (IJCAI), pp. 4271–4277 (2019)
18. Zhou, S., Nie, D., Adeli, E., Yin, J., Lian, J., Shen, D.: High-resolution encoder-decoder networks for low-contrast medical image segmentation. IEEE Trans. Image Process. 29, 461–475 (2019)

O-Net: An Overall Convolutional Network for Segmentation Tasks

Omid Haji Maghsoudi[✉], Aimilia Gastounioti, Lauren Pantalone,
Christos Davatzikos, Spyridon Bakas, and Despina Kontos

Center for Biomedical Image Computing and Analytics, University of Pennsylvania,
Philadelphia, PA 19104, USA
omid.hajimaghsoudi@pennmedicine.upenn.edu

Abstract. Convolutional neural networks (CNNs) have recently been popular for classification and segmentation through numerous network architectures offering a substantial performance improvement. Their value has been particularly appreciated in the domain of biomedical applications, where even a small improvement in the predicted segmented region (e.g., a malignancy) compared to the ground truth can potentially lead to better diagnosis or treatment planning. Here, we introduce a novel architecture, namely the Overall Convolutional Network (O-Net), which takes advantage of different pooling levels and convolutional layers to extract more deeper local and containing global context. Our quantitative results on 2D images from two distinct datasets show that O-Net can achieve a higher dice coefficient when compared to either a U-Net or a Pyramid Scene Parsing Net. We also look into the stability of results for training and validation sets which can show the robustness of model compared with new datasets. In addition to comparison to the decoder, we use different encoders including simple, VGG Net, and ResNet. The ResNet encoder could help to improve the results in most of the cases.

Keywords: Deep learning · Segmentation · Biomedical imaging

1 Introduction

Training a Convolutional neural networks (CNNs) usually needs thousands of images that can be beyond reach in biomedical applications [1,2]. A sliding-window pattern (patch processing) [3] can make a network to be quite slow, and it is prone to localization accuracy. Therefore, more advanced CNNs are developed to address these issues [4,5]. Two of the frequently used CNNs are U-Net [1] and Pyramid Scene Parsing (PSP) Net [6]. PSP Net uses parallel layers

Electronic supplementary material The online version of this chapter (https://doi.org/10.1007/978-3-030-59861-7_21) contains supplementary material, which is available to authorized users.

© Springer Nature Switzerland AG 2020
M. Liu et al. (Eds.): MLMI 2020, LNCS 12436, pp. 199–209, 2020.
https://doi.org/10.1007/978-3-030-59861-7_21

to pool information with different resolutions. This network combines local and global clues to make the final prediction more reliable. However, it can miss information by not extracting higher-order features using deeper layers. On the other hand, U-Net is based on highly deep layers providing depth information from an image. It uses successive layers, where upsampling operators replace pooling operators. These successive layers can increase the resolution of the final outcome while high-resolution features from the contracting path are combined with the upsampled output to increase localization int the final output.

For general segmentation applications, the PASCAL VOC dataset has been considered as one of the best resources for segmentation [7], while the COCO dataset is presented to help instance segmentation [8]. COCO leads to many advanced general segmentation methods [9]. For biomedical images, considering different layers connections to have various segmentation patterns [5], adding residual layers to extract deeper information [10], applying different pooling values to maximize the global context [6], and patch searching in an image [11] are some of the proposed approaches to improve the performance for segmentation. Furthermore, a fully 3D segmentation algorithm has been proposed based on 2D slices and U-Net [12] while V-net [13], which is based on 3D-variant of U-Net analyzed images based on 3D convolutional filters. A combination of DL method and distance regularized level set (DLRS) is proposed to segment lung in computed tomography (CT) images [14]. Breast [15,16] and brain [17,18] cancers have been subjects undergoing intense studies.

In this paper, we present a new CNN architecture for semantic segmentation; specifically designed for biomedical segmentation tasks. Our proposed architecture is built upon the advantages of PSP Net, which has been used frequently for various applications. We add more local context to enrich the information required for final segmentation by considering different encoders and improving the decoder side. The O-Net decoder uses different convolutional and pooling kernels to acquire deeper information from images. The novel contributions of the hereby proposed work are two-fold. First, our effective modification by enriching the local context improves PSP Net and U-Net performances for biomedical tasks. Accordingly, we evaluate the performance of our proposed method compared to two well-established segmentation architectures. Each of these three networks are trained with simple encoder, VGG Net encoder [19], and ResNet encoder [20]. These encoders can add residual or more in-depth information from an image that can help segmentation. Therefore, a total of nine networks are compared here. Our method performs favorably against state-of-the-art methods. Second, we train the CNNs from scratch, do not use already trained model, and do not split train in "pre-train" and "fine-tune" stages. We also consider the complexity of task in our work to evaluate the performance of our method for different tasks. Finally, our code is publicly available through GitHub.

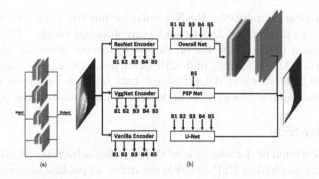

Fig. 1. O-Net decoder and other CNNs architectures are shown in this figure. The O-Net decoder layers are illustrated in (a). The brown layer shows the resizing function to return the convoluted result to the original image size. It combines different pooling layers inspired by PSP Net. Detailed information on how the CNNs are connected using encoder and decoder is shown in (b). The top right side of panel (b) provide details about the decision making layer for O-Net. (Color figure online)

2   Proposed Methods

2.1   O-Net Architecture

A CNN for segmentation contains three major components: encoder, decoder sides, and decision making layers. The encoder layers extract features while the decoder layers try to map the extracted features to pixels level of an input image. The decision-making layers can combine different layers and apply the final decision for the segmentation task based on the extracted features. In addition, training parameters and data augmentation can significantly affect the results. Therefore, in this section, we introduce our proposed network components following by the parameters being used in training. Finally, we briefly discuss the methods used for comparison and the experimental design.

2.2   Encoder Side

We consider three convolutional or encoder side, encoder, for each network (O-Net, U-Net, and PSP Net). Simple encoder, VGG Net encoder [19], and ResNet encoder [20]. The differences between these three encoders can be seen in Fig. 1. Each of these encoders generates five outputs, referred to as branches (B) as B1, B2, B3, B4, and B5, which is used at different levels of the decoder side.

For the simple encoder, the pooling layers size is (2, 2) while the convolutional layers have a kernel of (3, 3). The filter size for the convolutional layers starts from 64 and increases by a factor of 2 when going to the next layer (deeper to the left). Only, the fifth layer has the same number as the fourth layer (64 × 8 = 1024).

The VGG Net encoder employs the same pooling size of (2, 2) and the same kernel of (3, 3). The filter size has the exact same pattern as described for the simple encoder. Finally, the ResNet encoder has five branches with various kernels. ResNet consists of identity and convolutional blocks. The number of the convolutional block is one for all of the branches (after the first branch). However, second, third, fourth, and fifth branches have 2, 3, 4, and 2 identity blocks. Figure 1 shows more details about two of these branches (the second branch has two identity blocks). More details can be found in the code.

2.3 Decoder Side

The de-convolutional or decoder side of O-Net takes advantage of different pooling layers being inspired by PSP Net. We use different pooling layers and combine the results with the original input to mix the local and global context. The original input for each layer helps to improve the localization of the outcome. This decoder module has been illustrated in Fig. 1.

The decoder module includes five divisions with four different pooling kernels (1, 2, 3, and 6) and one layer which passes the input to improve the final localization. Each layer has one average pooling layer, one convolutional layer, one batch normalization layer, and one activation layer. The convolutional layer is designed by a kernel size of (1, 1) and 512 filters. These layers are followed by a resizing component to return all the images to the original input size.

2.4 Decision Making Layers

As explained in Sects. 2.2 and 2.3, five branches from one of the three encoders are the input of the decoder module. The output of the decoder module is five branches. We combine these branches and apply a convolutional step (one convolutional layer, one batch normalization, and one activation layer), as shown in Fig. 1. The convolutional layer has a kernel size of (3, 3) with 512 filters.

We use a drop out layer to reduce the chance of overfitting. Finally, another convolutional layer following by the image resizing component is used to have the original image resolution in output. Finally, an activation layer with the softmax function is used to differentiate the segmentation classes.

2.5 Methods for Comparison

We compare our method with U-Net [1] and PSP Net [6]. How these two networks and O-Net are used in this study have been shown in Fig. 1. O-Net and U-Net use all five branches generated by the encoder side while the PSP Net uses the last branch (B5) from each of the encoders. Therefore, we have a total of nine CNNs (three networks and three encoders) for comparison.

We use Adam optimizer with a learning rate of $1e^{-4}$ for all nine CNNs.

3 Experimental Setup

3.1 Datasets

In this work, we use two datasets: breast and brain scans. The breast dataset is in gray-scale (one channel) while for the brain dataset we considered gray-scale (one channel) and color images (three channels) to make different complexity levels. All of the images are resized to 256 × 256 pixels. Therefore, a total of three image sets are used in this study.

1) Gray-scale images for breast tissue segmentation: Segmentation of breast and calculating breast density percentage can is helpful for assessing breast cancer risk [21]. The breast dataset consists of 1,100 digital mammography images from 1,100 patients. 550 images are screened from left and the other half from right breast at the Hospital of the University of Pennsylvania between 2010 and 2014. Women were imaged per U.S. Food and Drug Administration approved protocol consisting of full-field digital mammography in both mediolateral oblique views using Selenia Dimensions, Hologic Inc. The breast area is manually differentiated from the background and pectoralis muscle using ImageJ software [22]. The background segmentation can be considered as a simple task while the pectoralis muscle can be challenging. This dataset includes gray-scale normalized images with 8-bit from the digital mammography images. We use half of the images to train and the other half to test the model. This dataset has two classes as breast and a combination of background and pectoralis muscle.

2) Gray-scale images for brain tumor segmentation: The brain dataset we used in this study describes the BraTS [17], [18] component of the publicly available Medical Segmentation Decathlon dataset [23]. The training dataset, which has images and labels, consists of four channels: 1) Fluid-attenuated inversion recovery (FLAIR), 2) native T1 weighted, 3) T1 post-contrast, and 4) T2-weighted MRI scans. The BraTS training set has 3D images from 484 patients with four classes of segmentation comprising 1) background, 2) edema, 3) non-enhancing tumor, and 4) enhancing tumor. Since the brain scans were 3D, we decided to extract 2D slices from each patient and randomly select five of them that encompass at least two out of the four segmentation classes. Therefore, we generate 1,200 images for training and 736 images for testing. In order to have a gray-scale, we considered the first channel (FLAIR).

3) Color Images for Brain Tumor Segmentation: We use the same BraTS dataset with the same number of images. However, we add two other channels (T1 and T1gd) to make color images.

3.2   Metric in Training and Measures for Comparisons

The segmentation performance is measured using two parameters: 1) dice similarity coefficient, and 2) dice weighted. We extend dice formula considering weights for each class based on the number of pixels for that class.

4   Results

This section presents comparisons between the nine CNNs using the three datasets mentioned in Sect. 3.1. All networks are trained using the dice weighted

Table 1. The dice results for all nine networks are summarized here. The name of networks shows encoder + decoder. The head and tail depict the results for the first and second half portions of training epochs. The best network is colored in blue for datasets (three datasets) and training phases (head and tail).

Networks	Head			Tail		
	Brain Color	Brain Gray	Breast	Brain Color	Brain Gray	Breast
ResNet + O-Net	54.611.3	48.910.5	91.45.0	61.70.9	58.51.7	96.01.4
Simple + O-Net	54.67.9	48.79.9	92.55.5	59.11.3	56.71.1	95.81.5
VGG Net + O-Net	55.59.8	49.69.6	91.44.7	60.60.9	58.91.1	96.30.8
ResNet + PSP Net	45.67.8	41.68.7	88.72.8	53.60.9	51.42.4	91.71.1
Simple + PSP Net	41.87.7	35.814.5	85.52.1	47.61.1	47.21.7	88.00.9
VGG Net + PSP Net	38.28.5	38.98.5	86.42.0	48.31.5	48.31.7	89.71.2
ResNet + U-Net	41.822.3	30.520.6	88.96.6	60.15.5	56.52.1	92.42.3
Simple + U-Net	50.614.6	48.98.1	88.52.1	58.71.5	56.91.6	91.01.5
VGG Net + U-Net	50.68.9	36.018.4	89.24.7	58.31.2	54.61.7	92.21.3

which is formulated in Sect. 3.2. We show training and testing sets results for all epochs for all training epochs, as illustrated in Fig. 2. The results for training and testing sets are compared using weighted dice and dice, respectively. The CNNs are trained till they show some signs of overfitting, e.g., Fig. 2 (b) depicts an increase while (d) reaches a plateau, or they reach a plateau for dice weighted, e.g., Fig. 2 (c) and (f). Therefore, using this strategy, we train the brain networks up to 200 epochs and the breast networks up to 50 epochs. The main reason for considering such a condition in training is that we can compare the top and bottom half of training epochs to visualize any possible patterns in the CNNs taring and testing phases.

It should be noted that we use the train and test sets (no validation set used for selecting an epoch). The reason is that we study the performance of networks during the whole training phases on our testing set without selecting one specific epoch. A stable network can be more reliable when an epoch is selected based on a measure on a validation set as the network shows fewer variations and is expected to perform the same on a test set. An unstable network can be highly dependent on the selected epoch and the dataset.

The comparisons are performed by combining the results for the CNNs based on two categories: 1) network-based comparison showing the results for all nine networks; 2) decoder-based and encoder-based comparisons illustrating the results for three decoders (O-Net, PSP Net, and U-Net) and three encoders (simple, VGG Net, and ResNet); In addition, we separate the analysis for the first and second half of the training epochs. This can help us to study a network performance while there is so much information to learn (the first half of training phase, referred to as head) and while a network is almost close to the plateau of learning (the second half of training phase, referred to as tail). In other words,

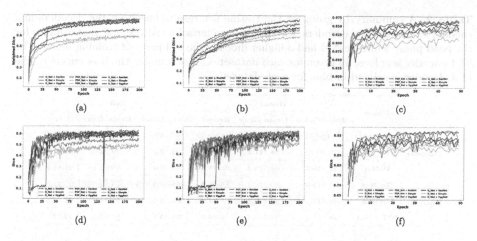

(a)   (b)   (c)

(d)   (e)   (f)

Fig. 2. The results for training and testing. Plots in (a), (b), and (c) show the training results for all epochs (200 for BRATS related datasets and 50 for the breast dataset). Panels in (d), (e), and (f) are the testing results corresponding to the training epochs. Each color shows one of the nine CNNs. Red, brown, and purple show the results for O-Net with ResNet, simple, and VGG Net encoders, respectively. Dark green, bright green, and yellow show the results for PSP Net with ResNet, simple, and VGG Net encoders, respectively. Bright blue, cyan, and dark blue show the results for U-Net with ResNet, simple, and VGG Net encoders, respectively. The color brain dataset results are shown in (a) and (d). The gray-scale brain dataset results are shown in (b) and (e). Finally, the breast dataset results are illustrated in (c) and (f). (Color figure online)

this type of comparison can show which network is more stable in the results. Therefore, the results can be studied as follow:

1) Networks-based Comparison: Table 1, which summarizes the testing set results in Fig. 2, illustrates the average and standard division of trained nine networks for the head and tail parts of training. O-Net achieved its best performance using VGG Net for the head and tail portion of the training. VGG Net shows about one percent higher dice measure for four out of six conditions (conditions are made by three datasets and two training phases). The ResNet encoder is usually the second network.

2) Decoder-based and Encoder-based Comparisons: A comprehensive comparison for the effect of decoders is performed and reported in Table 2. The results indicate that O-Net decoder remains on top of all conditions. An almost five percentage difference between O-Net and U-Net for the tail of the breast dataset might suggest the advantages of our network. In addition, Table 2 illustrates the results for encoder side of CNNs. The results show an average of better performance for ResNet (about one percent) while the simple encoder showed better performance at the earlier stage.

Table 2. A summary by grouping the testing set results based on the decoders and encoders. Amongst the encoders, the simple encoder achieved the best performance for the head phase while ResNet had a higher dice for the tail parts of training phase. The best encoder is colored in green for each dataset. O-Net remains the best encoder. The best decoder is colored in blue for each dataset.

		Name	Head			Tail		
			Brain Color	Brain Gray	Breast	Brain Color	Brain Gray	Breast
		O-Net	54.99.7	49.010.0	91.85.0	60.41.5	58.11.7	96.11.3
Decoder		PSP Net	41.98.5	38.711.2	86.92.7	49.83.0	49.02.6	89.81.9
		U-Net	47.616.7	38.518.3	88.94.8	59.03.4	56.02.1	91.81.8
		ResNet	47.316.0	40.316.1	89.75.2	58.54.8	55.53.6	93.42.5
Encoder		Simple	49.011.8	44.412.7	88.84.6	55.15.5	53.64.8	91.63.5
		VGG Net	48.111.6	41.514.2	89.04.5	55.75.5	54.04.6	92.73.0

5   Conclusions

In this work we introduced a new DL architecture for semantic segmentation, namely O-Net (Fig. 1). The presented CNN is compared with two popular architectures, U-Net and PSP Net. The comparisons are performed by changing the encoder and decoder possibilities. Figure 2 shows the results for such a comparison. In addition, we analyzed the nine CNNs more in detail for the early and late phases of training in Table 1 and Table 2.

We train and present the results for training set based on weighted dice while we report the testing results by dice, as the latter is the most common measure used for all segmentation tasks in the literature. However, it should be noted that the weighted dice had similar patterns with dice on the testing dataset. Figure 2 shows that the O-Net could achieve a higher weighted dice (less loss function) in the training set. This can be more obvious in Fig. 2 (b) and (c).

On the other hand, for the testing set, we analyzed more in depth, shown in Fig. 2, Table 1, and Table 2. We have six conditions based on the training phases (head and tail) and datasets (three datasets). Table 1 and Table 2 are derived from Fig. 2; however, they suggest important notes as follow:

1) O-Net remains the best network in all six conditions, shown in Table 2.
2) ResNet shows to be the best encoder in overall, shown in Table 2, especially for the tail portion of training. A reason for such a pattern can be the fact that ResNet tends to go deeper, and it needs a larger number of epochs to converge. However, when it converges it is shown to be more accurate. However, O-Net shows a higher performance for the VGG Net encoder for four out of six conditions. Although the ResNet and VGG Net results are just about one percent different from each other, the reason for such a difference can be the rich feature being extracted in the decoder parts of O-Net.
3) In the earlier stages of the training, the head phase, we can see that the simple encoder performed slightly better. This can be because of the need

for fewer iterations for learning some patterns from images when using the simple encoder compared with the other encoders.

4) In the earlier stages of the training, the head phase, we can see that the O-Net achieve significantly higher average dice compared to U-Net and PSP Net for all three datasets. This pattern is more obvious in Fig. 2, panels (d) and (e). This suggests that O-Net can reach it's best performance with fewer iteration.

5) We can conclude that O-Net with VGG Net encoder can be the best network amongst these nine CNNs. Notably, O-Net seems to be the most stable network on the testing set revealing its reliability. A robust and stable network results on validation set during the entire training phase can be really important because a new variations can cause the network performing worst than our expectations.

One of the limitations for O-Net is the required time for training that might be up to twice of U-Net. Also, saving the weights needs twice more space. In our future works, we intend to extend this work for 3D segmentation tasks as the current version of code is limited solely to 2D. It will let us attend and compare our results with the available challenges, e.g., BraTS. In addition, we plan to evaluate the method for the general segmentation tasks and compare the results with the medical datasets. Last but not least, we can comprehensively investigate the stability of network during the training phase on larger datasets.

Note: Sample images showing segmented area using nine networks and the code can be found in supplementary materials (which will be added on GitHub).

Acknowledgments. Research reported in this publication was partly supported by the National Institutes of Health (NIH) under award numbers NINDS:R01NS042645, NCI: R01CA161749, NCI:U24CA189523, NCI:U01CA242871. The content of this publication is solely the responsibility of the authors and does not represent the official views of the NIH. This work was also supported by the Susan G. Komen for the Cure® Breast Cancer Foundation [PDF17479714]. Also, we appreciate NVIDIA support for a donation of GPU to OHM.

References

1. Ronneberger, O., Fischer, P., Brox, T.: U-net: convolutional networks for biomedical image segmentation. In: Navab, N., Hornegger, J., Wells, W., Frangi, A. (eds.) MICCAI 2015. LNCS, pp. 234–241. Springer, Heidelberg (2015). https://doi.org/10.1007/978-3-319-24574-4_28

2. Mortazi, A., Bagci, U.: Automatically designing CNN architectures for medical image segmentation. In: Shi, Y., Suk, H.-I., Liu, M. (eds.) MLMI 2018. LNCS, vol. 11046, pp. 98–106. Springer, Cham (2018). https://doi.org/10.1007/978-3-030-00919-9_12

3. Ciresan, D., Giusti, A., Gambardella, L.M., Schmidhuber, J.: Deep neural networks segment neuronal membranes in electron microscopy images. In: Advances in Neural Information Processing Systems, pp. 2843–2851 (2012)

4. Iglovikov, V., Shvets, A.: Ternausnet: U-net with VGG11 encoder pre-trained on imagenet for image segmentation. arXiv preprint arXiv:1801.05746 (2018)

5. Murugesan, B., Sarveswaran, K., Shankaranarayana, S.M., Ram, K., Sivaprakasam, M.: Psi-net: Shape and boundary aware joint multi-task deep network for medical image segmentation. arXiv preprint arXiv:1902.04099 (2019)
6. Zhao, H., Shi, J., Qi, X., Wang, X., Jia, J.: Pyramid scene parsing network. In: Proceedings of the IEEE Conference on Computer Vision and Pattern Recognition, pp. 2881–2890 (2017)
7. Everingham, M., Eslami, S.M.A., Van Gool, L., Williams, C.K.I., Winn, J., Zisserman, A.: The Pascal visual object classes challenge: a retrospective. Int. J. Comput. Vis. **111**(1), 98–136 (2015)
8. Lin, T.-Y., et al.: Microsoft COCO: common objects in context. In: Fleet, D., Pajdla, T., Schiele, B., Tuytelaars, T. (eds.) ECCV 2014. LNCS, vol. 8693, pp. 740–755. Springer, Cham (2014). https://doi.org/10.1007/978-3-319-10602-1_48
9. Li, Y., Qi, H., Dai, J., Ji, X., Wei, Y.: Fully convolutional instance-aware semantic segmentation. In: Proceedings of the IEEE Conference on Computer Vision and Pattern Recognition, pp. 2359–2367 (2017)
10. Zhu, Z., Liu, C., Yang, D., Yuille, A., Xu, D.: V-NAS: Neural architecture search for volumetric medical image segmentation. arXiv preprint arXiv:1906.02817 (2019)
11. Liu, W., Rabinovich, A., Berg, A.C.: Parsenet: Looking wider to see better. arXiv preprint arXiv:1506.04579 (2015)
12. Çiçek, Ö., Abdulkadir, A., Lienkamp, S.S., Brox, T., Ronneberger, O.: 3D U-Net: learning dense volumetric segmentation from sparse annotation. In: Ourselin, S., Joskowicz, L., Sabuncu, M.R., Unal, G., Wells, W. (eds.) MICCAI 2016. LNCS, vol. 9901, pp. 424–432. Springer, Cham (2016). https://doi.org/10.1007/978-3-319-46723-8_49
13. Milletari, F., et al.: Hough-CNN: deep learning for segmentation of deep brain regions in MRI and ultrasound. Comput. Vis. Image Understand. **164**, 92–102 (2017)
14. Ngo, T.A., Carneiro, G.: Fully automated segmentation using distance regularised level set and deep-structured learning and inference. In: Lu, L., Zheng, Y., Carneiro, G., Yang, L. (eds.) Deep Learning and Convolutional Neural Networks for Medical Image Computing. ACVPR, pp. 197–224. Springer, Cham (2017). https://doi.org/10.1007/978-3-319-42999-1_12
15. Kallenberg, M., et al.: Unsupervised deep learning applied to breast density segmentation and mammographic risk scoring. IEEE Trans. Med. Imaging **35**(5), 1322–1331 (2016)
16. Maghsoudi, O.H., Gastounioti, A., Pantalone, L., Conant, E., Kontos, D.: Automatic breast segmentation in digital mammography using a convolutional neural network. In: 15th International Workshop on Breast Imaging (IWBI2020), vol. 11513, p. 1151322 (2020)
17. Bakas, S., et al.: Advancing the cancer genome atlas glioma MRI collections with expert segmentation labels and radiomic features. Sci. Data **4**, 170117 (2017)
18. Bakas, S., et al.: Identifying the best machine learning algorithms for brain tumor segmentation, progression assessment, and overall survival prediction in the brats challenge. arXiv preprint arXiv:1811.02629 (2018)
19. Simonyan, K., Zisserman, A.: Very deep convolutional networks for large-scale image recognition. arXiv preprint arXiv:1409.1556 (2014)
20. Szegedy, C., Ioffe, S., Vanhoucke, V., Alemi, A.A.: Inception-v4, inception-resnet and the impact of residual connections on learning. In: Thirty-First AAAI Conference on Artificial Intelligence (2017)

21. Kontos, D., et al.: Radiomic phenotypes of mammographic parenchymal complexity: toward augmenting breast density in breast cancer risk assessment. Radiology **290**(1), 41–49 (2018)
22. Rueden, C.T., et al.: Imagej 2: Imagej for the next generation of scientific image data. BMC Bioinform. **18**(1), 529 (2017)
23. Simpson, A.L., et al.: A large annotated medical image dataset for the development and evaluation of segmentation algorithms. arXiv preprint arXiv:1902.09063 (2019)

Label-Driven Brain Deformable Registration Using Structural Similarity and Nonoverlap Constraints

Shunbo Hu[1](✉), Lintao Zhang[1], Yan Xu[1], and Dinggang Shen[2](✉)

[1] School of Information Science and Engineering, Linyi University, Linyi, Shandong, China
hushunbo@lyu.edu.cn
[2] Department of Research and Development, Shanghai United Imaging Intelligence Co., Ltd., Shanghai, China
Dinggang.Shen@gmail.com

Abstract. Accurate deformable image registration is important for brain analysis. However, there are two challenges in deformation registration of brain magnetic resonance (MR) images. First, the global cerebrospinal fluid (CSF) regions are rarely aligned since most of them are located in narrow regions outside of gray matter (GM) tissue. Second, the small complex morphological structures in tissues are rarely aligned since dense deformation fields are too blurred. In this work, we use a weakly supervised registration scheme, which is driven by global segmentation labels and local segmentation labels via two special loss functions. Specifically, multiscale double Dice similarity is used to maximize the overlap of the same labels and also minimize the overlap of regions with different labels. The structural similarity loss function is further used to enhance registration performance of small structures, thus enhancing the whole image registration accuracy. Experimental results on inter-subject registration of T1-weighted MR brain images from the OASIS-1 dataset show that the proposed scheme achieves higher accuracy on CSF, GM and white matter (WM) compared with the baseline learning model.

Keywords: MR brain images · Deformable registration · Label-driven learning · Structural similarity

1 Introduction

Deformable image registration is very important for studying brain development, diagnosing developmental disorders, and building population atlases. The registration issues include aligning two or more images for the same or different subjects with different views, timepoints, or modalities. In recent years, deep learning-based methods have become a popular research topic in image registration communities [1–3].

Some deep learning-based registration algorithms utilize a convolution neural network (CNN) to estimate dense deformation field (DDF) between moving images and fixed images. These deep learning-based works decrease computational burdens during

© Springer Nature Switzerland AG 2020
M. Liu et al. (Eds.): MLMI 2020, LNCS 12436, pp. 210–219, 2020.
https://doi.org/10.1007/978-3-030-59861-7_22

inference time since they can estimate DDF fast through the forward mapping network. According to how the DDFs are predicted through the network, these works are divided into three groups: supervised registration, unsupervised registration, and weakly supervised registration. Supervised registration methods train the network by minimizing the errors between the ground-truth and estimated DDFs. However, the ground-truth DDFs are rarely obtained for real medical images. If the obtained DDFs are not precise, they may introduce new registration errors [4]. Unsupervised registration methods use the intensity similarity of two input images to derive DDFs, and they do not require ground-truth deformation or segmentation label information [5, 6]. However, intensity-similarity-driven learning methods inherit the key shortcomings of classical intensity-based registration algorithms [7], e.g., many local optima [23] or modal requirements. Weakly supervised registration methods use two input images to estimate DDFs via a forward pass through the network, and use the loss function between the warped moving segmentation *labels* and the fixed segmentation *labels* to refine network parameters via backpropagation of errors. Hu *et al.* proposed a label-driven weakly supervised registration framework to align intraoperative transrectal ultrasound images and MR images [7, 8]. Their method does not need to consider intensity variations or inhomogeneity, and also needs no ground-truth DDFs. The disadvantages of these weakly supervised registration methods include that precise segmentation labels are required, and also implausible DDFs may exist inside the segmented labels. To mitigate the above issues, Mansilla *et al.* proposed AC-RegNet architecture to incorporate global anatomical constraints from the encoders into the learning process for producing more realistic and accurate results [9]. The segmentation task (network) and the registration task can be combined and enhanced each other [10–12]. Generally, the registration performance will be enhanced by leveraging more prior knowledges [24] from inputs (multi-inputs or multimodalities) [13], outputs (multi-outputs or multitasks) [14], loss functions [15, 16], or network itself [17, 18].

However, there are some issues with deep learning-based registration of MR images. In this work, we mainly consider two detailed issues about brain MR image registration. The first issue is that the outermost tissue, CSF, is rarely aligned. There is a *single-force* problem at the boundaries between CSF and background. For example, in Fig. 1.*g*, there

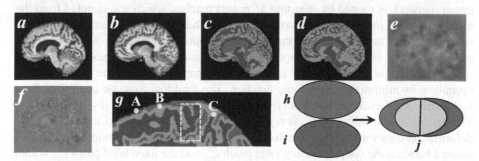

Fig. 1. Subfigures *a, b, c, d, e, f* are slices from moving images, fixed images, the segmentation labels of *a*, the labels of *b*, DDFs via the baseline learning scheme, and via our method, respectively. *g* is a detailed show of *c*. *h, i, j* are illustrations of (non) overlapping regions.

are three points, namely A, B and C, which are located at different boundaries. During the label-driven registration process, there are two forces in point B (i.e., CSF force and GM force) and C (i.e., GM force and WM force), while there is only a single force in point A (i.e., CSF force). As seen in Fig. 1.*e*, the single force produces blurred and enlarged DDFs in CSF regions, which may cause the warped CSF to expand beyond the brain skull. The second issue is the *small structure registration* problem. As seen in the dot white box in Fig. 1.*g*, there are small morphological structures in WM and GM. Many learning-based registration methods produce blurred DDFs being similar to Fig. 1.*e*, which rarely reflect the deformations in small morphological regions and then cause imprecise registration in these regions.

To mitigate the two above issues in this work, we applied a weakly supervised patch-based registration scheme for brain MR images, namely, Label-driven Registration scheme using Global labels and Local labels with multiscale Double Dice similarity and Structural similarity (LRGL-DDS). As seen in Fig. 1.*f*, the DDFs using our method are clear in many small morphological regions and CSF regions. The major contributions of our method can be summarized as follows:

1) The double Dice similarity is used as to maximize the same tissue overlap (i.e., yellow region in Fig. 1*j*) and minimize the nonoverlapping regions (i.e., green and red regions in Fig. 1*j*). This similarity can be seen as a constraint force to limit deformation of tissue within a reasonable range.
2) Small structure tissues are aligned by incorporating the structural similarity loss function during the training process, which also helps improve registration performance in global regions. The double Dice similarity and the structural similarity of segmentation labels are combined to align images in a coarse-to-fine fashion.
3) We use a path selector to accelerate the training process of local labels. Only if the local labels have enough voxels in the sampled patches, they are connected to the network to guide the training process.

2   Methods

Our deformable registration framework is shown in Fig. 2. A deep regression registration network is trained by inputting M paired patches, which are sampled from the training moving image A and the fixed image B. When the mth 3D patch pair (I_m^A, I_m^B) is inputted into the network $\mathcal{M}$, the network outputs the DDF, ϕ_m, which indicates the voxel dense coordinate correspondences between two m^{th} patches. The network functions as $\phi_m = \mathcal{M}(I_m^A, I_m^B, \theta)$. θ is the learnable parameter set of the network and is optimized by minimizing a total loss function. The total loss function comprises three loss terms: regularization loss, label dissimilarity loss, and structural dissimilarity loss. The deformation bending energy is regarded as the regularization loss term to preserve deformation smoothness. The label dissimilarity and the structural dissimilarity are calculated between the warped moving label patch l_{mn}^W and the fixed label patch l_{mn}^B within the mth patch. Here, $m = 1, \cdots, M$ and $n = 1, \cdots, N$, where M is the total number of sampled patches for each image and N is the total number of labels.

The network $\mathcal{M}$ is trained according to the following steps. First, two $64 \times 64 \times 64$ patches are sampled from a moving image and a fixed image at the same position. Then,

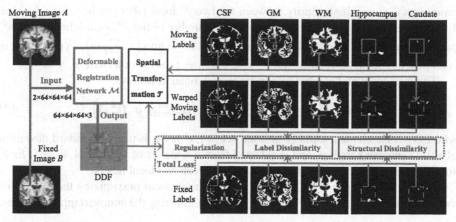

Fig. 2. The training framework of the proposed patch-based deformable image registration scheme, LRGL-DDS.

they are concentrated together and inputted into the network $\mathcal{M}$. After a forward pass through the network, a DDF patch is outputted with the size of $64 \times 64 \times 64 \times 3$. The moving label patches at the same position are warped to obtain the warped moving label patches by the DDF. Next, the double Dice (dis)similarity loss (i.e., label (dis)similarity loss) and the structural (dis)similarity loss of paired label patches are calculated. Finally, the total loss function is obtained by summing up the regularization term and the two above (dis)similarity losses. The network parameters are optimized by minimizing the total loss function for all sampled patches of all training images.

2.1 Total Loss Function

The total loss function of the mth pair of label patches is defined as:

$$E = \alpha E_D\left(l_m^W, l_m^B\right) + \beta E_S\left(l_m^W, l_m^B\right) + \gamma E_R(\phi_m), \tag{1}$$

where E_D measures the label dissimilarity between the warped moving label patch l_m^W and the corresponding fixed label patch l_m^B, E_S measures the structural dissimilarity between them, and E_R denotes the regularization term for DDF ϕ_m. $l_m^W = \mathcal{T}\left(\phi_m, l_m^A\right)$ is obtained by warping the moving label patch l_m^A via DDF ϕ_m. α, β and γ are hyperparameters that control the ratios of the three terms.

The label dissimilarity E_D is defined as follows:

$$E_D\left(l_m^W, l_m^B\right) = \frac{1}{|\{i\}|}\sum_i E_G\left(l_{mi}^W, l_{mi}^B\right) + \frac{1}{N_1}\sum_j \varepsilon_j E_L\left(l_{mj}^W, l_{mj}^B\right), \tag{2}$$

where i and j denote the ordinal numbers of the global labels and the local labels, respectively. $|\{i\}| + |\{j\}| = N$. $E_G\left(l_{mi}^W, l_{mi}^B\right)$ measures the global dissimilarity between the ith warped moving global label patch l_{mi}^W and the fixed global label patch l_{mi}^B. $E_L\left(l_{mj}^W, l_{mj}^B\right)$

represents the local dissimilarity between the two j^{th} local label patches. We take $\varepsilon_j = 1$ via connecting the path selector if the voxel number of the jth local label in the mth patch is larger than a threshold; otherwise, $\varepsilon_j = 0$. $N_1 = \max\left(1, \sum_j \varepsilon_j\right)$. In this work, α is empirically set to be 1. Note that β, $\gamma = 1$ if $\varepsilon_j = 1$ exists; otherwise β, $\gamma = 0.5$.

The multiscale global label dissimilarity is defined as follows:

$$E_G(l_{mi}^W, l_{mi}^B) = 1 - \frac{1}{N_2}\sum_\sigma D_{DDice}\left(g_\sigma(l_{mi}^W), g_\sigma(l_{mi}^B)\right), \tag{3}$$

where N_2 is the element number in scale set $\{\sigma\}$. σ is the isotropic standard deviation of a 3D Gaussian kernel g_σ and is selected from a scale set of $\{0, 1, 2, 4, 8, 16\}$. E_L is similar to Eq. (3) except that it is calculated between two local labels.

D_{DDice} is the double Dice similarity, which functions as maximizing the overlap of the same labels of two to-be-aligned images and minimizing the nonoverlapping regions.

$$D_{DDice}(g_\sigma(l_{mi}^W), g_\sigma(l_{mi}^B)) = \frac{2\|g_\sigma(l_{mi}^W)\circ g_\sigma(l_{mi}^B)\|_1 - \|(1-g_\sigma(l_{mi}^W))\circ g_\sigma(l_{mi}^B)\|_1 - \|g_\sigma(l_{mi}^W)\circ(1-g_\sigma(l_{mi}^B))\|_1}{\|g_\sigma(l_{mi}^W)\|_1 + \|g_\sigma(l_{mi}^B)\|_1}, \tag{4}$$

where $\|$ $\|_1$ denotes the ℓ^1 norm, and 'o' denotes Hadamard multiplication. The filtered labels of l_{mi}^W and l_{mi}^B are denoted as $g_\sigma(l_{mi}^W)$ and $g_\sigma(l_{mi}^B)$, which can be obtained by a 3D convolution with Gaussian kernel g_σ.

The multiscale structural dissimilarity is defined as follows:

$$E_S\left(l_m^W, l_m^B\right) = \frac{1}{|\{i\}|}\sum_i E_{SG}\left(l_{mi}^W, l_{mi}^B\right) + \frac{1}{N_1}\sum_j \varepsilon_j E_{SL}\left(l_{mj}^W, l_{mj}^B\right), \tag{5}$$

where E_{SG} and E_{SL} denote the multiscale structural dissimilarity of global labels and local labels, respectively. i, j, ε_j, and N_1 have the same meaning as in Eq. (2).

E_{SG} is the minus mean of the multiscale Mean Structural SIMilarity (MSSIM) for multi-scale global labels.

$$E_{SG}(l_{mi}^W, l_{mi}^B) = -\frac{1}{N_2}\sum_\sigma \text{MSSIM}\left(g_\sigma(l_{mi}^W), g_\sigma(l_{mi}^B)\right), \tag{6}$$

where N_2 and σ have the same meaning as in Eq. (3). E_{SL} is similar to Eq. (6) except that it is defined between two local labels.

MSSIM is the mean of the local weighted SSIM index volume [19, 20].

$$\text{MSSIM}\left(g_\sigma(l_{mi}^W), g_\sigma(l_{mi}^B)\right) = \text{mean}\left(\text{SSIM}\left(g_\sigma(l_{mi}^W), g_\sigma(l_{mi}^B)\right)\right), \tag{7}$$

$$\text{SSIM}(g_\sigma(l_{mi}^W), g_\sigma(l_{mi}^B)) = \frac{2\mu_{g_\sigma(l_{mi}^W)}\circ\mu_{g_\sigma(l_{mi}^B)}+C_1}{\mu_{g_\sigma(l_{mi}^W)}\circ\mu_{g_\sigma(l_{mi}^W)}+\mu_{g_\sigma(l_{mi}^B)}\circ\mu_{g_\sigma(l_{mi}^B)}+C_1}\circ\frac{2\delta_{g_\sigma(l_{mi}^W)}\circ g_\sigma(l_{mi}^B)+C_2}{\delta_{g_\sigma(l_{mi}^W)}\circ\delta_{g_\sigma(l_{mi}^W)}+\delta_{g_\sigma(l_{mi}^B)}\circ\delta_{g_\sigma(l_{mi}^B)}+C_2}, \tag{8}$$

where the constants $C_1 = (K_1 L)^2$ and $C_2 = (K_2 L)^2$ are used to avoid zero denominators. L is the dynamic range of the voxel intensities. As in the original paper [20], we set $K_1 = 0.01$, $K_2 = 0.03$ and $L = 1$ for normalized images. The elements of matrix μ are the weighted mean intensities in a local cubic window. The elements of matrix δ in denominator and in numerator denote the standard deviations and the covariances, respectively. μ and δ can be obtained via a 3D convolution with a Gaussian filter.

Additionally, the DDF should be smooth enough to preserve the topological correspondences. A regularization term of the bending energy is also used in this work.

2.2 Deformable Registration Network

Figure 3 depicts the brain MR deformable registration network that takes two patches as inputs. The UNet-style network consists of an encoder and decoder with skip connections. In the encoder, we use four ResNet blocks, each followed by a down-sampling max-pooling layer, to capture the hierarchical features of images. Each ResNet block consists of a $3 \times 3 \times 3$ convolution, batch normalization (BN), and rectified linear unit (ReLU) layer. The middle convolution block between the encoder and the decoder operates over coarser deformation representations between two input patches.

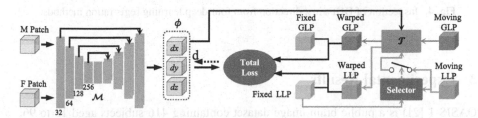

Fig. 3. Detailed architecture of our patch-based deformable registration network.

In the decoder, there are four up-sampling ResNet blocks. Each block consists of a transpose convolution layer with a stride of two voxels, a BN layer, a ReLU layer, and convolution layers. Successive blocks of the decoder operate on finer scales, doubling the feature map size and halving the number of channels. This multilevel decoder learns a coarse-to-fine deformation field. Finally, the DDF is predicted after an additional layer summing up the trilinearly up-sampled deformations on five scales.

Since the global labels can be found in all sampled patches, the moving global label patches (GLP) are directly connected to the transformation module $\mathcal{T}$. However, the local labels are small anatomical segmentations, and they only exist in some patches. Hence, we use a path selector to switch the network path of the moving local label patch (LLP). When the voxel numbers of the moving LLP and the fixed LLP are large enough, the selector connects the switch path; otherwise, it disconnects the path.

2.3 Comparison of the Whole DDFs

In Fig. 4, the axial slices of DDFs in x direction are compared by four label-driven deep learning registration methods: 1) Baseline Label-Reg using Dice similarity of Global labels (LRG) [7, 8]; 2) Label-Reg using Global labels and Local labels (LRGL) with Dice similarity (LRGL-D); 3) LRGL with Double Dice similarity (LRGL-DD); 4) LRGL with Double Dice similarity and Structural similarity (LRGL-DDS). The LRGL-DDS method corresponds to Eq. (1). If the structural dissimilarity of Eq. (1) is omitted, LRGL-DDS is reduced to LRGL-DD. The whole DDFs between new paired images are obtained by averaging the DDF patches, which are the outputs of the registration network. By comparing the DDF sharpness at the edges of different labels, we find the sort order: LRG < LRGL-D < LRGL-DD < LRGL-DDS. The DDFs using our LRGL-DDS are distinct *not only* at the boundaries *but also* in the small morphological regions, which implies that the LRGL-DDS method can align both the global label regions and the small inner morphological regions.

Fig. 4. Inspection of DDFs in *x* direction from four deep learning registration methods.

3 Experimental Results

OASIS-1 [21] is a public brain image dataset containing 416 subjects aged 18 to 96, where 385 subjects are randomly chosen for the moving images, one for the fixed image, and 30 for the testing images. For each subject, the dataset contains T1-weighted MR images and their global segmentation labels (WM, GM and CSF). The local hippocampus and caudate labels are further segmented by FSL package [22]. All images and labels are cropped to the same size of $176 \times 208 \times 176$ with 1-mm isotropic voxels.

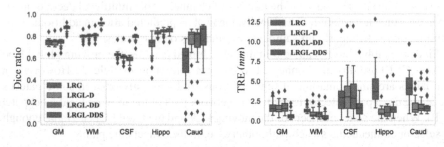

Fig. 5. Results of five labels via four patch-based label-driven deep learning methods.

The registration network was trained on a 12 GB Nvidia TitanX GPU for approximately 72 h, using an Adam optimizer starting at a learning rate of 10^{-5} with a minibatch size of 4 during the training. The training process took 10,000 iterations. The data augmentation was used via random linearly warping MR images and labels, and each image and each label were further uniformly sampled to patches with a stride of 32 voxels. 800,000 patches were used with 80 patches per iteration. In each training cycle, we shuffled the orders of subjects and patches. During inference, it took only ~11 s to calculate the whole DDF with the same stride.

Dice ratio (DR) and target registration error (TRE) were applied to quantify the alignment between the warped images and the fixed image. The quantitative results were illustrated in Fig. 5. For three global regions, especially for the CSF region (*p*

$< 9.32e^{-10}$ in DR and $p < 8.42e^{-7}$ in TRE via Wilcoxon signed-rank test), the registration performance of our LRGL-DDS method outperformed the other three learning-based methods. Compared with the best results of the other three methods, the medians of DRs of LRGL-DDS were enhanced by approximately 17% for GM, 14% for WM, and 26% for CSF; the medians of TREs of LRGL-DDS were reduced approximately 0.88 mm for GM, 0.38 mm for WM, and 1.25 mm for CSF, respectively. For two local regions, namely, the caudate and the hippocampus, all three kinds of LRGL methods achieved better registration accuracy than the LRG method.

We show some qualitative results in Fig. 6. The 104th (1st row) and 131st coronal slices (2nd row) highlight the local yellow hippocampal regions and local red caudate regions, respectively. Our LRGL-DDS method (6th column) can better align these local label regions than the other three methods, which is due to the fact that these regions are more consistent with the solid boundary curves in the fixed image (2nd column). Our LRGL-DDS method can better align global GM, WM and CSF tissues, especially the pink CSF regions as indicated by the arrows and the green detailed WM regions as circled by the four white dot curves.

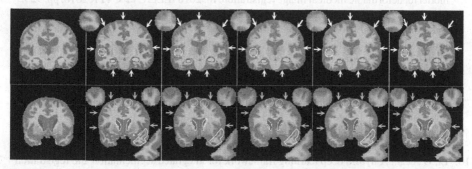

Fig. 6. Visualization of the inter-subject registration of T1-weighted MR images. From left to right: moving image, fixed image, and results of LRG, LRGL-D, LRGL-DD, and LRGL-DDS.

4 Conclusion

In this work, we use double Dice similarity to enhance brain MR image registration performances in narrow regions, and use structural similarity to further enhance registration accuracy in small detailed tissue regions. The two special loss functions can mitigate the *single force* issue in the outermost CSF regions and also the *small structure registration* issue. The total loss function is used to train the parameters of the UNet-style registration network. The path selector is used to accelerate the training process of local labels. Experimental results show that our LRGL-DDS registration method demonstrates promising registration performance *not only* for global GM and WM tissues, *but also* for global CSF. The registration accuracy of local tissues with three kinds of LRGL methods is also enhanced in comparison with the baseline LRG method. More deformation constraints and experiments, e.g., reducing negative Jacobian determinants, will be investigated in the future.

Acknowledgment. This work was supported in part by NSFC 61771230, 61773244, Shandong Provincial Natural Science Foundation ZR2019PF005, and Shandong Key R&D Program Project 2019GGX101006, 2019GNC106027. And we also thank for the open source code of Label-reg published by Hu Y *et al.*

References

1. Viergever, M.A., Maintz, J.B.A., Klein, S., Murphy, K., Staring, M., Pluim, J.P.W.: A survey of medical image registration – under review. Med. Image Anal. **33**, 140–144 (2016)
2. Litjens, G., et al.: A survey on deep learning in medical image analysis. Med. Image Anal. **42**, 60–88 (2017)
3. Haskins, G., Kruger, U., Yan, P.: Deep learning in medical image registration: a survey. Mach. Vis. Appl. **31**, 8 (2020). https://doi.org/10.1007/s00138-020-01060-x
4. Eppenhof, K.A.J., Lafarge, M.W., Pluim, J.P.W.: Progressively growing convolutional networks for end-to-end deformable image registration, vol. 48 (2019)
5. Balakrishnan, G., Zhao, A., Sabuncu, M.R., Dalca, A.V., Guttag, J.: An unsupervised learning model for deformable medical image registration. In: 2018 IEEE/CVF CVPR 2018, pp. 9252–9260. https://doi.org/10.1109/CVPR.2018.00964
6. Balakrishnan, G., Zhao, A., Sabuncu, M.R., Guttag, J., Dalca, A.V.: VoxelMorph: a learning framework for deformable medical image registration. IEEE Trans. Med. Imaging **38**, 1788–1800 (2019). https://doi.org/10.1109/TMI.2019.2897538
7. Hu, Y., et al.: Label-driven weakly-supervised learning for multimodal deformarle image registration. In: IEEE ISBI 2018, pp. 1070–1074 (2018)
8. Hu, Y., et al.: Weakly-supervised convolutional neural networks for multimodal image registration. Med. Image Anal. **49**, 1–13 (2018). https://doi.org/10.1016/j.media.2018.07.002
9. Mansilla, L., Milone, D.H., Ferrante, E.: Learning deformable registration of medical images with anatomical constraints. Neural Netw. **124**, 269–279 (2020)
10. Li, B., et al.: A hybrid deep learning framework for integrated segmentation and registration: evaluation on longitudinal white matter tract changes. In: Shen, D., et al. (eds.) MICCAI 2019. LNCS, vol. 11766, pp. 645–653. Springer, Cham (2019). https://doi.org/10.1007/978-3-030-32248-9_72
11. Lee, M.C.H., Oktay, O., Schuh, A., Schaap, M., Glocker, B.: Image-and-spatial transformer networks for structure-guided image registration. In: Shen, D., et al. (eds.) MICCAI 2019. LNCS, vol. 11765, pp. 337–345. Springer, Cham (2019). https://doi.org/10.1007/978-3-030-32245-8_38
12. Xu, Z., Niethammer, M.: DeepAtlas: joint semi-supervised learning of image registration and segmentation (2019). http://arxiv.org/abs/1904.08465
13. Hoffmann, M., Billot, B., Iglesias, J.E., Fischl, B., Dalca, A.V.: Learning multi-modal image registration without real data. arXiv Prepr. 2004, pp. 1–12 (2020)
14. Estienne, T., et al.: U-ReSNet: ultimate coupling of registration and segmentation with deep nets. In: Shen, D., et al. (eds.) MICCAI 2019. LNCS, vol. 11766, pp. 310–319. Springer, Cham (2019). https://doi.org/10.1007/978-3-030-32248-9_35
15. Yang, X., Kwitt, R., Styner, M., Niethammer, M.: Quicksilver: fast predictive image registration – a deep learning approach. Neuroimage **158**, 378–396 (2017)
16. Dalca, A.V., Balakrishnan, G., Guttag, J., Sabuncu, M.R.: Unsupervised learning of probabilistic diffeomorphic registration for images and surfaces. Med. Image Anal. **57**, 226–236 (2019). https://doi.org/10.1016/j.media.2019.07.006

17. Heinrich, M.P.: Closing the gap between deep and conventional image registration using probabilistic dense displacement networks. In: Shen, D., et al. (eds.) MICCAI 2019. LNCS, vol. 11769, pp. 50–58. Springer, Cham (2019). https://doi.org/10.1007/978-3-030-32226-7_6

18. Ha, I.Y., Heinrich, M.P.: Comparing deep learning strategies and attention mechanisms of discrete registration for multimodal image-guided interventions. In: Zhou, L., et al. (eds.) LABELS/HAL-MICCAI/CuRIOUS-2019. LNCS, vol. 11851, pp. 145–151. Springer, Cham (2019). https://doi.org/10.1007/978-3-030-33642-4_16

19. Sassi, O.B., Delleji, T., Taleb-Ahmed, A., Feki, I., Hamida, A.B.: MR image monomodal registration using structure similarity index. In: 2008 First Workshops on Image Processing Theory, Tools and Applications. pp. 1–5. IEEE (2008)

20. Wang, Z., Bovik, A.C., Sheikh, H.R., Simoncelli, E.P.: Image quality assessment: from error visibility to structural similarity. IEEE Trans. Image Process. **13**, 600–612 (2004)

21. Marcus, D.S., Fotenos, A.F., Csernansky, J.G., Morris, J.C., Buckner, R.L.: Open access series of imaging studies: longitudinal MRI data in nondemented and demented older adults. J. Cogn. Neurosci. **22**(12), 2677–2684 (2010)

22. Jenkinson, M., Beckmann, C.F., Behrens, T.E., Woolrich, M.W., Smith, S.M.: FSL. NeuroImage **62**, 782–790 (2012)

23. Luan, H., Qi, F., Xue, Z., Chen, L., Shen, D.: Multimodality image registration by maximization of quantitative–qualitative measure of mutual information. Pattern Recogn. **41**(1), 285–298 (2008)

24. Wu, G., Qi, F., Shen, D.: Learning-based deformable registration of MR brain images. IEEE Trans. Med. Imaging **25**(9), 1145–1157 (2006)

EczemaNet: Automating Detection and Severity Assessment of Atopic Dermatitis

Kevin Pan[1]⬤, Guillem Hurault[1]⬤, Kai Arulkumaran[1]⬤,
Hywel C. Williams[2]⬤, and Reiko J. Tanaka[1](✉)⬤

[1] Imperial College London, London SW7 2AZ, UK
r.tanaka@imperial.ac.uk
[2] University of Nottingham, Nottingham NG7 2UH, UK

Abstract. Atopic dermatitis (AD), also known as eczema, is one of
the most common chronic skin diseases. AD severity is primarily evaluated based on visual inspections by clinicians, but is subjective and has
large inter- and intra-observer variability in many clinical study settings.
To aid the standardisation and automating the evaluation of AD severity, this paper introduces a CNN computer vision pipeline, EczemaNet,
that first detects areas of AD from photographs and then makes probabilistic predictions on the severity of the disease. EczemaNet combines
transfer and multitask learning, ordinal classification, and ensembling
over crops to make its final predictions. We test EczemaNet using a set
of images acquired in a published clinical trial, and demonstrate low
RMSE with well-calibrated prediction intervals. We show the effectiveness of using CNNs for non-neoplastic dermatological diseases with a
medium-size dataset, and their potential for more efficiently and objectively evaluating AD severity, which has greater clinical relevance than
mere classification.

Keywords: Eczema · Multitask · Uncertainty

1 Introduction

Atopic dermatitis (or ezcema; AD) is a chronic skin disease affecting 15–30%
of children and 2–10% of adults worldwide [25]. It is characterised by recurrent
skin inflammation that can severely impact patients' lifestyles, with detrimental
effects on social, academic, and occupational aspects of their lives. While current treatments aim to manage dynamic and unpredictable fluctuations of AD
symptoms, only 24% of patients and caregivers feel confident that they can manage AD symptoms adequately [29]. Automating the evaluation of AD severity
would allow us to assist research into the disease and enable patients to become

Electronic supplementary material The online version of this chapter (https://
doi.org/10.1007/978-3-030-59861-7_23) contains supplementary material, which is
available to authorized users.

© Springer Nature Switzerland AG 2020
M. Liu et al. (Eds.): MLMI 2020, LNCS 12436, pp. 220–230, 2020.
https://doi.org/10.1007/978-3-030-59861-7_23

more involved in the management of their condition. Remote assessment of AD symptoms by automated evaluation would enhance data-enabled efficient clinical trials by reducing the burden of parties involved and minimise detection bias in clinical trials that test interventions.

Several clinical scores are commonly used to grade the severity of AD, including the Six Area, Six Sign Atopic Dermatitis (SASSAD) score [4], the Three Item Severity Score (TISS) [26], and the Eczema Area and Severity Index (EASI) [11], the latter of which is recommended by the Harmonising Outcome Measure for Eczema organisation [19]. Each of these are defined according to a combination of the severities of 7 disease signs[1] (Fig. 1): cracking (Cra.), dryness (Dry.), erythema (Ery.), excoriation (Exc.), exudation (Exu.), lichenification (Lic.) and oedema (Oed.). However, due to the lack of sufficient clinical training materials, and the non-intuitive nature of some disease signs (e.g., "dryness" versus "cracking"), inter- and intra-rater reliability is poor [18]. Our goal is to improve the reliability of these scoring systems through computer-aided evaluation of the different disease signs.

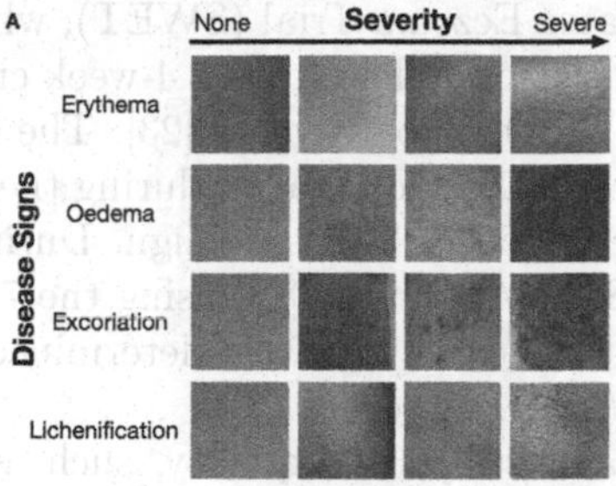

B

Disease Signs	Severity Score		
	SASSAD	TISS	EASI
Cracking (Cra.)	x		
Dryness (Dry.)	x		
Erythema (Ery.)	x	x	x
Excoriation (Exc.)	x	x	x
Exudation (Exu.)	x		
Lichenification (Lic.)	x		x
Oedema (Oed.)		x	x

Fig. 1. Disease signs and their relationship to severity scores. A) Examples of the 4 disease signs associated with EASI. Reproduced from [11]. B) A list of disease signs used for calculating SASSAD, TISS and EASI.

In recent years, machine-learning-based methods using convolutional neural networks (CNNs) have reached dermatologist-level performance on classifying skin cancers [5,7]. However, due to the lack of standardised clinical datasets beyond skin cancer, applications of CNNs for non-cancerous diseases have mostly been limited to automatic disease diagnosis of skin lesions [10,15,27]. Whether a lesion can be attributed to AD is of limited value to already diagnosed patients, and does not address the important challenge of assessing the overall severity of the disease, whose lesions are spatially distributed over the entire body and can exhibit multiple symptoms of varying intensities.

In this paper, we introduce a novel computer vision pipeline, EczemaNet, that is capable of detecting and evaluating the severity of AD from camera images. In comparison to prior work [2], we use deep learning to learn relevant features

[1] As well as the area of the affected region in the case of EASI.

from the data (as opposed to hand-engineered features), produce probabilistic predictions, and evaluate our method on a far larger dataset. Our pipeline uses CNNs to first detect regions-of-interest (RoI) from an image to make image crops, and then evaluate the severity of the 7 disease signs in each crop. Our input images often include background, clothes, etc. while most pipelines expect closely cropped images [24]. Similarly to recent work on psoriatic plaque severity assessment [16], we use ordinal classification to predict the severity of multiple disease signs simultaneously. However, we also propagate the uncertainties over these predictions to produce a final set of severity scores (SASSAD, TISS and EASI) simultaneously, and show that using multiple crops and probabilistic predictions allows us to make well-calibrated predictions with low root mean squared error (RMSE). These properties make EczemaNet a promising proof-of-concept for the use of CNNs in clinical trials, with downstream applications in personalised therapies for AD.

2   Data

Our data originates from the Softened Water Eczema Trial (SWET), which is a randomised controlled trial of 12 weeks duration followed by a 4-week crossover period, for 310 AD children aged from 6 months to 16 years [23]. The original data contains 1393 photos of representative AD regions taken during their clinic visits, along with the corresponding severity of each disease sign. During each visit, a disease assessment was made for SASSAD and TISS, using the 7 disease signs labelled for each image. The severity of each sign was determined on an ordinal scale: *none* (0), *mild* (1), *moderate* (2), or *severe* (3).

The photos vary both in resolution and subjective quality, such as focus, lighting, and blur. In addition, as the photos can contain significant areas of background or areas that are otherwise irrelevant for diagnosis, we manually curated 962 of the original photos, generating 1748 image crops of representative diseased regions by visual inspection[2]. We used these crops to fine-tune an RoI detection network, and then bootstrapped our dataset by running this network on all images, extracting a further 2178 image crops. Both sets of image crops were then combined and paired with the labels for the 7 disease signs, resulting in a final dataset of 933 diagnoses from 285 patients, including 1237 original photos with corresponding 3926 image crops[3].

This final dataset was used to train our severity prediction network (Subsect. 3.2). All crops were labelled with the overall diagnosis for the entire image, as we did not have labels for the individual crops. Despite this noisy labelling, the use of RoI detection and severity prediction in EczemaNet led to better performance than using the entire image (Subsect. 4.2).

---

[2] RoI, of arbitrary size, were labelled by 3 volunteers given a set of 50 expert-labelled images, where 1 volunteer was instructed directly by an expert. 431 photos were deemed difficult to label by the volunteers and hence left out of our dataset.

[3] The full data pipeline is provided in Supp. Fig. 1.

3   Method

Our EczemaNet pipeline consists of detecting RoI, making probabilistic predictions on all 7 disease signs over all crops simultaneously, and then combining these to predict the AD severity scores per image (Fig. 2). We made heavy use of transfer learning [28] to train on our medium-size dataset successfully: we fine-tuned both our RoI detection and severity prediction CNNs. The RoI detection was trained first, as otherwise it would not be able to provide relevant crops for the severity prediction network for end-to-end training. We used TensorFlow [1] for training and evaluation, starting with pretrained models in TensorFlow. Our code is available at https://github.com/Tanaka-Group/EczemaNet.

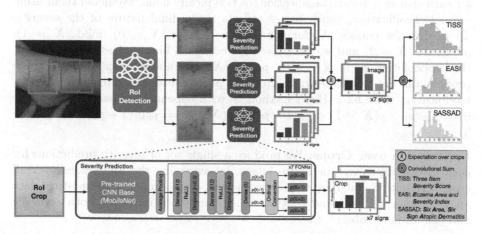

Fig. 2. EczemaNet overview. The RoI detection network extracts crops from an image. The severity prediction network makes probabilistic predictions for each disease sign in each crop. The averaged prediction over crops are then combined to form the final probabilistic prediction of the severity scores for the image.

3.1   RoI (Region of Interest) Detection

Following the speed/memory/accuracy model selection guidelines from Huang et al. [14], we chose the Faster R-CNN model [17] to perform RoI detection for diseased areas.

3.2   Severity Prediction

Our severity prediction pipeline is composed of a pretrained CNN base and 7 fully-connected neural networks (FCNNs), each of which predicts the severity of one of the 7 disease signs. We reflect the ordinal nature of the labels by training the FCNNs with ordinal classification. The predicted severities are averaged over all crops to calculate a probabilistic distribution of the severity of each disease sign for the image. Finally, the predictions for the disease signs are combined to produce a probability distribution of the regional[4] severity scores (SASSAD, TISS and EASI) per image.

Here we describe characteristic features of EczemaNet in more detail.

Pretrained CNN Base: Our base consists of all convolutional and pooling layers within MobileNet [13].

Separate FCNNs: We use separate FCNNs per disease sign, as opposed to using one FCNN to predict all disease signs simultaneously.

Ordinal Classification: Instead of predicting the 4 severities independently for each sign as a 4-way classification, as is typically done, we model them using ordinal classification, which better reflects the ordinal nature of the severity. To predict the classes, X, for the diagnoses none ($X = 0$), mild ($X = 1$), moderate ($X = 2$) and severe ($X = 3$), we train 3 binary classifiers to output the probabilities, $p_0 = p(X > 0)$, $p_1 = p(X > 1)$ and $p_2 = p(X > 2)$. These probabilities are then converted into class probabilities for outcome X using a modification of Frank & Hall's method [8] with dependent classifiers [6]: $p(X = 0) = 1 - p_0$, $p(X = 1) = p_0(1 - p_1)$, $p(X = 2) = p_0 p_1(1 - p_2)$, and $p(X = 3) = p_0 p_1 p_2$.

Expectation over Crops: We produce a single set of severity predictions for each disease sign over the entire image, by averaging the predictions over all crops[5]. Despite the high overlap between most crops, similarly to test-time data augmentation [3], we found that averaging over crops improved both accuracy and calibration (Subsect. 4.2).

Multitask Prediction: All 3 regional severity scores (TISS, EASI, SASSAD) are sums of subsets of the 7 disease signs (Fig. 1B). While it is possible to directly predict each of the regional severity scores, we treat prediction as a multitask problem, predicting the severity of all disease signs simultaneously, and then sum them[6] to calculate the final regional severity scores.

4   Experiments and Evaluation

Inference for a single image on CPU (Intel i9-9980HK) took 15.6s for the detection network and 1.6 s for the severity prediction network. Our work is a proof-of-concept, and could feasibly run on a smartphone in a few seconds with, e.g., model compression techniques.

---

[4] In practice, EASI and SASSAD are assessed across different regions of the body, which we do not consider in this work.

[5] Crops were preprocessed by bilinearly resampling to 224 × 224px.

[6] We convolve the probability mass functions of the predicted severity of the 7 disease signs, assuming that the predictions are independent random variables.

4.1 RoI (Region of Interest) Detection

We fine-tuned a pretrained Faster R-CNN model using the 962 manually curated original photos. With a train/validation/test ratio of 60:20:20, the manually curated photos were randomly split into 578:192:192 photos. It resulted in 1069:378:346 corresponding image crops, as each photo can contain a different number of image crops. The model was trained for 10^5 steps with a batch size of 1, using SGD with momentum $= 0.9$, with an initial learning rate of 3×10^{-4}, dropped to 3×10^{-5} after 90000 steps; no data augmentation was used. We weighted the localisation loss by a factor of 1.2, as our focus was to improve detection, rather than classification by Faster R-CNN, which was trained to detect the presence of AD.

We evaluated our model using the average precision (AP) score, the standard measure in object detection. The AP score measures the intersection between the ground truth and predicted boundaries, with a default overlap threshold of 50%. After tuning hyperparameters on our validation set, we tested our model using the test set of 192 images and obtained the AP score of 40.15%. We also performed a more qualitative evaluation to validate our trained model, and estimated that our model achieved a 10% false positive rate per image. We therefore concluded that our RoI detection network could generalise sufficiently well, and used it to extract more crops from the original data (Sect. 2).

4.2 Severity Prediction

We combined a pretrained MobileNet with 7 separate randomly initialised FCNNs (for each disease sign), and trained all parameters to predict the severity of the 7 disease signs on the final pre-processed dataset, which contained 933 diagnoses from 285 patients, including 1237 original photos with 3926 corresponding image crops. We used 10-fold cross-validation with a 90:10 train/test split, stratified on patients, to train and assess severity prediction models. The models were trained for a maximum of 50 epochs (using early stopping) with a batch size of 32, using SGD with a learning rate of 1×10^{-4} and momentum $= 0.9$; no data augmentation was used. Dropout with $p = 0.5$ and a max ℓ_2-norm weight constraint with $c = 3$ were used to regularise all fully-connected layers [21]. To combat severe class imbalance, we weighted all prediction losses by the inverse of the empirical class probabilities.

We evaluated RMSE on EASI (the recommended severity score [19]) for EczemaNet (1.929 ± 0.019) and for its variations listed below to confirm the use of each characteristic aspect of our model design (Fig. 3A and Table 1).

Pretrained CNN Base: The choice of pretrained CNN base significantly impacts the performance of the prediction model. We evaluated a range of commonly used CNN architectures for the base: Inception-v3 [22], MobileNet [13], ResNet-50 [12], VGG-16, and VGG-19 [20]. Only EczemaNet with MobileNet consistently achieved an RMSE on EASI of <2 including standard error.

Bootstrapped Dataset: Training EczemaNet with the 1748 manually labelled crops, plus the 2178 additional crops automatically extracted by our trained

RoI detection network, achieved the lowest RMSE across all of our experimental conditions (1.929 ± 0.019), compared to 2.003 ± 0.024 when EczemaNet was trained with only the manually labelled crops.

Model Architectures: We used a set of baselines (baseline and intercept-only) and ablations (listed in order of performance, Fig. 3A; Supp. Fig. 2):

EczemaNet	Our full model.
−Ordinal	4-way categorical classification *vs.* ordinal classification.
+Interaction	Sign interaction added by concatenating FCNN features *vs.* separate FCNN per sign.
−Separate FCNNs	A single FCNN for all 7 signs *vs.* separate FCNNs per sign.
−Crops	Using the entire image *vs.* averaging predictions over crops.
−Pretrained	Starting with random CNN weights *vs.* pretrained CNN weights.
Intercept-only	Predicting the average EASI in the training set.
Baseline	Predicting EASI from the whole image using regression.
−Multitask	Predicting EASI directly *vs.* summing predicted disease signs.

The full EczemaNet performs best, although some components have a lesser effect on the RMSE on EASI (Fig. 3A)[7]. In reverse order, multitask learning is the most important modelling choice, which possibly mitigates overfitting. The baseline model, which is a naive CNN-based approach, using regression on the whole image, performs almost the same as the intercept-only model, indicating the difficulty of our problem. Using pretrained weights and averaging over crops also play a large role in the good predictive performance of EczemaNet. Sharing FCNN parameters when modelling the 7 disease signs hurts performance slightly,

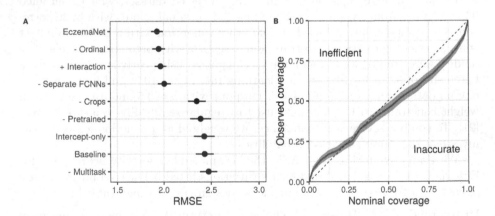

Fig. 3. A) RMSE (mean $\pm$ 1 standard error over cross-validation) on EASI across models. B) EASI calibration of highest density prediction intervals (coverage).

---

[7] We also observed a similar ranking across models for SASSAD (Supp. Figure 3) and TISS (Supp. Figure 4), as well as across the individual signs.

perhaps due to interference between the 7 tasks. Finally, ordinal classification provides a small boost over categorical classification with MobileNet[13][8].

The coverage of EczemaNet (Fig. 3B) indicates well-calibrated prediction intervals for a NN [9]. The performance could be further improved by post-processing, such as quantile calibration, to make the predictive distribution sharper at the mode and with longer tails.

Achieving high accuracy on the regional severity scores is a major aim of our work for clinical relevance. It is also important to examine other metrics as well, particularly because of the class imbalance in the data. We calculated F_1 scores and Ranked Probability Scores (RPS) for all disease signs for all models that predict all 7 disease signs (Table 1). The F_1 score is the harmonic mean of precision and recall, and hence is less sensitive to class imbalance than recall. RPS is a strictly proper scoring rule corresponding to the MSE of the cumulative forecast distribution and the cumulative outcome distribution, and measures the calibration of ordinal forecasts. We observed approximately the same ranking of baselines/ablations as for RMSE on EASI, with no clear outliers, supporting our earlier assessment on their relative importance.

Table 1. F_1 score (top; ↑ is better) and RPS (bottom; ↓ is better) for models that predict all 7 disease signs. Mean ± 1 standard error over cross-validation.

Model	Cra.	Dry.	Ery.	Exc.	Exu.	Lic.	Oed.
Full	0.707 ± 0.013	0.443 ± 0.006	0.419 ± 0.004	0.480 ± 0.007	0.769 ± 0.008	0.404 ± 0.005	0.694 ± 0.007
−Pretrained	0.671 ± 0.013	0.242 ± 0.008	0.250 ± 0.009	0.269 ± 0.004	0.759 ± 0.008	0.234 ± 0.003	0.694 ± 0.007
−Separate FCNNs	0.696 ± 0.013	0.422 ± 0.006	0.405 ± 0.006	0.473 ± 0.005	0.768 ± 0.008	0.390 ± 0.005	0.690 ± 0.007
+Interaction	0.704 ± 0.013	0.454 ± 0.005	0.437 ± 0.005	0.491 ± 0.007	0.767 ± 0.008	0.388 ± 0.007	0.697 ± 0.007
−Ordinal	0.696 ± 0.013	0.453 ± 0.006	0.428 ± 0.007	0.470 ± 0.004	0.772 ± 0.008	0.404 ± 0.006	0.692 ± 0.008
−Crops	0.686 ± 0.012	0.369 ± 0.004	0.370 ± 0.006	0.289 ± 0.007	0.765 ± 0.007	0.317 ± 0.006	0.700 ± 0.007
Full	0.076 ± 0.003	0.136 ± 0.001	0.137 ± 0.001	0.128 ± 0.001	0.056 ± 0.002	0.151 ± 0.002	0.077 ± 0.002
−Pretrained	0.098 ± 0.003	0.164 ± 0.001	0.160 ± 0.002	0.178 ± 0.001	0.077 ± 0.002	0.181 ± 0.001	0.085 ± 0.002
−Separate FCNNs	0.080 ± 0.003	0.140 ± 0.001	0.142 ± 0.001	0.132 ± 0.001	0.057 ± 0.002	0.156 ± 0.002	0.079 ± 0.002
+Interaction	0.080 ± 0.003	0.141 ± 0.001	0.141 ± 0.001	0.131 ± 0.002	0.056 ± 0.002	0.156 ± 0.002	0.079 ± 0.002
−Ordinal	0.079 ± 0.003	0.139 ± 0.001	0.136 ± 0.001	0.130 ± 0.001	0.055 ± 0.002	0.149 ± 0.001	0.079 ± 0.002
−Crops	0.083 ± 0.004	0.154 ± 0.001	0.155 ± 0.002	0.163 ± 0.002	0.063 ± 0.002	0.165 ± 0.002	0.081 ± 0.002

5 Discussion

This paper presented EczemaNet, a CNN-based pipeline for evaluating eczema severity directly from camera images. EczemaNet consists of an RoI detection network, which extracts relevant crops from each image, and a severity prediction network, which predicts the severity of 7 disease signs for each crop. The probability distributions of severities are averaged over crops, and then combined to form a prediction of the 3 regional severity scores. EczemaNet achieved

---

[8] The selection of base architecture was determined experimentally. MobileNet [13] provided greater benefits over other base architectures including VGG-16/19 [20], ResNet-50 [12], and Inception-v3 [22] (Supp. Fig. 5).

a low RMSE on EASI on a medium-size clinical dataset, and demonstrated well-calibrated prediction intervals. These results present a step towards standardising evaluation of objective AD severity scores for diverse dermatological research purposes, and could be applied to similar conditions, such as psoriasis.

Multiple sources of systematic errors, aside from random errors, can be considered to limit the performance of EczemaNet: mis-labelling due to inter- and intra-rater variability, discretisation error over a continuous outcome (severity), and errors arising from partial/noisy information (e.g., tactile diagnoses, out-of-focus images). While it is difficult to evaluate the effects of all of these sources of errors, Monte Carlo simulations of the measurement process suggested that rounding error alone could account for an RMSE of 0.6, which makes it unclear how much performance could be further improved on EczemaNet trained with our data. Future work could involve data augmentation while tackling the issue of the class imbalance.

A natural extension of the work presented here is to move beyond regional severity scores to predicting the overall severity scores. For a given area, EASI is the product of the intensity score (which we currently predict), and the area score. The area score could be predicted simultaneously with the intensity scores given the box labels identified by our RoI network. We encourage future clinical trials to collect and share richer labels, such as pixel-level segmentations, to increase the breadth of tasks, such as segmentation, that can be automated using machine learning.

References

1. Abadi, M., et al.: TensorFlow: a system for large-scale machine learning. In: USENIX Symposium on Operating Systems Design and Implementation, pp. 265–283 (2016)
2. Alam, M.N., Munia, T.T.K., Tavakolian, K., Vasefi, F., MacKinnon, N., Fazel-Rezai, R.: Automatic detection and severity measurement of eczema using image processing. In: EMBC, pp. 1365–1368. IEEE (2016)
3. Ashukha, A., Lyzhov, A., Molchanov, D., Vetrov, D.: Pitfalls of in-domain uncertainty estimation and ensembling in deep learning. In: International Conference on Learning Representations (2020)
4. Berth-Jones, J.: Six area, six sign atopic dermatitis (SASSAD) severity score: a simple system for monitoring disease activity in atopic dermatitis. Br. J. Dermatol. **135**, 25–30 (1996)
5. Brinker, T.J., et al.: Deep learning outperformed 136 of 157 dermatologists in a head-to-head dermoscopic melanoma image classification task. Eur. J. Cancer **113**, 47–54 (2019)
6. Cardoso, J.S., Costa, J.F.: Learning to classify ordinal data: the data replication method. JMLR **8**(Jul), 1393–1429 (2007)
7. Esteva, A., et al.: Dermatologist-level classification of skin cancer with deep neural networks. Nature **542**(7639), 115–118 (2017)
8. Frank, E., Hall, M.: A simple approach to ordinal classification. In: De Raedt, L., Flach, P. (eds.) ECML 2001. LNCS (LNAI), vol. 2167, pp. 145–156. Springer, Heidelberg (2001). https://doi.org/10.1007/3-540-44795-4_13

9. Guo, C., Pleiss, G., Sun, Y., Weinberger, K.Q.: On calibration of modern neural networks. In: ICML, pp. 1321–1330 (2017)

10. Hameed, N., Shabut, A.M., Hossain, M.A.: Multi-class skin diseases classification using deep convolutional neural network and support vector machine. In: SKIMA, pp. 1–7. IEEE (2018)

11. Hanifin, J., et al.: The eczema area and severity index (EASI): assessment of reliability in atopic dermatitis. Exp. Dermatol. **10**(1), 11–18 (2001)

12. He, K., Zhang, X., Ren, S., Sun, J.: Deep residual learning for image recognition. In: CVPR, pp. 770–778 (2016)

13. Howard, A.G., et al.: MobileNets: efficient convolutional neural networks for mobile vision applications. arXiv:1704.04861 (2017)

14. Huang, J., et al.: Speed/accuracy trade-offs for modern convolutional object detectors. In: CVPR, pp. 7310–7311 (2017)

15. Padilla, D., Yumang, A., Diaz, A.L., Inlong, G.: Differentiating atopic dermatitis and psoriasis chronic plaque using convolutional neural network mobilenet architecture. In: HNICEM, pp. 1–6 (2019)

16. Pal, A., Chaturvedi, A., Garain, U., Chandra, A., Chatterjee, R., Senapati, S.: Severity assessment of psoriatic plaques using deep CNN based ordinal classification. In: Stoyanov, D., et al. (eds.) CARE/CLIP/OR 2.0/ISIC -2018. LNCS, vol. 11041, pp. 252–259. Springer, Cham (2018). https://doi.org/10.1007/978-3-030-01201-4_27

17. Ren, S., He, K., Girshick, R., Sun, J.: Faster R-CNN: towards real-time object detection with region proposal networks. In: NeurIPS, pp. 91–99 (2015)

18. Schmitt, J., et al.: Assessment of clinical signs of atopic dermatitis: a systematic review and recommendation. J. Allergy Clin. Immunol. **132**(6), 1337–1347 (2013)

19. Schmitt, J., et al.: The Harmonising Outcome Measures for Eczema (HOME) statement to assess clinical signs of atopic eczema in trials. J. Allergy Clin. Immunol. **134**(4), 800–807 (2014)

20. Simonyan, K., Zisserman, A.: Very deep convolutional networks for large-scale image recognition. In: International Conference on Learning Representations (2015)

21. Srivastava, N., Hinton, G., Krizhevsky, A., Sutskever, I., Salakhutdinov, R.: Dropout: a simple way to prevent neural networks from overfitting. JMLR **15**(1), 1929–1958 (2014)

22. Szegedy, C., Vanhoucke, V., Ioffe, S., Shlens, J., Wojna, Z.: Rethinking the inception architecture for computer vision. In: CVPR, pp. 2818–2826 (2016)

23. Thomas, K., et al.: A multicentre randomised controlled trial and economic evaluation of ion-exchange water softeners for the treatment of eczema in children: the softened water eczema trial (SWET). Health Technol. Assess. **15**(8), 1–156 (2011)

24. Tschandl, P., Rosendahl, C., Kittler, H.: The ham10000 dataset, a large collection of multi-source dermatoscopic images of common pigmented skin lesions. Sci. Data **5**, 180161 (2018)

25. Weidinger, S., Beck, L.A., Bieber, T., Kabashima, K., Irvine, A.D.: Atopic dermatitis. Nat. Rev. Dis. Primers **4**(1), 1 (2018)

26. Wolkerstorfer, A., De Waard van der Spek, F., Glazenburg, E., Mulder, P., Oranje, A.: Scoring the severity of atopic dermatitis: three item severity score as a rough system for daily practice and as a pre-screening tool for studies. Acta Dermato-Venereologica **79**, 356–359 (1999)

27. Wu, H., et al.: A deep learning, image based approach for automated diagnosis for inflammatory skin diseases. Ann. Transl. Med. **8**(9) (2020)

28. Yosinski, J., Clune, J., Bengio, Y., Lipson, H.: How transferable are features in deep neural networks? In: NeurIPS, pp. 3320–3328 (2014)
29. Zuberbier, T., et al.: Patient perspectives on the management of atopic dermatitis. J. Allergy Clin. Immunol. **118**(1), 226–232 (2006)

Deep Distance Map Regression Network with Shape-Aware Loss for Imbalanced Medical Image Segmentation

Huiyu Li[1], Xiabi Liu[1(✉)], Said Boumaraf[1], Xiaopeng Gong[1], Donghai Liao[1], and Xiaohong Ma[2]

[1] Beijing Lab of Intelligent Information Technology, School of Computer Science, Beijing Institute of Technology, Beijing, China
liuxiabi@bit.edu.cn
[2] National Clinical Research Center for Caner, Chinese Academy of Medical Sciences, Beijing, China

Abstract. Small object segmentation, like tumor segmentation, is a difficult and critical task in the field of medical image analysis. Although deep learning based methods have achieved promising performance, they are restricted to the use of binary segmentation mask and suffer from the imbalance problem. In this research, we aim to tackle this limitation by adopting distance map as a novel ground truth and employing distance map regression as a proxy of the existing segmentation framework. Specially, we propose a new segmentation framework that incorporates the existing binary segmentation network and a light weight regression network (dubbed as LR-Net). Thus, the LR-Net can convert the conventional classification-based segmentation into a regression task and leverage the rich information of distance maps. Additionally, we derive a shape-aware loss by employing distance maps as penalty map to capture the complete shape of an object. We evaluated our approach on MICCAI 2017 Liver Tumor Segmentation (LiTS) Challenge dataset and a clinical dataset. Experimental results show that our approach outperforms the classification-based methods as well as other existing state-of-the-arts. Code is available at https://github.com/Huiyu-Li/Deep-Distance-Map-Regression.

Keywords: Deep network · Distance map · Data imbalance · 3D liver · Tumor segmentation

1 Introduction

In medical image analysis, automatic segmentation of small object is an active research area. This is the case, for instance, with liver tumor segmentation, where the accurate segmentation of the liver tumor from CT images provides useful information for liver cancer diagnosis and treatment. Due to the fact that liver tumors usually occupy a very small fraction of the input volume, there are

© Springer Nature Switzerland AG 2020
M. Liu et al. (Eds.): MLMI 2020, LNCS 12436, pp. 231–240, 2020.
https://doi.org/10.1007/978-3-030-59861-7_24

two major challenges involved. The first challenge is to segment the tumor from a huge and complex background, where the large variation in shape and location, as well as the unclear boundaries of tumors make segmentation much more complicated. The second challenge is to combat the problem of data imbalance. Without mitigating this problem, the training process will bias toward majority class and continue to fully neglect the minority class. Recently, several methods have been developed to deal with these two major challenges including cascaded training, class re-weighting, and balancing classification difficulties.

Cascaded training aims to mitigate the difficulty of small object segmentation by removing the irrelevant information outside the target object, in which the output of the former network is treated as an additional input for a subsequent network [6,7,10,15]. However, relying on the cascaded architecture to locate the small object from the huge background is computationally expensive and the ill-segmented results of the former network may deteriorate the small object segmentation.

Class re-weighting strategy modified the existing loss with the weights inversely proportional to the label frequencies, thus reducing the correlation between region size and loss contribution [4,13]. Furthermore, to achieve a better tradeoff between precision and recall, Salehi et al. [14] proposed a new loss based on the Tversky index. Inspired by the focal loss [11], Dice and Tvserky losses also integrated with an exponential factor to balances the labels not only by their relative sizes but also by their segmentation difficulties [1,16]. Despite their satisfactory performance for relatively imbalance data segmentation, they do not take into account any geometric properties and lack awareness of the overall shape.

In this paper, we propose to use the distance map regression to alleviate the data imbalance and derive a shape-aware loss to encourage the network to capture spatial information during training. Different from the existing methods of distance map usage, which only employ the ground-truth distance map or predict the distance map directly from the input image [12], we obtain distance map from the segmentation mask. This is more natural and intuitive according to the concept of distance map. Our main contributions are summarized as follows. (1) We employ the LR-Net to fulfill the computation of distance map. The LR-Net learns the strict mapping between the binary segmentation mask and the distance map. (2) We proposed a shape aware loss by introducing the rich information of distance map into the Dice loss, which places higher weights to the boundary and enforces the network to infer more accurate shape especially for small object. (3) We validate the effectiveness of our approach on two datasets and achieve the state-of-the-art or competitive performance over other baselines.

2   Methods

In this section, we first introduce a more informative ground truth beyond the binary segmentation mask. Then we construct a segmentation system capable of capturing the distinct geometric properties of the small object by distance map regression. An illustration of the overall segmentation system is shown in Fig. 1.

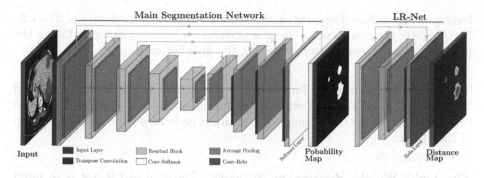

Fig. 1. Illustration of the main segmentation network with the LR-Net.

2.1 Distance Map

Considering that the generic binary segmentation mask assumes the same importance for each class, we adopt the distance map that incorporates both semantic information about different class and geometric properties of the object. Given a point (voxel) in an image space, the value of distance map is defined by the distance between the point and the closest boundary of the target object, through which the distance map embeds shape and boundary information into higher dimensional space. As a result, training the network to regress the distance map is equivalent to enforce the network to capture the shape and boundary properties.

In this work, we suggest to use norm inverse distance map (NI-DM), in which the inverse operation assign more weight to the voxels in proximity of the object boundary. The norm operation brings the distance map values within [0, 1] by normalization, which is more easily processed by the network.

Given a binary segmentation mask, we first calculate the original distance map (O-DM) $D(x)$. Then, each connected component C of O-DM is subtracted by its local maximum distance value plus 1 for inverse and, then divided by the local maximum distance for normalization. For every voxel x in the 3D medical image, we compute the NI-DM $\varphi(x)$ as

$$D(x) = \min_{\forall b \in B} d(x, b)$$
$$\varphi(x) = \frac{\max_{\forall x \in C}(D(x)) + 1 - D(x)}{\max_{\forall x \in C}(D(x))} \tag{1}$$

where $d(x, b)$ is the Euclidean distance between point x and b, B denotes the set of points on the object boundary.

2.2 Network Architecture

As shown in Fig. 1. The overall architecture contains a main segmentation network (M-Net) and the LR-Net, which are connected in tandem. The M-Net leverages the success of conventional classification-based segmentation. The LR-Net converts the classification-based segmentation into regression by taking the probability map as input and predicting the distance map.

The Main Segmentation Network. The backbone of the M-Net is inspired by the widely used 3D UNet with residual connections. For classification-based segmentation, we use the softmax as the output layer to get the probability map of the M-Net.

The Light Weight Regression Network. The goal of LR-Net is to fulfill the computation of distance map in a differentiable manner. By leveraging the rigorous mapping between binary segmentation mask and distance map, the LR-Ne bias the network to favor semantically meaningful regions and infer better spatial consistency maps.

Since each point of the distance map owns a precise spatial proximity of the object boundary, the mapping between the predicted and the ground truth of distance map is more rigorous than that of the binary segmentation map. A minor mismatch between the predicted and the ground truth distance map can exert large penalty to the network optimization. Thus, the LR-Net can improve the learning process and enforce the whole network to predict a perfect distance map as well as a more precise segmentation mask.

Motivated by the fact that the lower layers of the CNN extract low-level features, like shape and edge [9], we adopt a light weight UNet to obtain competitive performance with low complexity. The LR-Net takes two-channel probability map as input. The encoder of LR-Net consists of only one down-sampling operation which halves the size of feature map at the beginning. Symmetrically, the decoder contains one up-sampling operation to reconstruct the feature maps to the original size. Depending on the nature of the norm inverse distance map, the output layer uses the ReLU activation function.

The Training and Inference Pipeline. The training of the LR-Net is detached from the M-Net and takes the ground truth segmentation mask as input. Unlike training the M-Net and LR-Net together, training the LR-Net independently prevents the incorrect segmentation maps from bringing disaster to the LR-Net as well as the whole network through backward optimization. By using the ground truth segmentation mask as input, the rigorous mapping between the segmentation mask and the distance map can be established in an effective manner. Benefiting from the elaborated training scheme, the regression loss can be quickly optimized to global minima with a Dice score around 0.99. This rigorous mapping can therefore guarantee the correspondence between the outputs of the M-Net and the LR-Net when connecting in tandem.

During the training of the whole network, we froze the parameters of the LR-Net since the rigorous mapping has been established by its pre-trained process. Such a pipeline has the advantages that (1) the LR-Net can be easily cooperated with any classification-based segmentation network; (2) the LR-Net can adjust the M-Net to strictly obey the semantic and shape priors by the rigorous mapping, so the classification-based segmentation and the distance map regression can compensate for each other. During reference, the LR-Net can be removed and the M-Net predict the segmentation mask directly.

2.3 Loss Functions

Since the distance map is a continuous representation of the segmentation mask, we can train the LR-Net to predict the distance map by a regression loss. Considering that smooth L1 loss is robust to outliers and differentiable around 0, we adopt it as the regression loss to measure the difference between the predicted and ground truth distance map.

To make the M-Net more sensitive to the misclassified points and fully utilize the spatial expressiveness of the distance map, we proposed a novel MapDice loss by using the ground truth distance map as a pixel-wise penalty map. During training, the MapDice loss encourage the LR-Net to capture the overall shape of the target object by penalizing the mismatch. The loss term $L_{MapDice}$ is defined as

$$L_{MapDice} = 1 - \sum_{c=1}^{C} \frac{2 \times (p^c \times \varphi^c) + \varepsilon}{p^c + \varphi^c + \varepsilon} \qquad (2)$$

where p^c and φ^c are the predicted probability map and the ground truth distance map belonging to class c, respectively; ε is a very small number to prevent the denominator being zero.

3   Experiments

Dataset and Preprocessing. Our proposed method is evaluated on two datasets. One is the public MICCAI 2017 Liver Tumor Segmentation (LiTS) Challenge dataset [12]. It contains 130 CT scans for training and 70 CT scans for testing, which have the same resolution of 512×512 pixels but with different numbers of axial slices and slice thicknesses. The available ground truth is provided only for the training dataset.

Another dataset is our clinical tumor dataset. It contains 137 cases of Contrast-Enhanced CT (CECT) with arterial phase, portal venous phase and delay phase. The axial slices have the same resolution of 512×512, but the number of slices differs among different modalities. The dataset contains the manually segmented liver tumors and the final annotation was validated by a senior radiologist with 15-years' experience in abdominal imaging.

We perform the experiments on these two datasets independently. On LiTS dataset, all cases are randomly divided into two non-overlapping groups, 117/13 cases in the training set are randomly divided for training and validation, respectively, and 70 testing cases are used to test the approaches. On our clinical tumor dataset, all the cases are used for testing.

In data preprocessing, we perform spacing interpolation, window transform, effective range extraction, and sub-image generation to get the applicable input. The ground truth distance map are calculated by the Euclidean distance transform algorithm.

Implementation Details. In our experiments, we use the same backbone network implemented with the PyTorch framework for fair comparison. All the models were trained from scratch, initialized with Kaiming uniform [8], and optimized by Adam. The initial learning rate is 0.001 and decayed by factor of 0.8 once learning stagnates. Training was continued till validation loss converged. All the experiments are conducted on an NVIDIA 2080Ti GPU.

Evaluation Criteria. We utilize seven metrics to evaluate the accuracy of segmentation results. These evaluation metrics include Dice per Case score (DC), Dice Global score (DG), volumetric overlap error (VOE), relative volume difference (RVD), average symmetric surface distance (ASSD), maximum surface distance (MSD), root means square symmetric surface distance (RMSD) [3]. For the last five evaluation metrics, the smaller the value, the better the segmentation result.

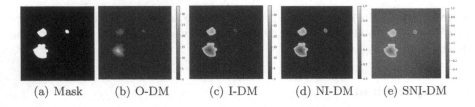

(a) Mask   (b) O-DM   (c) I-DM   (d) NI-DM   (e) SNI-DM

Fig. 2. An illustration of different kinds of distance maps.

3.1   Comparison of Various Distance Maps Regression

A simple illustration of distance maps is shown in Fig. 2, which contains the binary segmentation mask, O-DM, inverse distance map (I-DM), NI-DM and sign norm inverse distance map (SNI-DM). I-DM is derived from the I-DM by taking inverse operation. SNI-DM is modified from the NI-DM, where the voxel inside the boundary of the target object is positive, otherwise is negative.

To analyze the learning behavior of our method with different distance maps, we conduct several comparative experiments on the LiTS training dataset and the results are reported in Table 1. Notably, we adopt different activation functions of the LR-Net output layer according to the nature of distance maps. In brief, the O-DM and I-DM regression employ ReLU activation; the NI-DM regression uses both ReLU and Sigmoid for comparison purposes; the SNI-DM regression employs Tanh activation. We take the M-Net with Dice loss and

MapDice loss as two baseline methods, yielding a Dice score of 0. 6581 and 0.6856, respectively.

As shown in Fig. 3, our method demonstrates superior qualitative results, especially in the notoriously small tumors segmentation. In Table 1, the results show that the M-Net with the LR-Net achieves better performance than M-Net alone on all the evaluation criteria. This indicates the significance of LR-Net on accuracy improvement. Then, we evaluate the performance of MapDice loss. By comparing the results with and without the MapDice loss, it is apparent that MapDice loss contributes a lot for segmentation accuracy improvement. In particular, the MapDice loss yields the superior results of NI-DM regression, while Dice loss shows a significant drop in the last four columns of Table 1. This indicates that distance map can help the network to capture semantically meaningful regions and produce more accurate results. The constant value α, used to balance the magnitude difference of two different losses, is also verified to be effective for the performance improvement.

Table 1. Comparison of DC for different combinations of baselines and distance maps on LiTS validation dataset. 'NI-DMs': NI-DM regression with Sigmoid activation.

Methods	O-DM	I-DM	NI-DM	NI-DMs	SNI-DM
MNet+LR-Net+$L_{smoothL1}$	0. 6993	**0.7310**	0.7420	0.7381	**0.7342**
MNet+L_{Dice}+LR-Net+$L_{smoothL1}$	0.6842	0.7003	0.7172	0.6914	0.6281
MNet+L_{Dice}+LR-Net+$\alpha \cdot L_{smoothL1}$	**0.7101**	0.7169	0.7375	0.7228	0.6510
MNet+$L_{MapDice}$+LR-Net+$L_{smoothL1}$	0.6874	0.7135	0.7289	0.7283	0.6384
MNet+$L_{MapDice}$+LR-Net+$\alpha \cdot L_{smoothL1}$	0.6904	0.7303	**0.7463**	**0.7445**	0.6961

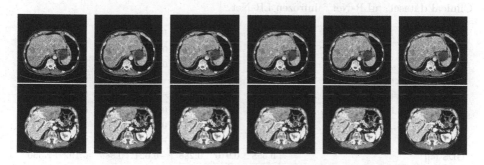

Fig. 3. Liver tumor segmentation results of different methods on the LiTS validation dataset. From left to right, ground truth, segmentation results by MNet+L_{Dice}, MNet+$L_{MapDice}$, MNet+LR-Net+$L_{smoothL1}$, MNet+L_{Dice}+LR-Net+$\alpha \cdot L_{smoothL1}$, MNet+$L_{MapDice}$+LR-Net+$\alpha \cdot L_{smoothL1}$ are shown respectively.

The results of different distance maps show that using I-DM and NI-DM is better than the O-DM, while the SNI-DM and sigmoid activation does not guarantee more improvement on the segmentation performance. This indicates that NI-DM with ReLU activation is the most powerful combination.

3.2 Effectiveness of the M-Net with LR-Net

We test our method and make comparison with other related approaches on the clinical dataset, with the checkpoint achieving the highest Dice score on the LiTS validation dataset. The experimental results are shown in Table 2. Firstly, we analyze the influence of each component of our method and list the results in row 2–7. Then we compare our method with Weighted cross-entropy (WCE) [13], Generalized Dice Score (GDS) [4], Tversky loss [14], Focal Tversky loss [1], and Exponential Logarithmic loss (Exp-Log) [16] that all proposed to combat the imbalance issue. The last two rows list the result of employing distance map regression as a proxy in multi-branch fashion and cascaded manner, respectively.

Despite the superior results of LR-Net and MapDice loss, demonstrating the effectiveness of our method, the significant drop in performance in row 4 indicates that our train scheme of LR-Net plays important roles in improving the segmentation performance. Compared to the methods for imbalanced data in row 8–12, our method achieves a significant increment in all the evaluation metrics. This demonstrates the effectiveness of our method in combating the imbalance issue. According to inferior performance of the last two rows, we can find that our method is more appropriate to fully utilize the geometric properties of distance map.

For fair performance comparison, we also submitted the result to the LiTS leaderboard. We reached a Dice per case of 0.679, Dice global of 0.830, VOE of 0.367, RVD of -0.052, ASSD of 1.058, MSD of 6.531, and RMSD of 1.580, which is a desirable performance on the LiTS challenge for tumor segmentation.

Table 2. Comparison with different baselines and other state-of-the-art methods on Clinical dataset. 'uLR-Net': unfrozen LR-Net.

Methods	DC	DG	VOE	RVD	ASSD	MSD	RMSD
MNet+L_{Dice}	0.647	0.888	0.292	0.065	0.809	6.201	1.292
MNet+$L_{MapDice}$	0.661	0.870	0.298	0.116	0.944	7.005	1.482
MNet+uLR-Net+$L_{smoothL1}$	0.628	0.715	0.395	−0.049	1.328	8.683	1.983
MNet+LR-Net+$L_{smoothL1}$	0.748	0.931	0.262	−0.016	0.674	**5.548**	1.100
MNet+L_{Dice}+LR-Net+$L_{smoothL1}$	0.721	0.913	0.273	0.118	0.754	6.134	1.218
MNet+$L_{MapDice}$+LR-Net+$L_{smoothL1}$	**0.751**	**0.935**	**0.252**	0.070	**0.654**	5.708	**1.079**
WCE [13]	0.622	0.883	0.379	**−0.253**	1.134	6.425	1.597
GDS [4]]	0.658	0.910	0.286	−0.024	0.886	6.192	1.350
Tversky [14]	0.738	0.930	0.261	0.059	0.667	5.589	1.094
Focal Tversky [1]	0.738	0.923	0.273	0.050	0.734	5.920	1.184
ExpLog [16]	0.737	0.921	0.255	0.126	0.708	6.152	1.160
Multi-branch Regression [5]	0.723	0.917	0.288	0.016	0.748	5.921	1.199
Cascaded Regression [2]	0.722	0.906	0.285	0.034	0.796	6.026	1.251

4   Conclusion

In this paper, we proposed a distance map regression network (LR-Net) to fulfill the computation of distance map, which makes distance map computation differentiable and applicable in deep learning. In virtue of the LR-Net and the rigorous mapping between the binary segmentation mask and the distance map, the conventional classification-based segmentation network and the regression network can be reciprocally influenced to produce more precise segmentation mask. Furthermore, a new shape-aware loss has been introduced to leverage the geometric and semantic information of distance map. Extensive experiments verified we can benefit from the distance map regression network and the shape-aware loss.

References

1. Abraham, N., Khan, N.M.: A novel focal Tversky loss function with improved attention U-Net for lesion segmentation. In: 2019 IEEE 16th International Symposium on Biomedical Imaging (ISBI 2019), pp. 683–687. IEEE (2019)
2. Audebert, N., Boulch, A., Le Saux, B., Lefèvre, S.: Distance transform regression for spatially-aware deep semantic segmentation. Comput. Vis. Image Underst. **189**, 102809 (2019)
3. Bilic, P., et al.: The liver tumor segmentation benchmark (LiTS). arXiv preprint arXiv:1901.04056 (2019)
4. Crum, W.R., Camara, O., Hill, D.L.: Generalized overlap measures for evaluation and validation in medical image analysis. IEEE Trans. Med. Imaging **25**(11), 1451–1461 (2006)
5. Dangi, S., Linte, C.A., Yaniv, Z.: A distance map regularized CNN for cardiac cine MR image segmentation. Med. Phys. **46**(12), 5637–5651 (2019)
6. Gao, Y., et al.: FocusNet: imbalanced large and small organ segmentation with an end-to-end deep neural network for head and neck CT images. In: Shen, D., et al. (eds.) MICCAI 2019. LNCS, vol. 11766, pp. 829–838. Springer, Cham (2019). https://doi.org/10.1007/978-3-030-32248-9_92
7. Havaei, M., et al.: Brain tumor segmentation with deep neural networks. Med. Image Anal. **35**, 18–31 (2017)
8. He, K., Zhang, X., Ren, S., Sun, J.: Delving deep into rectifiers: surpassing human-level performance on imagenet classification. In: Proceedings of the IEEE International Conference on Computer Vision, pp. 1026–1034 (2015)
9. Huang, Y., et al.: A liver fibrosis staging method using cross-contrast network. Expert Syst. Appl. **130**, 124–131 (2019)
10. Jiang, H., Shi, T., Bai, Z., Huang, L.: AHCNet: an application of attention mechanism and hybrid connection for liver tumor segmentation in CT volumes. IEEE Access **7**, 24898–24909 (2019)
11. Lin, T.Y., Goyal, P., Girshick, R., He, K., Dollár, P.: Focal loss for dense object detection. In: Proceedings of the IEEE International Conference on Computer Vision, pp. 2980–2988 (2017)
12. Ma, J., et al.: How distance transform maps boost segmentation CNNs: an empirical study. In: Medical Imaging with Deep Learning (2020)
13. Ronneberger, O., Fischer, P., Brox, T.: U-Net: convolutional networks for biomedical image segmentation. In: Navab, N., Hornegger, J., Wells, W.M., Frangi, A.F. (eds.) MICCAI 2015. LNCS, vol. 9351, pp. 234–241. Springer, Cham (2015). https://doi.org/10.1007/978-3-319-24574-4_28

14. Salehi, S.S.M., Erdogmus, D., Gholipour, A.: Tversky loss function for image segmentation using 3D fully convolutional deep networks. In: Wang, Q., Shi, Y., Suk, H.-I., Suzuki, K. (eds.) MLMI 2017. LNCS, vol. 10541, pp. 379–387. Springer, Cham (2017). https://doi.org/10.1007/978-3-319-67389-9_44

15. Valverde, S., et al.: Improving automated multiple sclerosis lesion segmentation with a cascaded 3D convolutional neural network approach. NeuroImage **155**, 159–168 (2017)

16. Wong, K.C.L., Moradi, M., Tang, H., Syeda-Mahmood, T.: 3D segmentation with exponential logarithmic loss for highly unbalanced object sizes. In: Frangi, A.F., Schnabel, J.A., Davatzikos, C., Alberola-López, C., Fichtinger, G. (eds.) MICCAI 2018. LNCS, vol. 11072, pp. 612–619. Springer, Cham (2018). https://doi.org/10.1007/978-3-030-00931-1_70

Joint Appearance-Feature Domain Adaptation: Application to QSM Segmentation Transfer

Bin Xiao[1,2], Naying He[3], Qian Wang[2(✉)], Zhong Xue[1], Lei Chen[1], Fuhua Yan[3], Feng Shi[1(✉)], and Dinggang Shen[1]

[1] Shanghai United Imaging Intelligence Co., Ltd., Shanghai, China
feng.shi@united-imaging.com
[2] Institute for Medical Imaging Technology, School of Biomedical Engineering, Shanghai Jiao Tong University, Shanghai, China
wang.qian@sjtu.edu.cn
[3] Department of Radiology, Ruijin Hospital, Shanghai Jiao Tong University School of Medicine, Shanghai, China

Abstract. Quantitative susceptibility mapping (QSM) is a magnetic resonance imaging technique used to quantitatively measure the iron content in the brain. Patients with Parkinson's disease are reported having increased iron deposition, especially in substantia nigra (SN) which is a relatively small gray matter structure located in the midbrain. The automatic segmentation of SN is a critical prerequisite step to facilitate the progression of evaluating the course of Parkinson's disease. However, the imaging protocol and reconstruction methods in QSM acquisition vary largely, rendering great challenges in constructing and applying image segmentation models. Thus, a model trained on a certain dataset often performs poorly on datasets from other scanners or reconstruction methods. To quickly transfer a trained segmentation model to a dataset acquired in a new instrument, we have developed a joint appearance-feature domain adaptation framework (JAFDAF) to transfer the knowledge from the source to the target domains for improved SN segmentation. In particular, we perform domain adaption in both appearance and feature spaces. In the appearance space, we use region-based histogram matching and a neural network to align the grayscale ranges of images between these two domains. In the feature space, we propose a domain regularization layer (DRL) by utilizing the idea of neural architecture search (NAS) to enforce the convolution kernels for learning features that are efficacious in both domains. Ablation experiments have been carried out to evaluate the proposed JAFDAF framework, and the experimental results on 27 subjects show that our method achieves up to 12% over the baseline model and about 5% over a fine-tuning approach.

Keywords: Domain adaptation · QSM · Substantia nigra · Segmentation · Region-based histogram matching · Domain regularization layer

1 Introduction

Parkinson's disease (PD) is a progressive neurodegenerative disease which leads to shaking, stiffness, and difficulty with walking, balance, and coordination. The main pathophysiological change is the loss of dopaminergic neurons in the substantia nigra (SN).

© Springer Nature Switzerland AG 2020
M. Liu et al. (Eds.): MLMI 2020, LNCS 12436, pp. 241–249, 2020.
https://doi.org/10.1007/978-3-030-59861-7_25

During this process, iron deposition in the SN of the midbrain increased significantly [1], which can be observed in quantitative susceptibility mapping (QSM) images.

To explore the relationship between signal changes in the SN and the course of Parkinson's disease [18], it is necessary to perform automatic segmentation of the SN. In practice, a fully convolutional neural network (FCN) [2] based segmentation algorithm can achieve excellent segmentation performance on the dataset from one data center. However, the quality of QSM images vary largely, and so challenges are being raised due to inconsistency of the scanner protocol and reconstruction algorithms used in different centers. All these factors may hold accountable for the phenomenon of domain transfer, e.g., the model trained in one data center often performs poorly on the data from another. Hence, when we apply a trained model to a new environment with only a few samples available for training, it is particularly desirable to implement fast domain transfer learning.

Domain adaptive algorithms have recently been developed to deal with such kind of reduced performance problems. Traditional domain adaptive methods combine maximum mean discrepancy (MMD) loss [3] and adaptation network layers [4–6]. These methods transfer the source and target domain images into a common feature space, while enforcing supervised learning on the source domain not to lose useful information for subsequent tasks. However, these methods rely on the design of the MMD loss and its variants. To overcome this shortcoming, inspired by the idea of adversarial learning [7], researchers replaced the MMD loss with a discriminative network to fulfill more complex domain adaptation tasks. In addition to performing domain adaptation on the feature space, some work [8] borrows CycleGAN's [9] method to transform between the source domain images and the target domain images. But all these methods require a sufficient number of samples in both domains to ensure the convergence of the network. They cannot perform well when the target domain has only a few samples for training.

In this article, in the case where the target domain has only a small number of samples, we eliminate the differences between the two domains in two spaces: appearance space and feature space. In the appearance space, we transform the target domain image into the source domain. We propose to use region-based histogram matching to simulate a source domain image for each target domain image, which turns the unsupervised mapping problem into a weakly-supervised problem. Then, we train a neural network to automate this process. In the feature space, inspired by Neural Architecture Search (NAS), we design a Domain Regularization Layer (DRL) which is decoupled into a convolution kernel and weighting coefficients. The convolution kernel of this layer was trained on the source domain to learn the knowledge used for segmentation and the weighting coefficient was trained on the target domain to enhance the learned convolution kernel useful for the target domain. Through alternate training, DRL can automatically select the convolution kernel that is valid for both domains. Comparative studies are performed to evaluate the performance of the proposed joint appearance-feature domain adaptation for SN segmentation in PD patients.

2 Method

For QSM images acquired from different instruments and reconstruction algorithms, we refer those to be transferred as in the target domain and those transferred as in the source domain. Figure 1 outlines our proposed joint appearance-feature domain adaptation framework (JAFDAF). The key technical contributions in our method are an appearance alignment neural network using region-based histogram matching, and a domain regularization layer using NAS.

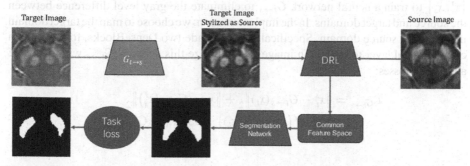

Fig. 1. The architecture of the proposed joint appearance-feature domain adaptation framework (JAFDAF). A neural network was first used to eliminate the differences between the appearance of the images. Subsequently, a domain regularization layer (DRL) is used to extract common features on the two image domains in the form of a regularization terms.

2.1 Appearance Space Adaptation

An image mapping is designed to eliminate difference between the two domains in the appearance space. Based on our observation, one significant finding between the source and target domains lies in the difference in the grayscale. For example, in the source domain, the mean intensity value of SN is 150, but it is about 220 in the target domain. Therefore, eliminating the grayscale difference between the source and target domains is necessary for the domain adaptation problem.

We first transform the problem into a weakly supervised problem through "region-based histogram matching" (RBHM). Formally, we define a source image set $\mathcal{X}_S \subset \mathbb{R}^{H \times W \times D}$ along with manually-labeled segmentation maps $\mathcal{Y}_S \subset \mathbb{R}^{H \times W \times D}$. Similarly, we have the image and segmentation images as $\mathcal{X}_T \subset \mathbb{R}^{H \times W \times D}$ and $\mathcal{Y}_T \subset \mathbb{R}^{H \times W \times D}$ in the target domain. For each segmentation map $p_s \in \mathcal{Y}_S$ (or $p_t \in \mathcal{Y}_T$), we have $p_s(i, j, k) = 1$ (or $p_t(i, j, k) = 1$) if the pixel at position (i, j, k) of image $x_s \in \mathcal{X}_S$ (or $x_t \in \mathcal{X}_T$) belongs to SN; otherwise, $p_s(i, j, k) = 0$ or $p_t(i, j, k) = 0$). We split the image into three parts: (1) pixels where $p_s(i, j, k) = 1$ (or $p_t(i, j, k) = 1$); (2) pixels where $p_s(i, j, k) = 0$ (or $p_t(i, j, k) = 0$) and $x_s(i, j, k) > 0$ (or $x_t(i, j, k) > 0$); (3) pixels where $p_s(i, j, k) = 0$ (or $p_t(i, j, k) = 0$) and $x_s(i, j, k) < 0$ (or $x_t(i, j, k) < 0$). Take the first part as an example, we extract all the pixels from the source domain and target domain to form two point sets, respectively. We apply histogram matching to the two point sets. Then the gray values of the SN region can be transformed from the target domain to the source domain. We call this operation "Region-based histogram matching" (RBHM). We apply RBHM to each of the three areas. In this way, for each $x_s \in \mathcal{X}_S$, we can get a simulated image that has the gray range of the source domain without changing the texture of the original image. We formulate the corresponding simulation image as x_s^t. Similarly, if we operate in a reverse direction, for each x_t we have x_t^s. After this, we can use x_s^t as a weakly supervised target to train the mapping model. Since the amount of data $\{x_t, x_t^s\}$ is very small, we include $\{x_s^t, x_s\}$ as data augmentation.

To make the above process automatic, we use the simulated data set $\{x_t, x_t^s\}$ and $\{x_s^t, x_s\}$ to train a neural network $G_{t \to s}$ to eliminate the gray level difference between the source and target domains. In the implementation, we choose to map the target domain image to the source domain. Specifically, we cascade two DenseBlocks, followed by a convolutional layer to output an image. We optimize this network $G_{t \to s}$ with the MSE and SSIM losses:

$$\mathcal{L}_{G_{t \to s}} = \left\| x_t^s - G_{t \to s}(x_t) \right\|_2 + \left\| x_s - G_{t \to s}(x_s^t) \right\|_2$$
$$+ SSIM\left(x_t^s, G_{t \to s}(x_t)\right) + SSIM\left(x_s, G_{t \to s}(x_s^t)\right)$$

2.2 Feature Space Adaptation

Just eliminating the appearance difference does not completely solve the problem of domain transfer. In fact, domain transfer is not only reflected in grayscale difference, but also in the feature space, i.e., in our data, an image in the target domain is sharper than that in the source domain. Therefore, it is necessary to guide the subsequent network to learn features that are valid for both domains.

Here we propose a domain regularization layer (DRL) to replace the first layer of the segmentation network as in Fig. 2. For DRL, unlike the conventional convolutional layers, it has two sets of learnable parameters: 1) convolution kernel parameter W and 2) convolution kernel combination parameter h. They are combined into the final convolution kernel by the following formula:

$$\widehat{W} = W \cdot softmax(h)$$

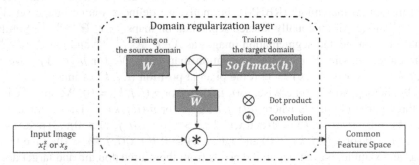

Fig. 2. The architecture of the domain regularization layer (DRL). W is the convolution kernel parameter, and h is the convolution kernel combination parameter. Image input is an QSM image or an image from the output of the $G_{t \to s}$ used in Sect. 2.1. After the convolution operation of the convolution kernel $\widehat{W}$, DRL outputs the feature map.

In the training stage, W is trained on the source-domain data along with the parameters of the subsequent segmentation network. Since the source-domain data has a large amount of labels, the network can learn the convolution kernels useful for segmentation task. After each iteration, we fix W and the parameters of the segmentation network, update h on the target domain image. In this way, h is equivalent to the regularization term in the training process of the network as it will automatically increase the weights of those convolution kernels that are valid for the target domain.

We use DenseBlock proposed in [13] as the backbone of our segmentation network S_θ (θ is the parameter to be trained). Although DenseBlock is not directly used to solve the segmentation task, as proved by [14], it is a good choice to use DenseBlock in the segmentation network for small target, such as SN in midbrain. The backbone of our segmentation network consists of three DenseBlock with the output channel of {8, 16, 32} followed by a convolution layer and softmax layer. Specifically, combined with DRL which is placed before S_θ, the objective function of S_θ is

$$\mathcal{L}_{(S_\theta, DRL)} = E_{(\theta, W)}(S_\theta(DRL_W(x_s)), p_s) + \underbrace{E_{(h)}(S_\theta(DRL_h(G_{t \to s}(x_t))), p_t)}_{\text{Regularization term}}$$

where E is the binary cross-entropy loss, and the subscripts of E, S and DRL is the parameters to be optimized. We optimize this objective function by alternating iterations, as summarized in Table 1.

Table 1. Pseudo code for training of segmentation network.

Algo. 1. Segmentation network with DRL
Require: A trained $G_{t \to s}$, S_θ, $DRL_{(w,h)}$, $\{x_s, p_s\}$, $\{x_t, p_t\}$
for $l = 0, \cdots, L-1$ **do**
Update (θ, W): $loss = E_{(\theta, W)}(S_\theta(DRL_W(x_s)), p_s)$
Update (h): $loss = E_{(h)}(S_\theta(DRL_h(G_{t \to s}(x_t))), p_t)$
end for
return $G_{t \to s}$, S_θ, $DRL_{(w,h)}$

The architecture of DRL is similar to that used in some previous work, but there are great differences in concept and implementation. Like the SE-net [10], each convolutional layer is decoupled into two parts: 1) convolution parameters W and 2) convolution kernel combination parameters h. For h in SE-net, it is a value returned by a neural network and can vary according to the input samples. At the same time, the SE-net is designed for image classification, which means ineffective for the domain adaptation problems. The main idea of DRL is borrowed from DARTS [11]. In order to find the best network architecture in a differentiable way, DARTS defines multiple convolution groups in each layer of the network. A weight α, which is analogous to h in DRL, is used to measure the effectiveness of each convolution group. The convolution group and α are alternately trained on the training set and the validation set, respectively. After the algorithm converges, the corresponding α_{max} convolution group in each layer is extracted as the final network architecture. In our work, we replace the training and validation data sets by the data of source and target domains. Meanwhile, the effectiveness of the convolution kernel is quantified, instead of the convolution group. In this way, the idea of searching for the best network architecture can be migrated to the search of a convolution kernels that are effective for both domains. Moreover, the work in the literature [12] is much similar to ours. It assigns different h to different data sets, and h will be trained along with the convolution kernel parameters. In our opinion, this method is only applicable when each data set has a large number of labeled samples. When there is little data in the target domain, there are too many model parameters to be trained, which could easily lead to overfitting.

3   Materials and Experiments

3.1   Materials

To verify our method, we collected 200 QSM images in our collaborated hospital with 3T GE equipment as the source domain. Data were collected using a 16 echo, gradient echo imaging sequence on a 3T GE Signa HDxt from an eight-channel receive-only head coil with the following imaging parameters: TE1 = 2.69 ms with ΔTE = 2.87 ms, TR = 59.3 ms, pixel bandwidth = 488 Hz/pixel, flip angle = 12°, a resolution of $0.86 \times 0.86 \times 1$ mm³. QSM images were reconstructed using a phase-wrap insensitive susceptibility mapping method [15]. At the same time, we collected 27 QSM images in the same hospital on their Philips instruments as the target domain data. The final high-resolution scan was acquired with the following imaging parameters: a flip angle of 9°, a resolution of $0.67 \times 0.67 \times 1.34$ mm³, a BW of 217 Hz/pixel and echo is 20 ms. QSM images were obtained following a threshold-based K-space/image domain iterative reconstruction approach [16]. It could be observed that the protocols of these two batches of data are quite different. At the same time, various reconstruction algorithms were employed, and their differences have been discussed in detail in [16].

We first sample all the images to $0.67 \times 0.67 \times 2$ mm³, and then use the registration algorithm [17] to locate the image patch containing SN, whose image size is $64 \times 64 \times 24$. This image patch will be used as the input for different methods.

3.2   Experimental Results

We performed an ablation experiment to demonstrate the effectiveness of our proposed method. As the baseline method, we first train a segmentation network on the source domain data and test it on the target domain. After that, we fine-tune the segmentation network on the target domain data as a benchmark method for comparison. Finally, we add the models proposed in Sects. 2.1 and 2.2, which are designed to eliminate the difference in both appearance space and feature space. Herein, we call these two models as JAFDAF (w/o DRL) and JAFDAF, respectively. After eliminating difference in appearance space and feature space, a fine-tune process is performed.

We used Pytroch to implement all the experiments. For all the networks, we used the same hyper-parameter with batch size = 10, input resolution = $24 \times 64 \times 64$, optimizer

= Adam, and max iteration = 200. The learning rate for all network is 0.001. One Titan XP with 12 GB is utilized to train the networks. In the training process, we use all data from the source domain and 2 images from the target domain as training data, and use 5 images and 20 images from the target domain, respectively, as the validation and testing data sets. We average the testing results from ten random trials.

We evaluated the accuracy of all segmentation methods in terms of Dice score. The quantitative result are showed in Table 2, along visualization results shown in Fig. 3.

Table 2. Segmentation result on the testing data set in terms of Dice score.

Method	Dice score	Hausdorff distance
Baseline	$0.670 \pm 2.66 \times 10^{-2}$	14.86mm
Fine-tune	$0.749 \pm 3.26 \times 10^{-2}$	14.41mm
JAFDAF (w/o DRL)	$0.768 \pm 4.02 \times 10^{-2}$	12.52mm
JAFDAF	$0.808 \pm 1.48 \times 10^{-2}$	11.89mm

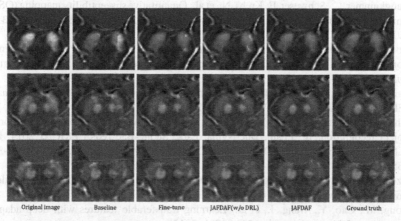

Original image   Baseline   Fine-tune   JAFDAF(w/o DRL)   JAFDAF   Ground truth

Fig. 3. Visual comparison of labeling results. We selected three subjects from the results obtained by different methods for visual comparison. Each row shows a subject. The first column is the original image. After that, from left to right are the results by the baseline model, fine-tuning, JAFDAF (w/o DRL), and JAFDAF, as well as the ground-truth results.

From the Dice score, Hausdorff distance, and visualization results of the baseline method, we can see that the performance of domain transfer is quite limited. After fine-turning, the segmentation performance of the network is improved, but still limited, due to overfitting when using only a small number of samples for fine-tuning. After eliminating appearance and feature differences, the segmentation performance is further improved. Results by our method (JAFDAF) is close to the ground-truth results.

4   Conclusion and Discussion

In this study, we have proposed the JAFDAF method to solve the problem of rapid transfer learning. To automatically transfer the trained segmentation model to the images acquired from new imaging device, we proposed to eliminate their appearance space and feature differences. To eliminate appearance difference, we transformed the task into a weakly labeled regression problem through region-based histogram matching, and implemented a corresponding image mapping through a neural network. To eliminate feature difference, we have borrowed the idea of DARTS to design the domain regularization layer and learn the convolution features that are applied to both domains by alternating iterations. With the help of the above models, we could migrate the existing models to the images acquired from new device with minimal labeling costs, thus greatly improving the generalization of the segmentation algorithm. Currently, the algorithm works on domain adaptation; in future work, we will consider introducing prior shape and location knowledge to train more robust segmentation model, and also improve the domain generalization performance of the segmentation model.

References

1. Langkammer, C., Schweser, F., Krebs, N., et al.: Quantitative susceptibility mapping (QSM) as a means to measure brain iron? A post mortem validation study. Neuroimage **62**(3), 1593–1599 (2012)
2. Long, J., Shelhamer, E., Darrell, T.: Fully convolutional networks for semantic segmentation. In: Proceedings of the IEEE Conference on Computer Vision and Pattern Recognition, pp. 3431–3440 (2015)
3. Pan, S.J., Tsang, I.W., Kwok, J.T., et al.: Domain adaptation via transfer component analysis. IEEE Trans. Neural Netw. **22**(2), 199–210 (2010)
4. Ghifary, Muhammad, Kleijn, W.B., Zhang, Mengjie: Domain adaptive neural networks for object recognition. In: Pham, Duc-Nghia, Park, Seong-Bae (eds.) PRICAI 2014. LNCS (LNAI), vol. 8862, pp. 898–904. Springer, Cham (2014). https://doi.org/10.1007/978-3-319-13560-1_76
5. Tzeng, E., Hoffman, J., Zhang, N., et al.: Deep domain confusion: Maximizing for domain invariance. arXiv preprint arXiv:1412.3474 (2014)
6. Long, M., Cao, Y., Wang, J., et al.: Learning transferable features with deep adaptation networks. arXiv preprint arXiv:1502.02791 (2015)
7. Goodfellow, I., Pouget-Abadie, J., Mirza, M., et al.: Generative adversarial nets. In: Advances in Neural Information Processing Systems, pp. 2672–2680 (2014)
8. Li, Minjun, Huang, Haozhi, Ma, Lin, Liu, Wei, Zhang, Tong, Jiang, Yugang: Unsupervised image-to-image translation with stacked cycle-consistent adversarial networks. In: Ferrari, Vittorio, Hebert, Martial, Sminchisescu, Cristian, Weiss, Yair (eds.) ECCV 2018. LNCS, vol. 11213, pp. 186–201. Springer, Cham (2018). https://doi.org/10.1007/978-3-030-01240-3_12
9. Zhu, J.Y., Park, T., Isola, P., et al.: Unpaired image-to-image translation using cycle-consistent adversarial networks. In: Proceedings of the IEEE International Conference on Computer Vision, pp. 2223–2232 (2017)
10. Hu, J., Shen, L., Sun, G.: Squeeze-and-excitation networks. In: Proceedings of the IEEE Conference on Computer Vision and Pattern Recognition, pp. 7132–7141 (2018)
11. Liu, H., Simonyan, K., Yang, Y.: Darts: Differentiable architecture search. arXiv preprint arXiv:1806.09055 (2018)

12. Bug, Daniel, et al.: Combined learning for similar tasks with domain-switching networks. In: Shen, Dinggang, Liu, Tianming, Peters, Terry M., Staib, Lawrence H., Essert, Caroline, Zhou, Sean, Yap, Pew-Thian, Khan, Ali (eds.) MICCAI 2019. LNCS, vol. 11768, pp. 565–572. Springer, Cham (2019). https://doi.org/10.1007/978-3-030-32254-0_63

13. Huang, G., Liu, Z., Van Der Maaten, L., et al.: Densely connected convolutional networks. In: Proceedings of the IEEE Conference on Computer Vision and Pattern Recognition, pp. 4700–4708 (2017)

14. Jégou, S., Drozdzal, M., Vazquez, D., et al.: The one hundred layers tiramisu: Fully convolutional densenets for semantic segmentation. In: Proceedings of the IEEE Conference on Computer Vision and Pattern Recognition Workshops, pp. 11–19 (2017)

15. Li, W., Wu, B., Liu, C.: Quantitative susceptibility mapping of human brain reflects spatial variation in tissue composition. Neuroimage **55**, 1645–1656 (2011)

16. Tang, J., Liu, S., Neelavalli, J., et al.: Improving susceptibility mapping using a threshold-based K-space/image domain iterative reconstruction approach. Magnet. Resonance Med. **69**(5), 1396–1407 (2013)

17. Avants, B.B., Tustison, N., Song, G.: Advanced normalization tools (ANTS). Insight J **2**(365), 1–35 (2009)

18. Xiao, B., He, N., Wang, Q., et al.: Quantitative susceptibility mapping based hybrid feature extraction for diagnosis of Parkinson's disease. NeuroImage: Clin. **24**, 102070 (2019)

Exploring Functional Difference Between Gyri and Sulci via Region-Specific 1D Convolutional Neural Networks

Mingxin Jiang[1], Shimin Yang[1], Jiadong Yan[1], Shu Zhang[2], Huan Liu[2], Lin Zhao[2,3], Haixing Dai[3], Jinglei Lv[4], Tuo Zhang[2], Tianming Liu[3], Keith M. Kendrick[1], and Xi Jiang[1(✉)]

[1] School of Life Science and Technology, MOE Key Lab for Neuroinformation, University of Electronic Science and Technology of China, Chengdu, China
xijiang@uestc.edu.cn
[2] School of Automation, Northwestern Polytechnical University, Xi'an, China
[3] Cortical Architecture Imaging and Discovery Lab, Department of Computer Science and Bioimaging Research Center, The University of Georgia, Athens, GA, USA
[4] Sydney Imaging and School of Biomedical Engineering, The University of Sydney, Camperdown, NSW, Australia

Abstract. The cerebral cortex is highly folded as convex gyri and concave sulci. Accumulating evidence has consistently suggested the morphological, structural, and functional differences between gyri and sulci, which are further supported by recent studies adopting deep learning methodologies. For instance, one of the pioneering studies demonstrated the intrinsic functional difference of neural activities between gyri and sulci by means of a convolutional neural network (CNN) based classifier on fMRI BOLD signals. While those studies revealed the holistic gyro-sulcal neural activity difference in the whole-brain scale, the characteristics of such gyro-sulcal difference within different brain regions, which account for specific brain functions, remains to be explored. In this study, we designed a region-specific one-dimensional (1D) CNN based classifier in order to differentiate gyro-sulcal resting state fMRI signals within each brain region. Time-frequency analysis was further performed on the learned 1D-CNN model to characterize the gyro-sulcal neural activity difference in different frequency scales of each brain region. Experiments results based on 900 subjects across 4 repeated resting-state fMRI scans from Human Connectome Project consistently showed that the gyral and sulcal signals could be differentiated within a majority of regions. Moreover, the gyral and sulcal filters exhibited different frequency characteristics in different scales across brain regions, suggesting that gyri and sulci may play different functional roles for different brain functions. To our best knowledge, this study provided one of the earliest mapping of the functional segregation of gyri/sulci for different brain regions, which helps better understand brain function mechanism.

Keywords: Cortical folding · Convolutional neural network · Functional MRI

© Springer Nature Switzerland AG 2020
M. Liu et al. (Eds.): MLMI 2020, LNCS 12436, pp. 250–259, 2020.
https://doi.org/10.1007/978-3-030-59861-7_26

1 Introduction

The human cerebral cortex is highly folded as convex gyri and concave sulci during the brain development [1, 2]. In the past decades, accumulating evidence from either micro- or macro- perspective has consistently suggested the genetic, morphological, and structural connection differences between gyri and sulci [2–5]. Given the close relationship between brain structure and function [6], increasing efforts have been devoted in recent years to unveiling the gyro-sulcal functional characteristics. With the help of advanced in-vivo functional neuroimaging such as functional MRI (fMRI), the gyro-sulcal functional difference in terms of functional connectivity strength [7], functional network properties [8–10], and temporal neural activity [11] has been extensively elucidated.

Thanks to the advancement of deep learning techniques in recent years, the gyro-sulcal functional difference has been further supported by applying deep learning methodologies on fMRI data. One of the pioneering studies revealed the intrinsic functional difference of neural activities between gyri and sulci by means of a convolutional neural network (CNN) based classifier on HCP grayordinate fMRI BOLD signals [12]. Another study demonstrated similar findings across human and macaque brains [13]. The 2-hinge and 3-hinge joints which were further categorized from gyral regions also showed different neural activities compared with sulci [14]. While those studies [12–14] revealed the holistic gyro-sulcal neural activity difference in the whole-brain scale, the characteristics of such gyro-sulcal difference within different brain regions, which account for specific brain functions, remains largely unknown.

To this end, this study designed a region-specific one-dimensional (1D) CNN based classifier in order to differentiate gyro-sulcal resting state fMRI signals within each predefined brain region [15] which account for different brain functions. Previous studies have shown the advantage of CNN in modeling fMRI BOLD signals [12–14, 16]. Given that human brains are likely to be a multi-frequency oscillation system [17], time-frequency analysis was further performed on the learned CNN model in order to characterize the neural activity difference between gyri and sulci in different frequency scales within each brain region. Based on 900 subjects with 4 repeated rsfMRI scans from Human Connectome Project S900 [18], we provide the detailed and reliable mapping of the functional segregation of gyri/sulci in different regions.

2 Methods

2.1 Data Acquisition and Preprocessing

In this study, we adopted the grayordinate resting-state fMRI (rsfMRI) data of 900 healthy subjects with 4 repeated rsfMRI scan runs from publicly released HCP S900 database [18]. 842 subjects (22–35 years old) with all 4 runs were adopted for test-retest validation in this study. More demographic information is referred to [18]. The main acquisition parameters of rsfMRI scans were as follows: 90×104 matrix, 72 slices, TR = 0.72 s, TE = 33.1 ms, FOV = 220 mm, flip angle = $52°$, in-plane FOV = 208×180 mm and 2.0 mm isotropic voxels. The major preprocessing steps of rsfMRI data were referred to [12, 19]. Note that the high temporal resolution of HCP rsfMRI data (TR = 0.72 s, corresponding to 1.39 Hz sampling frequency) not only helped directly record the oscillatory neural activity in higher frequencies [20], but also covered the major brain activity frequency bands (0.01–0.69 Hz) [21], thus helping us characterize the gyro-sulcal neural activity difference in different frequency scales in this study.

2.2 Cortical Surface Parcellation and Signal Extraction

The individual cortical surface is composed of cortical vertices. Each cortical vertex has associated geometric measurement and corresponding rsfMRI signal. We first parcellated individual cortical surface into 35 regions (symmetrical in left and right hemispheres) using the widely adopted brain atlas [15] as shown in Fig. 1a. Once the parcellation is performed on the atlas space, it can be directly mapped to all subjects due to the intrinsic correspondence established by the HCP grayordinate system [18]. In order to investigate the gyro-sulcal difference within each of the region, we further divided all vertices within each region (Fig. 1b) into gyri and sulci (Fig. 1c). Specifically, the signed distance that each vertex moves was quantified as average convexity (i.e., 'sulc' map in FreeSurfer) during the inflation process [20]. After sorting the average convexity values of all vertices within a region, the 20% vertices with highest average convexity values were labeled as gyri and the 20% with lowest values were labeled as sulci in order to provide a balanced dataset for gyri and sulci which were in line with previous studies [11, 12]. The remaining 60% vertices were intermediate regions between gyri and sulci and discarded in order to avoid any ambiguity and to provide an accurate ground truth database of gyri and sulci. Finally, the corresponding rsfMRI signals of labeled gyri/sulci within each region serve as the input of the following CNN based classification.

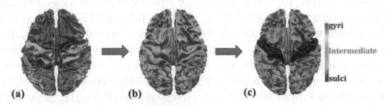

Fig. 1. (a) Cortical parcellation into 35 regions. Each color represents one region. (b) An example brain region (precentral cortex) colored in yellow. (c) The example region in (b) is parcellated into gyri, sulci and intermediate. (Color figure online)

2.3 Configuration of 1D-CNN Model

As illustrated in Fig. 2, a 1D-CNN model is proposed to classify the input gyral/sulcal signals. The proposed model consisted of a 1D convolution layer with the activation function ReLU, a batch-normalization layer, a max-pooling layer, a global average pooling (GAP) layer and a dense layer with the activation function Softmax, which has been demonstrated effective in differentiating 1D signals in [12]. Note that the dropout layer in [12] was not adopted given the relatively smaller sample size of each region compared to the whole brain. Specifically, the 64 convolution kernels with length 32 of the convolution layer were considered as filters, which tended to retain those discriminative features between input gyral and sulcal signals. Then the output feature vectors were fed to the max-pooling layer in order to better represent the characteristics of input signals and to reduce the number of parameters, making the model's convergence easier. The GAP layer was adopted to address the overfitting problem, instead of directly adding a fully connected layer [12]. Finally, the corresponding vertices of input signals were classified as gyri or sulci as the output of the model after following the dense layer. Note that the labels of gyri and sulci were encoded by [0 1] and [1 0] respectively using one-hot method in order to characterize the class-specific 1D-CNN features for gyri and sulci. The 1D-CNN model was implemented based on Keras and trained on NVIDIA GeForce GTX1080Ti GPU.

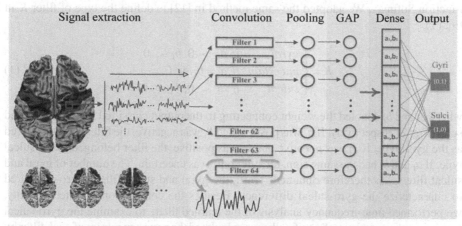

Fig. 2. The architecture of the region-specific 1D-CNN classification model. All gyral/sulcal signals across subjects within a brain region are the model input. The model sequentially consists of a convolution layer of 64 filters, a pooling layer, a GAP layer, and a dense layer with Softmax. The corresponding vertices within a region are classified into gyri/sulci as output.

We trained the model at group level in order to identify the commonly shared gyro-sulcal characteristics across different subjects. Note that the amount of rsfMRI signals ranged from hundreds of thousands to millions within each of the parcellated brain regions (Fig. 1a) across subjects, guaranteeing a reasonable large number of samples for model training and testing. We randomly divided all subjects into two equal subsets. For each brain region, the rsfMRI signals of one subset were used for model training, while those of the other subset were the testing samples, and vice versa. Note that the number of gyral and sulcal labels was balanced in both training and testing samples. In this way, we performed 8 independent training procedures using 4 repeated rsfMRI scans in order to confirm the test-retest validity of the gyro-sulcal functional difference. By repeating above-mentioned procedures on each of the brain region separately, we obtained region-specific CNN gyro-sulcal classification model.

We adopted similar hyperparameter settings of CNN model as in [12]. We utilized stochastic gradient descent (SGD) as an optimizer with a momentum coefficient at 0.9 and adopted categorical cross-entropy as loss function. We randomly initialized the weights on filters with unit normal distribution. To improve classification accuracy, learning rate was set to 0.01 at the beginning of the training, which decayed by 1e−6 after each iteration. Batch size was set to 128 and epoch size was set to 20.

2.4 Interpretation of 1D-CNN Model

We interpreted the learned CNN model for each region from three perspectives. First, the output gyri/sulci labels were used to evaluate the gyro-sulcal classification accuracy. Second, we divided the filters in convolution layer into gyral, sulcal, and uncertain types in order to analyze the characteristics of filter types between gyri and sulci. Specifically, each filter i corresponded to the pair of weights (a_i, b_i) in dense layer with the activation function Softmax. We adopted the same method in [12] to define the type of filter K in Eq. (1):

$$K = \begin{cases} gyral, & if\ a_i > 0, b_i < 0 \\ uncertain, & if\ a_i * b_i > 0 \\ sulcal, & if\ a_i < 0,\ b_i > 0 \end{cases} \tag{1}$$

where a_i and b_i denoted the weight connecting to the output classified labels of gyri and sulci (Fig. 2), respectively. If a_i was positive and b_i was negative, the filter was considered as the gyral type. If a_i was negative and b_i was positive, the filter belonged to the sulcal type. If a_i and b_i had the same sign, the filter type was uncertain. The number of gyral and sulcal filters was therefore obtained. Third, the gyral and sulcal filters were compared to characterize the gyro-sulcal difference. Besides the comparison of filter quantity, we performed time-frequency analysis of the learned filters to examine the gyro-sulcal frequency characteristics. Specifically, we calculated the power spectrum of each filter by performing Fourier transformation and examined power spectrum differences between gyral and sulcal filters. The discrete Fourier transform was defined in Eq. (2). N was set to the same number as filter length ($N = 32$). Since the obtained power spectrums were two-sided, we only took the first half of power spectrums (16 discrete frequency points plus zero frequency point) for frequency-specific analysis.

$$X(k) = \sum_{n=0}^{N-1} x(n) e^{-j\frac{2\pi}{N} kn} (k = 0, 1, 2 \ldots N - 1) \tag{2}$$

3 Results

3.1 1D-CNN Classification Performance

The gyro-sulcal rsfMRI signal classification accuracy of each brain region was illustrated in Fig. 3. As detailed in Fig. 3c, the accuracy values ranged from 51.87% (region #21, Pericalcarine cortex) to 81.14% (region #14, Medial orbital frontal cortex) with an averaged value of 65.62% across all regions, which were comparable with previous studies [12]. Based on the cortical mapping in Fig. 3a, we could see that compared with

Frontal lobe, Limbic lobe, and medial surface of Parietal and Occipital lobes, there was higher classification accuracy in Temporal lobe, lateral surface of Parietal and Occipital lobes, Orbitofrontal cortex, and Insula, indicating that those regions might have higher gyro-sulcal functional segregation.

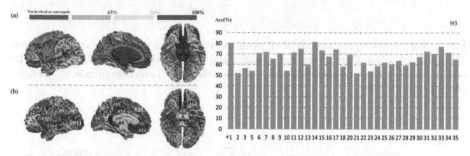

Fig. 3. Gyro-sulcal rsfMRI signal classification accuracy of each brain region. (a) A cortical map showing the classification accuracies of each region. Regions with different accuracy ranges are colored by green, yellow, and red, respectively. (b) A cortical map showing the 35 brain regions with their indices labeled in white/black. Each color represents one region. (c) Bar chart of detailed accuracy of each region. Regions which were not included in the study (#4, Corpus callosum without rsfMRI signals) or did not converge in training fashion (#19, Pars orbitalis) are colored by blue in (b) and not shown in (c). (Color figure online)

3.2 Time Series and Quantity Analysis of Gyral/Sulcal Filters

Figure 4 illustrated the time series representations of gyral and sulcal filters (defined in Eq. (1)) in two representative brain regions. In region #10, typical gyral filters contained more intense oscillations, while typical sulcal ones had relatively smooth time-series shapes. On the contrary, in region #24, typical sulcal filters contained more intense oscillations compared to the typical gyral ones. We further explored whether there was any quantity difference between the gyro-sulcal filters in each region. The two-sample t-test based on the 8 independent training procedures (Sect. 2.3) showed that there was no significant difference between the number of gyral and sulcal filters in each region ($p < 0.05$, Bonferroni correction for multiple comparison).

3.3 Frequency Analysis of Gyral/Sulcal Filters

We analyzed average frequency power spectrums of gyral and sulcal filters in each brain region. For the same two representative regions in Fig. 4, Fig. 5a showed that the power spectrum amplitude of the gyral filter increased sharply as the frequency increased, while that of the sulcal filter decreased slowly as the frequency increased in region #10. On the contrary, the gyral/sulcal filter had decreased/increased power spectrum amplitude as the frequency increased in region #24. In short, the frequency power spectrums findings of the two regions were consistent with the time series analysis in Fig. 4. Figure 5b

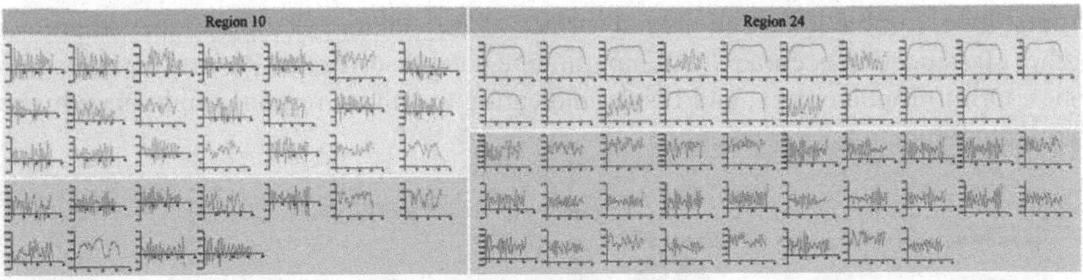

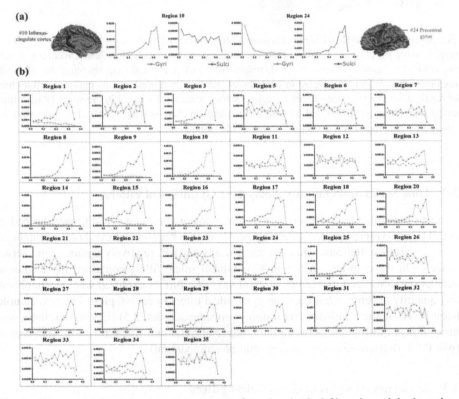

Fig. 4. Time-series representations of all gyral and sulcal filters in two representative regions. The gyral and sulcal filters are colored in orange and blue, respectively. In each sub-figure, the horizontal axis is temporal point (filter length 32) and the vertical axis is amplitude. (Color figure online)

Fig. 5. The average frequency power spectrums of gyral and sulcal filters in each brain region. (a) The location and detailed average power spectrum of gyral/sulcal filter in region #10 and #24. (b) Co-visualization of the average power spectrums of gyral and sulcal filters of each region. The distribution of the average power spectrums of gyral and sulcal filters are colored in orange and blue, respectively. In each sub-figure, the horizontal axis is frequency (0–0.69 Hz) and the vertical axis is amplitude. (Color figure online)

presented the average frequency power spectrums of gyral and sulcal filters of all 33 regions. In a majority of these regions, we observed a boost in power spectrums of sulcal filter in high-frequency band. The power spectrum amplitude of gyral/sulcal filters decreased/increased with the frequency increasing. There were two regions (#10 and #16) showing increased/decreased amplitude as the frequency increased in gyral/sulcal filter. There were also certain regions (e.g., #2, #5, #12, etc.) whose gyral and sulcal filters did not show obvious amplitude difference as the frequency increased.

We further investigated whether there was significant power spectrum amplitude difference between gyral and sulcal filters at each frequency point (Sect. 2.4) of each region. The statistical results (two-sample t-test, $p < 0.05$, Bonferroni correction for multiple comparison) of each region at two representative low and high frequency points (0.04 Hz and 0.48 Hz) across four repeated rsfMRI scan runs were visualized in Fig. 6a–b, respectively. At the low-frequency point 0.04 Hz (Fig. 6a), the average power spectrum amplitude of sulcal filters was significantly larger than that of gyral filters in Frontal lobe

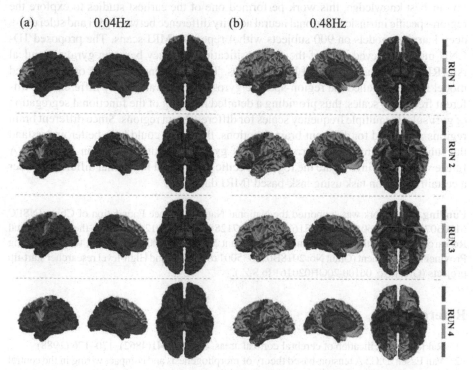

Fig. 6. Visualization of the power spectrum amplitude difference between gyral and sulcal filters in different brain regions at two representative frequency points (0.04 Hz in Fig. 6a and 0.48 Hz in Fig. 6b) across four repeated rsfMRI scan runs. Regions without significant difference in power spectrum between gyral and sulcal filters are colored by purple. Regions with significantly larger power spectrum of sulcal filters than that of gyral ones are colored by pink. Regions with significantly larger power spectrum of gyral filters than that of sulcal ones are colored by green. Two-sample t-test ($p < 0.05$, Bonferroni correction for multiple comparison) was adopted. The blue regions are not involved in the study as detailed in Sect. 3.1. (Color figure online)

including Rostral middle frontal and Superior frontal cortex, while the Pre- and Post-central gyrus showed opposite characteristics. There was no significant power spectrum amplitude difference between gyral-sulcal filters in a majority of regions. At the high-frequency point 0.48 Hz (Fig. 6b), the average power spectrum amplitude of sulcal filters was significantly larger than that of gyral filters in most regions of Frontal and Temporal lobe, and lateral surface of Parietal lobe, while the Isthmus cingulate cortex (#10) and Para hippocampal region (#16) showed larger amplitude of gyral filters than sulcal ones. These findings together with Figs. 4 and 5 were relatively consistent across the four repeated rsfMRI scans and provided a comprehensive mapping of the characteristics of gyro-sulcal neural activity difference in different frequency scales within each brain region.

4 Conclusion

To our best knowledge, this work performed one of the earliest studies to explore the region-specific intrinsic functional neural activity difference between gyri and sulci using deep learning models on 900 subjects with 4 repeated fMRI scans. The proposed 1D-CNN model achieved state-of-the-art classification accuracy between gyral and sulcal rsfMRI signals in a majority of brain regions. Time-frequency analysis on the learned model further unveiled the region-specific gyro-sulcal neural activity difference in different frequency scales, thus providing a detailed mapping of the functional segregation of gyri/sulci in multiple frequency scales for different brain regions. Since different brain regions accounted for different brain functions, this study could help better understand the functional segregation characteristics of gyri/sulci in different brain functions. A future work could investigate the region-specific gyro-sulcal functional difference under a certain cognition task using task-based fMRI data.

Funding. This work was supported the National Natural Science Foundation of China (NSFC 61703073 and 61976045 to X.J., 31671005, 31971288, and U1801265 to T.Z.), the Fundamental Research Funds for the Central Universities (Grant No. D5000200555 to S.Z.), the Guangdong Provincial Government (Grant No. 2018B030335001 to K.M.K) and High-level researcher start-up projects (Grant No. 06100-20GH020161 to S.Z.).

References

1. Rakic, P.: Specification of cerebral cortical areas. Science **241**(4862), 170–176 (1988)
2. Van Essen, D.C.: A tension-based theory of morphogenesis and compact wiring in the central nervous system. Nature **385**(6614), 313–318 (1997)
3. Hilgetag, C.C., Barbas, H.: Developmental mechanics of the primate cerebral cortex. Anat. Embryol. **210**(5–6), 411–417 (2005)
4. Stahl, R., et al.: Trnp1 regulates expansion and folding of the mammalian cerebral cortex by control of radial glial fate. Cell **153**(3), 535–549 (2013)
5. Nie, J.X., et al.: Axonal fiber terminations concentrate on gyri. Cereb. Cortex **22**(12), 2831–2839 (2012)
6. Passingham, R.E., Stephan, K.E., Kotter, R.: The anatomical basis of functional localization in the cortex. Nat. Rev. Neurosci. **3**(8), 606–616 (2002)

7. Deng, F., et al.: A functional model of cortical gyri and sulci. Brain Struct. Funct. **219**(4), 1473–1491 (2013). https://doi.org/10.1007/s00429-013-0581-z
8. Jiang, X., et al.: Sparse representation of HCP grayordinate data reveals novel functional architecture of cerebral cortex. Hum. Brain Mapp. **36**(12), 5301–5319 (2015)
9. Jiang, X., et al.: Temporal dynamics assessment of spatial overlap pattern of functional brain networks reveals novel functional architecture of cerebral cortex. IEEE Trans. Biomed. Eng. **65**(6), 1183–1192 (2018)
10. Jiang, X., Zhao, L., Liu, H., Guo, L., Kendrick, K.M., Liu, T.M.: A cortical folding pattern-guided model of intrinsic functional brain networks in emotion processing. Front. Neurosci. **12**, 575 (2018)
11. Yang, S.M., et al.: Temporal variability of cortical gyral-sulcal resting-state functional activity correlates with fluid intelligence. Front. Neural Circ. **13**(36), 1–12 (2019)
12. Liu, H., et al.: The cerebral cortex is bisectionally segregated into two fundamentally different functional units of gyri and sulci. Cereb. Cortex **29**(10), 4238–4252 (2018)
13. Zhang, S., et al.: Deep learning models unveiled functional difference between cortical gyri and sulci. IEEE Trans. Biomed. Eng. **66**(5), 1297–1308 (2019)
14. Ge, F.F., et al.: Exploring intrinsic functional difference of gyri, sulci and 2-hinge, 3-hinge joints on cerebral cortex. In: IEEE 16th International Symposium on Biomedical Imaging 2019, pp. 1585–1589 (2019)
15. Desikan, R.S., et al.: An automated labeling system for subdividing the human cerebral cortex on MRI scans into gyral based regions of interest. NeuroImage **31**(3), 968–980 (2006)
16. Huang, H., et al.: Modeling task fMRI data via deep convolutional autoencoder. IEEE Trans. Med. Imaging **37**(7), 1551–1561 (2018)
17. Gohel, S.R., Biswal, B.B.: Functional integration between brain regions at rest occurs in multiple-frequency bands. Brain Connect **5**(1), 23–34 (2015)
18. Van Essen, D.C., Smith, S.M., Barch, D.M., Behrens, T.E.J., Yacoub, E., Ugurbil, K.: The WU-Minn human connectome project: an overview. Neuroimage **80**, 62–79 (2013)
19. Smith, S.M., et al.: Resting-state fMRI in the human connectome project. Neuroimage **80**, 144–168 (2013)
20. Lewis, L.D., Setsompop, K., Rosen, B.R., Polimeni, J.R.: Fast fMRI can detect oscillatory neural activity in humans. Proc. Natl. Acad. Sci. **113**(43), E6679–E6685 (2016)
21. Buzsáki, G., Logothetis, N., Singer, W.: Scaling brain size, keeping timing: evolutionary preservation of brain rhythms. Neuron **80**(3), 751–764 (2013)

Detection of Ischemic Infarct Core in Non-contrast Computed Tomography

Maximilian Hornung[1,2], Oliver Taubmann[3(✉)], Hendrik Ditt[3], Björn Menze[1],
Pawel Herman[2], and Erik Fransén[2]

[1] Image-Based Biomedical Modeling, Technical University of Munich,
Munich, Germany
[2] Division of Computational Science and Technology, Royal Institute of Technology,
Stockholm, Sweden
[3] Computed Tomography, Siemens Healthcare GmbH, Forchheim, Germany
oliver.taubmann@siemens-healthineers.com

Abstract. Fast diagnosis is of critical importance for stroke treatment. In clinical routine, a non-contrast computed tomography scan (NCCT) is typically acquired immediately to determine whether the stroke is ischemic or hemorrhagic and plan therapy accordingly. In case of ischemia, early signs of infarction may appear due to increased water uptake. These signs may be subtle, especially if observed only shortly after symptom onset, but hold the potential to provide a crucial first assessment of the location and extent of the infarction. In this paper, we train a deep neural network to predict the infarct core from NCCT in an image-to-image fashion. To facilitate exploitation of anatomic correspondences, learning is carried out in the standardized coordinate system of a brain atlas to which all images are deformably registered. Apart from binary infarct core masks, perfusion maps such as cerebral blood volume and flow are employed as additional training targets to enrich the physiologic information available to the model. This extension is demonstrated to substantially improve the predictions of our model, which is trained on a data set consisting of 141 cases. It achieves a higher volumetric overlap (statistically significant, $p < 0.02$) of the predicted core with the reference mask as well as a better localization, although significance could not be shown ($p = 0.36$) for the latter. Agreement with human and automatic assessment of affected ASPECTS regions is likewise improved, measured as an increase of the area under the receiver operating characteristic curve from 72.7% to 75.1% and 71.9% to 83.5%, respectively.

Keywords: Ischemic stroke · Infarct core · Non-contrast CT

1 Introduction

Stroke is the second leading cause of death and the third leading cause of disability worldwide [9]. Ischemic stroke, i.e. lack of blood supply to brain tissue

M. Hornung and O. Taubmann—These authors contributed equally to this work.

© Springer Nature Switzerland AG 2020
M. Liu et al. (Eds.): MLMI 2020, LNCS 12436, pp. 260–269, 2020.
https://doi.org/10.1007/978-3-030-59861-7_27

due to atherosclerotic and thromboembolic events, accounts for 84.4% of prevalent strokes [6]. In patients suspected of suffering from acute stroke, NCCT is typically acquired as quickly as possible to determine the type of stroke and plan treatment accordingly. In case of ischemia, it is followed up with contrast-enhanced scans. However, it remains a valuable and immediately available resource for assessment of stroke severity, as is reflected prominently in the well-established ASPECTS (Alberta Stroke Program Early CT Score) [3]. Among other effects, increased water uptake in necrotic tissue leads to changes in brain appearance that are usually very subtle in the first few hours after stroke onset. This subtlety renders an initial visual assessment based on NCCT, as done in clinical practice, both time-consuming and highly subjective.

In this paper, we propose and evaluate a deep-learning based system for automatic assessment of the location and extent of the infarct core in the form of a dense, voxel-level prediction—based only on such early signs in NCCT. Potentially due to the difficulty of the task, little is found regarding this topic in existing literature besides recent, promising work by Qiu et al. [14]. Aside from a different algorithmic approach, our study differs from theirs in that we do not rely on expert segmentations as reference. Instead, as target output we use information automatically derived from a corresponding CT perfusion scan [12], which many sites acquire in practice as it could be shown to improve clinical confidence [2]. This offers the possibility to scale our approach to larger data sets without the need for manual annotation. It also allows us to provide the model with quantitative blood flow measurements, in addition to the infarct core mask, during a joint multi-target training. Other related prior work is concerned with onset time classification [23], infarct core determination in CT angiography [17] and in *follow-up* NCCT [4]. Other approaches are based directly on ASPECTS regions [18–20] or on a box-level localization and extent assessment [13]. An analysis of the variability of infarct core volumes derived from CT perfusion within NCCT ASPECTS strata is found in [7]. Much effort has also gone into tackling related tasks in magnetic resonance imaging (MRI) [8,24]; diffusion-weighted MRI in particular is the gold standard for infarct assessment [11,24]. However, as it is uncommon in routine to acquire both CT and MRI pre-treatment [11], suitable data set pairs that could be used to train a model for the task at hand are hard to come by. Hence, we propose to rely on CT perfusion instead.

2   Methods

2.1   Preprocessing

From the CT perfusion scan of each patient, maps containing the cerebral blood flow (CBF), cerebral blood volume (CBV), time to maximum enhancement (TMAX) as well as the infarct core mask are computed with a slice thickness of 1.5 mm using commercial software (syngo.CT Neuro Perfusion, version VB40, Siemens Healthineers, Forchheim, Germany). The infarct core is defined as tissue with a CBV below 1.2 ml/100 ml [1].

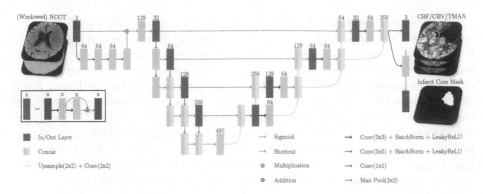

Fig. 1. Proposed network architecture for ischemic infarct core detection.

As vessels are masked out in the resulting perfusion maps, which leads to strong intensity discontinuities we assume to be detrimental to learning, we first perform inpainting to fill in the masked-out pixels [21]. Subsequently, both the perfusion scan and the NCCT scan are non-rigidly registered onto a brain atlas constructed from 150 independent patient data sets [10] with an isotropic voxel resolution of $1\,\mathrm{mm}^3$. In addition to correcting for patient motion between both scans, this step constitutes an anatomical normalization to reduce variation that is not essential for the task. The transformed slices are then downsampled to 128×128 pixels to reduce the model input/output space dimensionality.

2.2   Model Architecture and Training

Our model, depicted in Fig. 1, is based on a variant of the U-Net architecture [16] due to its widely reported success in medical image-to-image tasks. As input, it receives an axial slice of the preprocessed NCCT with two channels; one contains the original CT values with the range $[-1024, 3072]\,\mathrm{HU}$ normalized to $[0, 1]$, the other a windowed version clipped to the range $[0, 100]\,\mathrm{HU}$ and likewise normalized to $[0, 1]$ to focus on tissue contrast in gray and white matter.

The network has two output paths: One corresponds to the core infarct mask (pixel-wise binary classification, sigmoid activation), the other is a 3-channel tensor predicting CBF, CBV and TMAX, (pixel-wise regression, linear activation), which are each normalized to $[0, 1]$ as well. At inference time, the regression output is ignored—its sole purpose is to guide learning during joint training of both targets. With 3 scalar properties related to blood flow per pixel, it contains much richer information than the binary mask alone and allows the model to associate NCCT appearance characteristics with corresponding hemodynamic behavior. Naturally, this is only possible to a very limited degree as blood flow is *not* observable in the NCCT. Nonetheless, we will demonstrate below that providing this information during training improves the model accuracy.

Training is performed using stochastic gradient descent for a maximum of 100 epochs with a batch size of 32 and employs early stopping with 10 epochs

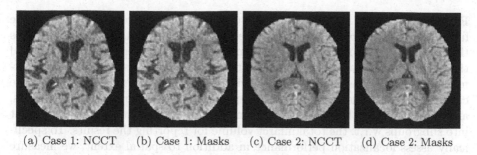

(a) Case 1: NCCT   (b) Case 1: Masks   (c) Case 2: NCCT   (d) Case 2: Masks

Fig. 2. Qualitative results of our proposed model. Two cases are shown without (a,c) and with (b,d) overlays indicating the predicted (red) and reference (green) infarct core masks as well as their overlap (ocre). (Color figure online)

patience. Class-frequency weighted binary cross-entropy is used as the classification loss, while the regression loss consists in the (unweighted) sum of the negative structural similarity index (SSIM) [22] and the mean absolute error (MAE). The total loss $\mathcal{L}(\mathbf{y}, \hat{\mathbf{y}})$ thus reads,

$$
\mathcal{L}(\mathbf{y}, \hat{\mathbf{y}}) = \overbrace{\lambda \sum_j \mathrm{w}_j^2}^{\text{Regularizer}} + \overbrace{\sum_{m \in \mathcal{M}} \left(1 - \mathrm{SSIM}(\mathbf{y}_m, \hat{\mathbf{y}_m})\right) + \tfrac{1}{N} \sum_{i=0}^{N} \left| \mathbf{y}_m^{(i)} - \hat{\mathbf{y}}_m^{(i)} \right|}^{\text{Regression loss (negative SSIM, MAE)}} -
$$
$$
\underbrace{\tfrac{1}{N} \sum_{i=0}^{N} w_{\mathrm{CM}}\, \mathbf{y}_{\mathrm{CM}}^{(i)} \log(\hat{\mathbf{y}}_{\mathrm{CM}}^{(i)}) + (1 - w_{\mathrm{CM}})\,(1 - \mathbf{y}_{\mathrm{CM}}^{(i)}) \log(1 - \hat{\mathbf{y}}_{\mathrm{CM}}^{(i)})}_{\text{Classification loss (class-frequency weighted binary cross-entropy)}},
$$

where $\hat{\mathbf{y}}_m$ and $\mathbf{y}_m$, $m \in \mathcal{M} = \{\mathrm{CBF}, \mathrm{CBV}, \mathrm{TMAX}\}$, are the predicted and actual perfusion maps, and $\hat{\mathbf{y}}_{\mathrm{CM}}$ and $\mathbf{y}_{\mathrm{CM}}$ are the predicted infarct core probability map and corresponding reference mask, respectively. N is the number of voxels per slice while the relative frequency of the infarct core class in the training data is denoted by w_{CM}. Additional moderate ℓ_2 regularization (weight $\lambda = 10^{-4}$) of the convolution layer weights w_j inside the encoder and decoder paths is applied.

2.3   Experiments

Data. Our data set consists of anonymized CT imaging studies from 141 patients suffering from acute ischemic stroke, which were collected retrospectively at Universitätsklinikum Schleswig-Holstein, Lübeck, Germany. Of these, 36 cases show a prior infarct. These cases were included in the training, but excluded for quantitative evaluation so as not to bias the results due to detections unrelated to the acute stroke. For the evaluated cases, the infarct cores derived from CT perfusion exhibit a volume of $16.0 \pm 31.1\,\mathrm{ml}$ (mean $\pm$ std.dev.), with the 25th, 50th and 75th percentiles at $0.964\,\mathrm{ml}$, $3.56\,\mathrm{ml}$ and $16.7\,\mathrm{ml}$, respectively. The NCCT slices are 1 mm thick and 0.8 mm apart, with an isotropic in-plane resolution of $(0.45 \times 0.45)\,\mathrm{mm}^2$. We randomly split the data sets on patient level to perform 5-fold cross validation with a 3/1/1 ratio for training/validation/test.

Figures of Merit. We perform three distinct quantitative evaluations on the full 3D probability maps predicted slice-wise by the model. The first measures the overlap of the predicted and reference infarct core. For this purpose, ideal thresholds for binarization of the output probability maps are previously determined on the validation set. Volumetric overlap is calculated using the Dice coefficient [5]. As it is known to be susceptible to degradation in smaller objects, and to account for the clinical significance of infarct severity, patients are split into subgroups w.r.t. the total infarct volume for reporting the results. To specifically assess localization performance in addition to spatial extent, we measure the 3D Euclidean distance, in mm, of the position of maximum predicted probability to the nearest reference infarct voxel. This is a robust indicator for whether the model has correctly determined the most salient brain region. Results are again reported for the aforementioned subgroups, excluding 4 patients for which the reference infarct mask was empty and the distance measure would thus be undefined. Lastly, we perform an evaluation based directly on ASPECTS [3]. In this scheme, 10 anatomic brain regions are defined and assessed for conspicuities in comparison to the their counterpart on the contralateral hemisphere. For each region that appears affected, one point is deducted from the initial score of 10. In our experiment, we consider binary classification performance for each of the ten ASPECTS regions on the affected side. To this end, the predicted scores are computed as the mean value of the per-voxel probabilities over the individual regions. We compare against two separate reference scorings: One is performed by an automated approach (syngo.CT ASPECTS, version VB40, Siemens Healthineers, Forchheim, Germany) [15], while the other is based on visual assessment of the NCCT by a human expert. In each evaluation, we compare our proposed multi-target model against a baseline variant that is trained using only the infarct mask output path, i.e. as a conventional segmentation model. All hyperparameters were otherwise equivalent apart from a small change to the class weights that was necessary to achieve stable training of the baseline segmentation network.

3   Results and Discussion

3.1   Volumetric Overlap

Figure 3a summarizes the evaluation of volumetric overlap. In accordance with expectation, the larger the area affected by necrosis, the more likely it is that the infarction can be correctly recognized based on the NCCT, although it remains challenging even then. When the infarct volume is less than 1 ml, Dice coefficients remain close to zero (mean ± std. dev.: 0.003 ± 0.005 for the proposed model, 0.002 ± 0.005 for the baseline), i.e. there is virtually no overlap with our model's prediction. Albeit unfortunate, this is in line with the understanding that the early changes visible in NCCT primarily manifest in already necrotic regions—as opposed to still remediable tissue just barely kept alive by blood supply from collateral vessels (penumbra). In contrast, for large infarcts (>70 ml), a median Dice coefficient of 53% is achieved (mean ± std. dev.: 0.466 ± 0.168 for the

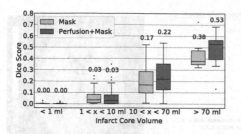 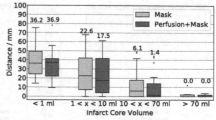

(a) Volumetric overlap of predicted and reference infarct core masks.

(b) Distance of peak probability location to nearest reference infarct core voxel.

Fig. 3. Quantitative evaluation of infarct core detection and localization performance for different actual infarct volumes. *Mask+Perfusion* denotes the proposed multi-task model while *Mask* refers to the baseline segmentation model. Boxes show the 25th (lower end), 50th (black line) and 75th (upper end) percentiles, with whiskers and circles indicating extrema and outliers, respectively. The median values (50th percentiles) are also given as numbers above the boxes.

proposed model, 0.438 ± 0.130 for the baseline). For the group with an infarct core volume between 1 and 10 ml (10 and 70 ml), we measured values of 0.059 ± 0.078 (0.242 ± 0.144) for the proposed and 0.057 ± 0.061 (0.197 ± 0.126) for the baseline model. Please note that the Dice values are expected to be much lower here than for, e.g., organ segmentation tasks, seeing as the infarct core does not appear as a clearly delineated structure in the NCCT (cf. Figs. 2a, c). While a very good match of the predicted and reference masks as for Case 1 can occur (Fig. 2b), we also frequently observe results as for Case 2 (Fig. 2d). Here, the predicted infarct core is plausible, yet the measured overlap with the reference is still small since the detection is coarser as well as slightly over-sensitive. It seems unlikely, however, that a segmentation as fine-grained as the reference is even attainable in most cases. In addition, not every change found in the perfusion scan must necessarily be detectable in the preceding NCCT at all. From a model design perspective, the results demonstrate the benefit of providing the perfusion masks as an additional training target; the improvement over the baseline segmentation network is statistically significant ($p < 0.02$, two-tailed paired-sample t-test over all cases, irrespective of infarct core size). Quantitatively, this corresponds to an increase of the overall Dice coefficient from 0.107 ± 0.143 to 0.122 ± 0.165.

3.2 Localization Performance

The localization performance displayed in Fig. 3b shows a similar picture overall. Here, for the group with the largest infarcts, the median distance is in fact zero (0.9 ± 1.4 mm for the proposed model, 2.2 ± 4.0 mm for the baseline), i.e. the location of maximum predicted probability lies inside the reference infarct mask. For all but the group with an infarct volume below 1 ml (34.9 ± 15.5 mm for the proposed model, 39.1 ± 18.4 mm for the baseline), the median distance stays

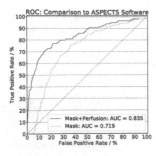
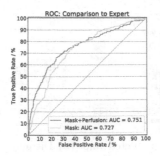
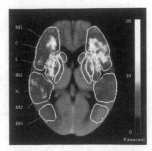

(a) Binary classification performance for ASPECTS regions against reference reading of NCCT by automatic ASPECTS evaluation.

(b) Binary classification performance for ASPECTS regions against reference reading of NCCT by a human expert.

(c) Atlas with ASPECTS regions (contours, cf. [3]), heatmap indicating no. of patients with infarct at corresponding location.

Fig. 4. Receiver operating characteristic (ROC) curves for ASPECTS region classification (a,b) and atlas with overlays (c). *Mask+Perfusion* denotes the proposed multi-task model while *Mask* refers to the baseline segmentation model.

below 2 cm. For the group with an infarct core volume between 1 and 10 ml (10 and 70 ml), the measured distances are 24.4 ± 21.3 mm (8.1 ± 12.8 mm) for the proposed and 25.4 ± 20.3 mm (12.3 ± 15.1 mm) for the baseline model. This measure helps provide a more complete picture for patients such as Case 2 in Fig. 2, which may have rather poor volumetric overlap as discussed above, but nevertheless localize the infarction correctly. Again, the multi-target model performs better than the baseline with an overall quantitative improvement of the distance from 23.2 ± 21.0 mm to 20.5 ± 20.4 mm. In this case, however, the difference is not statistically significant ($p = 0.36$, same test as before) on account of the baseline model performing reasonably well, too.

3.3 ASPECTS Classification

The receiver-operating characteristic (ROC) curves in Figs. 4a and b are obtained by pooling all ASPECTS regions of each patient and treating them as individual samples for binary classification. For this purpose, the distributions of predicted values for each region are calibrated by dividing them by the individual, region-specific thresholds that optimize the F-score on the training and validation sets. The curves demonstrate a good agreement with both references, especially considering that the model itself has no explicit notion of the regions. The prediction is slightly more similar to the automatic ASPECT scoring than the human expert. Although we assume the difference to be smaller than the effect of inter-reader variability, further investigation will be required to determine if there is a bias, such as the automatic methods potentially being less sensitive to certain radiologic signs than others as compared to a human reader.

It should also be noted that some regions are more frequently affected than others (cf. Fig. 4c), with, e.g., the M3 region (lower posterior cortical region supplied by the middle cerebral artery) only being labeled positive in 4 patients according to both references, which hinders both the overall model performance as well as its robust evaluation. For instance, when comparing against the automatic ASPECT scoring, the ROC area-under-curve (AUC) for the M3 region individually is 0.72, while it is 0.85 for the L region (lentiform nucleus, part of the basal ganglia) with the proposed model. Regardless of these caveats, the improvement over the baseline is consistently reflected in this evaluation as well.

3.4 Alternative Models

Besides the presented model we have also tested network architectures that are tailored to exploit the left-right brain symmetry even further, as similarly seen in recent work by Sheth et al. [17]. Specifically, we have tried "stacking" the hemispheres such that corresponding, contralateral regions fall within the same receptive fields, as well as architectures that have two parameter-tied encoder paths for the hemispheres. However, none of them yielded an improvement over the conventional U-Net applied in atlas space as described above. Thus, for the sake of conciseness, we opted not to include those results in this paper. A limitation of our model is that it operates on slices only. While this approach worked better than 3D models due to the smaller input space, identifying feasible ways to analyze the whole volume simultaneously is likely a goal worth pursuing in further experiments.

4   Conclusion

We describe and evaluate a deep-learning model for automatic detection of the ischemic infarct core in NCCT for improved stroke diagnosis. To this end, it needs to rely on the often subtle, early radiologic signs caused by increased water uptake in necrotic tissue. The model employs a state-of-the-art encoder-decoder architecture trained in a standardized image space obtained by non-rigid registration to a brain atlas. Aside from predicting a mask indicating the infarct core, we propose to simultaneously regress perfusion maps describing, e.g., cerebral blood flow and volume in order to supply richer information for learning meaningful features. All training targets are automatically derived from corresponding perfusion scans, foregoing the need for manual annotation. We demonstrate that this multi-target approach yields substantially improved results compared to a baseline trained only for binary segmentation. In quantitative evaluations, the model exhibits reasonable volumetric overlap of predicted and reference infarcted tissue, achieves a reliable localization of the infarction and is largely in agreement with both manual and automatic ASPECTS assessment.

In future work, our method will need to be trained and tested on larger data sets with external validation cohorts, to improve both generalization of the model as well as the robustness of its evaluation. In particular, a more in-depth clinical assessment will be necessary. Nonetheless, we believe the approach holds promise for providing radiologists and clinicians with highly valuable information at the first step along the imaging-based stroke diagnosis workflow.

References

1. Abels, B., Klotz, E., Tomandl, B., Kloska, S., Lell, M.: Perfusion CT in acute ischemic stroke: a qualitative and quantitative comparison of deconvolution and maximum slope approach. Am. J. Neuroradiol. **31**(9), 1690–1698 (2010)
2. Adebayo, O.D., Culpan, G.: Diagnostic accuracy of computed tomography perfusion in the prediction of haemorrhagic transformation and patient outcome in acute ischaemic stroke: a systematic review and meta-analysis. Eur. Stroke J. **5**(1), 4–16 (2020)
3. Barber, P.A., Demchuk, A.M., Zhang, J., Buchan, A.M., Group, A.S., et al.: Validity and reliability of a quantitative computed tomography score in predicting outcome of hyperacute stroke before thrombolytic therapy. Lancet, **355**(9216), 1670–1674 (2000)
4. Boers, A.M., et al.: Automated cerebral infarct volume measurement in follow-up noncontrast CT scans of patients with acute ischemic stroke. Am. J. Neuroradiol. **34**(8), 1522–1527 (2013)
5. Dice, L.R.: Measures of the amount of ecologic association between species. Ecology **26**(3), 297–302 (1945)
6. Feigin, V.L., et al.: Global, regional, and national burden of neurological disorders, 1990–2016: a systematic analysis for the Global Burden of Disease Study 2016. Lancet Neurol. **18**(5), 459–480 (2019)
7. Haussen, D.C., et al.: Automated CT perfusion ischemic core volume and noncontrast CT ASPECTS (Alberta Stroke Program Early CT Score): correlation and clinical outcome prediction in large vessel stroke. Stroke **47**(9), 2318–2322 (2016)
8. Ho, K.C., Speier, W., El-Saden, S., Arnold, C.W.: Classifying acute ischemic stroke onset time using deep imaging features. In: AMIA Annual Symposium Proceedings, vol. 2017, p. 892. American Medical Informatics Association (2017)
9. Johnson, W., Onuma, O., Owolabi, M., Sachdev, S.: Stroke: a global response is needed. Bull. World Health Organ. **94**(9), 634 (2016)
10. Kemmling, A., Wersching, H., Berger, K., Knecht, S., Groden, C., Nölte, I.: Decomposing the hounsfield unit: probabilistic segmentation of brain tissue in computed tomography. Clin. Neuroradiol. **22**(1), 79–91 (2012)
11. Mair, G., Wardlaw, J.: Imaging of acute stroke prior to treatment: current practice and evolving techniques. Br. J. Radiol. **87**(1040), 20140216 (2014)
12. Miles, K.A., Griffiths, M.R.: Perfusion CT: a worthwhile enhancement? Br. J. Radiol. **76**(904), 220–231 (2003)
13. Nowinski, W.L., et al.: Automatic detection, localization, and volume estimation of ischemic infarcts in noncontrast computed tomographic scans: method and preliminary results. Invest. Radiol. **48**(9), 661–670 (2013)
14. Qiu, W., et al.: Machine learning for detecting early infarction in acute stroke with non-contrast-enhanced CT. Radiology **294**, 191193 (2020)
15. Reidler, P.: Attenuation changes in ASPECTS regions: a surrogate for CT perfusion-based ischemic core in acute ischemic stroke. Radiology **291**(2), 451–458 (2019)
16. Ronneberger, O., Fischer, P., Brox, T.: U-Net: convolutional networks for biomedical image segmentation. In: Navab, N., Hornegger, J., Wells, W.M., Frangi, A.F. (eds.) MICCAI 2015. LNCS, vol. 9351, pp. 234–241. Springer, Cham (2015). https://doi.org/10.1007/978-3-319-24574-4_28
17. Sheth, S.A., et al.: Machine learning-enabled automated determination of acute ischemic core from computed tomography angiography. Stroke **50**(11), 3093–3100 (2019)

18. Shieh, Y., et al.: Computer-aided diagnosis of hyperacute stroke with thrombolysis decision support using a contralateral comparative method of CT image analysis. J. Digit. Imaging **27**(3), 392–406 (2014)

19. Stoel, B.C., et al.: Automated brain computed tomographic densitometry of early ischemic changes in acute stroke. J. Med. Imaging **2**(1), 014004 (2015)

20. Takahashi, N., et al.: Computerized identification of early ischemic changes in acute stroke in noncontrast CT using deep learning. In: Medical Imaging 2019: Computer-Aided Diagnosis, vol. 10950, p. 109503A. International Society for Optics and Photonics (2019)

21. Telea, A.: An image inpainting technique based on the fast marching method. J. Graph. Tools **9**(1), 23–34 (2004)

22. Wang, Z., Bovik, A.C., Sheikh, H.R., Simoncelli, E.P.: Image quality assessment: from error visibility to structural similarity. IEEE Trans. Image Process. **13**(4), 600–612 (2004)

23. Yao, X., Mao, L., Lv, S., Ren, Z., Li, W., Ren, K.: CT radiomics features as a diagnostic tool for classifying basal ganglia infarction onset time. J. Neurol. Sci. **412**, 116730 (2020)

24. Zhang, R.: Automatic segmentation of acute ischemic stroke from DWI using 3-D fully convolutional DenseNets. IEEE Trans. Med. Imaging **37**(9), 2149–2160 (2018)

Bayesian Neural Networks for Uncertainty Estimation of Imaging Biomarkers

Jyotirmay Senapati[1], Abhijit Guha Roy[1], Sebastian Pölsterl[1],
Daniel Gutmann[2], Sergios Gatidis[2], Christopher Schlett[3], Anette Peters[4],
Fabian Bamberg[3], and Christian Wachinger[1(✉)]

[1] Artificial Intelligence in Medical Imaging (AI-Med), KJP, LMU München,
Munich, Germany
senapati.jyotirmay@gmail.com, cwaching@med.lmu.de
[2] Department of Diagnostic and Interventional Radiology, University of Tübingen,
Tübingen, Germany
[3] Department of Diagnostic and Interventional Radiology, University Freiburg,
Freiburg im Breisgau, Germany
[4] Institute of Epidemiology, Helmholtz Zentrum München, Munich, Germany

Abstract. Image segmentation enables to extract quantitative measures from scans that can serve as imaging biomarkers for diseases. However, segmentation quality can vary substantially across scans, and therefore yield unfaithful estimates in the follow-up statistical analysis of biomarkers. The core problem is that segmentation and biomarker analysis are performed independently. We propose to propagate segmentation uncertainty to the statistical analysis to account for variations in segmentation confidence. To this end, we evaluate four Bayesian neural networks to sample from the posterior distribution and estimate the uncertainty. We then assign confidence measures to the biomarker and propose statistical models for its integration in group analysis and disease classification. Our results for segmenting the liver in patients with diabetes mellitus clearly demonstrate the improvement of integrating biomarker uncertainty in the statistical inference.

1 Introduction

Imaging biomarkers play a crucial role in tracking disease progression, in supporting an automated prediction of diagnosis, and in providing novel insights in the pathophysiology of diseases [5,23,24]. A prerequisite for many image-based markers is image segmentation, which provides access to morphological features like volume, thickness and shape information [6,7,22]. Despite a boost in segmentation accuracy by deep learning [15], automated segmentations are not perfect and their quality can vary substantially across scans. As a consequence, segmentation errors propagate to errors in the derived biomarker. To reduce the impact of erroneous segmentations in follow-up analyses and to infer

© Springer Nature Switzerland AG 2020
M. Liu et al. (Eds.): MLMI 2020, LNCS 12436, pp. 270–280, 2020.
https://doi.org/10.1007/978-3-030-59861-7_28

faithful estimates, a manual quality control is advised to identify segmentations of sufficient quality. However, the manual quality assessment is subject to intra- and inter-rater variability and time consuming, particularly for large datasets.

Fortunately, Bayesian neural networks for image segmentation [10,13,14] have been developed that do not only provide the mode (i.e., the most likely segmentation) but also the posterior distribution of the segmentation. Monte Carlo (MC) dropout [3,10] or the probabilistic U-Net [13,14] enable to sample multiple possible segmentations instead of only a single segmentation. Typically, a voxel-wise uncertainty is then computed and displayed to the user to detect regions with lower segmentation confidence In contrast, we want to use the segmentation uncertainty to derive a biomarker uncertainty. With such a measure, we could directly determine the scans from which biomarkers have been extracted reliably without the need for a manual quality control. However, the integration of the segmentation uncertainty into follow-up analyses of extracted biomarkers, such as group analyses or disease classification, has not yet been well studied. In addition, it is not clear which Bayesian segmentation method is best suited for inferring the uncertainty of the biomarker, capturing different aspects of aleatoric and epistemic uncertainty.

To address these issues, we present statistical models that integrate segmentation confidence measures in the parameter inference of the biomarker. Further, we compare four state-of-the-art Bayesian neural networks for computing the segmentation and confidence measures. We perform experiments for the segmentation of the liver in abdominal magnetic resonance imaging (MRI) scans in subjects with diabetes mellitus. Our results demonstrate that the integration of biomarker uncertainty yields estimates that are closer to the manual reference and higher classification accuracy.

Related Work. Several approaches have been proposed to compute uncertainty for the segmentation of medical images [1,2,8,9,16,18,21,25]. We have previously used MC dropout to compute the uncertainty in whole-brain segmentation [17,18]. Nair et al. [16] provide four different voxel-based uncertainty measures based on MC dropout. The reliability of uncertainty estimations for image segmentation has been evaluated in [9]. Eaton et al. [2] presented uncertainty for calibrating confidence boundary for robust predictions of tumor segmentations. Hu et al. [8] used calibrated inter-grader variability as a target for training a CNN model to predict aleatoric uncertainty. Sedai et al. [21] used uncertainty guided domain alignment to train a model for retinal and choroidal layers segmentation in OCT images. In [25], Yu et al. incorporate uncertainty in a teacher CNN to guide a student CNN in a semi-supervised segmentation setup. The architecture for multi-scale ambiguity detection and uncertainty quantification proposed by Baumgartner et al. [1] is similar to the hierarchical model in [14], which we also use in this work. Uncertainty-driven bootstrapping for data selection and model training was proposed in [4]. In contrast to prior work, we focus on propagating segmentation to the statistical analysis of imaging biomarkers.

2   Methods

2.1   Bayesian Neural Networks for Image Segmentation

Essential for our approach of estimating the biomarker uncertainty are Bayesian segmentation networks that enable to sample from the predictive posterior distribution. Several strategies to perform variational inference within fully convolutional neural networks (F-CNNs) have been proposed in the literature, where we describe four commonly used and promising approaches in the following.

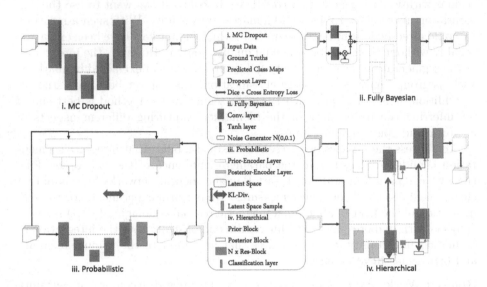

Fig. 1. Schematic illustration of the four Bayesian neural networks that we use for segmentation.

Monte-Carlo Dropout. Dropout layers were first adapted within deep neural networks to perform variational inference by Gal et al. [3]. This was later adopted for image segmentation in computer vision [10] and medical imaging [18]. The main idea is to keep the dropout layers active during inference, see Fig. 1(i). This enforces the neurons to be stochastic within the network and generates multiple segmentation maps for a single image. These multiple Monte-Carlo segmentation samples are aggregated to generate the final segmentation and its corresponding uncertainty map.

Fully-Bayesian F-CNN with Re-parameterization. We replace the convolutional layers in the segmentation network with a Bayesian convolution layer, see Fig. 1(ii), which has been developed using the re-parameterization trick [11,12]. We are not aware of a previous application of this approach for segmentation.

The Bayesian layer consists of two convolution layers, whose outputs are further processed to add non-linearity by adding a tanh activation at each layer. We consider the outputs from the tanh layers as μ_θ and σ_θ. A Gaussian white noise ε is multiplied with σ_θ to introduce stochasticity and the product is added to μ_θ

$$g_\theta(\varepsilon) = \mu_\theta + \varepsilon\sigma_\theta \qquad \text{and} \qquad \varepsilon \sim \mathcal{N}(0, 0.1). \qquad (1)$$

Kingma et al. [11,12] used a Gaussian distribution with mean 0 and standard deviation 1 in their experiments. We reduce the standard deviation to 0.1 to restrict higher variation in σ_θ.

Probabilistic U-Net. Kohl et al. [13] proposed the probabilistic U-Net. They suggested that ambiguous medical images can have multiple plausible segmentations based on multiple graders and that capturing this spectrum of variability is more meaningful than estimating the uncertainty maps. In this regard, along with the base segmentation network, they train a separate network termed prior net, which maps the input to an embedding hypothesis space, see Fig. 1(iii). One sample from this hypothesis space is concatenated to the last feature map of the base segmentation network to generate one segmentation output. Thus, multiple plausible segmentations are generated with sampling different points from the learnt hypothesis embedding space.

Hierarchical Probabilistic U-Net. Kohl et al. [14] further improved the probabilistic U-Net [13] to incorporate multi-scale ambiguity. In case the target organ exists in multiple scales, it is important to capture the spectrum of variation across all the scales. The previous work from the authors successfully captured only the variation across one scale. Thus, they modified the network to capture the underlying variation across multiple scales. The main idea is to learn multiple hypothesis embedding spaces, each one specific to a specific target scale, see Fig. 1(iv). In every encoder-decoder based F-CNN, it is assumed that different scale-specific features are learnt at each stage of the decoder with different spatial resolution. Therefore, during inference, multiple scale specific samples generated from different hypothesis embedding spaces are concatenated to their corresponding decoder feature map of appropriate scale. Consequently, different sets of samples from different embeddings generate multiple plausible segmentation maps.

2.2 Confidence Measure

Bayesian neural networks commonly provide a measure of uncertainty per voxel. As many biomarkers are associated to organs, we need an uncertainty measure per organ. To this end, we will use the intersection over union (IoU) and the coefficient of variation (CV) [18]. For the IoU, we consider N segmentation samples $S_1, \ldots, S_N$ from the network for the organ o

$$\mathrm{IoU} = \frac{|(S_1 == o) \cap (S_2 == o) \cap ...(S_N == o)|}{|(S_1 == o) \cup (S_2 == o) \cup ...(S_N == o)|}. \tag{2}$$

In our application, we use $N = 10$ and $o =$ liver.

In our analyses, we focus on the volume of the liver. Instead of quantifying uncertainty with regards to segmentation, we can also directly measure the variation of the volume across the segmentation samples. Considering volumes $V_1, ..., V_N$ computed from the N segmentation maps and the mean volume μ, the coefficient of variation is

$$\mathrm{CV} = \sqrt{\frac{\sum (V_i - \mu)^2}{N \cdot \mu^2}}. \tag{3}$$

Note that this estimate is agnostic to the size of the structure. As a high coefficient of variation indicates an erroneous segmentation, we use the inverse, CV^{-1}, as confidence measure, while the IoU can be used directly.

2.3 Statistical Methods

We want to integrate the segmentation confidence measures in the biomarker analysis to enable a more faithful and reliable estimation of model parameters. We present statistical models for group analysis and disease classification in the following.

Group Analysis. In the group analysis, we evaluate the association of the biomarker with respect to non-imaging variables. For our application of diabetes, we consider the age A_i, sex S_i, BMI B_i, and diabetes status D_i for subject i. The base model for the liver volume V_i is

$$\text{Base Model:} \quad V_i = \beta_0 + \beta_1 A_i + \beta_2 S_i + \beta_3 B_i + \beta_4 D_i + \varepsilon, \tag{4}$$

where $\beta_0, ..., \beta_4$ are regression coefficients and ε is the noise term.

We now want to integrate the confidence measure C_i that is associated to the volume V_i and comes from the Bayesian segmentation into the model. As first approach, we propose to add the confidence measure as additional variable to the model

$$\text{Variable:} \quad V_i = \beta_0 + \beta_1 A_i + \beta_2 S_i + \beta_3 B_i + \beta_4 D_i + \beta_5 C_i + \varepsilon. \tag{5}$$

As alternative, we use the confidence measure as instance weight in the regression model. Instead of giving equal importance to each subject i, subjects with higher confidence in the liver segmentation will be given higher importance in the estimation of the coefficients

$$\text{Instance Weighting:} \quad [V_i = \beta_0 + \beta_1 A_i + \beta_2 S_i + \beta_3 B_i + \beta_4 D_i + \varepsilon] \cdot C_i. \tag{6}$$

Weighted least squares is used for estimating the model coefficients, where the confidence measures are used as weights. Note that manual quality control is a special case of instance weighting with a binary confidence measure, where only those segmentations with passing quality are set to one and the rest to zero.

Disease Classification. For the prediction of the diabetes status, we use logistic regression. In the base model, we use the liver volume as input feature. For the integration of the confidence measure in the classification model, we consider three variants. First, we add the confidence measure C_i as additional variable to the model. Second, we do not only consider the additive effect of the confidence measure but also the interaction, so that $V_i \cdot C_i$ is also added to the model. Third, we use instance weighting based on the confidence measure to emphasize subjects with good segmentations.

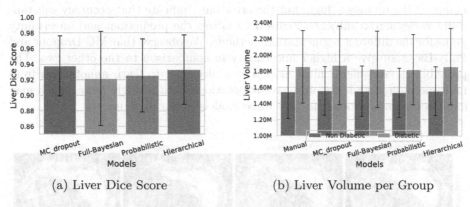

(a) Liver Dice Score   (b) Liver Volume per Group

Fig. 2. (a) Bars show mean Dice score of liver and error bars show standard deviation for different segmentation networks. (b) Bars show the mean liver volume of diabetic and non-diabetic subjects for manual and automated segmentation, error bars indicate standard deviation.

3   Results

3.1   Data

Experiments are performed on a set of whole-body Magnetic Resonance Images (MRI) obtained from the Cooperative Health Research in the Region Augsburg project (KORA). We work with 308 subjects (109 diabetic, 199 non-diabetic) that have a manual annotation of the liver. We resample all volumes to a standard resolution of $2 \times 2 \times 3$ mm^3 and $53 \times 256 \times 144$ voxels.

3.2   Bayesian Segmentation Results

We use QuickNAT [19,20] as base architecture for implementing Bayesian networks in Fig. 1. We use common network parameters across models with learning rate 1e-5, batch size 5, and 50 epochs. For MC Dropout, we use a dropout rate of 0.2. For Fully-Bayesian, we do not use a batch normalization layer. Instead, we use uni-variate KL-Divergence loss to regularize the distribution of weights from each Bayesian layer. For the probabilistic and hierarchical models, a latent variable of dimension 12 has been used to estimate the posterior embedding. We split the dataset into 155 training (56 diabetic, 99 non-diabetic) and 153 testing (53 diabetic, 100 non-diabetic) subjects by equally distributing diabetic and non-diabetic subjects.

Figure 2(a) shows a boxplot of the Dice score of the liver for different segmentation methods. We observe that MC dropout yields the highest accuracy, followed by hierarchical, probabilistic, and Fully-Bayesian. Overall, the performance of the models is high, but the error bars indicate that accuracy substantially varies across subjects. Figure 3 visualizes the predictions and uncertainty maps for the different segmentation methods. We observe that MC Dropout and Fully-Bayesian give a higher uncertainty in comparison to the other two. The probabilistic and hierarchical models were designed to learn annotations from multiple raters, while we only have annotations from a single rater, which may explain the lower stochasticity of these models in our experiments.

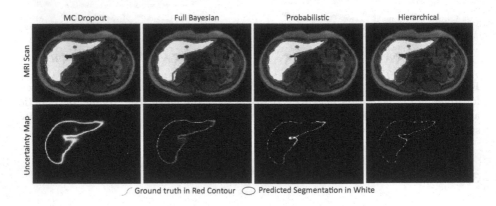

Fig. 3. Top: MRI scan overlaid by segmentation map (white) and manual annotation (red contour). Bottom: Voxel-wise uncertainty map of the segmentation. (Color figure online)

3.3   Group Analysis

Table 1 reports the regression coefficient of the diabetes status β_4, which is of primary interest for studying diabetes, where Fig. 2(b) illustrates that diabetic subjects tend to have a higher liver volume. The table shows the coefficient for different segmentation methods and statistical models. Next to the base model, and the integration of the confidence measure as additional variable and instance weight, we also estimate the coefficient from the manual segmentation, which serves as reference. All regression coefficients are estimated on the segmentation test set.

MC Dropout with IoU as additional variable or instance weight yields coefficients that are closest to the manual estimate. For the probabilistic and hierarchical models, adding IoU to the model leads to the best results. The coefficient of the Fully-Bayesian network has the highest divergence from the manual estimate across segmentation methods, but inclusion of confidence measures as variables helps to improve the estimate.

Table 1. Regression coefficient of diabetes status, β_4, for different segmentation approaches and statistical models, together with the manual estimate.

	Base	Variable		Instance		Manual
		IoU	CV^{-1}	IoU	CV^{-1}	
MC Dropout	0.308	**0.318**	0.308	0.316	0.268	
Fully-Bayesian	0.255	0.269	**0.271**	0.254	0.229	0.328
Probabilistic	0.287	**0.302**	0.297	0.287	0.192	
Hierarchical	0.294	**0.306**	0.288	0.295	0.249	

Table 2. Accuracy for diabetes classification with logistic regression for different segmentation methods and manual segmentation. The base model is compared to several approaches of including the confidence measure in the estimation.

	Base	Variable		Interaction		Instance		Manual
		IoU	CV^{-1}	IoU	CV^{-1}	IoU	CV^{-1}	
MC Dropout	0.702	**0.719**	0.709	0.716	0.712	0.706	0.708	
Fully-Bayesian	0.692	**0.705**	0.696	**0.705**	0.695	0.695	0.696	0.713
Probabilistic	0.691	0.719	0.696	**0.732**	0.694	0.691	0.696	
Hierarchical	0.702	**0.714**	0.694	**0.714**	0.695	0.703	0.699	

3.4 Disease Classification

For the classification experiment, we split the segmentation test set further into a classification training set (77 subjects, 27 diabetic, 50 non-diabetic) and a classification test set (76 subjects, 26 diabetic, 50 non-diabetic) randomly 1,000 times. Table 2 reports the mean classification accuracy across all runs. We compare different methods for segmentation and integration of the confidence measures.

The accuracy for volumes derived from manual annotations is 0.713; the accuracy decreases for all automated segmentations in the base model. The inclusion of the confidence measures in the classification helps to recover the accuracy and even pass the one from the manual segmentation. The likely reason for this behaviour is that the confidence measures vary between diagnostic groups and therefore provide additional information for the classification. We observe the best performance for the variable and interaction models with IoU. The overall best result is obtained by the probabilistic model with IoU interaction term.

4   Conclusion

In this work, we proposed to propagate segmentation uncertainty to the biomarker analysis as the segmentation quality can vary substantially between scans. Our results have demonstrated that assigning a confidence score to an imaging biomarker can yield a more faithful estimation of model parameters and a higher classification accuracy. We have evaluated four Bayesian neural networks with the best results for MC dropout and the probabilistic model, each one in combination with IoU as confidence measure. These results show a clear improvement over a base model that does not consider segmentation uncertainty, and therefore confirms the necessity of propagating uncertainty to the final biomarker analysis.

Acknowledgement. This research was supported by DFG, BMBF (project Deep-Mentia), and the Bavarian State Ministry of Science and the Arts and coordinated by the Bavarian Research Institute for Digital Transformation (bidt).

References

1. Baumgartner, C.F., et al.: PHiSeg: capturing uncertainty in medical image segmentation. In: Shen, D., et al. (eds.) MICCAI 2019. LNCS, vol. 11765, pp. 119–127. Springer, Cham (2019). https://doi.org/10.1007/978-3-030-32245-8_14
2. Eaton-Rosen, Z., Bragman, F., Bisdas, S., Ourselin, S., Cardoso, M.J.: Towards safe deep learning: accurately quantifying biomarker uncertainty in neural network predictions. In: Frangi, A.F., Schnabel, J.A., Davatzikos, C., Alberola-López, C., Fichtinger, G. (eds.) MICCAI 2018. LNCS, vol. 11070, pp. 691–699. Springer, Cham (2018). https://doi.org/10.1007/978-3-030-00928-1_78
3. Gal, Y., Ghahramani, Z.: Dropout as a Bayesian approximation: representing model uncertainty in deep learning. In: International Conference on Machine Learning, pp. 1050–1059 (2016)
4. Ghesu, F.C., et al.: Quantifying and leveraging classification uncertainty for chest radiograph assessment. In: Shen, D., et al. (eds.) MICCAI 2019. LNCS, vol. 11769, pp. 676–684. Springer, Cham (2019). https://doi.org/10.1007/978-3-030-32226-7_75
5. Gutiérrez-Becker, B., Klein, T., Wachinger, C.: Gaussian process uncertainty in age estimation as a measure of brain abnormality. NeuroImage **175**, 246–258 (2018)

6. Gutiérrez-Becker, B., Wachinger, C.: Deep multi-structural shape analysis: application to neuroanatomy. In: Frangi, A.F., Schnabel, J.A., Davatzikos, C., Alberola-López, C., Fichtinger, G. (eds.) MICCAI 2018. LNCS, vol. 11072, pp. 523–531. Springer, Cham (2018). https://doi.org/10.1007/978-3-030-00931-1_60

7. Gutiérrez-Becker, B., Wachinger, C.: Learning a conditional generative model for anatomical shape analysis. In: IPMI 2019, pp. 505–516. Springer, Heidelberg (2019). https://doi.org/10.1007/978-3-030-20351-1_39

8. Hu, S., Worrall, D., Knegt, S., Veeling, B., Huisman, H., Welling, M.: Supervised uncertainty quantification for segmentation with multiple annotations. In: Shen, D., et al. (eds.) MICCAI 2019. LNCS, vol. 11765, pp. 137–145. Springer, Cham (2019). https://doi.org/10.1007/978-3-030-32245-8_16

9. Jungo, A., Reyes, M.: Assessing reliability and challenges of uncertainty estimations for medical image segmentation. In: Shen, D., et al. (eds.) MICCAI 2019. LNCS, vol. 11765, pp. 48–56. Springer, Cham (2019). https://doi.org/10.1007/978-3-030-32245-8_6

10. Kendall, A., Gal, Y.: What uncertainties do we need in Bayesian deep learning for computer vision? In: Advances in Neural Information Processing Systems, pp. 5574–5584 (2017)

11. Kingma, D.P., Welling, M.: Auto-encoding variational Bayes. arXiv preprint arXiv:1312.6114 (2013)

12. Kingma, D.P., Salimans, T., Welling, M.: Variational dropout and the local reparameterization trick. In: Advances in Neural Information Processing Systems, pp. 2575–2583 (2015)

13. Kohl, S., et al.: A probabilistic u-net for segmentation of ambiguous images. In: Advances in Neural Information Processing Systems, pp. 6965–6975 (2018)

14. Kohl, S.A., et al.: A hierarchical probabilistic u-net for modeling multi-scale ambiguities. arXiv preprint arXiv:1905.13077 (2019)

15. Minaee, S., Boykov, Y., Porikli, F., Plaza, A., Kehtarnavaz, N., Terzopoulos, D.: Image segmentation using deep learning: A survey. arXiv preprint arXiv:2001.05566 (2020)

16. Nair, T., Precup, D., Arnold, D.L., Arbel, T.: Exploring uncertainty measures in deep networks for multiple sclerosis lesion detection and segmentation. Med. Image Anal. **59**, 101557 (2020)

17. Roy, A.G., Conjeti, S., Navab, N., Wachinger, C.: Inherent brain segmentation quality control from fully ConvNet Monte Carlo sampling. In: Frangi, A.F., Schnabel, J.A., Davatzikos, C., Alberola-López, C., Fichtinger, G. (eds.) MICCAI 2018. LNCS, vol. 11070, pp. 664–672. Springer, Cham (2018). https://doi.org/10.1007/978-3-030-00928-1_75

18. Roy, A.G., Conjeti, S., Navab, N., Wachinger, C.: Bayesian quicknat: model uncertainty in deep whole-brain segmentation for structure-wise quality control. NeuroImage **195**, 11–22 (2019)

19. Roy, A.G., Conjeti, S., Navab, N., Wachinger, C.: Quicknat: a fully convolutional network for quick and accurate segmentation of neuroanatomy. NeuroImage **186**, 713–727 (2019)

20. Roy, A.G., Conjeti, S., Sheet, D., Katouzian, A., Navab, N., Wachinger, C.: Error corrective boosting for learning fully convolutional networks with limited data. In: Descoteaux, M., Maier-Hein, L., Franz, A., Jannin, P., Collins, D.L., Duchesne, S. (eds.) MICCAI 2017. LNCS, vol. 10435, pp. 231–239. Springer, Cham (2017). https://doi.org/10.1007/978-3-319-66179-7_27

21. Sedai, S., Antony, B., Rai, R., Jones, K., Ishikawa, H., Schuman, J., Gadi, W., Garnavi, R.: Uncertainty guided semi-supervised segmentation of retinal layers in OCT images. In: Shen, D., et al. (eds.) MICCAI 2019. LNCS, vol. 11764, pp. 282–290. Springer, Cham (2019). https://doi.org/10.1007/978-3-030-32239-7_32
22. Wachinger, C., Golland, P., Kremen, W., Fischl, B., Reuter, M.: Brainprint: a discriminative characterization of brain morphology. NeuroImage **109**, 232–248 (2015)
23. Wachinger, C., Reuter, M.: Domain adaptation for Alzheimer's disease diagnostics. Neuroimage **139**, 470–479 (2016)
24. Wachinger, C., Salat, D.H., Weiner, M., Reuter, M.: Whole-brain analysis reveals increased neuroanatomical asymmetries in dementia for hippocampus and amygdala. Brain **139**(12), 3253–3266 (2016)
25. Yu, L., Wang, S., Li, X., Fu, C.-W., Heng, P.-A.: Uncertainty-aware self-ensembling model for semi-supervised 3D left atrium segmentation. In: Shen, D., et al. (eds.) MICCAI 2019. LNCS, vol. 11765, pp. 605–613. Springer, Cham (2019). https://doi.org/10.1007/978-3-030-32245-8_67

Extended Capture Range of Rigid 2D/3D Registration by Estimating Riemannian Pose Gradients

Wenhao Gu$^{(\boxtimes)}$, Cong Gao, Robert Grupp, Javad Fotouhi,
and Mathias Unberath

Johns Hopkins University, Baltimore, MD 21218, USA
wgu11@jhu.edu

Abstract. Traditional intensity-based 2D/3D registration requires near-perfect initialization in order for image similarity metrics to yield meaningful updates of X-ray pose and reduce the likelihood of getting trapped in a local minimum. The conventional approaches strongly depend on image appearance rather than content, and therefore, fail in revealing large pose offsets that substantially alter the appearance of the same structure. We complement traditional similarity metrics with a convolutional neural network-based (CNN-based) registration solution that captures large-range pose relations by extracting both local and contextual information, yielding meaningful X-ray pose updates without the need for accurate initialization. To register a 2D X-ray image and a 3D CT scan, our CNN accepts a target X-ray image and a digitally reconstructed radiograph at the current pose estimate as input and iteratively outputs pose updates in the direction of the pose gradient on the Riemannian Manifold. Our approach integrates seamlessly with conventional image-based registration frameworks, where long-range relations are captured primarily by our CNN-based method while short-range offsets are recovered accurately with an image similarity-based method. On both synthetic and real X-ray images of the human pelvis, we demonstrate that the proposed method can successfully recover large rotational and translational offsets, irrespective of initialization.

Keywords: Image-guided surgery · Machine learning · X-ray · CT

1 Introduction

The localization of patient anatomy during surgical procedures is an integral part of navigation for computer-assisted surgical interventions. Traditional navigation systems use specialized sensors and fiducial objects to recover the pose

Electronic supplementary material The online version of this chapter (https://doi.org/10.1007/978-3-030-59861-7_29) contains supplementary material, which is available to authorized users.

M. Liu et al. (Eds.): MLMI 2020, LNCS 12436, pp. 281–291, 2020.
https://doi.org/10.1007/978-3-030-59861-7_29

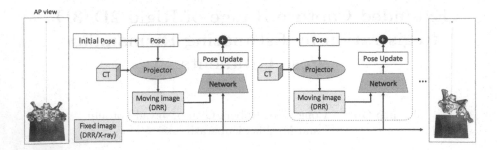

Fig. 1. Context-based registration workflow in an iterative scheme. The registration pipeline initiates with a fixed 2-D image, a 3-D CT, and a pose guess. The anterior-posterior pose of the anatomy is used for all images as an initial guess. The pose of the X-ray camera is updated in each iteration and forward projected to generate the moving image as part of the input of the network.

of patient anatomy [17,25,28], which are often invasive, sensitive to occlusion, and complicate surgical workflows.

Fluoroscopic imaging provides an alternative method for navigation and localization. Fluoroscopy is widely used during surgery and is not sensitive to the limitations imposed by other surgical navigation sensors. Therefore, a 2D/3D registration between the intra-operative 2D X-ray imaging system and a 3D CT volume may be used to perform navigation [19]. Such tracking approaches based on 2D/3D registration find applications in a wide spectrum of surgical interventions including orthopedics [10,23,29], trauma [8] and spine surgery [14].

1.1 Background

The two main variants of 2D/3D registration are split between intensity-based and feature-based approaches. Feature-based approaches require manual or automated segmentation or feature extraction in both of the imaging modalities and are optimized in a point-to-point, etc. fashion [24]. The accuracy of the feature-based methods directly relies on the accuracy of the feature extraction pipeline.

Intensity-based approaches, on the other hand, directly use the information contained in pixels of 2D images and voxels of 3D volumes. A typical intensity-based registration technique iteratively optimizes the similarity measure between simulated X-ray images known as digitally reconstructed radiographs (DRRs) that are generated by forward projecting the pre-operative 3D volume, and the real X-ray image [15]. The optimization problem for registering a single view image is described as:

$$\min_{\theta \in SE(3)} \mathcal{S}\left(I, \mathcal{P}\left(\theta; V\right)\right) + \mathcal{R}\left(\theta\right) \tag{1}$$

In Eq. 1, I denotes the 2D fluoroscopic image, V the preoperative 3D model, θ the pose of the volume with respect to the projective coordinate frame, $\mathcal{P}$ the projection operator used to create DRRs, $\mathcal{S}$ the similarity metric used to compare DRRs and I, and $\mathcal{R}$ the regularization over the plausible poses.

1.2   Related Work

A reasonable initial pose estimate is required for any intensity-based registration to find the true pose. A common technique used for initialization is to annotate corresponding anatomical landmarks in the 2D and 3D images and solve the PnP problem [3,19]. Another technique requires a user to manually adjust an object's pose and visually compare the estimated DRR to the intraoperative 2D image. These methods are time-consuming and challenging for inexperienced users, which makes them impractical during surgery. Alternatively, some restrictions may be imposed on plausible poses to significantly reduce, or eliminate, the number of landmarks required for initialization [19]. SLAM-based inside-out tracking solutions were suggested to provide re-initialization in 2D/3D registration settings. These group of methods only provide relative pose updates and do not contribute to the estimation of the absolute pose between the 2D and 3D data [7,11].

In [10], a single-landmark was used to initialize the registration of a 2D anterior-posterior (AP) view of the pelvis, and further views were initialized by restricting any additional C-arm movement to orbital rotations. However, for certain applications, such as the chiseling of bone at near-lateral views, it is not feasible to impose such restrictions on the initial view or C-arm movements.

Several works attempted to solve the ill-posed 2D/3D registration problem using convolutional neural networks (CNN). An early work by Miao et al. directly regressed the pose between simulated radiographs and X-ray images using CNNs [20]. Recent works combined the geometric principles from multi-view geometry and the semantic information extracted from CNNs to improve the capture range of 2D/3D registration. In [2,3,6], distinct anatomical landmarks were extracted from 2D X-ray images using CNNs and were matched with their corresponding locations on the 3D data. These 2D/3D correspondences were then used to estimate the relative projection matrix in a least-squares fashion. Similarly, a multi-view CNN-based registration approach used CNNs for correspondence establishment and triangulation between multiple X-ray images and a single 3D CT [16].

To overcome current shortcomings, we propose a novel CNN-based approach that is capable of learning large scale pose updates between a 2D X-ray image and the corresponding 3D CT volume. For large offsets, the network effectively learns the pose adjustment process that a human could conduct to initialize an intensity-based optimization. When close to the ground truth pose, updates will be derived by a classic intensity-based method for fine adjustments. Our proposed method exhibits a substantially extended capture range compared to conventional image-based registration [10,19]. Although similar effort to achieve robustness to poor initialization is made in [14] by using a multi-start optimization strategy within an intensity-based registration framework, their method was limited to level-check in spine surgery and the 2D radiographs acquired using a portable X-ray unit have a large field-of-view of the anatomy which is not suitable for interventions where only local radiographs is available (for example, those using mobile C-arms).

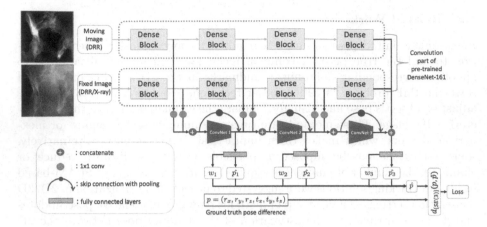

Fig. 2. A high-level overview of the proposed network architecture. The input images include a fixed, target image and a moving DRR image that is generated based on the current pose estimate of each iteration. To train the network, both input images are synthetically generated DRR images with precisely known camera poses with respect to the 3D CT volume. p represents the pose difference between the two image viewpoints in twist form, which establishes the target of the network. The relative pose $\hat{p}_i$ and respective "certainty" w_i is estimated at three different depths i in our CNN to capture both global and local information.

2   Methods

Similar to previous approaches, we employ an iterative strategy to sequentially approach the correct relative pose. In each iteration, a DRR is rendered from CT using the current pose estimate and compared to the fixed, target X-ray image using a CNN (Fig. 1). The network is trained to predict the relative 3D pose between the two 2D input fluoroscopy images using an untangled representation of 3D location and 3D orientation. While the proposed approach still requires the selection of a starting pose, the selection thereof is no longer critical because the image similarity metric estimated by our CNN approximates the geodesic distance between the respective image poses, which in theory, makes the registration problem globally convex (Sect. 2.1).

2.1   Image Similarity, the Riemannian Manifold, and Geodesic Gradients

Among the biggest challenges in 2D/3D image registration is the question of how to properly model the similarity between two images. This is because pose updates of iterative registration algorithms are generally derived from the gradient of the selected image similarity function. Conventional image similarity metrics, such as cross correlation [10] or normalized gradient information [1], only evaluate local intensity patterns that may agree in some areas while being substantially different in others. Since the changes in transmission image appearance can be substantial even for small pose differences, the aforementioned property of conventional image-based similarity metrics gives rise to a highly non-convex optimization landscape that is characterized by many local minima even far from the ground truth. It would be appealing to express 2D image similarity as the relative pose difference between the two viewpoints. Expressed in terms of the Riemannian tangent space, this image similarity metric defined over viewpoints is convex and thus effectively overcomes the aforementioned challenges. Given $SE(3)$ as Special Euclidean Group in 3D space, the distance between two rigid-body poses $T = \exp{(\hat{p})} \in SE(3)$ and $T' = \exp{(\hat{p'})} \in SE(3)$ can be defined as the gradient of the geodesic distance on the Riemannian manifold as [12,21]:

$$g(p, p') = \nabla \text{dist}(p, p') = -2\log_{p'}(p), \qquad (2)$$

where $\log_{p'}(.)$ denotes the Riemannian logarithm at p'; $\hat{p}$ and $\hat{p'}$ are the elements of the Lie algebra $se(3)$, the tangent space to $SE(3)$; $(p, p') \in \mathbb{R}^6$ are the twist coordinates. The geodesic gradient $g(p, p')$ indicates the direction of update from one viewpoint to the other, considering the structure of $SE(3)$. It is the generalization of straight lines of Euclidean geometry on Riemannian manifolds. We refer to [22] for a more detailed description and use the implementation provided in [21] for the experiments reported here.

In the case of 2D/3D image registration, only the pose of the moving DRR is known while the pose of the fixed, target X-ray image must be recovered and is thus unknown *a priori*. This means that Eq. 2 cannot be computed in practice to evaluate image similarity. However, if many images of similar 3D scenes with accurate viewpoint pose information are available then this image similarity function can be approximated with a CNN that processes both 2D images. Given two images I and $\hat{I}$ with viewpoints p and $\hat{p}$, respectively, we seek to learn the parameters θ of a CNN $f(I, \hat{I}, \theta)$ such that

$$f(I, \hat{I}, \theta) = g(p, \hat{p}) + \epsilon, \qquad (3)$$

where ϵ is an irreducible error.

2.2   Network Structure

We design a CNN architecture that takes two images of the same size as an input and predicts the gradient of the geodesic distance on the Riemannian manifold between the respective viewpoints, as per Sect. 2.1. An overview of the architecture is provided in Fig. 2. The images first pass through the convolutional part of a Siamese DenseNet-161 [13] pre-trained on ImageNet [5].

Feature maps of deeper layers are widely assumed to contain higher-level semantic information, while most information on spatial configuration and local image appearance is lost; yet, local features are likely informative for predicting pose updates as relative image poses get closer. We hypothesize that both – global and local – representations carry information that is relevant for regressing relative pose solely based on image content. Therefore, we 1) extract feature maps of both images at three different depths i of DenseNet, 2) concatenate them, and 3) pass them through additional CNNs and fully connected layers to individually estimate the geodesic gradient $\hat{p}_i$. During inference, it is unclear which of these three estimates $\hat{p}_i$ will be most appropriate at any given scenario and we surrender this importance weighting task to the CNN itself. This is realized by simultaneously regressing a weight w_i corresponding to the geodesic gradient prediction $\hat{p}_i$ at the respective depth i. After applying softmax to the weights w_i for normalization, the final output of the CNN $\hat{p}_i = \sum_{i=1}^{3} w_i \cdot \hat{p}_i$ is evaluated end-to-end together with the other three predictions.

During experimentation, we found that rotational pose changes were captured quite well while purely translational displacements could not be recovered accurately. Following [18], we replace all convolution layers after feature extraction from DenseNet by coordinate convolution (CoordConv) layers [18], which gives convolution filters access to the input image coordinate by appending a normalized coordinate channel to the respective feature representation.

We use the proposed method [10] as an effective initialization strategy to quickly approach the desired X-ray camera pose from an arbitrary initialization but then rely on a recent image-based method [10] to fine-tune the final pose once after convergence. Once the gradient update is below a certain threshold that is comparable with the capture range of the image-based registration method, we surrender to purely image-based registration to achieve very high accuracy.

3   Experiments and Results

3.1   Datasets

We select 7 high-resolution CT volumes from the NIH Cancer Imaging Archive [4] as the basis for our synthetic dataset and split data on the CT level into 5 volumes for training, 1 for validation, and 1 for testing. For each CT volume, a total of 4311 synthetic DRR images were generated from different positions (randomly sampling poses with rotations in LAO/RAO $\in [-40°, 40°]$ and CRAN/CAUD $\in [-20, 20]$, and translations of ± 75 mm in all directions). DRRs and corresponding ground truth poses are generated using DeepDRR [26,27].

During training, we then sample two DRRs generated from the same 3D CT volume with random and different perspectives and optimize the parameters of our network to regress the geodesic gradient that represents the relative pose difference. We use the open-source *geomstats* package to perform all calculations pertaining to the Riemannian tangent space [21]. Each image input to the model is log-corrected followed by Contrast Limited Adaptive Histogram Equalization and Gaussian filter to blur out high-frequency signal. Images are then normalized within $[-1, 1]$ and a maximum 40% random contrast and intensity to increase the robustness of generalization on real X-ray data. The training was performed on a single Nvidia Quadro P6000 GPU. Batch size used for training was 16; the learning rate starts from $1e-6$, and decreases to 30% after every $30,000$ iterations.

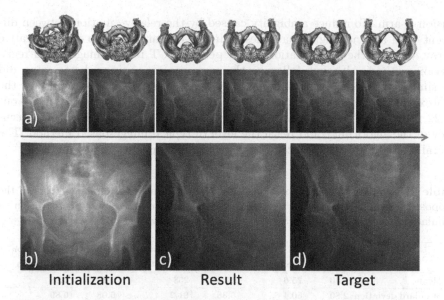

Initialization   Result   Target

Fig. 3. Example of pose update and registration on synthetic data. In **(a)**, intermediate DRRs are rendered from initialization towards the final estimation. In **(b-d)** the initial DRR in AP view, the final predicted DRR view, and the target image are shown respectively.

3.2 Registration of Simulated X-Ray Images

While the registration is conducted in its iterative scheme, as long as the gradients are driving in a coherent direction, we allow the network to predict gradients with minor errors during the intermediate steps to compensate small errors and make our registration method robust. An example is shown in Fig. 3.

In Table 1 we present the rotational and translational misalignment errors for the 196 synthetic test cases with known ground truth. Violin plot of distribution for the misalignment with three methods are attached in the supplementary material. We compare the final pose of our CNN-based registration to intensity-based registration using the covariance matrix adaptation evolution strategy (CMA-ES) [10]; both initialized at AP View. Among all the 196 test cases, 15 cases failed due to their non-typical appearance which were not seen in the images of the training set. Only the numerical comparison of the 181 success case using our method with the other two approaches is included in Table 1. Since the testing images mostly have large offset from the AP view (initialization), the image-based registration method fails in all tested cases and results are trapped in local minima near the initialization.

3.3 Registration Results on Real X-Ray Images

The registration of a real X-ray image to pre-operative CT is more complicated than simulated images. The X-ray images were acquired from a Siemens CIOS

Fusion C-arm. To reduce ambiguity caused by the relative motion between different rigid and non-rigid anatomies from pre-operative CT to intra-operative X-ray, we used the segmentation of the pelvis in CT in the image-based registration method. Although following the same pre-processing scheme as we did on simulated image during training, the domain shifting still deteriorates the context-based prediction compared with simulated data. As a result, only 8 out of 22 tested real X-ray converge in our experiment. Once converged, the accuracy of the algorithm could reach the level of typical image-based method. The overall statistics of all 22 tested real X-ray images are shown in Table 2.

Table 1. Comparison of the rotational and translational misalignment errors of the proposed sequential, contextual registration with standard image-based registration on simulated images. All methods are initialized at AP view.

	Contextual registration		Image-based registration		Sequential registration	
	Rotation	Translation	Rotation	Translation	Rotation	Translation
Mean	4.80	75.6	17.4	258	0.12	1.58
Standard deviation	2.80	60.4	5.38	81.2	0.08	0.89
Median	4.23	62.2	17.8	265	0.10	1.39
Minimum	1.01	10.9	1.72	37.5	0.01	0.29
Maximum	11.6	342	26.0	385	0.35	3.93

Table 2. Comparison of the rotational and translational misalignment errors of the proposed sequential, contextual registration with standard image-based registration on real X-ray images. All methods are initialized at AP view.

	Contextual registration		Image-based registration		Sequential registration	
	Rotation	Translation	Rotation	Translation	Rotation	Translation
Mean	11.5	61.7	14.3	200	6.95	39.4
Standard deviation	6.16	27.4	8.46	118	5.13	34.1
Median	12.3	60.0	11.9	171	8.13	43.2
Minimum	1.48	16.4	4.15	61.5	0.25	1.17
Maximum	24.4	113	35.5	473	14.7	104

4   Discussion and Conclusion

Our method is not compared with other CNN-based prior work because we consider our work sufficiently different from the prior works. [20] only demonstrates successful pose regression for artificial, metallic, objects. The use of the sum-of-squared distances similarity loss during training most likely does not generalize to natural anatomical objects. [2,3,6] all rely on manually identified anatomically relevant landmarks in 3D. [16] requires multiple views - the method proposed in this paper is compatible with applications limited to single views.

Our method largely increases the capture range of the 2D/3D registration algorithm as shown in Table 1, and indicates robustness against arbitrary view initialization. The proposed sequential registration strategy benefits from both the effective global search of the learning-based approaches as well as the accurate local search of the image-based methods, which jointly overcome the limitation of previous methods.

Currently, our pipeline combines pose update proposals obtained from three learning-based sub-networks. Upon convergence, the recovered poses are reasonably close to the desired target view. This learning-based architecture is capable of integrating pose updates provided by an intensity-based registration algorithm, the corresponding weight of which could be learned end-to-end. Since such algorithm cannot provide an estimate of the geodesic gradient, careful design of the overall loss function is necessary in a future work. A prospective cadaver study would allow implantation of radiopaque fiducial markers that can provide accurate ground truth, enabling these investigations and retraining of the CNN on real data.

In conclusion, we have shown that our CNN model is capable of learning pose relations in the presence of large rigid body distances. This is achieved by approximating a globally convex similarity metric in our CNN-based registration pipeline. The proposed network regresses a geodesic loss function over $SE(3)$ and produces promising results on the simulated X-ray images.

While our solution produces updates along the correct direction when tested on real data, the performance is compromised, particularly if tools and implants are present in the field of view. As the next step, we plan on more carefully analyzing the performance and failure modes of our method on clinical data. Improving generalization of our method to clinical X-rays is of highest importance. While pre-processing or style-transfer may be feasible, unsupervised domain adaptation or retraining on small clinical datasets that could be annotated using approach similar to [9] can also be considered.

Acknowledgement. This work is supported in part by NIH grant (R21EB028505).

References

1. Berger, M., et al.: Marker-free motion correction in weight-bearing cone-beam CT of the knee joint. Med. Phys. **43**(3), 1235–1248 (2016)
2. Bier, B., et al.: Learning to detect anatomical landmarks of the pelvis in X-rays from arbitrary views. Int. J. Comput. Assist. Radiol. Surg. 1–11 (2019)
3. Bier, B., et al.: X-ray-transform invariant anatomical landmark detection for pelvic trauma surgery. In: Frangi, A.F., Schnabel, J.A., Davatzikos, C., Alberola-López, C., Fichtinger, G. (eds.) MICCAI 2018. LNCS, vol. 11073, pp. 55–63. Springer, Cham (2018). https://doi.org/10.1007/978-3-030-00937-3_7
4. Clark, K., et al.: The cancer imaging archive (TCIA): maintaining and operating a public information repository. J. Digit. Imaging **26**(6), 1045–1057 (2013)
5. Deng, J., Dong, W., Socher, R., Li, L.J., Li, K., Fei-Fei, L.: Imagenet: a large-scale hierarchical image database. In: 2009 IEEE Conference on Computer Vision and Pattern Recognition, pp. 248–255. IEEE (2009)

6. Esteban, J., Grimm, M., Unberath, M., Zahnd, G., Navab, N.: Towards fully automatic X-ray to CT registration. In: Shen, D., et al. (eds.) MICCAI 2019. LNCS, pp. 631–639. Springer, Heidelberg (2019). https://doi.org/10.1007/978-3-030-32226-7_70

7. Fotouhi, J., et al.: Pose-aware C-arm for automatic re-initialization of interventional 2D/3D image registration. Int. J. Comput. Assist. Radiol. Surg. **12**(7), 1221–1230 (2017)

8. Gong, R.H., Stewart, J., Abolmaesumi, P.: Multiple-object 2-D-3-D registration for noninvasive pose identification of fracture fragments. IEEE Trans. Biomed. Eng. **58**(6), 1592–1601 (2011)

9. Grupp, R., et al.: Automatic annotation of hip anatomy in fluoroscopy for robust and efficient 2D/3D registration. arXiv preprint arXiv:1911.07042 (2019)

10. Grupp, R.B., et al.: Pose estimation of periacetabular osteotomy fragments with intraoperative X-ray navigation. arXiv preprint arXiv:1903.09339 (2019)

11. Hajek, J., Unberath, M., Fotouhi, J., Bier, B., Lee, S.C., Osgood, G., Maier, A., Armand, M., Navab, N.: Closing the calibration loop: an inside-out-tracking paradigm for augmented reality in orthopedic surgery. In: Frangi, A.F., Schnabel, J.A., Davatzikos, C., Alberola-López, C., Fichtinger, G. (eds.) MICCAI 2018. LNCS, vol. 11073, pp. 299–306. Springer, Cham (2018). https://doi.org/10.1007/978-3-030-00937-3_35

12. Hou, B., et al.: Deep pose estimation for image-based registration. AR (2018)

13. Huang, G., Liu, Z., Van Der Maaten, L., Weinberger, K.Q.: Densely connected convolutional networks. In: Proceedings of the IEEE Conference on Computer Vision and Pattern Recognition, pp. 4700–4708 (2017)

14. Ketcha, M., et al.: Multi-stage 3D–2D registration for correction of anatomical deformation in image-guided spine surgery. Phys. Med. Biol. **62**(11), 4604 (2017)

15. Lemieux, L., Jagoe, R., Fish, D., Kitchen, N., Thomas, D.: A patient-to-computed-tomography image registration method based on digitally reconstructed radiographs. Med. Phys. **21**(11), 1749–1760 (1994)

16. Liao, H., Lin, W.A., Zhang, J., Zhang, J., Luo, J., Zhou, S.K.: Multiview 2D/3D rigid registration via a point-of-interest network for tracking and triangulation. In: Proceedings of the IEEE Conference on Computer Vision and Pattern Recognition, pp. 12638–12647 (2019)

17. Liu, L., Ecker, T., Schumann, S., Siebenrock, K., Nolte, L., Zheng, G.: Computer assisted planning and navigation of periacetabular osteotomy with range of motion optimization. In: Golland, P., Hata, N., Barillot, C., Hornegger, J., Howe, R. (eds.) MICCAI 2014. LNCS, vol. 8674, pp. 643–650. Springer, Cham (2014). https://doi.org/10.1007/978-3-319-10470-6_80

18. Liu, R., et al.: An intriguing failing of convolutional neural networks and the CoordConv solution. In: Advances in Neural Information Processing Systems, pp. 9628–9639 (2018)

19. Markelj, P., Tomaževič, D., Likar, B., Pernuš, F.: A review of 3D/2D registration methods for image-guided interventions. Med. Image Anal. **16**(3), 642–661 (2012)

20. Miao, S., Wang, Z.J., Liao, R.: A CNN regression approach for real-time 2D/3D registration. IEEE Trans. Med. Imaging **35**(5), 1352–1363 (2016)

21. Miolane, N., Mathe, J., Donnat, C., Jorda, M., Pennec, X.: Geomstats: a python package for Riemannian geometry in machine learning (2018)

22. Murray, R.M.: A Mathematical Introduction to Robotic Manipulation. CRC Press, Boca Raton (2017)

23. Otake, Y., et al.: Intraoperative image-based multiview 2D/3D registration for image-guided orthopaedic surgery: incorporation of fiducial-based C-arm tracking and GPU-acceleration. IEEE Trans. Med. Imaging **31**(4), 948–962 (2012)

24. Ruijters, D., ter Haar Romeny, B.M., Suetens, P.: Vesselness-based 2D–3D registration of the coronary arteries. Int. J. Comput. Assist. Radiol. Surg. **4**(4), 391–397 (2009)

25. Troelsen, A., Elmengaard, B., Søballe, K.: A new minimally invasive transsartorial approach for periacetabular osteotomy. JBJS **90**(3), 493–498 (2008)

26. Unberath, M., et al.: Enabling machine learning in X-ray-based procedures via realistic simulation of image formation. Int. J. Comput. Assist. Radiol. Surg. 1–12 (2019)

27. Unberath, M., et al.: DeepDRR – a catalyst for machine learning in fluoroscopy-guided procedures. In: Frangi, A.F., Schnabel, J.A., Davatzikos, C., Alberola-López, C., Fichtinger, G. (eds.) MICCAI 2018. LNCS, vol. 11073, pp. 98–106. Springer, Cham (2018). https://doi.org/10.1007/978-3-030-00937-3_12

28. Yaniv, Z.: Registration for orthopaedic interventions. In: Zheng, G., Li, S. (eds.) Computational Radiology for Orthopaedic Interventions. LNCVB, vol. 23, pp. 41–70. Springer, Cham (2016). https://doi.org/10.1007/978-3-319-23482-3_3

29. Yao, J., et al.: A C-arm fluoroscopy-guided progressive cut refinement strategy using a surgical robot. Comput. Aided Surg.: Official J. Int. Soc. Comput. Aided Surg. (ISCAS) **5**(6), 373–390 (2000)

Structural Connectivity Enriched Functional Brain Network Using Simplex Regression with GraphNet

Mansu Kim[1], Jingxaun Bao[2], Kefei Liu[1], Bo-yong Park[3], Hyunjin Park[4,5], and Li Shen[1($\boxtimes$)]

[1] Department of Biostatistics, Epidemiology, and Informatics, University of Pennsylvania, Philadelphia, USA
li.shen@pennmedicine.upenn.edu

[2] School of Arts and Sciences, University of Pennsylvania, Philadelphia, USA

[3] McConnell Brain Imaging Centre, Montreal Neurological Institute, McGill University, Montreal, Canada

[4] School of Electronic and Electrical Engineering, Sungkyunkwan University, Suwon, Korea

[5] Center for Neuroscience Imaging Research, Institute for Basic Science, Suwon, Korea

Abstract. The connectivity analysis is a powerful technique for investigating a hard-wired brain architecture as well as flexible, functional dynamics tied to human cognition. Recent multi-modal connectivity studies had the challenge of combining functional and structural connectivity information into one integrated network. In this paper, we proposed a simplex regression model with graph-constrained Elastic Net (GraphNet) to estimate functional networks enriched by structural connectivity in a biologically meaningful way with a low model complexity. Our model constructed the functional networks using sparse simplex regression framework and enriched structural connectivity information based on GraphNet constraint. We applied our model on the real neuroimaging datasets to show its ability for predicting a clinical score. Our results demonstrated that integrating multi-modal features could detect more sensitive and subtle brain biomarkers than using a single modality.

Keywords: Structural connectivity · Functional connectivity · Simplex regression · GraphNet · Depression

L. Shen—This work was supported by the National Institutes of Health [R01 EB022574] and National Science Foundation [IIS 1837964]. Data were provided by the Human Connectome Project, WU-Minn Consortium (Principal Investigators: David Van Essen and Kamil Ugurbil; 1U54MH091657) funded by the 16 NIH Institutes and Centers that support the NIH Blueprint for Neuroscience Research; and by the McDonnell Center for Systems Neuroscience at Washington University.

M. Liu et al. (Eds.): MLMI 2020, LNCS 12436, pp. 292–302, 2020.
https://doi.org/10.1007/978-3-030-59861-7_30

1 Introduction

Connectivity analysis is a powerful technique for investigating a hard-wired brain architecture as well as flexible functional dynamics tied to human cognition [16,23]. Indeed, the whole-brain structural connectome can be measured via diffusion magnetic resonance imaging (dMRI) data through tractography algorithms by approximating structural wiring in white matter. Functional connectivity is constructed by measuring statistical associations of temporal coherence between different brain regions, and often computed from the resting-state functional MRI (rs-fMRI) data.

In the functional domain, various network modeling methods were introduced to measure the degree of coherence in the functional network [3,14,19], such as Pearson correlation (PearC), partial correlation (PartC), and graphical LASSO (GL). These approaches provided a novel perspective for understanding a large-scale functional organization of the brain, which was often used for distinguishing healthy and diseased brains in the studies of psychiatric and neurological disorders [2,13,20]. Unlike functional connectivity that infers statistical association, structural connectivity provides information of physical neuronal connections of the complex brain network, which can be used for identifying disrupted physical wiring between distinct brain regions. Recent multi-modal studies found that imaging features combining structural and functional connectivity information provided better imaging biomarkers for common diseases [21,22], indicating the integration of multi-modal features may help detect more sensitive and subtle brain biomarkers than using a single modality alone.

Recently, some studies have proposed various sparse models to estimate brain networks from structural, functional and/or genomic data. *Huang et al.* proposed a sparse simplex model (Simplex) to build a brain network using whole brain gene expression data, but their methods did not consider spatial proximity and structural connectivity [7]. *Pineda-Pardo et al.* applied adaptive GL to estimate an MEG connectivity network guided by a structural connectivity network [15]. *Li et al.* proposed an ultra-weighted-LASSO approach to efficiently estimate functional networks by considering structural connectivity and derivatives of the temporal signal [10]. These methods incorporated the adaptive LASSO regularization approach to incorporate multi-modal information. However, if one node is linked to two highly connected regions, this approach tends to select only one of the two regions randomly, thus inadequate to capture all the signals.

To over these limitations, in this paper, we proposed a simplex regression model with graph-constrained Elastic Net (GraphNet) to estimate functional networks enriched by structural connectivity in a biologically meaningful way with low model complexity. Our major contributions are as follows: i) We designed a simplex regression model to build a functional network. ii) We extended the simplex regression model to include the GraphNet penalty to incorporate structural connectivity computed from dMRI data using a tractography algorithm. iii) We applied our proposed algorithm to the Human Connectome Project (HCP) database to demonstrate its ability to predict a clinical score and showed the promise of our algorithm compared with multiple competing methods.

2   Materials

2.1   Data Description

We obtained neuroimaging (i.e., fMRI and dMRI) and genotyping datasets from the HCP database. Specifically, genetically unrelated, non-twins, non-Hispanic, white participants with full demographic information were considered in this study; see Table 1 for their characteristics. Of those, we randomly selected 100 participants and divided them into two groups (depression vs healthy) with equal size based on the Diagnostic and Statistical Manual of Mental Disorders 5th edition depression (DSM-dep) scores. Participants with a DSM-dep larger than 6 were classified as depression subjects, and the remaining participants were classified as healthy subjects [12]. The age, sex, and mini-mental state examination were matched between healthy and depression groups.

Table 1. Participant characteristics.

	Healthy	Depression	p-value
Number of subjects	50	50	–
Age	29.06 ± 3.89	28.66 ± 3.54	0.5925
Sex	M:28, F:22	M:24, F:26	0.4284
DSM-dep	0.66 ± 0.47	8.44 ± 2.22	<0.0001
Mini-Mental State Examination	29.16 ± 0.91	28.86 ± 1.16	0.1538

2.2   Data Pre-processing

HCP database provided minimally pre-processed neuroimaging (i.e., rs-fMRI and dMRI) and genotyping datasets. For the rs-fMRI data, the CIFTI dense time series data in standard grayordinate space were obtained using the minimal pre-processing pipeline, which includes corrections for EPI distortions and head motion, registration to the T1-weighted data and subsequently MNI space, skull removal, and intensity normalization [5]. Then, the artifacts of head movement, white matter, cardiac pulsation, arterial, and large vein related contributions were removed by FMRIB's ICA-based X-noisifier (FIX) [17]. Finally, we averaged the vertex-wise time-series into parcel-level using HCP multi-modal parcellation atlas (HCP-MMP) [4]. We added 12 subcortical regions to the 360 cortical areas yielding a total of 372 brain regions.

The dMRI data were processed using a procedure similar to the one described by Kim et al. [8]. Head motion and eddy current were corrected and then probabilistic tractography was performed to build structural connectivity using FSL

[18]. Graph nodes were defined by HCP-MMP atlas and the edges were defined using connection density between the nodes. Finally, the structural connectivity information was used as the constraint in our proposed approach described later.

3 Methods

3.1 Simplex Representation

Herein, we used the boldface lowercase letter to denote a vector, and the boldface uppercase letter to denote a matrix. Specifically, given the datasets $X \in \mathbb{R}^{n \times p}$, where X corresponded to the pre-processed rs-fMRI data as described in Sect. 2.2. n denoted time points of rs-fMRI data, and p denoted number of brain regions. The sparse simplex learning model proposed by *Huang et al.* was originally proposed to construct the neuroanatomical and transcriptomic networks [7]. The model is defined as follows:

$$\tilde{\beta}_i = \min_{\beta_i} ||X_{(:,i)} - X_{(:,\neq i)}\beta_i||_2^2 + \lambda||\beta_i||_1 \quad s.t. \quad \beta_i \geq 0, \beta_i^T \mathbf{1} = 1, \quad (1)$$

where $X_{(:,\neq i)}$ is the matrix X with the i-th column (i.e., i-th region) removed, $X_{(:,i)}$ is the i-th column of X, β_i is $p-1$ dimensional coefficient vector for the i-th brain region, and $\geq$ denotes "componentwise larger than or equal to". One advantage of the simplex regression model is that the simplex constraint yields network edge weights (i.e., regression coefficients) that can be treated as probability values.

3.2 Functional Brain Network Construction with Simplex Regression Framework and GraphNet Constraint

We herein proposed an algorithm for constructing functional network enriched by structural connectivity. Figure 1 showed overall procedure of our approach. Specifically, we proposed a sparse simplex regression model penalized by Graph-Net penalty. GraphNet penalty, proposed by *Grosenick et al.*, has an advantage for integrating biological graph constraint, such as structural connectivity, by encouraging the coefficients to be similar between two highly connected nodes [6]. For example, when the structural connectivity between the i-th and j-th regions is high, the GraphNet penalty forces the corresponding coefficients to be similar. Additionally, the structural connectivity contains white matter fiber information, which is a good source for a biological constraint. Thus, we applied the GraphNet penalty on the sparse simplex regression model. The formula for the algorithm is defined as follows:

$$\tilde{\beta}_i = \min_{\beta_i} ||X_{(:,i)} - X_{(:,\neq i)}\beta_i||_2^2 + \lambda||\beta_i||_1 + \lambda_G \beta_i^T L_{SC}\beta_i \quad s.t. \quad \beta_i \geq 0, \beta_i^T \mathbf{1} = 1,$$

$$(2)$$

where, L_{SC} is the Laplacian matrix of the structural connectivity C with the i-th brain region excluded. The Laplacian matrix is defined as $L_{SC} = D - C$, where D is the degree matrix of structural connectivity. Since simplex constraint yield l_1 penalty to be the constant term, we can rewrite Eq. (2) as the following:

$$\tilde{\beta}_i = \min_{\beta_i} \|X_{(:,i)} - X_{(:,\neq i)}\beta_i\|_2^2 + \lambda_G \beta_i^T L_{SC} \beta_i \quad s.t. \quad \beta_i \geq 0, \beta_i^T 1 = 1. \quad (3)$$

The constraints in Eq. (3) is also simplex, so we can optimize it using the accelerated projected gradient method, as described in the next section.

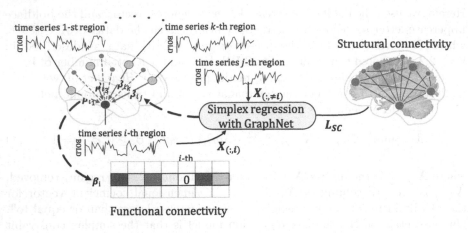

Fig. 1. The overall procedures of proposed algorithm.

We constructed the functional network by repeating the proposed algorithm p times for every brain region. The constructed network $S = [\tilde{\beta}_1, \tilde{\beta}_2, ..., \tilde{\beta}_p]$ is sparse and asymmetric. The $\tilde{\beta}_i$ denoted a p dimensional vector, zero was inserted for the i-th coefficient of estimated coefficients vector β_i. We defined the symmetric functional network by replacing $S_{(i,j)}$ and $S_{(j,i)}$ with the maximum value between them.

3.3   Optimization Details and the Proposed Algorithm

In this section, we describe an iterative algorithm for minimizing the cost function. The cost function, Eq. (3), can be solved by taking the derivative with respect to β_i and setting it to zero:

$$X_{(:,\neq i)}^T X_{(:,\neq i)}\beta_i + \lambda_G L_{SC}\beta_i - X_{(:,\neq i)}^T X_{(:,i)} = 0. \quad (4)$$

Thus, the solution can be obtained by solving Eq. (4) as follows:

$$\tilde{\beta}_i = \left(X_{(:,\neq i)}^T X_{(:,\neq i)} + \lambda_G L_{SC}\right)^{-1} X_{(:,\neq i)}^T X_{(:,i)}. \quad (5)$$

Next, we applied the accelerated projected gradient methods to solve the simplex problem as follow:

$$\min_{\beta_i} \frac{1}{2}\|\beta_i - v\|_2^2 \quad s.t. \quad \beta_i \geq 0, \beta_i^T 1 = 1, \tag{6}$$

where v denoted $\tilde{\beta}_i$. We rewrite the Eq. (6) using unconstrained formulation as

$$\frac{1}{2}\|\beta_i - v\|_2^2 - \gamma(\beta_i^T 1 - 1) - \lambda^T \beta_i, \tag{7}$$

where γ and λ is a Lagrangian multiplier and Lagrangian multiplier vector, respectively, both of which are to be determined. Suppose the optimal solution to the proximal problem (6) is β^*, the associated Lagrangian multipliers are γ^* and λ^*. We then derived the following equations, according to the KKT conditions [1]:

$$\forall j, \beta_{i_j}^* - v_j - \gamma^* - \lambda_j^* = 0, \tag{8}$$

$$\forall j, \beta_{i_j}^* \geq 0, \tag{9}$$

$$\forall j, \lambda_j^* \geq 0, \tag{10}$$

$$\forall j, \beta_{i_j}^* \lambda_j^* = 0, \tag{11}$$

where $\beta_{i_j}^*$ denoted the j-th element of β_i^*. We can rewrite Eq. (8) as $\beta_{i_j}^* - v_j - \gamma^* 1 - \lambda_j^* = 0$. We have $\gamma^* = \frac{1 - 1^T v - 1^T \lambda^*}{n}$ using the constraint $\beta_i^T 1 = 1$ and derive $\beta^* = (v - \frac{1}{n}1^T v + \frac{1}{n}1 - \frac{1^T \lambda^*}{n}1) + \lambda^*$. We rewrite it as $\beta^* = u + \lambda^* - \overline{\lambda^*}1$, where $\overline{\lambda^*} = \frac{1^T \lambda^*}{n}$ and $u = v - \frac{1}{n}1^T v + \frac{1}{n}1$. Thus, $\forall j$ we have

$$\beta_{i_j}^* = u_j + \lambda_j^* - \overline{\lambda^*}. \tag{12}$$

According to Eqs. (9)–(12), we have $u_j + \lambda_j^* - \overline{\lambda^*} = (u_j - \overline{\lambda^*})_+$, where $x_+ = \max(x, 0)$. We then have $\beta_{i_j}^* = (u_j - \overline{\lambda^*})_+$. Therefore, given we know $\overline{\lambda^*}$, we can compute the optimal solution β^*.

To obtain $\overline{\lambda^*}$, we rewrite Eq. (12) as $\lambda_j^* = \overline{\lambda^*} + \beta_{i_j}^* - u_j$. According to Eqs. (9)–(11), we have $\lambda_j^* = (\overline{\lambda^*} - u_j)_+$. Since v is a $p - 1$ dimensional vector, we have $\overline{\lambda^*} = \frac{1}{p-1}\sum_{j=1}^{p-1}(\overline{\lambda^*} - u_j)_+$. Thus, we define a function as follow:

$$f(\overline{\lambda^*}) = \frac{1}{p-1}\sum_{j=1}^{p-1}(\overline{\lambda^*} - u_j)_+ - \overline{\lambda}, \tag{13}$$

and we obtain $\overline{\lambda^*}$ by solving Eq. (13) to be zero. Since $\lambda^* \geq 0$, $f'(\overline{\lambda^*}) \leq 0$, and $f'(\overline{\lambda^*})$ is a piecewise linear and convex function, we can compute the root of $f'(\overline{\lambda^*}) = 0$ using Newton method efficiently.

4 Experiments and Results

4.1 Experimental Results on Human Connectome Project Data

In our experiments, we used pre-processed rs-fMRI and dMRI data, as described in Sect. 2.2. The rs-fMRI pre-processing procedure resulted in 2, 400 time points for 372 regions, and the dMRI pre-processing yielded structural connectivity matrix (i.e., 372×372 matrix) based on probability tractography for each subject.

We applied the proposed model to construct functional networks. We compared our approach with five different functional network construction methods (i.e., PearC, PartC, GL, GL with structural connectivity [GLs], and simplex) according to previous studies [3,9,11]. When we constructed functional networks using our algorithm, GL, and GLs, we applied different sets of hyper-parameters for each model. We used [1, 10, 100, 1000, 10000] for the proposed algorithm, [0.01, 0.1, 1, 10, 100] for GL and GLs.

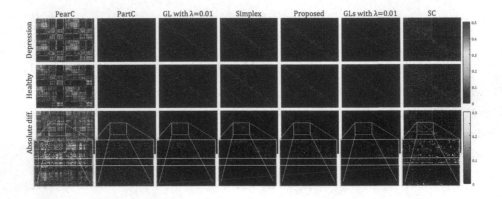

Fig. 2. Example of functional network map for each model. The first and second row are the functional network for depression and healthy group, respectively. The third row shows the absolute difference map between depression and healthy group. The fourth row shows an enlarged portion of each absolute difference map.

Overall, the constructed functional networks showed similar patterns except the PerC and SC, as shown in Fig. 2. We noted that our approach yielded more relevant and sparser patterns in sub-cortical structures compared to the methods using either fMRI and dMRI alone, as shown in the white box of Fig. 2. We compared the sparsity (ratio of non-zero connections in the functional network) for all methods. Figure 3(a) shows the boxplots of sparsity across all subjects for each method. The sparsity decreased for every method, as we increase the hyper-parameter value. For our approach, the sparsity did not change much when λ was larger than 100. The GL and GLs resulted in networks with almost zero sparsity, when λ was larger than 1. We also evaluated the similarity of the network patterns by reporting the pair-wise correlation among each method. We

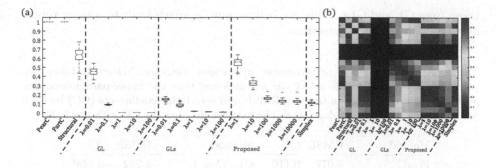

Fig. 3. The sparsity and similarity comparison of networks. Sub-figure (a) and (b) denoted a boxplot of the sparsity for each model and pair-wise correlation between models with varying hyper-parameters.

computed the correlation for network edge weights across subjects between two different methods (Fig. 3-(b)). Interestingly, the networks based on our approach were very similar to those of partial correlation networks and the networks with GL. Finally, our results suggested that our approach constructed relatively sparse networks that are to some extent consist with existing methods but with better enriched sub-cortical structural connectivity information.

4.2   Evaluations Using Prediction Task

In this section, we demonstrated and compared the efficacy of the constructed networks. However, there is no ground-truth for network constructions, thus we cannot directly compare the performances of all tested methods. Instead, we used the prediction task to compare the performances among different functional network construction methods. We first selected relevant features based on two-sample t-tests and built the ridge regression model to predict a DSM-dep score on the training set. A nested 10-fold-cross-validation was conducted to test the prediction performance. Specifically, the hyper-parameter for ridge regression was tuned using 10-fold-cross-validation on the training set. The trained prediction model was applied to testing set to measure the prediction performance.

After 10-fold-cross-validation, there were 349.98 ± 6.87 features were selected with $\lambda = 1000$. The lowest root-mean-square-error (RMSE) of 3.783 was obtained using our algorithm with $\lambda = 1000$. Our algorithm also led to the highest correlation of 0.475 between the actual and predicted DSM5-Depression scores. Additionally, the GLs with $\lambda = 0.01$ yielded a RMSE of 5.117 and a correlation of 0.279, the GL with $\lambda = 0.01$ yielded a RMSE of 4.113 and correlation of 0.208, and the PartC yielded a RMSE 4.218 and correlation of 0.227. The detailed performances of seven different models with varying parameters were shown in Table 2. Interestingly, functional networks from GL and GLs with $\lambda = 0.01$, and our algorithm with $\lambda = 1000$ showed similar network pattern and sparsity. However, our algorithm showed higher prediction performance than those from GL and GLs. Thus, we believe our approach leads to a more robust network with sparser connections.

Table 2. The prediction performances of various methods. Nested 10-fold-cross-validation was conducted to select the features and tune the hyper-parameters. The performance was reported in terms of RMSE and correlation coefficients (CC) between actual and predicted DSM-dep score. The asterisk denoted the CC with $p < 0.05$.

Method	RMSE	CC	Method	RMSE	CC
PearC	5.077	0.110	GLs ($\lambda = 1$)	5.252	-0.248*
PartC	4.218	0.227*	GLs ($\lambda = 10$)	-	-
SC	4.597	0.139	GL ($\lambda = 100$)	-	-
GL ($\lambda = 0.01$)	4.113	0.208*	Ours ($\lambda = 1$)	4.799	0.119
GL ($\lambda = 0.1$)	5.153	−0.065	Ours ($\lambda = 10$)	4.557	0.261*
GL ($\lambda = 1$)	-	-	Ours ($\lambda = 100$)	4.191	0.240*
GL ($\lambda = 10$)	-	-	Ours ($\lambda = 1000$)	3.783	0.475*
GL ($\lambda = 100$)	-	-	Ours ($\lambda = 10000$)	4.119	0.232*
GLs ($\lambda = 0.01$)	5.117	0.279*	Simplex	4.548	0.110
GLs ($\lambda = 0.1$)	4.711	0.152			

5 Conclusion

In this work, we proposed a simplex regression model with GraphNet penalty to estimate functional networks enriched by structural connectivity. We demonstrated the feasibility of our algorithm on the HCP database. Compared to the existing methods, our model has two advantages. First, the functional network based on simplex regression can be interpreted as a probability, which can help further analysis. Second, the simplex representation with GraphNet can efficiently combine structural and functional information. Furthermore, we validated our proposed algorithm on real neuroimaging data and compared the results with those obtained using the existing competing methods.

In the future, we will further look into generating the whole-brain connectivity at once by applying the matrix optimization algorithm. Furthermore, there is no ground-truth for network constructions. Thus, our results should be further confirmed by future independent replications.

References

1. Boyd, S., Vandenberghe, L.: Convex Optimization. Cambridge University Press, Cambridge (2004)
2. Damaraju, E., et al.: Dynamic functional connectivity analysis reveals transient states of dysconnectivity in schizophrenia. NeuroImage: Clin. **5**, 298–308 (2014)
3. Friedman, J., Hastie, T., Tibshirani, R.: Sparse inverse covariance estimation with the graphical lasso. Biostatistics **9**(3), 432–441 (2008)
4. Glasser, M., et al.: A multi-modal parcellation of human cerebral cortex. Nature **536**, 171–178 (2016)
5. Glasser, M.F., et al.: The minimal preprocessing pipelines for the human connectome project. Neuroimage **80**, 105–124 (2013)
6. Grosenick, L., Klingenberg, B., Katovich, K., Knutson, B., Taylor, J.E.: Interpretable whole-brain prediction analysis with graphnet. NeuroImage **72**, 304–321 (2013)
7. Huang, H., et al.: A new sparse simplex model for brain anatomical and genetic network analysis. In: International Conference on Medical Image Computing and Computer-Assisted Intervention, pp. 625–632 (2013)
8. Kim, M., Won, J.H., Youn, J., Park, H.: Joint-connectivity-based sparse canonical correlation analysis of imaging genetics for detecting biomarkers of Parkinson's disease. IEEE Trans. Med. Imaging **39**(1), 23–34 (2020)
9. Li, K., Guo, L., Nie, J., Li, G., Liu, T.: Review of methods for functional brain connectivity detection using fMRI. Comput. Med. Imaging Graph. **33**(2), 131–139 (2009)
10. Li, Y., et al.: Structural connectivity guided sparse effective connectivity for MCI identification. In: Wang, Q., Shi, Y., Suk, H.-I., Suzuki, K. (eds.) MLMI 2017. LNCS, vol. 10541, pp. 299–306. Springer, Cham (2017). https://doi.org/10.1007/978-3-319-67389-9_35
11. Marrelec, G., et al.: Partial correlation for functional brain interactivity investigation in functional MRI. Neuroimage **32**(1), 228–237 (2006)
12. Nedley, N., Ramirez, F.E.: Nedley depression hit hypothesis: identifying depression and its causes. Am. J. Lifestyle Med. **10**(6), 422–428 (2016)
13. Park, B.Y., Seo, J., Park, H.: Functional brain networks associated with eating behaviors in obesity. Sci. Rep. **6**(1), 1–8 (2016)
14. Pervaiz, U., Vidaurre, D., Woolrich, M.W., Smith, S.M.: Optimising network modelling methods for fMRI. NeuroImage **211**, 116604 (2020)
15. Pineda-Pardo, J.A., et al.: Guiding functional connectivity estimation by structural connectivity in MEG: an application to discrimination of conditions of mild cognitive impairment. Neuroimage **101**, 765–777 (2014)
16. Rubinov, M., Sporns, O.: Complex network measures of brain connectivity: uses and interpretations. Neuroimage **52**(3), 1059–1069 (2010)
17. Salimi-Khorshidi, G., Douaud, G., Beckmann, C.F., Glasser, M.F., Griffanti, L., Smith, S.M.: Automatic denoising of functional MRI data: combining independent component analysis and hierarchical fusion of classifiers. Neuroimage **90**, 449–468 (2014)
18. Smith, S.M., et al.: Advances in functional and structural MR image analysis and implementation as FSL. NeuroImage **23**, S208–S219 (2004)
19. Smith, S.M., et al.: Network modelling methods for fMRI. NeuroImage **54**(2), 875–891 (2011)

20. Stam, C.J., Jones, B., Nolte, G., Breakspear, M., Scheltens, P.: Small-world networks and functional connectivity in Alzheimer's disease. Cerebral Cortex **17**(1), 92–99 (2007)
21. Wee, C.Y., et al.: Identification of MCI individuals using structural and functional connectivity networks. Neuroimage **59**(3), 2045–2056 (2012)
22. Werring, D., et al.: The structural and functional mechanisms of motor recovery: complementary use of diffusion tensor and functional magnetic resonance imaging in a traumatic injury of the internal capsule. J. Neurol. Neurosurg. Psychiatry **65**(6), 863–869 (1998)
23. Zhang, Z., et al.: Altered functional-structural coupling of large-scale brain networks in idiopathic generalized epilepsy. Brain **134**(10), 2912–2928 (2011)

Constructing High-Order Dynamic Functional Connectivity Networks from Resting-State fMRI for Brain Dementia Identification

Chunxiang Feng[1], Biao Jie[1(✉)], Xintao Ding[1], Daoqiang Zhang[3], and Mingxia Liu[2(✉)]

[1] School of Computer and Information, Anhui Normal University, Wuhu 241003, Anhui, China
jbiao@ahnu.edu.cn

[2] Department of Radiology and BRIC, University of North Carolina at Chapel Hill, Chapel Hill, NC 27599, USA
mxliu@med.unc.edu

[3] College of Computer Science and Technology, Nanjing University of Aeronautics and Astronautics, Nanjing, China

Abstract. Functional connectivity (FC) networks with the resting-state functional magnetic resonance imaging (rs-fMRI) help advance our understanding of brain disorders, such as Alzheimer's disease (AD) and its prodromal stage, i.e., mild cognitive impairment (MCI). Recent studies have shown that FC networks demonstrate significant dynamic changes even in the resting state. However, previous studies typically focus on model the low-order (e.g., second-order) dynamics, without exploring the high-order dynamic properties of FC networks. In this paper, we propose to build a high-order dynamic functional connectivity network (hoDFCN) from the second-order FC networks, and define two novel measures to characterize the temporal and spatial variability of hoDFCN. Furthermore, we employ both spatial and temporal variability features for brain disease classification. Experimental results on 149 subjects with baseline resting-state functional MRI (rs-fMRI) data from the Alzheimer's Disease Neuroimaging Initiative (ADNI) suggest the effectiveness of our proposed method in brain dementia identification.

1 Introduction

Functional magnetic resonance imaging (fMRI) using the blood-oxygenation-level-dependent (BOLD) signal is emerging as an advanced imaging technique for the study of brain function and activity [1]. Resting-state fMRI (rs-fMRI) has great potential to serve as a biomarker for neurophysiological diseases. Brain functional connectivity (FC) networks constructed from rs-fMRI data can characterize the inter-region neural interactions of the brain, and has been

The original version of this chapter was revised: an additional acknowledgment has been added to the Acknowledgement section. The correction to this chapter is available at https://doi.org/10.1007/978-3-030-59861-7_69

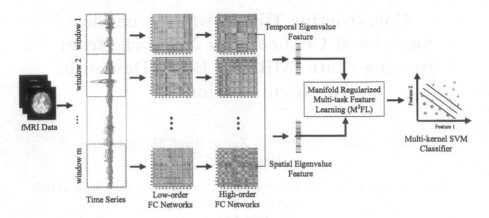

Fig. 1. Illustration of the proposed high-order dynamic functional connectivity network learning framework, including four main steps: image pre-processing, high-order dynamic connectivity networks construction, feature learning and classification.

successfully used to the computer-aided diagnosis of various brain diseases, *e.g.*, Alzheimer's disease (AD) and its prodromal stage (*i.e.*, mild cognitive impairment, MCI) [2]. Many studies have indicated that the structure of FC networks is associated with cognitive state [3] and brain diseases [4].

In traditional methods for FC network analysis, it is implicitly assumed that the FC between distinct brain regions is constant (*i.e.*, temporally stationary) throughout the recording period in rs-fMRI [5]. However, recent studies have suggested that the brain region correlations demonstrate significant dynamic changes even in the resting state [6], and changes in FC networks may contain a wealth of information for better understanding the brain's functional organization [5]. Increasing evidence has shown that the dynamics of FCs are associate with cognitive brain states [7], and altered dynamics are reported in patients with brain diseases [4]. In the literature, dynamic functional connectivity networks derived from rs-fMRI have been successfully used for classification of brain diseases [8,9]. Existing studies usually construct the low-order (*i.e.*, second-order) dynamic FC networks (DFCN) by using sliding windows, in which the FCs are estimated using the original BOLD signals of brain regions, characterizing just the correlation of paired brain regions. In fact, studies in neuroscience have found significant high-order interactions in cortical activities [10]. However, few works explore the high-order dynamic interaction among multiple brain regions based on rs-fMRI data. Intuitively, modeling the high-order dynamics of brain FC networks can provide more prior knowledge that can be potentially used to boost the diagnosis performance.

Accordingly, in this paper, we propose to construct a high-order dynamic FC network (hoDFCN) from the conventional second-order FC networks. We further define two new measures to characterize the temporal variability and spatial variability of hoDFCN for brain disease classification. Figure 1 illustrates the framework of the proposed hoDFCN method. Specifically, we first construct a set of traditional (*i.e.*, second-order) FC networks by computing the Pearson correlation coefficient (PCC) of BOLD signals from paired brain regions based

Table 1. Characteristics of the studied subjects (Mean ± Standard Deviation). MMSE: Mini-Mental State Examination; SD: Standard Deviation.

Group	lMCI	eMCI	NC
Male/Female	26/17	21/35	21/29
Age (Mean ± SD)	72.1 ± 8.2	71.1 ± 6.8	75.0 ± 6.9
MMSE (Mean ± SD)	27.2 ± 2.0	28.1 ± 1.5	28.9 ± 1.6

on a non-overlapping sliding window strategy. Then, for each FC network, we further compute the correlation between two functional architectures (*i.e.*, all FCs associated with the brain region) of brain regions. With this strategy, we can construct the high-order dynamic FC networks. Here, the obtained FCs are high-order since they are computed based on two functional architectures involving all brain regions. Then, both spatial and temporal eigenvalue features are extracted as feature representations of each subject, followed by a manifold regularized multi-task feature learning (M^2FL) for feature selection. Based on the selected features, a multi-kernel support vector machine (SVM) is employed for classification. The experimental results on 149 subjects with baseline rs-fMRI data from Alzheimer's Disease Neuroimaging Initiative (ADNI[1]) demonstrate the effectiveness of our proposed method.

2 Method

2.1 Subjects and Image Preprocessing

In this study, we use 149 subjects with rs-fMRI data from the ADNI database, including 43 late MCI (lMCI), 56 early MCI (eMCI) and 50 health controls (HCs). Data acquisition was performed as follows: the image resolution is 2.29-3.31 mm for inplane, and slice thickness is 3.31 mm, TE = 30 ms and TR = 2.2-3.1 s. The clinical and demographic information of these subjects is given in Table 1.

Following [8], we use the standard pipeline to preprocess the rs-fMRI data, including (1) discarding the first 10 rs-fMRI volumes, (2) slice timing correction, and (3) head motion correction. The brain space of fMRI scans is partitioned into 116 regions-of-interest (ROIs) using the Automated Anatomical Labeling (AAL) template [11] with a deformable registration method [12]. The band-pass filtering is performed within a frequency interval of [0.025 Hz, 0.100 Hz]. The BOLD signals from the gray matter tissue are extracted, and the mean time series of each ROI is calculated to construct the FC network.

2.2 High-Order Dynamic FC Network Construction

In this section, we first introduce the construction process of traditional dynamic FC networks, and then present the details of the proposed method for construction of high-order dynamic FC network.

---

[1] http://adni.loni.usc.edu.

Traditional Dynamic FC Network Construction. Based on the mean time series of ROIs, we first construct the traditional dynamic FC networks (DFCN) based on successive and non-overlapping time windows. As illustrated in Fig. 1, the PCC is used as a measure of functional connectivity between a pair of brain regions. Specifically, for each subject, we first segment the whole time series of ROIs equally into m successive and non-overlapping time windows. Then, an FC network (corresponding to an adjacency matrix) $\mathbf{C}^t$ ($t = 1, \cdots, m$) is constructed by calculating the PCC between time series of paired ROIs at the tth window, as follows

$$\mathbf{C}^t(i,j) = corr(x_i^t, x_j^t) \tag{1}$$

where $corr$ denotes the correlation between two time series (the PCC is used in this study). Here, x_i^t and x_j^t denote segments of the BOLD signals of the ith and the jth ROIs within the tth time window.

According to definition in Eq. 1, $\mathbf{C}^t(i,j)$ can only characterize the second-order interaction of paired brain regions. Therefore, given m time windows, we can generate a set of FC networks $\mathcal{C} = \{\mathbf{C}^1, \mathbf{C}^2, \cdots, \mathbf{C}^m\}$, which could implicitly characterize the dynamics of second-order FC networks.

High-Order Dynamic FC Network Construction. Based on the second-order FC network at the tth time window, we proposed to construct a high-order FC network $\mathbf{H}^t$ by calculating the correlation between functional architectures of paired region r and q as follows

$$\mathbf{H}^t(r,q) = corr(\mathbf{C}^t(r,:), \mathbf{C}^t(q,:)) \tag{2}$$

where $\mathbf{C}^t(r,:) = [\mathbf{C}^t(r,1), \mathbf{C}^t(r,2), \cdots, \mathbf{C}^t(r,R)]$ is a functional architecture of brain region r, corresponding to the rth row entity in $\mathbf{C}^t$, reflecting the correlation between the rth ($r = 1, \cdots, R$) region and all the other brain regions, and R is the number of brain regions.

According to Eq. 2, $\mathbf{H}^t(r,q)$ characterizes the high-order correlation between brain regions r and q, considering that it is calculated based on functional architectures of the regions r and q. Since such functional architectures involve the relationship between each ROI and all the other ROIs, our constructed $\mathbf{H}^t(r,q)$ can explicitly capture the high-order information among ROIs. Given m time windows, we can obtain a set of high-order FC networks, *i.e.*, $\mathcal{H} = \{\mathbf{H}^1, \mathbf{H}^2, \cdots, \mathbf{H}^m\}$, characterizing the dynamics of high-order FC networks.

2.3   Temporal and Spatial Variability of hoDFCN

Recent studies have suggested that the temporal and spatial properties of FC networks may contain a wealth of information to help understand the brain networks and brain diseases [6]. Motivated by [8], we define two new metrics to characterize the temporal and spatial variability of a given brain region, and then use these metrics to assess the temporal and spatial variability of high-order dynamic FC networks. Figure 2 illustrates the construction process of temporal

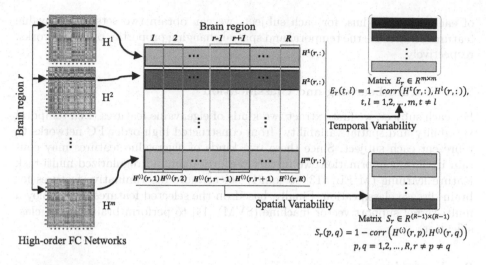

Fig. 2. Illustration of construction process of the temporal/spatial variability for the brain region r.

and spatial variability matrices associated with a specific brain region r. Specifically, given the set of high-order dynamic FC networks $\mathcal{H} = \{\mathbf{H}^1, \mathbf{H}^2, \cdots, \mathbf{H}^m\}$, to characterize the temporal changing properties of hoDFCN at a specific brain region r, we first construct a matrix $\mathbf{E}_r \in R^{m \times m}$ as follows

$$\mathbf{E}_r(t, l) = 1 - corr(\mathbf{H}^t(r, :), \mathbf{H}^l(r, :)) \tag{3}$$

where $corr(\mathbf{H}^t(r, :), \mathbf{H}^l(r, :))$ computes the correlation (*i.e.*, similarity) between functional architectures of brain regions r across time windows t and l. Thus, the matrix $\mathbf{E}_r$ characterizes the temporal variability of functional architectures of a specific brain region r across all time windows.

Using a similar strategy, we construct another matrix $\mathbf{S}_r \in R^{(R-1) \times (R-1)}$ to reflect the spatial variability of a given brain region r, which is defined as

$$\mathbf{S}_r(p, q) = 1 - corr(\mathbf{H}^{(:)}(r, p), \mathbf{H}^{(:)}(r, q)) \tag{4}$$

where $\mathbf{H}^{(:)}(r, p) = [\mathbf{H}^1(r, p), \mathbf{H}^2(r, p), \cdots, \mathbf{H}^m(r, p)]^T$ is defined as the functional sequence between a pair of specific brain regions, denoting changing profile of FC between brain regions r and p within all time windows. Besides, the term $corr(\mathbf{H}^{(:)}(r, p), \mathbf{H}^{(:)}(r, q)$ defines the similarity between two functional sequence associate with region r across different brain regions. Therefore, the matrix $\mathbf{S}_r$ reflects the spatial variability of functional sequences associated with a specific region r across all brain regions.

To further model the dynamic changes of high-order FC networks, for each brain region r, we calculate the eigenvalues of the corresponding matrices $\mathbf{E}_r$ and $\mathbf{S}_r$, and select two maximum eigenvalues as features to measure the temporal variability and spatial variability of brain region r, respectively. For each type of variability, we extract a set of eigenvalue features from constructed hoDFCN of each subject. Thus, for each subject, we can obtain two sets of eigenvalue features to measure the temporal and spatial changing properties of FC networks, respectively.

2.4 Feature Learning and Classification

For each subject, we first extract two kinds of eigenvalue features (*i.e.*, temporal variability and spatial variability) from constructed high-order FC networks to represent each subject. Since these two kinds of eigenvalue features may contain irrelevant information, we further perform manifold regularized multi-task feature learning (M^2FL) [13] to jointly select more discriminative features for brain disease classification. Finally, based on the selected features, we employ a multi-kernel support vector machine (SVM) [14] to perform brain disease classification.

3 Experiment

3.1 Experimental Setting

In this work, we perform two classification tasks: 1) lMCI vs. eMCI classification, and 2) eMCI vs. NC classification, by using a leave-one-out (LOO) cross-validation strategy. Following [8], we construct the hoDFCN using different values of m (*i.e.*, $m = \{5, 6, \cdots, 12\}$), and compute the average value of temporal/spatial eigenvalue features for all values of m to avoid the effect of different window lengths. In the process of multi-kernel SVM classification, we adopt a grid search strategy on training subjects to find optimal combination of multiple kernels, and use a linear SVM classifier with default parameter values for classification. To evaluate performance of different methods, we employ four metrics, *i.e.*, accuracy (ACC), sensitivity (SEN), specificity (SPE), and the area under the receiver operating characteristic (ROC) curve (AUC).

We first compare the proposed hoDFCN method with low-order DFCN methods, including 1) the method proposed in [8] (denoted as **DFCN-mean**), and 2) the method that integrates temporal and spatial eigenvalue features extracted from low-order DFCN networks (denoted as **DFCN-eigen**). Moreover, we compare the proposed method with three hoDFCN-based methods, including 1) the method that combines temporal and spatial mean features extracted from hoDFCNs (denoted **hoDFCN-mean**), 2) the method using only the temporal eigenvalue features (denoted **hoDFCN-temporal**), and 3) the method using only the spatial eigenvalue features (denoted **hoDFCN-spatial**). In addition, we compare our hoDFCN with the **Baseline** method using clustering coefficient features from stationary FC networks.

3.2 Classification Results

The results of all seven methods are summarized in Table 2. Figure 3 plots the ROC curves of all methods. From Table 2 and Fig. 3, we can see that our proposed

Table 2. Results of seven methods in two classification tasks. ACC: accuracy; SEN: sensitivity; SPE: specificity.

Method	lMCI vs. eMCI (%)				eMCI vs. NC (%)			
	ACC	SEN	SPE	AUC	ACC	SEN	SPE	AUC
Baseline	56.6	55.8	57.1	55.1	59.4	66.1	52.0	56.9
DFCN-mean	78.8	74.4	82.1	78.3	78.3	82.1	74.0	77.1
DFCN-eigen	78.8	74.4	82.1	81.5	78.3	83.9	72.0	78.3
hoDFCN-temporal	72.7	74.4	71.4	77.1	71.7	75.0	68.0	75.5
hoDFCN-spatial	73.7	74.4	73.2	78.1	72.6	76.8	68.0	75.8
hoDFCN-mean	80.8	79.1	82.1	80.3	80.2	80.4	80.0	80.7
hoDFCN (Ours)	**81.8**	**79.1**	**83.9**	**81.9**	**81.1**	**85.7**	**76.0**	**79.3**

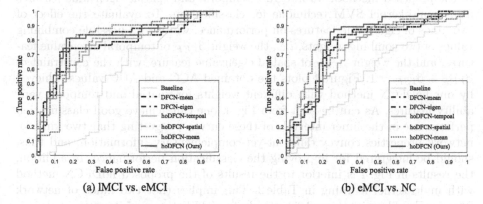

(a) lMCI vs. eMCI   (b) eMCI vs. NC

Fig. 3. ROC curves of seven methods on tasks of (a) lMCI vs. eMCI classification, and (b) eMCI vs. NC classification.

hoDFCN method achieves better classification performance when compared to six competing methods. For example, the proposed hoDFCN achieves the ACC values of 81.8% and 81.1% in two classification tasks (*i.e.*, lMCI vs. eMCI and eMCI vs. NC), respectively, while the best accuracy of the competing methods are 80.8% and 80.2% (by hoDFCN-mean). This suggests the efficacy of our proposed method in rs-fMRI based brain disease classification.

In addition, from Table 2 and Fig. 3, we could observe that two hoDFCN-based methods (*i.e.*, hoDFCN-mean and hoDFCN) consistently outperform the two DFCN-based methods (*i.e.*, DFCN-mean and DFCN-eigen), suggesting the advantages of high-order FC network over traditional (*i.e.*, second-order) FC networks. In addition, the proposed hoDFCN method consistently outperforms the competing methods that use only single eigenvalue features (*i.e.*, hoDFCN-temporal, and hoDFCN-spatial). These results imply that the proposed spatial variability and temporal variability features contain complementary information to further improve the classification performance.

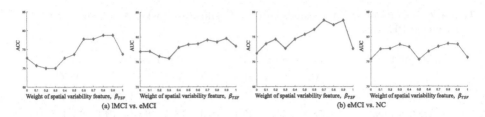

Fig. 4. Results achieved by our proposed method using different combining weights of temporal and spatial eigenvalue features on (a) lMCI vs. eMCI classification, and (b) eMCI vs. NC classification. Here, $\beta_{TEF} = 1 - \beta_{TSF}$.

3.3 Influence of Different Combining Schemes

In the proposed method, we integrate temporal and spatial eigenvalue features using multi-kernel SVM technique for classification. To evaluate the effect of two kinds of eigenvalue features on performance, we test all possible combining values of two combing weights, *i.e.*, the weight β_{TEF} of temporal eigenvalue features, and the weight β_{TSF} of spatial eigenvalue feature, with the constraint of $\beta_{TEF} + \beta_{TSF} = 1$. Figure 4 plots the obtained ACC and AUC values achieved by our hoDFCN method with different weights for spatial and temporal variability features. As can be seen from Fig. 4, one can achieve good classification performance in the inner intervals of these curves, suggesting that two kinds of network properties convey different-yet-complementary information, and thus, should be integrated for improving the classification performance. In addition, the results in Fig. 4 is inferior to the results of the proposed hoDFCN method with multi-kernel learning in Table 2. This implies that two kinds of network features should be integrated adaptively to yield better performance.

4   Conclusion

In this work, we propose a novel method to construct the high-order dynamic FC network, and also define two measures to characterize the temporal and spatial variability of FC networks for brain disease classification. Specifically, we construct the high-order FC networks based on the traditional (*i.e.*, second-order) dynamic FC networks, by calculating the correlation between functional architectures of pairs of brain regions. Then, we construct two matrices to reflect the temporal and spatial variability of high-order FC networks, and extract two eigenvalue features to assess the dynamic properties of FC networks. Finally, we propose to select discriminative features and use a multi-kernel SVM to integrate two kinds of network features for the classification of brain diseases. The experimental results on 149 subjects with baseline rs-fMRI data from ADNI demonstrate the effectiveness of our proposed method.

Acknowledgment. This study was supported by NSFC (61976006, 61573023, 61703301, 61902003), Anhui-NSFC (1708085MF145, 1808085MF171), AHNU-FOYHE (gxyqZD2017010), CERNET Innovation Project (NGII20190621).

References

1. Cribben, I., Haraldsdottir, R., Atlas, L.Y., Wager, T.D., Lindquist, M.A.: Dynamic connectivity regression: determining state-related changes in brain connectivity. NeuroImage **61**(4), 907–920 (2012)
2. Supekar, K., Menon, V., Rubin, D., Musen, M., Greicius, M.D.: Network analysis of intrinsic functional brain connectivity in Alzheimer's disease. PLoS Comput. Biol. **4**(6), e1000100:1–11 (2008)
3. Sharp, D.J., Scott, G., Leech, R.: Network dysfunction after traumatic brain injury. Nat. Rev. Neurol. **10**(3), 156–166 (2014)
4. Jones, D.T., et al.: Non-stationarity in the "resting brain's" modular architecture. PloS One **7**(6), e39731:1–15 (2012)
5. Hutchison, R.M., et al.: Dynamic functional connectivity: promise, issues, and interpretations. NeuroImage **80**, 360–378 (2013)
6. Kudela, M., Harezlak, J., Lindquist, M.A.: Assessing uncertainty in dynamic functional connectivity. NeuroImage **149**, 165–177 (2017)
7. Thompson, G.J., et al.: Short-time windows of correlation between large-scale functional brain networks predict vigilance intraindividually and interindividually. Hum. Brain Mapping **34**(12), 3280–3298 (2013)
8. Jie, B., Liu, M., Shen, D.: Integration of temporal and spatial properties of dynamic connectivity networks for automatic diagnosis of brain disease. Med. Image Anal. **47**, 81–94 (2018)
9. Wang, M., Lian, C., Yao, D., Zhang, D., Liu, M., Shen, D.: Spatial-temporal dependency modeling and network hub detection for functional MRI analysis via convolutional-recurrent network. IEEE Trans. Biomed. Eng. **67**(8), 2241–2252 (2019)
10. Montani, F., Ince, R.A.A., Senatore, R., Arabzadeh, E., Diamond, M.E., Panzeri, S.: The impact of high-order interactions on the rate of synchronous discharge and information transmission in somatosensory cortex. Philos. Trans. **367**(1901), 3297–3310 (2009)
11. Tzourio-Mazoyer, N., et al.: Automated anatomical labeling of activations in SPM using a macroscopic anatomical parcellation of the MNI MRI single-subject brain. NeuroImage **15**(1), 273–289 (2002)
12. Vercauteren, T., Pennec, X., Perchant, A., Ayache, N.: Diffeomorphic demons: efficient non-parametric image registration. NeuroImage **45**(1), S61–S72 (2009)
13. Jie, B., Zhang, D., Cheng, B., Shen, D.: Manifold regularized multitask feature learning for multimodality disease classification. Hum. Brain Mapping **36**(2), 489–507 (2015)
14. Zhang, D., Wang, Y., Zhou, L., Yuan, H., Shen, D.: Multimodal classification of Alzheimer's disease and mild cognitive impairment. NeuroImage **55**(3), 856–867 (2011)

Multi-tasking Siamese Networks for Breast Mass Detection Using Dual-View Mammogram Matching

Yutong Yan[1,2,3], Pierre-Henri Conze[2,3]($\boxtimes$), Mathieu Lamard[1,2],
Gwenolé Quellec[2], Béatrice Cochener[1,2,4], and Gouenou Coatrieux[2,3]

[1] Université de Bretagne Occidentale, Brest, France
[2] LaTIM UMR 1101, Inserm, Brest, France
[3] IMT Atlantique, Brest, France
{yutong.yan,pierre-henri.conze}@imt-atlantique.fr
[4] University Hospital of Brest, Brest, France

Abstract. In clinical practice, radiologists use multiple views of routine mammograms for breast cancer screening. Similarly, computer-aided diagnosis (CAD) systems could be enhanced by integrating information arising from pairs of views. In this work, we present a new multi-tasking framework that combines craniocaudal (CC) and mediolateral-oblique (MLO) mammograms. We exploit multi-tasking properties of deep networks to jointly learn mass matching and classification, towards better detection performance. A combined Siamese model that includes patch-level mass classification and dual-view mass matching is used to take full advantage of multi-view information. This network is exploited in a full image detection pipeline based on You-Only-Look-Once (YOLO) region proposals. Experiments highlight the benefits of dual-view analysis for both patch-level classification and examination-level detection scenarios. Our pipeline outperforms conventional single-task deep models with 94.78% as Area Under the Curve (AUC) score and a classification accuracy of 0.8791. Additionally to these gains, our method further guides clinicians by providing accurate multi-view mass correspondences. This suggests that it could act as a relevant automatic second opinion for mammogram interpretation and breast cancer diagnosis.

Keywords: Breast cancer · Mass detection · Dual-view mammogram matching · Information fusion · Deep learning · Computer-aided diagnosis

1 Introduction

At early stage, mammography is the main imaging modality for breast abnormality detection. Bilateral craniocaudal (CC) and mediolateral-oblique (MLO) views comprise routine screening mammography. Compared to single-view screening, the clinical use of dual-view techniques reduces false-positive cases and improves

© Springer Nature Switzerland AG 2020
M. Liu et al. (Eds.): MLMI 2020, LNCS 12436, pp. 312–321, 2020.
https://doi.org/10.1007/978-3-030-59861-7_32

cancer detection rates [23]. This analysis is essentially related to the detection and classification of breast masses, the main clinical symptoms of carcinomas. Manual mammogram analysis is a time-consuming and tedious task for radiologists. Computer-aided diagnosis (CAD) systems have been designed as double reading for mammogram interpretation. However, conventional CAD systems are inefficient and not automatic enough to improve diagnosis performance [11]. The use of multi-view context is a known weakness of current CAD technology.

In recent years, deep learning has achieved remarkable breakthroughs in medical image analysis through convolutional neural networks (CNN). CAD systems that employ CNN demonstrate better performance in clinical implementation. Nevertheless, breast mass detection and classification are still open issues due to strong variations in mass appearance, size, shape and texture [24]. Some studies [4,27] focus on whole mammograms by providing a unique image-level label (normal, benign or malignant). The drawback is that it avoids conducting a comprehensive analysis comprising lesion types and locations. Other works are mostly region-based methods [1,2,12,22,26], where images are decomposed into regions to further distinguish between normal and abnormal tissues. However, most of the above methods use single-view mammogram information only, thus neglecting the rich representation that can be extracted from multi-view images.

To address the limitation of single-view processing, we aim at taking advantage of information arising from both CC and MLO mammograms, as do clinicians when making decisions in clinical practice [21]. There is a huge potential to improve the performance of CAD systems by integrating information from paired views. The concept of multi-view information fusion was recently introduced to improve the performance of detection, classification or content-based mammogram retrieval [8]. Several multi-view fusion schemes learn on full images from each view separately and concatenate respective features afterwards. Geras et al. [4] proposed to apply CNN models to each view separately to obtain view-specific representations for further classification purposes. Nevertheless, such late-fusion schemes only exploit image-level view-specific representations.

Alternatively, we propose a novel multi-tasking Siamese deep model that combines CC and MLO mammograms to improve breast mass detection. A Siamese model includes two identical sub-networks with shared weights such that multiple inputs can be trained simultaneously. Previous related works [14,16] also employ Siamese networks [9] for multi-view study. However, these are single-task studies (mass detection [14] or mass matching [16] only). To design a more comprehensive and efficient CAD system, we aim at exploiting the multi-tasking properties of deep CNN. Multi-task learning processes multiple tasks jointly with many advantages such as saving computation time and resources as well as improving robustness against overfitting [18]. The network parameters from feature extraction layers are updated through the optimization of a combined loss dealing with both mass classification and matching. Contrary to [14,16], our method can provide both classification and matching results. Specifically, our contributions are two-folds. First, we propose a new deep learning algorithm that capitalizes on multi-view fusion and multi-task learning to improve breast

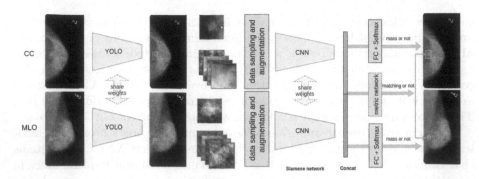

Fig. 1. Proposed multi-tasking deep framework. Within images, green lines indicate ground truth delineations, red and yellow boxes indicate false and true detections. (Color figure online)

mass detection. To the best of our knowledge, our framework is the first that exploits multi-tasking abilities of deep learning models to improve mass detection through multi-view matching. Second, we conduct a comprehensive evaluation of various networks towards multi-task learning on public datasets. Both quantitative and visual results prove the effectiveness of the proposed strategy.

2   Methods

Overview. Our multi-tasking framework (Fig. 1) takes unregistered CC/MLO pairs as inputs and provides as outputs accurate mass detections along with correspondences between mass regions from two views. Candidate patch selection is based on YOLOv3 [17] which offers, among existing deep detectors, a good trade-off between accuracy and efficiency. Given a pair of mammogram $\{I_{CC}, I_{MLO}\}$, YOLOv3 predicts two sets of candidate mass patches $P_{CC} = \{p_{CC}^1, ..., p_{CC}^N\}$ and $P_{MLO} = \{p_{MLO}^1, ..., p_{MLO}^M\}$. To further identify target mass regions and discover the latent relation between CC/MLO views, we design a combined model through a Siamese network that jointly performs patch-level classification and matching (Fig. 1). We sample candidate mass patches P_{CC} and P_{MLO} to the same size, while performing data augmentation to prevent overfitting. These samples are then fed into the combined network. Based on robust generic feature extraction, the results of our model is whether each patch contains mass and the correspondence between patches from the two views.

Dual-View Mammogram Matching. Due to breast deformation and different acquisition conditions, dual-view mammogram analysis is a challenging task. Inspired by [6,16], we employ a Siamese model to identify correspondences between masses in both CC/MLO views (Fig. 2). Patch pairs from CC and MLO views are inserted separately to the two branches of the network. The feature network A is a Siamese network in which two fully convolutional networks are connected with shared weights for feature extraction. For illustration, we use

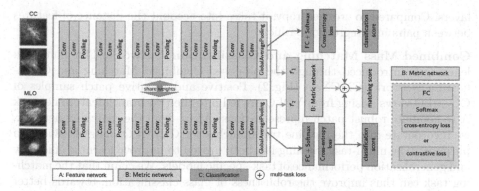

Fig. 2. Proposed combined matching and classification network (CMCNet). A: two-branch feature network which takes as input both positive (green patch) and negative (red patch) patch samples of CC and MLO views separately to compute effective features. Resulting features f_1 and f_2 are concatenated for patch comparison. B: metric network. C: single-view classification based on multi-task loss. FC = fully-connected. (Color figure online)

in Fig. 2 a VGG16 architecture [19]. To reduce the number of parameters and avoid overfitting, we apply a global average pooling layer before subsequent fully-connected (FC) layers. Particularly, different widely used deep convolutional models such as VGG16 [19], ResNet50, ResNet101 [7] and InceptionV3 [20] can be exploited for feature extraction purposes.

Contrastive Loss for Matching. For feature comparison, two manners are explored based on different loss functions. First, one can use a metric network [6, 16] consisting of several FC and softmax layers, trained with a cross-entropy loss. Alternatively, we can rather employ a contrastive loss [5] to improve the ability of network A to extract discriminative features. Contrastive learning is employed to learn powerful data representations where labels are used to guide the choice of positive and negative pairs. The contrastive loss is usually exploited for image retrieval tasks along with Siamese networks to learn paired data relationships. During training, an image pair is fed into the model with their ground truth relationship Y. The loss function is as follows:

$$L_{mat}\left(W,(Y,X_1,X_2)\right) = \frac{1}{2N} \sum_{n=1}^{N} Y D_W^2 + (1-Y)\max\left(m - D_W, 0\right)^2 \quad (1)$$

where $D_W(X_1, X_2) = \|f_1 - f_2\|_2$ is the Euclidean distance between sample features f_1 and f_2. Y is the label of whether the two samples match. Y = 1 if the two samples are similar and 0 otherwise. $m > 0$ is a margin that defines a radius: dissimilar pairs contribute to the loss only if their distance is within this radius. N is the number of samples. Unlike conventional learning systems where the loss function is a sum over samples, the contrastive loss runs over pairs of feature vectors $\{f_1, f_2\}$ such that there is no more need for FC and softmax layers. Compared to cross-entropy, it takes into account the distance of features between pairs in a regression fashion.

Combined Mass Matching and Classification Network. The multi-task learning is introduced through the proposed Combined Matching and Classification Network (CMCNet) (Fig. 2). Positive and negative patch samples of CC/MLO views arising from YOLO are fed into the two-branch feature network A to compute robust patch representations. Apart from the matching network, we incorporate into the pipeline two branches for CC/MLO mass classification purposes. The multi-task learning has been proven to improve learning efficiency and generalization performance of task-specific models. We claim that the matching task can thus improve the robustness of mass classification, towards better predictive results than classification-only strategies. The designed loss L is the sum of three losses to optimize the entire CMCNet parameters through SGD:

$$L = \alpha L_{cls,CC} + \beta L_{cls,MLO} + \gamma L_{mat} \tag{2}$$

where $L_{cls,CC}$ and $L_{cls,MLO}$ represent the classification loss for CC and MLO view respectively. L_{mat} is the matching loss which can be cross-entropy or contrastive loss (Eq. 1). α, β and γ are coefficients balancing the loss terms.

3   Experiments and Results

3.1   Experimental Settings

Datasets. Two publicly-available datasets are used for experiments: INbreast [15] and DDSM-CBIS (Digital Database for Screening Mammography) [10]. We target the 1514 (107) DDSM-CBIS (INbreast) 2048×1024 images containing ground truth mass delineations. Since not all images are pairwise, only 586 (35) CC/MLO mammograms pairs from DDSM-CBIS (INbreast) are selected. Due to the lack of multi-mass correspondence information, we select pairs containing one mass only in the training process. However, this is not a limitation for classifying multiple masses. Among 586 DDSM-CBIS pairs, 80% are used for training and the remaining 20% for validation. The 35 INbreast pairs are employed in the testing stage only since it is too small to be representative as training data.

Data Sampling and Augmentation. In our multi-task framework, sampling in training is crucial. Healthy tissue areas are much larger than mass regions, leading to inevitable false positive YOLO proposals. Sample imbalance can therefore make the classification model biased. To alleviate this limitation, we sample our data as follows. For classification training, positive samples are taken according to provided groundtruth masks, while negative patches are generated by YOLO [25]. In particular, we randomly generate K patches per image with an intersection over union (IoU) with respect to the ground truth box larger than 0.5. In practice, $K = 5$ (10) for DDSM-CBIS (INbreast) since INbreast is

Table 1. Data distribution setting for experiments. Each cell has the following format: number of positive samplings/number of negative samplings.

	DDSM-CBIS [10]			INbreast [15]
	Training	Validation	Test	Full-pipeline test
Classification	4690/4690	1170/1170	700/700	125/225
Matching	2345/4690	585/1170	350/700	125/225

Table 2. Multi-task learning versus classification-only. Results include CC, MLO and overall classification accuracy (acc) as well as statistical significance p-values.

Methods	Matching	Matching loss	CC acc	MLO acc	overall acc	p-value
VGG16 [19]	×	–	0.8558	0.8857	0.8699	–
	√	Cross entropy	0.8796	**0.9163**	0.8958	$<1e^{-6}$
	√	Contrastive	**0.9061**	0.9156	**0.9084**	$<1e^{-6}$
ResNet50 [7]	×	–	0.8517	0.9034	0.8734	–
	√	Cross entropy	0.8958	0.9116	0.9014	$4e^{-4}$
	√	Contrastive	**0.9010**	**0.9122**	**0.9049**	$<1e^{-6}$
ResNet101 [7]	×	–	0.8680	0.9097	0.8823	–
	√	Cross entropy	**0.8980**	**0.9265**	**0.9098**	0.007
	√	Contrastive	0.8891	0.9252	0.9049	0.003
InceptionV3 [20]	×	–	0.8238	0.8980	0.8601	–
	√	Cross entropy	0.8776	**0.9184**	0.8972	$<1e^{-6}$
	√	Contrastive	**0.8946**	0.9095	**0.9000**	$4e^{-4}$

much smaller. Likewise, we choose K negative patches from false YOLO predictions. We thus use a very small threshold ($<10^{-4}$) on detection probabilities to retain as many predictions as possible and select the K false candidates with the highest scores. All patches are resized to 64 × 64 pixels, as in [6,16]. Random rotation, translation and flip are applied for data augmentation. For matching, we consider a pair of positive patches of the same mass from the two views as a matching sample. If one of the patches is labeled negative, they are considered as a negative match. Detailed data distribution is shown in Table 1.

Training Patch-Level Classification and Matching. We conduct experiments using various baselines for feature network: VGG16, ResNet50, ResNet101 and InceptionV3. All models employ pre-trained weights [13] from ImageNet [3] and are trained using SGD. Optimal hyper-parameters vary depending on the network: learning rate $\in \{0.0001, 0.0005, 0.001, 0.005, 0.01\}$ with a decay of 0.1 and batch size $\in \{32, 64, 128\}$. The influence of α, β, and γ has been studied to balance the multi-task loss. We finally choose $\alpha = \beta = \gamma = 1$ for cross-entropy, $\gamma = 0.1$ and margin $m \in \{5, 10, 15\}$ for contrastive loss (Eq. 1).

Table 3. Full detection pipeline results including overall classification accuracy (acc) and AUC (area under the receiver operating characteristics curve) scores.

Methods	Matching	Matching loss	Overall acc	AUC (%)
VGG16 [19]	×	–	0.8260	90.47
	√	Cross entropy	0.8761	94.17
	√	Contrastive	**0.8791**	**94.78**
Resnet50 [7]	×	–	0.6814	70.03
	√	Cross entropy	**0.8555**	**91.98**
	√	Contrastive	0.8496	90.30
Resnet101 [7]	×	–	0.7080	71.46
	√	Cross entropy	0.8555	91.74
	√	Contrastive	**0.8584**	**92.82**
InceptionV3 [20]	×	–	0.8112	89.75
	√	Cross entropy	0.8201	89.86
	√	Contrastive	**0.8702**	**93.61**

3.2   Evaluation on Clinical Data

Multi-task Learning Versus Classification-Only. Classification performance are measured using classification accuracy (acc). The statistical significance of the multi-tasking model with respect to the classification-only baseline is estimated using Student's t-tests. In most cases, multi-tasking models that combine classification and matching are better than classification-only from 2% to 4% in accuracy with statistical significance ($p < 0.05$), which reflects the benefits of dual-view matching (Table 2). Except for ResNet101, we obtain slight gains with the contrastive loss compared to cross-entropy. The difference between networks is not obvious. The ResNet101 achieves the best overall accuracy with statistical significance (acc = 0.9098, $p = 0.007$). The improvement obtained by VGG16 using the contrastive loss is also significant (acc = 0.9084), followed by ResNet50 (0.9049) and InceptionV3 (0.90), demonstrating that deeper networks are not necessary required. We get better results on MLO than on CC (Table 2), which shows that mass identification is simpler on MLO and justifies the integration of the matching task in the pipeline to benefit from multi-view information.

Full Detection Pipeline. To further prove the effectiveness of our method, we conduct experiments through a full detection pipeline. Firstly, coarse mass YOLO detections [25] are performed on INbreast images to generate testing samples. YOLO is pre-trained on ImageNet and fine-tuned on DDSM-CBIS images. Thereafter, we use a small threshold (10^{-4}) on detection probabilities to ensure that predictions with high/low confidence are both selected. We obtain 350 candidates, labeled as positive (125 cases) or negative (225 cases) according to IoU ($\geq$ or <0.5) between RoIs and ground truth. The performance of each setting

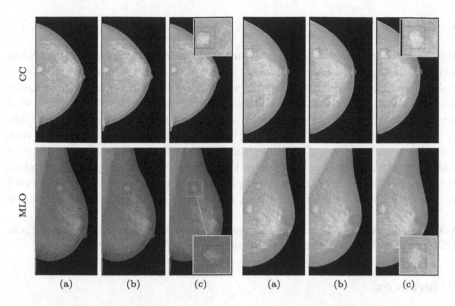

Fig. 3. Full-pipeline mass detection: (a) YOLO detection only, (b) YOLO followed by a classification-only model, (c) YOLO followed by the proposed combined model. Red boxes are detected mass bounding boxes. Green represents ground truth annotations. Blue boxes show the matching pair selected through dual-view matching. (Color figure online)

(classification-only, CMCNet with cross-entropy or contrastive loss) is measured using the AUC (Area Under the receiver operating characteristics Curve).

For full-pipeline experiments, the classification performance is highly improved over the baseline models by exploiting dual-view matching (Table 3), with improvements from 4.31% to 21.36% in accuracy. The best AUC score (94.78%) is obtained using VGG16 trained with contrastive loss, with an overall accuracy of 0.8791. The results using the contrastive loss are slightly better than cross-entropy in most cases, except for ResNet50. Higher AUC scores indicate that we can significantly reduce the false positive proposals resulting from YOLO.

According to visual results (Fig. 3), the additional classification stage (b) helps in eliminating most of false YOLO detections (a). The improvement reached by the combined network (c) compared to the classification-only model (b) is highlighted with further wrong proposal removals. The dual-view matching improves the accuracy of detection and successfully identifies matching patches in both views. All these findings suggest that exploiting multi-view relationships and multi-tasking learning could greatly help clinicians for multi-view mammogram interpretation, towards better breast cancer diagnosis and management.

4   Conclusion

In this paper, we propose a multi-tasking approach that combines mass classification with dual-view mass matching. We prove the effectiveness of integrating multi-view information within the breast mass detection pipeline by extensive experiments on public datasets. The method generalizes well using different deep networks and shows impressive results as an integrated CAD system. Therefore, we reduce false detections without struggling with difficult whole image mass detection schemes. Even if multiple masses can still be detected using the classification network, dealing with more than one mass with respect to matching purposes should deserve further investigation. Furthermore, it is essential to push further data fusion by integrating both multi-view and longitudinal information.

Acknowledgements. This work was partly funded by France Life Imaging (grant ANR-11-INBS-0006 from the French Investissements d'Avenir program).

References

1. Arevalo, J., González, F.A., Ramos-Pollán, R., Oliveira, J.L., Lopez, M.A.G.: Convolutional neural networks for mammography mass lesion classification. In: IEEE Engineering in Medicine and Biology Society, pp. 797–800 (2015)
2. Choukroun, Y., Bakalo, R., Ben-Ari, R., Akselrod-Ballin, A., Barkan, E., Kisilev, P.: Mammogram classification and abnormality detection from non-local labels using deep multiple instance neural network. In: Eurographics Workshop on Visual Computing for Biology and Medicine (2017)
3. Deng, J., Dong, W., Socher, R., Li, L.J., Li, K., Fei-Fei, L.: ImageNet: a large-scale hierarchical image database. In: IEEE Conference on Computer Vision and Pattern Recognition, pp. 248–255 (2009)
4. Geras, K.J., et al.: High-resolution breast cancer screening with multi-view deep convolutional neural networks. arXiv preprint arXiv:1703.07047 (2017)
5. Hadsell, R., Chopra, S., LeCun, Y.: Dimensionality reduction by learning an invariant mapping. In: IEEE Conference on Computer Vision and Pattern Recognition, pp. 1735–1742 (2006)
6. Han, X., Leung, T., Jia, Y., Sukthankar, R., Berg, A.C.: MatchNet: unifying feature and metric learning for patch-based matching. In: IEEE Conference on Computer Vision and Pattern Recognition, pp. 3279–3286 (2015)
7. He, K., Zhang, X., Ren, S., Sun, J.: Deep residual learning for image recognition. In: IEEE Conference on Computer Vision and Pattern Recognition, pp. 770–778 (2016)
8. Jouirou, A., Baâzaoui, A., Barhoumi, W.: Multi-view information fusion in mammograms: a comprehensive overview. Inf. Fusion **52**, 308–321 (2019)
9. Koch, G., Zemel, R., Salakhutdinov, R.: Siamese neural networks for one-shot image recognition. In: ICML Deep Learning Workshop (2015)
10. Lee, R., Gimenez, F., Hoogi, A., Miyake, K.K., Gorovoy, M., Rubin, D.: A curated mammography data set for use in computer-aided detection and diagnosis research. Sci. Data **4** (2017). Article number: 170177. https://doi.org/10.1038/sdata.2017.177

11. Lehman, C.D., Wellman, R.D., Buist, D.S., Kerlikowske, K., Tosteson, A.N., Miglioretti, D.L.: Diagnostic accuracy of digital screening mammography with and without computer-aided detection. J. Am. Med. Assoc. Intern. Med. **175**(11), 1828–1837 (2015)
12. Lévy, D., Jain, A.: Breast mass classification from mammograms using deep convolutional neural networks. arXiv preprint arXiv:1612.00542 (2016)
13. Litjens, G., et al.: A survey on deep learning in medical image analysis. Med. Image Anal. **42**, 60–88 (2017)
14. Ma, J., et al.: Cross-view relation networks for mammogram mass detection. arXiv preprint arXiv:1907.00528 (2019)
15. Moreira, I.C., Amaral, I.F., Domingues, I., Cardoso, A.J.M., Cardoso, M.J., Cardoso, J.S.: INbreast: toward a full-field digital mammographic database. Acad. Radiol. **19**, 236–248 (2012)
16. Perek, S., Hazan, A., Barkan, E., Akselrod-Ballin, A.: Mammography dual view mass correspondence. arXiv preprint arXiv:1807.00637 (2018)
17. Redmon, J., Farhadi, A.: YOLOv3: an incremental improvement. arXiv preprint arXiv:1804.02767 (2018)
18. Ruder, S.: An overview of multi-task learning in deep neural networks. arXiv preprint arXiv:1706.05098 (2017)
19. Simonyan, K., Zisserman, A.: Very deep convolutional networks for large-scale image recognition. arXiv preprint arXiv:1409.1556 (2014)
20. Szegedy, C., Vanhoucke, V., Ioffe, S., Shlens, J., Wojna, Z.: Rethinking the inception architecture for computer vision. In: IEEE Conference on Computer Vision and Pattern Recognition, pp. 2818–2826 (2016)
21. Vijayarajan, S., Jaganathan, P.: Breast cancer segmentation and detection using multi-view mammogram. Acad. J. Cancer Res. **7**(2), 131–140 (2014)
22. Wang, H., et al.: Breast mass classification via deeply integrating the contextual information from multi-view data. Pattern Recogn. **80**, 42–52 (2018)
23. Warren, R.M., Duffy, S., Bashir, S.: The value of the second view in screening mammography. Br. J. Radiol. **69**(818), 105–108 (1996)
24. Yan, Y., et al.: Cascaded multi-scale convolutional encoder-decoders for breast mass segmentation in high-resolution mammograms. In: International Conference of the IEEE Engineering in Medicine and Biology Society, pp. 6738–6741 (2019)
25. Yan, Y., Conze, P.H., Quellec, G., Lamard, M., Cochener, B., Coatrieux, G.: Two-stage breast mass detection and segmentation system towards automated high-resolution full mammogram analysis. arXiv preprint arXiv:2002.12079 (2020)
26. Zhou, H., Zaninovich, Y., Gregory, C.: Mammogram classification using convolutional neural networks. In: International Conference on Technology Trends (2017)
27. Zhu, W., Lou, Q., Vang, Y.S., Xie, X.: Deep multi-instance networks with sparse label assignment for whole mammogram classification. In: Descoteaux, M., Maier-Hein, L., Franz, A., Jannin, P., Collins, D.L., Duchesne, S. (eds.) MICCAI 2017. LNCS, vol. 10435, pp. 603–611. Springer, Cham (2017). https://doi.org/10.1007/978-3-319-66179-7_69

3D Volume Reconstruction from Single Lateral X-Ray Image via Cross-Modal Discrete Embedding Transition

Yikun Jiang[1], Peixin Li[1], Yungeng Zhang[1], Yuru Pei[1(✉)], Yuke Guo[2], Tianmin Xu[3], and Xiaoru Yuan[1]

[1] Key Laboratory of Machine Perception (MOE),
Department of Machine Intelligence, Peking University, Beijing, China
peiyuru@cis.pku.edu.cn
[2] Luoyang Institute of Science and Technology, Luoyang, China
[3] School of Stomatology, Peking University, Beijing, China

Abstract. In this paper, we propose a deep neural network (DNN)-based volumetric image reconstruction framework, enabling an end-to-end volume inference from a 2D X-ray image. The proposed framework is built upon the vector quantised-variational autoencoders of the 2D X-ray images and the 3D cone-beam CT (CBCT) images. We present a bi-directional cross-modal transition module between the discrete latent variables of the 2D and 3D images. In the X-ray-to-CBCT pass, the transition module takes the feature maps of the X-ray images as an input and outputs the discrete volumetric embedding, which is combined with the codebook in the embedding space for the reconstruction of CBCT images. On the other hand, the CBCT-to-X-ray pass realizes the DNN-based volume rendering. Given real clinically-obtained X-ray images without paired volumetric images, we devise an unsupervised learning scheme to optimize the discrete embedding transition module. Our approach utilizes the quantised latent representation and the cross-modality transition module to infer volumetric images. The proposed method has been applied to the lateral X-ray-based CBCT image reconstruction in clinical orthodontics, achieving performance improvements over compared methods.

Keywords: 3D volumetric image reconstruction · Single lateral X-ray image · Cross-modality transition

1 Introduction

3D volumetric image reconstruction is an essential step in image-guided therapy for treatment planning and evaluation. For instance, the reconstructed 3D volumetric CBCT images in the longitudinal orthodontic treatment facilitate assessments of 3D structure variations while reducing radiation exposure hazards. The lateral X-ray images are clinically widely used due to low ironizing

© Springer Nature Switzerland AG 2020
M. Liu et al. (Eds.): MLMI 2020, LNCS 12436, pp. 322–331, 2020.
https://doi.org/10.1007/978-3-030-59861-7_33

radiation and price compared with CBCT images. Nevertheless, prior knowledge and carefully designed regularization are required to estimate 3D volumes from 2D X-ray images.

Existing deep neural network (DNN)-based methods rely on the synthetic 2D and 3D image pairs to generate the nonlinear mapping between the 2D X-ray image and the 3D volumetric transformation parameters [2,7,9,12,13,22], similar to traditional regression-based methods [4,16,29]. Additional domain adaption is required when handling the real X-ray images [17,27,30]. Domain randomization added unrealistic perturbations to handle the reality gap between synthetic and real X-ray images to generate training data [21]. The low-dimensional statistical model of volumetric images or deformation vector fields simplifies the parametric space while being limited to cover the fine-grained anatomical structures in the subspace spanned by reduced principal components [10,17,25,28]. The DNN is employed in low-dose and low-sample volume reconstruction [3,23,24,31]. Syben et al. [20] realized the filter-back project reconstruction (FBP) via a Tensorflow-based framework. The DNN makes it possible to reconstruct volumetric CT images from 2-view X-ray images [14,26]. The DNN also realizes the pixel-wise image reconstruction from the latent representation of a single X-ray image [6,19]. Nevertheless, the resulted 3D volume is blurry and additional fusion with the input X-ray images is required for volume refinement [6]. The vector quantised-variational autoencoder (VQ-VAE) [18] took advantage of an autoregressive codebook of the latent embedding space for the preservation of image details, showing great potentials to reconstruct realistic images.

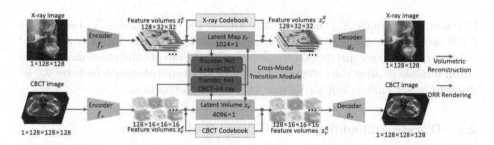

Fig. 1. The proposed cross-modal volumetric image reconstruction framework. We build the VQ-VAE for both the 2D X-ray images and 3D CBCT images. We present a bidirectional cross-modal transition module with the mapping to the discrete latent variables, enabling both volumetric reconstruction and DRR rendering.

In this paper, we propose a cross-modal volumetric image reconstruction framework to predict the volumetric CBCT image and ensure its digitally reconstructed radiograph (DRR) projection consistent with the 2D X-ray image (Fig. 1). The proposed framework is stacked on the VQ-VAE of the 2D X-ray images and the 3D CBCT images. The encoders map the images to the discrete codes in the latent space by the vector quantification using the codebooks concerning the X-ray and CBCT images, respectively. We present a bi-directional cross-modal transition module to couple the latent representations of the 2D and 3D images. In the X-ray-to-CBCT pass, the transition module takes the concatenation of multi-scale feature maps of the X-ray images as an input and outputs the discrete codes of the CBCT images, which are combined with the latent volumetric codebook for the reconstruction of CBCT images. On the other hand, the CBCT-to-X-ray pass takes the features of CBCT images as the input and infers the discrete code for X-ray image simulation. We present an unsupervised learning scheme to optimize the bi-directional cross-modal transition module using real X-ray images, requiring the DRR to be consistent with the input X-ray image in both the image level and the latent continuous and discrete embedding level. Our approach integrates the quantised latent representation and the cross-modality transition module to infer the CBCT image. The proposed method has been applied to clinically-obtained lateral X-ray images in orthodontics for CBCT reconstruction. The main contributions of this work are as follows:

- We present an end-to-end volumetric image reconstruction network by the cross-modal deep neural network, utilizing both continuous and discrete latent embedding and codebooks for high-quality volume estimation.
- We propose bi-directional cross-modal categorical mapping to infer discrete latent variables, facilitating both the X-ray-based volume reconstruction and radiograph rendering.

2   Method

Given an X-ray image X_r, the goal is to estimate the CBCT image X_v bearing the DRR projection consistent with the X-ray image X_r. We introduce a cross-modal volumetric image reconstruction framework. The bi-directional cross-modal transition module realizes the categorical mapping from concatenated features to the discrete latent embedding for further volume reconstruction.

2.1   Discete Embedding of CBCT and X-Ray Images

We learn the discrete embedding of the CBCT and X-ray images utilizing the VQ-VAE [15]-based network. A codebook is learned to quantise the continuous feature embedding into a discrete one by the nearest neighbor search scheme. Compared with the variational autoencoder, there are no such Gaussian distribution assumptions of the latent variables. The codebook $C = \{c_1, \ldots, c_K\} \in \mathbb{R}^{m \times K}$ is composed of K codes with the dimension of m, the same as the channel number of continuous feature embedding. The CNN-based encoder f maps the input image $X \in \mathbb{R}^N$ with N pixels to continuous feature embedding $Z^e \in \mathbb{R}^{N_z \times m}$, and $Z^e = f(X)$. Then entry $z^e \in \mathbb{R}^m$ is discretized using codebook C, where the posterior distribution of the discrete latent variable $p(z = i|x)$ is set to 1 when the $i = \arg\min_j \|z^e - c_j\|$, and 0 otherwise. The value of the discrete pixel/voxel code z is computed as $c(z) = \sum_{i=1}^{K} p(z = i|x)c_i$, using the codebook entry with the shortest distance.

In the decoding process, the discrete latent variables are combined with the codebook to recover the continuous feature embedding Z^q, which is sent to the decoder g for image reconstruction, and $X' = g(Z^q)$. The objective function of the autoencoder is defined as follows:

$$L_{vq} = -\log p(X|Z^q(X)) + \|sg(Z^e) - C\|_2^2 + \alpha\|Z^e - sg(C)\|_2^2. \qquad (1)$$

The stopping-gradient function $sg(x) = x$ and $\partial sg(x)/\partial x = 0$. The first term is the image reconstruction loss defined by the log likelihood to optimize both the encoder and the decoder. The second term is used to learn the codebook C in the embedding space by moving the embedding codebook towards the image encoding Z^e. The third term is the commitment loss to minimize the difference between the codebook and the output of the encoder to ensure the encoder commits to the embedding codebook with the weight of α of 0.25. We train the encoder-decoder networks and the codebooks concerning both X-ray and CBCT images by minimizing L_{vq}.

2.2   Bi-directional Cross-Modal Discrete Embedding Transition

The proposed volumetric image reconstruction framework has bi-directional cross-modal passes. The forward X-ray-to-CBCT pass maps the 2D X-ray image to the CBCT image. The backward CBCT-to-X-ray pass simulates the volume rendering of the CBCT image to the DRR.

In the forward X-ray-to-CBCT pass, when given X-ray images, the convolutional encoder gives the continuous feature embedding $Z_r^e \in \mathbb{R}^{N_z^r \times m_r}$ with m_r feature channels. The transition function h_f is modeled by the fully connected network-based multi-category classifier, which takes the feature volumes as the input and outputs the discrete code probability distribution of the volumetric images. Considering the CBCT codebook with K_v codes, the classifier output $Q \in R^{N_z^v \times K_v}$, with an entry q_{ij} indicating the probability of voxel i being assigned the j-th code. The classifier determines the discrete latent variable $Z_v \in \mathbb{R}^{N_z^v}$ of volumetric images. We train the network using paired synthetic X-ray and CBCT images (X_r, X_v). The loss function is defined as follows:

$$L_f = \|X_v - g_v(\Theta_v(h_f(f_r(X_r)), C_v))\|_2^2 - \Phi_v(f_v(X_v), C_v)\log(h_f(f_r(X_r))), \quad (2)$$

where operator Θ_v recover the continuous embedding of the volumetric images from the discrete one combined with the CBCT codebook C_v. The first data term measures the difference between volume X_v and the one reconstructed from X-ray image X_r using the X-ray image encoder f_r, the forward mapping h_f, and the volume decoder g_v. The second term is the cross entropy-based image difference in the discrete latent embedding space. $\Phi_v \in \mathbb{R}^{N_z^v \times K_v}$ denotes the discrete latent representation. The entry $\Phi_{v,ij} = 1$ when voxel i is set to the j-th code, and 0 otherwise.

The backward mapping function h_b from the CBCT image to the discrete latent variable of the X-ray image is learned analogously.

$$L_b = \|X_r - g_r(\Theta_r(h_b(f_v(X_v))), C_r))\|_2^2 - \Phi_r(f_r(X_r), C_r) \log(h_b(f_v(X_v))), \quad (3)$$

where Θ_r recovers the continuous embedding of the X-ray images from discrete latent variables. $\Phi_r \in \mathbb{R}^{N_z^r \times K_r}$ denotes the discrete latent representation of the X-ray image. The second cross-entropy-based term measures difference in the discrete latent space of the X-ray image. Function h_b, combined with the volumetric encoder f_v and the X-ray decoder g_r, enables the DRR rendering from the CBCT image.

We learn the bi-directional cross-modal latent variable transition module using the synthetic data with paired X-ray and CBCT images by minimizing L_f and L_b. As we know, it is not easy to get real paired X-ray and CBCT images of patients considering the radiation exposure hazards. In this paper, we present an unsupervised learning scheme to optimize the cross-modal transition module using real X-ray images.

2.3   Learning from Real X-Ray Images

Given the autoencoders of the X-ray and CBCT images and the cross-modal transition module, we utilize the real X-ray images without paired CBCT images to optimize the parameters of the autoencoders and the multi-category classifiers of the transition module. The loss function L_{rec} is designed as the difference between the DRR projection of the reconstructed volumes X_v and the real X-ray images in both the image-level and the latent embedding level.

$$L_{rec} = \underbrace{\|X_r - g_r(\Theta_r(h_b(f_v(X_v))), C_r))\|_{NCC}^2}_{Image\ level}$$
$$\underbrace{-\Phi_r(f_r(X_r), C_r)\log(h_b(f_v(X_v))) - \Phi_v(f_v(X_v), C_v)\log(h_f(f_r(X_r)))}_{Discrete\ embedding\ level} \quad (4)$$
$$+ \underbrace{\|sg(f_r(X_r)) - \Theta_r(h_b(f_v(X_v))), C_r)\|_2^2 + \|f_r(X_r) - sg(\Theta_r(h_b(f_v(X_v))), C_r)\|_2^2}_{Continuous\ embedding\ level},$$

where $X_v = g_v(\Theta_v(h_f(f_r(X_r))), C_v))$ denotes the estimated volumetric image. Operator Φ_r and Φ_v returns the discrete latent representations from the continuous embedding concerning the X-ray and CBCT images, respectively. The first term measures the normalized cross-correlation (NCC)-based distance between the DRR of the reconstructed volume and the X-ray image. The second and third terms measure the cross-entropy-based image difference in the discrete embedding space of the X-ray and CBCT images, respectively. The last two terms measure the image difference in the continuous embedding level. We fix the encoder f_v of CBCT images and the decoder g_r of X-ray images, and fine-tune the parameters of X-ray image encoder f_r, the volumetric decoder g_v, and the forward transition function h_f.

In the online testing process, when given the X-ray image, the volumetric image is reconstructed as $X_v = g_v(\Theta_v(h_f(f_r(X_r)), C_v))$, utilizing the X-ray encoder f_r for image embedding, the transition function h_f for cross-modal latent variable inference, and the volume decoder g_v for volumetric reconstruction. The proposed framework realizes an end-to-end volumetric image reconstruction without online iterative optimizations and DRR evaluations.

3 Experiments

Dataset and Evaluation. We evaluate the proposed methods on both synthetic and real X-ray images. We sample $40k$ volumes images in a subspace spanned by 100 clinically-obtained CBCT images with a resolution of $128 \times 128 \times 128$, and then employ the ray-casting-based DRR algorithm to generate the synthetic X-ray images. The real X-ray image dataset has $4k$ clinically-obtained X-ray images. Both the synthetic and real X-ray images are resized to a resolution of 128×128, which are split with 80% for training and the remaining for testing.

As to the quantitative evaluation, we employ the NCC-based metric to measure the 3D and 2D image distance between the estimated volume and its DRR projection with the ground-truth. We also use the 2D landmark registration errors (LRE), $e_{LRE} = \frac{1}{n}\sum_{i=1}^{n} \|x_{li} - x_{li}^*\|$. x and x^* are 2D coordinates of 32 landmark on 2D DRRs and real X-ray images. The CNN enables the semantic annotation of 2D X-ray images [1,5]. Here we utilize a similar CNN-based framework for landmark detection for evaluation of e_{LRE}.

Implementation Details. The X-ray encoder consists of two 4×4 convolutional layers with a stride of 2 and two 3×3 convolutional layers with a stride of 1, as well as one residual block (with ReLU, 3×3 convolution, ReLU, 1×1 convolution). The X-ray decoder has symmetric residual blocks and convolutional layers. The CBCT autoencoder replaces the 2D convolution of the X-ray image autoencoder with the 3D convolution analogously and uses an additional $4 \times 4 \times 4$ convolutional layer with a stride of 2. The multi-category classifier in the cross-modal transition module has three fully connected layers. We implement the proposed network using the open-source PyTorch with the ADAM optimizer [8] on a PC with one NVIDIA GeForce RTX 2080Ti GPU. The X-ray autoencoder, the CBCT autoencoder, the transition module, and the real X-ray-based fine-tuning use the learning rates of 1e−3, 1e−4, 1e−4, and 1e−6, with the mini-batch of 8, 4, 1, and 1. They need the training time of approx. 2, 40, 80, 20 h, respectively. The momentum is set to 0.999. The end-to-end volumetric image reconstruction takes 0.526 s in the online testing process.

Qualitative Assessment. The proposed method realizes an end-to-end volumetric image estimation from a 2D X-ray image. Figure 2 shows the volumetric image reconstruction from a synthetic X-ray image. The overlappings of the estimated volumetric images and the ground-truth are illustrated in the axial, sagittal, and coronal views. As we can see, the resulted volumetric image is consistent with the ground-truth. Moreover, the landmarks on the boundaries of craniofacial structures in the DRR are consistent with those on the input X-ray image. We quantitatively evaluate the registration using both the 3D and 2D NCC-based metrics, as shown in Table 1. As to the synthetic testing dataset, the proposed method outperforms the traditional registration-based method using the normalized cross-correlation (OP_{NCC}) and the mutual information (OP_{MI}) metrics [11] with the B-spline-based nonrigid transformation model, and the partial least square regression (PLSR) model [29]. We also compare with the deep-learning-based methods, including the ResNet-based regression between the X-ray images and the volumetric deformation parameters [17], and the U-net-based volume estimation from a single-view X-ray image [6]. The proposed method achieves the average LRE of 1.08 mm, outperforming the compared methods.

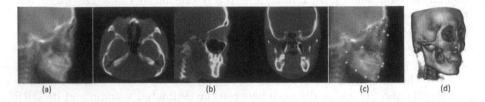

Fig. 2. Volumetric image reconstruction of a synthetic X-ray image. (a) Input X-ray image. (b) Overlapping of the reconstructed volume (green) with the ground truth (grey) in axial, sagittal, and coronal views. (c) Landmark overlapping on DRR of the reconstructed volume (red-input X-ray image, green-DRR). (d) The reconstructed volume. (Color figure online)

Table 1. Errors of the proposed method, traditional registration-based methods of the OP_{MI} and the OP_{NCC} [11], the PLSR [29], the ResNet [17], and Henzlers [6] method on synthetic and real X-ray images. († with B-spline-based nonrigid transformation model)

	Synthetic X-ray							Real X-ray						
	LRE	LRE percentile				NCC_2	NCC_3	LRE	LRE percentile				NCC_2
		25	50	75	90				25	50	75	90	
OP_{MI} [11]†	1.91	0.89	1.58	2.15	3.54	0.89	0.88	3.11	1.54	2.84	3.71	6.24	0.75
OP_{NCC} [11]†	1.82	0.81	1.54	2.15	3.16	0.96	0.92	2.21	0.97	1.95	2.84	4.83	0.81
PLSR [29]	1.60	0.74	1.41	2.07	3.08	0.98	0.96	6.04	3.45	5.38	8.83	11.7	0.42
ResNet [17]	1.11	0.72	1.09	1.55	2.18	0.99	**0.98**	3.20	2.07	3.08	4.36	5.71	0.69
Henzler's [6]	2.06	1.38	1.95	2.84	3.71	0.95	0.95	3.68	1.54	2.84	5.58	8.07	0.61
Ours $C_{v,128}$	1.39	0.74	1.38	1.54	2.48	0.99	**0.98**	2.21	0.97	1.54	2.48	5.56	0.82
$C_{v,192}$	1.25	0.74	1.15	1.51	2.41	0.99	**0.98**	1.96	0.98	1.51	2.51	4.02	0.83
$C_{v,256}$	1.10	0.71	1.07	1.49	**2.38**	**1.00**	**0.98**	**1.84**	**0.78**	**1.48**	**2.34**	**3.97**	**0.84**
$C_{v,512}$	**1.08**	**0.69**	**0.99**	**1.45**	2.39	0.99	**0.98**	2.13	0.87	1.56	2.76	4.87	0.82

We also evaluate volumetric image reconstruction from real X-ray images. As shown in Fig. 3, the DRR projection of the estimated volume images is consistent with real X-ray images regarding landmarks on anatomical structures. We think the performance improvements can be ascribed to the deep learning-based nonlinear transition functions and the vector quantisation scheme for the high-quality image reconstruction. Moreover, the unsupervised fine-tuning of the cross-modal transition module enables reliable volumetric reconstruction from real X-ray images, without additional operations on the domain adaptation.

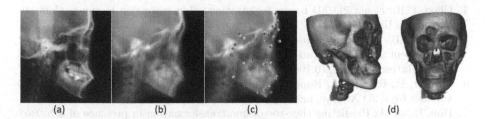

Fig. 3. Volumetric image reconstruction from a real X-ray image. (a) Input X-ray image. (b) The DRR of the reconstructed volume. (c) Landmark overlapping on the DRR of the reconstructed volume (red-input X-ray image, green-DRR). (d) The reconstructed volume in two views. (Color figure online)

Our cross-modal framework relies on the codebook in the embedding space for quantisation and image decoding. In our experiments, we evaluate the volumetric image reconstruction using codebooks ranging from 128–512, as shown in Table 1. The volumetric image quality improves with the increasing sizes of codebooks. We think it can be ascribed to the larger codebook, enabling image quantisation with the preservation of more image details. In our experiments, the code number is set to 256 for both the X-ray and CBCT autoencoders to balance the image reconstruction accuracy and the complexity of the multi-category classifier-based transition module.

4 Discussion and Conclusion

In this paper, we propose a cross-modal framework for the volumetric image reconstruction from a 2D lateral X-ray. We present a multi-category classifier-based transition module and realize the cross-modal mapping to the latent representations of X-ray and CBCT images. The bidirectional transition passes enable the X-ray image-based volume reconstruction and simulate the DRR rendering. The qualitative and quantitative experiments on synthetic and real clinically-obtained X-ray images demonstrate that the transition module in the latent space enables the effective and efficient volume estimation from a single 2D X-ray image.

Acknowledgments. This work was supported by NSFC 61876008.

References

1. Bier, B., et al.: Learning to detect anatomical landmarks of the pelvis in x-rays from arbitrary views. Int. J. Comput. Assist. Radiol. Surg. **14**, 1463–1473 (2019). https://doi.org/10.1007/s11548-019-01975-5
2. Bui, M., Albarqouni, S., Schrapp, M., Navab, N., Ilic, S.: X-Ray PoseNet: 6 DoF pose estimation for mobile x-Ray devices. In: 2017 IEEE Winter Conference on Applications of Computer Vision (WACV), pp. 1036–1044 (2017)
3. Chen, H., et al.: LEARN: learned experts assessment-based reconstruction network for sparse-data CT. IEEE Trans. Med. Imaging **37**, 1333–1347 (2018)
4. Chou, C.R., et al.: 2D/3D image registration using regression learning. Comput. Vis. Image Underst. **117**(9), 1095–1106 (2013)
5. Grupp, R.B., et al.: Automatic annotation of hip anatomy in fluoroscopy for robust and efficient 2D/3D registration. Int. J. Comput. Assist. Radiol. Surg. **15**, 759–769 (2020). https://doi.org/10.1007/s11548-020-02162-7
6. Henzler, P., Rasche, V., Ropinski, T., Ritschel, T.: Single-image tomography: 3D volumes from 2D X-Rays. arXiv preprint arXiv:1710.04867 (2017)
7. Hou, B., et al.: Predicting slice-to-volume transformation in presence of arbitrary subject motion. In: Descoteaux, M., Maier-Hein, L., Franz, A., Jannin, P., Collins, D.L., Duchesne, S. (eds.) MICCAI 2017. LNCS, vol. 10434, pp. 296–304. Springer, Cham (2017). https://doi.org/10.1007/978-3-319-66185-8_34
8. Kingma, D.P., Ba, J.: Adam: a method for stochastic optimization. arXiv preprint arXiv:1412.6980 (2014)
9. Kügler, D., Stefanov, A., Mukhopadhyay, A.: i3PosNet: instrument pose estimation from X-ray. arXiv preprint arXiv:1802.09575 (2018)
10. Li, R., et al.: 3D tumor localization through real-time volumetric X-ray imaging for lung cancer radiotherapy. Med. Phys. **38**(5), 2783–94 (2011)
11. Likar, B.: A review of 3D/2D registration methods for image-guided interventions. Med. Image Anal. **16**(3), 642–661 (2012)
12. Miao, S., et al.: Dilated FCN for multi-agent 2D/3D medical image registration. In: AAAI (2018)
13. Miao, S., Wang, Z.J., Liao, R.: A CNN regression approach for real-time 2D/3D registration. IEEE Trans. MI **35**(5), 1352–1363 (2016)
14. Montoya, J., Zhang, C., Li, K., Chen, G.H.: Volumetric scout CT images reconstructed from conventional two-view radiograph localizers using deep learning (Conference Presentation) (2019)
15. van den Oord, A., Vinyals, O., et al.: Neural discrete representation learning. In: Advances in Neural Information Processing Systems, pp. 6306–6315 (2017)
16. Pei, Y., Dai, F., Xu, T., Zha, H., Ma, G.: Volumetric reconstruction of craniofacial structures from 2D lateral cephalograms by regression forest. In: IEEE ICIP, pp. 4052–4056 (2016)
17. Pei, Y., et al.: Non-rigid craniofacial 2D-3D registration using CNN-based regression. In: Cardoso, M.J., et al. (eds.) DLMIA/ML-CDS -2017. LNCS, vol. 10553, pp. 117–125. Springer, Cham (2017). https://doi.org/10.1007/978-3-319-67558-9_14
18. Razavi, A., van den Oord, A., Vinyals, O.: Generating diverse high-fidelity images with VQ-VAE-2. In: Advances in Neural Information Processing Systems, pp. 14837–14847 (2019)
19. Shen, L., Zhao, W., Xing, L.: Patient-specific reconstruction of volumetric computed tomography images from a single projection view via deep learning. Nat. Biomed. Eng. **3**, 880–888 (2019)

20. Syben, C., Michen, M., Stimpel, B., Seitz, S., Ploner, S.B., Maier, A.K.: PYRO-NN: python reconstruction operators in neural networks. Med. Phys. **46**, 5110–5115 (2019)
21. Toth, D., Cimen, S., Ceccaldi, P., Kurzendorfer, T., Rhode, K.S., Mountney, P.: Training deep networks on domain randomized synthetic X-ray data for cardiac interventions. In: MIDL (2019)
22. Toth, D., et al.: 3D/2D model-to-image registration by imitation learning for cardiac procedures. Int. J. Comput. Assist. Radiol. Surg. **13**(8), 1141–1149 (2018). https://doi.org/10.1007/s11548-018-1774-y
23. Wu, Y., et al.: Incorporating prior knowledge via volumetric deep residual network to optimize the reconstruction of sparsely sampled MRI. Magn. Reson. Imaging **66**, 93–103 (2019)
24. Würfl, T., et al.: Deep learning computed tomography: learning projection-domain weights from image domain in limited angle problems. IEEE Trans. Med. Imaging **37**, 1454–1463 (2018)
25. Xu, Y., et al.: A method for volumetric imaging in radiotherapy using single X-ray projection. Med. Phys. **42**(5), 2498–509 (2014)
26. Ying, X., Guo, H., Ma, K., Wu, J.Y., Weng, Z., Zheng, Y.: X2CT-GAN: reconstructing CT from biplanar X-rays with generative adversarial networks. In: 2019 IEEE/CVF Conference on Computer Vision and Pattern Recognition (CVPR), pp. 10611–10620 (2019)
27. Zhang, Y., Miao, S., Mansi, T., Liao, R.: Task driven generative modeling for unsupervised domain adaptation: application to X-ray image segmentation. In: Frangi, A.F., Schnabel, J.A., Davatzikos, C., Alberola-López, C., Fichtinger, G. (eds.) MICCAI 2018. LNCS, vol. 11071, pp. 599–607. Springer, Cham (2018). https://doi.org/10.1007/978-3-030-00934-2_67
28. Zhang, Y., et al.: Temporal consistent 2D-3D registration of lateral cephalograms and cone-beam computed tomography images. In: Shi, Y., Suk, H.-I., Liu, M. (eds.) MLMI 2018. LNCS, vol. 11046, pp. 371–379. Springer, Cham (2018). https://doi.org/10.1007/978-3-030-00919-9_43
29. Zheng, G.: 3D volumetric intensity reconsturction from 2D X-ray images using partial least squares regression. In: IEEE ISBI, pp. 1268–1271 (2013)
30. Zheng, J., Miao, S., Liao, R.: Learning CNNs with pairwise domain adaption for real-time 6DoF ultrasound transducer detection and tracking from X-ray images. In: Descoteaux, M., Maier-Hein, L., Franz, A., Jannin, P., Collins, D.L., Duchesne, S. (eds.) MICCAI 2017. LNCS, vol. 10434, pp. 646–654. Springer, Cham (2017). https://doi.org/10.1007/978-3-319-66185-8_73
31. Zhu, B., Liu, J.Z., Rosen, B.R., Rosen, M.S.: Image reconstruction by domain-transform manifold learning. Nature **555**, 487–492 (2018)

Cleft Volume Estimation and Maxilla Completion Using Cascaded Deep Neural Networks

Yungeng Zhang[1], Yuru Pei[1(✉)], Yuke Guo[2], Si Chen[3], Tianmin Xu[3], and Hongbin Zha[1]

[1] Key Laboratory of Machine Perception (MOE),
Department of Machine Intelligence, Peking University, Beijing, China
peiyuru@cis.pku.edu.cn
[2] Luoyang Institute of Science and Technology, Luoyang, China
[3] School of Stomatology, Peking University, Beijing, China

Abstract. In this paper, we propose an end-to-end cascaded deep neural network based-framework for the prediction of cleft volume and maxilla completion in the alveolar cleft grafting procedures. We devise the coupled cascaded deformable volumetric registration and cleft prediction networks with progressively refined cleft masks. The framework can be stacked on an existing volumetric registration network for partial registration between the template volume with the complete maxilla and the one with cleft lips and palates (CLP). Instead of one-shot registration-based volume completion for the cleft volume prediction, we present a cascaded registration network to accommodate coarse-to-fine volumetric transformations, enabling the refinement of the cleft volume and fine-tuning of cleft prediction network. The resulting dense displacement fields facilitate the cleft defect location and virtual maxilla completion. The iteratively updated cleft volume from the partial registration is utilized to refine the end-to-end cleft prediction network, which avoids the Boolean operation-based cleft estimation in the online testing process. We devise an alternating optimization approach to fine-tune the registration and cleft prediction networks. Qualitative and quantitative comparisons of the proposed approach on clinically-obtained CLP CBCT images demonstrate that our method is effective for cleft volume estimation and virtual maxilla completion.

Keywords: Cleft volume estimation · Partial registration · Alternating optimization

1 Introduction

Applications of the cone-beam CT (CBCT) images in the secondary alveolar bone grafts operation to cleft lips and palates (CLP) patients create virtual cleft volumes, which enable quantitative assessment of the cleft defect volume and

M. Liu et al. (Eds.): MLMI 2020, LNCS 12436, pp. 332–341, 2020.
https://doi.org/10.1007/978-3-030-59861-7_34

grafting material [8,21]. Such virtual maxilla completion and cleft volume estimation play an essential role in the treatment management of the CLP patients for a continuous maxillary arch, which facilitates tooth eruption and bony support of the anterior teeth and the alar base. The effective and accurate estimation of the volumetric cleft from CBCT images avoids the waste or deficient bone harvesting for the grafting procedure. However, considering the absence of the cranio-caudal and bucco-palatal boundaries with soft tissues, as well as the low images contrast of CBCT images, it is a challenging task to discriminate cleft defect from surrounding tissues.

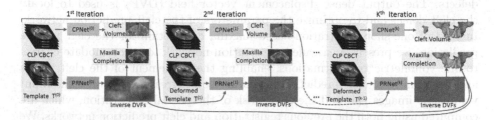

Fig. 1. Cleft volume estimation and maxilla completion by the proposed c-RCN, the cascaded partial registration and cleft volume prediction networks. The volumetric template with the complete maxilla is deformed progressively by the inverse displacement vector fields (DVFs) resulted from the cascaded coarse-to-fine registration networks (PRNet). The cleft volumes obtained by the cascaded registrations are used to train the cleft volume prediction network (CPNet), which takes the CLP CBCT image as an input and outputs the cleft volumes. The masks used in the partial registration are iteratively updated by both the previous registration and cleft prediction networks.

Existing work on cleft estimation relies on the interactive demarcation tools to outline labial and palatal cortices on 2D slices from the cemento-enamel junction or the alveolar bone crest to the anterior nasal spine [2,9,18,19]. The interactive operation depends on the practitioner's experiences and prone to inter-observer labeling variations. The semi-automatic methods use the mirroring of the symmetric unaffected maxillary contours [12,13], the thresholding [10], and the region-growing [10,25] methods to infer the contours of cleft defects. However, the mirroring operation is limited to handle the asymmetric maxillar and fails in the bilateral CLP cases. The thresholding and the region growing methods are incapable of locating cranio-caudal and bucco-palatal boundaries. The recent data-driven deep learning-based framework handles completion of shapes with different representations, such as the voxel grid [6,11,23,24], 3D point clouds [1,22], and meshes [14,15]. The deep-learning-based shape completion models usually adopt the autoencoder framework, where encoder learns a latent representation of partial input, and further this representation is used to reconstruct the missing parts [16,17]. The decoder is augments by the generative adversarial generator [23], the semantic labels [20], or the long short-term memorized context fusion [11] for the shape refinement. The above work mainly addresses the simple human-made objects with the relatively low-resolution representation of the voxel grid or point clouds. The deep learning-based registration models [4,7] produce dense voxel-wise correspondence, showing possibilities for shape completion by the alignment of the template to the target volumetric image with incomplete structures.

In this paper, we propose an end-to-end cascaded partial registration and cleft volume prediction networks (c-RCN) for the prediction of the volumetric cleft and maxilla completion as shown in Fig. 1. The framework can be stacked on an existing volumetric registration network for partial registration between the template with the complete maxilla and the CLP CBCT image with cleft defects. The output dense displacement vector field (DVF) is used to locate the cleft defect and to optimize the parameters of the cleft prediction network. Instead of one-shot registration-based maxilla completion for the cleft volume prediction, we present a cascaded registration network to accommodate coarse-to-fine volumetric transformations, enabling the refinement of the cleft masks and fine-tuning of cleft prediction network. We progressively update the input volumetric images pair and the cleft mask of the partial registration, which are computed using both the previous registration and cleft prediction networks. We devise an alternating optimization approach to fine-tune the proposed framework. Qualitative and quantitative comparisons of the proposed approach on clinically-obtained CLP CBCT images demonstrate that our method is effective for online cleft volume estimation and virtual maxilla completion with performance improvement over the compared one-shot learning-based models. The main contributions of this work are as follows:

- We present an end-to-end registration-based framework for virtual cleft volume estimation and maxilla completion. By the cascaded registration and the cleft prediction networks, our model produces plausible predictions of irregular cleft defects.
- We introduce an alternating optimization approach to optimize the framework, which is resilient to a large range of maxilla shape variations between the template and target CLP CBCT images.

2   Method

Given a volumetric CLP CBCT image $V \in \mathbb{R}^N$ with N voxel, the goal is to predict the cleft volumetric image $Y \in \mathbb{R}^N$ with entry set to 1 indicating the cleft defect, and 0 otherwise. Moreover, our framework outputs the virtual complete maxilla $Z \in \mathbb{R}^N$ with respect to the target CLP CBCT image. We propose an end-to-end registration-based framework, which integrates cascaded partial registration network (PRNet) and the cleft prediction network (CPNet) as shown in Fig. 1. Our framework is stacked on the existing base volumetric image registration network, the CVN [26]. Instead of one-shot registration-based volume completion and the postprocessing operation for the cleft volume, we utilize the cascaded coarse-to-fine registration to update the cleft volume and the CPNet progressively.

2.1 Partial Registration

Given the template volume T and the target CLP CBCT image V, the goal of the PRNet is to infer the dense deformation field ϕ, and minimize the masked image distance $\|M(V - T \circ \phi)\|$. The template CBCT image T is selected randomly from the CBCT dataset with a complete maxilla. We adapt the CVN [26] for the partial registration, where the volume masked by the cleft does not contribute to the registration. The PRNet parameterizes a nonlinear mapping function from the image pair(V, T) to invertible displacement fields (ϕ, ϕ_{inv}).

The mask volume M of the cleft defect is initialized as a regular bounding box as shown in Fig. 2. The six planes of the bounding box are defined by the lower part of the piriform aperture, the proximal central incisors cement-enamel junction, a pair of planes parallel to the median plane, and the surrounding maxillary bony structures. The PRNet is optimized by minimizing the volumetric image difference after the nonrigid deformation determined by (ϕ, ϕ_{inv}). The partial registration loss function

$$L_{pr} = \|M(T \circ \phi - V)\|_F + \|M \circ \phi_{inv}(V \circ \phi_{inv} - T)\|_F + \gamma(\|\nabla\phi\|_F + \|\nabla\phi_{inv}\|_F),$$
(1)

where $\|\cdot\|_F$ denotes the Frobenius norm. The bidirectional DVFs are regularized by minimizing the first-order gradients $\nabla\phi$ and $\nabla\phi_{inv}$ with the weight γ of 0.1. Let $Z_T \in \mathbb{R}^N$ denote the predefined complete maxilla mask of the template, where the entry is set to 1 for the voxel inside the maxilla and 0 otherwise. The deformed maxilla mask $Z_T \circ \phi$ gives a virtual complete maxilla of the target CLP CBCT image.

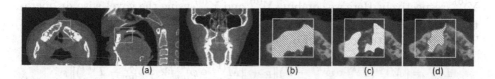

Fig. 2. (a) Initial cleft mask (bounding box) definition in the axial, sagittal, and coronal views. (b) Intersection of the cleft mask and the virtual complete maxilla. (c) Removal of the maxillary bony structures by thresholding. (d) Extracted cleft.

A Boolean operation combined with thresholding is used to extract the cleft volume when given the virtual complete maxilla (see Fig. 2). First, compute the intersection of the cleft mask M and the virtual complete maxilla $Z_T \circ \phi$. Second, use the thresholding operation to remove the maxillary bony structure inside the cleft mask. The cleft volume is computed as

$$Y_r = M \oplus (Z_T \circ \phi) \ominus Z_r,$$
(2)

where $\oplus$ and $\ominus$ denote the voxel-wise *and* and *minus* operations. $Z_r \in \mathbb{R}^N$ with entry $Z_{r,i} = 1$, when voxel i is in the cleft mask M and with the intensity value greater than the threshold η of 300 Hounsfield units (HU) in experiments. Z_r denotes the remaining maxillary bony structure inside the cleft mask.

2.2   Cleft Volume Prediction

The CPNet is built upon the 3D-Unet [5] to parameterize the mapping function, $f : V \rightarrow Y$, from the target CLP CBCT V to the cleft defect volume Y. Given the cleft volume Y_r obtained from the PRNet, the parameters of the CPNet are optimized in a supervised manner by minimizing the distance between the predicted cleft volume Y_c and Y_r. The loss function

$$L_{cp} = \|Y_c - Y_r\|_F + \|\nabla Y_c\|_F. \tag{3}$$

The second term is used to regularize the cleft volume by minimizing the surface area of the cleft, which encourages a smooth cleft surface. Cleft prediction is different from the ordinary segmentation in that there are no cranio-caudal and bucco-palatal boundaries of cleft defects in the regions padded with soft tissues. Note that the function f parameterized by the CPNet realizes online end-to-end cleft volume estimation without volumetric Boolean operations.

2.3   Alternating Optimization

Instead of one-shot registration-based maxilla completion and cleft volume prediction, we present a cascaded framework to accommodate coarse-to-fine volumetric transformations, which enables the refinement of the cleft volumes and the CPNet. We devise an alternating optimization scheme to optimize the PRNet and CPNet al.ternately. Given the CLP CBCT image dataset, the initial PRNet$^{(0)}$ (Sect. 2.1) and CPNet$^{(0)}$ (Sect. 2.2) produce the cleft volumes $Y_r^{(0)}$ and $Y_c^{(0)}$, respectively. Here we combine $Y_r^{(0)}$ and $Y_c^{(0)}$ using the voxel-wise or operation $\odot$ to update the mask M in the partial registration, and $M^{(1)} = Y_r^{(0)} \odot Y_c^{(0)}$. The partial registration loss (Eq. 1) is rewritten as follows:

$$
\begin{aligned}
L_{pr}^{(k)} &= \|M^{(k)}(T^{(k)} \circ \phi^{(k)} - V)\|_F + \|M^{(k)} \circ \phi_{inv}^{(k)}(V \circ \phi_{inv}^{(k)} - T^{(k)})\|_F \\
&+ \gamma(\|\nabla \phi^{(k)}\|_F + \|\nabla \phi_{inv}^{(k)}\|_F).
\end{aligned}
\tag{4}
$$

Algorithm 1. Alternating Optimization of c-RCN

Input: CLP CBCT image dataset V, Template T, Cascade depth K, Cleft bounding box $M^{(0)}$;

Output: PRNet$^{(0 \cdots K)}$, CPNet$^{(K)}$;

1: Train PRNet$^{(0)}$ (Eq. 1);
2: **for** $i = 1 : K$ **do**
3:    Compute the cleft volume $Y^{(i-1)}$ (Eq. 2)
4:    Train CPNet$^{(i-1)}$ using $(V, Y^{(i-1)})$ (Eq. 3);
5:    Update template $T^{(i)}$ using concatenated DVFs;
6:    Update cleft defect mask $M^{(i)}$;
7:    Train PRNet$^{(i)}$ using $(V, T^{(i)}, M^{(i)})$ (Eq. 4);
8: **end for**

We iteratively train the $PRNet^{(k)}$ using the image pair $(V, T^{(k)})$ with newly updated template $T^{(k)}$ and mask $M^{(k)}$, where $T^{(k)} = T \circ \Pi_{i=1}^{k} \phi^{(i-1)}$. The resulted cleft volumes from the $PRNet^{(k)}$ is used to further refine the $CPNet^{(k)}$. We summarize the alternating optimization in Algorithm 1.

In the testing process, when given the target CLP CBCT image, we utilize the final $CPNet^{(K)}$ to get the cleft defect volume $Y = f^{(K)}(V)$. The virtual complete maxilla Z is computed using concatenated displacement fields.

$$Z = Z_T \circ \Pi_{i=0}^{K} \phi^{(i)}, \tag{5}$$

where the DVFs obtained from the cascaded registration networks account for the coarse-to-fine volumetric deformation of the complete maxilla of the template to fit the maxilla of the target CLP CBCT image.

3 Experiments

Dataset and Evaluation. The proposed c-RCN is applied to clinically-obtained CLP images. The dataset consists of 25 CBCT images of CLP patients with lateral or bilateral cleft defects to undergo the secondary alveolar cleft grafting procedures. The dataset is split with 15 CLP images for training and the remaining for testing. We perform the data augmentation by applying 30 randomly perturbed nonrigid volumetric deformations to each volume, resulting in 450 volumetric images. The volumetric images are re-sampled to a resolution of $128 \times 128 \times 96$. The isometric voxel size is $1.2 \times 1.2 \times 1.2\,\mathrm{mm}^3$.

The maxilla completion and cleft volume estimation are evaluated using the Dice similarity coefficient (DSC), where $DSC_m = \frac{2\|Z \oplus Z_{gt}\|_0}{\|Z\|_0 + \|Z_{gt}\|_0}$, and $DSC_c = \frac{2\|Y \oplus Y_{gt}\|_0}{\|Y\|_0 + \|Y_{gt}\|_0}$. Z_{gt} and Y_{gt} denote the ground truth complete maxilla and the cleft defect. Here the 0-norm measures the number of nonzero elements. We also evaluate the cleft volume using the relative error $e_v = \frac{\|\|Y\|_0 - \|Y_{gt}\|_0\|}{\|Y_{gt}\|_0}$.

Implementation Details. In our system, the partial registration network is stacked on an existing registration network of the CVN [26]. The cleft volume prediction network is built on the U-Net [5]. The depth of the cascaded network K is set to 3. The framework is implemented using the open-source PyTorch with the Adam optimizer on a PC with one GeForce GTX TITAN Xp GPU. The momentum is set to 0.999. The initial learning rate is $1e - 4$ for the first epochs and reduced in half after every 50 epochs. The mini-batch has 1 volume image for both the PRNet and CPNet. The training of the cascaded model takes $4.5\,\mathrm{h}$ with 200 epochs for both the PRNet and the CPNet in one stage. The online cleft defect volume estimation takes $0.079\,\mathrm{s}$, and the maxilla completion takes $0.12\,\mathrm{s}$.

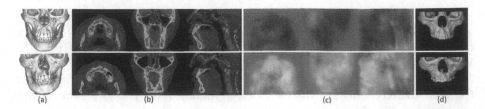

Fig. 3. (a) Template volume with the complete maxilla and the target CLP CBCT image with cleft defects. (b) Overlapping of the template and the target volume before and after registration in axial, coronal, and sagittal views. (c) Inverse displacement fields in the axial, coronal, and sagittal views. (d) Template maxilla surfaces before and after registration.

Qualitative Assessment. Our approach utilizes the cascaded partial registration for virtual maxilla completion. Figure 3 shows the nonrigid registration of the template with the complete maxilla and the target CLP CBCT image. The deformed template is consistent with the target, especially surrounding the clefts, by virtue of the progressive registrations. The deformed maxilla of the template provides a virtual view of the maxilla completion for the target CLP image.

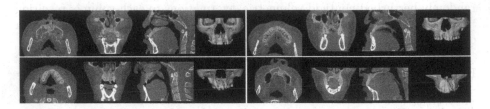

Fig. 4. Cleft defect mask estimation of four CLP CBCT image. From left to right: the cleft defect overlapping in the axial, coronal, and sagittal views, and the partial maxilla and cleft defect surface models.

The end-to-end CPNet predicts the cleft defect when given a CLP CBCT image. Figure 4 shows the overlapping of the estimated cleft with the target CLP volumes. The proposed method predicts both the lateral and bilateral cleft defects, avoiding the limitation of traditional symmetric mirroring methods. Note that the cranio-caudal and bucco-palatal boundaries with soft tissue padding are obtained automatically by the CPNet without interactive demarcation.

Our approach relies on cascaded coarse-to-fine registration for the refinement of the maxilla completion and cleft volumes. Figure 5(a–b) shows the registration fields and estimated cleft volumes with increasing cascade depths. Table 1 reports the maxilla completion and cleft volume estimation errors. As we can see, the cascaded framework produces performance improvements on all backbone registration models, including the SyN [3], the VM [4], and the CVN [26].

Table 1. Cleft volume and maxilla completion accuracies with increasing cascade depths using backbone registration models of the SyN [3], VM [4], and CVN [26].

Cascade depth		SyN			VM			CVN		
		One	Two	Three	One	Two	Three	One	Two	Three
DSC_m	Mean	0.859	0.880	**0.889**	0.846	0.881	**0.889**	0.864	0.892	**0.901**
	STD	0.046	0.047	0.045	0.048	0.026	0.026	0.043	0.025	0.019
DSC_c	Mean	0.777	0.811	**0.821**	0.769	0.805	**0.812**	0.803	0.831	**0.841**
	STD	0.075	0.066	0.061	0.067	0.056	0.050	0.073	0.045	0.042
e_v	Mean	0.160	0.133	**0.129**	0.179	0.156	**0.150**	0.122	0.091	**0.080**
	STD	0.128	0.112	0.100	0.105	0.077	0.090	0.076	0.072	0.071

For instance, the relative cleft volume error reduces from 0.122 of one-shot model to 0.080 of the cascaded model with the depth of 3. In our experiments, the cleft volume and maxilla completion accuracies reach a plateau at the depth of three (Fig. 5(c–e)). The proposed cascaded framework facilitates the consistent registration of the template and target CLP CBCT image, allowing reliable cleft estimation and maxilla completion.

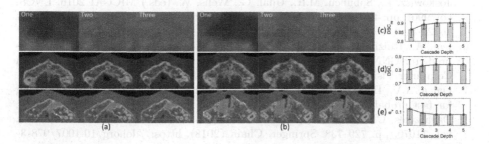

Fig. 5. (a) and (b) are cleft volume estimation with increasing cascade depths of two cases. Top: registration fields. Middle: overlapping of the deformed template (grey) and the target CLP CBCT (red). Bottom: predicted cleft volume (green) and the maxilla (pink). Means and STDs of (c) the DSC_m, (d) the DSC_c, and (e) the e_v with increasing depths. (Color figure online)

4   Discussion and Conclusion

In this paper, we present the unsupervised c-RCN, utilizing the cascaded PRNet and CPNet for the end-to-end maxilla completion and the cleft volume estimation. The coarse-to-fine partial registration facilitates the reliable fitting of the template with the target CLP image for the virtual maxilla completion and the refinement of the CPNet. We devise an alternating optimization scheme and progressively refine the neural networks. Our approach is applied to clinically-obtained CLP CBCT images. Qualitative and quantitative comparisons demonstrate that the cascaded framework realizes reliable and efficient online maxilla completion and cleft volume computation.

Acknowledgments. This work was supported by NSFC 61876008.

References

1. Achlioptas, P., Diamanti, O., Mitliagkas, I., Guibas, L.: Learning representations and generative models for 3D point clouds. arXiv preprint arXiv:1707.02392 (2017)
2. Amirlak, B., Tang, C.J., Becker, D., Palomo, J.M., Gosain, A.K.: Volumetric analysis of simulated alveolar cleft defects and bone grafts using cone beam computed tomography. Plast. Reconstr. Surg. **131**(4), 854–859 (2013)
3. Avants, B., Epstein, C., Grossman, M., Gee, J.: Symmetric diffeomorphic image registration with cross-correlation: evaluating automated labeling of elderly and neurodegenerative brain. Med. Image Anal. **12**(1), 26–41 (2008)
4. Balakrishnan, G., Zhao, A., Sabuncu, M.R., Guttag, J., Dalca, A.V.: VoxelMorph: a learning framework for deformable medical image registration. IEEE Trans. Med. Imaging **38**(8), 1788–1800 (2019)
5. Çiçek, Ö., Abdulkadir, A., Lienkamp, S.S., Brox, T., Ronneberger, O.: 3D U-Net: learning dense volumetric segmentation from sparse annotation. In: Ourselin, S., Joskowicz, L., Sabuncu, M.R., Unal, G., Wells, W. (eds.) MICCAI 2016. LNCS, vol. 9901, pp. 424–432. Springer, Cham (2016). https://doi.org/10.1007/978-3-319-46723-8_49
6. Dai, A., Ruizhongtai Qi, C., Nießner, M.: Shape completion using 3D-encoder-predictor CNNs and shape synthesis. In: Proceedings of the IEEE Conference on Computer Vision and Pattern Recognition, pp. 5868–5877 (2017)
7. Dalca, A.V., Balakrishnan, G., Guttag, J., Sabuncu, M.R.: Unsupervised learning for fast probabilistic diffeomorphic registration. In: Frangi, A.F., Schnabel, J.A., Davatzikos, C., Alberola-López, C., Fichtinger, G. (eds.) MICCAI 2018. LNCS, vol. 11070, pp. 729–738. Springer, Cham (2018). https://doi.org/10.1007/978-3-030-00928-1_82
8. De Mulder, D., Cadenas de Llano-Pérula, M., Jacobs, R., Verdonck, A., Willems, G.: Three-dimensional radiological evaluation of secondary alveolar bone grafting in cleft lip and palate patients: a systematic review. Dentomaxillofacial Radiol. **48**(1) (2019). https://doi.org/10.1259/dmfr.20180047
9. De Ruiter, A., Janssen, N., Van Es, R., Frank, M., Meijer, G., Koole, R., Rosenberg, T.: Micro-structured beta-tricalcium phosphate for repair of the alveolar cleft in cleft lip and palate patients: a pilot study. Cleft Palate-Craniofac. J. **52**(3), 336–340 (2015)
10. Feng, B., Jiang, M., Xu, X., Li, J.: A new method of volumetric assessment of alveolar bone grafting for cleft patients using cone beam computed tomography. Oral Surg. Oral Med. Oral Pathol. Oral Radiol. **124**(2), e171–e182 (2017)
11. Han, X., Li, Z., Huang, H., Kalogerakis, E., Yu, Y.: High-resolution shape completion using deep neural networks for global structure and local geometry inference. In: Proceedings of the IEEE International Conference on Computer Vision, pp. 85–93 (2017)

12. Janssen, N.G., et al.: A novel semi-automatic segmentation protocol for volumetric assessment of alveolar cleft grafting procedures. J. Cranio-Maxillofac. Surg. **45**(5), 685–689 (2017)
13. Linderup, B.W., Küseler, A., Jensen, J., Cattaneo, P.M.: A novel semiautomatic technique for volumetric assessment of the alveolar bone defect using cone beam computed tomography. Cleft Palate-Craniofac. J. **52**(3), 47–55 (2015)
14. Litany, O., Bronstein, A., Bronstein, M., Makadia, A.: Deformable shape completion with graph convolutional autoencoders. In: Proceedings of the IEEE Conference on Computer Vision and Pattern Recognition, pp. 1886–1895 (2018)
15. Monti, F., Boscaini, D., Masci, J., Rodola, E., Svoboda, J., Bronstein, M.M.: Geometric deep learning on graphs and manifolds using mixture model CNNs. In: Proceedings of the IEEE Conference on Computer Vision and Pattern Recognition, pp. 5115–5124 (2017)
16. Morais, A., Egger, J., Alves, V.: Automated computer-aided design of cranial implants using a deep volumetric convolutional denoising autoencoder. In: Rocha, Á., Adeli, H., Reis, L.P., Costanzo, S. (eds.) WorldCIST'19 2019. AISC, vol. 932, pp. 151–160. Springer, Cham (2019). https://doi.org/10.1007/978-3-030-16187-3_15
17. Sharma, A., Grau, O., Fritz, M.: VConv-DAE: deep volumetric shape learning without object labels. In: Hua, G., Jégou, H. (eds.) ECCV 2016. LNCS, vol. 9915, pp. 236–250. Springer, Cham (2016). https://doi.org/10.1007/978-3-319-49409-8_20
18. Shawky, H., Seifeldin, S.A.: Does platelet-rich fibrin enhance bone quality and quantity of alveolar cleft reconstruction? Cleft Palate-Craniofac. J. **53**(5), 597–606 (2016)
19. Shirota, T., Kurabayashi, H., Ogura, H., Seki, K., Maki, K., Shintani, S.: Analysis of bone volume using computer simulation system for secondary bone graft in alveolar cleft. Int. J. Oral Maxillofac. Surg. **39**(9), 904–908 (2010)
20. Song, S., Yu, F., Zeng, A., Chang, A.X., Savva, M., Funkhouser, T.: Semantic scene completion from a single depth image. In: Proceedings of the IEEE Conference on Computer Vision and Pattern Recognition, pp. 1746–1754 (2017)
21. Stasiak, M., Wojtaszek-Słomińska, A., Racka-Pilszak, B.: Current methods for secondary alveolar bone grafting assessment in cleft lip and palate patients - a systematic review. J. Cranio-Maxillofac. Surg. **47**(4), 578–585 (2019)
22. Stutz, D., Geiger, A.: Learning 3D shape completion from laser scan data with weak supervision. In: Proceedings of the IEEE Conference on Computer Vision and Pattern Recognition, pp. 1955–1964 (2018)
23. Wang, W., Huang, Q., You, S., Yang, C., Neumann, U.: Shape inpainting using 3D generative adversarial network and recurrent convolutional networks. In: Proceedings of the IEEE International Conference on Computer Vision, pp. 2298–2306 (2017)
24. Wu, Z., et al.: 3D ShapeNets: a deep representation for volumetric shapes. In: Proceedings of the IEEE Conference on Computer Vision and Pattern Recognition, pp. 1912–1920 (2015)
25. Xi, T., Schreurs, R., Heerink, W.J., Berge, S.J., Maal, T.J.: A novel region-growing based semi-automatic segmentation protocol for three-dimensional condylar reconstruction using cone beam computed tomography (CBCT). PLoS ONE **9**(11), e111126 (2014)
26. Zhang, Y., Pei, Y., Guo, Y., Ma, G., Xu, T., Zha, H.: Fully convolutional network for consistent voxel-wise correspondence. In: Thirty-Fourth AAAI Conference on Artificial Intelligence (AAAI 2020) (2020)

A Deep Network for Joint Registration and Reconstruction of Images with Pathologies

Xu Han[1]([✉]), Zhengyang Shen[1], Zhenlin Xu[1], Spyridon Bakas[2],
Hamed Akbari[2], Michel Bilello[2], Christos Davatzikos[2], and Marc Niethammer[1]

[1] Department of Computer Science, UNC Chapel Hill, Chapel Hill, NC, USA
xhs400@cs.unc.edu
[2] Center for Biomedical Image Computing and Analytics, Perelman School
of Medicine, University of Pennsylvania, Philadelphia, PA, USA

Abstract. Registration of images with pathologies is challenging due
to tissue appearance changes and missing correspondences caused by
the pathologies. Moreover, mass effects as observed for brain tumors
may displace tissue, creating larger deformations over time than what is
observed in a healthy brain. Deep learning models have successfully been
applied to image registration to offer dramatic speed up and to use surrogate information (e.g., segmentations) during training. However, existing approaches focus on learning registration models using images from
healthy patients. They are therefore not designed for the registration
of images with strong pathologies for example in the context of brain
tumors, and traumatic brain injuries. In this work, we explore a deep
learning approach to register images with brain tumors to an atlas. Our
model learns an appearance mapping from images with tumors to the
atlas, while simultaneously predicting the transformation to atlas space.
Using separate decoders, the network disentangles the tumor mass effect
from the reconstruction of quasi-normal images. Results on both synthetic and real brain tumor scans show that our approach outperforms
cost function masking for registration to the atlas and that reconstructed
quasi-normal images can be used for better longitudinal registrations.

1 Introduction

Registration is a fundamental problem in medical image analysis [26]. It aims
at finding spatial correspondences between two images that are useful for many
tasks, e.g., for atlas-based segmentation [2]. Particularly for patients with brain
tumors, an accurate image registration between the pre-operative and the post-
recurrence images can help analyze the characteristics of tissue resulting in tumor
recurrence [1,10,14,20]. Traditionally, image registration is formulated as an

---

Electronic supplementary material The online version of this chapter (https://
doi.org/10.1007/978-3-030-59861-7_35) contains supplementary material, which is
available to authorized users.

M. Liu et al. (Eds.): MLMI 2020, LNCS 12436, pp. 342–352, 2020.
https://doi.org/10.1007/978-3-030-59861-7_35

optimization problem seeking to minimize the dissimilarity between a warped source image and a target image while simultaneously encouraging spatially regular transformations. To capture large deformations, fluid-based registration models are frequently used [18], e.g., stationary velocity field (SVF) [27] or large deformation diffeomorphic metric mapping (LDDMM) approaches [3,7], which can guarantee diffeomorphic transformations if sufficiently regularized. Non-parametric image registration models [18] such as SVF and LDDMM require optimizing over millions of parameters in 3D, which is usually very slow. Hence, deep learning (DL) approaches have been proposed for such registration models [6,23,24,29]. By shifting the computational cost to the training time, DL approaches are orders of magnitudes faster at test time than numerical optimization, while retaining registration accuracy.

While many registration approaches for normal images or images with similar appearance have been proposed, a limited body of literature exists for the registration of images with pathologies, which is challenging due to tissue appearance differences and missing correspondences. Possible approaches include a) cost-function masking [8] (masking out tumor regions when calculating the similarity measure), b) use of robust similarity measures [21], or c) replacing the pathology with quasi-normal appearance [11,12,16,28]. Masking out the tumor requires an accurate segmentation of the tumor region, and if it is large or in anatomically critical locations cost function masking may hide too much of the underlying brain structure, which should guide the registration [28]. Reconstruction of quasi-normal appearance, on the other hand, does not require a prior segmentation and tumor-to-quasi-normal appearance can be learned via quasi-lesions with a variational autoencoder [28], or from a statistical model of a healthy population [11,12,16]. The quasi-lesion approach [28] introduces synthetic tumors and learns to reconstruct the underlying normal appearance, but the resulting reconstructions are still subject to mass effects and therefore do not properly disentangle appearance from such deformation changes. Existing approaches based on statistical models require underlying registrations to a common space for quasi-normal image reconstruction. But as a good alignment in cases of mass effect cannot be obtained without reconstruction, registration and reconstruction need to be interleaved in a costly iterative scheme.

A conceptually attractive approach would be to separate the mass effect and appearance changes and to reconstruct quasi-normal images in an atlas space, where appearance variability is expected to be lower. Inspired by a previous work on shape and appearance disentangling [25], we propose a deep neural network to simultaneously register a brain tumor[1] image to an atlas while reconstructing a quasi-normal image *in atlas space*. The reconstructed quasi-normal image is in turn used in the similarity loss to guide our network to learn the spatial transformation from the image to the atlas.

Contributions. 1) *Joint reconstruction and registration network.* To the best of our knowledge, this is the first deep network trained jointly to reconstruct and

---

[1] Our goal is to register images with strong pathologies, e.g., tumors, traumatic brain injuries, or strokes. We focus on tumors in this work, but our approach is general.

register brain images with strong pathologies to an atlas. The network recovers the missing correspondences between the pathologies and the atlas space. Our approach is also more computationally efficient than previous approaches by avoiding the interleaving of registrations and reconstructions, resulting in rapid predictions at test time. 2) *Reconstruction of quasi-normal appearance in atlas space.* As we disentangle the transformation to the atlas from the reconstruction, we obtain tumor-to-quasi-normal image appearances in atlas space, thereby simplifying the appearance modeling. 3) *Vector-momentum parameterized fluid-based registration.* Our network incorporates a vector-momentum parameterized stationary velocity field (vSVF) [23], which can capture large deformations while retaining diffeomorphic transformations. We use the reconstructed quasi-normal image to drive the registration, instead of the input tumor image. 4) *Validation.* We show that our network successfully learns to reconstruct quasi-normal appearance simultaneously with the transformation of the tumor image to atlas space. Specifically, we show improvements over cost function masking, demonstrating that modeling quasi-normal image structure is beneficial for the registration of images with pathologies.

Organization. Section 2 describes our registration and reconstruction network. Section 3 presents experimental details and results on both a synthetic brain tumor dataset and on paired sets of pre-operative and post-recurrence brain tumor scans. Section 4 concludes with a summary and an outlook on future work.

2   Methodologies

This section describes our deep network, including its architecture and the associated loss functions. Figure 1 shows an overview of our network. The network takes a tumor image I_T and an atlas A as its inputs and outputs a vector-momentum parameterization of the transformation Φ^{-1}, a reconstructed quasi-normal image I_R and a segmentation of the tumor region I_S. The network jointly learns both the registration and reconstruction, which is more efficient than approaches that interleave registrations and reconstructions. Importantly, the transformation warps the tumor image to the atlas for a better reconstruction in *atlas space*, while the *reconstructed image* guides the similarity measure so that the network learns a better transformation as it is no longer perturbed by the pathology.

Registration. We use a vector-momentum parameterized stationary velocity field (vSVF) model [19,23]. Instead of directly predicting the transformation field, our network predicts a momentum vector field, m, which gets smoothed by a multi-Gaussian kernel [22] resulting in a velocity vector field, v, from which the transformation map, Φ^{-1}, is computed via integration. The benefit of this indirect way is that it can assure diffeomorphic transformations at *test* time.

The registration loss consists of a regularization loss and a similarity loss:

$$L_{rgs}(m_0) = \langle m_0, v_0 \rangle + \frac{1}{\sigma^2} Sim[I_R \circ \Phi^{-1}(1), A],$$

$$\Phi_t^{-1} + D\Phi^{-1}v_0 = 0, \quad \text{s.t.} \quad \Phi^{-1}(0) = \Phi_{(0)}^{-1}, \quad v_0 = (L^\dagger L)^{-1} m_0, \tag{1}$$

where D denotes the Jacobian, m_0 is the initial vector momentum, $\sigma > 0$ balances the two terms, and $\Phi_{(0)}^{-1}$ is the initial condition for the transformation map, Φ^{-1}, which can be set to identity or to the transformation of a pre-registration, for example, an affine registration. $\|v\|_L^2 = \langle L^\dagger L v, v \rangle$ is a norm defined by a differential operator L and its adjoint $L^\dagger$ [7]. We use localized normalized cross correlation (LNCC) as our similarity loss as in [23]. A significant difference from existing registration networks is that instead of using the input tumor image I_T to evaluate the similarity loss, we use the reconstructed image I_R. The reconstructed I_R recovers image correspondences which can guide image registration. The registration loss only backpropagates through the registration decoder.

Reconstruction. The reconstruction decoder predicts a quasi-normal image from the tumor image. We directly learn this mapping from the atlas appearance. Specifically, for a given tumor image, we use its manually segmented tumor mask, S, to separate the tumor and the normal region. The tumor mask is only used during training. In the normal region, the warped reconstruction image $I_{RW} =$

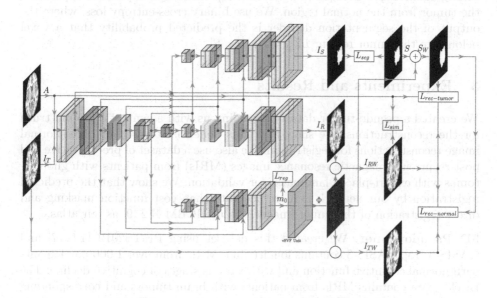

Fig. 1. Overview of the proposed network. The network outputs a mask I_S, a reconstructed quasi-normal image I_R and a vector momentum m_0 which is used to obtain the transformation map Φ^{-1}. The regularization loss L_{reg} penalizes m_0, while the similarity loss L_{sim} penalizes the warped reconstructed image I_{RW} with respect to the atlas A. The reconstruction loss penalizes the warped quasi-normal image in the tumor region and the normal region.

$I_R \circ \Phi^{-1}(1)$ should be close to the warped original image $I_{TW} = I_T \circ \Phi^{-1}(1)$. In the tumor region, the reconstruction should be close to the atlas A. The warped tumor mask is $S_W = S \circ \Phi^{-1}(1)$. We define the reconstruction loss as follows:

$$L_{rec} = \frac{1}{|\Omega_N|} \int_{\Omega_N} (I_{RW} - I_{TW})^2 \, dx + \frac{1}{|\Omega_T|} \int_{\Omega_T} (I_{RW} - A)^2 \, dx, \qquad (2)$$

where $\Omega_N = \{x : S_W(x) = 0\}$ is the normal domain, $\Omega_T = \{x : S_W(x) = 1\}$ is the tumor domain, and $|\Omega|$ denotes the volume of domain Ω. The loss captures the sum of the mean-squared errors over the normal region and the tumor region. We use atlas appearance to learn the tumor-to-quasi-normal mapping since the atlas is our target image. This can be considered a highly simplified statistical model only represented by its mean, the atlas. Combinations with more advanced statistical models, for example based on principal component analysis [12,16] or variational autoencoders [13], are conceivable. The reconstruction loss only backpropagates through the reconstruction decoder.

Segmentation. In principle, the segmentation decoder is not required for registration and reconstruction. Since we use the segmentation mask during training for reconstruction, we also add a segmentation decoder which outputs a predicted segmentation of the tumor. This is similar to [25], where an instance class can also be predicted. Intuitively, by providing direct supervision on the segmentation, the network is required to learn a representation capable of separating the tumor from the normal region. We use binary cross-entropy loss, where the output of the segmentation decoder is the predicted probability that a voxel belongs to the tumor region: $L_{seg} = Bce[I_S, S]$.

3   Experiments and Results

We created a pseudo-tumor dataset providing us with a synthetic ground-truth for the reconstructions. We show that it is beneficial to use our quasi-normal image reconstructions for registration. We also use a dataset of pre-operative and post-recurrence magnetic resonance images (MRIs) from patients with glioblastomas with expert-placed landmarks for validation. We show that the predicted registration by our network is more accurate than cost function masking and direct registration of the tumor images. We use ICBM 152 [9] as our atlas.

3D Pseudo-tumor. We created this dataset using BraTS2019 [4,5,17] and OASIS-3 [15]. OASIS-3 contains longitudinal MRIs from over 1,000 participants with normal cognitive function and with various stages of cognitive decline. The BraTS data contains MRIs from patients with brain tumors and corresponding tumor segmentations. We randomly selected 280 pairs of T1w-images; one from OASIS (we only use one scan for each patient) and one from BraTS. To mimic the mass effect of the brain tumor, we registered the OASIS T1w scan to the BraTS T1w scan with cost function masking and pasted the brain tumor from the BraTS scan onto the deformed OASIS scan. The resulting 280 simulated images are our pseudo-tumor dataset. We randomly select 40 for testing, 40 for validation and 200 for training. Images are affinely aligned to the atlas, which is resampled to $128 \times 128 \times 128$ with $1.5 \times 1.5 \times 1.5 \, \text{mm}^3$ isotropic voxels.

Since this dataset is simulated, we have the images without the added tumor but including the spatial transformation. We register the atlas to these images. As these registrations are not impacted by the tumors, but might not reflect the exact correspondence (due to possible registration errors), we regard the resulting registrations as the gold-standard to which we compare in the following. We register the atlas to: 1) the tumor images (TUMOR), 2) the tumor images using cost function masking, 3) the quasi-normal images predicted by a network with a quasi-lesion layer [28] (REC_QL) and 4) the quasi-normal images predicted by our network. As the gold-standard is obtained through optimization, we perform all the registrations using the same *optimization* model for the pseudo-tumor dataset and do not compare to the predicted registrations. For cost function masking, we conduct two experiments using different masks, one using the groundtruth masks (CFM_GM) and one using the predicted masks by our network (CFM_PM). Using the predicted masks (CFM_PM) allows us to evaluate the performance of cost function masking, when groundtruth (or manually segmented) masks are not available at test time, which is often the case. For our model, we train with (REC_RRS) and without (REC_RR) the segmentation decoder. In addition, for the predicted quasi-normal images, we can keep the normal tissue unchanged by using the predicted segmentation (REC_RRS_PM). We compare the deformation differences between the results obtained by each of the optimization-based registrations and our gold standard registration result.

Figure 2 shows the results for the pseudo-tumor dataset. For each case, we evaluate the mean deformation differences in three regions: 1) the tumor region, 2) the normal region near the tumor (within 30 mm), and 3) the normal region far from the tumor (over 30 mm). Our network performs much better when the segmentation decoder is used, because of the additional supervision (REC_RRS vs. REC_RR). The network using the quasi-lesion layer (REC_QL) works well in the normal region but performs poorly in the tumor region. This might be because at test time the real tumor region is subject to larger mass effects than what was captured during training, as quasi-lesions can never be introduced inside the actual tumor region. Compared to cost function masking, our method (REC_RRS_PM), on average, improves by 0.5 mm in the tumor region when the groundtruth masks are available (CFM_GM) and 0.8 mm when the groundtruth masks are not available (CFM_PM). In the normal regions, improvements over cost function masking are relatively small, around 0.3 mm.

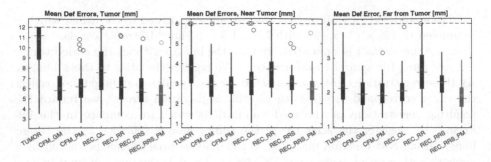

Fig. 2. Boxplots of mean deformation differences with respect to the gold standard deformations. TUMOR: directly registering to the tumor image; CFM: cost function masking, where _GM and _PM refer to using the groundtruth masks and predicted masks, respectively; REC_*s: registering to the reconstructed images, where REC_QL uses the quasi-lesion layer, REC_RR only uses the registration and reconstruction decoders. REC_RRS: proposed network using registration, reconstruction, and segmentation decoders. In addition, REC_RRS_PM (in red) retains the normal region in areas predicted by the masks obtained by our network. (Color figure online)

3D Real Brain Tumor. This dataset consists of images for 22 patients with brain glioblastoma. Each patient has scans from two time-points, one before the surgery (pre-operative) and one after surgery (post-recurrence). All images are of size $155 \times 240 \times 240$ with isotropic voxels $1 \times 1 \times 1$ mm^3. We only use the T1w images in the dataset. For each patient, a radiologist placed 10 landmarks near the tumor (within 30 mm) and 10 landmarks far from the tumor (over 30 mm) in both the pre- and post-scans. We train our network using a subset of the BraTS2019 training data with 120 training images and 20 validation images. Testing is performed via our glioblastoma dataset. To limit dataset variability, we selected a subset of the BraTS training data, which was acquired by one institution and which is similar in acquisition to our test data. Ideally, our test dataset is used for longitudinal registration, i.e., registering between the pre- and post-scans from the same patient. As our network predictions are with respect to an atlas we conduct the following two experiments:

- **Atlas Registration.** For each patient, we feed both scans into our network and obtain respective transformations to the atlas. We then compose the forward map of the pre-scan and the inverse map of the post-scan, resulting in a pre-atlas-post (REC_PAP) map. To compare, we also perform an optimization-based atlas-registration directly using the tumor images (TUMOR_PAP) and with cost function masking (CFM_PAP). In both cases, we obtain the composited transformation. Using the resulting transformations, we warp the landmarks from the post-scan to the pre-scan space and evaluate the landmark differences. As we do not have manual tumor segmentations, we use predicted masks for cost function masking.
- **Longitudinal Registration.** We perform optimization-based vSVF registrations between reconstructed quasi-normal images of both the scans,

predicted by our network (REC_PP). We compare with longitudinally registering directly using tumor images (TUMOR_PP) and using cost function masking
(CFM_PP).

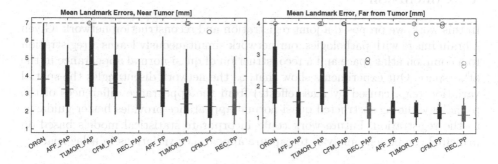

Fig. 3. Boxplots of mean landmark errors for registration of glioblastoma patients.
(ORGN) is the landmark differences before registration. The next four are results via
the atlas, i.e, pre-atlas-post (_PAP); the last four are longitudinal results, i.e., pre-post
(_PP). We compare to affine registration, registration of tumor images, and cost function
masking.

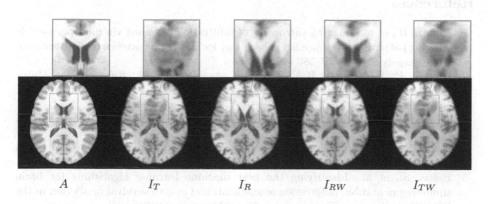

Fig. 4. One example network result for a brain tumor image. The 5 columns show: 1)
the atlas; 2) the tumor image; 3) the reconstructed quasi-normal image, predicted by
our network; 4) the warped quasi-normal image; and 5) the warped tumor by applying
the transformation.

Figure 3 shows landmark errors in two different regions for the different registration approaches. When registrations are composed through the atlas, errors
are much larger than direct longitudinal registration. However, our method shows
improvements over cost function masking in both cases. Finally, Fig. 4 shows an
example for a brain tumor image. The 3rd column is the predicted quasi-normal
image, and the 4th column is the warped image in atlas space. We observe some

contrast differences between the tumor and the normal region. However, as our goal is registration, it is not an issue as the correspondences can be established between the reconstructed image and the atlas.

4   Conclusion

In this work, we proposed a joint registration and reconstruction network. Given a brain image with pathologies, our network simultaneously learns a registration to a common atlas space and a reconstruction of quasi-normal appearance in the atlas space. Our experiments show that, as the network disentangles the spatial variation (e.g., caused by mass effects) from the appearance differences of the pathology, the reconstructed quasi-normal appearance provides better guidance to the registration. Future work could incorporate statistical models based on principal component analysis to capture appearance variations in atlas space.

Acknowledgments. Research reported in this publication was supported by the National Institutes of Health (NIH) and the National Science Foundation (NSF) under award numbers NINDS: R01NS042645, NCI: U24CA189523/U01CA242871, NSF: EECS1711776, and NIH: 1R21CA22330401. The content is solely the responsibility of the authors and does not represent the official views of the NIH or the NSF.

References

1. Akbari, H., et al.: Imaging surrogates of infiltration obtained via multiparametric imaging pattern analysis predict subsequent location of recurrence of glioblastoma. Neurosurgery **78**(4), 572–580 (2016)
2. Aljabar, P., Heckemann, R.A., Hammers, A., Hajnal, J.V., Rueckert, D.: Multi-atlas based segmentation of brain images: atlas selection and its effect on accuracy. Neuroimage **46**(3), 726–738 (2009)
3. Avants, B.B., Tustison, N., Song, G.: Advanced normalization tools (ANTS). Insight J. **2**(365), 1–35 (2009)
4. Bakas, S., et al.: Advancing the cancer genome atlas glioma MRI collections with expert segmentation labels and radiomic features. Sci. Data **4**, 170117 (2017)
5. Bakas, S., et al.: Identifying the best machine learning algorithms for brain tumor segmentation, progression assessment, and overall survival prediction in the BRATS challenge. arXiv preprint arXiv:1811.02629 (2018)
6. Balakrishnan, G., Zhao, A., Sabuncu, M.R., Guttag, J., Dalca, A.V.: VoxelMorph: a learning framework for deformable medical image registration. IEEE Trans. Med. Imaging **38**(8), 1788–1800 (2019)
7. Beg, M.F., Miller, M.I., Trouvé, A., Younes, L.: Computing large deformation metric mappings via geodesic flows of diffeomorphisms. Int. J. Comput. Vis. **61**(2), 139–157 (2005)
8. Brett, M., Leff, A.P., Rorden, C., Ashburner, J.: Spatial normalization of brain images with focal lesions using cost function masking. Neuroimage **14**(2), 486–500 (2001)
9. Fonov, V.S., Evans, A.C., McKinstry, R.C., Almli, C., Collins, D.: Unbiased nonlinear average age-appropriate brain templates from birth to adulthood. NeuroImage (47), S102 (2009)

10. Han, X., et al.: Patient-specific registration of pre-operative and post-recurrence brain tumor MRI scans. In: Crimi, A., Bakas, S., Kuijf, H., Keyvan, F., Reyes, M., van Walsum, T. (eds.) BrainLes 2018. LNCS, vol. 11383, pp. 105–114. Springer, Cham (2019). https://doi.org/10.1007/978-3-030-11723-8_10

11. Han, X., et al.: Brain extraction from normal and pathological images: a joint PCA/image-reconstruction approach. NeuroImage **176**, 431–445 (2018)

12. Han, X., Yang, X., Aylward, S., Kwitt, R., Niethammer, M.: Efficient registration of pathological images: a joint PCA/image-reconstruction approach. In: 2017 IEEE 14th International Symposium on Biomedical Imaging (ISBI 2017), pp. 10–14. IEEE (2017)

13. Kingma, D.P., Welling, M.: Auto-encoding variational bayes. arXiv preprint arXiv:1312.6114 (2013)

14. Kwon, D., Niethammer, M., Akbari, H., Bilello, M., Davatzikos, C., Pohl, K.M.: PORTR: pre-operative and post-recurrence brain tumor registration. IEEE Trans. Med. Imaging **33**(3), 651–667 (2013)

15. LaMontagne, P.J., et al.: OASIS-3: longitudinal neuroimaging, clinical, and cognitive dataset for normal aging and alzheimer's disease. Alzheimer's Dementia: J. Alzheimer's Assoc. **14**(7), P1097 (2018)

16. Liu, X., Niethammer, M., Kwitt, R., McCormick, M., Aylward, S.: Low-rank to the rescue – atlas-based analyses in the presence of pathologies. In: Golland, P., Hata, N., Barillot, C., Hornegger, J., Howe, R. (eds.) MICCAI 2014. LNCS, vol. 8675, pp. 97–104. Springer, Cham (2014). https://doi.org/10.1007/978-3-319-10443-0_13

17. Menze, B.H., et al.: The multimodal brain tumor image segmentation benchmark (BRATS). IEEE Trans. Med. Imaging **34**(10), 1993–2024 (2014)

18. Modersitzki, J.: Numerical Methods for Image Registration. Oxford University (2004, Press on Demand)

19. Niethammer, M., Kwitt, R., Vialard, F.X.: Metric learning for image registration. In: Proceedings of the IEEE Conference on Computer Vision and Pattern Recognition, pp. 8463–8472 (2019)

20. Provenzale, J.M., Mukundan, S., Barboriak, D.P.: Diffusion-weighted and perfusion MR imaging for brain tumor characterization and assessment of treatment response. Radiology **239**(3), 632–649 (2006)

21. Reuter, M., Rosas, H.D., Fischl, B.: Highly accurate inverse consistent registration: a robust approach. Neuroimage **53**(4), 1181–1196 (2010)

22. Risser, L., Vialard, F.X., Wolz, R., Murgasova, M., Holm, D.D., Rueckert, D.: Simultaneous multi-scale registration using large deformation diffeomorphic metric mapping. IEEE Trans. Med. Imaging **30**(10), 1746–1759 (2011)

23. Shen, Z., Han, X., Xu, Z., Niethammer, M.: Networks for joint affine and non-parametric image registration. In: Proceedings of the IEEE Conference on Computer Vision and Pattern Recognition, pp. 4224–4233 (2019)

24. Shen, Z., Vialard, F.X., Niethammer, M.: Region-specific diffeomorphic metric mapping. In: Advances in Neural Information Processing Systems, pp. 1096–1106 (2019)

25. Shu, Z., Sahasrabudhe, M., Alp Güler, R., Samaras, D., Paragios, N., Kokkinos, I.: Deforming autoencoders: unsupervised disentangling of shape and appearance. In: Ferrari, V., Hebert, M., Sminchisescu, C., Weiss, Y. (eds.) ECCV 2018. LNCS, vol. 11214, pp. 664–680. Springer, Cham (2018). https://doi.org/10.1007/978-3-030-01249-6_40

26. Sotiras, A., Davatzikos, C., Paragios, N.: Deformable medical image registration: a survey. IEEE Trans. Med. Imaging **32**(7), 1153–1190 (2013)

27. Vercauteren, T., Pennec, X., Perchant, A., Ayache, N.: Diffeomorphic demons: efficient non-parametric image registration. NeuroImage **45**(1), S61–S72 (2009)
28. Yang, X., Han, X., Park, E., Aylward, S., Kwitt, R., Niethammer, M.: Registration of pathological images. In: Tsaftaris, S.A., Gooya, A., Frangi, A.F., Prince, J.L. (eds.) SASHIMI 2016. LNCS, vol. 9968, pp. 97–107. Springer, Cham (2016). https://doi.org/10.1007/978-3-319-46630-9_10
29. Yang, X., Kwitt, R., Styner, M., Niethammer, M.: Quicksilver: fast predictive image registration–a deep learning approach. NeuroImage **158**, 378–396 (2017)

Learning Conditional Deformable Shape Templates for Brain Anatomy

Evan M. Yu[1]([✉]), Adrian V. Dalca[2,3], and Mert R. Sabuncu[1,4]

[1] Nancy E. and Peter C. Meinig School of Biomedical Engineering,
Cornell University, Ithaca, USA
`emy24@cornell.edu`
[2] Martinos Center for Biomedical Imaging, Massachusetts General Hospital,
Harvard Medical School, Boston, USA
[3] Computer Science and Artificial Intelligence Laboratory (CSAIL),
MIT, Cambridge, USA
[4] School of Electrical and Computer Engineering, Cornell University, Ithaca, USA

Abstract. A brain template that describes the anatomical layout of an "average" brain is an essential building block of neuroimage analysis pipelines. However, a single template is often not sufficient to fully capture the variability in a heterogeneous population. Brain structures have very different shapes and sizes in different clinical and demographic groups. In this paper, we develop a novel neural network model that captures this morphometric variability. Our model learns to compute an attribute-specific spatial deformation that warps a brain template. We train this model on individual brain MRI segmentations in an end-to-end fashion, allowing for fast inference during testing. We demonstrate the ability of our model to deform a brain template given a wide range of ages, presence of disease and different sexes. Detailed qualitative and quantitative experiments are provided in order to demonstrate the flexibility of our model. Finally, we study the surface of the deformed template's hippocampus to show how our model can be used for shape analysis. The code is freely available at https://github.com/evanmy/conditional_deformation.

Keywords: Deformable templates · Conditional deformation · Neuroimaging

1 Introduction

Advances in neuroimaging have enabled examination of the brain at an unprecedented scale. The shapes and sizes of brain regions are an important area of neuroscientific study. Changes associated with factors such as aging, sexual dimorphism, and neurological diseases have been analyzed in many studies [1–7].

Today, conventional brain analysis pipelines rely on a probabilistic template (or atlas), which assigns anatomical label probabilities at each voxel. Once constructed, imaging data from different individuals are spatially registered to the

© Springer Nature Switzerland AG 2020
M. Liu et al. (Eds.): MLMI 2020, LNCS 12436, pp. 353–362, 2020.
https://doi.org/10.1007/978-3-030-59861-7_36

template for statistical analysis. However, demographic, clinical, or other confounding factors can influence the shapes and sizes of brain regions. As a result, a single and fixed template can struggle to accommodate complex structural differences across a heterogeneous group of individuals, which can complicate downstream statistical analyses. One approach to address this issue is to explicitly endow the template with more flexibility that might account for subject-specific characteristics [29,30].

In this paper, we consider modeling attribute-specific neuroanatomical variability via a deformable template model, where the deformation is an explicit function of a given attribute vector. We present an end-to-end learning strategy to train the proposed neural network model and present empirical results that demonstrate utility and reveal interesting neuroanatomical shape variability associated with aging, sex, and Alzheimer's disease (AD).

2   Background and Related Work

There are many ways to construct a template or atlas that assigns labels on a voxel grid. The segmentation of a representative brain MRI from a dataset can be used as a naive reference by applying spatial blurring to account for inter-subject variability at the boundaries. However, today, most atlases are constructed from multi-subject data [10,11]. A common approach involves co-registering the subjects and computing the frequency of anatomical labels at each voxel. It is widely recognized that a single atlas has difficulty accounting for the morphological variability across a heterogeneous group of individuals [16,29,30]. Multiple atlases can be constructed for different subgroups. However, this would demand a significant amount of time, funds, and expertise.

Given a template, the morphological variability in the population is largely captured via deformations [15]. Deformation models can include global affine transformations or more flexible non-linear transformations. A popular parameterization employs B-slines [17]. Non-parametric deformation strategies can build on an elastic model [18] or diffusion model [19,20]. A popular approach is to use diffeomorphic transformations, which ensures that the underlying topology is preserved through the use of continuous, invertible, and differentiable deformations [21–25].

Recently, deep learning based approaches to image registration have showed a lot of promise. Instead of solving an optimization problem for a pair of images, these methods use a neural network that learns to directly compute the transformation that aligns two input images [26–28]. By obviating the need of optimization during inference, these methods are significantly faster than non-learning-based approaches.

A recent paper closely related to ours, proposed a method to construct image templates in a learning-based framework using convolutional neural networks (CNN) [29]. The network synthesizes a conditional template for a given attribute value and produces a deformation field that aligns the conditional template with an input image. Our paper builds on this prior work but introduces a different approach. Unlike [29], we learn a function that computes a deformation field that warps a universal (unconditional) population template. This way, we are explicitly modeling morphological changes associated with the attributes as a diffeomorphic deformation (i.e. shape and size variation). In contrast, previous works involving the estimation of multiple (conditional) templates, including [29] allowed these templates to have different appearances.

3 Proposed Method

We adopt a template t that assigns probabilistic labels at each voxel. This can describe an unconditional prior on an individual segmentation image s:

$$p(s; t) = \frac{1}{Z} \exp \left(\text{SoftDice}(s, t) \right), \tag{1}$$

where SoftDice is the soft Dice between the two segmentation maps [32] and Z is the partition function. We are interested in modifying the prior as a function of demographic and/or clinical variables that are collected in an attribute vector a. Thus, our objective is to learn the conditional distribution of s given a set of attributes and a template $p(s|a; t)$:

$$p(s|a; t) = \int p(s|z; t) p(z|a) dz. \tag{2}$$

where z is a latent embedding vector that parameterizes the attribute-specific deformation of the template, i.e., ϕ_z. In our implementation, z is of size $5 \times 6 \times 7 \times 128$ and follows a Gaussian distribution

$$p(z|a) = \mathcal{N}(z; \mu_a, \Sigma_a), \tag{3}$$

where μ_a and Σ_a are the mean and diagonal covariance matrix, respectively. ϕ_z is computed via a series of up-sampling and convolution layers (details below).

For the likelihood term $p(s|z; t)$, we assume that s is generated by warping the template t with the deformation field ϕ_z:

$$p(s|z; t) \propto \exp \left(\text{SoftDice}(s, t \circ \phi_z) \right). \tag{4}$$

The conditional prior $p(z|a)$ captures the dependency between the template and attributes. Equation (2) is computationally intractable, and we rely on Monte Carlo samples to approximate the expectation:

$$p(s|a; t) = \mathop{\mathbb{E}}_{z \sim p(z|a)} p(s|z; t) \approx \frac{1}{K} \sum_{k=1}^{K} p(s|z_k; t), \text{ where } z_k \sim p(z|a). \tag{5}$$

We implemented parts of the model with neural networks. Details of our architecture can be found in Fig. 1. We use a fully-connected layer to parameterize $p(z|a)$. For a given set of attributes, the network outputs a mean μ_a, and

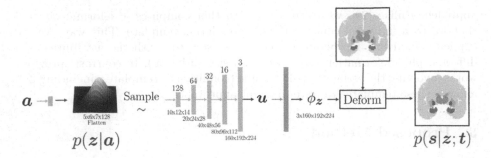

→ FC, ReLU
⇢ T.Conv, ReLU
⤳ Integration Layer (Scaling and Squaring)

Fig. 1. Proposed architecture. Attributes are passed to a fully-connected network (FC) and rectified linear unit (ReLU) to obtain the mean and variance of a multivariate Gaussian. Samples from z are up-sampled using $2 \times 2 \times 2$ transpose convolution (T.Conv) with a stride of 2. The last layer before the velocity field u does not have a ReLU. Scaling and squaring are used to integrate u [31]. The deformed template is obtained by $t \circ \phi_z$

variance Σ_a. As is common in Monte Carlo based deep learning techniques, a single instance of z is sampled using the reparametrization trick [35]. The sample is reshaped to a small cube. Then, a series of convolutional layers with kernel $2 \times 2 \times 2$ and stride of 2 are used to upsample the latent space z. We repeat this process until we have a tensor with the same size as the template t. This tensor is the "stationary" velocity field u, which parameterizes a diffeomorphic deformation, as in [31]. Thus the final deformation can be computed via applying the following ordinary differential equation:

$$\frac{\partial \phi_z}{\partial \tau} = u\left(\phi_z^{\tau}\right), \tag{6}$$

which describes a particle flowing according to a stationary velocity field. As we integrate over time, we start from an identity transformation at $\tau = 0$ to the final deformation ϕ_z at $\tau = 1$. This integration can be approximated in a neural network with a scaling and squaring layer [31,39].

4   Experiments

4.1   Dataset

To demonstrate the ability of our model to deform a brain template given a wide range of attributes, we used 3D brain segmentations of T1-weighted

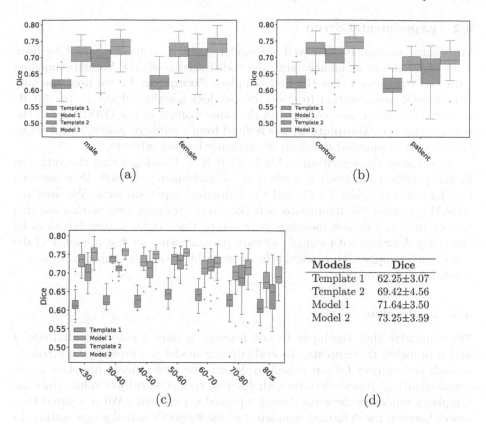

Fig. 2. Dice scores between individual segmentations and templates. **Template 1** is the un-deformed template from a single subject. **Template 2** uses un-deformed template from a multi-subject probabilitistic atlas. **Model 1** or **2** learns to apply an attribute-specific deformation to Template 1 or 2, respectively. Similarly, (A-C) Box-plot of Dice score across different groups of attributes. (D) Overall Dice score for different models. Mean ± standard deviation.

MRI scans from the OASIS-1 dataset[1] [33]. Using FreeSurfer [34], we performed skull stripping, bias-field correction, intensity normalization, affine registration to Talairach space, resampling to 1mm^3 isotropic resolution, and segmentation into 12 regions of interest (listed in caption of Fig. 3). Each segmentation was visually inspected for quality assurance. We used 415 subjects (255 females), with ages ranging from 18 to 96 years old (52.8 ± 25 years). The dataset includes 100 subjects diagnosed with probable Alzheimer's disease (AD). We randomly picked 375 subjects for training and the remaining 40 were reserved for testing. We ensured that the age distribution was consistent between the training the test samples.

---

[1] https://www.oasis-brains.org/.

4.2   Experimental Setup

We wanted to evaluate how well our model is able to deform a template given a set of attributes a, namely: sex, age and diagnosis of AD. We experimented with two templates t. For the first template (**Template 1**), we used the one-hot encoded segmentation from an independent healthy subject in the MCIC dataset [37], which was processed in the same manner as the OASIS data. The second template (**Template 2**) was derived from a publicly available probabilistic atlas [38], computed based on 20 manually labeled subjects.

Optimizing the logarithm of Eq. 5 (with $K = 1$ and ignoring the variation in the partition function) is equivalent to maximizing the soft Dice between the deformed template $t \circ \phi_z$ and the individual input subjects. We used the ADAM optimizer [36] to optimize soft Dice in the training data, with a learning rate of 10^{-4} and default moments parameters. Once trained, templates can be efficiently deformed with a single forward pass, allowing for fast inference of the conditional template. Our model is freely available https://github.com/evanmy/conditional_deformation.

4.3   Evaluation

We emphasize that the input to our network is only a subject's attribute a and a probabilistic template. To evaluate our model, we provide the attribute of each test subject for our model to deform the probabilistic template t. We repeated all experiments 5 times with different train/test subject splits. Only the templates remained the same during repeated experiments. We computed Dice scores between the deformed template and the subject's actual segmentation. In Fig. 2d, we can see that our model is able individualize the template in order to account attribute specific characteristics. The performance of the model depends on the quality of the template. The model that learns to deform a single subject template (**Model 1**) does not perform as well as a model using the probabilistic template that was constructed from multiple subjects (**Model 2**). In Fig. 2a-c, we show the boxplots of grouped Dice scores according to different attribute configurations. Regardless of the grouping, the deformed templates achieved better alignment of regions than the corresponding templates.

4.4   Visualization of Attribute-Specific Templates

Our framework enables us to efficiently create a template for any configuration of attribute values, which we think is a unique way to interrogate associations between brain anatomy and demographic or clinical variables. In Fig. 3a, **Model 2** is used to deform the template for a range of attributes. For example, ventricular enlargement (green regions) is substantial in a healthy female, going from 20 to 70 years old. Similarly, AD-associated deformation of ventricles in a 70y old female is evident. Other brain regions' shapes and sizes vary with age and AD too. In Fig. 3b, we visualize the change in total normalized[2] grey matter (GM)

---

[2] Divided by the total WM/GM volume of a 20 year old male or female.

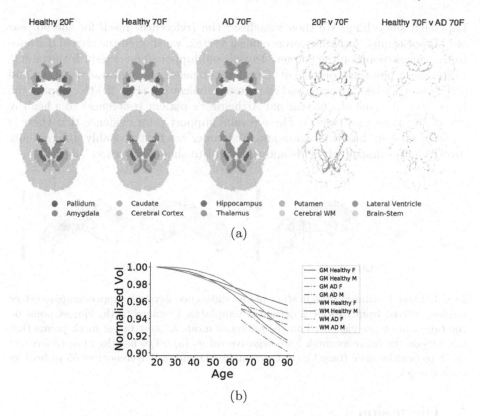

Healthy 20F   Healthy 70F   AD 70F   20F v 70F   Healthy 70F v AD 70F

● Pallidum   ● Caudate   ● Hippocampus   ● Putamen   ● Lateral Ventricle
● Amygdala   ● Cerebral Cortex   ● Thalamus   ● Cerebral WM   ● Brain-Stem

(a)

(b)

Fig. 3. (A) Coronal and axial views of **Model 2** deformed templates for 20 and 70 year old healthy female, and 70 year old female AD patient. Difference maps between pairs of deformed templates are shown in last two columns. White pixels indicate that the compared templates have same label. Colored pixels show the label for the second template. (B) Changes of deformed template's grey matter (GM) and white matter (WM) volumes over age for different attributes. Each regional volume was normalized with respect to a 20 year old healthy male or female. (Color figure online)

or white matter (WM) volume as a function of age and AD status. Associated monotonic and non-linear atrophy patterns are apparent.

4.5   Shape Analysis

We can use the learned model to further investigate and visualize shape changes associated with specific variables. In this experiment, we wanted to capture the effect of aging and AD on the shape of the hippocampus, an anatomical structure that is strongly associated with both attributes [40]. In Fig. 4a, we visualize the difference in hippocampal shape between 18 and 90 years, for a healthy male. We used **Model 2** to create a whole-brain, volumetric template for these attribute values. We isolated the hippocampi and applied morphological opening to remove noise. The binary masks were then converted to a mesh and was smoothed with

Laplacian smoothing. We then visualized the (reference) mesh for the 90-year old hippocampus. At each reference mesh vertex, we showed the signed distance to the closest point on the (target) 18-year old hippocampus mesh. If the closest target mesh point was outside of the reference mesh, the sign was negative; and otherwise positive. We employed the same visualization (Fig. 4b) to compare the hippocampal shape of a 65 year old Alzheimer's patient (reference) to a healthy one of the same age (target). These results support prior evidence that there is regional atrophy linked to aging and Alzheimer's, which probably differentially involve hippocampal sub-fields and thus lead to shape differences [40].

(a)   (b)

Fig. 4. Signed distance visualization of the difference between hippcocampal surface meshes derived from **Model 2** deformed templates. Distance to the closest point on the target mesh are visualized on the reference mesh. Closest target mesh points that fall outside the reference mesh have negative value. (a) 90 yo healthy male (reference) vs 18 yo healthy male (target); (b) 65 yo male AD patient (reference) vs 65 yo healthy male (target).

5 Discussion

We introduced a novel framework to learn a deformable template, where the deformation is a function of attributes such as age, sex or diseases status. We believe our modeling approach has at least three different use cases. First, this model can be used as a subject-specific prior in a segmentation framework. Our results suggest that a subject-specific prior can yield improved quality segmentations than a model based on a single global prior. Second, our framework can be used to interrogate morphological changes associated with certain variables of interest. In our experiments, we demonstrated how we can visualize shape changes linked to aging and Alzheimer's disease. Finally, we believe that the proposed framework can be useful to normalize for confounding variables. The conventional approach in computational anatomy is to spatially register with a single template and then control for confounding variables such as aging by including them as regresors in subsequent statistical analyses. This approach cannot account for non-linear effects. Instead, one can use the proposed framework that would allow us to directly normalize for nuisance variation in shape and size. We will explore this direction in future research.

References

1. Passe, T.J., et al.: Age and sex effects on brain morphology. Prog. Neuropsychopharmacol. Biol. Psychiatry **21**, 1231–1237 (1997)

2. Raz, N., et al.: Aging, sexual dimorphism, and hemispheric asymmetry of the cerebral cortex: replicability of regional differences in volume. Neurobiol. Aging **25**(3), 377–396 (2004)
3. Raz, N., et al.: Regional brain changes in aging healthy adults: general trends, individual differences and modifiers. Cereb. Cortex **15**(11), 1676–1689 (2005)
4. Hedden, T., Gabrieli, J.D.E.: Insights into the ageing mind: a view from cognitive neuroscience. Nat. Rev. Neurosci. **5**(2), 87–96 (2004)
5. Fotenos, A.F., et al.: Normative estimates of cross-sectional and longitudinal brain volume decline in aging and AD. Neurology **64**(6), 1032–1039 (2005)
6. Serrano-Pozo, A., et al.: Neuropathological alterations in Alzheimer disease. Cold Spring Harbor Perspect. Med. **1**(1), a006189 (2011)
7. Vita, A., et al.: Brain morphology in first-episode schizophrenia: a meta-analysis of quantitative magnetic resonance imaging studies. Schizophr. Res. **82**(1), 75–88 (2006)
8. Ng, B., Toews, M., Durrleman, S., Shi, Y.: Shape analysis for brain structures. In: Li, S., Tavares, J.M.R.S. (eds.) Shape Analysis in Medical Image Analysis. LNCVB, vol. 14, pp. 3–49. Springer, Cham (2014). https://doi.org/10.1007/978-3-319-03813-1_1
9. Frisoni, G.B., et al.: The clinical use of structural MRI in Alzheimer disease. Nat. Rev. Neurol. **6**(2), 67–77 (2010)
10. Joshi, S., et al.: Unbiased diffeomorphic atlas construction for computational anatomy. NeuroImage **23**, S151–S160 (2004)
11. Ma, J., et al.: Bayesian template estimation in computational anatomy. NeuroImage **42**(1), 252–261 (2008)
12. Grenander, U., Miller, M.I.: Computational anatomy: an emerging discipline. Q. Appl. Math. **56**(4), 617–694 (1998)
13. Sandor, S., Leahy, R.: Surface-based labeling of cortical anatomy using a deformable atlas. IEEE Trans. Med. Imaging **16**(1), 41–54 (1997)
14. Ashburner, J., Friston, K.J.: Voxel-based morphometry-the methods. Neuroimage **11**(6), 805–821 (2000)
15. Oliveira, F.P., Tavares, J.M.R.: Medical image registration: a review. Comput. Methods Biomech. Biomed. Eng. **17**(2), 73–93 (2014)
16. Ribbens, A., et al.: Unsupervised segmentation, clustering, and groupwise registration of heterogeneous populations of brain MR images. IEEE Trans. Med. Imaging **33**(2), 201–224 (2013)
17. Rueckert, D., et al.: Nonrigid registration using free-form deformations: application to breast MR images. IEEE Trans. Med. Imaging **18**(8), 712–721 (1999)
18. Bajcsy, R., Kovačič, S.: Multiresolution elastic matching. Comput. Vis. Graph. Image Process. **46**(1), 1–21 (1989)
19. Horn, B.K.P, Schunck, B.G.: Determining optical flow. In: Techniques and Applications of Image Understanding, vol. 281. International Society for Optics and Photonics (1981)
20. Thirion, J.-P.: Image matching as a diffusion process: an analogy with Maxwell's demons. Med. Image Anal. **2**, 243–260 (1998)
21. Beg, M.F., et al.: Computing large deformation metric mappings via geodesic flows of diffeomorphisms. Int. J. Comput. Vis. **61**(2), 139–157 (2005)
22. Joshi, S.C., Miller, M.I.: Landmark matching via large deformation diffeomorphisms. IEEE Trans. Image Process. **9**(8), 1357–1370 (2000)
23. Ashburner, J.: A fast diffeomorphic image registration algorithm. Neuroimage **38**(1), 95–113 (2007)

24. Avants, B.B., et al.: Symmetric diffeomorphic image registration with cross-correlation: evaluating automated labeling of elderly and neurodegenerative brain. Med. Image Anal. **12**(1), 26–41 (2008)
25. Vercauteren, T., et al.: Diffeomorphic demons: efficient non-parametric image registration. NeuroImage **45**(1), S61–S72 (2009)
26. Balakrishnan, G., et al.: VoxelMorph: a learning framework for deformable medical image registration. IEEE Trans. Med. Imaging **38**(8), 1788–1800 (2019)
27. de Vos, B.D., Berendsen, F.F., Viergever, M.A., Staring, M., Išgum, I.: End-to-end unsupervised deformable image registration with a convolutional neural network. In: Cardoso, M.J., et al. (eds.) DLMIA/ML-CDS -2017. LNCS, vol. 10553, pp. 204–212. Springer, Cham (2017). https://doi.org/10.1007/978-3-319-67558-9_24
28. Sokooti, H., de Vos, B., Berendsen, F., Lelieveldt, B.P.F., Išgum, I., Staring, M.: Nonrigid image registration using multi-scale 3D convolutional neural networks. In: Descoteaux, M., Maier-Hein, L., Franz, A., Jannin, P., Collins, D.L., Duchesne, S. (eds.) MICCAI 2017. LNCS, vol. 10433, pp. 232–239. Springer, Cham (2017). https://doi.org/10.1007/978-3-319-66182-7_27
29. Dalca, A., et al.: Learning conditional deformable templates with convolutional networks. In: Advances in Neural Information Processing Systems (2019)
30. Sabuncu, M.R., Balci, S.K., Golland, P.: Discovering modes of an image population through mixture modeling. In: Metaxas, D., Axel, L., Fichtinger, G., Székely, G. (eds.) MICCAI 2008. LNCS, vol. 5242, pp. 381–389. Springer, Heidelberg (2008). https://doi.org/10.1007/978-3-540-85990-1_46
31. Dalca, A.V., et al.: Unsupervised learning of probabilistic diffeomorphic registration for images and surfaces. Med. Image Anal. **57**, 226–236 (2019)
32. Milletari, F., Navab, N., Ahmadi, S.-A.: V-net: fully convolutional neural networks for volumetric medical image segmentation. In: 2016 Fourth International Conference on 3D Vision (3DV). IEEE (2016)
33. Marcus, D.S., et al.: Open access series of imaging studies (OASIS): cross-sectional MRI data in young, middle aged, nondemented, and demented older adults. J. Cogn. Neurosci. **19**, 1498–1507 (2007)
34. Fischl, B.: Freesurfer. Neuroimage **62**(2), 774–781 (2012)
35. Kingma, D.P., Welling, M.: Auto-encoding variational bayes. arXiv preprint arXiv:1312.6114 (2013)
36. Kingma, D.P., Ba, J.: Adam: a method for stochastic optimization. arXiv preprint arXiv:1412.6980 (2014)
37. Gollub, R.L., et al.: The MCIC collection: a shared repository of multi-modal, multi-site brain image data from a clinical investigation of schizophrenia. Neuroinformatics **11**(3), 367–388 (2013)
38. Puonti, O., Iglesias, J.E., Van Leemput, K.: Fast and sequence-adaptivewhole-brain segmentation using parametric bayesian modeling. NeuroImage **143**, 235–249 (2016)
39. Arsigny, V., Commowick, O., Pennec, X., Ayache, N.: A log-euclidean framework for statistics on diffeomorphisms. In: Larsen, R., Nielsen, M., Sporring, J. (eds.) MICCAI 2006. LNCS, vol. 4190, pp. 924–931. Springer, Heidelberg (2006). https://doi.org/10.1007/11866565_113
40. Adler, D.H., et al.: Characterizing the human hippocampus in aging and Alzheimer's disease using a computational atlas derived from ex vivo MRI and histology. Proc. Nat. Acad. Sci. **115**(16), 4252–4257 (2018)

Demographic-Guided Attention in Recurrent Neural Networks for Modeling Neuropathophysiological Heterogeneity

Nicha C. Dvornek[1,2]([⊠]), Xiaoxiao Li[2], Juntang Zhuang[2], Pamela Ventola[3], and James S. Duncan[1,2,4,5]

[1] Radiology & Biomedical Imaging, Yale School of Medicine, New Haven, CT, USA
nicha.dvornek@yale.edu
[2] Biomedical Engineering, Yale University, New Haven, CT, USA
[3] Child Study Center, Yale School of Medicine, New Haven, CT, USA
[4] Electrical Engineering, Yale University, New Haven, CT, USA
[5] Statistics and Data Science, Yale University, New Haven, CT, USA

Abstract. Heterogeneous presentation of a neurological disorder suggests potential differences in the underlying pathophysiological changes that occur in the brain. We propose to model heterogeneous patterns of functional network differences using a demographic-guided attention (DGA) mechanism for recurrent neural network models for prediction from functional magnetic resonance imaging (fMRI) time-series data. The context computed from the DGA head is used to help focus on the appropriate functional networks based on individual demographic information. We demonstrate improved classification on 3 subsets of the ABIDE I dataset used in published studies that have previously produced state-of-the-art results, evaluating performance under a leave-one-site-out cross-validation framework for better generalizeability to new data. Finally, we provide examples of interpreting functional network differences based on individual demographic variables.

1 Introduction

Functional magnetic resonance imaging (fMRI) has begun to play a large role in characterizing the neuropathophysiology of psychiatric disorders. One example is in the characterization of autism spectrum disorder (ASD), a neurodevelopmental disorder that affects communication and behavior. ASD is extremely heterogeneous, presenting with a wide range of symptoms and severity of impairments. Early fMRI studies investigated small datasets with imposed homogeneity, e.g., restricting to one gender, age group, or level of functioning. However, this resulted in smaller datasets, largely irreproducible results and lack of generalization to new datasets. More recently, the popular large public Autism Brain Imaging Data Exchange (ABIDE) I resting-state fMRI dataset [4] has undergone extensive analysis, including the application of machine learning to classify

© Springer Nature Switzerland AG 2020
M. Liu et al. (Eds.): MLMI 2020, LNCS 12436, pp. 363–372, 2020.
https://doi.org/10.1007/978-3-030-59861-7_37

ASD and healthy controls (HC) for the purpose of discovering neuroimaging biomarkers of ASD. However, even with the large amount of neuroimaging data, achieving high classification performance has been a challenge, likely due in part to both the heterogeneity of the sample populations of each imaging site and the heterogeneity of the underlying neurological mechanisms of the disorder itself. Evidence for these potential reasons includes the much poorer performance of leave-one-site-out cross-validation (LOSO CV) compared to intrasite k-fold cross-validation [1,9].

One approach to mitigating the heterogeneity is to incorporate demographic information into the classification problem. Here, we refer to demographic variables as non-imaging, scalar variables that are often measured and easy to obtain, such as gender, age, or IQ. Demographic information can be incorporated in different ways depending on the classification model. For example, the demographic information can be fused at different layers in a standard feedforward neural network [7,12] or used as targets for prediction [7]. Furthermore, demographic information can be combined in model specific ways, e.g., to define the edges in graph-based models [13] or to set the initial state of recurrent neural network models [6,11]. However, none of these approaches aim to modulate the underlying neurological differences that may be describing the heterogeneity in ASD.

To model disorder heterogeneity in terms of changes in the underlying functional processing, we propose a demographic-guided attention module to enhance a recurrent neural network model for processing fMRI time-series data. While the attention scores are computed across time, we can interpret the resulting context as guiding attention to different functional networks. In addition to using the demographic information to help identify which functional networks to attend to in classifying ASD or HC, we propose a novel loss for computing more diverse queries for each attention head to better model the sample heterogeneity. We compare our proposed methods to other ways of handling demographic data on 3 subsets of the ABIDE dataset, matched to previous studies that have previously demonstrated state-of-the-art results from the fMRI data alone. We achieve some of the highest accuracy of ABIDE classification under LOSO CV. Finally, we give examples of functional networks that may undergo diverse processing in ASD based on individual demographic factors.

2   Methods

We build on recent models for predicting from fMRI time-series data that use recurrent neural networks with long short-term memory (LSTM). To model the heterogeneity of ASD, we apply a generalized attention mechanism that is guided by individual demographic characteristics. The context learned from the attention mechanism is then used to bias the LSTM outputs, allowing the model to focus on different functional networks based on individual non-imaging characteristics (Fig. 1).

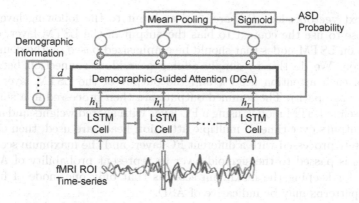

Fig. 1. Demographic-guided attention network for classification of ASD/HC from fMRI. (Color figure online)

2.1 Network Architecture

Baseline LSTM for fMRI Time-Series. The baseline LSTM network to predict from fMRI time-series was first proposed by Dvornek et al. [5]. The fMRI time-series with length T from regions of interest (ROIs) in a predefined brain parcellation is first input to the LSTM layer. Then the output of the LSTM cell at each timepoint $h_t \in R^n$ is input to a fully connected (FC) layer with weights shared across time. The outputs of the FC layer are averaged across time and input to a sigmoid activation function to produce the probability of ASD label.

Demographic-Guided Attention. We propose to incorporate functional network differences resulting from disease heterogeneity through a generalized attention mechanism [14]. The attention mechanism can be described as a function mapping a query and key-value pair to some output, often referred to as the context or a head. In our work, the query is defined by the demographic information, and the key and value are defined by the outputs of the LSTM layer h_t. Applying the scaled dot product attention [14], the context vector c is computed by

$$c = att\,(d, \{h_t\}) = \sum_{t=1}^{T} softmax\left[(W_q d)^T (W_k h_t)/\sqrt{m}\right] W_v h_t, \qquad (1)$$

where $d \in R^l$ is the vector of demographic information; $softmax\,[a_t] = \exp(a_t)/\sum_{j=1}^{T} \exp(a_j)$ with $a_t = (W_q d)^T (W_k h_t)/\sqrt{m}$; and $W_q \in R^{m \times l}$, $W_k \in R^{m \times n}$, and $W_v \in R^{m \times n}$ are weight matrices that operate on d or h_t to define the query, key, and value vectors, respectively. In this work, we set $m = n$.

Residual Connection for Modeling Heterogeneity. In standard attention approaches, the context vector is concatenated with the LSTM output [2] or the context vectors alone [14] are used as input to the following layers. Here, we propose to use the context to bias the output of the LSTM layer, changing the focus on LSTM nodes that should be emphasized based on the demographic information. We do this by simply adding a residual connection between the output of each attention head k and the output of the LSTM layer, $c_k + h_t$ (Fig. 1, orange path). The summed outputs are then processed in a similar way as the baseline LSTM model, using a FC layer with shared weights and averaging the FC outputs over time. If multiple attention heads are used, then each head is separately processed with a different FC layer, and the maximum score across the heads is passed to the sigmoid layer to represent probability of ASD. The rationale for keeping the maximum score is that only one mode of functional network patterns may be indicative of ASD.

2.2 Query Diversity Loss

A single attention module allows for attending to different LSTM nodes based on the demographic information. However, this assumes then that two individuals with the same demographic profile must share the same underlying neuropathology. To allow for even greater diversity in modeling disease heterogeneity, we can include more attention heads that will learn different contexts. To encourage the different attention heads to capture different underlying neuropathological modes, we propose the following query diversity loss (QDL):

$$L_{QD} = \sum_{i=1}^{N} \sum_{j=1}^{K-1} \sum_{k=j+1}^{K} \left| \frac{q_{ij}^T q_{ik}}{\|q_{ij}\| \|q_{ik}\|} \right| \tag{2}$$

where N is the number of subjects and $q_{ij} = W_{q_j} d_i$ is the n-dimensional query vector for attention head j. QDL computes the cosine proximity for all query vectors q_{ij} for subject i. Minimizing QDL thus encourages projection of the demographic information into orthogonal subspaces, which capture complementary information, before comparing to the keys to compute the attention scores.

The total loss L is then

$$L = L_C + \lambda L_{QD}, \tag{3}$$

where L_C is the classification loss (e.g., binary cross-entropy) and λ is a hyperpara meter controlling the contribution of QDL.

2.3 Interpretation of Attention as Neuropathological Heterogeneity

We first interpret each node of the LSTM as modeling a functional network. While different attribution methods can be applied, we follow Dvornek et al. and assign ROIs to a network if the LSTM weights for the ROI inputs have large magnitude (>3 standard deviations above mean weight magnitude) [5].

The proposed model uses the context computed by the demographic-guided attention module as a bias for the LSTM outputs. Since each node of the LSTM is interpreted as processing the signal corresponding to some functional network, we interpret the demographic information as providing context for deciding which functional networks should be given more attention in performing ASD classification, i.e., we measure the demographic-guided attention to a functional network f as $c(f)$. We then assess the coupling between a functional network and a demographic variable by computing the correlation between the demographic variable $d(i)$ and the context $c(f)$ for functional network f across subjects. Different patterns of attention for a functional network in different attention heads allows for modeling greater neuropathological heterogeneity.

3 Experiments

3.1 Data

We use resting-state fMRI data from the multisite ABIDE I dataset [4] which was released by the Preprocessed Connectomes Project [3]. To demonstrate robustness of our approach and directly compare with results from the literature, we analyzed the same subsets of data under the same preprocessing conditions as in 3 prior studies: Dataset 1 (DS1) from [5], with $N = 1100$ subjects, preprocessed using the Connectome Computation System pipeline, band-pass filtering and no global signal regression, and parcellated with the CC200 atlas; Dataset 2 (DS2) from [9], with $N = 1035$ subjects, preprocessed using the Configurable Pipeline for the Analysis of Connectomes, band-pass filtering and global signal regression, and parcellated with the CC200 atlas; and Dataset 3 (DS3) from [1], with $N = 870$ subjects, preprocessed using the same pipeline as in [9] but parcellated with the HO atlas.

The time-series for each ROI of each subject was standardized by subtracting the mean and dividing by the standard deviation and resampled to 2s intervals between time points to harmonize the sampling across acquisition sites. We augmented the dataset by a factor of 10 during training by extracting 10 randomly cropped windows with length $T = 90$ timepoints from each subject during each epoch. At test time, every possible window of 90 timepoints is extracted from the time-series data for each subject and input to the trained network. The predicted probability of ASD for a given subject was then computed as the proportion of windowed samples classified as ASD.

Demographic information included gender, age, handedness, full IQ, verbal IQ, performance IQ, and eye status during scanning. Missing IQ data were imputed based on other available IQ scores for the subject, where we approximated full IQ as the average of verbal IQ and performance IQ, and subjects with no available IQ scores were assigned scores of 100, which is the mean population IQ. Each demographic variable was standardized to lie in the range of $[-1,1]$.

3.2 Experimental Methods

Models for classification of ASD vs. HC were trained for each subset of the ABIDE dataset. We compared and implemented the following models which have the same underlying LSTM baseline architecture and incorporate demographic information: the proposed demographic-guided attention network (DGA); the DGA network without the residual connection, i.e. using the computed context alone (DGA-C); the baseline LSTM network combined with separately processed demographic information through late fusion as proposed in [7] (DFuse); the baseline LSTM network with the hidden state and cell state of the LSTM initialized based on the demographic information as proposed in [6] (DInit). Models were implemented in Keras, with 32 nodes for the LSTM. For regularziation, models were trained using a dropout layer before each fully connected layer (with 0.5 probability of node dropout). Optimization was performed using the Adam optimizer, with binary cross-entropy loss or with QDL as in Eq. 3 for DGA2, a batch size of 32, and early stopping based on validation loss and a patience of 5 epochs. DGA-based models were tested with 1 (DGA1) or 2 (DGA2) attention heads and QDL with $\lambda = 0.5$ (DGA2-QDL). In addition, we compared the original study for each dataset that used only imaging information.

To assess the implemented models, we used LOSO CV, repeating the CV 5 times and averaging the performance measures for each site across CV runs both with and without weighting by the number of subjects per test site. We chose the LOSO framework to better estimate the model generalizeability compared to the commonly employed stratified k-fold cross-validation, which gives overoptimistic results. We measured classification performance by computing the accuracy (ACC), true positive rate (TPR), true negative rate (TNR), and area under the receiver operating characteristic curve (AUC). We tested for differences against the baseline LSTM model by comparing the performance for the same left-out sites using two-tailed paired t-tests with a significance level of 0.05.

We also evaluated functional networks that were attended to based on individual demographic factors by applying the Neurosynth decoder [15], which correlates over 14000 fMRI studies with 1300 descriptors. For the 2-head attention model with QDL loss, we computed the correlation between the demographic variable $d(i)$ and the context for functional network f from each head $c_1(f)$ and $c_2(f)$ across the test ASD subjects. We analyzed the US and Yale site as their test accuracy was high (>75%) and they contained significant heterogeneity for the investigated demographic variables of age, gender, handedness, and full IQ. We then found the functional network f that resulted in the largest difference in correlation values for the 2 heads. The binary mask of the functional network of interest was then input to Neurosynth to assess neurocognitive processes associated with different modes of heterogeneity in ASD.

3.3   Classification Results

Classification results for each dataset are summarized in Tables 1, 2 and 3. The results using the method from the original study for DS1 and published in the original study for DS2 and DS3 use only fMRI data and are shown in the first entry. We notice that generally, the fusion model DFuse and LSTM initialization model DInit do not perform significantly differently from the baseline LSTM model, particularly for DS3. The DGA-based models that use the context alone

Table 1. DS1 classification results (N = 1100, 48.1% ASD)

Model	Leave-one-site-out				Weighted by # subjects/site		
	Mean (std) ACC (%)	Mean (std) TPR (%)	Mean (std) TNR (%)	Mean (std) AUC	Mean (std) ACC (%)	Mean (Std) TPR (%)	Mean (std) TNR (%)
Orig (LSTM) [5]	63.4 (0.7)	60.9 (1.2)	66.2 (0.5)	0.695 (0.006)	65.0 (0.7)	61.3 (1.3)	68.4 (1.2)
DFuse [7]	63.3 (1.2)	55.7 (3.3)$^\diamond$	70.7 (2.5)*	0.701 (0.017)	65.4 (1.3)	57.7 (3.3)	72.5 (3.3)
DInit [6]	65.4 (0.6)*	60.7 (1.2)	69.9 (0.6)*	0.709 (0.006)	**67.1 (0.7)***	62.6 (2.4)	71.3 (2.5)*
DGA1-C	64.4 (0.7)	**62.5 (0.6)**	66.3 (1.5)	0.710 (0.009)	65.9 (0.5)	**63.5 (1.4)**	68.1 (0.9)
DGA2-C	64.3 (1.2)	56.2 (2.3)$^\diamond$	71.8 (3.0)*	0.703 (0.006)	65.8 (1.1)	57.3 (1.7)$^\diamond$	73.8 (3.0)*
DGA1	63.8 (0.9)	61.5 (2.9)	66.1 (1.9)	0.702 (0.009)	65.7 (1.1)	**63.5 (3.0)**	67.7 (2.7)
DGA2	64.8 (2.4)	56.1 (3.8)	**73.1 (2.1)***	0.710 (0.011)	66.3 (1.6)	57.1 (3.2)$^\diamond$	**74.8 (2.5)***
DGA2-QDL	**65.5 (0.8)***	59.1 (2.3)	72.0 (2.4)*	**0.711 (0.006)**	66.8 (0.7)*	60.7 (1.3)	72.4 (1.9)

* Significantly different compared to LSTM with no demographic input ($p < 0.05$), with larger mean value.
$\diamond$ Significantly different compared to LSTM with no demographic input ($p < 0.05$), with smaller mean value.

Table 2. DS2 classification results (N = 1035, 48.8% ASD)

Model	Leave-one-site-out				Weighted by # subjects/site		
	Mean (std) ACC (%)	Mean (std) TPR (%)	Mean (std) TNR (%)	Mean (std) AUC	Mean (std) ACC (%)	Mean (std) TPR (%)	Mean (std) TNR (%)
Orig[†] [9]	65 (1.5)	69 (2.6)	62 (2.7)	–	65.4 (1.3)	68.1 (2.6)	62.3 (2.6)
LSTM [5]	63.6 (0.5)	55.2 (1.6)	71.9 (0.6)	0.709 (0.006)	65.6 (0.6)	58.2 (1.7)	72.7 (0.9)
DFuse [7]	65.5 (0.9)*	57.1 (0.6)	73.5 (1.6)	0.713 (0.006)	67.2 (0.6)	61.2 (1.2)	72.8 (1.0)
DInit [6]	65.8 (0.8)*	58.1 (0.4)	72.9 (1.4)	0.720 (0.009)	**67.5 (1.1)***	61.8 (1.6)*	72.9 (3.2)
DGA1-C	65.6 (1.7)*	61.1 (1.6)	69.6 (1.1)	0.713 (0.011)	66.8 (1.6)	**64.1 (2.0)***	69.3 (1.9)
DGA2-C	65.8 (0.9)*	52.6 (2.4)	**78.3 (1.7)***	0.719 (0.009)	67.2 (1.2)*	55.9 (2.4)	**78.0 (0.8)***
DGA1	66.1 (1.5)*	**61.3 (2.5)***	70.4 (1.4)	0.719 (0.011)	67.4 (1.7)*	63.6 (2.3)*	70.9 (1.7)
DGA2	65.5 (1.0)*	54.3 (1.5)	76.5 (1.4)*	0.716 (0.015)	67.1 (1.4)	57.6 (1.3)	76.1 (2.3)*
DGA2-QDL	**66.4 (0.4)***	58.0 (1.9)*	74.2 (2.0)	**0.722 (0.006)**	67.4 (0.5)*	61.3 (1.7)*	73.1 (1.9)

[†] Values taken from the literature, reflecting one round of LOSO CV.
* Significantly different compared to LSTM with no demographic input ($p < 0.05$).

Table 3. DS3 classification results (N = 860, 46.1% ASD)

Model	Leave-one-site-out				Weighted by # subjects/site		
	Mean (std) ACC (%)	Mean (std) TPR (%)	Mean (std) TNR (%)	Mean (std) AUC	Mean (std) ACC (%)	Mean (std) TPR (%)	Mean (std) TNR (%)
Orig[†] [1]	63.6 (6.2)	59.8 (10.3)	66.7 (12.8)	–	–	–	–
LSTM [5]	63.8 (0.4)	50.3 (1.9)	75.5 (1.4)	0.694 (0.012)	65.3 (0.6)	53.9 (2.3)	75.0 (1.9)
DFuse [7]	65.6 (1.6)	52.7 (1.8)	76.4 (3.0)	0.714 (0.007)	67.1 (0.8)*	56.9 (2.5)	75.8 (1.4)
DInit [6]	64.5 (1.2)	50.5 (2.2)	76.4 (1.9)	0.702 (0.013)	66.3 (0.8)	55.5 (2.4)	75.5 (2.4)
DGA1-C	65.5 (1.2)*	**55.3 (1.6)***	74.5 (2.1)	0.708 (0.010)	66.8 (0.9)*	59.0 (2.4)*	73.5 (3.4)
DGA2-C	65.9 (1.6)	52.6 (1.7)	78.6 (2.0)	**0.717 (0.014)**	67.2 (1.2)	55.2 (1.8)	78.6 (1.5)
DGA1	65.8 (0.1)*	**55.3 (1.1)***	75.2 (1.2)	0.712 (0.006)	66.8 (0.7)*	**59.1 (1.8)***	73.3 (1.5)
DGA2	**66.8 (1.0)***	51.2 (2.1)	**80.0 (2.7)***	0.714 (0.005)	**68.0 (1.0)***	54.0 (2.5)	**80.0 (2.7)***
DGA2-QDL	66.0 (1.1)	53.5 (1.4)	76.8 (3)	0.709 (0.006)	67.0 (0.9)*	57.6 (2.9)	75.2 (3.3)

[†] Values obtained from corresponding author of [1]reflecting one round of LOSO CV.
*Significantly different compared to LSTM with no demographic input ($p < 0.05$).

as the input to the FC (DGA1-C and DGA2-C) tend to perform about the same (DS1) or better (DS2 and DS3) than the non-DGA models. Adding in the residual connection for DGA1 and DGA2 results in similar (DS1 and DS2) or better (DS3) results than the DGA-C models. Finally, the DGA2-QDL model resulted in the top performance for DS1 and DS2 as measured by accuracy and AUC.

To better understand the performance over all the datasets, we scored each model by the number of performance measures that significantly improved over the baseline LSTM, minus the number of measures that significantly worsened compared to baseline, plus the number of top ranked measures. The models ranked in order of increasing performance was then DFuse, DGA2-C, DInit, DGA1-C, DGA1, DGA2-QDL, DGA2. Thus, DGA-based models generally performed better than other demographic models; 2-headed attention was generally better than 1; and the proposed residual connection for using the context as a bias to the LSTM outputs generally performed better than using the context alone. The reason for DGA2-QDL's lower ranking is due to the performance on DS3; we posit that the lower number of subjects in this dataset led to less heterogeneity, thus making it difficult to find two disparate attention modes, which QDL is trying to recover by minimizing the projection space similarity.

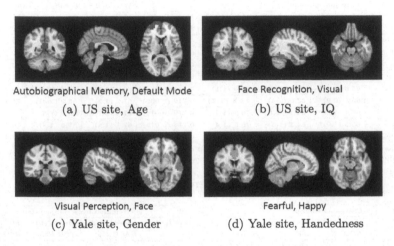

Autobiographical Memory, Default Mode

(a) US site, Age

Face Recognition, Visual

(b) US site, IQ

Visual Perception, Face

(c) Yale site, Gender

Fearful, Happy

(d) Yale site, Handedness

Fig. 2. Functional networks from the DGA2-QDL model trained on DS2 which had largest difference between the correlations of the listed demographic variable with the two attention measures $c_1(f)$ and $c_2(f)$ for ASD subjects in the listed test site. The top associated cognitive functions decoded by Neurosynth for each network are shown.

3.4 Demographic-Guided Heterogeneity of Functional Processing

We explored the functional networks from the best model for DS2, DGA2-QDL, that corresponded to the most diverse outputs by the 2 attention heads. These different modes of the model's response to a functional network may correspond to potentially different mechanisms of ASD pathophysiology. Resulting functional networks and the top 2 associated Neurosynth cognitive terms are shown in Fig. 2. The functional networks highlight regions that are often associated with ASD (e.g., Fig. 2(b) and (c), visual perception and face processing [10]), and are also potentially associated with the demographic variable of interest (e.g., Fig. 2(a), default mode network changes with age [8]).

4 Conclusions

We have presented a novel demographic-guided attention mechanism for modeling the heterogeneity in neuropathophysiology of ASD. We achieved higher ASD classification performance on several ABIDE datasets and preprocessing conditions under a leave-one-site-out cross-validation framework, demonstrating improved generalization to data from new imaging sites. The success of having multiple attention modes for modeling the different neural mechanisms associated with ASD may help partially explain some of the conflicting results in the ASD literature (e.g., hyper- vs. hypo-connectivity), as our classification models improve once we account for the heterogeneity of the disorder.

References

1. Abraham, A., et al.: Deriving reproducible biomarkers from multi-site resting-state data: an autism-based example. Neuroimage **147**, 736–745 (2017)
2. Bahdanau, D., Cho, K., Bengio, Y.: Neural machine translation by jointly learning to align and translate. In: ICLR 2015 (2015)
3. Craddock, C., et al.: The neuro bureau preprocessing initiative: open sharing of preprocessed neuroimaging data and derivatives. In: Neuroinformatics (2013)
4. Martino, D., et al.: The autism brain imaging data exchange: towards a large-scale evaluation of the intrinsic brain architecture in autism. Mol. Psychiatry **19**, 659–667 (2014)
5. Dvornek, N.C., Ventola, P., Pelphrey, K.A., Duncan, J.S.: Identifying autism from resting-state fMRI using long short-term memory networks. In: Wang, Q., Shi, Y., Suk, H.-I., Suzuki, K. (eds.) MLMI 2017. LNCS, vol. 10541, pp. 362–370. Springer, Cham (2017). https://doi.org/10.1007/978-3-319-67389-9_42
6. Dvornek, N.C., Yang, D., Ventola, P., Duncan, J.S.: Learning generalizable recurrent neural networks from small task-fMRI datasets. In: Frangi, A.F., Schnabel, J.A., Davatzikos, C., Alberola-López, C., Fichtinger, G. (eds.) MICCAI 2018. LNCS, vol. 11072, pp. 329–337. Springer, Cham (2018). https://doi.org/10.1007/978-3-030-00931-1_38
7. Dvornek, N.C., Ventola, P., Duncan, J.S.: Combining phenotypic and resting-state fMRI data for autism classification with recurrent neural networks. In: ISBI (2018)
8. Fair, D.A., et al.: The maturing architecture of the brain's default network. Proc. Nat. Acad. Sci. **105**(10), 4028–4032 (2008)
9. Heinsfeld, A.S., Franco, A.R., Craddock, R.C., Buchweitz, A., Meneguzzi, F.: Identification of autism spectrum disorder using deep learning and the abide dataset. Neuroimage Clin. **17**, 16–23 (2018)
10. Kaiser, M., et al.: Neural signatures of autism. Proc. Natl. Acad. Sci. U S A **107**, 21223–21228 (2010)
11. Karpathy, A., Fei-Fei, L.: Deep visual-semantic alignments for generating image descriptions. IEEE Trans. Pattern Anal. Mach. Intell. **39**, 664–676 (2016)
12. Ngiam, J., Khosla, A., Kim, M., Nam, J., Lee, H., Ng, A.Y.: Multimodal deep learning. In: The 28th International Conference on Machine Learning (2011)

13. Parisot, S., et al.: Spectral graph convolutions for population-based disease prediction. In: Descoteaux, M., Maier-Hein, L., Franz, A., Jannin, P., Collins, D.L., Duchesne, S. (eds.) MICCAI 2017. LNCS, vol. 10435, pp. 177–185. Springer, Cham (2017). https://doi.org/10.1007/978-3-319-66179-7_21
14. Vaswani, A., et al.: Attention is all you need. In: 31st Conference on Neural Information Processing Systems (NIPS 2017) (2017)
15. Yarkoni, T., Poldrack, R.A., Nichols, T.E., Van Essen, D.C., Wagerss, T.D.: Large-scale automated synthesis of human functional neuroimaging data. Nat. Methods 8, 665–670 (2011). www.neurosynth.org

Unsupervised Learning for Spherical Surface Registration

Fenqiang Zhao[1,2], Zhengwang Wu[2], Li Wang[2], Weili Lin[2], Shunren Xia[1],
Dinggang Shen[2], Gang Li[2(✉)], and The UNC/UMN Baby Connectome
Project Consortium

[1] Key Laboratory of Biomedical Engineering of Ministry of Education,
Zhejiang University, Hangzhou, China
[2] Department of Radiology and BRIC, University of North Carolina at Chapel Hill,
Chapel Hill, NC, USA
gang_li@med.unc.edu

Abstract. Current spherical surface registration methods achieve good
performance on alignment and spatial normalization of cortical surfaces
across individuals in neuroimaging analysis. However, they are computationally intensive, since they have to optimize an objective function
independently for each pair of surfaces. In this paper, we present a
fast learning-based algorithm that makes use of the recent development
in spherical Convolutional Neural Networks (CNNs) for spherical cortical surface registration. Given a set of surface pairs without supervised
information such as ground truth deformation fields or anatomical landmarks, we formulate the registration as a parametric function and learn
its parameters by enforcing the feature similarity between one surface
and the other one warped by the estimated deformation field using the
function. Then, given a new pair of surfaces, we can quickly infer the
spherical deformation field registering one surface to the other one. We
model this parametric function using three orthogonal Spherical U-Nets
and use spherical transform layers to warp the spherical surfaces, while
imposing smoothness constraints on the deformation field. All the layers
in the network are well-defined and differentiable, thus the parameters
can be effectively learned. We show that our method achieves accurate
cortical alignment results on 102 subjects, comparable to two state-of-
the-art methods: Spherical Demons and MSM, while runs much faster.

Keywords: Spherical U-Net · Cortical surface registration

1 Introduction

Cortical surface registration is a fundamental task in population-based neuroimaging studies and has been an important research topic for decades. Accurate registration of the convoluted cerebral cortex is important for establishing
cortical correspondences across individuals and time points, thus facilitating the
subsequent analysis, e.g.., group comparison or longitudinal studies [8].

© Springer Nature Switzerland AG 2020
M. Liu et al. (Eds.): MLMI 2020, LNCS 12436, pp. 373–383, 2020.
https://doi.org/10.1007/978-3-030-59861-7_38

Motivated by the inherent spherical topology of the cerebral cortex, many surface registration methods [3,14,19] model the cortical surface as a 2D closed manifold and map it to a sphere, which can thus offer a simpler and more accurate geometry for aligning cortical structure and function than 3D volumetric registration approaches [13]. These conventional methods are designed to solve an optimization problem in spherical space that aligns vertices with similar feature patterns, while enforcing smoothness constraints on the spherical deformation. For example, the popular FreeSurfer [3] registration algorithm calculates a dense displacement field for all the vertices by minimizing the mean squared distance between the source and target feature maps. Another popular registration method, Spherical Demons [19], uses the same similarity measure as FreeSurfer, but utilizes Demons algorithm [16] to greedily seek the locally optimal displacement vectors on the tangent space by Gauss-Newton method. The fast convergence rate of Gauss-Newton method speeds up the registration process by a large margin, up to 2 min for registering two surfaces. Alternatively, MSM [14] solved a Markov Random Field (MRF) labelling model using discrete optimization for surface registration. Based on the rotation deformations, the regularization term in MSM penalizes the differences between adjacent vertices' rotation matrices. Some other related works have tried to enhance feature description more distinctively with spectral embedding features [9], use higher-order smoothness constraints [13], extend Demons to functional connectivity alignment [11], or perform intrinsic surface registration in the Laplacian embedding space [4].

However, all these methods have to optimize their objective functions and smooth the deformation fields for each pair of surfaces independently. This process is computationally intensive, and therefore very slow. According to our experiences, even the fastest Spherical Demons takes 2 min for registration of a pair of surfaces. In large-scale neuroimaging studies with hundreds or thousands of subjects, it still takes days for registering all the surfaces to an atlas.

Recently, learning-based methods have greatly advanced and accelerated 3D volumetric image registration in medical imaging [18], especially using the Convolutional Neural Network (CNN) models with GPU implementations [1,2,12]. These methods formulate the registration as a parametric function that maps all voxels of one volume to another volume. Some or all the parameters are learned by minimizing the loss function composed of similarity metric and smoothness constraint on a training set of volume pairs. Then given a new pair of volumes, the model can quickly compute the deformation field by evaluating the function using the learned parameters.

Inspired by this, in this paper, we propose the *first* learning-based framework for cortical surface registration. We extend the framework of VoxelMorph [1], previously demonstrated in the Euclidean space that learns deformation field for volumetric image registration, to the spherical space. We reformulate it to fit the spherical coordinate system using three orthogonal Spherical U-Nets [20]. Consequently, our method only needs to learn one global optimization function for aligning any pair of surfaces, thus yielding a fast registration process. We evaluate our method on registering 102 surfaces to an atlas. Results show that

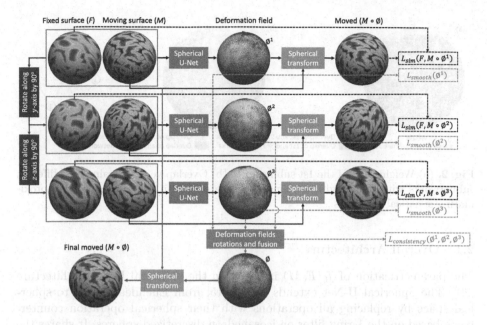

Fig. 1. Overview of our method. At training stage, we learn the registration function using three orthogonal Spherical U-Nets and transform layers. At inference stage, we fuse the three deformation fields together and obtain the final warped surface.

our method achieves comparable accuracy with state-of-the-art methods, while runs much faster, with less than 17 s for registration of a pair of surfaces.

2   Method

Let F, M be two spherical surface maps defined on the sphere S^2, discretized using icosahedron subdivisions [3]. For simplicity, we assume that F and M contain single-channel feature data, e.g.., mean curvature or average convexity. We model the registration function $f_\theta(F, M) = \phi$, where ϕ is a spherical deformation field and θ are the learnable parameters of function f. For each vertex $v \in S^2$, $\phi(v)$ maps v on M to $\phi(v)$ on F. Then we can express the objective as:

$$\mathcal{L}(F, M, \phi) = \mathcal{L}_{sim}(F, M \circ \phi) + \lambda_s \mathcal{L}_{smooth}(\phi), \qquad (1)$$

where $\mathcal{L}_{sim}(\cdot, \cdot)$ measures surfaces feature similarity, $\mathcal{L}_{smooth}(\cdot)$ imposes smoothness on ϕ and λ_s is a regularization parameter. The goal of registration is thus to find optimal parameters $\hat{\theta}$ that minimizes $\mathcal{L}(F, M, \phi)$ on a training set D: $\hat{\theta} = \arg\min_\theta \mathbb{E}_{(F,M) \sim D}[\mathcal{L}(F, M, f_\theta(F, M))]$.

Therefore, this learning-based framework provides great flexibility to the choices of similarity measure and smoothness constraint by stochastic gradient descent or Adam optimizer [5] in deep learning.

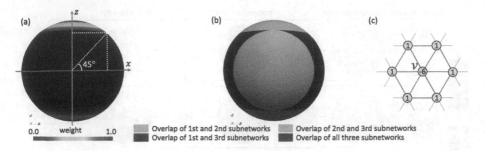

Fig. 2. (a) Weight map of the 1st subnetwork. (b) Overlap vertices trained by different subnetworks with full weight. (c) Smooth operator ∇_s on spherical surface approximating spherical gradients.

2.1 Overall Architecture

The parametrization of $f_\theta(F, M)$ is based on the Spherical U-Net architecture [20]. The Spherical U-Net extends U-Net [15] from Euclidean space to spherical space by replacing all operations with their spherical operation counterparts based on the 1-ring filter on icosahedron discretized spheres. It shares the same architecture with standard U-Net and further possesses the same excellent ability to learn both contextual and localization information for segmentation/parcellation tasks. We use the default Spherical U-Net architecture in [20] with input channels 2 for F and M, respectively, and output channels 2 for deformation field represented by tangent vectors. However, the 1-ring filter in Spherical U-Net was originally designed to be azimuthally rotation equivariant/invariant. In this design, to establish a reference direction on sphere, the local coordinates are inversed across poles, thus introducing inherent discontinuity at poles. When predicting the displacement vector (or rotation matrix) that traverses across poles using unsupervised learning, this design leads to severe distortions in the prediction results, especially for the vertices near poles.

To address this issue, we propose to rotate the sphere to other 2 orthogonal orientations. Suppose for a spherical surface with N vertices $\{v_n\}_{n=1}^N$, we first rotate the sphere along y-axis by 90° to get v_n^2 and then along z-axis by 90° to get v_n^3, i.e., $v_n^2 = R_y(\pi/2)v_n$, $v_n^3 = R_z(\pi/2)v_n^2$, where R is the rotation matrix, v_n^i represents the vertices on i-th sphere. For convenience, we now also represent $\{v_n\}_{n=1}^N$ as $\{v_n^1\}_{n=1}^N$. Accordingly, we construct three subnetworks independently for the spheres at 3 orientations, as shown in Fig. 1. Each subnetwork predicts a separate deformation field (ϕ^1, ϕ^2, ϕ^3 in Fig. 1) for registering the corresponding rotated moving surface and the rotated atlas surface. Then in each subnetwork, a weighting function is added to the loss function to disregard the influences of vertices near poles: $W(v) = \begin{cases} 1 & |v(z)| \leq r/\sqrt{2} \\ (2+\sqrt{2})(1-|v(z)|/r) & r/\sqrt{2} < |v(z)| \leq r \end{cases}$, where r is the radius of the sphere, $v(z)$ is the z value of vertex v. Figure 2 (a) shows the weights for vertices in the 1st subnetwork. Besides the regular similarity and smoothness term in loss function, we additionally enforce the consistency among ϕ^1, ϕ^2 and ϕ^3, in which only vertices trained with full weight are considered:

$$
\begin{aligned}
\mathcal{L}_{consistency}(\phi^1, \phi^2, \phi^3) = {} & \frac{1}{|O^{1,2}|} \sum\nolimits_{n \in O^{1,2}} \left| R_y(\frac{\pi}{2})\phi^1(v_n^1) - \phi^2(v_n^2) \right| \\
& + \frac{1}{|O^{2,3}|} \sum\nolimits_{n \in O^{2,3}} \left| R_z(\frac{\pi}{2})\phi^2(v_n^2) - \phi^3(v_n^3) \right| \\
& + \frac{1}{|O^{1,3}|} \sum\nolimits_{n \in O^{1,3}} \left| R_z(\frac{\pi}{2})R_y(\frac{\pi}{2})\phi^1(v_n^1) - \phi^3(v_n^3) \right|,
\end{aligned}
\tag{2}
$$

where $O^{i,j}$ represents the overlap vertices of i-th and j-th sphere trained with full weight, e.g.., $O^{1,2} = \{n|W(v_n^1) = 1 \text{ and } W(v_n^2) = 1\}$, $|O^{i,j}|$ is the number of vertices in $O^{i,j}$. Figure 2 (b) intuitively shows the overlap vertices trained by different subnetworks with full weight. At inference stage, we will also use this overlap map for deformations fusion.

2.2 Spherical Transform Layer

Since the spherical deformation is inherently constrained to S^2, it only has 2 degrees of freedom. We choose to represent the deformation using tangent vectors as in Spherical Demons [19]. The tangent vector field $\{\overrightarrow{\phi_n}\}_{n=1}^N$ is predicted from Spherical U-Net with 2 channels output, where $\overrightarrow{\phi_n} \in T_{v_n}R^2$ and $T_{v_n}R^2$ is the local 2D coordinate tangent to v_n (for simplicity, we formulate this only for the 1st sphere). Recall that the spherical deformation $\phi = \{\phi(v_n)\}_{n=1}^N$ maps a vertex $v_n \in S^2$ to a point $\phi(v_n) \in S^2$. Then on a unit sphere, we define $\phi(v_n) = \frac{v_n + E_n \overrightarrow{\phi_n}}{\left\| v_n + E_n \overrightarrow{\phi_n} \right\|}$, where $E_n = [\overrightarrow{e_n^1}, \overrightarrow{e_n^2}]$ is a 3×2 orthonormal basis on $T_{v_n}S^2$ and $T_{v_n}S^2$ is the tangent space at v_n, and $E_n\overrightarrow{\phi_n}$ maps tangent vector field from tangent bundles TR^2 to TS^2 [19]. With this definition, we establish a 1-to-1 correspondence between $\{\overrightarrow{\phi_n}\}_{n=1}^N$ and $\{\phi(v_n)\}_{n=1}^N$, when the angle α between v_n and $\phi(v_n)$ is less than $\pi/2$. Hence, given a surface with N vertices $\{v_n\}_{n=1}^N$, the spherical deformation $\{\phi(v_n)\}_{n=1}^N$, or equivalently the tangent vector field $\{\overrightarrow{\phi_n}\}_{n=1}^N$, together with a choice of an interpolation function define the deformation ϕ everywhere on S^2. It is worth noting that the length of $\overrightarrow{\phi_n}$ in our definition is equal to $tan(\alpha)$ rather than $sin(\alpha)$ in Spherical Demons or the geodesic distance α. Though these three definitions are approximately equal when α is very small, we show that our definition is more convenient and suitable for our framework as stated above and in Sect. 2.3.

Now for each deformed vertex $\phi(v_n)$, we choose to directly warp moving surface M so that the feature value at $\phi(v_n)$ on fixed surface $F(\phi(v_n))$ is computed using barycentric interpolation [19]. Then we can directly compare $M(v_n)$ and $F(\phi(v_n))$ in the loss function. Conclusively, all the operations in the spherical transform layer are differentiable and thus can backpropagate error to train the parameters of Spherical U-Net.

2.3 Loss Functions

With the above definition, now we can rewrite the objective as:

$$\mathcal{L}(F, M, \phi, W) = \sum_{i=1}^{3} \mathcal{L}_{sim}(F(\phi^i(v_n^i)), M(v_n^i), W)$$

$$+ \lambda_s \sum_{i=1}^{3} \mathcal{L}_{smooth}(\vec{\phi_n^i}, W) + \lambda_{con} \mathcal{L}_{consistency}(\phi^1, \phi^2, \phi^3). \tag{3}$$

For the similarity term, we choose the mean squared distance (MSD) used in Spherical Demons and correlation in MSM:

$$\mathcal{L}_{sim}(F(\phi^i(v_n^i)), M(v_n^i), W) = \frac{1}{N} \sum_{n=1}^{N} W(v_n^i) \left\| F(\phi^i(v_n^i)) - M(v_n^i) \right\|^2$$

$$- \lambda_{cc} \frac{\text{cov}(F(\phi^i(v_n^i)), M(v_n^i); W(v_n^i))}{\sqrt{\text{cov}(F(\phi^i(v_n^i)), F(\phi^i(v_n^i)); W(v_n^i)) \, \text{cov}(M(v_n^i), M(v_n^i); W(v_n^i))}} \tag{4}$$

where λ_{cc} is the weight for correlation term and $\text{cov}(\cdot, \cdot; W)$ is the weighted covariance.

Based on the tangent vector deformations, we propose a new operator ∇_s approximating the spherical gradients on spherical surface, as shown in Fig. 2 (c). Accordingly,

$$\mathcal{L}_{smooth}(\vec{\phi_n^i}, W) = \frac{1}{N} \sum_{n=1}^{N} W(v_n^i) \left| \nabla_s Q(\vec{\phi_n^i}) \right| \tag{5}$$

where $Q(\vec{\phi_n^i})$ represents the local 1-ring deformations of vertex v_n. We note that the operator ∇_s does not strictly guarantee a topology-preserving deformation. Therefore, in inference stage, we restrict $|\vec{\phi_n^i}|$ to be not greater than 0.45 times the minimum edge distance d of the surface mesh. Such a constraint is motivated and proven to be effective by MSM [14]. With our definition of the deformation field, since $\alpha = \tan^{-1}(|\vec{\phi_n^i}|) \leq \tan^{-1}(0.45 \times d) < \tan^{-1}(d/2) < \sin^{-1}(d/2)$ on a unit sphere, $\phi(v_n)$ is restricted in a small circle around v_n and will not intersect with its neighborhood vertices. Therefore, it is also sufficient to guarantee a topology-preserving registration.

3   Experiments and Results

3.1   Experimental Setting

We demonstrate our method on an atlas-based registration task, although our method is obviously not limited to that. We used a dataset with 102 pediatric subjects. The cortical surfaces were reconstructed with iBEAT V2.0 Cloud

Table 1. Comparison of registration performance using different methods.

	Spherical demons	MSM	Our method
Correlation of sulc	0.6982 ± 0.0521	0.7103 ± 0.0431	$\mathbf{0.7359 \pm 0.0526}$
Correlation of curv	0.2749 ± 0.0811	$\mathbf{0.3268 \pm 0.0762}$	0.2955 ± 0.0810
MAE of sulc	2.7669 ± 0.3528	2.6660 ± 0.3168	$\mathbf{2.3730 \pm 0.3362}$
MAE of curv	0.1933 ± 0.0205	$\mathbf{0.1790 \pm 0.0189}$	0.1853 ± 0.0197
Dice	0.7858 ± 0.0583	0.7659 ± 0.0552	$\mathbf{0.7903 \pm 0.0566}$
Folded triangles	0	0	0
Run-time	$\sim$1.5 min	$\sim$8 min (4 min for sulc + 4 min for curv)	$\sim$17 s

(http://www.ibeat.cloud/), an online infant-dedicated computational pipeline [6,7,17] and then mapped onto the sphere using FreeSurfer [3]. Each surface was coded with 2 geometric features at each vertex, i.e., 'sulc' (average convexity) and 'curv' (mean curvature), and a parcellation map also obtained and manually corrected to remove obvious errors. We used an atlas constructed from other 83 subjects with similar ages by co-registering them using Spherical Demons [19].

We compared our method with two popular surface registration methods: Spherical Demons [19] and MSM [14] in the context of registering 102 moving surfaces to the fixed atlas surface. The evaluation metrics we adopted for the registration performance are mean absolute error (MAE), correlation and Dice of parcellation results. We evaluated these metrics by comparing any two registered surfaces, as all surfaces should be in the same spherical space after registration.

We used the official codes of Spherical Demons[1] and MSM[2] for their experiments. We run Spherical Demons with its default parameters: registering two surfaces at 4 levels (4, 5, 6, 7, with 2,562, 10,242, 40,962, 163,842 vertices, respectively) of icosahedron subdivisions to align curvature of inflated surface, sulc, sulc, curv, respectively. For MSM, we used a set of optimized parameters for our dataset. We made the default regularization term several times larger and the input smoothing term smaller. It was still run by default with 2 features (first sulc then curv) at four levels (4, 4, 5, 6 for sulc, 4, 5, 5, 6 for curv) using 3 iterations in each level. To have a fair comparison with our method, we run Spherical Demons and MSM on an Intel Core i7-8700 CPU.

3.2   Implementation of Our Method

As in Spherical Demons and MSM, we also performed the registration in a coarse-to-fine multi-level style. We implemented our method using PyTorch. We trained 4 models at 4 levels (3, 4, 5, 6) for aligning sulc, sulc, sulc, curv, respectively. We used Adam optimizer with a learning rate decreasing from 1e−3 to 1e−6 in 100 epochs. Feature values were firstly normalized between $[-1, 1]$. λ_{cc} for training 4 models is consistently 0.1; λ_{con} is set to 0.06, 0.1, 0.2, 0.4; λ_s is 0.05, 0.06, 0.1, 0.3. After training, we registered the moving surface using 3, 2, 2, 3 iterations at

---

[1] https://sites.google.com/site/yeoyeo02/software/sphericaldemonsrelease.
[2] We used the MSM algorithm in fsl/6.0.0.

380   F. Zhao et al.

Fig. 3. Group-average maps of registered surfaces by different methods.

each level. We used 70 surfaces for training and 32 surfaces for validation. Since
the model is essentially an unsupervised learning model, we do not need a test
set. The registration results of training and validation sets verified that there
is no significant difference between them. We run our method on a PC with a
NVIDIA RTX2080 Ti GPU and an Intel Core i7-8700 CPU.

3.3 Results

Table 1 presents the overall performance in cortical surface registration using
different methods, as well as the folded triangles [10] computed for each warped
surface for validating a topology-preserving registration. It is reasonable that our
method achieves better performance on sulc alignment, because we registered
sulc on 3 levels and designed particular MSD and correlation loss matching
the evaluation metrics. On the other hand, MSM achieves better alignment on
curv. This is because MSM aligns curv 4 times at 4 levels based on the sulc-
driven registration. Visual inspection of MSM registration results confirms that
there is more squeeze of structures than Spherical Demons and our method.
Nevertheless, as these methods all provide flexible regularization or smoothness
parameters to trade off alignment accuracy against area distortion, the results
are still tunable, especially for MSM. However, in terms of run-time, our method
declares an overwhelming victory.

Figure 3 shows group-average maps of the 102 surfaces after registration to
the atlas using different methods. As can be seen, in many regions, e.g.., the
rostral middle frontal gyrus and temporal-occipital junction cortex, our method
presents sharper folding patterns, indicating a better alignment among subjects.
Figure 4 provides a visual comparison between registration results using different
methods. We can see that all three methods achieve very similar results. As
for the warped parcellation maps of this surface, our method leads to better
alignment with the atlas at the postcentral gyrus boundary.

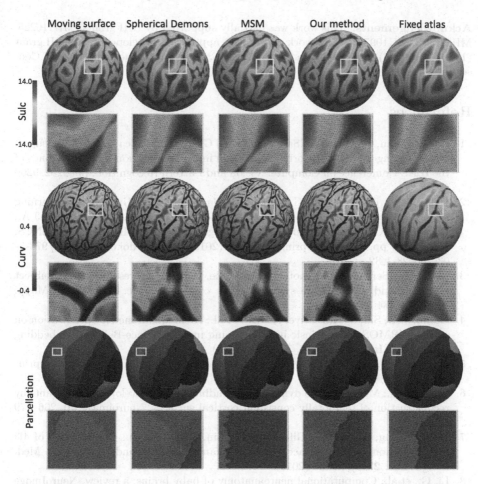

Fig. 4. Representative results of registering moving surfaces to an atlas using different methods.

4   Conclusion

In this paper, we propose the *first* deep learning-based model for spherical cortical surface registration. We showed that the characteristics of unsupervised learning, combined with 3 orthogonal Spherical U-Nets can effectively solve the gauge variance near poles and learn the deformation field on sphere. Compared to state-of-the-art non-learning-based methods, our method achieves similar registration accuracy, while needs much less run-time, making it preferable for large-scale neuroimaging data analyses. Importantly, our method is independent of the choices of similarity metrics and smoothness constraints, thus providing many potential directions on learning-based spherical surface registration.

Acknowledgements. This work was partially supported by NIH grants (MH116225, MH117943, MH109773). This work also utilizes approaches developed by an NIH grant (1U01MH110274) and the efforts of the UNC/UMN Baby Connectome Project Consortium.

References

1. Balakrishnan, G., Zhao, A., Sabuncu, M.R., Guttag, J., Dalca, A.V.: An unsupervised learning model for deformable medical image registration. In: Proceedings of the IEEE Conference on Computer Vision and Pattern Recognition, pp. 9252–9260 (2018)
2. Dalca, A.V., Balakrishnan, G., Guttag, J., Sabuncu, M.R.: Unsupervised learning for fast probabilistic diffeomorphic registration. In: Frangi, A.F., Schnabel, J.A., Davatzikos, C., Alberola-López, C., Fichtinger, G. (eds.) MICCAI 2018. LNCS, vol. 11070, pp. 729–738. Springer, Cham (2018). https://doi.org/10.1007/978-3-030-00928-1_82
3. Fischl, B., Sereno, M.I., Tootell, R.B., Dale, A.M.: High-resolution intersubject averaging and a coordinate system for the cortical surface. Hum. Brain Mapp. **8**(4), 272–284 (1999)
4. Gahm, J.K., Shi, Y., Initiative, A.D.N., et al.: Riemannian metric optimization on surfaces (RMOS) for intrinsic brain mapping in the Laplace-Beltrami embedding space. Med. Image Anal. **46**, 189–201 (2018)
5. Kingma, D.P., Ba, J.: Adam: a method for stochastic optimization. arXiv preprint arXiv:1412.6980 (2014)
6. Li, G., et al.: Measuring the dynamic longitudinal cortex development in infants by reconstruction of temporally consistent cortical surfaces. Neuroimage **90**, 266–279 (2014)
7. Li, G., Wang, L., Shi, F., Gilmore, J.H., Lin, W., Shen, D.: Construction of 4D high-definition cortical surface atlases of infants: methods and applications. Med. Image Anal. **25**(1), 22–36 (2015)
8. Li, G., et al.: Computational neuroanatomy of baby brains: a review. NeuroImage **185**, 906–925 (2019)
9. Lombaert, H., Sporring, J., Siddiqi, K.: Diffeomorphic spectral matching of cortical surfaces. In: Gee, J.C., Joshi, S., Pohl, K.M., Wells, W.M., Zöllei, L. (eds.) IPMI 2013. LNCS, vol. 7917, pp. 376–389. Springer, Heidelberg (2013). https://doi.org/10.1007/978-3-642-38868-2_32
10. Möller, T.: A fast triangle-triangle intersection test. J. Graph. Tools **2**(2), 25–30 (1997)
11. Nenning, K.H., Liu, H., Ghosh, S.S., Sabuncu, M.R., Schwartz, E., Langs, G.: Diffeomorphic functional brain surface alignment: functional demons. NeuroImage **156**, 456–465 (2017)
12. Niethammer, M., Kwitt, R., Vialard, F.X.: Metric learning for image registration. In: Proceedings of the IEEE Conference on Computer Vision and Pattern Recognition, pp. 8463–8472 (2019)
13. Robinson, E.C., et al.: Multimodal surface matching with higher-order smoothness constraints. NeuroImage **167**, 453–465 (2018)
14. Robinson, E.C., et al.: MSM: a new flexible framework for multimodal surface matching. Neuroimage **100**, 414–426 (2014)

15. Ronneberger, O., Fischer, P., Brox, T.: U-net: convolutional networks for biomedical image segmentation. In: Navab, N., Hornegger, J., Wells, W.M., Frangi, A.F. (eds.) MICCAI 2015. LNCS, vol. 9351, pp. 234–241. Springer, Cham (2015). https://doi.org/10.1007/978-3-319-24574-4_28
16. Vercauteren, T., Pennec, X., Perchant, A., Ayache, N.: Diffeomorphic demons: efficient non-parametric image registration. NeuroImage **45**(1), S61–S72 (2009)
17. Wang, L., et al.: Volume-based analysis of 6-month-old infant brain MRI for Autism biomarker identification and early diagnosis. In: Frangi, A.F., Schnabel, J.A., Davatzikos, C., Alberola-López, C., Fichtinger, G. (eds.) MICCAI 2018. LNCS, vol. 11072, pp. 411–419. Springer, Cham (2018). https://doi.org/10.1007/978-3-030-00931-1_47
18. Wang, Q., Kim, M., Shi, Y., Wu, G., Shen, D., Initiative, A.D.N., et al.: Predict brain MR image registration via sparse learning of appearance and transformation. Med. Image Anal. **20**(1), 61–75 (2015)
19. Yeo, B.T., Sabuncu, M.R., Vercauteren, T., Ayache, N., Fischl, B., Golland, P.: Spherical demons: fast diffeomorphic landmark-free surface registration. IEEE Trans. Med. Imaging **29**(3), 650–668 (2009)
20. Zhao, F., et al.: Spherical U-net on cortical surfaces: methods and applications. In: Chung, A.C.S., Gee, J.C., Yushkevich, P.A., Bao, S. (eds.) IPMI 2019. LNCS, vol. 11492, pp. 855–866. Springer, Cham (2019). https://doi.org/10.1007/978-3-030-20351-1_67

Anatomy-Guided Convolutional Neural Network for Motion Correction in Fetal Brain MRI

Yuchen Pei[1,2], Lisheng Wang[1], Fenqiang Zhao[2], Tao Zhong[2], Lufan Liao[2],
Dinggang Shen[2], and Gang Li[2(✉)]

[1] Institute of Image Processing and Pattern Recognition,
Department of Automation, Shanghai Jiao Tong University, Shanghai, China
[2] Department of Radiology and BRIC, University of North Carolina at Chapel Hill,
Chapel Hill, USA
gang_li@med.unc.edu

Abstract. Fetal Magnetic Resonance Imaging (MRI) is challenged by the fetal movements and maternal breathing. Although fast MRI sequences allow artifact free acquisition of individual 2D slices, motion commonly occurs in between slices acquisitions. Motion correction for each slice is thus very important for reconstruction of 3D fetal brain MRI, but is highly operator-dependent and time-consuming. Approaches based on convolutional neural networks (CNNs) have achieved encouraging performance on prediction of 3D motion parameters of arbitrarily oriented 2D slices, which, however, does not capitalize on important brain structural information. To address this problem, we propose a new multi-task learning framework to jointly learn the transformation parameters and tissue segmentation map of each slice, for providing brain anatomical information to guide the mapping from 2D slices to 3D volumetric space in a coarse to fine manner. In the coarse stage, the first network learns the features shared for both regression and segmentation tasks. In the refinement stage, to fully utilize the anatomical information, distance maps constructed based on the coarse segmentation are introduced to the second network. Finally, incorporation of the signed distance maps to guide the regression and segmentation together improves the performance in both tasks. Experimental results indicate that the proposed method achieves superior performance in reducing the motion prediction error and obtaining satisfactory tissue segmentation results simultaneously, compared with state-of-the-art methods.

Keywords: Fetal brain · Motion correction · Anatomical knowledge

1 Introduction

Reconstruction of 3D fetal brain images from multiple motion-corrupted stacks of 2D slices plays an important role for modeling and quantification of prenatal brain development [1, 19]. However, high-quality volume reconstruction remains

© Springer Nature Switzerland AG 2020
M. Liu et al. (Eds.): MLMI 2020, LNCS 12436, pp. 384–393, 2020.
https://doi.org/10.1007/978-3-030-59861-7_39

a challenging task due to motion commonly occurring between slice acquisitions. Particularly, fetuses in mid-gestation have relatively large space to stretc.h and rotate. Arbitrary fetal motion can invalidate slice alignment and manual intervention may be necessary. However, manual motion correction in each slice often becomes unfeasible in practice, due to the magnitude of image data involved. Although many methods such as slice-to-volume registration [3,12] are successfully applied to reconstruct fetal brain, they require a coarsely aligned initialization of slices to initialize reconstruction process. Therefore, good initial alignment of 2D slices is critical to reconstruct brain volumetric images.

Recently, there has been an increasing interest in applying deep learning techniques in medical image computing, inspired by the promising results that have been achieved in computer vision. In an effort to speed up slice-to-volume rigid registration and improve its capture range, Miao et al. [9,10] firstly proposed a registration algorithm using CNN regressors in X-ray images. In fetal MRI, deep-learning based methods [4,5,13] have been also used to improve the prediction of slice transformation parameters for motion correction. These approaches share similarity with [7] in computer vision, which relied upon image retrieval [14] that matches the testing image and retrieved image's intensity information to predict the camera pose. While they are powerful in learning to predict brain position based on intensity information, the multi-layer CNNs only implicitly learn the contour and shape of the brain. Since the brain tissue maps have more explicit semantic information about the anatomical boundary, it can provide key compensatory information to intensity for establishing matching across slices, thus is critical to the robustness of motion correction methods in the fetal brain. The anatomical knowledge can be also applied to improve the segmentation performance in MRI, which has been proved to be effective in [17].

Therefore, in this paper, for the first time, we present a multi-task learning framework to jointly predict the position and tissue segmentation map of each 2D slice in fetal MRI stacks. Instead of treating these two tasks as independent problems, we optimize the network by simultaneously features shared within regression and segmentation tasks. We show that brain motion correction can be improved by utilizing the association between two tasks. Moreover, the complementary anatomical information from the tissue maps is incorporated in refinement segmentation network to improve the regression and segmentation results. We quantitatively evaluate the regression and segmentation performance using simulated 2D slice data extracted from reconstructed 3D fetal brain MRI. The comparison with other CNN-based 3D motion correction methods indicates that our method is effective in reducing the motion prediction error and obtaining superior tissue segmentation results simultaneously.

2   Method

As illustrated in Fig. 1, our framework is composed of a coarse regression and segmentation network and a multi-stream refinement network. In coarse stage, a multi-output network is designed to predict the transformation parameters and segmentation results jointly. In the refinement stage, signed distance maps of tissue boundaries are introduced to provide additional anatomical contour information. Multi-stream inputs are convoluted by the same encoder structure and shared representation module is added to fuse multiple high-level features to refine predictions and segmentations.

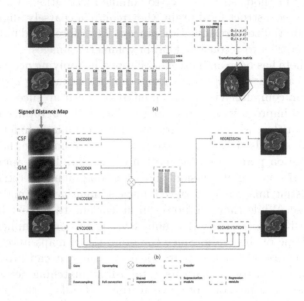

Fig. 1. An illustration of our framework. (a) Coarse regression and segmentation network. (b) Refinement network that uses multi-stream to extract anatomy features and shared representation module to combine multi-source features to make accurate prediction and segmentation.

2.1 Coarse Regression and Segmentation Network

The coarse regression and segmentation network has two branches: one for regression of 2D slice transformation parameters and the other for segmentation of brain tissues. The encoder part learns common features shared by two tasks, learning valid deep representation for position and segmentation. In decoder parts, we design the regression module and segmentation module, separately, which further learn task-specific features for each task. This network architecture can thus avoid training individual network for each task, by utilizing the association between two tasks and more oversight on learning shared features. Afterwards, in the training process, the joint optimization is employed, which ensures learning common features between the regression and segmentation tasks and also avoids over-fitting to one particular task.

Encoder Module. As shown in Fig. 1 (a), all the layers in the encoder module and segmentation module use a fixed kernel size 3×3, the last convolution layer in regression module uses a kernel size 1×1. The downsampling is achieved by setting stride size of the convolution kernel to 2. The batch normalization (BN) layers are used after each convolution layer in our network to accelerate the training process. We employ rectified linear unit (ReLU) activations after each BN layer. Finally, our network branches from the pooling layer to produce outputs for each specific task.

Regression Module. The architecture of this part is derived from the VGG [15], in which two fully connected layers are used to transfer feature from the encoder to regress a desired output. The movement of the fetal brain can be considered as a rigid transformation. Thus, the slices are transformed rigidly in 3D space. Parameterization of each slice therefore lies within the bounds of the SE(3) Lie group. The parameterization includes: a rotation component as well as a translation component. Similar to [5], we define three Cartesian anchor points within a plane (nine parameters) as 3D transformation presentation. Any three non-linear or non-identical points in a 3D space form a plane and their order defines the orientation. In this way, the rotation and translation components of the labels are combined together. For an $L \times L$ 2D slice, we define P_1 as the center of the slice $(\frac{L}{2}, \frac{L}{2}, 0)$, P_2 as the up-right corner of the slice $(L, 0, 0)$, P_3 as the bottom-right corner of the slice $(L, L, 0)$. The regression module will estimate the transformed positions $Q_1 = TP_1$, $Q_2 = TP_2$, $Q_3 = TP_3$ for these three points, where T is the transformation matrix. Then, we can calculate the transformation matrix T based on the predicted points. Finally, we transform the corresponding slice to its corrected position in 3D volumetric space.

Segmentation Module. In the segmentation module, motivated by the outstanding performance of U-net [8,11,18] in segmentation, we also use skip connection which can extract holistic and local feature jointly from the intensity image. In order to get more anatomical knowledge, we segment fetal brain into cerebrospinal fluid (CSF), gray matter (GM) and white matter (WM). The stride size of deconvolution kernel is set to 2 to achieve upsampling of feature maps 2 times.

2.2 Anatomy-Guided Refinement Network

Anatomical Knowledge. In the coarse stage, the architecture only takes the intensity information as the input and finally outputs the transformation parameters and tissue segmentation maps. Therefore, in the refinement stage, we add the anatomical prior knowledge to guide the regression and segmentation tasks as shown in Fig. 1 (b). Based on the coarse segmentation results, we can directly construct the Signed Distance Map (SDM) [2] for three tissue types CSF, GM, WM, respectively. Given a target tissue and a pixel x in the image, the SDM is defined as:

$$D_{SDM}(x, B) = \begin{cases} 0, & if \quad x\epsilon B, \\ -\|x - y\|_2, & if \quad x\epsilon\Omega_{in}, \\ +\|x - y\|_2, & if \quad x\epsilon\Omega_{out} \end{cases} \tag{1}$$

where B represents the boundary of the target tissue, Ω_{in} and Ω_{out} denote the region inside and outside the target tissue, y denotes the closest pixel on B to x. The absolute value of SDM indicates the distance from the pixel to the closest pixel on boundary of tissue, while the sign indicates either inside (negative) or outside (positive) the tissue. Note that the zero distance or zero level set means that the pixel is on the boundary of the tissue. We normalize the $D_{SDM}(x,B)$ to be in the range $[-1, 1]$ for each tissue.

Multi-stream Network Architecture. The anatomy-guided refinement network takes the intensity as well as three types of structural knowledge as inputs. Since our distance maps include different tissue information, straightforward concatenation of extracted features from them is not reasonable. To effectively leverage features from different brain tissues to guide regression and segmentation tasks, we propose a multi-stream network architecture. By using individual stream for each tissue, we can investigate when it is best to merge the streams. [16] shows that cross-modality convolution can effectively aggregate the information between modalities to produce better results. Inspired by that, after concatenating the features from the encoder part, we designed the shared representation module composed of 2 convolution layers and 1 pooling layer to better fuse different tissue anatomical features. It is worth noting that only the low-level features of the intensity image pass to upsampling stream by skip connection, while the anatomical knowledge does not, thus noise and irrelevant information is not introduced. Similar to the coarse stage, the regression and segmentation tasks are split in decoder part and make predictions separately.

2.3   Loss Function Design

In essence, we aim to jointly perform the 3D position regression for mapping a 2D slice to 3D volumetric space and segmentation of the 2D slice into different types of tissues: CSF, GM, and WM. To train the multi-task model, we define the loss of the regression module and segmentation module as L_{reg} and L_{seg}, respectively.

For regression task, the anchor points consist of 9 parameters: (Q_1 (x,y,z), Q_2 (x,y,z), Q_3 (x,y,z)). As [6] presented, we calculate the Euclidean distance between the points and predicted points as loss function. This approach keeps the nature of the network loss consistent and avoids the balance of rotation loss and translation loss. As each point is Cartesian, the optimization is guaranteed to be balanced. The 3D transformation loss is defined as:

$$L_{reg} = \|\hat{Q}_1 - Q_1\|_2 + \|\hat{Q}_2 - Q_2\|_2 + \|\hat{Q}_3 - Q_3\|_2 \tag{2}$$

where $\hat{Q}_1, \hat{Q}_2, \hat{Q}_3$ are the predicted anchor points.

In segmentation stream, we choose the cross-entropy loss for training stability. In addition to this, we apply weights to each class to offset the imbalance of pixel frequency across different classes.

$$L_{seg} = -\sum_i \sum_c w_c l_{ic} \log(p_{ic}) \tag{3}$$

where w_c represents the proportions of different classes in input data, $c \in \{WM, GM, CSF\}$, l_{ic} is 1 if the pixel i belongs to class c, otherwise 0, and the p_{ic} is the probability of the pixel i predicted as c.

Incorporation of the multi-loss framework [20], the combined loss for regression and segmentation networks can therefore be written as:

$$L = L_{reg} + \beta L_{seg} \tag{4}$$

where β controls the relative importance of the segmentation loss term. In our experiments, β is set as 20 in coarse stage and 10 in refinement stage.

3 Experiments and Discussion

3.1 Dataset and Evaluation Metrics

Since there is no ground truth in motion correction, we simulate 2D slices with random motion based on 3D fetal brain volumes, as in [5]. Specifically, experiments were conducted on a dataset with 48 fetal brain MRI volumes with manual tissue segmentation results [1], which were reconstructed to have an isotropic resolution of $0.75\,\text{mm} \times 0.75\,\text{mm} \times 0.75\,\text{mm}$. 2D slices were extracted from the high-resolution 3D volumes. A stack of 120×120 sampling planes was aligned with the brain. Using random sampling, the entire stack was rotated randomly with the fetal brain's isocenter, with z-axis offs et al. so sampled randomly. 2000 random rotations were made between $-\pi/2$ and $+\pi/2$ in x, y, z axes. Since the rotation matrices were known, the anchor points Q_1, Q_2, Q_3 can be computed and used as the ground truth. Each volume generated 32,000 2D slices in total. This method covered half of all possible orientations, and provided different views in the training set. Therefore, for training the network, the separation of different views (i.e., axial, coronal, and sagittal) was unnecessary. We did not span the whole space in this experiment, because some 2D brain slices do not have enough information to distinguish they belong to the right or left hemisphere, due to the relatively symmetric shape of the brain.

We performed 4-fold cross-validation. To evaluate the regression performance, we tested the network with a 2D image slice ω_i, as extracted from the volume $\mathbf{V}$. By using the parameters predicted from the network, we extract a new slice ω_p from the same $\mathbf{V}$ and compare it to slice ω_i. We chose several standard image similarity metrics: Cross Correlation (CC), Peak Signal-to-Noise Ratio (PSNR), Mean Squared Error (MSE), and Structural Similarity (SSIM).

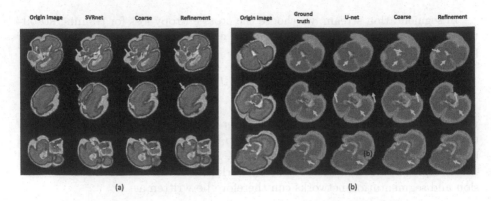

Fig. 2. (a) The origin slices inputted to the network and slices extracted from the respective fetal volume using parameters predicted by different methods. (b) The segmentation results. (red: CSF, green: GM, blue: WM) (Color figure online)

3.2 Motion Correction Results on Fetal Brain

We present the results of the single regression task, regression in coarse stage and regression in anatomy-guided refinement stage including single-stream network and multi-stream network to validate the effectiveness of different parts in our proposed method. In addition, we applied the state-of-the-art method, SVRnet [5], which used anchor points as the regression loss, to our dataset for comparison. The CC, MSE, PSNR and SSIM values of different methods are shown in Table 1. For CC, PSNR and SSIM, the higher values indicate higher accuracy. As for MSE, the lower value means higher accuracy.

As shown in Table 1, our multi-task learning approach achieves better performance than the single task. For refinement stage, single-stream which directly the anatomical information and intensity information achieves worse result than only intensity information. In multi-stream network, anatomy-guided learning improves the accuracy significantly, which indicates that the anatomical clue helps the network to predict the transformation parameters more accurately and multi-stream architecture facilitates fusing anatomical feature. Our proposed method also outperforms the state-of-the-art method [5], which only utilizes the intensity information. In Fig. 2(a), we present some experimental results, with some distinct regions highlighted by yellow arrows. Compared with other methods, the results of refinement-multi are more similar to the original images. It further validates that our method is effective in predicting the transformation parameters more accurately.

3.3 Segmentation Results

In Table 2, we present the segmentation results of the coarse stage, anatomy-guided refinement stage including single-stream network and multi-stream network and U-net [11]. Compared with the U-net and the coarse stage, MHD in

Table 1. Regression results of different methods.

Method	CC	MSE	PSNR	SSIM
SVRnet [5]	0.822 ± 0.029	1095.12 ± 203.02	17.854 ± 0.867	0.600 ± 0.051
Single Regression	0.822 ± 0.036	1114.33 ± 234.41	17.821 ± 0.953	0.598 ± 0.044
Coarse Stage	0.828 ± 0.024	1058.77 ± 206.73	18.033 ± 0.861	0.608 ± 0.052
Refinement-single	0.803 ± 0.043	1263.32 ± 335.47	17.293 ± 1.100	0.598 ± 0.054
Refinement-multi	$\mathbf{0.837 \pm 0.024}$	$\mathbf{1013.09 \pm 199.14}$	$\mathbf{18.253 \pm 0.804}$	$\mathbf{0.618 \pm 0.050}$

anatomy-guided refinement-multi stage has been significantly improved. DSC does not improve significantly, as it is not sensitive to change of details near contours. The results of refinement-multi are better than the refinement-single which demonstrate the contribution of the multi-network for extracting mutli-source feature. As shown in Fig. 2(b), some qualitative results of anatomy-guided refinement stage are superior to other methods.

Table 2. Segmentation results of different methods.

Method	U-net [11]	Coarse stage	Refinement-single	Refinement-multi
DSC_{CSF}	0.954 ± 0.004	0.955 ± 0.003	0.952 ± 0.006	$\mathbf{0.956 \pm 0.003}$
DSC_{GM}	0.908 ± 0.008	0.908 ± 0.007	0.897 ± 0.011	$\mathbf{0.909 \pm 0.007}$
DSC_{WM}	0.976 ± 0.003	0.976 ± 0.003	0.963 ± 0.010	$\mathbf{0.977 \pm 0.003}$
$MHD_{CSF}(mm)$	0.676 ± 0.073	0.674 ± 0.070	0.685 ± 0.082	$\mathbf{0.661 \pm 0.069}$
$MHD_{GM}(mm)$	0.608 ± 0.079	0.605 ± 0.079	0.616 ± 0.098	$\mathbf{0.600 \pm 0.079}$
$MHD_{WM}(mm)$	0.421 ± 0.069	0.412 ± 0.069	0.424 ± 0.078	$\mathbf{0.403 \pm 0.062}$

3.4 Discussion

In our method, the segmentation task actually helps the regression task to improve the prediction performance by providing boundary information. Meanwhile, since the regression task takes boundary information for better slice matching in 3D space, it in turn improves the performance of segmentations. Further, the anatomical knowledge makes the regression of transformation parameters and tissue segmentation more accurately in refinement stage. Consequently, the proposed method can leverage the shared information in both tasks in one pass and achieve satisfactory regression and segmentation results simultaneously.

4 Conclusion

This paper proposes a coarse-to-fine framework for fetal brain motion correction and tissue segmentation. In the coarse stage, our multi-task model jointly predicts the transformation parameters and tissue maps. In the refinement stage, the signed distance maps of segmented tissues are introduced to provide additional tissue boundary features. Experiments demonstrate that motion correction can be improved by multi-task learning and additional anatomical information further enchances the performance of regression and segmentation tasks. In future, we will evaluate on more datasets and make our model predict more accurately.

Acknowledgements. This work was partially supported by NIH grants (MH117943).

References

1. Benkarim, O.M., et al.: A novel approach to multiple anatomical shape analysis: application to fetal ventriculomegaly. Med. Image Anal. **64**, 101750 (2020)
2. Danielsson, P.E.: Euclidean distance mapping. Comput. Graph. Image Process. **14**(3), 227–248 (1980)
3. Gholipour, A., Estroff, J.A., Barnewolt, C.E., Connolly, S.A., Warfield, S.K.: Fetal brain volumetry through MRI volumetric reconstruction and segmentation. Int. J. Comput. Assist. Radiol. Surg. **6**(3), 329–339 (2011)
4. Hou, B., et al.: Predicting slice-to-volume transformation in presence of arbitrary subject motion. In: Descoteaux, M., Maier-Hein, L., Franz, A., Jannin, P., Collins, D.L., Duchesne, S. (eds.) MICCAI 2017. LNCS, vol. 10434, pp. 296–304. Springer, Cham (2017). https://doi.org/10.1007/978-3-319-66185-8_34
5. Hou, B.: 3-D reconstruction in canonical co-ordinate space from arbitrarily oriented 2-D images. IEEE Trans. Med. Imaging **37**(8), 1737–1750 (2018)
6. Hou, B., et al.: Computing CNN loss and gradients for pose estimation with Riemannian geometry. In: Frangi, A.F., Schnabel, J.A., Davatzikos, C., Alberola-López, C., Fichtinger, G. (eds.) MICCAI 2018. LNCS, vol. 11070, pp. 756–764. Springer, Cham (2018). https://doi.org/10.1007/978-3-030-00928-1_85
7. Kendall, A., Grimes, M., Cipolla, R.: PoseNet: a convolutional network for real-time 6-DOF camera relocalization. In: Proceedings of the IEEE International Conference on Computer Vision, pp. 2938–2946 (2015)
8. Li, G., et al.: Computational neuroanatomy of baby brains: a review. NeuroImage **185**, 906–925 (2019)
9. Miao, S., Wang, Z.J., Liao, R.: A CNN regression approach for real-time 2D/3D registration. IEEE Trans. Med. Imaging **35**(5), 1352–1363 (2016)
10. Miao, S., Wang, Z.J., Zheng, Y., Liao, R.: Real-time 2D/3D registration via CNN regression. In: 2016 IEEE 13th International Symposium on Biomedical Imaging (ISBI), pp. 1430–1434. IEEE (2016)
11. Ronneberger, O., Fischer, P., Brox, T.: U-Net: convolutional networks for biomedical image segmentation. In: Navab, N., Hornegger, J., Wells, W.M., Frangi, A.F. (eds.) MICCAI 2015. LNCS, vol. 9351, pp. 234–241. Springer, Cham (2015). https://doi.org/10.1007/978-3-319-24574-4_28
12. Rousseau, F., Glenn, O.A., Iordanova, B., Barkovich, J.A., Studholme, C.: Registration-based approach for reconstruction of high-resolution in utero fetal MR brain images. Acad. Radiol. **13**(9), 1072–1081 (2006)
13. Salehi, S.S.M., Khan, S., Erdogmus, D., Gholipour, A.: Real-time deep pose estimation with geodesic loss for image-to-template rigid registration. IEEE Trans. Med. Imaging **38**(2), 470–481 (2018)
14. Sattler, T., Zhou, Q., Pollefeys, M., Leal-Taixe, L.: Understanding the limitations of CNN-based absolute camera pose regression. In: Proceedings of the IEEE Conference on Computer Vision and Pattern Recognition, pp. 3302–3312 (2019)

15. Simonyan, K., Zisserman, A.: Very deep convolutional networks for large-scale image recognition. arXiv preprint arXiv:1409.1556 (2014)
16. Tseng, K.L., Lin, Y.L., Hsu, W., Huang, C.Y.: Joint sequence learning and cross-modality convolution for 3D biomedical segmentation. In: Proceedings of the IEEE Conference on Computer Vision and Pattern Recognition, pp. 6393–6400 (2017)
17. Wang, L., et al.: Volume-based analysis of 6-month-old infant brain MRI for autism biomarker identification and early diagnosis. In: Frangi, A.F., Schnabel, J.A., Davatzikos, C., Alberola-López, C., Fichtinger, G. (eds.) MICCAI 2018. LNCS, vol. 11072, pp. 411–419. Springer, Cham (2018). https://doi.org/10.1007/978-3-030-00931-1_47
18. Wang, L., et al.: Benchmark on automatic six-month-old infant brain segmentation algorithms: the iSeg-2017 challenge. IEEE Trans. Med. Imaging **38**(9), 2219–2230 (2019)
19. Xia, J., et al.: Fetal cortical surface atlas parcellation based on growth patterns. Hum. Brain Mapp. **40**(13), 3881–3899 (2019)
20. Xu, C., et al.: Multi-loss regularized deep neural network. IEEE Trans. Circuits Syst. Video Technol. **26**(12), 2273–2283 (2015)

Gyral Growth Patterns of Macaque Brains Revealed by Scattered Orthogonal Nonnegative Matrix Factorization

Songyao Zhang[1], Lei Du[1], Jinglei Lv[2], Zhibin He[1], Xi Jiang[3], Lei Guo[1], Li Wang[4], Tianming Liu[5], Dinggang Shen[4], Gang Li[4], and Tuo Zhang[1($\boxtimes$)]

[1] School of Automation, Northwestern Polytechnical University, Xi'an, China
tuozhang@nwpu.edu.cn
[2] Sydney Imaging, Brain and Mind Centre and School of Biomedical Engineering, The University of Sydney, Camperdown, Australia
[3] School of Life Science and Technology, MOE Key Lab for Neuroinformation, University of Electronic Science and Technology of China, Chengdu, China
[4] Department of Radiology, University of North Carolina, Chapel Hill, NC 27599, USA
[5] Cortical Architecture Imaging and Discovery Lab, Department of Computer Science and Bioimaging Research Center, The University of Georgia, Athens, GA, USA

Abstract. Cerebral cortex development undergoes a variety of alternate processes, providing valuable information to study the developmental mechanism of the cortical folding and the structural and functional architectures. Many longitudinal studies are performed on the development of sulci using features like sulcal depth, but the gyral system is less studied. To fill the gap, we propose a novel feature, termed gyral height, to quantify the longitudinal developmental patterns of gyri. Another practical problem is the difficulty of obtaining data for all time points for all subjects, even in animal datasets, such as the macaque neurodevelopment dataset in this work. Therefore, we develop a novel method by introducing a scattered factor to the orthogonal nonnegative matrix factorization to align data both longitudinally and cross-sectionally. By this method, the gyral height feature maps are decomposed into orthogonal cortical clusters which encode spatiotemporal patterns. Close relations are found between these clusters and anatomical, structural connective and functional metrics, suggesting the potential of the novel cortical feature and the method in investigating the brain development.

Keywords: Gyral height · Orthogonal nonnegative matrix factorization

1 Introduction

Postnatal brains undergo interwound complex processes of maturation, such as maturation of neurons and axonal myelination [1–3]. Therefore, information during this period is valuable in understanding the development of both normal and abnormal brain architectures [1]. In practice, it is challenging to recruit human subjects for data collections at the early stage, and developmental animal models are thus widely used [4]. Among

© Springer Nature Switzerland AG 2020
M. Liu et al. (Eds.): MLMI 2020, LNCS 12436, pp. 394–403, 2020.
https://doi.org/10.1007/978-3-030-59861-7_40

the animal models, macaque monkeys attract special attentions because of their close phylogenetic relation to humans [5–7]. One of such datasets is the public rhesus macaque neurodevelopment dataset with 156 scans from 32 macaques [8].

Changes in cortex is one of the most pronounced characteristics of developing macaque brains, and have been related to brain functions [9, 10, 12]. Among a variety of cortical features, sulcal depth is used to quantify cortical folding patterns. The deepest sulcal regions, known as sulcal pits, were found follow the alignment of lateral ventricle, the origin of neuron migration [10]. They were also suggested to be the earliest developed regions such that their locations and functions are more consistent cross subjects [10]. In fact, as counterparts of sulci, gyri have also been demonstrated to have potential in presenting the cortical folding patterns as an organization system [13]. However, very few longitudinal studies were found to specifically focus on the development of gyral systems and the relation with the maturation of the underlying connective systems and brain functions.

To fill the gap, we propose a novel folding pattern metric complementary to sulcal depth, termed gyral height. This metric measures the radial distance between a cortical region and the inner core [10], and is expected to be related to the maturation of both cortex and axons, which have been suggested to dynamically impose their impact to gyrification [14, 15] and the formation of functions. To learn the spatiotemporal patterns of gyral heights, we develop a scattered orthogonal nonnegative matrix factorization (S-ONMF) method based on [16] to identify cortical clusters. In each cluster, cortical regions share the same pattern of gyral height developmental trajectory. The proposed scattered constraint is to align the scans both longitudinally and cross-sectionally, because even in this macaque dataset [8] it is still difficult to find a timepoint on which all subjects were scheduled to scan. We compare the gyral height trajectories of the identified cortical clusters with the ones from cortical thickness and the white matter fiber density, and find the interpretable coherence among them. Functionally defined cortical parcellation atlases are also used to compare with the identified cortical clusters to reveal the close relationship between them. All these results demonstrate the soundness of both the novel folding pattern metric and the algorithm.

2 Materials and Methods

2.1 Datasets and Data Preprocessing

Thirty-two healthy rhesus macaques used in this study were from the University of Wisconsin-Madison [8]. Each subject has four or five longitudinal brain MRI scans (GE MR750 3.0T) at scheduled intervals, resulting a total of 156 scans (scanning schedule in Fig. 1). The parameters of T1-weighted MRI are: TI $= 450$ ms, TR $= 8.684$ ms, TE $= 3.652$ ms, FOV $= 140 \times 140$ mm^2, flip angle $= 12°$, acquisition matrix $= 256 \times 256$ and voxel size $= 0.55 \times 0.55 \times 0.8$ mm^3. The parameters of diffusion MRI are: TR $= 8000$ ms, TE $= 65.7$ ms, FOV $= 16.7$ mm, matrix $= 128 \times 128$, slice thickness $= 2.6$ mm, with 1.3 mm slice overlap, 120 gradient directions with $b = 1000$ s/mm^2 and ten images with $b = 0$ s/mm^2.

We rigidly align one subject's T2-weighted image onto its T1-weighted image, and resampled all images to be isotropic ($0.55 \times 0.55 \times 0.55$ mm^3). After removing skull,

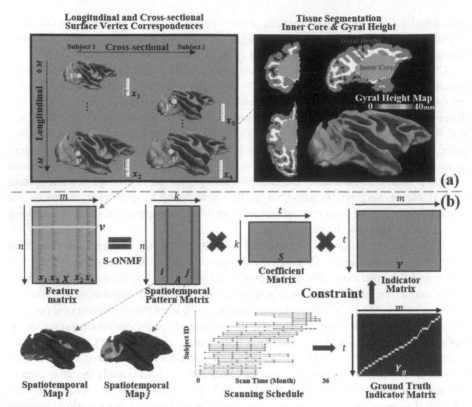

Fig. 1. (a) The flow chart of data preprocessing. (b) The flow chart of S-ONMF. (Color figure online)

brain stem, and cerebellum, we use an infant-dedicated learning-based method, coupled with longitudinal guidance [17–19] to perform brain tissue segmentation (white matter, WM; gray matter, GM; cerebrospinal fluid, CSF; right panel in Fig. 1(a)). On the segmentation result, we reconstruct the inner (WM) and outer (GM) cortical surfaces by using the method in [20, 21]. For dMRI, we perform skull-strip and eddy current correction *via* FSL [22, 23]. DSI-Studio is used to estimate the voxel-wise distribution of water diffusion [24] and track 4×10^4 deterministic fibers for the whole-brain [25] with default parameters (max turning angle: 60°, streamline length: 30 mm–300 mm, step length: 1 mm, quantitative anisotropy threshold: 0.2).

2.2 Definition of Gyral Height and Other Cortical Features

Similar to sulcal depth [10], we use image opening and closing operations to WM map to yield the inner core (Fig. 1(a)). We define the distance from each vertex on the white matter surface to the nearest corresponding voxel on the inner core as the gyral height (see the illustrative red arrows and the gyral height surface map in Fig. 1(a)). Cortical thickness is defined as the minimum distance between the inner and outer surfaces. Fiber density is defined as the number of fibers penetrating a unit (1 mm^2) surface area.

2.3 Longitudinal and Cross-Sectional Surface Vertex Correspondences

As illustrated in Fig. 1(a), longitudinal (intra-subject) cortical correspondences are established by aligning longitudinal surfaces and generating the mean intra-subject cortical folding map *via* spherical demons [11]. Cross-sectional (inter-subject) correspondences are established by aligning all the intra-subject mean cortical folding maps and generating the group-mean cortical folding maps. We resample the aligned cortical surfaces along with their cortical thickness and gyral height maps to a standard-mesh tessellation with 10242 vertices, establishing vertex-to-vertex correspondences across the cohort (see yellow dots in Fig. 1(a)). The cortical features, such as gyral heights or cortical thicknesses, of a surface is present as a vector $\mathbf{x}$, and $\mathbf{x}$s of the entire cohort give a feature matrix $\mathbf{X} \in R^{n \times m}$ (see illustrative features in Fig. 1(a)&(b)), where $n = 10242$, $m = 156$ (scans).

2.4 Scattered Orthogonal Matrix Factorization

The orthogonal matrix factorization [16] aims at minimizing the following function:

$$\min_{A \geq 0, G \geq 0} \|X - AG\|^2, s.t. A^T A = I \tag{1}$$

where $\mathbf{X} \in R^{n \times m}$ is the feature matrix. $\mathbf{A} \in R^{n \times k}$ consists of k nonnegative columns, each of which encodes a spatiotemporal pattern of the cortical feature (left-bottom in Fig. 1(b)). The orthogonality $\mathbf{A}^T \mathbf{A} = \mathbf{I}$ ensures the columns are distinct from each other. $\mathbf{G} \in R^{k \times m}$ is the coefficient matrix but is difficult to interpret, because there are multiple columns in $\mathbf{X}$ and $\mathbf{G}$ that correspond to the same month. We thus decompose $\mathbf{G}$ as the product of $\mathbf{S} \in R^{k \times t}$ and $\mathbf{Y} \in R^{t \times m}$ (t is the month). $y_{i,j}$ is supposed to indicate that the jth scan is conducted in the ith month. As so, the ith column of $\mathbf{S}$ can be interpreted as the weights corresponding to the k components/columns of $\mathbf{A}$ and indicating how they are summed to estimate the feature in the ith month. Therefore, function (1) is rewritten as:

$$\min_{A \geq 0, S \geq 0, Y \geq 0} \left\| X - ASY^2 \right\| + \left\| Y - Y_g^2 \right\|, s.t. A^T A = I \tag{2}$$

where $\mathbf{Y}_g$ is the "ground-truth" indicator matrix converted from the scanning schedule (Fig. 1(b)). The $y_{g(i,j)} = 1$ if the jth scan was performed in the ith month. Because different months have different numbers of scans, each row of $\mathbf{Y}_g$ was normalized by dividing by its total number, such that the scans from different subjects have equal contributions.

The S-ONMF in Eq. (2) is solved by an iterative update algorithm. Because the update algorithm for $\mathbf{A}$ and $\mathbf{S}$ have been detailed in [16], we focused on the update algorithm $\mathbf{Y}$. By fixing fix $\mathbf{A}$ and $\mathbf{S}$, the function in Eq. (2) can be written as:

$$J(\mathbf{Y}) = Tr\left(\mathbf{X}^T \mathbf{X} - 2\mathbf{X}^T \mathbf{ASY} + \mathbf{Y}^T \mathbf{S}^T \mathbf{A}^T \mathbf{ASY} \right) + Tr\left(\mathbf{Y}^T \mathbf{Y} - 2\mathbf{Y}^T \mathbf{Y}_g + \mathbf{Y}_g^T \mathbf{Y}_g \right) \tag{3}$$

The gradient is

$$\partial J / \partial Y = -2\mathbf{S}^T \mathbf{A}^T \mathbf{X} + 2\mathbf{S}^T \mathbf{A}^T \mathbf{ASY} + 2\mathbf{Y} - 2\mathbf{Y}_g \tag{4}$$

The KKT complementarity condition for the nonnegativity of Y_{ik} gives

$$\left(-2S^T A^T X + 2S^T A^T ASY + 2Y - 2Y_g\right)_{ik} Y_{ik} = 0 \tag{5}$$

Given an initial guess of Y, update of

$$Y_{ik}^{t+1} = Y_{ik}^t \left(S^T A^T X + Y_g\right)_{ik} / \left(\left(S^T A^T ASY\right)_{ik} + Y_{ik}\right) \tag{6}$$

will converges to a local minimum. To demonstrate this, we use $Z\left(Y, \tilde{Y}\right)$ as an auxiliary function of $J(Y)$ if it satisfies the following conditions for any Y and $\tilde{Y}$:

$$Z\left(Y, \tilde{Y}\right) \geq J(Y), \ Z(Y, Y) = J(Y) \tag{7}$$

Define

$$Y^{t+1} = arg \ \min_Y Z\left(Y, Y^t\right) \tag{8}$$

Then, $J\left(Y^t\right) = Z\left(Y^t, Y^t\right) \geq Z\left(Y^{t+1}, Y^t\right) \geq J\left(Y^{t+1}\right)$. $J\left(Y^t\right)$ is thus monotonic decreasing. The key is to define $Z\left(Y, \tilde{Y}\right)$ and find its global minimum. The auxiliary function of Eq. (3) is

$$Z(Y, Y') = -\sum_{ik} 2(X^T ASY)_{ik} + \sum_{ik} \left(Y^T S^T A^T AS\right)_{ik} Y_{ik}^2 / Y_{ik}' + \sum_{ik} \left(Y^T\right)_{ik} Y_{ik}^2 / Y_{ik}' - \sum_{ik} 2\left(Y_g^T Y\right)_{ik} \tag{9}$$

Y^{t+1} is obtained by minimizing $Z(Y, Y')$ while fixing $Y' = Y^t$. This minimum is given by

$$0 = \partial Z(Y, Y') / \partial Y_{ik} = -2\left(S^T A^T X\right)_{ik} + 2\left(S^T A^T ASY\right)_{ik} Y_{ik} / Y_{ik}' + 2(Y)_{ik} Y_{ik} / Y_{ik}' - 2(Y_g)_{ik} \tag{10}$$

which is equal to

$$Y_{ik} = Y_{ik}' \left(S^T A^T X + Y_g\right)_{ik} / \left(\left(S^T A^T ASY\right)_{ik} + Y_{ik}\right) \tag{11}$$

Solving A and S follow a similar way [16]. The final update rules are:

$$A_{ik} \leftarrow A_{ik} \left(XY^T S^T\right)_{ik} / \left(AA^T XY^T S^T\right)_{ik} \tag{12}$$

$$S_{ik} \leftarrow S_{ik} \left(A^T XY^T\right)_{ik} / \left(A^T AS\right)_{ik} \tag{13}$$

$$Y_{ik} \leftarrow Y_{ik} \left(S^T A^T X + Y_g\right)_{ik} / \left(S^T A^T ASY + Y\right)_{ik} \tag{14}$$

3 Results

3.1 Parameter Settings

To determine the cluster (or column of A) number k, three criteria are used: 1) a smaller reconstruction error $r = \|X - ASY\|^2$; 2) a higher mean silhouette coefficient s among clusters over all vertices; and 3) a small reproducibility metric c. For c, we subdivide the subjects to two groups while keeping each one covers the full range of ages. Both sub-groups yield k clusters (or columns) in A. We compute Euclidian distance among the clusters across the two groups, yielding a $k \times k$ distance matrix. Then, we apply Hungarian algorithm to the distance matrix, to estimate a one-to-one assignment for the k clusters of the two sub-groups. Finally, we compute the same Euclidian distance for the k assigned pairs and the mean distance c is used to quantify the reproducibility.

On gyral height matrix A, we compute rs, ss and cs for ks ranging from 5 to 20. We use $-s$ instead of s because both r and k are expected to be smaller. We normalized rs, ss and cs, respectively, by subtracting the mean and dividing by the standard deviation. After this normalization, $k = 7$ is determined as it yields the smallest $(r + s + c)/3$. To further evaluate the reproducibility of the algorithm, we apply the algorithm with the determined k to two hemispheres, separately. Similar Hungarian algorithm is used to yield a one-to-one assignment of the clusters between hemispheres. The cross-hemisphere similarity between assigned clusters is observable in Fig. 2, and the Pearson correlation coefficient between them is 0.61 ± 0.17, on average.

3.2 Evaluation of the Identified Components

The 7 clusters of spatiotemporal patterns of gyral heights are mapped back to the surface (inflated with blue color as the background in Fig. 2). Cluster #1 (Fig. 2(a)) consists of five regions: three long gyri including superior temporal gyrus (#III) and inferior front gyrus (#II) and supramarginal and angular gyri (#IV); two isolated regions including frontal pole (#I) and the conjunction of middle temporal gyrus and lateral occipital gyrus (#V). Cluster #2 (Fig. 2(b)) highlights two sensory regions including primary somatosensory region (#I, 3b) and auditory cortex (#II), one lower-order visual regions (part of V2, #V) and three higher-order visual regions including MT (or V5, #III), dorsal part of V4 (#IV) and V3 (#VI). Most regions in Cluster #1 reside on gyri while most regions in cluster #2 (except #IV) reside on the walls between gyri and sulci. Note that we use longitudinal patterns of gyral height but not the height itself to separate gyral crests in Cluster #1 from gyral walls in Cluster #2. The mean gyral height does not significantly differ between the two clusters (around 16 mm and 18 mm in Table 1, and $p > 0.05$ by t-test) while the developmental trend of the two clusters are totally different (Fig. 2(i)). Cluster #1 possess the lowest absolute height (around 16 mm) but its height grows while the ones of Cluster #2-#7 decrease. Not all gyral crests grow as Cluster #1 does not cover all gyral crests. For example, precentral gyrus and superior gyrus are not in Cluster #1 while Cluster #2 includes the middle temporal gyrus (#IV).

The other five clusters align with visual regions from V1 to V3. Gyral heights of most of them decrease over time except that Cluster #3 and #7 have a slight increase at tails. The decreasing speed accelerates from V1 (Cluster #3) to V3 (Cluster #7) while

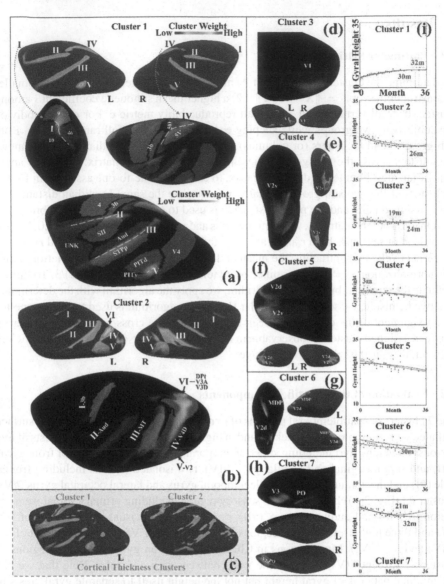

Fig. 2. (a)–(b) Two clusters on gyral height that cover multiple cortical areas. (c) Two clusters obtained on cortical thickness that find their correspondence to gyral height clusters in (a) and (b). (d)–(h) The other five clusters obtained based on gyral height. In all clusters, the weights in **X** are shown on the inflated surfaces with blue background. Brain sites (color patches) from PH00 or LVE atlases are overlaid on the inflated surface of the left hemisphere with black ground (The weights on these surfaces are present by gray scales). White dashed curves in (a) highlight the locations with heavy weight. Surfaces are scaled and rotated to have the best view. (i) Longitudinal gyral height values (scattered dots) for each cluster (blue for left hemispheres; red for right hemispheres). Polynomial curves are used to fit the dots. We show the quadratic ones. Other fitting models yield similar results. Extrema are highlighted by digits. (Color figure online)

Table 1. Statistics of cortical, structural connective and functional metrics on clusters.

Cluster	Gyral height		Curve slope *Figure 2(i)*	Cortical thickness		Function involvement		Avg. fiber density over all timepoints
	L	R	L/R	L	R	PH00	LVE	
1	15.67 ±0.93	15.54 ±0.96	0.08 0.09	2.14 ±0.07	2.12 ±0.08	4.69	3.38	1.85 ±0.39
2	18.79 ±1.38	19.23 ±1.58	−0.11 −0.11	1.60 ±0.11	1.54 ±0.13	3.52	2.93	0.86 ±0.08
3	18.60 ±0.64	19.08 ±0.73	−0.02 −0.02	1.99 ±0.13	1.93 ±0.11	3.66	3.11	1.75 ±0.29
4	21.90 ±1.29	21.86 ±1.31	−0.07 −0.04	1.80 ±0.18	1.91 ±0.16	3.54	2.14	1.59 ±0.23
5	25.24 ±1.64	25.26 ±1.62	−0.07 −0.12	1.65 ±0.11	1.63 ±0.15	3.02	1.97	1.32 ±0.24
6	25.80 ±1.59	24.57 ±0.96	−0.09 −0.05	1.68 ±0.14	1.70 ±0.10	3.09	2.74	1.41 ±0.37
7	30.12 ±1.30	30.53 ±1.20	−0.11 −0.07	1.67 ±0.10	1.59 ±0.09	2.28	2.49	1.04 ±0.24

V1 has the lowest gyral height and V3 has the highest height (see "Slope" and "Gyral height" columns in Table 1).

3.3 The Relation to Brain Anatomy, Structural Connection and Function

Clusters having higher heights have thinner cortex. This relation is observable in Table 1. The Pearson correlation coefficients between the two metrics are −0.68 and −0.67 for the left and right hemispheres, respectively. By applying the S-ONMF algorithm to longitudinal cortical thickness features, we also identify seven clusters and find two thickness clusters that have similar spatial patterns (Fig. 2(c)) with Cluster #1&#2 of gyral height clusters. The Pearson correlation coefficients between the spatial patterns of them are 0.41 for Cluster #1 and 0.43 for Clusters #2.

Regions in Cluster #2-#7 are well covered by functionally defined brain sites (Fig. 2(b)) while region in Cluster #1 appear to be at the borders between or among them (see the brain sites and white dashed curves on the inflated surface in Fig. 2). We compute the Dice coefficient between the cortical regions and the brain sites (from PH00 atlas [27]) they touch. On average, the coefficient is 0.67 ± 0.15 for Cluster #2-#7, demonstrating the alignment between them. Meanwhile, the Dice coefficient between the regions in Cluster #1 and their neighboring brain sites (Fig. 2(a)) is 0.12. It is inferred that regions in Cluster #1 could be involved in more brain functions. To quantify the function involvement, we compute the numbers of brain sites within the neighborhood (a sphere, radius = 3 mm) of each vertex. The weights (values in **A**) in each cluster is normalized by dividing the sum. The product of the numbers and weights is defined as the functional involvement of a cluster. We used the brain sites in PH00 [27] and LVE [28] atlases to quantify the functional involvement (Table 1). On average, regions in Cluster #1 are involved in 4.69 brain sites in PH00 atlas and 3.38 sites in LVE atlas, higher than all the other clusters ($p < 0.05$). Higher functional involvement of Cluster #1 is supported by its higher structural connective density (1.85 ± 0.39) averaged over all timepoints (Table 1) than all the other clusters ($p < 0.05$ for all).

In summary, regions in Cluster #1 have the lowest gyral height but they are the only cortical regions that keep growing in height. They have the thickest cortex, the densest fiber connections and the most diverse functional involvement.

4 Conclusions

We develop a S-ONMF method to decompose the cortex into clusters by the gyral height developmental trajectory. The Cortical thickness, the white matter fiber density and functionally defined cortical parcellation atlases are compared to these clusters, revealing the close and interpretable relationship between them. All these results demonstrate the soundness of both the definition of gyral height and the algorithm in brain development analysis.

Acknowledgements. T Zhang, L Du, X Jiang and L Guo were supported by the National Natural Science Foundation of China (31971288, 61973255, 61703073, 61976045, 61936007 and U1801265).

References

1. Toga, A.W., Thompson, P.M., Sowell, E.R.: Mapping brain maturation. Focus **29**(3), 148–390 (2006)
2. Lebel, C., Walker, L., Leemans, A., Phillips, L., Beaulieu, C.: Microstructural maturation of the human brain from childhood to adulthood. Neuroimage **40**(3), 1044–1055 (2008)
3. Paus, T.: Mapping brain maturation and cognitive development during adolescence. Trends Cogn. Sci. **9**(2), 60–68 (2005)
4. Williams, R., Bokhari, S., Silverstein, P., Pinson, D., Kumar, A., Buch, S.: Nonhuman primate models of NeuroAIDS. J. NeuroVirol. **14**(4), 292–300 (2008). https://doi.org/10.1080/135502 80802074539
5. Lacreuse, A., Herndon, J.G.: Nonhuman primate models of cognitive aging. In: Animal Models of Human Cognitive Aging, pp. 1–30. Humana Press (2009)
6. Rilling, J.K.: Comparative primate neuroimaging: insights into human brain evolution. Trends Cogn. Sci. **18**(1), 46–55 (2014)
7. Price, K.C., Coe, C.L.: Maternal constraint on fetal growth patterns in the rhesus monkey (Macaca mulatta): the intergenerational link between mothers and daughters. Hum. Reprod. **15**(2), 452–457 (2000)
8. Young, J.T., et al.: The UNC-Wisconsin rhesus macaque neurodevelopment database: a structural MRI and DTI database of early postnatal development. Front. Neurosci. **11**, 29 (2017)
9. Wang, F., et al.: Developmental topography of cortical thickness during infancy. Proc. Natl. Acad. Sci. **116**(32), 15855–15860 (2019)

10. Lohmann, G., Von Cramon, D.Y., Colchester, A.C.: Deep sulcal landmarks provide an organizing framework for human cortical folding. Cereb. Cortex **18**(6), 1415–1420 (2008)
11. Yeo, B.T., Sabuncu, M.R., Vercauteren, T., Ayache, N., Fischl, B., Golland, P.: Spherical demons: fast diffeomorphic landmark-free surface registration. IEEE Trans. Med. Imaging **29**(3), 650–668 (2009)
12. Reardon, P.K., et al.: Normative brain size variation and brain shape diversity in humans. Science **360**(6394), 1222–1227 (2018)
13. Chen, H., Li, Y., Ge, F., Li, G., Shen, D., Liu, T.: Gyral net: a new representation of cortical folding organization. Med. Image Anal. **42**, 14–25 (2017)
14. Nie, J., et al.: Axonal fiber terminations concentrate on gyri. Cereb. Cortex **22**(12), 2831–2839 (2012)
15. Van Essen, D.C.: A tension-based theory of morphogenesis and compact wiring in the central nervous system. Nature **385**(6614), 313–318 (1997)
16. Ding, C., Li, T., Peng, W., Park, H.: Orthogonal nonnegative matrix t-factorizations for clustering. In Proceedings of the 12th ACM SIGKDD International Conference on Knowledge Discovery and Data Mining, pp. 126–135, August 2006
17. Wang, L., et al.: LINKS: learning-based multi-source IntegratioN frameworK for Segmentation of infant brain images. NeuroImage **108**, 160–172 (2015)
18. Wang, L., et al.: Segmentation of neonatal brain MR images using patch-driven level sets. NeuroImage **84**, 141–158 (2014)
19. Wang, L., Shi, F., Yap, P.T., Lin, W., Gilmore, J.H., Shen, D.: Longitudinally guided level sets for consistent tissue segmentation of neonates. Hum. Brain Mapp. **34**(4), 956–972 (2013)
20. Li, G., Nie, J., Wu, G., Wang, Y., Shen, D., Initiative, A.D.N.: Consistent reconstruction of cortical surfaces from longitudinal brain MR images. Neuroimage **59**(4), 3805–3820 (2012)
21. Li, G., et al.: Measuring the dynamic longitudinal cortex development in infants by reconstruction of temporally consistent cortical surfaces. Neuroimage **90**, 266–279 (2014)
22. Andersson, J.L., Sotiropoulos, S.N.: An integrated approach to correction for off-resonance effects and subject movement in diffusion MR imaging. Neuroimage **125**, 1063–1078 (2016)
23. Jenkinson, M., Beckmann, C.F., Behrens, T.E., Woolrich, M.W., Smith, S.M.: Fsl. Neuroimage, **62**(2), 782–790 (2012)
24. Yeh, F.C., Wedeen, V.J., Tseng, W.Y.I.: Generalized q-sampling imaging. IEEE Trans. Med. Imaging **29**(9), 1626–1635 (2010)
25. Yeh, F.C., Verstynen, T.D., Wang, Y., Fernández-Miranda, J.C., Tseng, W.Y.I.: Deterministic diffusion fiber tracking improved by quantitative anisotropy. PLoS ONE **8**(11), e80713 (2013)
26. Xia, J., et al.: Mapping hemispheric asymmetries of the macaque cerebral cortex during early brain development. Hum. Brain Mapp. **41**(1), 95–106 (2020)
27. Paxinos, G., Huang, X.F., Toga, A.W.: The rhesus monkey brain in stereotaxic coordinates (2000)
28. Lewis, J.W., Van Essen, D.C.: Corticocortical connections of visual, sensorimotor, and multimodal processing areas in the parietal lobe of the macaque monkey. J. Comp. Neurol. **428**(1), 112–137 (2000)

Inhomogeneity Correction in Magnetic Resonance Images Using Deep Image Priors

Shuo Han[✉], Jerry L. Prince, and Aaron Carass

Johns Hopkins Whiting School of Engineering, Baltimore, MD 21218, USA
{shan50,prince,aaron_carass}@jhu.edu

Abstract. Intensity inhomogeneity in magnetic resonance (MR) images can decrease the performance of image processing, such as segmentation and registration. In this work, we propose an unsupervised learning approach to correct the inhomogeneity of an MR image based on deep image priors (DIPs). In DIPs, the structure of the convolutional neural networks was previously shown to capture the prior probability of an image, which has been demonstrated in several applications such as image denoising, segmentation, and super resolution. To obtain an inhomogeneity-free MR image, the problem was formulated in a Bayesian inference framework. The priors of the image and inhomogeneity field were captured by two DIPs and their likelihood was modeled based on the observed image. The approximated expectation of the posterior was calculated to get the corrected image using a stochastic gradient Langevin dynamics algorithm. Since we modeled the noise distribution, the proposed method is simultaneously capable of denoising to some extent. We compared our method with N4, a popular inhomogeneity correction method, in a simulated data set and a couple of real data sets, statistically showing that it has comparable or even superior performance than N4 when the inhomogeneity is severe or noise is high.

1 Introduction

As a noninvasive and nonradioactive modality, magnetic resonance (MR) imaging provides good soft tissue contrast and is widely used in medical studies and clinical practice. However, spatially varying intensity inhomogeneity—different intensities for the same tissue across different locations—is often present in MR images and hinders automatic image processing and analysis methods such as segmentation and registration [18]. As a result, the correction of inhomogeneity is usually performed as a pre-processing step in many algorithms [8,13].

MR inhomogeneity can often be viewed as a slowly-varying multiplicative field that is applied to the underlying uncorrupted image. The retrospective correction methods, which are only based on the observed image instead of extra acquisition or hardware calibration, can broadly fall into five categories [7,18]. (1) Filtering. The low frequency content of the image is extracted to get the inhomogeneity field. (2) Statistical modeling. Prior knowledge is incorporated into

© Springer Nature Switzerland AG 2020
M. Liu et al. (Eds.): MLMI 2020, LNCS 12436, pp. 404–413, 2020.
https://doi.org/10.1007/978-3-030-59861-7_41

an energy minimization framework. As an example, George and Kalaivani [6] incorporated l^1 norm to impose a sparsity constraint on the uncorrupted image within the framelet domain and a sparsity constraint on the inhomogeneity field within the Fourier domain. (3) Surface fitting. A parametric smooth surface is fitted to model the inhomogeneity field. As an example, Zhao et al. [22] fit a smooth polynomial surface using voxels with similar structures matched with a non-local means algorithm. (4) Segmentation based. The tissue segmentation and inhomogeneity correction are obtained simultaneously to benefit each other. As an example, Zhang and Song [21] modeled the inhomogeneity field as a linear combination of smooth basis functions whose coefficients were jointly optimized with tissue classification. (5) Histogram based. The correction is directly based on image intensity histograms. N3 [15] and its improvement N4 [16] are the most popular inhomogeneity correction algorithms. N3 models the probability distributions via the image histograms and obtains the inhomogeneity field iteratively by maximizing frequency content of the image. N4 improves N3 by using advantageous B-spline smoothing and an alternative optimization scheme. Readers are referred to [7,18] for more comprehensive reviews.

Convolutional neural networks (CNNs) have been applied to various image processing problems, but mostly in a supervised fashion, i.e., ground truth is available for training the networks. In contrast, the deep image prior (DIP) [11] does not rely on any training data, and thus is considered an unsupervised approach. It acts as a prior or regularization during loss minimization, by capturing the internal patch recurrence of an image with the structure of a CNN. As opposed to conventional networks, this CNN takes a randomly initialized tensor as input rather than an image, and the network parameters are optimized so that it can output an estimate of the uncorrupted image. DIP has been applied to various image processing problems, such as image denoising, super resolution, inpainting, segmentation, and blind deconvolution [3,4,11,12].

In this work, we applied this technique to inhomogeneity correction of MR images. In particular, two DIPs were used to estimate the uncorrupted image and the inhomogeneity field, respectively. By extending previous work, we derived the objective function with DIPs in a Bayesian inference framework. A stochastic gradient Langevin dynamics (SGLD) algorithm [19] was used to find the expectations of the uncorrupted image and inhomogeneity field. By modeling the noise distribution, the proposed method is robust to noise and simultaneously capable of denoising to some extent. It was compared with N4 on a simulated data set and a couple of real data sets, and statistically shows on a par or even superior performance when the inhomogeneity is severe or noise is high.

2   Methods

2.1   Theory

Suppose that the observed image is v, the underlying uncorrupted image is u, and the inhomogeneity field is b. The image formation [18] is modeled as

$$v_i = u_i b_i + n_i, \qquad \forall i = 1, 2, ..., N, \tag{1}$$

where i indicates the ith pixel of an image, N is the total number of pixels, and n is i.i.d. zero-mean Gaussian noise with variance σ^2. Given v, prior knowledge is usually required to estimate u and b. Common choices include minimizing the total variation norm for u, where u is assumed to be piece-wise constant [6], and interpolating b with B-spline, where b is assumed to be smoothly varying [16].

The DIP [11], however, imposes the prior using the structure of a CNN, whose output is proven to approximate a stationary Gaussian process [3]. The CNN takes a randomly initialized tensor as input, and the network parameters are optimized to minimize the l^2 norm of the difference between the network output and the observed image. Extending previous work [3,4,11], we mathematically derive the objective function of DIPs in a Bayesian framework below.

Assume that the uncorrupted image u and the inhomogeneity field b are parameterized as $u = f_u(z_u; \theta_u)$ and $b = f_b(z_b; \theta_b)$, where f_u and f_b are two CNNs, and the network inputs z_u and z_b and network weights θ_u and θ_b are modeled as four i.i.d. zero-mean Gaussian random variables with variances $\gamma_u{}^2$, $\gamma_b{}^2$, $\eta_u{}^2$, and $\eta_b{}^2$, respectively. Instead of finding the maximum a posteriori, we estimate the posterior expectation for better accuracy [3]. In particular, according to the law of the unconscious statistician[1], the expectation can be calculated as

$$\mathbb{E}_{u,b \sim p(u,b|v)}[u, b] = \mathbb{E}_{z_u,z_b,\theta_u,\theta_b \sim p(z_u,z_b,\theta_u,\theta_b|v)}[f_u(z_u; \theta_u), f_b(z_b; \theta_b)]. \quad (2)$$

For the posterior $p(z_u, z_b, \theta_u, \theta_b \mid v)$, the corresponding likelihood is

$$p(v \mid z_u, z_b, \theta_u, \theta_b) \propto \exp\left(-\frac{1}{2\sigma^2} \sum_{i=1}^{N} (v_i - f_u(z_u; \theta_u)_i f_b(z_b; \theta_b)_i)^2\right), \quad (3)$$

according to Eq. (1). Since the $z_u, z_b, \theta_u, \theta_b$ are Gaussian distributed, their prior

$$p(z_u, z_b, \theta_u, \theta_b) \propto \exp\left(-\frac{\sum_j z_{uj}{}^2}{2\gamma_u{}^2} - \frac{\sum_k z_{bk}{}^2}{2\gamma_b{}^2} - \frac{\sum_s \theta_{us}{}^2}{2\eta_u{}^2} - \frac{\sum_r \theta_{br}{}^2}{2\eta_b{}^2}\right). \quad (4)$$

In order to estimate the expectation, we adopted an SGLD algorithm [19]. This algorithm uses the negative logarithm of the posterior as its objective function. Noise sampled from a Gaussian distribution is injected to the parameter updates during each iteration, and the expectation is calculated as a weighted average of the outputs of each iteration to approximate a Markov Chain Monte Carlo process. As in [3], we used Adam [9] to calculate the parameter updates, drew the noise from a zero-mean i.i.d. Gaussian distribution with constant variance, and weighted each iteration equally to calculate the expectation. According to Bayes's theorem and Eqs. (3) and (4), the objective function J of our problem can be written as

$$J = \frac{\sum_i (v_i - f_{ui} f_{bi})^2}{2\sigma^2} + \frac{\sum_j z_{uj}{}^2}{2\gamma_u{}^2} + \frac{\sum_k z_{bk}{}^2}{2\gamma_b{}^2} + \frac{\sum_s \theta_{us}{}^2}{2\eta_u{}^2} + \frac{\sum_r \theta_{br}{}^2}{2\eta_b{}^2}. \quad (5)$$

Note that the first term on the right hand side of Eq. (5) is the sum of squared error loss between the observed image and the network outputs, and the last

---

[1] https://en.wikipedia.org/wiki/Law_of_the_unconscious_statistician.

four terms coincide with l^2 weight decay which is not implemented in the original work [11]. We further used cubic interpolation to impose a smoothly-varying constraint on b. The corrected image and the estimated inhomogeneity are optimized as the expectations of network outputs and the image noise is reduced in theory during this process.

Following the proof in [3], we chose the variance of network weights η_u^2 and η_b^2 directly related to the number of convolution channels H and kernel size d^2 as $\eta_u^2 = \eta_b^2 = 1/(Hd^2)$, the same for both CNNs in the 2D situation. Rather than using fixed weighting between the loss and the weight decay, Eq. (5) suggests that this should depend on the noise level of the image, which can be estimated using other algorithms such as [2]. In contrast to previous work [3,11], we chose to optimize the network inputs z_u and z_b as well, and the values of γ_u^2 and γ_b^2 are left tunable, which can affect the algorithm performance according to our preliminary experiments.

2.2 Implementation Details

Although the aforementioned algorithm can be applied to 3D images, we used 2D CNNs implemented with PyTorch 1.4 for demonstration purposes. Two modified 2D U-Nets [14] were used to estimate u and b, respectively. Instead of channel-wise concatenation, we used element-wise summation for the skip connections. All convolutions have the same number of input channels $H = 128$ and kernel size $d = 3$. The input and output of f_u have the same spatial size as the observed image v. The input and output of f_b are 32 times smaller than each dimension of v and the output is upsampled with cubic interpolation to the same size as v. f_u and f_b have 6 and 2 pooling layers, respectively. During parameter initialization, the convolution bias was set to 0, and network inputs and the convolution kernels were randomly drawn from their corresponding prior distributions. Instance normalization [17] with learnable affine parameters (using default initialization) were used. To use these U-Nets, the images were zero-padded when it had background (e.g., a typical brain image) or reflection-padded otherwise.

For SGLD, Adam was used with default parameters [9] except that the learning rate $= 5 \times 10^{-4}$. The variance of the injected noise was 1. To encourage the outputs to have positive values, f_u was optimized for 10 iterations without incorporating f_b. f_b was then optimized for 10 iterations with f_u fixed. The two were optimized together for 480 iterations before averaging the outputs and then for another 1500 iterations for expectation estimation. In practice, we found that the optimization may diverge during the loss plateau; therefore, we stopped optimization when the loss exceeded three times its moving average. We set $\gamma_u^2 = 1 \times 10^{-5}$ and $\gamma_b^2 = 1 \times 10^{-10}$ according to our preliminary results.

To estimate the image noise variance, the algorithm in [2] was used. For testing on brain MR images, only the foreground region should be used to estimate the noise. Therefore, we used k-means to estimate a head mask and only use relatively smooth regions (judging from their gradient magnitudes) within this mask for more accurate noise estimation. The image was divided by its standard deviation to stabilize the optimization.

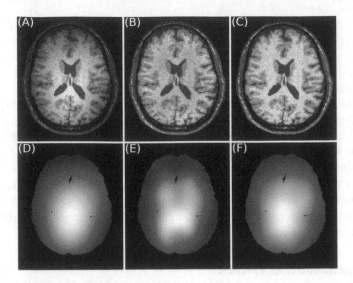

Fig. 1. Visual comparison between N4 and DIP-Bias on a BrainWeb image with 8% noise and 80% inhomogeneity. (A) the observed image, (B) the corrected image from N4, (C) the corrected image from DIP-Bias, (D) the true inhomogeneity field, (E) the estimated inhomogeneity field from N4, and (F) the estimated inhomogeneity field from DIP-Bias. (F) is visually more similar to (D) than (E).

3   Experiments and Results

3.1   BrainWeb Simulation

The BrainWeb [1] data set provides simulated brain phantoms with known inhomogeneity fields and Rician noise. To quantitatively compare the proposed method, termed as DIP-Bias, with N4, twenty subjects[2] were simulated[3] with T1-weighted (T1w) contrast. Three noise levels 2%, 4%, and 8% measured against white matter (WM) intensity and three shapes of inhomogeneity fields were included. We extracted the 80th and 90th axial slices from each subject, and applied three different inhomogeneity levels 20%, 40%, and 80%, meaning that the intensity of an inhomogeneity field was linearly scaled to $[0.9, 1.1]$, $[0.8, 1.2]$, and $[0.6, 1.4]$, respectively, within the brain region of each slice. As suggested by [5], these three types of severity can reflect the inhomogeneity from 1.5 T, 3 T, and 7 T scanners, respectively. As a result, this setup included $20 \times 2 \times 3 \times 3 \times 3 = 1080$ images. Note that N4 was performed with the parameters suggested in [16].

The image and inhomogeneity can only be estimated up to an intensity scaling factor. Therefore, to compare these two methods, we used normalized cross correlation (NCC) to measure the agreement between estimated and true inho-

---

[2] https://brainweb.bic.mni.mcgill.ca/anatomic_normal_20.html.

[3] https://github.com/BIC-MNI/mrisim.

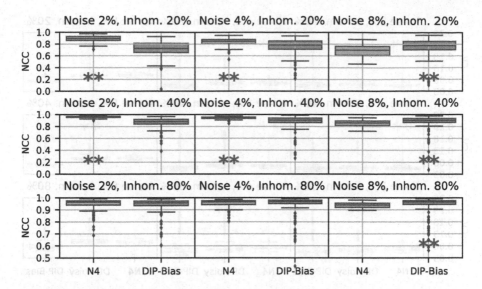

Fig. 2. NCC comparison between N4 and DIP-Bias. NCC measures the agreement between estimated and true inhomogeneity. Statistically better method is marked with asterisks (** for $p < 0.01$ and * for $p < 0.05$). DIP-Bias is comparable or better when the noise or inhomogeneity is severe. **Inhom.**: inhomogeneity.

mogeneity within the brain region and the coefficient of variation (CV) to assess the uniformity within WM of the corrected image. They are defined as

$$\text{NCC} = \frac{\sum_{i \in \Omega_m}(x_i - \bar{x}_m)(y_i - \bar{y}_m)}{\sqrt{\sum_{i \in \Omega_m}(x_i - \bar{x}_m)^2}\sqrt{\sum_{i \in \Omega_m}(y_i - \bar{y}_m)^2}} \quad \text{and} \quad \text{CV} = \frac{s_w}{\bar{z}_w}, \quad (6)$$

where x is the estimated inhomogeneity field, y is the true inhomogeneity field, Ω_m is the brain mask, $\bar{x}_m$ and $\bar{y}_m$ are the intensity means within Ω_m, z is the corrected image, $\bar{z}_w$ is the mean within WM mask Ω_w, and s_w is the standard deviation within Ω_w.

We further conducted paired Wilcoxon tests between DIP-Bias and N4 for each combination of noise and inhomogeneity levels. We used two-sided tests to determine whether there is significance and one-sided to determine which one is better. The NCC and CV of both methods with the statistical significance (** for $p < 0.01$ and * for $0.01 \leq p < 0.05$) are shown in Figs. 2 and 3, respectively. Note that since our method denoises images simultaneously, we instead compared DIP-Bias without noise reduction—by dividing the observed image with the estimated inhomogeneity field—or DB noisy, with N4 in Fig. 3. These results indicate that N4 is significantly better than DIP-Bias when the noise or inhomogeneity is mild, while DIP-Bias is comparable to or even better than N4 when the noise or inhomogeneity is severe. A visual comparison in a 8% noise and 80% inhomogeneity image is shown in Fig. 1.

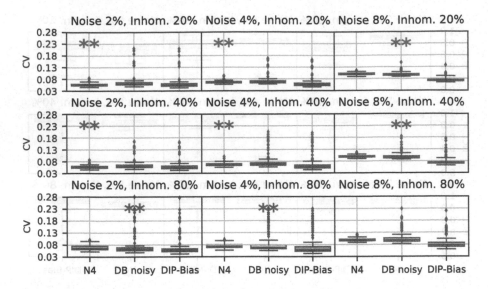

Fig. 3. CV comparison between N4 and DIP-Bias. Lower CV indicates more uniform WM. Statistically better method between N4 and DB noisy is marked with asterisks (∗∗ for $p < 0.01$ and ∗ for $p < 0.05$). DB noisy is comparable or better than N4 when the noise or inhomogeneity is severe. DIP-Bias provides more uniform WM due to noise reduction. **DB noisy**: the observed image divided by the inhomogeneity estimate from DIP-Bias. **Inhom.**: inhomogeneity.

3.2 Real Data Sets

The proposed method was qualitatively compared to N4 using a couple of real data sets. The comparison using an OASIS3 [10] T1w axial slice is shown in Fig. 4. DIP-Bias visually produced more uniform intensities than N4. The comparison using a sagittal slice of a postmortem hippocampus specimen [20] acquired from a 9.4 T scanner is shown in Fig. 5. The two methods have comparable performance. Note that the suggested parameters of N4 [16] for this particular data set were adopted.

4 Discussion and Conclusions

In this work, we proposed an inhomogeneity correction method in MR images based on DIPs. We derived the objective function in a Bayesian framework and estimated the uncorrupted image and inhomogeneity field via expectations of the posterior using SGLD optimization. The proposed method was compared with N4 quantitatively and qualitatively, showing statistically comparable or even better performance when the noise or inhomogeneity is severe, and thus it can be an alternative approach to N4 in such scenarios.

We found that the optimization is unstable and produced many outliers as shown in Figs. 2 and 3. It could be trapped into undesired local minima with

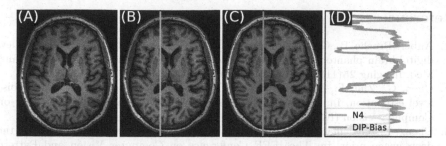

Fig. 4. Qualitative comparison between N4 and DIP-Bias on an OASIS3 image. (A) the observed image, **(B)** the corrected image from N4, **(C)** the corrected image from DIP-Bias, and **(D)** the intensities at the selected position as indicated in (B) and (C). DIP-Bias is more uniform compared with N4 at the selected position.

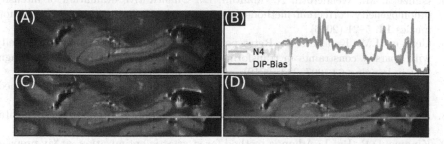

Fig. 5. Qualitative comparison between N4 and DIP-Bias on a hippocampus specimen image. (A) the observed image, **(B)** the intensities at the selected position as indicated in (C) and (D), **(C)** the corrected image from N4, and **(D)** the corrected image from DIP-Bias. DIP-Bias is comparable to N4 at the selected position.

bad inhomogeneity correction quality, and could even diverge. A better optimization that is capable of approximating expectations should be studied in the future. Meanwhile, more accurate noise estimation could potentially improve our method. Additional regularization could also be tested to encourage better separation between the image and inhomogeneity. The proposed algorithm would also be implemented for 3D images and evaluated for more image contrasts in the future.

Acknowledgments. The authors would thank colleagues from the Image Analysis and Communications Laboratory at the Johns Hopkins University for their support and help.

Data were provided in part by OASIS-3: Principal Investigators: T. Benzinger, D. Marcus, J. Morris; NIH P50AG00561, P30NS09857781, P01AG026276, P01AG003991, R01AG043434, UL1TR000448, R01EB009352. AV-45 doses were provided by Avid Radiopharmaceuticals, a wholly owned subsidiary of Eli Lilly.

References

1. Aubert-Broche, B., Griffin, M., Pike, G.B., Evans, A.C., Collins, D.L.: Twenty new digital brain phantoms for creation of validation image data bases. IEEE Trans. Med. Imaging **25**(11), 1410–1416 (2006)
2. Chen, G., Zhu, F., Heng, P.A.: An efficient statistical method for image noise level estimation. In: Proceedings of the 2015 IEEE International Conference on Computer Vision (ICCV), pp. 477–485. IEEE Computer Society (2015)
3. Cheng, Z., Gadelha, M., Maji, S., Sheldon, D.: A Bayesian perspective on the deep image prior. In: The IEEE Conference on Computer Vision and Pattern Recognition (CVPR), June 2019
4. Gandelsman, Y., Shocher, A., Irani, M.: "Double-DIP": unsupervised image decomposition via coupled deep-image-priors. In: The IEEE Conference on Computer Vision and Pattern Recognition (CVPR), June 2019
5. Ganzetti, M., Wenderoth, N., Mantini, D.: Quantitative evaluation of intensity inhomogeneity correction methods for structural MR brain images. Neuroinformatics **14**, 5–21 (2016)
6. George, M.M., Kalaivani, S.: Retrospective correction of intensity inhomogeneity with sparsity constraints in transform-domain: application to brain MRI. Magn. Reson. Imaging **61**, 207–223 (2019)
7. Hou, Z.: A review on MR image intensity inhomogeneity correction. Int. J. Biomed. Imaging **2006**, 1–11 (2006)
8. Huo, Y., et al.: Consistent cortical reconstruction and multi-atlas brain segmentation. NeuroImage **138**, 197–210 (2016)
9. Kingma, D.P., Ba, J.: Adam: a method for stochastic optimization. arXiv preprint arXiv:1412.6980 (2014)
10. LaMontagne, P.J., et al.: OASIS-3: longitudinal neuroimaging, clinical, and cognitive dataset for normal aging and Alzheimer disease. medRxiv (2019)
11. Lempitsky, V., Vedaldi, A., Ulyanov, D.: Deep image prior. In: The IEEE Conference on Computer Vision and Pattern Recognition (CVPR), pp. 9446–9454 (2018)
12. Ren, D., Zhang, K., Wang, Q., Hu, Q., Zuo, W.: Neural blind deconvolution using deep priors. arXiv preprint arXiv:1908.02197 (2019)
13. Romero, J.E., et al.: CERES: a new cerebellum lobule segmentation method. NeuroImage **147**, 916–924 (2017)
14. Ronneberger, O., Fischer, P., Brox, T.: U-Net: convolutional networks for biomedical image segmentation. In: Medical Image Computing and Computer-Assisted Intervention (MICCAI), pp. 234–241 (2015)
15. Sled, J.G., Zijdenbos, A.P., Evans, A.C.: A nonparametric method for automatic correction of intensity nonuniformity in MRI data. IEEE Trans. Med. Imaging **17**(1), 87–97 (1998)
16. Tustison, N.J., et al.: N4ITK: improved N3 bias correction. IEEE Trans. Med. Imaging **29**(6), 1310–1320 (2010)
17. Ulyanov, D., Vedaldi, A., Lempitsky, V.: Improved texture networks: maximizing quality and diversity in feed-forward stylization and texture synthesis. In: The IEEE Conference on Computer Vision and Pattern Recognition (CVPR), pp. 6924–6932 (2017)
18. Vovk, U., Pernus, F., Likar, B.: A review of methods for correction of intensity inhomogeneity in MRI. IEEE Trans. Med. Imaging **26**(3), 405–421 (2007)
19. Welling, M., Teh, Y.W.: Bayesian learning via stochastic gradient Langevin dynamics. In: Proceedings of the 28th International Conference on International Conference on Machine Learning, pp. 681–688 (2011)

20. Yushkevich, P.A., et al.: A high-resolution computational atlas of the human hippocampus from postmortem magnetic resonance imaging at 9.4 T. NeuroImage **44**(2), 385–398 (2009)
21. Zhang, Z., Song, J.: A robust brain MRI segmentation and bias field correction method integrating local contextual information into a clustering model. Appl. Sci. **9**(7), 1332 (2019)
22. Zhao, X., Xie, H., Li, W., Yang, G., Yan, X.: MRI intensity inhomogeneity correction based on similar points. In: 2017 10th International Congress on Image and Signal Processing, BioMedical Engineering and Informatics (CISP-BMEI), pp. 1–6 (2017)

Hierarchical and Robust Pathology Image Reading for High-Throughput Cervical Abnormality Screening

Ming Zhou, Lichi Zhang, Xiaping Du, Xi Ouyang, Xin Zhang, Qijia Shen, and Qian Wang[✉]

Institute for Medical Imaging Technology, School of Biomedical Engineering, Shanghai Jiao Tong University, Shanghai, China
wang.qian@sjtu.edu.cn

Abstract. Cervical smear screening is an imaging-based cancer detection tool which is of pivotal importance for the early-stage warning. A computer-aided screening system can automatically decide if the images with cervical cells are classified as "abnormal" or "normal", and then alert pathologists. It can significantly reduce the workload for human experts and is therefore highly-demanded in clinical practice. Most of the screening methods are based on automatic cervical cell detection and classification, but the accuracy is generally limited due to the high variation of cell appearance and lacking of the context information from the surroundings. Here we propose a novel and complete framework for pathology image classification, which can provide a robust screening performance. We commence by implementing the cervical cell detection method to the pathology image from the whole-slide image (WSI) and extract representative patches from the detected "abnormal" cells with corresponding confidence information. The patches are fed into our novel classification model for a more comprehensive analysis, and conduct the classification for the overall target pathology image. It can be demonstrated in experiments that our two-stage method can effectively suppress the errors from cell-level classification, and provide a robust way for pathology image classification.

1 Introduction

Cervical cancer [1] is the second most common cancer among women of all ages. Since the disease can be cured if diagnosed in the early stage, cervical smear screening plays an important role in the prevention and treatment of cervical cancer. Specifically, the most common physical technique for early screening is pap smear, which is firstly staining the cervical cells, and presenting them onto a glass slide for examination following "The Bethesda System (TBS)" [2] rules. Pap smear [3] is one of the common staining methods for cervical cancer screening. Currently, the examinations are generally manual by an expert pathologist, which is labor-intensive and influenced by the personal subjectivities of pathologists. Such an issue is further deteriorated for developing countries with a

---

M. Zhou and L. Zhang—Contributed equally in this work.

© Springer Nature Switzerland AG 2020
M. Liu et al. (Eds.): MLMI 2020, LNCS 12436, pp. 414–422, 2020.
https://doi.org/10.1007/978-3-030-59861-7_42

large population, where the pathologists need to face much larger amounts of cervical screening works. Therefore, it is highly demanded the automatic computer-aided screening system, which can provide fast and efficient screening system, and aims at reducing the mortality rate from cervical cancer.

The developments of automatic cervical screening have been extensively investigated, and the majority attempts are generally focused on cervical cell detection, segmentation, and classification [4–6]. For example, Zhang et al. [7] proposed a method namely DeepPap that uses convolutional neural networks to extract features and then uses additional data sets for fine-tuning. Zhao et al. [8] proposed the Deformable Multipath Ensemble Model (D-MEM) for cervical cell nuclear segmentation. Zhang et al. [9] proposed a binary-tree-structured cervical cell nuclear segmentation network incorporating attention mechanisms. Hussain et al. [10] proposed a fusion method that merged multiple convolutional neural networks. Taha et al. [11] proposed a method to classify cervical-cancer cells by employing a pre-trained CNN architecture as a feature extractor and an SVM as a classifier. However, the cell-level detection and classification remain challenging due to the high complexity and variation of cervical cells, which are therefore impractical to be directly used for cervical screening. Besides, our input image is relatively large in size and contains a huge number of cervical cells. Effective image classification is also needed to deal with this situation.

In this paper, we propose a novel hierarchical framework for cervical screening of given pathology images aiming at resolving the above-mentioned issues. There are two stages in our method. The first stage intends to incorporate the cell detection technique to find the "abnormal" cells from the pathology images, with their confidence information of detection works. Then, we utilize the detected cell location to extract the corresponding patches from the images, along with their confidence as the context information for image-level classification. In this way, our novel classification framework can effectively utilize the low-level cell detection output, and further guarantee the robustness of classification by a more comprehensive investigation of all high-level appearance from the patches with potentially detected abnormal cells. Our novel screening system can guarantee high efficiency and robustness, making it eligible to be embedded into the overall pipeline of WSI-level cervical screening works and further improving its performance.

2   Method

As previously mentioned, our hierarchical pathology classification method consists of two stages, which are the cell-level detection and image-level classification. The overall pipeline of our framework is presented in Fig. 1. All of our pathology images are extracted from the collected whole-slide images (WSIs), which are cropped with the image size of 1024×1024 pixels. Note that further details of image acquisition and dataset collection are presented in Sect. 3. The methodology details of the two stages are illustrated in the subsequent sections.

2.1   Cell-Level Detection

Our pathology image classification requires the cell-level detection as context information, and therefore its accuracy is also highly dependent on the performance of cell

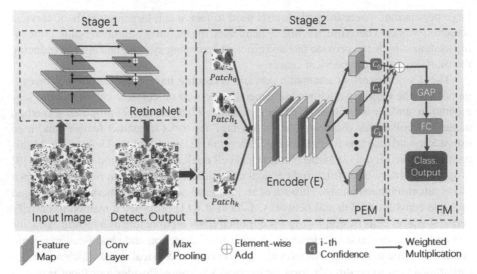

Fig. 1. The overall pipeline of our hierarchical pathology image classification framework. Stage 1 is the cell-level detection process. Stage 2 is the image-level classification process, including two modules PEM (Patch Encoder Module) and FM (Fusion Module).

detection. In this way, it is quite important to choose a reliable object detection which can best fit with our needs in finding abnormal cervical cells. With the advent of deep learning technology, there are many object detection methods developed and widely applied in these years, such as FasterRCNN [12], RetinaNet [13], FCOS [14], Grid RCNN [15], SSD [16]. We have undergone all the mentioned methods and compared their performance in cell detection, the details are presented in Sect. 3.1.

Specifically, we have found RetinaNet to be our top choice in this work, with advantages of both high accuracy and efficiency compared with the alternatives. The network architecture of RetinaNet mainly includes a backbone network of Residual Network (ResNet) [17] and Feature Pyramid Network (FPN), which is used to extract features and obtain a feature pyramid at the same time. After obtaining the feature pyramid, two subnetworks (classification network + detection position regression) are used for each layer of feature pyramid to achieve localization and classification of objects. Note that the output of cell detection using RetinaNet consists of bounding boxes with their corresponding confidence information. Here we only choose k bounding boxes with highest confidence values, which are fed into the subsequent stage for the further image-level classification process.

2.2 Image-Level Classification

The second stage of our framework is the classification of the pathology image based on object detection results. Specifically, we commence by extracting patches that their center locations are the same as these detected bounding boxes, and their patch sizes are all set as 224×224. After feature extraction, there are in all k patches obtained for the classification works, where we denote the i-th patch with its confidence value as $Patch_i$ and c_i.

As shown in Fig. 1, the image-level classification of our framework can be further divided into two component modules. The first module is PEM (Patch Encoder Module), which is designed to use a backbone architecture network (encoder E) that shares weights to extract the feature map of each patch in k patches. Then, the confidence of the detection network is passed in as context information, which represents the weight of the amount of information represented by different patches. The confidence of the object detection network usually represents the probability of classification. For example, a high-confidence area indicates that the corresponding patch has a high probability of belonging to this category. Then the feature information extracted by different patches should be given different weights. The patch with relatively higher anomalies needs to be given higher weights. The confidence of the detection network has a similar characterization function. We simply let the weight of $Patch_i$ equal to the confidence c_i (confidence of $Patch_i$) of the detection network.

Then each patch passes through the feature extractor E to obtain the feature map corresponding to the current patch, and then multiply them by the corresponding weight to obtain the weighted feature map PEM_i of the k patches after weighting. The specific formula is as follows:

$$PEM_i = E(Patch_i) * c_i \tag{1}$$

The second module in the second stage is Fusion Module (FM). The function of this module is to fuse k weighted patches for information fusion. Here we aim to add element-level additions to each weighted patch feature map, then do a global average pooling (GAP) of the results, and finally pass the pooled results through a fully connected layer (FC) to achieve the final classification result.

3   Experiments and Results

In this section, we compare the detection performance of 5 different detection methods and establish the performance gap between the two-stage image classification method and the single-stage image classification. Finally, the effectiveness of the feature fusion method in the PEM module is verified. Our annotations are all manually marked by expert pathologists. Some details in the experimental evaluation are presented as follows:

- All the collected pathology images are obtained from the WSI, with the same size of 1024×1024 pixels as shown in Fig. 2.
- In the cell-level detection stage, we use 10619 annotated pathology images to evaluate the performance of different models, e.g., FasterRCNN [12], RetinaNet [13], FCOS [14], Grid RCNN [15], SSD [16].
- In the image-level classification stage, we use other 4928 normal images and 1612 abnormal images for the experiments. ResNet50 [17], DenseNet121 [18], and our pathology image classification model are evaluated on these data.
- Our model is implemented by PyTorch, with the machine of a CPU of Intel Core i7-4790 K and a GPU of Nvidia GTX 1080Ti.

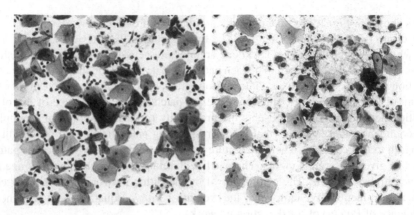

Fig. 2. Pathology images of samples. The left one is normal and the right one is abnormal.

3.1   Abnormal Cell Detection in Pathology Image

The first experiment conducted is to investigate the current widely-applied object detection methods and compare the performance in abnormal pathology image. We use Average Precision (AP) as the evaluation metric. AP is computed based on the precision and the recall, which is the area surrounded by the precision-recall curve and the x-axis.

We apply 5 above-mentioned models for cell-level detection and compare the AP results along with their inference time per image, which are all presented in Table 1:

Table 1.   AP and Runtime of different models for abnormal cell detection.

Method	FasterRCNN	SSD	GridRCNN	FCOS	RetinaNet
AP	0.706	0.661	0.689	0.697	0.715
Runtime (s)	0.170	0.292	0.163	0.125	0.128

As shown in Table 1, RetinaNet model achieves the best AP scores, while as the performance of SSD are relatively poor. As for the runtime, FCOS has the fastest computation performance. By comprehensively considering the factors of AP and runtime of these methods, we decide to choose RetinaNet for the abnormal cell detection task. We also show some visualization results of abnormal cell detection in pathology images using RetinaNet in Fig. 3.

3.2   The Experiment of Pathology Image Classification

As previously mentioned, although the cell-level detection method can locate the suspected lesion areas, it cannot be directly used to classify the corresponding images due to the possible detection errors. To overcome this issue, we instead use the detection results as an auxiliary context information to guide the subsequent classification task. Specifically, we select k bounding boxes with top confidence values to be identified as

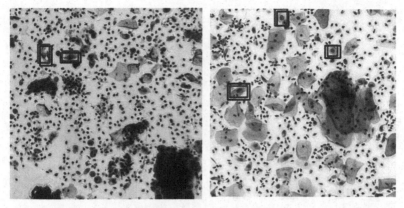

Fig. 3. Results of object detection of two pathology images. The red rectangles are the annotations of the pathologist, and the blue rectangles are the result of our detection network. (Color figure online)

"abnormal", and use their locations and confidences as the input to the pathology image classification network.

In order to find the optimal value of k, here we conduct another experiment shown in Fig. 4, which is the statistical analysis based on the annotated training set. First, we denote hit images as the images whose selected patches contain real lesion cervical cells. For example, the column with the number 5 indicates the proportion of hit images to all images, when 5 patches are selected for a pathology image. As the number of selected patches increases, more and more images emerge areas that coincide with the patches annotated by the pathologist. It can be observed in Fig. 4 that when we choose $k = 5$, almost all pathology images can hit at least one region that is consistent with the pathologist's labeling results. Besides, even if we choose more patches, there is no great enhancement. Therefore, we choose $k = 5$ as the patch number based on the balance of network complexity and detection performance.

Besides, in the PEM module, we use the confidence from the detection model as a weight coefficient for the corresponding patch. To illustrate this effect, we set up a set of ablation experiments. First, the weight coefficients of all patches are all assigned to be 1, which is used to verify the function of the confidence generated by the detection network in the fusion of patch information. Second, the other settings are the same. We briefly check the accuracy of two different weighting methods. The model using 1 as a weight to weight different feature maps can get the accuracy of 85% as a consequence. Compared with the model without the confidence generated by the detection network, the model improves the accuracy of the classification task by 7% after utilizing the confidences of detection network as the fusion weights. It proves that the confidences generated by the detection network are the importance context cues for the pathology image classification task.

To verify the effectiveness of the proposed method, we also use the pathology images under study as input of different backbone networks (e.g., ResNet50, DenseNet121). In these experiments, we do not use the detection model to generate the abnormal patches

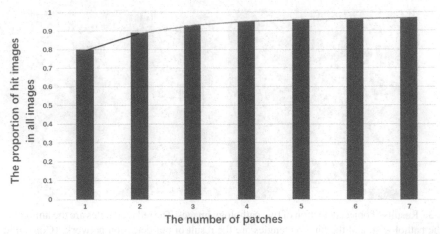

Fig. 4. The relationship between the number of patches with the ratio of the hit images to all images. The horizontal axis is the number of patches that we use, and the ordinate axis is the proportion of hit images in all images. The green line indicates the trends when choosing different number of patches. Therefore, we choose k = 5 as the patch number in experiments. (Color figure online)

firstly. At the same time, to prove that the proposed model is more effective than the direct classification model, we use the confidence of the object detection network as the benchmark for pathology image classification. For pathology images after detection, if a patch with a confidence greater than the threshold appears in this image, we will treat this image as an abnormal image. Here, we set the threshold as 0.4. In this way, we can also classify pathology images, we simply use "Only Confidence" to represent this method. The specific experimental results are shown in the Table 2. We use accuracy and F1-score to characterize different models.

Table 2. Accuracy and F1-score of different pathology image classification models

Method	Only Confidence	DenseNet121 [17]	ResNet50 [18]	Proposed Method
Accuracy	0.69	0.85	0.86	0.92
F1-score	0.63	0.78	0.80	0.87

From the table, we can see that just using the detection results to make a classification task is relatively insufficient. It also reveals that the detection models produce too much failure cases. However, the information from the detection can be integrated into other methods as context knowledge. Then, the proposed two-stage method can achieve better performance than the one-stage method, such as ResNet and DenseNet, with about 7% of accuracy improvement. We also compare the ROC curves of three different classification methods as shown in Fig. 5.

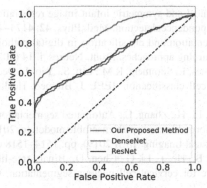

Fig. 5. The ROC curves of different methods. The red curve is the ResNet, the blue curve is DenseNet and the orange one is our proposed method. (Color figure online)

4   Conclusion

In this paper, we propose a novel framework to achieve cervical cancer classification based on the provided large pathology images, which is consisted of two steps. The first step is to locate the "abnormal" cervical cells and the corresponding confidence information using the object detection technique. The second step is to utilize the output of cell detection for patch extraction, which is further fused in a novel pathology image classification network for obtaining the final results. For this large pathology image, our method achieves better accuracy than directly using object detection and applying a classification network directly on the original image. The main goal is to provide a more robust resolution to the cervical cancer screening process and to resolve the current limitations in the cell-level detection and classification. Our future plan includes further investigation of our method's validity using more pathology images available. We will also look into the solution to apply our method to the pipeline of cervical cancer screening using the whole WSI image, in order to finally improve its performance.

Acknowledgement. This work was supported by the National Key Research and Development Program of China (2018YFC0116400), STCSM (19QC1400600, 17411953300, 18JC1420305), Shanghai Pujiang Program (19PJ1406800), and Interdisciplinary Program of Shanghai Jiao Tong University.

References

1. Schiffman, M., Castle, P.E., Jeronimo, J., Rodriguez, A.C., Wacholder, S.: Human papillomavirus and cervical cancer. Lancet **370**, 890–907 (2007)
2. Nayar, R., Wilbur, D.C.: The Pap test and Bethesda 2014. Acta Cytol. **59**, 121–132 (2015)
3. Koss, L.G.: The papanicolaou test for cervical cancer detection: a triumph and a tragedy. JAMA **261**, 737–743 (1989)
4. Chen, X., et al.: A graph-based approach to automated EUS image layer segmentation and abnormal region detection. Neurocomputing **336**, 79–91 (2019)

5. Wu, Y., et al.: Hierarchical and symmetric infant image registration by robust longitudinal-example-guided correspondence detection. Med. Phys. **42**, 4174–4189 (2015)
6. Kurc, T., et al.: Segmentation and classification in digital pathology for glioma research: challenges and deep learning approaches. Front. Neurosci. **14** (2020)
7. Zhang, L., Lu, L., Nogues, I., Summers, R.M., Liu, S., Yao, J.: DeepPap: deep convolutional networks for cervical cell classification. IEEE J. Biomed. Health Inform. **21**, 1633–1643 (2017)
8. Zhao, J., Li, Q., Li, X., Li, H., Zhang, L.: Automated segmentation of cervical nuclei in pap smear images using deformable multi-path ensemble model. In: 2019 IEEE 16th International Symposium on Biomedical Imaging (ISBI 2019), pp. 1514–1518 (2019)
9. Zhang, J., Liu, Z., Du, B., He, J., Li, G., Chen, D.: Binary tree-like network with two-path fusion attention feature for cervical cell nucleus segmentation. Comput. Biol. Med. **108**, 223–233 (2019)
10. Hussain, E., Mahanta, L.B., Das, C.R., Talukdar, R.K.: A comprehensive study on the multi-class cervical cancer diagnostic prediction on pap smear images using a fusion-based decision from ensemble deep convolutional neural network. Tissue Cell **65**, 101347 (2020)
11. Taha, B., Dias, J., Werghi, N.: Classification of cervical-cancer using Pap-smear images: a convolutional neural network approach. In: Valdés Hernández, M., González-Castro, V. (eds.) MIUA 2017. CCIS, vol. 723, pp. 261–272. Springer, Cham (2017). https://doi.org/10.1007/978-3-319-60964-5_23
12. Ren, S., He, K., Girshick, R., Sun, J.: Faster R-CNN: towards real-time object detection with region proposal networks. In: Cortes, C., Lawrence, N.D., Lee, D.D., Sugiyama, M., Garnett, R. (eds.) Advances in Neural Information Processing Systems, vol. 28, pp. 91–99. Curran Associates, Inc. (2015)
13. Lin, T., Goyal, P., Girshick, R., He, K., Dollár, P.: Focal loss for dense object detection. IEEE Trans. Pattern Anal. Mach. Intell. **42**, 318–327 (2020)
14. Tian, Z., Shen, C., Chen, H., He, T.: FCOS: fully convolutional one-stage object detection. In: 2019 IEEE/CVF International Conference on Computer Vision (ICCV), pp. 9626–9635 (2019)
15. Lu, X., Li, B., Yue, Y., Li, Q., Yan, J.: Grid R-CNN. In: 2019 IEEE/CVF Conference on Computer Vision and Pattern Recognition (CVPR), pp. 7355–7364 (2019)
16. Liu, W., et al.: SSD: Single shot multibox detector. In: Leibe, B., Matas, J., Sebe, N., Welling, M. (eds.) ECCV 2016. LNCS, vol. 9905, pp. 21–37. Springer, Cham (2016). https://doi.org/10.1007/978-3-319-46448-0_2
17. He, K., Zhang, X., Ren, S., Sun, J.,: Deep residual learning for image recognition. In: 2016 IEEE Conference on Computer Vision and Pattern Recognition (CVPR), pp. 770–778. IEEE, Las Vegas (2016)
18. Huang, G., Liu, Z., Van Der Maaten, L., Weinberger, K.Q.: Densely connected convolutional networks. In: 2017 IEEE Conference on Computer Vision and Pattern Recognition (CVPR), pp. 2261–2269 (2017)

Importance Driven Continual Learning
for Segmentation Across Domains

Sinan Özgün, Anne-Marie Rickmann[✉], Abhijit Guha Roy,
and Christian Wachinger

Artificial Intelligence in Medical Imaging (AI-Med), KJP, LMU München,
München, Germany
arickman@med.lmu.de

Abstract. The ability of neural networks to continuously learn and
adapt to new tasks while retaining prior knowledge is crucial for many
applications. However, current neural networks tend to forget previously
learned tasks when trained on new ones, i.e., they suffer from Catastrophic Forgetting (CF). The objective of Continual Learning (CL) is to
alleviate this problem, which is particularly relevant for medical applications, where it may not be feasible to store and access previously used
sensitive patient data. In this work, we propose a Continual Learning
approach for brain segmentation, where a single network is consecutively
trained on samples from different domains. We build upon an importance
driven approach and adapt it for medical image segmentation. Particularly, we introduce a learning rate regularization to prevent the loss of the
network's knowledge. Our results demonstrate that directly restricting
the adaptation of important network parameters clearly reduces Catastrophic Forgetting for segmentation across domains. Our code is publicly
available on https://github.com/ai-med/MAS-LR.

1 Introduction

After the breakthrough of Convolutional Neural Networks (CNN) [14], deep
learning methods have become the technique of choice for medical image analysis
tasks such as disease classification, lesion detection, or image segmentation [17,
22]. Common deep architectures require large sets of training data, which are
often gathered over time and across institutions. Ideally, a system would be
continuously re-trained on a consolidated set of incoming data samples. However,
this sequential learning requires the storage of large datasets over a long period,
which can be infeasible. Particularly in the medical field, privacy restrictions
can prohibit the sharing of clinical data so that a trained model may be easily

---

S. Özgün and A.-M. Rickmann—The authors contributed equally.

Electronic supplementary material The online version of this chapter (https://
doi.org/10.1007/978-3-030-59861-7_43) contains supplementary material, which is
available to authorized users.

M. Liu et al. (Eds.): MLMI 2020, LNCS 12436, pp. 423–433, 2020.
https://doi.org/10.1007/978-3-030-59861-7_43

passed among institutions, but not the data itself. Continuously fine-tuning a neural network without access to old data often results in a deterioration of the performance on prior datasets [20]. Neural Networks are especially prone to this phenomenon known as *Catastrophic Forgetting* (CF), which emerges from the stability-plasticity trade-off [11]. *Continual Learning* (CL) aims to overcome this dilemma. The focus of CL methods has mainly been on classification [13,32], object detection [28], or reinforcement learning [25]. We have found that a naïve translation of such approaches to medical image segmentation is yielding suboptimal performance. In this work, we explore the effect of importance driven regularization methods in an incremental domain learning setting [8], where at each point in time, a new magnetic resonance imaging (MRI) scan is retrieved. This setting poses a challenge, as neural networks are sensitive to shifts in the input distribution that emerge from changes in the acquisition protocol, the use of different scanners, or age differences of subjects. To overcome these problems, we define learning rate regularization that utilizes importance weights defined in Memory Aware Synapses (MAS) [1]. In contrast to the soft penalty applied in MAS, we show that directly restricting the adaptation of important network parameters clearly reduces Catastrophic Forgetting, while preserving the ability to learn new domains.

Desiderata: To define the Continual Learning setting and distinguish it from other learning paradigms, several desiderata have been formulated in the literature [3,6,26]. The most important ones are that CL methods should be able to (i) adapt to new datasets, while retaining knowledge about old domains, (ii) without the access to old data samples, and (iii) over a long period. Furthermore, (iv) the model should not be aware of the task or domain a data sample belongs to, i.e., the network should not have access to so-called task labels. We strictly follow these desiderata in our Continual Learning approach for brain segmentation.

Related Work: In the literature, different techniques for CL have been proposed that can be grouped into three main categories [3].

Replay-based methods range from naïve rehearsal methods that store a subset of old data [21] to pseudo-rehearsal methods that approximate previous samples using generative models [27].

Parameter isolation-based methods assign different parameters in a network to each task. This can be achieved by either fixing the architecture [19] or dynamically extending the network [31]. Fixed architectures are limited by the network's capacity, whereas dynamic architectures need more memory with every new task.

Regularization-based methods can be divided into data-focused and prior-focused approaches. Data-focused approaches [29] distill the knowledge of old tasks to enhance the CL capabilities of the present model, whereas prior-based approaches such as [1,13,32] define importance weights for the network's parameters. Based on these weights, a regularization loss is introduced that penalizes the shift of important parameters.

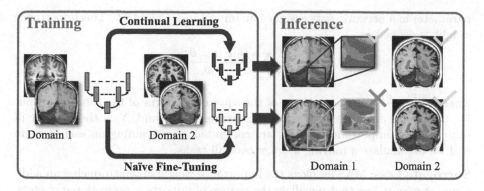

Fig. 1. Illustration of Catastrophic Forgetting. Left: The Segmentation network is trained on the first domain and adapted to the second using naïve fine-tuning (bottom) and our Continual Learning method MAS-LR (top). Right: Whereas both models adapted well to the second domain, naïvely fine-tuning the network leads to higher CF (red X), than CL. (Color figure online)

CL approaches have also been proposed in medical imaging [2,10], but they do not follow the desiderata formulated above. In [10], only batch normalization (BN) layers are fine-tuned to handle differences between domains. As this approach dedicates specific BN parameters to each dataset, task labels are necessary that determine to which dataset each sample belongs. In [2], the application of Elastic Weight Consolidation (EWC) [13] was proposed. The authors evaluate the method on only two consecutive tasks, in an incremental class learning setting.

2 Methods

Our objective is to sequentially fine-tune a segmentation network on new domains without decreasing the performance on previous domains. Figure 1 illustrates the effect of Catastrophic Forgetting with normal fine-tuning and the improvement with our Continual Learning approach described in the following.

2.1 Memory Aware Synapses

We are building on top of Memory Aware Synapses (MAS) [1], which is one of the best performing prior-based CL methods [3]. As other prior-based CL methods [13,32], MAS also defines a weight for each network parameter that reflects its importance for a specific task. For the computation of the importance weights, MAS uses an unsupervised approach, where weights measure the sensitivity of the network's output to changes in its parameters.

Importance Metric: Let F be the learned function of the model that maps the input X to the output Y. Each weight θ_i, where i denotes the index of the parameter in a network, gets assigned an importance weight Ω_i. This importance weight is defined as:

$$\Omega_i = \frac{1}{N} \sum_{n=1}^{N} \frac{\partial \|F(x_n; \boldsymbol{\theta})\|_2^2}{\partial \theta_i}, \tag{1}$$

where $\frac{\partial \|F(x_n;\boldsymbol{\theta})\|_2^2}{\partial \theta_i}$ is the gradient of the squared $\ell 2$ norm of the softmax output for data point x_n with respect to the parameter θ_i and N is the number of samples. The importance weights are computed after training on each domain and we accumulate a moving average over all tasks.

Surrogate Loss: MAS employs the importance weights by introducing an additional surrogate loss that penalizes the change of important network parameters. The total loss function is then defined as:

$$L(\boldsymbol{\theta}) = L_d(\boldsymbol{\theta}) + \lambda \sum_i \Omega_i (\theta_i - \theta_i^*)^2, \tag{2}$$

where L_d describes the loss of the current domain e.g. Cross-Entropy Loss, $\boldsymbol{\Omega}$ the important weights, $\boldsymbol{\theta}$ the current network parameters and $\boldsymbol{\theta}^*$ the parameters of the old network, trained on the previous task. The hyperparameter λ controls the impact of the regularization term on the loss function.

2.2 Learning Rate Regularization

In this section, we propose an alternative regularization approach for MAS. In contrast to regularizing changes of important parameters using a surrogate loss, we define a parameter-specific learning rate such that the learning rate becomes a function of a parameter's importance [5]. Hence, the learning rate of important parameters will be reduced, while the learning rate for non-important parameters will be kept the same. While the surrogate loss in MAS indirectly penalizes changes of the parameters, learning rate regularization provides a more direct means to avoid changes to important parameters. Let α^d be the initial learning rate for training domain d, the parameter-specific learning rate is:

$$\alpha_i^d = (1 - \Omega_i^k)\alpha^d. \tag{3}$$

We refer to this approach as **MAS-LR**. Another advantage is its lack of additional hyperparameters.

Parameter Freezing: A soft penalty might not be sufficient to enforce the network to retain old knowledge. Taking inspiration from network pruning methods [16,19], we propose **MAS-LR$^\beta$**, which freezes important parameters during the training of a new task and only fine-tunes unimportant parameters. This approach can be interpreted as an alternative of Eq. (3) by either setting $\alpha_i^d = \alpha^d$ or $\alpha_i^d = 0$. We define hyperparameters β_d for each domain d that define a threshold of how much of the network can be frozen in each step. If all important parameters of a succeeding task were already fixed in earlier stages, the network

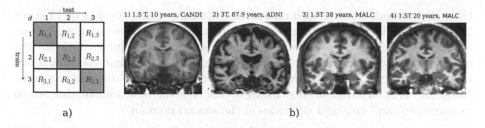

Fig. 2. a) Train-Test-Accuracy-Matrix. b) Slices of brain scans from the four different domains with magnetic field strength, age and original dataset.

will remain as is. In doing so, we do not enforce the network to freeze unimportant parameters and thus extend the remaining capacity of the network and the number of forthcoming tasks.

Filter and Kernel Importance: MAS defines importance weights for each parameter of a network. This can be cumbersome for larger networks, as it doubles the amount of memory needed to save the model. In our experiments, we observed that importance values within a $k \times k$ convolutional kernel are similar, which is expected due to the shared functionality of the parameters within a kernel. In addition, importance weights of a convolutional layer of shape $n_{out} \times n_{in} \times k \times k$, where n_{in} and n_{out} describe the number of input and output channels, also had similar values, even though the similarity within a kernel was higher. Hence, we additionally defined an importance metric on a filter level by averaging the values of every $n_{in} \times k \times k$ filter, so that each n_{out} filter gets assigned an importance weight. The filter and kernel importance can be easily integrated into the proposed regularization of the learning rate by averaging all weights within a kernel or filter, respectively.

3 Experiments and Results

3.1 Experimental Setup

Datasets: We use MRI T1 brain scans from three different datasets: Child and Adolescent NeuroDevelopment Initiative (CANDI) [12], Multi-Atlas Labelling Challenge (MALC) [15], and Alzheimer's Disease Neuroimaging Initiative (ADNI) [9]. The datasets differ in their age ranges, MRI field strengths and presence of pathologies or motion artifacts. All datasets were re-sampled to have an isotropic resolution of $1\,mm^3$. Manual segmentations of all brain scans were provided by Neuromorphometrics, Inc. and follow the same delineation protocol. In our experiments we segment the brain into 32 structures.

Domains: We adopt an online learning approach, where at each point in time, a new volume is used to update the network. For our setting, we define four different domains that we train on consecutively. We assume that to build a working system, it has to be initially trained on a larger dataset. Therefore, we train the network from scratch on our first domain, which consists of 13 scans from the CANDI dataset. The next domains contain one training scan from other datasets. We chose this setting, as we assume that volumes are collected one at a time because annotating medical scans is not only time-consuming but also costly. Figure 2 shows slices of brain scans of the four different domains. Noticeable are, for example, the ringing artifacts in the first domain, differences in intensities, and enlarged ventricles in the second domain.

Network Architecture and Training Parameters: We choose Quick-NAT [23,24] as our baseline architecture as it achieves state-of-the-art performance in brain segmentation. We train the models on coronal slices optimizing a combined Dice and Cross-Entropy Loss function using SGD with momentum of 0.95 for 12 epochs on each domain. The initial learning rate is set to 0.1 and reduced every 4 epochs by a factor of 0.5 during the training of the first domain. For all succeeding domains, the learning rate is not further reduced, unless specified by parameter-specific learning rates. For CL methods, we conducted a hyperparameter grid-search where necessary. To balance the surrogate loss proposed in the original MAS method, we set λ to 10^4. In MAS-LR$^\beta$, we set β_d to 0.25 for $d \in [1, D]$, to freeze 25% of the network after the first stage. For every consecutive training step, we allow the model to fix up to an additional 25%. MAS-LR does not require an additional hyperparameter. We use kernel-level importance weights for MAS-LR$^\beta$ and filter level importance weights for MAS-LR. We did not observe an improvement for aggregating weights in MAS.

Adaptation of MAS to Brain Segmentation: The original surrogate loss in Eq. (2) is dependent on the size of the network, which makes it unstable for large networks. Consequently, we divide the surrogate loss by the number of network parameters. Moreover, directly applying the importance calculation of MAS to brain segmentation was not feasible, as highly skewed importance weights resulted in an unstable training process. To counter this problem, we detected outliers based on the interquartile range criterion and set them to their respective boundaries. We normalized the resulting importance values between zero and one to increase their interpretability.

3.2   Evaluation Metrics

To evaluate CL methods, it is important to not only focus on the improvement of Catastrophic Forgetting but also to consider the accuracy over time and knowledge transfer to unseen domains. Hence, we adopt some of the metrics proposed in [4]. Fundamental is the train-test-accuracy-matrix, $R \in \mathbb{R}^{D \times D}$, illustrated in Fig. 2a, where D determines the number of domains and each entry $R_{i,j}$ is the mean Dice score (DSC) of the model on domain j after consecutively fine-tuning on domains $1, .., i$ [18]. The entry $R_{2,1}$, e.g., represents the DSC for a model initially trained on domain 1, fine-tuned on domain 2, and evaluated on domain 1. *Transfer Learning* (TL) is the average of the diagonal of R and measures the plasticity, i.e., the ability to adapt to new tasks. In a CL setting we are mainly interested in the effect that learning a new task has on the performance on older

Table 1. Comparison of baselines (top) and our importance based training methods (bottom). The CL metrics are calculated on the average Dice scores over all segmented structures.

	Method	▨CL DSC	▨REM	▨BWT$^+$	▨TL	▨FWT
Baseline	Fine-tuning	0.716 ± 0.138	0.903 ± 0.054	0.010 ± 0.016	0.770 ± 0.118	0.605 ± 0.174
	Joint training	0.783 ± 0.108	0.997 ± 0.003	0.029 ± 0.024	0.776 ± 0.114	0.650 ± 0.161
CL Methods	MAS	0.742 ± 0.129	0.929 ± 0.045	0.007 ± 0.011	0.783 ± 0.112	0.625 ± 0.166
	MAS-LR (ours)	0.756 ± 0.128	0.960 ± 0.032	$\mathbf{0.012 \pm 0.016}$	0.778 ± 0.117	0.637 ± 0.164
	MAS-LR$^\beta$ (ours)	0.755 ± 0.130	0.954 ± 0.036	0.010 ± 0.014	0.781 ± 0.116	0.634 ± 0.166
Regularization $\ell 2$		0.726 ± 0.135	0.913 ± 0.054	0.011 ± 0.012	0.778 ± 0.108	0.614 ± 0.185
	Dropout	0.744 ± 0.146	0.931 ± 0.055	0.007 ± 0.008	$\mathbf{0.786 \pm 0.121}$	0.690 ± 0.169
Combination	MAS-LR-Dropout	$\mathbf{0.761 \pm 0.132}$	$\mathbf{0.965 \pm 0.026}$	0.009 ± 0.008	0.778 ± 0.124	$\mathbf{0.693 \pm 0.170}$

tasks. The performance can either degrade, in case of CF, or ideally increase. To measure this backward transfer, we slightly modify the metrics introduced in [18], as shown in Eq. 4 and Eq. 5. *Remembering* (REM) measures the stability of the model, i.e., the ability of the network to retain its knowledge. This metric assesses the effect of a CL method on Catastrophic Forgetting.

$$REM = \frac{2\sum_{i=2}^{D}\sum_{j=1}^{i-1} 1 - |\min(R_{i,j} - R_{j,j}, 0)|}{D(D-1)}. \tag{4}$$

Positive Backward Transfer (BWT$^+$) measures the improvement of the network on old domains by accommodating new knowledge.

$$BWT^+ = \frac{2\sum_{i=2}^{D}\sum_{j=1}^{i-1} \max(R_{i,j} - R_{j,j}, 0)}{D(D-1)}. \tag{5}$$

CL Dice Score (CL DSC) combines the transfer learning and backward transfer abilities of the network and is the most generic metric to evaluate Continual Learning. This metric is calculated as the average of the entries of the diagonal and below the diagonal of R. *Forward Transfer* (FT) is the average performance of the network on unseen domains (entries above the diagonal). This metric does not explicitly measure the Continual Learning abilities of the system, but it is an essential indicator of the network's ability to generalize well on unseen data.

3.3 Results

We compare our methods to naïve fine-tuning of the network (lower bound) and joint training of the network on a combined dataset (upper bound for REM and BWT$^+$) as baselines and report the results in Table 1. The train-test-accuracy matrices can be found in the Supplementary Material. We observe an increase in

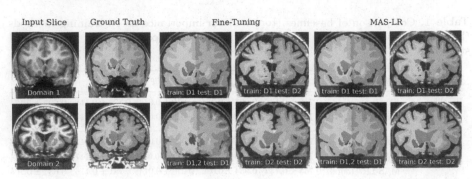

Fig. 3. Comparison of segmentation results on the first two domains for the naïve fine-tuning baseline and our proposed method MAS-LR. Train $D1, 2$ refers to training a model on domain 1 and fine-tuning on domain 2. Most striking are the improvements in Backward Transfer.

the overall CL Dice score for all CL methods, where learning rate regularization (MAS-LR and MAS-LR$^\beta$) performs better than regularization using a surrogate loss as proposed in MAS. As both of our methods provide the ability to set the learning rate to zero for important parameters, they lead to higher stability (better remembering), while the ability to learn new knowledge is comparable to MAS. Interestingly, in contrast to the stability-plasticity trade-off, we observe not only a better Remembering (REM) but also an increase of the Transfer Learning (TL) performance for all CL methods. We believe this is due to the regularization effect of the methods, that help the model to generalize better and thus achieve higher performance. The ability to generalize well on unseen data (FWT), also increases using regularization techniques. Positive Backward Transfer (BWT$^+$) does not differ much between the CL methods. MAS leads to a slight decrease in BWT$^+$, which could be caused by the higher Transfer Learning capability. In general, BWT$^+$ is hard to achieve, as even the upper bound has a low score in this metric. We show segmentation results in Fig. 3, where we compare the effect of naïve fine-tuning and MAS-LR on Backward Transfer, Forward Transfer and Transfer Learning for the first two domains. As many modern networks are trained using regularization techniques like $\ell2$ regularization and dropout [30], which can reduce Catastrophic Forgetting [1, 7,13], we also compare to models using these techniques. We observe a slight improvement using $\ell2$ regularization, whereas dropout even outperforms MAS. Dropout specifically leads to the highest increase in Forward Transfer. Finally, to determine how dropout influences CL methods, we trained a network with dropout and our best performing CL-method (MAS-LR), which further increased the Remembering and FWT performance.

4 Conclusion

We proposed an Importance Driven Continual Learning approach for brain segmentation across domains. We adapted the importance weights introduced in MAS to our medical setting. We observed that detecting outliers in the importance weights and normalizing them, lead to more stable training and higher performance. In contrast to the surrogate loss used in MAS, we proposed learning rate regularization to restrain changes to important network parameters. MAS-LR outperformed MAS by clearly reducing catastrophic forgetting, without the need for additional hyperparameters. We further demonstrated that learning rate regularization can be combined with standard regularization approaches like dropout.

Acknowledgements. This research was partially supported by the Bavarian State Ministry of Science and the Arts and co-ordinated by the bidt, and the BMBF (Deep-Mentia, 031L0200A).

References

1. Aljundi, R., Babiloni, F., Elhoseiny, M., Rohrbach, M., Tuytelaars, T.: Memory aware synapses: learning what (not) to forget. In: Proceedings of the European Conference on Computer Vision (ECCV), pp. 139–154 (2018)
2. Baweja, C., Glocker, B., Kamnitsas, K.: Towards continual learning in medical imaging. arXiv preprint arXiv:1811.02496 (2018)
3. De Lange, M., et al.: Continual learning: a comparative study on how to defy forgetting in classification tasks. arXiv preprint arXiv:1909.08383 (2019)
4. Díaz-Rodríguez, N., Lomonaco, V., Filliat, D., Maltoni, D.: Don't forget, there is more than forgetting: new metrics for continual learning. In: Continual Learning Workshop, 32nd Conference on Neural Information Processing Systems (2018)
5. Ebrahimi, S., Elhoseiny, M., Darrell, T., Rohrbach, M.: Uncertainty-guided continual learning with Bayesian neural networks. arXiv preprint arXiv:1906.02425 (2019)
6. Farquhar, S., Gal, Y.: Towards robust evaluations of continual learning. arXiv preprint arXiv:1805.09733 (2018)
7. Goodfellow, I.J., Mirza, M., Xiao, D., Courville, A., Bengio, Y.: An empirical investigation of catastrophic forgetting in gradient-based neural networks. arXiv preprint arXiv:1312.6211 (2013)
8. Hsu, Y.C., Liu, Y.C., Ramasamy, A., Kira, Z.: Re-evaluating continual learning scenarios: a categorization and case for strong baselines. In: Continual Learning Workshop, 32nd Conference on Neural Information Processing Systems (2018)
9. Jack, C.R., et al.: The alzheimer's disease neuroimaging initiative (ADNI): MRI methods. J. Magn. Reson. Imaging **27**(4), 685–691 (2008)
10. Karani, N., Chaitanya, K., Baumgartner, C., Konukoglu, E.: A lifelong learning approach to brain MR segmentation across scanners and protocols. In: Frangi, A.F., Schnabel, J.A., Davatzikos, C., Alberola-López, C., Fichtinger, G. (eds.) MICCAI 2018. LNCS, vol. 11070, pp. 476–484. Springer, Cham (2018). https://doi.org/10.1007/978-3-030-00928-1_54

11. Kemker, R., McClure, M., Abitino, A., Hayes, T.L., Kanan, C.: Measuring catastrophic forgetting in neural networks. In: Thirty-second AAAI Conference on Artificial Intelligence (2018)
12. Kennedy, D.N., Haselgrove, C., Hodge, S.M., Rane, P.S., Makris, N., Frazier, J.A.: Candishare: a resource for pediatric neuroimaging data. Neuroinformatics 10(3), 319–322 (2012)
13. Kirkpatrick, J., et al.: Overcoming catastrophic forgetting in neural networks. Proc. Nat. Acad. Sci. 114(13), 3521–3526 (2017)
14. Krizhevsky, A., Sutskever, I., Hinton, G.E.: Imagenet classification with deep convolutional neural networks. In: Advances in Neural Information Processing Systems, pp. 1097–1105 (2012)
15. Landman, B., Warfield, S.: Miccai 2012 workshop on multi-atlas labeling. In: Medical Image Computing and Computer Assisted Intervention Conference (2012)
16. Li, H., Kadav, A., Durdanovic, I., Samet, H., Graf, H.P.: Pruning filters for efficient convnets. arXiv preprint arXiv:1608.08710 (2016)
17. Litjens, G., et al.: A survey on deep learning in medical image analysis. Med. Image Anal. 42, 60–88 (2017)
18. Lopez-Paz, D., Ranzato, M.: Gradient episodic memory for continual learning. In: Advances in Neural Information Processing Systems, pp. 6467–6476 (2017)
19. Mallya, A., Lazebnik, S.: Packnet: Adding multiple tasks to a single network by iterative pruning. In: Proceedings of the IEEE Conference on Computer Vision and Pattern Recognition, pp. 7765–7773 (2018)
20. Parisi, G.I., Kemker, R., Part, J.L., Kanan, C., Wermter, S.: Continual lifelong learning with neural networks: a review. Neural Netw. 113, 54–71 (2019)
21. Rebuffi, S.A., Kolesnikov, A., Sperl, G., Lampert, C.H.: icarl: incremental classifier and representation learning. In: Proceedings of the IEEE Conference on Computer Vision and Pattern Recognition, pp. 2001–2010 (2017)
22. Ronneberger, O., Fischer, P., Brox, T.: U-Net: convolutional networks for biomedical image segmentation. In: Navab, N., Hornegger, J., Wells, W.M., Frangi, A.F. (eds.) MICCAI 2015. LNCS, vol. 9351, pp. 234–241. Springer, Cham (2015). https://doi.org/10.1007/978-3-319-24574-4_28
23. Roy, A.G., Conjeti, S., Navab, N., Wachinger, C.: Quicknat: a fully convolutional network for quick and accurate segmentation of neuroanatomy. NeuroImage 186, 713–727 (2019)
24. Roy, A.G., Conjeti, S., Sheet, D., Katouzian, A., Navab, N., Wachinger, C.: Error corrective boosting for learning fully convolutional networks with limited data. In: Descoteaux, M., Maier-Hein, L., Franz, A., Jannin, P., Collins, D.L., Duchesne, S. (eds.) MICCAI 2017. LNCS, vol. 10435, pp. 231–239. Springer, Cham (2017). https://doi.org/10.1007/978-3-319-66179-7_27
25. Rusu, A.A., et al.: Progressive neural networks. arXiv preprint arXiv:1606.04671 (2016)
26. Schwarz, J., et al.: Progress & compress: a scalable framework for continual learning. In: International Conference on Machine Learning, pp. 4528–4537 (2018)
27. Shin, H., Lee, J.K., Kim, J., Kim, J.: Continual learning with deep generative replay. In: Advances in Neural Information Processing Systems, pp. 2990–2999 (2017)
28. Shmelkov, K., Schmid, C., Alahari, K.: Incremental learning of object detectors without catastrophic forgetting. In: Proceedings of the IEEE International Conference on Computer Vision, pp. 3400–3409 (2017)

29. Silver, D.L., Mercer, R.E.: The task rehearsal method of life-long learning: overcoming impoverished data. In: Cohen, R., Spencer, B. (eds.) AI 2002. LNCS (LNAI), vol. 2338, pp. 90–101. Springer, Heidelberg (2002). https://doi.org/10.1007/3-540-47922-8_8

30. Srivastava, N., Hinton, G., Krizhevsky, A., Sutskever, I., Salakhutdinov, R.: Dropout: a simple way to prevent neural networks from overfitting. J. Mach. Learn. Res. **15**(1), 1929–1958 (2014)

31. Xu, J., Zhu, Z.: Reinforced continual learning. In: Advances in Neural Information Processing Systems, pp. 899–908 (2018)

32. Zenke, F., Poole, B., Ganguli, S.: Continual learning through synaptic intelligence. In: Proceedings of the 34th International Conference on Machine Learning-Volume 70, pp. 3987–3995. JMLR. org (2017)

RDCNet: Instance Segmentation with a Minimalist Recurrent Residual Network

Raphael Ortiz[1]([✉]), Gustavo de Medeiros[1], Antoine H. F. M. Peters[1,2], Prisca Liberali[1,2], and Markus Rempfler[1]

[1] Friedrich Miescher Institute for Biomedical Research (FMI), Basel, Switzerland
raphael.ortiz@fmi.ch
[2] Faculty of Sciences, University of Basel, Basel, Switzerland

Abstract. Instance segmentation is a key step for quantitative microscopy. While several machine learning based methods have been proposed for this problem, most of them rely on computationally complex models that are trained on surrogate tasks. Building on recent developments towards end-to-end trainable instance segmentation, we propose a minimalist recurrent network called recurrent dilated convolutional network (RDCNet), consisting of a shared stacked dilated convolution (sSDC) layer that iteratively refines its output and thereby generates interpretable intermediate predictions. It is light-weight and has few critical hyperparameters, which can be related to physical aspects such as object size or density. We perform a sensitivity analysis of its main parameters and we demonstrate its versatility on 3 tasks with different imaging modalities: nuclear segmentation of H&E slides, of 3D anisotropic stacks from light-sheet fluorescence microscopy and leaf segmentation of top-view images of plants. It achieves state-of-the-art on 2 of the 3 datasets.

1 Introduction

Instance segmentation is the task of detecting and outlining different objects of the same class within an image, *e.g.* cells or nuclei. As such, it is a key step in many biomedical image analysis workflows and has recently received increased attention in the community [1,2,5,12,13,17,22].

Instance segmentation was traditionally tackled with pipelines based on watershedding, while more recent approaches rely mostly on machine learning. However due to the permutation invariance of instance labels, training machine-learning based models end-to-end is non-trivial, and remains an active area of research. A first class of methods are proposal-driven and follow a detect, then segment paradigm. For instance, Mask-RCNN [3] first predict object bounding

Electronic supplementary material The online version of this chapter (https://doi.org/10.1007/978-3-030-59861-7_44) contains supplementary material, which is available to authorized users.

M. Liu et al. (Eds.): MLMI 2020, LNCS 12436, pp. 434–443, 2020.
https://doi.org/10.1007/978-3-030-59861-7_44

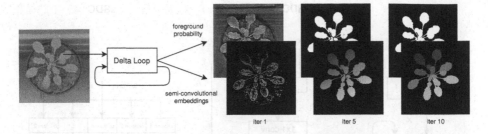

Fig. 1. Our approach to instance segmentation illustrated on an example of leaf segmentation. A minimalistic network is applied recursively to the input, refining its predictions of foreground and instance embeddings iteratively. Foreground probabilities are depicted in greyscale (white $\simeq P(\text{foreground}) = 1$), embeddings are shown in pseudocolor. While the outputs of the first iteration $i = 1$ are not very coherent yet, they quickly converge until, in the last iteration $i = 10$, the embeddings sharply distinguish even the slim stalk of the individual leafs.

boxes and then perform mask segmentation within each box. StarDist [17,22], removes this last step by predicting a star-convex polyhedron instead of rectangular boxes. This is often more robust, but the fact that a fixed shape representation approximates the object, limits the accuracy of the segmentation boundary and restricts its application to roundish shapes.

The second class of methods tackles the problem in reverse, segment first, then detect. Early approaches were often trained on surrogate outputs such as foreground vs background vs boundary, which are then combined during post-processing, *i.e.* not end-to-end [5,16]. More recently, *Instance embedding* methods [1,2,9,12,13] aiming to predict pixel embeddings that are similar within an instance and dissimilar across different instances have been proposed. However, losses like the ones used [1,2,12,13] are also surrogates. Only lately, Neven et al. [9] proposed to optimize a segmentation loss to learn the instance embedding.

As argued in [11], embedding methods like [1,2,12,13] that rely on fully convolutional models have to rely on texture to generate embeddings that satisfy the (dis-)similarity requirements because of their translation invariance. In turn, this makes the task of modelling the embedding considerably more complex and, for example, creates problems when having to process an input image in a tiled fashion.

Besides specifying an appropriate loss to optimize for the given task, the network architecture also plays a crucial role. U-Net-like [16] architectures are at the core of many state-of-the-art biomedical segmentation methods. While increasingly complex architectures are being proposed, state-of-the-art results in segmentation tasks have recently been demonstrated with a more light-weight U-Net applied recurrently to refine its output [20].

In this paper, we take it a step further and propose a minimalist recurrent dilated convolutional network (RDCNet) for instance segmentation in biomedical instance segmentation. We distill knowledge from a few recent key works on instance embeddings, namely 1) to use semi-convolutional [11] or its special

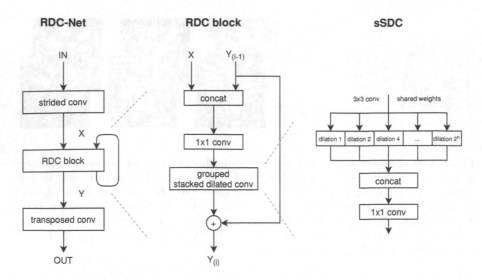

Fig. 2. Our overall network architecture (*left*), the recursive module (*center*) that refines a previous prediction $Y^{(i-1)}$ for X in a residual fashion, and (*right*) its core component, a stacked, dilated convolution block with shared weights (sSDC) followed by a 1×1 convolution to project the stacked features back to the same number of channels as the input.

case, the additive semi-convolutional layer to generate the embeddings, and 2) train the embedding output on an instance segmentation loss similar to [9]. Combining those, the instance segmentation task becomes much simpler and we propose 3) to address it with a light-weight, recurrent architecture which is applied iteratively to input and its latest prediction. This minimalist RDCNet has only a fraction of the parameters of a common U-Net [16] and is much easier to interpret since the output at every iteration can easily be visualized (see Fig. 1).

Finally, we conduct experiments on three different datasets and show that our approaches matches state-of-the-art without extra domain-specific adjustments.

2   Methods

Architecture Rational. Our architecture consists of a single shallow recurrent block sandwiched between learnable downsampling and upsampling layers respectively as depicted in Fig. 2 (left). In the 3D case, these layers have a different stride in XY than in Z to compensate for anisotropy of typical microscopic Z-stacks. At the heart of this (Fig. 2, center) is a recurrent block that follows a residual formulation and is comprised of grouped convolutions of kernel 3. A point-wise, *i.e.* 1×1, convolution is also added to mix group information between iterations. To bring global context in early iterations, each group uses stacked dilated convolutions [18] with shared weights and a point-wise convolution for channel reduction, hereafter called shared stacked dilated convolution (sSDC) and depicted in Fig. 2 (right). Note that this procedure enables the network to determine when to use narrow/wide convolutions based on training data. All convolutional layers except the first one are preceded by leaky ReLU "pre-activation" to keep the residual path clear [4].

Formally, our RDCNet generates the output of iteration i based on input X and its previous output Y^{i-1}

$$Y^i = f_\theta(X, Y^{i-1}) + Y^{i-1}, \tag{1}$$

where f_θ is the transform of the recurrent block and Y^0 is initialized to zero.

The raw network output is split in two branches. The first predicts the semantic class with a softmax activation, i.e. in this work simply foreground-background. The other predicts the instance embeddings and is chosen to be an additive semi-convolutional layer [11] that sums pixel/voxel coordinates to the convolutional output, leading to semi-convolutional instance embeddings in 2D or 3D, respectively. An illustration of the semi-convolutional layer is provided in supplement, Fig. 1.

Objective Functions. At training time, we follow [9] and convert embeddings y into probabilities for pixel u being part of instance k as

$$P(u = k) = \exp\left(-\frac{\|y_u - \hat{y}_k\|^2}{2\sigma^2}\right), \tag{2}$$

where $\sigma > 0$ is the bandwidth parameter and the centroids $\hat{y}_k$ are estimated as the mean embedding under the *true* mask of instance k denoted with $\mathcal{S}_k$, i.e. $\hat{y}_k = \frac{1}{|\mathcal{S}_k|}\sum_{u\in\mathcal{S}_k} y_u$. Note that the bandwidth σ can be reformulated as a more interpretable *margin* parameter defined by the distance from the centroid where $P(u = k) = 0.5$:

$$margin = \sigma\sqrt{-2\ln 0.5}. \tag{3}$$

Ultimately, this generates a probability map for each instance such that it can be directly compared to the one-hot encoded *true* segmentation $\mathbb{1}\{u = k\}$. In our workflow, we choose to optimize the soft Jaccard loss as defined in [14] for both class and instance predictions (i.e. an embedding soft jaccard (ESJ)) as it inherently handles class imbalance. Using the same loss function for both tasks also facilitates multi-task training such that we found uniform loss weighting to be sufficient. Finally, since we only use the instance embeddings to split the predicted foreground mask into instances, the embedding loss is not applied over background regions.

Post-processing. At inference time, the *true* centroids used in (2) are not available. Hence, we have to estimate them from the embeddings. We do this by a computationally inexpensive Hough voting scheme as illustrated in supplement, Fig. 2. Embeddings are binned in a 2D/3D histogram where each bin corresponds to a pixel/voxel in the input image. Local maxima with a window size related to *margin* are taken as centres. With a perfect zero loss, the inter-center distance

Input image   Ground truth   Prediction

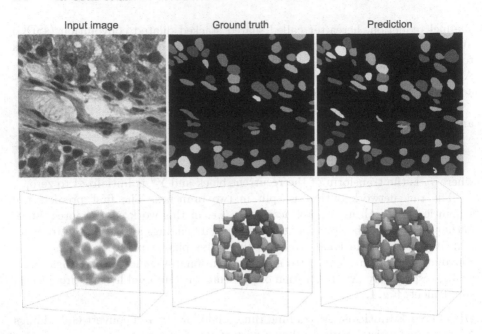

Fig. 3. Qualitative results of our RDCNet on images from MoNuSeg (top row) and 3D-ORG (bottom row). For 3D-ORG, *unlabeled* pixels at the object boundary are not depicted in the ground truth and therefore appear slightly smaller than the predictions.

would be at least 2 *margin*, however in practice we find it beneficial to fine tune the window size on the validation split. Finally, instance labels are obtained by assigning foreground pixels to their nearest center in the embedding space.

3   Experiments and Results

We conduct experiments on three datasets of different modalities and compare our results to the literature where available as detailed below. For all experiments, we train a RDCNet with 8 parallel sSDC blocks, *i.e.* groups, each having 64 channels. The number of iterations is varied from 1 to 10 and the set of dilation rates of the sSDC block from 1 up to the largest that can fit in the training patch size. A scaling factor s_d is chosen according to the instances size and image resolution of each dataset d as detailed below. The strided convolution input layer has both kernel size and stride of s_d and 32 channels while the output transposed convolution has a kernel size of $2s_d$ and stride s_d. We train all networks with Adam optimizer and cosine scheduler with learning rates from 10^{-3} to 10^{-5}, 10% spatial dropout on the input of the recurrent block and a batch size of 2. We also perform online data augmentation as detailed in supporting information. To assess the benefits of our architecture, we also train a U-Net [16] baseline using the same ESJ loss and a additive semi-convolutional layer for the embedding. We report the instance precision, recall and F_1 scores at

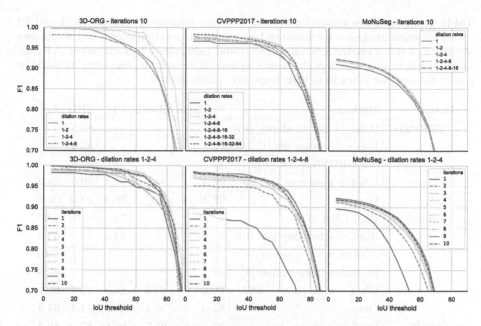

Fig. 4. Hyperparameter analysis. We compare the effect of different dilation ranges in the sSDC block (top) and varying number of iterations (bottom) on all three datasets (columns). Curves depict instance F1-score with varying IoU threshold. Dilation rate = 1 corresponds to the base case of regular 3×3 convolution.

50% IoU threshold per-image unless otherwise specified. In accordance with relevant literature, we also report the symetric best dice (SBD) [8] and aggregated Jaccard index (AJI) [5].

3.1   Datasets

CVPPP2017: A plant leaf segmentation dataset from [7,8]. Leafs exhibit more complex shapes than nuclei and are therefore an excellent test case for a general instance segmentation method. An example can be found in Fig. 1. Since ground-truth for the test set is not publicly available, we randomly split the 128 images of the A1 subset into 60% training, 20% validation and 20% test. We train on 480×480 crops and use a scaling factor of 4. The *margin* in the ESJ is set to 10 px. Note that this drives centers of close-by, central leaves apart while centers of mass of large leaves remain valid solutions. We compare our results with 3 methods reported in the literature: cosine embedding that uses local constraints [13], recurrent attention that models a human-like counting process [15] and a recent work based on Mask-RCNN with domain-tailored data augmentation [21].

MoNuSeg: A nuclei segmentation dataset composed of digital pathology images originating from seven different organs [5]. The training set contains 30 images that we re-split into 23 and 7 images for training and validation respectively.

Table 1. Quantitative evaluation of instance segmentations. Precision, recall and F1 scores are calculated on a per-instance basis at an intersection-over-union acceptance threshold of 0.5. Symetric best dice (SBD) and aggregated Jaccard index (AJI) are calculated as in the respective challenges [8] and [5]. Scores for competing methods on public datasets are taken from their respective publication.

Dataset	Method	Precision	Recall	F1	SBD	AJI
CVPPP2017	Hglass + cos similarity [13]	–	–	–	84.5	–
	Recurrent attention [15]	–	–	–	84.9	–
	Mask-RCNN + synth [21]	–	–	–	90.0	–
	UNet + semi-conv + ESJ	96.9	94.1	95.4	89.6	89.9
	Ours	97.3	96.7	96.9	**91.4**	96.9
MoNuSeg	Dual UNet [6]	–	–	79.1	–	59.0
	ResNet + bending loss [19]	–	–	77.2	–	63.0
	MoNuSeg top score [5]	–	–	–	–	**69.1**
	MoNuSeg inter-human [5]	–	–	–	–	65.3
	UNet + semi-conv + ESJ	79.8	90.8	84.8	72.7	66.1
	Ours	82.0	90.3	85.8	74.2	67.3
3D-ORG	StarDist [22]	97.5	95.7	96.6	87.7	80.2
	UNet + semi-conv + ESJ	98.1	94.6	96.2	92.1	86.2
	Ours	**99.4**	**99.1**	**99.3**	**95.5**	**92.4**

We report results on the 14 test images as described in the original challenge. We train on 256 × 256 crops, using a scaling factor of 4 and 5 px *margin* for the ESJ loss. Due to the smaller field of view required for this dataset, the U-Net baseline is trained with 4 levels instead of the original 5 which provided better results. We compare our result to the MoNuSeg competition [5] top rank as well as published work relying on boundary prediction [6] and a curvature regularization technique [19].

3D-ORG: A 3D nuclei segmentation dataset comprised of 49 3D image stacks of developing organoids acquired with light-sheet microscopy. The stacks have a voxel spacing of 0.26 × 0.26 × 2 μm. An example is depicted in Fig. 3. We split the dataset into 32, 9 and 8 images for training, validation and testing respectively. Annotations were obtained in a semi-automatic fashion with manual corrections. Cell boundaries sometimes appear fuzzy due to low signal-to-noise and scattering. In these ambiguous regions, the annotation labels were set as *undefined*, which can be elegantly handled in our approach by zeroing the loss in these regions. We train on 20 × 160 × 160 crops, using a scaling factor of (1, 8, 8), *i.e.* no downscaling along Z to compensate for anisotropy. In this case the semi-convolutional layer also uses physical coordinates rather than voxel indices. The ESJ loss *margin* is set to 3 μm. Anisotropy in the U-Net baseline is compensated by omitting max-pooling along the Z-axis. During post-processing, we clean jagged edges with a label-wise morphological opening of 0.5 μm. Finally, we compare our method against StarDist [22]. Since StarDist relies on explicit boundaries for training, voxels in undefined regions are assigned to the nearest label.

3.2   Hyperparameter Analysis

We examine the behavior of our RDCNet with varying hyperparameters. To this end, we vary the dilation rates from 1 (*i.e.* none) up to 64, depending on the dataset, and the number of iterations in the range $i \in \{1, \ldots 10\}$. The results are depicted in Fig. 4.

We observe that for a fixed number of iterations $i = 10$, the F1 score increases with higher dilation rates. Since the weights of the spatial convolutions are shared, the network complexity is only slightly increased due to the subsequent point-wise convolution. Therefore, improvement is likely due to the larger receptive field available during early iterations. This is in line with observations that several small stacked hourglass networks perform better than a large one as reported in [10]. One exception we notice is on the 3D-ORG dataset, where increasing dilations up to 8 decreases F1. We account this to a field of view that is too big for the available patch size.

Looking at the effect of the number of iterations (Fig. 4 bottom row), we note that the increased context from dilations alone (*i.e.* only one iteration) is not sufficient. Clear improvements are observed with increasing number of iterations, plateauing at around 5 iterations for the three datasets. This indicates that 5 iterations would be a good choice to balance performance with computational complexity, resulting in 68% Multiply-Add operations of the baseline UNet.

3.3   Comparison

Quantitative evaluation results on all 3 datasets (described in Sect. 3.1) are shown in Table 1. We report state-of-the-art results on CVPPP2017 and 3D-ORG in terms of SBD and AJI, respectively. On MoNuSeg, our result falls between rank 5 and 6 reported in [5] without any extra domain-specific modelling. Note that this is already better than the reported inter-human agreement level. With all 3 datasets we observe an improvement across all metrics when swapping the baseline U-Net for our RDCNet, despite having ≈ 30× less parameters. Importantly, it has a reduced memory footprint, which is particularly useful for processing 3D datasets. For example, predicting a single 3D patch of $32 \times 256 \times 256$ with RDCNet uses only 3.8 GB VRAM while the baseline UNet uses 8.8 GB. Furthermore, the memory footprint at prediction is constant w.r.t. the number of iterations.

4   Conclusions

We have presented a minimalist recursive network for instance segmentation in biomedical images called RDCNet. We have shown that it achieves state-of-the-art results on 2 out of 3 datasets and is highly competitive on the other. This is achieved by optimizing an instance segmentation loss instead of a surrogate and by relying on semi-convolutional embeddings. We also advocated for grounding hyperparameters in physical space which is made possible by the tight relationship between embeddings and the spatial domain and provided rules of thumb to adapt the method to different modalities. The iterative nature of the RDCNet facilitates the interpretation of intermediate predictions, while the light-weight aspect of the architecture makes it an ideal candidate to process volumetric data. This could, potentially, even incorporate the temporal dimension, which we plan to investigate in future work.

References

1. Chen, L., Strauch, M., Merhof, D.: Instance segmentation of biomedical images with an object-aware embedding learned with local constraints. In: Shen, D., et al. (eds.) MICCAI 2019. LNCS, vol. 11764, pp. 451–459. Springer, Cham (2019). https://doi.org/10.1007/978-3-030-32239-7_50
2. De Brabandere, B., Neven, D., Van Gool, L.: Semantic instance segmentation with a discriminative loss function. arXiv preprint arXiv:1708.02551 (2017)
3. He, K., Gkioxari, G., Dollár, P., Girshick, R.: Mask R-CNN. In: Proceedings of the IEEE International Conference on Computer Vision, pp. 2961–2969 (2017)
4. He, K., Zhang, X., Ren, S., Sun, J.: Identity mappings in deep residual networks. In: Leibe, B., Matas, J., Sebe, N., Welling, M. (eds.) ECCV 2016. LNCS, vol. 9908, pp. 630–645. Springer, Cham (2016). https://doi.org/10.1007/978-3-319-46493-0_38
5. Kumar, N., Verma, R., Anand, D., et al.: A multi-organ nucleus segmentation challenge. IEEE Trans. Med. Imaging 39(5), 1380–1391 (2019)
6. Li, X., Wang, Y., Tang, Q., Fan, Z., Yu, J.: Dual U-Net for the segmentation of overlapping glioma nuclei. IEEE Access 7, 84040–84052 (2019)
7. Minervini, M., Fischbach, A., Scharr, H., Tsaftaris, S.: Plant phenotyping datasets (2015). http://www.plant-phenotyping.org/datasets
8. Minervini, M., Fischbach, A., Scharr, H., Tsaftaris, S.A.: Finely-grained annotated datasets for image-based plant phenotyping (2016)
9. Neven, D., Brabandere, B.D., Proesmans, M., Van Gool, L.: Instance segmentation by jointly optimizing spatial embeddings and clustering bandwidth. In: Proceedings of the IEEE Computer Society Conference on Computer Vision and Pattern Recognition, June 2019, pp. 8829–8837 (2019)
10. Newell, A., Yang, K., Deng, J.: Stacked hourglass networks for human pose estimation. In: Leibe, B., Matas, J., Sebe, N., Welling, M. (eds.) ECCV 2016. LNCS, vol. 9912, pp. 483–499. Springer, Cham (2016). https://doi.org/10.1007/978-3-319-46484-8_29
11. Novotny, D., Albanie, S., Larlus, D., Vedaldi, A.: Semi-convolutional operators for instance segmentation. In: Proceedings of the European Conference on Computer Vision (ECCV), pp. 86–102 (2018)
12. Payer, C., Štern, D., Feiner, M., Bischof, H., Urschler, M.: Segmenting and tracking cell instances with cosine embeddings and recurrent hourglass networks. Med. Image Anal. 57, 106–119 (2019)
13. Payer, C., Štern, D., Neff, T., Bischof, H., Urschler, M.: Instance segmentation and tracking with cosine embeddings and recurrent hourglass networks. In: Frangi, A.F., Schnabel, J.A., Davatzikos, C., Alberola-López, C., Fichtinger, G. (eds.) MICCAI 2018. LNCS, vol. 11071, pp. 3–11. Springer, Cham (2018). https://doi.org/10.1007/978-3-030-00934-2_1

14. Rahman, M.A., Wang, Y.: Optimizing intersection-over-union in deep neural networks for image segmentation. In: Bebis, G., et al. (eds.) ISVC 2016. LNCS, vol. 10072, pp. 234–244. Springer, Cham (2016). https://doi.org/10.1007/978-3-319-50835-1_22

15. Ren, M., Zemel, R.S.: End-to-end instance segmentation with recurrent attention. In: Proceedings of the 30th IEEE Conference on Computer Vision and Pattern Recognition, CVPR 2017, January 2017, pp. 293–301. Institute of Electrical and Electronics Engineers Inc., November 2017

16. Ronneberger, O., Fischer, P., Brox, T.: U-Net: convolutional networks for biomedical image segmentation. In: Navab, N., Hornegger, J., Wells, W.M., Frangi, A.F. (eds.) MICCAI 2015. LNCS, vol. 9351, pp. 234–241. Springer, Cham (2015). https://doi.org/10.1007/978-3-319-24574-4_28

17. Schmidt, U., Weigert, M., Broaddus, C., Myers, G.: Cell detection with star-convex polygons. In: Frangi, A.F., Schnabel, J.A., Davatzikos, C., Alberola-López, C., Fichtinger, G. (eds.) MICCAI 2018. LNCS, vol. 11071, pp. 265–273. Springer, Cham (2018). https://doi.org/10.1007/978-3-030-00934-2_30

18. Schuster, R., Wasenmuller, O., Unger, C., Stricker, D.: SDC-stacked dilated convolution: a unified descriptor network for dense matching tasks. In: Proceedings of the IEEE Computer Society Conference on Computer Vision and Pattern Recognition (2019)

19. Wang, H., Xian, M., Vakanski, A.: Bending loss regularized network for nuclei segmentation in histopathology images (2020)

20. Wang, W., Yu, K., Hugonot, J., Fua, P., Salzmann, M.: Recurrent U-Net for resource-constrained segmentation. In: The IEEE International Conference on Computer Vision (ICCV), October 2019

21. Ward, D., Moghadam, P., Hudson, N.: Deep leaf segmentation using synthetic data. In: British Machine Vision Conference 2018, BMVC 2018 (2019)

22. Weigert, M., Schmidt, U., Haase, R., Sugawara, K., Myers, G.: Star-convex polyhedra for 3D object detection and segmentation in microscopy. In: The IEEE Winter Conference on Applications of Computer Vision (WACV), March 2020

Automatic Segmentation of Achilles Tendon Tissues Using Deep Convolutional Neural Network

Tariq Alzyadat[1(✉)], Stephan Praet[3], Girija Chetty[1], Roland Goecke[1],
David Hughes[4], Dinesh Kumar[1], Marijke Welvaert[5], Nicole Vlahovich[2],
and Gordon Waddington[2,3]

[1] Faculty of Science and Technology, University of Canberra,
Canberra, ACT 2617, Australia
Tariq.Alzyadat@canberra.edu.au
[2] Faculty of Health, University of Canberra, Canberra, ACT, Australia
[3] UCRISE, University of Canberra, Canberra, ACT 2617, Australia
[4] Department of Sports Medicine and Physiotherapy, Australian Institute of Sport,
Canberra, ACT 2617, Australia
[5] The Australian National University, Canberra, ACT 0200, Australia

Abstract. The automatic segmentation of Achilles tendon tissues is one
of the preliminary steps towards creating a tool for diagnosing, prog-
nosing, or monitoring changes in tendon organization over time. Manual delineation is the current approach of identifying Achilles region-of-
interest (*ROI*), it is a tedious and time-consuming task. In this respect,
the current work describes the first steps taken towards creating an
automatic approach for Achilles tendon segmentation that utilize the
capabilities of Deep Convolutional Neural Networks (CNNs). Firstly, the
dataset has been pre-processed and manually segmented to be used as
the ground-truth in the training and testing of the proposed automated
model. Secondly, the model was trained and validated using three CNN
architectures SegNet, ResNet-18 and ResNet-50. Finally, Tversky loss
function, 3D augmentation and network ensembling approaches were
used to improve the segmentation performance and to tackle challenges
such as the limited size of the training dataset and data imbalance. The
proposed fully automated segmentation method reached average Dice
score of 0.904. In conclusion, this novel study demonstrates that a CNN
approach is useful for performing accurate Achilles tendon segmentation
in musculoskeletal imaging.

Keywords: Deep learning · Achilles segmentation · Musculoskeletal
imaging

1 Introduction

According to the growing numbers of participants at running events, the popularity of recreational running is still increasing. Unfortunately, the incidence

M. Liu et al. (Eds.): MLMI 2020, LNCS 12436, pp. 444–454, 2020.
https://doi.org/10.1007/978-3-030-59861-7_45

of sports injuries is high [1,2]. A frequent running-related injury is *Achilles Tendinopathy*. The prevalence of Achilles Tendinopathy in general running-related musculoskeletal injuries ranging from 6.2% to 9.5% and the annual incidence ranging from 9.1% to 10.9% for main cases, and prevalence ranging from 2.0% to 18.5% in the main ultra-marathon cases [3]. The use of non-invasive sensitive imaging technique is very crucial to identify Achilles tendinopathy and measuring the efficacy of therapeutic interventions. Therefore, Ultrasonography (US) and Magnetic Resonance Imaging (MRI) are the first-choice diagnostic modalities in the evaluation of Achilles Tendinopathy because of their abilities to visualize soft tissue structures [4]. It is possible to quantify the tissues' signal through the use of Ultrashort Time to Echo pulse sequence (UTE-sequence), it can achieve as short as 0.05–0.5 ms relaxation time, which makes it capable to detect very short T2 values from different tissues [1,5].

Measuring the tendon volume has been used to identify tissues' degeneration in Achilles tendon [6]. There are two approaches to measure the tendon volume: the manual approach, which is a time-consuming and user-dependent task. The other approach is the automatic segmentation, which is a computer-dependent task, hence it is faster and less biased. A thorough search of the relevant literature yielded only few articles related to automatic segmentation [6,7]. The segmentation used in the literature was the 3D seed growing, and the volume of tendon was extracted from seven consecutive sagittal slices on T1-WI MRI. The limitations of this approach were the extra preparation steps, the manual correction and the limited number of slices used to extract the volume.

Another reported approach [8] was based on 3D T2-weighted (T2w) Fast Spin-Echo (FSE) MRI sequence, this study used the seed growing in the transverse plain controlled by the outer boundary of the leg to prevent seed growing leakage, after the seed growing stops, the resulted outer border is used to produce the initial contour, which will be used by the 2D active contour algorithm to enhance the tendon region border. This study used 26 Achilles tendons of 13 healthy volunteers and another two subjects with proven Achilles Tendinopathy. Despite the segmentation accuracy of this approach, most of its population are of healthy subjects, and this limits the efficiency of this approach when it is used with pathological cases where the tendon border disappears, hence the performance of the active contour algorithm will be affected.

The purpose of the current study is to develop a fully automated Achilles tendon segmentation pipeline that utilizes the capabilities of Deep Convolutional Neural Networks (CNN) based on Ultrashort Echo Time Magnetic Resonance (MRI-UTE). The performance of the proposed approach is tested by comparing its results against manually segmented dataset, serving as gold standard.

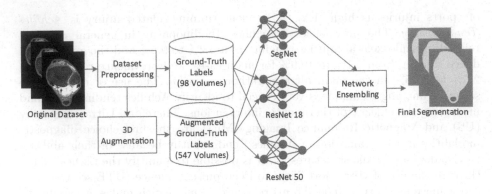

Fig. 1. Achilles tendon segmentation workflow

2   Method

2.1   Image Dataset

The first dataset, a total of 20 patients (13 men/7 women, age: 44 ± 3 years, BMI: $24.4 \pm 3.3 \, \text{kg.m}^2$) with clinical symptoms (duration 54 ± 90 months) of uni ($n = 7$) or bilateral ($n = 13$) mid-portion Achilles Tendinopathy were formally included in the study following a detailed medical history and physical examination by a sport and exercise physician (SP) [9].

UTE-MRI measurements were performed for both ankles at baseline (T1) and after 3 (T2) and 6 months (T3) on 3.0 T clinical whole-body MR system (Ingenia 3.0 T, Philips Healthcare, Best, The Netherlands) using a T/R knee coil with 16 elements for receive.

Axial UTE T2* weighted images were acquired using a 3D radial FID stack of stars technique. For RF excitation a non-selective pulse was used to achieve a shorter echo time. A series of inphase TEs (0.18 ms, 2.3 ms, 4.6 ms, 6.9 ms, 9.2 ms) were acquired for T2* quantification. Typical UTE acquisition parameters were: FOV = 140×140 mm, slice thickness = 1.5 mm (3 mm over contiguous), 120 slices, TR = 15 ms, acquisition matrix = 200×200 (recon matrix = 256×256), flip angle = 10 degs, BW = 500 Hz/pixel, scan time = 4 min.

The second dataset, consisted of a healthy control cohort of twenty participants (elite and sub-elite runners), age: 27 ± 6 years. A total of 10 healthy track athletes with subclinical mid-portion Achilles Tendinopathy (Achilles pain) and a total of 10 healthy track athletes with no reported Achilles Tendinopathy will form the two groups for analysis. The same MRI sequence for the previous cohort is used with this dataset, except it is used for the right ankle only.

2.2   Data Preprocessing

Bias-Field Correction. In this pipeline, the inhomogeneity correction proposed by Manjón et. al [10] has been used.

Denoising. For the present study, we adopted two approaches to denoise the MR images; the baseline subtraction [11] and the truncation model [12,13].

T2* Relaxation Map Calculation. A voxel-wise monoexponential least-square fitting approach with two variable parameters was used to calculate T2* relaxation [14].

The Segmentation of the Ground-Truth Dataset. To segement the ground-truth dataset, we used a semi-automated segmentation method according to the seed growing technique [6] in the transverse plane. Based on anatomical knowledge, the operator could use the manual correction by adding or removing voxels if needed. The segmentation was performed using the aforementioned method by an assesor trained by a sport and exercise physician with over 15 years' experience in musculoskeletal imaging. The whole dataset was segmented by the assesor, then verified and corrected by the sport and exercise physician.

Dataset Augmentation. In order to increase the dataset size in this experiment, for each volume of the original dataset new different deformed volumes were reconstructed by applying 3D registration with respect to a randomly selected volume for another subject, this guarantees different volumes deformation. A rigid transformation model was used in all registrations, which was performed using in-house developed MatLab software (MatLab R2019b; Mathworks). By using the abovementioned approach, we increased the size of our training/validation dataset from (98) volumes to (547) volumes, and the testing dataset from (43) volumes to (187) volumes. The exact registration settings can be found in Table 1.

2.3   Network Architecture

In this paper, in order to test our proposed ensemble model, we used ResNet and SegNet as our segmentation networks, below is the description of the two models.

ResNet. Proposed by [15], Residual Networks (ResNet) is a popular CNN architecture that is widely used in applications areas involving object detection and face recognition. This network is said to model the pyramidal cortex in the cerebral cortex by introducing *skip* connection or *jumps* between one or several convolution layers. In our work, we experimented with two variants of ResNet, namely ResNet-18 and ResNet-50 containing 18 and 50 layers, respectively. The reasons for using two variants of ResNet is to experiment the relationship of network depth on our dataset.

SegNet. Proposed by [16], SegNets were one of the first networks that emerged in the category of segmentation networks. In our experiments the SegNet network contained the same layers as in the benchmark VGG16 network [17] but without the fully connected layers. In addition, our model was compiled using the same network convolution and max pooling layer parameters. The encoder network comprised of 5 distinct blocks with 2 convolution layers in the first 2 blocks and 3 convolution layers in the rest of the blocks. A max pooling layer was placed at the end of each block resulting in a total of 5 max pooling layers used. Filter counts of 64, 128 and 256 were applied to the convolution layers in the 1st, 2nd and 3rd blocks while the convolution layers in the remaining last two blocks had a filter count of 512 respectively. Across the model for all convolution layers the receptive field size of 3×3 was applied with stride of 1. For each max pooling layer in the model pool size of 2×2 was used with stride of 2. This allowed a spatial reduction of the height and width dimensions feature maps by a factor of 2.

2.4   Network Training

As illustrated in Fig. 1, our Achilles tendon image dataset was resized to 256×256 to conform to the VGG16, ResNet input data shape dimensions. Further, all images were normalized using contrast normalization as a pre-processing step [18]. Each model in our network was trained with the original and augmented datasets respectively. The composition of our dataset is given in Table 2. All networks were trained end-to-end (without transfer learning) and summarised using specific parameters in Table 3. The models were implemented in MatLab (MatLab R2019b; Mathworks) and executed on a Dell Precision Xeon 3.5 GHz CPU, 64GB of memory with GPU support utilizing Nvidia Quadro K2200 graphics card.

Table 1. The 3D registration settings

Parameters	Values
Modality	Monomodal
Optimizer	Regular Step Gradient Descent
Metric	MeanSquares
Transform Type	Rigid
Gradient magnitude tolerance	1e-4 (default)
MinimumStepLength—Tolerance for convergence	1e-5 (default)
MaximumStepLength—Initial step length	0.00625
MaximumIterations—Maximum number of iterations	300
RelaxationFactor—Step length reduction factor	0.5 (default)

Table 2. Composition of images for datasets 1 and 2.

	Original dataset	Augmented dataset
Training	3708(45%)*	18964(45%)*
Validation	2472(30%)*	12643(30%)*
Testing	10862**	10862(25%)*

*The percentages here are compared to the whole dataset size, if we exclude the testing dataset, they will be (60%) Training and (40%) Validation.
**We used the augmented dataset for the tesing in order to compare the performance of all models using the same testing cases.

Table 3. Network parameters.

Parameter	ResNet-18	ResNet-50	ResNet-50	SegNet	SegNet
Dataset	Original	Both	Augmented	Original	Augmented
Optimisation function	sgdm	sgdm	sgdm	sgdm	sgdm
Loss function	entropy	entropy	tversky	entropy	entropy
Learning rate	0.001*	0.001*	0.001*	0.01	0.001
L2 regularization	0.005	0.005	0.005	0.0005	0.0005
Momentum	0.9	0.9	0.9	0.9	0.9
Epochs	20	20	20	20	20

sgdm, Stochastic Gradient Descent With Momentum Optimizer.
Both, The Original and the Augmented datasets
*learning rate was reduced by 0.3 every 5 epochs

2.5   Loss Functions

Initially, we trained our 2-class networks using the cross entropy loss function. After examining the results, specifically Precision and Sensitivity, we discovered that all the models have a high Sensitivity but low Precision. It is expected because the dataset is imbalanced, this is due to the difference between the number of voxels of Achilles tendon class compared to the number of voxels of the background class. This imbalance resulted in the segmented volumes larger than the ground-truth volumes as a result of the large number of false positives of Achilles class. To tackle this issue, we retrained the network with best performance (ResNet-50 trained with augmented dataset), using Tversky loss function which has shown promising results in case of imbalance data. In network training, we used the parameters $\alpha = 0.3$ and $\beta = 0.7$. These parameters control the weights of false positives and false negatives, and by increasing the value of β the loss function will generalize and improve the performance in case of imbalanced data [19].

2.6   Network Ensemble

The process of network ensemble started after finalizing the network training. The output of the softmax layer was obtained for every trained network, in total 12 activations(six activations for Entropy loss and six for Tversky loss). After that, three network ensemble approaches were used; Averaging (Avg), Weighted Average (wAvg) and Majority Voting (mVot). The weight of the average has been assigned according to the performance of the network, and the voting was given to the class when all the networks agree upon the same classification for that class.

2.7   Evaluation Metrics

Several quantitative metrics have been used to measure the segmentation accuracy and to evaluate the proposed model. Among the overlap-based metrics, volumetric overlap error (VOE) [20] and Dice similarity coefficient (DSR) [21] were used. Higher DSR value yields better segmentation accuracy, whilst lower VOE value yields better segmentation accuracy.

Other metrics were used to evaluate the performance in this experiment, namely; Accuracy, Specificity, Precision and Sensitivity (Recall) [22].

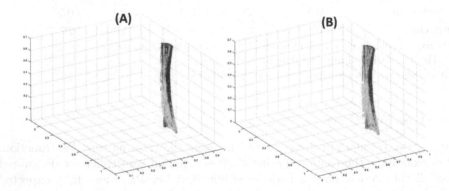

Fig. 2. Segmentation example demonstrates 3D view for the best segmentation result **(A)**Ground-Truth Segmentation **(B)**Network Prediction $(DSR) = 0.943$ and $(VOE) = 10.616$.

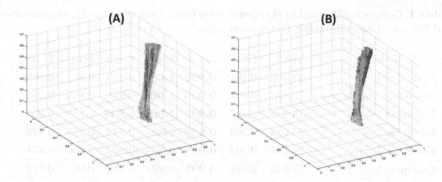

Fig. 3. Segmentation example demonstrates 3D view for the worst segmentation result **(A)**Ground-Truth Segmentation **(B)**Network Prediction $(DSR) = 0.803$ and $(VOE) = 32.481$.

3   Results and Discussion

The Dice score (DSR) was used to evaluate the performance of the automatic segmentation. Based on that, combinations of network ensembles were obtained, and the segmentation performance was evaluated for every combination. In total, 7 networks were trained from scratch, six with entropy loss and then the best performing one of them (ResNet-50 trained using augmented data and Entropy loss) was retrained using Tversky loss. Table 4 shows the results of those 7 trained networks in addition to 5 results of network ensembles with highest scores out of 28 investigated ensembles resulted from combining the loss function, the network ensemble and the trained networks. For the ensemble with best performance (Ensemble 1), 3D volumes for the best and worst segmentation examples compared to the ground-truth are shown in Figs. 2 and 3, respectively. The augmentation has improved the performance for SegNet and ResNet-50, whilst for ResNet-18 the original data network performs better than the augmented data network. As expected, the use of Tversky loss in training the ResNet-50 network improved the Dice score from 0.828 to 0.901, in comparison the same network trained with cross entropy loss. It also improved the Precision score from 0.715 to 0.945 as a result of reducing the number of False positives' classification.

Table 4. Comparing the quality of segmentation (with/without Tversky, augmentation and Network Ensemble) using metrics' averages.

CNN Model	VOE	DSR	Acc.	Speci.	Preci.	Sensi.	SPAvg
Ensemble 1	**17.342**	**0.904**	**0.999**	**1.000**	0.940	0.873	**0.906**
ResNet-50Aug Tversky	17.826	0.901	**0.999**	**1.000**	0.945	0.863	0.904
Ensemble 2	18.350	0.897	**0.999**	**1.000**	**0.947**	0.856	0.901
Ensemble 3	23.620	0.864	**0.999**	0.999	0.793	0.953	0.873
Ensemble 4	23.737	0.863	**0.999**	0.999	0.802	0.940	0.871
Ensemble 5	23.940	0.861	**0.999**	0.999	0.783	0.961	0.872
ResNet-50Aug Entropy	28.803	0.828	0.998	0.998	0.715	0.987	0.851
ResNet-50Org Entropy	30.896	0.805	0.988	0.998	0.686	0.980	0.833
ResNet-18Org Entropy	31.281	0.803	0.988	0.998	0.684	0.978	0.831
ResNet-18Aug Entropy	34.944	0.780	0.998	0.998	0.644	**0.993**	0.819
SegNetAug Entropy	44.175	0.700	0.996	0.996	0.547	0.982	0.764
SegNetOrg Entropy	56.678	0.583	0.994	0.994	0.422	0.966	0.694

VOE, Volumetric overlap error; **DSR**, Dice Score; **Acc.**, Accuracy; **Speci.**, Specificity; **Preci.**, Precision; **Sensi.**, Sensitivity; **SPAvg**, Sensitivity and Precision Average; **Ensemble 1**, Tversky loss weighted with average ensemble for the best 4 networks; **Ensemble 2**, Tversky loss with majority voting ensemble for the best 4 networks; **Ensemble 3**, Entropy loss with majority voting ensemble for the best 5 networks; **Ensemble 4**, Entropy loss with majority voting ensemble for all networks;
Ensemble 5, Entropy loss with majority voting ensemble for the best 4 networks.

4 Conclusion

In this study, we introduced an end-to-end pipeline to segment Achilles tendon region using deep CNN model, which is to the best of our knowledge, the first reported study that exploits the deep CNN capabilities to perform automatic segmentation of Achilles tissues using UTE-MRI data record at 3T. The segmentation was performed automatically in transverse slices. One limitation of this study was the limited size of the training dataset, it was mitigated successfully by using the data augmentation approach. The other limitation was imbalance data, the remedy was the use of Tversky loss instead of cross entropy. Finally, the segmentation was improved further by using the network ensemble approach. Further study is planned to improve the accuracy and performance of the automatic segmentation by performing postprocessing to the segmentation output of the Deep CNN.

References

1. Gallo, R., Plakke, M., Silvis, M.: Common leg injuries of long-distance runners. Sports Health **4**, 485–495 (2012)
2. Maffulli, N., Wong, J., Almekinders, L.: Types and epidemiology of tendinopathy. Clin. Sports Med. **22**, 675–692 (2003)
3. Lopes, A., Hespanhol, L., Yeung, S., Costa, L.O.: What are the main running-related musculoskeletal injuries? Sports Med. **42**, 891–905 (2012). https://doi.org/10.1007/BF03262301
4. Bleakney, R., White, L.: Imaging of the Achilles tendon. Foot Ankle Clin. **10**, 239–254 (2005)
5. Filho, G., et al.: Quantitative characterization of the Achilles tendon in cadaveric specimens: T1 and t2* measurements using ultrashort-te mri at 3 t. Am. J. Roentgenol. **192**, 117–124 (2009)
6. Shalabi, A., Movin, T., Kristoffersen-Wiberg, M., Aspelin, P., Svensson, L.: Reliability in the assessment of tendon volume and intratendinous signal of the Achilles tendon on MRI: a methodological description. Knee Surg. Sports Traumatol. Arthrosc. **13**, 492–498 (2005). https://doi.org/10.1007/s00167-004-0546-0
7. Gärdin, A., Bruno, J., Movin, T., Kristoffersen-Wiberg, M., Shalabi, A.: Magnetic resonance signal, rather than tendon volume, correlates to pain and functional impairment in chronic Achilles tendinopathy. Acta Radiol. **47**, 718–724 (2006)
8. Syha, R.: Automated volumetric assessment of the Achilles tendon (AVAT) using a 3D T2 weighted space sequence at 3T in healthy and pathologic cases. Eur. J. Radiol. **81**, 1612–1617 (2012)
9. Praet, S., et al.: Oral supplementation of specific collagen peptides combined with calf-strengthening exercises enhances function and reduces pain in Achilles tendinopathy patients. Nutrients **11**, 76 (2019)
10. Manjón, J.V., Lull, J.J., Carbonell-Caballero, J., García-Martí, G., Martí-Bonmatí, L., Robles, M.: A nonparametric MRI inhomogeneity correction method. Med. Image Anal. **11**, 336–345 (2007)
11. Henkelman, R.: Measurement of signal intensities in the presence of noise in MR images. Med. Phys. **12**, 232–233 (1985)
12. Westwood, M., et al.: A single breath-hold multiecho T2* cardiovascular magnetic resonance technique for diagnosis of myocardial iron overload. J. Magn. Reson. Imaging **18**, 33–39 (2003)
13. Westwood, M., et al.: Interscanner reproducibility of cardiovascular magnetic resonance T2* measurements of tissue iron in thalassemia. J. Magn. Reson. Imaging **18**, 616–620 (2003)
14. Grosse, U., et al.: Influence of physical activity on T1 and T2* relaxation times of healthy Achilles tendons at 3T. J. Magn. Reson. Imaging **41**(1), 193–201 (2015)
15. He, K., Zhang, X., Ren, S., Sun, J.: Deep residual learning for image recognition. In: 2016 IEEE Conference on Computer Vision and Pattern Recognition (CVPR), pp. 770–778 (2016)
16. Badrinarayanan, V., Kendall, A., Cipolla, R.: Segnet: a deep convolutional encoder-decoder architecture for image segmentation. IEEE Trans. Pattern Anal. Mach. Intell. **39**(12), 2481–2495 (2017)
17. Szegedy, C., et al.: Going deeper with convolutions. In: 2015 IEEE Conference on Computer Vision and Pattern Recognition (CVPR), pp. 1–9 (2015)
18. Jarrett, K., Kavukcuoglu, K., Ranzato, M., LeCun, Y.: What is the best multistage architecture for object recognition?" In: 12th IEEE International Conference on Computer Vision, pp. 2146–2153 (2009)

19. Salehi, S.S.M., Erdoğmuş, D., Gholipour, A.: Tversky loss function for image segmentation using 3D fully convolutional deep networks. CoRR, vol. abs/1706.05721 (2017)
20. Heimann, T., et al.: Comparison and evaluation of methods for liver segmentation from CT datasets. IEEE Trans. Med. Imaging **28**, 1251–1265 (2009)
21. Sørensen, T.: A Method of establishing groups of equal amplitude in plant sociology based on similarity of species content and its application to analyses of the vegetation on Danish commons. Munksgaard, I kommission hos E (1948)
22. Silva, G., Oliveira, L., Pithon, M.: Automatic segmenting teeth in x-ray images: trends, a novel data set, benchmarking and future perspectives. Expert Syst. Appl. **107**, 15–31 (2018)

An End to End System for Measuring Axon Growth

Zewen Liu[1]($\boxtimes$), Timothy Cootes[1], and Christoph Ballestrem[2]

[1] Division of Informatics, Imaging and Data Sciences, Stopford Building,
The University of Manchester, Manchester M13 9PT, UK
zewen.liu@postgrad.manchester.ac.uk
[2] Wellcome Trust Centre for Cell-Matrix Research, Faculty of Biology,
Medicine and Health, University of Manchester, Manchester M13 9PT, UK

Abstract. To study how axon growth is affected by the local environment biologists perform extensive experiments, watching the axons develop on different substrates. As axons grow from the neuron cell body they form tree-like structures, with branches forming and withering as they explore their surroundings. In this paper, we propose a system which can track individual axons as they grow and branch over time, enabling quantitative evaluation of different aspects of the axon behaviour. The system includes a novel segmentation network with Gabor kernels. It uses less than 0.5% of the number of parameters required in an equivalent U-Net or other related CNN but gives better overall performance on a standard test set. We evaluate the complete axon tracking system and demonstrating that it achieves results comparable to a human annotator, but gives a far richer description and is much faster.

Keywords: Axon tracking · Vessel segmentation · Microscopy image analysis

1 Introduction

Nerve cells (neurons) have axons which enable them to communicate with other neurons. During development these axons grow out from the cell body, forming tree like branching structures. Branches are formed and wither away as the cells explore their local environment. Many biomedical and biochemical factors can affect the way the axons grow, and understanding the mechanisms is an important challenge to biologists. To better understand the factors influencing their behavior, sequences of microscope images are taken, watching the axons grow on different types of media. Currently these images are analyzed by an expert marking the tip of the growth cone (at the end of the axon) on every frame, then estimating the growth speed and direction on different chemical substrates. This annotation is very time consuming, limiting the numbers of experiments which can be analyzed practically. It also ignores potentially important information about the shape and structure of the axon trees. There are many promising methods for solving large 3D neuron reconstruction where the strategy of

© Springer Nature Switzerland AG 2020
M. Liu et al. (Eds.): MLMI 2020, LNCS 12436, pp. 455–464, 2020.
https://doi.org/10.1007/978-3-030-59861-7_46

boundary segmentation with flood-filling is widely used [1]. These methods are computationally expensive and require manual verification of the result. This approach is not appropriate for our 2D videos in which the axons are thin and often broken by occlusions. We propose a complete system for extracting axon morphology data from microscopy videos. The system first segments the axon fibres using a novel convolutional neural network (CNN). The fibres are grouped into trees, then matched from one image to the next to enable temporal analysis (Fig. 1).

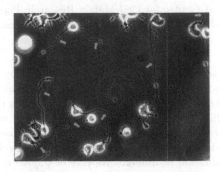

Fig. 1. Axons (black, vessel-like structures) in a microscope image.

Segmentation: CNN models such as U-Net [2] and R2U-Net [3] have been shown to produce good results in many scenarios, including the curvilinear structures such as the axons. However, such an architecture usually has hundreds of thousands of parameters so needs a lot of training data (which may be augmented versions of a modest number of images). Networks specialized for curvilinear structures, such as Vessel-Net [5] also have many parameters to learn. In [6], the network starts from generated filters instead of training from random. The idea of convolutional Gabor orientation filters (GoF) was first introduced in [7], where a convolutional kernel is made by multiplying a bank of Gabor filters with a set of normal weights of the same size. Experiments on CIFAR100 [8] showed such a model can achieve a better classification rate with fewer parameters than other approaches. In this paper, a similar, but much lighter structure, GConv, is proposed for axon image segmentation. We enable the training of the Gabor part of the kernel. We also update the weights to rotate with the Gabor part and scale over different sizes. This new features saved more than 99.5% parameters when comparing to the ordinary fully convolutional networks (FCN) [2,9,10] and thus requires less training data to achieve comparable performance.

Having segmented the axons as a binary mask, we run a path following algorithm in order to find the branches of the axon tree. The images are collected over several days as the neurons grow so there can be distractors such as fleeting blobs, shadows or camera jitter. We derive a method of tracking the tree structures from one frame to the next which provides tolerance for such factors.

The result is a detailed description of the tree for each axon at each frame, enabling analysis of the way that it is growing. In the following we describe the components of the system and results of experiments evaluating them.

2 Method

2.1 The Proposed Structure

The full system is composed of three modules to be applied to raw microscopy axon videos (Fig. 2). The first module segments the video frames, the second extracts the axon trees from the binary maps. The last links axons from one frame to the next.

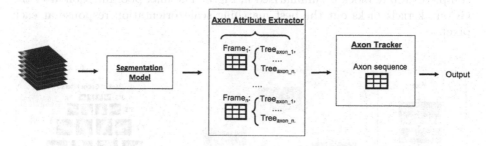

Fig. 2. Workflow of the system.

2.2 Axon Segmentation

When segmenting tree like objects, small or thin branches are usually harder to detect. For the segmentation stage of the system, we introduce a novel method, the Gabor-Convolutional layer (GConv), which is designed for detecting thin curvilinear structures with low contrast.

Inspired by [6] and [7], at the heart of our GConv module is a bank of filters constructed from Gabor kernels at n_s scales and n_a orientations, each multiplied (pixel-wise) by a grid of learned weights. The same grid of weights is scaled and rotated to match all kernels. The (x, y) value of a Gabor kernel at angle zero is given by

$$G(x, y; \lambda, \gamma, \sigma) = exp(-(x^2 + \gamma^2 y^2)/(2\sigma^2))cos(2\pi x/\lambda) \tag{1}$$

where λ is wavelength, σ^2 denotes variance and γ represents axis ratio.

If $G_{s,\theta}(i, j)$ are the elements of a Gabor filter rotated to angle θ and scaled to $s \times s$, and $W_{s,\theta}(i, j)$ are the elements of a grid of weights obtained by scaling and rotating the base weights, W, then the elements of the resulting convolution kernel are given by $K_{s,\theta}(i, j) = G_{s,\theta}(i, j)W_{s,\theta}(i, j)$. The base weights are all initialized to 1. The scale/angle parameters in 16 kernels are set to $(\theta = \pi/8, 3\pi/8, 5\pi/8, 7\pi/8) \times (s = 3, 5, 7, 9)$, which were found to be a memory efficient combination. During optimization the 9×9 base weights and the 3 parameters of the base Gabor kernel $(\lambda, \gamma, \sigma)$ are modified. Normalized correlation is calculated between a GConv kernel and input patches rather than standard convolution procedure, so that the output of different scaled kernels is comparable. The Gabor part constrains the interested pattern and the convolutional part provides some flexibility during training. By sharing parameters and weights across all orientations and scales we significantly reduce the overall number of parameters (84 + 1 bias term per scale) to define all 16 kernels. In order to keep model relatively light, the number of hidden layers is limited. This means a standard U-shape design is not necessary, in part because the structures of interest are relatively thin so disappear at coarser resolutions. A complete GConv block is summarized in Fig. 3. The max pool function after the GConv kernels picks out the best matching scale/orientation response at each pixel.

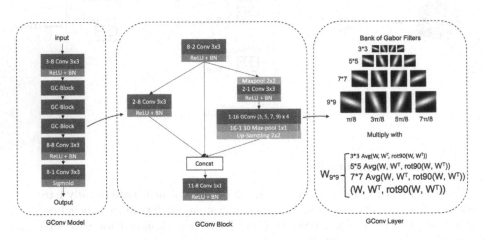

Fig. 3. Diagram of proposed GConv-Net.

2.3   Extracting Axon Trees

The segmentation module produces an axon probability image, which must be further processed to extract the individual axon trees. Currently we are particularly interested in the growth direction, the speed of growth cones and the distribution of branching events. These attributes are widely involved in the studies of biochemical factors of axon growth.

Also, for the vessel-shaped object, one challenge is determining the branch connection errors caused by false-positive pixel classification. Given the position of the tip of a branch (an axon pixel with only one neighbouring axon pixel), we can trace the axon back to its source cell body by finding the path, $\{x_i\}$, which minimizes $\sum_{i=0}^{n}(1 - P(x_i))$ such that x_0 is the axon tip, x_n is on the cell body and $1 \leq |x_{i+1} - x_i| \leq \sqrt{2}$, and $P(x_i)$ is the axon likelihood at the position x_i. These paths are the axon trace candidates with high confidence. The tip farthest from the root node (on the cell body) gives the main branch, and other tips will connect either to the main branch or branches off it.

2.4   Frame to Frame Tracking

Since the biological experiments last several days (with several minutes between each frame), there can be significant changes between frames including occlusions due to objects floating above the cells of interest. This can make creating a complete axon trace challenging. The module above derives a draft tree structure for each axon. The next step is to track and complete the tree by bridging the gaps and pruning any unrelated branches.

Given a new frame, we have a set of candidate axon pieces (each a continuous line of pixels, ending at branch points). Each axon piece is compared to the target axon in previous frames and the one with the largest overlap is selected. We then connect other pieces to it, and prune branches without sufficient support. To do this we first construct a history image as a weighted sum of the previous n_f binary segmentation maps.

$$H(x) = \sum_{t=1}^{n_f} w_t \times f(map_t(x)) \tag{2}$$

$$w_t = \frac{IoU(map_t, map_{t-1})}{\sum_{t'=1}^{n_f} IoU(map'_t, map_{t'-1})} \tag{3}$$

$$f(map(x)) = \{1, 0, -1 | x_i \in \{\text{selected axon, background, other axon}\}\} \tag{4}$$

Here map_t is the binary segmentation result of frame t. $f(map)$ is an image indicating whether each pixel is part of the current axon $(+1)$, background (0) or another axon (-1). IoU is the Intersection over Union of the two binary images (a value in $[0,1]$). The weights mean that less attention is paid to frames which are not consistent with their neighbours, which usually means that there was an acquisition problem.

If a candidate piece is given by the n pixels $\{x_i\}$, then a value P_{path} is assigned to the piece indicating its consistency with the history,

$$P_{path} = \frac{1}{n} \sum_{i=1}^{n} map(x_i) \tag{5}$$

Each unassigned piece in turn is evaluated and connected to the current axon tree if it is close enough to a current branch and has $P_{path} > P_t$ for some threshold P_t. Gaps in branches caused by occlusions are filled as long as the ends are consistent. The pieces with P_{path} greater than P_t will be merged to the tree, and a branches with P_{path} less than P_t will be removed.

The axon tree is complete when no unassigned pieces can be added to it. Axons always grow from cells, and since cells don't move much the root cell is the closest in the current frame to that in the previous frame. The root of the tree is initialised as the node closest to the centre of the root cell.

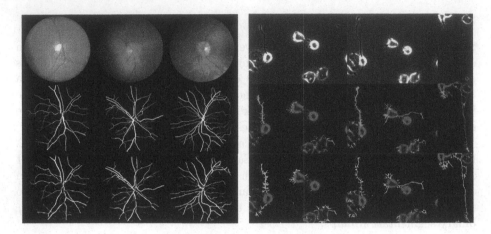

Fig. 4. Examples of segmentatoin results on CHASE_DB1 (left) and Axon images (right). Top to bottom: original image, ground truth and segmentation result.

3   Experiments

We evaluate the novel GConv-based segmentation on two databases, (1) the CHASE-DB1 [9,10] database of retina vessels and (2) our own axon dataset. The GConv model has only 2862 parameters. For CHASE-DB1 database, which has 28 RGB images (999 × 960), we take the images indexed from 1 to 20 as training set and the rest 8 images as test set [11–13]. The annotation from the first observer was used as ground truth. The field of view (FOV) for the images is determined manually as it is not included in the database. There are 30 1096 × 1100 greyscale microscopy images in the axon dataset. 20 were used for training, 10 for testing. We used binary cross-entropy as a loss function and the Adam optimizer for training the CNN.

For each training set image, 400 partly overlapped 48 × 48 patches were randomly cropped, giving 8,000 training patches. The training batch size was set 32. A plateau learning rate scheduler was preferred with a decaying rate of 0.1 starting from 0.01 when its patience was set to 10 epochs. Examples of segmentation results from two datasets are show in Fig. 4.

4   Results

The segmentation model was evaluated by the indicators of per-pixel F1 scores, sensitivity (SE), specificity (SP), accuracy (Acc) and Area under the ROC curve (AUC). Table 1 shows the performance of our model against the other state-of-the-art algorithms on the dataset of CHASE_BD1 and on our axon dataset. In the retina vessel dataset CHASE_DB1, our model achieved the best F1 score and sensitivity despite having far fewer parameters than the other methods. On the axon dataset, our model also achieves and AUC 2.7% higher than U-Net with less than 0.5% of the parameters.

Table 1. Comparison with state-of-the-art methods on CHASE_DB1 and axon dataset. (*results are obtained from [12])

Datasets	Methods	F1	Se	Sp	Acc	AUC
CHASE_DB1	U-Net [1]	0.792	0.791	0.974	0.954	0.953
	Residual U-Net [2]*	0.780	0.773	0.982	0.955	0.978
	Reccurent U-Net [2]	0.781	0.746	0.984	0.962	0.980
	R2U-Net [2]*	0.793	0.776	0.982	0.963	0.981
	LadderNet [12]*	0.790	0.786	0.980	0.962	0.977
	VesselNet [4]*	0.791	0.782	0.981	0.962	0.976
	Ours (2,862 parameters)	0.795	0.797	0.975	0.955	0.972
Axon dataset	U-Net [1]	0.88	0.87	0.997	0.995	0.935
	Ours (2,862 parameters)	0.81	0.80	0.997	0.996	0.961

Table 2. Ablation studies using the same experiment settings on CHASE_DB1.

Dataset	CHASE_DB1					
Indicator	F1	Se	Sp	Acc	AUC	Parameters
U-Net[1]	0.792	0.791	0.974	0.954	0.953	573,537
w/o GConv block	0.779	0.748	0.978	0.953	0.969	2,598
w/o Gabor kernel	0.785	0.765	0.977	0.954	0.970	2,847
Ours	0.795	0.797	0.975	0.955	0.972	2,862

An ablation experiment was conducted on the CHASE_DB1 dataset. The standard model was compared with the version without GConv Blocks and a version without the Gabor filters in GConv layers. Results are summarised in Table 2. This shows that the full version is better able to detect the positive class (3.2% and 4.9% higher than the other two in sensitivity). The segmentation results over the non-vessel areas are similar between all three versions.

For the general indicators of F1, accuracy and AUC, our model, with only 2862 parameters, also outperformed the other two versions as well as the U-Net model which requires 573,537 parameters.

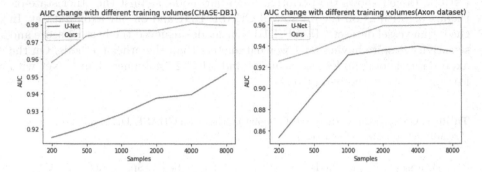

Fig. 5. AUC changes for different training set size on CHASE_DB1 and axon datasets.

We explored how the training set size affected performance. Figure 5 shows our model can perform relatively better comparing to a U-Net model with training set sizes of 200, 500, 1K, 2K, 4K 8K examples. The accuracy of GConv model improved rapidly as the training sample volume increased, eventually plateauing. This plateau phenomenon usually happens when over-sampled from limited data source, in which case our model works well and has relatively smaller fluctuations relative to the changes in training volume.

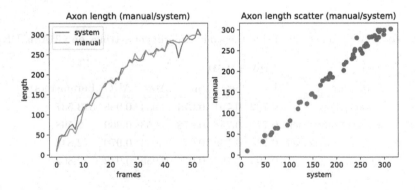

Fig. 6. Axon length measure (system output vs manual annotation).

Axon Tracking. The system is able to track axon growth over time. It can thus efficiently reproduce measures of growth normally produced by an expert manually marking the growth cone position in each frame of a video. In Fig. 6

we compare the length measures produced from manual annotation and the result of the automatic system (using $P_t = 0.3, n_f = 5$). The system output is closely correlated with the manual measurements. The differences can be found in particular frames are normally caused by growth cone ambiguity where, in some frames, growth cone is an ambiguous area not a concrete point. In this case, the algorithm will locate the growth cone at the furthest tip of the area.

5 Conclusion

We present a complete system for tracing axon trees and monitoring their growth over time. We also introduce a novel CNN structure, GConv, for vessel-like object segmentation. Experiments on two data sets (vessels and axons) show that this produces results which are better than alternative methods that use far more parameters, and that the GConv based system can achieve good results with fewer training examples. The overall system is able to locate and track axons as well as human experts, and produces a much richer description which will enable more extensive analysis of how the structures respond to their environment.

References

1. Januszewski, M., et al.: High-precision automated reconstruction of neurons with flood-filling networks. Nat. Methods **15**(8), 605–610 (2018)
2. Ronneberger, O., Fischer, P., Brox, T.: U-Net: convolutional networks for biomedical image segmentation. In: Navab, N., Hornegger, J., Wells, W.M., Frangi, A.F. (eds.) MICCAI 2015. LNCS, vol. 9351, pp. 234–241. Springer, Cham (2015). https://doi.org/10.1007/978-3-319-24574-4_28
3. Alom, M.Z., Hasan, M., Yakopcic, C., Taha, T.M., Asari, V.K.: Recurrent residual convolutional neural network based on u-net (r2u-net) for medical image segmentation. arXiv preprint arXiv:1802.06955 (2018)
4. Fu, H., Xu, Y., Lin, S., Kee Wong, D.W., Liu, J.: DeepVessel: retinal vessel segmentation via deep learning and conditional random field. In: Ourselin, S., Joskowicz, L., Sabuncu, M.R., Unal, G., Wells, W. (eds.) MICCAI 2016. LNCS, vol. 9901, pp. 132–139. Springer, Cham (2016). https://doi.org/10.1007/978-3-319-46723-8_16
5. Kitrungrotsakul, T., et al.: VesselNet: a deep convolutional neural network with multi pathways for robust hepatic vessel segmentation. Comput. Med. Imaging Graph. **75**, 74–83 (2019)
6. Chan, T.-H., Jia, K., Gao, S., Lu, J., Zeng, Z., Ma, Y.: PCANet: a simple deep learning baseline for image classification? IEEE Trans. Image Process. **24**(12), 5017–5032 (2015)
7. Luan, S., Chen, C., Zhang, B., Han, J., Liu, J.: Gabor convolutional networks. IEEE Trans. Image Process. **27**(9), 4357–4366 (2018)
8. Krizhevsky, A., Hinton, G.: Learning multiple layers of features from tiny images, p. 7 (2009)
9. Owen, C.G., et al.: Measuring retinal vessel tortuosity in 10-year-old children: validation of the computer-assisted image analysis of the retina (CAIAR) program. Invest. Ophthalmol. Vis. Sci. **50**(5), 2004–2010 (2009)

10. Owen, C.G., et al.: Retinal arteriolar tortuosity and cardiovascular risk factors in a multi-ethnic population study of 10-year-old children; the Child Heart and Health Study in England (CHASE). Arterioscler. Thromb. Vasc. Biol. **31**(8), 1933–1938 (2011)

11. Zhang, Z., Liu, Q., Wang, Y.: Road extraction by deep residual U-Net. IEEE Geosci. Remote Sens. Lett. **15**(5), 749–753 (2018)

12. Liu, B., Gu, L., Lu, F.: Unsupervised ensemble strategy for retinal vessel segmentation. In: Shen, D., et al. (eds.) MICCAI 2019. LNCS, vol. 11764, pp. 111–119. Springer, Cham (2019). https://doi.org/10.1007/978-3-030-32239-7_13

13. Zhuang, J.: LadderNet: multi-path networks based on U-Net for medical image segmentation. arXiv preprint arXiv:1810.07810 (2018)

Interwound Structural and Functional Difference Between Preterm and Term Infant Brains Revealed by Multi-view CCA

Zhibin He[1], Shu Zhang[2], Songyao Zhang[1], Yin Zhang[1], Xintao Hu[1], Xi Jiang[3], Lei Guo[1], Tianming Liu[4], Lei Du[1], and Tuo Zhang[1(✉)]

[1] School of Automation, Northwestern Polytechnical University, Xi'an, China
tuozhang@nwpu.edu.cn
[2] School of Computer Science, Northwestern Polytechnical University, Xi'an, China
[3] School of Life Science and Technology, MOE Key Lab for Neuroinformation,
University of Electronic Science and Technology of China, Chengdu, China
[4] Cortical Architecture Imaging and Discovery Lab, Department of Computer
Science and Bioimaging Research Center, The University of Georgia, Athens, GA, USA

Abstract. The perinatal period is a critical time of development of brain cortex, structural connection and function. Therefore, A premature exposure to the extrauterine environment is suggested to have the downstream consequences of abnormality in brain structure, function and cognition. A comparative study between the preterm infant brains and term ones at the term-equivalent age provides a valuable window to investigate the normal and abnormal developmental mechanism of these interwound developmental processes. Most of works focused only on one of these processes, and very few studies are found to interpret how these processes interact with each other and how such interactions have been altered on preterm infants' brains. To fill this gap, we propose a multi-view canonical correlation analysis (CCA) method with the locality preserving projection (LPP) constraint and the age regression constraint, by which interactions between these interwound structural and functional features are identified to maximize the discrimination between preterm and term groups. Our findings on the interaction patterns among structural and functional features find supports from previous reports and provide new knowledge to the development patterns of infant brains.

Keywords: Preterm · Multi-view CCA · Locality preserving projection

1 Introduction

The perinatal period is a critical time of development of brain cortex, structural connection and function [1]. It has been reported that the generation of most cortical neurons and long-range white matter connections are finished prenatally [1, 2], and even the repertoire of resting-state networks is present at term-equivalent age [3]. However, many important developmental processes continue to the postnatal period, such as migration of inhibitory neurons and generation of astrocytes in the cortex, and myelination and

© Springer Nature Switzerland AG 2020
M. Liu et al. (Eds.): MLMI 2020, LNCS 12436, pp. 465–473, 2020.
https://doi.org/10.1007/978-3-030-59861-7_47

the development of short-range cortico-cortical connections in white matters [1, 4]. Due to these important developmental processes during the perinatal period, a premature exposure to the extrauterine environment is suggested to have the downstream consequences of abnormality in cortex, connection, function and cognition [5, 6], such as autism spectrum disorder (ASD) and attention deficit hyperactivity disorder (ADHD) [8]. In this sense, a comparative study between the preterm infant brains and term ones at the term-equivalent age provides a valuable window to decipher the developmental mechanisms of the interwound developmental processes.

Many comparative studies have been conducted to this field [1]. However, most of them focus on one developmental process, such as cortical variations [7], alteration of white matters [8] or the abnormality of functional interactions [12]. Few studies explicitly interpret how these processes interact with each other and how the preterm infant brains are altered by such interactions, such as the coupling and the decoupling between structural wiring patterns and the functional activation patterns. The study on such interaction patterns and their difference between term and preterm groups could provide new clues to how preterm infants become susceptible to cognitive disorders [1].

To this end, we selected 59 subjects from dHCP datasets [13]. The MRI scans of all of them are obtained at the term-equivalent age (40 ± 0.50 wk) while 29 of them are preterm infants (35.35 ± 3.67 wk). We develop a novel algorithm to detect how the interactions between cortical features, structural and functional connective features are different between preterm and term groups. The interactions are modeled by multi-view canonical correlations between any two features projected to the canonical spaces [9, 10], while a locality preserving projection [11] constraint is added to ensure the subjects from two groups are distinct by projected features. Also, considering that features of a preterm infant with earlier birth age could be more different from term infants, we let the projected features in canonical space regress to their ages. By this way, the interactions between multiple features that separate preterm infants from the term ones have been quantified and encoded in the weights of canonical correlation analysis. We analyze the features highlighted by heavy weights, as well as the coupling or de-coupling patterns that contribute to the between-group discrimination. Our results are in line with previous reports and new findings on the coupling/de-coupling patterns among structural and functional features demonstrate the effectiveness of the method and provide new knowledge to the interwound developmental mechanisms of infant brains.

2   Materials and Methods

2.1   Dataset and Preprocessing

We select 59 infant brains, including structural MRI, diffusion MRI (dMRI) and resting state functional MRI (rsfMRI), from the Developing Human Connectome Project (dHCP) [13] to develop our algorithms. These selected individuals were scanning at the 40th week (40 ± 0.50 wk). Twenty-nine of them are preterm infants (35.35 ± 3.67 wk). The other are term infants. The parameters of T2-weighted structural MRI are as flows: TR = 12000 ms, TE = 156 ms, SENSE factor 2.11 (axial) and 2.60 (sagittal), image matrix = 290 × 290 × 203 and resolution = 0.5 × 0.5 × 0.5 mm^3. DMRI consisted of 3 shells of b = 400, 1000, and 2600 s/mm^2 interspersed with an approximately equal number of acquisitions on each shell within each run, matrix $= 128 \times 128 \times 64$, TR/TE $= 3800/90$ ms, resolution $= 1.17 \times 1.17 \times 1.5$ mm^3. The parameters of rsfMRI are as flows: TE $= 38$ ms, TR $= 392$ ms, 2300 volumes, resolution $= 2.15 \times 2.15 \times 2.15$ mm^3, matrix $= 67 \times 67 \times 45$.

Cortical surfaces have been reconstructed from T2-weighted MRI data and provided in dHCP dataset, following the steps of skull removal, tissue segmentation and surface reconstruction. More details for these steps are referred to [13]. On dMRI data, skull-strip and eddy currents *via* FSL [15] are applied, followed by deterministic fiber tracking (6×10^4 fibers in each subjects) *via* DSI Studio [14]. The pre-processing of rsfMRI data includes skull removal, motion correction, slice time correction, and spatial smoothing. These steps are implemented by FSL-FEAT [15].

T2 weighted MRI volumes are linearly registered to FA map of dMRI by using FSL-flirt [15]. Then, the surface is transposed to dMRI space by applying the transformation matrix to it. T2 weighted MRI volumes as well as the surface are registered to the rsfMRI data *via* the same way. The multimodal features are all present on the surface.

2.2 Definition of Cortical, Structural and Functional Features

The definitions in this section are illustrated in Fig. 1(a). A white matter surface is parcellated to the resolution of 500 patches of equal area on each hemisphere. The cortical patches are used as graphic nodes. We select the cortical thickness provided by dHCP dataset as the cortical feature for nodes, denoted by $\mathbf{z} \in R^{m \times 1}$ ($m = 500$). A structural connectivity matrix is constructed on these nodes by further defining the number of fiber tracts connecting two nodes as connective strength. Nodal degree of this

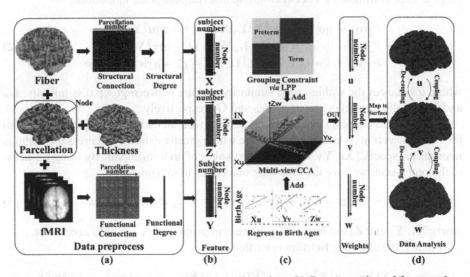

Fig. 1. Flow charts of this work. (a) Data preprocessing; (b) Reconstruction of features from cortex, structural and functional connections; (c) Multi-view CCA with the LPP constraint and the birth-age regression constraint; (d) the learnt weights are mapped back to surface as spatial patterns. Their relation to the between-group discrimination is analyzed.

matrix (by zeroing the element below a threshold t_s) is defined as the structural connective feature, denoted by $\mathbf{x} \in \mathbf{R}^{m \times 1}$. Similarly, we construct a functional connective matrix by defining the Pearson correlation coefficient between the mean rsfMRI signals from two nodes as the connective strength. Its nodal degree (a threshold of t_f) vector $\mathbf{y} \in \mathbf{R}^{m \times 1}$ is used to represent the functional connective patterns. Piling the features across all subjects give the feature matrices $(\mathbf{X}, \mathbf{Y}, \mathbf{Z} \in \mathbf{R}^{m \times n}, n = 59$, Fig. 1(b)) of the cohort.

2.3 Multi-view CCA with Locality Preserving Projection

Canonical correlation analysis (CCA) is to achieve the maximal correlation between $\mathbf{Xu}$ and $\mathbf{Yv}$ by linear transforming $\mathbf{X}$ and $\mathbf{Y}$. $\mathbf{u}$ and $\mathbf{v}$ are the weights, encoding the importance of each feature in the correlation. Because we aim at investigating such correlations among three features, including the structural and functional connective feature and cortical thickness, a multi-view CCA is adopted, which learns the bi-multivariate associations among more than three views of data $\{\mathbf{Xu}, \mathbf{Yv}, \mathbf{Zw}\}$. That is

$$\max_{\mathbf{u},\mathbf{v},\mathbf{w}} \mathbf{u}^T\mathbf{X}^T\mathbf{Yv} + \mathbf{u}^T\mathbf{X}^T\mathbf{Zw} + \mathbf{v}^T\mathbf{Y}^T\mathbf{Zw}$$
$$s.t.\, \mathbf{u}^T\mathbf{X}^T\mathbf{Xu} = 1, \mathbf{v}^T\mathbf{Y}^T\mathbf{Yv} = 1 \text{ and } \mathbf{w}^T\mathbf{Z}^T\mathbf{Zw} = 1 \tag{1}$$

Another aim is to distinguish term infants from preterm ones. To this end, the locality preserving projection (LPP) constraint in [16] is introduced. Specifically, we construct two graphs $\mathbf{G}_w$ and $\mathbf{G}_b$ (size of $n \times n, n = 59$) to quantify the relationship between subjects from the two groups. In $\mathbf{G}_w$, subjects within the same group are connected, while those from different groups are connected in In $\mathbf{G}_b$ (upper panel of Fig. 1(c)). Based on these graphs, three constraints for between-group discrimination are introduced:

$$P_1(\mathbf{u}) = \|\mathbf{u}\|_D = \alpha\mathbf{u}^T\mathbf{X}^T\mathbf{L}_w\mathbf{Xu} - (1 - \alpha)\mathbf{u}^T\mathbf{X}^T\mathbf{L}_b\mathbf{Xu}$$
$$P_2(\mathbf{v}) = \|\mathbf{v}\|_D = \alpha\mathbf{v}^T\mathbf{Y}^T\mathbf{L}_w\mathbf{Yu} - (1 - \alpha)\mathbf{v}^T\mathbf{Y}^T\mathbf{L}_b\mathbf{Yv} \tag{2}$$
$$P_3(\mathbf{w}) = \|\mathbf{w}\|_D = \alpha\mathbf{w}^T\mathbf{Z}^T\mathbf{L}_w\mathbf{Zw} - (1 - \alpha)\mathbf{w}^T\mathbf{Z}^T\mathbf{L}_b\mathbf{Zw}$$

where α balances the within-group similarity and the between-group dissimilarity. $\mathbf{L}_w$ and $\mathbf{L}_w$ are the Laplacian graphs of $\mathbf{G}_w$ and $\mathbf{G}_b$ respectively.

Under the assumption that a preterm subject with an earlier birth age variates from the term subjects at its term-equivalent age with a greater extent, we regress the features in projected spaces $\{\mathbf{Xu}, \mathbf{Yv}, \mathbf{Zw}\}$ to the birth ages of preterm infants. By using L2-norm to the regression, we have the following objectives to maximize:

$$R_1(\mathbf{u}) = \|\mathbf{X}_1\mathbf{u} - \mathbf{A}\|_2^2, R_2(\mathbf{v}) = \|\mathbf{Y}_1\mathbf{v} - \mathbf{A}\|_2^2, R_3(\mathbf{w}) = \|\mathbf{Z}_1\mathbf{w} - \mathbf{A}\|_2^2 \tag{3}$$

where $\mathbf{X}_1$, $\mathbf{Y}_1$ and $\mathbf{Z}_1$ are features from preterm group and $\mathbf{A}$ is a birth age vector.

Finally, the objective function is written as

$$\min_{\mathbf{u},\mathbf{v},\mathbf{w}} -\mathbf{u}^T\mathbf{X}^T\mathbf{Yv} - \mathbf{u}^T\mathbf{X}^T\mathbf{Zw} - \mathbf{v}\mathbf{Y}^T\mathbf{Zw} + \lambda_1\|\mathbf{Xu}\|_2^2 + \lambda_2\|\mathbf{Yv}\|_2^2 + \lambda_3\|\mathbf{Zw}\|_2^2$$
$$+ \sum_{i=1}^3 \beta_i P_i + \sum_{i=1}^3 \gamma_i R_i + \omega_1\|\mathbf{u}\|_1 + \omega_2\|\mathbf{v}\|_1 + \omega_3\|\mathbf{w}\|_1 \tag{4}$$
$$s.t.\, \mathbf{u}^T\mathbf{X}^T\mathbf{Xu} = 1, \mathbf{v}^T\mathbf{Y}^T\mathbf{Yv} = 1 \text{ and } \mathbf{w}^T\mathbf{Z}^T\mathbf{Zw} = 1$$

This objective is convex in $\mathbf{u}$ if we fix $\mathbf{v}$ and $\mathbf{w}$, and is the same for both $\mathbf{v}$ and $\mathbf{w}$. Thus, we can solve Eq. (4) by the alternating iteration algorithm [7]. By fixing $\mathbf{u}$, $\mathbf{v}$ and $\mathbf{w}$, alternatively, we solve three minimization problems as follows:

$$
\begin{aligned}
\min_{\mathbf{u}} &-\mathbf{u}^T\mathbf{X}^T\mathbf{Y}\mathbf{v} - \mathbf{u}^T\mathbf{X}^T\mathbf{Z}\mathbf{w} + \lambda_1\|\mathbf{X}\mathbf{u}\|_2^2 + \beta_1 P_1 + \gamma_1 R_1 + \omega_1\|\mathbf{u}\|_1 \\
\min_{\mathbf{v}} &-\mathbf{u}^T\mathbf{X}^T\mathbf{Y}\mathbf{v} - \mathbf{v}^T\mathbf{Y}^T\mathbf{Z}\mathbf{w} + \lambda_2\|\mathbf{Y}\mathbf{v}\|_2^2 + \beta_2 P_2 + \gamma_2 R_2 + \omega_2\|\mathbf{v}\|_1 \\
\min_{\mathbf{w}} &-\mathbf{u}^T\mathbf{X}^T\mathbf{Z}\mathbf{w} - \mathbf{v}^T\mathbf{Y}^T\mathbf{Z}\mathbf{w} + \lambda_3\|\mathbf{Z}\mathbf{w}\|_2^2 + \beta_3 P_3 + \gamma_3 R_3 + \omega_3\|\mathbf{w}\|_1
\end{aligned}
\tag{5}
$$

Algorithm 1 shows the procedure, where we use 10^{-6} as stop criteria.

Algorithm 1. Locality Preserving Projection Multi-view CCA

1: Given the normalize feature $\mathbf{X}$, $\mathbf{Y}$, $\mathbf{Z}$, parameter λ, β, γ, ω, group-relation matrices $\mathbf{G_w}$ and $\mathbf{G_b}$ and preterm age vector $\mathbf{A}$.

2: Calculate $\mathbf{L_w}$ and $\mathbf{L_b}$ that the Laplacian graphs of $\mathbf{G_w}$ and $\mathbf{G_b}$ respectively

3: Calculate gradient of LPP in Eq. (2)

4: Set t=1, Initialize $\mathbf{u}, \mathbf{v}, \mathbf{w} \in \Re^N$

5: **while** not converge $\|$ t<100 **do**

6:    Solve Eq. (5) alternately to obtain $\mathbf{u}$, $\mathbf{v}$ and $\mathbf{w}$;

7:    Scale $\mathbf{u} = \mathbf{u}./\sqrt{\mathbf{u}^T\mathbf{X}^T\mathbf{X}\mathbf{u}}$, $\mathbf{v} = \mathbf{v}./\sqrt{\mathbf{v}^T\mathbf{Y}^T\mathbf{Y}\mathbf{v}}$, $\mathbf{w} = \mathbf{w}./\sqrt{\mathbf{w}^T\mathbf{Z}^T\mathbf{Z}\mathbf{w}}$

8:    t=t+1;

9: **end while**

2.4 Determination of Parameters

To determine the parameters in Algorithm 1, we use five-fold cross-validation scheme where the results on the testing datasets satisfy three criteria: 1) the projected features yield the best classification results between preterm and term groups; 2) the projected features are strongly correlated with each other; 3) the preterm infants' birth ages are well fitted by the projected features. By using the subjects' labels (preterm or term) as the classification results, silhouette coefficient is used to features [$\mathbf{Xu}$ $\mathbf{Yv}$ $\mathbf{Zw}$] to measure their performance in separating the two groups. Because each subject has a silhouette coefficient, a mean silhouette coefficient s averaged over all individual coefficient and over all cross-validation tests is used to measure the overall classification performance. Pearson correlation is used to measure the similarity among $\{\mathbf{Xu}\,\mathbf{Yv}\,\mathbf{Zw}\}$ in 2) and between $\mathbf{Xu}/\mathbf{Yv}/\mathbf{Zw}$ and birth age in 3). The correlation coefficients are averaged over all cross-validation tests.

2.5 Brain Atlases Used to Validate and Interpret the Results

Weights in $\{\mathbf{u}\,\mathbf{v}\,\mathbf{w}\}$ are mapped back to a randomly selected surface (as the template surface) to show their spatial distributions (Fig. 1(d)). To interpret the results, we use the atlas derived from the fetal cortical developmental datasets [7, 17–19] and the templates of nine intrinsic networks derived from rsfMRI [20] as references (Fig. 2(d)). The label tags on these atlases are warped to our surfaces *via* linear registration [15]. A bipolar cortical organization system of the cortex is established based on the cortical developmental atlas [21], where trans-modal regions in default mode networks, including medial temporal lobe, the medial prefrontal cortex, the posterior cingulate cortex, the ventral precuneus and parts of the parietal cortex, (red dots Fig. 2(d)) are defined as one pole and early sensory regions (or unimodal), such as central sulcus and calcarine sulcus (white dots), are the other pole, leaving the rest as multimodal regions. By setting the sensorimotor regions as 0 and trans-modal regions as 1, the distance between them is computed to yield the gradient map in Fig. 2(d).

3 Results

3.1 Parameter Settings

By using the criteria in Sect. 2.4, the parameters are determined as $t_f = 0.3$, $t_s = 6.8$, $\lambda = 0.88$, $\alpha = 0.7$, $\beta = 0.8$, $\gamma = 0.68$. In contrast to other parameter combinations, they yield a better classification performance ($s = 0.85$), higher similarity among the projected features ($R_{(Xu,Yv)} = 0.91$, $R_{(Xu,Zw)} = 0.86$, $R_{(Zw,Yv)} = 0.93$) and a better regression to preterm birth ages ($R_{(Xu,A)} = 0.45$, $R_{(Xu,A)} = 0.49$, $R_{(Xu,A)} = 0.48$), as illustrated in Fig. 2(a).

3.2 Interpretation of the Results

Figure 2(b) shows the spatial distribution patterns of regions with nonnegative values in **u**, **v** and **w**. It is noteworthy that **u**, **v** and **w** jointly impose their impact to distinguish preterm and term groups. Therefore, they only reflect one profile of the interwound interactions. Figure 2(c) shows their interactions patterns by detecting the simultaneously positive/negative weights in pairs in {**u**, **v**, **w**} and defined them as the coupling patterns while the inconsistent (one positive and one negative) weights in pairs as decoupling.

It is reported that the preterm infants' brains generate more local white matter connections than term ones, resulting a higher clustering coefficient (CC) in peripheral cortex [6]. In our analysis, we identified the cortical regions where CC on preterm brains significantly greater than the one on term brains. We find that this spatial pattern resembles the spatial pattern of the structural (**u**) map (dice coefficient of 0.35) in Fig. 2(b), demonstrating the effectiveness of the work. On average, the structural connective degrees of the contributive regions (red) in **u** map are significantly greater that other regions (blue) on both preterm group (37.65 ± 5.58 vs. 19.82 ± 2.66, $p < 0.05$) and term group (41.90 ± 6.07 vs. 19.47 ± 2.63, $p < 0.05$). The preterm group has higher degrees in red region than term group while the degrees of blue regions are similar (19.82 ± 2.66 vs. 19.47 ± 2.63, $p>0.05$). Functional connective degrees on **v** map (preterm group: 156.08 vs. 90.04; term group: 226.36 vs. 133.26) and cortical thickness profiles on **w** map (preterm group: 0.93 ± 0.05 vs. 0.92 ± 0.05; term group: 0.89 ± 0.05 vs. 0.89 ± 0.04) are less distinctive between preterm and term groups in this sense. These results demonstrate that all features of preterm have been altered, but the decrease of structural degrees is limited within high degree regions but the decrease in functional networks and increase in cortical thickness are global. This suggests the dis-coupling between them is found in preterm especially in regions of lower degrees. Finally, the spatial distributions of **u**, **v**, **w** maps are either positively or negatively correlated with the bipolar gradient map (Fig. 2(d), Pearson correlation coefficients are 0.51, −0.41 and −0.27), demonstrating that brain structure is more distinctive between preterm and term brains in higher-order cortex while function and thickness are more distinctive in primary cortex.

We also analyze the coupling and de-coupling patterns in Fig. 2(c). By overlapping them with intrinsic network atlases (Table 1, light shade) quantified by dice coefficients, we find that most coupling and de-coupling patterns are found within visual cortex

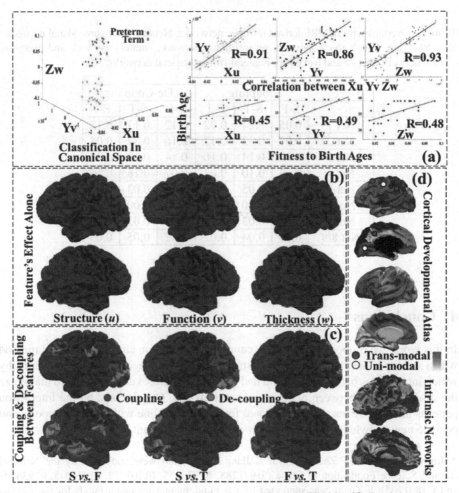

Fig. 2. (a) The selected parameters satisfy the three criteria. (b) The identified weights for structural/functional connective degrees and cortical thickness that work together to distinguish preterm infants from term ones. (c) Coupling and De-coupling patterns between features; (d) Fetal brain developmental atlas, unimodal-transmodal bipolar system and intrinsic networks are used as references. S for structure, F for function and T for cortical thickness. (Color figure online)

(#1–#3), in line with the aforementioned disparity between the alternation of structural profiles and functional/cortical profiles in regions of lower degrees. It is also interesting to see the coupling/de-coupling patterns between structure and function on frontal/parietal networks (#8 and #9, dark shade), in line with reports in [6]. These short connections develop later than the core network, and are abnormally more in preterm brains than term brains due to their altered connections to deep gray matters [1, 6]. Function-cortex and structure-cortex decoupling with relatively higher overlap ratio is found in default mode network (#4, dark shade). All these decoupling patterns found in higher-level networks (#4, #8 and #9) are in line with, and could partially explain, that preterm infants are more susceptible to malfunctions in cognitions in their adolescence and adulthood [1, 6].

Table 1. Overlaps with rsfMRI derived intrinsic networks. Nets #1–3 are three visual networks. Nets #4–7 are default mode network, sensorimotor network, auditory network and executive control network. Net #8 and Net #9 are bilateral frontal/parietal networks.

	Coupling			De-Coupling		
	S-F	S-T	F-T	S-F	S-T	F-T
Net 1	0.05	0.24	0.02	0.12	0.17	0.13
Net 2	0.07	0.33	0.17	0.16	0.32	0.04
Net 3	0.07	0.14	0.10	0.14	0.19	0.07
Net 4	0.03	0.10	0.03	0.07	0.16	0.10
Net 5	0.07	0.05	0.02	0.06	0.03	0.03
Net 6	0.03	0.00	0.00	0.11	0.00	0.00
Net 7	0.05	0.03	0.03	0.05	0.03	0.04
Net 8/9	0.10	0.04	0.02	0.12	0.05	0.03

4 Conclusions

In this work, we propose a multi-view canonical correlation analysis (MCCA) method with a locality preserving projection constraint (LPP) and an age regression constraint, by which interactions between structural and functional features are identified to maximize the discrimination between preterm and term groups. Our findings on the interaction patterns among structural and functional features are in line with previous reports and provide new knowledge to the development patterns of infant brains.

Acknowledgements. T Zhang, L Du, X Jiang and L Guo were supported by the National Natural Science Foundation of China (31971288, 61973255, 61703073, 61976045, 61936007 and U1801265); S Zhang was supported by the Fundamental Research Funds for the Central Universities (D5000200555) and High-level researcher start-up projects (06100-20GH020161).

References

1. Batalle, D., Edwards, A.D., O'Muircheartaigh, J.: Annual research review: not just a small adult brain: understanding later neurodevelopment through imaging the neonatal brain. J. Child Psychol. Psychiatry **59**(4), 350–371 (2018)
2. Kjær, M., Fabricius, K., Sigaard, R.K., Pakkenberg, B.: Neocortical development in brain of young children– a stereological study. Cereb. Cortex **27**, 5477–5484 (2017)
3. Ball, G., et al.: Machine-learning to characterize neonatal functional connectivity in the preterm brain. NeuroImage **124**, 267–275 (2016)
4. Kostovic, I., Jovanov-Milosevic, N.: The development of cerebral connections during the first 20–45 weeks' gestation. Semin. Fetal Neonatal Med. **11**, 415–422 (2006)
5. Marlow, N., Wolke, D., Bracewell, M.A., Samara, M.: Neurologic and developmental disability at six years of age after extremely preterm birth. New Engl. J. Med. **352**, 9–19 (2005)
6. Ball, G., et al.: Rich-club organization of the newborn human brain. Proc. Natl. Acad. Sci. **111**(20), 7456–7461 (2014)
7. Wang, F., et al.: Developmental topography of cortical thickness during infancy. Proc. Natl. Acad. Sci. **116**(32), 15855–15860 (2019)
8. Johnson, S., Marlow, N.: Growing up after extremely preterm birth: lifespan mental health outcomes. Semin. Fetal Neonatal Med. **19**, 97–104 (2014)
9. Witten, D.M., Tibshirani, R., Hastie, T.: A penalized matrix decomposition, with applications to sparse principal components and canonical correlation analysis. Biostatistics **10**(3), 515–534 (2009)
10. Du, L.: Detecting genetic associations with brain imaging phenotypes in Alzheimer's disease via a novel structured SCCA approach. Med. Image Anal. **61**, 101656 (2020)
11. Yan, J., Risacher, S.L., Nho, K., Saykin, A. J., Shen, L.: Identification of discriminative imaging proteomics associations in Alzheimer's disease via a novel sparse correlation model. In: Pacific Symposium on Biocomputing 2017, pp. 94–104 (2017)
12. Smyser, C.D., et al.: Longitudinal analysis of neural network development in preterm infants. Cereb. Cortex **20**, 2852–2862 (2010)
13. Makropoulos, A., et al.: The developing human connectome project: a minimal processing pipeline for neonatal cortical surface reconstruction. Neuroimage **173**, 88–112 (2018)
14. http://dsi-studio.labsolver.org/
15. Jenkinson, M., Beckmann, C.F., Behrens, T.E., Woolrich, M.W., Smith, S.M.: Fsl. Neuroimage **62**(2), 782–790 (2012)
16. Lu, K., Ding, Z., Ge, S.: Sparse-representation-based graph embedding for traffic sign recognition. IEEE Trans. Intell. Transp. Syst. **13**(4), 1515–1524 (2012)
17. Li, G., Wang, L., Shi, F., Gilmore, J.H., Lin, W., Shen, D.: Construction of 4D high-definition cortical surface atlases of infants: methods and applications. Med. Image Anal. **25**(1), 22–36 (2015)
18. Wu, Z., Li, G., Meng, Y., Wang, L., Lin, W., Shen, D.: 4D infant cortical surface atlas construction using spherical patch-based sparse representation. In: International Conference on Medical Image Computing and Computer-Assisted Intervention, pp. 57–65. Springer, Cham, September 2017
19. Wu, Z., Wang, L., Lin, W., Gilmore, J.H., Li, G., Shen, D.: Construction of 4D infant cortical surface atlases with sharp folding patterns via spherical patch-based group-wise sparse representation. Hum. Brain Mapp. **40**(13), 3860–3880 (2019)
20. Smith, S.M., et al.: Correspondence of the brain's functional architecture during activation and rest. Proc. Natl. Acad. Sci. **106**(31), 13040–13045 (2009)
21. Huntenburg, J.M., Bazin, P.L., Margulies, D.S.: Large-scale gradients in human cortical organization. Trends Cogn. Sci. **22**(1), 21–31 (2018)

Graph Convolutional Network Based Point Cloud for Head and Neck Vessel Labeling

Linlin Yao[1,2], Pengbo Jiang[1], Zhong Xue[1], Yiqiang Zhan[1], Dijia Wu[1], Lichi Zhang[2], Qian Wang[2(✉)], Feng Shi[1(✉)], and Dinggang Shen[1]

[1] Shanghai United Imaging Intelligence Co., Ltd., Shanghai, China
feng.shi@united-imaging.com, Dinggang.Shen@gmail.com
[2] Institute for Medical Imaging Technology, School of Biomedical Engineering,
Shanghai Jiao Tong University, Shanghai, China
wang.qian@sjtu.edu.cn

Abstract. Vessel segmentation and anatomical labeling are of great significance for vascular disease analysis. Because vessels in 3D images are the tree-like tubular structures with diverse shapes and sizes, and direct use of convolutional neural networks (CNNs, based on spatial convolutional kernels) for vessel segmentation often encounters great challenges. To tackle this problem, we propose a graph convolutional network (GCN)-based point cloud approach to improve vessel segmentation over the conventional CNN-based method and further conduct semantic labeling on 13 major head and neck vessels. The proposed method can *not only* learn the global shape representation *but also* precisely adapt to local vascular shapes by utilizing the prior knowledge of tubular structures to explicitly learn anatomical shape. Specifically, starting from rough segmentation using V-Net, our approach further refines the segmentation and performs labeling on the refined segmentations, with two steps. First, a point cloud network is applied to the points formed by initial vessel voxels to refine vessel segmentation. Then, GCN is employed on the point cloud to further label vessels into 13 major segments. To evaluate the performance of our proposed method, CT angiography images (covering heads and necks) of 72 subjects are used in our experiment. Using four-fold cross-validation, an average Dice coefficient of 0.965 can be achieved for vessel segmentation compared to that of 0.885 obtained by the conventional V-Net based segmentation. Also, for vessel labeling, our proposed algorithm achieves an average Dice coefficient of 0.899 for 13 vessel segments compared to that of 0.829 by V-Net. These results show that our proposed method could facilitate head and neck vessel analysis by providing automatic and accurate vessel segmentation and labeling results.

Keywords: Head and neck vessels · Anatomical labeling · Point cloud · Graph convolutional network · Shape representation

© Springer Nature Switzerland AG 2020
M. Liu et al. (Eds.): MLMI 2020, LNCS 12436, pp. 474–483, 2020.
https://doi.org/10.1007/978-3-030-59861-7_48

1   Introduction

Vascular disease has been one of the top and severe diseases with high mortality, morbidity and medical risk [1]. Blood vessel binary segmentation and anatomical labeling are of high interest in medical image analysis, since vessel quantification is crucial for diagnosis, treatment planning, prognosis and clinical outcome evaluation. In clinical practice, users have to manually edit or correct tracking error by defining the starting and ending points of each vessel segment, which is a time-consuming effort. It is therefore desirable to automatically and accurately segment and label vessels to facilitate vessel quantification. Computed tomography angiography (CTA) is the commonly used modality for studying vascular diseases. As shown in Fig. 1, head and neck vessels have long and tortuous tubular-like vascular structures with diverse shapes and sizes, and span across the entire image volume. Particularly, vessels inside the head are much thinner than those going through the neck. Therefore, it is challenging to handle vessels with varied shapes and size.

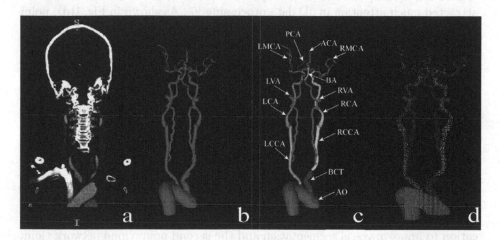

Fig. 1. An example of head and neck CTA image, along with major vessels. (a) A coronal slice of CTA; (b) A 3D vessel mask consisting of all major head and neck vessels; (c) 13 annotated segments: AO, BCT, L/R CCA, L/R ICA, L/R VA, and BA in the neck and L/R MCA, ACA and PCA in the head; (d) Point cloud representation of the head and neck vessels.

In the literature, traditional techniques have been developed for head and neck vessels segmentation [1,2] from CTA images, as well as for cerebral vasculature segmentation and labeling [3,4] from MRA images. Convolutional neural networks (CNNs) have also been developed for this purpose [5]. However, despite of these efforts, CNN-based segmentation still encounters great challenges in handling complicated structures. Particularly, although, because of the nature of spatial convolution, CNN-based techniques outperform many traditional algorithms for blob or larger region segmentation, the complicated shapes

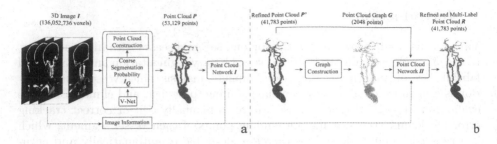

Fig. 2. Overview of the proposed method.

such as vessels and surfaces have to be considered specifically by re-designing the networks or the loss functions. Thus, head and neck vessel segmentation and labeling from CTA images remain an open field to be explored.

Possible vital techniques to tackle this problem is to effectively consider spatial relationship among vascular points. Recently, point cloud learning has attracted much attention in 3D data processing [6]. As shown in Fig. 1(d), point cloud representation of head and neck vessels allows for quantification of spatial relationship among points in vascular structures, as well as effective extraction of vessel by leveraging their spatial information in the entire volume. Previous point cloud methods [7–9] have shown impressive performance in 3D classification and segmentation. Balsiger *et al.* [10] reported the improved volumetric segmentation of peripheral nerves from magnetic resonance neurography (MRN) images by point cloud learning. However, compared to peripheral nerves, head and neck vessels have more complicated structures. On the other hand, graph convolutional network (GCN) has already been used in vessel segmentation in the literature [11–14], for learning tree-like graph structures in the images.

In this paper, we propose a GCN-based point cloud learning framework to improve CNN-based vessel segmentation and further perform vessel labeling. Specially, the first point cloud network, named as I, is used for two-class classification to improve vessel segmentation and the second point cloud network (joint with GCN), names as II, is employed for thirteen-class classification to label vessel segments. The proposed method incorporates 1) the advantage of GCN to utilize the prior knowledge of tree-like tubular structures of vessels and 2) the advantage of point cloud-based networks to handle the whole image volume, and learns anatomical shapes to obtain accurate vessel segmentation and labeling. The performance of our proposed method is evaluated on 72 subjects, by using the overlapping ratio as a metric to evaluate binary segmentation and labeling of vessels.

2 Method

Figure 2 shows the overall workflow of the proposed method, with two stages:

1) Vessel segmentation with point cloud refinement. In particular, a V-Net [16] model is first applied for coarse vessel segmentation, from which the point

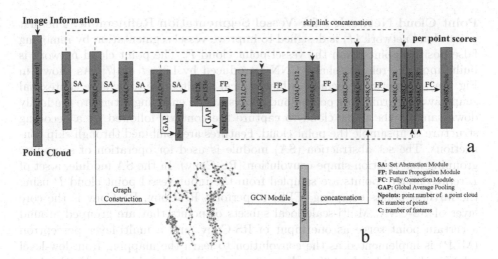

Fig. 3. The proposed GCN-based point cloud network (the point cloud network II). (a) The point cloud network I utilized to improve binary segmentation of vessels, and (b) GCN branch.

cloud is constructed. Then, the first point cloud network I is applied to refining the coarse segmentation.

2) Anatomical labeling with GCN-based point cloud network. A GCN-based point cloud network II is constructed to further label the vessels into 13 major segments. The detailed architecture of the GCN-based point cloud network is shown in Fig. 3.

2.1 Vessel Segmentation Refinement with Point Cloud Network

Coarse Vessel Segmentation. A V-Net is trained to delineate the coarse head and neck vessels as initialization of our proposed method. In particular, we dilate the ground-truth mask (labeled by radiologists) to expand the vessel segmentation area for ensuring inclusion of all vessel voxels (even with high false positive segmentations). Using the dilated masks to train the V-Net network, vessel segmentation can be performed, for generating a probability map I_Q for each image.

Point Cloud Construction. A vessel point cloud P as shown in Fig. 2(a) can be constructed from the aforementioned probability map I_Q by setting a threshold θ. Note that the amount of points depends on the output of V-Net and also the size of the object to be segmented. We denote the point cloud P as $P = [p_1, p_2, ..., p_N]$ with N points $p_i \in R^3$. Each voxel $v \in I_Q$ with its probability $q \in [0, 1]$ larger than θ is set as a point $p_i = (x, y, z)$, which are the Cartesian coordinates of v.

Point Cloud Network I for Vessel Segmentation Refinement. The first point cloud network (I) is designed to improve vessel segmentation by removing false positive points from the vessel point cloud P. The point cloud network is built upon the relation-shape CNN introduced by Liu *et al.* [7]. As shown in Fig. 3(a), the network includes a hierarchical architecture to achieve contextual shape-aware learning for point cloud analysis. The encoding structure gradually down-samples the point cloud to capture the context, followed by a decoding structure to upsample the point cloud. Features are combined through skip connections. The set abstraction (SA) module is used for operation of sampling, grouping and relation shape convolution (RS-Conv). In the SA module, a set of L representative points are sampled from the input vessel point cloud P using the farthest points sampling (FPS) to perform RS-Conv. RS-Conv is the core layer of RS-CNN. Multi-scale local subsets of points that are grouped around a certain point serve as one input of RS-Conv, and a multi-layer perceptron (MLP) is implemented as the convolution to learn the mapping from low-level relations to high-level relations between points in the local subset. Further, the feature propagation (FP) module propagates features from subsampled points to the original points for set segmentation. Then, two fully-connected (FC) layers decrease the features of each point to the number of classes. Finally, a softmax function gives the class probabilities of each point. Image information, contained in the original images and the probability map I_Q, are fed into the first SA operator with the point Cartesian coordinates. Image information of each point is extracted from a nearby volume of interest $I_p \in R^{X \times Y \times Z}$ using a sequence of two 3D convolutions, and then transformed into a vector of input point cloud size to be fed into the network. The trained point cloud network I is applied on the point cloud P, and a refined point cloud P' shown in Fig. 2(b) can be obtained and converted into 3D volumetric image as the refined binary segmentation of vessels.

2.2 Vessel Labeling with GCN-based Point Cloud Network

Point Cloud Construction. Vessel labeling is carried out on the refined vessel point cloud P' acquired from the first stage. For training labeling model, the point cloud representation $O = [o_1, o_2, ..., o_M]$ with M points $o_i \in R^3$, namely the refined vessel point cloud, can be established from the ground-truth anatomical mask M_{al} annotated by radiologists. Labels of points are represented using numbers $l_1, l_2, ..., l_{13}$. Anatomical point cloud O with labels and constructed graphs are employed to train the point cloud network II for vessel labeling.

Graph Construction. Point cloud graph G as shown in Fig. 2(b) is built from the L representative points, namely the vertices, sampled from the point cloud P' using aforementioned FPS. Edges of graph are set as the Euclidean distance after normalization of coordinates of points. According to the varying diameters of vessels, a threshold of d is set to determine whether two vertices are connected. Therefore, vertices and edges are acquired. The output features of the first SA operator shown in Fig. 3(b) are utilized as the input features of vertices.

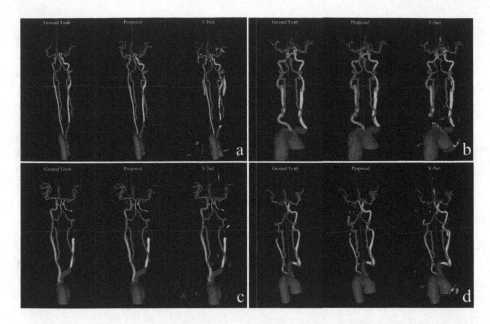

Fig. 4. Qualitative results. Each panel (a, b, c, d) shows the ground-truth vessel segment, the vessel labeling results by our proposed method, and the corresponding segmentation results by V-Net.

GCN-based Point Cloud Network *II* for Labeling. The architecture of the point cloud network *III* used in Fig. 2(b) is shown in Fig. 3, which is built upon the point cloud network *I*. The training process of the second stage is similar to the first stage, apart from three aspects. First, the input is the point cloud *O* and the output is 13 classes (representing 13 labels). Second, image information of only the original image is used to enrich each point's representation. Third, graph branch is constructed to extract structural and spatial features of vessels. The constructed graph is trained using the two-layer GCN [15]. The output is concatenated to the input of the last FP operation as additional features to help labeling. Finally, these features are employed to improve the classification of every point. The anatomical point cloud *R* shown in Fig. 2(b) can be obtained and transformed to 3D image as the final labeling result of vessels.

3 Experiments and Results

3.1 Materials and Parameters Setting

In our experiment, CT angiography images (covering heads and necks) of 72 subjects are used to evaluate our proposed method. The size of the CTA image is $512 \times 512 \times 533$ and the voxel spacing is $0.4063 \times 0.4063 \times 0.7000 \, \text{mm}^3$. The head and neck vessels have been manually annotated by a radiologist and reviewed by a senior radiologist. Four-fold cross-validation is used in the experiment. An ellipse kernel size k is set as 5 for the dilation of ground-truth segmentation. Threshold θ is set to 0.1 to construct the point cloud P from the V-Net-based probability map. L is set to 2048, which stands for the number of the representative points to perform RS-Conv and also the vertex number of the graph. The size of a volume of interest I_p is set to $X = 5, Y = 5, Z = 5$ in both the point cloud networks I and II. In the point cloud network I, we train the network for 85 epochs using Adam optimizer with a learning rate of 0.001 and cross-entropy loss. Notice that, during the testing, we also randomly extract subsets of 2048 points until all the points of a point cloud have been classified. The labels of vessel segments $l_1, l_2, ..., l_{13}$ are set to $1, 2, ..., 13$ in experiment, corresponding to the vessel segment labels. The threshold d used for edge connection is set to 0.05 after normalization of coordinates of points.

3.2   Results

To make fair comparison between vessel labeling results, both the proposed method and the V-Net use the same data set and the four-fold validation setting. Qualitative and quantitative evaluations are performed.

Qualitative Results. The qualitative results for vessel labeling of four patients are demonstrated in Fig. 4. For each patient, annotations on the images from left to right stand for the ground-truth vessel labeling, and the vessel labeling results by our proposed method and the V-Net, respectively. Specially, the V-Net used to train the labeling model takes the 3D original image as input, the ground-truth vessel labeling as supervision information, and Dice ratio as loss. As shown in Fig. 4(a) and Fig. 4(b), the complete head and neck vessel structures can be segmented and labeled accurately using our proposed method. As illustrated in Fig. 4(c) and Fig. 4(d), the multi-label segmentation results are obtained without RCA and LCA. Compared to the ground truth, the corresponding labels are missing too. This shows that our proposed method has good performance on both healthy cases and diseased cases. Compared to the labeling results with direct use of the V-Net, our proposed method has better performance on both binary segmentation and labeling. As shown in Fig. 4, for head vessels with small diameter, our proposed method can achieve better performance on their segmentations.

Quantitative Results. For vessel binary segmentation, the first point cloud network I is used to improve over the V-Net based segmentation. Points in the point cloud P can be classified into the vessel points belonging to the target and the outliers not belonging to the target. Average accuracy (ACC) and intersection over union (IOU) are used to evaluate the performance of the first point cloud network I. The average ACC in the four-fold cross-validation is 0.972 and 0.986 for the outlier and the vessel points, respectively, and IOU is 0.964 and 0.976, respectively. The Dice coefficient is used to evaluate the binary segmentation of vessels. The refined point cloud P' can be transformed into volumetric

Table 1. Quantitative evaluation of multi-label segmentation; here, the *Proposed w/o* represents the proposed point cloud network without GCN.

Label				Dice		
Index	Abbreviation	ACC	IOU	V-Net [16]	Proposed w/o	Proposed
1	AO	0.989	0.983	0.961	0.972	0.986
2	BCT	0.903	0.880	0.852	0.865	0.883
3	RCCA	0.937	0.913	0.912	0.915	0.928
4	LCCA	0.937	0.874	0.917	0.924	0.942
5	RCA	0.950	0.920	0.861	0.887	0.902
6	LCA	0.949	0.953	0.789	0.873	0.925
7	LVA	0.968	0.951	0.902	0.913	0.937
8	RVA	0.959	0.890	0.903	0.928	0.941
9	BA	0.792	0.781	0.782	0.798	0.813
Average-neck	–	0.932	0.905	0.875	0.897	0.917
10	PCA	0.993	0.854	0.706	0.783	0.832
11	ACA	0.944	0.903	0.785	0.851	0.885
12	RMCA	0.988	0.971	0.719	0.822	0.846
13	LMCA	0.973	0.933	0.684	0.819	0.872
Average-head	–	0.975	0.915	0.724	0.819	0.859
Average	-	0.945	0.910	0.829	0.873	0.899

images as the binary segmentation of result of vessels. The average Dice coefficient is 0.965 for the refined binary segmentation result of vessels, which is improved by 0.08 compared to the result of 0.885 by the V-Net. This shows large improvement of binary segmentation of vessels by the first point cloud network I, which contributes significantly to the vessel labeling.

Vessel labeling is carried out on the binary segmentation results. The quantitative results of vessel labeling are presented in Table 1. The $1st$ column is the label index and its corresponding abbreviations of vessel segments. The $2nd$ column consists of average accuracy (ACC) and intersection over union (IOU) used to evaluate the performance of the second point cloud network II. The $3rd$ column shows the Dice coefficient used to evaluate vessel labeling. Three methods, i.e., 1) V-Net, 2) the proposed point cloud method without GCN, and 3) the proposed method, are evaluated. Compared to the V-Net and our proposed method without GCN, the performance of our proposed method is increased by 0.07 and 0.026, respectively, for the average Dice coefficient of all vessel segments. Taking various diameters of different segments into account, two groups of head and neck are separated. Compared to the V-Net, the average Dice coefficient of the proposed method is increased by 0.042 for neck vessels, while 0.135 for head vessels. This shows that our proposed method has better performance both on neck vessels and head vessels with small diameter, and also our proposed method is robust.

4   Conclusion

In this paper, we have proposed a GCN-based point cloud framework for labeling of head and neck vessels from CTA images. Specifically, we formulated vessel segmentation problem into a point-wise classification problem, for improving over the CNN-based binary segmentation results. Then, the GCN-based point cloud learning can further leverage the vascular structures and anatomical shapes to improve vessel labeling. Experiment results indicate that our proposed method is effective in improving volumetric image segmentation and learning complex structures for anatomical labeling. Future work will focus on the construction of graph as well as more efficient point-based sparse learning for volumetric image segmentation.

References

1. Hedblom, A.: Blood vessel segmentation for neck and head computed tomography angiography (2013)
2. Cuisenaire, O., Virmani, S., Olszewski, M.E., Ardon, R.: Fully automated segmentation of carotid and vertebral arteries from contrast-enhanced CTA. In: Medical Imaging 2008: Image Processing, vol. 6914, p. 69143R. International Society for Optics and Photonics (2008)
3. Bogunovic, H., Pozo, J.M., Cardenes, R., San Roman, L., Frangi, A.F.: Anatomical labeling of the circle of willis using maximum a posteriori probability estimation. IEEE Trans. Medi. Imaging 32(9), 1587–1599 (2013)
4. Robben, D., et al.: Simultaneous segmentation and anatomical labeling of the cerebral vasculature. Med. Image Anal. 32, 201–215 (2016)
5. Moccia, S., De Momi, E., El Hadji, S., Mattos, L.S.: Blood vessel segmentation algorithms-review of methods, datasets and evaluation metrics. Comput. Methods Programs Biomed. 158, 71–91 (2018)
6. Liu, W., Sun, J., Li, W., Hu, T., Wang, P.: Deep learning on point clouds and its application: a survey. Sensors 19(19), 4188 (2019)
7. Liu, Y., Fan, B., Xiang, S., Pan, C.: Relation-shape convolutional neural network for point cloud analysis. In: Proceedings of the IEEE Conference on Computer Vision and Pattern Recognition, pp. 8895–8904 (2019)
8. Liu, Z., Tang, H., Lin, Y., Han, S.: Point-voxel CNN for efficient 3D deep learning. In: Advances in Neural Information Processing Systems, pp. 963–973 (2019)
9. Qi, C.R., Su, H., Mo, K., Guibas, L.J.: Pointnet: deep learning on point sets for 3D classification and segmentation. In: Proceedings of the IEEE Conference on Computer Vision and Pattern Recognition, pp. 652–660 (2017)
10. Balsiger, F., Soom, Y., Scheidegger, O., Reyes, M.: Learning shape representation on sparse point clouds for volumetric image segmentation. In: Shen, D., et al. (eds.) MICCAI 2019. LNCS, vol. 11765, pp. 273–281. Springer, Cham (2019). https://doi.org/10.1007/978-3-030-32245-8_31
11. Garcia-Uceda Juarez, A., Selvan, R., Saghir, Z., de Bruijne, M.: A joint 3D UNet-graph neural network-based method for airway segmentation from chest CTs. In: Suk, H.-I., Liu, M., Yan, P., Lian, C. (eds.) MLMI 2019. LNCS, vol. 11861, pp. 583–591. Springer, Cham (2019). https://doi.org/10.1007/978-3-030-32692-0_67
12. Shin, S.Y., Lee, S., Yun, I.D., Lee, K.M.: Deep vessel segmentation by learning graphical connectivity. Med. Image Anal. 58, 101556 (2019)

13. Wolterink, J.M., Leiner, T., Išgum, I.: Graph convolutional networks for coronary artery segmentation in cardiac CT angiography. In: Zhang, D., Zhou, L., Jie, B., Liu, M. (eds.) GLMI 2019. LNCS, vol. 11849, pp. 62–69. Springer, Cham (2019). https://doi.org/10.1007/978-3-030-35817-4_8

14. Zhai, Z., et al.: Linking convolutional neural networks with graph convolutional networks: application in pulmonary artery-vein separation. In: Zhang, D., Zhou, L., Jie, B., Liu, M. (eds.) GLMI 2019. LNCS, vol. 11849, pp. 36–43. Springer, Cham (2019). https://doi.org/10.1007/978-3-030-35817-4_5

15. Kipf, T.N., Welling, M.: Semi-supervised classification with graph convolutional networks. arXiv preprint arXiv:1609.02907 (2016)

16. Milletari, F., Navab, N., Ahmadi, S.A.: V-net: fully convolutional neural networks for volumetric medical image segmentation. In: 2016 Fourth International Conference on 3D Vision (3DV), pp. 565–571. IEEE (2016)

Unsupervised Learning-Based Nonrigid Registration of High Resolution Histology Images

Marek Wodzinski[1]([✉])[ID] and Henning Müller[2][ID]

[1] Department of Measurement and Electronics,
AGH University of Science and Technology, Krakow, Poland
wodzinski@agh.edu.pl
[2] Information Systems Institute,
University of Applied Sciences Western Switzerland (HES-SO Valais),
Sierre, Switzerland
henning.mueller@hevs.ch

Abstract. The use of different dyes during histological sample preparation reveals distinct tissue properties and may improve the diagnosis. Nonetheless, the staining process deforms the tissue slides and registration is necessary before further processing. The importance of this problem led to organizing an open challenge named Automatic Non-rigid Histological Image Registration Challenge (ANHIR), organized jointly with the IEEE ISBI 2019 conference. The challenge organizers provided 481 image pairs and a server-side evaluation platform making it possible to reliably compare the proposed algorithms. The majority of the methods proposed for the challenge were based on the classical, iterative image registration, resulting in high computational load and arguable usefulness in clinical practice due to the long analysis time. In this work, we propose a deep learning-based unsupervised nonrigid registration method, that provides results comparable to the solutions of the best scoring teams, while being significantly faster during the inference. We propose a multilevel, patch-based training and inference scheme that makes it possible to register images of almost any size, up to the highest resolution provided by the challenge organizers. The median target registration error is close to 0.2% of the image diagonal while the average registration time, including the data loading and initial alignment, is below 3 s. We freely release both the training and inference code making the results fully reproducible.

Keywords: Image registration · Deep learning · Histology · ANHIR

1 Introduction

Registration of histology images acquired using different stains is a difficult and important task that makes it possible to fuse information and improve further

© Springer Nature Switzerland AG 2020
M. Liu et al. (Eds.): MLMI 2020, LNCS 12436, pp. 484–493, 2020.
https://doi.org/10.1007/978-3-030-59861-7_49

processing and diagnosis. The problem is challenging due to: (i) a very high resolution of the images, (ii) complex, large deformations, (iii) difference in the appearance and partially missing data. A dedicated challenge named Automatic Non-rigid Histological Image Registration Challenge (ANHIR) [1–3] was organized in conjunction with the IEEE ISBI 2019 conference to address the problem and compare algorithms developed by different researchers. The challenge organizers provided a high quality and open dataset [1,4–7], manually annotated by experts and reasonably divided into training and evaluation sets. Moreover, an independent, server-side evaluation platform was developed that made it possible to reliably compare the participant's solutions [3].

The challenge participants proposed several different algorithms, mostly using the classical, iterative approach to the image registration [2]. The three best scoring methods were quite similar. The winner team (MEVIS) [8] proposed a method consisting of brute-force initial alignment followed by affine and B-Splines-based nonrigid registration. The researchers used the normalized gradient field (NGF) similarity metric [9] and strongly optimized code resulting in undoubtedly the best and clinically applicable method. The team with the second-best score (UPENN) [10] proposed an algorithm consisting of background removal by stain deconvolution, random initial alignment, affine registration and diffeomorphic, nonrigid registration based on the Greedy tool [11,12]. The third best team (AGH) [13] developed a method similar to the winners with the differences that instead of the NGF they used the modality independent neighborhood descriptor (MIND) [14], and used the Demons algorithm to directly optimize the dense deformation field replacing the B-Spline deformation model, as in [8]. Interestingly, only a single team proposed a method based on deep learning [15]. However, the team first re-sampled the images to a relatively low resolution and second, they fine-tuned the deep network using the landmarks provided for the evaluation, thus introducing strong bias into the results. Nonetheless, since their method was amazingly fast and therefore potentially the most useful in real-world applications, we feel inspired to propose a method based on deep learning that works for high resolution images without the requirement to fine-tune the network using manually annotated landmarks to achieve results comparable to the best scoring solutions based on the classical approach.

One of the challenges related to deep learning registration is connected to image size. High resolution images cannot be simply propagated through the network because the number of parameters required to provide an appropriate receptive field and accurate registration results would be too high to fit in the GPU memory. There are several approaches that decrease the GPU memory consumption by e.g. using B-Splines transformation model instead of the dense deformation field [16] or using a patch-based approach [17]. However, it is not well-established how to deal with patches that cannot be directly propagated through the network after unfolding due to the GPU memory constraints, which is the case for the high resolution histology images (full images are in the range of 100k × 100x pixels).

In this work, we propose a nonrigid registration method based on deep networks trained in an unsupervised way in a multi-level, patch-based and multi-iteration framework. The proposed approach works for images with any resolution using a single GPU, both during the training and the inference. The results are comparable to the best scoring teams using a traditional, iterative approach while being significantly faster during the inference. We make the source code freely available that, together with the open access to the data set, makes the results fully reproducible [18].

2   Methods

We assume that the input to the proposed method consists of images initially aligned by an affine registration. In this work, we used the affine registration method described in [19] that accurately aligns the large majority of the image pairs.

The first step is to transfer the source and target images to the GPU memory. The image transfer is being done only if a single GPU is used and both images fit into the memory. Otherwise, if a multi-GPU computing cluster is used and the memory transfer is done later. Second, the images are re-sampled to a pre-defined number of levels, building a classical resolution pyramid. This approach allows the method to calculate significantly larger deformations. Then, starting at the lowest resolution, the images are unfolded into overlapping patches with a given size and stride. The patches overlap because we use only the centers of the calculated displacement fields. The displacement vectors calculated at patch boundaries are not reliable because the real displacement may point outside the given image patch. The unfolded patches are grouped in the tensor batch dimension with a pre-defined size. This parameter controls the GPU memory usage and can be adjusted differently during the training and inference. If a multi-GPU computing cluster is used, the groups are divided between the GPUs. For each group, the patches are passed through the deep network.

We used the encoder/decoder U-Net-like architecture [20] with the batch normalization replaced by the group normalization [21] and max-pooling replaced by strided convolutions. The network architecture is part of Fig. 1.

As the next step, the current group is warped with the resulting displacement field and the loss is calculated, backpropagated and the optimizer is updated. In this work, we use the negative NCC as the cost function and the curvature as the displacement field regularization term [15,22]. The objective function can be defined as:

$$S(M, F, u) = -\text{NCC}(M, F) + \alpha\text{CURV}(u) \to min, \qquad (1)$$

where NCC denotes the normalized cross-correlation, CURV is the curvature regularization, α is the regularization parameter controlling the deformation smoothness, and M, F, u are the warped moving patches, target patches and the displacement fields respectively.

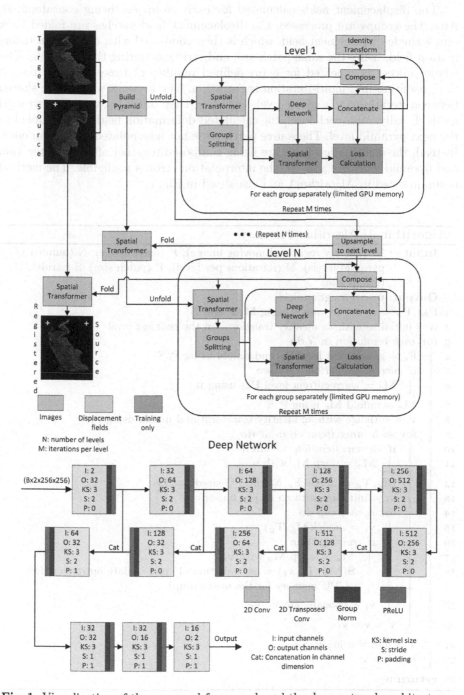

Fig. 1. Visualization of the proposed framework and the deep network architecture.

The displacement fields calculated for each group are being concatenated. After the groups are processed, the displacement field patches are folded back into a single displacement field, which is then composed with the current deformation field, using the same patch size and stride as during the unfolding. The whole process is repeated for a pre-defined number of times for each resolution, resulting in a multi-iteration registration. The network weights are shared between iterations at a given level. However, they differ between the pyramid levels. Finally, after each level, the calculated deformation field is up-sampled to the next pyramid level. The source patches are not interpolated more than once. Instead, the deformation fields are being composed together after each iteration and pyramid level. As a result, the interpolation error is negligible. The method is summarized in Algorithm 1 and visualized in Fig. 1.

Algorithm 1: Algorithm Summary.

Input : $\mathbf{M}$ (affinely registered moving image), $\mathbf{F}$ (fixed image), N (number of pyramid levels), M (iterations per level), P (patch size), S (stride), G (group size)

Output: $\mathbf{u}$ (deformation field)

1   $\mathbf{P_M}, \mathbf{P_F}$ = create pyramids using $\mathbf{M}, \mathbf{F}$ and N

2   $\mathbf{u}$ = initialize with an identity transform on the coarsest level

3   **for** *each resolution in N* **do**

4      $\mathbf{F_c}$ = get current level $\mathbf{P_F}$ and unfold using P, S

5   **if** *current resolution > 0* **then**

6         $\mathbf{M_c}$ = warp current level $\mathbf{P_M}$ using $\mathbf{u}$

7      $\mathbf{M_c}$ = unfold $\mathbf{M_c}$ using P, S

8      $\mathbf{v}$ = initialize with an identity transform and unfold using P, S

9   **for** *each inner iteration in M* **do**

10   **if** *current iteration > 0* **then**

11            $\mathbf{M_c}$ = warp $\mathbf{M_c}$ with $\mathbf{v}$

12         $\mathbf{M_g}, \mathbf{T_g}$ = divide $\mathbf{F_c}, \mathbf{M_c}$ into G-sized batches

13         $\mathbf{v_i}$ = initialize with an empty tensor

14   **for** *each group* **do**

15            $\mathbf{v_t}$ = model($\mathbf{M_g}, \mathbf{T_g}$)

16   **if** *training* **then**

17               $\mathbf{M_w}$ = warp $\mathbf{M_g}$ with $\mathbf{v_t}$

18               $S(\mathbf{M_w}, \mathbf{T_g}, \mathbf{v_t})$ = use equation (1) and update optimizer (free GPU memory for the next group)

19            $\mathbf{v_i}$ = concatenate($\mathbf{v_i}, \mathbf{v_t}$)

20         $\mathbf{v} = \mathbf{v} \circ \mathbf{v_i}$

21      $\mathbf{v}$ = fold $\mathbf{v}$ using P, S

22      $\mathbf{u} = \mathbf{u} \circ \mathbf{v}$

23 **return** $\mathbf{u}$

The proposed method has 5 main parameters: (i) number of pyramid levels, (ii) number of iterations per level, (iii) patch size, (iv) stride, and (v) group size. Increasing the number of pyramid levels makes it possible to calculate larger deformations, however, at the cost of increasing the registration time. The number of iterations per level is important for registering fine details, but similarly to the number of resolutions, increasing the value leads to longer registration time. The patch size is connected with the deep network architecture, its value should be chosen to correctly utilize the network receptive field. The stride defines how much the unfolded patches overlap. Finally, the group size defines the number of patches registered simultaneously. The larger the value, the faster the registration, as well as the GPU memory consumption. The patch size, stride and group size were established by calculating the theoretically required receptive field. The number of pyramid levels and number of iterations per level were tuned by a simple brute force search (the range of reasonable value is low).

The framework was trained using the Adam optimizer, with a fixed number of epochs, without using the early stopping technique. Only the images denoted as training by the challenge organizers were used during training, while the evaluation set was used for the validation. However, no decision was made based on the validation set results. Overfitting was not observed. The training set was augmented by small, random affine and color transformations. Schedulers were used, different for each pyramid level, decreasing the learning rate by a given factor after each epoch. No information about the landmarks was used during training. We make the source code freely available [18].

3 Results

The dataset consists of 481 image pairs, 230 in the training and 251 in the evaluation set. The landmarks are provided only for the training set, the evaluation of the remaining images must be done using the challenge platform, independently of the method authors. There are 8 different tissue types stained using 10 distinct dyes. The images vary from 8k to 16k pixels in one dimension. The full dataset description, including details about the acquisition, landmarks annotation, tissue abbreviations, and image size, is available at the challenge website [3].

Table 1. The normalized average processing time (in minutes) calculated by the automatic ANHIR evaluation system. The registration time is reported for RTX 2080 Ti.

Ours	MEVIS	AGH	UPENN	TUNI	CASIA	DROP	CKVST	BTP
0.033	0.141	8.596	1.374	8.977	4.824	3.388	7.488	0.684

The evaluation metric used to compare the participant's method is based on the target registration error, divided by the image diagonal, defined as:

$$rTRE = \frac{TRE}{\sqrt{w^2 + h^2}}, \tag{2}$$

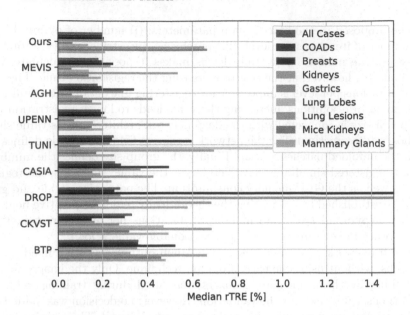

Fig. 2. The median rTRE calculated by the ANHIR evaluation system for all cases and each tissue separately. For team and tissue abbreviations see [2,3].

where TRE denotes the target registration error, w is the image width and h is the image height. We use the median of rTRE to compare the methods, following the original challenge rules. The average difference between two landmarks annotators was 0.05% while the best scoring methods achieve accuracy at the level of 0.2% of the image diagonal [2].

In Fig. 2, we compare our method to the best solutions in terms of the median rTRE, for all cases together and for each tissue type separately. We also show the normalized average registration time in Table 1. An example checkerboard visualization of the images before the registration, after the affine registration and after the proposed nonrigid method is shown in Fig. 3. We decided to compare only the solutions submitted using the automatic, server-side evaluation tool. We chose to not use other classical/deep algorithms and tune the parameters because the results would be unintentionally biased towards our method.

4   Discussion and Conclusion

The proposed framework achieves results comparable to other well-performing methods proposed for the nonrigid histological registration. The results in terms of the median rTRE are comparable to the best-scoring methods. Only the results for mice kidneys are considerably worse. The reason for this is an extremely low number of training samples available for the mice kidneys. In general, it can be observed that the larger the number of training samples for a particular tissue type, the more accurate the results. Similar challenges are

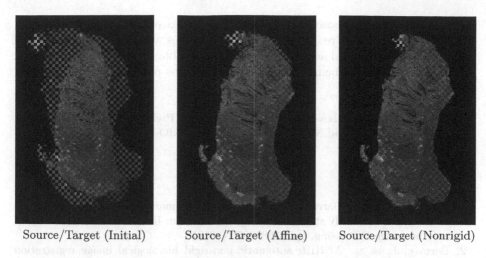

Source/Target (Initial)   Source/Target (Affine)   Source/Target (Nonrigid)

Fig. 3. Exemplary checkerboards for visual quality assessment at different registration stages (high quality pictures, best viewed zoomed in electronic format).

related to the lung lesions. However, there is also a problem connected with the regularization parameter that should be different for this type of tissue. An adaptive regularization would be beneficial.

The proposed solution is significantly faster and thus potentially more useful in practice since registration time above several minutes for a single pair is usually unacceptable. The only method that can be directly compared to our solution in terms of the computational time was proposed by the MEVIS team [8]. They proposed not only the most accurate but also a greatly optimized method. Unfortunately, their solution is commercial and the source code is unavailable. All other methods used rather home-designed software and we think that their computational time could be significantly decreased. However, most probably even the most efficient optimizations and use of GPU would not shorten the processing below time required by just few passes through a deep network.

In future work, we plan to investigate other similarity metrics like MIND [14] or NGF [9] since NCC is less resistant to missing structures and without a proper regularization or diffeomorpishm enforcement may introduce folding in such regions. Nonetheless, both similarity metrics are hard to use in patch-based deep frameworks and require an adaptive regularization. What is more, the noise parameter in NGF needs to be tuned, as well as the radius and the neighborhood type of the MIND descriptor. Moreover, we will investigate the network itself, since recent advances in encoder-decoder architectures may further improve the results. Finally, the curvature regularization is not perfect for tissues like lung lesions or mammary glands. We will look for alternative, adaptive regularization possibilities.

To conclude, we propose a fully automatic deep learning-based nonrigid registration method for high resolution histological images, working independently of the image resolution and achieving results comparable to other well-performing ANHIR methods while being significantly faster, thus potentially more useful in clinical practice.

Acknowledgments. This work was funded by NCN Preludium project no. UMO-2018/29/N/ST6/00143 and NCN Etiuda project no. UMO-2019/32/T/ST6/00065.

References

1. Borovec, J., Munoz-Barrutia, A., Kybic, J.: Benchmarking of image registration methods for differently stained histological slides. In: IEEE International Conference on Image Processing, pp. 3368–3372 (2018)
2. Borovec, J., et al.: ANHIR: automatic non-rigid histological image registration challenge. IEEE Trans. Med. Imaging (2020)
3. Borovec, J., et al.: ANHIR Website. https://anhir.grand-challenge.org
4. Fernandez-Gonzalez, R., et al.: System for combined three-dimensional morphological and molecular analysis of thick tissue specimens. Microsc. Res. Tech. **59**(6), 522–530 (2002)
5. Gupta, L., Klinkhammer, B., Boor, P., Merhof, D., Gadermayr, M.: Stain independent segmentation of whole slide images: a case study in renal histology. In: IEEE ISBI, pp. 1360–1364 (2018)
6. Mikhailov, I., Danilova, N., Malkov, P.: The immune microenvironment of various histological types of EBV-associated gastric cancer. Virchows Archiv (2018)
7. Bueno, G., Deniz, O.: AIDPATH: Academia and Industry Collaboration for Digital Pathology. http://aidpath.eu
8. Lotz, J., Weiss, N., Heldmann, S.: Robust, fast and accurate: a 3-step method for automatic histological image registration. arXiv:1903.12063 (2019)
9. Haber, E., Modersitzki, J.: Intensity gradient based registration and fusion of multi-modal images. In: Larsen, R., Nielsen, M., Sporring, J. (eds.) MICCAI 2006. LNCS, vol. 4191, pp. 726–733. Springer, Heidelberg (2006). https://doi.org/10.1007/11866763_89
10. Venet, L., Pati, S., Yushkevich, P., Bakas, S.: Accurate and robust alignment of variable-stained histologic images using a general-purpose greedy diffeomorphic registration tool. arXiv:1904.11929 (2019)
11. Joshi, S., Davis, B., Jomier, M., Gerig, G.: Unbiased diffeomorphic atlas construction for computational anatomy. NeuroImage **23**, 151–160 (2004)
12. Yushkevich, P., et al.: Fast automatic segmentation of hippocampal subfields and medial temporal lobe subregions in 3 Tesla and 7 Tesla T2-weighted MRI. Alzheimer's Dementia **12**, 126–127 (2016)
13. Wodzinski, M., Skalski, A.: Automatic nonrigid histological image registration with adaptive multistep algorithm. arXiv:1904.00982 (2019)
14. Heinrich, M., et al.: MIND: modality independent neighbourhood descriptor for multi-modal deformable registration. Med. Image Anal. **16**(7), 1423–1435 (2012)
15. Zhao, S., Lau, T., Luo, J., Chang, E., Xu, Y.: Unsupervised 3D end-to-end medical image registration with volume tweening network. IEEE J. Biomed. Health Inform. (2019). (Early Access)

16. de Vos, B., Berendsen, F., Viergever, M., Sokooti, H., Staring, M., Isgum, I.: A deep learning framework for unsupervised affine and deformable image registration. Med. Image Anal. **52**, 128–143 (2019)
17. Fan, J., Cao, X., Wang, Q., Yap, P., Shen, D.: Adversarial learning for mono- or multi-modal registration. Med. Image Anal. **58** (2019)
18. Wodzinski, M.: The Source Code. https://github.com/lNefarin/DeepHistReg
19. Wodzinski, M., Müller, H.: Learning-based affine registration of histological images. In: Špiclin, Ž., McClelland, J., Kybic, J., Goksel, O. (eds.) WBIR 2020. LNCS, vol. 12120, pp. 12–22. Springer, Cham (2020). https://doi.org/10.1007/978-3-030-50120-4_2
20. Ronneberger, O., Fischer, P., Brox, T.: U-Net: convolutional networks for biomedical image segmentation. In: Navab, N., Hornegger, J., Wells, W.M., Frangi, A.F. (eds.) MICCAI 2015. LNCS, vol. 9351, pp. 234–241. Springer, Cham (2015). https://doi.org/10.1007/978-3-319-24574-4_28
21. Wu, Y., He, K.: Group normalization. arXiv:1803.084943 (2018)
22. Fischer, B., Modersitzki, J.: Curvature based image registration. J. Math. Imaging Vis. **18**(1), 81–85 (2003)

Additive Angular Margin for Few Shot Learning to Classify Clinical Endoscopy Images

Sharib Ali[1(✉)], Binod Bhattarai[2], Tae-Kyun Kim[2], and Jens Rittscher[1]

[1] Institute of Biomedical Engineering, University of Oxford, Oxford, UK
sharib.ali@eng.ox.ac.uk
[2] Department of Electrical and Electronics Engineering,
Imperial College London, London, UK

Abstract. Endoscopy is a widely used imaging modality to diagnose and treat diseases in gastrointestinal tract. However, varied modalities and use of different imaging protocols at various clinical centers impose significant challenges when generalising deep learning models. Moreover, the assembly of large datasets from different clinical centers can introduce a huge label biases in multi-center studies that renders any learnt model unusable. Additionally, when using new modality or presence of images with rare pattern abnormalities such as dysplasia; a bulk amount of similar image data and their corresponding labels may not be available for training these models. In this work, we propose to use a few-shot learning approach that requires less training data and can be used to predict class labels of test samples from an unseen dataset. We propose a novel additive angular margin metric in the framework of the prototypical network in few-shot learning setting. We compare our approach to the several established methods on a large cohort of multi-center, multi-organ, multi-disease, and multi-modal gastroendoscopy data. The proposed algorithm outperforms existing state-of-the-art methods.

Keywords: Few shot · Endoscopy · Classification

1 Introduction

The use of deep and non-linear models for medical applications is exponentially growing [2]. The major bottleneck in training such data voracious models is the lack of abundant (expert) labeled data. Due to the requirement of large volume of labels, the possibility of surging incorrect labels is another problem. It is even more challenging on gastrointestinal endoscopy data due to: 1) difficulty to get domain experts to perform annotations, 2) could consist of multiple organs [10]

Electronic supplementary material The online version of this chapter (https://doi.org/10.1007/978-3-030-59861-7_50) contains supplementary material, which is available to authorized users.

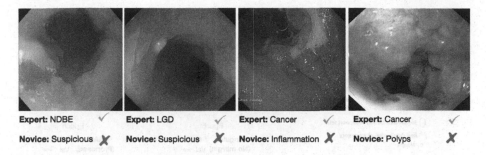

Fig. 1. Expert vs Novice. Examples of comparing expert (>20 years experience) labels with novice (<3 years experience) for some subtle cases in our dataset. Non-dysplastic (NDBE) and dysplastic (LGD) Barrett's are both graded as suspicious by the novice practitioner for two cases on the left. Similarly, some of the less subtle cases such as cancer are miss labelled as well by the novice annotator.

(*the oesophagus, stomach and the colon*) and varied disease types, and 3) large variability between expert and novice/trainee annotations (see Fig. 1). The lack of publicly available datasets as well as their quality (*e.g.*, missing and erroneous labels) pose additional challenges. Supporting new imaging protocols, such as new fluorescent (FL) or narrow-band imaging (NBI) for endoscopy, is a case in which the entire training data would need to be collected, curated and annotated from scratch and in larger numbers.

Given a training dataset with a large number of labeled samples we consider the case where one particular class with clinically relevant pattern is severely underrepresented. In this context, it is extremely challenging to train a model that will achieve an acceptable accuracy for such underrepresented class due to over-fitting. To overcome this problem, we propose to exploit the available annotated examples from related existing classes and use it to learn a metric parameter that can map test samples of an underrepresented and new class/classes without requiring large number of images and labels. Few-shot learning methods [14,15] which have been successfully used in the context of natural images, aim to learn a model with a very small amount of labelled data. Some of the notable computer vision applications are in classification [5,6],semantic segmentation [18], object detection [16], image segmentation [4], and image-to-image translation [7]. For more information, we suggest readers to refer to [17].

Here, we utilise this approach to overcome the problem of reliably detecting underrepresented classes. To date, few-shot learning has only been applied in a few selected medical image analysis applications. Mendela *et al.* [9] utilised this technique to classify a set of 8 different histology patterns. However, their work lacks a systematic comparison of the state-of-the-art methods. Punch and colleagues [12] proposed to train Siamese network to minimise the triplet loss on Euclidean sub-space for brain imaging.

Metric based few-shot learning algorithms have successfully been used in several tasks [14,15]. Studies have shown that the success of these approaches

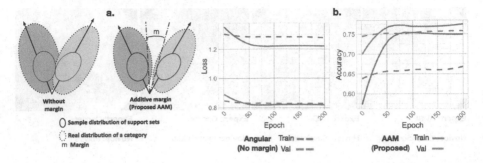

Fig. 2. Proposed Angular Additive Margin (AAM). a) Geometric interpretation of Soft max without margin (left) and with the margin (right). b) Loss and accuracy during training and validation with and without additive angular margin in (a).

are due to the discriminative behaviour of the metric subspace [12,14,15]. Most existing methods rely on either minimising a triplet loss function [15] or use of *softmax* on Euclidean and subspace spanned by *cosine* function [14,15]. Qian *et al.* [13] have recently demonstrated that the triplet loss is equivalent to using a *softmax* loss. However, the *softmax* loss is ineffective when number of classes becomes large and in presence of limited training examples. The drawback of these loss functions has been successfully addressed by incorporating an extra margin in metric subspace functions and was validated for face verification task [3,8]. Adding margin in the metric-based loss function helps to generate more discriminative representations by widening the inter-class separation. Figure 2 shows the geometric interpretation of *softmax* loss with and without the incorporated margin. Inspired by these ideas we introduce a margin on the objective function used in metric based few-shot learning [14,15] approach. To the best of our knowledge, this is the first work to introduce such an objective for few shot learning. In this paper, we introduce a novel *additive angular metric* (AAM) metric loss function in the prototypical network framework [14] to perform few-shot learning based classification of diverse endoscopy samples that consists of multi-center, multi-modal (white light, narrow-band modality), underrepresented (e.g., low-grade dysplasia (LGD)), and hard samples (e.g., rare cancer samples, refer Fig. 1). Figure 1 illustrates cases which are differently labeled by an expert compared to a trainee: (Left) subtle images with NDBE and LGD, and (right) hard samples for cancer. This becomes more challenging when multi-center and multi-modality data are fused as in our case. We present extensive experiments for meta-training strategies and meta-testing performances on a diverse endoscopic data with 25 classes. In summary, we make the following contributions:

– Formulate a few-short learning approach to reliably classify multi-center, underrepresented, and hard samples in the context of endoscopy data

- Proposed a novel and generic angular distance metric for few-shot learning that improves the classification accuracy compared to the existing state-of-the-art methods
- An extensive evaluation of the proposed method and existing arts is done on the endoscopy benchmark.

2 Method

In this section, first we introduce few-shot learning and prototypical networks. Then, we introduce our proposed Additive Angular Margin loss in the framework of such prototypical networks.

Few Shot Learning: Let us consider a scenario where there are two disjoint sets: $C_{train} \cap C_{test} = \emptyset$. There are a large number of training examples $(X_{train}^N, Y_{train}^N)$ for the classes belonging to C_{train} and only few training examples are available for the classes in C_{test}. In medical domains, we can derive analogies between these two sets with the well studied resource that have rich class categories compared to underrepresented classes that are clinically relevant patterns such as low-grade dysplasia in gastrointestinal endoscopy (see Fig. 1). To enable model to generalise with such limited training examples, few shot learning algorithm can be used to train the model in an episodic paradigm. In an episode trained in n-**shot and** k-**way manner**, n training examples belonging to k classes are used to learn the parameters of the model. Here, $n \ll N$ is a very small number of randomly sampled examples from the training set without replacement from a sub set of classes $n \times k \ll |C_{train}|$. These subset of annotated examples are called support set $\mathbb{S}_b$. At the same time, from the same sub-set of classes, we set aside few examples, not present in $\mathbb{S}_b$, as query set $\mathbb{Q}_b$. These are equivalent to the validation examples on supervised learning algorithms. However, the examples on query set $\mathbb{Q}_b$ changes in every episode, *i.e.*, with the change in support sets $\mathbb{S}_b$. The model parameters ϕ are learnt $f_\phi : R^D \to R^d$ ($D \gg d$) to make the correct predictions on the query set $\mathbb{Q}_b$. This procedure is repeated until the model selection criteria is met which is the accuracy on query set $\mathbb{Q}_b$ (for details please refer [16]).

Prototypical Network [14]: This few-shot learning model is simple yet obtains state-of-the-art performance on several natural image benchmarks. The network computes a d-dimensional prototype representation $\phi \in R^d$ for every class k from the representations of support set $\mathbb{S}_b$ as shown in Eq. (1). It then calculates distance $d(.)$ between the query example X and the prototype representations ϕ of any class k (see Eq. 2) and assign probability as shown in the Eq. (3).

$$L_k = \frac{1}{|S_b^k|} \sum_{(\mathbf{x}_i, Y_i) \in S_b^k} f_\phi(\mathbf{x}_i) \tag{1}$$

$$d(f_\phi(X), L_k) = \arccos \frac{f_\phi(X).L_k}{|f_\phi(X)|.|L_k|} \tag{2}$$

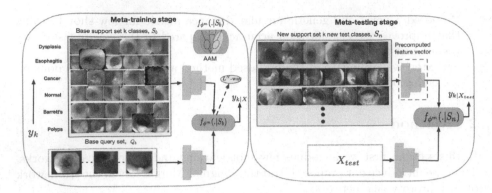

Fig. 3. Training and test strategies for few-shot classification for endoscopy. (Left) Meta-training stage utilizes randomly generated sub-sets of base support and base query samples to learn the metric parameter $f(\phi)$ for which we propose an additive angular margin (AAM).

$$p_\phi(y_k|X) = \frac{e^{\cos(d(f_\phi(X), L_k))}}{\sum_{k'} e^{\cos(d(f_\phi(X), L_{k'}))}}, \quad k' \in [1, ..., k] \tag{3}$$

$$J_\phi = -\log p_\phi(y_k|X) \tag{4}$$

We have evaluated on both commonly used distance metrics: Euclidean (l_2) and *cosine* [14]. Given the subtle differences or the continuous nature of disease progression *cosine* metric is more effective to our purpose (see Sect. 3). The parameters are estimated via stochastic gradient descent (SGD) to minimise average negative log likelihood (see Eq. (4)) of target label y_k for the query example ($X \in Q_b$). **Proposed framework:** Figure 3 shows schematic diagram of the proposed approach with two separate blocks outline the training and testing stages. Here, we utilise a prototypical network but introduce an additive angular margin on the *cosine* function.

Training Stage: There are two different sets of images: support set $\mathbb{S}_b$ and query set $\mathbb{Q}_b$ which we refer as base sets for our training stage. $\mathbb{S}_b$ consists of few randomly sampled images n from a subset of k classes. Embedding of these images computes their respective class prototypical representations ϕ. These representations are compared with the query images $X^i \in Q_b$. Baseline prototypical model [14] computes their probability p_ϕ of belonging to any class k as in Eq. (3). As we argue that the limitations of such an approach can introduce restricted inter-class boundaries. To approximate the exact class distributions, we propose to incorporate an *additive angular marginal* (AAM) with penalty margin m as shown in Eq. (5). m is an additive angular margin in radians and ϕ^m is the learnable parameter. This margin pushes samples apart which helps to approximate the real class distribution (see Fig. 2 (a, right)).

$$p_{\phi^m}(y_k|X) = \frac{e^{\cos(d(f_\phi(X),L_k)+m)}}{e^{\cos(d(f_\phi(X),L_k)+m)} + \sum_{k',k'\neq k} e^{\cos(d(f_\phi(X),L_{k'}))}} \quad (5)$$

During training, only few n-train examples (e.g., $n = 5$ in 5-shot) for k-classes (e.g., $k = 5$ in 5-way) are used. Thus, requiring very small amount of data samples to learn the mapping function ϕ^m. **Testing Stage:** Figure 3 (right) outlines the testing stage of the proposed approach. During inference time, we use the learnt ϕ^m to map both the support sets S_n and query example X_{test} to a embedding sub-space $f(\phi^m|S_n)$. It is to be noted that these class categories *were not present in the training set*. From the embedding of the support set S_n with n examples for each class k, prototype representation are computed. Query examples X^i_{test} are compared to the prototype representations of every classes k^{test} which are later used to compute their distances. From these distances, first probability of target support class is computed and then the class with the highest probability p_{ϕ^m} is assigned to the target label.

3 Experiments and Results

3.1 Dataset, Training and Evaluation Metrics

The dataset consists of **25 classes** with 60 images per class (1500 images) that has been collected from both in-house, international collaborators and online sources [1,11] and consists of **multi-modal** (white light, narrow-band imaging and chromo-Endoscopy), **multi-center** (UK, France, Italy) and **multi-organ** (oesophagus, stomach, colon-rectum). We refer to this dataset as the *miniEndoGI* classification dataset. The dataset consists of 8 classes from Kvasir [11], 5 classes from EDD2020 [1], and an additional 12 classes from our collected dataset from in-house and our collaborators (see **Supplementary materials Fig. 1**). Most of these classes are not publicly available and often found in scarce (e.g., gastric cancer or inflammation samples). The dataset was labelled independently by two expert endoscopists who have more than 20 years of experience. Since, the built dataset is from different sources, it captures a large variability in the clinical endoscopy imaging. Also, the use of the entire gastrointestinal tract (notably 3 organs: *oesophagus, stomach, colon and rectum*) provides the evidence of robustness of our proposed approach. From this data cohort, we have used 15 classes for training, 5 for validation and 5 classes for testing. It is to be noted that *no test class is present in the training set* and only sub-set of training data was used during meta-training stage (e.g., 1 sample for 1-shot and 5 samples for 5-shot).

The images were resized to 84 × 84 (similar to state-of-the-art methods that were applied on *mini*ImageNet dataset). We have also used the four-block embedding architecture [14,15] for a fair comparison with other existing metric distances. Each baseline block consisted of 64-filter 3 × 3 convolution, batch normalisation layer, a ReLU non-linearity and a 2×2 max-pooling layer. The same encoding layer that produces 1024−dimensional image features was used for both support and query samples (Fig. 3). All models were trained for 200 epochs with 100 episodes per epoch and a learning rate (lr) of 10^{-3} in SGD optimiser. We introduced a cutting rate of $1/3 \times lr$ for every 500 episodes. A stopping criteria was set if validation loss stops improving. For training, validation and test, same n−shot (samples) and k−way (classes) were chosen with set of 5 query samples for each experiment (see Sect. 2 for details).

3.2 Quantitative Evaluation

Table 1 shows that the baseline CNN architecture poorly performs on small samples. However, when trained using prototypical network with metric learning approaches the classification performance improves significantly. Notably, our proposed AAM surpasses all the state-of-the-art methods [14]). We also have compared Siamese with triplet loss recently used technique in medical imaging [9]. The improvements over few-shot approaches are more than 6% for 5-way and 1-shot, and 5-way and 5-shot. It is >2% each for 3-way and >1% for the 2-way classification cases for both 1-shot and 5-shot cases. Also, the standard deviation is the least for most cases which suggests that the proposed metric is able to well capture the inter-class variability present in the dataset. Nearly 80%, and 90% classification accuracies for 3-way, and 2-way settings shows a boost of more than 25%, and 37%, respectively, compared to the traditional deep-learning framework demonstrating the strength of our approach for classification of new

Table 1. Few-shot classification using Conv-4 backbone on *Endoscopy* dataset. Training was performed using n-shot, 5-query and k-way for every epoch and was tested on 5 new test class dataset, where $n = [1, 5]$ and $k = [5, 3, 2]$. The entire training was done for 200 epochs with stopping criteria of minimum loss drop of 0.01.

Method	dist.	5-way		3-way		2-way	
		1-shot	5-shot	1-shot	5-shot	1-shot	5-shot
Baseline	–	34.40	47.08	47.53	54.80	52.59	53.16
Siamese	Trip. loss [9]	–	–	–	–	79.00 ± 4.24	–
ProtoNet	Euclid. [14]	50.76 ± 2.78	59.40 ± 1.55	54.44 ± 2.72	73.80 ± 1.66	68.80 ± 1.51	83.70 ± 3.70
	cosine [15]	52.48 ± 1.95	60.60 ± 1.73	73.67 ± 1.88	78.60 ± 1.84	84.50 ± 2.01	88.80 ± 1.77
	AAM (our)	**58.76 ± 1.64**	**66.72 ± 1.35**	**75.06 ± 1.87**	**81.20 ± 1.72**	**85.60 ± 2.21**	**90.60 ± 1.70**

Table 2. Few-shot classification on *Endoscopyy* dataset for different backbone architectures. Networks were pretrained on *ImageNet*. Test results are provided for 5-shot, 5-way, and 5-query.

Method	dist.	Network backbones				
		VGG-19	ResNet18	ResNet34	ResNet50	DenseNet
ProtoNet	Euclid. [15]	20.00 ± 2.77	64.40 ± 1.35	67.84 ± 1.47	62.60 ± 1.21	63.32 ± 1.64
	cosine [14]	22.04 ± 1.70	67.44 ± 1.62	67.44 ± 1.86	66.00 ± 1.71	69.00 ± 1.44
	AAM (ours)	**24.16 ± 1.80**	**69.08 ± 2.18**	**70.00 ± 2.58**	**66.20 ± 2.91**	**71.00 ± 1.85**

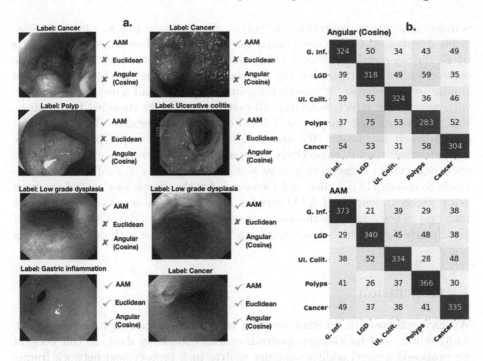

Fig. 4. Qualitative results on the test dataset for 5-shot, 5-way classification. (a) Classification using different metric distances, and (b) confusion matrix showing outcome for each class for proposed AAM and angular (*cosine*).

classes and under representative samples on few samples (*i.e.*, 1-shot referring to just 1 sample and 5-shot referring to just 5 samples). Additionally, the proposed AAM based prototypical network has an increased accuracy by nearly 7% compared to the state-of-the-art Siamese network with triplet loss.

We also perform a comparative analysis on different network backbones shown in Table 2. It can be observed that our proposed method with embedded AAM gap on the *cosine* outperforms all the state-of-the-art metrics. There is a 2% improvement for VGG-19, ResNet18, ResNet34 and DenseNet architectures compared to the baseline *cosine* metric. Figure 2b demonstrates that the proposed AAM approach with additive margin minimises the categorical cross-entropy loss function better and have a large accuracy improvement over the classical *cosine* metric without the angular margin. As illustrated in the Fig. 2a, the learnt margin boosts the discriminating capability of the network.

3.3 Qualitative Evaluation

From Fig. 4a (1st row) it can be observed that 'cancer' and 'polyps' are confused by both Euclidean and angular metrics. This may be due to the protrusion seen in these images. While for the (2nd row), Euclidean metric miss classifies 'cancer' and 'ulcerative colitis' as 'polyp'. Similarly, in Fig. 4a (3rd row) low-grade dysplasia (LGD) in oesophagus was miss classified as cancer in both cases by Euclidean metric while *cosine* and the proposed method with AAM metric correctly identified them. For the Fig. 4a (4th row), due to the abundance of similar pyloric images for 'gastric inflammation' (left) and a distinct protrusion with wound like structure (right), all methods correctly classified these labels. Figure 4b shows that the proposed AAM outperforms per class classification for all classes. It has nearly 20% and 10% improvement for 'polyps' and 'gastric inflammation' classes, respectively, compared with the *cosine* metric. Also, this confusion matrix suggests that most samples for 'polyps' is confused with low-grade dysplasia (LGD) class and vice-versa for the *cosine* case which has been dealt widely by our novel AAM metric. The qualitative results in Fig. 4 shows that due to the added discriminative margin proposed in our AAM approach it can classify both hard and easy labels and do not confuse with more closer class types.

4 Conclusion

We have proposed a few-shot learning approach for classifying multi-modal, multi-center, and multi-organ gastrointestinal endoscopy data. In this context we proposed a novel additive angular metric in a prototypical network framework that surpasses other state-of-the-art methods. Our experiments on both traditionally used Conv-4 backbone and other widely used backbones showed an improved performance of our method in some cases by up to 7% compared to recent works on few-shot learning approach. In future, we plan to add more underrepresented classes in clinical endoscopy and explore other non-linear functions for improved inter-class separation.

Acknowledgement. S. Ali is supported by the National Institute for Health Research (NIHR) Oxford Biomedical Research Centre (BRC). The views expressed are those of the author(s) and not necessarily those of the NHS, the NIHR or the Department of Health. J. Rittscher is supported by Ludwig Institute for Cancer Research and EPSRC Seebibyte Programme Grant (EP/M0133774/1).

References

1. Ali, S., et al.: Endoscopy disease detection challenge 2020. CoRR abs/2003.03376 (2020). https://arxiv.org/abs/2003.03376
2. Biswas, M., et al.: State-of-the-art review on deep learning in medical imaging. Front. Biosci. **24**, 392–426 (2019)
3. Deng, J., Guo, J., Xue, N., Zafeiriou, S.: ArcFace: additive angular margin loss for deep face recognition. In: CVPR (2019)
4. Dong, N., Xing, E.: Few-shot semantic segmentation with prototype learning. In: BMVC (2018)
5. Garcia, V., Bruna, J.: Few-shot learning with graph neural networks. In: ICLR (2018)

6. Liu, B., Yu, X., Yu, A., Zhang, P., Wan, G., Wang, R.: Deep few-shot learning for hyperspectral image classification. IEEE Trans. Geosci. Remote Sens. **57**(4), 2290–2304 (2018)
7. Liu, M.Y., et al.: Few-shot unsupervised image-to-image translation. In: ICCV (2019)
8. Liu, W., Wen, Y., Yu, Z., Li, M., Raj, B., Song, L.: SphereFace: deep hypersphere embedding for face recognition. In: CVPR (2017)
9. Medela, A., et al.: Few shot learning in histopathological images: reducing the need of labeled data on biological datasets, pp. 1860–1864 (2019)
10. Min, J.K., Kwak, M.S., Cha, J.M.: Overview of deep learning in gastrointestinal endoscopy. Gut Liver **13**, 388–393 (2019)
11. Pogorelov, K., et al.: KVASIR: a multi-class image dataset for computer aided gastrointestinal disease detection. In: Proceedings of the 8th ACM on Multimedia Systems Conference, MMSys 2017, pp. 164–169 (2017)
12. Puch, S., Sánchez, I., Rowe, M.: Few-shot learning with deep triplet networks for brain imaging modality recognition. In: Wang, Q., et al. (eds.) DART/MIL3ID -2019. LNCS, vol. 11795, pp. 181–189. Springer, Cham (2019). https://doi.org/10.1007/978-3-030-33391-1_21
13. Qian, Q., Shang, L., Sun, B., Hu, J., Li, H., Jin, R.: SoftTriple loss: deep metric learning without triplet sampling. In: ICCV (2019)
14. Snell, J., Swersky, K., Zemel, R.: Prototypical networks for few-shot learning. In: NIPS, pp. 4077–4087 (2017)
15. Vinyals, O., Blundell, C., Lillicrap, T., Wierstra, D., et al.: Matching networks for one shot learning. In: NIPS, pp. 3630–3638 (2016)
16. Wang, Y., Yao, Q.: Few-shot learning: a survey. arXiv:1904.05046 (2019)
17. Wang, Y., Yao, Q., Kwok, J.T., Ni, L.M.: Generalizing from a few examples: a survey on few-shot learning. ACM Comput. Surv. (CSUR) **53**, 1–34 (2019)
18. Zhang, C., Lin, G., Liu, F., Yao, R., Shen, C.: CANet: class-agnostic segmentation networks with iterative refinement and attentive few-shot learning. In: CVPR (2019)

Extracting and Leveraging Nodule Features with Lung Inpainting for Local Feature Augmentation

Sebastian Gündel[1,3]([⊠]), Arnaud A. A. Setio[1], Sasa Grbic[2], Andreas Maier[3], and Dorin Comaniciu[2]

[1] Digital Technology and Innovation, Siemens Healthineers, Erlangen, Germany
[2] Digital Technology and Innovation, Siemens Healthineers, Princeton, NJ, USA
[3] Pattern Recognition Lab, Friedrich-Alexander-Universität Erlangen, Erlangen, Germany
sebastian.guendel@fau.de

Abstract. Chest X-ray (CXR) is the most common examination for fast detection of pulmonary abnormalities. Recently, automated algorithms have been developed to classify multiple diseases and abnormalities in CXR scans. However, because of the limited availability of scans containing nodules and the subtle properties of nodules in CXRs, state-of-the-art methods do not perform well on nodule classification. To create additional data for the training process, standard augmentation techniques are applied. However, the variance introduced by these methods are limited as the images are typically modified globally. In this paper, we propose a method for local feature augmentation by extracting local nodule features using a generative inpainting network. The network is applied to generate realistic, healthy tissue and structures in patches containing nodules. The nodules are entirely removed in the inpainted representation. The extraction of the nodule features is processed by subtraction of the inpainted patch from the nodule patch. With arbitrary displacement of the extracted nodules in the lung area across different CXR scans and further local modifications during training, we significantly increase the nodule classification performance and outperform state-of-the-art augmentation methods.

Keywords: Nodule classification · Local feature augmentation · Context encoder · Chest X-ray

1 Introduction

Lung cancer is one of the most frequent cancer worldwide. Combined with the high mortality rate, the efficiency of lung cancer diagnosis and treatment is of paramount importance. In 2019, over 228,000 new cases and over 140,000 estimated deaths are predicted in the US [10]. The chance of surviving is higher when lung cancer is diagnosed in early cancer stages. The overall 5-year survival

© Springer Nature Switzerland AG 2020
M. Liu et al. (Eds.): MLMI 2020, LNCS 12436, pp. 504–512, 2020.
https://doi.org/10.1007/978-3-030-59861-7_51

rate is approximately 70% for people with stage *IA/B* and 50% for people with stage *IIA/B* non-small lung cancer [2].

In the past years, automated systems have been established to support the radiologists in diagnosing abnormalities on CXR images. Recent study shows that tremendous amount of nodule X-rays are required to compete with the nodule detection performance of radiologists [6]. State-of-the art augmentation methods can be used to increase the amount of training data [3,6]. However, most of the augmentation methods hardly improve model performances as most techniques are applied on the whole image [9].

We present a method to extract nodules from the image and apply local, patch-based augmentation approaches to improve the system in nodule versus non-nodule image classification. A trained image inpainting network of CXR patches is used to replace a patch containing a nodule with authentic background structures. By subtracting the inpainted patch from the nodule patch, nodules can be separated from normal structures (e.g., tissues, bones, etc.). The extraction of nodules leads to various approaches which can be applied on the local nodule apart from the global CXR image. We show that a novel idea of augmentation - namely local feature augmentation - improves the system and can be defined as a better variant for nodule image augmentation based on CXRs.

2   Background and Motivation

2.1   Computer-Aided Systems on Pulmonary X-ray Scans

In 2017, NIH released the first public CXR dataset with over 112,000 images and corresponding abnormality labels [13] which has led to various publications in classifying multiple abnormalities. The NIH group defines the baseline performance with an area under the curve (AUC) average of 0.75 across the abnormalities on their official evaluation set [13]. Hereafter, several groups increase the abnormality classification performance based on novel training strategies and network designs [3,5]. State-of-the-art results show that the performance for all 14 abnormalities raise to 0.82 AUC on average whereas the nodule classification score is improved to 0.78 AUC [6]. However, over 6,000 nodule images are required to achieve such performance. Less training images significantly downgrade the performance as shown by Ausawalaithong et al. [1]. Often, standard augmentation techniques are applied, e.g., horizontal flipping of the image [3,14]. These methods imply some major drawbacks as the global modifications limit the degree of freedom to change the image. As nodules are small abnormalities with less than or equal to 30 mm in diameter, relevant features for nodule classification are only present locally, on a small fraction of the image. Accessing these local features of the image which contributes to the class prediction allows us to expand the augmentation space.

2.2   Lung Region Inpainting for Classifier Deception

Recent analysis shows that adversarial attacks can easily change classification predictions. Taghanaki et al. created a comprehensive evaluation how CXR abnormality classification networks act on adversarial perturbations [12]. Given image data $D = \{x_1, x_2 \ldots x_n\}$ and its corresponding labels $Y = \{y_1, y_2 \ldots y_n\}$, a classification model C can be trained by minimization of a loss function l. (1a)

$$\arg \min_{C} \sum_{x_i \in D} l(C(x_i), y_i) \tag{1a}$$

$$\arg \min_{G} \sum_{x_i \in D} l(C(G(x_i), y_i')) \tag{1b}$$

The classification model can be attacked, e.g., with adversarial examples, generated from a model or method G to change the prediction of model C where $y_i \neq y_i'$. (1b)

Our novel approach builds on this basic idea generating realistic-looking patches in a supervised fashion which are placed in the image and change the nodule classification prediction. Local nodule features contributing to the class prediction which are covered by the inpainting frame can be entirely removed. The isolation process of the local features leads to various ideas; we focus on augmentation techniques to improve the classification system.

3   Proposed Method

Our local feature augmentation system is composed of two parts. First, we extract nodule features using a patch inpainting method (left side of Fig. 1). In a second step, with the help of the isolated nodules patches based on a nodule extraction process, we are able to displace nodules and apply further local augmentation techniques (right side).

3.1   Nodule Inpainting with Context Encoders

Inspired by the work of Sogancioglu et al., we generate a patch inpainting network by using context encoders for our baseline model [11].

We perform several modifications to improve the performance. As the context encoders do not perform well on predicting borders such that the rectangular contours of the mask are slightly visible after inpainting [11], we modify the system by applying the spatially discounted reconstruction loss introduced by Yu et al. [15]. Missing pixels at the border have less ambiguity, hence, those pixels are weighted stronger during training. We predict the weight for each pixel with γ^r, where r denotes the nearest distance to the mask border. As our mask size is smaller than the one in the reference work, we adapt γ from 0.99 to 0.97. Further, we increase the network capacity of the network with channel size $c_l = 2^{(8+l)}$ for encoder and adversarial part and $c_l = 2^{(12-l)}$ for the decoder. The layer index l is correspondingly $l_{enc} = \{0, 1, 2, 3, 4\}$ and $l_{dec/adv} = \{0, 1, 2, 3\}$. From the full image, we extract patches with size 64×64. A mask is overlayed with half as large in each dimension as the input patch.

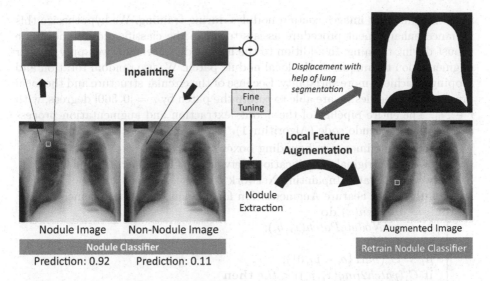

Fig. 1. Overview of our proposed method: We extract nodule patches from CXR images. The inpainting network predicts pixels for the mask. The nodule which has no correlation to the given frame surrounding that mask is entirely removed and lung tissue is predicted. Local augmentation techniques are applied on the isolated nodules to increase the classification performance. One augmentation method, the displacement of the nodule, can be arranged with given lung segmentation masks.

After training, the nodules can be extracted with $n_i^{pre} = o_i - I(o_i^M)$ where o_i denotes the original patches including the nodule and o_i^M the same patches including the mask which is fed into the patch inpainting network I. Post-processing steps are applied to remove noises: $n_i = \Theta_s(max\{n_i^{pre}, 0\}), \forall i$. As pixels with nodules are brighter than pixels without nodules, we truncate all negative values to zero. Parameter Θ_s stands for the bilateral filter with a filter size of $s = 3$. We hypothesize that the filter smooths the nodule patches and removes undesired background noise.

3.2 Local Feature Augmentation Techniques for Chest X-ray Classification

The isolated nodule patches can be implanted in different ways to augment the dataset. In this study, we applied the extracted nodules on non-nodule images and not on the images where the nodules are derived from. In this way, the original nodule images are kept unchanged and more *synthetic* nodule images are produced. According to this augmentation procedure, the dataset is more balanced with respect to the labels.

Based on the given lung segmentation masks, we randomly insert a nodule patch in the lung region of an image with probability k. The corresponding class label is modified adequately. This process is performed for each epoch such that different images contain nodules during training. We hypothesize this variance enhancement procedure assists to make the classification model more robust during training. In addition to the nodule displacement, we apply further augmentation techniques to the local nodule patch: We use random rotation and flipping to achieve more variability. Because of the circular structure and the local properties of nodules we are able to rotate the patch by $r = [0, 360[$ degrees, with $r \in \mathbb{N}_0$. The entire pipeline of the nodule extraction and augmentation process can be seen in pseudo code (Algorithm 1).

> **Data:** nodule images x; bounding boxes b
> **Networks:** Original Classification Network C_1; Retrained Classification Network C_2; Patch Inpainting Network I
> **Result:** Local Feature Augmentation for Classification Improvement
> **for** $i \leftarrow 0$ **to** $len(x)$ **do**
> $\quad$ $o_i := getNodulePatch(x_i, b_i)$;
> $\quad$ $p_i := I(o_i^M)$;   // inpaint patch
> $\quad$ $n_i := \Theta_s(max\{o_i - p_i, 0\})$;
> $\quad$ **if** $C_1(patch2img(x_i, p_i)) < thr$ **then**
> $\quad\quad$ | consider n_i for augmentation;
> $\quad$ **end**
> **end**
> **while** $Train(C_2)$ **do**
> $\quad$ **if** $random([0, 1]) < k$ **then**
> $\quad\quad$ | $AugmentImg(n_{rand})$;   // insert nodule patch to image
> $\quad$ **end**
> $\quad$ train epoch with modified images;
> **end**

Algorithm 1. Local Feature Extraction for Classification Augmentation

4   Experiments

For our experiments, we use the ChestX-ray14 [13] and the JSRT [8] database. The combined database contains 112,367 images with 6,485 nodule images. Nodule bounding boxes for 233 images are provided in the datasets. We have lung segmentation masks available for all images retrieved from a standard U-Net segmentation network [7]. The classification network is trained by using the architecture and hyperparameters from the work in [4]. However, we upscale the input image size to 512×512 to increase the resolution of the overall images and nodules.

At first, we trained the inpainting network I. We randomly collected 1 million, 10,000, and 800 patches for training, validation, and testing, respectively. The patches are extracted at random position from non-nodule images. The quantitative evaluation can be seen in Table 1.

In Fig. 2, we illustrate 4 example patches (first row). The inpainted image can be seen in the second row and the subtracted patch after the post-processing steps in the third row.

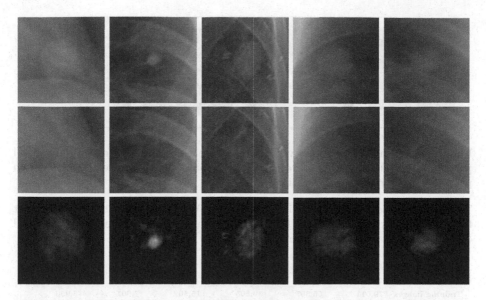

Fig. 2. Qualitative performance of our inpainting method for 4 different examples (Columns): Original nodule patch (Row 1); Inpainted Patch without nodule (Row 2); and subtracted patch including post-processing (Row 3)

Table 1. Peak-Signal-to-Noise Ratio (PSNR) on a test set of 800 patches. CE: Context Encoder

	CE [11]	CE*	CE* [ours]
PSNR (mean ± std)	26.31 ± 4.48	31.24 ± 3.77	**34.22 ± 3.95**

*Evaluated on a different test set

In addition to the quantitative and qualitative evaluation in Table 1 and Fig. 2, we show attention maps in Fig. 3 based on 2 CXR images. Each possible patch of an image was inpainted sequentially, fed into the classification network, and the prediction is placed on the map. Figure 3 shows that the image classification drops substantially when nodule regions were inpainted. We argue that the inpainting network is able to successfully remove nodules and replace it with background tissue to change the classifier prediction. Moreover, the prediction score remained stable when regions without nodules were inpainted, indicating that the inpainting network could generate normal patches robustly.

In order to ensure that nodules are reliably removed for augmentation purposes, the inpainting CXR images were individually validated. If the classification prediction was lower than the threshold $thr = 0.5$, we considered the corresponding patch for the augmentation process. In addition to the training images, hence, we can include 178 nodule patches. The model was trained in following way: For each image and epoch we inserted a nodule patch with probability k. Accordingly, we changed the corresponding nodule label.

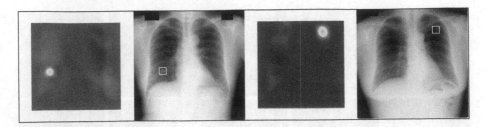

Fig. 3. Classification prediction visualized as attention: We sequentially inpaint all patches in nodule images and create attention maps based on the class prediction placed on the corresponding position.

Table 2. AUC scores of the classification system. We show results based on different training set sizes for training the baseline model, adding standard augmentation and our proposed local features augmentation.

	Area Under the Curve					
Train set size [%]	100	70	50	20	10	5
Training images	79,011	55,307	39,505	15,802	7,901	3,950
Baseline	0.792 ± 0.010	0.776 ± 0.012	0.763 ± 0.009	0.722 ± 0.019	0.667 ± 0.007	0.649 ± 0.009
Standard augmentation	0.795 ± 0.004	0.775 ± 0.008	0.769 ± 0.010	0.728 ± 0.013	0.681 ± 0.005	0.655 ± 0.007
Local feature augmentation	0.805 ± 0.004	0.790 ± 0.005	0.781 ± 0.004	0.746 ± 0.005	0.705 ± 0.017	0.669 ± 0.013

To evaluate the benefit of using the local augmentation method on varying size of the training set, we performed learning curve analysis. We trained the network with t% images of the training set and evaluated the performance. The dataset was split patient-wise into 70%, 10%, and 20% for training, validation, and testing, respectively. We ensured that the images from the extracted nodule patches were present in the training set. For all experiments, we used a nodule insertion rate $k = 0.05$. Each experiment was conducted 3 times. We show the resulting mean and standard deviation of the 3 runs in Table 2.

We defined the baseline without any augmentation techniques (Row 1). Then, we conducted experiments with state-of-the-art augmentation on the full image. We applied random horizontal flipping and random rotation with a degree range of $[-15, 15]$. No significant improvement can be seen compared to the baseline model (Row 2). The evaluation of our local feature augmentation method can be seen in Row 3. For each column the same training set was applied. For all training set sizes we state that our augmentation method consistently achieves better performance, compared to the baseline and standard augmentation method.

5   Discussion

In the proposed work, we demonstrated a novel image augmentation approach. We showed increased performance scores on nodule classification by applying augmentation locally. The advantage of the context model was the nearly unlimited training data as the local patches were retrieved from the full image. In this study, we collected 1 million patches for training, derived from a big data collection. However, only few images include information about nodule detection. Additionally, some nodules had to be sorted out during the retrieving process such that 178 nodules could be considered for the augmentation process. An additional radiologist validation process may decrease the amount of rejected samples as the current process was solely based on the classification system.

The limited amount of nodules led to an improved nodule classification system on different training set sizes. In future work, more nodule annotations can be considered which may further increase the performance with local feature augmentation. The size of the full images was resized to 512 in each dimension. Especially small nodules may entirely disappear with this resolution change. Experiments on the original image size may result in an increased collection of valid nodule patches.

We demonstrated the proposed method based on the classification of nodules. The system can be expanded to apply local feature augmentation on other local lung abnormalities, e.g., mass. Furthermore, we see no limitations to handle 3-dimensional image data, e.g., applying our local feature augmentation method on lung CT scans.

6 Conclusion

In this paper, we presented a novel idea of image augmentation to improve the nodule classification system on chest X-ray images. Instead of transforming the global image with standard augmentation techniques, we created an enhanced system of an inpainting model with context encoders to directly access nodule features. The extracted nodules were modified with our novel local feature augmentation method. Experiments conducted on different training set sizes showed significantly improved performance scores on nodule classification.

Disclaimer. The concepts and information presented in this paper are based on research results that are not commercially available.

References

1. Ausawalaithong, W., Thirach, A., Marukatat, S., Wilaiprasitporn, T.: Automatic lung cancer prediction from chest X-ray images using the deep learning approach. In: 11th Biomedical Engineering International Conference (BMEiCON), pp. 1–5 (2018)
2. Goldstraw, P., et al.: The IASLC lung cancer staging project: proposals for the revision of the TNM stage groupings in the forthcoming (seventh) edition of the TNM classification of Malignant Tumours. J. Thorac. Oncol. 2(8), 706–714 (2007)
3. Guan, Q., Huang, Y., Zhong, Z., Zheng, Z., Zheng, L., Yang, Y.: Diagnose like a radiologist: attention guided convolutional neural network for thorax disease classification. arXiv:1801.09927 (2018)

4. Gündel, S., Grbic, S., Georgescu, B., Liu, S., Maier, A., Comaniciu, D.: Learning to recognize abnormalities in chest X-rays with location-aware dense networks. In: Vera-Rodriguez, R., Fierrez, J., Morales, A. (eds.) CIARP 2018. LNCS, vol. 11401, pp. 757–765. Springer, Cham (2019). https://doi.org/10.1007/978-3-030-13469-3_88

5. Li, Z., et al.: Thoracic disease identification and localization with limited supervision. In: 2018 IEEE/CVF Conference on Computer Vision and Pattern Recognition (CVPR), pp. 8290–8299 (2018)

6. Rajpurkar, P., et al.: CheXNet: radiologist-level pneumonia detection on chest x-rays with deep learning. arXiv:1711.05225 (2017)

7. Ronneberger, O., Fischer, P., Brox, T.: U-Net: convolutional networks for biomedical image segmentation. In: Navab, N., Hornegger, J., Wells, W.M., Frangi, A.F. (eds.) MICCAI 2015. LNCS, vol. 9351, pp. 234–241. Springer, Cham (2015). https://doi.org/10.1007/978-3-319-24574-4_28

8. Shiraishi, J., et al.: Development of a digital image database for chest radiographs with and without a lung nodule: receiver operating characteristic analysis of radiologists' detection of pulmonary nodules. In: AJR, pp. 71–74 (2000)

9. Shorten, C., Khoshgoftaar, T.M.: A survey on image data augmentation for deep learning. J. Big Data 6, 1–48 (2019)

10. Siegel, R.L., Miller, K.D., Jemal, A.: Cancer statistics, 2019. CA: Cancer J. Clin. 69(1), 7–34 (2019)

11. Sogancioglu, E., Hu, S., Belli, D., van Ginneken, B.: Chest X-ray inpainting with deep generative models. arXiv:1809.01471 (2018)

12. Asgari Taghanaki, S., Das, A., Hamarneh, G.: Vulnerability analysis of chest X-ray image classification against adversarial attacks. In: Stoyanov, D., et al. (eds.) MLCN/DLF/IMIMIC -2018. LNCS, vol. 11038, pp. 87–94. Springer, Cham (2018). https://doi.org/10.1007/978-3-030-02628-8_10

13. Wang, X., Peng, Y., Lu, L., Lu, Z., Bagheri, M., Summers, R.: ChestX-ray8: hospital-scale chest X-ray database and benchmarks on weakly-supervised classification and localization of common thorax diseases. In: 2017 IEEE Conference on Computer Vision and Pattern Recognition (CVPR), pp. 3462–3471 (2017)

14. Yao, L., Poblenz, E., Dagunts, D., Covington, B., Bernard, D., Lyman, K.: Learning to diagnose from scratch by exploiting dependencies among labels. arXiv:1710.10501 (2018)

15. Yu, J., Lin, Z.L., Yang, J., Shen, X., Lu, X., Huang, T.S.: Generative image inpainting with contextual attention. In: 2018 IEEE/CVF Conference on Computer Vision and Pattern Recognition, pp. 5505–5514 (2018)

Gambling Adversarial Nets for Hard Sample Mining and Structured Prediction: Application in Ultrasound Thyroid Nodule Segmentation

Masoumeh Bakhtiariziabari[1,2(✉)] and Mohsen Ghafoorian[3]

[1] University of Amsterdam, Amsterdam, The Netherlands
[2] 3DUniversum, Amsterdam, The Netherlands
mbakhtiariz@gmail.com
[3] TomTom, Amsterdam, The Netherlands

Abstract. Most real-world datasets are characterized by long-tail distributions over classes or, more generally, over underlying visual representations. Consequently, not all samples contribute equally to the training of a model and therefore, methods properly evaluating the importance/difficulty of the samples can considerably improve the training efficiency and effectivity. Moreover, preserving certain inter-pixel/voxel structural qualities and consistencies in the dense predictions of semantic segmentation models is often highly desirable; accordingly, a recent trend of using adversarial training is clearly observable in the literature that aims for achieving higher-level structural qualities. However, as we argue and show, the common formulation of adversarial training for semantic segmentation is ill-posed, sub-optimal, and may result in side-effects, such as the disability to express uncertainties.

In this paper, we suggest using recently introduced Gambling Adversarial Networks that revise the conventional adversarial training for semantic segmentation, by reformulating the fake/real discrimination task into a correct/wrong distinction. This forms then a more effective training strategy that simultaneously serves for both hard sample mining as well as structured prediction. Applying the gambling networks to the ultrasound thyroid nodule segmentation task, the new adversarial training dynamics consistently improve the qualities of the predictions shown over different state-of-the-art semantic segmentation architectures and various metrics.

Keywords: Adversarial training · Hard sample mining · Structured prediction · Ultrasound thyroid nodule segmentation

Electronic supplementary material The online version of this chapter (https://doi.org/10.1007/978-3-030-59861-7_52) contains supplementary material, which is available to authorized users.

© Springer Nature Switzerland AG 2020
M. Liu et al. (Eds.): MLMI 2020, LNCS 12436, pp. 513–522, 2020.
https://doi.org/10.1007/978-3-030-59861-7_52

1 Introduction

Semantic segmentation is arguably among the longest-standing and most important problems in medical image analysis. Despite the significant improvements in semantic segmentation, due to much better representation learning capabilities of modern deep learning architectures [1], the task is still facing inherent challenges that remain not fully resolved. In the following, we briefly discuss two such important challenges, namely the hard sample mining and structured prediction.

Hard Sample Mining. Most of the real-world datasets exhibit long-tail distributions as certain categories are observed much more frequently than others; This issue becomes even more pronounced in the world of medical image analysis, where the pathological observations are generally much less abundant compared to the normal. Arguing beyond the class-imbalance problem, even within the same category of a frequent or an infrequent class, not all samples are of the same difficulty and therefore are not equally informative for the model to attend while being trained [2]. Thus, identically treating different samples is potentially inefficient and should be avoided. While some methods modify the sampling distribution of the training data [3], many others, including [4–10], approximate the sampling process by re-weighting the sample contributions to the objective function to be minimized. For instance, class-based re-weighting, among the most simple and popular approaches, uses the class infrequency as a proxy metric for the sample difficulty/importance. Some other approaches [4,5,11,12] directly use the corresponding errors as a measure of sample importance. Such methods, however, may suffer from their strategy when dealing with noisy labels [13].

Structured Prediction. Semantic segmentation models not only do need to optimize for per-pixel accuracy, but also certain inter-pixel/voxel structural qualities should be preserved in many cases. For instance, the predictions should be smooth, preserve certain shapes, geometries, and be semantically consistent. Besides using graphical models such as dense CRFs [14], adversarial semantic segmentation [7,15–21] has been widely employed recently, where a discriminator is incorporated to provide higher-level feedback by learning to distinguish model predictions (fake) from the GT annotations (real). However, GAN models are notoriously difficult to train and are very sensitive to the hyperparameters. More importantly, a major issue when applying adversarial training to semantic segmentation is an inherent triviality of the distinction between real and fake predictions using only low-level cues. An obvious example of this is using value-based clues to contrast the soft values of the model predictions with the bimodal sharp GT labels. This not only hinders learning to improve on high-level structural qualities but also pushes the model to be overconfident, even in the presence of high uncertainties, to close this low-level unimportant gap.

In this paper, we propose to use Gambling adversarial networks [6], a recent method that tackles the aforementioned shortcomings and simultaneously serves as an adversarial hard sample mining and structured semantic segmentation strategy. We demonstrate that applying the proposed method to the task of ultrasound thyroid nodule segmentation, consistently improves results compared to the state-of-the-art hard sample mining and structured prediction approaches, measured over various segmentation architectures and metrics.

2   Methods

Consider $\mathcal{D} = \{(x^i, y^i)\}_{i\in\{1..N\}}$, a dataset of N supervised samples in which $x^i \in \mathbb{R}^{W\times H}$ and $y^i \in \{0,1\}^{W\times H\times C}$ represent the i-th image and the corresponding pixel-wise one-hot labels of size $W \times H$ on a C-class problem. A standard approach to solve such a problem is to train a deep neural network F_θ by minimizing a (weighted) aggregation of pixel-wise loss terms, e.g., categorical cross-entropy:

$$\mathcal{L}_{ce}(x, y; \theta) = -\frac{1}{W \times H \times N} \sum_{i,j,k} \sum_c w(x^i, y^i)_{j,k}\, y^i_{j,k,c} \ln(F_\theta(x^i)_{j,k,c}), \qquad (1)$$

where $w(x^i, y^i)$ is a sample weighting function. The weighting function w is, in a vast majority of cases, a uniform weighting of 1 for each sample or is set based on class frequencies as a heuristic, agnostic to the structure and difficulty of the input sample x^i. On the other hand, focal loss [4] sets this weighting based on the sample error, but still ignores the structure in samples x^i:

$$w_{focal}(x^i, y^i)_{j,k} = \sum_c y^i_{j,k,c}(1 - F_\theta(x^i)_{j,k,c})^\gamma, \qquad (2)$$

Here γ is a hyperparameter factor that controls the extent to which the faultier sample predictions would contribute more to the final loss. Adversarial confidence learning [7], a recently proposed method, suggests to use sample confidences taken from a discriminator D_ϕ, trained to distinguish GT labels (real) from the network predictions (fake) to extract such sample weighting function:

$$w_{conf}(x^i, y^i)_{j,k} = (1 - D_\phi(x^i, F_\theta(x^i))_{j,k})^\gamma. \qquad (3)$$

Meanwhile, a multitude of methods further add adversarial loss terms by incorporating discriminators distinguishing real and fake predictions, to improve the structural qualities of the predictions:

$$\mathcal{L}(x, y; \theta, \phi) = \mathcal{L}_{ce}(x, y; \theta) + \alpha\mathcal{L}_{adv}(x, y; \theta, \phi), \qquad (4)$$

where the adversarial loss is either computed with the standard non-saturated cross-entropy loss [15] as $\mathcal{L}_{adv}(x, y; \theta, \phi) = \mathbb{E}_i \ln(D_\phi(x^i, F_\theta(x^i)))$, or as a distance to be minimized in the embedding space [16,21] mapped by the discriminator: $\mathcal{L}_{adv}(x, y; \theta, \phi) = \mathbb{E}_i ||D_\phi(x^i, F_\theta(x^i)) - D_\phi(x^i, y^i)||$. However, as discussed, there is an inherent ill-posedness in the real/fake distinction task for semantic segmentation. Therefore, we propose to use gambling adversarial nets [6], reformulating the real/fake discrimination task into a *correct/wrong* distinction, to overcome this shortcoming.

This is achieved by replacing a conventional discriminator with a gambler model (G_φ) generating dense $W \times H$ betting/investment maps, where $G_\varphi(x^i, F_\theta(x^i))_{j,k}$, i.e. the betting map at position (j, k), aims to predict how likely the prediction $F_\theta(x^i)$ is *wrong* (rather than fake). The gambler attempts to maximize the weighted cross-entropy loss for the segmenter network as in Eq. (1), where its betting map forms the weight terms (w_gam). This translates into the following loss function for the gambler:

$$\mathcal{L}_g(x, y; \varphi, \theta) = \frac{1}{W \times H \times N} \sum_{i,j,k} \sum_c w_\text{gam}(x^i)_{j,k} \, y^i_{j,k,c} \, \ln(F_\theta(x^i)_{j,k,c}), \quad (5)$$

A trivial solution now for the gambler to minimize its loss is to infinitely bet on every single location. To prevent this, we make the analogy to a real-world gambler complete, by giving the gambler a limited budget, so that the gambler needs to learn the mistake patterns to efficiently distribute its limited budget. This is obtained by spatially normalizing the betting maps, in the following form:

$$w_\text{gam}(x^i)_{j,k} = \frac{e^{G_\varphi(x^i, F_\theta(x^i))_{j,k} + \beta}}{\sum_{m,n} e^{G_\varphi(x^i, F_\theta(x^i))_{m,n} + \beta}}, \quad (6)$$

where β is a regularizing smoothing factor, ensuring that the weights are smoothly distributed over the different samples. The segmenter network F_θ is involved in a minimax game:

$$\mathcal{L}_f(x, y; \varphi, \theta) = -\mathcal{L}_g(x, y; \varphi, \theta). \quad (7)$$

Note that with such an adversarial game between the semantic segmentation model and the gambler network, the proposed method implements two strategies, hard-sample mining as well as improving structural qualities. Note that using this formulation, gambling nets do not suffer from the inherent problems of real/fake distinction, e.g. value-based discrimination. Structural inconsistencies are reliable investments and often easy-to-find clues for the gambler to bet on; therefore the resulting gradients will encourage the segmenter network to avoid structurally wrong predictions. An overview of the gambling adversarial nets is presented in Fig. 1.

Notice that in contrast to all the aforementioned adversarial methods, our critic, i.e. the gambler, never perceives real ground-truth images as input and therefore learns the mistake patterns only through the structure of the model predictions, in combination with the input image. We argue that this an important aspect in not letting the critic learn to misuse some of the inherent and sometimes even desirable discrepancies between the GT labels and model predictions, such as soft values and uncertainties.

3   Experimental Setup

We evaluate and compare the proposed method with focal loss [4] and adversarial confidence learning [7,8], as well as adversarial training [15] and SegAN [16],

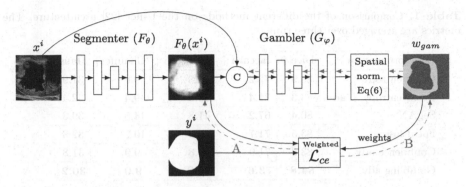

Fig. 1. A schematic of the gambling adversarial networks for semantic segmentation, where the node marked with C represents concatenation operation. Note the two gradient flows specified with the red dashed lines, A and B. While the gradients on path A support hard sample reweighting, the gradients on path B help improving structural qualities as containing information on why the gambler has picked certain regions to upweight.

representing the hard sample mining and structured prediction literature respectively. To ensure fair comparisons, all the common hyperparameters are kept the same and the models only differ in the corresponding loss formulation, and the specific hyperparameters are tuned separately. To show the consistency of the comparison beyond a single network architecture, all the models are trained and evaluated with three state-of-the-art semantic segmentation network architectures, namely U-net [22], PSPNet [23] with ResNet-101 [24] backbone, and DeepLabV3+ [25] with an Xception [26] backbone network. The details of the training process and the hyperparameters are available in the supplementary materials. Please note that all reported metrics are averaged over three runs to suppress possible fluctuations due to random initialization.

3.1 Dataset

The dataset used in this study is obtained from the TN-SCUI challenge [27] on Thyroid nodule segmentation and classification on ultrasound images. The dataset contains 3644 images of various resolutions each provided with a binary mask of the corresponding thyroid nodule, annotated by experienced doctors. We divide the data into training, validation, and test sets of 80%, 10%, and 10%. We tune the models on the validation set, and then use the full training and validation samples to train the final models to be evaluated on the test set.

Table 1. Comparison of the different methods on the U-net [22] architecture. The metrics are averaged over three runs.

Loss formulation	Dice ↑	Jaccard ↑	BF-score ↑	Chamfer↓	Hausdorff↓
Cross-entropy	83.9	72.2	55.8	9.8	31.9
Cross-entropy + adv.	83.3	71.4	53.6	9.4	32.4
SegAN	80.4	67.2	41.8	14.5	39.3
Focal loss	83.5	71.7	54.0	10.2	32.3
Confidence adv.	83.6	71.9	54.8	9.9	31.8
Gambling adv.	**84.8**	**73.6**	**59.8**	**9.0**	**30.2**

3.2   Metrics

In addition to using Dice similarity score, and Jaccard index, widely used for semantic segmentation, we further assess our trained models with BF-score [28], Chamfer distance and Hausdorff distance that are commonly used in the structured semantic segmentation literature. These metrics mainly deal with the quality of prediction boundaries that, compared to pixel-wise metrics, better correlate with structural qualities. These metrics are computed as follows:

$$d_{\text{Chamfer}}(X,Y) = \frac{1}{2} \sum \left\{ \frac{1}{|X|} \sum_{x \in X} \min_{y \in Y} d(x,y), \frac{1}{|Y|} \sum_{y \in Y} \min_{x \in X} d(x,y) \right\}, \qquad (8)$$

$$d_\tau(X,Y) = \frac{1}{|X|} \sum_{x \in X} [\min_{y \in Y} d(x,y) < \tau], \qquad (9)$$

$$BF(X,Y) = \frac{2 d_\tau(X,Y) d_\tau(Y,X)}{d_\tau(X,Y) + d_\tau(Y,X)}, \qquad (10)$$

where X and Y are the boundaries of the corresponding classes for the predictions and the ground-truth and τ represents a max tolerable distance. Note that the Hausdorff distance is quite similar to the Chamfer distance with the difference that the maximum of surface distances is computed rather than the average, which makes it more sensitive to the outliers. To assess the ability of the model to express uncertainties, we also report the mean maximum class likelihood (MMCL), representing the average likelihood of the most likely class, where the max likelihoods are averaged across the spatial dimensions and different samples.

4   Experimental Results and Discussion

Tables 1, 2 and 3 show the Dice, Jaccard, BF-score, Chamfer and Hausdorff distance metrics on the test set, on models trained with U-net, PSPNet and DeepLabV3+ architectures, respectively. Table 4 demonstrates and compares the MMCL values for the different methods. Extensive qualitative comparisons are

Table 2. Comparison of the different methods on the PSPNet [23] architecture, with Resnet101 backbone. The metrics are averaged over three runs.

Loss formulation	Dice ↑	Jaccard ↑	BF-score ↑	Chamfer↓	Hausdorff↓
Cross-entropy	86.6	76.4	65.4	6.9	23.8
Cross-entropy + adv.	85.7	74.9	64.4	7.6	26.0
SegAN	85.7	75.1	62.9	7.1	24.2
Focal loss	86.8	76.7	64.8	7.1	23.6
Confidence adv.	85.9	75.3	63.8	7.6	25.1
Gambling adv.	**87.4**	**77.6**	**68.5**	**6.7**	**22.1**

Table 3. Comparison of the different methods on the DeeplabV3+ [25] architecture with an Xception [26] backbone. The metrics are averaged over three runs.

Loss formulation	Dice ↑	Jaccard ↑	BF-score ↑	Chamfer↓	Hausdorff↓
Cross-entropy	86.6	76.4	64.8	7.3	24.7
Cross-entropy + adv.	87.2	77.4	66.6	8.0	43.2
SegAN	86.9	76.8	66.5	6.8	23.1
Focal loss	86.3	76.0	64.6	7.3	24.2
Confidence adv.	86.5	76.2	64.7	7.2	23.3
Gambling adv.	**87.5**	**77.7**	**69.3**	**6.5**	**21.6**

Table 4. The mean maximum class likelihoods from U-net reported for the different training methods.

Loss formulation	CE	Focal	CE + Adv.	SegAN	Gambling
MMCL	0.846	0.705	0.930	0.985	0.862

available in Figs. 1, 2, and 3 in the supplementary materials. As observed in the reported empirical results, models using gambling adversarial nets as the loss formulation consistently outperform the other adversarial and hard sample mining methods over different network architectures and metrics. In the following, we present a brief analysis for comparing the gambling nets to each of the other methods.

Focal Loss. Even though a normalized focal error map can be thought of as the minimization solution for the problem that the gambler deals with, training the segmenter network with the gambler sample weights has two clear advantages: Firstly, as illustrated in Fig. 1, in addition to the plain up-weighting of the difficult samples, the gambler also provides structural information, representing why certain areas are considered investment-worthy. Secondly, focal loss can suffer from noisy labels, where a possibly correct prediction from the model is harshly penalized due to a noisy label. The gambling nets, on the other hand, suffer less

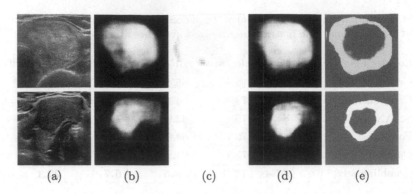

(a)   (b)   (c)   (d)   (e)

Fig. 2. Sample comparison of the obtained uncertainty maps from adv. confidence learning and adv. gambling nets. (a) input image, (b) adv. conf. learning prediction, (c) uncertainty map from adv. conf. learning (d) prediction from gambling nets, (e) betting map from the gambler.

from this, as the possibly incorrect labels only indirectly influence the resulting weights. Therefore as long as the gambler network is not overfitted to the noise patterns, the training framework is more resilient to label noise compared to the focal loss.

Conventional Adversarial Training. As suggested by the MMCL comparison in Table 4, the critic in both adversarial models push the model to fake to be more certain. However, we can also note that the segmentation models do not fully close the value-based gap, likely because otherwise, the pixel-wise loss would harshly penalize a confident wrong prediction. Therefore, with the remaining gap, the discriminator still has an easy job distinguishing the real and fake and thus will likely not go beyond such low-level remaining clues. This would obviously hinder learning higher-level structural qualities and consistencies. In contrast, a smooth likelihood, e.g. 0.8, is not a good investment for the gambler as long as the prediction is correct.

Adversarial Confidence Learning. Even though adversarial confidence learning [7] is the closest work to the gambling networks, in the regard that it similarly aims to extract the samples' difficulty weights in a learnable fashion, there is still a major difference in how the critic is trained. This method still trains a discriminator to distinguish the real and fake labels. Apart from the argued ill-posedness of such formulation for semantic segmentation, we found it very difficult in practice to get meaningful confidence maps from the discriminator. As visible in Fig. 2, the uncertainty map values were almost always very close to one. This can be attributed to the confidence model loss formulation [7] that forces the model to predict fake at 'every' spatial position in the network predictions; therefore finding any single clue, the confidence model is encouraged to propagate the fake prediction all over the spatial locations, no matter if the corresponding predictions were correct or wrong.

5   Conclusion and Future Work

In this paper, we showed that a simple but fundamental reformulation of the critic in adversarial training can consistently and effectively improve semantic segmentation results on the thyroid nodule segmentation task and the advantages were intuitively and empirically analyzed. We believe that not only using gambling nets as a 'learned' hard sample learning policy is potentially useful for (medical) image segmentation tasks, but also can be studied in combination with other image recognition tasks such as detection and classification; for instance in presence of controlled noise for comparison with other hard sample mining methods, which is left as future work.

References

1. Litjens, G., et al.: A survey on deep learning in medical image analysis. Med. Image Anal. **42**, 60–88 (2017)
2. Katharopoulos, A., Fleuret, F.: Not all samples are created equal: deep learning with importance sampling. arXiv preprint arXiv:1803.00942 (2018)
3. Van Grinsven, M.J.J.P., van Ginneken, B., Hoyng, C.B., Theelen, T., Sánchez, C.I.: Fast convolutional neural network training using selective data sampling: application to hemorrhage detection in color fundus images. IEEE Trans. Med. Imaging **35**(5), 1273–1284 (2016)
4. Lin, T.-Y., Goyal, P., Girshick, R., He, K., Dollár, P.: Focal loss for dense object detection. In: Proceedings of the IEEE International Conference on Computer Vision, pp. 2980–2988 (2017)
5. Bulo, S.R., Neuhold, G., Kontschieder, P.: Loss max-pooling for semantic image segmentation. In: Proceedings of the IEEE Conference on Computer Vision and Pattern Recognition, pp. 2126–2135 (2017)
6. Samson, L., van Noord, N., Booij, O., Hofmann, M., Gavves, E., Ghafoorian, M.: I bet you are wrong: gambling adversarial networks for structured semantic segmentation. In: Proceedings of the IEEE International Conference on Computer Vision Workshops (2019)
7. Nie, D., Wang, L., Xiang, L., Zhou, S., Adeli, E., Shen, D.: Difficulty-aware attention network with confidence learning for medical image segmentation. In: Proceedings of the AAAI Conference on Artificial Intelligence, vol. 33, pp. 1085–1092 (2019)
8. Nie, D., Shen, D.: Adversarial confidence learning for medical image segmentation and synthesis. Int. J. Comput. Vis. 1–20 (2020)
9. Mehrtash, A., Wells III, W.M., Tempany, C.M., Abolmaesumi, P., Kapur, T.: Confidence calibration and predictive uncertainty estimation for deep medical image segmentation. arXiv preprint arXiv:1911.13273 (2019)
10. Ghafoorian, M., et al.: Student beats the teacher: deep neural networks for lateral ventricles segmentation in brain MR. In: Medical Imaging 2018: Image Processing, vol. 10574, p. 105742U. International Society for Optics and Photonics (2018)
11. Wang, P., Chung, A.C.S.: Focal dice loss and image dilation for brain tumor segmentation. In: Stoyanov, D., et al. (eds.) DLMIA/ML-CDS -2018. LNCS, vol. 11045, pp. 119–127. Springer, Cham (2018). https://doi.org/10.1007/978-3-030-00889-5_14

12. Abulnaga, S.M., Rubin, J.: Ischemic stroke lesion segmentation in CT perfusion scans using pyramid pooling and focal loss. In: Crimi, A., Bakas, S., Kuijf, H., Keyvan, F., Reyes, M., van Walsum, T. (eds.) BrainLes 2018. LNCS, vol. 11383, pp. 352–363. Springer, Cham (2019). https://doi.org/10.1007/978-3-030-11723-8_36
13. Ren, M., Zeng, W., Yang, B., Urtasun, R.: Learning to reweight examples for robust deep learning. arXiv preprint arXiv:1803.09050 (2018)
14. Kamnitsas, K., et al.: Efficient multi-scale 3D CNN with fully connected CRF for accurate brain lesion segmentation. Med. Image Anal. **36**, 61–78 (2017)
15. Luc, P., Couprie, C., Chintala, S., Verbeek, J.: Semantic segmentation using adversarial networks. In: NIPS Workshop on Adversarial Training (2016)
16. Xue, Y., Xu, T., Zhang, H., Long, L.R., Huang, X.: SegAN: adversarial network with multi-scale L_1 loss for medical image segmentation. Neuroinformatics **16**(3–4), 383–392 (2018)
17. Isola, P., Zhu, J.-Y., Zhou, T., Efros, A.A.: Image-to-image translation with conditional adversarial networks. In: Proceedings of the IEEE Conference on Computer Vision and Pattern Recognition, pp. 1125–1134 (2017)
18. Rezaei, M., et al.: A conditional adversarial network for semantic segmentation of brain tumor. In: Crimi, A., Bakas, S., Kuijf, H., Menze, B., Reyes, M. (eds.) BrainLes 2017. LNCS, vol. 10670, pp. 241–252. Springer, Cham (2018). https://doi.org/10.1007/978-3-319-75238-9_21
19. Zanjani, F.G., et al.: Deep learning approach to semantic segmentation in 3D point cloud intra-oral scans of teeth. In: International Conference on Medical Imaging with Deep Learning, pp. 557–571 (2019)
20. Moeskops, P., Veta, M., Lafarge, M.W., Eppenhof, K.A.J., Pluim, J.P.W.: Adversarial training and dilated convolutions for brain MRI segmentation. In: Cardoso, M.J., et al. (eds.) DLMIA/ML-CDS -2017. LNCS, vol. 10553, pp. 56–64. Springer, Cham (2017). https://doi.org/10.1007/978-3-319-67558-9_7
21. Ghafoorian, M., Nugteren, C., Baka, N., Booij, O., Hofmann, M.: EL-GAN: embedding loss driven generative adversarial networks for lane detection. In: Leal-Taixé, L., Roth, S. (eds.) ECCV 2018. LNCS, vol. 11129, pp. 256–272. Springer, Cham (2019). https://doi.org/10.1007/978-3-030-11009-3_15
22. Ronneberger, O., Fischer, P., Brox, T.: U-Net: convolutional networks for biomedical image segmentation. In: Navab, N., Hornegger, J., Wells, W.M., Frangi, A.F. (eds.) MICCAI 2015. LNCS, vol. 9351, pp. 234–241. Springer, Cham (2015). https://doi.org/10.1007/978-3-319-24574-4_28
23. Zhao, H., Shi, J., Qi, X., Wang, X., Jia, J.: Pyramid scene parsing network. In: Proceedings of the IEEE Conference on Computer Vision and Pattern Recognition, pp. 2881–2890 (2017)
24. He, K., Zhang, X., Ren, S., Sun, J.: Deep residual learning for image recognition. In: Proceedings of the IEEE Conference on Computer Vision and Pattern Recognition, pp. 770–778 (2016)
25. Chen, L.-C., Zhu, Y., Papandreou, G., Schroff, F., Adam, H.: Encoder-decoder with atrous separable convolution for semantic image segmentation. In: Proceedings of the European Conference on Computer Vision (ECCV), pp. 801–818 (2018)
26. Chollet, F.: Xception: deep learning with depthwise separable convolutions. In: Proceedings of the IEEE Conference on Computer Vision and Pattern Recognition, pp. 1251–1258 (2017)
27. Zhou, J., et al.: Thyroid nodule segmentation and classification in ultrasound images, March 2020
28. Csurka, G., Larlus, D., Perronnin, F., Meylan, F.: What is a good evaluation measure for semantic segmentation?. In: BMVC, vol. 27, p. 2013 (2013)

Mammographic Image Conversion Between Source and Target Acquisition Systems Using cGAN

Zahra Ghanian(✉) ⓘ, Andreu Badal ⓘ, Kenny Cha ⓘ, Mohammad Mehdi Farhangi ⓘ,
Nicholas Petrick ⓘ, and Berkman Sahiner ⓘ

U.S. Food and Drug Administration, Center for Devices and Radiological Health,
Division of Imaging, Diagnostics and Software Reliability, Silver Spring, MD, USA
Zahra.Ghanian@fda.hhs.gov

Abstract. Our work aims at developing a machine learning-based image conversion algorithm to adjust quantum noise, sharpness, scattering, and other characteristics of radiographic images acquired with a given imaging system as if they had been acquired with a different acquisition system. Purely physics-based methods which have previously been developed for image conversion rely on the measurement of the physical properties of the acquisition devices, which limit the range of their applicability. In this study, we focused on the conversion of mammographic images from a source acquisition system into a target system using a conditional Generative Adversarial Network (cGAN). This network penalizes any possible structural differences between network-generated and target images. The optimization process was enhanced by designing new reconstruction loss terms which emphasized the quality of high frequency image contents. We trained our cGAN model on a dataset of paired synthetic mammograms and slanted edge phantom images. We coupled one independent slanted edge phantom image with each anthropomorphic breast image and presented the pair as a combined input into the network. To improve network performance at high frequencies, we incorporated an edge-based loss function into the reconstruction loss. Qualitative results demonstrated the feasibility of our method to adjust the sharpness of mammograms acquired with a source system to appear as if the they were acquired with a different target system. Our method was validated by comparing the presampled modulation transfer function (MTF) of the network-generated edge image and the MTF of the source and target mammography acquisition systems at different spatial frequencies. This image conversion technique may help training of machine learning algorithms so that their applicability generalizes to a larger set of medical image acquisition devices. Our work may also facilitate performance assessment of computer-aided detection systems.

Keywords: Mammogram · Acquisition system · Neural network · Conditional GAN · Composite loss · Edge learning · Modulation transfer function

Electronic supplementary material The online version of this chapter (https://doi.org/10.1007/978-3-030-59861-7_53) contains supplementary material, which is available to authorized users.

M. Liu et al. (Eds.): MLMI 2020, LNCS 12436, pp. 523–531, 2020.
https://doi.org/10.1007/978-3-030-59861-7_53

1 Introduction

Generative adversarial networks (GANs) have recently shown great promise in generating realistic images. Originally, GANs were used to generate images from random inputs [1–3]. Later developments incorporated guidance conditioned on auxiliary information such as class labels or data from other modalities. These models are known as conditional GANs (cGANs) [4] and are applied for various applications of image-to-image translation such as semantic maps to real images, sketch of image edge pixels to full images, and grayscale to color images [5].

Our work aims at using the cGAN framework to simulate image acquisition with different mammography devices and provide an image conversion methodology that incorporates commonly-used concepts in the medical physics field, such as image sharpness and noise properties. Such an image conversion algorithm would have a range of uses in the development of machine learning-based algorithms, including data augmentation techniques that increase the number of annotated images representing image properties from different image acquisition devices. In addition, our proposed technique may be useful for computer-aided detection and diagnosis (CAD) device evaluation. Mammographic CAD devices are typically first developed and assessed for a specific "original" acquisition system. When developers are ready to apply their CAD device to a new mammographic acquisition system, they typically assess the device with images acquired using the new system. Collecting large repositories of clinical images containing verified lesion locations acquired by a new system is costly and time consuming. Converting mammographic images acquired by the original mammographic acquisition system into images that appear as if they were acquired by the new system (e.g., in terms of sharpness, noise and scatter properties) will facilitate CAD device performance assessment [6]. Moreover, the generated dataset may be helpful to improve the training of CAD devices. Therefore, our technique may be useful for reducing the clinical data burden in the training and assessment of a CAD device for use with a new image acquisition system.

Training of a cGAN requires a sufficient number of paired training examples. Using real patient data to obtain such a paired dataset is unethical because it would expose patients to double dose of radiation. Moreover, two different compressions of the breast will change the projected anatomy and prevent the acquisition of a paired dataset. The limited number of available breast phantom configurations makes it difficult to obtain a large dataset of independent phantom images for training. Due to these reasons, we focused on generating synthetic mammograms in this initial step. We used procedurally-generated images using biology inspired object models, and physics-based image acquisition simulation by two mammography systems. A method for simulating the image acquisition with a Siemens Mammomat Inspiration has previously been developed [7]. In this study, we first developed a method for the simulation of image acquisition by a Hologic Lorad Selenia that incorporates an amorphous selenium detector and a HTC (High Transmission Cellular) anti-scatter grid. Paired datasets of the simulated mammograms were generated using these two simulated mammography systems and utilized for training, validation and testing of the cGAN.

The main contributions of this study are summarized as follows:

– A novel machine learning-based method was developed for generation of images, which preserves the anatomical content of the source image but physical characteristics of the target image acquisition system. This method proposes to:

• incorporate slanted edge images to the training dataset and improve the edge learning process of the network by appropriately combining breast and edge images in training
• add an edge-based loss function term, which helps to optimize the MTF of the model, match with the MTF of the target system, and adapt the network with the structural details of the breast images
• extend the loss function from a simple adversarial loss to a composite loss that includes adversarial, reconstruction, and high-frequency error norm normalized (*HFENN*) loss terms, to emphasize the reconstruction of the fine details

– Synthetic images were generated using state-of-the-art simulation to model a commercial x-ray image acquisition system that incorporated an amorphous selenium detector and a HTC (High Transmission Cellular) 2D anti-scatter grid. The use of simulated radiographic images was essential to create pairs of images that display the exact same anatomy acquired by competing acquisition systems.

2 Materials and Methods

2.1 Synthetic Images

Synthetic mammogram images were generated using methods described by Badano et al. [7]. The methods are briefly described in the following. First, virtual 3D anthropomorphic phantoms were produced using a procedural analytic model in which major anatomical structures (fat and glandular tissues, ductal tree, vasculature, and ligaments) are randomly generated within a predefined breast volume. The anthropomorphic phantoms were generated across the four BI-RADS breast density categories (dense, heterogeneous, scattered, and fatty). A Monte Carlo-based x-ray transport simulation code, MC-GPU [7, 8], was used to project the 3D phantoms, voxelized at 50 μm resolution, into realistic-looking synthetic mammograms. The Monte Carlo algorithm correctly models the x-ray scatter, quantum noise and the image formation process in the detector. Two full-field digital mammography (FFDM) acquisition systems were modeled (Source System and Target System in Fig. 1). These digital breast imaging systems both have an amorphous-selenium direct conversion detector but differ in pixel size and anti-scatter grid. Source system has a detector with pixel size of 70 μm and a 2D, focused anti-scatter grid with 30 μm copper septa, 4:1 ratio, and 23 line pairs/mm. Target system has a detector with pixel size of 85 μm and a 1D, focused anti-scatter grid with 65 μm lead septa, 5:1 ratio, and 31 line pairs/mm. Source system has a 30 μm rhodium and 30 μm molybdenum x ray filter, and source to detector distance of 66 cm. Target system has a 50 μm rhodium filter, and source to detector distance of 65 cm. Therefore, the x-ray energy spectra emitted from the two systems and the image magnification are different. Additional information regarding the generation of the synthetic mammogram images can be found in literature [7]. The code for generating the synthetic mammograms and the computational breast phantom are publicly available (https://github.com/DIDSR/VICTRE). A total of 700 paired synthetic mammogram images were generated and used for network training.

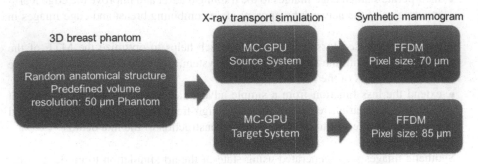

Fig. 1. Workflow for generating paired synthetic mammograms

A validation set of 100 synthetic images, and a test set of 200 synthetic mammogram images were also generated. Paired simulated mammograms share the same breast/edge structures but differ in image size, pixel size, resolution, noise, and scattering. In addition to synthetic mammograms generated starting from our virtual 3D anthropomorphic phantoms, we also generated images of a slanted edge steel plate. These two image types were simulated with different conditions that conform to the International Electrotechnical Commission (IEC) standard. A two millimeters thick aluminum filter was simulated in front of the x-ray collimator when the slanted edge images were acquired. Our dataset included 700, 100 and 200 slanted edge images for training, validation, and testing. Both image types (anthropomorphic and slanted edge) were simulated in the presence of the anti-scatter grid, and the system settings between the two image types were consistent. After paired mammograms were generated and registered, they were cropped to patches of size 256 × 256 with 30% overlap.

2.2 Conditional GAN

In an unconditional generative model, there is no control on modes of the data being generated. In a cGAN, however, the generator learns to generate a fake sample with specific conditions or characteristics. In the image conversion application, we conditioned the output of the network on the input image and hence cGAN forces the output image to be loyal to the input image in terms of the subtle anatomical details and hence preserves the diagnostic features of the breast. The condition was imposed on both the generator and discriminator inputs. An overview of our method is presented in Fig. 2. In our design and assessment, we included anthropomorphic breast images and edge images in training, validation and test sets. Within each mini-batch, a training sample includes two pairs of two images, (x, S_x) and (y, S_y), one anthropomorphic breast image and one corresponding edge image both of which were generated with one of the two simulated image acquisition systems and with consistent settings. During back propagation the weights were updated after both the anthropomorphic breast image and the corresponding edge image were passed separately through the system. Our proposed architecture builds off of Isola et al.'s work [5]. Details of the architecture is provided in supplementary material. Our cGAN formulation and training strategy, however, are explained in the following section.

2.3 cGAN Formulation and Training

Our goal is to generate synthetic mammograms of different pixel size, resolution, noise, and scattering to appear as if they had been acquired with a different x-ray system (target system). For this purpose, the cGAN was conditioned on the source images x, and S_x, which are ROIs cropped from a mammogram and a slanted edge image generated with the source system. While it is possible to also condition on a random vector z, using dropout instead to inject randomness into the generator [5] has shown better performance [9]. The adversarial loss for cGANs is then formulated as:

$$L_{cGAN}(G, D) = E_{x,y}\big[\log D(x, y)\big] + E_x\big[\log(1 - D(x, G(x)))\big], \tag{1}$$

where y is the original ROI acquired with the target system (ground-truth) and G tries to minimize the loss function above against an adversarial discriminator, D, that tries to maximize it. Similar to other studies [5, 10], we observed that an additional reconstruction loss term in the form of $E_{x,y}\big[\|y - G(x)\|_2\big]$ is beneficial, as it helps to learn the latent representation from ground-truth image context to regenerate the same structure. Moreover, adding this reconstruction loss helps to stabilize training and speed convergence. However, this type of reconstruction loss tends to produce blurred results because it averages multiple modes in the data distribution [5, 9]. Therefore, we combined the reconstruction and adversarial loss with a "High-Frequency Error Norm Normalized" (*HFENN*) loss, making the former responsible for capturing the overall structure of the ground-truth image and source image while the latter learns to emphasize the reconstruction of high-frequency details.

Let $S_{G(x)}$ be the generated edge image and S_y be the edge image patch acquired with the target system. Then, the composite L_2 loss for our network is defined as:

$$L_{L2}(G) = E_{x,y}\big[\|y - G(x)\|_2\big] + \alpha * E_{x,y}[HFENN] + \beta * E_{x,y}\big[\|S_y - S_{G(x)}\|_2\big], \tag{2}$$

where α and $\beta \geq 1$ are weight factors, and *HFENN* is defined as:

$$HFENN = \|LoG(y - G(x))\|_2, \quad LoG = \text{Laplacian of Gaussian}, \tag{3}$$

In the formulation of composite L_2 loss, the first term is calculated over all (anthropomorphic and edge) image patches, while the last term corresponds to only edge patches and it is equal to pixel-wise mean squared error between the cGAN-generated and the target edge patches. By adding this specific composite L_2 loss, final loss is:

$$G^* = arg\ min_G\ max_D\ L_{cGAN}(G, D) + \lambda * L_{L2}(G). \tag{4}$$

For each batch of training, one mammographic breast patch and one edge patch are presented separately into our network and the corresponding terms of the L_2 loss

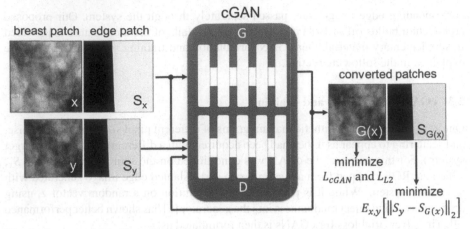

Fig. 2. Same model (with anti-scatter grid) was used to convert the edge and breast images. In conversion from source system to target system, the generator was conditioned on images x and S_x and generated a converted version of the anthropomorphic breast image, $G(x) = y'$, and a converted version of the edge image, $S_{G(x)} = S'_y$.

are calculated. In this way, only after passing one breast patch and one edge patch, the final G^* loss (Eq. 4) is calculated and then the network weights are updated through the back-propagation pathway. We empirically found that α, $\beta = 10$, and $\lambda = 100$ work well in our experiments. Hyperparameter λ was examined between the two extremes [0 ∞]. Using loss from cGAN alone (setting $\lambda = 0$ in Eq. 4) introduces visual artifacts and adding reconstruction loss with $\lambda = 100$ reduces these artifacts. $\lambda = \infty$ (setting discriminator loss weight to zero in adversarial loss and considering only reconstruction loss) resulted in poorer validation (tuning) results compared to $\lambda = 100$ and revealed the positive contribution of the discriminator in learning process and MTF matching. α, and β were examined using the validation (tuning) set in the range of 2 to 100 and were determined empirically to achieve a balance in the reconstruction of the low and high frequency contents. $\beta = 10$ helped with the fine matching of the MTF at middle and high frequencies. We used Adam optimizer [11] to train both the generator and discriminator with a learning rate of 0.0002 and momentum parameter of 0.5.

3   Results and Discussion

To characterize the spatial resolution of the generated images, we used the modulation transfer function (MTF) as a metric. MTF is measured from the slanted edge images using the methodology described in Saunders et al. [12]. Presampled MTF of the cGAN-generated edge image and MTF of the source and target systems were displayed in Fig. 3. This figure illustrates the importance of including the slanted edge images as part of the training data. Figure 3a shows what happens when the slanted edge images are excluded from training. The neural network has difficulty to learn the edge profiles and hence the MTF measured from the network-generated edge images (shown in green) is not close to the MTF of the target system (shown in red in Fig. 3a). However, including the slanted edge images in the training and minimizing the corresponding loss function of the edge images (third term in Eq. 2) in the course of training progressively improves cGAN performance (Fig. 3b). This mix-training method helps the network learn the edges and more accurately reconstruct not only the edge images but also the anthropomorphic breast images (specifically patches at the boundary of the breast). As a result, the MTF of the cGAN model improves and provides a better match with the MTF of the target system (Fig. 3b). This figure also illustrates that $MTF_y - MTF_{G(x)}$ increases at higher frequencies. This issue might be addressed by considering the third term of the L_2 loss as weighted sum of $\left\| S_y - S_{G(x)} \right\|_2$ with a larger weight for higher frequencies. Therefore, the maximum weight is assigned to the slanted edge pixels of the edge patch.

Using the same model and hyperparameter set, structural similarity index (SSIM) for the test set was measured between the target and generated breast patches, when edge patches were present and absent in the training dataset. The result shows a statistically significant improvement of 0.17 in SSIM of the generated and target breast patches when edge patches were added to the training dataset and supports our claim that adding edge images helps the network learn high frequency details.

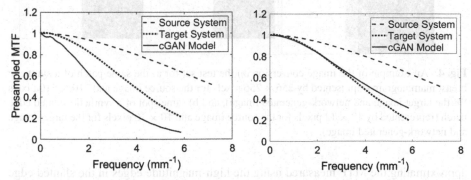

Fig. 3. An example of the MTF of two mammographic systems and MTF of the cGAN while the training dataset includes mammograms of a) only anthropomorphic breast phantoms, b) both anthropomorphic breast phantoms and slanted edge phantoms

Figure 4a shows the anthropomorphic breast patches generated with source system, target system, and cGAN, respectively. At the bottom panel, Fig. 4b, a small area of the corresponding edge images is presented for each aforementioned category. Comparing the cGAN-generated breast image with the target breast patch illustrates that the cGAN has learned the structures and details of the anthropomorphic breast. The SSIM measured between the target and cGAN-generated breast image patches and averaged over all test patches was 0.89 ± 0.23. However, the high-frequency noise is smoothed, giving the generated image a slightly different appearance than the target image. Figure 4b confirms that network thrives in generating an edge similar to the target edge (gray pixels in the middle of the right panel are similar to those of middle panel). However, as it can be observed by comparing the pixels in the lighter regions of the right and middle panels, the network has not adequately modeled the noise in the target image. Combined with our results for the MTF, this observation indicates that the current network succeeds in

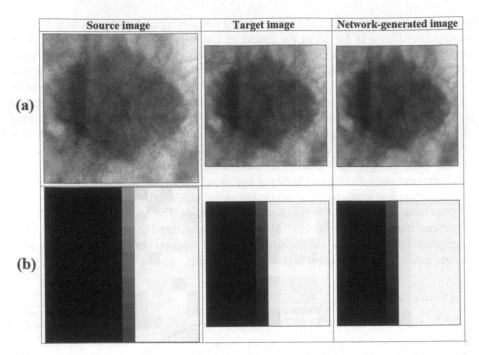

Fig. 4. An example of the image conversion on the test set for a) the same patch of a synthetic breast mammogram (represented by 256 × 256 pixels for the source image and 210 × 210 pixels for the target image and network-generated image), and b) same spot of a synthetic slanted edge patch (represented by 12 × 12 pixels for the source image and 10 × 10 pixels for the target image and network-generated image).

approximating the MTF measured using the high-magnitude edges in the slanted edge phantom. However, without controlling noise during the training, it tends to smooth smaller magnitude and high frequency noise components.

4   Conclusion

A GAN-based image conversion method was developed to allow a mammogram from a source imaging system to appear with similar spatial resolution properties as that from a target imaging system. The cGAN was simultaneously trained with edge images as well as anthropomorphic breast images to progressively improve the reconstruction of both types of the images. To emphasize the reconstruction of the high frequency details, high frequency error norm was defined as part of the loss function. Moreover, L_2 loss of the edge image was added to the total loss to improve edge learning. To validate the method, the presampled MTF measured from the cGAN generated edge image was compared with the MTF of the source and target mammography acquisition systems up to Nyquist frequency of the target system. The results suggest that with the proposed conversion technique, we were able to simulate the MTF of the target system and hence the sharpness of the target mammogram.

Although our experimental results focused on image resolution, matching the MTF is not the only consideration in our image conversion technique. Our overall goal is to match all appropriate characteristics of the two image acquisition systems, including spatial resolution, scattering and noise that may result from differences in detector and grid types, and other acquisition properties. Our future work includes incorporating representative examples of noise (flat filed images) into training dataset and utilizing a term to characterize the noise power spectrum in the composite L_2 loss function to improve noise characteristics of our image conversion technique. The results of this work show that it may be possible to convert images of the same modality from one system to another using a GAN-based method. This study may lead to increased number of images for development and validation of machine learning-based algorithms and also may facilitate evaluation of devices that uses mammography images.

Acknowledgment. This work was supported in part through an Office of Women's Health grant from the U.S. Food and Drug Administration.

References

1. Denton, E., Chintala, S., Fergus, R.: Deep generative image models using a Laplacian pyramid of adversarial networks. In: Advances in Neural Information Processing Systems, pp. 1486–1494 (2015)
2. Radford, A., Metz, L., Chintala, S.: Unsupervised representation learning with deep convolutional generative adversarial networks. arXiv preprint arXiv:1511.06434 (2015)
3. Ledig, C., et al.: Photo-realistic single image superresolution using a generative adversarial network. arXiv preprint (2016)
4. Mirza, M., Osindero, S.: Conditional generative adversarial nets. arXiv preprint arXiv:1411.1784 (2014)
5. Isola, P., Zhu, J., Zhou, T., Efros, A.: Image-to-image translation with conditional adversarial networks. In: The IEEE Conference on Computer Vision and Pattern Recognition (CVPR), pp. 1125–1134 (2017)
6. Ghanian, Z., Pezeshk, A., Petrick, N., Sahiner, B.: Computational insertion of microcalcification clusters on mammograms: reader differentiation from native clusters and computer-aided detection comparison. J. Med. Imaging **5**(4), 044502 (2018)
7. Badano, A., Graff, C.G., Badal, A.: Evaluation of digital breast tomosynthesis as replacement of fullfield digital mammography using an in-silico imaging trial. JAMA Netw. Open **1**(7), e185474 (2018)
8. Badal, A., Badano, A.: Accelerating Monte Carlo simulations of photon transport in a voxelized geometry using a massively parallel graphics processing unit. Med. Phys. **36**, 4878–4880 (2009)
9. Jin, D., Xu, Z., Tang, Y., Harrison, A.P., Mollura, D.J.: CT-Realistic lung nodule simulation from 3d conditional generative adversarial networks for robust lung segmentation. In: Frangi, A., Schnabel, J., Davatzikos, C., Alberola-López, C., Fichtinger, G. (eds.) Medical Image Computing and Computer Assisted Intervention – MICCAI 2018. LNCS, vol. 11071, pp 732–740. Springer, Cham.https://doi.org/10.1007/978-3-030-00934-2_81
10. Pathak, D., Krahenbuhl, P., Donahue, J.: Context encoders: feature learning by inpainting. In: Proceedings of the IEEE CVPR, pp. 2536–2544 (2016)
11. Kingma, D.P., Ba, J.: Adam: a method for stochastic optimization. arXiv preprint arXiv:1412.6980 (2014)
12. Saunders, R., Samei, E.: A method for modifying the image quality parameters of digital radiographic images. Med. Phys. **30**, 3006–3017 (2003)

An End-to-End Learnable Flow Regularized Model for Brain Tumor Segmentation

Yan Shen, Zhanghexuan Ji, and Mingchen Gao[✉]

Department of Computer Science and Engineering, University at Buffalo,
The State University of New York, Buffalo, USA
mgao8@buffalo.edu

Abstract. Many segmentation tasks for biomedical images can be modeled as the minimization of an energy function and solved by a class of max-flow and min-cut optimization algorithms. However, the segmentation accuracy is sensitive to the contrasting of semantic features of different segmenting objects, as the traditional energy function usually uses hand-crafted features in their energy functions. To address these limitations, we propose to incorporate end-to-end trainable neural network features into the energy functions. Our deep neural network features are extracted from the down-sampling and up-sampling layers with skip-connections of a U-net. In the inference stage, the learned features are fed into the energy functions. And the segmentations are solved in a primal-dual form by ADMM solvers. In the training stage, we train our neural networks by optimizing the energy function in the primal form with regularizations on the min-cut and flow-conservation functions, which are derived from the optimal conditions in the dual form. We evaluate our methods, both qualitatively and quantitatively, in a brain tumor segmentation task. As the energy minimization model achieves a balance on sensitivity and smooth boundaries, we would show how our segmentation contours evolve actively through iterations as ensemble references for doctor diagnosis.

1 Introduction

Brain Tumors are fatal diseases affecting more than 25,000 new patients every year in the US. Most brain tumors are not diagnosed until symptoms appear, which would significantly reduce the expected life span of patients. Having early diagnosis and access to proper treatments is a vital factor to increase the survival rate of patients. MRI image has been very useful in differentiating sub-regions of the brain tumor. Computer-aided automatic segmentation distinguishing those sub-regions would be a substantial tool to help diagnosis.

Among these automatic medical imaging algorithms, the advent of deep learning is a milestone. These multi-layer neural networks have been widely deployed on brain tumor segmentation systems. Chen *et al.* [3] uses a densely connected 3D-CNN to segment brain tumor hierarchically. Karimaghaloo *et al.* [10]

M. Liu et al. (Eds.): MLMI 2020, LNCS 12436, pp. 532–541, 2020.
https://doi.org/10.1007/978-3-030-59861-7_54

proposes an adaptive CRF following the network output to further produce a smooth segmentation. Qin *et al.* [15] and Dey *et al.* [5] use attention model as modulations on network model. Zhou *et al.* [18] uses transfer learning from different tasks. Spizer *et al.* [16] and Ganaye *et al.* [6] use spatial correspondence among images for segmentation. Le *et al.* [12] proposes a level-set layer as a recurrent neural network to iteratively minimize segmentation energy functions. These methods combine the benefit of low inductive bias of deep neural network with smooth segmentation boundaries.

One fundamental difficulty with distinguishing tumor segmentation is that their boundaries have large variations. For some extreme conditions, even experienced doctors have to vote for agreements for a final decision. Under those circumstances, a unique deterministic output of segmentation result is insufficient. Active contour models (ACMs), which is firstly proposed by Kass *et al.* [11], are widely applied in biomedical image segmentation before the era of deep learning. ACMs treat segmentation as an energy minimization problem. They are able to handle various topology changes naturally by providing multiple optimal solutions as a level set with different thresholds. In the past two decades, quite a number of variations of ACMs have been proposed, such as active contour without edge [2], with balloon term [4]. Yuan *et al.* [17] proposes a flow based track for deriving active segmentation boundaries. The evolving boundaries provide a coarse to fine separation boundary from the background.

In this paper, we present a trainable deep network based active contour method. Deep neural network has tremendous advantages in providing global statistics at semantic level. However, deep features do not preserve the boundary geometry, such as topology and shapes. In our model, we explicitly use the active contour to model the boundary and optimize its flow information. Different from traditional active contour methods, the energy function takes neural network trained features. The energy minimization problems are reformulated as a max-flow/min-cut problem by introducing an auxiliary dual variable indicating the flow transportation. We link the optimal segmentation conditions with the saturated flow edges with minimal capacities. By utilizing this property, we design a trainable objective function with extra flow regularization terms on these saturated edges. Our work combines the benefit of deep neural network and active contour models.

Our contributions can be summarized as follows: (1) We present a trainable flow regularized loss combined with neural network architecture, leveraging the benefits of feature learning from neural networks and the advantages of regularizing geometry from active contour models. (2) Our results achieve comparable results with state-of-the-art, and more importantly, show that they are flexible to be adjusted to meet the ambiguity nature of biomedical image segmentation.

2   Methods

2.1   Image Segmentation as Energy Minimization Problem

Chan *et al.* [1] considered image segmentation with minimizing the following energy functions

$$\min_{\lambda(x)\in\{0,1\}} \int_\Omega (1-\lambda(x))C_s(x)dx + \int_\Omega \lambda(x)C_t(x)dx + \int_\Omega C_g(x)|\nabla\lambda(x)|dx \quad (1)$$

where $C_s(x)$ is foreground pixels, $C_t(x)$ is background pixels and $C_g(x)$ is edge pixels. As a naive treatment, $C_s(x)$ and $C_t(x)$ could use a simple thresholding of original image, $C_g(x)$ could use a filtered version of original image by Sobel edge detectors.

Relation to Level Set. Chan *et al.* [1] constructs a relationship between the global optimum of the binary relaxed problem of $\lambda(x) \in [0,1]$ with the original binary problem (1). Specifically, let $\lambda^*(x)$ be a global optimum of (1), its thresholding $\lambda^l(x)$ defined as

$$\lambda^l(x) = \begin{cases} 0 & \text{when} \lambda^*(x) > l \\ 1 & \text{when} \lambda^*(x) \leq l \end{cases} \quad (2)$$

is a global solution for (1) with any $l \in [0,1]$. The function $\lambda^l(x)$ indicates the level set S^l.

2.2   Reformulation as Max-Flow/Min-Cut Problem

The above energy minimization model for image segmentation could be transformed as the well-known max-flow/min-cut [7] problems

$$\max_{p_s,p_t,\mathbf{P}} \min_{\lambda(x)\in\{0,1\}} \int_\Omega p_s(x)dx + \int_\Omega \lambda(x)(divp(x) - p_s(x) + p_t(x))dx$$
$$\text{s.t} \quad p_s(x) \leq C_s(x), p_t(x) \leq C_t(x), |p| \leq C_g(x) \quad (3)$$

where p_s, p_t and $divp$ are inflow, outflow and edgeflow capacity with constraints up to the term C_s, C_t and C_g in energy minimization functions. The correlations with flow model are shown in Fig. 1. We give a ADMM [13] solution in Algorithm 1.

Algorithm 1: ADMM Algorithm for Segmentation Inference

Input: $C_s(x), C_t(x), C_g(x), N_t$

Output: $p_s^*(x), p_t^*(x), p, \lambda^*(x)$

1 Initialize $p_s^1(x), p_t^1(x), p^1, \lambda^1(x)$

2 **for** $i = 1: N_t$ **do**

3 $\quad$ Optimizing p by fixing other variables

$\quad\quad p^{i+1} =: \arg\max_{|p| \leq C_g(x)} -\frac{c}{2}|divp - p_s + p_t|^2 + \int_\Omega \lambda divp dx$

4 $\quad\quad p^{i+1} =: \text{Proj } [p^i + \alpha\nabla(divp - p_s + p_t)]_{|p^{i+1}(x)| \leq C_g(x)}$

5 $\quad$ Optimizing p_s by fixing other variables

$\quad\quad p_s^{i+1} =: \arg\max_{p_s \leq C_s(x)} -\frac{c}{2}|divpp - p_s + p_t|^2 + \int_\Omega (1-\lambda)p_s dx$

6 $\quad\quad p_s^{i+1} = \text{Proj } [p_s^i + \alpha(divp + p_t - -p_s - (\lambda - 1)/c)]_{p^{i+1}(s) \leq C_s(x)}$

7 $\quad$ Optimizing p_t by fixing other variables

$\quad\quad p_t^{i+1} =: \arg\max_{p_t \leq C_t(x)} -\frac{c}{2}|divpp - p_s + p_t|^2 + \int_\Omega \lambda p_t dx$

8 $\quad\quad p_t^{i+1} = \text{Proj } [p_t^i + \alpha(-divp - p_t + p_s + \lambda/c)]_{p^{i+1}(s) \leq C_s(x)}$

9 $\quad$ Optimizing λ by fixing other variables

$\quad\quad \lambda^{i+1} =: \arg\min_\lambda \int_\Omega \lambda(divp - p_s + p_t)dx$

10 $\quad\quad \lambda^{i+1} =: \lambda^i - \alpha(divp - p_s + p_t)$

11 $p_s^* := p_s^{N_t+1}, p_t^* := p_t^{N_t+1}, p^* := p^{N_t+1}, \lambda^* := \lambda^{N_t+1}$

2.3 Optimal Conditions for Max-flow/min-cut Model

The optimal condition for max-flow/min-cut model could be given by

$$\lambda^*(x) = 0 \implies p_s^*(x) = C_s(x) \tag{4}$$

$$\lambda^*(x) = 1 \implies p_t^*(x) = C_t(x) \tag{5}$$

$$|\nabla\lambda^*(x)| \neq 0 \implies |p| = C_g(x) \tag{6}$$

As it is shown in Fig. 1, an intuitive explanation for the optimal condition is that the incoming flow saturates at the optimal segmentation masks of background, the outgoing flow saturates at the optimal segmentation masks of foreground and the spatial flow saturates at the segmentation boundaries.

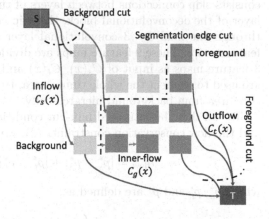

Fig. 1. The max-flow/min-cut model for segmentation.

2.4 Proposed Flow Regularized Training Losses

In our proposed methods, $C_s(x)$, $C_t(x)$ and $C_g(x)$ are taken from

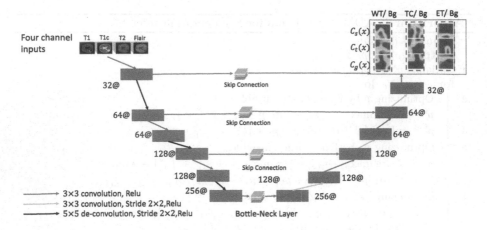

Fig. 2. Our U-Net takes all four modalities MRI input and produces 9 feature maps output into 3 groups of $C_s(x)$, $C_t(x)$ and $C_g(x)$.

neural network output features rather than handcrafted features in traditional methods. Specifically, our $C_s(x)$, $C_t(x)$ and $C_g(x)$ come from the parameterized outputs of a deep U-Net as shown in Fig. 2.

Our U-Net takes the standardized input of four-modalities (T1, T2, Flair and T1c) MRI images. Then it passes through three down-sampling blocks. Each down-sampling block consists of a cascade of a 3×3 convolutional layer of stride 2 and another 3×3 convolutional layer of stride 1 to reduce the size of feature map by half. The number of feature maps downward are 32, 64, 64, 128, 128 and 256. Following the bottle-neck layers, our U-Net takes three up-sampling blocks. Each up-sampling block consists of a cascade of a 5×5 deconvolutional layer of stride 2 and another 3×3 convolutional layer of stride 1 to increase the size of feature map one time. Besides the feed-forward connections, our U-Net also consists skip connections between layers of the same horizon. Following the last layer of the deconvolutional block, the skip-connected feature maps are passing through the final 3×3 convolutional layer of stride 1 to the final layer of 9 feature maps. These 9 feature maps are divided into 3 groups. Each group takes 3 feature maps as input of $C_s(x)$, $C_t(x)$ and $C_g(x)$. The three different groups are used to segment the whole tumor area, tumor core area and enhanced tumor core area from background hierarchically.

Recall that the saturated min-cut condition at optimal $\lambda^*(x)$ in (4), (5), (6) and the flow conservation constraints (3), we have the followings

$$l_{\text{flow}} = |\hat{p}_s^* - p_s^*| + |\hat{p}_t^* - p_t^*| + |\hat{p}^* - p^*| = 0 \qquad (7)$$

where $\hat{p}_s^*$, $\hat{p}_t^*$ and $\hat{p}^*$ are defined as

$$\hat{p}_s^* = \begin{cases} C_s(x) & \text{if} \quad \lambda^*(x) = 0 \\ p_s^* & \text{if} \quad \lambda^*(x) = 1 \end{cases} \qquad (8)$$

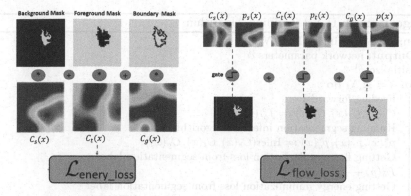

Fig. 3. Our loss term includes two terms of energy loss and flow loss. The energy loss is in the same form as energy minimization function. The flow loss is in the form of primal-duality gaps between flows p_s, p_t and p and segmentation feature maps $C_g(x)$, $C_t(x)$ and $C_s(x)$. We enforce the constraints of optimal condition in the form of background mask on inflow $C_s(x)$ and p_s, foreground mask in outflow $C_t(x)$ and p_t and boundary masks in edgeflow $C_g(x)$ and p.

$$\hat{p}_t^* = \begin{cases} C_t(x) & \text{if} \quad \lambda^*(x) = 1 \\ p_t^* & \text{if} \quad \lambda^*(x) = 0 \end{cases} \tag{9}$$

$$\hat{p}^* = \begin{cases} p^* & \text{if} \quad |\nabla\lambda^*(x)| = 0 \\ p^* C_g(x)/|p^*| & \text{if} \quad |\nabla\lambda^*(x)| \neq 0 \end{cases} \tag{10}$$

The above equation holds as a result of joint optimal conditions of prime and duality. At the optimal points of primal variables λ^* saturated flows at cutting edges equal to its maximum capacity constraints. And at the optimal points of dual variables p_s^*, p_t^* and p^*, the flow conservation function holds. By training on l_{flow}, we close both the primal and duality gaps at the point of ground truth segmentation λ^*. In our training function, we use Huber loss on l_{flow}.

Our whole training loss function consists of an energy minimization term and a flow-regularized term as shown in Fig. 3.

$$L_{\text{train}} = \underbrace{L_\delta(l_{\text{flow}})}_{\text{flow loss}} \underbrace{- \int_\Omega \lambda^*(x)C_s(x)dx + \int_\Omega \lambda^*(x)C_t(x)dx + \int_\Omega C_g(x)|\nabla\lambda^*(x)|dx}_{\text{energy loss}}$$

$$\tag{11}$$

Our U-net is trained end-to-end by Algorithm 2.

Algorithm 2: U-Net Training Algorithm

   Input: $\lambda^*(x)$, Image **I**, α, N_t
   Output: network parameters ϕ
1 Initialize ϕ^1
2 **for** $i = 1:\ N_t$ **do**
3 $\quad$ Feeding forward **I**
4 $\quad$ $C_s(x), C_t(x), C_g(x) := f_{\phi^i}(\mathbf{I})$
5 $\quad$ Running segmentation inference algorithm
6 $\quad$ $p_s^*(x), p_t^*(x), p_g^*(x) := \mathrm{Infer}(C_s(x), C_t(x), C_g(x))$
7 $\quad$ Getting flow regularization loss from segmentation label
8 $\quad$ $L_\delta(\hat{p}_s^* + -\hat{p}_t^* - div\hat{p}^*)$
9 $\quad$ Getting energy minimization loss from segmentation label
10 $\quad$ $\int_\Omega -\lambda^*(x)C_s(x)dx + \int_\Omega \lambda(x)^*C_t(x)dx + \int_\Omega C_g(x)|\nabla\lambda^*(x)|dx$
11 $\quad$ Updating ϕ from loss gradient
12 $\quad$ $\phi^{i+1} := \phi^i - \alpha\nabla(L_{train})$
13 $\phi := \phi^{N_t+1}$

---

3   Experiments

Experiment Settings. We evaluate our proposed methods in BRATS2018 [14] dataset and compare it with other state-of-the-art methods. We randomly split the dataset of 262 glioblastoma scans of 199 lower grade glioma scans into training (80%) and testing (20%). We evaluate our methods following the BRATS challenge suggested evaluation metrics of Dice, Sensitivity (Sens) and Specificity (Spec) and Hausdorff. And we report our segmentation scores in three categories of whole tumor area (WT), tumor core (TC) and enhance tumor core (EC).

Implementation Details. In training phase, we use a weight decay of $1e-6$ convolutional kernels with a drop-out probability of 0.3. We use momentum optimizer of learning rate 0.002. The optimal dual p_s, p_t and p used in our training are instantly run from 15 steps of iterations with a descent rate of $\alpha = 0.16$ and $c = 0.3$. In our quantitative evaluation, we empirically select to use the 15th iteration result $\lambda^{15}(x)$ and thresholds it with $l = 0.5$.

Table 1. Segmentation results in the measurements of Dice score, Sensitivity and Specificity.

	Dice score			Sensitivity			Specificity		
	WT	TC	EC	WT	TC	EC	WT	TC	EC
Deep Medic [8]	0.896	0.754	0.718	0.903	0.73	0.73	N/A	N/A	N/A
DMRes [9]	**0.896**	0.763	0.724	**0.922**	0.754	0.763	N/A	N/A	N/A
DRLS [12]	0.88	0.82	0.73	0.91	0.76	0.78	0.90	0.81	0.71
Proposed	0.89	**0.85**	**0.78**	0.92	**0.79**	**0.78**	**0.93**	**0.83**	**0.75**

Table 2. We report result of our proposed methods with ACM loss in the lower section of our table and comparing it with the result of the baseline without ACM loss the upper section of our table.

	Dice Score			Hausdorff		
w/o ACM	WT	TC	EC	WT	TC	EC
Mean	0.87	0.82	0.74	5.03	9.23	5.58
Std	0.13	0.18	0.26	6.54	11.78	6.27
Medium	0.89	0.87	0.83	4.78	8.59	4.92
25 Quantile	0.86	0.77	0.73	4.23	8.12	4.21
75 Quantile	0.95	0.88	0.85	4.91	8.87	5.24
w/ ACM	WT	TC	EC	WT	TC	EC
Mean	**0.89**	**0.85**	**0.78**	**4.52**	**6.14**	**3.78**
Std	0.12	0.21	0.28	5.92	7.13	4.18
Medium	0.91	0.88	0.77	2.73	3.82	3.13
25 Quantile	0.87	0.83	0.75	1.83	2.93	2.84
75 Quantile	0.93	0.90	0.80	3.18	5.12	3.52

3.1 Quantitative Results

A quantitative evaluation of results obtained from our implementation of proposed methods is shown in Table 1. The experiment results show that our performances are comparable with state-of-the-art results in the categories of all metrics of sensitivity, specificity and dice score. We perform data ablation experiments by substituting our ACM in Eq. 11 with standard cross-entropy loss. The comparison of our proposed methods with the one without ACM loss is shown in Table 2. The trainable active contour model would increase performance on the same U-Net structure.

3.2 Qualitative Results

Figure 4 shows the active contours evolving with different number of iterations and different level set thresholds. The figure shows two examples with one iteration, five iterations, and ten iterations, and with level set thresholds of 0.5 and 0.3, respectively. Increasing the number of iterations tends to have smoothing effects of the boundaries and filtering outlying dots and holes. Changing the level set threshold values would cause a trade-off between specificity and sensitivity. The combination of deep learning models and active contour models provides the flexibility to adjust the results.

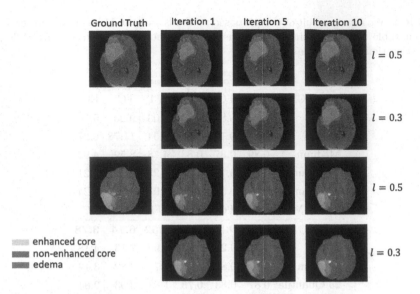

Fig. 4. Segmentation results with various number of iterations and level set thresholds.

4   Conclusion

We propose an active contour model with deep U-Net extracted features. Our model is trainable end-to-end on an energy minimization function with flow-regularized optimal constraints. In the experiments, we show that the performance of our methods is comparable with state-of-the-art. And we also demonstrate how the segmentation evolves with the number of iterations and level set thresholds.

References

1. Chan, T.F., Esedoglu, S., Nikolova, M.: Algorithms for finding global minimizers of image segmentation and denoising models. SIAM J. Appl. Math. **66**(5), 1632–1648 (2006)
2. Chan, T.F., Vese, L.A.: Active contours without edges. IEEE Trans. Image Process. **10**(2), 266–277 (2001)
3. Chen, L., Wu, Y., DSouza, A.M., Abidin, A.Z., Wismüller, A., Xu, C.: MRI tumor segmentation with densely connected 3D CNN. In: Medical Imaging 2018: Image Processing, vol. 10574, p. 105741F. International Society for Optics and Photonics (2018)
4. Cohen, L.D.: On active contour models and balloons. CVGIP Image Underst. **53**(2), 211–218 (1991)
5. Dey, R., Hong, Y.: CompNet: complementary segmentation network for brain MRI extraction. In: Frangi, A.F., Schnabel, J.A., Davatzikos, C., Alberola-López, C., Fichtinger, G. (eds.) MICCAI 2018. LNCS, vol. 11072, pp. 628–636. Springer, Cham (2018). https://doi.org/10.1007/978-3-030-00931-1_72

6. Ganaye, P.-A., Sdika, M., Benoit-Cattin, H.: Semi-supervised learning for segmentation under semantic constraint. In: Frangi, A.F., Schnabel, J.A., Davatzikos, C., Alberola-López, C., Fichtinger, G. (eds.) MICCAI 2018. LNCS, vol. 11072, pp. 595–602. Springer, Cham (2018). https://doi.org/10.1007/978-3-030-00931-1_68

7. Greig, D.M., Porteous, B.T., Seheult, A.H.: Exact maximum a posteriori estimation for binary images. J. Roy. Stat. Soc.: Ser. B (Methodol.) **51**(2), 271–279 (1989)

8. Kamnitsas, K., Chen, L., Ledig, C., Rueckert, D., Glocker, B.: Multi-scale 3D CNNs for segmentation of brain lesions in multi-modal MRI. In: Proceeding of Isles Challenge, MICCAI (2015)

9. Kamnitsas, K., et al.: Efficient multi-scale 3D CNN with fully connected CRF for accurate brain lesion segmentation. Med. Image Anal. **36**, 61–78 (2017)

10. Karimaghaloo, Z., Arnold, D.L., Arbel, T.: Adaptive multi-level conditional random fields for detection and segmentation of small enhanced pathology in medical images. Med. Image Anal. **27**, 17–30 (2016)

11. Kass, M., Witkin, A., Terzopoulos, D.: Snakes: active contour models. Int. J. Comput. Vis. **1**(4), 321–331 (1988)

12. Le, T.H.N., Gummadi, R., Savvides, M.: Deep recurrent level set for segmenting brain tumors. In: Frangi, A.F., Schnabel, J.A., Davatzikos, C., Alberola-López, C., Fichtinger, G. (eds.) MICCAI 2018. LNCS, vol. 11072, pp. 646–653. Springer, Cham (2018). https://doi.org/10.1007/978-3-030-00931-1_74

13. Mangasarian, O.L.: Nonlinear Programming. SIAM (1994)

14. Menze, B.H., et al.: The multimodal brain tumor image segmentation benchmark (BRATS). IEEE Trans. Med. Imaging **34**(10), 1993–2024 (2014)

15. Qin, Y., et al.: Autofocus layer for semantic segmentation. In: Frangi, A.F., Schnabel, J.A., Davatzikos, C., Alberola-López, C., Fichtinger, G. (eds.) MICCAI 2018. LNCS, vol. 11072, pp. 603–611. Springer, Cham (2018). https://doi.org/10.1007/978-3-030-00931-1_69

16. Spitzer, H., Kiwitz, K., Amunts, K., Harmeling, S., Dickscheid, T.: Improving cytoarchitectonic segmentation of human brain areas with self-supervised Siamese networks. In: Frangi, A.F., Schnabel, J.A., Davatzikos, C., Alberola-López, C., Fichtinger, G. (eds.) MICCAI 2018. LNCS, vol. 11072, pp. 663–671. Springer, Cham (2018). https://doi.org/10.1007/978-3-030-00931-1_76

17. Yuan, J., Bae, E., Tai, X.-C.: A study on continuous max-flow and min-cut approaches. In: 2010 IEEE Computer Society Conference on Computer Vision and Pattern Recognition, pp. 2217–2224. IEEE (2010)

18. Zhou, C., Ding, C., Lu, Z., Wang, X., Tao, D.: One-pass multi-task convolutional neural networks for efficient brain tumor segmentation. In: Frangi, A.F., Schnabel, J.A., Davatzikos, C., Alberola-López, C., Fichtinger, G. (eds.) MICCAI 2018. LNCS, vol. 11072, pp. 637–645. Springer, Cham (2018). https://doi.org/10.1007/978-3-030-00931-1_73

Neural Architecture Search
for Microscopy Cell Segmentation

Yanming Zhu[✉] and Erik Meijering

School of Computer Science and Engineering and Graduate School of Biomedical
Engineering, University of New South Wales, Sydney, NSW 2052, Australia
{yanming.zhu,erik.meijering}@unsw.edu.au

Abstract. Live microscopy cell segmentation is a crucial step and challenging task in biological research. In recent years, numerous deep learning based techniques have been proposed to tackle this task and obtained
promising results. However, designing a network with excellent performance is time-consuming and labor-intensive, which limits the progress
of biological research. In this paper, we propose a neural architecture
search (NAS) based solution for cell segmentation in microscopy images.
Different from most of the current NAS-based solutions that search the
network using basic operations, we restrict the search space by exploring sophisticated network blocks. In this way, both expert knowledge and
NAS are considered to facilitate the network searching. We attempt NAS
with two prevailing backbone networks of U-net and Unet++. The experimental results on seven cell tracking challenge (CTC) microscopy cell
data sets demonstrate that the searched networks achieve better performances with much fewer parameters than the baseline method. Thanks
to its simplicity and transportability, the proposed method is applicable
to many deep learning based cell segmentation methods.

Keywords: Microscopy cell segmentation · Neural architecture
search · Auto hyper-parameter tuning · CLSTM-Unet · Unet++

1 Introduction

Cell segmentation has received increasing attention in past years due to its
key importance for further progress in biological research [18,25]. Live cells in
time-lapse microscopy images usually exhibit complex spatial structures and
complicated temporal behavior, which makes their segmentation a challenging
task. Many researchers have made substantial efforts for tackling this task and
achieved promising results [6,14]. Recently, with the huge success of deep learning
in various image processing problems, deep neural networks have been proposed
for microscopy cell segmentation [1,3,24]. Among them, U-net [20] is one of the
most renowned and frequently chosen architecture due to its demonstrated effectiveness and efficiency. After that, various variants and improvements on U-net

© Springer Nature Switzerland AG 2020
M. Liu et al. (Eds.): MLMI 2020, LNCS 12436, pp. 542–551, 2020.
https://doi.org/10.1007/978-3-030-59861-7_55

have been made by researchers for better performance. For example, Drozdzal et al. [8] proposed using both long and short skip connections to benefit the segmentation. Hollandi et al. [10] proposed combining both Mask R-CNN and U-net to predict the segmentation and thus to improve the accuracy. Arbelle et al. [4] proposed an integration of convolutional long short term memory (CLSTM) and U-net to exploit temporal information to support the segmentation decisions. Long et al. [16] proposed an enhanced U-net with a modified encoded branch to work with low-resources computing. Despite their excellent performance, these popular network architectures are currently designed manually by experts, which is a very time-consuming and labor-intensive process. Also, designing such networks requires a large amount of professional knowledge and expert experiences, and thus traps the average researchers without such capability.

To tackle the above issues, neural architecture search (NAS), which can be seen as a subfield of automated machine learning, has emerged in recent years [9,11]. NAS research focuses on three main aspects: search space, search strategy, and performance estimation strategy. The search space defines which architectures can be represented in principle. Generally, it includes the selection of basic operations used to build a network block and the prior backbone architecture used to define the outer network. Most of the recent works [5,17,26] tend to search repeatable block structure while keeping the backbone network fixed, and among them, the NASNet [29] is a representative. The search strategy details how to explore the search space, which mainly includes Bayesian optimization, heuristic algorithm, reinforcement learning, and gradient-based methods. The performance evaluation refers to the process of estimating the performance of the searched architecture and aims to find the optimal architecture that achieves high predictive performance. One major issue of NAS is the resource cost, and thus reducing the consumption on time and memory space while simultaneously maintaining high effectiveness is an important focus in NAS research.

Since NAS was proposed, it has mainly solved natural image tasks. Only a few works have applied NAS to medical imaging tasks due to the diversity and complexity of the medical scenarios. Concerning medical image segmentation, the current practice of applying NAS is to respectively search for the optimal design of each layer in down-sampling and up-sampling modules, and construct a U-net shaped architecture. For example, Weng et al. [23] proposed a NAS-Unet for 2D prostate MRI (magnetic resonance imaging), liver CT (computed tomography), and nerve ultrasound images. Zhu et al. [28] proposed a V-NAS, which is a DARTS-style differentiable NAS U-net, for lung and pancreas 2D CT image segmentation. Kim et al. [13] proposed a scalable NAS for 3D medical image segmentation based on 3D U-net. Wang et al. [22] proposed a NAS solution for MRI gliomas image segmentation. Generally, the underlying idea of these methods is introducing common basic operations (e.g. convolution, down/up convolution, down/up depth convolution, max/average pooling, etc.) for searching an optimal block architecture within a fixed U-net-like backbone network. Also, there are a few works designed for non-U-net-like backbone networks such as adversarial network [7] and deep belief network [19]. Since they are designed for specific medical scenarios, they are not widely applicable.

To the best of our knowledge, NAS has not yet been applied in the field of microscopy cell segmentation. To fill this gap, in this paper, we propose a NAS based solution for microscopy cell segmentation, which aims to automatically design a neural network with better performance than the handcrafted network. Based on the above analysis and according to Elsken et al. [9], incorporating prior knowledge about typical properties of architectures well-suited for a task can reduce the size of the search space and simplify the search. Therefore, in this paper, we focus on starting the NAS search from sophisticated block candidates demonstrated in the latest literature (e.g. the CLSTM and convolution block in [4]) and investigating NAS with two backbone networks (U-net and Unet++ [27]). We conduct experiments on seven cell tracking challenge (CTC)[1] data sets [21] and experimental results demonstrate that the searched networks achieve better performances with fewer parameters than the baseline method in all cases.

The contributions of this work are:

- This is the first study to apply NAS to microscopy cell segmentation, which could liberate researchers from the laborious network designing and parameter tuning work.
- Incorporating expert knowledge about block construction for defining search space, which reduces the size of the search space and simplifies the search.
- Demonstrated stable performance improvement and NAS application to two popular backbone networks, which make the proposed method applicable to various scenarios.

The rest of the paper is organized as follows: Sect. 2 presents the proposed methods in detail. Experimental results and analysis are provided in Sect. 3. The paper is concluded and the future work is discussed in Sect. 4.

2   Method

In the field of cell segmentation, U-net [20] is a reputable and frequently chosen network. Unet++ [27] is an evolution of U-net with redesigned skip connections and ensemble architecture of U-nets, and outperforms the baseline U-net. Therefore, in this paper, we investigate the NAS with these two backbone networks of U-net (detailed in Sect. 2.1) and Unet++ (detailed in Sect. 2.2).

2.1   NAS-U-net

Among the U-net-based microscopy cell segmentation methods, the one proposed by Arbelle et al. [4] has shown excellent performance. It integrates CLSTM with U-net to exploit cell dynamics by capturing spatio-temporal encoding in the CLSTM memory units. For convenience, we name this network CLSTM-Unet. The essence of the CLSTM-Unet is a U-shaped architecture composed of mutually connected down-sampling (encoder) and up-sampling (decoder) blocks.

---

[1] http://celltrackingchallenge.net/.

More specifically, the CLSTM-Unet comprises four encoder and four decoder blocks. Each block in the encoder is composed of a CLSTM layer, a convolution layer, a down convolution layer, leaky ReLU and batch normalization; each block in the decoder is composed of a convolution layers, a up convolution layer, leaky ReLU and batch normalization; and the skip connection is implemented by a concatenation with a bilinear interpolation. As a result, this is a fully convolutional architecture. The introduction of a CLSTM layer in each encoder block allows considering past cell appearances at multiple scales for better segmentation while the fully convolutional architecture ensures the network is applicable to any image size during both training and testing. Inspired by the CLSTM-Unet, our NAS-U-net is defined as follows.

Backbone Network. Slightly different from the U-net that has an additional convolution layer at the middle of the network, the CLSTM-Unet has a symmetric architecture. In our NAS-U-net, the backbone network is also following this design. To be consistent with the convention of NAS, the encoder and decoder blocks are named encoder cell (EC) and decoder cell (DC), respectively. For the EC, its input is defined as the output of the previous EC, and for the DC, its input is defined as the concatenation of the output of the previous DC and the output of the horizontally corresponding EC. The NAS is responsible for the EC/DC construction management. Figure 1 illustrates the constitution of our NAS-U-net. The input is a time-lapse sequence of microscopy cell images and the output is the final segmentation map. For better segmentation, an auxiliary block, which contains only one convolution layer, is added to the last DC. This auxiliary block is adopted to solve the problem of multiple adjacent cells in a microscopy image by calculating an additional loss [2], and is fixed during the NAS.

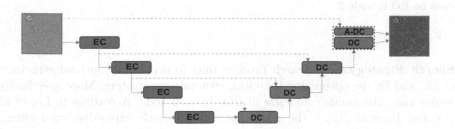

Fig. 1. Schematic of the NAS-U-net. This is an example of a network with four ECs and DCs, but during the NAS, the number of ECs and DCs can vary.

Search Space. Generally, the explanation of the search space starts with the definition of a basic operation (BO) set which is the fundamental computing unit in EC and DC. The current practice in medical image segmentation is designing different types of BO sets (usually down/up/normal BO sets) for searching the EC and DC architecture, and the BOs in these sets are empirically selected from some prevalent operations (e.g. convolution, depth convolution, max pooling, average pooling, etc.) in NAS methods. Although former works show good architectures can be searched for medical image segmentation tasks, they do not incorporate prior knowledge about typical properties of architectures well-suited for the task which can simplify the search and reduce the size of the search space [9]. In this paper, based on the success of the CLSTM-Unet, we define two types of BO sets for the EC and DC, respectively. The BO set for EC contains operations of only CLSTM, convolution, and down convolution; and the BO set for DC contains operations of only convolution and up convolution. Moreover, considering the necessity of the CLSTM operation and for further simplifying the search, we add constraints that: 1) the EC/DC structure is restricted to a sequential structure; and 2) each EC has three nodes which are CLSTM node, convolution node, and down convolution node; and each DC has two nodes which are convolution node and up convolution node. The CLSTM and convolution nodes contain only CLSTM and convolution operations, respectively, and their numbers and sizes are to be searched. The down/up convolution node contains only one down/up convolution and its size is to be searched. Figure 2 illustrates the fundamental structure of an EC. Note that all BOs in EC/DC involve batch normalization and ReLU activation. Also, the number of ECs and DCs (the depth of the network) is to be searched, which is different from the fixed setting in current works.

Fig. 2. Diagram of an EC. The conception of the node is illustrated with dashed lines and labels. During NAS, the number of BOs in the nodes may be fewer or more, and even no BO in node 2.

Search Strategy. The search process aims to decide the optimal structures of EC and DC by optimizing the block structure parameters. More specifically, in our case, the number and size of BOs in each node. According to Liu et al. [15] and Jin et al. [12], if the search space is not overly expansive, even using a random search may achieve strong results. Considering our constrained search space, we formulate our NAS as an auto hyper-parameter tuning by treating the block structure parameters as hyper-parameters, and use a tree-structured Parzen estimator (TPE) for the optimization.

2.2   NAS-Unet++

The recently proposed Unet++ is an evolution of U-net and has achieved huge success in medical image segmentation tasks [27]. Given its flexibility and potential in various segmentation scenarios, in this paper, we also attempt NAS with a

Unet++ backbone network for microscopy cell segmentation. The essence of the Unet++ is an ensemble architecture, which combines U-nets of varying depths into one unified architecture, as illustrated in Fig. 3(a). All U-nets in the Unet++ partially share the same encoder, but have their own decoders. Also, the decoders are connected for the deeper decoders to supervise the shallower decoders. As a result, each layer in the UNet++ decoders, from a horizontal perspective, combines multi-scale features from all its preceding layers at the same resolution, and from a vertical perspective, integrates multi-scale features across different resolutions from its preceding layer. This multi-scale feature aggregation of UNet++ gradually synthesizes the segmentation, leading to increased accuracy and faster convergence. Considering the advantages of both Unet++ and CLSTM-Unet, our NAS-Unet++ is defined as follows.

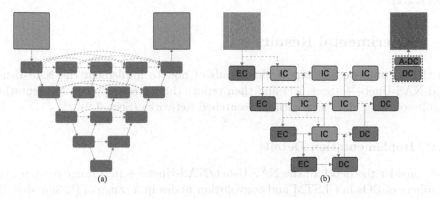

Fig. 3. Schematic of (a) Unet++, where each node in the graph represents a convolution block, downward arrows indicate down-sampling, up-ward arrows indicate up-sampling, and dashed arrows indicate skip connections; and (b) NAS-Unet++, where the input is a time-lapse sequence of microscopy cell images and the output is the final segmentation map.

Backbone Network. Slightly different from the Unet++, our backbone network has a symmetric architecture and removes the dense skip connections. Figure 3(b) illustrate the constitution of our NAS-Unet++. Following the NAS naming mechanism, the outer encoder and decoder blocks are still named as ECs and DCs, respectively, and the intermediate blocks are named as intermediate cells (ICs). For the EC, its input is defined as the output of the previous EC. For the IC/DC, its input is defined as the concatenation of the output of the previous IC/DC and the output of the horizontally corresponding EC/IC. The NAS is responsible for the EC/IC/DC structure management. Also, as shown in the figure, an auxiliary block, which contains only one convolution operation, is added to the last DC. The purpose of this auxiliary block is the same as in NAS-U-net, and is also fixed during the NAS.

Search Space. Similar to the NAS-U-net search space, there are two types of BO sets for the EC, IC, and DC. The BO set for the EC contains operations of only CLSTM, convolution, and down convolution. The IC and DC share a same BO set which contains operations of only convolution and up convolution. Also, the EC/IC/DC structure is restricted to a sequential structure. Each EC has three nodes which are CLSTM node, convolution node, and down convolution node; and each IC/DC has two nodes which are convolution node and up convolution node. All these nodes are defined the same as those in NAS-U-net (Sect. 2.1). The number n of ECs is to be searched, and for n ECs, the numbers of DCs and ICs are n and $n(n - 1)/2$, respectively.

Search Strategy. The search strategy is the same as the one used in NAS-U-net (Sect. 2.1).

3   Experimental Results

In this section, we first report the details of how to implement the NAS-U-net and NAS-Unet++ (Sect. 3.1) and then report the microscopy cell segmentation results on CTC data sets with our searched networks (Sect. 3.2).

3.1   Implementation Details

We consider the depth of the NAS-U-net/NAS-Unet++ in a range of [3, 6], the numbers of BOs in CLSTM and convolution nodes in a range of [1, 3] and [0, 2], respectively, and the filter size of BOs in a set of [3, 5, 7]. Note that the same filter size is adopted for all BOs in a network. We follow the practice of doubling the number of filters when halving the size of feature map for first four layers, and the start number ranges from 8 to 128 with a step of 8. After the fourth layer, the number of filters remains the same as the fourth layer. Also, we adopt a strategy with different numbers of filters for different BOs. The network is trained using truncated back propagation through time (TBPTT). At each back propagation step, the network is unrolled to a time-step ranged in [3, 10]. The learning rate decays from 0.0001 to 0.01, and batch size ranges from 3 to 10. The last DC in the network generates a 3-channel output, which is correspondingly responsible for the cell background, cell foreground, and cell boundary. The weights of these three channels are denoted as $w, w + \varepsilon$, and $1 - 2w - \varepsilon$, respectively. The w and ε are in ranges of [0.08, 0.15] and [0.1, 0.15], respectively. Due to the data scarcity, we conduct architecture search on image crops whose sizes range from 64 to 256 with a step of 32.

3.2   Microscopy Cell Segmentation

To evaluate the performance of our NAS-U-net and NAS-Unet++, we conduct NAS on seven CTC data sets (see [21] for full details on the data) for microscopy cell segmentation. Prior to experiments, for each data set, the images were

Table 1. SEG Results and searched networks of NAS-U-net and NAS-Unet++ on seven data sets, compared with the results of the baseline method.

Data set	Method				
	Baseline SEG	NAS-U-net		NAS-Unet++	
		SEG	Searched network	SEG	Searched network
DIC-C2DH-HeLa	0.8275	0.8457	depth: 4 fsize: 5	0.8538	depth: 4 fsize: 3
			clstm1: 2 clstm2: 8		clstm1: 2 clstm2: 8
			econv1: 1 econv2: 16		econv1: 0 econv2: 16
			dconv1: 1 dconv2: 24		dconv1: 1 dconv2: 24
					iconv1: 1 iconv2: 8
Fluo-C2DL-MSC	0.5983	0.6138	depth: 6 fsize: 3	0.6193	depth: 4 fsize: 5
			clstm1: 2 clstm2: 16		clstm1: 2 clstm2: 8
			econv1: 1 econv2: 8		econv1: 1 econv2: 8
			dconv1: 0 dconv2: 8		dconv1: 1 dconv2: 24
					iconv1: 0 iconv2: 8
Fluo-N2DH-GOWT1	0.8975	0.9228	depth: 4 fsize: 5	0.9381	depth: 3 fsize: 3
			clstm1: 1 clstm2: 8		clstm1: 2 clstm2: 8
			econv1: 0 econv2: 8		econv1: 0 econv2: 8
			dconv1: 1 dconv2: 24		dconv1: 1 dconv2: 24
					iconv1: 1 iconv2: 24
Fluo-N2DL-HeLa	0.8219	0.8376	depth: 5 fsize: 5	0.8432	depth: 3 fsize: 5
			clstm1: 2 clstm2: 16		clstm1: 1 clstm2: 24
			econv1: 1 econv2: 16		econv1: 0 econv2: 16
			dconv1: 1 dconv2: 24		dconv1: 1 dconv2: 8
					iconv1: 0 iconv2: 24
PhC-C2DH-U373	0.8248	0.8519	depth: 3 fsize: 5	0.8617	depth: 3 fsize: 5
			clstm1: 2 clstm2: 24		clstm1: 2 clstm2: 16
			econv1: 0 econv2: 8		econv1: 1 econv2: 24
			dconv1: 1 dconv2: 24		dconv1: 1 dconv2: 16
					iconv1: 1 iconv2: 8
PhC-C2DL-PSC	0.5853	0.5962	depth: 3 fsize: 3	0.6044	depth: 4 fsize: 3
			clstm1: 2 clstm2: 16		clstm1: 2 clstm2: 8
			econv1: 1 econv2: 16		econv1: 1 econv2: 8
			dconv1: 1 dconv2: 8		dconv1: 0 dconv2: 16
					iconv1: 1 iconv2: 8
Fluo-N2DH-SIM+	0.8196	0.8370	depth: 6 fsize: 3	0.8447	depth: 5 fsize: 5
			clstm1: 1 clstm2: 8		clstm2: 1 clstm2: 24
			econv1: 0 econv2: 24		econv1: 1 econv2: 16
			dconv1: 0 dconv2: 8		dconv1: 0 dconv2: 8
					iconv1: 0 iconv2: 16

fsize: filter size; clstm1: the number of CLSTMs in EC; clstm2: the number of filters of a CLSTM; econv1: the number of convolutions in EC; econv2: the number filters of a convolution/down convolution in EC; and dconv1, dconv2, iconv1, and iconv2: corresponding definitions in DC and IC, respectively.

divided into separate 75% training and 25% testing sets. We use the training set for the search and the testing set for segmentation performance evaluation. The baseline method is CLSTM-Unet [4], because our backbone networks are derived from it. We use the metric "SEG" proposed in [21] to evaluate segmentation performance. For the sake of fairness, we retrain the CLSTM-Unet using the reported configurations on the training set for 200,000 epochs. Table 1 presents the SEG results and searched networks of the NAS-U-net and NAS-Unet++ on the testing set for all the seven data sets. As shown in the table, our searched networks achieve stable performance improvements in all cases. The results also show that NAS-Unet++ consistently outperforms both the baseline and NAS-U-net.

4   Conclusion

In this paper, we proposed a NAS based solution for microscopy cell segmentation. Different from most of the current NAS-based solutions that search the network from common basic operations, we restrict the search space by searching sophisticated blocks. This way, both expert knowledge and NAS are considered to facilitate the network searching. We investigated NAS with two prevailing backbone networks of U-net and Unet++. Experimental results on seven CTC microscopy cell data sets demonstrated the performance of our method. Thanks to its simplicity and transportability, the proposed method is applicable to many deep learning based cell segmentation methods. Future works can be done by exploring more effective search spaces by defining more well-suited block structures.

References

1. Al-Kofahi, Y., Zaltsman, A., Graves, R., Marshall, W., Rusu, M.: A deep learning-based algorithm for 2D cell segmentation in microscopy images. BMC Bioinform. **19**(1), 1–11 (2018)
2. Arbelle, A., Raviv, T.R.: Weakly supervised microscopy cell segmentation via convolutional LSTM networks. https://public.celltrackingchallenge.net/participants/BGU-IL
3. Arbelle, A., Raviv, T.R.: Microscopy cell segmentation via adversarial neural networks. In: 15th International Symposium on Biomedical Imaging (ISBI 2018), pp. 645–648. IEEE (2018)
4. Arbelle, A., Raviv, T.R.: Microscopy cell segmentation via convolutional LSTM networks. In: 16th International Symposium on Biomedical Imaging (ISBI 2019), pp. 1008–1012. IEEE (2019)
5. Cai, H., Zhu, L., Han, S.: ProxylessNAS: direct neural architecture search on target task and hardware. arXiv preprint arXiv:1812.00332 (2018)
6. Dimopoulos, S., Mayer, C.E., Rudolf, F., Stelling, J.: Accurate cell segmentation in microscopy images using membrane patterns. Bioinformatics **30**(18), 2644–2651 (2014)
7. Dong, N., Xu, M., Liang, X., Jiang, Y., Dai, W., Xing, E.: Neural architecture search for adversarial medical image segmentation. In: Shen, D., et al. (eds.) MICCAI 2019. LNCS, vol. 11769, pp. 828–836. Springer, Cham (2019). https://doi.org/10.1007/978-3-030-32226-7_92
8. Drozdzal, M., Vorontsov, E., Chartrand, G., Kadoury, S., Pal, C.: The importance of skip connections in biomedical image segmentation. In: Carneiro, G., et al. (eds.) LABELS/DLMIA -2016. LNCS, vol. 10008, pp. 179–187. Springer, Cham (2016). https://doi.org/10.1007/978-3-319-46976-8_19
9. Elsken, T., Metzen, J.H., Hutter, F.: Neural architecture search: a survey. J. Mach. Learn. Res. **20**(55), 1–21 (2019)
10. Hollandi, R., et al.: A deep learning framework for nucleus segmentation using image style transfer. bioRxiv, p. 580605 (2019)

11. Hutter, F., Kotthoff, L., Vanschoren, J.: Automated Machine Learning: Methods, Systems, Challenges. Springer, Heidelberg (2019). https://doi.org/10.1007/978-3-030-05318-5
12. Jin, H., Song, Q., Hu, X.: Auto-keras: efficient neural architecture search with network morphism. arXiv preprint arXiv:1806.10282 5 (2018)
13. Kim, S., et al.: Scalable neural architecture search for 3D medical image segmentation. In: Shen, D., et al. (eds.) MICCAI 2019. LNCS, vol. 11766, pp. 220–228. Springer, Cham (2019). https://doi.org/10.1007/978-3-030-32248-9_25
14. Kong, J., et al.: Automated cell segmentation with 3D fluorescence microscopy images. In: 12th International Symposium on Biomedical Imaging (ISBI), pp. 1212–1215. IEEE (2015)
15. Liu, H., Simonyan, K., Yang, Y.: Darts: differentiable architecture search. arXiv preprint arXiv:1806.09055 (2018)
16. Long, F.: Microscopy cell nuclei segmentation with enhanced U-Net. BMC Bioinform. **21**(1), 1–12 (2020)
17. Luo, R., Tian, F., Qin, T., Chen, E., Liu, T.Y.: Neural architecture optimization. In: Advances in Neural Information Processing Systems, pp. 7816–7827 (2018)
18. Meijering, E.: Cell segmentation: 50 years down the road. IEEE Signal Process. Mag. **29**(5), 140–145 (2012)
19. Qiang, N., Ge, B., Dong, Q., Ge, F., Liu, T.: Neural architecture search for optimizing deep belief network models of fMRI data. In: Li, Q., Leahy, R., Dong, B., Li, X. (eds.) MMMI 2019. LNCS, vol. 11977, pp. 26–34. Springer, Cham (2020). https://doi.org/10.1007/978-3-030-37969-8_4
20. Ronneberger, O., Fischer, P., Brox, T.: U-Net: convolutional networks for biomedical image segmentation. In: Navab, N., Hornegger, J., Wells, W.M., Frangi, A.F. (eds.) MICCAI 2015. LNCS, vol. 9351, pp. 234–241. Springer, Cham (2015). https://doi.org/10.1007/978-3-319-24574-4_28
21. Ulman, V., et al.: An objective comparison of cell-tracking algorithms. Nat. Methods **14**(12), 1141–1152 (2017)
22. Wang, F., Biswal, B.: Neural architecture search for gliomas segmentation on multimodal magnetic resonance imaging. arXiv preprint arXiv:2005.06338 (2020)
23. Weng, Y., Zhou, T., Li, Y., Qiu, X.: NAS-UNet: neural architecture search for medical image segmentation. IEEE Access **7**, 44247–44257 (2019)
24. Xing, F., Xie, Y., Su, H., Liu, F., Yang, L.: Deep learning in microscopy image analysis: a survey. IEEE Trans. Neural Netw. Learn. Syst. **29**(10), 4550–4568 (2017)
25. Xing, F., Yang, L.: Robust nucleus/cell detection and segmentation in digital pathology and microscopy images: a comprehensive review. IEEE Rev. Biomed. Eng. **9**, 234–263 (2016)
26. Zela, A., Elsken, T., Saikia, T., Marrakchi, Y., Brox, T., Hutter, F.: Understanding and robustifying differentiable architecture search. arXiv preprint arXiv:1909.09656 (2019)
27. Zhou, Z., Siddiquee, M.M.R., Tajbakhsh, N., Liang, J.: UNet++: redesigning skip connections to exploit multiscale features in image segmentation. IEEE Trans. Med. Imaging **39**(6), 1856–1867 (2019)
28. Zhu, Z., Liu, C., Yang, D., Yuille, A., Xu, D.: V-NAS: neural architecture search for volumetric medical image segmentation. In: International Conference on 3D Vision (3DV), pp. 240–248. IEEE (2019)
29. Zoph, B., Vasudevan, V., Shlens, J., Le, Q.V.: Learning transferable architectures for scalable image recognition. In: IEEE Conference on Computer Vision and Pattern Recognition, pp. 8697–8710 (2018)

Classification of Ulcerative Colitis Severity in Colonoscopy Videos Using Vascular Pattern Detection

Md Farhad Mokter[1], JungHwan Oh[1(✉)], Wallapak Tavanapong[2], Johnny Wong[2], and Piet C. de Groen[3]

[1] Department of Computer Science and Engineering, University of North Texas, Denton, TX 76203, USA
Junghwan.Oh@unt.edu
[2] Computer Science Department, Iowa State University, Ames, IA 50011, USA
tavanapo@iastate.edu
[3] Department of Medicine, University of Minnesota, Minneapolis, MN, USA
degroen@umn.edu

Abstract. Endoscopic measurement of ulcerative colitis (UC) severity is important since endoscopic disease severity may better predict future outcomes in UC than symptoms. However, it is difficult to evaluate the endoscopic severity of UC objectively because of the non-uniform nature of endoscopic features associated with UC, and large variations in their patterns. In this paper, we propose a method to classify UC severity in colonoscopy videos by detecting the vascular (vein) patterns which are defined specifically in this paper as the amounts of blood vessels in the video frames. To detect these vascular patterns, we use Convolutional Neural Network (CNN) and image preprocessing methods. The experiments show that the proposed method for classifying UC severity by detecting these vascular patterns increases classification effectiveness significantly.

Keywords: Convolutional Neural Network · Medical image classification · Ulcerative colitis severity · Colonoscopy video

1 Introduction

Ulcerative colitis (UC) is a chronic inflammatory disease of the colon characterized by periods of relapses and remissions affecting more than 750,000 people in the United States [1]. As mucosal healing is a specific treatment goal in UC, the importance of endoscopic evaluation of disease activity in predicting outcomes is being increasingly recognized [2]. Disease activity in UC has been extensively evaluated using various scoring systems incorporating both clinical and endoscopic features [3]. These scoring systems have been developed to evaluate systematically the responses to treatments being studied in UC patients [4]. Many scoring systems exist, but mainly two endoscopic score systems of mucosal inflammation are used currently in clinical practice, which are the Mayo Endoscopic Score (MES) and the Ulcerative Colitis Endoscopic Index of Severity

© Springer Nature Switzerland AG 2020
M. Liu et al. (Eds.): MLMI 2020, LNCS 12436, pp. 552–562, 2020.
https://doi.org/10.1007/978-3-030-59861-7_56

(UCEIS) [3]. In Table 1 we compare these two scoring systems and divide the disease activity features into four different classes, Normal (Score 0), Mild (Score 1), Moderate (Score 2) and Severe (Score 3), based on their endoscopic features.

Since disease severity may better predict future outcomes in UC than symptoms, UC severity measurement by endoscopy is very important [5, 6]. However, even if we have the scoring systems mentioned above, it is very difficult to evaluate the severity of UC objectively because of non-uniform nature of endoscopic findings associated with UC, and large variations in their patterns [7]. To objectively apply these scoring systems, we focus on one common feature in both scoring systems as seen in Table 1, which is 'vascular (predominantly vein) pattern'. In Normal and Mild disease activity, the vascular pattern is either clearly or somewhat visible, but it is either mostly or completely lost in Moderate and Severe disease activity.

Table 1. Comparison of the Mayo Endoscopic Score (MES) and the Ulcerative Colitis Endoscopic Index of Severity (UCEIS) features

Score	Disease activity	Features for MES	Features for UCEIS
0	Normal	No abnormality, clear vascular pattern	No abnormality, clear vascular pattern
1	Mild	Erythema, Decreased vascular pattern, Mild friability	Patchy obliteration of vascular pattern, Mucosal bleeding, Erosions
2	Moderate	Marked erythema, Absent vascular pattern, Friability, Erosions	Complete obliteration of vascular pattern, Luminal mild bleeding, Superficial ulcer
3	Severe	Absent vascular pattern, Spontaneous bleeding, Ulceration	Complete obliteration of vascular pattern, Luminal moderate or severe bleeding, Deep ulcer

We propose a method for classifying UC severity in colonoscopy videos by detecting these vascular patterns which are defined specifically in this paper as the amount of blood vessels in the video frames. First, we implement a classifier using Convolutional Neural Network (CNN) to detect the amount of blood vessels in a colonoscopy video frame. For convenience, we call this first CNN as Vascular Convolutional Neural Network Number 1 (VCNN1). VCNN1 classifies a frame to one of two different classes in which one has high amount of blood vessels (the vascular pattern is either clearly or somewhat visible), and the other has low amount of blood vessels (the vascular pattern is either mostly or completely lost). A frame with high amount of blood vessels is fed into Vascular Convolutional Neural Network Number 2 (VCNN2) which classifies it to either Normal or Mild class. A frame with low amount of blood vessels is fed into Vascular Convolutional Neural Network Number 3 (VCNN3) which classifies it to either Moderate or Severe class. VCNN2 and VCNN3 are implemented using CNN similar with VNNC1. Then, we verify the accuracies of VCNN1, VCNN2 and VCNN3 on our colonoscopy video dataset, and compare the results with the previous method [8].

Contributions: (1) To the best of our knowledge, this is the first published result of vascular pattern (defined as the amount of blood vessels in the video frames) detection in colonoscopy video frames. (2) The proposed method for classifying UC severity by detecting these vascular patterns increases classification effectiveness by about 17% compared to our previous work [8] and achieves a 42% improvement in time analysis.

The remainder of this paper is organized as follows. Related work is presented in Sect. 2. The data preparation is discussed in Sect. 3. The proposed technique is described in Sect. 4. In Sect. 5, we discuss our experimental setup and results. Finally, Sect. 6 presents some concluding remarks and future works.

2   Related Work

We proposed a CNN based approach evaluating the severity of UC [9]. Its accuracy was reasonable at the video level, but its frame level accuracy was very low (around 45%). We improved this CNN based approach in two ways to provide better accuracy for the classification [8]. First, we added more thorough and essential preprocessing. Second, we subdivided each class of UC severity based on visual appearance and generated more sub-classes for the classification to accommodate large variations in UC severity patterns. This method provided an improved frame-level accuracy (around 60%) to evaluate the severity of UC.

A method using 159-layer convolutional neural network (CNN) based on Inception V3 was constructed as a deep learning model to train and categorize colonoscopy frames based on UC severity [10]. The accuracies reported were 75.3%, 67.6%, 64.3%, and 67.9% for normal, mild, moderate and severe classes respectively, based on their testing dataset with 11,492 colonoscopy video frames in which 8,148 (70.9%) frames of normal, 1,574 (13.7%) frames of mild, 1,126 (9.8%) frames of moderate, and 3,644 (5.6%) of severe frames. A computer aided diagnosis (CAD) system was developed based on the GoogleNet architecture along with Caffe deep learning framework to identify the endoscopic activities and was validated using the datasets of colonoscopy images from patients with UC [11]. 26,304 colonoscopy images from 841 patients were used to train the CNN and 3981 images from 114 patients were used for testing. The performance was evaluated by calculating the areas under the receiver operating characteristics curves (AUROCs). The CNN showed a remarkable performance with AUROCs of 0.86 to identify normal mucosa (Mayo score 0) and 0.98 to identify mucosa healing state (Mayo score 0–1).

3   Data Preparation

In this section, we discuss the data preparation including the image preprocessing, and the patch extraction and filtering from the colonoscopy video frames.

3.1   Image Preprocessing

The colonoscopy videos were captured at 29.97 frames per second with 720 × 480-pixel resolution. In our previous work [8], the captured videos were labeled by a domain expert into four UC classes such as Normal, Mild, Moderate, and Severe based on the MES as seen in Table 1. From each captured video, we extracted a sequence of frames at the rate of three frames per second. Then, we crop an area (224 × 224 pixels) centered on the center pixel of the original frame (720 × 480 pixels). After the cropping, we perform preprocessing using the three steps which were developed previously [8]. The preprocessing discards unnecessary frames. More details can be found in [8].

3.2 Patch Extraction and Filtering

The frames after all processing are divided into a number of non-overlapping patches. The patch size that we chose is 28 × 28 pixels. Since the frame size is 224 × 224 pixels after the preprocessing mentioned above, 64 patches are generated from one frame. These patches are used to detect the vascular patterns. Blood vessels can be mostly found in some parts of frames. Dividing a whole frame into smaller patches makes it possible to distinguish the blood vessel patches (Fig. 1(a)) from non-blood vessel patches (Fig. 1(b)) and ensures the extraction of different blood vessel patterns.

The next step is to distinguish non-informative patches (i.e., patches without usable information) from informative ones and discard them for the further processing. An informative patch can be defined as a patch which has a subject of interest, i.e., visible blood vessels, for our purpose. A non-informative patch has an opposite definition. Typical non-informative patches contain very dark and/or very bright portions.

To distinguish these non-informative patches, a Gaussian blur filter is applied first to remove high frequency noises [12]. Then we count very bright and dark pixels in a patch. A pixel is considered to be very bright if its grey scale pixel value is greater than a certain threshold ($TH_{bright} \geq 195$) and considered to be very dark if its grey scale pixel value is less than a certain threshold ($TH_{dark} \leq 90$). We calculate a ratio of the total number of bright pixels in a patch to the total number of pixels in the patch. Also, we calculate another ratio of the total number of dark pixels in a patch to the total number of pixels in the patch. If either ratio is above a certain threshold ($TH_{informative} = 0.5$), we consider it as a non-informative patch. Threshold values were chosen experimentally to ensure the informative patches are not being compromised. Non-informative patches (Fig. 1(c)) are discarded.

After we applied all the preprocessing steps mentioned above, the dataset in Table 2 remained. We used 67,599 frames for training (52,674 frames), and testing (14,925 frames). The training dataset is mutually exclusive from the testing dataset. We extracted 4,326,336 patches from these frames. 30,692 non-informative patches were excluded, and the remaining 4,295,444 patches were used to train and evaluate the proposed method.

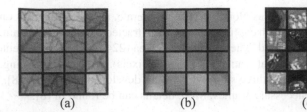

(a)   (b)   (c)

Fig. 1. Examples of patches (a) with blood vessels, (b) without blood vessels, and (c) without usable information.

Table 2. Details of the dataset after patch extraction and filtering

Classes	Video clips	Frames	Patches
Normal	47	16,348	1,038,456
Mild	63	19,890	1,264,034
Moderate	43	17,088	1,085,709
Severe	25	14,273	907,245
Total	178	67,599	4,295,444

4 Proposed Method

This section describes the architecture of the proposed method using our Vascular Convolutional Neural Networks (VCNNs) for frame classification, and the process of assigning severity scores to the video clips based on the CNN results.

4.1 Vascular Convolutional Neural Networks

The main objective is classifying a colonoscopy video frame to one of the four UC severity classes: Normal (Score 0), Mild (Score 1), Moderate (Score 2), and Severe (Score 3) by detecting the vascular patterns. To achieve this objective, we implement three CNNs: VCNN1, VCNN2, and VCNN3 as previously discussed.

The first CNN, VCNN1 is trained using significant numbers of blood vessel and non-blood vessel patches. It classifies the video frames into one of two different classes in which one has high amount of blood vessels, and the other has low amount of blood vessels. Each patch in a frame is classified by VCNN1 first. If the ratio (R_{blood}: the number of blood vessel patches in a frame to the total number of informative patches in a frame) is larger than a certain threshold (TH_{blood}: 0.25 in our case, which was chosen experimentally), it is considered as a frame with high amount of blood vessels. Otherwise, it is considered as a frame with low amount of blood vessels. A frame with high amount of blood vessels is expected to be either Normal (Score 0) or Mild (Score 1) class, and a frame with low amount of blood vessels is expected to be Moderate (Score 2) or Severe (Score 3) class as seen in Table 1.

VCNN2 is trained using significant numbers of informative patches from Normal and Mild frames to classify an input frame to one of the two classes (Normal and Mild). All informative patches in the frame with high amount of blood vessels, which is determined by VCNN1 are fed into VCNN2. A frame is classified as Normal if the number of patches predicted as Normal is greater than the number of patches predicted as Mild. Otherwise, the frame is classified as Mild.

Similarly, VCNN3 is trained using significant numbers of informative patches from Moderate and Severe frames to classify an input frame to one of the two classes (Moderate and Severe). All informative patches in the frame with low amount of blood vessels, which is determined by VCNN1 are fed into VCNN3. A frame is classified as Moderate if the number of patches predicted as Moderate is greater than the number of patches predicted as Severe. Otherwise, the frame is classified as Severe. The overall procedure of the proposed method using the three CNNs can be seen in Fig. 2, in which an input frame is eventually classified to one of four UC Severity classes.

The proposed VCNN1, VCNN2 and VCNN3 all have the same CNN architecture. It is a 6-layer CNN with a dense layer and a flatten layer, in which each convolutional layer is followed by a pooling layer. The first convolutional layer filters the input with 16 filters of size 3×3. The next convolutional layer filters it with 32 filters of same size as the previous layer, and the third convolutional layer uses 64 filters. The same max-pooling is performed after each convolutional layer over a 2×2-pixel window with the 2 strides to avoid excessive computation and overfitting. To preserve the spatial resolution between the convolutional layers, we use zero-padding in borders as necessary. ReLU, Tanh and sigmoid are typical activation functions [13]. Among them, ReLU is used for all convolutional layers. A dense layer is added that acts as a fully connected layer. A flatten layer is used to convert the data into a 1-dimensional array ready for feeding into the next layer. The output layer is a layer with the Sigmoid function that returns class probabilities for given classes.

4.2 Assigning Severity Scores

The next step is to assign a severity score for a whole video clip of a patient. Here, we assign a severity score for a whole video clip automatically based on the class label assigned to each frame. We calculate severity score, S_v for a given video clip as an average of class labels of all frames as follows,

$$S_V = \frac{\sum_{i=1}^{n} C_i}{n}, \tag{1}$$

where n is a total number of frames, and C_i is a class label (such as 0 for normal, 1 for mild, 2 for moderate, and 3 for severe) assigned to frame i of a given video clip.

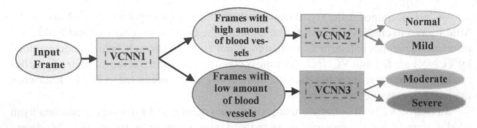

Fig. 2. Overview of the proposed method

5   Experimental Results

In this section, we discuss performance evaluation of the proposed method.

5.1   Training and Testing

We implemented the three CNNs (VCNN1, VCNN2, and VCNN3) using Keras [14] which is an open-source library for neural networks written in Python and runs on top of Tensorflow [15]. We trained VCNN1 using the training dataset in Table 3. These frames were preprocessed as discussed in Sect. 3.2, and 3,347,846 patches were obtained as seen in Table 3. These patches were divided manually into two categories: blood vessel and non-blood vessel patches, confirmed by our domain expert. VCNN1 was trained based on these two types of patches, so it can eventually classify an input frame to one of two classes in which one has a high amount of blood vessels, and the other has a low amount of blood vessels as discussed in the previous section. The training parameters were set as a batch size of 32 with an epoch number of 50, and a learning rate of 0.001. We used 'Adam' as an optimizer and 'binary cross-entropy' as a loss function of the network.

VCNN2 was trained on the dataset in Table 4. A total of 1,662,935 patches were obtained from these frames and used to train VCNN2. We used the same training parameters used in VCNN1 for VCNN2 except for the epoch number which was set to 35 since the learning rate was not improved after 35 epochs.

Table 3. Details of the training dataset for VCNN1

Classes	Video clips	Frames	Patches
Normal	35	12,725	808,341
Mild	51	15,490	984,631
Moderate	30	14,027	891,908
Severe	19	10,432	662,966
Total	135	52,674	3,347,846

Table 4. Details of the training dataset for VCNN2

Classes	Video clips	Frames	Patches
Normal	35	11,962	758,279
Mild	51	14,258	904,656
Total	86	26,220	1,662,935

VCNN3 was trained on the dataset in Table 5. A total of 1,480,939 patches were obtained from these frames and used to train VCNN3. We used the same training parameters in VCNN2 for VCNN3 including 35 epochs.

To evaluate an overall performance of the proposed method, we tested VCNN1, VCNN2 and VCNN3 using the test dataset described in Table 6. Each frame is divided into 64 patches as discussed in Sect. 3.2, which are fed to VCNN1 which calculates the ratio (R_{blood}) as discussed in the previous section. If the R_{blood} is larger than TH_{blood} (0.25 in our case), the input frame is considered to have high amount of blood vessels and will be an input for VCNN2. Otherwise, it is considered to have low amount of blood vessels and will be an input for VCNN3. Recall that VCNN2 classifies an input frame to either Normal (Score 0) or Mild (Score 1) classes, and VCNN3 classifies it to either Moderate (Score 2) or Severe (Score 3) classes.

Table 5. Details of the training dataset for VCNN3

Classes	Video clips	Frames	Patches
Moderate	30	13,336	849,374
Severe	19	9,912	631,565
Total	49	23,248	1,480,939

Table 6. Details of the test dataset for VCNN1, VCNN2 and VCNN3

Classes	Video clips	Frames	Patches
Normal	12	3,623	230,115
Mild	12	4,400	279,403
Moderate	13	3,061	193,801
Severe	06	3,841	244,279
Total	43	14,925	947,598

5.2 Patch Level and Frame Level Accuracies

The patch level accuracy of VCNN1 is the number of correctly classified blood-vessel patches and non-blood vessel patches to the total number of patches. The patch level accuracy of VCNN2 is the number of correctly classified Normal and Mild patches to the total number of actual Normal and Mild patches. Similarly, the patch level accuracy of VCNN3 is the ratio of the number of correctly classified Moderate and Severe patches to the total number of actual Moderate and Severe patches. As seen in Table 7, all three VCNNs performed reasonably (77%–82%). We calculated the frame level accuracies using four performance evaluation matrices: Accuracy, Sensitivity (Recall), Specificity, and Precision which are defined as:

$$\text{Acc} = \frac{TP + TN}{TP + TN + FP + FN}, \text{ Sens} = \frac{TP}{TP + FN}, \text{ Spec} = \frac{TN}{TN + FP} \text{ and Prec} = \frac{TP}{TP + FP},$$

where TP (True Positive) represents the number of correctly detected positive samples; FP (False Positive) represents the number of incorrectly detected negative samples. TN (True Negative) counts the number of correctly detected negative samples, and FN (False Negative) is the number of incorrectly detected positive samples.

For VCNN2, the frames of Normal class were considered as positive, and the frames of Mild class were considered as negative. For VCNN3, the frames of Moderate class were considered as positive, and the frames of Severe class were considered as negative. The decision is based on the output of the sigmoid unit of the output layer which predicts a patch to be positive when the output function returns a score greater than 0.50 or larger and predicts negative otherwise. As shown in Table 8, our proposed VCCN2 and VCNN3 show promising performance with 79.4% and 80.8% of accuracy, respectively. We also compared the frame level accuracy of proposed method with that of our previous work [8] in Table 9. For convenience, the proposed method is called as VCNN1+2+3, and the previous method is called as UCS-AlexNet. VCNN1+2+3 outperforms UCS-AlexNet by around 17%, which is a significant improvement. One reason for the improvement is that the proposed method is combining three different CNNs in which each CNN is a simple two class classifier performing its own function.

Table 7. Patch level accuracies for test set in Table 6

Methods	Accuracy (%)
VCNN1	82.2
VCNN2	77.1
VCNN3	78.2

Table 8. Frame level performance for the test set in Table 6 (unit: %)

Methods	Acc	Sens	Spec	Prec
VCNN2	79.4	78.9	80.2	81.3
VCNN3	80.8	78.7	82.8	79.1

5.3 Comparison of Severity Scores

We calculated the severity scores for the test dataset in Table 6 using Eq. (1) in Sect. 4.2. The results are shown in Table 10. The third and fourth columns show the severity scores generated from our previous work UCS-AlexNet [8]) and the proposed method (VCNN1+2+3), respectively. All severity scores generated from the proposed method are closer to our domain expert's manual evaluations (the second column) compared to those from our previous work.

To calculate how much they are closer, we calculated two Pearson correlation coefficients (PCC) by class level (Normal, Mild, Moderate and Severe) for the entire set of video clips in the test dataset in Table 6. The first one is between the severity scores generated from our domain expert's manual evaluations (the second column) and those generated from our previous work [8]. The second one is between the severity scores generated from our domain expert's manual evaluations and those generated from the proposed method. These two Pearson correlation coefficients are 0.94 and 0.96 respectively as seen in Table 10. Also, we calculated two Pearson correlation coefficients by frame level using all testing frames in Table 6 using the same way used for the class level. These two Pearson correlation coefficients are 0.80 and 0.86 respectively as seen in Table 10. These PCCs indicate the proposed method is closer to the domain's expert classification than our previous work. A reason why the proposed method is closer to the domain's expert classification is that it provides better frame-level accuracies as seen in Table 9.

5.4 Time Analysis

The experiments were run on a 3.20 GHz machine with 32 GB of memory and 2 GB Nvidia GPU. They were implemented using Keras [14] which is an open-source library for neural networks written in Python and runs on top of Tensorflow [15]. The proposed VCNN1+2+3 could classify a single frame in 8.23 ms (milli-second) on average, which was an improvement of around 42% in time analysis when compared with our previous work (UCS-AlexNet [8] - 14.13 ms on average).

Table 9 Comparison of frame level accuracies with our previous work (UCS-AlexNet [8]) (unit: %)

Methods	UCS-AlexNet [8]	VCNN1+2+3
Normal	63.2	81.2
Mild	61.4	74.6
Moderate	45.7	78.4
Severe	72.3	80.1
Average	61.5	78.4

Table 10. Average severity scores and Pearson correlation coefficients (PCC)

Methods	Manual evaluation	USC-Alexnet [8]	VCNN1+2+3
Normal	0	0.44	0.27
Mild	1	1.09	0.95
Moderate	2	2.42	2.09
Severe	3	2.68	2.75
PCC by class		0.94	0.96
PCC by frame		0.80	0.86

6 Concluding Remarks and Future Works

Our proposed method has an additional benefit of model interpretability that most CNN models do not have; by using two models for low and high amounts of visible vessels, and using patches as sub-classification of frame classification, we can interpret how UC severity class prediction is reached for each frame. Interpretability is desirable since it increases trust in the model. Since each VCNN is not of a recurrent architecture, we can apply on each VCNN interpretation methods recently reported in [16]. These methods are shown to be quite effective for non-recurrent deep models. Understanding of the inner working of deep recurrent models like Inception V3 remains a challenging problem, and we will consider other methods in [17–20] in future work.

The current results may be sufficient for use in clinical practice. However, when used in clinical practice, we will have to calculate segmental as well as whole colon UC scores in order to distinguish a mostly normal colon with severe proctitis from mild pan-colitis which both may have a similar whole colon UC score. Clearly, our current CNN-based application needs formal evaluation in clinical practice.

References

1. U.S. National Library of Medicine: Ulcerative colitis. https://ghr.nlm.nih.gov/condition/ulcerative-colitis. Accessed 04 Apr 2020

2. Xie, T., et al.: Ulcerative Colitis Endoscopic Index of Severity (UCEIS) versus Mayo Endoscopic Score (MES) in guiding the need for colectomy in patients with acute severe colitis. Gastroenterol. Rep. **6**(1), 38–44 (2018)

3. Paine, E.: Colonoscopic evaluation in ulcerative colitis. Gastroenterol. Rep. **2**(3), 161–168 (2014)

4. D'Haens, G., et al.: A review of activity indices and efficacy end points for clinical trials of medical therapy in adults with ulcerative colitis. Gastroenterology **132**(2), 763–786 (2007)

5. Kappelman, M.D., Rifas-Shiman, S.L., Kleinman, K., et al.: The prevalence and geographic distribution of Crohn's disease and ulcerative colitis in the United States. Clin. Gastroenterol. Hepatol. **5**(12), 1424–1429 (2007)

6. Rutter, M., Saunders, B., et al.: Severity of inflammation is a risk factor for colorectal neoplasia in ulcerative colitis. Gastroenterology **126**(2), 451–459 (2004)

7. Nosato, H., Sakanashi, H., Takahashi, E., Murakawa, M.: An objective evaluation method of ulcerative colitis with optical colonoscopy images based on higher order local auto-correlation features. In: 2014 IEEE 11th International Symposium on Biomedical Imaging (ISBI), pp. 89–92. IEEE (2014)

8. Tejaswini, S.V.L.L., Mittal, B., Oh, J., Tavanapong, W., Wong, J., de Groen, P.C.: Enhanced approach for classification of ulcerative colitis severity in colonoscopy videos using CNN. In: Bebis, G., et al. (eds.) ISVC 2019. LNCS, vol. 11845, pp. 25–37. Springer, Cham (2019). https://doi.org/10.1007/978-3-030-33723-0_3

9. Alammari, A., Islam, A.R., Oh, J., Tavanapong, W., Wong, J., De Groen, P.C.: Classification of ulcerative colitis severity in colonoscopy videos using CNN. In: Proceedings of the 9th International Conference on Information Management and Engineering, Barcelona, Spain, pp. 139–144 (2017)

10. Stidham, R.W., et al.: Performance of a deep learning model vs human reviewers in grading endoscopic disease severity of patients with ulcerative colitis. JAMA Netw. Open **2**(5), e193963 (2019)

11. Ozawa, T., et al.: Novel computer-assisted diagnosis system for endoscopic disease activity in patients with ulcerative colitis. Gastrointest. Endosc. **89**(2), 416–421 (2019)

12. Fan, L., Zhang, F., Fan, H., Zhang, C.: Brief review of image denoising techniques. Vis. Comput. Ind. Biomed. Art **2**(1) (2019). Article number: 7. https://doi.org/10.1186/s42492-019-0016-7

13. Lo, S.C., Lou, S.L., Lin, J.S., Freedman, M.T., Chien, M.V., Mun, S.K.: Artificial convolution neural network techniques and applications for lung nodule detection. IEEE Trans. Med. Imaging **14**(4), 711–718 (1995)

14. Ramasubramanian, K., Singh, A.: Deep learning using Keras and TensorFlow. In: Machine Learning Using R, pp. 667–688. Apress, Berkeley (2019)

15. Abadi, M., et al.: TensorFlow: large-scale machine learning on heterogeneous distributed systems. arXiv preprint arXiv:1603.04467 (2016)

16. Gilpin, L.H., Bau, D., Yuan, B.Z., Bajwa, A., Specter, M., Kagal, L.: Explaining explanations: an overview of interpretability of machine learning. In: 2018 IEEE 5th International Conference on Data Science and Advanced Analytics (DSAA), pp. 80–89 (2018)

17. He, K., Gkioxari, G., Dollár, P., Girshick, R.: Mask R-CNN. In: Proceedings of the IEEE International Conference on Computer Vision, pp. 2961–2969 (2017)

18. Zhang, W., Tang, P., Zhao, L.: Remote sensing image scene classification using CNN-CapsNet. Remote Sens. **11**(5), 494 (2019)

19. Turan, M., Almalioglu, Y., Araujo, H., Konukoglu, E., Sitti, M.: Deep EndoVO: a recurrent convolutional neural network (RCNN) based visual odometry approach for endoscopic capsule robots. Neurocomputing **275**, 1861–1870 (2017)

20. Liskowski, P., Krawiec, K.: Segmenting retinal blood vessels with deep neural networks. IEEE Trans. Med. Imaging **35**(11), 2369–2380 (2016)

Predicting Catheter Ablation Outcomes with Pre-ablation Heart Rhythm Data: Less Is More

Lisa Y. W. Tang[1]([✉]), Kendall Ho[1], Roger C. Tam[2,3], Nathaniel M. Hawkins[4,5], Michael Lim[1], and Jason G. Andrade[4,5]

[1] Department of Emergency Medicine, UBC, Vancouver, Canada
lisa.yw.tang@gmail.com
[2] Department of Radiology, UBC, Vancouver, Canada
[3] School of Biomedical Engineering, UBC, Vancouver, Canada
[4] Center for Cardiovascular Innovation, Vancouver, Canada
[5] Heart Rhythm Services, Department of Medicine, UBC, Vancouver, Canada

Abstract. While numerous studies have shown that catheter ablation is superior to anti-arrhythmic drug (AAD) in treating atrial fibrillation (AF), its long-term outcomes have been limited by arrhythmia recurrence, which is considered a negative outcome per current clinical standard. This gives rise to difficulty in choosing between AAD and catheter ablation, which pose risks of complications but may achieve higher efficacy when compared to the former. As an effort to overcome this dilemma, we evaluate in this work the joint utility of machine learning methods and cardiac data measured prior to ablation for outcome prediction. We advanced research along two fronts. On the clinical front, we evaluated the plausibility of developing models that take as input pre-ablation heart rhythm time-series data to predict future outcome of ablation. On the technical front, we conducted extensive experiments to address the following questions: 1) Could the use of recurrent neural networks achieve the best predictive performance for this application? 2) How would multi-layer perceptron (MLP) compare to recurrent networks? 3) How might the design of bottleneck in MLPs affect performance? 4) How would traditional classification algorithms compare to (deep) neural networks? As an initial attempt to answer these questions, we conducted over 100 sets of cross-validation experiments and found that the top-performing predictive model achieved 71.0 ± 2.1 in area under receiver operating characteristic curve (AUC), with sensitivity of 63.0 ± 4.3 and specificity of 64.2 ± 4.5, as evaluated on a cohort of 343 samples. We also found that all models evaluated in this work achieved greater predictive performance than two risk scores commonly cited in the clinical research literature.

1 Introduction

Atrial fibrillation (AF) is the most common heart rhythm disorder worldwide, affecting 33.5 million people globally, with an expected doubling in prevalence

© Springer Nature Switzerland AG 2020
M. Liu et al. (Eds.): MLMI 2020, LNCS 12436, pp. 563–571, 2020.
https://doi.org/10.1007/978-3-030-59861-7_57

rate by 2030 [17]. Clinical presentations and symptoms of AF include rapid, irregular and inefficient heartbeats, as well as palpitations, shortness of breath, nausea, dizziness, fatigue, depressed mood, and anxiety [13]. Individuals with AF have higher risks of stroke, heart failure, and sudden death.

Treatment strategies for AF management are generally categorized under ventricular rate control or rhythm control [2]. **Rate control** aims to slow the rapid, irregular conduction to the ventricles and is typically facilitated by medications slowing conduction through the atrio-ventricular node [13]. **Rhythm control**, on the other hand, aims to correct the source of the abnormal rhythm within the atria to restore the normal sinus rhythm. It is generally facilitated by cardioversions (electrical and/or pharmacological) and catheter ablations, in combination with chronic anti-arrhythmic drug (AAD) therapy.

Selecting the best treatment option, especially for rhythm control, can be difficult as it involves choosing between the use of AAD versus invasive methods (i.e. catheter ablation), which pose higher risks but can be more effective in eliminating arrhythmia when compared to AAD. The treatment decision requires joint considerations of numerous data sources, including quantitative data from rhythm monitoring (e.g. the frequency and duration of AF episodes), imaging data for the examination of the cardiac structure, as well as the clinical reasoning of symptoms, complications and comorbidities. Currently, these factors are qualitatively examined by physicians on a case-by-case basis. On the other hand, while few risk scores have been proposed in the clinical literature, their prognostic values are poor, as shown in a recent study by Black et al. [4]. In fact, a 2020 systematic review [6] concludes that none of these risk scores in the research literature are adequate because the performance of each score was highly variable and none had consistently good performance.

In this work, we hypothesize that the use of baseline variables such as age, sex, and medical history, may be inadequate for ablation-outcome prediction and thus propose in this work the novel combination of longitudinal data acquired by heart rhythm monitors and machine learning methods for treatment prediction. As the paper later presents, we searched over a large selection of model architectures by comparing five types of neural network architectures and their variants along with traditional algorithms.

2   Materials and Methods

2.1   Data: Heart Rhythm Data Collected Using Implanted Monitors

We retrospectively obtained data acquired from a randomized clinical trial [1] that continuously recorded seven sets of biomeasures on a daily basis. In brief, 343 patients were referred for first catheter ablation due to AF refractory to at least one AAD and subsequently arranged for a placement of an implanted cardiac monitor (ICM) at least one month prior to a planned ablation procedure.

The ICM recorded the following measures on a daily basis: degree of AF burden (AFB), heart rate variability (HRV), mean ventricular rate (mnVR), maximum ventricular rate (mxVR), cardiac activity (CA), daytime heart rate (DHR), and nighttime heart rate (NHR). AFB was measured based on AF duration,

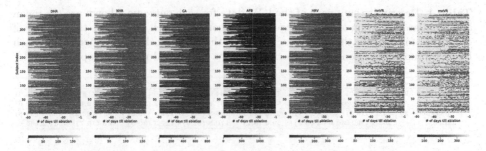

Fig. 1. ICM data visualized collectively. X-axis represents time. Missing values are denoted with gray colors. Subjects with indices 1 to 184 are those who experienced AF recurrence after ablation as defined in Sect. 2.2.

which was defined as the total minutes of all AF episodes detected each day. Both DHR and NHR measured ventricular rate, with nighttime defined as the time from midnight to 4 a.m. CA was computed using a proprietary algorithm to detect activity count as commonly done in pacemakers. In a nutshell, the algorithm counts the number of fluctuations in an accelerometer signal during each minute and classify each instant as active if the signal exceeded a threshold of 70 steps/minute. Subsequently, activity was defined as the number of active minutes per day. HRV was defined as the standard deviation of R-R medians (measured in 5-min intervals) over 24-h periods [1]. Data over periods of detected AF episodes were omitted from the calculations. More details of this dataset and patient characteristics can be found at [1].

2.2 Outcome and Patient Characteristics

Following standard clinical guidelines, ablation is considered unsuccessful for patients who experienced at least one AF episode of longer than 30s during the post-ablation period, which started and ended on day 91 and 365 post ablation, respectively. Based on this definition, our dataset is considered class-balanced (175 successful vs. 180 failed ablations).

Roughly 33% of patients were female; mean ages of females and males were 60.9 ± 9.1 and 57.7 ± 10.2, respectively. The body mass indices of females and males were 29.01 ± 5.18 and 29.15 ± 5.30, respectively.

After standardizing all ICM data, each patient sample is characterized by a 7-dimensional time-series with maximum length of $d = 90$ (days). About 80 patients had complete data for 90 days while 206 patients had more than 60 days of pre-ablation ICM recordings. The extent of missing data in this cohort is captured in Fig. 1; Table 1 presents a descriptive summary of the ICM measures.

2.3 Data Pre-processing and Splits

We performed k-fold cross-validations where we divided the entire dataset into non-overlapping subsets of training, validation, and testing, with each fold consisting of the same procedure involving the following steps.

Table 1. Descriptive summary of the ICM data for each outcome. Shown are the mean and standard deviation of the average values recorded of each group. d is the number of days used to calculate the statistics. Values of the colored cells are higher within each block (group comparison). The coloring suggests that d had minimal impact overall.

Group	d	AFB	DHR	NHR	CA	HRV	mnVR	mxVR
Succeeded	90	84.7 (167.0)	61.2 (9.6)	70.0 (9.6)	184.9 (87.4)	121.6 (32.9)	102.9 (18.6)	192.7 (56.9)
Failed		207.6 (320.0)	67.7 (10.8)	59.3 (7.8)	167.9 (78.9)	121.2 (29.8)	97.2 (14.6)	209.9 (62.6)
Succeeded	30	89.2 (178.5)	70.4 (9.7)	61.5 (10.1)	185.3 (90.3)	122.1 (33.3)	104.1 (20.2)	193.5 (53.8)
Failed		208.2 (320.9)	68.2 (9.8)	59.4 (8.2)	170.8 (81.3)	122.5 (30.5)	98.3 (15.7)	211.2 (65.4)

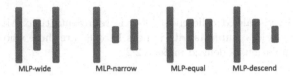

MLP-wide　　MLP-narrow　　MLP-equal　　MLP-descend

Fig. 2. MLP architectures explored in this work. Each blue bar denotes a layer; the length of each bar is proportional to the number of units used at each layer.

First, all time-series were temporally aligned so that the last entry of each time-series was the measure recorded on the day before each patient's ablation date. ICM recordings shorter than 90 days were appended with constant value of $\gamma = -1$. Second, the time-series were re-scaled to the range of [0, 1] based on the maximum and minimum values of all time-series t computed from the training subset. Third, missing values were replaced with γ. The test set in each fold was processed in the same manner.

We performed model training using the training set and evaluated each trained model using the test set (left-out set) in terms of sensitivity, specificity, and area under the receiver operating characteristic curve (AUC).

2.4　Tuning Neural Network Architectures: Number of Layers, Bottleneck Design Development, Hyper-parameter Tuning

We implemented five types of neural networks that have been deployed for time-series analyses in previous works; these include 1-dimensional convolutional neural network (1D-CNN) [10], multi-layer perceptrons (MLP) [3], long-short term memory (LSTM) networks, bi-directional LSTM (BiLSTM) [12], and the gated recurrent network (GRU) [16]. We further optimized the MLP architecture by exploring four bottleneck designs: 1) in **MLP-narrow**, the intermediate layer has $n/4$ units while the last layer has $n/2$ units; 2) in **MLP-equal**, both the last and intermediate layers use $n/2$ units; 3) **MLP-wide** has an intermediate layer of $n/2$ units; 4) **MLP-descend** has an intermediate layer of $n/2$ units and last layer of $n/4$ units. In this work, we set $n = d$. Visual summary of these bottleneck designs are shown in Fig. 2.

All examined neural networks and their variants employed ReLu [16] as the activation function as done in [7] for MLPs and [11] for LSTMs. For initialization of network weights, we explored methods of He and Xavier [9] (it has

Table 2. Preliminary analysis conducted to evaluate the importance of each measure. Cells with AUC greater than 63 are highlighted in purple, which collectively suggests the importance of AFB.

Algorithm		#1: AFB	#2: mxVR	#3: mnVR	#4: DHR	#5: NHR	#6: HRV	#7: CA
RF	AUC	66.4±3.0	63.9±4.5	59.1±6.0	58.4±5.0	57.8±1.6	55.9±3.0	54.5±4.7
	Sensitivity	60.2±1.1	59.6±3.6	56.7±3.8	55.6±3.5	53.8±3.6	53.8±3.6	54.1±3.0
	Specificity	61.4±6.2	60.3±7.1	57.8±9.3	54.7±5.9	52.8±2.5	52.8±2.5	52.9±5.6
SVM-linear	AUC	63.5±5.3	61.2±5.7	53.4±4.4	50.0±6.5	53.4±4.4	50.0±6.5	51.7±5.4
	Sensitivity	66.4±2.3	53.5±3.1	53.1±2.4	54.3±4.0	53.1±2.4	54.3±4.0	54.4±7.2
	Specificity	57.8±3.4	55.9±8.2	62.3±18.1	53.1±3.5	62.3±18.1	53.1±3.5	52.0±2.3
SVM-poly	AUC	68.9±2.3	62.1±2.6	52.6±2.0	46.4±3.3	47.2±2.6	52.6±2.0	68.9±2.3
	Sensitivity	67.8±7.3	56.7±1.1	56.4±0.9	49.4±0.2	49.1±0.4	56.4±0.9	67.8±7.3
	Specificity	59.8±1.7	95.8±5.9	100±0	56.4±10.2	51.0±11.4	100±0	59.8±1.7
SVM-RBF	AUC	70.8±2.8	62.1±4.8	68.6±5.6	61.5±5.5	58.3±1.1	49.5±5.7	45.1±2.8
	Sensitivity	67.4±5.4	56.5±1.8	62.5±3.9	57.1±2.1	55.6±3.9	49.4±3.1	47.9±2.2
	Specificity	62.3±1.7	66.1±11.8	69.4±5.9	58.2±5.7	65.3±5.6	52.7±11.6	48.9±4.2

been suggested to use Xavier's uniform for weight initialization of MPLs [7]). We also explored impact of including and omitting batch normalization and dropout layers. When we added dropout layers, we explored using a fixed dropout probability of 0.15 and the monotonically increasing scheme of Fawaz et al. [7].

In all trials, we left-out 30% of the development set as validation set, which was used to determine termination and early-stopping as similarly done in [20]. Following the analyses of Change et al. [5], we also explored two optimization algorithms (stochastic gradient descent and RMSprop) and two learning rate schedules (exponential decay and step-decay, i.e. reducing the learning rate by factor of 10 every 10 epochs). We set initial learning rate to a value of 0.0001 in most cases and experimented with batch sizes of $\{1, 4, 16\}$.

3 Results

3.1 Preliminary Analyses on the Individual ICM Measures

We first explored the value of individual measure using simple classifiers. As shown in Table 2 where cells with AUC greater than 63 are highlighted, use of all other measures alone generally did not lead to classification performance of greater than 60%. This was true regardless of model choice.

3.2 Comparative Analyses

We next examined the performance of all explored models using all seven biomeasures as well as using a single biomeasure. Table 3 reports a representative subset of all comparisons conducted in this study. In this table, models based on neural networks are highlighted in red cells whereas simpler models such as random forest, gradient boosted trees, and support vector machine using radial basis kernel (SVM-RBF) or polynomial kernel (SVM-poly-degree3) are shown on white

Table 3. Performance evaluations of different classification algorithms. Cells with blue background indicate top value of the group as calculated based on the achieved average value. RF used 1000 trees unless otherwise stated. "DO" denotes use of dropout layers while "BN" denotes use of batch normalization.

Input	Classifier settings		Performance		
	Algorithm	P	Sensitivity	Specificity	AUC
AFB	Random forest (50 trees)	2	58.3±3.0	59.2±6.9	64.8±3.0
	Random forest	2	60.2±1.1	61.4±6.2	66.4±3.0
	SVM-poly-degree3	2	67.8±7.3	59.8±1.7	68.9±2.3
	SVM-RBF	2	67.4±5.4	62.3±1.7	70.8±2.8
	MLP-narrow	11,092	66.6±16.1	45.7±18.2	62.3±8.1
	MLP-equal	14,040	61.6±18.7	50.6±28.2	58.1±11.3
	MLP-wide	16,155	66.0±4.7	56.0±0.3	66.7±2.1
	MLP-descend	16,599+444	62.4±20.2	33.5±23.7	51.8±3.6
	LSTM3	103,864	56.7±5.8	58.4±2.5	67.1±2.1
	LSTM3-DO	103,864	56.7±6.9	79.4±20.6	67.2±1.9
	BiLSTM3-DO	270,382	61.6±9.0	61.8±4.9	64.8±2.7
	GRU-DO	78,609	61.6±9.0	61.8±4.9	64.8±2.7
	GRU-BN-Xa	79,053+444	58.0±5.8	48.7±10.9	54.0±5.9
	GRU-BN-He	79,053+444	68.2±12.0	53.8±0.9	61.6±4.2
mnVR	Random forest		56.7±3.8	57.8±9.3	59.1±6.0
	SVM-linear		53.1±2.4	62.3±18.1	53.4±4.4
	SVM-poly-degree3		56.4±0.9	100±0	52.6±2.0
	SVM-RBF		62.5±3.9	69.4±5.9	68.6±5.6
	MLP-wide-DO-Xa-b8		56.7±1.2	94.2±5.1	56.7±7.1
	MLP-wide-DO-xa		56.5±0.8	82.0±21.8	54.3±1.9
	MLP-wide-DO-He-b8		58.4±3.7	71.4±11.4	60.0±7.7
	MLP-wide-DO-he	Same as above	55.9±0.4	73.1±19.1	57.6±6.0
	MLP-descend-xa		55.9±0.6	64.6±7.3	62.1±2.1
	MLP-descend-he		57.1±2.9	73.1±19.9	58.9±8.5
	LSTM-Xa, b8		51.6±3.4	77.8±25.9	51.3±2.5
	LSTM-DO-Xa-SDG-b1		55.9±5.0	81.1±18.9	64.0±10.4
	BiLSTM-DO-Xa		54.0±4.0	94.3±0	67.8±6.8
	GRU-DO-Xa		53.5±3.4	100.0±0.0	62.9±9.7
mxVR	Random forest		61.8±2.1	63.5±6.5	65.6±3.2
	SVM-poly-degree3		56.7±1.1	95.8±5.9	62.1±2.6
	SVM-RBF		56.5±1.8	66.1±11.8	62.1±4.8
	MLP-narrow	Same as above	56.6±0.8	62.9±8.4	62.5±2.7
	MLP-equal		55.6±1.6	60.9±8.0	61.6±3.2
	MLP-wide		55.1±1.7	58.5±6.7	63.1±2.8
All 7 measures	Random forest	2	63.1±4.3	67.5±10.2	67.8±5.0
	SVM-linear	2	61.8±2.6	62.0±5.1	63.3±2.7
	SVM-poly-degree3	2	56.7±1.1	95.8±5.9	66.1±4.1
	SVM-RBF	2	61.5±3.3	65.6±7.7	68.4±4.3
	Gradient boosted trees	2	57.2±4.9	56.1±17.8	56.7±8.3
	MLP-narrow	534,612	63.2±3.3	63.0±0.4	69.8±2.7
	MLP-equal	680,472	63.0±4.3	64.2±4.4	71.0±2.1
	MLP-wide	778,440	63.7±3.6	67.6±2.9	69.9±3.4
	MLP-descend	631,488	63.3±4.3	59.5±1.7	70.9±3.8
	BiLSTM-DO	13,233,766	57.6±2.2	86.7±6.8	68.2±0.3
	GRU-DO-Xa-SDG-b16	80,211	51.0±4.4	45.4±8.5	48.1±7.8
	GRU-DO-He-SDG-b16	80,111	55.4±1.8	65.2±12.8	58.0±4.7
	GRU-DO-Xa-SDG	80,211	50.0±5.8	56.4±16.0	57.2±3.4
	1D-CNN (3 layers)	583,170	61.3±11.8	49.5 ±17.5	55.4±3.2
	1D-CNN (deep) [10]	3,213,634+64	73.3±32.8	26.9±32.9	50.0±2.4
	1D-ResNet51 [18]	7,228,496+15,246	65.1±13.2	56.2±11.0	60.1±3.8
	1D-ResNet101 [18]	13,939,280+32,654	50.3±27.6	55.9±30.4	53.1±5.5
	AutoML [8]	N/A	55.0	52.0	53.0

Table 4. Predictive performance of APPLE [14] and CAAP-AF [19] scores.

Score	Performance		
	Sensitivity	Specificity	AUC
APPLE [14]	43.7	40.0	59.1
CAAP-AF [19]	49.0	33.3	45.9

cells. For direct comparison with deep learning algorithms, we also included in some of our experiments the AutoML pipeline [8], the deep 1-D CNN of [10] and 1-D variant of residual networks [18]. We highlighted AFB, mxVR and mnVR in this table based on results of Sect. 3.1 that suggested the inferiority of other biomeasures.

From this table, we highlight a summary of key findings as follows. First, comparing the four bottleneck designs explored, MLP-wide generally achieved better performance than the other variants. Second, using only the time-series capturing AF burden, traditional machine learning algorithms such as random forest and SVM achieved AUC of 64.8% to 70.8% while models based on recurrent neural networks achieved 54% to 67.2%. MLPs achieved AUC of 51.8 to 66.7%. Thirdly, BiLSTM, did not always achieve the most competitive results when compared with other recurrent networks such as LSTM. Lastly, using all seven time-series, MLP-equal gave the best performance (71.0 ± 2.1 in AUC) while deep networks such as the residual networks and the deep 1D-CNN of [10] gave inferior results most likely because these models need significantly more training samples when trained from scratch, given that they have significantly more model parameters than those of MLPs.

3.3 Comparison to Risk Scores Proposed in Recent Literature

As alluded in the introduction, the APPLE [14] and CAAP-AF [19] risk scores are routinely implemented in the clinical research literature to stratify AF patients. The APPLE risk score examines five baseline variables dichotomously: age, sex, left atrial diameter (LAD), left ventricular ejection fraction, and a measure of kidney function (i.e. estimated glomerular filtration rate). Similarly, the CAAP-AF [19] score maps the following 6 variables into different scales and subsequently totalled to yield an integer ranging from 0 to 13: age, sex, coronary artery disease, LAD, type of AF (persistent or longstanding), and the number of AAD failed.

The predictive performances of APPLE and CAAP-AF for our cohort are reported in Table 4. As reported in a recent study [4], the variables examined by these scores were also not predictive of treatment outcomes for our cohort.

3.4 Impact of Observation Period on Classification Performance

As a secondary analysis, we questioned whether the duration of cardiac monitoring could be shortened from 90 days. In other words, if we were to monitor heart

Table 5. Predictive performance when observation window of pre-ablation period was shortened from 90 days to d days. Start and end dates are expressed relative to the index date of ablation (negative values refer to days prior to ablation). Standard deviations are shown in brackets in this table.

Observation window			Classification algorithm	Performance		
d	Start date	End date		Sensitivity	Specificity	AUC
30	-45	-15	SVM-RBF	66.9 (5.1)	62.1 (2.1)	68.7 (2.7)
			SVM-poly-degree3	66.5 (5.3)	59.1 (1.1)	67.8 (3.6)
			RF	61.2 (3.7)	57.9 (0.6)	62.5 (3.9)
15	-30	-15	SVM-RBF	63.5 (5.5)	57.6 (2.5)	65.6 (2.4)
			SVM-poly-degree3	63.4 (5.0)	56.7 (2.6)	65.9 (2.6)
			RF	57.7 (1.9)	53.9 (1.7)	54.9 (3.3)
15	-45	-30	SVM-poly-degree3	68.2 (7.4)	58.7 (2.0)	66.5 (3.0)
			SVM-RBF	64.7 (4.3)	59.2 (3.6)	65.7 (3.2)
			RF	62.6 (5.6)	56.6 (0.7)	61.9 (6.1)

rhythm continuously for only 30 or 15 days, could there still be sufficient information to cast outcome prediction reliably? We answered this question empirically. From Table 5, one could see that shortening the monitoring period to as few as 15 days would lead to a slight decline in performance. The top-performing model achieved 68.7% and 65.6% in AUC for $d = 30$ and $d = 15$, respectively. This might be an encouraging result as the noninvasive cardiac monitors that record heart rhythm data continuously for up to 15 days may be used as an alternative to invasive ICMs [15].

4   Conclusions

Based on over 100 cross-validation trials, we conclude that the sole use of heart rhythm data collected prior to ablation treatment can predict treatment outcome with clinically acceptable performance. In particular, the top-performing predictive model achieved 71.0 ± 2.1 in AUC. All predictive models evaluated in this work achieved greater predictive performance than those achieved by APPLE [14] and CAAP-AF [19], two risk scores that are commonly implemented in the clinical research literature but achieving lower than 0.50 in AUC for our cohort, which is similar to findings of a recent evaluation study [4]. Future work will validate the trained models using an independent dataset.

Acknowledgements. We thank UBC's Data Science Institute-Huawei Research Program for funding support, CIRCA-DOSE investigators for provision of the data, Natural Sciences and Engineering Research Council of Canada, Compute Canada, and Calcul Québec for in-kind support.

References

1. Andrade, J.G., et al.: Cryoballoon or radiofrequency ablation for atrial fibrillation assessed by continuous monitoring: a randomized clinical trial. Circulation **140**(22), 1779–1788 (2019)

2. Beed, M.: Bennett's cardiac arrhythmias, practical notes on interpretation and treatment (2014)
3. Bellingegni, A.D., et al.: NLR, MLP, SVM, and LDA: a comparative analysis on EMG data from people with trans-radial amputation. J. Neuroeng. Rehabil. 14(1) (2017). Article number: 82. https://doi.org/10.1186/s12984-017-0290-6
4. Black-Maier, E., et al.: Predicting atrial fibrillation recurrence after ablation in patients with heart failure: validity of the APPLE and CAAP-AF risk scoring systems. Pacing Clin. Electrophysiol. 42(11), 1440–1447 (2019)
5. Chang, Z., Zhang, Y., Chen, W.: Effective adam-optimized LSTM neural network for electricity price forecasting. In: 2018 IEEE 9th International Conference on Software Engineering and Service Science (ICSESS), pp. 245–248. IEEE (2018)
6. Dretzke, J., et al.: Predicting recurrent atrial fibrillation after catheter ablation: a systematic review of prognostic models. EP Europace 22(5), 748–760 (2020)
7. Fawaz, H.I., et al.: Deep learning for time series classification: a review. Data Min. Knowl. Discov. 33(4), 917–963 (2019). https://doi.org/10.1007/s10618-019-00619-1
8. Feurer, M., Hutter, F.: Towards further automation in automl. In: ICML AutoML Workshop, p. 13 (2018)
9. Hou, L., et al.: Normalization helps training of quantized LSTM. In: Advances in Neural Information Processing Systems, pp. 7344–7354 (2019)
10. Hsieh, C.-H., et al.: Detection of atrial fibrillation using 1D convolutional neural network. Sensors 20(7), 2136 (2020)
11. Kent, D., Salem, F.: Performance of three slim variants of the long short-term memory (LSTM) layer. In: IEEE 62nd International Midwest Symposium on Circuits and Systems (MWSCAS), pp. 307–310. IEEE (2019)
12. Kim, J., Moon, N.: BiLSTM model based on multivariate time series data in multiple field for forecasting trading area. J. Ambient Intell. Hum. Comput. 1–10 (2019). https://doi.org/10.1007/s12652-019-01398-9
13. Kirchhof, P.: The future of atrial fibrillation management: integrated care and stratified therapy. The Lancet 390(10105), 1873–1887 (2017)
14. Kornej, J., et al.: The APPLE score: a novel and simple score for the prediction of rhythm outcomes after catheter ablation of atrial fibrillation. Clin. Res. Cardiol. 104(10), 871–876 (2015). https://doi.org/10.1007/s00392-015-0856-x
15. Lee, S.P., et al.: Highly flexible, wearable, and disposable cardiac biosensors for remote and ambulatory monitoring. NPJ Digit. Med. 1(1), 1–8 (2018)
16. Neyshabur, B., et al.: Exploring generalization in deep learning. In: Advances in Neural Information Processing Systems, pp. 5947–5956 (2017)
17. Patel, N.J., et al.: Global rising trends of atrial fibrillation: a major public health concern (2018)
18. Strodthoff, N., et al.: Deep learning for ECG analysis: benchmarks and insights from PTB-XL. arXiv preprint arXiv:2004.13701 (2020)
19. Winkle, R.A., et al.: Predicting atrial fibrillation ablation outcome: the CAAP-AF score. Heart Rhythm 13(11), 2119–2125 (2016)
20. Yoo, Y., et al.: Deep learning of brain lesion patterns and user-defined clinical and MRI features for predicting conversion to multiple sclerosis from clinically isolated syndrome. Comput. Methods Biomech. Biomed. Eng. Imaging Vis. 7(3), 250–259 (2019)

AdaBoosted Deep Ensembles: Getting Maximum Performance Out of Small Training Datasets

Syed M. S. Reza[1]($\boxtimes$), John A. Butman[2], Deric M. Park[3], Dzung L. Pham[1], and Snehashis Roy[1]

[1] Center for Neuroscience and Regenerative Medicine, Henry Jackson Foundation, Bethesda, MD 20817, USA
{syed.reza,dzung.pham,snehashis.roy}@nih.gov
[2] Radiology and Imaging Sciences, Clinical Center,National Institute of Health, Bethesda, MD 20892, USA
jbutmana@cc.nih.gov
[3] Department of Neurology, The University of Chicago, Chicago, IL 60637, USA
parkd@uchicago.edu

Abstract. Even though state-of-the-art convolutional neural networks (CNNs) have shown outstanding performance in a wide range of imaging applications, they typically require large amounts of high-quality training data to prevent over fitting. In the case of medical image segmentation, it is often difficult to gain access to large data sets, particularly those involving rare diseases, such as skull-based chordoma tumors. This challenge is exacerbated by the difficulty in performing manual delineations, which are time-consuming and can have inconsistent quality. In this work, we propose a deep ensemble method that learns multiple models, trained using a leave-one-out strategy, and then aggregates the outputs for test data through a boosting strategy. The proposed method was evaluated for chordoma tumor segmentation in head magnetic resonance images using three well-known CNN architectures; VNET, UNET, and Feature pyramid network (FPN). Significantly improved Dice scores (up to 27%) were obtained using the proposed ensemble method when compared to a single model trained with all available training subjects. The proposed ensemble method can be applied to any neural network based segmentation method to potentially improve generalizability when learning from a small sized dataset.

1 Introduction

Over the last couple of decades, ensemble learning has been shown to be an effective technique to improve the performance of both classical machine learning (ML) and deep learning approaches. The ensembling technique was first introduced by Dasarathy and Sheela [6] with the idea of combining multiple classifiers to improve performance over a single approach. Later, Hansen et al. [9] proposed an ensemble of similarly configured neural networks to improve the

M. Liu et al. (Eds.): MLMI 2020, LNCS 12436, pp. 572–582, 2020.
https://doi.org/10.1007/978-3-030-59861-7_58

performance for random pattern classification. Subsequently, many ensemble-based techniques such as boosting [24], AdaBoost [8], mixture of experts [10], consensus aggregation [2], and random forest [4] have been proposed for classification and regression analysis.

With the advent of deep learning [13] and enhanced computational resources, CNNs [14] have become the dominant ML approach in most image analysis tasks because of its superior performance. Inevitably, different variants of ensemble techniques have emerged with CNN-based methods for segmenting ischemic stroke lesions [5], the optic cup [28] for glaucoma detection, white matter lesions [17], and infant brains [7] from magnetic resonance imaging (MRI). Bnouni et al. [3] used an ensemble of ten multi-scale CNNs for cervical cancer segmentation. Kamnitsas et al. [11] proposed an ensemble method that aggregates predictions from multiple models and architectures for tumor segmentation. The above techniques typically differ from each other based on the selection of individual classifiers, the specific fusion levels (e.g., feature, classifier, output), and/or the aggregation rule for obtaining the ensemble decision. However, these techniques were designed to learn from adequately sized training data sets and may suffer from over fitting when learning from small training sets. Data augmentation [25] techniques is commonly used to deal with limited data by synthesizing under-represented samples. However, quality improvements with augmentation techniques are generally small and they do not sufficiently address the inconsistency in the ground-truth data.

In medical image analysis, automated segmentation of pathologies is often challenging due to insufficient training data, particularly for rare diseases such as chordoma, which is a rare cancer resulting in tumors at the skull-base. In addition, the diverse size, shape, and location of chordomas, as well as the overlapping intensity distribution of nearby anatomical structures, cause even experts to disagree on the ground truth. Therefore, inconsistencies can be evident in chordoma manual delineations to a higher degree than other pathologies. Although a number of state-of-the-art brain tumor segmentation methods have been reported in the BRATS [18] challenge workshops, none of them have been applied for chordoma segmentation. Recently, a cascaded CNN-based method [22] has been reported with a primary focus on reducing the false positives which strongly appear outside the brain. However, the method did not address the two issues of limited training data size and inconsistency in the ground-truth. Unlike the BRATS [18] datasets, which has hundreds of images with manually delineated labels, smaller datasets pose difficulty in training, because CNN algorithms typically need large amounts of training data.

In this work, we propose an ensemble method to address these issues. The proposed method uses a leave-one-out type strategy to construct multiple, relatively weaker classifiers and then aggregates the probability maps of the test case by means of a boosting strategy. Our proposed method can be applied to any supervised machine learning-based segmentation task to potentially improve generalizability when learning from a small training dataset.

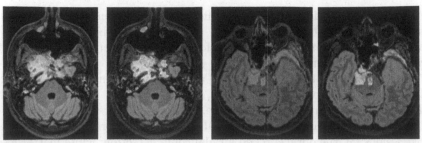

FLAIR Subj A FLAIRC Subj A   FLAIR Subj B   FLAIRC Subj B

Fig. 1. Example FLAIR and FLAIRC images for two subjects with chordomas are shown. The tumor margins are shown on FLAIRC images with red outline. (Color figure online)

2 Method

2.1 Dataset

The chordoma tumor dataset used in this study was reported in [22] which consists of only 8 patients, each with one to five time points, totaling 22 scans. Each time point included T_1-w, T_2-w, post-contrast T_1 (called T_1C), FLAIR, and post-contrast FLAIR (called FLAIRC). In this study, we chose only FLAIR and FLAIRC because, (a) training time increases with each additional contrast, and (b) we evaluated every possible combination of two contrasts on one image, and found the FLAIR+FLAIRC combination gave the best result. All images were acquired on a Siemens 1.5T MRI scanner. The image acquisition parameters for FLAIR and FLAIRC were set as follows: $TR/TE/TI = 8000/335/2280$ ms, flip angle 120°, resolution $1.02 \times 1.02 \times 1$ mm³. Manual delineations of the chordomas were performed by a trained operator and verified by a radiologist.

2.2 Pre-processing

To define a canonical space across patients, the MNI atlas was used as a template. All FLAIR images of the 22 scans were rigidly registered to this template image [1]. The corresponding FLAIRC images were also placed in the same space by using the same transformation from FLAIR. Figure 1 shows some example images. Intensity inhomogeneity correction was carried out using N4 [26]. Finally, the intensity of each image was independently normalized so that the modes of the white matter intensities were unity. The modes were automatically detected by a kernel density estimator from the intensity histograms [21]. Note that because chordomas are outside the parenchyma, brain extraction can not be not performed.

2.3 CNN Architectures and Hyper-parameters

To demonstrate that our ensemble approach is not specific to a particular CNN approach, we employed three well-known architectures; VNET [19], UNET [23], and FPN [15]. The hyper-parameters of all three networks were the same, learning rate 0.0001 with optimizer Adam [12], batch-size 60, patch-size $32 \times 32 \times 32$. Considering the variation of class-ratios (foreground/background) among the subjects and hard-to-detect pathologies from nearby tissues, we chose focal loss [16] as the loss function. To train each model, an equal number of positive and negative patches are provided as input, where positive or negative patches is defined on whether the center voxel falls on tumor or non-tumor regions, respectively. However, our primary focus in this work is not in the CNN architecture design, but in their use when working with limited data.

2.4 Ensemble Learning

A schematic of the training, testing, and ensemble learning setup is shown in Fig. 2. A subject-wise leave-one-out cross-validation (LOOCV) was conducted using the images from the $N = 8$ subjects. In other words, all longitudinal scans of one subject were kept out of training while using it as validation. The LOOCV with ensembling strategy is described as follows. Assume the ith subject is considered as a validation data. Usually a model is trained with all of the remaining $(N-1)$ atlas images, i.e., $\{1, \ldots, i-1, i+1, \ldots, N\}$. However, instead of creating one model with $(N-1)$ images, we create an ensemble of $(N-1)$ "weak" classifier models with $(N-2)$ images, excluding one from the $(N-1)$ atlases at a time. The assumption is that with a limited number of training atlases, it is highly likely that the subject (i.e. the validation) image is inconsistent with some of the atlases (i.e. the tumors have a very different appearance). This leave-one-out training strategy ensures the generalizability of the models with a "fault tolerance" of at most one atlas. Since most neural networks are not able to overcome the inconsistency when the amount of data is small, excluding some from training helps the network converge better. This assumption is especially important for small scale training data.

Consequently, for a test subject, there are $(N-1) = 7$ weak classifiers, each trained with $(N-2) = 6$ images. The $(N-1)$ classifiers are boosted to create a stronger prediction, as described in the next section. This procedure is repeated as leave-one-out cross validation for all of the $N = 8$ subjects, resulting in total $N \times (N-1) \times 3 = 168$ trainings for each of the VNET, UNET, and FPN models.

2.5 Boosting

Boosting algorithms fuse the outputs of multiple methods; consensus-based majority voting, simple averaging or weighted averaging are some popular forms of boosting used to combine classifier outputs. STAPLE [27] is another method to fuse multiple hard segmentations to estimate the ground truth. We performed a weighted averaging inspired by AdaBoost [8] where the weight parameters are calculated based on an accuracy metric of the classifiers. The weight parameter α_j for the corresponding j^{th} weak classifier, $j \in \{1, \ldots, N-2\}, j \neq i$, is measured by $\alpha_j = \frac{1}{2} \log(\frac{1-\epsilon_j}{\epsilon_j})$, where ϵ_j is (1-TPR), TPR being the true positive rate of

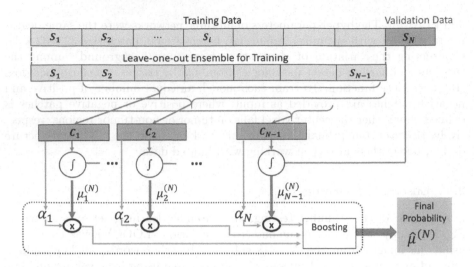

Fig. 2. Training, testing, and cross-validated ensemble learning setup.

the jth classifier. TPR was selected to prioritize high segmentation sensitivity. The final membership of the ith test image is calculated by,

$$\hat{\mu}^{(i)} = \frac{1}{\sum_{j=1}^{N-2} \alpha_j} \sum_{j=1}^{N-2} \alpha_j \mu_j^{(i)},$$

where $\mu_j^{(i)}$ is the membership of the ith image obtained by applying the jth classifier, $j \neq i$. This approach therefore weighs the models with higher cross-validated true positive rate more heavily in the ensemble.

3   Results

The training was performed on a 16 core Intel Xeon E5 3.2GHz CPU and 4 NVIDIA GeForce 12GB TitanX GPUs. The cross-validation procedure for one subject, i.e. with 7 patients as training data, and one as validation, took approximately 9 days for all 3 networks, compared to only a day of standard training with all subjects. Note that while a normal LOOCV procedure is $\mathcal{O}(N)$ in training time, our ensembling strategy is $\mathcal{O}(N^2)$, N being the number of subjects. The inference time is N ($N = 7$ here) times the inference time for one model, which is $\sim$1 min for a $1\,\text{mm}^3$ 3D image.

The probability maps of a test subject (call it i^{th} image) obtained by several weak classifiers are shown in Fig. 3. C-j indicates that the membership is obtained by the jth weak classifier, which is synonymous with having the training set of images $\{1, \ldots, N\} \setminus \{i, j\}$. Significant variability among the memberships are observed because of the diverse nature of chordomas in a very small dataset, and possibly some inconsistency in the ground-truth or image quality. Classifiers that show good performance means that excluding the data from that patient during training did not greatly impact the model performance. Similarly, classifiers that show poor performance suggests that the inclusion of that subject is critically important for obtaining an accurate segmentation and should be weighted more strongly. For example, C-5 of VNET and FPN produces a poor segmentation that includes only a small part of the chordoma. Since exclusion of the 5th image results in poor segmentation, it is assumed to be similar to the test subject and important for training of this i^{th} subject image. Any training that excludes the 5th image should be weighted less to compute the final segmentation of the ith image.

Example images of the segmentations for three subjects are shown in Fig. 4. Chordoma patients frequently develop sinus infections, which look very similar to the tumor itself in all contrasts. This is a frequent area of false positives (yellow arrows). The ensembling approach clearly provides more accurate segmentation with fewer false positives.

Quantitative evaluation was performed using 5 metrics of the segmented tumor, namely Dice similarity, sensitivity, positive predictive value (PPV),

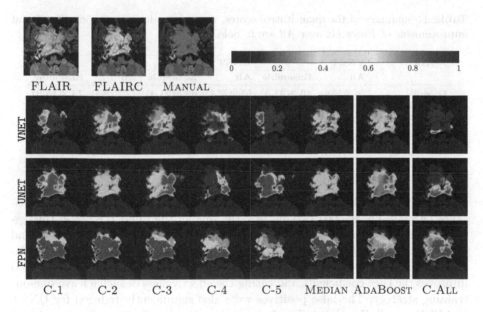

Fig. 3. The output probability maps of the weak and boosted classifiers are shown. Top row shows FLAIRC, FLAIR, and manual mask of a subject i. Rows 2–4 show probability maps for 5 (out of total 7) weak classifiers. C-j indicates the membership $\mu_j^{(i)}$ i.e. the membership of the ith image obtained by the jth weak classifier, which was trained with images $\{1, \ldots, N\} \setminus \{i, j\}$. Two boosting techniques using the median of memberships and weighted average with Adaboost weights, as well as the single classifier (named as C-All) trained on all available training subjects are shown for VNET, UNET, and FPN, respectively. All images are cropped and zoomed for better visualization.

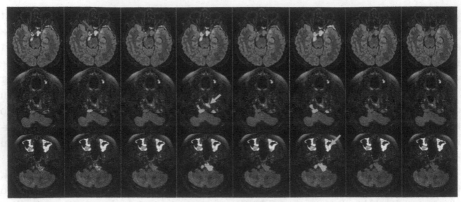

FLAIRC   VNET-All VNET-En   UNET-All UNET-En   FPN-All   FPN-En   Manual

Fig. 4. Example images of segmented tumor using cross-validated ensemble learning. *All* indicates training with all available subjects and *En* corresponds to the proposed ensemble learning. The yellow and red arrows show the presence of false positives and false negatives, respectively. (Color figure online)

Table 1. Summary of the quantitative scores, mean (standard deviation). Significant improvements of *Ensemble* over *All* are in bold.

Metric	VNET		UNET		FPN	
	All	Ensemble	All	Ensemble	All	Ensemble
Dice(%)	36.8(25.6)	**46.9(21.3)**	53.9(27.7)	**63.3(21.4)**	72.2(16.3)	**74.2(15.9)**
Sensitivity(%)	30.3(26.2)	**38.0(23.5)**	51.9(28.1)	57.0(22.5)	78.9(14.4)	79.4(14.4)
PPV(%)	71.6(37.5)	80.2(29.6)	69.2(33.1)	**79.1(27.2)**	71.7(21.1)	**74.3(20.3)**
RAVD	0.68(0.28)	**0.60(0.20)**	1.04(1.71)	**0.45(0.32)**	0.59(1.19)	0.55(1.15)
ASSD(mm)	8.81(16.3)	8.34(12.9)	7.02(9.70)	**4.47(7.09)**	4.68(8.19)	4.33(7.71)

relative absolute volume difference (RAVD), and average symmetric surface distance (ASSD). For the last two metrics, the smaller the value, the better the segmentation. The average and standard deviations of these metrics can be found in Table 1. A Wilcoxon signed-rank test was performed to measure the statistical significance. For all three networks, having ensembles significantly ($p < 0.05$) improves the Dice coefficients, indicating the effectiveness of such a leave-one-out training strategy. The false positives were also significantly reduced for UNET and FPN as well. Boxplots in Fig. 5(a)-(c) show the distributions of the statistics.

Comparisons between different boosting strategies such as STAPLE, simple mean or median of the membership functions, and Adaboost was also carried out for all three networks, but shown in Fig. 5(d) for FPN only. Adaboost with memberships improved the Dice coefficients compared to STAPLE with hard segmentations, and had similar mean performance with lower standard deviation than Median and Mean.

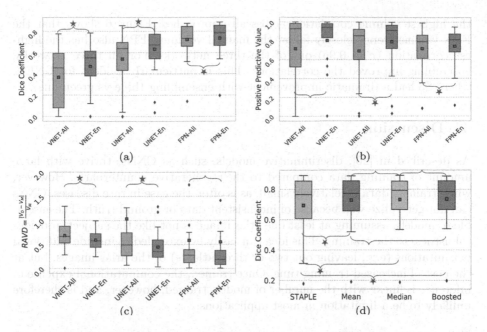

Fig. 5. Boxplots **(a)-(c)** show Dice, PPV, and volume difference of the proposed ensemble method over traditional LOOCV for the 3 networks. The small red squares show the average. The ∗ corresponds to $p < 0.05$ according to the Wilcoxon signed-rank test. Curly braces without ∗ corresponds to $p \geq 0.05$. Comparison among different boosting techniques using FPN is shown in **(d)**. (Color figure online)

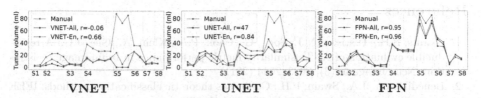

Fig. 6. Subject-wise volumetric plots for the segmented tumors by the CNNs are shown. The x-axis shows contiguous time-points for 8 subjects, denoted by Sj. Pearson's correlation coefficients, r, between each CNN-based method and the manual segmentation are shown inset. (Color figure online)

It is evident that the ensemble based training was effective in learning from a very small atlas set of only 7 subjects, indicated by 27%, 17%, and 3% improvement of Dice for VNET, UNET, and FPN. Compared to VNET or UNET, FPN is significantly better as seen in Fig. 5. FPN-En provides smaller, albeit statistically significant improvement from ensembling over FPN-All.

Subject-wise segmented tumor volumes are shown in Fig. 6 with Pearson's linear correlation coefficient computed between each CNN-based method and the manual segmentations. We found the Adaboost Ensemble technique to provide the highest volume correlation across all approaches. Figure 6 shows that the FPN volume trends closely follow the manual volumes. FPN also has the highest correlation ($r = 0.96$) out of the three networks. For all three networks, ensembling improved the correlations. This is particularly evident for UNET, where S3 had a dramatic improvement with ensembling (blue vs green line).

4 Discussion

As described in [20], discriminative models, such as CNNs, thrive with large amount of training data compared to their generative counterparts. However, when training data is relatively small, as is often the case in rare diseases, CNNs can not generalize well because of inconsistent data or ground truth. The ensemble of models, assuming at least one atlas image is not like the subject, provides robustness to the training. This idea can easily be extended to include additional permutations (e.g., leaving out two or three atlases) of the atlas images, but at the cost of increased training time. Once trained, the computational expense of inference is linear with the number of models trained, however, and is therefore unlikely to be a limitation in most applications.

Acknowledgments. This works was partially supported by the Department of Defense in the Center for Neuroscience and Regenerative Medicine, by grant RG-1507–05243 from the National Multiple Sclerosis Society, and by the Intramural Research Program of the National Institutes of Health, Clinical Center.

References

1. Avants, B.B., Tustison, N.J., Song, G., Cook, P.A., Klein, A., Gee, J.C.: A reproducible evaluation of ANTs similarity metric performance in brain image registration. Neuroimage **54**(3), 2033–2044 (2011)
2. Benediktsson, J.A., Swain, P.H.: Consensus theoretic classification methods. IEEE Trans. Syst. Man Cybern. **22**(4), 688–704 (1992)
3. Bnouni, N., Rekik, I., Rhim, M.S., Amara, N.E.B.: Dynamic multi-scale CNN forest learning for automatic cervical cancer segmentation. In: Shi, Y., Suk, H-Il, Liu, M. (eds.) MLMI 2018. LNCS, vol. 11046, pp. 19–27. Springer, Cham (2018). https://doi.org/10.1007/978-3-030-00919-9_3
4. Breiman, L.: Random forests. Mach. Learn **45**(1), 5–32 (2001)
5. Chen, L., Bentley, P., Rueckert, D.: Fully automatic acute ischemic lesion segmentation in DWI using convolutional neural networks. NeuroImage Clin. **15**, 633–643 (2017)
6. Dasarathy, B.V., Sheela, B.V.: A composite classifier system design: concepts and methodology. Proc. IEEE **67**(5), 708–713 (1979)
7. Dolz, J., Desrosiers, C., Wang, L., Yuan, J., Shen, D., Ayed, I.B.: Deep CNN ensembles and suggestive annotations for infant brain MRI segmentation. Comput. Med. Imaging Graph. **79**, 101660 (2020)
8. Freung, Y., Shapire, R.: A decision-theoretic generalization of on-line learning and an application to boosting. J. Comput. Syst. Sci. **55**, 119–139 (1997)

9. Hansen, L.K., Salamon, P.: Neural network ensembles. IEEE Trans. Pattern Anal. Mach. Intell. **12**(10), 993–1001 (1990)

10. Jordan, M.I., Jacobs, R.A.: Hierarchical mixtures of experts and the EM algorithm. Neural Comput. **6**(2), 181–214 (1994)

11. Kamnitsas, K., et al.: Ensembles of multiple models and architectures for robust brain tumour segmentation. In: Crimi, A., Bakas, S., Kuijf, H., Menze, B., Reyes, M. (eds.) BrainLes 2017. LNCS, vol. 10670, pp. 450–462. Springer, Cham (2018). https://doi.org/10.1007/978-3-319-75238-9_38

12. Kingma, D.P., Ba, J.: Adam: a method for stochastic optimization. arXiv preprint, (2014) arXiv:1412.6980

13. LeCun, Y., Bengio, Y., Hinton, G.: Deep learning. Nature **521**(7553), 436–444 (2015)

14. LeCun, Y., Bengio, Y., et al.: Convolutional networks for images, speech, and time series. Handb. Brain Theory Neural Netw. **3361**(10), 1995 (1995)

15. Lin, T.Y., Dollár, P., Girshick, R., He, K., Hariharan, B., Belongie, S.: Feature pyramid networks for object detection. In: Proceedings of the IEEE conference on computer vision and pattern recognition, pp. 2117–2125. IEEE (2017)

16. Lin, T.Y., Goyal, P., Girshick, R., He, K., Dollár, P.: Focal loss for dense object detection. In: Proceedings of the IEEE international conference on computer vision, pp. 2980–2988. IEEE (2017)

17. Manjón, J.V., et al.: MRI white matter lesion segmentation using an ensemble of neural networks and overcomplete patch-based voting. Comput. Med. Imaging Graph. **69**, 43–51 (2018)

18. Menze, B.H., et al.: The multimodal brain tumor image segmentation benchmark (BRATS). IEEE Trans. Med. Imaging **34**(10), 1993–2024 (2014)

19. Milletari, F., Navab, N., Ahmadi, S.A.: V-net: fully convolutional neural networks for volumetric medical image segmentation. In: 2016 Fourth International Conference on 3D Vision (3DV), pp. 565–571. IEEE (2016)

20. Ng, A., Jordan, M.I.: On discriminative vs. generative classifiers: a comparison of logistic regression and naive Bayes. In: Intl. Conf. on Neural Information Processing Systems (NIPS), pp. 841–848 (2002)

21. Pham, D.L., Prince, J.L.: An adaptive fuzzy C-means algorithm for image segmentation in the presence of intensity inhomogeneities. Pattern Recogn. Lett. **20**(1), 57–68 (1999)

22. Reza, S.M.S., Roy, S., Park, D.M., Pham, D.L., Butman, J.A.: Cascaded convolutional neural networks for spine chordoma tumor segmentation from MRI. In: Medical Imaging 2019: Biomedical Applications in Molecular, Structural, and Functional Imaging, International Society for Optics and Photonics. **10953**, p. 1095325 (2019)

23. Ronneberger, O., Fischer, P., Brox, T.: U-Net: convolutional networks for biomedical image segmentation. In: Navab, N., Hornegger, J., Wells, W.M., Frangi, A.F. (eds.) MICCAI 2015. LNCS, vol. 9351, pp. 234–241. Springer, Cham (2015). https://doi.org/10.1007/978-3-319-24574-4_28

24. Schapire, R.E.: The strength of weak learnability. Mach. Learn. **5**(2), 197–227 (1990)

25. Shorten, C., Khoshgoftaar, T.M.: A survey on image data augmentation for deep learning. J. Big Data **6**(1), 60 (2019)

26. Tustison, N.J., et al.: N4ITK: improved N3 bias correction. IEEE Trans. Med. Imaging **29**(6), 1310–1320 (2010)

27. Warfield, S.K., Zou, K.H., Wells, W.M.: Simultaneous truth and performance level estimation (STAPLE): an algorithm for the validation of image segmentation. IEEE Trans. Med. Imaging **23**(7), 903–921 (2004)
28. Zilly, J., Buhmann, J.M., Mahapatra, D.: Glaucoma detection using entropy sampling and ensemble learning for automatic optic cup and disc segmentation. Comput. Med. Imaging Graph. **55**, 28–41 (2017)

Cross-Task Representation Learning
for Anatomical Landmark Detection

Zeyu Fu[1](✉), Jianbo Jiao[1], Michael Suttie[2], and J. Alison Noble[1]

[1] Department of Engineering Science, University of Oxford, Oxford, UK
zeyu.fu@eng.ox.ac.uk
[2] Nuffield Department of Women's and Reproductive Health, University of Oxford, Oxford, UK

Abstract. Recently, there is an increasing demand for automatically detecting anatomical landmarks which provide rich structural information to facilitate subsequent medical image analysis. Current methods related to this task often leverage the power of deep neural networks, while a major challenge in fine tuning such models in medical applications arises from insufficient number of labeled samples. To address this, we propose to regularize the knowledge transfer across source and target tasks through cross-task representation learning. The proposed method is demonstrated for extracting facial natomical landmarks which facilitate the diagnosis of fetal alcohol syndrome. The source and target tasks in this work are face recognition and landmark detection, respectively. The main idea of the proposed method is to retain the feature representations of the source model on the target task data, and to leverage them as an additional source of supervisory signals for regularizing the target model learning, thereby improving its performance under limited training samples. Concretely, we present two approaches for the proposed representation learning by constraining either final or intermediate model features on the target model. Experimental results on a clinical face image dataset demonstrate that the proposed approach works well with few labeled data, and outperforms other compared approaches.

Keywords: Anatomical landmark detection · Knowledge transfer

1 Introduction

Accurate localization of anatomical landmarks plays an important role for medical image analysis and applications such as image registration and shape analysis [3]. It also has the potential to facilitate the early diagnosis of Fetal Alcohol Syndrome (FAS) [11]. An FAS diagnosis requires the identification of at least 2 of 3 cardinal facial features; a thin upper lip, a smooth philtrum and a reduced palpebral fissure length (PFL) [10], which means that even a small inaccuracy in the PFL measurement can easily result in misdiagnosis. Conventional approaches for extracting anatomical landmarks mostly rely on manual examination, which is

© Springer Nature Switzerland AG 2020
M. Liu et al. (Eds.): MLMI 2020, LNCS 12436, pp. 583–592, 2020.
https://doi.org/10.1007/978-3-030-59861-7_59

tedious and subject to inter-operator variability. To automate landmark detection, recent methods in computer vision [16,22,25] and medical image analysis [3,11,26] have extensively relied on convolutional neural networks (CNN) for keypoint regression. Although these models have achieved promising performance, this task still remains challenging especially when handling the labeled data scarcity in medical domain, due to expensive and inefficient annotation process. Transfer learning, in particular fine-tuning pre-trained models from similar domains have been widely used to help reduce over-fitting by providing a better initialization [17]. However, merely fine-tuning the existing parameters may arguably lead to a suboptimal local minimum for the target task, because much knowledge of the pre-trained model in the feature space is barely explored [13,14]. To address this, we explore the following question: *Is it possible to leverage the abundant knowledge from a domain-similar source task to guide or regularize the training of the target task with limited training samples?*

We investigate this hypothesis via cross-task representation learning, where "cross-task" here means that the learning process is made between the source and target tasks with different objectives. In this work, the proposed cross-task representation learning approach is illustrated for localizing anatomical landmarks in clinical face images to facilitate early recognition of fetal alcohol syndrome [1], where the source and target tasks are face recognition and landmark detection. Intuitively, the proposed representation learning is interpreted as preserving feature representations of a source classification model on the target task data, which serves as a regularization constraint for learning the landmark detector. Two approaches for the proposed representation learning are developed by constraining either final or intermediate network features on the target model.

Related Work. Current state-of-art methods formulate the landmark detection as a CNN based regression problem, including two main frameworks: direct coordinate regression [6,24] and heatmap regression [16,22]. Heatmap regression usually outperforms its counterpart as it preserves high spatial resolution during regression. In medical imaging, several CNN architectures have been developed based on attention mechanisms [3,26], and cascaded processing [23] for the enhancement of anatomical landmark detection. However, the proposed learning approach in this paper focuses on internally enriching the feature representations for the keypoint localization without complicating the network design.

Among existing knowledge transfer approaches, fine-tuning [22], as a standard practice initializes from a pre-trained model and shifts its original capability towards a target task, where a small learning rate is often applied and some model parameters may need to be frozen to avoid over fitting. However, empirically modifying the existing parameters may not generalize well over the small training dataset. Knowledge distillation originally proposed for model compression [9] is also related to knowledge transfer. This technique has been successfully extended and applied to various applications, including hint learning [20], incremental learning [5,15], privileged learning [4], domain adaptation [7] and human expert knowledge distillation [19]. These distillation methods focused on training a compact model by operating the knowledge transfer across the same tasks [9,19,20]. However, our proposed learning approach aims to regularize the transfer learning across different tasks.

Contributions. We propose a new deep learning framework for anatomical landmark detection under limited training samples. The main contributions are: (1) we propose a cross-task representation learning approach whereby the feature representations of a pre-trained classification model are leveraged for regularizing the optimization of landmark detection. (2) We present two approaches for the proposed representation learning by constraining either final or intermediate network features on the target task data. In addition, a cosine similarity inspired by metric learning is adopted as a regularization loss to transfer the relational knowledge between tasks. (3) We experimentally show that the proposed learning approach performs well in anatomical landmark detection with limited training samples and is superior to standard transfer learning approaches.

2   Method

In this section, we first present the problem formulation of anatomical landmark detection, and then describe the design of the proposed cross-task representation learning to address this task.

2.1   Problem Formulation

In this paper, our target task is anatomical landmark detection, which aims to localize a set of pre-defined anatomical landmarks given a facial image. Let $\mathcal{D}^t = \{\mathbf{I}_i^t, \mathbf{p}_i^t\}_{i=1}^{N_t}$ be the training dataset with N_t pairs of training samples in the target domain. $\mathbf{I}_i^t \in \mathbb{R}^{H \times W \times 3}$ represents a 2D RGB image with height H and width W, $\mathbf{p}_i^t = [(x_1, y_1), (x_2, y_2), ..., (x_K, y_K)] \in \mathbb{R}^{2 \times K}$ denotes the corresponding labeled landmark coordinates, and K is the number of anatomical landmarks ($K = 14$). We formulate this task using heatmap regression, inspired by its recent success in keypoint localization [16,22]. Following prior work [16], we downscale the labeled coordinates to $1/4$ of the input size ($\mathbf{p}_i^t = \mathbf{p}_i^t/4$), and then transform them to a set of heatmaps $\mathbf{G}_i^t \in \mathbb{R}^{(H/4) \times (W/4) \times K}$. Each heatmap $\mathbf{g}_k^t \in \mathbb{R}^{(H/4) \times (W/4)}, k \in \{1, ..., K\}$ is defined as a 2D Gaussian kernel centered on the k-th landmark coordinate (x_k, y_k). The (a, b) entry of $\mathbf{g}_k^t$ is computed as $\mathbf{g}_k^t(a, b) = \exp(-\frac{(a-x_k)^2+(b-y_k)^2}{2\sigma^2})$, where σ denotes the kernel width ($\sigma = 1.5$ pixels). Consequently, the goal is to learn a network which regresses each input image to a set of heatmaps, based on the updated dataset $\mathcal{D}^t = \{\mathbf{I}_i^t, \mathbf{G}_i^t\}_{i=1}^{N_t}$.

For this regression problem, most state-the-of-the-art methods [22,25] follow the encoder-decoder design, in which a pre-trained network (e.g. ResNet50 [8]) is usually utilized in the encoder for feature extraction, and then the entire network or only the decoder is fine-tuned during training. However, due to the limited number of training samples in our case, merely relying on standard fine-tuning may not always provide a good localization accuracy. Therefore, we present the proposed solution to address this problem in the next section.

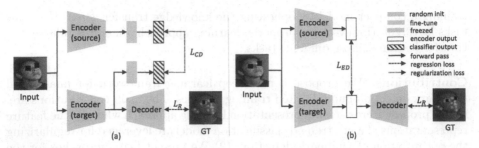

Fig. 1. Illustration of proposed approaches for learning the anatomical landmark detection models, where (a) presents the regularization constraint on the final layer output (L_{CD}), and (b) is to constrain the predictions on the encoder output (L_{ED}).

2.2   Cross-Task Representation Learning

Overview. Fig. 1 depicts the overall design of the proposed cross-task representation learning approach. Firstly, the source model pre-trained on a face classification task is operated in the inference mode to predict rich feature representations from either classification or intermediate layers for the target task data. The target model is then initialized from the source model and extended with a task-specific decoder for the task of landmark detection (L_R). Obtained feature representations are then transferred by regularization losses (L_{CD} or L_{ED}) for regularizing the target model learning.

Source Model. We consider a pre-trained face classification network as our source model, since generic facial representations generated from this domain-similar task have been demonstrated to be helpful for other facial analysis [21]. Formally, let $\mathcal{S}_{\theta_1,\theta_2} : \mathbb{R}^{H \times W \times 3} \to \mathbb{R}^C$ be the source network for a face classification task with C classes, where θ_1 and θ_2 are the learnable parameters. The network consists of a feature extractor (encoder) $f_{\theta_1}^s : \mathbb{R}^{H \times W \times 3} \to \mathbb{R}^d$ and a classifier $g_{\theta_2}^s : \mathbb{R}^d \to \mathbb{R}^C$, where d denotes the dimensionality of the encoder output. A cross-entropy loss is typically used to train the network $\mathcal{S}_{\theta_1,\theta_2} := g_{\theta_2}^s(f_{\theta_1}^s(\mathbf{I}))$ which maps a facial image to classification scores based on a rich labeled dataset $\mathcal{D}^s$. In practice, we adopt a pre-trained ResNet-50 [8] model from VGGFace2 [2] for the source network. Other available deep network architectures could also be utilized for this purpose.

Target Model. For the task of heatmap regression, the target network $\mathcal{T}_{\theta_1,\theta_2}$ is firstly initialized from the pre-trained source network. We then follow the design of [22], employing three deconvolutional layers after the encoder output $f_{\theta_1}^t(\mathbf{I})$ to recover the desired spatial resolution, where each layer has the dimension of 256 and 4×4 kernel with the stride of 2. Finally, a 1×1 convolutional layer is added to complete this task-specific decoder $h_{\theta_3}^t(f_{\theta_1}^t(\mathbf{I})) : \mathbb{R}^d \to \mathbb{R}^{(H/4) \times (W/4) \times K}$. The primary learning objective is to minimize the following loss between the decoder

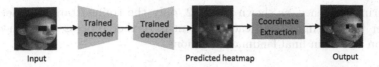

Input　　　　　　　　　　　　　　　Predicted heatmap　　　　　　Output

Fig. 2. Illustration of proposed framework for testing landmark detection models.

outputs and the labeled heatmaps,

$$L_R = \frac{1}{N_t} \sum_{i=1}^{N_t} \left\| \mathbf{G}_i^t - h_{\theta_3}^t (f_{\theta_1}^t (\mathbf{I}_i^t)) \right\|_F^2 \tag{1}$$

where F denotes the Frobenius norm.

Regularized Knowledge Transfer. Motivated by knowledge distillation, we aim to regularize the network training by directly acquiring the source model's predictions for the target task data $\mathcal{D}^t$, which are further transferred through a regularization loss L_D. Hence, the total loss is defined as,

$$L = L_R + \lambda L_D \tag{2}$$

where λ is a weighting parameter. If $\lambda = 0$, the knowledge transfer becomes standard fine-tuning, as no regularization is included.

For the design of L_D, we firstly consider constraining the distance between the final layer outputs of the two networks, as shown in Fig. 1 (a). Similar to the distillation loss in [9], we use a temperature parameter μ with *softmax* function to smooth the predictions, but the original cross-entropy function is replaced by the following term,

$$L_{CD} = \frac{1}{N_t} \sum_{i=1}^{N_t} \left\| softmax \left(\frac{g_{\theta_2}^s (f_{\theta_1}^s (\mathbf{I}_i^t))}{\mu} \right) - softmax \left(\frac{g_{\theta_2}^t (f_{\theta_1}^t (\mathbf{I}_i^t))}{\mu} \right) \right\|_2^2. \tag{3}$$

The purpose of this design of L_{CD} is to directly align the facial embeddings between instances, instead of preserving the original classification ability.

Moreover, we consider matching the features maps produced from both encoders as another choice, as shown in Fig. 1 (b). Motivated by the work in [18], we adopt the cosine similarity for the feature alignment as described below,

$$L_{ED} = 1 - \sum_{i=1}^{N_t} \cos(f_{\theta_1}^s (\mathbf{I}_i^t), f_{\theta_1}^t (\mathbf{I}_i^t)). \tag{4}$$

We conjecture that penalizing higher-order angular differences in this context would help transfer the relational information across different tasks, and also give more flexibility for the target model learning. Besides, both regularization terms can be combined together to regularize the learning process. Different approaches of the proposed learning strategy will be evaluated in the experimental section.

During inference, as shown in Fig. 2, only the trained target model is used to infer the heatmaps, and each of them is further processed via an *argmax* function to obtain final landmark locations.

3   Experiments

3.1   Dataset and Implementation Details

We evaluate the proposed approach for extracting facial anatomical landmarks. Images used for training and test datasets were collected by the Collaborative Initiative on Fetal Alcohol Spectrum Disorders (CIFASD)[1], a global multidisciplinary consortium focused on furthering the understanding of FASD. It contains subjects from 4 sites across the USA, aged between 4 and 18 years. Each subject was imaged using a commercially available static 3D photogrammetry system from 3dMD[2]. For this study, we utilize the high-resolution 2D images captured during 3D acquisition, which are used as UV mapped textures for the 3D surfaces.

Specifically, we acquired in total 1549 facial images annotated by an expert, and randomly split them into training/validation set (80%), and test set (20%). All the images were cropped and resized to 256×256 for the network training and evaluation. Standard data augmentation was performed with randomly horizontal flip (50%) and scaling (0.8). During training, the Adam optimizer [12] was used for the optimization with the mini-batch size of 2 for 150 epochs. A polynomial decay learning rate was used with the initial value of 0.001. Parameters of λ and μ used in (2) and (3) were set to 0.002 and 2, respectively.

3.2   Evaluation Metrics

For the evaluation, we firstly employ the Mean Error (ME), which is a commonly-used evaluation metric in the task of facial landmark detection. It is defined as, $\text{ME} = \frac{1}{N_e} \sum_{i=1}^{N_e} \frac{1}{K} \|\mathbf{p}_i - \hat{\mathbf{p}}_i\|_2$, where N_e is the number of images in the test set, and $\mathbf{p}_i$ and $\hat{\mathbf{p}}_i$ denote the manual annotations and predictions, respectively. Note that the original normalization factor measured by inter-ocular distance (Euclidean distance between outer eye corners) is not included in this evaluation, due to the unavailable annotations for the other eye, as illustrated in Fig. 3. In addition, we use the Cumulative Errors Distribution (CED) curve with the metrics of Area-Under-the-Curve (AUC) and Failure Rate (FR), where a failure case is considered if the point-to-point Euclidean error is greater than 1.2. Higher scores of AUC or lower scores of FR demonstrate the larger proportion of the test set is well predicted.

---

[1] https://cifasd.org/.
[2] http://www.3dmd.com/.

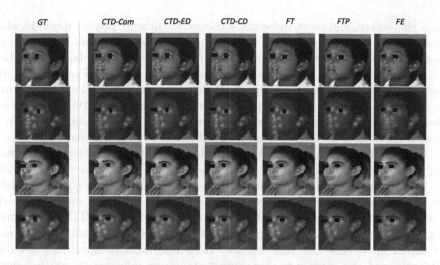

Fig. 3. Qualitative performance of landmark prediction and heatmap regression on the test set. Subjects' eyes are masked for privacy preservation. Better viewed in color.

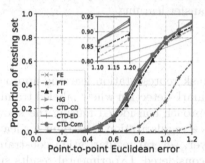

Fig. 4. Evaluation of CED curve on the test set. Better viewed in color.

Table 1. Quantitative evaluation on the test set.

Method	ME ± SD	FR	AUC
FE [22]	1.822 ± 0.501	94.52%	0.01
FTP [22]	1.161 ± 0.261	40.32%	0.10
FT [22]	0.858 ± **0.238**	10.65%	0.29
HG [16]	0.879 ± 0.386	12.58%	0.30
CTD-CD	0.842 ± 0.246	**5.81%**	0.31
CTD-ED	0.830 ± 0.245	7.74%	**0.32**
CTD-Com	**0.829** ± 0.253	6.45%	**0.32**

3.3 Results and Discussions

To verify the effectiveness of the proposed cross-task representation learning (CTD) approach, we compare to a widely-used CNN model: stacked Hourglass (HG) [16] and three variants of fine-tuning [22] without regularization ($\lambda = 0$): Feature Extraction (FE) with freezing the encoder, Fine Tuning Parts (FTP) without freezing the final convolutional layer of the encoder, and Fine Tuning (FT) without freezing any layer. In addition, we present an ablation study to examine the significance of each approach in our proposed CTD, including the regularization on the classifier output (CTD-CD), the regularization on the encoder output (CTD-ED), and the regularization on both outputs (CTD-Com).

Figure 3 shows the qualitative comparisons between different models on the test set. As we can see, the predicted landmarks from the proposed methods generally achieve the better alignment with the ground truth (the first left column) than the others, and seem to be more robust to difficult pixels especially when landmarks are in close proximity (upper lip). One possible reason is that feature representations generated from the source model encode richer facial semantics, which make landmark spatial locations more discriminative. Furthermore, the visualization of predicted heatmaps explains how each compared model responds to the desired task. We observe that our cross-task representation learning can effectively suppress spurious responses and improve the feature confidence in related regions, so that more accurate predictions can be achieved.

On the other hand, Table 1 summarizes the quantitative evaluation by reporting the statistics for each model. Figure 4 depicts the CED curve which provides an intuitive understanding of the overall performance of the compared models. These evaluations above demonstrate that the proposed methods consistently outperform standard fine-tuning solutions. Moreover, CTD-ED performs slightly better than CTD-CD considering the scores of ME and AUC. This may be explained by the fact that features from intermediate layers are not only semantic, and also contain to some extent structural information which is beneficial for localization [7]. Interestingly, CTD-Com using both regularization losses achieves similar results in CTD-ED, as a result, CTD-ED may be considered as a better choice for the regularization of transfer learning.

4   Conclusions

In this paper, we presented a new cross-task representation learning approach to address the problem of anatomical landmark detection where labeled training data is limited. The proposed learning approach considered reusing the knowledge from a domain-similar source task as a regularization constraint for learning the target landmark detector. Moreover, several regularization constraints for the proposed learning approach were considered. Experimental results suggested that the proposed learning approach works well with limited training samples and outperforms other compared solutions. The proposed approach can be potentially applied to other related applications in the clinical domain where the target task has small training set and the source task data is not accessible.

Acknowledgements. This work was done in conjunction with the Collaborative Initiative on Fetal Alcohol Spectrum Disorders (CIFASD), which is funded by grants from the National Institute on Alcohol Abuse and Alcoholism (NIAAA). This work was supported by NIH grant U01AA014809 and EPSRC grant EP/M013774/1.

References

1. Astley, S.J.: Palpebral fissure length measurement: accuracy of the FAS facial photographic analysis software and inaccuracy of the ruler. J. Popul. Ther. Clin. Pharmacol. **22**(1), e9–e26 (2015)
2. Cao, Q., Shen, L., Xie, W., Parkhi, O.M., Zisserman, A.: Vggface2: a dataset for recognising faces across pose and age. In: IEEE International Conference on Automatic Face Gesture Recognition, pp. 67–74. IEEE (2018)

3. Chen, R., Ma, Y., Chen, N., Lee, D., Wang, W.: Cephalometric landmark detection by attentive feature pyramid fusion and regression-voting. In: Medical Image Computing and Computer Assisted Intervention (MICCAI), pp. 873–881 (2019)
4. Lopez-Paz, D., Bottou, L., Schölkopf, B., Vapnik, V.: Unifying distillation and privileged information, pp. 1–10 (2016)
5. Dhar, P., Singh, R.V., Peng, K.C., Wu, Z., Chellappa, R.: Learning without memorizing. In: IEEE Conference on Computer Vision and Pattern Recognition (CVPR), pp. 5138–5146. IEEE (2019)
6. Feng, Z.H., Kittler, J., Awais, M., Huber, P., Wu, X.J.: Wing loss for robust facial landmark localisation with convolutional neural networks. In: The IEEE Conference on Computer Vision and Pattern Recognition (CVPR), pp. 2235–2245. IEEE (2018)
7. Gupta, S., Hoffman, J., Malik, J.: Cross modal distillation for supervision transfer. In: IEEE Conference on Computer Vision and Pattern Recognition (CVPR), pp. 2827–2836. IEEE (2016)
8. He, K., Zhang, X., Ren, S., Sun, J.: Deep residual learning for image recognition. In: IEEE Conference on Computer Vision and Pattern Recognition (CVPR), pp. 770–778. IEEE (2016)
9. Hinton, G., Vinyals, O., Dean, J.: Distilling the knowledge in a neural network. In: Conference on Neural Information Processing Systems (NeurIPS) Workshops, (2015)
10. Hoyme, H.E., May, P.A., Kalberg, W.O., et al.: A practical clinical approach to diagnosis of fetal alcohol spectrum disorders: clarification of the 1996 institute of medicine criteria. Pediatr. 115(1), 39–47 (2006)
11. Huang, R., Suttie, M., Noble, J.A.: An automated CNN-based 3D anatomical landmark detection method to facilitate surface-based 3D facial shape analysis. In: Medical Image Computing and Computer-Assisted Intervention (MICCAI) Workshops, pp. 163–171 (2019)
12. Kingma, D.P., Ba, J.: Adam: a method for stochastic optimization. In: Proc. of International Conference on Learning Representations (ICLR), pp. 1–15 (2015)
13. Li, X., et al.: DELTA: deep learning transfer using feature map with attention for convolutional networks. In: Proc. of International Conference on Learning Representations (ICLR), pp. 1–13 (2019)
14. Li, X., Grandvalet, Y., Davoine, F.: Explicit inductive bias for transfer learning with convolutional networks. Int. Conf. Mach. Learn. (ICML). 80, 2830–2839 (2018)
15. Li, Z., Hoiem, D.: Learning without forgetting. IEEE Trans. Pattern Anal. Mach. Intell. 40(12), 2935–2947 (2018)
16. Newell, A., Yang, K., Deng, J.: Stacked hourglass networks for human pose estimation. In: European Conference on Computer Vision (ECCV), pp. 483–499 (2016)
17. Pan, S.J., Yang, Q.: A survey on transfer learning. IEEE Trans. Knowl. Data Eng. 22(10), 1345–1359 (2010)
18. Park, W., Kim, D., Lu, Y., Cho, M.: Relational knowledge distillation. In: IEEE Conference on Computer Vision and Pattern Recognition (CVPR), pp. 3967–3976. IEEE (2019)
19. Patra, A., et al.: Efficient ultrasound image analysis models with sonographer gaze assisted distillation. In: Proc. of Medical Image Computing and Computer-Assisted Intervention (MICCAI), pp. 394–402 (2019)
20. Romero, A., Ballas, N., Kahou, S.E., Chassang, A., Gatta, C., Bengio, Y.: Fitnets: hints for thin deep nets. In: Proc. of International Conference on Learning Representations (ICLR), pp. 1–13 (2015)

21. Wiles, O., Koepke, A., Zisserman, A.: Self-supervised learning of a facial attribute embedding from video. In: British Machine Vision Conference (BMVC), (2018)
22. Xiao, B., Wu, H., Wei, Y.: Simple baselines for human pose estimation and tracking. In: European Conference on Computer Vision (ECCV), pp. 472–487 (2018)
23. Zhang, J., Liu, M., Shen, D.: Detecting anatomical landmarks from limited medical imaging data using two-stage task-oriented deep neural networks. IEEE Trans. Image Process. **26**(10), 4753–4764 (2017)
24. Zhang, Z., Luo, P., Loy, C.C., Tang, X.: Learning deep representation for face alignment with auxiliary attributes. IEEE Trans. Pattern Anal. Mach. Intell. **38**(5), 918–930 (2016)
25. Zhao, Y., Liu, Y., Shen, C., Gao, Y., Xiong, S.: MobileFAN: transferring deep hidden representation for face alignment. Pattern Recogn. **100**, 107–114 (2020)
26. Zhong, Z., Li, J., Zhang, Z., Jiao, Z., Gao, X.: An attention-guided deep regression model for landmark detection in cephalograms. In: Proc. of Medical Image Computing and Computer-Assisted Intervention (MICCAI), pp. 540–548 (2019)

Cycle Ynet: Semi-supervised Tracking of 3D Anatomical Landmarks

Jianzhe Lin[1,2(✉)], Yue Zhang[2], Abdoul-aziz Amadou[2], Ingmar Voigt[3], Tommaso Mansi[2], and Rui Liao[2]

[1] Department of Electrical and Computer Engineering, University of British Columbia, Vancouver, Canada
jianzhelin@ece.ubc.ca
[2] Digital Technology and Innovation, Siemens Healthineers, Princeton, NJ, Germany
[3] Digital Technology and Innovation, Siemens Healthineers, Erlangen, Germany

Abstract. Real-time tracking of anatomical landmarks in 3D medical images is of great importance, ranging from live quantification to optimal visualization.Existing deep network models have shown promising performance but typically require a large amount of annotated data for training. However, obtaining accurate and consistent annotations on sequences of 3D medical images can be very challenging even for skilled clinicians. In this paper, we propose a semi-supervised spatial-temporal modeling framework for real-time anatomical landmark tracking in 3D transesophageal echocardiography (TEE) images, which requires annotations on only a small fraction of frames in a sequence. Specifically, a spatial discriminative feature encoder is first trained via deep Q-learning on static images across all patients. Then we introduce a Cycle Ynet framework that integrates the encoded spatial features and learns temporal landmark correspondence over a sequence using a generative model by enforcing both cycle-consistency and accurate prediction on a couple of annotated frames. We validate the proposed model using 738 TEE sequences with around 15,000 frames and demonstrate that by combining a discriminative feature extractor with a generative tracking model, we could achieve superior performance using a small number of annotated data compared to state-of-the-art methods.

1 Introduction

Transesophageal echocardiography (TEE) is one of the most frequently used image modalities for cardiac disease diagnosis. Compared with other modalities such as Computed Tomography (CT) and Magnetic Resonance Imaging (MRI), TEE does not involve radiation and/or contrast medium, and can provide real-time motion imaging of the heart. Compared with 2D echo images, 3D echography has shown to provide additional anatomical details and improved spatial relationships, and thus is rapidly becoming part of the clinical mainstream. Real-time tracking of anatomical landmarks in 3D echocardiography

© Springer Nature Switzerland AG 2020
M. Liu et al. (Eds.): MLMI 2020, LNCS 12436, pp. 593–602, 2020.
https://doi.org/10.1007/978-3-030-59861-7_60

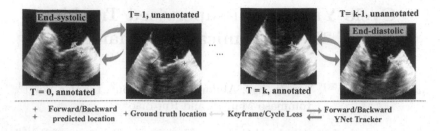

Fig. 1. Overview of cycle tracking process. Tracker tracks landmarks between the first annotated keyframe (end-systolic) and the second annotated keyframe (end-diastolic). The cycle loss and the keyframe loss compare the predicted location at its ground truth on these two frames accordingly.

could potentially enable a wide range of applications, including live quantification of heart chambers, semantically enhanced imaging for optimal visualization of anatomical structures, and dynamic guidance for catheter-based procedures.

Deep learning has shown its advantages in various applications including real-time object motion tracking, which typically requires a large amount of annotated data for training. However, annotating on 3D medical images is very time-consuming and relies heavily on expert knowledge, especially for 3D echography with a relatively low signal-to-noise ratio. As a result, most 3D TEE sequences from clinical sites have only a few keyframes (e.g. end-systolic and end-diastolic frames) annotated. Such a shortage of annotation limits the potentials of the deep network models in object tracking for 3D medical applications. In terms of methodology, existing frameworks of deep learning based visual tracking can be generally divided into two categories: generative methods and discriminative methods. Generative methods predict the location of the target by exploiting the correlation among temporal frames [7], while discriminative methods solves the tracking problem by detection framework [9,11]. Discriminative methods can explore information better on single frame by regarding the tracking as a binary classification task, but they fail to consider temporal correlations of consecutive frames [5,6]. In comparison, generative methods can explore the consistency of motions of consecutive frames, but sudden occlusions for several frames might lead to a total lose of target without a re-identification module [13].

In this paper, we propose a semi-supervised Cycle Ynet framework for spatial-temporal 3D anatomical landmark tracking, to fully utilize both the annotated keyframes of 3D TEE images and the unannotated ones with temporal coherence. In addition, our method combines the advantages of both discriminative methods and generative methods by incorporating a discriminative feature extractor into a generative tracking framework. Specifically, the proposed Cycle Ynet framework takes advantage of cycle consistency of video frames, by adding a backward tracking process, see Fig. 1. The supervision of such a framework is three-fold. First, the correspondence between the start point of the forward tracking and the endpoint of the backward tracking serves as the cycle-consistent self-supervision

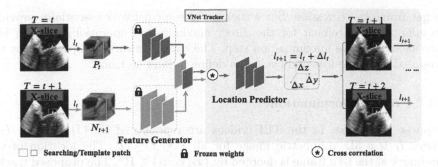

Fig. 2. The flowchart of the proposed "Y-shaped" tracker. The 3D landmark at location l_t would be the target for tracking. The inputs are the searching patch at $T = t+1$ and the landmark template patch in the previous frame at $T = t$. The output of the model would be the predicted motion, from which we get the updated landmark location l_{t+1}.

[2,10,12]. As a tracker that never moves would be inherently cycle-consistent, we mitigate this by introducing the second supervision by long-distance tracking between the annotated keyframes. We further introduce the third supervision to let the tracker be aware of the contextual information of the target, by introducing a pre-trained deep Q-Network (DQN) feature encoder based on annotated keyframes [4]. Therefore, the model learns not only a data-driven discriminative feature extractor but also a task-driven tracking policy.

In summary, our technical contributions are: 1) The framework is semi-supervised requiring only a few annotated keyframes in a sequence for training. To our knowledge, this is the first method on semi-supervised deep learning for tracking using generative models, and the first semi-supervised deep learning for 3D landmark tracking in general; 2) A novel Ynet tracker involving adaptive maximization is proposed, which transforms a tracking problem into a motion learning problem without explicit feature matching; 3) Two complementary losses, cycle loss and keyframe loss, are introduced for the model training; 4) A novel pre-trained discriminative DQN feature for spatial supervision is utilized in a generative tracking framework.

2 Methodology

The proposed Ynet tracker consists of two parts, a siamese pre-trained feature extractor and an adaptive maximization location predictor, as is depicted in Fig. 2. The siamese feature generator is first pre-trained with deep Q-learning on static volumes to produce robust feature embeddings of spatial information. It is frozen during the training of the location predictor utilizing a correlation filter and a fully-convolutional regressor network. Specifically after the features are generated, the location predictor constructs a feature affinity map by feature correlation and uses it to predict the 3D translation of the landmark in the target frame by regression. Since such a regressor network essentially provides an adaptive replacement for the direct maximization operation, we refer this step as an adaptive maximization step. The entire network is supervised by the proposed keyframe loss and cycle loss define in later sections.

2.1 Problem Formulation

Suppose the frames in the TEE videos are represented by $\{I_1, I_2, I_3, ..., I_T\}$, where I_t is a 3D volumetric image for all $1 \leq t \leq T$. The location of the landmark at the t-th frame is denoted by $\{x_t, y_t, z_t\} \in \mathbf{R}^3$. The proposed tracker takes 3D local patches from two consecutive frames as inputs and predicts the location deviation of the landmarks in these two frames. Given frames I_t and I_{t+1}, we denote the local patch centered around the landmark at I_t by P_t and the consecutive searching patch from I_{t+1} by N_{t+1}. N_{t+1} is set to be larger than P_t to accommodate the possible motion of the landmarks between two consecutive frames.

2.2 Feature Generator

In order to obtain meaningful feature encoding of spatial information, we train an artificial agent via deep Q-learning for landmark detection in individual frames. The trained agent is able to learn the anatomical structures presented in the 3D volumes and navigate towards the target landmark. We then leverage the first layers of the agent to generate the features for the tracking module. Following the setup of Q-learning for landmark detection in [4], we consider a set of Markov decision process defined by the tuple $\{S, \mathcal{A}, \tau, r\}$, where

- S stands for the state of the agent, corresponds to the sub-volume of the 3D image centered at p, where $p \in R^3$ is the current location of the agent.
- $\mathcal{A}$ represents a finite set of actions executed by the agent. In the 3D navigation problem, we consider A as an action space of displacements along each axis $\{x, y, z\}$.
- $\tau : S \times A \times S \rightarrow [0; 1]$ is a stochastic transition function, describing the probability of arriving in a certain state with a given action.
- r is the reward collected by the agent by interacting with the environment. Following the previous work, we define $r = \|p^c - p^{gt}\|_2^2 - \|p^n - p^{gt}\|_2^2$. Here p^c represents the current location of the agent, p^{gt} is the ground truth location of the landmark it is pursuing, p^n is the next location of the agent after it executes an action.

We use the standard deep Q-learning strategy to train the agent. The agent is represented by a six-layer fully convolutional network. Given any 3D local landmark, the network outputs a 6×1 vector, corresponding to the Q-value evaluation of the actions in space $\mathcal{A}$. The agent is trained to collect the maximum amount of rewards. Since a well-trained agent can always move closer to the target landmark starting from any location, the feature extractor of the agent efficiently encodes the spatial information associated with the underlying anatomical structures. Therefore it can serve as a good feature generator for the object tracking model. In this paper, we use the first 3 layers of the agent network as the feature generator and denote it by ϕ. Given the local patches P_t and N_{t+1}, we denote their encoded features by ϕ_{N_t} and $\phi_{P_{t-1}}$. For the entire network, we use $3 \times 3 \times 3$ kernels with stride as 1 and zero padding.

2.3   Location Predictor

Next, we propose a location predictor module $h(\cdot)$ with adaptive maximization to infer the motions of the landmarks from the encoded features. Given frame I_t and frame I_{t+1}, it takes the encoded features ϕ_{P_t} and $\phi_{N_{t+1}}$ as inputs, generates a feature affinity map, and predicts the translation of the landmark location between these two frames, $i.e.$,

$$\Delta l_{t+1} = h(\phi_{P_t}, \phi_{N_{t+1}}).$$

The predicted location of the landmark at frame I_{t+1} is $l_t + \Delta l_{t+1}$. We then define P_{t+1} as an image patch centered at this detected location and continue this prediction process for all the frames in the sequence.

We leverage the standard convolutional operation to compute the affinity between each sub-patch of ϕ_{N_t} and $\phi_{P_{t-1}}$. Specifically, $\phi_{P_{t-1}}$ and ϕ_{N_t} are combined using a cross correlation layer

$$f(\phi_{N_t}, \phi_{P_{t-1}}) = \phi_{P_{t-1}} * \phi_{N_t} \tag{1}$$

Instead of directly taking the pixel location with maximal correlation, we further forward this constructed feature map into a three-layer convolutional network to map the affinity score to the landmark motion. We refer this regression step as adaptive maximization. It considers the contextual information in the feature map and thus is able to provide more robustness predictions. The formulation is as follows,

$$\Delta l_t = m(f(\phi_{N_t}, \phi_{P_{i-t}}); \theta_f) \tag{2}$$

where m is the location predictor, and θ_f represents the parameters for the fully connected network. The new landmark location would be calculated by combining its previous location with the predicted motion.

2.4   Cycle-Consistency with Key-Frame Loss

To tackle the challenge of limited annotations, we leverage the cycle tracking process [12] for model training, as is illustrated in Fig. 2. Furthermore, if any image sequence is annotated on more than one frame, we incorporate these additional annotations into the loss function to semi-supervise the training process of the tracker. Such frames are referred as keyframes.

Without loss of generality, we set the first annotated frame in each image sequence to be I_1^* and the corresponding annotated landmark location as l_1^*.

Here we use * to mark the annotated landmark locations as well as the frames. For any frame t, $t > 1$, we have the following recursive formulation,

$$
\begin{aligned}
l_t &= h(\phi_{P_{t-1}}, \phi_{N_t}) + l_{t-1} \\
&= h(\phi_{P_{t-1}}, \phi_{N_t}) + h(\phi_{P_{t-2}}, \phi_{N_{t-1}}) + l_{t-2} \\
&= h(\phi_{P_{t-1}}, \phi_{N_t}) + \ldots + h(\phi_{P_1}, \phi_{N_2}) + l_1^*.
\end{aligned}
\tag{3}
$$

Starting from l_1^*, we can continuously forward the patches through the composition of h and ϕ to predict the landmark locations at any frame t. Similarly, if frame k is annotated, we can derive the formulation for l_1 in a backward manner,

$$
\begin{aligned}
l_1 &= h(\phi_{P_2}, \phi_{N_1}) + l_2 \\
&= h(\phi_{P_2}, \phi_{N_1}) + h(\phi_{P_3}, \phi_{N_2}) + l_3 \\
&= h(\phi_{P_2}, \phi_{N_1}) + \ldots + h(\phi_{P_t}, \phi_{N_{t-1}}) + l_k^*.
\end{aligned}
\tag{4}
$$

During training, we use the annotated diastolic frame as the beginning frame for tracking (I_1^*), and the annotated systolic frame as the end frame (I_1^*).

Let $1 \to k$ be the forward tracking process where we track the landmark from I_1^* and predict its location in I_k^*. Note here $I_2, I_3, ..., I_{k-1}$ are all unannotated. The key-frame loss $\mathcal{L}_{1 \to k}$ is defined by the deviation between the predicted landmark location and its ground truth at frame k,

$$
\begin{aligned}
\mathcal{L}_{1 \to k} &= \| l_k^* - l_k \|^2 \\
&= \| l_k^* - (h(\phi_{P_{k-1}}, \phi_{N_k}) + \ldots + l_1) \|^2.
\end{aligned}
\tag{5}
$$

We can derive similar formula for the loss $\mathcal{L}_{k \to 1}$. In addition to these single directional supervision, we add cycle-consistency loss to help stabilize the training process. The idea behind is simple: starting from I_1^*, while the tracker tracks the landmark to I_k^* and then performs tracking in reverse direction, the predicted location at I_1^* should be identical to the starting position, i.e. l_1^*. By combining Eq. 3 and Eq. 4, we have the cycle-consistency loss $\mathcal{L}_{1 \to k \to 1}$ as follows,

$$
\begin{aligned}
\mathcal{L}_{1 \to k \to 1} &= \| l_1 - l_1^* \|^2 \\
&= \| h(\phi_{P_1}, \phi_{N_2}) + \ldots + h(\phi_{P_{k-1}}, \phi_{N_k}) + \\
&\quad\; h(\phi_{P_k}, \phi_{N_{t-1}}) + \ldots + h(\phi_{P_2}, \phi_{N_1}) \|^2
\end{aligned}
\tag{6}
$$

Similar formulation can be derived for $\mathcal{L}_{k \to 1 \to k}$. Such cycle-consistency losses enforce the network to have consistent predictions from the embedded features cross the frames. The key-frame losses help to avoid degenerated solutions and improve the tracking accuracy. Finally, the overall training objective is a weighted aggregation of all the aforementioned losses,

$$
\mathcal{L}_{total} = \mathcal{L}_{1 \to k} + \mathcal{L}_{k \to 1} + \lambda_1 \mathcal{L}_{1 \to k \to 1} + \lambda_2 \mathcal{L}_{k \to 1 \to k},
\tag{7}
$$

where λ_1 and λ_2 are scalars to balance different losses, and we empirically set $\lambda_1 / \lambda_2 = 1$.

3   Experiments

The dataset consists of 738 TEE ultrasound sequences with around 15,000 frames collected from 6 different clinical sites, and is then augmented using rotation within [-16 16] degrees and rescaling within [0.8 1.2] scaling factor, resulting in 5,570 TEE sequence (97,660 frames) for training and 1,490 sequences (51,510 frames) for testing, with each sequence containing on average 2 annotated keyframes. We ignore the sparse extent of the annotation (the length of sequence between the two keyframes mostly ranges from 5 20) as we find it will not influence our model training. All the data has a field of view containing the entire mitral valve with varying sizes, and the image resolution is 1 mm isotropic. The ground truth landmarks of the left trigone and right trigone are labeled by echocardiogram specialists using our specialized 3D TEE image visualization and editing software, see Fig. 3 for an example.

We make quantitative comparison with three different deep learning based SOTA baselines: 1) Tracking by DQN Detection (TDD) [3,4] (supervised discriminative tracking method); 2) SiamFC [1] (supervised generative tracking method); and 3) Self-supervised Cycle tracking (SCT) [12] (unsupervised generative tracking method). The evaluation criteria are **Location Deviation(LD)** (in millimeter) and **Intersection over Union (IoU)**. For IoU, we use a $9 \times 9 \times 9$ 3D bounding box to represent the landmark and measure the region overlap between predicted and ground truth landmarks[1]. The above deep learning based methods are based on the same basic network settings and have a similar speed for tracking. We also benchmark the speed of our method against traditional optical flow based methods [8]. The CPU is Intel Xeon Gold 6128, and GPU is NVIDIA Quadro M2200 GPU with 16MB memory.

In Table 1, we make comparisons based on LD and IoU for left and right trigones respectively. Comparison for precision by using different LD thresholds can be found in Fig. 4. For both LD and IoU, the C-Ynet gets the best performance in mean values, with C-Ynet exceeding SCT by *15%* for left trigone and *9.6%* for right trigone, demonstrating the advantage of our semi-supervised spatial-temporal modeling framework over fully-unsupervised method. By comparing with SiamFC, we demonstrate the importance of making use of the information on unannotated frames to augment the training data for improved tracking accuracy, when the number of annotate data is limited. TDD achieves the minimum median value but much higher mean value because such a discriminative method may result in a large number of grossly failed tracking, as it fails to consider the temporal correlation between consecutive frames.

Furthermore, we analyze the speed by comparing with optical flow based tracking, which is one of the fastest traditional tracking methods and used in ([8]) for speedup when combined with machine-learning based detection

---

[1] Such criterion is only for generative tracking methods but is not applicable to TDD, which uses no bounding box in tracking process.

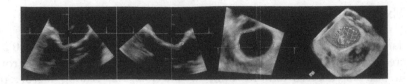

Fig. 3. Example of the 3D mitral valve dataset, annotation (colored) and the multi-planar reconstructions.

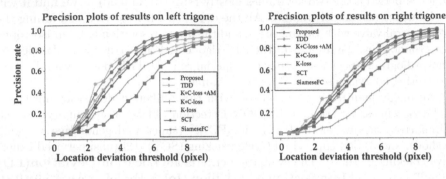

Fig. 4. Precision plots for left and right trigones.

algorithm. The speed for our proposed tracker is 9.14ms per frame (109.14 FPS), in comparison to 30.0ms per frame (33.3 FPS) for traditional optical flow method in our implementation, all on the same hardware configuration. This clearly demonstrates the advantage of deep neural network-based solutions for real-time 3D tracking applications.

We also perform an ablation study to verify the effectiveness of each component of our proposed C-Ynet, and the results are shown in Table 2 and Fig. 4. From the loss level, it is clear that using both the keyframe loss and cycle loss improves the tracking accuracy for both left and right trigones, demonstrating the complementary information provided by these two types of losses. From the model level, we can verify the effectiveness of such an adaptive maximization component that considers the contextual information in an adaptive way over simple maximization. We achieve additional performance gain by introducing the discriminative pre-trained DQN feature, which explores the spatial information for tracking in our spatial-temporal framework.

Table 1. Quantitative comparison between different methods on trigone landmark tracking.

Method	Left				Right			
	LD (mm)		IoU		LD (mm)		IoU	
	Mean± std	Median	Mean	Median	Mean± std	Median	Mean	Median
TDD (L)	4.53 ± 5.94	**2.83**	-	-	4.87 ± 4.48	**3.74**	-	-
SiamFC (L)	6.26 ± 3.38	5.74	0.294	0.288	5.85 ± 3.64	5.20	0.331	0.329
SCT (L)	4.08 ± 2.09	3.67	0.473	0.490	4.67 ± 2.48	4.30	0.418	0.425
C-Ynet (L)	**3.46 ± 2.05**	2.99	**0.538**	**0.569**	**4.22 ± 2.24**	3.85	**0.461**	**0.479**

Table 2. Tracking accuracy (mean) with different model formulations.

losses		model		L-Trigone		R-Trigone	
K-Loss	C-Loss	AM	DQN	LD	IoU	LD	IoU
✓	✗	✓	✗	6.01	0.271	5.19	0.387
✗	✓	✓	✗	4.08	0.473	4.67	0.425
✓	✓	✗	✗	5.94	0.403	8.07	0.222
✓	✓	✓	✗	3.82	0.509	4.66	0.434
✓	✓	✓	✓	**3.46**	**0.538**	**4.22**	**0.461**

4 Discussions and Conclusion

In this paper we propose a novel semi-supervised Cycle Ynet framework for 3D Mitral Valve landmark tracking. To overcome the annotation scarcity problem of the 3D TEE sequence data, the model is semi-supervised by utilizing both the annotations of a few keyframes and the temporal correlation of unannotated ones in a sequence. The proposed framework combines the advantages of both discriminative feature encoder and generative tracking model to achieve an additional gain in tracking accuracy, and is able to recover the underlying heart motion with the highest fidelity compared to the state-of-the-art. Our future work includes an extension to other anatomical structures and image modalities, as well as real-world applications like cardiac motion analysis based on the proposed Cycle Ynet framework.

References

1. Bertinetto, L., Valmadre, J., Henriques, J.F., Vedaldi, A., Torr, P.H.S.: Fully-convolutional siamese networks for object tracking. In: Hua, G., Jégou, H. (eds.) ECCV 2016. LNCS, vol. 9914, pp. 850–865. Springer, Cham (2016). https://doi.org/10.1007/978-3-319-48881-3_56
2. Dwibedi, D., Aytar, Y., Tompson, J., Sermanet, P., Zisserman, A.: Temporal cycle-consistency learning. In: Proceedings of the IEEE Conference on Computer Vision and Pattern Recognition, pp. 1801–1810 (2019)

3. Ghesu, F.C., Georgescu, B., Mansi, T., Neumann, D., Hornegger, J., Comaniciu, D.: An artificial agent for anatomical landmark detection in medical images. In: Ourselin, S., Joskowicz, L., Sabuncu, M.R., Unal, G., Wells, W. (eds.) MICCAI 2016. LNCS, vol. 9902, pp. 229–237. Springer, Cham (2016). https://doi.org/10.1007/978-3-319-46726-9_27

4. Ghesu, F.C., et al.: Multi-scale deep reinforcement learning for real-time 3d-landmark detection in ct scans. IEEE Trans. Pattern Anal. Mach. Intell. **41**(1), 176–189 (2017)

5. Henriques, J.F., Caseiro, R., Martins, P., Batista, J.: High-speed tracking with kernelized correlation filters. IEEE Trans. Pattern Anal. Mach. Intell. **37**(3), 583–596 (2014)

6. Lukezic, A., Vojir, T., Cehovin Zajc, L., Matas, J., Kristan, M.: Discriminative correlation filter with channel and spatial reliability. In: Proceedings of the IEEE Conference on Computer Vision and Pattern Recognition, pp. 6309–6318 (2017)

7. Misra, I., Zitnick, C.L., Hebert, M.: Shuffle and learn: unsupervised learning using temporal order verification. In: Leibe, B., Matas, J., Sebe, N., Welling, M. (eds.) ECCV 2016. LNCS, vol. 9905, pp. 527–544. Springer, Cham (2016). https://doi.org/10.1007/978-3-319-46448-0_32

8. Voigt, I., et al.: Robust live tracking of mitral valve annulus for minimally-invasive intervention guidance. In: Navab, N., Hornegger, J., Wells, W.M., Frangi, A.F. (eds.) MICCAI 2015. LNCS, vol. 9349, pp. 439–446. Springer, Cham (2015). https://doi.org/10.1007/978-3-319-24553-9_54

9. Wang, G., Luo, C., Sun, X., Xiong, Z., Zeng, W.: Tracking by instance detection: a meta-learning approach. In: Proceedings of the IEEE conference on computer vision and pattern recognition, (2020)

10. Wang, N., Song, Y., Ma, C., Zhou, W., Liu, W., Li, H.: Unsupervised deep tracking. In: Proceedings of the IEEE Conference on Computer Vision and Pattern Recognition, pp. 1308–1317 (2019)

11. Wang, W., Shen, J., Shao, L.: Video salient object detection via fully convolutional networks. IEEE Trans. Image Process. **27**(1), 38–49 (2017)

12. Wang, X., Jabri, A., Efros, A.A.: Learning correspondence from the cycle-consistency of time. In: Proceedings of the IEEE Conference on Computer Vision and Pattern Recognition, pp. 2566–2576 (2019)

13. Wojke, N., Bewley, A., Paulus, D.: Simple online and realtime tracking with a deep association metric. In: 2017 IEEE international conference on image processing (ICIP), pp. 3645–3649. IEEE (2017)

Learning Hierarchical Semantic Correspondence and Gland Instance Segmentation

Pei Wang$^{(\boxtimes)}$ and Albert C. S. Chung

Lo Kwee -Seong Medical Image Analysis Laboratory, Department of Computer Science and Engineering, The Hong Kong University of Science and Technology, Kowloon, Hong Kong SAR
pei.wang@connect.ust.hk

Abstract. The morphology statistics of colon glands is a key feature for pathologists to diagnose colorectal cancer. Current gland instance segmentation methods show good overall performances, but accurate segmentation of extremely deformed glands in highly malignant cases or some rare benign cases remains to be challenging . In this paper, we propose a hybrid model that learns hierarchical semantic feature matching from histological pairs in an attentive process, where both spatial details and morphological appearances can be well preserved and balanced, especially for the glands with severe deformation. A consistency loss function is also introduced to enforce simultaneous satisfaction of semantic correspondence and gland instance segmentation on the pixel-level. The novel proposed model is validated on two publicly available colon gland datasets GlaS and CRAG. The model successfully boosts the segmentation performances on greatly mutated or deformed cases, and outperforms the state-of-the-art approaches.

Keywords: Hierarchical semantic correspondence · Consistency loss · Attentive process · Gland instance segmentation

1 Introduction

Colorectal cancer is the third most common cancer worldwide [16]. In clinical practice, the morphological statistics of intestinal glands is one of the primary features to colorectal cancer diagnosis and further treatment plan [3]. Automated gland segmentation is essential to provide morphological statistics to raise assessing efficiency and reliability, reduce inter- and intra-observer variability, and handle the ever-increasing image quantity.

Recently, CNN plays a significant role in the gland instance segmentation of histology images. To separate gland clusters, DCAN [4] performs gland segmentation and boundary detection in a unified network, and won the 2015 MICCAI GlaS challenge [15]. Based on the architecture of DCAN, MILD-Net [6] adopts maximal information loss to retain more spatial details in the feature extraction. A multi-channel multi-task network is proposed by Xu et al. [19,20], where

© Springer Nature Switzerland AG 2020
M. Liu et al. (Eds.): MLMI 2020, LNCS 12436, pp. 603–613, 2020.
https://doi.org/10.1007/978-3-030-59861-7_61

benign cases   malignant cases

Fig. 1. Examples of gland histology images. Great morphological changes in some benign cases and highly malignant cases remain to be a challenge in gland segmentation.

the foreground segmentation, edge detection, and object detection for glandular objects are conducted simultaneously. Besides, a loss function for boundary regularization is introduced by Yan et al. [21] to focus on the gland shape. Similarly, Qu et al. [13] abandoned pooling layers to improve the localization accuracy and applied a variance constraint on the loss function to explore more spatial features. DSE [17] is a nested network that first segments the gland and then refines the results by learning the inconsistency between ground truth and predicted masks. Furthermore, some methods also achieve competitive results by utilizing less manual annotations [22,24,25] and network quantization [18].

However, the accurate segmentation of gland instance with great diversity in shape, structure, and appearance remains to be a challenge, as shown in Fig. 1. Basically, current methods focus more on exploiting the boundaries [4,19–21] and spatial information [6,13], where the huge morphological changes can undermine their performances. Another important reason is that these greatly deformed cases take up a small proportion [5] of the population/dataset (a few benign cases and some highly malignant cases), which results in insufficient training samples for these complex cases. To address these problems, we propose a model that learns semantically related features from histological pairs with a hierarchical attention process, where the multi-level features from spatial information to morphological appearance can be emphasized and balanced even for complicated cases with severe gland deformation. A consistency loss is also proposed to enforce pixel-wise satisfaction of semantic feature correspondence and gland instance segmentation. The proposed method is validated on two publicly available colon gland datasets and outperforms the state-of-the-art approaches.

2   Methodology

A pair of histologic image pairs are fed into our model to learn the hierarchical semantic correspondence and gland instance segmentation simultaneously, as shown in Fig.2.

2.1   Feature Extraction and Matching

The source and target input images (I^s, I^t) are fed into a siamese network branch for extracting semantic features with shared learning weights. The feature extractor and decoder consist of dilated [23] residual blocks [7] following the U-Net

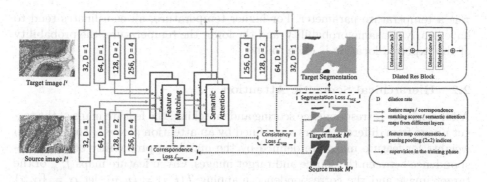

Fig. 2. Overview of the proposed model. A pair of source and target images are fed into the model, and features are extracted by a siamese network encoder. Pairwise feature matching and attentive modules are established hierarchically for instance segmentation. At training time, corresponding foreground masks are used to compute gland segmentation, semantic correspondence, and consistency loss terms.

architecture [14], and the feature maps of different layers contain information of different levels. For a certain layer of the feature extractor, the output features maps (f^s, f^t) with size $h \times w \times d$ for each image, can be represented as $h \times w$ grids of local features $f^s_{i,j}$ and $f^t_{u,v}$ in d-dimension. L2 normalization is applied to the individual d-dimensional features. The matching between local features of two images can be computed by the dot product operation. The matching scores are calculated by a normalized correlation function and defined as:

$$\mathcal{M} : \mathbb{R}^{h \times w \times d} \times \mathbb{R}^{h \times w \times d} \to \mathbb{R}^{h \times w \times h \times w}, \tag{1}$$

$$m_{ijuv} = \mathcal{M}(f^s, f^t)_{ijuv} = \frac{\langle f^s_{i,j}, f^t_{u,v} \rangle}{\sqrt{\sum_{i',j'} \langle f^s_{i',j'}, f^t_{u,v} \rangle^2}}. \tag{2}$$

The normalization operation emphasizes the similarity scores of highly-related local features and also penalizes the other ambiguous matches. The resulting $m = \{m_{ijuv}\}$ contains all the normalized match scores between two features.

The soft argmax function [8,10] is adopted to calculate the best matches based on the similarity scores. The differentiable soft argmax is applied to the 2-dimensional correlation map m for feature $f^s_{i,j}$ with coordinate (i, j). To be more specific, the coordinates of semantic correspondence to feature $f^s_{i,j}$ are calculated by a weighted average of matching scores of all spatial locations (u, v) in the target feature maps. The matching probability w is assigned to different locations by applying softmax function to our correlation map m. The matching function and corresponding probability map is defined as:

$$\mathcal{T} : \mathbb{R}^2 \to \mathbb{R}^2, \quad \mathcal{T}(i, j) = \sum_{u,v} w_{i,j}(u, v) \, (u, v), \tag{3}$$

$$w_{i,j}(u, v) = \frac{exp(m_{ijuv}/\tau)}{\sum_{u',v'} exp(m_{iju'v'}/\tau)}. \tag{4}$$

τ is a temperature parameter. For higher temperature, all coordinates tend to have nearly the same probability, and the lower the temperature, the probability of the expected location is close to one.

2.2 Hierarchical Semantic Attention

After semantic correspondence scoring and matching, the feature maps of the target image from different layers are refined by an attention process. The attention weights for feature maps are defined by the matching probability of the correspondence between the source and target images. Given feature maps $f_{u,v}^t$ of the target image and the correspondence mapping $T(i,j) = (u,v)$, let $\alpha = \{\alpha_{i,j}\}$ be the attention probability distribution over the feature maps, we compute the attended feature $f_{u,v}^{att}$ by element-wise multiplication:

$$f_{u,v}^{att} = \alpha_{i,j} f_{u,v}^t, \quad \alpha_{i,j} = \frac{exp(m_{ijT(i,j)}/\tau)}{\sum_{i',j'} exp(m_{i'j'T(i',j')}/\tau)}. \tag{5}$$

The attention weight is formed by the similarity scores of semantic correspondence between feature maps and then gone through a softmax function. In the feature extractor, deeper layers have larger receptive fields and result in more features related to shape and appearance in the corresponding feature maps and attention maps. A series of hierarchical attention maps are generated to emphasize features from spatial to appearance level. In Fig. 3, we visualize the semantic correspondence of the input image pair with different feature levels and the corresponding segmentation performance.

2.3 Loss

The binary foreground masks of histology images are employed for the supervision of both segmentation and correspondence tasks in training the proposed network. The loss function can be expressed as:

$$\mathcal{L} = \lambda_{seg}\mathcal{L}_{seg} + \lambda_{cor}\mathcal{L}_{cor} + \lambda_{con}\mathcal{L}_{con}. \tag{6}$$

It consists of loss function for gland segmentation $\mathcal{L}_{seg}$, semantic correspondence $\mathcal{L}_{cor}$, and our proposed $\mathcal{L}_{con}$ for the consistency of these two tasks. We use cross entropy for the gland instance segmentation:

$$\mathcal{L}_{seg} = w \, \mathcal{L}_{seg}' = -\sum_{u,v} w(u,v) \log p((u,v), y(u,v); \boldsymbol{\theta}_{seg}), \tag{7}$$

$$w(u,v) = \max(w_0(d_0 - dist^2(u,v)), 1). \tag{8}$$

$p((u,v), y(u,v); \boldsymbol{\theta}_{seg})$ represents the pixel-based softmax classification for true labels $y(u,v)$ of pixel (u,v). A weight map w is applied to better identify the closing glands, where $dist(u,v)$ is the Euclidean distance of a pixel to the nearest gland. In our experiments w_0 and d_0 are set to 0.037 and 55 respectively.

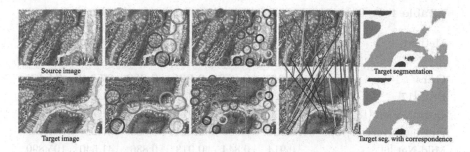

Fig. 3. Visualization of hierarchical semantic correspondence on histological pairs (feature matchings are visualized with thresholding for a clearer view).

We adapt the mask consistence loss [11] to regularize the semantic matching on foreground only. The flow field $\mathcal{F}^s$ from source to target image can be expressed as $\mathcal{F}^s(i,j) = \mathcal{T}(i,j) - (i,j)$. Similarly, $\mathcal{F}^t$ is defined as $\mathcal{T}(u,v) - (u,v)$. Let M^s and M^t be the binary masks of source and target images. We estimate the source mask by warping [9] using the flow field as $\hat{M}^s = \mathcal{W}(M^t; \mathcal{F}^s)$. The warping operator can be formulated as $\mathcal{W}(M^t; \mathcal{F}^s)(i,j) = M^t((i,j) + \mathcal{F}^s(i,j))$. Finally, our loss for semantic correspondence can be expressed as:

$$\mathcal{L}_{cor} = \frac{1}{|N^s|}\sum_{i,j}(M^s(i,j) - \hat{M}^s(i,j))^2 + \frac{1}{|N^t|}\sum_{u,v}(M^t(u,v) - \hat{M}^t(u,v))^2, \quad (9)$$

where $|N|$ is the number of pixels in the mask. The function encourages matches between foreground pixels and penalizes other matching cases. For the semantic feature matching of different layers, we resize the masks and take the average of loss terms from different feature maps. Besides, due to the nature of histology images that contain multiple gland objects and complex background, the proposed model learns feature matching instead of warping the entire image.

Besides, we introduce a consistency loss to encourage simultaneous sanctification of the two tasks based on the target flow field and the softmax classification for segmentation, and with the same weight focusing on the boundary area:

$$\mathcal{L}_{con} = -\sum_{u,v} w(u,v)[(M^t(u,v) - \hat{M}^t(u,v))^2 + k]\log p((u,v), y(u,v); \boldsymbol{\theta}_{seg}), \quad (10)$$

where k is a parameter for the consistency level of two tasks. In our cases we set k to 0.5. The function enforces correct prediction of foreground objects and precise matching within the same class for each pixel of the target images.

3   Experiments

We evaluate the proposed method on two public datasets for gland instance segmentation. The experiments demonstrate that our attentive model with hierarchical semantic matching and consistency loss substantially improves the performance of extremely complex cases and achieves state-of-the-art results.

Table 1. Performance on GlaS dataset in comparison with other methods.

Method	F1 Score		Object Dice		Object Hausdorff	
	Part A	Part B	Part A	Part B	Part A	Part B
Ours	**0.931**	**0.872**	**0.929**	**0.882**	**27.143**	**74.175**
DSE [17]	0.926	0.862	0.927	0.871	31.209	80.509
Quantization [18]	0.930	0.862	0.914	0.859	41.783	97.390
FullNet & varCE [13]	0.924	0.853	0.914	0.856	37.28	88.75
Mild-Net [6]	0.914	0.844	0.913	0.836	41.540	105.890
Shape Loss [21]	0.924	0.844	0.902	0.840	49.881	106.075
Suggestive Annotation [22]	0.921	0.855	0.904	0.858	44.736	96.976
Multi-channel [20]	0.893	0.843	0.908	0.833	44.129	116.821
DCAN [4]	0.912	0.716	0.897	0.781	45.418	160.347

Datasets & Evaluation. We validate the proposed model on GlaS dataset [15] from 2015 MICCAI challenge, and CRAG dataset [6] from Awan et al. [2]. GlaS consists of 85 training (37 benign (BN) and 48 malignant (MT)) and 80 test images (33 BN and 27 MT in Part A, 4 BN and 16 MT in Part B as on-site test of the challenge). In CRAG dataset there are 173 training and 40 testing images. The official metrics of GlaS are for different aspects: F1 score for object detection, *object-level* Dice index for instance segmentation, and *object-level* Hausdorff distance for glandular shape similarity [15]. The dense semantic correspondence is evaluated by the number of correctly labeled pixels: label transfer accuracy (LT-ACC) and the intersection-over-union (IoU) [11].

Training & Implementation Details. In the testing phase, we find the best matched image pairs by a simple and fast entropy-histogram approach [1]. In order to alleviate the over-fitting issue, we use random pairs from groups in training. Images with higher similarity are assigned into one group, and random image pairs are formed from the group for training. In our experiments, the images are augmented by elastic transformation, rotation, flip, Gaussian blur, and color distortion. Eventually, we randomly crop patches of size 480×480. Our method is implemented with PyTorch [12]. We adopt Gaussian distribution ($\mu = 0, \sigma = 0.01$) for weight initialization and train with Adam optimization of initial learning rate 8×10^{-4}, with batch size of 2. For loss function, we assign the coefficients for segmentation, correspondence, and consistency as 1.5, 1.0 and 0.85. For both datasets, we split 20% of the training images for validation. The model is trained and tested on an NVIDIA Titan X Pascal for both datasets.

3.1   Results

Table 1 shows the comparative results on GlaS dataset. It includes methods using nested network DSE [17], and multi-channel multi-task model [20]; approaches

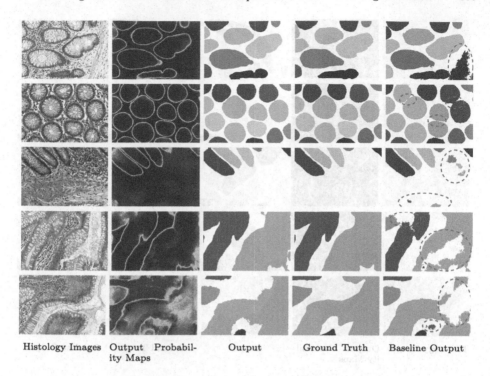

Histology Images   Output Probabil-   Output   Ground Truth   Baseline Output
              ity Maps

Fig. 4. Segmentation examples of benign cases on GlaS dataset (top three from part A, bottom two from part B).

Table 2. Ablation study on GlaS dataset.

Method	F1 Score		Object Dice		Object Hausdorff		LT-ACC		IoU	
	Part A	Part B	Part A	Part B	Part A	Part B	Part A	Part B	Part A	Part B
Baseline	0.923	0.854	0.916	0.862	40.456	88.463	-	-	-	-
+ Semantic Attn	0.927	0.860	0.923	0.870	34.421	79.245	0.948	0.863	0.876	0.808
+ Semantic Attn. & $\mathcal{L}_{con}$	0.931	0.872	0.929	0.882	27.143	74.175	0.962	0.908	0. 894	0.831

with boundary segmentation like Shape Loss [21] and the challenge winner DCAN [4]; methods for more spatial information like Mild-Net [6] and FullNet with varCE [13]; and methods with suggestive annotation [22] and quantization [18]. As shown in Table 1, the proposed model outperforms all the other methods that are directly comparable. All three evaluation metrics for segmentation are promoted simultaneously, and substantial improvement lies in Part B for F1 score and object Dice, and object Hausdorff for Part A and B. These advancement indicates better performance for rather complex cases (75% of Part B are malignant cases) and better recognition of overall gland structures.

Figure 4 and Fig. 5 visualize the exemplar segmentation results of benign and malignant cases in GlaS dataset. The common issues in segmenting benign

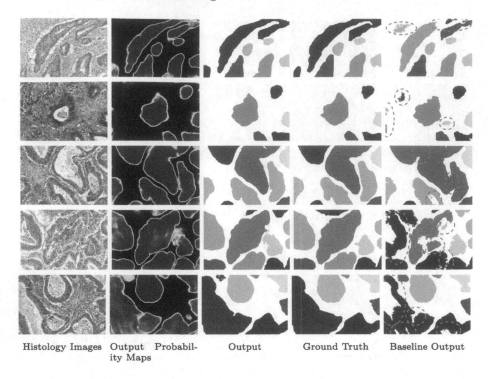

Histology Images   Output Probabil-   Output   Ground Truth   Baseline Output
ity Maps

Fig. 5. Segmentation examples of malignant cases on GlaS dataset (top two from part A, bottom three from part B).

Table 3. Performance on CRAG dataset in comparison with other methods.

Method	F1 Score	Object Dice	Object Hausdorff
Ours	**0.840**	**0.898**	**109.02**
DSE [17]	0.835	0.889	120.127
Mild-Net [6]	0.825	0.875	160.14
DCAN [4]	0.736	0.794	218.76

cases include the touching glands, the misleading background, and the structural changes in a few cases. As shown in Fig. 4, the proposed method shows better performances in handling the details and the recognition of overall glandular structures. Noticed that the baseline method is the proposed one without semantic feature matching and $\mathcal{L}_{con}$. For malignant cases in Fig. 5, the gland morphology appears to be more complicated, where the majority of them have no regular shape or structure. With the visual aids from the semantically related images, the morphological change is well captured by the proposed model.

Table 2 demonstrates the ablation study on GlaS dataset. The baseline method achieves promising performance. With the addition of the proposed hierarchal semantic attention module, an 5% improvement can be observed on average for all three metrics of segmentation, and especially the Hausdorff distance that measures glandular shape similarity. With the consistency loss, the proposed method further promotes the results by 4% on average for segmentation and semantic correspondence simultaneously with better shape recognition. The hards cases are greatly improved in terms of the glandular shape.

Table 3 lists the comparative results on CRAG dataset. It is a more recent dataset and we have reported all results to the best of our knowledge. Similarly, the advancements in segmentation metrics and especially the Hausdorff distance validate the effectiveness of our proposed method in shape recognition.

In our experiments, it takes about 6 h to train the model, and 0.4s to 0.9s to segment the test image, depending on the image size. We have also tested the performance of the model with two decoders and performed simultaneous segmentation of both source and target images, which is more efficient but downgrades the overall performances. The possible reason could be the siamese encoder fails to extract sufficient features for both images for pixel-level classification, especially when the similarity of the histologic pairs are not high enough. This problem can be further discussed and studied in the future.

4   Conclusion

In this paper, we tackle the problem of morphology diversity in highly deformed gland cases by an attentive model with hierarchical semantic feature matching, where both spatial and appearance features are well preserved for accurate gland segmentation. A consistency loss is introduced to supervise the simultaneous fulfillment of feature matching and segmentation on pixel-level. The proposed model is validated on two public gland datasets and outperforms the state-of-the-art approaches with a major improvement in the greatly deformed cases.

References

1. Aljanabi, M.A., Hussain, Z.M., Lu, S.F.: An entropy-histogram approach forimage similarity and face recognition. Mathematical Problems in Engineering **2018**, (2018)
2. Awan, R., Sirinukunwattana, K., Epstein, D., Jefferyes, S., Qidwai, U., Aftab, Z., Mujeeb, I., Snead, D., Rajpoot, N.: Glandular morphometrics for objective grading of colorectal adenocarcinoma histology images. Sci. Reports **7**(1), 16852 (2017)
3. Bosman, F.T., Carneiro, F., Hruban, R.H., Theise, N.D., et al.: WHO classification of tumours of the digestive system. No. 4 En., World Health Organization, (2010)
4. Chen, H., Qi, X., Yu, L., Heng, P.A.: DCAN: deep contour-aware networks for accurate gland segmentation. In: Proceedings of the IEEE Conference on Computer Vision and Pattern Recognition, pp. 2487–2496 (2016)
5. Fleming, M., Ravula, S., Tatishchev, S.F., Wang, H.L.: Colorectal carcinoma: pathologic aspects. J. Gastrointestinal Oncol. **3**(3), 153 (2012)
6. Graham, S., et al.: Mild-net: minimal information loss dilated network for gland instance segmentation in colon histology images. Med. Image Anal. **52**, 199–211 (2019)

7. He, K., Zhang, X., Ren, S., Sun, J.: Deep residual learning for image recognition. In: Proceedings of the IEEE Conference on Computer Vision and Pattern Recognition, pp. 770–778 (2016)
8. Honari, S., Molchanov, P., Tyree, S., Vincent, P., Pal, C., Kautz, J.: Improving landmark localization with semi-supervised learning. In: Proceedings of the IEEE Conference on Computer Vision and Pattern Recognition, pp. 1546–1555 (2018)
9. Jaderberg, M., Simonyan, K., Zisserman, A., et al.: Spatial transformer networks. In: Advances in Neural Information Processing Systems, pp. 2017–2025 (2015)
10. Kendall, A., et al.: End-to-end learning of geometry and context for deep stereo regression. In: Proceedings of the IEEE International Conference on Computer Vision, pp. 66–75 (2017)
11. Lee, J., Kim, D., Ponce, J., Ham, B.: Sfnet: learning object-aware semantic correspondence. In: Proceedings of the IEEE Conference on Computer Vision and Pattern Recognition, pp. 2278–2287 (2019)
12. Paszke, A., et al.: Pytorch: an imperative style, high-performance deep learning library. In: Advances in Neural Information Processing Systems, pp. 8024–8035 (2019)
13. Qu, H., Yan, Z., Riedlinger, G.M., De, S., Metaxas, D.N.: Improving nuclei/gland instance segmentation in histopathology images by full resolution neural network and spatial constrained loss. In: Shen, D., et al. (eds.) MICCAI 2019. LNCS, vol. 11764, pp. 378–386. Springer, Cham (2019). https://doi.org/10.1007/978-3-030-32239-7_42
14. Ronneberger, O., Fischer, P., Brox, T.: U-Net: convolutional networks for biomedical image segmentation. In: Navab, N., Hornegger, J., Wells, W., Frangi, A. (eds.) MICCAI 2015. LNCS, vol. 9351, pp. 234–241. Springer, Cham (2015). https://doi.org/10.1007/978-3-319-24574-4_28
15. Sirinukunwattana, K., Pluim, J.P., Chen, H., Qi, X., Heng, P.A., Guo, Y.B., Wang, L.Y., Matuszewski, B.J., Bruni, E., Sanchez, U., et al.: Gland segmentation in colon histology images: the glas challenge contest. Med. Image Anal. 35, 489–502 (2017)
16. Torre, L.A., Bray, F., Siegel, R.L., Ferlay, J., Lortet-Tieulent, J., Jemal, A.: Global cancer statistics, 2012. CA: A Cancer J. Clin. 65(2), 87–108 (2015)
17. Xie, Y., Lu, H., Zhang, J., Shen, C., Xia, Y.: Deep segmentation-emendation model for gland instance segmentation. In: Shen, D., et al. (eds.) MICCAI 2019. LNCS, vol. 11764, pp. 469–477. Springer, Cham (2019). https://doi.org/10.1007/978-3-030-32239-7_52
18. Xu, X., et al.: Quantization of fully convolutional networks for accurate biomedical image segmentation. In: Proceedings of the IEEE Conference on Computer Vision and Pattern Recognition, pp. 8300–8308. IEEE (2018)
19. Xu, Y., Li, Y., Liu, M., Wang, Y., Lai, M., Eric, I., Chang, C.: Gland instance segmentation by deep multichannel side supervision. In: Ourselin, S., Joskowicz, L., Sabuncu, M., Unal, G., Wells, W. (eds.) MICCAI 2016. LNCS, vol. 9901, pp. 496–504. Springer, Cham (2016). https://doi.org/10.1007/978-3-319-46723-8_57
20. Xu, Y., Li, Y., Wang, Y., Liu, M., Fan, Y., Lai, M., Eric, I., Chang, C.: Gland instance segmentation using deep multichannel neural networks. IEEE Trans. Biomed. Eng. 64(12), 2901–2912 (2017)

21. Yan, Z., Yang, X., Cheng, K.T.T.: A deep model with shape-preserving loss for gland instance segmentation. In: Frangi, A., Schnabel, J., Davatzikos, C., Alberola-López, C., Fichtinger, G. (eds.) MICCAI 2018. LNCS, vol. 11071, pp. 138–146. Springer, Cham (2018). https://doi.org/10.1007/978-3-030-00934-2_16

22. Yang, L., Zhang, Y., Chen, J., Zhang, S., Chen, D.Z.: Suggestive annotation: a deep active learning framework for biomedical image segmentation. In: Descoteaux, M., Maier-Hein, L., Franz, A., Jannin, P., Collins, D., Duchesne, S. (eds.) MICCAI 2017. LNCS, vol. 10435, pp. 399–407. Springer, Cham (2017). https://doi.org/10. 1007/978-3-319-66179-7_46

23. Yu, F., Koltun, V.: Multi-scale context aggregation by dilated convolutions. arXiv preprint, (2015) arXiv:1511.07122

24. Zhang, Y., Yang, L., Chen, J., Fredericksen, M., Hughes, D.P., Chen, D.Z.: Deep adversarial networks for biomedical image segmentation utilizing unannotated images. In: Descoteaux, M., Maier-Hein, L., Franz, A., Jannin, P., Collins, D., Duchesne, S. (eds.) MICCAI 2017. LNCS, vol. 10435, pp. 408–416. Springer, Cham (2017). https://doi.org/10.1007/978-3-319-66179-7_47

25. Zheng, H., et al.: Biomedical image segmentation via representative annotation. In: Proceedings of the AAAI Conference on Artificial Intelligence, vol. 33, pp. 5901–5908 (2019)

Open-Set Recognition for Skin Lesions Using Dermoscopic Images

Pranav Budhwant⬤, Sumeet Shinde⬤, and Madhura Ingalhalikar$^{(\boxtimes)}$⬤

Symbiosis Center for Medical Image Analysis, Symbiosis International University,
Pune 412115, Lavale, India
head@scmia.edu

Abstract. Application of deep neural networks in learning underlying dermoscopic patterns and classifying skin-lesion pathology is crucial. It can help in early diagnosis which can lead to timely therapeutic intervention and efficacy. To establish the clinical applicability of such techniques it is important to delineate each pathology with superior accuracy. However, with innumerable types of skin conditions and supervised closed class classification methods trained on limited classes, applicability into clinical workflow could be unattainable. To mitigate this issue our work considers this as an open-set recognition problem. The technique is divided into two stages, closed-set classification of labelled data and open-set recognition for unknown classes which employs an autoencoder for conditional reconstruction of the input image. We compare our technique to a traditional baseline method and demonstrate on ISIC and Derm7pt data, higher accuracy and sensitivity for known as well as unknown classes. In summary, our open-set recognition method for dermoscopic images illustrates high clinical applicability.

Keywords: Open-set recognition · Out-of-distribution detection · Medical imaging · ISIC · Dermoscopy

1 Introduction

Melanoma and non-melanoma skin cancers are the most common worldwide malignancies with a 5-fold increasing trend over last 3 decades [9]. Most of the non-melanoma cancers are highly curable if diagnosed in early stage while melanomas can be highly infiltrative and can be a cause of future metastasis, particularly if diagnosed in later stages. Overall, early identification of the skin cancer is fundamental as it can lead to timely treatment and therapeutic interventions consequently resulting into better outcomes.

Dermoscopy is a non-invasive in-vivo skin surface microscopy technique that facilitates extremely high resolution images [19]. The underlying pigment and vascular patterns in the derma-images for conditions like melanoma and multiple non-melanoma cancers can be visually interpreted by the dermatologists, however have illustrated poor inter-rater agreement as visually evaluating these

© Springer Nature Switzerland AG 2020
M. Liu et al. (Eds.): MLMI 2020, LNCS 12436, pp. 614–623, 2020.
https://doi.org/10.1007/978-3-030-59861-7_62

patterns requires considerable experience [19]. To this end, with better pattern analysis using learning techniques, computer aided diagnostic systems can be built upon these images that may identify the pathology consequently avoiding the need for invasive methods such as skin biopsy.

With the introduction of deep learning (DL), computational models have been increasingly employed in detecting the type of skin lesion, especially in case of melanomas on dermoscopic images [20]. However, these techniques have not yet been established for routine clinical usage as the accuracies are lower [5,13] and the techniques are more specific in identifying a single lesion or limited lesion types, and therefore are not robust enough to detect and diagnose dermoscopic images from innumerable other conditions that may include pigmentations, blisters, keratosis, lentigo, ulcers etc. Hence, there is a wide opportunity to progress over the existing learning models not only to improve prediction accuracies but also to accommodate open-sets where any dermoscopic test image will be classified either into the known set of classes or into an anonymous class and shall be more applicable in a clinical setting.

Open-set recognition (OSR) framework presumes that samples encountered during testing may belong to classes other than what the model has been trained on, referred to as *"unknown unknowns"* [15]. Traditional classifiers fail to adapt to such a scenarios. Score thresholding could be one way to tackle this [1,14,16,23], however, deciding the operating threshold for the model generally relies on adjusting the Softmax scores which may consequently affect the prediction accuracy of the known classes [1,4,10,16]. Our method alleviates these issues by dividing the problem into closed-set classification and open-set recognition. For the closed-set classification stage, we train a standard classifier on the known classes and for the open-set recognition stage, we train a conditional autoencoder which reconstructs original inputs for known class images and random image for unknown class images. We then perform thresholding on the reconstruction errors to determine if a sample belongs to unknown class. This allows us to retain the performance on known classes, while boosting the performance of unknown class detection. We evaluate our performance on natural dermoscopic images for open-set recognition of skin lesions and show that our method performs significantly better when compared to the traditional Softmax thresholding based techniques.

2   Proposed Method

Our proposed method is loosely based on the C2AE (Class Conditoned Auto-Encoder) method [11], however we make substantial modifications. First, we divide the problem in two stages, closed-set classification and open-set recognition. The closed-set classification uses a deep convolutional neural network (CNN) while for the open-set recognition, we train an autoencoder to perform conditional reconstruction of the given input image based on condition vectors defined for each class. For each input image, the *match condition vector* is the condition vector defined for the class to which the image belongs, and the condition vectors for all other classes are referred to as *non-match condition vectors*.

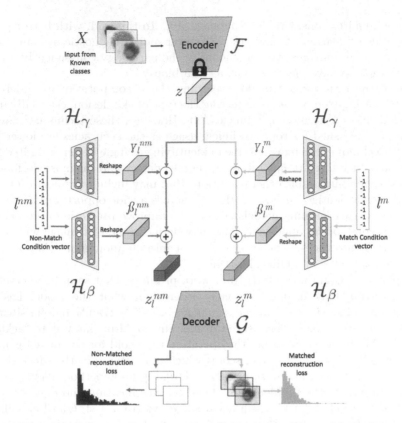

Fig. 1. Overview of the conditional autoencoder training. The weights of encoder $\mathcal{F}$ are frozen. Here the two $\mathcal{H}_\gamma$ and $\mathcal{H}_\beta$ are the same networks.

The decoder is trained to reconstruct the input image for the latent representation conditioned on the match condition vector, and to reconstruct a random image for the latent representation conditioned on a non-match condition vector. Thresholding on the reconstruction error is performed to determine the image class.

Closed Set Training. We consider various pre-trained models for the closed-set classification stage. To address the imbalance in the data, we use a weighted cross-entropy loss to train the network. The weight for a class is calculated from N_{class}, the number of samples belonging to the class and N_{total}, the total number of samples present in the training set as

$$(1 - \frac{N_{class}}{N_{total}}) * 10 \tag{1}$$

Conditional Autoencoder Training. The autoencoder (Fig. 1) consists of a pre-trained DenseNet121 without the Softmax and Global Average Pooling (GAP) layers fine-tuned for ISIC 8-way classification (without UNK) as the encoder ($\mathcal{F}$), and a deep CNN decoder ($\mathcal{G}$). We map the input image to a 3D volume as a 1D tensor is not able to capture enough meaningful information for complex images as present in our data. We freeze the weights of $\mathcal{F}$ while training the conditional autoencoder. This is done to ensure that the decoder learns reconstructions based on the information used to classify the input. During training, $\mathcal{F}$ is used to generate the latent representation z for a batch of images. This latent representation batch is conditioned using FiLM [12], which transforms the input feature map by performing feature-wise linear modulations based on the condition vector. Considering k classes, the k-dimensional condition vector l_j for a class j is computed as $l_j = +1, \forall x = j$, and $l_j = -1, \forall x \neq j$, where $x, j \in \{1, 2, ...k\}$. We then obtain the class conditioned latent representation z_{l_j} using the following set of equations

$$\gamma_j = \mathcal{H}_\gamma(l_j), \qquad\qquad \beta_j = \mathcal{H}_\beta(l_j) \qquad (2)$$
$$z_{l_j} = \gamma_j \odot z + \beta_j \qquad\qquad\qquad\qquad (3)$$

Here $\mathcal{H}_\gamma$ and $\mathcal{H}_\beta$ are single layer neural networks, the tensors γ_j, β_j, and z_{l_j} have the same shape and $\odot$ represents the Hadamard product. The decoder is expected to reconstruct the original input image when z is conditioned on the *match condition vector* or l_m. The decoder is simultaneously trained to poorly reconstruct the original input when z is conditioned on the *non-match condition vector*, l_{nm}. For the rest of the paper, m is used to represent match, and nm is used to represent non-match. Consider a given input X_i from the batch. It's corresponding class is denoted as y_i^m, and y_i^{nm} is any other class. The match and non-match condition vectors, therefore, are $l_m = l_{y_i^m}$ and $l_{nm} = l_{y_i^{nm}}$ respectively, where $y_i^{nm}, y_i^m \in \{1, 2, ...k\}$ such that $y_i^{nm} \neq y_i^m$ and y_i^{nm} is randomly sampled. Let z_i represent the latent representation $\mathcal{F}(X_i)$. We then generate the *match conditioned latent representation* $z_{i_{lm}}$ and the *non-match conditioned latent representation* $z_{i_{l_{nm}}}$ using equations (2) and (3). The reconstructions are then generated as $\tilde{X}_i^m = \mathcal{G}(z_{i_{l_m}})$ and $\tilde{X}_i^{nm} = \mathcal{G}(z_{i_{l_{nm}}})$. Here $\tilde{X}_i^m$ and $\tilde{X}_i^{nm}$ represent the reconstructions for the *match conditioned latent representation* and the *non-match conditioned latent representation* respectively. The reconstruction error $\mathcal{R}$ is calculated as the mean squared error between the input image and the generated reconstruction as $\mathcal{R}(X_i, \tilde{X}_i) = MSE(X_i, \tilde{X}_i)$. We want $\mathcal{R}(X_i, \tilde{X}_i^m)$ to be near 0, and $\mathcal{R}(X_i, X_i^{\tilde{n}m})$ to be far from 0. Following the feed-forward path summarized above, $\mathcal{G}, H_\gamma, H_\beta$ with parameters $\Theta_g, \Theta_\gamma, \Theta_\beta$ respectively, are trained to on the following loss function

$$\min_{\{\Theta_g, \Theta_\gamma, \Theta_\beta\}} \alpha \mathcal{L}_r^m(\{\Theta_g, \Theta_\gamma, \Theta_\beta\}) + (1 - \alpha)\mathcal{L}_r^{nm}(\{\Theta_g, \Theta_\gamma, \Theta_\beta\}) \qquad (4)$$

Here $\mathcal{L}_r^m, \mathcal{L}_r^{nm}$ calculate the perceptual loss [6] using a VGG-16 [17] network pretrained on ImageNet dataset. We prefer perceptual loss over a simple mean

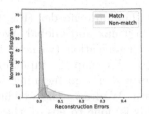
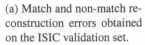
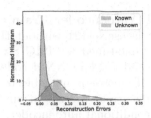

(a) Match and non-match reconstruction errors obtained on the ISIC validation set.

(b) Known and unknown reconstruction errors obtained on the Derm7pt dataset.

Fig. 2. Normalized histograms of reconstruction errors

absolute error (MAE) or mean squared error (MSE) as it results in significantly better reconstructions. We use the activations of layers 2,9 and 17 from the pretrained network. The loss function $\mathcal{L}_r^m$ imposes the constraint that the reconstruction for match condition vector $\tilde{X}_i^m$ should be the input image X_i, whereas the loss function $\mathcal{L}_r^{nm}$ imposes the constraint that the reconstruction for non-match condition vector $\tilde{X}_i^{nm}$ should be poor. For this, we minimize the distance between $\tilde{X}_i^{nm}$ and a random image X_i^{nm}. We use a complete white image as X_i^{nm} as we found that it improves the performance as opposed to the method used in [11]. Equation (4) gives the final training objective, where $\mathcal{L}_r^m$ and $\mathcal{L}_r^{nm}$ are weighted with $\alpha \in [0, 1]$. As this trains $\mathcal{G}$ to reconstruct poor images if the condition vector does not match the input image class, at test time, ideally, none of the condition vectors will match the unknown class image, thus resulting in poor reconstruction. In this way, this training methodology facilitates open-set recognition.

Threshold Calculation and Inference. After the conditional autoencoder has been trained following the procedure described above, we generate a set of match and non-match reconstruction errors $(\mathcal{R})$ S_m and S_{nm} from the validation set $\{X_1, X_2, ..X_{N_{val}}\}$, and their corresponding match and non-match condition vectors $\{l_{y_1^m}, l_{y_2^m}, ..l_{y_{val}^m}\}$ and $\{l_{y_1^{nm}}, l_{y_2^{nm}}, ..l_{y_{val}^{nm}}\}$ using the following equations

$$\tilde{X}_i^m = \mathcal{G}(\mathcal{H}_\gamma(l_{y_i^m}) \odot \mathcal{F}(X_i) + \mathcal{H}_\beta(l_{y_i^m})), \tag{5}$$

$$\tilde{X}_i^{nm} = \mathcal{G}(\mathcal{H}_\gamma(l_{y_i^{nm}}) \odot \mathcal{F}(X_i) + \mathcal{H}_\beta(l_{y_i^{nm}})), \tag{6}$$

$$S_m = \{r_i^m \in \mathbb{R}^+ \cup \{0\} | r_i^m = \mathcal{R}(X_i, \tilde{X}_i^m)\}, \tag{7}$$

$$S_{nm} = \{r_i^{nm} \in \mathbb{R}^+ \cup \{0\} | r_i^{nm} = \mathcal{R}(X_i, \tilde{X}_i^{nm})\}, \tag{8}$$

$$\forall i \in \{1, 2, ...N_{val}\}$$

We utilize the reconstruction errors generated on the validation set, and not the training set as proposed by [11]. This is because the autoencoder is directly trained to minimize the loss on the training set. This would result in more clearly separated distributions, but the distributions obtained on the validation data would more closely resemble the distributions obtained on the unknown classes. The histogram of S_m and S_{nm} are shown in Fig. 2a for the validation set. The threshold τ for deciding whether a sample belongs to the known class lies in the region $S_m \cap S_{nm}$. We manually decide the threshold for rejection, such that almost all of the validation set (over 99%) is accepted as belonging to one of the known classes. This threshold employed is 0.05.

The open-set inference algorithm used for testing is described in Algorithm 1. Our inference method significantly reduces the time required, as we only check if the input belongs to the predicted class distribution, as opposed to checking it with every known class as proposed by [11].

3 Experiments and Results

In this section we compare the performance of various classifiers for the closed-set classification, and evaluate the performance of our open-set recognition method and compare it with a baseline method of Softmax thresholding [10]. An important factor that affects open-set performance is the openness of the problem [15] given by

$$\mathbf{O} = 1 - \sqrt{\frac{2 * N_{train}}{N_{test} + N_{target}}} \qquad (9)$$

where, N_{train} is the number of known classes used for training, N_{test} is the number of classes that will be observed during testing, and N_{target} is the number of classes that should be identified correctly during testing. Generally, the performance of open-set recognition approaches drops as the openness of the problem setting increases [11]. However, we argue that this openness measure may not be the best evaluation metric for our problem. This is because equation (9) computes the openness based on the number of unknown classes, and in our case multiple classes are clubbed together as unknown as a result of innumerable diagnoses that cannot be accounted for as well as unavailability of sufficient samples. For instance, the class *reed or spitz nevus* could be separated in two, or the class *miscellaneous* could be split into multiple sub-classes. Therefore in such cases, equation (9) fails to provide the true openness measure. The openness for our problem computed this way is 23%.

3.1 Datasets

We employ the ISIC 2019 Training Dataset [2, 3, 22] and the Derm7pt [7] dataset to build a dataset for the open-set recognition framework. The ISIC 2019 Training Set consists of 9 classes: MEL, NV, BCC, AK, BKL, DF, VASC, SCC and UNK. The Derm7pt dataset is a dermoscopic and clinical skin disease image dataset, containing 20 different diseases. The classes common to Derm7pt and

---

Algorithm 1: Open-set Inference Algorithm

Require: Trained network models $\mathcal{C}, \mathcal{F}, \mathcal{G}, \mathcal{H}_\gamma, \mathcal{H}_\beta$
Require: Threshold τ
Require: Test image X, k condition vectors $\{l_1, ..., l_k\}$
1 Prediction probabilities, $p_y = \mathcal{C}(X)$;
2 Predicted known label, $\hat{y} = argmax(p_y)$;
3 Latent representation, $z = \mathcal{F}(X)$;
4 $z_{l_{\hat{y}}} = \mathcal{H}_\gamma(l_{\hat{y}}) \odot z + \mathcal{H}_\beta(l_{\hat{y}})$;
5 $\tilde{X}_{\hat{y}} = \mathcal{G}(z_{l_{\hat{y}}})$;
6 Reconstruction Error $r = \mathcal{R}(X, \tilde{X}_{\hat{y}})$;
7 **if** $r < \tau$ **then**
8 | predict X as Known, with label $\hat{y}$;
9 **else**
10 | predict X as Unknown;
11 **end**

ISIC data are eliminated from the Derm7pt dataset to obtain a set of unknown classes. This leaves us with 11 classes, namely melanosis, clark nevus, lentigo, congenital nevus, reed or spitz nevus, miscellaneous, blue nevus, recurrent nevus, seborrheic keratosis, dermal nevus, combined nevus. Figure 3 shows sample images belonging to the known and unknown classes.

3.2   Implementation Details and Results

We train the closed-set classifiers to minimize the weighted crossentropy loss using the Adam [8] optimizer with an initial learning rate of 10^{-5}. Furthermore, we employ early stopping by monitoring the validation loss to prevent overfitting. For training the open-set models, we make use of Cyclical Learning Rate with triangular2 policy and the method to automatically find optimal learning rates described in [18]. We make use of the Adam optimizer and early stopping by monitoring the validation loss. The decoder uses nearest neighbor upsampling, and 2D Spatial Dropout [21]. α in equation (4) is set to 0.8.

Closed-Set Classification. For training the closed-set classifiers, we split the ISIC data (without the UNK class) into training, validation and testing sets with 80%, 4% and 16% of samples respectively. We then train and evaluate various models for closed-set classification, namely DenseNet121, EfficientNet B2, EfficientNet B3, and EfficientNet B4 to minimize a weighted crossentropy loss. We adopt data augmentation by randomly flipping the images vertically and horizontally, performing random rotations and translations on the images. Table 1 summarizes the results of these classifiers on the test set. EfficientNet B4 is then chosen as the classification model $\mathcal{C}$ for further experiments.

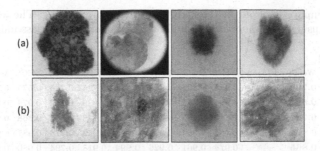

Fig. 3. Sample images from the dataset. **(a)** Images belonging to the known classes. **(b)** Images belonging to the unknown classes.

Open-Set Recognition. As discussed in subsection 3.1 we consider 11 classes from the Derm7pt dataset as the unknown class for testing, along with the test set containing 16% of the samples from ISIC data. The autoencoder maps input image of shape (224,224,3) to a latent representation of (7,7,1024) then upsamples this back to (224,224,3). We evaluate and compare our method with a baseline of Softmax thresholding.

Figure 2a depicts the distribution of reconstruction errors on the ISIC validation set for the match and non-match condition vectors, and Fig. 2b depicts the observed known and unknown class reconstruction errors on the test set containing the ISIC test set and the Derm7pt dataset. As can be seen from the figures, the distributions for the match and non-match reconstruction errors closely resemble the true distributions observed for the known and unknown reconstruction errors. This indicates that the training methodology does in fact emulate open-set behaviour, and the reconstruction errors can be utilized to detect unknown samples. Table 2 summarizes the results of our method and Softmax thresholding on various metrics. Most per-class metrics are similar, and our method achieves significantly better results on the unknown class, resulting in better overall performance without hampering closed-set classification accuracy.

Table 1. Performance of closed-set classifiers on the test set. The weighted mean is calculated using the support for each class to account for the class imbalance.

Model	Weighted Mean				
	F1	ROC AUC	Sensitivity	Specificity	Accuracy
DenseNet121	0.754	0.938	0.763	0.91	0.888
EfficientNet B2	0.775	0.946	0.786	0.918	0.898
EfficientNet B3	0.788	0.952	0.798	**0.92**	0.906
EfficientNet B4	**0.809**	**0.96**	**0.818**	0.917	**0.913**

Table 2. Comparison of our method with Softmax Thresholding. The weighted mean is calculated using the support for each class to account for the class imbalance.

Our method										
Metric	Weighted Mean	AK	BCC	BKL	DF	MEL	NV	SCC	VASC	UNK
F1	**0.709**	0.537	0.823	0.654	0.683	0.725	0.746	0.575	0.738	**0.585**
ROC AUC	**0.892**	0.966	0.987	0.948	0.983	0.939	0.863	0.978	0.998	**0.789**
Sensitivity	**0.729**	0.585	0.785	0.571	0.622	0.738	0.822	0.868	0.613	**0.511**
Specificity	0.882	0.984	0.984	0.976	0.998	0.949	0.778	0.987	0.999	**0.945**
Accuracy	**0.865**	0.974	0.961	0.926	0.994	0.918	0.794	0.986	0.994	**0.863**
Softmax Thresholding (0.5)										
Metric	Weighted Mean	AK	BCC	BKL	DF	MEL	NV	SCC	VASC	UNK
F1	0.643	0.535	0.826	0.649	0.675	0.721	0.779	0.523	0.733	0.036
ROC AUC	0.849	0.966	0.987	0.948	0.983	0.939	0.863	0.978	0.998	0.479
Sensitivity	0.629	0.663	0.811	0.572	0.65	0.759	0.718	0.929	0.617	0.059
Specificity	**0.905**	0.983	0.981	0.974	0.998	0.945	0.862	0.985	0.999	0.853
Accuracy	0.854	0.976	0.963	0.926	0.995	0.92	0.786	0.985	0.994	0.805

4 Conclusion and Future Work

Our work illustrated that the novel open-set recognition algorithm for detecting unknown classes is highly applicable in clinical settings. Our results on dermoscopic skin lesion images were significantly superior at detecting unknowns than softmax thresholding. Existing approaches that achieve superior results on closed-set classification can easily adapt to this method without compromising the performance on known classes.

References

1. Bendale, A., Boult, T.E.: Towards open set deep networks. In: Proceedings of the IEEE Conference on Computer Vision and Pattern Recognition, pp. 1563–1572. IEEE (2016). https://doi.org/10.1109/CVPR.2016.173
2. Codella, N.C.F., et al.: Skin lesion analysis toward melanoma detection: a challenge at the 2017 international symposium on biomedical imaging (ISBI), hosted by the international skin imaging collaboration (ISIC). CoRR abs/1710.05006 (2017). http://arxiv.org/abs/1710.05006
3. Combalia, M., et al.: Bcn20000: dermoscopic lesions in the wild, August 2019
4. Ge, Z., Demyanov, S., Chen, Z., Garnavi, R.: Generative openmax for multi-class open set classification. arXiv preprint (2017). arXiv:1707.07418
5. Gessert, N., Nielsen, M., Shaikh, M., Werner, R., Schlaefer, A.: Skin lesion classification using ensembles of multi-resolution efficientnets with meta data (2019)
6. Johnson, J., Alahi, A., Fei-Fei, L.: Perceptual losses for real-time style transfer and super-resolution. In: Leibe, B., Matas, J., Sebe, N., Welling, M. (eds.) ECCV 2016. LNCS, vol. 9906, pp. 694–711. Springer, Cham (2016). https://doi.org/10.1007/978-3-319-46475-6_43
7. Kawahara, J., Daneshvar, S., Argenziano, G., Hamarneh, G.: 7-point checklist and skin lesion classification using multi-task multi-modal neural nets. IEEE J. Biomed. Health Inform. 1–1, April 2018. https://doi.org/10.1109/JBHI.2018.2824327

8. Kingma, D., Ba, J.: Adam: a method for stochastic optimization. Int. Conf. Learn. Represent. December 2014
9. Leiter, U., Garbe, C.: Epidemiology of melanoma and nonmelanoma skin cancer-the role of sunlight. Sunlight, Vitamin D and Skin Cancer, pp. 89–103. Springer, Berlin (2008). https://doi.org/10.1007/978-0-387-77574-6_8
10. Neal, L., Olson, M., Fern, X., Wong, W.K., Li, F.: Open set learning with counterfactual images. In: Proceedings of the European Conference on Computer Vision (ECCV), pp. 613–628 (2018)
11. Oza, P., Patel, V.M.: C2ae: class conditioned auto-encoder for open-set recognition. In: Proceedings of the IEEE Conference on Computer Vision and Pattern Recognition, pp. 2302–2311. IEEE (2019). https://doi.org/10.1109/CVPR.2019.00241
12. Perez, E., Strub, F., de Vries, H., Dumoulin, V., Courville, A.: Film: visual reasoning with a general conditioning layer (2017)
13. di Ruffano, L.F., et al.: Computer-assisted diagnosis techniques (dermoscopy and spectroscopy-based) for diagnosing skin cancer in adults. Cochrane Database Syst. Rev. (2018). https://doi.org/10.1002/14651858.cd013186
14. Scheirer, W.J., Jain, L.P., Boult, T.E.: Probability models for open set recognition. IEEE Trans. Pattern Anal. Mach. Intell. **36**, 2317–2324 (2014). https://doi.org/10.1109/TPAMI.2014.2321392
15. Scheirer, W.J., de Rezende Rocha, A., Sapkota, A., Boult, T.E.: Toward open set recognition. IEEE Trans. Pattern Anal. Mach. Intell. **35**, 1757–1772 (2013). https://doi.org/10.1109/TPAMI.2012.256
16. Shu, L., Xu, H., Liu, B.: Doc: deep open classification of text documents. arXiv preprint (2017). arXiv:1709.08716
17. Simonyan, K., Zisserman, A.: Very deep convolutional networks for large-scale image recognition (2014)
18. Smith, L.N.: Cyclical learning rates for training neural networks (2015)
19. Sonthalia, F.: Dermoscopy overview and extradiagnostic applications. StatPearls Publishing, StatPearls (2020)
20. Sultana, N.N., Puhan, N.B.: Recent deep learning methods for melanoma detection: a review. In: International Conference on Mathematics and Computing (2018). https://doi.org/10.1007/978-981-13-0023-3_12
21. Tompson, J., Goroshin, R., Jain, A., LeCun, Y., Bregler, C.: Efficient object localization using convolutional networks. In: Proceedings of the IEEE Conference on Computer Vision and Pattern Recognition, pp. 648–656 (2015). https://doi.org/10.1109/cvpr.2015.7298664
22. Tschandl, P., Rosendahl, C., Kittler, H.: The ham10000 dataset: a large collection of multi-source dermatoscopic images of common pigmented skin lesions. Sci. Data **5**, 180161 (2018). https://doi.org/10.1038/sdata.2018.161
23. Zhang, H., Patel, V.M.: Sparse representation-based open set recognition. IEEE Trans. Pattern Anal. Mach. Intell. **39**, 1690–1696 (2017). https://doi.org/10.1109/TPAMI.2016.2613924

End-to-End Coordinate Regression Model with Attention-Guided Mechanism for Landmark Localization in 3D Medical Images

Jupeng Li[1(✉)], Yinghui Wang[2], Junbo Mao[1], Gang Li[2], and Ruohan Ma[2]

[1] School of Electronic and Information Engineering, Beijing Jiaotong University, Beijing 100044, China
lijupeng@bjtu.edu.cn
[2] Department of Oral and Maxillofacial Radiology, Peking University School and Hospital of Stomatology, Beijing 100081, China

Abstract. In this paper, we propose a deep learning based framework for accurate anatomical landmark localization in 3D medical volumes. An end-to-end coordinate regression model with attention-guided mechanism was designed for landmark detection, which combines global landmark configuration with local high-resolution feature responses. This framework regress multiple landmarks coordinates for landmark localization directly, instead of the traditional heat-maps regression. Global stage informs spatial information on the coarse low resolution images to regress landmarks attention, which improve landmarks localization accuracy in the local stage. We have evaluated the proposed framework on our Temporomandibular Joints (TMJs) dataset with 102 image subjects. With less computation and manually tuning, the proposed framework achieves state-of-the-art results.

Keywords: Landmark localization · Coordinate regression · End-to-end learning · Attention mechanism · Medical images analysis

1 Introduction

Localization of anatomical landmarks is an important step in medical image analysis, e.g., image segmentation, registration, anatomical structures detection, et al. [1]. Unfortunately, diversity between images and locally similar structures often introduce difficulties into landmark localization. To deal with these difficulties, machine learning based approaches are predominantly used to automatically localize anatomical landmarks in images. These approaches often combine spatial information and local landmark predictions with explicit handcrafted graphical models, aiming to improve landmark localization accuracy.

Here, we will take TMJs 3D-CBCT images as an example to study the difficult problems of landmark detection in medical images. TMJs are the most complex and delicate joints in the maxillofacial region, often affected by many factors, such as abnormal oral

© Springer Nature Switzerland AG 2020
M. Liu et al. (Eds.): MLMI 2020, LNCS 12436, pp. 624–633, 2020.
https://doi.org/10.1007/978-3-030-59861-7_63

occlusion, habits and force changes, etc. These will be resulted in adaptive changes and compensations of TMJs or the occurrence of related diseases in the high loading activities [2–4]. The accurate localization of landmarks is the fundamental step in the quantification of TMJs deformity. At present, in routine clinical practice all anatomical landmarks are still more often manually marked in 3D images, but this is an extremely time-consuming work. In addition, the reliability between and within the inspectors and the repeatability of manual landmarks localization are also very limited. There are two major challenges that make landmark localization still a difficult task in medical image analysis.

The first challenge is related to the morphological changes between different patients, which will lead to significant changes in the anatomical landmarks of the entire patient. As shown in Fig. 1(a), the local morphology of patient A and patient B near the same tooth boundary may be significantly different [5]. These different performances will be a huge challenge for traditional template-based detection methods. The second challenge is related to the ambiguity in the shape of bone tissue in CBCT images. Such ambiguities make it hard to achieve low landmark localization error, defined both high robustness towards landmark misidentification and high accuracy locally at each identified landmark. For example, the image in Fig. 1(b) shows the CBCT image of patient A and the corresponding 3D reconstructed image. The approximately circular shape change of the top of the condyle will reduce the positioning accuracy of landmarks.

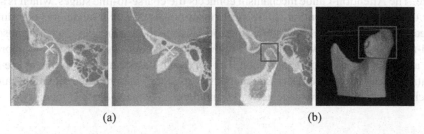

(a) (b)

Fig. 1. TMJs 3D CBCT image landmark's appearance feature analysis, "×" indicates the condylar head coordinate localization. The two images in (a) are from sagittal slices of two patients, and the shapes of condyle heads are obviously different. Figure (b) is another patient's sagittal slice and corresponding 3D reconstructed image. There is obvious shape ambiguity in the condyle.

Related Works: Because manually labeling landmarks of 3D CBCT images is a time-consuming task, researchers have proposed a variety of computer-aided automated detection methods. In the past few years, learning-based methods have been successfully applied to this task from random forest-based methods. A detailed review of this work will not be within the scope of this article, but includes some representative papers [6]. Recently, convolutional neural networks (CNNs) have been used for a range of image processing applications. Originally developed for 2D images, they have been expanded to 3D and the 3D U-Net proposed by Çiçek has been widely used for medical image segmentation and detection tasks [7]. A complete coverage of this work would be outside the scope of our article but examples that are germane to our work include the work of

Liu (2017) whose two-stage task-oriented deep learning (T^2DL) framework to detect landmarks in the brain for disease diagnosis [8], and of Payer (2019) who have proposed a "Spatial Configuration Net" to detect landmarks in MR volumes [1], of Zhang (2020) who have designed a multi-task network that consists of two 3D fully convolutional networks (FCN) for both bone segmentation and landmark digitization [9], of Zhang (2020) who used "HeadLocNet" to detect 7 landmarks located around each inner ear [10].

Inspired by the coarse-to-fine two-stage method widely used in image processing, some methods have shown encouraging results in medical landmark detection tasks. Zhong (2019) propose a two-stage U-Net deep learning framework to automatically detect anatomical landmarks in cephalometric X-ray and achieved state-of-the-art results [11]. During inference, numerical coordinates are obtained from the model's output by computing the *argmax* of pixel values, which is a non-differentiable operation. It should be noted that making predictions based on the *argmax* also introduces quantization issues, since the coordinates have their precision tied to the heat-map's resolution.

Contribution: In this paper, we propose a novel deep learning framework for automatically locating the anatomical landmarks in 3D CBCT image of TMJs. The proposed method regress coordinates of landmarks directly instead of heat-maps to improve the localization accuracy of landmarks. Also, our model consists of two stages from coarse to fine tasks, informing global configuration as well as accurately describing local appearance. The Attention-Guide mechanism connects the coarse-to-fine stages, which is similar to [11] but our Attention-Guide mechanism makes effect on landmarks coordinate directly. The high efficiency of our framework owes to these strategies: (i) we propose an end-to-end learning network for direct regression of landmarks coordinates to improve the accuracy of landmark localization; (ii) our patch-based strategy optimizes the utilization of the network to learn landmarks features; (iii) the proposed attention-guided mechanism connects two-stage networks and reduces demand of GPU memory.

2   Method

2.1   Overall Framework

As shown in Fig. 2, our overall framework for landmark detection includes two stages, regressing N-channel coordinate $L(x, y, z)$ of landmark from coarse to fine localization, instead of heat-maps regression. The two landmark detection stages share end-to-end L^2Net structure designed specially that regress landmarks coordinates directly (Fig. 3). Global-Stage takes a low-resolution CBCT image as input to learn the global information of the image, and outputs coarse coordinates, $L_{att}^i(x, y, z), i = 0, 1, ..., N-1$. Local-stage trains the patch-based End-to-End L^2Net model with high-resolution image patches centered on coordinate points $L_{att}^i(x, y, z)$, $i = 0, 1, ..., N-1$. Guided by the coarse attention points $L_{att}^i(x, y, z)$, local stage learning the proposal local image information to regress the fine landmarks' coordinates $L_{inf}^i(x, y, z), i = 0, 1, ..., N-1$ in a high-resolution scale.

Global Stage and Attention Regression: The global stage takes the entire images with low dimensions as input, and informs the underlying global landmark configuration. We train the Global End-to-End L^2Net to regress N landmarks coordinate coarsely, which are Attention-Guide information for the next stage. The output is the N landmarks coordinate, $L_{att}^i(x, y, z)$, $i = 0, 1, ..., N-1$, as shown in Fig. 2a. Although, the large size of distributions limits the accuracy of prediction. The convolution kernels cannot distinguish subtle features from low resolution data, and the network cannot regress coordinates with the small distributions. Besides, the prediction errors increase as sizing back to the original scale. So, we take those highlights as the coarse attention for local stage, and design a patch-based structure to narrow the learning scope, in order to process data and feature maps in a higher resolution.

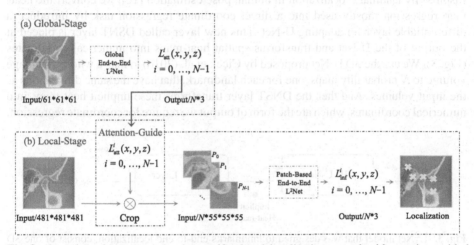

Fig. 2. Overview of the proposed end-to-end landmark localization network with attention-guided mechanism, including two-stage (i.e., global-stage, and local-stage). The global-stage estimates the coarse landmark attention location, while local-stage performs landmark localization with the attention-guided information output from global stage. Each sub-stage shares the same end-to-end landmark localization network to regress landmarks coordinate directly.

Local stage and Landmarks Coordinates Inference: The local stage guided by the coarse attention given by global stage, focuses on learning local appearance around landmarks. The patch-based End-to-End L^2Net shares the same structure with global stage. It is trained with the high-dimension image patches, $P_0, P_1, ..., P_{N-1}$, which are cropped around ground-truth annotation $L_{GT}^i(x, y, z)$ with a random offset $L_{off}^i(x, y, z)$, $i = 0, 1, ..., N-1$ for each image subject. The local stage learns to inference landmark coordinate $L_{inf}^i(x, y, z)$ for each patches P_i, $i = 0, 1, ..., N-1$ within higher dimension than global stage. So, the patch-based End-to-End L^2Net informs the high-resolution local features and has better localization ability than global stage. Our patch-based strategy optimizes the efficiency of local training process, avoiding the negative impact of the areas without landmarks.

Attention-Guided Mechanism: The Attention-Guide mechanism connects global and local stages, and embedded in the local stage inference. Global stage firstly regresses N coarse landmark coordinates as the centers of the attention regions for local stage. As shown in Fig. 2b, high resolution image patches guided by these attention coordinates, by cropping image patches in the high dimension CBCT image at the corresponding centers. So, the Attention-Guide mechanism acts as an information extractor for local stage, to improve landmarks localization accuracy. Local stage takes these concatenated N image patches as input, regressing N local landmarks coordinates.

2.2 End-to-End L^2Net

Inspired by landmark localization in human pose estimation [12], we convert the heat-map regression mostly used into a direct coordinate regression task by introduce a differentiable layer for adapting U-Net. This new layer called DSNT layer is placed at the output of the U-Net and transforms spatial heat-maps into numerical coordinates (Fig. 3). We use the 3D U-Net proposed by Çiçek et al. (2016) to map a whole 3D image volume to N probability maps, one for each landmark, that have the same dimensions as the input volumes. And then the DNST layer transforms these implicit heat-maps into numerical coordinates, which are the form of output we require for coordinate regression.

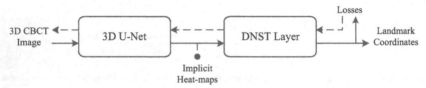

Fig. 3. L^2Net model that was designed to landmarks end-to-end localization, consist of one 3D U-Net and DNST layer.

In contrast to heat-map matching techniques, we do not require applying a loss directly to the landmarks coordinates output by the L^2Net. Instead, the heat-map is learned indirectly by optimizing a loss applied to the predicted coordinates output by the model as a whole. For more technical details of the DNST layer, you can read reference paper [12]. Here, we will give another explanation of the DSNT coordinate regression transform with a differentiable way, allowing us to back-propagate through the DSNT layer. Given an input image I, the implicit normalized heat-map, $H(I; \omega)$, represented as an $m \times n \times k$ matrix where m, n and k correspond to the heat-map resolution. By taking the probabilistic interpretation of $H(I; \omega)$ we can represent the landmark coordinates, $L(x, y, z)$ as gray weighted centroid function $DSNT(H)$ defined as

$$DSNT(H) = L(x, y, z) = \frac{\sum\limits_{(x,y,z)\in v}(x, y, z) * H(I; \omega)}{\sum\limits_{v} H(I; \omega)} \tag{1}$$

This gray weighted centroid is the result μ calculated by Frobenius inner product in [12]. From this aspect, the technical principle of the DSNT layer can be more intuitively understood.

Regression Loss Functions: Since the DSNT layer outputs numerical coordinates, it is possible to directly calculate the two-dimensional Euclidean distance between the prediction u and ground truth p. We take advantage of this fact to formulate the core term of our loss function (Eq. 2). The Euclidean loss function has the advantage of directly optimizing the metric we are interested in the distance between the predicted and actual locations. Contrast this with the mean-square-error (MSE) loss used in heat-map matching, which optimizes the pixel-wise similarity between the output and a synthetic heat-map generated from ground truth locations. The pixel-wise MSE loss is a much less direct way of optimizing the metric that we actually care about.

$$L_{euc}(L_{GT}, L_{inf}) = \|L_{inf} - L_{GT}\|_2 \tag{2}$$

The shape of the output heat-map implicit in the network also affects the regression accuracy of key point coordinates. Here, the implicit heat-map is constrained to a 3D Gaussian distribution, thereby defining the regular term of the loss function. Alternatively, we can impose even stricter regularization on the appearance of the heat-map to directly encourage a certain shape. More specifically, to force the heat-map to resemble a spherical Gaussian, we can minimize the divergence between the generated heat-map and an appropriate target normal distribution. Equation 3 defines the distribution regularization term, where $D(\cdot\|\cdot)$ is a divergence measure (e.g. Jensen-Shannon divergence).

$$L_{reg}(H, L) = D(L\|N(L, \sigma_t^2 H_2)) \tag{3}$$

Equation 4 shows how regularization is incorporated into the DSNT loss function. A regularization coefficient, λ, is used to set the strength of the regularizer, L_{reg}. In our experiments, we picked $\lambda = 1$ using cross validation.

$$L = L_{euc}(L_{GT}, L_{inf}) + \lambda L_{reg}(H, L_{inf}) \tag{4}$$

3 Experiments

3.1 Data and Training

The data used in this study were images of 102 TMJs CBCTs (left TMJ of 103 patients) collected from Peking University School and Hospital of Stomatology. 3D Accuitomo 170 (J. Morita MFG. Corp., Kyoto, Japan) was used to acquire these images.

The device is a flat-panel low-dose cone-beam CT scanner used to diagnose apical lesions, fractures, cysts, tumors, TMJ problems, Dental caries, and allow implant treatment plans, etc. The volume resolution is $0.125 \times 0.125 \times 0.125$ mm^3, and image size is $481 \times 481 \times 481$. Each patient captures the left and right condyles respectively. When acquiring images, the patient the head is fixed and the joint is adjusted to be approximately in the center of the 3D image. For each individual data, there are artificially pre-defined $N = 5$ landmarks around the condyle shown in Fig. 4.

For global stage training, we resample the original image from initial resolution to $61 * 61 * 61$, and ground-truth of coordinates annotated by doctors is also scaled by the same ratio. So, these images and landmarks coordinate data were used for end-to-end

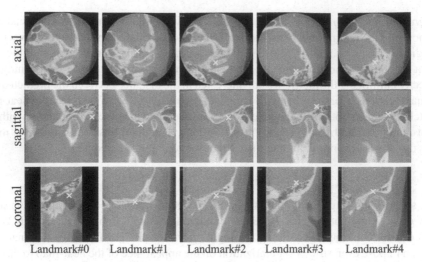

Fig. 4. Five landmarks selected in this study, from left to right are the external auditory meatus apex, lowest point of the articular nodule, condyle apex, mastoid apex, and joint fossa apex.

training of the global end-to-end L^2Net. The implicit heat-maps are the same size as the resampled input image with $\sigma = 5$.

On the basis of completing the global-stage model, its parameters are fixed and local-stage network training is performed. We take the ground truth plus a random offset as the center on the original image to intercept 5 image patches, and concatenate these image blocks into size of 5 * 55 * 55 * 55. Using these data to train the network causes the network to converge to the ground truth position. All the internal heat-maps are as large as the input image, and from the entire heat map to the corresponding 5 coordinates through the DNST layer regression. The two-stage network is trained by our regression loss respectively. Training was completed on single Maxwell-architecture NVIDIA Titan X GPUs.

3.2 Results

Gaussian distribution heat-map is a widely used method for landmark detection. Regardless of whether it is heat-map regression or the coordinate regression method proposed in this article, the distribution of heat-map directly determines the final landmark localization accuracy. We selected two landmarks on the same subject, and the distribution gave the heat point maps of the coordinate points inferred by the two methods, Fig. 5. After inferring from the network, our method can obtain heat-maps more similar to the Gaussian distribution.

The mean radial error (MRE, in mm) and the successful detection rate (SDR, in %) are the evaluation indexes of medical image landmark detection task. The MRE is defined by

$$\text{MRE} = \left(\sum\nolimits_{i=1}^{n} R_i\right)/n$$

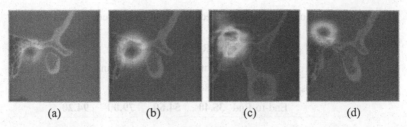

(a)   (b)   (c)   (d)

Fig. 5. Heat-map comparison of different methods, heat-map regression (a, c) and coordinate regression (b, d). Heat-map in a/b locates Landmark#0, and both fit the Gaussian distribution. But inference heat-map (c) is poor, conversely, our method can achieve good result (d).

where n indicates the number of data and R indcates the Euclidean distance between ground truths L_{GT} and prediction L_{inf}. The Std indicates the error's standard deviation in dataset.

As mentioned in the introduction, the detection of landmarks near the nearly circular bone structure has poor accuracy. It can be seen from Table 1 that detection accuracy of landmark#3 with less ambiguity is lower than others. The SDR shows the percentage of landmarks successfully detected in a range of 1.0 mm, 2.0 mm, 4.0 mm, and 8.0 mm (Table 2).

Table 1. Comparison on proposed end-to-end regression model (End-to-End) with heat-map regression approaches (HMR) on landmarks localization.

Test data	Methods	MRE ± Std (mm)				
		Lmk#0	Lmk#1	Lmk#2	Lmk#3	Lmk#4
Group#1	HMR	3.90 ± 2.77	3.47 ± 1.88	3.62 ± 1.76	8.16 ± 4.57	3.27 ± 2.29
	End-to-End	**0.79 ± 0.54**	**0.73 ± 0.46**	**1.25 ± 0.85**	**0.89 ± 1.17**	**0.73 ± 0.54**
Group#2	HMR	4.54 ± 3.08	3.42 ± 2.55	3.91 ± 2.81	7.22 ± 5.08	4.10 ± 3.00
	End-to-End	**2.86 ± 2.53**	**2.36 ± 2.01**	**2.06 ± 1.14**	**4.88 ± 4.24**	**2.08 ± 1.43**
Group#3	HMR	3.89 ± 2.64	2.97 ± 2.04	2.88 ± 1.36	**5.81 ± 4.07**	**2.88 ± 1.62**
	End-to-End	**3.70 ± 3.38**	**2.44 ± 2.38**	**2.70 ± 2.62**	6.19 ± 4.37	3.10 ± 2.80
Group#4	HMR	3.65 ± 1.79	3.58 ± 1.65	3.78 ± 1.75	6.95 ± 3.69	3.96 ± 1.94
	End-to-End	**2.90 ± 2.57**	**2.37 ± 1.95**	**2.50 ± 1.95**	**6.74 ± 4.91**	**2.37 ± 1.88**
4-fold cross	HMR	3.99 ± 2.59	3.36 ± 2.04	3.55 ± 2.00	7.04 ± 4.40	3.56 ± 2.29
	End-to-End	**2.56 ± 2.68**	**1.98 ± 1.96**	**2.13 ± 1.84**	**4.67 ± 4.52**	**2.07 ± 2.02**

Table 2. Comparison on successful detection rate (%) between different methods.

Test data	Methods	SDR (%)			
		1.0 mm	2.0 mm	4.0 mm	8.0 mm
4-fold cross	HMR	7.80	20.40	55.40	90.00
	End-to-End	**35.40**	**54.60**	**79.00**	**94.20**

4   Conclusion

We present a method for the localization of multiple landmarks in 3D medical images and for physiological or pathological changes assessment. In our framework, two-stage models share the same end-to-end L^2Net to regress coordinates directly. The attention-guide mechanism makes sure that searching fields is smaller and data resolution is higher with minimum information redundancy. Our model with higher efficiency but less manual tuning achieves a state-of-the-art result on automatic landmark detection in TMJs 3D-CBCT images.

Acknowledgments. This work was supported by the National Natural Science Foundation of China with Project No. 81671034 and the Foundation of China Scholarship Council for Study Abroad. Computations used the Department of Radiology and Biomedical Research Imaging Center (BRIC), University of North Carolina at Chapel Hill facility.

References

1. Payer, C., Štern, D., Bischof, H., et al.: Integrating spatial configuration into heatmap regression based CNNs for landmark localization. Med. Image Anal. **54**, 207–219 (2019)
2. Schilling, J., Gomes, L.C., Benavides, E., et al.: Regional 3D superimposition to assess temporomandibular joint condylar morphology. Dentomaxillofac. Radiol. **43**(1), 1–12 (2014)
3. Han, Y.S., Jung, Y.E., Song, I.S., et al.: Three-dimensional computed tomographic assessment of temporomandibular joint stability after orthognathic surgery. J. Oral Maxillofac. Surg. **74**(7), 1454–1462 (2016)
4. Al-Saleh, M.A., Jaremko, J.L., Alsufyani, N., et al.: Assessing the reliability of MRI-CBCT image registration to visualize temporomandibular joints. Dentomaxillofac. Radiol. **44**(6), 1–8 (2015)
5. Hanaoka, S., Akinobu, S., Nemoto, M., et al.: Automatic detection of over 100 anatomical landmarks in medical CT images: a framework with independent detectors and combinatorial optimization. Med. Image Anal. **35**, 192–214 (2017)
6. Donner, R., Menze, B.H., Bischof, H., et al.: Global localization of 3D anatomical structures by pre-filtered hough forests and discrete optimization. Med. Image Anal. **17**(8), 1304–1314 (2013)
7. Çiçek, Ö., Abdulkadir, A., Lienkamp, S.S., Brox, T., Ronneberger, O.: 3D U-Net: learning dense volumetric segmentation from sparse annotation. In: Ourselin, S., Joskowicz, L., Sabuncu, Mert R., Unal, G., Wells, W. (eds.) MICCAI 2016. LNCS, vol. 9901, pp. 424–432. Springer, Cham (2016). https://doi.org/10.1007/978-3-319-46723-8_49

8. Zhang, J., Liu, M., Shen, D.: Detecting anatomical landmarks from limited medical imaging data using two-stage task-oriented deep neural networks. IEEE Trans. Image Process. **26**(10), 4753–4764 (2017)

9. Zhang, J., Liu, M., Wang, L., et al.: Context-guided fully convolutional networks for joint craniomaxillofacial bone segmentation and landmark digitization. Med. Image Anal. **60**, 1–10 (2020)

10. Zhang, D., Wang, J., Noble, J.H., et al.: HeadLocNet: deep convolutional neural networks for accurate classification and multi-landmark localization of head CTs. Med. Image Anal. **61**, 1–10 (2020)

11. Zhong, Z., Li, J., Zhang, Z., Jiao, Z., Gao, X.: An attention-guided deep regression model for landmark detection in cephalograms. In: Shen, D., et al. (eds.) MICCAI 2019. LNCS, vol. 11769, pp. 540–548. Springer, Cham (2019). https://doi.org/10.1007/978-3-030-32226-7_60

12. Nibali, A, He, Z., Morgan, S., et al.: Numerical coordinate regression with convolutional neural networks. arXiv preprint arXiv: 1801.07372 (2018)

Enhanced MRI Reconstruction Network Using Neural Architecture Search

Qiaoying Huang[1](✉), Dong yang[2], Yikun Xian[1], Pengxiang Wu[1], Jingru Yi[1], Hui Qu[1], and Dimitris Metaxas[1]

[1] Department of Computer Science, Rutgers University, Piscataway, NJ, USA
[2] NVIDIA, Bethesda, MD, USA

Abstract. The accurate reconstruction of under-sampled magnetic resonance imaging (MRI) data using modern deep learning technology, requires significant effort to design the necessary complex neural network architectures. The cascaded network architecture for MRI reconstruction has been widely used, while it suffers from the "vanishing gradient" problem when the network becomes deep. In addition, the homogeneous architecture degrades the representation capacity of the network. In this work, we present an enhanced MRI reconstruction network using a residual in residual basic block. For each cell in the basic block, we use the differentiable neural architecture search (NAS) technique to automatically choose the optimal operation among eight variants of the dense block. This new heterogeneous network is evaluated on two publicly available datasets and outperforms all current state-of-the-art methods, which demonstrates the effectiveness of our proposed method.

1 Introduction

Magnetic resonance imaging (MRI) is widely used in many clinical applications. However, acquiring a fully-sampled MRI scan is time consuming, which is expensive and often uncomfortable to the patient. In clinical practice, MR data are often undersampled in the Fourier domain to speed up the acquisition process. Many researchers have focused on developing new methods to accelerate MRI reconstruction, including a series of compressed sensing methods [4,12,13,20,21] and deep learning-based methods [5–9,16,18,22].

Recently, deep learning-based methods have achieved promising high-quality image reconstruction results. These methods use a similar framework, as shown in Fig. 1, by stacking the same modules to form a very deep network to directly map the undersampled data to fully-sampled data. For example, Schlemper *et al.* [16] propose a deep neural network using cascaded convolutional layers with data consistency (DC) layers to compensate the reconstructed data with the original k-space data. A UNet combined with DC layers has been shown to achieve good results in MRI reconstruction [9]. Sun *et al.* [18] propose a recursive dilated network (RDN) and prove that dilated convolution in each recursive block can aggregate multi-scale information within the MRI. The most recent work [22]

© Springer Nature Switzerland AG 2020
M. Liu et al. (Eds.): MLMI 2020, LNCS 12436, pp. 634–643, 2020.
https://doi.org/10.1007/978-3-030-59861-7_64

uses repeated dilated dense blocks in the framework and improves the DC layer via a two-step compensation in both k-space and image domains. The common feature of these works is to employ a very deep architecture with homogeneous computing blocks. However, as the depth of the network increases, the model may suffer from the gradient vanishing problem. Besides, the homogeneous blocks may limit the feature representation capacity of the network.

To the end, we propose a deep neural model called **EMR-NAS** featured by residual-in-residual (RIR) structure and heterogeneous blocks. The RIR structure [19] is shown to be effective in alleviating gradient vanishing in tasks such as super resolution. For heterogeneity, we design various candidate operations inside blocks. To avoid huge manual effort of tuning the best composition of operations, we employ neural architecture search (NAS) technique to automatically decide which one is optimal to improve the ability of feature learning. NAS achieves promising performance in classification tasks but is seldom explored in the MRI reconstuction domain. It is ideal for those tasks that need arduous architecture design, such as in MRI reconstruction. NAS methods can be separated into two different types: optimizing by reinforcement learning algorithm or by being differentiable with the use of back-propagation. The differentiable ones are more effective and cost less computational resource. They alternatively train the shared weights of the network [2,15] and parameters of the architecture design. For example, DARTS [11] propose a continuous relaxation of the architecture parameters by a softmax function, allowing an efficient search of the architecture using gradient descent. However, it still depends on very large GPU memory and needs a long training time. Therefore, they can only search the architecture on a smaller dataset and then transfer it to the a large dataset. ProxylessNAS [3] aims to overcome this limitation, by proposing a binarization strategy that activates only specific paths during training to decrease training memory and time dramatically. Since this NAS technique can replace human efforts, we apply it in the MRI reconstruction problem to automatically choose the optimal block for boosting the performance.

Our major contributions are listed below: (1) To the best of our knowledge, this is the first work to study Neural Architecture Search techniques for MRI reconstruction. (2) We propose to use a residual in residual (RIR) basic block for the deep reconstruction network. (3) We design a new search space with eight novel cell-level operations adapted to MRI reconstruction and they are placed in the RIR basic block to boost the network capacity and performance. (4) The searched heterogeneous architecture achieves superior performance over current state-of-the-art reconstruction methods in two public datasets. We also experiment extensive ablation studies to validate the impact of each component of the searched model.

2   Method

In this section, we first introduce the common neural network architecture adopted by existing works on MRI reconstruction and the residual-in-residual

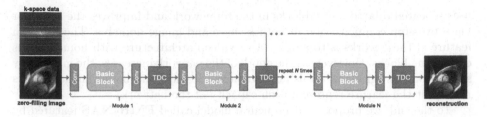

Fig. 1. The common network architecture of MRI reconstruction.

block adapted to the network. Then, we describe the possible operations inside the block and the detail of how to automatically find the optimal composition of these operations via the differentiable NAS.

2.1 Common Network Architecture for MRI Reconstruction

The goal of MRI reconstruction problem is to learn a function f that maps from undersampled data x to fully-sampled data y. Recent works attempt to approximate the function via a deep neural network, which has achieved promising reconstruction results [16,18,22]. Although various deep neural networks have been proposed to increasingly boost the reconstruction performance, we find that most of these networks share the same backbone of neural architectures. An example of a common architecture is illustrated in Fig. 1. The input x is a zero-filled image and output y is a reconstructed image, and we have $x, y \in \mathbb{R}^{2 \times w \times h}$, where channel 2 represents the real and imaginary parts, w and h are the width and height of the image, respectively. The common architecture consists of N stacked components that have the same *Conv–BasicBlock–Conv–TDC* structure but are optimized separately. In each component, the first convolutional layer *Conv* extracts feature maps of size $c \times w \times h$ from the original input. Then the *BasicBlock* is a customized operation to further capture deep features of the input and the common choices are sequential convolutional layers [16], recursive dilated block [18] and dense block [22]. The second *Conv* maps c channel features back to the original input size. The last *TDC* is a two-step data consistency layer [22]: (i) replace specific k-space value with the original sampled one; (ii) convert the result to real-valued format by calculating its absolute value and then apply step one again. The *TDC* layer aims to overcome the inconsistency problem in both k-space and image domains. Let $\mathbf{w}$ be the network parameters, which are usually optimized by a l_2 loss function $L(\mathbf{w}) = \|y - f(x; \mathbf{w})\|_2^2$.

Ideally, deeper neural networks (in terms of both N and depth of *BasicBlock*) are more likely to approximate complex functions and expected to achieve better reconstruction performance. However, in practice, stacking such components many times may suffer the vanishing gradient problem, which in turn degrades the performance. Most works in MRI reconstruction adopt skip connection and residual operation in the *BasicBlock* to alleviate the issue of vanishing gradient. In this work, we adapt the residual-in-residual (RIR) technique [19] to the

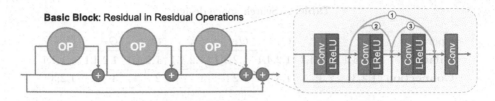

Fig. 2. Illustration of residual in residual operations.

BasicBlock, which has been recently shown to be effective in very deep neural networks used in super resolution applications. As shown in Fig. 2, the *RIR BasicBlock* is made of three operation units (OP) and they are sequentially composited via "residual in residual". In each OP, Batch Norm layers (BN) are not placed after Leaky ReLU since existing works have proven such a design can further boost performance and reduce computational complexity in different PSNR-oriented tasks [10,14]. Meanwhile, multi-level residual dense blocks are adopted, which employ a deeper and more complex structure to learn different level representations, resulting in a higher network capacity [19].

Beyond going deeper, the composition of the network can also become more "heterogeneous". Note that existing works usually adopt the homogeneous structure for all *BasicBlocks*, which may limit the ability of feature representation. In this work, we attempt to explore if heterogeneous structures of these *BasicBlocks* can further improve the reconstruction performance. Instead of manually experimenting different compositions of OPs, we use differentiable NAS techniques to automatically determine the optimal combinations of cells.

2.2   Neural Architecture Search for MRI Reconstruction

We introduce the **EMR-NAS** (Enhanced MRI Reconstruction Network via neural architecture search) for automatically determining operations in the blocks.

Search Space. In NAS, the first step is to design the search space. Our search space is based on the OP structure in Fig. 2 (right). We introduce eight different cells $\mathcal{O} = \{O_i, i = 1 \cdots 8\}$ that are listed in Table 1. Specifically, all convolutional layers in OP have the same kernel size of 3×3, but different dilation rate and the connection between them. The dilation rate of each convolutional layer are listed in the second row of Table 1. The dilation rates of $O_1 \ldots, O_7$ are 1–2–4–1, which induce larger receptive fields than that of 1–1–1–1, and are proven to benefit the reconstruction performance [18,22]. For connection, we only consider the connections numbered with "1", "2" and "3" in Fig. 2 (right). As the third row in Table 1 shows that, O_1 and O_8 are densely connected. O_2 to O_4 have two connections while O_5 to O_7 have only one connection. Our goal is to boost the representation capacity of the network by automatically choosing the best operation within each cell.

Table 1. Search space design.

Operation	O_1	O_2	O_3	O_4	O_5	O_6	O_7	O_8
Dilation	1,2,4,1	1,2,4,1	1,2,4,1	1,2,4,1	1,2,4,1	1,2,4,1	1,2,4,1	1,1,1,1
Connection	1,2,3	2,3	1,3	1,2	1	2	3	1,2,3

Search Strategy. Suppose there are T OP cells in the network, where every three cells form a *RIR BasicBlock*. This results in totally 8^T different architectures. Let O_i^l be the ith operation of the lth cell ($i \in [8], l \in [T]$). We relax the categorical choice of an operation to the softmax over all possible operations [11]:

$$x^{l+1} = \sum_{i=1}^{8} p_i^l O_i^l(x^l) = \sum_{i=1}^{8} \frac{\exp(\alpha_i^l)}{\sum_{j=1}^{8} \exp(\alpha_j^l)} O_i^l(x^l), \tag{1}$$

where x^l and x^{l+1} denote the input and output of the lth cell respectively. The probability p_i^l of choosing the corresponding operation is calculated by the softmax over the architecture parameters $\alpha^l \in \mathbb{R}^8$ for the lth cell.

Due to the huge search space, optimizing all the architecture parameters $\alpha = \{\alpha^1, \dots, \alpha^T\}$ requires lots of computation and large storage in the memory. To save memory and speed up the search process, we follow the path binarization strategy proposed in [3]. In particular, the probability p of a specific cell is transformed into binary gates:

$$g = \text{binarize}(p_1, \dots, p_8) = \begin{cases} [1, 0, \cdots, 0] & \text{if } p_1 = \text{argmax}_i p_i \\ \cdots \\ [0, 0, \cdots, 1] & \text{if } p_8 = \text{argmax}_i p_i \end{cases} \tag{2}$$

Based on the binary gates g, the output of mixed operations of the lth cell is given by $x^{l+1} = \sum_{i=1}^{8} g_i^l O_i^l(x^l)$. After binarization of probabilities, only one path is activated in memory at run-time and the memory decreases to the same level of training a single model. The relaxation of Eq. 1 makes the network's training and search possible to be differentiable. We partition the whole dataset into: $\{S_{train}, S_{val}, S_{test}\}$. Note that the network weights are optimized on S_{train} and the architecture parameters α are optimized on S_{val}. We search and optimize the network **w** in an alternative way, which is given in Algorithm 1. After obtaining the optimal α and discretizing it by $argmax$, we fix the architecture and retrain the network on the $S_{trainval} = \{S_{train}, S_{val}\}$ and then test it on S_{test}.

3   Experiments

We evaluate the performance of our proposed model on two public datasets.

(1) **Cardiac.** We use the same short axis cardiac datasets as in work [22], which is created by the work of Alexander *et al.* [1]. Each subject's sequence consists of 20 frames and 8–15 slices along the long axis. In all, it contains 4480 cardiac real-valued MR images from 33 subjects. The image size is 256×256.

Algorithm 1. EMR-NAS

1: **Input:** training set $\mathcal{S}_{train}$, validation set $\mathcal{S}_{val}$, mixed operations $\mathcal{O}$.
2: **Output:** network weights $\mathbf{w}$, architecture parameters α.
3: Warmup the training for M epochs.
4: **while** training not converged **do**
5:     // Train $\mathbf{w}$
6:     Reset binary gates by $p = softmax(\alpha)$, active chosen paths.
7:     Update network weights $\mathbf{w}$ by gradient descent $\nabla_{\mathbf{w}} L_{train}(\mathbf{w}, \alpha)$.
8:     // Train α
9:     Reset binary gates by $p = softmax(\alpha)$, active chosen paths.
10:     Update architecture parameters α by gradient descent $\nabla_{\alpha} L_{val}(\mathbf{w}, \alpha)$.
11: **return** $\mathbf{w}$ and α

---

(2) **Brain.** The Calgary-Campinas-359 dataset is provided by the work [17]. It includes 35 fully-sampled subjects of T1-weighted MR, which are acquired on a clinical MR scanner. The original raw data are acquired with a 12-channel imaging coil and are reconstructed using vendor supplied tools to make them into a single coil image. The matrix size is also 256×256. We use random Cartesian masks with 15% sampling rate for both datasets.

To fully validate the proposed method, we perform a 3-fold cross-validation in the following experiments. One fold $\mathcal{S}_{test}$ is for testing and the remaining two folds are separated into $\mathcal{S}_{train}$ and $\mathcal{S}_{val}$ with a ratio around 9:2. Three different architectures are achieved due to different $\{\mathcal{S}_{train}, \mathcal{S}_{val}\}$ of each fold. We adopt an ensemble method by summing up probabilities p of three folds and discretizing the aggregated probabilities to form the optimal architecture. We set $N = 5$ and $T = 3 \times N = 15$. The size of search space is 8^{15}. The warmup training epochs $M = 50$ and the search process takes another 50 epochs. For training the network parameter $\mathbf{w}$, we use the Adam optimizer with a base learning rate 10^{-3} with a cosine annealing schedule, a 0.9 momentum and weight decay of 10^{-7}. For training the architecture parameters α, we also adopt Adam optimizer with a learning rate of 10^{-3} and weight decay 10^{-6}. All models are trained with a batch size of 8. It takes around 0.5 Quadro RTX 8000 GPU day for one fold training.

3.1 Comparisons to State-of-the-Art

In this experiment, we show the reconstruction performance of our proposed model compared with some state-of-the-art methods, including UNet [9], DCCNN [16], RDN [18] and CDDNTDC [22]. For our model, the resulting operations in each OP cell after the architecture search is as follows. We obtain $[O_5\ O_8\ O_8|O_8\ O_8\ O_8|O_4\ O_1\ O_2|O_8\ O_8\ O_8|O_6\ O_8\ O_8]$ for Cardiac dataset, and $[O_6\ O_6\ O_2|O_4\ O_1\ O_2|O_3\ O_8\ O_1|O_3\ O_6\ O_3|O_3\ O_1\ O_3]$ for Brain dataset.

We also found that O_8 is the most frequent one in the Cardiac dataset, while O_3 is the most frequent one in the Brain dataset. Dense connections are not optimal in most cases nor the dilated convolution since useless information may be filtered by using fewer connections. For both datasets, good cell diversity

Table 2. Results of the proposed method on Cardiac and Brain datasets. The mean ± std values of 3-fold cross validation indices (PSNR and SSIM) are presented.

Model	Cardiac		Brain	
	PSNR	SSIM	PSNR	SSIM
UNet [9]	30.9877 ± 0.9676	0.8516 ± 0.0110	29.8066 ± 0.0767	0.8408 ± 0.0031
DCCNN [16]	34.1993 ± 0.8519	0.9235 ± 0.0025	30.9349 ± 0.2271	0.8687 ± 0.0082
RDN [18]	34.0686 ± 0.9440	0.9224 ± 0.0055	31.1769 ± 0.4659	0.8717 ± 0.0068
CDDNTDC [22]	34.4631 ± 0.9161	0.9291 ± 0.0029	29.9225 ± 0.1042	0.8389 ± 0.0027
Ours	**34.8653 ± 0.9126**	**0.9342 ± 0.0028**	**31.7616 ± 0.0774**	**0.8882 ± 0.0011**

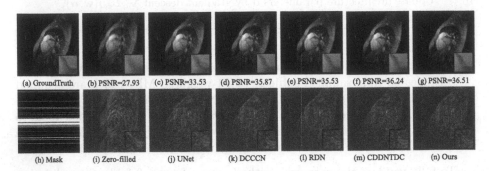

Fig. 3. Example of reconstructed images of all methods on the Cardiac dataset.(Color figure online)

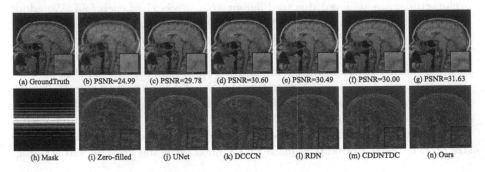

Fig. 4. Example of reconstructed images of all methods on the Brain dataset.(Color figure online)

may achieve better results as the searched architectures are heterogeneous across different RIR BasicBlocks. In fact, in Sect. 3.2, the model with repeated blocks underperforms our searched heterogeneous architecture.

The 3-fold cross-validation test performance of all methods are reported in Table 2. For both datasets, our proposed model achieves the best performance in terms of both PSNR and SSIM. Especially for the Brain dataset, our approach outperforms other methods by a large margin. Example reconstruction results and the corresponding errors are shown in Fig. 3 and Fig. 4. Improvements achieved by our method are highlighted by the red box .

3.2 Ablation Study

We study the contributions of different components of our model on the Cardiac dataset. Seven variants (column A to G) are designed and listed in Table 3 with six different factors related to our model. *Batch Norm* or *RIR* indicate if BN layer or residual-in-residual is adopted. *Search* represents whether the architecture is searched by the strategy in Sect. 2.2 or randomly assembled using operations $\mathcal{O}$. *Ensemble* means if we ensemble three different architectures from 3-folds or adopt the architecture searched from the corresponding fold. *Deeper* means 4 cells in each *BasicBlock* rather than the original 3 cells. *Homogeneous* means if the *BasicBlocks* consist of single operation or multiple opearations.

The PSNR and SSIM results of seven variants are plotted in Fig. 5. Basically, we see that the optimal combination is given by the default model A, whose structure is searched by NAS and equipped with RIR and ensemble. RIR improves deep network training and NAS helps improve the representation capacity of the network. In addition, we observe that the ensemble (E) and the deeper architectures (F) play a less important role in the reconstruction performance, since the corresponding scores are very close to the one by model (A).

3.3 Discussion on Model Size and Efficiency

For the number of parameters, we observed that U-Net is the largest model with 1.57M parameters, but it achieves the worst performance. Our model achieves the best performance using much fewer parameters (0.33M). This shows higher model complexity does not always lead to better performance. The key is how to design an effective architecture, and the NAS technique can automate this process. Other models like DCCNN, RDN and CDDNTDC originally use fewer parameters, however, for a fair comparison, we increased their parameters to around 0.33M (same as ours) by adding convolutional layers between each DC layer. Note that our method still dominates others over PSNR and SSIM on two datasets, for example, our model achieves 34.865 in PSNR while DCCNN, RDN and CDDNTDC gain 34.301, 33.257 and 33.981, respectively, which means the searched architecture is better. The RIR structure also helps to prevent the gradient vanishing problem when the network goes deep while other methods' performance is improved when we increase the capacity of the network. Besides, our model costs 310s per epoch in training and 0.055 s/frame in inference, which is faster than RDN (370s, 0.060s) and CDDNTDC models (441s, 0.065s), but slower than the U-Net (280s, 0.036s) and DCCNN models (288s, 0.026s).

Table 3. Contribution of each component in our model. Model A is the proposed combination and the contradicted component in other variants is marked in red.

Component	A	B	C	D	E	F	G
Batch Norm?	No	Yes	No	No	No	No	No
RIR?	Yes	Yes	No	Yes	Yes	Yes	Yes
Search?	Yes	Yes	Yes	No	Yes	Yes	Yes
Ensemble?	Yes	Yes	Yes	Yes	No	Yes	Yes
Deeper?	No	No	No	No	No	Yes	No
Homogeneous?	No	No	No	No	No	Yes	Yes

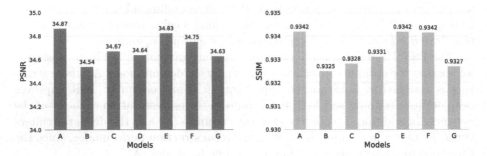

Fig. 5. The PSNR (left) and SSIM (right) results of ablation studies.

4   Conclusion

In this work, we present an enhanced MRI reconstruction network using NAS technique. In particular, we use the residual in residual structure as the basic block and design eight different choices in each block. An automatic differentiable search technique is used to decide the optimal composition of operations. We conduct extensive experiments to compare our methods to the state-of-the-art methods and also perform an ablation study to prove the importance of each component of the proposed method. The results show the superior performance of our proposed method and the effectiveness of our architectures design.

References

1. Andreopoulos, A., Tsotsos, J.K.: Efficient and generalizable statistical models of shape and appearance for analysis of cardiac MRI. Med. Image Anal. **12**(3), 335–357 (2008)
2. Bender, G.: Understanding and simplifying one-shot architecture search (2019)
3. Cai, H., Zhu, L., Han, S.: Proxylessnas: direct neural architecture search on target task and hardware. arXiv preprint (2018). arXiv:1812.00332
4. Huang, J., Zhang, S., Metaxas, D.: Efficient MR image reconstruction for compressed MR imaging. Med. Image Anal. **15**(5), 670–679 (2011)

5. Huang, Q., Chen, X., Metaxas, D., Nadar, M.S.: Brain segmentation from k-space with end-to-end recurrent attention network. In: Shen, D., et al. (eds.) MICCAI 2019. LNCS, vol. 11766, pp. 275–283. Springer, Cham (2019). https://doi.org/10.1007/978-3-030-32248-9_31

6. Huang, Q., Yang, D., Qu, H., Yi, J., Wu, P., Metaxas, D.: Dynamic MRI reconstruction with motion-guided network. In: International Conference on Medical Imaging with Deep Learning, vol. 102, pp. 275–284 (2019)

7. Huang, Q., Yang, D., Wu, P., Qu, H., Yi, J., Metaxas, D.: MRI reconstruction via cascaded channel-wise attention network. In: 2019 IEEE 16th International Symposium on Biomedical Imaging (ISBI 2019), pp. 1622–1626 (2019)

8. Huang, Q., Yang, D., Yi, J., Axel, L., Metaxas, D.: FR-Net: joint reconstruction and segmentation in compressed sensing cardiac MRI. In: Coudière, Y., Ozenne, V., Vigmond, E., Zemzemi, Nejib (eds.) FIMH 2019. LNCS, vol. 11504, pp. 352–360. Springer, Cham (2019). https://doi.org/10.1007/978-3-030-21949-9_38

9. Hyun, C.M., Kim, H.P., Lee, S.M., Lee, S., Seo, J.K.: Deep learning for undersampled MRI reconstruction. Phys. Med. Biol. **63**(13), 135007 (2018)

10. Lim, B., Son, S., Kim, H., Nah, S., Mu Lee, K.: Enhanced deep residual networks for single image super-resolution. In: Proceedings of the IEEE conference on computer vision and pattern recognition workshops, pp. 136–144 (2017)

11. Liu, H., Simonyan, K., Yang, Y.: Darts: differentiable architecture search. arXiv preprint (2018). arXiv:1806.09055

12. Lustig, M., Donoho, D., Pauly, J.M.: Sparse MRI: the application of compressed sensing for rapid MR imaging. Magn. Reson. Med. **58**(6), 1182–1195 (2007)

13. Lustig, M., Donoho, D.L., Santos, J.M., Pauly, J.M.: Compressed sensing MRI. IEEE Signal Process. Mag. **25**(2), 72–82 (2008)

14. Nah, S., Hyun Kim, T., Mu Lee, K.: Deep multi-scale convolutional neural network for dynamic scene deblurring. In: Proceedings of the IEEE Conference on Computer Vision and Pattern Recognition, pp. 3883–3891 (2017)

15. Pham, H., Guan, M.Y., Zoph, B., Le, Q.V., Dean, J.: Efficient neural architecture search via parameter sharing. arXiv preprint (2018). arXiv:1802.03268

16. Schlemper, J., Caballero, J., Hajnal, J.V., Price, A., Rueckert, D.: A deep cascade of convolutional neural networks for MR image reconstruction. In: International Conference on Information Processing in Medical Imaging, pp. 647–658. Springer (2017)

17. Souza, R., et al.: An open, multi-vendor, multi-field-strength brain MR dataset and analysis of publicly available skull stripping methods agreement. NeuroImage **170**, 482–494 (2018)

18. Sun, L., Fan, Z., Huang, Y., Ding, X., Paisley, J.: Compressed sensing MRI using a recursive dilated network. In: Thirty-Second AAAI Conference on Artificial Intelligence (2018)

19. Wang, X., et al.: Esrgan: enhanced super-resolution generative adversarial networks. In: Proceedings of the European Conference on Computer Vision (ECCV), pp. 0–0 (2018)

20. Yang, A.C.Y., Kretzler, M., Sudarski, S., Gulani, V., Seiberlich, N.: Sparse reconstruction techniques in MRI: methods, applications, and challenges to clinical adoption. Invest. Radiol. **51**(6), 349 (2016)

21. Yang, J., Zhang, Y., Yin, W.: A fast alternating direction method for tvl1-l2 signal reconstruction from partial fourier data. IEEE J. Selected Topics Signal Process. **4**(2), 288–297 (2010)

22. Zheng, H., Fang, F., Zhang, G.: Cascaded dilated dense network with two-step data consistency for MRI reconstruction. In: Advances in Neural Information Processing Systems, pp. 1742–1752 (2019)

Learning Invariant Feature Representation to Improve Generalization Across Chest X-Ray Datasets

Sandesh Ghimire[1,2], Satyananda Kashyap[1], Joy T. Wu[1],
Alexandros Karargyris[1], and Mehdi Moradi[1(✉)]

[1] IBM Almaden Research Center, San Jose, CA, USA
mmoradi@us.ibm.com
[2] Rochester Institute of Technology, Rochester, NY, USA

Abstract. Chest radiography is the most common medical image examination for screening and diagnosis in hospitals. Automatic interpretation of chest X-rays at the level of an entry-level radiologist can greatly benefit work prioritization and assist in analyzing a larger population. Subsequently, several datasets and deep learning-based solutions have been proposed to identify diseases based on chest X-ray images. However, these methods are shown to be vulnerable to shift in the source of data: a deep learning model performing well when tested on the same dataset as training data, starts to perform poorly when it is tested on a dataset from a different source. In this work, we address this challenge of generalization to a new source by forcing the network to learn a source-invariant representation. By employing an adversarial training strategy, we show that a network can be forced to learn a source-invariant representation. Through pneumonia-classification experiments on multi-source chest X-ray datasets, we show that this algorithm helps in improving classification accuracy on a new source of X-ray dataset.

Keywords: Generalization · Adversarial training · Learning theory · Domain adaptation

1 Introduction

Automatic interpretation and disease detection in chest X-ray images is a potential use case for artificial intelligence in reducing the costs and improving access to healthcare. It is one of the most commonly requested imaging procedures not only in the context of clinical examination but also for routine screening and even legal procedures such as health surveys for immigration purposes. Therefore, analysis of X-ray images through several computer vision algorithms has been an important topic of research in the past. Recently, with the release of several large open source public datasets, deep learning-based image classification [10,22] has found important applications in this area. Our team aslo has

© Springer Nature Switzerland AG 2020
M. Liu et al. (Eds.): MLMI 2020, LNCS 12436, pp. 644–653, 2020.
https://doi.org/10.1007/978-3-030-59861-7_65

worked in this area extensively [21,25]. The recent outbreak of COVID-19 pandemic and the need for widespread screening has further amplified the need for identification of pneumonia and consolidation findings on X-ray radiographs.

Most of the reported deep learning approaches are trained and tested on the same dataset and/or a single source. This is an unrealistic assumption in the case of medical image analysis with widespread screening applications. In radiology, we can always expect different images coming from different scanners, population, or image settings and therefore we can expect test images are different from the ones used in training. In non-quantitative imaging modalities, such as X-ray, this inconsistency of images across datasets is even more drastic. This is a significant hurdle for the adaptation of automated disease classification algorithms in the practice of radiology. Generalization across X-ray sources is therefore necessary to make deep learning algorithms viable in clinical practice. Recently this has been recognized with the radiology editorial board encouraging testing in *external* test set [2]. Some works have tried to answer the question of generalization by intensity normalization and adding Gaussian noise layers to neural networks [14] while others use simple ensemble strategy as in [20].

Drawing ideas from causality and invariant risk minimization [1], we propose that the key to resolve this issue is to learn features that are invariant in several X-ray datasets, and would be valid features even for the new test cases. *The main contribution of our work is that we enforce feature invariance to source of data by using an adversarial penalization strategy.* We show thus with different X-ray datasets that exhibit similar diseases, but come from different sources/institutions. We have access to four public chest X-ray datasets and validate our method by leave-one-dataset-out experiments of training and testing [12,22,27]. Given the recent interest in pneumonia like conditions, we chose to target pneumonia and consolidation. *We show that the out of source testing error can be reduced with our proposed adversarial penalization method.* We also perform experiments using Grad-CAM [23] to create activation maps and qualitatively evaluate and compare the behavior of the baseline and the proposed method in terms of focus on relevant area of the image.

2   Related Work

Earlier works on generalization concentrated on statistical learning theory [3,26], studying the worst-case generalization bound based on the capacity of the classifier. Later on, differing viewpoints emerged like PAC Bayes [19], information-theoretic [28] and stability based methods [4]. Modern works on generalization, however, find statistical learning theory insufficient [29] and propose other theories from an analytical perspectives [13]. Our work is quite different from these works. Most of these works are about in-source generalization and assume that data is independent and identically distributed (i.i.d) both in training and testing. We, however, start with the assumption that the training and testing could be from different distributions but share some common, causal features. Based on the principles of Invariant Risk Minimization [1], we propose the idea that learning invariant features from multiple sources could lead to learning causal features that would help in generalization to new sources.

Another closely related area to our work is that of domain adaptation [7,24], and its application in medical imaging [5]. In a domain adaptation setting, the data is available from source and target domains; but, the labels are available only from the source domain. The objective is to learn to adapt knowledge from the source to predict the label of the target. Although similar in spirit, our work is quite different from domain adaptation in that we do not have target data to adapt to during training. Other ideas of distribution matching like Maximum Mean Discrepancy (MMD) [15,16] are related to our work. In comparison, the adversarial approach is very powerful and easily extendable to more than two sources, which is cumbersome to realize using MMD.

3   Method

Causation as Invariance: Following reasoning similar to [1], we argue that extracting invariant features from many different sources would help the network focus on the causal features. This would help the network generalize to new sources in the future assuming that it would extract causal features from the new X-ray images obtained in the future.

To force a network to learn invariant features, we propose an architecture as shown in Fig. 1 based on adversarial penalization strategy. It has three major components: Feature extractor, Discriminator and Classifier. Drawing ideas from unsupervised domain adaptation [7], we train the discriminator to classify which source the image was obtained from just using the latent features extracted by the feature extractor. The discriminator is trained to well identify the source from the features. The feature extractor, however, is trained adversarially to make it very difficult for the discriminator to classify among sources. This way, we force the feature extractor network to extract features from the X-ray images that are invariant across different sources for if there were any element in the latent feature that is indicative of the source, it would be easier for the discriminator to identify the sources. In the end, we expect the feature extractor and discriminator to reach an equilibrium where the feature extractor generates features that are invariant to the sources. Meanwhile, the same features are fed to the disease classifier which is trained to properly identify disease. Hence, the features must be source invariant and at the same time discriminative enough of the disease. Next, we describe three main components of our network.

1. Feature extractor: The feature extractor is the first component that takes in the input X-ray image and gives a latent representation. In Fig. 1, the feature extractor consists of a Resnet 34 [9] architecture up to layer 4 followed by a global average pooling layer.

2. Discriminator: The discriminator consists of fully connected layers that take in features after the global average pooling layer and tries to classify which of

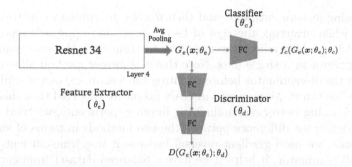

Fig. 1. Proposed architecture to learn source invariant representation while simultaneously classifying disease labels

the sources the image is obtained from. If adversarial training reaches equilibrium, it would mean that feature representation from different sources are indistinguishable (source invariant).

3. Classifier: The output of the feature extractor network should not only be source invariant but also be discriminative to simultaneously classify X-ray images according to the presence or absence of disease. In our simple model, we simply use a fully connected layer followed by sigmoid as the classifier.

3.1 Training

From Fig. 1, the disease classification loss and source classification (discrimination) loss are respectively defined as:

$$\mathcal{L}_p(\theta_e, \theta_c) = \underset{p(x,y)}{E}[\ell_{BCE}(f_c(G_e(x; \theta_e); \theta_c), y)] \tag{1}$$

$$\mathcal{L}_s(\theta_e, \theta_d) = \underset{p(x,y_s)}{E}[\ell_{CE}(D(G_e(x; \theta_e); \theta_d), y_s)] \tag{2}$$

where $\ell_{BCE}(\hat{y}, y) = y \log \hat{y} + (1 - y) \log(1 - \hat{y})$ is the binary cross entropy loss and similarly $\ell_{CE}(\hat{y}, y) = \sum_i (y_s)_i \log(\hat{y}_s)_i + (1 - (y_s)_i) \log(1 - (\hat{y}_s)_i)$ is the cross entropy loss. We train extractor, classifier and discriminator by solving following min-max problem.

$$\hat{\theta}_e, \hat{\theta}_c = \underset{\theta_e, \theta_c}{argmin} \ \mathcal{L}_p(\theta_e, \theta_c) - \lambda \mathcal{L}_s(\theta_e, \hat{\theta}_d), \qquad \hat{\theta}_d = \underset{\theta_d}{argmin} \ \mathcal{L}_s(\hat{\theta}_e, \theta_d) \tag{3}$$

It is easy to note that this is a two player min-max game where two players are trying to optimize an objective in opposite directions: note the negative sign and positive sign in front of loss $\mathcal{L}_s$ in eq.(3). Such min-max games in GAN literature are notorious for being difficult to optimize. However, in our case optimization was smooth as there was no issue with stability.

To perform adversarial optimization, two methods are prevalent in the literature. The first method, originally proposed in [8], trains the discriminator while freezing feature extractor and then freezes discriminator to train feature extractor while inverting the sign of loss. The second approach was proposed in [7], which uses a gradient reversal layer to train both the discriminator and feature extractor in a single pass. Note that the former method allows multiple updates of the discriminator before updating the feature extractor while the latter method does not. Many works in GAN literature reported that this strategy helped in learning better discriminators. In our experiments, we tried both and found no significant difference between the two methods in terms of stability or result. Hence, we used gradient reversal because it was time-efficient. To optimize the discriminator, it helps if we have a balanced dataset from each source. To account for the imbalanced dataset from each source, we resample data from the source with the small size until the source of the largest size is exhausted. By such resampling, we ensure that there is a balanced stream of data from each source to train the discriminator.

3.2 Grad-CAM Visualization

Grad-CAM [23] identifies important locations in an image for the downstream tasks like classification. It visualizes the last feature extraction layer of a neural network scaled by the backpropagated gradient and interpolated to the actual image size. In this paper, we use Grad-CAM to visualize which location in the X-ray is being attended by the neural network when we train with and without adversarial penalization. We hypothesize that a method that extracts source invariant features should be extracting more relevant features for the disease to be identified, whereas a network which was trained without specific guidance to extract source invariant features would be less focused in the specific diseases and may be attending to irrelevant features in the input X-ray image. Using Grad-CAM, we qualitatively verify this hypothesis.

4 Datasets and Labeling Scheme

We used three publicly available datasets for our study, NIH ChestXray14 [27], MIMIC-CXR dataset [12], and Stanford CheXpert dataset [10]. Further, a smaller internally curated dataset of images originating from Deccan Hospital in India was used.

We are interested in the classification task detecting signs of pneumonia and consolidation in chest X-ray images. Consolidation is a sign of the disease (occurring when alveoli are filled with something other than air, such as blood) whereas Pneumonia is a disease often causing consolidation. Radiologists use consolidation, potentially with other signs and symptoms, to diagnose pneumonia. In a radiology report, both of these may be mentioned. Therefore, we have used both to build a dataset of pneumonia/consolidation.

We have used all four datasets listed above. The Stanford CheXpert dataset [10] is released with images and labels, but without accompanying reports. The NIH dataset is also publicly available with only images and no reports. A subset

Table 1. The distribution of the datasets used in the paper. The breakdown of the Positive (pneumonia/consolidation) and Negative (not pneumonia/consolidation) cases.

Leave out Dataset	Train		Test	
	Positive	Negative	Positive	Negative
Stanford	15183	123493	1686	13720
MIMIC	83288	49335	23478	13704
NIH	1588	6374	363	1868
Deccan Hospital	50	1306	12	379
Total	**100109**	**180508**	**25539**	**29671**

of 16,000 images from this dataset were de novo reported by crowd-sourced radiologists. For the MIMIC dataset, we have full-fledged de-identified reports provided under a consortium agreement to us for the MIMIC-4 collection recently released [11]. For Deccan collection, we have the de-identified reports along with images. For the NIH, MIMIC and Deccan datasets, we used our natural language processing (NLP) labeling pipeline, described below, to find positive and negative examples in the reports; whereas, for the Stanford dataset, we used the labels provided. The pipeline utilizes a CXR ontology curated by our clinicians from a large corpus of CXR reports using a concept expansion tool [6] applied to a large collection of radiology reports. Abnormal terminologies from reports are lexically and semantically grouped into radiology finding concepts. Each concept is then ontologically categorized under major anatomical structures in the chest (lungs, pleura, mediastinum, bones, major airways, and other soft tissues), or medical devices (including various prosthesis, post-surgical material, support tubes, and lines). Given a CXR report, the text pipeline 1) tokenizes the sentences with NLTK [17], 2) excludes any sentence from the history and indication sections of the report via key section phrases so only the main body of the text is considered, 3) extracts finding mentions from the remaining sentences, and 4) finally performs negation and hypothetical context detection on the last relevant sentence for each finding label. Finally, clinician driven filtering rules are applied to some finding labels to increase specificity (e.g. "collapse" means "fracture" if mentioned with bones, but should mean "lobar/segmental collapse" if mentioned with lungs).

Using NLP generated and available labels (for CheXpert), we created a training dataset by including images with a positive indication of pneumonia or consolidation in our positive set and those with no indication of pneumonia or consolidation in the negative set. Table 1 lists the number of images from each class for each dataset.

5   Experiments and Results

We use four datasets as shown in Table 1. We use a simple Resnet-34 architecture with classifier as our baseline so that enforcement of invariance through

Table 2. The classification results in terms of area under ROC curve from baseline ResNet34 model, and our proposed architecture. Each row lists a leave-one-dataset-out experiment.

Leave out Dataset	Baseline		Proposed Architecture	
	In-source	Out-of-source	In-source	Out-of-source
Stanford	0.74	0.65	0.74	0.70
MIMIC	0.80	0.64	0.80	0.64
NIH	0.82	0.73	0.71	0.76
Deccan Hospital	0.73	0.67	0.75	0.70

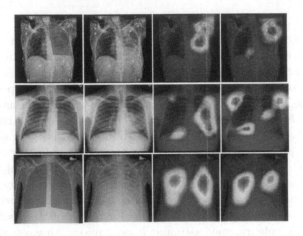

Fig. 2. The qualitative comparison of the activation maps of the proposed and the baseline models with the annotation of an expert radiologist. The first column shows the region marked by the expert as the area of the lung affected by pneumonia. The second column shows the original image for reference. The third and fourth columns are the Grad-CAM activation of the proposed and baseline models respectively.

discriminator is the only difference between baseline and proposed method. Experiments using both the architectures use a leave-one-dataset-out strategy: we trained on three of the four datasets and left one out. Each experiment has two test sets: 1)in-source test that draws from only the unseen samples from datasets used for training, 2) out-of-source test set, only including test samples from the fourth dataset that is not used in training. Note that all images from all sources are resized to 512 × 512.

The results of the classification experiments are listed in Table 2. We have chosen the area under the ROC curve (AUC-ROC) as the classification metric since this is the standard metric in computer-aided diagnosis. The first observation is that in all experiments, both for baseline and our proposed architecture, the AUC-ROC curve decreases as we move from the in-source test set to the out-of-source test set as expected. However, this drop in accuracy is generally smaller in our proposed architecture. For example, when the Stanford dataset is left out of training, in the baseline method the difference between in-source and out-of-source tests is 0.09 (from 0.74 to 0.65), whereas, in our proposed architecture, the drop in AUC-ROC is only 0.05 (from 0.74 to 0.70). While the performance on the in-source test stays flat, we gain a 5% improvement in area under the ROC curve, from 0.65 to 0.70 for the out-of-source test.

A similar pattern holds in both the case of NIH and Deccan datasets: in both cases, the drop in performance due to out-of-source testing is smaller for the proposed architecture compared with the baseline classifier. For the NIH dataset, the out-of-source testing results in higher accuracy, which we interpret as heavy regularization during training. In the case of the MIMIC dataset, the performance remains the same for the baseline and the proposed method.

Figure 2 shows Grad-CAM visualization to qualitatively differentiate between the regions or features focused by a baseline model and the proposed model while classifying X-ray images. Three positive examples and their activation maps are shown. The interpretation of activation maps in chest X-ray images is generally challenging. However, the evident pattern is that the heatmaps from the proposed method (third column) tend to agree more than the baseline (fourth column) with the clinician's marking in the first column. The proposed method shows fewer spurious activations. This is especially true in Row 2 wherein the opacity from the shoulder blades is falsely highlighted as lung pneumonia.

To compare our algorithm with domain generalization approach, we tested on the method in [18] using pseudo clusters. This methods has the state of the art performance on natural images. On testing with the Stanford leave-out set, the ROC for in-source and out-of-source tests were 0.74 and 0.68 respectively which is slightly below the performance reported here in row 1 of Table 2.

6   Conclusion and Future Work

We tackled the problem of out of source generalization in the context of a chest X-ray image classification by proposing an adversarial penalization strategy to obtain a source-invariant representation. In experiments, we show that the proposed algorithm provides improved generalization compared to the baseline.

It is important to note that the performance on the in-source test set does not necessarily increase in our method. Mostly it stays flat except in one case, namely the NIH set, where the baseline beats the proposed method in the in-source test. This can be understood as a trade-off between in-source and out-of-source performance induced by the strategy to learn invariant representation. By learning invariant features our objective is to improve on the out-of-source test cases even if in-source performance degrades. A possible route for further examination is the impact of the size of the training datasets and left-out set on the behavior of the model. It is noteworthy that we have kept the feature extractor and classifier components of our current architecture fairly simple to avoid excessive computational cost owing to adversarial training and large data and image size. A more sophisticated architecture might enhance the disease classification performance and is left as future work.

References

1. Arjovsky, M., Bottou, L., Gulrajani, I., Lopez-Paz, D.: Invariant risk minimization. arXiv preprint (2019). arXiv:1907.02893
2. Bluemke, D.A., et al.: Assessing radiology research on artificial intelligence: a brief guide for authors, reviewers, and readers-from the radiology editorial board (2020)
3. Bousquet, O., Boucheron, S., Lugosi, G.: Introduction to statistical learning theory. In: Bousquet, O., von Luxburg, U., Rätsch, G. (eds.) ML -2003. LNCS (LNAI), vol. 3176, pp. 169–207. Springer, Heidelberg (2004). https://doi.org/10.1007/978-3-540-28650-9_8
4. Bousquet, O., Elisseeff, A.: Stability and generalization. J. Mach. Learn. Res. **2**(Mar), 499–526 (2002)
5. Chen, C., Dou, Q., Chen, H., Heng, P.-A.: Semantic-aware generative adversarial nets for unsupervised domain adaptation in chest X-ray segmentation. In: Shi, Y., Suk, H-Il, Liu, Mingxia (eds.) MLMI 2018. LNCS, vol. 11046, pp. 143–151. Springer, Cham (2018). https://doi.org/10.1007/978-3-030-00919-9_17
6. Coden, A., Gruhl, D., Lewis, N., Tanenblatt, M., Terdiman, J.: Spot the drug! An unsupervised pattern matching method to extract drug names from very large clinical corpora. In: 2012 IEEE Second International Conference on Healthcare Informatics, Imaging and Systems Biology, pp. 33–39. IEEE (2012)
7. Ganin, Y., Lempitsky, V.: Unsupervised domain adaptation by backpropagation. In: Proceedings of the 32nd International Conference on International Conference on Machine Learning-Volume 37, pp. 1180–1189. JMLR. org (2015)
8. Goodfellow, I., et al.: Generative adversarial nets. In: Advances in Neural Information Processing Systems, pp. 2672–2680 (2014)
9. He, K., Zhang, X., Ren, S., Sun, J.: Deep residual learning for image recognition. In: 2016 IEEE Conference on Computer Vision and Pattern Recognition (cvpr), vol. 5, p. 6 (2015)
10. Irvin, J., et al.: Chexpert: a large chest radiograph dataset with uncertainty labels and expert comparison. CoRR abs/1901.07031 (2019). http://arxiv.org/abs/1901.07031
11. Johnson, A.E.W., et al.: MIMIC-CXR: a large publicly available database of labeled chest radiographs (2019). arXiv:1901.07042 [cs.CV]
12. Johnson, A.E., Pollard, T.J., Shen, L., Li-wei, H.L., Feng, M., Ghassemi, M., Moody, B., Szolovits, P., Celi, L.A., Mark, R.G.: MIMIC-III, a freely accessible critical care database. Sci. Data **3**, 160035 (2016)
13. Kawaguchi, K., Bengio, Y., Verma, V., Kaelbling, L.P.: Towards understanding generalization via analytical learning theory. arXiv preprint (2018). arXiv:1802.07426
14. Klambauer, G., Unterthiner, T., Mayr, A., Hochreiter, S.: Self-normalizing neural networks. CoRR abs/1706.02515 (2017). http://arxiv.org/abs/1706.02515
15. Li, C.L., Chang, W.C., Cheng, Y., Yang, Y., Póczos, B.: Mmd gan: towards deeper understanding of moment matching network. In: Advances in Neural Information Processing Systems, pp. 2203–2213 (2017)
16. Li, Y., Swersky, K., Zemel, R.: Generative moment matching networks. In: International Conference on Machine Learning, pp. 1718–1727 (2015)
17. Loper, E., Bird, S.: NLTK: the natural language toolkit (2002). arXiv:cs/0205028 [cs.CL]
18. Matsuura, T., Harada, T.: Domain generalization using a mixture of multiple latent domains. arXiv preprint (2019). arXiv:1911.07661

19. McAllester, D.A.: Some pac-bayesian theorems. Mach. Learn. **37**(3), 355–363 (1999)
20. McKinney, S.M., et al.: International evaluation of an AI system for breast cancer screening. Nature **577**(7788), 89–94 (2020)
21. Moradi, M., Madani, A., Gur, Y., Guo, Y., Syeda-Mahmood, T.: Bimodal network architectures for automatic generation of image annotation from text. In: Frangi, A.F., Schnabel, J.A., Davatzikos, C., Alberola-López, C., Fichtinger, Gabor (eds.) MICCAI 2018. LNCS, vol. 11070, pp. 449–456. Springer, Cham (2018). https://doi.org/10.1007/978-3-030-00928-1_51
22. Rajpurkar, P., et al.: Chexnet: radiologist-level pneumonia detection on chest x-rays with deep learning. arXiv preprint (2017). arXiv:1711.05225
23. Selvaraju, R.R., Cogswell, M., Das, A., Vedantam, R., Parikh, D., Batra, D.: Grad-cam: visual explanations from deep networks via gradient-based localization. In: Proceedings of the IEEE International Conference on Computer Vision, pp. 618–626 (2017)
24. Sener, O., Song, H.O., Saxena, A., Savarese, S.: Learning transferrable representations for unsupervised domain adaptation. In: Advances in Neural Information Processing Systems, pp. 2110–2118 (2016)
25. Syeda-Mahmood, T., et al.: Chest x-ray report generation through fine-grained label learning. MICCAI 2020, arXiv preprint (2020). arXiv:2007.13831
26. Vapnik, V.: The Nature of Statistical Learning Theory. Springer science & business media, Berlin (2013)
27. Wang, X., Peng, Y., Lu, L., Lu, Z., Bagheri, M., Summers, R.M.: ChestX-ray8: hospital-scale chest X-ray database and benchmarks on weakly-supervised classification and localization of common thorax diseases. In: IEEE Conference on Computer Vision and Pattern Recognition, pp. 2097–2106 (2017)
28. Xu, A., Raginsky, M.: Information-theoretic analysis of generalization capability of learning algorithms. In: Advances in Neural Information Processing Systems, pp. 2524–2533 (2017)
29. Zhang, C., Bengio, S., Hardt, M., Recht, B., Vinyals, O.: Understanding deep learning requires rethinking generalization. In: International Conference in Learning and Representation (2017)

Noise-Aware Standard-Dose PET Reconstruction Using General and Adaptive Robust Loss

Lei Xiang[1]([⊠]), Long Wang[1], Enhao Gong[1], Greg Zaharchuk[1,2], and Tao Zhang[1]

[1] Subtle Medical Inc., Menlo Park, USA
{lei,long,enhao,greg,tao}@subtlemedical.com
[2] Department of Radiology, Stanford University, Stanford, USA

Abstract. Positron Emission Tomography (PET) has been widely applied in clinics for diagnosis of cancer, cardiovascular disease, neurological disorder, and other challenging diseases. Radiotracers are injected into patients prior to PET exams, introducing inevitable radiation risks. While recent deep learning methods have shown to enable low-dose PET without compromising image quality, their performance are often limited when the amplified noise in low-dose scans becomes indistinguishable from high-intensity small abnormality. In this paper, we propose a noise-aware dual Res-UNet framework to enable low dose PET scans and achieve the image quality comparable to that from standard-dose PET scans. Specifically, noise-aware dual Res-UNets are designed to identify the location of high intensity noise in the low dose PET images first, followed by an image reconstruction network incorporating the estimated noise attention map to reconstruct the high quality standard-dose PET image. In order to better reduce the Poisson distribution noise, a general and adaptive robust loss is applied. Experimental results show that our method can outperform other state-of-the-art methods quantitatively and qualitatively and can be applied on real clinical application.

1 Introduction

In recent years, the use of positron emission tomography (PET) for molecular and diagnostic imaging has been rising steadily. PET is widely applied in clinics for diagnosis of cancer, cardiovascular disease, neurological disorder, and other challenging diseases, as well as for assessment of the effectiveness of treatment plans. In order to acquire high quality PET image to satisfy the diagnostic needs, a certain amount of radiotracer needs to be injected into the patients. The radiation exposure inevitably introduces associated imaging risks. These risks also accumulate if multiple PET scans are required throughout the treatment and follow-ups.

To tackle this issue, researchers have proposed low dose PET scans and applied image enhancement methods to recover the image quality loss due to the reduced dose counts. An et al. [1] presented a data-driven multi-level canonical correlation analysis (MCCA) scheme to generate the high quality PET

© Springer Nature Switzerland AG 2020
M. Liu et al. (Eds.): MLMI 2020, LNCS 12436, pp. 654–662, 2020.
https://doi.org/10.1007/978-3-030-59861-7_66

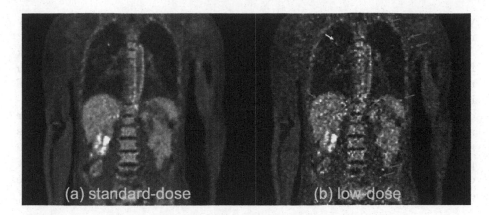

Fig. 1. Example of standard-dose PET and 14 low-dose PET. Best viewed zoomed-in on digital copy

image from low dose PET data using patch-based sparse representation. Xiang et al. [13] proposed an auto-context convolutional neural network (CNN) method for standard-dose PET image estimation from low-dose PET and the simultaneously acquired MR image. Xu et al. [14] adopted a fully convolutional encoder-decoder residual deep neural network model to reconstruct standard-dose PET images from ultra low-dose images (99.5% dose reduction). In order to obtain better image synthesis, Wang et al. [12] developed a 3D auto-context-based locality adaptive multi-modality generative adversarial networks model (LA-GANs) to synthesize high quality PET image from the low dose image and guided anatomical information from the accompanying MRI images.

These aforementioned methods are effective when the image noise from low dose scans follows a Gaussian distribution. However, depending on the PET image reconstruction used, the Gaussian noise assumption may not always hold. There are two common PET reconstruction algorithms integrated in state of the art PET scanners: the ordered subset expectation maximization (OSEM) algorithm [3] and the block sequential regularized expectation maximization (BSREM) algorithm [10]. OSEM and its variations generate PET image with Gaussian noise. BSREM and its variations incorporate a Bayesian likelihood that improves image quality and quantification by controlling or penalizing noise during iterative image reconstruction. When low-dose PET image is reconstructed by BSREM, image noise approximately follows a Poisson distribution, and high intensity noise can be observed in the reconstructed images. The aforementioned image enhancement methods are unable to distinguish high intensity small abnormality (e.g., small lesions) and high intensity noise, and therefore cannot achieve similar performance as removing Gaussian noise. An example of standard-dose PET and low-dose PET reconstructed by BSREM is shown in Fig. 1. A lot of high intensity noise in the low-dose PET image can be observed, which dramatically decrease the diagnostic image quality as the high intensity noise could be misdiagnosed as small lesions or vice versa.

In this work, we develop a Noise-Aware Dual Res-UNet (NADRU) framework for low-dose PET reconstruction. This framework first identifies an attention map corresponding to the location of high intensity noise in the low-dose PET images. Then, the noise attention map is incorporated with the original low-dose PET image and passed onto the second reconstruction network. To further address the Poisson noise distribution, a general and adaptive robust loss is applied to achieve superior image quality. Experimental results suggest that the proposed method can dramatically remove the high intensity noise in the low dose PET images and generate high quality PET image compared to other image enhancement methods.

2   Methods

To address the challenges in low dose PET with BSREM image reconstruction, we propose a NADRU framework by cascading two Res-UNets, as is shown in Fig. 2(a).

2.1   Noise-Aware Dual Res-UNets

This framework mainly consists of two components: a first Res-UNet for identifying high intensity noise (attention map), and a second Res-UNet for image enhancement. The architecture of the two Res-UNets are almost the same, except the network input and output. Res-UNet is an extension of UNet with residual blocks in each resolution stage. This network takes advantage of two popular network architectures, UNet [9] and Res-Net [4], which have been proven effective in many low level computer vision tasks, such as image denoising [11,15], image super-resolution [7,8] and image-to-image translation [5,16]. The first Res-UNet takes low-dose PET image as input and generates a noise attention probability map. The attention map is concatenated with the original low-dose PET image and passed on to the second Res-UNet for image reconstruction. The noise attention map helps the second Res-UNet to pay close attention to the high intensity noise. The detailed network settings for the first and second Res-UNets are illustrated in Fig. 2 (b) and (c), respectively. The details of the network setting can be found in Sect. 2.3.

2.2   Loss Function

Training Noise-aware Network: We treat the noise detection problem as a segmentation task, with the noise attention as the foreground. Because the foreground of noise mask only occupies a small percentage of the entire image, it creates a typical class imbalance problem. We utilized the Dice loss (L_{Dice}) to overcome this problem. Furthermore, we also used the binary cross entropy loss

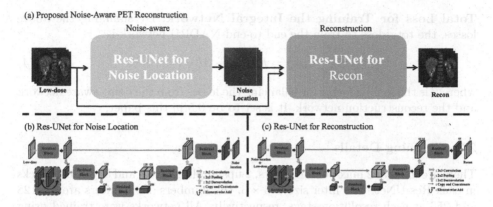

Fig. 2. Illustration of proposed noise-aware PET reconstruction network - NADRU.

(L_{BCE}) to form the voxel-wise measurement to stabilize the training process. The total loss (L_{NA}) for noise-aware network can be formulated as in Eq. 1:

$$L_{NA} = L_{Dice} + L_{BCE} \tag{1}$$

Training Image Enhancement Network: After the noise-aware network, the noise attention map is passed on to the second Res-UNet network along with the original low-dose PET image. When the noise distribution in the low dose PET image is Poisson distributed, L_1 loss, commonly used in image enhancement, is not a suitable loss for training the second network. Instead, we applied a general and adaptive robust loss proposed in [2] to automatically determine the loss function during training without any manual parameter tuning. This approach can adjust the optimal loss function according to the data distribution. The general and adaptive robust loss function is defined as:

$$L_{GAR}(p, \hat{p}, \alpha, c) = \frac{|\alpha - 2|}{\alpha} \left(\left(\frac{\left(\frac{(p - \hat{p})}{c}\right)^2}{|\alpha - 2|} + 1 \right)^{\frac{\alpha}{2}} - 1 \right), \tag{2}$$

where α and c are two parameters that need to be learned during training. α controls the robustness of the loss, and c controls the size of the loss's quadratic bowl near $p - \hat{p} = 0$. p is the standard dose PET image (ground-truth) and $\hat{p}$ is the reconstructed result by the proposed method.

To ensure the sharpness of the reconstructed PET image, we also included structural similarity (SSIM) loss (L_{SSIM}) in the loss function. The loss for training the second Res-UNet is defined as:

$$L_{recon} = L_{GAR} + L_{SSIM} \tag{3}$$

Total Loss for Training the Integral Network: By summing the above losses, the total loss to train the end-to-end NADRU network is:

$$L_{total} = L_{Recon} + \beta L_{NA} \tag{4}$$

where β is the scaling factor for balancing the losses from the noise-aware network and the reconstruction network. It is set to be 0.5 in this paper.

2.3 Training Details

There are in total 2 max pooling layers, 2 upsampling layers and 5 residual blocks in each Res-UNet. The filter size is 3×3, the numbers of the filters are 64, 128 and 256 at each resolution stage, respectively. All networks were trained using the Adam optimizer with momentum of 0.9. We set 100 epochs for the training stage. The batch size was set to 4 and the initial learning rate was set to 0.0001, which was then divided by 10 after 50 epochs. The code was implemented using the PyTorch library[1]. We used consecutive 2D axial slices (2.5D) as the input of the network so the model could get 3D local context information from upper and lower slices. This strategy using consecutive 2D axial slices could prevent reformat artifacts in coronal or sagittal planes (see Fig. 4) even though only axial images were used for training.

3   Experiments and Results

Dataset: With IRB approval and patient consent, ten subjects referred for whole-body FDG-18 PET/CT scan on a GE Discovery 710 scanner (GE Healthcare, Waukesha, WI) were recruited for this study. The voxel size is $2.73 \times 2.73 \times 2.77$ mm^3. The final matrix size of each PET image is $256 \times 256 \times 332$. The standard PET exam was performed with a 3.5 min/bed setting and 6 beds in total. List-mode data from the standard exams were saved. fourfold lower dose PET images were obtained by image reconstruction using only 1/4 of the dose count from the List-mode data. We utilized the mean value of all voxels to normalize the PET image. As all the amplified noise in the low dose PET image is of extreme high intensity value compared to the standard dose PET image, we set two criteria to get the ground-truth segmentation map. One criterion is an empirical thresholding: a threshold value of 30 after mean normalization was applied, only voxels with intensity above the threshold were considered as foreground candidates. The other criterion is that these intensity values in the candidate locations must be at least twice larger than those of the standard dose PET in the same locations. This is to avoid including high intensity small lesions in the noise attention map and other high-intensity region (e.g., brain or kidney). After applying these criteria, an initial segmentation map was achieved. We also applied Gaussion low pass filter on the initial segmentation map for better robustness.

---

[1] https://github.com/pytorch/pytorch.

Five-fold cross-validation was used to evaluate the proposed method. To quantitatively evaluate the reconstruction performance, we used the peak signal-noise ratio (PSNR) and structural similarity (SSIM) as the evaluation metrics. To demonstrate the advantage of the proposed method in terms of reconstruction accuracy, we compared it with four widely-used deep learning image enhancement methods: UNet, Res-UNet, EDSR [8], and SRGAN [6].

3.1   Impact of Proposed Noise-Aware Strategy

Res-UNet with L_1 loss was included as the baseline method. An example of PET reconstruction using the proposed method (with L_1 loss, refer as NADRU_L1) and baseline method is shown in Fig. 3 along with the low-dose PET image and standard-dose PET image (ground-truth). High intensity noise (pointed by red arrows) is visible in low dose PET image. The baseline model only partially eliminated image noise, with high intensity noise still visible in the processed images. For the PET reconstruction result with proposed noise-aware strategy, the high intensity noise has been fully removed and the resulted image quality is comparable to the ground truth. The noise probability map is also presented in Fig. 3 to demonstrate the effectiveness of noise-aware network that can identify the attention map of high intensity noise accurately. Quantitative results of PSNR and SSIM are presented in Table 1.

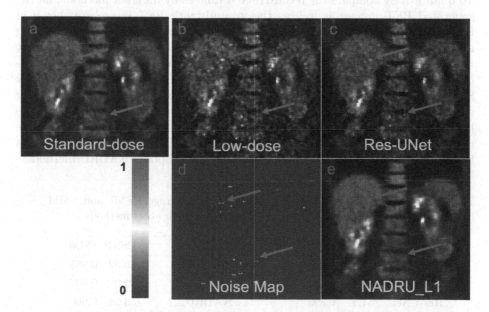

Fig. 3. Visual comparison of results by baseline model and proposed noise-aware strategy.(a) standard-dose PET image, (b) low dose PET of fourfold dose reduction, (c) result by baseline model, (d) noise map from proposed method and (e) result by proposed noise-aware strategy.

3.2   Impact of General and Adaptive Robust Loss

To show the impact of the adopted general and adaptive robust loss, we conducted experiments to compare the performance with GAR loss and with L_1 loss. The experimental results (shown in Table 2) indicated that the performance could be improved by 0.33dB and 0.008 in terms of PSNR and SSIM using the advanced loss function. After training, α was determined as 0.0012 and c 4×10^{-5}. When the lowest possible value of α is set to 0.001, Eq. 2 becomes as follow:

$$\lim_{\alpha \to 0} L_{GAR}(p, \hat{p}, \alpha, c) = log\left(\frac{1}{2}(\frac{p-\hat{p}}{c})^2 + 1\right), \qquad (5)$$

This yields Cauchy loss. We also conducted experiments using our proposed method with Cauchy loss, shown in Table 2. The SSIM and PSNR for NADRU and NADRU_Cauchy was almost the same and both were better than NADRU_L1. Therefore, it further verify the fact that noise produced by BSREM follows a Poisson distribution. This also indicates L_1 may not the best loss function when the noise satisfy Poission distribution.

3.3   Comparison with Other Methods

To qualitatively compare the reconstructed images by different methods, all the generated PET images as well as the ground-truth PET image are shown in Fig. 4. We can see that the proposed algorithm can better preserve the lung nodule (a lesion pointed by yellow arrow) while suppressing other high intensity noise (pointed by red arrow), since it used information provided from the attention noise map (also shown in Fig. 4 (f)). Whilst, the reconstructed result by SRGAN mistakenly removed the lung nodule as it likely had treated this lung nodule as other high intensity noise. In the reconstructed result by EDSR, some high-intensity noise was still visible (pointed by red arrow). The quantitative results of all the methods are given in Table 2. The PSNR and SSIM evaluation further indicated the superior performance of the proposed NADRU method.

Table 1. Average PSNR and SSIM comparing with baseline.

Method	PSNR	SSIM
Low-dose	50.52	0.872
UNet	51.04	0.887
Res-UNet	51.37	0.893
NADRU_L1	**53.33**	**0.906**

Table 2. Average PSNR and SSIM comparing with other methods.

Method	PSNR	SSIM
SRGAN	50.92	0.885
EDSR	52.39	0.907
NADRU_L1	53.33	0.906
NADRU_Cauchy	53.58	**0.916**
NADRU	**53.66**	0.914

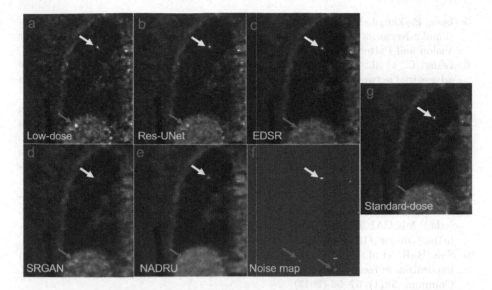

Fig. 4. Visual comparison of results by different methods. (a) low-dose PET of fourfold dose reduction, (b) result by Res-UNet, (c) result by EDSR, (d) result by SRGAN, (e) result by proposed method (NADRU), (f) noise map from proposed method and (g) standard-dose PET image.

4   Conclusion

In this work, we proposed a noise-aware network architecture for reconstructing high quality PET image from the low-dose PET scans. Different from traditional deep learning methods, which directly find the mapping between low dose PET image and standard dose PET image, we proposed a two-stage network to identify the high intensity noise attention map at the first stage, and then to reconstruct the high quality PET image at the second stage. Experiment results demonstrated that our method significantly outperformed traditional single stage deep learning methods.

References

1. An, L., et al.: Multi-level canonical correlation analysis for standard-dose PET image estimation. IEEE Trans. Image Process. **25**(7), 3303–3315 (2016)
2. Barron, J.T.: A general and adaptive robust loss function. In: Proceedings of the IEEE Conference on Computer Vision and Pattern Recognition, pp. 4331–4339 (2019)
3. Boellaard, R., Van Lingen, A., Lammertsma, A.A.: Experimental and clinical evaluation of iterative reconstruction (OSEM) in dynamic PET: quantitative characteristics and effects on kinetic modeling. J. Nucl. Med. **42**(5), 808–817 (2001)
4. He, K., Zhang, X., Ren, S., Sun, J.: Deep residual learning for image recognition. In: Proceedings of the IEEE Conference on Computer Vision and Pattern Recognition, pp. 770–778 (2016)

5. Isola, P., Zhu, J.-Y., Zhou, T., Efros, A.A.: Image-to-image translation with conditional adversarial networks. In: Proceedings of the IEEE Conference on Computer Vision and Pattern Recognition, pp. 1125–1134 (2017)
6. Ledig, C., et al.: Photo-realistic single image super-resolution using a generative adversarial network. In: Proceedings of the IEEE Conference on Computer Vision and Pattern Recognition, pp. 4681–4690 (2017)
7. Li, J., Fang, F., Mei, K., Zhang, G.: Multi-scale residual network for image super-resolution. In Proceedings of the European Conference on Computer Vision (ECCV), pp. 517–532 (2018)
8. Lim, B., Son, S., Kim, H., Nah, S., Mu Lee, K.: Enhanced deep residual networks for single image super-resolution. In: Proceedings of the IEEE Conference on Computer Vision and Pattern Recognition Workshops, pp. 136–144 (2017)
9. Ronneberger, O., Fischer, P., Brox, T.: U-Net: convolutional networks for biomedical image segmentation. In: Navab, N., Hornegger, J., Wells, W.M., Frangi, A.F. (eds.) MICCAI 2015. LNCS, vol. 9351, pp. 234–241. Springer, Cham (2015). https://doi.org/10.1007/978-3-319-24574-4_28
10. Sah, B.-R., et al.: Clinical evaluation of a block sequential regularized expectation maximization reconstruction algorithm in 18F-FDG PET/CT studies. Nucl. Med. Commun. **38**(1), 57–66 (2017)
11. Shen, X., Chen, Y-C., Tao, X., Jia, J.: Convolutional neural pyramid for image processing. arXiv preprint (2017). arXiv:1704.02071
12. Wang, Y., et al.: 3D conditional generative adversarial networks for high-quality PET image estimation at low dose. Neuroimage **174**, 550–562 (2018)
13. Xiang, L., et al.: Deep auto-context convolutional neural networks for standard-dose PET image estimation from low-dose PET/MRI. Neurocomputing **267**, 406–416 (2017)
14. Xu, J., Gong, E., Pauly, J., Zaharchuk, G.: 200x low-dose PET reconstruction using deep learning. arXiv preprint (2017). arXiv:1712.04119
15. Zhang, K., Zuo, W., Chen, Y., Meng, D., Zhang, L.: Beyond a gaussian denoiser: residual learning of deep CNN for image denoising. IEEE Trans. Image Process. **26**(7), 3142–3155 (2017)
16. Zhu, J-Y., Park, T., Isola, P., Efros, A.A.: Unpaired image-to-image translation using cycle-consistent adversarial networks. In: Proceedings of the IEEE International Conference on Computer Vision, pp. 2223–2232 (2017)

Semi-supervised Transfer Learning for Infant Cerebellum Tissue Segmentation

Yue Sun, Kun Gao, Sijie Niu, Weili Lin, Gang Li, Li Wang[✉],
and The UNC/UMN Baby Connectome Project Consortium

Department of Radiology and Biomedical Research Imaging Center,
University of North Carolina at Chapel Hill, Chapel Hill, USA
li_wang@med.unc.edu

Abstract. To characterize early cerebellum development, accurate segmentation of the cerebellum into white matter (WM), gray matter (GM), and cerebrospinal fluid (CSF) tissues is one of the most pivotal steps. However, due to the weak tissue contrast, extremely folded tiny structures, and severe partial volume effect, infant cerebellum tissue segmentation is especially challenging, and the manual labels are hard to obtain and correct for learning-based methods. To the best of our knowledge, there is no work on the cerebellum segmentation for infant subjects less than 24 months of age. In this work, we develop a semi-supervised transfer learning framework guided by a confidence map for tissue segmentation of cerebellum MR images from 24-month-old to 6-month-old infants. Note that only 24-month-old subjects have reliable manual labels for training, due to their high tissue contrast. Through the proposed semi-supervised transfer learning, the labels from 24-month-old subjects are gradually propagated to the 18-, 12-, and 6-month-old subjects, which have a low tissue contrast. Comparison with the state-of-the-art methods demonstrates the superior performance of the proposed method, especially for 6-month-old subjects.

Keywords: Infant cerebellum segmentation · Confidence map · Semi-supervised learning

1 Introduction

The first 2 years of life is the most dynamic postnatal period of the human cerebellum development [1], with the cerebellum volume increasing by 240% from 2 weeks to 1 year, and by 15% from 1 to 2 years of age [2]. Cerebellum plays an important role in motor control, and is also involved in some cognitive functions as well as emotional control [3]. For instance, recent cerebellar findings in autism suggest developmental differences at multiple levels of neural structure and function, indicating that the cerebellum is an important player in the complex neural underpinnings of autism spectrum disorder, with behavioral implications beyond the motor domain [4]. To characterize early cerebellum development, accurate segmentation of the cerebellum into white matter (WM), gray

© Springer Nature Switzerland AG 2020
M. Liu et al. (Eds.): MLMI 2020, LNCS 12436, pp. 663–673, 2020.
https://doi.org/10.1007/978-3-030-59861-7_67

matter (GM), and cerebrospinal fluid (CSF) is one of the most pivotal steps. However, compared with adult cerebellum, infant cerebellum is much more challenging in tissue segmentation, due to the low tissue contrast caused by ongoing myelination, extremely folded tiny structures, and severe partial volume effect.

Most of the previous brain development studies have focused on the cerebral cortex [5–10]. For instance, Wang *et al.* proposed an anatomy-guided Densely-connected U-Net (ADU-Net) [11] for the cerebrum image segmentation of 6-month-old infants. However, there are very few works proposed for pediatric cerebellum tissue segmentation [12–16]. Chen *et al.* [17] proposed an ensemble sparse learning method for cerebellum tissue segmentation of 24-month-old subjects. Romero *et al.* [15] presented a patch-based multi-atlas segmentation tool called CERES, that is able to automatically parcellate the cerebellum lobules, and is the winner of a MICCAI cerebellum segmentation challenge. To the best of our knowledge, there is no work on cerebellum tissue segmentation for infant subjects less than 24 months of age. Figure 1 shows an example of T1-weighted (T1w) and T2-weighted (T2w) MR images (MRIs) of cerebellum at 6, 12, 18 and 24 months of age, and the corresponding segmentations are obtained by ADU-Net [11] and the proposed semi-supervised method in the last two rows. From 6 months to 24 months, we can observe that the cerebellum volume increases rapidly, and the tissue contrast is varying remarkably, i.e., 6-month-old cerebellum exhibits an extremely low tissue contrast, while 24-month-old cerebellum shows a much high contrast. As also confirmed from the previous work [14], 24-month-old cerebellum can be automatically or manually segmented due to its high contrast. However, for other early ages, especially for 6-month-old cerebellum, it is challenging even for manual segmentation by experienced experts. Directly applying the model trained on 24-month-old subjects to younger infants cannot derive satisfactory segmentation results. For example, we directly apply a trained model on 24-month-old subjects using ADU-Net [11] to other time points, and show the derived results in the third row of Fig. 1. It can be seen that the results are not accurate, due to distinct tissue contrast and distribution between 24-month-old subjects and other younger subjects. Therefore, in this work, we will investigate how to effectively utilize the labels from 24-month-old subjects with high contrast to the other time-point subjects with low contrast. This is a general yet challenging transfer learning task, if we consider 24-month-old subjects as a source site while the remaining time-point subjects as a target site. Note that all studied subjects in this paper are cross-sectional.

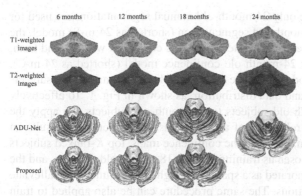

In this paper, we propose a semi-supervised transfer learning framework guided by the a confidence map for tissue segmentation of cerebellum MRIs from 24-month-old to 6-month-old infants, where only 24-month-old subjects with high tissue contrast have manual labels for training. Then, for other younger subjects without manual labels, we retrain the segmentation models to handle the different tissue contrast and distribution guided by the confidence map. Specifically, in order to

Fig. 1. T1- and T2-weighted MRIs of the cerebellum at 6, 12, 18 and 24 months of age, with the corresponding segmentation results obtained by ADU-Net [9] and the proposed semi-supervised method.

select reliable segmentations as training datasets at 18, 12, and 6 months of age, a confidence network is trained to estimate the reliability of automatic tissue segmentation results [18]. Second, the confidence map is further incorporated as a spatially-weighted loss function to alleviate the effect from these regions with unreliable segmentations. This paper is organized as follows. Section 2 introduces the dataset and related preprocessing. Then, the proposed semi-supervised framework is detailed in Sect. 3. In Sect. 4, experimental results and analyses are presented to demonstrate the superior performance of our method. Finally, Sect. 5 concludes the paper.

2   Dataset and Preprocessing

T1w and T2w infant brain MRIs used in this study were from the UNC/UMN Baby Connectome Project (BCP) [19] and were acquired at around 24, 18, 12, and 6 months of age on Siemens Prisma scanners. During scanning, infants were naturally sleeping, fitted with ear protection, and their heads were secured in a vacuum-fixation device. T1w MRIs were acquired with 160 sagittal slices using parameters: TR/TE = 2400/2.2 ms and voxel resolution = $0.8 \times 0.8 \times 0.8$ mm^3. T2w MRIs were obtained with 160 sagittal slices using parameters: TR/TE = 3200/564 ms and voxel resolution = $0.8 \times 0.8 \times 0.8$ mm^3.

Accurate manual segmentation, providing labels for training and testing, is of great importance for learning-based segmentation methods. In this paper, we manually edited eighteen 24-month-old subjects to train the segmentation model. Limited number of 18-, 12-, and 6-month-old subjects are manually edited for validation. From 24- to 6-month-old subjects, the label editing becomes gradually difficult and more time-consuming due to the low tissue contrast and extremely folded tiny structures.

3   Method

Figure 2 illustrates the flowchart of the proposed semi-supervised segmentation framework guided by a confidence map. As we can see, there are infant subjects at 6, 12,

18, and 24 months of age, while only 24-month-old manual segmentations are used for training. After training the 24-month-old segmentation (shorted as 24 m-S) model, the automatic segmentations are used to generate error maps compared with ground truth, which are viewed as targets for 24-month-old confidence model (shorted as 24 m-C). However, the trained 24 m-S model cannot be directly applied to 18-month-old subjects due to different tissue contrast and data distribution, as shown in Fig. 1. To effectively utilize the labels from 24-month-old subjects to 18-month-old subjects, we apply the 24 m-C model to estimate the reliability of automatic tissue segmentation results on the 18-month-old subjects. Then, based on the confidence maps, top K-ranked subjects with good segmentations are chosen as training sets for 18-month-old subjects, and the confidence map is further incorporated as a spatially-weighted loss function to alleviate possible errors in the segmentations. The same procedure can be also applied to train 12-month-old segmentation (12 m-S) model and 6-month-old segmentation (6 m-S) model.

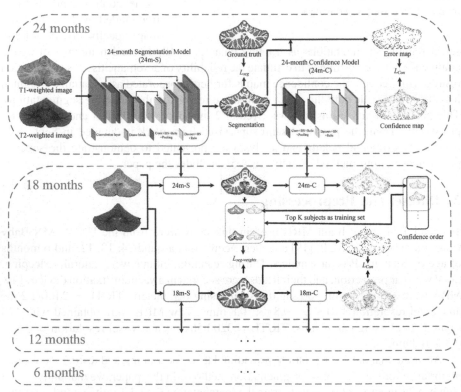

Fig. 2. Flowchart of the proposed semi-supervised segmentation framework guided by confidence map. For 24-month-old subjects, the ground truth is edited manually, the loss function of the segmentation model L_{seg} is cross entropy, and the loss function of the confidence network L_{cp} is multi-task cross-entropy. For other months, the ground truth is chosen from automatic segmentations, the loss function of the segmentation model $L_{seg-weights}$ is the proposed spatially-weighted cross entropy.

3.1 Confidence Map of Automatic Segmentations

To derive reliable 18- (12-, 6-) month cerebellum segmentations, we first employ the confidence map to evaluate the automatic segmentations generated by the trained 24 m-S (18 m-S, 12 m-S) model. Inspired by [18], we apply U-Net structure [20] with the contracting path and expansive path to achieve the confidence map. Instead of using adversarial learning, the error map (Fig. 3 (a)) generated based on the differences between manual results and automatic segmentations, is regarded as ground truth to train the confidence model. We employ a multi-task softmax loss function, which is more effective to learn whether the segmentation results are reasonable or not voxel-by-voxel, as shown in Fig. 3 (b). Note that the darker the color, the worse the segmentation. The 3D zoomed view of WM segmentation is shown in Fig. 3 (c), where the intersection of red lines denotes a missing gyrus that is the same region with Fig. 3 (b), and the corresponding ground truth is also displayed in Fig. 3 (d).

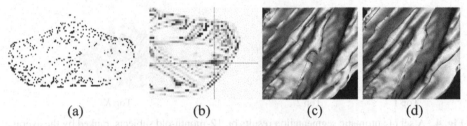

(a)   (b)   (c)   (d)

Fig. 3. (a) is the error map generated based on the differences between ground truth and automatic segmentations. (b) shows the confidence map (a probability map), where the intersection of red lines points out a low confidence region, which means the segmentation is relatively unreasonable. (c) is the corresponding 3D surface rendering results, i.e., the missing gyrus as indicated in (b), and (d) is the ground truth.

3.2 Semi-supervised Learning

After training the 24 m-S model with manual labels, we retrain the 18 m-S, 12 m-S and 6 m-S models based on 18-, 12-, and 6-month-old subjects, respectively. In particular, the training labels are automatically generated from the automatic segmentations, and a spatially-weighted cross-entropy loss is proposed to learn from reasonable segmentations guided by the confidence map.

Training Segmentation Model for 24-month-old Subjects: We employ the ADU-Net architecture [11] as the segmentation model, which combines the advantages of U-Net and Dense block, and demonstrates outstanding performance on infant brain segmentation. As shown in Fig. 2, the ADU-Net includes a down-sampling path and an up-sampling path, going through seven dense blocks. Then, eighteen paired T1w and T2w images with their corresponding manual segmentations are as inputs of ADU-Net to train the 24 m-S model. We evaluate the performance of the 24 m-S model in terms of Dice ratio on five 24-month-old testing subjects, with the accuracy of $90.46 \pm 1.56\%$, $91.83 \pm 0.62\%$ and $94.11 \pm 0.38\%$ for CSF, GM and WM, respectively.

Automatic Generation of Training Labels for 18-, 12-, 6-month-old Subjects:
With the guidance of the confidence map, we select K top-ranked subjects with good segmentations as training sets for each month. The rank is based on the average confidence values of each confidence map. Figure 4 shows a set of automatic segmentation results on 12-month-old subjects, ranked by the average confidence values. Specifically, the 12-month-old cerebellum segmentations and confidence maps are obtained by 18 m-S and 18 m-C models, respectively. From Fig. 4, we can observe that the confidence order is consistent with the accuracy of segmentations, which also proves the effectiveness of the confidence network. Therefore, according to the confidence order, the chosen K top-ranked subjects are reliable for training the segmentation model of other months.

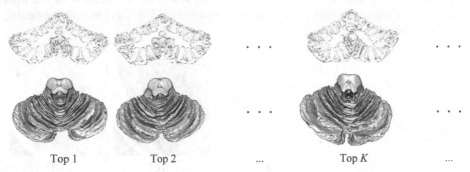

Top 1   Top 2   ...   Top K ...

Fig. 4. A set of automatic segmentation results on 12-month-old subjects, ranked by the average confidence values. The first row is the confidence maps, and the second row is the automatic 3D WM segmentations, which are obtained from 18 m-S and 18 m-C model, respectively.

Spatially-Weighted Cross-entropy Loss with Confidence Map: Although we select reliable segmentation results as the training labels for 18-, 12- and 6-month-old subjects based on the confidence map, for each selected subject, there are still many locations with unreliable labels. Considering this issue, we further incorporate the confidence map into the loss function, therefore, the segmentation model would pay more attention to reliable labels, while less attention to unreliable labels. The spatially-weighted cross-entropy loss function is written as,

$$L_{seg-weights} = -w \sum_{i=C} y_i \ln x_i$$

where C is the class number, x_i represents the predicted probability map, y_i is the ground truth, and w denotes the weights from the confidence map.

Implementation Details: We randomly extract 1,000 $32 \times 32 \times 32$ 3D patches from each training subject. The loss L_{cp} for the confidence network is multi-task cross-entropy. The kernels are initialized by Xavier [38]. We use SGD optimization strategy. The learning rate is 0.005 and multiplies by 0.1 after each epoch.

4 Experimental Results

In this section, we first investigate the optimal choice of number K of training subjects, then make a comparison of semi-supervised learning and supervised learning to demonstrate the effectiveness of the proposed method. Later, we perform an ablation study of confidence weights. Finally, the performance of our method is compared with vol-Brain [21] and ADU-Net method [11] on five 18-month-old subjects, five 12-month-old subjects, and five 6-month-old subjects with manual labels.

Selection of the Number K of Training Subjects: According to the confidence map, we select the K top-ranked subjects as training images for the 18 m-S (12 m-S and 6 m-S) models. Considering that the reliability of ordered segmentations gradually decreases, we compare the performance associated with the different number K to choose the best one, as shown in Fig. 5. It is expected with the increase of K (<10), the Dice ratio is gradually improved in terms of CSF, GM and WM results, whereas the value begins to drop after $K > 10$, due to introducing too many unreliable labels into the training. Therefore, we set $K = 10$ in all experiments.

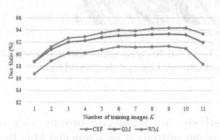

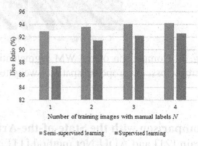

Fig. 5. Comparison of different K top-ranked training subjects, in terms of Dice ratio.

Fig. 6. Comparison of the supervised and semi-supervised learning on 6-month-old subjects, in terms of Dice ratio in WM segmentation.

Semi-supervised vs. Supervised Learning: Although the limited number of manual segmentation results for 18-, 12- and 6-month-old subjects are purposely created for validation only, we are wondering whether the performance with the semi-supervised learning is better than the supervised learning or not. To this end, for the supervised learning, we select N subjects with manual labels as the training subjects. Similarly, for the semi-supervised learning, we select the same N training subjects as the supervised learning, plus additional top K-ranked subjects based on the confidence. The same remaining subjects with manual labels are used for testing. The comparison is shown in Fig. 6 in terms of WM segmentation, along with the number of training subjects N. The number of training subjects with manual labels for the supervised learning is N, while N + top K for the semi-supervised learning. As we can see, compared with the supervised learning, the semi-supervised learning (i.e., the proposed method) greatly improves the accuracy of tissue segmentations, especially when the number of training subjects with manual labels is highly limited.

Ablation Study: To demonstrate the advantage of the proposed spatially-weighted cross-entropy loss, we make a comparison between the results using the cross-entropy loss without/with confidence weights. Figure 7 shows the comparison of WM segmentations, where the first (second) column shows the surface rendering results without (with) confidence weights. We can see that without the guidance of confidence weights, there are many topological and geometric errors as indicated by red arrow in the first column, whereas these errors are alleviated as shown in the second column, which is also more consistent with the corresponding manual labels in the last column.

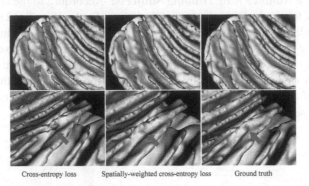

Cross-entropy loss   Spatially-weighted cross-entropy loss   Ground truth

Fig. 7. Comparison of the WM segmentations. From left to right: segmentations using cross-entropy loss, the proposed spatially-weighted cross-entropy loss, and the ground truth.

Comparison with the State-of-the-Art Methods: We make comparisons with vol-Brain [21] and ADU-Net method [11], where the volBrain is an automated MRI Brain Volumetry System (https://volbrain.upv.es/index.php) and the ADU-Net architecture is the backbone of our segmentation model. In the volBrain system, we choose the CERES pipeline [15] to automatically analyze the cerebellum, which wins a MICCAI cerebellum segmentation challenge. Figure 8 displays the comparison among these methods on 18-, 12-, and 6-month-old testing subjects. Tissue segmentations of the proposed method are much more consistent with the ground truth, which can be observed from both 2D slices and 3D surface rendering results.

Furthermore, we compute the Dice ratio of tissue segmentation (i.e., CSF, GM, and WM) on 15 infant subjects (i.e., five 18-month-old subjects, five 12-month-old subjects, and five 6-month-old subjects), to evaluate the performance of our method. In order to compare the difference of segmentation results, Wilcoxon signed-rank tests are also calculated for statistical analysis in Table 1. The proposed method achieves a significantly better performance in terms of Dice ratio on CSF and GM for 18-month-old subjects and CSF, GM, and WM for 12- and 6-month-old subjects.

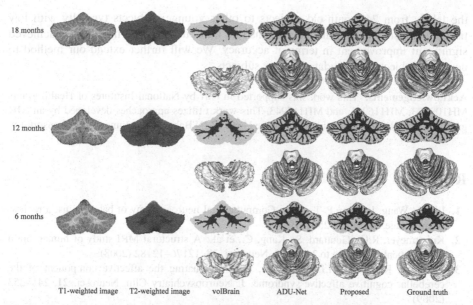

Fig. 8. Segmentation results of the volBrain [21], ADU-Net [11] and the proposed method on 18-, 12-, and 6-month-old infant subjects from BCP, with the corresponding 3D WM surface rendering views. The red/green/blue color denotes CSF/GM/WM. (Color figure online)

Table 1. Dice ratio (%) of cerebellum segmentation results on testing subjects at 18 months, 12 months, and 6 months of age. "$^+$" indicates that our proposed method is significantly better than both volBrain and ADU-Net methods with p-value < 0.05.

Age in month	Method	CSF	GM	WM
18	volBrain	N/A	78.23 ± 1.10	54.43 ± 3.87
	ADU-Net	87.57 ± 1.70	91.57 ± 0.43	93.52 ± 0.65
	Proposed	$91.36 \pm 1.11^+$	$93.40 \pm 0.75^+$	94.39 ± 0.69
12	volBrain	N/A	70.80 ± 13.54	49.86 ± 4.70
	ADU-Net	84.06 ± 2.40	89.83 ± 0.88	91.89 ± 0.68
	Proposed	$90.50 \pm 1.25^+$	$93.08 \pm 0.47^+$	$94.14 \pm 0.48^+$
6	volBrain	N/A	77.76 ± 1.24	50.96 ± 3.91
	ADU-Net	76.68 ± 0.76	86.30 ± 0.79	88.98 ± 1.87
	Proposed	$85.35 \pm 0.76^+$	$90.23 \pm 1.15^+$	$92.02 \pm 1.92^+$

5 Conclusion

To deal with the challenging task of infant cerebellum tissue segmentation, we proposed a semi-supervised transfer learning framework guided by the confidence map. We took advantage of 24-month-old subjects with high tissue contrast and effectively transferred the labels from 24-month-old subjects to other younger subjects typically with low tissue contrast. The experiments demonstrate that our proposed method has achieved significant improvement in terms of accuracy. We will further extend our method to newborn subjects and validate on more subjects.

Acknowledgements. This work was supported in part by National Institutes of Health grants MH109773, MH116225, and MH117943. This work utilizes approaches developed by an NIH grant (1U01MH110274) and the efforts of the UNC/UMN Baby Connectome Project Consortium.

References

1. Li, G., Wang, L., Yap, P.-T., et al.: Computational neuroanatomy of baby brains: a review. NeuroImage **185**, 906–925 (2019)
2. Knickmeyer, R.C., Gouttard, S., Kang, C., et al.: A structural MRI study of human brain development from birth to 2 years. J. Neurosci. **28**, 12176–12182 (2008)
3. Wolf, U., Rapoport, M.J., Schweizer, T.A.: Evaluating the affective component of the cerebellar cognitive affective syndrome. J. Neuropsychiatry Clin. Neurosci. **21**, 245–253 (2009)
4. Becker, E.B.E., Stoodley, C.J.: Autism spectrum disorder and the cerebellum. Int. Rev. Neurobiol. **113**, 1–34 (2013)
5. Wang, F., Lian, C., Wu, Z., et al.: Developmental topography of cortical thickness during infancy. Proc. Nat. Acad. Sci. **116**, 15855 (2019)
6. Duan, D., Xia, S., Rekik, I., et al.: Exploring folding patterns of infant cerebral cortex based on multi-view curvature features: methods and applications. NeuroImage **185**, 575–592 (2019)
7. Li, G., Nie, J., Wang, L., et al.: Measuring the dynamic longitudinal cortex development in infants by reconstruction of temporally consistent cortical surfaces. NeuroImage **90**, 266–279 (2014)
8. Li, G., Nie, J., Wang, L., et al.: Mapping longitudinal hemispheric structural asymmetries of the human cerebral cortex from birth to 2 years of age. Cereb Cortex **24**, 1289–1300 (2014)
9. Sun, Y., Gao, K., Wu, Z., et al.: Multi-site infant brain segmentation algorithms: The iSeg-2019 Challenge. arXiv preprint arXiv:2007.02096 (2020)
10. Wang, L., Nie, D., Li, G., et al.: Benchmark on automatic six-month-old infant brain segmentation algorithms: the iSeg-2017 Challenge. IEEE Trans. Med. Imaging **38**, 2219–2230 (2019)
11. Wang, L., Li, G., Shi, F., et al.: Volume-based analysis of 6-month-old infant brain MRI for autism biomarker identification and early diagnosis. Med. Image Comput. Comput. Assist. Interv. **11072**, 411–419 (2018)
12. Cettour-Janet, P., et al.: Hierarchical approach for neonate cerebellum segmentation from MRI: an experimental study. In: Burgeth, B., Kleefeld, A., Naegel, B., Passat, N., Perret, B. (eds.) ISMM 2019. LNCS, vol. 11564, pp. 483–495. Springer, Cham (2019). https://doi.org/10.1007/978-3-030-20867-7_37
13. Bogovic, J.A., Bazin, P.-L., Ying, S.H., Prince, J.L.: Automated segmentation of the cerebellar lobules using boundary specific classification and evolution. Inf. Process Med. Imaging **23**, 62–73 (2013)
14. Chen, J., Wang, L., Shen, D.: Cerebellum tissue segmentation with ensemble sparse learning. Proc. Int. Soc. Magn. Reson. Med. Sci. Meet Exhib. Int. **25**, 0266 (2017)
15. Romero, J.E., Coupé, P., Giraud, R., et al.: CERES: a new cerebellum lobule segmentation method. NeuroImage **147**, 916–924 (2017)

16. Hwang, J., Kim, J., Han, Y., Park, H.: An automatic cerebellum extraction method in T1-weighted brain MR images using an active contour model with a shape prior. Magn. Reson. Imaging **29**, 1014–1022 (2011)

17. Chen, J., et al.: Automatic accurate infant cerebellar tissue segmentation with densely connected convolutional network. In: Shi, Y., Suk, H.-I., Liu, M. (eds.) MLMI 2018. LNCS, vol. 11046, pp. 233–240. Springer, Cham (2018). https://doi.org/10.1007/978-3-030-00919-9_27

18. Nie, D., Gao, Y., Wang, L., Shen, D.: ASDNet: attention based semi-supervised deep networks for medical image segmentation. In: Frangi, A.F., Schnabel, J.A., Davatzikos, C., Alberola-López, C., Fichtinger, G. (eds.) MICCAI 2018. LNCS, vol. 11073, pp. 370–378. Springer, Cham (2018). https://doi.org/10.1007/978-3-030-00937-3_43

19. Howell, B.R., Styner, M.A., Gao, W., et al.: The UNC/UMN Baby Connectome Project (BCP): an overview of the study design and protocol development. NeuroImage **185**, 891–905 (2019)

20. Ronneberger, O., Fischer, P., Brox, T.: U-Net: convolutional networks for biomedical image segmentation. In: Navab, N., Hornegger, J., Wells, W.M., Frangi, A.F. (eds.) MICCAI 2015. LNCS, vol. 9351, pp. 234–241. Springer, Cham (2015). https://doi.org/10.1007/978-3-319-24574-4_28

21. Manjón, J.V., Coupé, P.: volBrain: an online MRI brain volumetry system. Front Neuroinform **10**, 30 (2016)

Informative Feature-Guided Siamese Network for Early Diagnosis of Autism

Kun Gao, Yue Sun, Sijie Niu, and Li Wang[✉]

Department of Radiology and Biomedical Research Imaging Center,
University of North Carolina at Chapel Hill, Chapel Hill, USA
li_wang@med.unc.edu

Abstract. Autism, or autism spectrum disorder (ASD), is a complex developmental disability, and usually diagnosed with observations at around 3-4 years old based on behaviors. Studies have indicated that the early treatment, especially during early brain development in the first two years of life, can significantly improve the symptoms, therefore, it is important to identify ASD as early as possible. Most previous works employed imaging-based biomarkers for the early diagnosis of ASD. However, they only focused on extracting features from the intensity images, ignoring the more informative guidance from segmentation and parcellation maps. Moreover, since the number of autistic subjects is always much smaller than that of normal subjects, this class-imbalance issue makes the ASD diagnosis more challenging. In this work, we propose an end-to-end informative feature-guided Siamese network for the early ASD diagnosis. Specifically, besides T1w and T2w images, the discriminative features from segmentation and parcellation maps are also employed to train the model. To alleviate the class-imbalance issue, the Siamese network is utilized to effectively learn what makes the pair of inputs belong to the same class or different classes. Furthermore, the subject-specific attention module is incorporated to identify the ASD-related regions in an end-to-end fully automatic learning manner. Both ablation study and comparisons demonstrate the effectiveness of the proposed method, achieving an overall accuracy of 85.4%, sensitivity of 80.8%, and specificity of 86.7%.

Keywords: Early diagnosis · Siamese network · Subject-specific attention · Autism spectrum disorder

1 Introduction

Autism spectrum disorder (ASD), a developmental disability, would occur in all ethnic, racial, and economic groups. People suffering from ASD always perform abnormally in behaviors, communication and interaction, such as difficult communication with other people and repetitive behaviors. According to the latest report from Centers for Disease Control and Prevention, one in 54 children aged 8 years in the U.S. was diagnosed as ASD [1]. However, due to the absence of early biomarkers, ASD cannot be reliably diagnosed until around 3–4 years of age [2], only through a long process that involves observing behaviors, including language, social interactions and physical movements.

© Springer Nature Switzerland AG 2020
M. Liu et al. (Eds.): MLMI 2020, LNCS 12436, pp. 674–682, 2020.
https://doi.org/10.1007/978-3-030-59861-7_68

Consequently, intervention efforts may miss a critical developmental window [3]. Given the potential diagnostic instability of ASD in infancy, it is critically important to develop a system for categorizing infants at risk of ASD, who do not yet meet criteria for behaviors-based diagnosis, thus helping prevent the development of ASD [4].

Currently, there are very few works focusing on the prediction of ASD at the early stage. Shen et al. predicted ASD at 12–15 months based on the ratio of extra-axial cerebrospinal fluid (EA-CSF) to total cerebral volume [5]. They found that the ratio of 0.14 yielded 78% sensitivity and 79% specificity in predicting ASD diagnosis. In addition to EA-CSF, some works [6–8] indicated that the abnormal development of cortical gray and white matter in the infants can be used to distinguish ASD and normal control (NC). The total brain volume enlargement reported in [9–11], especially between 12 and 24 months of age, was also viewed as a crucial difference between ASD and NC. Besides, high risk-ASD infants showed a faster increasing rate in terms of cortical surface area expansion, compared with NC [10, 11]. Furthermore, Shen et al. [12] combined extra-axial CSF volume, total brain volume, age, and sex information for prediction, achieving accuracy of 78%, sensitivity of 84%, and specificity of 65%. Recently, a multi-channel convolutional neural network with a patch-level data-expanding strategy was proposed to automatically identify infants with risk of ASD at 24 months of age [13], achieving accuracy of 76.2%.

However, there are three key limitations of previous works. 1) Pre-defined brain landmarks/biomarkers isolated to the subsequent learning stage may lead to sub-optimal prediction performance due to potential heterogeneity in two standalone stages. 2) Previous works typically only relied on intensity images for classification, ignoring the more informative guidance from segmentation and parcellation maps, e.g., Li et al. [14] found many regions of interest (ROIs) with significant differences between ASD and NC groups. 3) There is a class-imbalance issue, i.e., the number of autistic subjects is far less than that of normal subjects. To address these limitations, we develop an end-to-end informative feature-guided Siamese network for the automated autism diagnosis at 24 months of age. In this work, besides T1w and T2w images, informative features from the segmentation map as well as the parcellation map are also used to train the model. Besides, inspired by [15], a subject-specific attention module is employed to locate the disease-related area in terms of ASD, which can make the prediction more reasonable. To alleviate the class-imbalance issue, we leverage the Siamese network [16] consisting of two identical subnetworks that share identical weights to learn what makes the pair of inputs belong to the same class or different classes, instead of directly classifying an input as ASD or NC in the conventional methods.

2 Dataset Acquisition and Preprocessing

There are a total of 247 subjects used in this work, including 52 ASD subjects and 195 NC subjects, which were gathered from National Database for Autism Research (NDAR) [17]. All images were acquired at 24 months of age on a Siemens 3T scanner. T1w images were acquired with parameters: TR/TE = 2400/3.16 ms and voxel resolution = $1 \times 1 \times 1$ mm^3. T2w images were acquired with parameters: TR/TE = 3200/499 ms and voxel resolution = $1 \times 1 \times 1$ mm^3. Besides T1w images and T2w images, we also employ the segmentation map and parcellation map for the diagnosis of ASD, which were generated by a publicly available software iBEAT V2.0 Cloud (http://www.ibeat. cloud). Note that iBEAT V2.0 Cloud has been validated on 4100+ infant brain images with various protocols and scanners from 60+ institutions, including Harvard Medical School, Stanford University, Yale University, and Princeton University. For the tissue segmentation [3], each infant brain image was segmented into white matter (WM), gray matter (GM) and cerebrospinal fluid (CSF). For the parcellation, each infant brain image was labeled into 151 ROIs, with 133 ROIs for cerebrum and 18 ROIs for cerebellum. After careful inspection, all the segmentation and parcellation maps generated by the iBEAT V2.0 Cloud passed the quality assurance. An example of T1w image, T2w image, and corresponding segmentation and parcellation maps is presented in Fig. 1. To facilitate the following diagnosis, all images/maps were rigidly aligned to an infant atlas [18] and further cropped to an identical size.

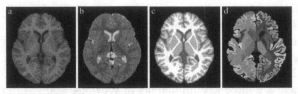

Fig. 1. An example of T1w image (a), T2w image (b), corresponding segmentation (c) and parcellation maps (d), generated by iBEAT V2.0 Cloud (http://www.ibeat.cloud).

3 Method

The proposed informative feature-guided Siamese network is shown in Fig. 2, which consists of four components: 1) feature extractor to extract discriminative features from T1w images, T2w images, segmentations and parcellation maps, 2) feature concatenation/fusion (FCF) module to fuse the extracted features, 3) subject-specific attention (SSA) module to identify ASD-related location, and 4) Siamese classifier to identify the class of the input subject.

Feature Extractor. We employ a convolution neural network as the feature extractor, to capture diverse features from T1w image, T2w image, segmentation, and parcellation maps. As a plug-in unit, the feature extractor could be implemented by any convolution neural network, such as VGGNet, ResNet or DenseNet. Besides, note that the extractors of different inputs are with the same structure but different weights. In this way, different extractors are used to learn the distinctive patterns from different inputs.

In details, there are six $3 \times 3 \times 3$ convolution layers (Conv), followed by batch normalization (BN) and parametric rectified linear unit (PReLu), and two $4 \times 4 \times 4$ downsampling layers for each extractor. The number of filters from Conv1 to Conv6 are 64, 64, 96, 128, 256, and 32, respectively. To reserve more information in the shallow stage/layer of the model, the convolution layer with stride of $4 \times 4 \times 4$ is used to downsample feature maps and increase receptive field, whereas the stride of other convolution layers is set as $1 \times 1 \times 1$.

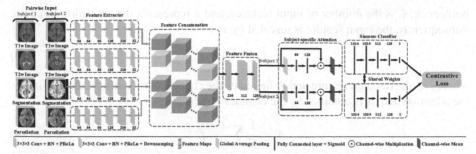

Fig. 2. Schematic diagram of the proposed end-to-end informative feature-guided Siamese network for the automated ASD diagnosis.

Feature Concatenation and Fusion Module. As shown in Fig. 2, there are four feature maps generated from the inputs, indicated by different colors. Considering that the features of each subject represent different information, we adopt concatenation operation for the informative features with the output channel, instead of element-wise addition. Subsequently, the concatenated features are fed into the fusion module for the further fusion and extraction. More specifically, the fusion module contains three convolution layers, with the kernel size of $4 \times 4 \times 4$ and the stride of $1 \times 1 \times 1$.

Subject-specific Attention Module. Previous works [9, 12, 13] have indicated the differences between ASD and NC subjects based on the MR images, such as the enlargement of total brain volume [9], the extra-axial CSF volume [12], and the detected ROIs with statistically significant difference between ASD and NC subjects. However, the predefined/detected landmarks/biomarkers are isolated to the subsequent ASD diagnosis procedure, which may lead to the sub-optimal performance. In this work, we deploy the SSA module to identify the ASD-related regions in an end-to-end fully automatic learning manner.

As shown in Fig. 2, the SSA module includes two parallel branches that consist of group average pooling, two fully connected layers, channel-wise multiplication, and channel-wise mean, where two branches with identical structure have different parameters. In details, the feature generated from FCF module is first squeezed as a vector using global average pooling to generate channel-wise statistics, regarding as a channel descriptor Z for the input feature, such that the i-th element of Z is calculated by:

$$Z_i = \frac{1}{H \times W \times L} \sum_{h=1}^{H} \sum_{w=1}^{W} \sum_{l=1}^{L} f_i^{h,w,l} \tag{1}$$

where f indicates the input features, $H \times W \times L$ is the spatial dimensions of the feature. To learn the nonlinear dependencies between channels better, a bottleneck with two fully connected layers are employed:

$$s = \delta\{W_2(\delta\{W_1 Z\})\} \tag{2}$$

where s is the scalar that will be applied to the input features, $W_1 \in \mathbb{R}^{\frac{C}{r} \times C}$ and $W_2 \in \mathbb{R}^{C \times \frac{C}{r}}$ are the weights of the fully connected layers, r is the reduction ratio for the bottleneck, C is the number of input features, and δ represents the activation function. Subsequently, the input feature is rescaled by s:

$$\tilde{f} = f \odot s \tag{3}$$

where $\tilde{f}$ is the rescaled feature and $\odot$ indicates the channel-wise multiplication. Finally, the attention map A is obtained by the channel-wise mean:

$$A = \frac{1}{C} \sum_{c=1}^{C} f_c \tag{4}$$

Siamese Classifier. To alleviate the class-imbalance issue, we employ the Siamese network to identify whether the pair-wise inputs are from the same class or not. In detail, the Siamese classifier is composed of two identical subnetworks that share identical weights, in which each subnetwork consists of five fully connected layers. After each fully connected layer, the sigmoid function is used as the activation function, followed by the dropout layer to alleviate the overfitting problem. It should be noted that the sigmoid function is more suitable than PReLu function in the Siamese network as it can regularize the outputs to the same range of 0–1 to accelerate the training procedure.

In our model, the first two modules (i.e., the feature extractor and FCF module) are built to non-linearly map the input images into a low dimensional space, and then the SSA module is established to make the model focus on the ASD-related region. At last, the Siamese classifier is used to calculate the distance of the pair-wise inputs in such a way that the distance is small if the inputs belong to the same class and large otherwise.

Let X_1 and X_2 be the pair-wise attention maps from two inputs (e.g., subject 1 and subject 2 in Fig. 2). Let Y be the binary label of the pair-wise inputs, $Y = 0$ if the inputs are from the same class and $Y = 1$ otherwise. Let w be the shared weights of the two subnetworks, and $G_w()$ indicates the Siamese classifier. Then the contrastive loss $\mathcal{L}_{contrastive}$ is applied to calculate the distance of pair-wise output and formulated as:

$$\mathcal{L}_{contrastive} = (1 - Y)(D)^2 + Y\{\max(0, m - D)\}^2, D = \sqrt{\{G_w(X_1) - G_w(X_2)\}^2} \tag{5}$$

where D is defined as the distance between the outputs $G_w(X_1)$ and $G_w(X_2)$. $m > 0$ is a margin value. Having a margin indicates that dissimilar pairs that are beyond this margin will not contribute to the loss.

Hence, for the diagnosis of ASD/NC, if the class of one input is pre-defined, the class of the other input can be determined according to the contrastive loss. Compared with classifying the subject as ASD/NC directly, the proposed method, which identifies the testing subject and each training subject as the same class or not, is more effective and reasonable.

4   Experiments and Results

4.1   Implementations

In our experiments, the margin m is set as 2. The Stochastic Gradient Descent (SGD) optimizer with momentum is used during the training stage. Besides, the initial learning rate is set as 0.001 and the cosine annealing decay is used to adjust the learning rate. In the testing phase, the distance between the given testing subject and each training subject is calculated to determine whether they are the same class or not, and the final result is obtained by majority voting. We use a 3-fold cross-validation strategy to evaluate the performance of the proposed method. More specifically, we choose two-thirds ASD subjects and two-thirds NC subjects as training set for each fold.

4.2 Ablation Study

In this part, we present the results of ablation experiments to explore the different combinations of T1w, T2w, segmentation and parcellation maps. The corresponding results in terms of sensitivity, specificity, and accuracy of each comparison and the corresponding p-values are listed in Table 1.

Table 1. The results of ablation comparisons. p-value is calculated between any input and the proposed input (T1w+T2w+Segmentation+Parcellation+Attention) with the Siamese network.

Input	Sensitivity	p-value	Specificity	p-value	Accuracy	p-value
T1w	76.9%	0.3389	81.5%	0.0272	80.6%	0.1810
T2w	73.1%	0.0560	80.0%	0.0418	78.6%	0.0307
T1w+T2w	75.0%	0.1377	82.1%	0.0313	80.6%	0.0311
T1w+T2w +Segmentation	82.7%	0.6481	83.1%	0.3375	83.0%	0.3515
T1w+T2w+Segmentation +Parcellation	82.7%	0.5476	84.6%	0.1347	84.2%	0.2729
Proposed method without Siamese network	71.2%	0.0417	77.9%	0.0339	76.5%	0.0192
Proposed method	80.8%	–	**86.7%**	–	**85.4%**	–

From Table 1, we can see that inputs with the segmentation map and parcellation map can improve the performance, which indicates the proposed informative guidance is effective for autism classification. In addition, we replaced the Siamese network with a conventional CNN for the finial classifier but kept others the same, with the performance listed in the last second row. It can be seen that the Siamese network can provide more accurate prediction compared with the conventional CNN. The p-values presented in Table 1 also show the effectiveness of the proposed method. Especially for the specificity, a statistically significant difference is reported for the result that is only trained on the intensity images (T1w, T2w, as well as T1w + T2w) and the result provided by conventional CNN (proposed method without the Siamese network), i.e., p-value < 0.05, compared with the proposed method.

Besides, we also show the attention maps generated from different inputs in Fig. 3. We can observe that the cerebellum area, which has been consistently reported in ASD [19], is highlighted in almost all attention maps. Additionally, the insular lobe is also pointed up in Fig. 3(f2), which has a role in different aspects, such as asymbolia for pain, sensory area and motor association area, showing the consistency with characteristics of ASD, e.g., indifference to pain/temperature and restricted/repetitive behaviors. Similar findings have been also reported in [20, 21].

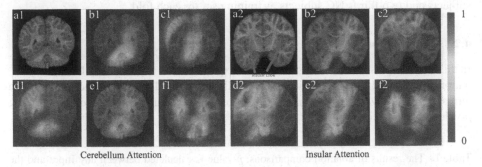

Cerebellum Attention   Insular Attention

Fig. 3. Typical attention maps generated by different inputs: T1w (b1, b2), T2w (c1, c2), T1w+T2w (d1, d2), T1w+T2w+segmentation (e1, e2), and T1w+T2w+segmentation+parcellation map (f1, f2). (a1, a2) is the T1w image with different slices.

4.3   Comparison with State-of-the-Art Methods

In addition, we also compare our method with random forest (RF)-based method [22], the multi-channel CNNs [13] that utilizes the patches from anatomical landmarks to predict the status (ASD/NC) of the given subject, the EA-CSF-based method [23], and the classification method based on EA-CSF volume, total brain volume, age, and sex information (EA-CSF-BAS) [12]. Although it is hard to directly make a comparison due to different subjects involved, as shown in Table 2, our proposed method can generally achieve more than 7% increase in terms of accuracy compared with other methods [12, 13, 23], benefiting from the informative features from four input data and the Siamese classifier. Specifically, the proposed method can extract more meaningful features from different inputs, and can alleviate the class-imbalance issue due to the learning strategy of pair-wise inputs. Although our method does not perform better than the results reported in [22], our method is validated on 247 subjects, which is much more than 38 subjects involved in [22]. Furthermore, our method is fully data-driven and does not need to rely on pre-defined brain landmarks [13] or the pre-defined biomarkers, e.g., cortex shape [22], EA-CSF [23] or total brain volume [12].

Table 2. Experimental comparison with state-of-the-art methods.

	Number of ASD/NC	Modality	Age (in month)	Accuracy
RF-based method [22]	19/19	DTI	6	86.8%
Multi-channel CNNs [13]	61/215	T1w + T2w	24	76.2%
EA-CSF-based method [23]	47/296	T1w	6	69.0%
EA-CSF-BAS [12]	159/77	T1w	6	78.0%
The proposed method	52/195	T1w+T2w	24	85.4%

5   Conclusion

In this paper, we propose an end-to-end informative feature-guided Siamese network for the ASD diagnosis at 24 months of age. Specifically, we utilize the features from T1w image, T2w image, segmentation map and parcellation map to distinguish the essential difference between ASD and NC subjects. Then the SSA module is employed to locate the ASD-related region, and finally we employ the Siamese network to learn what makes the pair of inputs belong to the same class or different classes. The ablation experiments and comparison with other methods demonstrate the effectiveness of the proposed method. In the future, we will extend our work to 6-month-old infant subjects and validate on multi-site datasets.

Acknowledgements. Data used in the preparation of this work were obtained from the NIH-supported National Database for Autism Research (NDAR). NDAR is a collaborative informatics system created by the National Institutes of Health to provide a national resource to support and accelerate research in autism. This paper reflects the views of the authors and may not reflect the opinions or views of the NIH or of the Submitters submitting original data to NDAR. This work was supported in part by National Institutes of Health grants MH109773 and MH117943.

References

1. Maenner, M.J., Shaw, K.A., Baio, J.: Prevalence of autism spectrum disorder among children aged 8 years—autism and developmental disabilities monitoring network, 11 sites, United States, 2016. MMWR Surveillance Summ. **69**, 1 (2020)
2. Damiano, C.R., Mazefsky, C.A., White, S.W., Dichter, G.S.: Future directions for research in autism spectrum disorders. J. Clin. Child Adolescent Psychol. **43**, 828–843 (2014)
3. Wang, L., et al.: Volume-based analysis of 6-month-old infant brain MRI for autism biomarker identification and early diagnosis. In: Frangi, Alejandro F., Schnabel, Julia A., Davatzikos, C., Alberola-López, C., Fichtinger, G. (eds.) MICCAI 2018. LNCS, vol. 11072, pp. 411–419. Springer, Cham (2018). https://doi.org/10.1007/978-3-030-00931-1_47
4. Committee on Educational Interventions for Children with Autism; Board on Behavioral, C., and Sensory Sciences; Board on Children, Youth and Families; Division of Behavioral and Social Sciences and Education; National Research Council (ed.): Educating Children with Autism. National Academy Press, Washington, DC (2001)

5. Shen, M.D., et al.: Early brain enlargement and elevated extra-axial fluid in infants who develop autism spectrum disorder (2013)
6. Wolff, J.J., et al.: Neural circuitry at age 6 months associated with later repetitive behavior and sensory responsiveness in autism. Molecular Autism **8**, 8 (2017)
7. Swanson, M.R., et al.: Subcortical brain and behavior phenotypes differentiate infants with autism versus language delay. Biol. Psychiatry: Cogn. Neurosci. Neuroimaging **2**, 664–672 (2017)
8. Emerson, R.W., et al.: Functional neuroimaging of high-risk 6-month-old infants predicts a diagnosis of autism at 24 months of age. Sci. Transl. Med. **9**, eaag2882 (2017)
9. Shen, M.D., et al.: Early brain enlargement and elevated extra-axial fluid in infants who develop autism spectrum disorder. Brain **136**, 2825–2835 (2013)
10. Hazlett, H.C., et al.: Early brain development in infants at high risk for autism spectrum disorder. Nature **542**, 348–351 (2017)
11. Panizzon, M.S., et al.: Distinct genetic influences on cortical surface area and cortical thickness. Cereb. Cortex **19**, 2728–2735 (2009)
12. Shen, M.D., et al.: Extra-axial cerebrospinal fluid in high-risk and normal-risk children with autism aged 2–4 years: a case-control study. The Lancet Psychiatry **5**, 895–904 (2018)
13. Li, G., Liu, M., Sun, Q., Shen, D., Wang, L.: Early diagnosis of autism disease by multi-channel CNNs. In: Shi, Y., Suk, H.-I., Liu, M. (eds.) MLMI 2018. LNCS, vol. 11046, pp. 303–309. Springer, Cham (2018). https://doi.org/10.1007/978-3-030-00919-9_35
14. Li, G., et al.: A preliminary volumetric MRI study of amygdala and hippocampal subfields in autism during infancy. In: 2019 IEEE 16th International Symposium on Biomedical Imaging (ISBI 2019), pp. 1052–1056. IEEE (2019)
15. Hu, J., Shen, L., Sun, G.: Squeeze-and-excitation networks. In: Proceedings of the IEEE Conference on Computer Vision and Pattern Recognition, pp. 7132–7141 (2018)
16. Chopra, S., Hadsell, R., LeCun, Y.: Learning a similarity metric discriminatively, with application to face verification. In: 2005 IEEE Computer Society Conference on Computer Vision and Pattern Recognition (CVPR 2005), vol. 1, pp. 539–546. IEEE (2005)
17. Payakachat, N., Tilford, J.M., Ungar, W.J.: National Database for Autism Research (NDAR): big data opportunities for health services research and health technology assessment. Pharmacoeconomics **34**, 127–138 (2016)
18. Shi, F., et al.: Infant brain atlases from neonates to 1-and 2-year-olds. PLoS ONE **6**, e18746 (2011)
19. Schmitt, L.M., Cook, E.H., Sweeney, J.A., Mosconi, M.W.: Saccadic eye movement abnormalities in autism spectrum disorder indicate dysfunctions in cerebellum and brainstem. Mol. Autism **5**, 47 (2014)
20. Caria, A., de Falco, S.: Anterior insular cortex regulation in autism spectrum disorders. Front. Behav. Neurosci. **9**, 38 (2015)
21. Yamada, T., et al.: Altered functional organization within the insular cortex in adult males with high-functioning autism spectrum disorder: evidence from connectivity-based parcellation. Mol. Autism **7**, 1–15 (2016)
22. Mostapha, M., Casanova, M.F., Gimel'farb, G., El-Baz, A.: Towards non-invasive image-based early diagnosis of autism. In: Navab, N., Hornegger, J., Wells, William M., Frangi, Alejandro F. (eds.) MICCAI 2015. LNCS, vol. 9350, pp. 160–168. Springer, Cham (2015). https://doi.org/10.1007/978-3-319-24571-3_20
23. Shen, M.D., et al.: Increased extra-axial cerebrospinal fluid in high-risk infants who later develop autism. Biol. Psychiatry **82**, 186–193 (2017)

Correction to: Constructing High-Order Dynamic Functional Connectivity Networks from Resting-State fMRI for Brain Dementia Identification

Chunxiang Feng, Biao Jie, Xintao Ding, Daoqiang Zhang, and Mingxia Liu

Correction to:
Chapter "Constructing High-Order Dynamic Functional Connectivity Networks from Resting-State fMRI for Brain Dementia Identification" in: M. Liu et al. (Eds.): *Machine Learning in Medical Imaging*, **LNCS 12436, https://doi.org/10.1007/978-3-030-59861-7_31**

In a former version of this paper, the CERNET Innovation Project (NGII20190621) was missing from the Acknowledgement section. This has been corrected.

The updated version of this chapter can be found at
https://doi.org/10.1007/978-3-030-59861-7_31

Correction to: Constructing High-Order Dynamic Functional Connectivity Networks from Resting-State fMRI for Brain Dementia Identification

Yingying Zhu, Xiao Jin, Xiaobo Zhang, Dongqing Zhou,
and Mingxia Liu

Correction to:
Chapter "Constructing High-Order Dynamic Functional
Connectivity Networks from Resting-State fMRI for Brain
Dementia Identification" in M. Liu et al. (Eds.): Machine
Learning in Medical Imaging, LNCS 12436,
https://doi.org/10.1007/978-3-030-59861-7_31

The funder section of this paper the DISNET funding Project NSFB2020000D
was left out of the Acknowledgement section. This has been corrected.

The updated version of this chapter can be found at
https://doi.org/10.1007/978-3-030-59861-7_31

Author Index

Printed in the United States
by Baker & Taylor Publisher Services